Senior

Biology 2

2004

Student Resource and Activity Manual

BIOZONE

Senior **Biology 2** 2004
Student Resource and Activity Manual

Previous editions 2002-2003
Third edition 2004

ISBN   1-877329-10-X

Copyright © **2003** Richard Allan
Published by **BIOZONE International Ltd**
Printed in New Zealand

About the Writing Team

Tracey Greenwood joined the staff of BIOZONE at the beginning of 1993. She has a Ph.D. in biology, specialising in lake ecology, and taught undergraduate and graduate biology at the University of Waikato for four years.

Richard Allan has had 11 years experience teaching senior biology at Hillcrest High School in Hamilton, New Zealand. He attained a Masters degree in biology at Waikato University, New Zealand.

The authors acknowledge and thank our graphic artist **Daniel Butler** for general assistance with production and his tireless pursuit of the perfect 3-D image.

This edition is dedicated to the late Ron Lind, who sadly passed away earlier this year. Ron contributed photographs used in this edition.

Purchases of this manual may be made direct from the publisher:

BIOZONE   **www.thebiozone.com**

EUROPE & MIDDLE EAST:
BIOZONE Learning Media (UK) Ltd.
P.O. Box 16710, Glasgow G12 9WS
United Kingdom
Telephone: +44 (141) 337 3355
FAX: +44 (141) 337 2266
E-mail: info@biozone.co.uk

ASIA & AUSTRALIA:
BIOZONE Learning Media Australia
P.O. Box 7523, GCMC 4217 QLD
Australia
Telephone: +61 (7) 5575 4615
FAX: +61 (7) 5572 0161
E-mail: info@biozone.com.au

NORTH & SOUTH AMERICA, AFRICA:
BIOZONE International Ltd.
P.O. Box 13-034, Hamilton
New Zealand
Telephone: +64 (7) 856 8104
FAX: +64 (7) 856 9243
E-mail: sales@biozone.co.nz

Preface to the Year 2004 Edition

This is the third edition of **Senior Biology 2**. It is designed to meet the needs of students undertaking biology at grades 11 and 12 or equivalent. It is particularly well suited to students taking **Advanced Placement** (AP), **Honors Biology**, or **International Baccalaureate** courses. Our Senior Biology 1 and 2 manuals cater for a wide audience, and may contain more material than is required by any one particular biology course. Due to the large amount of material covered, and the inconvenience that one large write-on resource would create, we have produced two smaller manuals. Note that the order in which topics are taught is usually at the discretion of each school; we therefore recommend purchasing both manuals at the commencement of the course. Previous editions have received very favorable reviews; see our web site: **www.the biozone.com** for details. This year we have continued to refine the stimulus material in the manual to improve its accessibility and interest level. In response to input from users, we have also removed the video and software listings from each topic and have included them in a supplementary product, the **Teacher Resource Handbook** (on CD-ROM), which is available free of charge with the first order of five or more manuals. This handbook also contains a detailed account of changes in the manual since the previous edition (previously provided as a looseleaf handout) and expanded and updated information on the suppliers of scientific equipment and the publishers of all listed software and video resources. Because supplier information is more appropriate to teachers, this information has also been removed from the introductory section in the manual. As in previous years, we have updated all our lists of resources: comprehensive and supplementary textbooks, video documentaries, computer software, periodicals, and internet sites. Most topics this year contain upgraded material, and there are a number of new activities. Check the contents pages for information on these. These annual upgrades are in keeping with our ongoing commitment to providing up-to-date, relevant, interesting, and accurate information to students and teachers.

A Note to the Teacher

This manual has been produced as a student-centered resource, aimed at facilitating independent learning. By providing a highly visual format, a clear map through the course, and a synopsis of available supplemental resources, these manuals will motivate and challenge a wide range of students. Today, many teachers are finding that a single textbook does not provide all of the information they need. This manual is **not a textbook**. It is a generic resource and, to this end, we have made a point of referencing texts from other publishers. Above all, we are committed to continually revising and improving this resource **each and every year**. The price, at only US$17 for student purchase, is a reflection of our commitment to providing high-quality, cost effective resources for biology. Please do not treat this resource as a *photocopy master* for your own handouts. We simply cannot afford to supply single copies of manuals to schools and continue to provide annual updates as we intend. Please **do not photocopy** from this manual. If you think it is worth using, then we recommend that the students themselves own this resource and keep it for their own use. A free model answer book is supplied, with the Teacher Resource Handbook, with your **first order** of 5 or more manuals.

How Teachers May Use This Manual

This manual may be used in the classroom to guide students through each topic. Some activities may be used to introduce topics while others may be used to consolidate and test concepts already covered by other means. The manual may be used as the primary tool in teaching some topics, but it should not be at the expense of good, 'hands-on' biology. Students may attempt the activities on their own or in groups. The latter provides opportunities for healthy discussion and peer-to-peer learning. Many of the activities may be set as homework exercises. Each page is perforated, allowing for easy removal of pages that must be submitted for formal marking. Teachers may prescribe the specific activities to be attempted by the students (using the check boxes next to the objectives for each topic), or they may allow students a degree of freedom with respect to the activities they attempt. The objectives for each topic will allow students to keep up to date even if they miss lessons. Teachers who are away from class may set work easily in their absence.

I thank you for your support.

Richard Allan

Acknowledgements

We would like to thank the people who have contributed to this edition: • Dan Butler for his cheerful attack on graphics • David Brill for permission to produce an artist's rendering of his reconstructed skeleton of 'Lucy' • Dr. John Green, Uni. of Waikato, for his input to the evolution and human evolution sections • Dr. John Craig for permission to use his material on the behavior of swamphen • Dr. John Stencil for his data on the albino gray squirrel population • Nathalie Loussert for proofreading • Mary McDougall and Sue FitzGerald for their efficient handling of the office • Jan Morrison for her diagrams • Raewyn Poole, University of Waikato, for information provided in her MSc thesis: Culture and transformation of *Acacia* • TechPool Studios, for their clipart collection of human anatomy: Copyright ©1994, TechPool Studios Corp. USA (some of these images were modified by R. Allan and T. Greenwood) • Totem Graphics, for their clipart collection • Corel Corporation, for use of their eps clipart of plants and animals from the Corel MEGAGALLERY collection • 3D modeling software, Poser IV (Curious Labs) and Bryce.

Photo Credits

Royalty free images, purchased by Biozone International Ltd, are used throughout this manual and have been obtained from the following sources: **Corel** Corporation from various titles in their Professional Photos CD-ROM collection; **IMSI** (International Microcomputer Software Inc.) images from IMSI's MasterClips® and MasterPhotosTM Collection, 1895 Francisco Blvd. East, San Rafael, CA 94901-5506, USA; ©1996 **Digital Stock**, Medicine and Health Care collection; ©**Hemera** Technologies Inc, 1999-2001 www.arttoday.com; **ArtToday** ©1999-2001 www.arttoday.com; ©Click Art, ©T/Maker Company; ©1994., ©**Digital Vision**; Gazelle Technologies Inc.; **PhotoDisc®**, Inc. USA, www.photodisc.com

We would like to thank the following individuals and institutions who kindly provided photographs: • Grotte de Rouffignac, for drawings and photographs of the Rouffignac Cave • Dr. John Dale, Defenders Ltd., www.defenders.co.uk for the photos on biological pest control • Janice Windsor, for photographs taken 'on safari' in East Africa • Simon Pollard, for his photograph of the naked mole rat • The late Ron Lind for his photograph of stromatolites • The late Dr. M Soper, for his photograph of the waxeye feeding chicks • Stephen Moore, for his photo of a hydrophyte, *Myriophyllum* and for his photos of stream invertebrates

Contributors identified by coded credits are as follows: **BF**: Brian Finerran (Uni. of Canterbury), **BH**: Brendan Hicks (Uni. of Waikato), **BOB**: Barry O'Brien (Uni. of Waikato), **CDC**: Centers for Disease Control and Prevention, Atlanta, USA, **COD**: Colin O'Donnell, **DEQ**: Dept of Environment Queensland Ltd., **DOC**: Dept of Conservation (NZ), **EII**: Education Interactive Imaging, **EW**: Environment Waikato, **Eyewire**: Eyewire, Inc © 1998-2001, www.eyewire.com **FRI**: Forest Research Institute, **GW**: Graham Walker, **JR-PE**: Jane Roskruge, **JW**: Janice Windsor, **RA**: Richard Allan, **RCN**: Ralph Cocklin, **RM-DOC**: Rod Morris, **RL**: Ron Lind, **TG**: Tracey Greenwood, **VM**: Villa Maria Wines, **WBS**: Warwick Silvester (Uni. of Waikato), **WMU**: Waikato Microscope Unit.

Special thanks to all the partners of the Biozone team for their support.

Cover Photographs

Main photograph: The solitary mountain lion (*Puma concolor*), also known as the cougar or puma, has proved adaptable to a wide range of habitats throughout the Americas. However, hunting pressure and environmental changes have now restricted their range to inhospitable mountainous areas. PHOTO: D. Robert Franz

Background photograph: SEM of the villi lining the ileum. PHOTO: ©1996 Digital Stock Corporation, Medicine and Healthcare collection.

Contents

CODES: Δ **Upgraded** this edition   ☆ **New** this edition   **Activity** is marked: ⬛ to be done;   ✔ when completed

CONTENTS *(continued)*

CODES: Δ **Upgraded** this edition   ☆ **New** this edition   **Activity** is marked: • to be done; ✓ when completed

CONTENTS *(continued)*

CODES: Δ **Upgraded** this edition ☆ **New** this edition   **Activity** is marked: ▪ to be done; ✔ when completed

How to Use this Manual

This manual is designed to provide you with a resource that will make the subject of biology more enjoyable and fun to study. The manual addresses the requirements for the **International Baccalaureate** (IB) and **Advanced Placement** (AP) courses. Consult the Syllabus Guides on pages 12-14 of this manual to establish where material for your syllabus is covered. It is hoped that this manual will reinforce and extend the ideas developed by your teacher. It must be emphasized that this manual is **not a textbook**. It is designed to complement the biology textbooks provided for your course. For each topic the manual provides the following useful resources:

Guidance Provided for Each Topic

Learning objectives:

These provide you with a map of the topic content. Completing the relevant learning objectives will help you to satisfy the knowledge requirements of your course. Your teacher may decide to leave out points or add to this list.

Topic outcomes:

This panel provides details of the learning objectives that need to be completed to satisfy requirements relevant to that topic for each designated course. Attempt to meet the objectives relating to your course only. See pages 12-14 for a listing of your syllabus requirements.

Key words:

Key words are displayed in **bold** type in the learning objectives and should be used to create a glossary as you study each topic. From your own reading and your teacher's descriptions, write your own definition for each word.

Note: Only the terms relevant to your learning objectives should be used to create your glossary. Free glossary worksheets are also available from our web site.

Textbook references:

Provides a list of current texts appropriate for your course. Go to the *Textbook Reference Grid* on page 8 to see the comprehensive textbooks listed (these are texts providing coverage of the majority of course topics at least). The grid provides the page numbers from each text relevant to each topic in the manual. Page numbers for supplementary texts, which have only a restricted topic coverage, are provided as appropriate in each topic.

Use the check boxes to mark objectives to be completed (use a **dot** to be done; use a **tick** when completed).

Internet addresses:

We provide a database of links to more than **800** web sites (updated regularly) that form an excellent source of additional information.

Go to Biozone's own internet site: **www.thebiozone.com** and link directly to these sites using the *'BioLinks'* button.

Video documentaries and computer software:

Listings of computer software and videos relevant to each topic in the manual are now provided in the "Teacher Resource Handbook", which is provided free of charge with your first order of five or more manuals.

Some of the titles listed may already be available in your school collections. If not, and you are interested in purchasing them, full supplier details are provided via the resource hub at Biozone's website.

Periodical articles:

For students who wish to find out more about the topic or examine the latest research in the topic area. Visit your school, public, or university library for these articles.

Activity Pages

The activities and exercises make up most of the content of this book. They are designed to reinforce the concepts you have learned about in the topic. Your teacher may use the activity pages to introduce a topic for the first time, or you may use them to revise ideas already covered. They are excellent for use in the classroom, and as homework exercises and revision. In most cases, the activities should not be attempted until you have carried out the necessary background reading from your textbook. Your teacher should have a model answer book with the answers to each activity. This manual caters for the needs of more than one syllabus, and you will find some activities and even whole topics that may not be relevant to your course. Although you will miss out these pages, our manuals still represent exceptional value.

Activity code:
To assist you in identifying the type of activities in this manual and the skills they require, activities are coded. Note that most activities will require some knowledge recall. Unless this is all that is required, this code is excluded from the coding list.

66

RDA2

* Material to assist with the activity may be found on other pages of the manual or in textbooks.

Activity Level

1 = Simple questions not requiring complex reasoning
2 = Some complex reasoning may be required
3 = More challenging, requiring integration of concepts

Type of Activity

D = Data handling and/or interpretation
P = Paper practical
R = Research outside the information on the page*
A = Application of knowledge to solve a problem
K = Knowledge recall from information on the page
E = Extension material

---

114   The Mechanisms of Evolution

DA3

Changes in a Gene Pool

The diagram below shows an imaginary population of beetles undergoing changes as it is subjected to two 'events'. The three phases represent a progression in time, i.e. the same gene pool, undergoing change. The beetles have three phenotypes determined by the amount of pigment deposited in the cuticle. Three versions of this trait exist: black, dark, and pale. The gene controlling this character is represented by two alleles **A** and **a**. Your task is to analyze the gene pool as it undergoes changes.

Phase 1: Initial gene pool
Calculate the frequencies of the *allele types* and *allele combinations* by counting the actual numbers, then working them out as percentages.

	A	a	AA	Aa	aa
	Black	Dark	Pale		
No.	27	7			
%	54	28			

Allele types   *Allele combinations*

Phase 2: Natural selection
In the same gene pool at a later time there was a change in the allele frequencies. This was due to the loss of certain allele combinations due to natural selection. Some of those with a genotype of aa were eliminated (poor fitness).
Calculate as for above. Do not include the individuals surrounded by small white arrows in your calculations; they are dead!

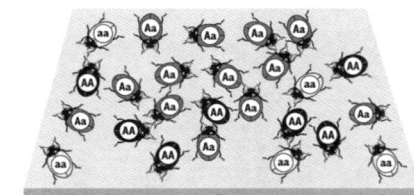

Two pale individuals died and therefore their alleles are removed from the gene pool.

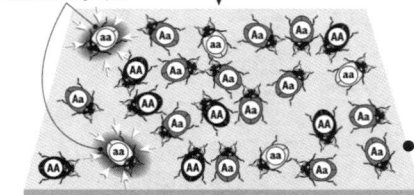

	A	a	AA	Aa	aa
No.					
%					

Phase 3: Immigration and emigration
This particular kind of beetle exhibits wandering behavior. The allele frequencies change again due to the introduction and departure of individual beetles, each carrying certain allele combinations.
Calculate as above. In your calculations, include the individual coming into the gene pool (AA), but remove the one leaving (aa).

This individual is entering the population and will add its alleles to the gene pool.

This individual is leaving the population, removing its alleles from the gene pool.

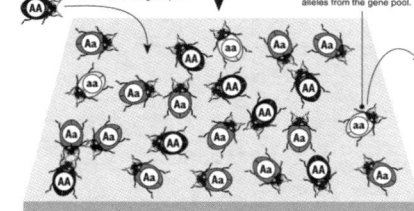

	A	a	AA	Aa	aa
No.					
%					

1. Explain how the number of dominant alleles (A) in the genotype of a beetle affects its phenotype:

_____

_____

2. For each phase in the gene pool above (place your answers in the tables provided; some have been done for you):
   (a) Determine the relative frequencies of the two alleles: A and a. Simply total the **A** alleles and **a** alleles separately.
   (b) Determine the frequency of how the alleles come together as allele pair combinations in the gene pool (AA, Aa and aa). Count the number of each type of combination.
   (c) For each of the above, work out the frequencies as percentages:
       Allele frequency = No. counted alleles ÷ Total no. of alleles x 100

Photocopying Prohibited   © Biozone International 2001-2003

Introductory paragraph:
The introductory paragraph sets the 'scene' for the focus of the page. Note any words that appear in **bold**, as they are 'key words' worthy of including in a glossary of biological terms for the topic.

Tear-out pages:
Each page of the book has a perforation that allows easy removal. Your teacher may ask you to remove activity pages from this manual for marking. Your teacher may also ask you to tear out the pages and place them in a folder with other work on the topic.

Easy to understand diagrams:
The main ideas of the topic are represented and explained by clear, informative diagrams.

Write-on format:
Your understanding of the main ideas of the topic are tested by asking you questions and providing spaces for your answers. Your answers should be concise (brief) and even a list of descriptive terms may be adequate to convey the answer. Writing your answers in pencil will allow you to easily make corrections.
Take care that you answer the questions adequately (see the facing page that explains the questioning terms used).

Explanation of Terms

Questions come in a variety of forms. Whether you are studying for an exam, or writing an essay, it is important to understand exactly what the question is asking. A question has two parts to it: one part of the question will provide you with information, the second part of the question will provide you with instructions as to how to answer the question. Following these instructions is most important. Often students in exams know the material but fail to follow instructions and therefore do not answer the question appropriately. Examiners often use certain key words to introduce questions. Look out for them and be absolutely clear as to what they mean. Below is a list of commonly used terms that you will come across and a brief explanation of each.

Commonly used Terms in Biology

The following terms are frequently used when asking questions in examinations and assessments. Most of these are listed in the IB syllabus document as action verbs indicating the depth of treatment required for a given statement. Students should have a clear understanding of each of the following terms and use this understanding to answer questions appropriately.

Analyze: Interpret data to reach stated conclusions.

Annotate: Add **brief** notes to a diagram, drawing or graph.

Apply: Use an idea, equation, principle, theory, or law in a new situation.

Appreciate: To understand the meaning or relevance of a particular situation.

Calculate: Find an answer using mathematical methods. Show the working unless instructed not to.

Compare: Give an account of similarities and differences between two or more items, referring to both (or all) of them throughout. Comparisons can be given using a table. Comparisons generally ask for similarities more than differences (see contrast).

Construct: Represent or develop in graphical form.

Contrast: Show differences. Set in opposition.

Deduce: Reach a conclusion from information given.

Define: Give the precise meaning of a word or phrase as concisely as possible.

Derive: Manipulate a mathematical equation to give a new equation or result.

Describe: Give a detailed account, including all the relevant information.

Design: Produce a plan, object, simulation or model.

Determine: Find the only possible answer.

Discuss: Give an account including, where possible, a range of arguments, assessments of the relative importance of various factors, or comparison of alternative hypotheses.

Distinguish: Give the difference(s) between two or more different items.

Draw: Represent by means of pencil lines. Add labels unless told not to do so.

Estimate: Find an approximate value for an unknown quantity, based on the information provided and application of scientific knowledge.

Evaluate: Assess the implications and limitations.

Explain: Give a clear account including causes, reasons, or mechanisms.

Identify: Find an answer from a number of possibilities.

Illustrate: Give concrete examples. Explain clearly by using comparisons or examples.

Interpret: Comment upon, give examples, describe relationships. Describe, then evaluate.

List: Give a sequence of names or other brief answers with no elaboration. Each one should be clearly distinguishable from the others.

Measure: Find a value for a quantity.

Outline: Give a brief account or summary. Include essential information only.

Predict: Give an expected result.

Solve: Obtain an answer using algebraic and/or numerical methods.

State: Give a specific name, value, or other answer. No supporting argument or calculation is necessary.

Suggest: Propose a hypothesis or other possible explanation.

Summarize: Give a brief, condensed account. Include conclusions and avoid unnecessary details.

In Conclusion

Students should familiarize themselves with this list of terms and, where necessary throughout the course, they should refer back to them when answering questions. The list of terms mentioned above is not exhaustive and students should compare this list with past examination papers and essays etc. and add any new terms (and their meaning) to the list above. The aim is to become familiar with interpreting the question and answering it appropriately.

Resources Information

Your set textbook should always be a starting point for information. There are also many other resources available, including scientific journals, magazine and newspaper articles, supplementary texts covering restricted topic areas, dictionaries, computer software and videos, and the internet.

A synopsis of currently available resources is provided below. Access to the publishers of these resources can be made directly from Biozone's web site through our resources hub: **www.thebiozonecom/resource-hub.html**, or by typing in the relevant addresses provided below. Most titles are also available through www.amazon.com. Please note that our listing any product in this manual does not, in any way, denote Biozone's endorsement of that product.

Comprehensive Biology Texts Referenced

Appropriate texts for this course are referenced in this manual. Page or chapter references for each text are provided in the text reference grid on page 8. These will enable you to identify the relevant reading as you progress through the activities in this manual. Publication details of texts referenced in the grid are provided below and opposite. For further details of text content, or to make purchases, link to the relevant publisher via Biozone's resources hub or by typing:
www.thebiozone.com/resources/us-comprehensive-pg1.html

Allott, Andrew, 2001
Biology for the IB Diploma - Standard and Higher Level
Publisher: Oxford University Press
Pages: 192
ISBN: 0-19-914818-X
Comments: *Book structure mirrors that of the new IB program. Includes core and option material.*

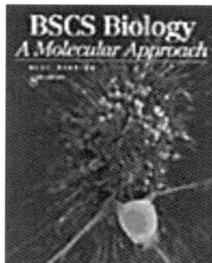

Bloom, M. and J. Greenberg, 2001
Biological Science: A Molecular Approach, (BSCS Blue Version), 8/edn
Publisher: Glencoe/McGraw Hill
Pages: 821 including glossary
ISBN: 0-538-69039-9 (student edition)
Comments: *A teacher's annotated edition, resource book, and overhead transparency booklet are also available.*

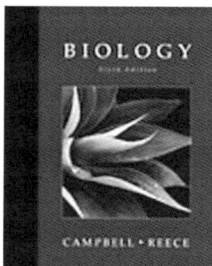

Campbell, N. A. and J.B. Reece, 2002
Biology , 6/edn
Publisher: Benjamin Cummings
Pages: 1175
ISBN: 0-8053-6624-5
Comments: *Comes with CD-ROM. A wide range of supplemental material is available. Also available in softback. The 5th edition is still in print and available.*

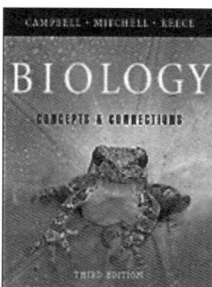

Campbell, N. A., L.G. Mitchell, and J.B. Reece, 2000
Biology; Concepts and Connections, 3/edn
Publisher: Benjamin Cummings
Pages: 807 plus appendices
ISBN: 0-8053-6625-3
Comments: *Set at a more introductory level than Campbell and Reece. Comes with an interactive study partner on CD-ROM. A CourseCompass version and an unbound flextext version are also available.*

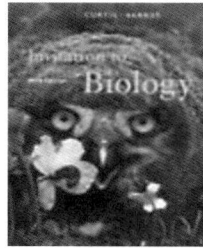

Curtis, H. and N. Sue Barnes, 1994
Invitation to Biology, 5 edn
Publisher: W.H. Freeman
Pages: 862
ISBN: 0-87901-679-5
Comments: *A well illustrated introduction to biology at this level. Evolution as a theme is integrated throughout. Also available as a split edition in two volumes.*

Freeman, S., 2002
Biological Science
Publisher: Prentice Hall
Pages: 1017 plus appendices and index
ISBN: 0-13-081923-9
Comments: *Aimed at the Advanced Placement audience, this book provides an introductory chapter, followed by nine units covering core themes. Each chapter concludes with a review, questions, and ideas for resources and additional reading.*

Ghalayini, 2000
Higher level Biology
Publisher: purchase from the author:
www.biology-books.com
P.O. Box 922333, Amman, Jordan
Pages: approx 450
ISBN: not available at the time of printing
Comments: *Written for both core and options for the IB course (higher level). A text for standard level is also available.*

Gould, J.L. and W.T. Keeton, 1996
Biological Science, 6 edn
Publisher: W.W. Norton
Pages: 1206
ISBN: 0-393-96920-7
Comments: *Also available as a two volume set in softback.*

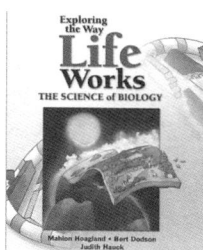

Hoagland, M., B. Dodson, & J. Hauck, 2001
Exploring the Way Life Works
Publisher: Jones & Bartlett Publishers, Inc.
Pages: 353 plus glossary and answers
ISBN: 0-7637-1688-X
Comments: *Ideal for those looking for a new approach. This text combines an innovative, student-friendly format with accurate information and clear presentation of ideas. Includes suggested web site links.*

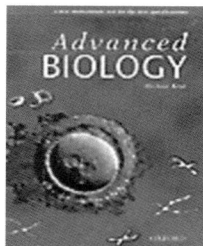

Kent, N. A. 2000
Advanced Biology
Publisher: Oxford University Press
Pages: 624
ISBN: 0-19-914195-9
Comments: *Each book comes with a free CD-ROM to help with specification planning. Book is formatted as a series of two page concept spreads.*

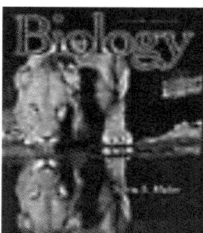

Mader, Sylvia, 2001
Biology, 7 edn
Publisher: McGraw Hill
Pages: 939 plus appendices
ISBN: 0-07-250819-1
Comments: *Comes with CD-ROM and OLC passcard. Also available as "Biology with study partner".*

Miller, R. and J. Levine, 2000
Biology, 5 edn
Publisher: Prentice-Hall
Pages: 1114 plus references
ISBN: 0134362659
Comments: *This edition also available on CD-ROM at slightly less cost.*

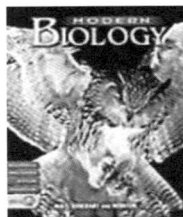

National Geographic Society, 2002
Biology: The Dynamics of Life
Publisher: Glencoe/McGraw-Hill
Pages: 1089 plus appendices
ISBN: 0-07-825925-8
Comments: *Highly colorful text, which uses a fairly large, easy-to-read format. A number of supplementary resources are also available to complement this text.*

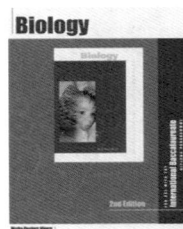

Purves, W.K., D. Sadava, G.H. Orians, and H.C. Heller, 2000
Life: The Science of Biology, 6/edn
Publisher: W.H. Freeman/Sinauer
Pages: 1100
ISBN: 0-7167-3873-2
Comments: *Available as a three volume set maintaining original pagination.*

Raven, P.H. and G.B. Johnson, 2002
Biology , 6 edn
Publisher: McGraw-Hill
Pages: 1238 plus appendices
ISBN: 0-07-249937-0
Comments: *Comes with OLC and biocourse.com password card. 5th edition (1999) is also available.*

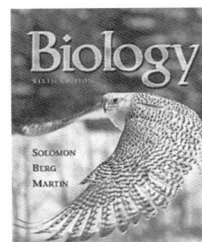

Solomon, E., L. Berg, and D.W. Martin, 2002
Biology , 6 edn
Publisher: Brooks/Cole
Pages: 1368
ISBN: 0-03-033503-5
Comments: *Significantly revised and updated. This edition is also available with CD-ROM & InfoTrac on-line library access.*

Starr, C. and R. Taggart, 2001
Biology: The Unity & Diversity of Life, 9 edn
Publisher: Brooks/Cole
Pages: 942
ISBN: 0-534-37795-5
Comments: *Comes with CD-ROM. Includes web links. Book is formatted as a series of two page concept spreads.*

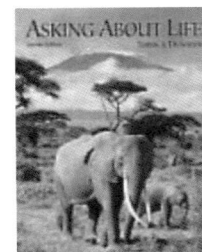

Tobin, A.J. and J. Dusheck, 2001
Asking About Life, 2 edn
Publisher: Brooks/Cole
Pages: 960
ISBN: 0-03-027044-8
Comments: *A recent revision aimed at making the writing style more concise and accessible to students at grades 11 and 12.*

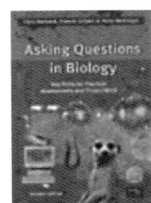

Towle, Albert, 2002
Modern Biology, 10/edn
Publisher: Holt, Rinehart, and Winston
Pages: 53 chapters
ISBN: 0030565413
Comments: *Annotated teacher's edition is also available. A wide range of resources complementary to this text is available. The earlier edition (2000) is also available.*

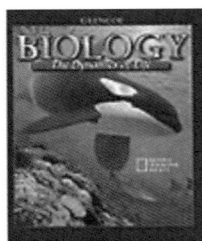

Weem, M.P., 2001
Biology, 2 edn
Publisher: IBID Press
Pages: 494
ISBN: 1-876659-47-5
Comments: *Written specifically to support the revised IB course, which began in September 2001. Contains theory and worked examples.*

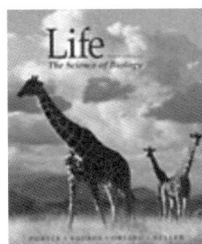

Supplementary Texts

For further details of text content, or to make purchases, link to the relevant publisher via Biozone's resources hub or by typing:
www.thebiozone.com/resources/us-supplementary-pg1.html

Barnard, C., F. Gilbert, F., and P. McGregor, 2001
Asking Questions in Biology: Key Skills for Practical Assessments & Project Work, 208 pp.
Publisher: Prentice Hall
ISBN: 0130-90370-1
Comments: *Covers many aspects of design, analysis and presentation of practical work in senior level biology.*

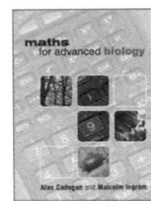

Cadogan, A. and Ingram, M., 2002
Maths for Advanced Biology
Publisher: NelsonThornes
ISBN: 0-7487-6506-9
Comments: *Provides coverage of basic mathematics requirements for biology at grades 11 and 12 (UK AS/A2). Includes worked examples.*

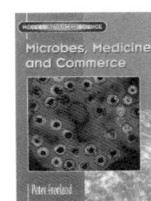

Freeland, P., 1999
Hodder Advanced Science: Microbes, Medicine, and Commerce, 160 pp.
Publisher: Hodder and Stoughton
ISBN: 0-340-73103-6
Comments: *Combines biotechnology, pathology, microbiology, and immunity in a thorough text.*

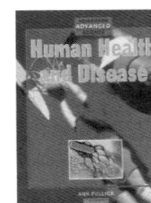

Fullick, A. , 1998
Human Health and Disease, 162 pp.
Publisher: Heinemann Educational Publishers
ISBN: 0435570919
Comments: *An accompanying text for courses with coverage of human health and disease. Covers both infectious and non-infectious disease.*

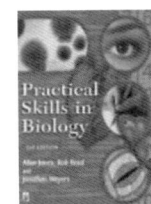

Jones, A., R. Reed, and J. Weyers, 1994
Practical Skills in Biology, 292 pp.
Publisher: Longman
ISBN: 0-582-06699-9
Comments: *Provides information on all aspects of experimental and field design, implementation, and data analysis. Available directly from www.amazon.com*

Advanced Biology Readers (John Murray Publishers)
Texts in a series designed as supplemental texts supporting a range of specific topics in biology. They are also useful as teacher reference and student extension reading.

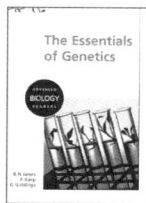

Jones, N., A. Karp., & G. Giddings, 2001.
Essentials of Genetics, 224 pp.
ISBN: 0-7195-8611-9
Thorough supplemental for genetics and evolution. Comprehensive coverage of cell division, molecular genetics, and genetic engineering is provided, and the application of new gene technologies to humans is discussed in a concluding chapter.

Collins Advanced Modular Sciences (HarperCollins)
Modular-style texts covering material related to specific topic options in the UK, but suitable as teacher reference and student extension reading for specific topic areas.

Hudson, T. and K. Mannion, 2001.
Microbes and Disease, 104 pp.
ISBN: 0-00-327742-9
Coverage of selected aspects of microbiology including the culture and applications of bacteria, and the role of bacteria and viruses in disease. Immunity, vaccination, and antimicrobial drug use are covered in the concluding chapter.

Murray, P. & N. Owens, 2001.
Behaviour & Populations, 82 pp.
ISBN: 0-00-327743-7
This text covers an eclectic range of topics including patterns of behavior, reproduction and its control, human growth and development, human populations, aspects of infectious disease, and issues related to health and lifestyle.

Illustrated Advanced Biology (John Murray Publishers)
One title in a modular-style series aimed as supplemental resources for biology students at grades 11 and 12.

Clegg, C.J., 1998.
Mammals: Structure & Function, 96 pp.
ISBN: 0-7195-7551-6
Includes an introduction to classification and diversity followed by a section on mammalian histology. Aspects of mammalian physiology are presented, including nutrition, exchange and transport, immunity, and reproduction.

Clegg, C.J., 1999.
Genetics and Evolution, 96 pp.
ISBN: 0-7195-7552-4
Concise but thorough coverage of molecular genetics, genetic engineering, inheritance, and evolution. An historical perspective is included by way of introduction, and a glossary and a list of abbreviations used are included.

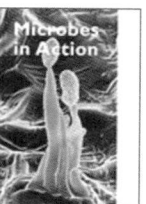

Clegg, C.J., 2002.
Microbes in Action, 97 pp.
ISBN: 0-71957-554-0
Microbes and their roles in disease and biotechnology. It includes material on the diversity of the microbial world, microbiological techniques, and a short, but useful, account of enzyme technology.

Clegg, C.J., 2003
Green Plants: The Inside Story, 96 pp.
ISBN: 0 7195 7553 2
The emphasis in this text is on flowering plants. Topics include leaf, stem, and root structure in relation to function, reproduction, economic botany, and sensitivity and adaptation. This text has not been included in chapter resources as the content details were not available when going to press.

Nelson Advanced Sciences (NelsonThornes)
Modular-style texts suitable as teacher reference and student extension reading for specific topics in grades 11 and 12 biology.

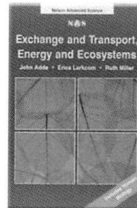

Adds, J., E. Larkcom & R. Miller, 2000.
Exchange and Transport, Energy and Ecosystems, 216 pp.
ISBN: 0-17-448294-9
Includes exchange processes (gas exchanges, digestion, absorption), transport systems, adaptation, sexual reproduction, energy and the environment, and human impact. Practical activities are included in several of the chapters.

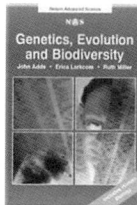

Adds, J., E. Larkcom & R. Miller, 2001.
Genetics, Evolution, and Biodiversity, 200 pp.
ISBN: 0-17-448296-5
A range of topics including photosynthesis and the control of growth in plants, classification and quantitative field ecology, populations and pest control, conservation, Mendelian genetics and evolution, gene technology and human evolution. Practical activities are included in many chapters.

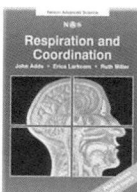

Adds, J., E. Larkcom & R. Miller, 2001.
Respiration and Coordination, 200 pp.
ISBN: 0-17-448295-7
This text covers Unit 4 and all option modules for Edexcel, providing material on metabolic pathways, internal regulation and nervous coordination, microbiology and biotechnology, food science, and aspects of health and exercise physiology.

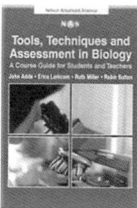

Adds, J., E. Larkcom, R. Miller, & R. Sutton, 1999.
Tools, Techniques and Assessment in Biology, 160 pp.
ISBN: 0-17-448273-6
A course guide covering basic lab protocols, microscopy, quantitative techniques in the lab and field, advanced DNA techniques and tissue culture, data handling and statistical tests, and exam preparation. Includes several useful appendices.

Periodicals, Magazines, and Journals
Articles in *Biological Sciences Review (Biol. Sci. Rev.)*, *New Scientist*, and *Scientific American* can be of great value in providing current information on specific topics. Periodicals may be accessed in your school, local, public, and university libraries. Listed below are the periodicals referenced in this manual. For general enquiries and further details regarding subscriptions, link to the relevant publisher via Biozone's resources hub or type:
www.thebiozone.com/resources/resource-journal.html

Biological Sciences Review: *An excellent quarterly publication for all teachers and students of biology. The content is current and the language is accessible.* Subscriptions available from Philip Allan Publishers, Market Place, Deddington, Oxfordshire OX 15 OSE.
Tel. 01869 338652
Fax 01869 338803
E-mail: sales@philipallan.co.uk

New Scientist: *Published weekly and found in many libraries. It often summarizes the findings published in other journals. Articles range from news releases to features.*
Subscription enquiries:
Tel. (UK and international): +44 (0)1444 475636. (US & Canada) 1 888 822 3242.
E-mail: ns.subs@qss-uk.com

Scientific American: *A monthly magazine containing mostly specialist feature articles. Articles range in level of reading difficulty and assumed knowledge.*
Subscription enquiries:
Tel. (US & Canada) 800-333-1199.
Tel. (outside North America): 515-247-7631
Web: www.sciam.com

The American Biology Teacher: *The official, peer-reviewed journal of the National Association of Biology Teachers. Published nine times a year and containing information and activities relevant to the teaching of biology in the US and elsewhere.*
Subscription enquiries:
NABT, 12030 Sunrise Valley Drive, #110, Reston, VA 20191-3409
Web: www.nabt.org

School Science Review: *A quarterly journal published by the ASE for science teachers in 11-19 education. SSR includes articles, reviews, and news on current research and curriculum development. Free to all Ordinary Members of the ASE or available on subscription.*
Subscription enquiries:
Tel: 01707 28300
Email: info@ase.org.uk *or visit their web site.*

Biology Dictionaries

Access to a good biology dictionary is of great value when dealing with the technical terms used in biology. Below are some biology dictionaries that you may wish to locate or purchase. They can usually be sourced directly from the publisher or they are all available (at the time of printing) from www.amazon.com. For further details of text content, or to make purchases, link to the relevant publisher via Biozone's resources hub or by typing:
www.thebiozone.com/resources/dictionaries-pg1.html

Allaby, M. (ed).
A Dictionary of Zoology 2 ed., 1999, 606 pp. Oxford University Press.
ISBN: 0192800760
Wide coverage of terms in animal behavior, ecology, physiology, genetics, cytology, evolution, and zoogeography. Full taxonomic coverage of most phyla and revised to cover extremophiles.

Hale, W.G. and J.P. Margham
HarperCollins: Dictionary of Biology, reprint ed., 1991, 576 pp. HarperCollins
ISBN: 0064610152
More than 5600 entries and nearly 300 diagrams. Entries go beyond basic definitions to provide in-depth explanations and examples. There are no pronunciation guidelines provided.

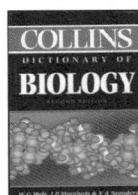

Hale, W.G., J.P. Margham, and V.A. Saunders
Collins: Dictionary of Biology, 2 ed., 1995, 656 pp. HarperCollins
ISBN: 0004708059
6500 entries covering all major fields within biology, and recently expanded to reflect recent developments in the science. There are no pronunciation guidelines provided.

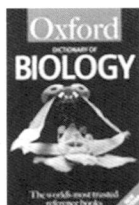

King, R.C. and W.D. Stansfield
A Dictionary of Genetics, 6 ed., 2002, 544 pp. Oxford University Press.
ISBN: 0195143256
A good source for the specialized terminology associated with genetics and related disciplines. Genera and species important to genetics are included, cross linked to an appendix.

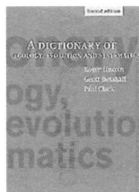

Lincoln, R.J., G.A. Boxshall, & P.F. Clark. **A Dictionary of Ecology, Evolution, and Systematics**, 2 ed., 1998, 371 pp. Cambridge Uni. Press.
ISBN: 052143842X
6500 entries covering all major fields within biology, and recently expanded to reflect recent developments in the science. There are no pronunciation guidelines provided.

Market House Books (compiled by).
Oxford Dictionary of Biology 4 ed., 2000, 648 pp. Oxford University Press.
ISBN: 0192801023.
Fully revised and updated, with many new entries. This edition contains biographical entries on key scientists and comprehensive coverage of terms in biology, biophysics, and biochemistry.

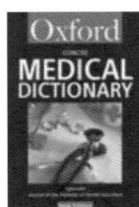

Market House Books (compiled by).
Oxford Concise Medical Dictionary 5 ed., 1998, 726 pp. Oxford University Press.
ISBN: 0192800752.
Revised edition includes 500 new entries and updates to preexisting ones. Full coverage of major medical and surgical specialties, and new entries for infectious and non-infectious disease, antibiotic resistance, and organ transplantation.

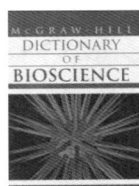

Parker, S. (ed).
McGraw-Hill Dictionary of Bioscience, International edn, 1996, 448 pp. McGraw-Hill.
ISBN: 0070524300
Provides explanatory detail of 16 000 essential terms in the biosciences. Contains a number of appendices and cross references. Pronunciation guidelines are also provided.

Rudin, N.
Dictionary of Modern Biology (1997), 504 pp. Barron's Educational Series Inc
ISBN: 0812095162.
More than 6000 terms in biosciences defined for college level students. Includes extensive cross referencing and several useful appendices.

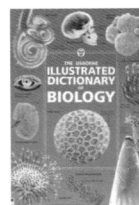

Stockley, C., 2000.
The Usborne Illustrated Dictionary of Biology 2nd ed., 128 pp. Usborne Publishing Ltd.
ISBN: 0746037929
Topics are arranged thematically so that words are explained in context. Includes cross referencing and a comprehensive index. Definitions are supported by detailed pictures and diagrams. Ideal for the visual learner.

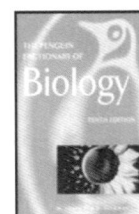

Thain, M. and M. Hickman.
Penguin Dictionary of Biology 10/e (2000), 704 pp. Penguin (USA).
ISBN: 0140513590
Pocket sized reference with definitions to more than 7500 terms, including more than 400 new entries. It includes explanations of fundamental concepts ad explorations of some of the more recent discoveries and developments in biology.

Internet Resources

The internet is a powerful tool for locating information. See pages 10-11 for details of how to access internet resources.

Textbook Reference Grid

Guide to use: Page or chapter numbers provided refer to material provided in each text relevant to the stated topic in the manual.

TOPIC IN MANUAL	Allott 2001	Bloom & Greenberg 2001	Campbell & Reece 2001	Campbell *et al.* 2000	
Pathogens and Disease	49	Chpt. 23 as reqd	330, 333-338, 344-345, 540, 556-557	203-206, 330, 500	
Defense Against Infectious Disease	50, 96-98	Chpt. 23 as reqd	Chpt. 43	Chpt. 24	
The Origin and Evolution of Life	124, 127	Chpt. 17 & 19 as reqd	Chpt. 26	Chpt. 15 & 16	
The Mechanisms of Evolution	125-126, 130, 132	Chpt. 17, 19-20 as reqd	Chpt. 22-24	Chpt. 13 & 14	
The Evolution of Humans	128-129	Chpt. 20 as reqd	707-715	Chpt. 19	
Diet and Animal Nutrition	47, 112-16, 165-68	Chpt. 2 as reqd	834-839, 850-869	Chpt. 21	
Animal Transport Systems	48, 169-70	Chpt. 7 as reqd	871-885	Chpt. 23	
Gas Exchange in Animals	51, 171-72	Chpt. 3 as reqd	886-897	Chpt. 22	
Reproduction and Development	54-57, 90-94	Chpt. 12 as reqd	Chpt. 46, & 47 (in part)	Chpt. 27	
Homeostasis and Excretion	53, 104-106, 164	Chpt. 3 as reqd	Chpt. 44	pp. 425-426, chpt. 25-26	
Nerves, Muscles, and Movement	99-102, 118-21, 135, 137, 140-41	Chpt. 21 as reqd	Chpt. 48-49	Chpt. 28 & 30	
Animal Behavior	134,136, 138-139	Chpt. 22 as reqd	Chpt. 51	Chpt. 37	
Plant Science	107-110, 151-152	Chpt. 11 & 12 as reqd	Chpt. 35-39 as required	Chpt.17 & 31-32	
Applied Plant and Animal Science	144-150	Chpt. 11 as reqd	406-410, 794-799, chpt. 39 as required, 995	Chpt. 33	

Figures refer to page number unless indicated otherwise

TOPIC IN MANUAL	Miller & Levine 2000	National Geo. Soc. 2002	Purves *et al.* 2000	Raven & Johnson 2002	
Pathogens and Disease	Chpt. 17 & 44, pp. 421-423	Chpt.18-19, pp. 562,1055-1062	466-467, 533	Chpt. 33-34	
Defences Against Infectious Disease	Chpt. 45	1063-1076	Chpt. 19	Chpt. 57	
The Origin and Evolution of Life	Chpt. 13, 16	Chpt. 14	Chpt.1, 20, 23, & 57	pp. 15-16, chpt. 4	
The Mechanisms of Evolution	Chpt. 14	Chpt. 15	Chpt. 21-22	Chpt. 21-22	
The Evolution of Humans	Chpt. 34	Chpt. 16	Chpt. 24-25	Chpt. 23	
Diet and Animal Nutrition	Chpt. 39	Chpt. 35 (in part)	Chpt. 50	Chpt. 51	
Animal Transport Systems	Chpt. 41 (in part)	1007-1016	Chpt. 49	Chpt. 52	
Gas Exchange in Animals	Chpt. 40	1003-1006, 1020-1021	Chpt. 48	Chpt. 53	
Reproduction and Development	Chpt. 43	Chpt. 38	Chpt. 42-43	Chpt. 59-60	
Homeostasis and Excretion	pp. 30-31,664-665, chpt. 41 (in part)	1017-1019	Chpt. 40 & 51	Chpt. 58	
Nerves, Muscles, and Movement	Chpt. 37-38	Chpt. 34, 36	Chpt. 44-47	Chpt. 50, 54-55	
Animal Behavior	Chpt. 35	Chpt. 33	Chpt. 52-53	Chpt. 26-27	
Plant Science	Chpt. 23 & 25	Chpt. 23-24	Chpt. 34-36, 38	Chpt. 37-40, 42	
Applied Plant and Animal Science	Chpt. 24	Chpt. 13, pp. 620, 642-645, 680	Chpt. 37	Chpt. 41 & 43	

Figures refer to page number unless indicated otherwise

Curtis & Barnes 1994	Freeman 2002	Ghalayini 2000	Gould & Keeton 1996	Kent 2000	Mader 2001
420-421	495-98, 501-516, 534	N/A	Chpt. 20	Chpt. 15, pp. 364-69	Chpt. 29
Chpt. 33	Chpt. 46	Chpt. 15	Chpt. 15	326-333	Chpt. 42
5-6, 71-75, 366	Chpt. 1-4, 21 as reqd	Chpt. 24 (in part)	Chpt. 19	160, 438-441	Chpt. 20
Chpt. 19-21	Chpt. 22-24 as reqd	Chpt. 24 (in part)	Chpt. 17-18	442-447, 450-453	Chpt. 18-19
490-503	596-600	Chpt. 24 (in part)	N/A	454-461	Chpt. 21
Chpt. 29	Chpt. 40	Chpt. 12 & 26 (in part)	Chpt. 27	Chpt. 9	Chpt. 43
Chpt. 31	793-801	Chpt. 13 & 26 (in part)	Chpt. 30	118-133	Chpt. 41
Chpt. 30	786-795	Chpt. 14 & 26 (in part)	Chpt. 28	112-117	Chpt. 44
Chpt. 37-38	Chpt. 45	Chpt. 20	Chpt. 34	Chpt. 12	Chpt. 50
Chpt. 32-34	739-742, chpt. 39, 44	Chpt. 18-19, 26 (in part)	Chpt. 31	Chpt. 8	Chpt. 40, 45
Chpt. 35-36	Chpt. 42-43 as reqd	Chpt. 16-17	Chpt. 35-37	Chpt. 10, pp. 212-225	Chpt. 46-48
Chpt. 22	Chpt. 47	N/A	Chpt. 38	226-241	Chpt. 22
Chpt. 25, pp. 39-41	Chpt. 31-36 as reqd	Chpt. 23	Chpt. 22, 26, 29, 32	Chpt. 13, pp. 290-301	Chpt. 36-37, 39
Chpt. 42	639, 686, 703, chpt. 35 as reqd	N/A	Chpt. 32	302-313, 448-449, 538-543	Chpt. 38

Solomon et al. 2002	Starr & Taggart 2001	Tobin & Dusheck 2001	Towle 2002	Weem 2001
Chpt. 23, pp. 550-551	Chpt. 22, pp. 382, 400, 434-435	Chpt.12 & 20, p. 468	N/A	123-124
Chpt. 43	Chpt. 40	Chpt. 40	Chpt. 48	125-126, 214-219
Chpt. 17 & 20	Chpt. 17, 20-21	Chpt. 18	Chpt. 14	314-328
Chpt. 18-19	Chpt. 18-19	Chpt.16-17 (in part)	Chpt. 15-16	98-100, 339-342
Chpt. 21	Chpt. 27 (in part)	Chpt.17 (in part)	Chpt. 17	329-335
Chpt. 45	Chpt. 42	Chpt. 35	Chpt. 49	258-276, 431-438
Chpt. 42	Chpt. 39	Chpt. 37	Chpt. 47	439-444
Chpt. 44	Chpt. 41	Chpt. 38		127-131, 445-450
Chpt. 48-49	Chpt. 45	Chpt. 43	Chpt. 52	136-143, 204-209
Chpt. 46	Chpt. 33 (in part) & 43	Chpt. 34 (in part) & 39	Chpt. 5	132-136, 234-239
Chpt. 38, 40-41	Chpt. 34-36, 38	Chpt. 34 & 42	Chpt. 46 & 50	222-230, 278-292, 349-354, 364-368
Chpt. 50	Chpt. 47	Chpt. 29		346-348, 355-363
Chpt. 31-35	Chpt. 25, 29-31	Chpt. 30-31	Chpt. 29, 31-32	242-253
Chpt. 36	Chpt. 32	Chpt. 33	Chpt. 33	372-391

Using the Internet

The internet is a vast global network of computers connected by a system that allows information to be passed through telephone connections. When people talk about the internet they usually mean the **World Wide Web** (WWW). The WWW is a service that has made the internet so simple to use that virtually anyone can find their way around, exchange messages, search libraries and perform all manner of tasks. The internet is a powerful resource for locating information. Listed below are two useful articles giving information on use of the internet, together with examples of useful web sites.

- **Click Here: Biology on the Internet** Biol. Sci. Rev., 10(2) November 1997, pp. 26-29.
- **Using the Internet as a Supplemental Instructional Tool for Biology Teachers** The American Biology Teacher 62(3), March 2000, pp. 171-176.

Using the Biozone Website: www.thebiozone.com

The **Back** and **Forward** buttons allow you to navigate between pages displayed on a WWW site

The current **internet address (URL)** for the web site is displayed here. You can type in a new address directly into this space.

Tool bar provides a row of buttons with shortcuts for some commonly performed tasks, such as printing a page or 'refreshing' the page (i.e. making the page load again).

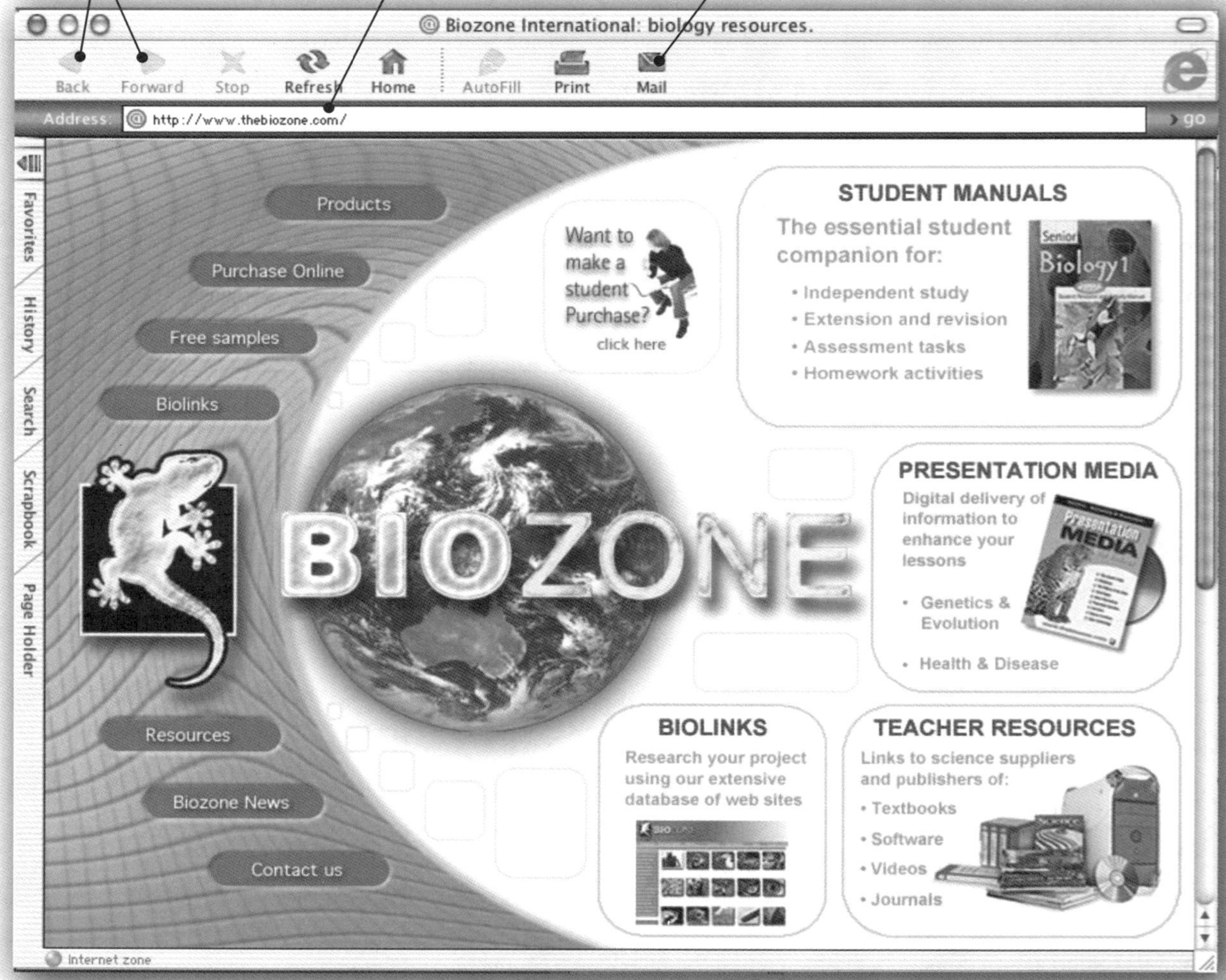

Searching the Net

The WWW addresses listed throughout the manual have been selected for their relevance to the topic in which they are listed. We believe they are good sites. Don't just rely on the sites that we have listed. Use the powerful 'search engines', which can scan the millions of sites for useful information. Here are some good ones to try:

Alta Vista:	**www.altavista.com**
Ask Jeeves:	**www.ask.com**
Excite:	**www.excite.com/search**
Google:	**www.google.com**
Go.com:	**www.go.com**
Lycos:	**www.lycos.com**
Metacrawler:	**www.metacrawler.com**
Yahoo:	**www.yahoo.com**

Biozone International provides a service on its web site that links to all internet sites listed in this manual. Our web site also provides regular updates with new sites listed as they come to our notice and defunct sites deleted. Our **BIO LINKS** page, shown below, will take you to a database of regularly updated links to more than 800 other quality biology web sites.

The **Resource Hub**, accessed via the homepage or publishers online, provides links to the supporting resources referenced in the manual and the *Teacher Resource Handbook*. These resources include *comprehensive* and *supplementary texts, biology dictionaries, computer software, videos,* and *science supplies*. These can be used to supplement and enhance your learning experience.

Click on each topic to see a list of all related biology links. Each topic has relevant subtopics to make searching easier and each link has a brief description.

Index of sub-topics on this page. Click on these to jump down to the desired section.

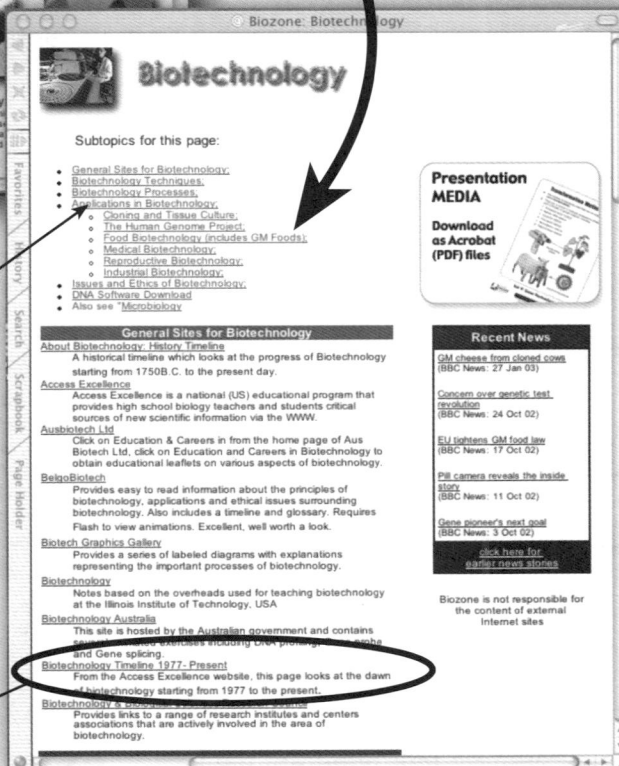

Click on the link to access the named site. The brief description tells you how the site may be of interest, as well as any country specific bias, if this is relevant.

International Baccalaureate Course

The IB biology course is divided into three sections: core, additional higher level material, and option material. All **IB candidates** must complete the **core** topics. Higher level students are also required to undertake Additional HL **(AHL)** material as part of the core. Options fall into three categories: those specific to standard level students **(OPT-SL)**, those specific to higher level students **(OPT-HL)** and those offered to both **(OPT-SL/HL)**. All candidates are required to study two options. All candidates must also carry out **practical work** and must participate in **the group 4 project**. In the guide below, we have indicated where the relevant material can be found: SB1 for Senior Biology 1 and SB2 for Senior Biology 2.

Topic	See manual

CORE: *(All Students)*

1   Cells

1.1   Cell theory. Viral structure. Cell sizes. Light and electron microscopy. SA:Volume ratio. Cell specialization. — SB1   Cell Structure, Cell Membranes and Transport

1.2   Prokaryotic cells: structure and function. — SB1   Cell Structure

1.3   Cell organelles. Plant vs animal cells. Prokaryotic vs eukaryotic cells. — SB1   Cell Structure

1.4   Membrane structure. Active and passive transport. Diffusion and osmosis. — SB1   Cell Membranes and Transport

1.5   Cell division and the origins of cancer. — SB1   Cell Structure

2   The chemistry of life

2.1   Elements of life. The properties and importance of water. — SB1   The Chemistry of Life

2.2   Structure and function of carbohydrates, lipids, and proteins. — SB1   The Chemistry of Life

2.3   Enzyme structure and function. — SB1   The Chemistry of Life

2.4   Nucleotides and the structure of DNA. — SB1   Molecular Genetics

2.5   Semi-conservative DNA replication. — SB1   Molecular Genetics

2.6   RNA and DNA structure. The genetic code. Transcription. Translation. — SB1   Molecular Genetics

2.7   Cellular respiration and ATP production. — SB1   Cellular Energetics

2.8   Biochemistry of photosynthesis. Factors affecting photosynthetic rates. — SB1   Cellular Energetics

3   Genetics

3.1   Eukaryote chromosomes. Karyotyping. Gene mutations and consequences. — SB1   Genes and Chromosomes

3.2   Meiosis and non-disjunction (Down syndrome). Law of segregation. — SB1   Genes and Chromosomes

3.3   Theoretical genetics: alleles and inheritance, sex linkage, pedigrees. — SB1   Inheritance

3.4   Genetic engineering and biotechnology: PCR, gel electrophoresis, DNA profiling, genetic screening. HGP. Transformation. GMOs. Gene therapy. Cloning. — SB1   Gene Technology

4   Ecology and evolution

4.1   Ecosystems. Food chains and webs. Trophic levels. Ecological pyramids. Carbon cycle. The role of decomposers. — SB1   Ecosystems, Energy Flow and Nutrient Cycles

4.2   Factors influencing population size. Population growth. Random sampling. Analyzing ecological data (mean & SD). — SB1   The Dynamics of Populations, Practical Ecology

4.3   Genetic variation. Sexual reproduction as a source of variation in species. Natural selection. Evolution in response to environmental change (e.g. antibiotic resistance in bacteria). — SB1   Genes and Chromosomes / SB2   Mechanisms of Evolution

4.4   The species concept. Classification of organisms. Binomial nomenclature. Five kingdom classification. Use of keys. — SB1   Classification

4.5   Human impact on the environment (e.g. greenhouse effect). Mitigation. — SB1   Human Impact and Conservation

5   Human health and physiology

5.1   Role of enzymes in digestion. Structure and function of the digestive system. — SB2   Diet and Animal Nutrition

5.2   Structure and function of the heart. The control of heart activity. Blood. — SB2   Animal Transport Systems

5.3   Pathogens and their transmission. Antimicrobial drugs. HIV/AIDS. — SB2   Pathogens and Disease

5.4   Role of skin as a barrier to infection. Role of phagocytic leukocytes. Antigens. Antibody production. Effects of HIV on the immune system. — SB2   Pathogens and Disease, Defence Against Infectious Disease

5.5   Ventilation systems. Control of breathing. — SB2   Gas Exchange

5.6   Principles of homeostasis. Control of blood glucose and body temperature. Role of the nervous and endocrine — SB2   Homeostasis and Excretion

systems in homeostasis. Role of the kidney in excretion and water balance.

5.7   Human reproduction: urinogenital systems. Role of hormones in birth and sexual development. Fertilization and embryonic development. The placenta. Contraception. Reproductive technologies and ethical issues. — SB2   Reproduction and Development

COMPULSORY: AHL Topics *(HL students only)*

6   Nucleic acids and proteins

6.1   DNA structure: nucleosomes, purines, pyrimidines. — SB1   Molecular Genetics

6.2   DNA replication including the role of enzymes and Okazaki fragments. — SB1   Molecular Genetics

6.3   Transcription and its control. Reverse transcriptase and its applications. — SB1   Molecular Genetics

6.4   The structure of tRNA and ribosomes. The process of translation. — SB1   Molecular Genetics

6.5   Protein structure and function. Fibrous and globular proteins. — SB1   The Chemistry of Life

6.6   Enzymes: induced fit model. Inhibition. Allostery in the control of metabolism. — SB1   The Chemistry of Life

7   Cell respiration and photosynthesis

7.1   Structure and function of mitochondria. Biochemistry of cellular respiration. — SB1   Cellular Energetics

7.2   Chloroplasts, the biochemistry of photosynthesis, chemiosmosis. Action and absorption spectra. Limiting factors. — SB1   Cellular Energetics

8   Genetics

8.1   Meiosis, and the process of crossing over. Recombination. Mendel's laws. — SB1   Genes and Chromosomes

8.2   Dihybrid crosses in unlinked genes. Using the chi-squared test in genetics. — SB1   Inheritance

8.3   Autosomes and sex chromosomes. Crossing over. Dihybrid crosses involving autosomal linkage. — SB1   Inheritance

8.4   Polygenic inheritance. — SB1   Inheritance

9   Human reproduction

9.1   Testis structure and spermatogenesis. Ovarian structure and oogenesis. — SB2   Reproduction and Development

9.2   Fertilization. The role of HCG in early development. Structure and function of the placenta, including its hormonal role. — SB2   Reproduction and Development

10   Defence against infectious disease

10.1 Blood clotting. Clonal selection. Acquired immunity. Antibodies. Monoclonal antibodies. Vaccination. — SB2   Defence Against Infectious Disease

11   Nerves, muscles, and movement

11.1 Structure and function of the human nervous system. Motor neuron structure. Action potential. Synapses. — SB2   Nerve, Muscles and Movement

11.2 Locomotion in animals. Roles of nerves, muscles, and bones in movement. Joints. Skeletal muscle and contraction. — SB2   Nerve, Muscles and Movement

12   Excretion

12.1 The need for excretion. The relationship between waste products and habitat. — SB2   Homeostasis and Excretion

12.2 Structure and function of the human kidney. Urine production. Kidney dialysis. — SB2   Homeostasis and Excretion

13   Plant science

13.1 Plant diversity. — SB1   Classification

Structure of a dicot plant. Function and distribution of tissues in stem, root, and leaves. Xerophytes and hydrophytes. — SB2   Plant Science

International Baccalaureate Course *continued*

Topic		See manual
13.2	Support in terrestrial plants. Transport in angiosperms: active ion uptake by roots, transpiration, translocation. Food storage.	SB2 Plant Science
13.3	Dicot flowers. Pollination and fertilization. Seeds: structure, germination, dispersal.	SB2 Plant Science

OPTION: OPT - SL *(SL students only)*

A   Diet and human nutrition

A.1	Main constituents of diet. A balanced diet. Interpretation of dietary information.	SB2 Diet and Animal Nutrition
A.2	The source and use of lipids, proteins, and carbohydrates in the diet. Energy requirements. Importance of fiber, vitamins, and minerals in the diet.	SB2 Aspects covered in Diet and Animal Nutrition
A.3	Health problems associated with high fat diets. Balanced diet. Malnutrition. Food additives. Food handling.	SB2 Aspects covered in Diet and Animal Nutrition

B   Physiology of exercise

B.1	Structure and function of the human skeleton. Muscle structure and contraction.	SB2 Nerve, Muscles and Movement
B.2	Human nervous system. Sensory and motor neurons. Synaptic transmission. Control of muscle function by the brain.	SB2 Aspects covered in Nerve, Muscles and Movement
B.3	Respiration and exercise intensity. Roles of myoglobin and adrenaline. Oxygen debt and lactate in muscle fatigue.	SB2 Nerve, Muscles and Movement, Gas Exchange
B.4	Principles of training. Measuring fitness. Training and the cardiovascular system.	SB2 Nerve, Muscles and Movement
B.5	Exercise induced injuries and treatment.	*Not yet covered*

C   Cells and energy

C.1	Protein structure and function. Fibrous and globular proteins.	SB1 The Chemistry of Life
C.2	Enzymes: induced fit model. Inhibition. Allostery in the control of metabolism.	SB1 The Chemistry of Life
C.3	Biochemistry of cellular respiration.	SB1 Cellular Energetics.
C.4	The biochemistry of photosynthesis including chemiosmosis. Action and absorption spectra. Limiting factors.	SB1 Cellular Energetics

OPTION: OPT - SL/HL *(SL and HL students)*

D   Evolution

D.1	Prebiotic experiments. Origins of prokaryotic cells. Endosymbiotic theory.	SB2 The Origins and Evolution of Life
D.2	Lamarck's theory of evolution by inheritance of acquired characteristics. Darwin-Wallace theory of evolution by natural selection. Other theories for the origins of life.	SB2 Aspects covered in The Origins and Evolution of Life, Mechanisms of Evolution
D.3	Evidence for evolution. Fossil dating. Modern day examples of evolution.	SB2 The Origins and Evolution of Life
D.4	Primate features. Hominid features. Genetic and cultural evolution.	SB2 The Evolution of Humans
D.5	Sources of mutations. Gene and chromosomal mutations (PKU, CF, Klinefelter syndrome). Gene pools and evolution. Speciation (migration, isolating mechanisms, adaptation). Gradualism and punctuated equilibrium.	SB1 Molecular Genetics SB2 Mechanisms of Evolution, also see SB1: Classification for the species concept
D.6	The Hardy-Weinberg principle. Transient and balanced polymorphism.	SB2 Mechanisms of Evolution

E   Neurobiology and behavior

E.1	Innate behavior. Behavior patterns in animals and the role of natural selection.	SB2 Animal Behavior
E.2	Sensory receptors. Structure and function of the human eye.	SB2 Nerves, Muscles and Movement
E.3	Innate behavior and its role in survival. The reflex arc: cranial & spinal reflexes. Brain structure. Taxes and kineses.	SB2 Nerves, Muscles and Movement, Animal Behavior
E.4	Types of learned behavior.	SB2 Animal Behavior
E.5	Social behavior and organization. The role of altruism in sociality.	SB2 Animal Behavior
E.6	Structure and function of the ANS. Conscious control of reflexes.	SB2 Nerves, Muscles and Movement
E.7	Neurotransmitters and synapses. Hormones as painkillers. Effects of drugs on synaptic transmission.	SB2 Nerves, Muscles and Movement

Topic		See manual
	Behavioral effects of excitatory and inhibitory psychoactive drugs.	*This area not covered.*

F   Applied plant and animal science

F.1	Plant productivity. Human control of plant growth. Farming methods and their implications. Pest control.	SB2 Applied Plant and Animal Science
F.2	Evaluation of animal rearing techniques (including misuse of growth promoters). Artificial insemination. Animal health.	SB2 Aspects covered in Applied Plant and Animal Science
F.3	Fertilization. Plant growth regulators. Auxin & plant growth. Micropropagation.	SB2 Applied Plant and Animal Science
F.4	Gene banks and genetic diversity. Production of cereal crops & livestock.	SB2 Applied Plant and Animal Science
F.5	Uses of transgenic techniques in agriculture (including ethics).	SB1 Aspects covered in Gene Technology
F.6	Monocot flowers. Wind and insect pollinated flowers. Asexual reproduction and artificial propagation. Phytochrome.	SB2 Plant Science Applied Plant and Animal Science

G   Ecology and conservation

G.1	Factors affecting plant and animal distribution. Ecological niche and the competitive exclusion principle. Analysis of ecological data (student t-test).	SB1 Ecosystems, Practical Ecology
G.2	Species interactions: competition, predation, herbivory, parasitism, and mutualism. Trophic levels. Ecological pyramids. Ecological succession and climax communities.	SB1 Ecosystems, Energy Flow and Nutrient Cycles, The Dynamics of Populations
	Plant productivity (includes calculating gross and net production, and biomass).	SB2 Applied Plant and Animal Science
G.3	Conservation of biodiversity. The Simpson diversity index. Human impact on ecosystems. Conservation strategies and the role of international agencies.	SB1 Ecosystems, Human Impact and Conservation

G.4-G.5 is extension for HL only

G.4	Details of the nitrogen cycle including the role of bacteria.	SB1 Energy Flow and Nutrient Cycles
	Use of fertilizers, crop rotation to increase nitrogen fertility of soil.	SB2 Applied Plant and Animal Science
G.5	Human impact: ozone depletion, water pollution (e.g. raw sewage, BOD), acid rain. Biomass as a source of fuel.	SB1 Human Impact and Conservation

OPTION: OPT - HL *(HL students only)*

H   Further human physiology

H.1	Hormones and their modes of action. Hypothalamus and pituitary gland. Control of thyroxine and ADH secretion.	SB2 Homeostasis and Excretion
H.2	Digestion and digestive enzymes. The role of bile in lipid digestion.	SB2 Diet and Animal Nutrition
H.3	Structure of villus. Absorption of nutrients and transport of digested food.	SB2 Diet and Animal Nutrition
H.4	The structure and function of the liver (including role in nutrient processing). Production and secretion of bile.	SB2 Homeostasis and Excretion, also Diet and Animal Nutrition
H.5	The cardiac cycle and control of heart rhythm. Lymph and the transport role of lymphatic system. Atherosclerosis and coronary heart disease.	SB2 Animal Transport System
H.6	Gas exchange: oxygen dissociation curves and the Bohr shift. Ventilation rate and exercise. Effects of lung cancer and asthma. Breathing at high altitude.	SB2 Gas Exchange

Practical Work *(All students)*

Practical work consists of short and long term investigations, and an interdisciplinary project (The Group 4 project). Also see the "Guide to Practical Work" on the last page of this introductory section.

Short and long term investigations

Investigations should reflect the breadth and depth of the subjects taught at each level, and include a spread of content material from the core, options, and AHL material, where relevant.

The Group 4 project

All candidates must participate in the group 4 project. In this project it is intended that students analyze a topic or problem suitable for investigation in each of the science disciplines offered by the school (not just in biology). This project emphasizes the processes involved in scientific investigations rather than the products of an investigation.

Advanced Placement Course

The AP biology course is designed to be equivalent to a college introductory biology course. It is to be taken by students after successful completion of first courses in high school biology and chemistry. In the guide below, we have indicated where the relevant material can be found: SB1 for Senior Biology 1 and SB2 for Senior Biology 2. Because of the general nature of the AP curriculum document, the detail provided here is based on the content in the manuals.

Topic	See manual

Topic I: Molecules and Cells

A   Chemistry of life

1	The chemical & physical properties of water. The importance of water to life.	SB1 The Chemistry of Life
2	The role of carbon. Structure and function of carbohydrates, lipids, nucleic acids, and proteins. The synthesis and breakdown of macromolecules.	SB1 The Chemistry of Life, Molecular Genetics, Cell membranes and Transport
3	The laws of thermodynamics and their relationship to biochemical processes. Free energy changes.	SB1 The Chemistry of Life
4	The action of enzymes and their role in the regulation of metabolism. Enzyme specificity. Factors affecting enzyme activity. Applications of enzymes.	SB1 The Chemistry of Life

B   Cells

1	Comparison of prokaryotic and eukaryotic cells, including their evolutionary relationships.	SB1 Cell Structure, SB2 The Origin and Evolution of Life
2	Membrane structure: fluid mosaic model. Active and passive transport.	SB1 Cell Membranes and Transport
3	Structure and function of organelles. Organization of cell function. Comparison of plant and animal cells. Cell size and surface area: volume ratio.	SB1 Cell Structure, Cell Membranes and Transport
4	Mitosis and the cell cycle. Mechanisms of cytokinesis. Cancer (tumor formation) as the result of uncontrolled cell division.	SB1 Cell Structure

C   Cellular energetics

1	Nature and role of ATP. Anabolic and catabolic processes. Chemiosmosis.	SB1 Cellular Energetics
2	Structure and function of mitochondria. Biochemistry of cellular respiration, including the role of oxygen in energy yielding pathways. Anaerobic generation of ATP.	SB1 Cellular Energetics
3	Structure and function of chloroplasts. The biochemistry of photosynthesis. Adaptations for photosynthesis in different environments.	SB1 Cellular Energetics

Topic II: Heredity and Evolution

A   Heredity

1	The importance of meiosis in heredity. Gametogenesis. Similarities and differences between gametogenesis in animals and plants.	SB1 Genes and Chromosomes SB2 Reproduction, Plant Science
2	Structure of eukaryotic chromosomes. Heredity of genetic information.	SB1 Genes and Chromosomes
3	Mendel's laws. Inheritance patterns.	SB1 Inheritance

B   Molecular genetics

1	RNA and DNA structure and function. Eukaryotic and prokaryotic genomes.	SB1 Molecular Genetics
2	Gene expression in prokaryotes and eukaryotes. The *Lac* operon model.	SB1 Molecular Genetics
3	Causes of mutations. Gene mutations (e.g. sickle cell disease). Chromosomal mutations (e.g. Down syndrome).	SB1 Genes and Chromosomes
4	Viral structure and replication.	SB2 Pathogens and Disease
5	Nucleic acid technology and applications. legal and ethical issues.	SB1 Gene Technology

C   Evolutionary biology

1	The origins of life on Earth. Prebiotic experiments. Origins of prokaryotic cells. Endosymbiotic theory.	SB2 The Origins and Evolution of Life
2	Evidence for evolution: comparative anatomy, vestigial organs, biochemistry, biogeography. Dating of fossils.	SB2 The Origins and Evolution of Life
3	Mechanisms of evolution: natural selection, speciation, macroevolution. The species concept.	SB2 Mechanisms of Evolution SB1 Classification

Topic III: Organisms and Populations

A   Diversity of organisms

1	Evolutionary patterns: major body plans of plants and animals.	SB1 Classification
2	Diversity of life: representative members from the five kingdoms Monera (=Prokaryotae), Fungi, Protista (=Protoctista), Animalia and Plantae.	SB1 Classification
3	Phylogenetic classification. Binomial nomenclature. Five kingdom classification. Use of dichotomous keys.	SB1 Classification
4	Evolutionary relationships: genetic and morphological characters. Phylogenies.	SB1 Classification SB2 The Origin and Evolution of Life

B   Structure and function of plants and animals

1	Plant and animal reproduction and development (includes humans). Adaptive significance of reproductive features and their regulation.	SB2 Reproduction, Plant Science
2	Organization of cells, tissues & organs.	SB1 Cell Structure
	The structure and function of animal and plant organ systems. Adaptive features that have contributed to the success of plants and animals in occupying particular terrestrial niches.	SB2 Plant Science, Diet and Animal Nutrition, Animal Transport Systems, Homeostasis and Excretion, Gas Exchange
3	Plant and animal responses to environmental cues. The role of hormones in these responses.	SB2 Animal Behavior, Applied Plant and Animal Science

C   Ecology

1	Factors influencing population size. Population growth curves.	SB1 The Dynamics of Populations
2	Abiotic and biotic factors: effects on community structure and ecosystem function. Trophic levels: energy flows through ecosystems and relationship to trophic structure. Nutrient cycles.	SB1 Ecosystems, Energy Flow and Nutrient Cycles
3	Human influence on biogeochemical cycles: (e.g. use of fertilizers).	SB1 Human Impact and Conservation

Practical Work

Integrated practicals as appropriate: see Senior Biology 1: Skills in Biology. Also see the page "Guide to Practical Work" on the last page of this introductory section.

Guide to Practical Work

A practical or laboratory component is an essential part of any biology course, especially at senior level. It is through your practical sessions that you are challenged to carry out experiments drawn from many areas within modern biology. Both AP and IB courses have a strong practical component, aimed at providing a framework for your laboratory experience. Well executed laboratory and field sessions will help you to understand problems, observe accurately, make hypotheses, design and implement controlled experiments, collect and analyze data, think analytically, and communicate your findings in an appropriate way using tables and graphs. The outline below provides some guidelines for AP and IB students undertaking their practical work. Be sure to follow required safety procedures at all times during practical work.

International Baccalaureate Practical Work

The practical work carried out by IB biology students should reflect the depth and breadth of the subject syllabus, although there may not be an investigation for every syllabus topic. All candidates must participate in the group 4 project, and the internal assessment (IA) requirements should be met via a spread of content from the core, options and, where relevant, AHL material. A wide range of IA investigations is possible: *short laboratory practicals and longer term practicals or projects, computer simulations, data gathering and analysis exercises, and general laboratory and field work.*

Suitable material, or background preparation, for this component can be found in this manual and its companion title, Senior Biology 2.

College Board's AP® Biology Lab Topics

Each of the 12 set laboratory sessions in the AP course is designed to complement a particular topic area within the course. The basic structure of the lab course is outlined below:

LAB 1:   Diffusion and osmosis
Overview: To investigate diffusion and osmosis in dialysis tubing. To investigate the effect of solute concentration on water potential (ψ) in plant tissues.

Aims: An understanding of passive transport mechanisms in cells, and an understanding of the concept of water potential, solute potential, and pressure potential, and how these are measured.

LAB 2:   Enzyme catalysis
Overview: To investigate the conversion of hydrogen peroxide to water and oxygen gas by catalase.

Aims: An understanding of the effects of environmental factors on the rate of enzyme catalyzed reactions.

LAB 3:   Mitosis and meiosis
Overview: To use prepared slides of onion root tips to study plant mitosis. To simulate the phases of meiosis by using chromosome models.

Aims: Recognition of stages in mitosis in plant cells and calculation of relative duration of cell cycle stages. An understanding of chromosome activity during meiosis and an ability to calculate map distances for genes.

LAB 4:   Plant pigments and photosynthesis
Overview: To separate plant pigments using chromatography. To measure photosynthetic rate in chloroplasts.

Aims: An understanding of Rf values. An understanding of the techniques used to determine photosynthetic rates. An ability to explain variations in photosynthetic rate under different environmental conditions.

LAB 5:   Cell(ular) respiration
Overview: To investigate oxygen consumption during germination (including the effect of temperature).

Aims: An understanding of how cell respiration rates can be calculated from experimental data. An understanding of the relationship between gas production and respiration rate, and the effect of temperature on this.

LAB 6:   Molecular biology
Overview: To investigate the basic principles of molecular biology through the transformation of *E.coli* cells. To investigate the use of restriction digestion and gel electrophoresis.

Aims: An understanding of the role of plasmids as vectors, and the use of gel electrophoresis to separate DNA fragments of varying size. An ability to design appropriate experimental procedures and use multiple experimental controls.

LAB 7:   Genetics of organisms
Overview: Use *Drosophila* to perform genetic crosses. To collect and analyze the data from these crosses.

Aims: An understanding of the independent assortment of two genes and an ability to determine if genes are autosomal or sex linked from the analysis of the results of multigeneration genetic crosses.

LAB 8:   Population genetics and evolution
Overview: To learn about the Hardy-Weinberg law of genetic equilibrium and study the relationship between evolution and changes in allele frequency.

Aims: An ability to calculate allele and genotype frequencies using the Hardy-Weinberg formula. An understanding of natural selection and other causes of microevolution.

LAB 9:   Transpiration
Overview: To investigate transpiration in plants under controlled conditions. To examine the organization of plant stems and leaves as they relate to this.

Aims: An understanding of the effects of environmental variables on transpiration rates. An understanding of the relationship between the structure and function of the tissues involved.

LAB 10:   Physiology of the circulatory system
Overview: To measure (human) blood pressure and pulse rate under different conditions. To analyze these variables and relate them to an index of fitness. To investigate the effect of temperature on heart rate in *Daphnia*.

Aims: An understanding of blood pressure and pulse rate, and their measurement and significance with respect to fitness. An understanding of the relationship between heart rate and temperature in a poikilotherm.

LAB 11:   Animal behavior
Overview: To investigate responses in pillbugs (woodlice). To investigate mating behavior in fruit flies.

Aims: To understand and describe aspects of animal behavior. To understand the adaptiveness of appropriate behaviors.

LAB 12:   Dissolved oxygen & aquatic primary productivity
Overview: To measure & analyze dissolved oxygen concentration in water samples. To measure and analyze the primary productivity of natural waters or lab cultures.

Aims: An understanding of primary productivity and its measurement. To use a controlled experiment to investigate the effect of changing light intensity on primary productivity.

Pathogens and Disease

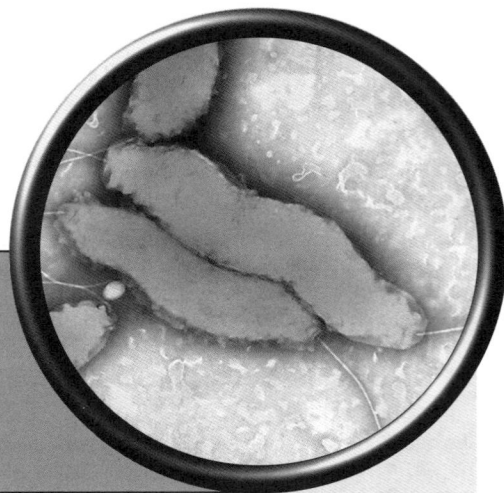

IB SL

Complete nos:
*1, 6-8, 12-14, 30-31
Extension: 2-5, 9-11,
22-27, 32 as
appropriate*

IB HL

Complete nos:
*1, 6-8, 12-14, 30-31
Extension: 2-5, 9-11,
22-27, 32 as
appropriate*

IB Options

Not applicable
to core

AP Biology

Not applicable
to AP biology

Learning Objectives

□ 1. Compile your own glossary from the **KEY WORDS** displayed in **bold type** in the learning objectives below.

The nature of disease

Classification of disease *(page 18)*

□ 2. Explain what is meant by the terms **health, disease**, **infection, symptom**. Distinguish between **acute** and **chronic diseases**.

□ 3. Explain, giving an example of each, how diseases can be classified. Recognize the following categories of disease: **infectious, non-infectious, deficiency, inherited** (genetic), **mental, degenerative, social, self-inflicted**. Understand that some diseases will fall into more than one category.

Patterns of disease *(pages 20-21)*

□ 4. Recognise patterns of disease distribution: **pandemic, epidemic**, and **endemic diseases**. Distinguish between **etiology** and **epidemiology**. Explain the role health statistics (including **prevalence, incidence, morbidity**, and **mortality**) in predicting and managing disease outbreaks.

□ 5. Describe and explain differences in the standards of health in developed and developing countries.

Treatment of disease *(pages 44-47)*

□ 6. Understand the role of the following in the treatment or prevention of disease: **antibiotics**, therapeutic **anti-microbial drugs** (other than antibiotics), **hygiene, diet**. Discuss these the context of a case study (#15-21).

Infectious disease *(pages 18-19)*

□ 7. Recall the difference between **infectious** and **non-infectious disease**. Define: **pathogen** and, if required, **infection**. Identify one example of a disease caused by a pathogenic member of each of the following taxa: **bacteria, viruses, fungi, protozoa, flatworms**, and **roundworms** (cross ref. with case studies).

□ 8. List six modes of **transmission** for some named pathogens. Appreciate the role of (improved) hygiene and sanitation in controlling some infectious diseases.

Bacterial diseases *(pages 22-26, 44-47)*

□ 9. Recognize that bacteria are widespread and only a small proportion ever cause disease. Identify the ways in which pathogenic bacteria cause disease. Giving examples, identify the ways in which bacterial diseases are transmitted. Relate the type and incidence of bacterial disease to the prevailing social conditions.

□ 10. Describe factors affecting bacterial **pathogenicity**, including: features of the cell wall and capsule, **toxin** production, **infectivity**, and **invasiveness**.

□ 11. Distinguish between different types of bacterial toxins and their actions: **exotoxins** (e.g. *Staphylococcus*) and **endotoxins** (e.g. *Salmonella*). Recognize **enterotoxins** as exotoxins that affect the gastrointestinal tract.

□ 12. With reference to **disinfectants, antiseptics**, and **antibiotics**, explain how bacterial pathogens are controlled and treated.

□ 13. Understand why antibiotics are not effective against viruses. Identify the ways in which different antibiotics work against specific bacteria. Describe the role of antibiotics in medicine and discuss the current problems associated with their use.

□ 14. Describe the cause, transmission, and effects of one bacterial disease affecting humans. You could choose from the case studies below (#15-21), or use an example of a locally occurring disease.

Case study: tuberculosis (TB)

□ 15. Describe the causes and modes of transmission of TB. Assess the global importance of TB and understand its history in the human population, including reference to its **prevalence**, decline, and reemergence.

□ 16. Discuss the factors important in the prevalence of TB in a population. Define the term **carrier** and explain the importance of carriers in the spread of TB.

□ 17. Discuss the treatment of TB, including the significance of increasing antibiotic resistance in *Mycobacterium*. Describe the roles of social, economic, and biological factors in the control and prevention of TB.

Contamination of food and water

□ 18. Identify factors important in transmitting food and water-borne pathogens. Examples spread by the **fecal-oral route** include: *Salmonella* (e.g. *Salmonella typhi*), *Vibrio cholerae*, and *E. coli* (including *E. coli* O157:H7).

Case study: food poisoning

□ 19. Describe the causes and modes of transmission of **salmonellosis** and/or **staphylococcal food poisoning**. Describe factors governing the occurrence, prevention, and severity of these diseases.

Case study: cholera

□ 20. Describe the agent involved and modes of transmission of **cholera**. Assess the past and current global importance of cholera and relate its distribution to factors such as levels of sanitation and general poverty.

□ 21. Describe the roles of social, economic, and biological factors in the control and prevention of cholera. Explain clearly how cholera of different severities is treated.

Fungal diseases *(page 27)*

□ 22. Only a few fungi are pathogenic to human and most of the diseases they cause tend to be superficial diseases of the skin and nails. List and describe some common fungal diseases, identifying the pathogen in each case.

Protozoan diseases *(pages 28-29)*

☐ 23. *Background:* Describe the nature of protozoa (ciliates, amoebae, sporozoans, and flagellates). Explain how some pathogenic **protozoans** are also parasites with part of their life cycle occurring within a human.

Case study: malaria

☐ 24. Describe the agent involved and modes of transmission of **malaria**. Assess the global importance of malaria and describe factors in its distribution.

☐ 25. Describe the roles of social, economic, and biological factors in the treatment, control, and prevention of malaria. Comment on the adequacy of these methods with reference to the difficulties associated with developing drugs against protozoans.

Multicellular pathogens *(pages 30-31)*

*NOTE: A number of different types of worm infect humans and cause disease. Most are **endoparasites** responsible for a variety of debilitating and sometimes life-threatening illnesses.*

☐ 26. Describe the disease caused by each of the following, including reference to the mode of transmission:
  • Flatworms, e.g. hydatid tapeworm, *Schistosoma*.
  • Roundworms, e.g. *Ascaris*, hookworm (*Necator)*, and the nematodes that cause trichinosis and elephantiasis.

*NOTE: Insects and other arthropods are major vectors of disease, even when they do not cause disease directly. Often they are **ectoparasites**, carrying infective particles (e.g. viruses) and transmitting them via their mouthparts.*

☐ 27. Describe a modern example of an insect-carried infection of humans. Name some ectoparasites and the conditions or diseases for which they are responsible.

Viral diseases *(pages 32-39 also see pages 64-65)*

☐ 28. Describe the host-specific, parasitic nature of viral pathogens. Using a named example or examples, describe how **viral diseases** are transmitted and how they infect a host and cause disease.

☐ 29. Identify some of the globally important viral diseases and their causative agents. Using illustrative examples, describe the role of **vaccination** in the past and present control of viral disease.

Case study: HIV/AIDS

☐ 30. Describe the cause, transmission, and social implications of **HIV/AIDS**. In your account:
  • Assess the global importance of HIV/AIDS and describe factors in its distribution and future spread.
  • Identify the role of social, economic, and biological factors in treating, controlling, and preventing AIDS.
  • Discuss the economic impact of the disease on the countries where incidence rates are very high.

☐ 31. Identify stages in the development of an HIV infection, including the effect of HIV on the immune system (cross ref. with 'Defense Against Infectious Disease').

☐ 32. Describe the probable origins of the two strains of HIV as cross species transfers (**zoonoses**).

Emerging diseases *(pages 40-43)*

☐ 33. Explain what is meant by an **emerging disease**. Giving an example, identify factors important in the emergence, spread, and **virulence** of an emerging disease.

☐ 34. Describe the nature of **prion diseases**, identifying the feature that distinguishes them from other pathogens. Describe how prions are thought to cause disease. Give examples of prion diseases, describing their mode of transmission, the incubation period, and the mortality.

Textbooks

See the 'Textbook Reference Grid' on pages 8-9 for textbook page references relating to material in this topic.

Supplementary Texts

See pages 5-6 for additional details of these texts:

■ Clegg, C.J., 2002. **Microbes in Action**, (John Murray), chpt 1-5, and chpt 10.

■ Fullick, A., 1998. **Human Health and Disease** (Heinemann), pp. 2-26, 36-53 as required.

■ Freeland, P., 1999. **Microbes, Medicine and Commerce** (Hodder & Stoughton), pp. 37-42, 102-108.

■ Hudson, T. & K. Mannion, 2001. **Microbes and Disease** (Collins), pp. 48-69, 82-85.

■ Murray, P. & N. Owens, 2001. **Behaviour and Populations** (Collins), pp. 72-95.

Periodicals

See page 6 for details of publishers of periodicals:

STUDENT'S REFERENCE

■ **War on Disease** National Geographic 201(2) February 2002, pp. 4-31. *An excellent update on the global importance of a range of infectious diseases. A great overview for students and teachers.*

■ **Koch's Postulates** Biol. Sci. Rev., 15(3) February 2003, pp. 24-25. *Koch's postulates and the diagnosis of infectious disease.*

■ **Food / How Safe?** National Geographic, May 2002, pp. 2-31. *An excellent account of the issue of food safety and bacterial contamination of food.*

■ **HIV and AIDS Update** Biol. Sci. Rev., 14(1) Sept. 2001, pp. 37-40. *A summary of the current state of knowledge on HIV/AIDS.*

■ **Search for a Cure** National Geographic 201(2) February 2002, pp. 32-43. *A current account of the global status of the AIDS epidemic, and an examination of the measures to stop it.*

■ **New Medicines for the Developing World** Biol. Sci. Rev., 14(1) Sept. 2001, pp. 22-26. *The challenges of controlling and treating infectious disease in the developing world.*

■ *Campylobacter jejuni* Biol. Sci. Rev., 15(1) Sept. 2002, pp. 26-28. *An account of the diseases caused by Campylobacter, an increasingly common contaminant. Preventative measures are discussed.*

■ **The White Plague** New Scientist (Inside Science), 9 Nov. 2002. *The causes and nature of TB, an update on the global incidence of this disease, and a discussion of the implications of increasing drug resistance to TB treatment.*

■ **Malaria** Biol. Sci. Rev., 15(1) Sept. 2002, pp. 29-33. *An account of the the world's most important parasitic infection of humans. The parasite's life cycle, disease symptoms, control and prevention, and future treatment options are all discussed.*

■ **Finding and Improving Antibiotics** Biol. Sci. Rev. 12(1) Sept. 1999, pp. 36-38. *Antibiotics, their production & testing, and the search for new drugs.*

TEACHER'S REFERENCE

■ **The New Polio** New Scientist, 7 June 2003, pp. 40-43. *An account of the causes, occurrence, and spread of West Nile fever in the US, and its disturbing similarity to post polio syndrome.*

■ **Epidemiology: Teaching the Fundamentals** The American Biology Teacher, 62(1), Jan. 2000, pp. 8-17. *Using computer simulations to model patterns of infection and spread of disease.*

■ **Is TB is your Curriculum?** The American Biology Teacher, 64(4), April 2002, pp. 280-284. *A look at TB: symptoms, epidemiology, and treatment.*

■ **Anthrax: A Guide for Biology Teachers** The American Biology Teacher, 64(1), Jan. 2002, pp. 11-19. *A synopsis of the cause, symptoms, presentation, prevention, and treatment of anthrax.*

■ **The Prion Diseases** Scientific American, Jan. 1995, pp. 30-37. *Prions are now recognized as the cause of a number of infectious diseases.*

■ **Hope in a Vial** Sci. American, June 2002, pp. 28-35. *The search for an AIDS vaccine, plus current research and the status of global infection rates. Also see the HIV special in the issue: 8 Feb. 2003.*

■ **To Kill a Superbug** New Scientist, 13 Feb. 1999, pp. 34-37. *New technology to counter the increasing antibiotic resistance in bacteria.*

■ **The Challenge of Antibiotic Resistance** Scientific American, March 1998, pp. 32-39. *The rise in antibiotic resistance: how it arises and the threat it poses to the treatment of bacterial disease.*

Internet

See pages 10-11 for details of how to access **Bio Links** from our web site: **www.thebiozone.com**. From Bio Links, access sites under the topics:

GENERAL BIOLOGY ONLINE RESOURCES > **Online Textbooks and Lecture Notes** • An on-line biology book • Learn.co.uk ... *and others*

HEALTH & DISEASE: • CDC Disease links • WHO/OMS: Health topics > **Infectious Diseases**: • Cholera and epidemic dysentery • Disease causing bacteria • HIV InSite ... *and many others* **Prevention and Treatment**: • Antibiotic resistance • Antimicrobial agents ... *and many others*

Software and video resources are now provided in the Teacher Resource Handbook

The Nature of Disease

K 1

Disease is more difficult to define than **health**, which is described as a state of complete physical, mental, and social well-being. A disease is usually associated with particular **symptoms** that help to define and diagnose it. The term **disease** is used to describe a condition whereby part or all of an organism's normal physiological function is upset. All diseases, with the exception of some mental diseases, can be classified as **physical diseases** (i.e. diseases that cause permanent or temporary damage to the body). Physical diseases can be subdivided into two major groups: **infectious diseases** caused by an infectious agent (**pathogen**) and **non-infectious diseases** (most of which are better described as disorders). Non-infectious diseases are often not clearly the result of any single factor. Environmental, genetic, and biological factors may all contribute to their development. Diseases can be further categorized into major subgroups according to their principal cause (outlined below). However, many diseases fall into more than one category, e.g. Alzheimer's disease and some cancers.

Infectious Disease

Pathogens and Parasites

Pathogens are organisms that cause disease. Some pathogens are also parasites and seek to exploit the rich food resources of our bodies and use them as incubators for their own reproduction. The invasion of the body by pathogens is called **infection**. Pathogens can be classified as microorganisms or macroorganisms.

Infectious microorganisms

The majority of pathogens are classified as microorganisms (organisms not visible to the naked eye) and many are parasites that include bacteria, fungi and viruses. These microorganisms (sometimes called microbes) can be:

- **Exogenous**: originating from outside the body.
- **Endogenous**: originating from inside the body.

Mature HIV viruses

Fungal nail infection

Infectious macroorganisms

Humans are exploited by a range of macroorganisms (organisms visible to the naked eye). These are classified as:

- **Endoparasites**: parasites that live inside the body.
- **Ectoparasites**: parasites that live freely on or attached to the outside the body.

Macroorganisms can cause disease as a direct result of their activity, or they can serve as **vectors** for the transmission of other infectious agents.

The head of *Taenia solium*, a parasitic tapeworm

Mouthparts of the hookworm, *Necator americanus*

Non-Infectious Disease

Inherited Diseases

Some diseases result from inherited malfunctions in a body system and have no external cause. Defective genes may cause the failure of a body system throughout a person's life, or the onset of disease may occur later in life. Examples include cystic fibrosis, multiple sclerosis, Alzheimer's, and Huntington's disease.

Deficiency Diseases

Deficiency diseases are caused by an inadequate or unbalanced diet, or by over eating. Examples include obesity, rickets, scurvy, marasmus, and kwashiorkor.

Degenerative Diseases

Degenerative diseases are caused by ageing and the inability of the body to carry out effective repairs and regeneration. Examples include osteoarthritis, Alzheimer's disease, and many cancers.

Mental Disorders

The term mental disorder encompasses a range of diseases that affect a persons thoughts, memory, emotions, and personal behavior. Examples include Alzheimer's, vCJD, schizophrenia, and depression.

Social Diseases

Social diseases include a wide range of disorders that are influenced by living conditions and personal behavior. They may or may not be caused by an infectious agent. Examples include pneumonia caused by overcrowded living conditions, sexually transmitted diseases, and lung cancer due to smoking.

1. Briefly explain the following terms:

   (a) **Pathogen**: _____

   (b) **Health**: _____

   (c) **Disease**: _____

   (d) An **exogenous** infectious microorganism: _____

   (e) An **ectoparasite**: _____

2. Outline the **key difference** between an infectious disease and a non-infectious disease:

   _____

   _____

Transmission of Disease

RA 2

The human body is no different to that of other large animals in that it is under constant attack by a wide range of organisms wanting to penetrate its defenses. Once inside us, these organisms will seek to reproduce and exploit us for food. Some of these organisms may be pathogens. Pathogens may be transferred from one individual to another by a number of methods (below). The transmission of infectious diseases can be virtually eliminated by observing appropriate personal hygiene procedures, providing adequate sanitation, and chlorinating drinking water.

Portals of Entry

Respiratory tract
The mouth and nose are major entry points for pathogens, particularly airborne viruses, which are inhaled from other people's expelled mucus.
Examples: diphtheria, meningococcal meningitis, tuberculosis, whooping cough, influenza, measles, German measles (rubella), chickenpox.

Gastrointestinal tract
The mouth is one of the few openings where we deliberately place foreign substances into our body. Food is often contaminated with microorganisms, but most of these are destroyed in the stomach.
Examples: cholera, typhoid fever, mumps, hepatitis A, poliomyelitis, bacillary dysentery, salmonellosis.

Urinogenital openings
The urinogenital openings provide entry points for the pathogens responsible for sexually transmitted infections (STIs) and other opportunistic infections (i.e. thrush).
Examples: gonorrhea, syphilis, HIV, and *E. coli* (a cause of urinary tract infections).

Breaking the skin surface
The skin provides an effective barrier to the entry of most pathogens. However, a cut or abrasion will allow easy entry for pathogens. Some parasites and pathogens have adaptive features that allow them to penetrate the skin surface.
Examples: tetanus, gas gangrene, bubonic plague, hepatitis B, rabies, malaria, leptospirosis, and HIV.

The Body Under Assault

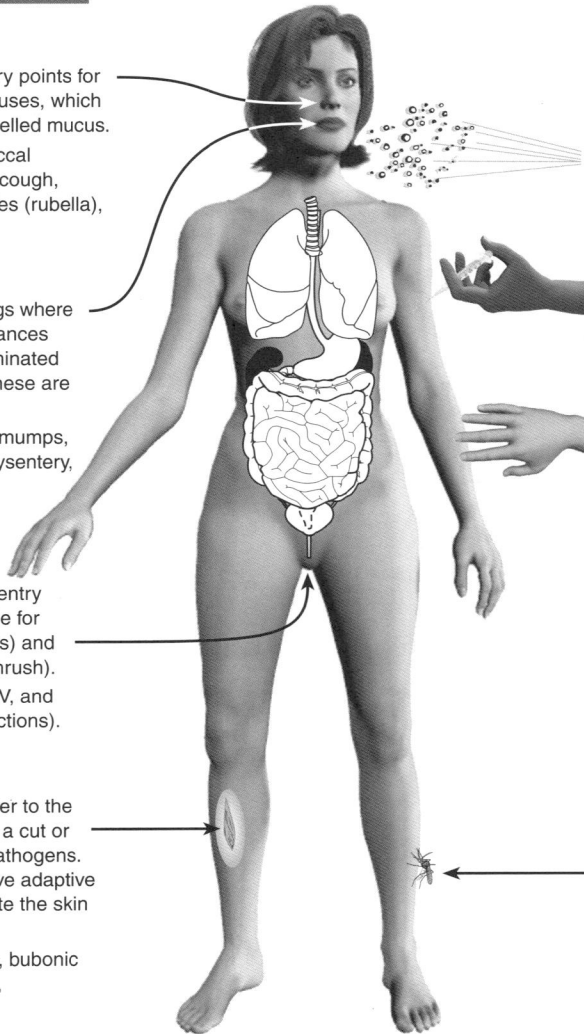

Modes of Transmission

Contact transmission
The agent of disease may occur by contact with other infected humans or animals:

Droplet transmission: Mucus droplets are discharged into the air by coughing, sneezing, laughing, or talking within a radius of 1 m.

Indirect contact: Includes touching objects that have been in contact with the source of infection. Examples include: eating utensils, drinking cups, bedding, toys, money, and used syringes.

Direct contact: Direct transmission of an agent by physical contact between its source and a potential host. Includes touching, kissing, and sexual intercourse. May be person to person, or between humans and other animals.

Vehicle transmission
Agents of disease may be transmitted by a medium such as food, blood, water, intravenous fluids (e.g., drugs), and air. Airborne transmission refers to the spread of fungal spores, some viruses, and bacteria that are transported on dust particles.

Animal vectors
Some pathogens are transmitted between hosts by other animals. Bites from arthropods (e.g., mosquitoes, ticks, fleas, and lice) and mammals (e.g., rodents) may introduce pathogens, while flies can carry pathogens on their feet.

1. Describe three personal hygiene practices that would minimize the risk of transmitting an infectious disease:

    (a) _____

    (b) _____

    (c) _____

2. Identify the common **mode of transmission** and the **portal of entry** for the following pathogens:

    (a) Protozoan causing malaria: _____

    (b) Tetanus bacteria: _____

    (c) Cholera bacteria: _____

    (d) Common cold virus: _____

    (e) Tuberculosis bacteria: _____

    (f) HIV (AIDS) virus: _____

    (g) Gonorrhea bacteria: _____

Patterns of Disease

Diseases present in low levels of a population at any time are known as **endemic** diseases. Occasionally there may be a sudden increase in the prevalence of a particular disease. On a local level this is known as an **outbreak**. Such an increase in prevalence on a national scale is called an **epidemic**. An epidemic occurs when an infectious disease spreads rapidly through a population and affects large numbers of people. One example is influenza, epidemics of which are relatively common and occur every two to three years. On rare occasions an epidemic disease will spread to other countries throughout the world. This is known as a **pandemic**. Examples of diseases that are known to have caused pandemics are bubonic plague, cholera, tuberculosis, HIV/AIDS, and influenza. **Epidemiology** is the study of the occurrence and the spread of a disease. Epidemiologists gather data on the number of infected people (**morbidity**) and the number of people that have died (**mortality**) within a population. These data help to provide information on the **incidence** (number of new cases) and **prevalence** (number of infected people) of the disease within the population at any given time. **Etiology** is the study of the cause of a particular disease. Etiology can assist in pinpointing the origin of new diseases as they arise in populations.

The HIV pandemic in Africa

1984

1989

1994

Percentage of
population infected
20 - 36%
10 - 20%
5 - 10%
1 - 5%
0 - 1%

Source: UNAIDS

1999

The figure above shows the spread of HIV through Africa as part of the current global pandemic. More than 36 million people are infected with HIV worldwide and 70% of those infected live in sub-Saharan Africa. In this region, seven countries have an adult prevalence of 20% or higher, including Botswana where 36% of the population is infected.

The *Vibrio cholerae 01* epidemic in Latin America

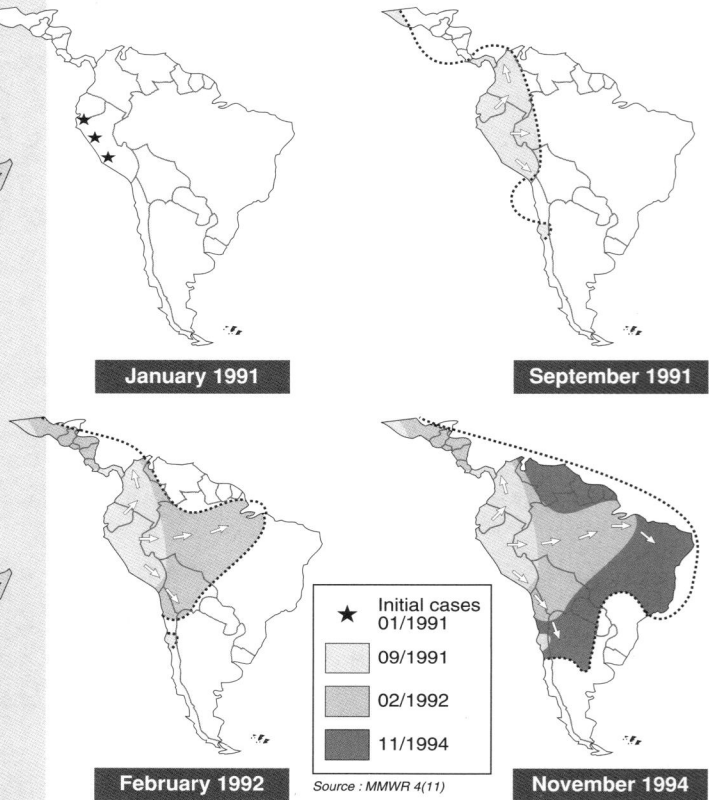

January 1991

September 1991

February 1992

★ Initial cases
01/1991
09/1991
02/1992
11/1994

Source : MMWR 4(11)

November 1994

Cholera had not been reported in Latin America for over a century before the initial outbreaks occurred in January, 1991. Cholera is transmitted through ingestion of food and beverages contaminated with feces, or by bathing in fecally contaminated water. By the time the epidemic began to subside in 1994, more than 1 million cases and nearly 10 000 deaths had been reported. Death rates were high as a result of inadequate provision for oral rehydration.

1. Explain the following terms providing an example in each case:

(a) **Epidemic:** _____

_____

(b) **Pandemic:** _____

_____

(c) **Endemic:** _____

_____

(d) **Outbreak:** _____

_____

Health statistics collected by epidemiologists and etiologists are used by various health authorities to identify patterns of disease within their country. They also enable the effectiveness of health policies and practices to be monitored. The World Health Organization (WHO) gathers data on an international basis to identify patterns of global importance.

Figure 1. Mean body mass index (BMI) for all ages by survey year
England (1993-1999)

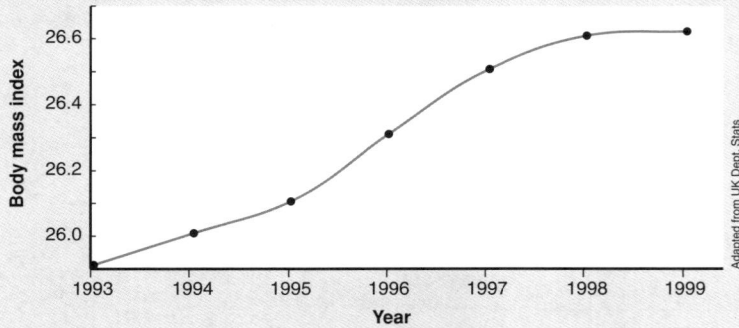

Adapted from UK Dept. Stats

Figure 2. Reported cases of *Haemophilus influenzae* Type B.
England and Wales (1989-1995)

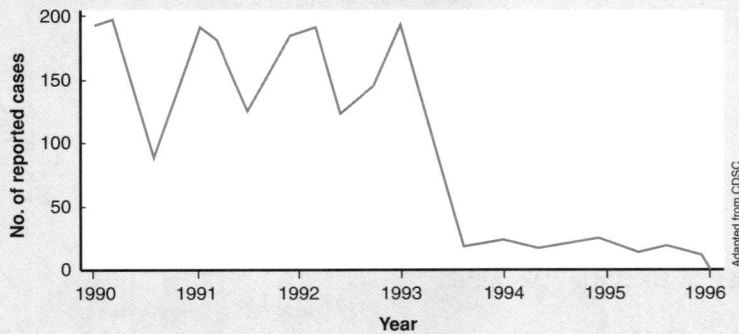

Adapted from CDSC

Figure 3. The causes of death in developed and developing countries, 1998

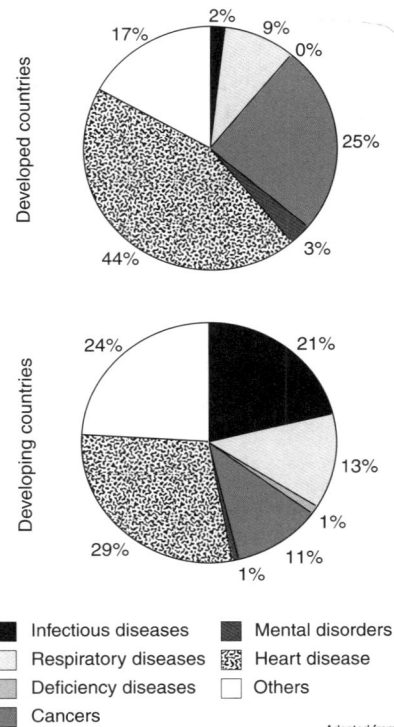

Developed countries: 2%, 9%, 0%, 25%, 3%, 44%, 17%

Developing countries: 21%, 13%, 1%, 11%, 1%, 29%, 24%

- ■ Infectious diseases
- □ Respiratory diseases
- ▨ Deficiency diseases
- ■ Cancers
- ▨ Mental disorders
- ▨ Heart disease
- □ Others

Adapted from WHO

2. Distinguish between **epidemiology** and **etiology**: _____

_____

_____

3. Explain why the **incidence** and **prevalence** are investigated when a disease begins to spread through a community:

_____

_____

_____

4. Outline the likely cause of the trend shown in Figure 1: _____

_____

5. (a) Suggest a probable reason for the pattern of reported cases of *Hemophilus influenzae* prior to 1993:

_____

(b) Suggest a possible cause for the decline in the incidence of *Hemophilus influenzae* after 1993:

_____

6. (a) Identify **two** differences between the cause of death between developed and developing countries:

_____

_____

(b) Suggest **two** reasons for these differences:

_____

_____

Bacterial Diseases

RA 2

Of the many species of bacteria that exist in the world, relatively few cause disease in humans, other animals, plants or any other organisms. The diagram below shows four adaptive features that help bacteria infect host tissue and cause disease. Bacteria infect a host to exploit the food potential of the host's body tissues. The fact that this exploitation causes disease is not in the interest of the bacteria – a healthy host is better than a sick one. Some well-known human diseases caused by bacteria are illustrated in the diagram below. The natural reservoir (source of infection) of a disease varies from species to species – ranging from humans, insects, and other animals, to sewage and contaminated water.

Bacterial Infection

Enzymes are released that digest the connective tissue of the host, allowing the spread of infection

Body tissue

Fibrin: Fibrous threads of protein are deposited when blood clots. This is designed to limit movement of pathogens in infected areas.

Fimbriae: Fine, threadlike extensions from the bacterial cell, called fimbriae, enable the bacteria to attach to the mucous membranes and thus allows it to concentrate its attack on nearby tissues of the host.

Bacterium

Enzymes are released that break down fibrin, allowing the bacteria greater freedom of movement.

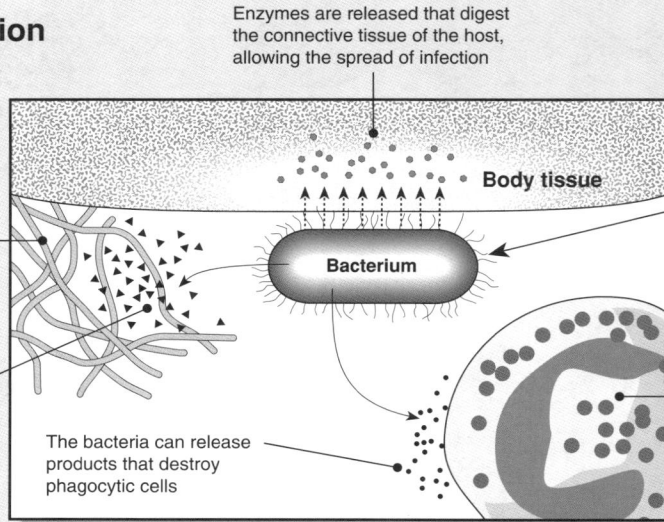

The bacteria can release products that destroy phagocytic cells

Phagocyte: These white blood cells are very effective in identifying and destroying foreign cells such as pathogens.

Examples of Bacterial Diseases

Streptococcus bacteria
These bacteria can cause scarlet fever, sore throats (pharyngitis) and a form of pneumonia. They exist as chains or in pairs. They cause more illness than any other group of bacteria.

Vibrio cholerae
These bacteria cause cholera, a disease common in Asia, caused by a temporary lapse in sanitation (where drinking water is contaminated with human waste).

Salmonella bacteria
This group is not divided up into species, but comprises over 2,000 varieties (called *serovars*). They cause gastrointestinal diseases such as typhoid.

Staphylococcus aureus
This bacterium inhabits noses, the surface of skin, and is also found growing in cured meats such as ham. One of the most common causes of food poisoning, it produces many toxins that increase its ability to invade the body or damage tissue. It has the ability to develop antibiotic resistance very quickly and for this reason is a common problem in hospitals.

Enterobacter cloacae
This bacterium can cause urinary tract infections and is widely distributed in humans and animals, as well as in water, sewage and soil. It is a common source of hospital-acquired infection.

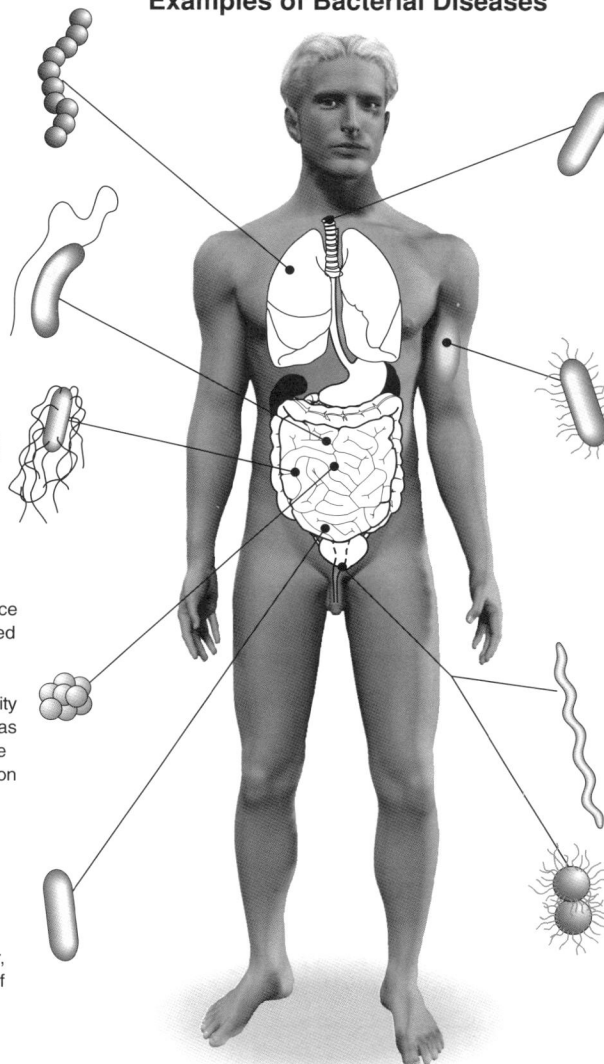

Hemophilus influenzae
Despite its name, this bacterium does not cause influenza. This organism inhabits the mucous membranes of the upper respiratory tract and mouth. It causes the most common form of meningitis in young children and is a frequent cause of earaches. It can also cause epiglottitis, bronchitis and pneumonia.

Yersinia pestis
This bacterium caused the Black Death or the bubonic plague of medieval Europe. Fleas from urban rats and ground squirrels transmit the bacteria among animals and to humans. Direct contact with animals and respiratory droplets from infected people can be involved in transmission.

Treponema pallidum
This spirochete bacterium causes syphilis and is transmitted through sexual intercourse. The helical shape allows it to move by a corkscrew rotation.

Neisseria gonorrhoeae
This bacterium exists in a paired arrangement and causes the sexually transmitted disease called gonorrhea. The fimbriae enable the organism to attach to the mucous membranes of the vagina and urethra of the penis.

Properties of Exotoxins

Exotoxins released

Bacterial source
Exotoxins are proteins produced by **gram-positive** bacteria and released as part of normal bacterial growth and metabolism.

Toxicity and lethal dose
Exotoxins are amongst the most toxic compounds known. Due to their solubility they can diffuse easily into the circulatory system and are then easily transported around the body. They are unstable and can usually (but not always) be destroyed easily by heat. However, they have a high infectivity and a very small dose causes symptoms in the infected person.

Diseases
Gas gangrene, tetanus, botulism, diphtheria, scarlet fever, and various staphylococcal infections.

Properties of Endotoxins

Dead bacterium releases endotoxins

Bacterial source
Endotoxins are part of the cell wall of **gram-negative** bacteria. They are composed primarily of lipids (in contrast to exotoxins, which are proteins). Endotoxins exert their effect only when the bacteria die.

Toxicity and lethal dose
Although endotoxins are less toxic than exotoxins, they are heat stable and withstand autoclaving ($121°C$ for one hour). The dose required to produce symptoms is relatively high, but the immune system cannot neutralize them with antitoxins.

Diseases
Typhoid fever, urinary tract infections, meningococcal meningitis, and *Salmonella* food poisoning.

1. Define the following terms:

   (a) **Natural reservoir** of disease-causing bacteria: _____

   _____

   (b) **Exotoxin**: _____

   _____

   (c) **Endotoxin**: _____

   _____

2. **Complete** the following table summarizing the features of selected bacterial diseases. Use the illustration at the bottom of the facing page to assist you (for disease symptoms, consult a textbook, good dictionary, or an encyclopedia):

Bacteria	Natural reservoir	Diseases caused	Symptoms
(a) *Streptococcus* bacteria	Infected humans	Scarlet fever, sore throats, a form of pneumonia	Scarlet fever: fever, red tongue, rash on neck, chest, abdomen and limbs. Pneumonia: inflamed lungs with fluid in air sacs. Sore throat: inflammation of the throat.
(b) *Vibrio cholerae*			
(c) *Salmonella* bacteria	Common inhabitants of the guts of many animals (esp. poultry and cattle)		
(d) *Staphylococcus aureus*	Infected humans		
(e) *Enterobacter cloacae*			
(f) *Clostridium botulinum*		Botulism (a form of food poisoning)	
(g) *Yersinia pestis*			
(h) *Bacillus anthracis*		Anthrax	

A 2

Cholera

Cholera is an acute intestinal infection caused by the bacterium *Vibrio cholerae*. The disease has a short incubation period, from one to five days. The bacterium produces an enterotoxin that causes a copious, painless, watery diarrhea that can quickly lead to severe dehydration and death if treatment is not promptly given. Most people infected with *V. cholerae* do not become ill, although the bacterium is present in their feces for 7-14 days. When cholera appears in a community it is essential to take measures against its spread. These include: **hygienic disposal of human feces**, provision of an adequate supply of **safe drinking water**, **safe food handling and preparation** (e.g. preventing contamination of food and cooking food thoroughly) , and **effective general hygiene** (e.g. hand washing with soap). Cholera has reemerged as a global health threat after virtually disappearing from the Americas and most of Africa and Europe for more than a century. Originally restricted to the Indian subcontinent, cholera spread to Europe in 1817 in the first of seven pandemics. The current pandemic (illustrated below) shows signs of increasing rather than abating.

Symptoms

More than 90% of cases are of mild or moderate severity and are difficult to distinguish from other types of acute diarrhea. Less than 10% of ill people develop typical cholera with signs of moderate or severe dehydration.

Treatment

Most cases of diarrhea can be treated by giving a solution of oral rehydration salts. During an epidemic, 80-90% of diarrhea patients can be treated by oral rehydration alone, but patients who become severely dehydrated must be given intravenous fluids. In severe cases, antibiotics can reduce the volume and duration of diarrhea and reduce the presence of *V. cholerae* in the feces.

Transmission

Cholera is spread by contaminated water and food. Sudden large outbreaks are usually caused by a contaminated water supply. *Vibrio cholerae* is often found in the aquatic environment and is part of the normal flora of brackish water and estuaries. Human beings are also one of the reservoirs of the pathogenic form of *Vibrio cholerae*.

The Cholera Pandemic: Cases and Deaths (2001)

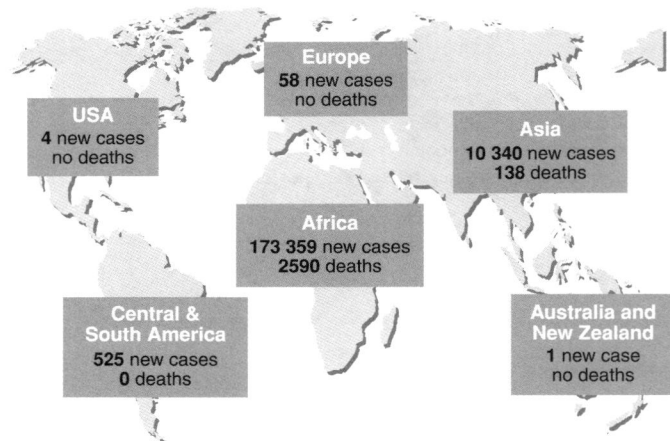

Europe
58 new cases
no deaths

USA
4 new cases
no deaths

Asia
10 340 new cases
138 deaths

Africa
173 359 new cases
2590 deaths

Central & South America
525 new cases
0 deaths

Australia and New Zealand
1 new case
no deaths

Source: WHO

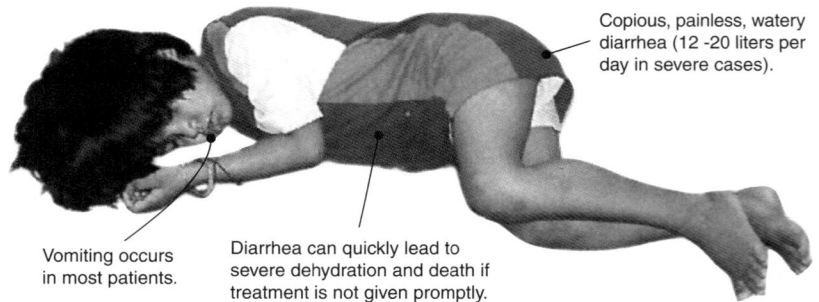

Copious, painless, watery diarrhea (12 -20 liters per day in severe cases).

Vomiting occurs in most patients.

Diarrhea can quickly lead to severe dehydration and death if treatment is not given promptly.

1. Name the pathogen that causes cholera: _____

2. List the symptoms of cholera: _____
_____

3. Explain why these symptoms are so dangerous if not treated quickly: _____
_____

4. State how cholera is transmitted between people: _____
_____

5. Describe the effective treatment of cholera at the following stages in the progression of the disease:

   (a) Mild onset of dehydration: _____

   (b) Severe symptoms: _____

6. Identify the risk factors associated with the incidence of cholera and relate these to social and economic conditions:
_____
_____
_____

A 2

Tuberculosis

Tuberculosis (TB) is a contagious disease caused by the *Mycobacterium tuberculosis* bacterium (**MTB**). The breakdown in health services in some countries, the spread of HIV/AIDS, and the emergence of **multidrug-resistant TB** are contributing to the increasingly harmful impact of this disease. In 1993, the World Health Organization (WHO) responded to the growing pandemic and declared TB a global emergency. By 1998, the WHO estimated that about a third of the world's population were already infected with MTB. They estimate that 8 million new cases are being added annually and that TB causes about 2 million deaths each year (note that in the figures given below, only *notified cases* are reported). If controls are not strengthened, it is anticipated that between 2002 and 2020, approximately 1000 million people will be newly infected, over 150 million people will get sick, and 36 million will die from TB.

Infection and Transmission

TB is a contagious disease, and is spread through the air when infectious people cough, sneeze, talk, or spit. A person needs only to inhale a small number of MTB to be infected.

Left untreated, each person with active TB will infect on average between 10 and 15 people every year. People infected with MTB will not necessarily get sick with the disease; the immune system 'walls off' the MTB which can lie dormant for years, protected by a thick waxy coat. When the immune system is weakened, the chance of getting sick (showing symptoms) is greater.

Symptoms

TB usually affects the lungs, but it can also affect other parts of the body, such as the brain, the kidneys, and the spine.

The general symptoms of TB disease include weakness and nausea, weight loss, fever, and night sweats. The symptoms of TB of the lungs include coughing, chest pain, and coughing up blood. The bacteria can spread from the bronchioles to other body systems, where the symptoms depend on the part of the body that is affected.

Treatment

TB is treated with an aggressive antibiotic regime. Since the early 1990s, the WHO has recommended the DOTS (Directly Observed Therapy, Short-course) strategy to control TB worldwide. This program improves the proportion of patients successfully completing therapy (taking their full course of antibiotics). Proper completion of treatment is the most effective way in which to combat increasing drug resistance.

Estimated TB Incidence Rates in 2001 (per 100 000)

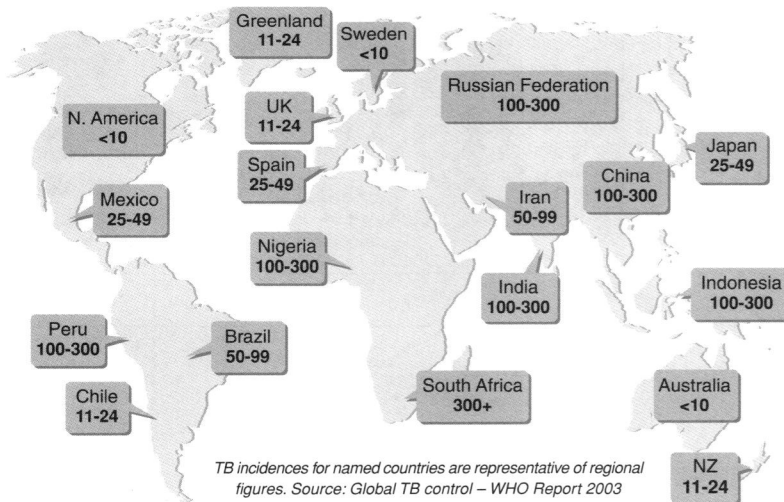

TB incidences for named countries are representative of regional figures. Source: Global TB control – WHO Report 2003

The Pathogenesis of Tuberculosis

The series below illustrates stages in MTB infection.

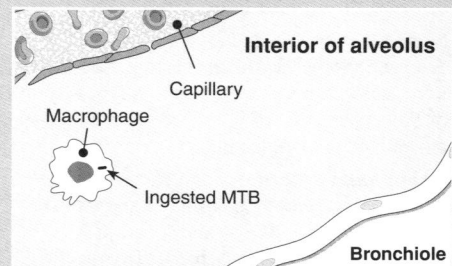

MTB enter the lung and are ingested by macrophages (phagocytic white blood cells).

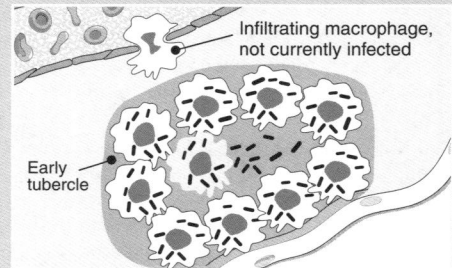

The multiplying bacteria cause the macrophages to swell and rupture. The newly released bacilli infect other macrophages. At this stage a tubercle may form and the disease may lie dormant.

Eventually the tubercle ruptures, allowing bacilli to spill into the bronchiole. The bacilli can now be transmitted when the infected person coughs.

1. Name the pathogen that causes tuberculosis (TB): _____

2. Explain how MTB may exist in a dormant state in a person for many years without causing disease symptoms:

_____

_____

3. State how TB is transmitted between people: _____

_____

4. Suggest how some strains of MTB have acquired **multi-drug resistance**: _____

_____

Foodborne Disease

K 1

Foodborne disease is caused by consuming contaminated foods or beverages. More than 250 food and water borne diseases have been identified. The symptoms and severity of these diseases vary according to the infectious agent, however diarrhea and vomiting are two universal symptoms. Food and water borne diseases cause an estimated 76 million illnesses in the USA alone. Food poisoning is a common cause of gastroenteritis; the inflammation of the stomach and intestines. Food poisoning is a term used for any gastrointestinal illness with sudden onset, usually accompanied by stomach pain, diarrhea, and vomiting, caused by eating **contaminated food**. Food poisoning usually results from food contaminated with viruses, or bacteria or their toxins. It may also result from contamination of food or water by chemicals such as nitrates.

Common Sources of Bacterial Food Poisoning

Salmonella Infections

Most serotypes of *Salmonella* bacteria are pathogenic. **Endotoxins** released from dead bacteria are a likely (but not proven) cause of the symptoms associated with infection.

Salmonella enteritidis can spread to humans via a variety of foods of animal origin (especially poultry products) and is the cause of **salmonellosis** (*Salmonella* food poisoning). Typical symptoms include fever, accompanied by diarrhea and abdominal cramps.

Salmonella typhi is a highly pathogenic *Salmonella* serotype and causes the life threatening disease, **typhoid fever**. *S.typhi* lives in humans and is shed in the feces. Transmission occurs through the ingestion of food or drink that has been handled by a person shedding the bacterium, or when water used to prepare of wash food is contaminated with sewage containing the pathogen. Recovered patients can become carriers and continue to shed the bacteria and spread infection. Typhoid fever is common in most regions of the world except in industrialized nations such as the USA, Canada, and western Europe.

E. coli Gastroenteritis

Escherichia coli is the most common form of infantile and travellers' diarrhea in developing countries. *E. coli* is the most abundant microbe in the intestinal tract and is normally harmless. However, certain strains are pathogenic and have specialized fimbriae allowing them to bind to the intestinal epithelial cells. They also release **exotoxins** which cause the production of copious watery diarrhea and symptoms similar to mild cholera. *E. coli* infection is caused by poor sanitation and can be very difficult to avoid in developing countries.

Staphylococcus aureus

S. aureus is a normal inhabitant of human nasal passages. From here, it can contaminate the hands, where it may cause skin lesions and/or contaminate food. Contaminated food held at room temperature will rapidly produce a population of about 1 million bacteria per gram of food and enough **exotoxin** to cause illness. Unusually, the toxin is heat stable and can survive up to 30 minutes of boiling. Reheating the contaminated food may destroy the bacteria but not the toxin itself.

Fecal contamination of the hands at meal times is a common cause of gastroenteritis.

Sharing food and utensils may transmit foodborne pathogens between individuals.

Inadequate supply of clean drinking water is a major problem in many parts of the world.

1. Define **gastroenteritis**: _____

2. List three ways in which food can become contaminated by *E. coli*: _____
   _____

3. Describe why food poisoning is more prevalent in developing countries: _____
   _____

4. Outline the basic precautions that should be taken with drinking water when travelling to developing countries:
   _____
   _____

5. (a) List the symptoms of salmonellosis: _____
   _____

   (b) Identify the method of transmission of this disease: _____

6. Explain why reheating food will still cause food poisoning if the food is contaminated with *Staphylococcus aureus*:
   _____
   _____

Fungal Diseases

The study of fungi (molds, yeasts, and fleshy fungi) is called **mycology**. All fungi are chemoheterotrophs, requiring organic compounds for energy and carbon. Most fungi are saprophytes, and are found in the soil and water, where they decompose organic matter using extracellular enzymes. Of the 100 000 species of fungi, only about 100 species are pathogenic to humans and other animals, although thousands of fungal species are pathogenic to plants. Any fungal infection is called a **mycosis**. They are generally **chronic** (long-lasting) infections because fungi grow slowly. Fungal infections are divided into three groups according to the degree of tissue involvement and the mode of entry into the host. Characteristics of these groups are summarized below. Some of these infections (e.g. candidiasis) can also be classed opportunistic, because they occur when the host is immune depressed or weakened in some way.

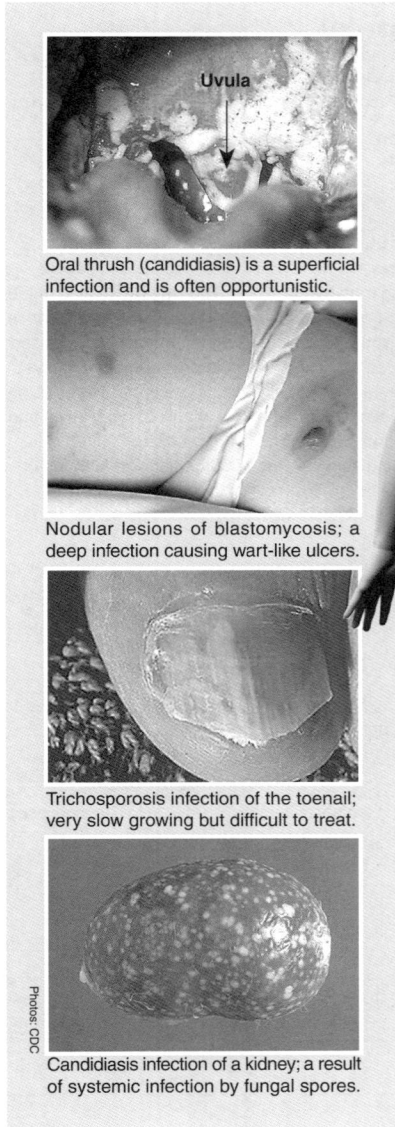

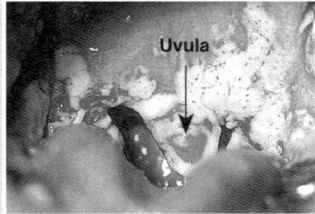

Uvula

Oral thrush (candidiasis) is a superficial infection and is often opportunistic.

Nodular lesions of blastomycosis; a deep infection causing wart-like ulcers.

Trichosporosis infection of the toenail; very slow growing but difficult to treat.

Candidiasis infection of a kidney; a result of systemic infection by fungal spores.

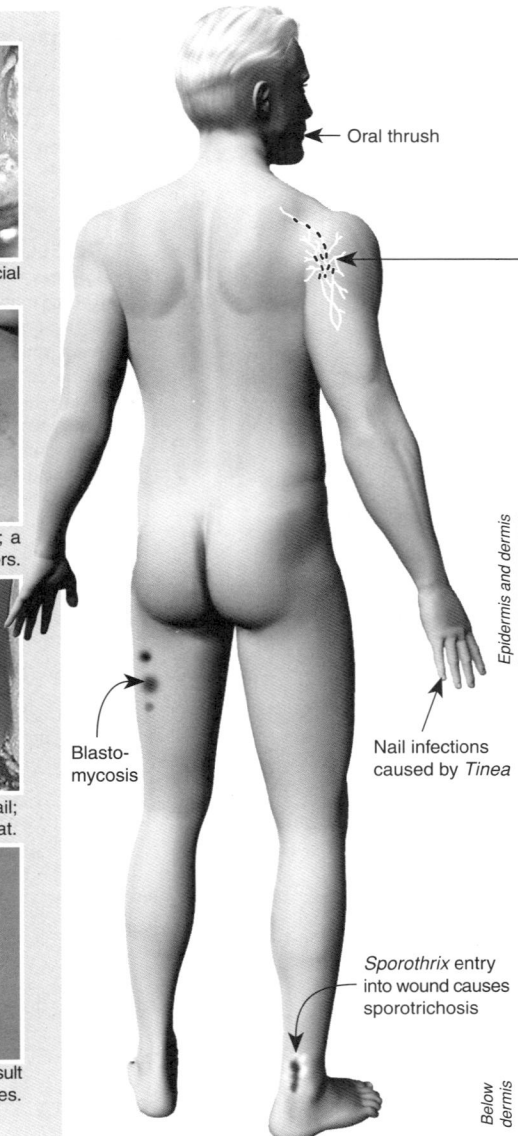

Photos: CDC

Oral thrush

Systemic infection

Infection occurring deep inside the body, affecting internal organs, such as the lungs, bones, lymph nodes, heart, and urinary tract. Often starting in the lungs and spreading throughout the body.

Depth of tissue affected: Internal tissues.

Transmission: Usually through inhalation of spores.

Examples: Histoplasmosis; a disease endemic to northern and central USA and parts of South America and Africa. Blastomycosis; a disease affecting various internal organs as well as the skin.

Cutaneous (superficial) infection

Infection affecting the skin, hair, nails, genital organs, and the inside of the mouth.

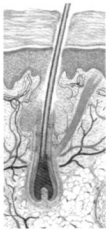

Epidermis and dermis

Depth of tissue affected: Superficial (affecting epidermis and dermis). Some more persistent infections (e.g. of the toenails) require long treatment with systemic, oral antifungal drugs.

Transmission: By contact with an infected person or spores.

Examples: Candidiasis (thrush) and *Tinea* (ringworm and athlete's foot)

Blasto-mycosis

Nail infections caused by *Tinea*

Subcutaneous infection

Rare infections caused by direct implantation of spores into the skin via a scratch or puncture wound.

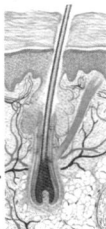

Depth of tissue affected: Subcutaneous i.e. beneath the dermis, affecting the layer of fatty connective tissue beneath the skin.

Transmission: Contact with plant material or soil (gardeners are at risk).

Examples: Sporotrichosis is the most common. Other conditions of this type occur mainly in tropical countries.

Sporothrix entry into wound causes sporotrichosis

Below dermis

1. Distinguish between cutaneous and subcutaneous fungal infections, identifying why subcutaneous infections are rarer:

_____

_____

2. Suggest which individuals would be at greatest risk from systemic fungal infections and why: _____

_____

_____

3. Explain why fungal infections tend to be **chronic**: _____

_____

4. Suggest how the spread of athlete's foot (*Tinea pedis*) can be limited by thorough drying of the feet: _____

_____

Protozoan Diseases

RA 2

Protozoa are one-celled, eukaryotic organisms that belong to the Kingdom Protista. Among the protozoans, there are many variations on cell structure. While most inhabit water and soil habitats, some are part of the natural microbiota of animals (i.e. they are microorganisms that live on or in animals). Relatively few of the nearly 20 000 species of protozoans cause disease; those that do are often highly specialized, intracellular parasites with complex life cycles involving one or more hosts. Under certain adverse conditions, some protozoans produce a protective capsule called a **cyst**. A cyst allows the protozoan to survive conditions unsuitable for survival. For specialized parasitic species, this includes survival for periods outside a host.

AMOEBAE

Amoebae move by extending projections of their cytoplasm. Several pathogenic amoebae infect humans and feed mainly on red blood cells. *Entamoeba* is transmitted through ingestion of cysts that are passed in the feces. People become infected with *Naegleria* while swimming, when the waterborne cysts pass across mucous membranes and infect blood, brain, and spinal cord.

Pathogen	Disease
Naegleria fowleri	Microencephalitis
Entamoeba histolytica	Amoebic dysentery

APICOMPLEXA

These protozoans are not mobile and tend to be intracellular parasites. They use special enzymes to penetrate the host's tissues. They have complex life cycles involving transmission between several host species.

Plasmodium vivax

Pathogen	Disease	Host species
Plasmodium vivax	Malaria	*Anopheles* mosquito
Toxoplasma gondii	Toxoplasmosis	Cats
Pneumocystis carinii	Pneumonia	Humans

MICROSPORA

This unusual group of protozoans lack mitochondria and live as intracellular parasites (within cells). They were first reported to cause human diseases in 1984.

Pathogen	Disease
Nosema	Chronic diarrhoea, kerato-conjunctivitis (in AIDS patients)

FLAGELLATES

Flagellates are usually spindle-shaped, with flagella projecting from the front end. The whiplike motion of the flagella pulls the cells through their environment. *Giardia* is found in the small intestine of mammals. It is passed in the feces and survives in the environment as a cyst until ingested by the next host. *Trichinomas* moves using an undulating membrane. It is unable to form a cyst and must be transferred directly from host to host quickly (e.g. during sexual intercourse or via toilet facilities or towels). Various *Trypanosoma* species, which cause African sleeping sickness, are spread by the tsetse fly.

Pathogen	Disease
Giardia lamblia	Giardia enteritis
Trichinomas vaginalis	Urethritis, vaginitis
Trypanosoma (in tsetse fly vector)	Sleeping sickness (African trypanosomiasis)

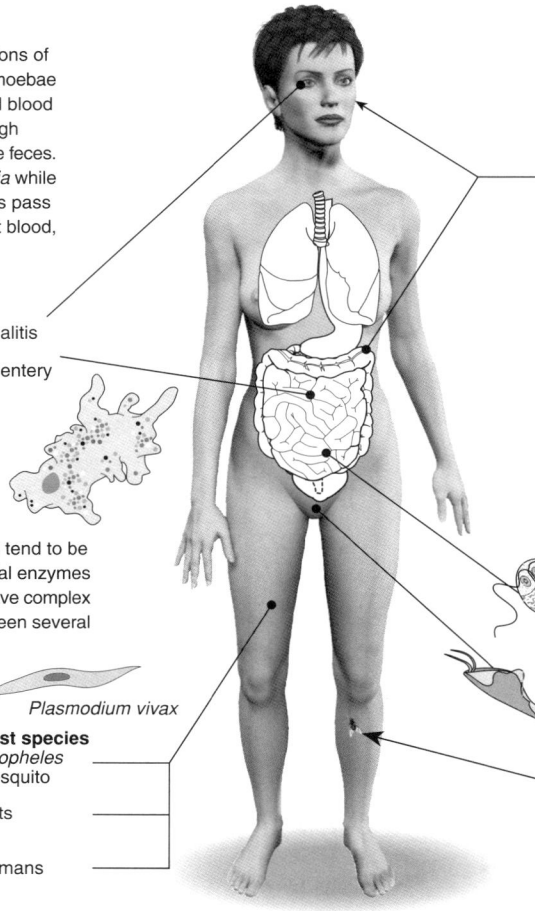

1. Some protozoans form cysts under certain conditions.

   (a) Explain what a **cyst** is: _____

   _____

   (b) Explain how the ability to form a cyst helps a parasitic protozoan to survive: _____

   _____

   _____

2. Several parasitic protozoans causing diseases in humans use other animal species as hosts for part of their life cycle. Identify the host (including class and genus) that is involved in part of the life cycle for each of the following diseases:

   (a) Sleeping sickness: _____

   (b) Malaria: _____

3. The disease known as **giardia** is an increasingly common problem for campers. In seemingly remote areas, campers may contract this disease by drinking water from streams and lakes. Briefly explain the likely reason for this:

   _____

4. Describe the likely conditions under which amoebic dysentery is transmitted: _____

   _____

Malaria

RA 2

Malaria is a serious parasitic disease, spread by bites of **Anopheles mosquitoes**, affecting up to 300 million people in the tropics each year. The parasites responsible for malaria are protozoa known as **plasmodia**. Four species can cause the disease in humans. Each spends part of its life cycle in humans and part in *Anopheles* mosquitoes. Even people who take antimalarial drugs and precautions against being bitten may contract malaria. Malaria, especially *falciparum* malaria, is often a medical emergency that requires hospitalization. Treatment involves the use of antimalarial drugs and, in severe cases, blood transfusions may be necessary. Symptoms, which appear one to two weeks after being bitten, include headache, shaking, chills, and fever. *Falciparum* malaria is more severe, with high fever, coma, and convulsions, and it can be fatal within a few days of the first symptoms. These more severe symptoms result from this plasmodium's ability to infect all ages of red blood cells (whereas other species attack only young or old cells). Destruction of a greater proportion of blood cells results in *hemolytic anemia*. The infected blood cells become sticky and block blood vessels to vital organs such as the kidneys and the brain.

Malaria

Malaria occurs in over 100 countries and territories. More than 40% of the people in the world are at risk. Large areas of Central and South America, Hispaniola (Haiti and the Dominican Republic), Africa, the Indian subcontinent, Southeast Asia, the Middle East, and Oceania are considered malaria-risk areas (an area of the world that has malaria).

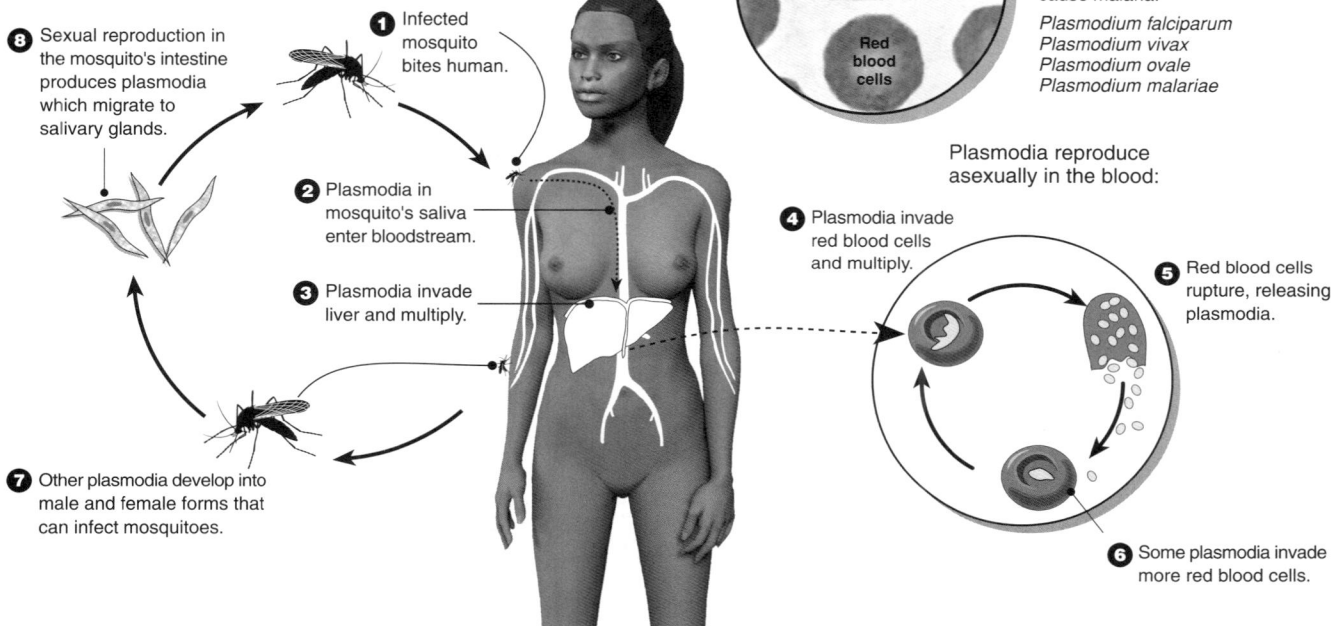

Four species of *Plasmodium* cause malaria:

Plasmodium falciparum
Plasmodium vivax
Plasmodium ovale
Plasmodium malariae

Red blood cells

Plasmodia reproduce asexually in the blood:

❶ Infected mosquito bites human.

❷ Plasmodia in mosquito's saliva enter bloodstream.

❸ Plasmodia invade liver and multiply.

❹ Plasmodia invade red blood cells and multiply.

❺ Red blood cells rupture, releasing plasmodia.

❻ Some plasmodia invade more red blood cells.

❼ Other plasmodia develop into male and female forms that can infect mosquitoes.

❽ Sexual reproduction in the mosquito's intestine produces plasmodia which migrate to salivary glands.

1. Explain how a plasmodium parasite enters the body: _____

_____

2. Suggest a way in which villagers could reduce the occurrence of malaria carrying mosquitoes in their immediate area:

_____

3. (a) Describe the symptoms of a malaria attack: _____

_____

   (b) Explain **why** the symptoms of *falciparum* malaria are more severe than other forms of malaria: _____

_____

_____

4. Global warming is expected to increase the geographical area of malaria infection. Explain why this is expected:

_____

_____

Multicellular Parasites

Multicellular parasites comprise more than a single cell and are relatively complex organisms. Some **endoparasites**, such as flatworms and roundworms, cause disease directly and are highly specialized to live inside their hosts. Parasitic forms differ from their free-living relatives in the following ways: they have no digestive system or one that is highly simplified, their nervous system is reduced, they have little or no means of locomotion, and their reproductive system is often complex, with an individual producing large numbers of fertilized eggs to infect a new host. Some insects and arachnids (especially ticks and mites), apart from being **ectoparasites**, can also carry disease-causing microorganisms between hosts. They act as **vectors**, picking up bacteria, viruses, or protozoans when they suck the blood of their host. Some vectors are just a mechanical means of transport for a pathogen. Other parasites multiply in their vectors and can accumulate in the vector's saliva or feces.

PLATYHELMINTHES (flatworms)

These flatworms, which include flukes and tapeworms, are flattened from front to back. They have no digestive system, or the digestive system is incomplete, with a single opening (mouth) through which they feed and expel wastes.

Parasite	Disease
Echinococcus granulosus	Hydatidosis (hydatids)
Taenia saginata	Tapeworm

Liver fluke

Tapeworm

Schistosoma	Schistosomiasis (also known as bilharzia)

NEMATODES (Roundworms)

Some species of nematode are free-living in soil or water, and others are parasitic on plants and animals. Roundworms have a complete digestive system; a mouth, intestine, and anus. Some parasitic nematodes pass their entire life cycle in a single host. Nematode infections of humans can be divided into two categories: those in which the larva is infective and those in which the egg is infective.

Parasite	Disease
Necator americanus	Hookworm infection
Enterobius vermicularis	Pinworm infection
Trichinella spirallis	Trichinosis

Pinworm

TICKS AND MITES

Ticks and mites (related to spiders) have four pairs of legs. They are blood sucking arthropods which can burrow into the skin, causing irritation. Their most important effect is that they may be vectors for disease-causing microorganisms.

Parasite	Disease	Pathogen
Ixodes	Lyme disease	Borrelia burgdorferi
Sarcoptes scabiei	Scabies	

Soft tick

Scabies mite

INSECTS

A number of biting insects are parasites on humans, feeding on blood which is rich in protein. As well as being an irritant, they may introduce dangerous pathogens into the bloodstream.

Parasite	Disease
Pediculus (human louse)	Epidemic typhus
Xenopsylla (rat flea)	Plague and endemic murine typhus
Aedes (mosquito)	Dengue fever and yellow fever
Anopheles (mosquito)	Malaria
Glossina (tsetse fly)	African sleeping sickness (African trypanosomiasis)

1. (a) Distinguish between endoparasites and ectoparasites: _____

_____

(b) State which of these are most likely to be vectors of disease rather than pathogens themselves and explain why:

_____

_____

2. Suggest why many of the diseases carried by insect vectors are restricted to tropical regions: _____

_____

_____

3. Trichinosis is spread by the ingestion of undercooked meat (e.g. pork) infected with the parasite. Explain why a human infection of trichinosis is a dead end for the parasite:

_____

_____

The Initial Spread of SARS in Toronto, Canada
(February – April, 2003)

How SARS Was Beaten

Kwan Sui-Chu
travels to Hong Kong in February, contracts SARS at the Metropole Hotel from a "super spreader", and returns home to Toronto where she infects her family. She later dies of SARS on March 5.

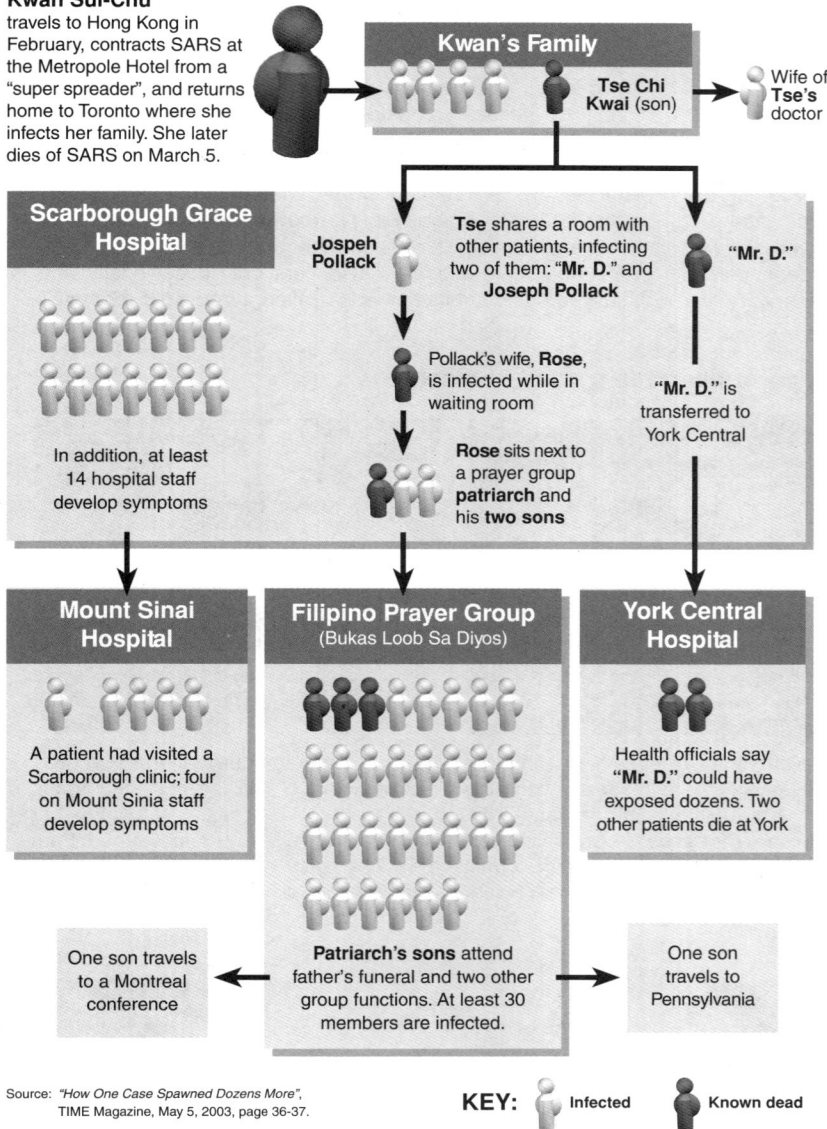

Kwan's Family

Tse Chi Kwai (son) → Wife of **Tse's** doctor

Scarborough Grace Hospital

Jospeh Pollack

Tse shares a room with other patients, infecting two of them: "**Mr. D.**" and **Joseph Pollack**

"Mr. D."

Pollack's wife, **Rose**, is infected while in waiting room

"Mr. D." is transferred to York Central

Rose sits next to a prayer group **patriarch** and his **two sons**

In addition, at least 14 hospital staff develop symptoms

Mount Sinai Hospital

A patient had visited a Scarborough clinic; four on Mount Sinia staff develop symptoms

Filipino Prayer Group
(Bukas Loob Sa Diyos)

York Central Hospital

Health officials say "**Mr. D.**" could have exposed dozens. Two other patients die at York

One son travels to a Montreal conference

Patriarch's sons attend father's funeral and two other group functions. At least 30 members are infected.

One son travels to Pennsylvania

Source: "How One Case Spawned Dozens More", TIME Magazine, May 5, 2003, page 36-37.

KEY: Infected   Known dead

The global SARS outbreak developed quickly and dramatically. The containment of SARS required heroic efforts and extraordinary measures. The last reported probable case of SARS was detected and isolated (in Taiwan) on 15 June 2003. Health systems at every major outbreak site were strained to the limits of their capacity.

Health authorities rapidly introduced a series of sweeping measures, including:

- Vigorous tracing of every possible contact with a SARS patient.
- Immediate quarantine of individuals suspected (but not confirmed) of having SARS (enforced with the threat of execution in the case of mainland China).
- Surveillance systems were upgraded and began to deliver the kind of information needed for prompt and targeted action.
- Hospital procedures for infection control were tightened, and procedures were developed to ensure the efficient delivery of protective equipment and other supplies.
- Mass education campaigns persuaded the population to check frequently for fever and report promptly at fever clinics. This greatly reduced the time between onset of symptoms and isolation of patients.
- A mechanism was established for coordinating the response of all relevant agencies.
- WHO issued rare travel advisories as evidence mounted that SARS was spreading by air travel along international routes. WHO recommended that persons traveling to certain regions/cities consider postponing all but essential travel until further notice. This was the most stringent travel advisory issued by WHO in its 55-year history.
- WHO set up three networks of leading laboratories around the world to investigate:
  - speeding up detection of the causative agent and developing a diagnostic test;
  - pooling clinical knowledge on symptoms, diagnosis, and management (treatment);
  - SARS epidemiology (how the disease is spread through a population).

Source: World Health Organisation (WHO)

1. List the biological and social factors important in the emergence and spread of a named **emerging disease**:

2. Define the term **zoonosis**:

3. Explain what a **re-emerging disease** is:

4. The Spanish influenza pandemic of 1917-18 was made worse by the return of troops from World War I to their home countries. More than 20 million people died in the pandemic, which had a death rate of about 3%. Explain how this pandemic differed from that of SARS in 2003, in terms of its **global spread** and **death rate**:

RA② The Control of Disease

Many factors can influence the spread of disease, including the social climate, diet, general health, and access to medical care. Human intervention and modification of behavior can reduce the transmission rate of some diseases and inhibit their spread. Examples include the use of personal physical barriers, such as condoms, to prevent sexually transmitted infections (STIs), and the use of **quarantine** to ensure that potential carriers of disease are isolated until incubation periods have elapsed. Cleaning up the environment also lowers the incidence of disease by reducing the likelihood that pathogens or their vectors will survive. The effective control of infectious disease depends on knowing the origin of the outbreak (its natural reservoir), its mode of transmission within the population, and the methods that can be feasibly employed to contain it. Diseases are often classified according to how they behave in a given population. Any disease that spreads from one host to another, either directly or indirectly, is said to be a **communicable disease**. Those that are easily spread from one person to another, such as chicken pox or measles, are said to be **contagious**. Such diseases are a threat to **public health** and many must be notified to health authorities. **Noncommunicable diseases** are not spread from one host to another and pose less of a threat to public health. A disease that occurs only occasionally and is usually restricted in its spread is called a **sporadic disease**.

Methods for controlling the spread of disease

Transmission of disease can be prevented or reduced by adopting 'safe' behaviors. Examples include using condoms to reduce the spread of STIs, isolation of people with a specific illness (such as SARS), or establishing quarantine procedures for people who may be infected, but are not yet ill.

The development of effective sanitation, sewage treatment, and treatment of drinking water has virtually eliminated dangerous waterborne diseases from developed countries. These practices disrupt the normal infection cycle of pathogens such as cholera and giardia.

Appropriate personal hygiene practices reduce the risk of infection and transmission. Soap may not destroy the pathogens but washing will dilute and remove them from the skin. Although popular, antibacterial soaps encourage development of strains resistant to antimicrobial agents.

The environment can be made less suitable for the growth and transmission of pathogens. For example, spraying drainage ditches and draining swamps eliminates breeding habitats for mosquitoes carrying diseases such as malaria and dengue fever.

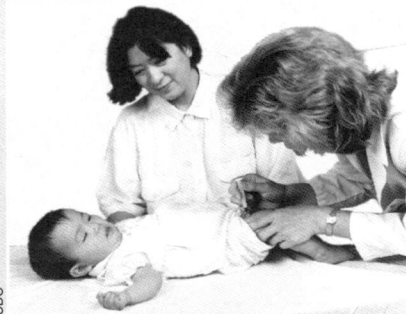

Immunization schedules form part of public health programs. If most of the population is immune, 'herd immunity' limits outbreaks to sporadic cases. In such populations there are too few susceptible individuals to support the spread of an epidemic.

Disinfectants and sterilization techniques, such as autoclaving, destroy pathogenic microbes before they have the opportunity to infect. The use of these techniques in medicine has significantly reduced post operative infections and associated deaths.

1. Distinguish between contagious and non-communicable diseases, providing an example of each:

_____

_____

2. (a) Explain the difference between **isolation** and **quarantine**: _____

_____

_____

_____

(b) Using the recent example of SARS, explain how isolation and quarantine operate to prevent the spread of disease:

_____

_____

3. Explain how the use of condoms reduces the spread of the human immunodeficiency virus (HIV) that causes AIDS:

_____

_____

4. Explain how the drainage of stagnant water in tropical regions may reduce the incidence of malaria in those countries:

_____

_____

5. Describe how each of the following methods is used to control the **growth** of disease-causing microbes:

(a) Disinfectants: _____

_____

(b) Antiseptics: _____

_____

(c) Heat: _____

_____

(d) Ionizing radiation (gamma rays): _____

_____

(e) Desiccation: _____

_____

(f) Cold: _____

_____

6. The **Human Genome Project** (HGP) was launched in 1990 with the aim of sequencing the entire human genome (the unique genetic code that makes us 'human'). On 26 June, 2000, scientists produced the first working draft of the genome. It is hoped that understanding the genome will revolutionize the treatment and prevention of disease.

Briefly discuss how the HGP will facilitate:

(a) Diagnosis of disease: _____

_____

_____

(b) Treatment of disease: _____

_____

_____

7. The first measles vaccine was introduced to Britain in 1964. However, in 1993 there were 9000 cases of measles notified to the health authorities in England and Wales.

(a) Suggest why measles has not been eliminated in Britain: _____

_____

(b) Explain how vaccination interrupts the transmission of measles within a population: _____

_____

_____

Antimicrobial Drugs

Antimicrobial drugs include synthetic (manufactured) **drugs** as well as drugs produced by bacteria and fungi, called **antibiotics**. Antibiotics are produced naturally by these microorganisms as a means of inhibiting competing microbes around them (a form of antibiosis, hence the name antibiotic). The first antibiotic, called penicillin, was discovered in 1928 by Alexander Fleming. Since then, similar inhibitory reactions between colonies growing on solid media have been commonly observed. Antibiotics are actually rather easy to discover, but few of them are of medical or commercial value. Many antibiotics are toxic to humans or lack any advantage over those already in use. More than half of our antibiotics are produced by species of filamentous bacteria that commonly inhabit the soil, called ***Streptomyces***. A few antibiotics are produced by bacteria of the genus ***Bacillus***. Others are produced by molds, mostly of the genera *Cephalosporium* and *Penicillium*. Antimicrobial drugs are used in **chemotherapy** programs to treat infectious diseases. Like disinfectants, these chemicals interfere with the growth of

microorganisms (see diagram below). They may either kill microbes directly (**bactericidal**) or prevent them from growing (**bacteriostatic**). To be effective, they must often act inside the host, so their effect on the host's cells and tissues is important. The ideal antimicrobial drug has **selective toxicity**, killing the pathogen without damaging the host. Some antimicrobial drugs have a narrow **spectrum of activity**, and affect only a limited number of microbial types. Others are **broad-spectrum drugs** and affect a large number of microbial species (see the table below). When the identity of a pathogen is not known, a broad-spectrum drug may be prescribed in order to save valuable time. There is a disadvantage with this, because broad spectrum drugs target not just the pathogen, but much of the host's normal microflora also. The normal microbial community usually controls the growth of pathogens and other microbes by competing with them. By selectively removing them with drugs, certain microbes in the community that do not normally cause problems, may flourish and become **opportunistic pathogens**.

An antibiotic capsule

How Antimicrobial Drugs Work

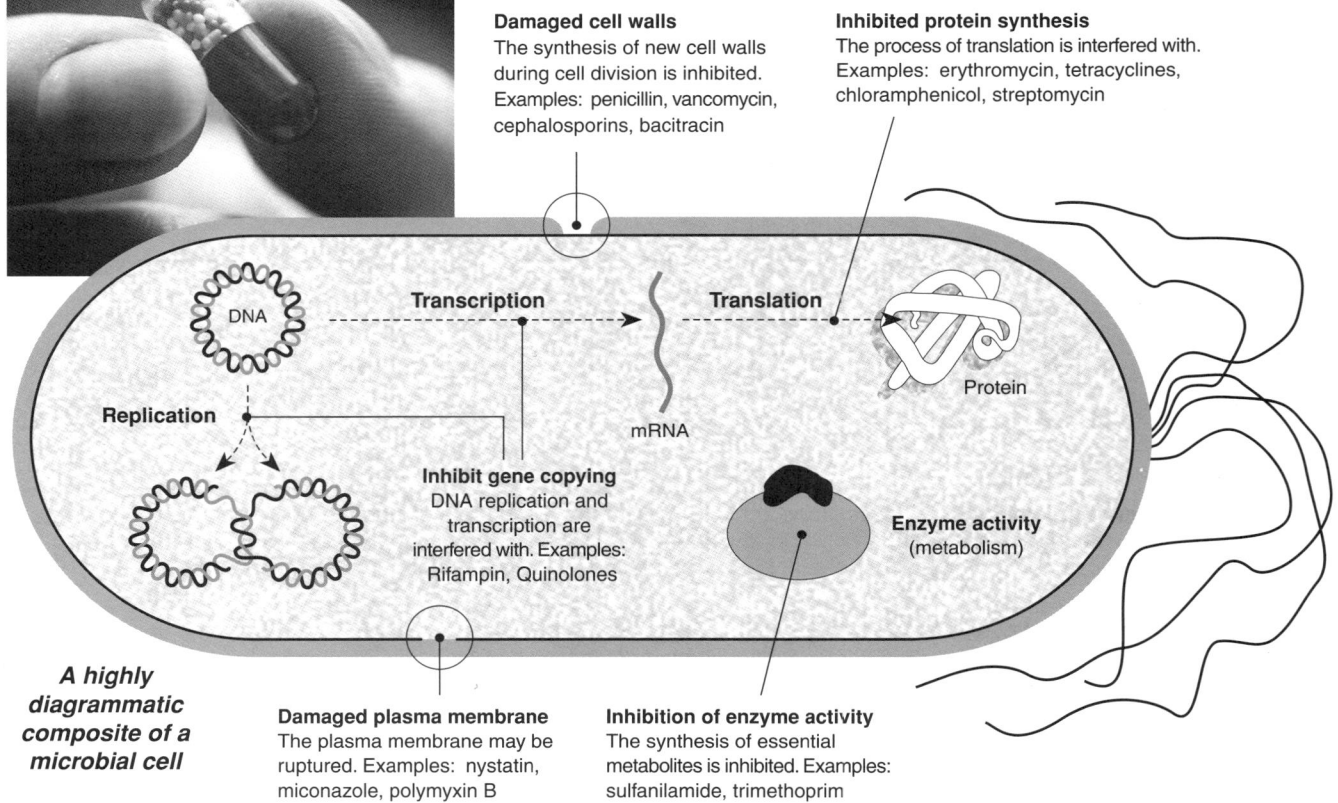

Damaged cell walls
The synthesis of new cell walls during cell division is inhibited. Examples: penicillin, vancomycin, cephalosporins, bacitracin

Inhibited protein synthesis
The process of translation is interfered with. Examples: erythromycin, tetracyclines, chloramphenicol, streptomycin

A highly diagrammatic composite of a microbial cell

DNA

Transcription

Translation

Protein

mRNA

Replication

Inhibit gene copying
DNA replication and transcription are interfered with. Examples: Rifampin, Quinolones

Enzyme activity
(metabolism)

Damaged plasma membrane
The plasma membrane may be ruptured. Examples: nystatin, miconazole, polymyxin B

Inhibition of enzyme activity
The synthesis of essential metabolites is inhibited. Examples: sulfanilamide, trimethoprim

Spectrum of antimicrobial activity of a number of chemotherapeutic drugs

Prokaryotes				Eukaryotes			
Mycobacteria	Gram-negative bacteria	Gram-positive bacteria	Rickettsias/ Chlamydias	Fungi	Protozoa	Tapeworms and flukes	Viruses
		Penicillin*		Ketoconazole		Nicosamide (tapeworms)	
Streptomycin							Acyclovir
		Tetracycline			Mefloquine (malaria)		
Isoniazid						Praziquantel (flukes)	
		Zyvox¶					

* There are some synthetic derivatives of penicillin that act effectively against gram-negative bacteria.
¶ The first new class of antibiotics to be used in 35 years.

Source: Totora, Funke, & Case: Microbiology: An IIntroduction (1998). The Benjamin/Cummings Publishing Co. Inc.

1. Distinguish between the following categories of antimicrobial drug:

    (a) Antibiotic: _____

    _____

    (b) Synthetic drug: _____

    _____

2. Some bacteria have ways of tolerating treatment by antibiotics, and are termed 'superbugs'.
    (a) Explain what is meant by **antibiotic resistance** in bacteria:

    _____

    _____

    (b) Explain why a course of antibiotics should be finished completely, even when the symptoms of infection have gone:

    _____

    _____

3. The spectrum of activity varies for different groups of drugs.
    (a) Explain the advantages and disadvantages of using a broad-spectrum drug on an unidentified bacterial infection:

    _____

    _____

    (b) Name two broad spectrum groups of drugs: _____

4. Although there are a few drugs that have some success in controlling viruses, antibiotics are ineffective. Explain why
    antibiotics do not work against viruses:

    _____

    _____

5. List four ways in which antimicrobial drugs kill or inhibit the growth of microbes: _____

    _____

    _____

6. The diagram below shows an experiment investigating the effectiveness of different antibiotics on a pure culture of a
    single species of bacteria. Giving a reason, state which antibiotic (A-D) is most effective in controlling the bacteria:

    _____

    _____

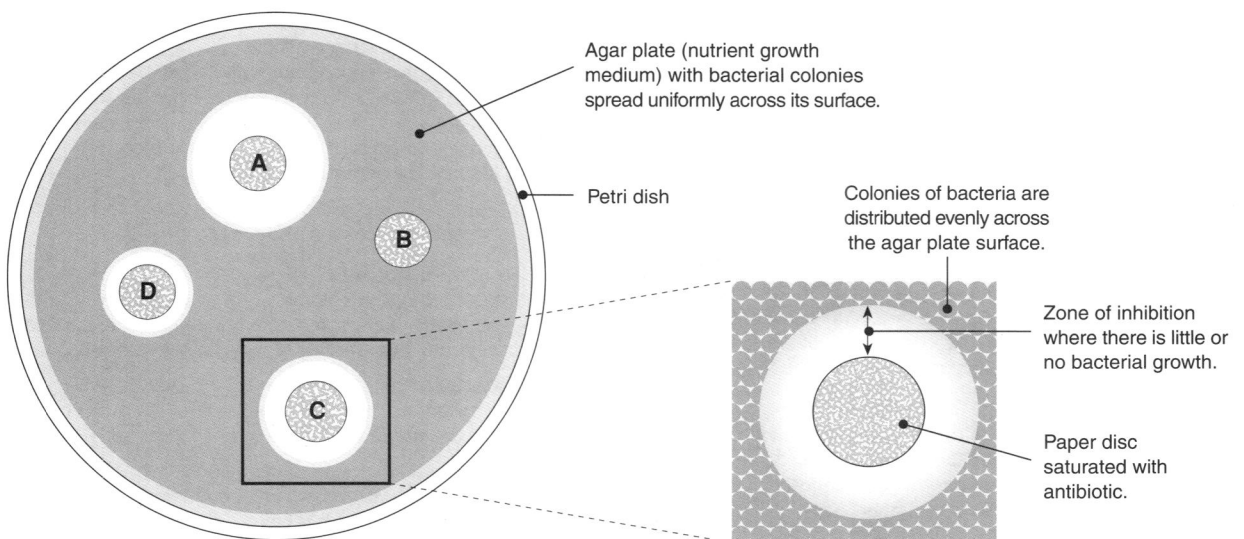

Agar plate (nutrient growth
medium) with bacterial colonies
spread uniformly across its surface.

Petri dish

Colonies of bacteria are
distributed evenly across
the agar plate surface.

Zone of inhibition
where there is little or
no bacterial growth.

Paper disc
saturated with
antibiotic.

Defense Against Infectious Disease

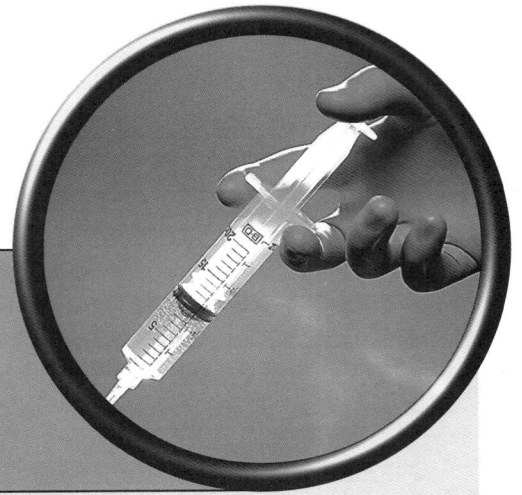

IB SL
Complete nos:
1, 7(a)-(b), (f),
19-21, 24
Extension:
7(c)-(e), 8-10

IB HL
Complete nos:
1, 6-12, 14-15, 17,
19-24, 27-29, 33, 35
Extension: 13, 16,
18, 30-32, 34

IB Options
Not applicable
to options

AP Biology
Complete nos:
1-35
Some numbers
extension as
appropriate

Learning Objectives

☐ 1. Compile your own glossary from the **KEY WORDS** displayed in **bold type** in the learning objectives below.

Recognizing self and non-self (pages 52-53)

☐ 2. Explain how a body is able to distinguish between self and non-self and comment on the importance of this.

☐ 3. Appreciate the nature of **major histocompatibility complex (MHC)** and its role in self-recognition and in determining tissue compatibility in transplant recipients.

☐ 4. Explain the basis of the **Rh** and **ABO blood group systems** in humans. Explain what is meant by **agglutination** and how this reaction forms the basis of blood grouping. Explain the consequences of blood type incompatibility in **blood transfusions**.

☐ 5. Discuss how self-recognition poses problems for tissue and organ transplants. Determine the physiological basis of transplant rejection and suggest how it may be avoided. Explain why it is so difficult to find compatible tissue and organ donors and suggest how this problem may be solved in the future.

Defense mechanisms

Blood clotting (page 54)

☐ 6. Describe the process of **blood clotting**, including the role of **clotting factors**, **thrombin**, and **fibrin**. Appreciate the role of blood clotting in the resistance of the body to infection by sealing off damage and restricting invasion of the tissues by microorganisms.

Non-specific defenses (pages 50-51, 55-57)

☐ 7. Explain what is meant by a **non-specific defense mechanism**. Distinguish between first and second lines of defense. Describe the nature and role of each of the following in protecting against pathogens:

Preventing pathogen entry
(a) Skin (including sweat and sebum production).
(b) Mucus-secreting and ciliated membranes.
(c) Body secretions (tears, urine, saliva, gastric juice).

Non-specific defense after pathogen entry
(d) Natural anti-bacterial and anti-viral proteins such as **interferon** and **complement.**
(e) The **inflammatory response**, **fever**, and cell death.
(f) **Phagocytosis** by phagocytes. Recognize the term phagocyte as referring to any of a number of phagocytic leukocytes (e.g. macrophages).

Specific defenses (page 50, 58-59)

☐ 8. Identify the role of **specific resistance** in body's resistance to infection. Contrast specific and non-specific defenses in terms of time for activation and specificity towards a pathogen.

☐ 9. Explain what is meant by an **immune response**. Explain how the immune response involves recognition and response to foreign material. Explain the significance of the immune system having both **specificity** and **memory**. Providing examples, distinguish between **naturally acquired** and **artificially acquired immunity** and between **active** and **passive immunity**. Compare the duration of the immunity gained by active and passive means.

☐ 10. Recognize the role of the **lymphatic system** in the production and transport of leukocytes.

The immune system (pages 60-63)

☐ 11. Distinguish between: **cell-mediated immunity** and **humoral (antibody-mediated) immunity**.

☐ 12. Recall that other types of white blood cells are involved in non-specific defense mechanisms.

☐ 13. Explain the role of the **thymus** in the immune response. Describe the nature, origin, and role of **macrophages** (a type of phagocyte). Appreciate the role of macrophages in processing and presenting foreign antigens and in stimulating lymphocyte activity.

☐ 14. Explain the origin and maturation of **B lymphocytes** (cells) and **T lymphocytes** (cells). Describe and distinguish between the activities of the B and T lymphocytes in the immune response.

☐ 15. With reference to immune system function, outline the principle of challenge and response. Outline **clonal selection** and the basis of **immunological memory**. Explain how the immune system is able to respond to the large and unpredictable range of potential antigens.

☐ 16. Appreciate that self-tolerance occurs during development as a result of the selective destruction of the B cells that react to self-antigens.

Cell-mediated immunity

☐ 17. T cells are responsible for **cell-mediated immunity**. Describe how T cells recognize **specific** foreign antigens. Describe the roles of named T cells, including **cytotoxic** (killer) **T cells** (T_C) and **helper T cells** (T_H). Identify the organisms against which these T cells act.

☐ 18. Appreciate the role of T lymphocytes in the rejection of transplanted tissues and organs.

Humoral immunity

☐ 19. Define the terms: **antibody** (immunoglobulin), and **antigen**. Name some common antigens and explain their role in provoking a specific immune response.

☐ 20. Describe the structure of an antibody identifying the constant and variable regions, and the antigen binding site. Relate the structure of antibodies to their function.

☐ 21. Explain antibody production, including how B cells bring about **humoral** (antibody-mediated) **immunity** to specific antigens. If required, provide an explanation of how antigens are presented, the role of **helper T-cells**, and the activation and differentiation of B-cells.

☐ 22. Describe and contrast the functional roles of **plasma cells** and **memory cells** and recall the basis for immunological memory. Discuss the role of **immunological memory** in long term immunity (ability to respond quickly to previously encountered antigens).

☐ 23. Describe the methods by which antibodies inactivate antigens and facilitate their destruction.

Immune dysfunction (pages 36-37, 219)

☐ 24. Outline the effects of **HIV** on the immune system, including reference to the reduction in the number of active lymphocytes and the loss of immune function.

☐ 25. Explain what is meant by an **autoimmune disease** and provide examples. Define the terms: **allergy** and **allergic response**, **allergen**, **hypersensitivity**, and **sensitized**. Name some of the common triggers for allergies in susceptible people.

☐ 26. With reference to **asthma** or **hayfever**, outline the role of the immune system in allergic reactions, including the role of **histamine** in these allergies.

Vaccines and immunization (pages 64-68)

☐ 27. Recognize that vaccination provides **artificially acquired immunity**. Recall the difference between **passive** and **active immunity**.

☐ 28. Outline the principle of **vaccination**. Explain what is meant by a **primary** and a **secondary response** to infection and identify the role of these, and the immune system memory, in the success of vaccines.

☐ 29. Appreciate that **immunization** involves the production of immunity by artificial means and that **vaccination** *usually* refers to immunization by inoculation. Know that these terms are frequently used synonymously.

☐ 30. Explain the role of **vaccination** programs in preventing disease. Discuss the role of aggressive vaccination programs in the eradication (or near-eradication) of some (named) infectious diseases.

☐ 31. Outline the vaccination schedule for your country, identifying critical times for vaccination against specific diseases. Comment on the role of effective vaccination programs in public health.

☐ 32. Describe the principles involved in vaccine production. Explain, with examples, how vaccines are administered. Distinguish between **subunit** and **whole-agent vaccines** and between **inactivated** (dead) and **live** (attenuated) **vaccines**. Contrast the risks and benefits associated with live and dead vaccines.

☐ 33. Discuss the benefits and risks of vaccination against bacterial and viral infection. Include reference to the MMR vaccine and two other examples. Evaluate the risks associated with immunization relative to the risks associated with contracting the disease itself.

☐ 34. Describe and comment on the role of genetic engineering in the development of new vaccines.

Monoclonal antibodies (page 69)

☐ 35. Describe the production of **monoclonal antibodies**. Explain why they are so useful in medicine and outline some of their applications. Describe one use of them in diagnosis and one use in treatment.

Textbooks

See the 'Textbook Reference Grid' on pages 8-9 for textbook page references relating to material in this topic.

Supplementary Texts

See pages 5-6 for additional details of these texts:

■ Clegg, C.J., 1998. **Mammals: Structure and Function** (John Murray), pp. 40-41.

■ Freeland, P., 1999. **Microbes, Medicine and Commerce** (Hodder & Stoughton), pp. 92-99.

■ Fullick, A., 1998. **Human Health and Disease** (Heinemann), pp. 27-36.

■ Hudson, T. & K. Mannion, 2001. **Microbes and Disease** (Collins), pp. 70-86.

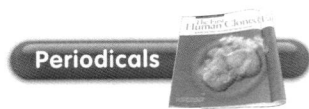

Periodicals

See page 6 for details of publishers of periodicals:

STUDENT'S REFERENCE

Self-recognition & the immune system

■ **Antibodies** Biol. Sci. Rev., 11(3) January 1999, pp. 34-35. *The operation of the immune system and the production of antibodies (including procedures for producing monoclonal antibodies).*

■ **Blood Group Antigens** Biol. Sci. Rev., 9(5) May 1997, pp. 10-13. *Human genetic diversity is expressed in blood group antigens: an account of the ABO and rhesus system in humans.*

■ **Lymphocytes - The Heart of the Immune System** Biol. Sci. Rev., 12 (1) September 1999 pp. 32-35. *An excellent account of the role of lymphocytes in the immune response (includes the types and actions of different lymphocytes).*

■ **Red Blood Cells** Biol. Sci. Rev., 11(2) November 1998, pp. 2-4. *The function of red blood cells, including their role in antigenic recognition.*

Vaccines and vaccine development

■ **HIV Focus** New Scientist, 8 Feb. 2003, pp. 33-44. *A special issue covering the latest IV research: why the immune system responds in different ways in different individuals, new hope in vaccine development, the new trend towards the use of protective microbiocides.*

■ **Immunotherapy** Biol. Sci. Rev., 15(1), Sept. 2002, pp. 39-41. *Medical research is uncovering ways in which our immune system can be used in developing vaccines for cancer.*

■ **Dirty Secrets** New Scientist, 2 November 1996, pp. 26-29. *Vaccine efficacy relies on contaminants. What do these do and why are they needed?*

Hypersensitivity and immune failure

■ **Beware! Allergens** New Scientist, 22 January 2000 (Inside Science). *The allergic response: sensitization and the role of the immune system.*

TEACHER'S REFERENCE

■ **Inside Trading** New Scientist, 26 June 1999, pp. 42-46. *How do we maintain a stable relationship with our microflora and protect ourselves from attack by pathogens?*

■ **Life, Death, and the Immune System** Scientific American, Sept. 1993. *An entire special issue on human infection, immune system, and disease.*

■ **The Long Arm of the Immune System** Sci. American, Nov. 2002, pp. 34-41. *The role of dendritic cells, a class of leukocyte with a role in activating the immune system (good extension).*

■ **Let Them Eat Dirt** New Scientist, 18 July 1998, pp. 26-31. *Effective, normal immune system function may require a certain level of early exposure to bacteria and microorganisms.*

■ **Edible Vaccines** Scientific American, Sept. 2000, pp. 48-53. *Vaccines in food may be the way of future immunization programs.*

■ **How Interferons Fight Disease** Scientific American, May 1994, pp. 40-47. *The interferons of the human immune system and their active role in immune system function. Interferons can even activate immune system cells to attack tumors.*

■ **Genetic Vaccines** Scientific American, July 1999, pp. 34-41. *This excellent article includes a description of how the vaccines work and a table of specific diseases treatable by this method.*

■ **Preparing for Battle** Scientific American, Feb. 2001, pp. 68-69. *Preparation and mode of action of the influenza vaccine. Includes discussion of the problems associated with the changing virus.*

■ **Disarming Flu Viruses** Scientific American, January 1999, pp. 56-65. *The influenza virus, its life cycle, and vaccine development for its control.*

Internet

See pages 10-11 for details of how to access **Bio Links** from our web site: **www.thebiozone.com**. From Bio Links, access sites under the topics:

GENERAL BIOLOGY ONLINE RESOURCES > Online Textbooks and Lecture Notes: • S-Cool! A level biology revision guide • Learn.co.uk • Mark Rothery's biology web site ... *and others*

ANIMAL BIOLOGY: • Anatomy and physiology • Human physiology lecture notes ... *and others*

HEALTH & DISEASE > Defense and the Immune System: • Blood group antigens • Inducible defenses against pathogens • Microbiology and immunology • Primary immunodeficiency diseases • The immune system: An overview • Understanding the immune system ... *and others*

Software and video resources are now provided in the Teacher Resource Handbook

The Body's Defenses

RA 2

If microorganisms never encountered resistance from our body defenses, we would be constantly ill and would eventually die of various diseases. Fortunately, in most cases our defenses prevent this from happening. Some of these defenses are designed to keep microorganisms from entering the body. Other defenses remove the microorganisms if they manage to get inside. Further defenses attack the microorganisms if they remain inside the body. The ability to ward off disease through the various defense mechanisms is called **resistance**. The lack of resistance, or vulnerability to disease, is known as

susceptibility. One form of defense is referred to as **non-specific resistance**, and includes defenses that protect us from any pathogen. This includes a first line of defense such as the physical barriers to infection (skin and mucous membranes) and a second line of defense (phagocytes, inflammation, fever, and antimicrobial substances). **Specific resistance** is a third line of defense that forms the **immune response** and targets specific pathogens. Specialized cells of the immune system, called lymphocytes, produce specific proteins called antibodies which are produced against specific antigens.

Most microorganisms find it difficult to get inside the body. If they succeed, they face a range of other defences.

The natural populations of harmless microbes living on the skin and mucous membranes inhibit the growth of most pathogenic microbes

Microorganisms are trapped in sticky mucus and expelled by cilia (tiny hairs that move in a wavelike fashion)

Intact skin

1st Line of Defense
The skin provides a formidable physical barrier to the entry of pathogens. Healthy skin is rarely penetrated by microorganisms. Certain chemical secretions are produced by skin that inhibit growth of bacteria and fungi. Tears, mucus and saliva also help to wash bacteria away.

Mucous membranes and their secretions:

Lining of the respiratory, urinary, reproductive and gastrointestinal tracts

2nd Line of Defence
A range of defense mechanisms operate inside the body to inhibit or destroy pathogens. These responses react to the presence of any pathogen, regardless of which species it is. White blood cells are involved in most of these responses.

Antimicrobial substances

Inflammation and fever

40°C

37°C

Phagocytic white blood cells

Eosinophils: Produce toxic proteins against certain parasites, some phagocytosis

Basophils: Release heparin (an anticoagulant) and histamine which promotes inflammation

Neutrophils, macrophages: These cells engulf and destroy foreign material (e.g. bacteria)

3rd Line of Defense
Once the pathogen has been *identified* by the immune system, a specific response from white blood cells called lymphocytes occurs. These coordinate a range of specific responses to the pathogen.

Specialized lymphocytes

B cell: Antibody production

T cell: Cell-mediated immunity

1. Describe the type of response against pathogens carried out by each of the following levels of defense:

(a) First line of defense: _____

_____

_____

(b) Second line of defense: _____

_____

_____

_____

(c) Third line of defense: _____

_____

_____

_____

2. Distinguish between the following categories of resistance to pathogens:

   (a) Non-specific resistance: _____

   _____

   (b) Specific resistance: _____

   _____

3. Briefly define the following terms and give a short explanation of their role in internal defense:

   (a) Susceptibility: _____

   _____

   (b) Resistance: _____

   _____

   (c) Phagocytosis: _____

   _____

   (d) Inflammation: _____

   _____

   (e) Fever: _____

   _____

4. Describe the functional role of each of the following defense mechanisms (the first one has been completed for you):

   (a) Skin (including sweat and sebum production): __Skin helps to prevent direct entry of pathogens__
   into the body. Sebum slows growth of bacteria and fungi.

   (b) Phagocytosis by white blood cells: _____

   _____

   (c) Mucus-secreting and ciliated membranes: _____

   _____

   (d) Body secretions: tears, urine, saliva, gastric juice: _____

   _____

   (e) Natural antimicrobial proteins (e.g. interferon): _____

   _____

   (f) Antibody production: _____

   _____

   (g) Fever: _____

   _____

   (h) Cell-mediated immunity: _____

   _____

   (i) The inflammatory response: _____

   _____

5. Infection with HIV results in the progressive destruction of T lymphocytes. Suggest why this leads to an increasing number of opportunistic infections in AIDS sufferers:

   _____

Targets for Defense

RA 2

In order for the body to present an effective defense against pathogens, it must first be able to recognize its own tissues (*self*). It must also ignore the normal microflora that inhabits parts of our bodies (e.g. skin and gastrointestinal tract). In addition, the body needs to be able to deal with abnormal cells that periodically appear in the body that, if not eliminated, develop into cancer. Failure of self/non-self recognition can lead to autoimmune disorders, in which the immune system mistakenly destroys its own tissues. The ability of the body to recognize its own molecules has implications for medical techniques such as tissue grafts, organ transplants, and blood transfusions. Incompatible tissues (correctly identified as foreign) are attacked by the body's immune system (rejection). Even a healthy pregnancy involves suppression of specific features of the self recognition system, allowing the mother to tolerate a nine month parasitic relationship with what is essentially a large foreign body.

The Body's Natural Microbiota

After birth, normal and characteristic microbial populations begin to establish themselves on and in the body. A typical human body contains 1×10^{13} body cells, yet harbors 1×10^{14} bacterial cells. These microorganisms establish more or less permanent residence but, under normal conditions, do not cause disease. In fact, this normal microflora can benefit the host by preventing the overgrowth of harmful pathogens. They are not found throughout the entire body, but are located in certain regions.

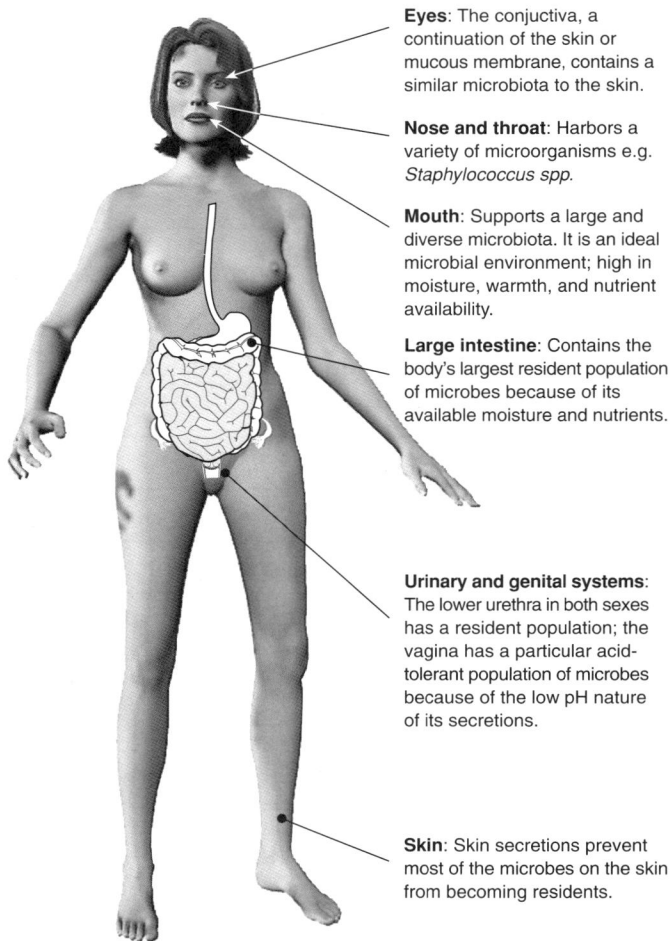

Eyes: The conjuctiva, a continuation of the skin or mucous membrane, contains a similar microbiota to the skin.

Nose and throat: Harbors a variety of microorganisms e.g. *Staphylococcus spp.*

Mouth: Supports a large and diverse microbiota. It is an ideal microbial environment; high in moisture, warmth, and nutrient availability.

Large intestine: Contains the body's largest resident population of microbes because of its available moisture and nutrients.

Urinary and genital systems: The lower urethra in both sexes has a resident population; the vagina has a particular acid-tolerant population of microbes because of the low pH nature of its secretions.

Skin: Skin secretions prevent most of the microbes on the skin from becoming residents.

Distinguishing Self from Non-Self

The human immune system achieves self-recognition through the **major histocompatibility complex** (MHC). This is a cluster of tightly linked genes on chromosome 6 in humans. These genes code for protein molecules (MHC antigens) that are attached to the surface of body cells. They are used by the immune system to recognize its own or foreign material. **Class I MHC** antigens are located on the surface of virtually all human cells, but **Class II MHC** antigens are restricted to macrophages and the antibody-producing B-lymphocytes.

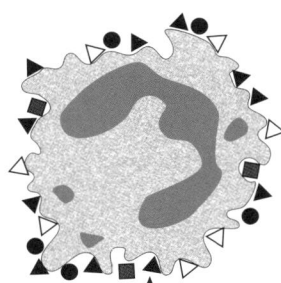

Class I HLA

Class II HLA

Genes for producing the HLA antigens

HLA surface proteins (antigens) provide a chemical signature that allows the immune system to recognize the body's own cells

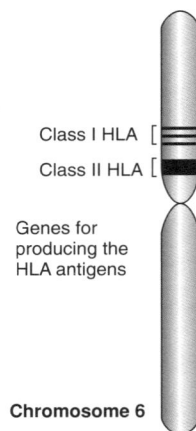

Chromosome 6

Tissue Transplants

The MHC is responsible for the rejection of tissue grafts and organ transplants. Foreign MHC molecules are antigenic, causing the immune system to respond in the following way:

- T cells directly lyse the foreign cells

- Macrophages are activated by T cells and engulf foreign cells

- Antibodies are released that attack the foreign cell

- The complement system injures blood vessels supplying the graft or transplanted organ

To minimize this rejection, attempts are made to match the MHC of the organ donor to that of the recipient as closely as possible.

1. Explain why it is healthy to have a natural population of microbes on and inside the body: _____

_____

2. (a) Explain the nature and purpose of the major histocompatibility complex (MHC): _____

_____

_____

_____

(b) Explain the importance of such a self-recognition system: _____

_____

3. Name two situations when the body's recognition of 'self' is undesirable: _____

Blood Group Antigens

Blood groups classify blood according to the different marker proteins on the surface of red blood cells (RBCs). These marker proteins act as **antigens** and affect the ability of RBCs to provoke an immune response. The **ABO blood group** is the most important blood typing system in medical practice, because of the presence of anti-A and anti-B antibodies in nearly all people who lack the corresponding red cell antigens (these antibodies are carried in the plasma and are present at birth). If a patient is to receive blood from a blood donor, that blood must be compatible otherwise the red blood cells of the donated blood will clump together (agglutinate), break apart, and block capillaries. There is a small margin of safety in certain blood group combinations, because the volume of donated blood is usually relatively small and the donor's antibodies are quickly diluted in the plasma. In practice, blood is carefully matched, not only for ABO types, but for other types as well. Although human RBCs have more than 500 known antigens, fewer than 30 (in 9 blood groups) are regularly tested for when blood is donated for transfusion. The blood groups involved are: *ABO, Rh, MNS, P, Lewis, Lutheran, Kell, Duffy,* and *Kidd.* The ABO and rhesus (Rh) are the best known. Although blood typing has important applications in medicine, it can also be used to rule out individuals in cases of crime (or paternity) and establish a list of potential suspects (or fathers).

	Blood Type A	Blood Type B	Blood Type AB	Blood Type O
Antigens present on the **red blood cells**	antigen *A*	antigen *B*	antigens *A* and *B*	Neither antigen *A* nor *B*
Antibodies present in the **plasma**	Contains **anti-B** antibodies; but no antibodies that would attack its own antigen *A*	Contains **anti-A** antibodies; but no antibodies that would attack its own antigen *B*	Contains neither **anti-A** nor **anti-B** antibodies	Contains both **anti-A** and **anti-B** antibodies

Blood type	Frequency in US Rh⁺	Frequency in US Rh⁻	Antigen	Antibody	Can donate blood to:	Can receive blood from:
A	34%	6%	*A*	*anti-B*	*A, AB*	*A, O*
B	9%	2%				
AB	3%	1%				
O	38%	7%				

1. Complete the table above to show the antibodies and antigens present in each blood group, and donor blood types:

2. In a hypothetical murder case, blood from both the victim and the murderer was left at the scene. There were five suspects under investigation:

   (a) Describe what blood typing **could** establish about the guilt or innocence of the suspects: _____

   _____

   (b) Identify what a blood typing could **not** establish: _____

   _____

   (c) Suggest how the murderer's identity could be firmly established (assuming that s/he was one of the five suspects):

   _____

   (d) Explain why blood typing is not used forensically to any great extent: _____

   _____

3. Explain why the discovery of the ABO system was such a significant medical breakthrough: _____

Blood Clotting and Defense

Apart from its transport role, **blood** has a role in the body's defense against infection and **hemostasis** (the prevention of bleeding and maintenance of blood volume). The tearing or puncturing of a blood vessel initiates **clotting**. Clotting is normally rapid process that seals off the tear, preventing blood loss and the invasion of bacteria into the site. Clot formation is triggered by the release of clotting factors from the damaged cells at the site of the tear or puncture. A hardened clot forms a scab, which acts to prevent further blood loss and acts as a mechanical barrier to the entry of pathogens.

Blood Clotting

1 Injury to the lining of a blood vessels exposes collagen fibers to the blood. Platelets stick to the collagen fibers.

3 Platelets clump together. The platelet plug forms an emergency protection against blood loss.

Endothelial cell
Red blood cell
Exposed collagen fibers

2 Platelet releases chemicals that make the surrounding platelets sticky

Blood vessel

Platelet plug

When tissue is wounded, the blood quickly coagulates to prevent further blood loss and maintain the integrity of the circulatory system. For external wounds, clotting also prevents the entry of pathogens. Blood clotting involves a cascade of reactions involving at least twelve clotting factors in the blood. The end result is the formation of an insoluble network of fibers, which traps red blood cells and seals the wound.

4 A fibrin clot reinforces the seal. The clot traps blood cells and the clot eventually dries to form a **scab**.

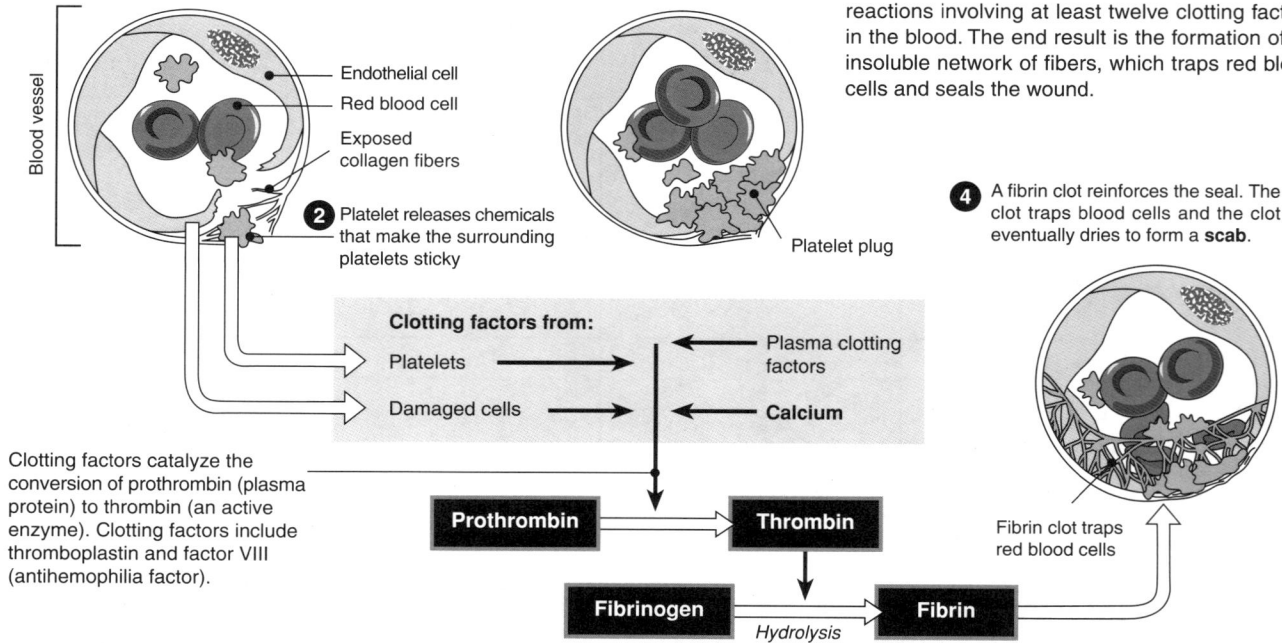

Clotting factors from:

Platelets ⟶   ⟵ Plasma clotting factors
Damaged cells ⟶   ⟵ **Calcium**

Clotting factors catalyze the conversion of prothrombin (plasma protein) to thrombin (an active enzyme). Clotting factors include thromboplastin and factor VIII (antihemophilia factor).

Prothrombin ⟶ **Thrombin**

Fibrinogen → *Hydrolysis* → **Fibrin**

Fibrin clot traps red blood cells

1. Explain two roles of the blood clotting system in internal defense and hemostasis:

   (a) _____

   (b) _____

2. Explain the role of each of the following in the sequence of events leading to a blood clot:

   (a) Injury: _____

   (b) Release of chemicals from platelets: _____

   _____

   (c) Clumping of platelets at the wound site: _____

   _____

   (d) Formation of a fibrin clot: _____

   _____

3. (a) Explain the role of clotting factors in the blood in formation of the clot: _____

   _____

   (b) Explain why these clotting factors are not normally present in the plasma: _____

   _____

4. (a) Name one inherited disease caused by the absence of a clotting factor: _____

   (b) Name the clotting factor involved: _____

The Action of Phagocytes

Human cells that ingest microbes and digest them by the process of **phagocytosis** are called **phagocytes**. All are types of white blood cells. During many kinds of infections, especially bacterial infections, the total number of white blood cells increases by two to four times the normal number. The ratio of various white blood cell types changes during the course of an infection.

How a Phagocyte Destroys Microbes

1 Detection
Phagocyte detects microbes by the chemicals they give off (chemotaxis) and sticks the microbes to its surface.

2 Ingestion
The microbe is engulfed by the phagocyte wrapping pseudopodia around it to form a vesicle.

3 Phagosome forms
A phagosome (phagocytic vesicle) is formed, which encloses the microbes in a membrane.

4 Fusion with lysosome
Phagosome fuses with a lysosome (which contains powerful enzymes that can digest the microbe).

5 Digestion
The microbes are broken down by enzymes into their chemical constituents.

6 Discharge
Indigestible material is discharged from the phagocyte cell.

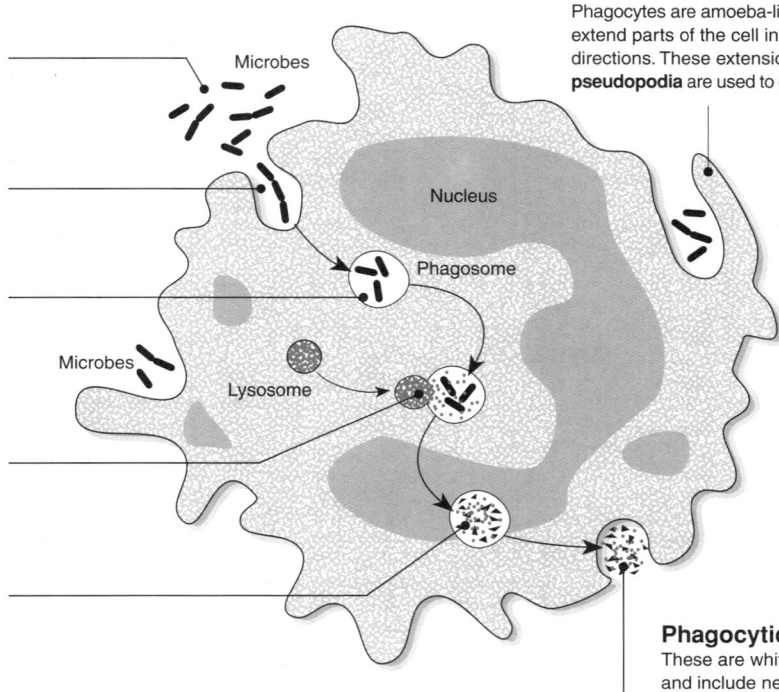

Phagocytes are amoeba-like cells that can extend parts of the cell in different directions. These extensions are called **pseudopodia** are used to engulf microbes.

Microbes

Nucleus

Phagosome

Microbes

Lysosome

Phagocytic cell
These are white blood cells and include neutrophils and eosinophils.

The Interaction of Microbes and Phagocytes

Some microbes kill phagocytes.

Microbes enter phagocytes and evade the immune response.

Dormant microbes may hide inside phagocytes.

Some microbes kill phagocytes
Some microbes produce toxins that can actually kill phagocytes, e.g., toxin-producing staphylococci and the dental plaque-forming bacteria *Actinobacillus*.

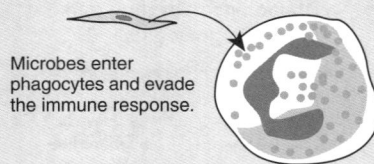

Microbes evade immune system
Some microbes can evade the immune system by entering phagocytes. The microbes prevent fusion of the lysosome with the phagosome and multiply inside the phagocyte, almost filling it. Examples include *Chlamydia, Mycobacterium tuberculosis, Shigella*, and malarial parasites.

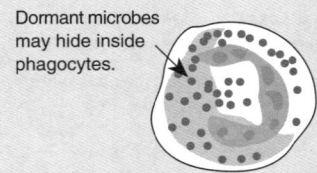

Dormant microbes hide inside
Some microbes can remain dormant inside the phagocyte for months or years at a time. Examples include the microbes that cause brucellosis and tularemia.

1. List the white blood cells that engage in the process of phagocytosis: _____

_____

2. Describe how a blood sample from a patient may be used to determine whether they have a microbial infection (without looking for the microbes themselves):

_____

_____

3. Explain how some microbes are able to overcome phagocytic cells and use them to their advantage:

_____

_____

Inflammation

Damage to the body's tissues can be caused by physical agents (e.g. sharp objects, heat, radiant energy, or electricity), microbial infection, or chemical agents (e.g. gases, acids and bases). The damage triggers a defensive response called **inflammation**. It is usually characterized by four symptoms: pain, redness, heat and swelling. The inflammatory response is beneficial and has the following functions: (1) to destroy the cause of the infection and remove it and its products from the body; (2) if this fails, to limit the effects on the body by confining the infection to a small area; (3) replacing or repairing tissue damaged by the infection. The process of inflammation can be divided into three distinct stages. These are described below.

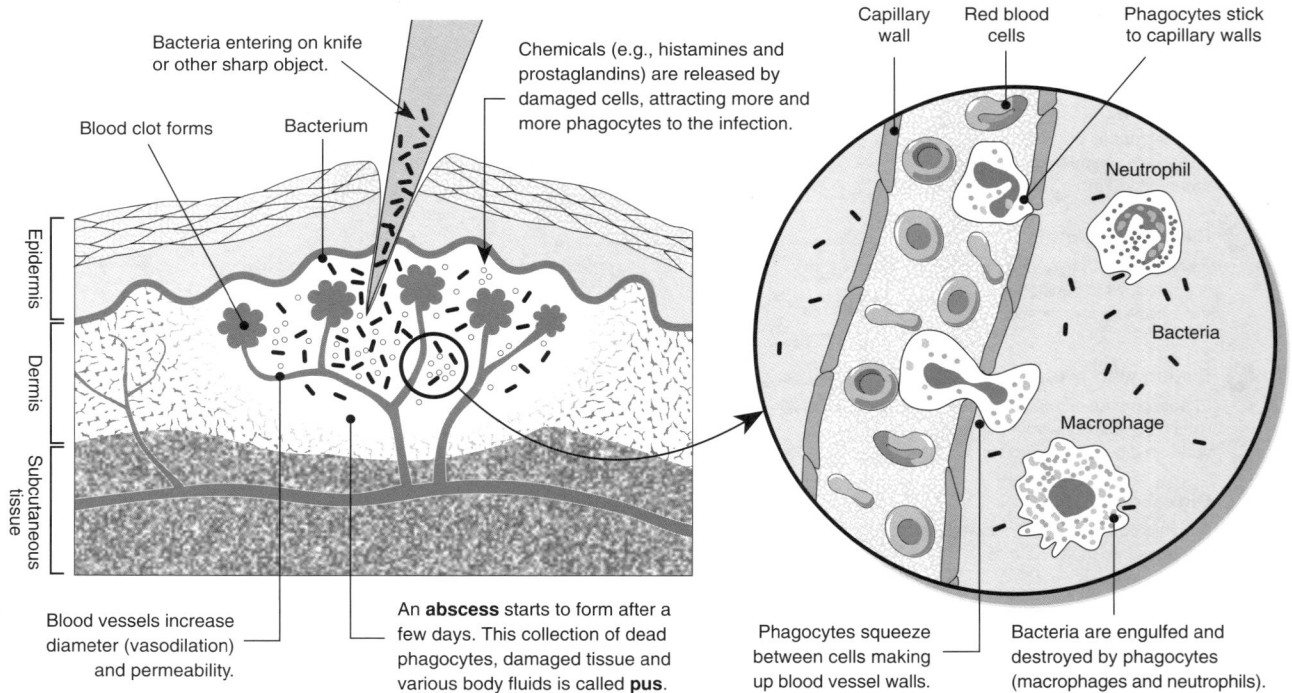

Bacteria entering on knife or other sharp object.

Chemicals (e.g., histamines and prostaglandins) are released by damaged cells, attracting more and more phagocytes to the infection.

Blood clot forms

Bacterium

Epidermis

Dermis

Subcutaneous tissue

Blood vessels increase diameter (vasodilation) and permeability.

An **abscess** starts to form after a few days. This collection of dead phagocytes, damaged tissue and various body fluids is called **pus**.

Capillary wall

Red blood cells

Phagocytes stick to capillary walls

Neutrophil

Bacteria

Macrophage

Phagocytes squeeze between cells making up blood vessel walls.

Bacteria are engulfed and destroyed by phagocytes (macrophages and neutrophils).

Stages in inflammation

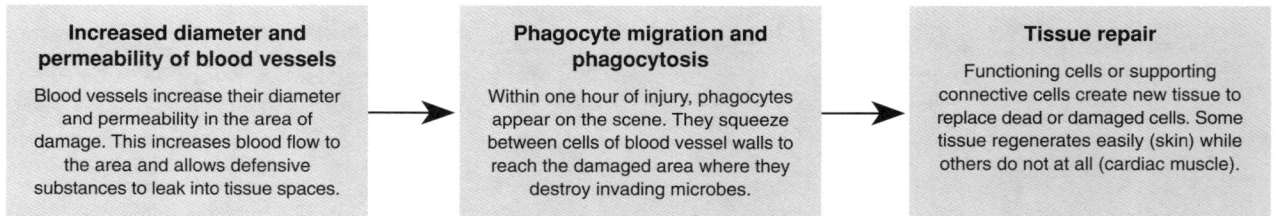

Increased diameter and permeability of blood vessels	**Phagocyte migration and phagocytosis**	**Tissue repair**
Blood vessels increase their diameter and permeability in the area of damage. This increases blood flow to the area and allows defensive substances to leak into tissue spaces.	Within one hour of injury, phagocytes appear on the scene. They squeeze between cells of blood vessel walls to reach the damaged area where they destroy invading microbes.	Functioning cells or supporting connective cells create new tissue to replace dead or damaged cells. Some tissue regenerates easily (skin) while others do not at all (cardiac muscle).

1. Outline the three **stages** of inflammation and identify the beneficial role of each stage:

(a) _____

_____

(b) _____

_____

(c) _____

_____

2. Identify two features of phagocytes important in the response to microbial invasion: _____

_____

3. State the role of histamines and prostaglandins in inflammation: _____

4. Explain why pus forms at the site of infection: _____

_____

Fever

A 2

Up to a point, fever is beneficial, since it assists a number of the defense processes. The release of the protein **interleukin-1** not only helps to reset the thermostat of the body to a higher level, but also helps step up production of **T cells** (lymphocytes). High body temperature also intensifies the effect of **interferon** (an antiviral protein) and is believed to inhibit the growth of some bacteria and viruses. Because high temperatures speed up the body's **metabolic reactions**, it may help body tissues to repair themselves more quickly. Fever also increases heart rate so that white blood cells are delivered to sites of infection more rapidly. The normal body temperature range for most people is 36.2 to 37.2°C. Fevers of less than 40°C do not need treatment for **hyperthermia**, but excessive fever requires prompt attention (particularly in children). Death usually results if body temperature rises to 44.4 to 45.5°C.

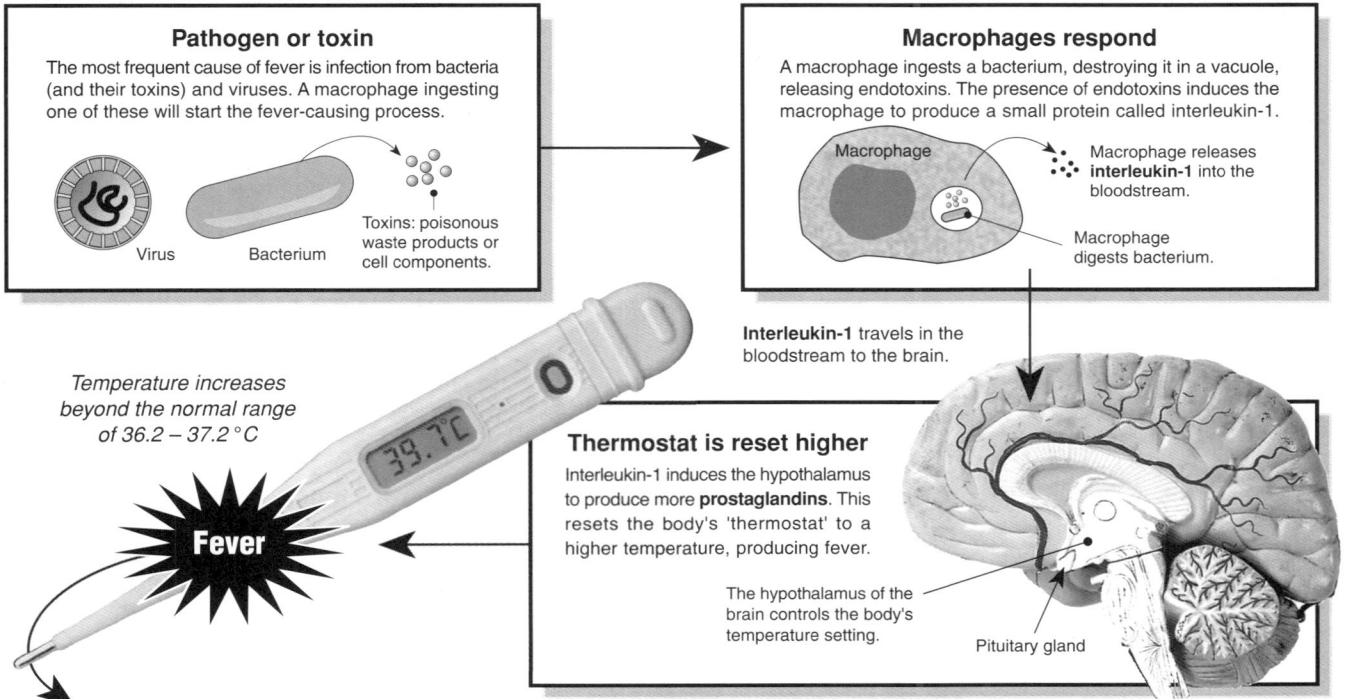

Pathogen or toxin
The most frequent cause of fever is infection from bacteria (and their toxins) and viruses. A macrophage ingesting one of these will start the fever-causing process.

Virus

Bacterium

Toxins: poisonous waste products or cell components.

Macrophages respond
A macrophage ingests a bacterium, destroying it in a vacuole, releasing endotoxins. The presence of endotoxins induces the macrophage to produce a small protein called interleukin-1.

Macrophage

Macrophage releases **interleukin-1** into the bloodstream.

Macrophage digests bacterium.

Interleukin-1 travels in the bloodstream to the brain.

Temperature increases beyond the normal range of 36.2 – 37.2 °C

Fever

Thermostat is reset higher
Interleukin-1 induces the hypothalamus to produce more **prostaglandins**. This resets the body's 'thermostat' to a higher temperature, producing fever.

The hypothalamus of the brain controls the body's temperature setting.

Pituitary gland

Fever onset
To adjust to the new thermostat setting, the body responds with the following which raise the body temperature:
• Blood vessel constriction
• Increased metabolic rate
• Shivering

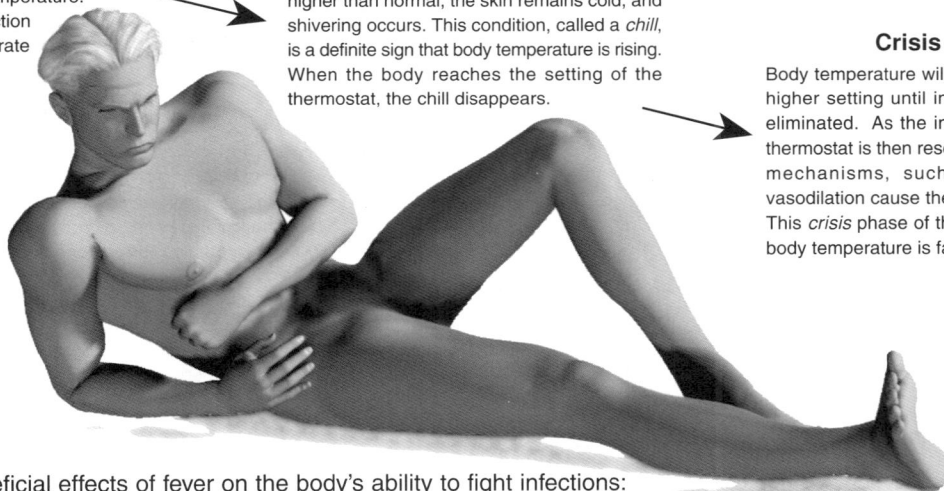

Chill phase
Even though the body temperature is climbing higher than normal, the skin remains cold, and shivering occurs. This condition, called a *chill*, is a definite sign that body temperature is rising. When the body reaches the setting of the thermostat, the chill disappears.

Crisis phase
Body temperature will be maintained at the higher setting until interleukin-1 has been eliminated. As the infection subsides, the thermostat is then reset to 37°C. Heat losing mechanisms, such as sweating and vasodilation cause the person to feel warm. This *crisis* phase of the fever indicates that body temperature is falling.

1. List **four** beneficial effects of fever on the body's ability to fight infections:

(a) _____

(b) _____

(c) _____

(d) _____

2. Summarize the key steps of how the body's thermostat is set at a higher level by infection: _____

_____

RA 2   The Lymphatic System

Fluid leaks out from capillaries and forms the tissue fluid, which is similar in composition to plasma but lacks large proteins. This fluid bathes the tissues, supplying them with nutrients and oxygen, and removing wastes. Some of the tissue fluid returns directly into the capillaries, but some drains back into the blood circulation through a network of lymph vessels. This fluid, called **lymph**, is similar to tissue fluid, but contains more leukocytes. Apart from its circulatory role, the lymphatic system also has an important function in the immune response. Lymph nodes are the primary sites where the destruction of pathogens and other foreign substances occurs. A lymph node that is fighting an infection becomes swollen and hard as the lymph cells reproduce rapidly to increase their numbers. The thymus, spleen, and bone marrow also contribute leukocyte to the lymphatic and circulatory systems.

Tonsils: Tonsils (and adenoids) comprise a collection of large lymphatic nodules at the back of the throat. They produce lymphocytes and antibodies and are well-placed to protect against invasion of pathogens.

Thymus gland: The thymus is a two-lobed organ located close to the heart. It is prominent in infants and diminishes after puberty to a fraction of its original size. Its role in immunity is to help produce **T cells** that destroy invading microbes directly or indirectly by producing various substances.

Spleen: The oval spleen is the largest mass of lymphatic tissue in the body, measuring about 12 cm in length. It stores and releases blood in case of demand (e.g., in cases of bleeding), produces mature **B cells**, and destroys bacteria by phagocytosis.

Bone marrow: Bone marrow produces red blood cells and many kinds of leukocytes: monocytes (and macrophages), neutrophils, eosinophils, basophils, and lymphocytes (B cells and T cells).

Lymphatic vessels: When tissue fluid is picked up by lymph capillaries, it is called **lymph**. The lymph is passed along lymphatic vessels to a series of lymph nodes. These vessels contain one-way valves that move the lymph in the direction of the heart until it is reintroduced to the blood at the subclavian veins.

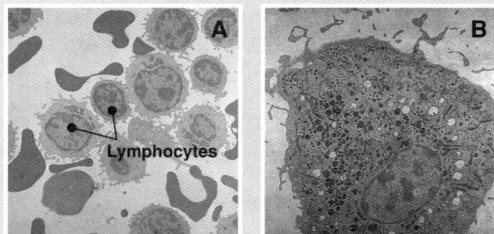

Many types of leukocytes are involved in internal defense. The photos above illustrate examples of leukocytes. **A** shows a cluster of **lymphocytes**. **B** shows a single **macrophage**: large, phagocytic cells that develop from monocytes and move from the blood to reside in many organs and tissues, including the spleen and lymph nodes.

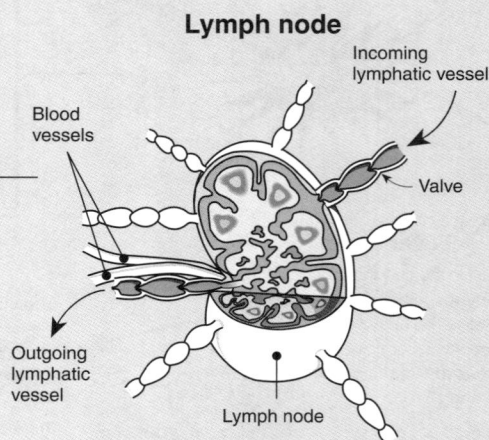

Lymph node

Lymph nodes are oval or bean-shaped structures, scattered throughout the body, usually in groups, along the length of lymphatic vessels. As lymph passes through the nodes, it filters foreign particles (including pathogens) by trapping them in fibres. Lymph nodes are also a "store" of **lymphocytes**, which may circulate to other parts of the body. Once trapped, macrophages destroy the foreign substances by phagocytosis. T cells may destroy them by releasing various products, and/or B cells may release antibodies that destroy them.

1. Briefly describe the composition of lymph: _____

   _____

2. Identify two roles of lymph:

   (a) _____

   (b) _____

3. Describe one role of each of the following in the lymphatic system:

   (a) Lymph nodes: _____

   (b) Bone marrow: _____

Acquired Immunity

A ②

We have natural or **innate resistance** to certain illnesses – examples include most diseases of other animal species. **Acquired immunity** refers to the protection an animal develops against certain types of microbes or foreign substances. Immunity can be acquired either passively or actively and is developed during an individual's lifetime. **Active immunity** develops when a person is exposed to microorganisms or foreign substances and the immune system responds. **Passive immunity** is acquired when antibodies are transferred from one person to another. Recipients do not make the antibodies themselves and the effect lasts only as long as the antibodies are present; usually several weeks or months. Immunity may also be **naturally acquired**, through natural exposure to microbes, or **artificially acquired** as a result of medical treatment.

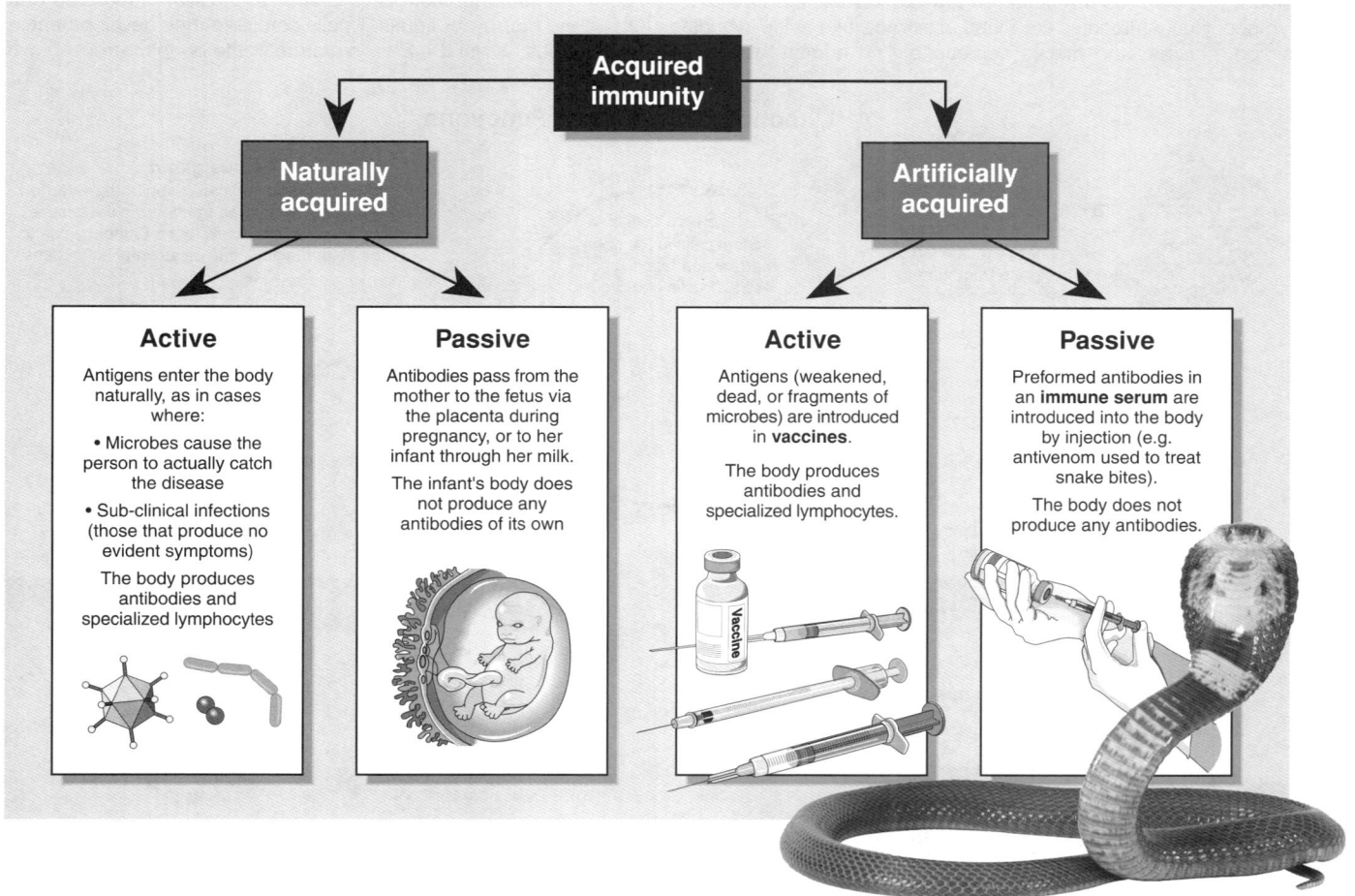

Acquired immunity

Naturally acquired

Artificially acquired

Active

Antigens enter the body naturally, as in cases where:

• Microbes cause the person to actually catch the disease

• Sub-clinical infections (those that produce no evident symptoms)

The body produces antibodies and specialized lymphocytes

Passive

Antibodies pass from the mother to the fetus via the placenta during pregnancy, or to her infant through her milk.

The infant's body does not produce any antibodies of its own

Active

Antigens (weakened, dead, or fragments of microbes) are introduced in **vaccines**.

The body produces antibodies and specialized lymphocytes.

Passive

Preformed antibodies in an **immune serum** are introduced into the body by injection (e.g. antivenom used to treat snake bites).

The body does not produce any antibodies.

1. (a) Explain what is meant by **active immunity**: _____

_____

(b) Distinguish between naturally and artificially acquired active immunity and give an example of each:

_____

_____

2. (a) Explain what is meant by **passive immunity**: _____

_____

(b) Distinguish between naturally and artificially acquired passive immunity and give an example of each:

_____

_____

3. Prior to birth, a baby receives antibodies across the placenta from its mother.
   (a) Explain why a newborn baby needs to have had a supply of maternal antibodies: _____

_____

(b) Explain why this supply is supplemented by antibodies provided in breast milk: _____

_____

The Immune System

The efficient internal defense provided by the immune system is based on its ability to respond specifically against a foreign substance and its ability to hold a memory of this response. There are two main components of the immune system: the humoral and the cell-mediated responses. They work separately and together to protect us from disease. The **humoral immune response** is associated with the serum (non-cellular part of the blood) and involves the action of **antibodies** secreted by B cell lymphocytes. Antibodies are found in extracellular fluids including lymph, plasma, and mucus secretions. The humoral response

protects the body against circulating viruses, and bacteria and their toxins. The **cell-mediated immune response** is associated with the production of specialized lymphocytes called **T cells**. It is most effective against bacteria and viruses located within host cells, as well as against parasitic protozoa, fungi, and worms. This system is also an important defense against cancer, and is responsible for the rejection of transplanted tissue. Both B and T cells develop from stem cells located in the liver of foetuses and the bone marrow of adults. T cells complete their development in the thymus, whilst the B cells mature in the bone marrow.

Lymphocytes and their Functions

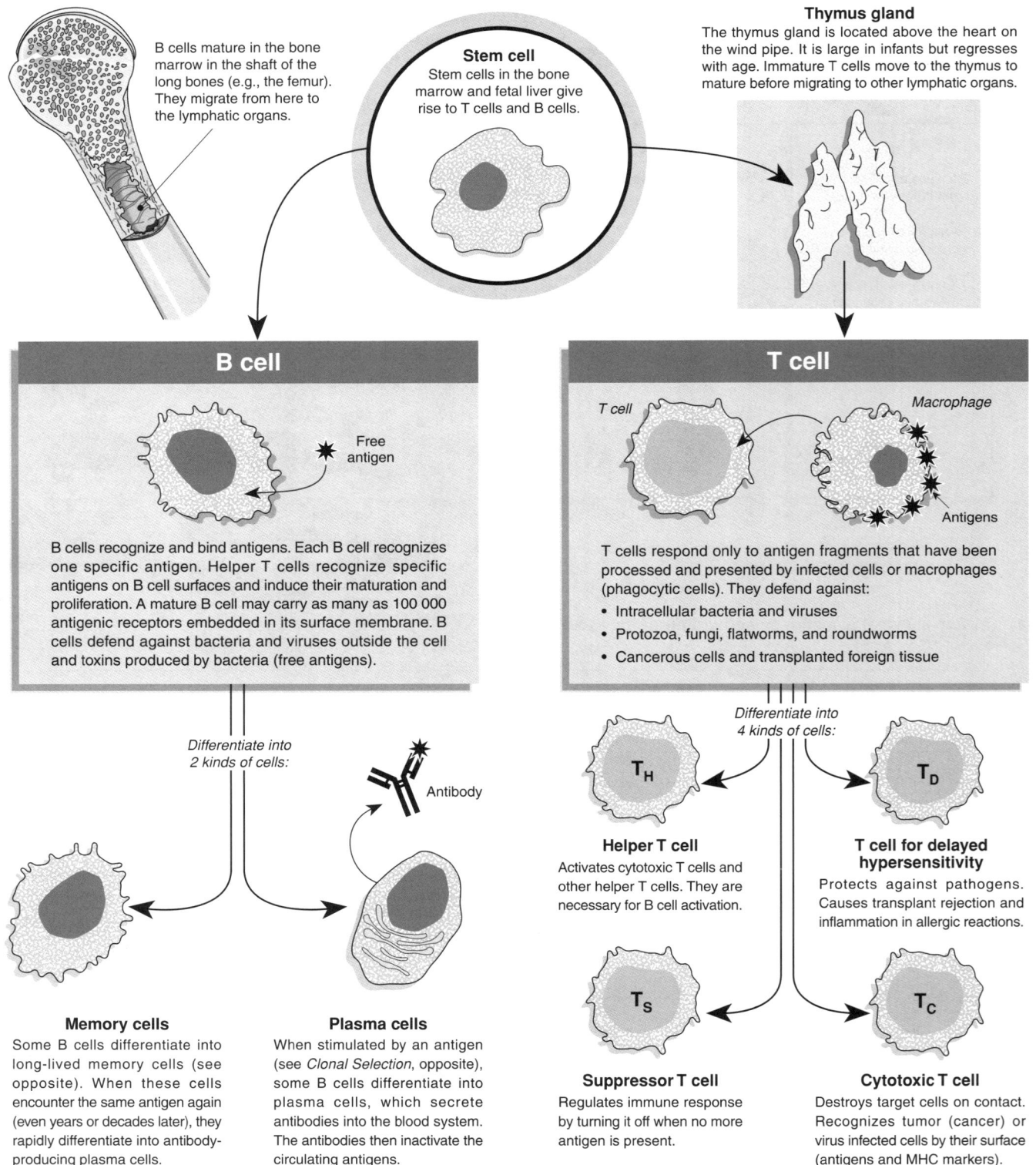

B cells mature in the bone marrow in the shaft of the long bones (e.g., the femur). They migrate from here to the lymphatic organs.

Stem cell
Stem cells in the bone marrow and fetal liver give rise to T cells and B cells.

Thymus gland
The thymus gland is located above the heart on the wind pipe. It is large in infants but regresses with age. Immature T cells move to the thymus to mature before migrating to other lymphatic organs.

B cell

Free antigen

B cells recognize and bind antigens. Each B cell recognizes one specific antigen. Helper T cells recognize specific antigens on B cell surfaces and induce their maturation and proliferation. A mature B cell may carry as many as 100 000 antigenic receptors embedded in its surface membrane. B cells defend against bacteria and viruses outside the cell and toxins produced by bacteria (free antigens).

T cell

T cell   *Macrophage*

Antigens

T cells respond only to antigen fragments that have been processed and presented by infected cells or macrophages (phagocytic cells). They defend against:
• Intracellular bacteria and viruses
• Protozoa, fungi, flatworms, and roundworms
• Cancerous cells and transplanted foreign tissue

Differentiate into 2 kinds of cells:

Antibody

Differentiate into 4 kinds of cells:

T_H

T_D

Helper T cell
Activates cytotoxic T cells and other helper T cells. They are necessary for B cell activation.

T cell for delayed hypersensitivity
Protects against pathogens. Causes transplant rejection and inflammation in allergic reactions.

Memory cells
Some B cells differentiate into long-lived memory cells (see opposite). When these cells encounter the same antigen again (even years or decades later), they rapidly differentiate into antibody-producing plasma cells.

Plasma cells
When stimulated by an antigen (see *Clonal Selection*, opposite), some B cells differentiate into plasma cells, which secrete antibodies into the blood system. The antibodies then inactivate the circulating antigens.

T_S

T_C

Suppressor T cell
Regulates immune response by turning it off when no more antigen is present.

Cytotoxic T cell
Destroys target cells on contact. Recognizes tumor (cancer) or virus infected cells by their surface (antigens and MHC markers).

The immune system has the ability to respond to the large and unpredictable range of potential antigens encountered in the environment. The diagram below explains how this ability is based on **clonal selection** after antigen exposure. The example illustrated is for B cell lymphocytes. In the same way, a T cell stimulated by a specific antigen will multiply and develop into different types of T cells. Clonal selection and differentiation of lymphocytes provide the basis for **immunological memory**.

Five (a-e) of the many, randomly generated B cells. Each one can recognize only one specific antigen.

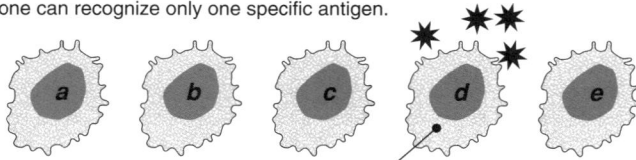

This B cell encounters and binds an antigen. It is then stimulated to proliferate.

Clonal Selection Theory

During development, millions of randomly generated B cells are formed. These are able to recognize many different antigens, including those never before encountered. Each B cell has one specific type of antigenic receptor on its surface whose shape is identical to the antibodies that the cell can make. The receptor will react only to a single antigen. When a B cell encounters its specific antigen, it responds by proliferating into a large clone of cells, all with the same genetic material and the same kind of antibody. This is called **clonal selection** because the antigen selects the B cells that will proliferate.

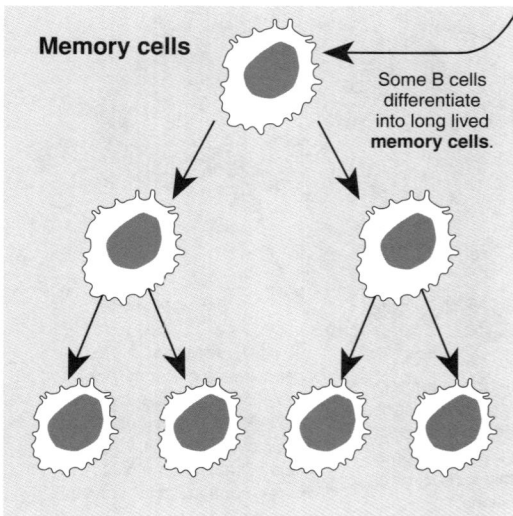

Memory cells

Some B cells differentiate into long lived **memory cells**.

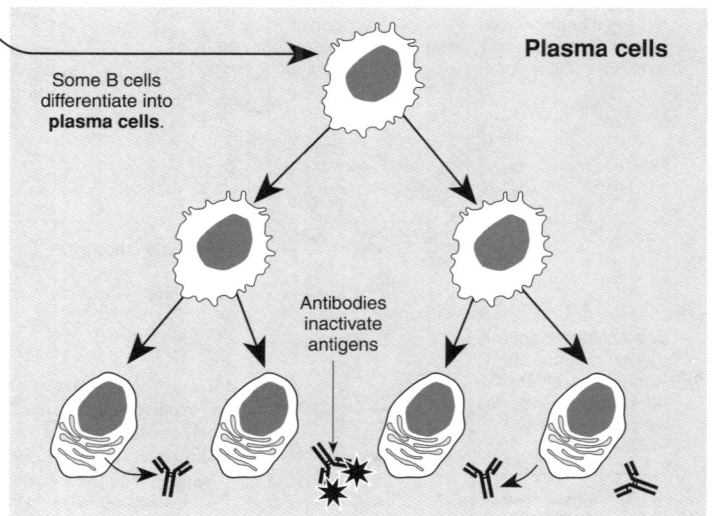

Plasma cells

Some B cells differentiate into **plasma cells**.

Antibodies inactivate antigens

Some B cells differentiate into long lived **memory cells**. These are retained in the lymph nodes to provide future immunity (**immunological memory**). In the event of a second infection, B-memory cells react more quickly and vigorously than the initial B-cell reaction to the first infection.

Plasma cells secrete antibodies specific to the antigen that stimulated their development. Each plasma cell lives for only a few days, but can produce about 2000 antibody molecules per second. Note that during development, any B cells that react to the body's own antigens are selectively destroyed in a process that leads to **self tolerance** (acceptance of the body's own tissues).

1. State briefly the general action of the two major divisions in the immune system:

    (a) Humoral immune system: _____

    (b) Cell-mediated immune system: _____

2. Name the origin of B cells and T cells (before maturing): _____

3. (a) State where B cells mature: _____ (b) State where T cells mature: _____

4. State briefly the function of each of the following cells in the immune system response:

    (a) Memory cells: _____

    (b) Plasma cells: _____

    (c) Helper T cells: _____

    (d) Suppressor T cells: _____

    (e) Delayed hypersensitivity T cells: _____

    (f) Cytotoxic T cells: _____

5. Briefly explain the basis of **immunological memory**: _____

    _____

    _____

Antibodies

Antibodies and antigens play key roles in the response of the immune system. Antigens are foreign molecules that are able to bind to antibodies (or T cell receptors) and provoke a specific immune response. Antigens include potentially damaging microbes and their toxins (see below) as well as substances such as pollen grains, blood cell surface molecules, and the surface proteins on transplanted tissues. **Antibodies** (also called immunoglobulins) are proteins that are made in response to antigens. They are secreted into the plasma where they circulate and can recognize, bind to, and help to destroy antigens. There are 5 classes of **immunoglobulins**. Each plays a different role in

the immune response (including destroying protozoan parasites, enhancing phagocytosis, protecting mucous surfaces, and neutralizing toxins and viruses). The human body can produce an estimated 100 million antibodies, recognizing many different antigens, including those it has never encountered. Each type of antibody is highly specific to only one particular antigen. The ability of the immune system to recognize and ignore the antigenic properties of its own tissues occurs early in development and is called **self-tolerance**. Exceptions occur when the immune system malfunctions and the body attacks its own tissues, causing an **autoimmune disorder**.

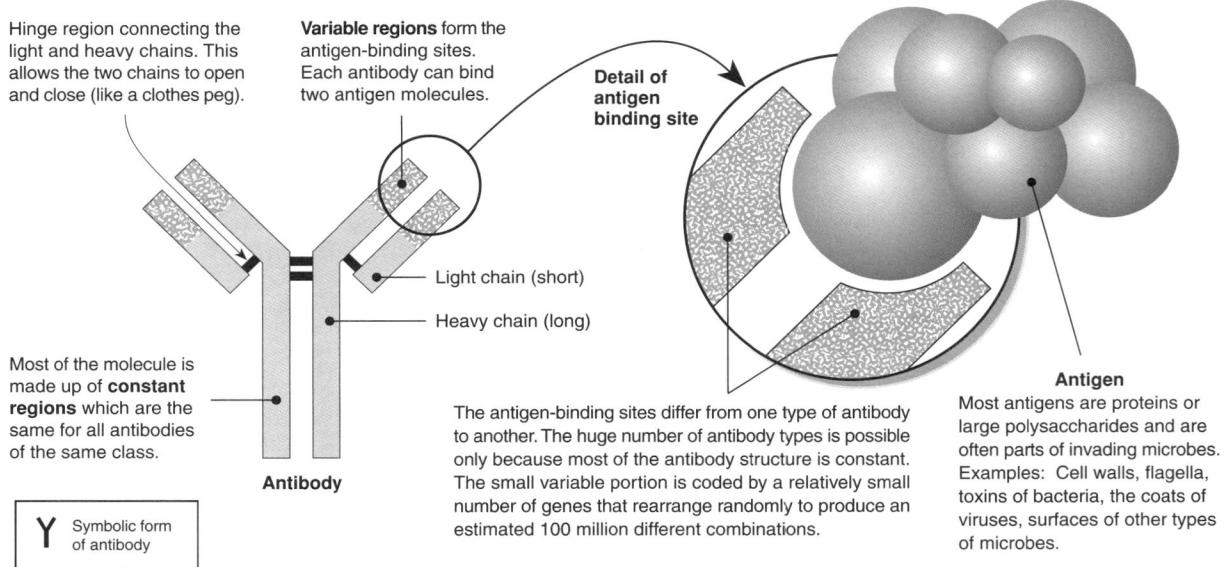

Hinge region connecting the light and heavy chains. This allows the two chains to open and close (like a clothes peg).

Variable regions form the antigen-binding sites. Each antibody can bind two antigen molecules.

Detail of antigen binding site

Light chain (short)

Heavy chain (long)

Most of the molecule is made up of **constant regions** which are the same for all antibodies of the same class.

Antibody

Y   Symbolic form of antibody

The antigen-binding sites differ from one type of antibody to another. The huge number of antibody types is possible only because most of the antibody structure is constant. The small variable portion is coded by a relatively small number of genes that rearrange randomly to produce an estimated 100 million different combinations.

Antigen
Most antigens are proteins or large polysaccharides and are often parts of invading microbes. Examples: Cell walls, flagella, toxins of bacteria, the coats of viruses, surfaces of other types of microbes.

How Antibodies Inactivate Antigens

Neutralization	Sticking together particulate antigens	Precipitation of soluble antigens	Activation of complement
Virus / Toxin	Bacterial cell	Soluble antigens	Complement / Bacterial cell
Antibodies bind to viral binding sites and coat bacterial toxins.	Solid antigens such as bacteria are stuck together in clumps.	Soluble antigens are stuck together to form precipitates.	Tags foreign cells for destruction by phagocytes and complement.

Enhances phagocytosis

Macrophage

Enhances inflammation

Blood vessel

Bacteria

Leads to rupture of cell

Lesion

Bacterial cell

1. Give a brief definition for each of the following:

   (a) Antibody: _____

   _____

   _____

   (b) Antigen: _____

   _____

   _____

2. It is necessary for the immune system to clearly distinguish cells and proteins made by the body, from foreign ones.

   (a) Explain why this is the case: _____

   _____

   _____

   (b) In simple terms, explain how self tolerance develops (see the activity "The Immune System" if you need help):

   _____

   _____

   (c) Name the type of disorder that results when this recognition system fails: _____

   (d) Name two examples of disorders that are caused in this way: _____

   _____

3. Briefly describe four ways in which antibodies work to inactivate antigens:

   (a) _____

   _____

   _____

   (b) _____

   _____

   _____

   (c) _____

   _____

   _____

   (d) _____

   _____

   _____

4. Explain how antibody activity enhances or leads to:

   (a) Phagocytosis: _____

   _____

   (b) Inflammation: _____

   _____

   (c) Bacterial cell lysis: _____

   _____

Immunization

RDA②

A vaccine is a suspension of microorganisms (or pieces of them) that protects against disease by stimulating the production of antibodies and inducing **immunity**. **Vaccination** (often used synonymously with **immunization**) is a procedure that provides **artificially acquired active immunity** in the recipient. A concerted vaccination campaign led to the eradication (in 1977) of **smallpox**, the only disease to have been eradicated in this way. Once eradicated, a pathogen is no longer present in the environment and vaccination is no longer necessary. Features of smallpox made it particularly suitable for complete eradication. It was a very recognizable and visible disease, with no long-term,

human carriers and no non-human carriers. In addition, people who had not been vaccinated against the disease were identifiable by the absence of a vaccination scar on the upper arm. Disease control (as opposed to eradication) does not necessarily require that everyone be immune. **Herd immunity**, where most of the population is immune, limits outbreaks to sporadic cases because there are too few susceptible individuals to support an epidemic. Vaccination provides effective control over many common bacterial and viral diseases. Viral diseases in particular are best prevented with vaccination, as they cannot be effectively treated once contracted.

Primary and Secondary Responses to Antigens

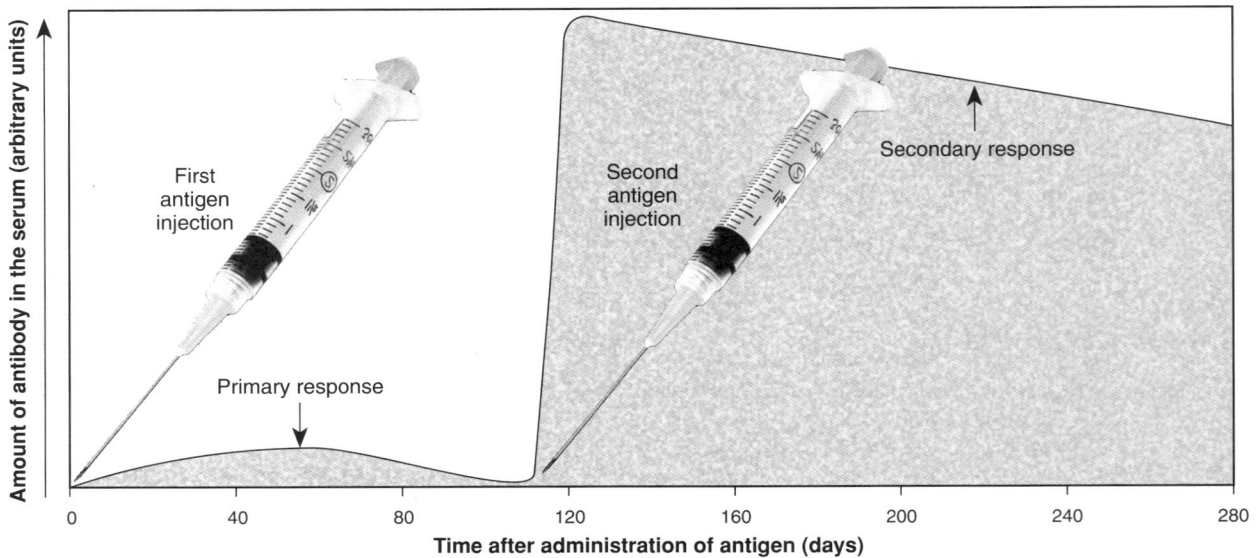

Graph: Amount of antibody in the serum (arbitrary units) vs Time after administration of antigen (days), x-axis from 0 to 280. First antigen injection — Primary response. Second antigen injection — Secondary response.

Vaccines to protect against common diseases are administered at various stages during childhood according to an immunization schedule.

While most vaccinations are given in childhood, adults may be vaccinated against specific diseases (e.g. tuberculosis) if they are in a high risk group or if they are travelling to a region in the world where a disease is prevalent.

Selected vaccines used to prevent diseases in humans

Disease	Type of vaccine	Recommendation
Diphtheria	Purified diphtheria toxoid	From early childhood and every 10 years for adults
Meningococcal meningitis	Purified polysaccharide of *Neisseria menigitidis*	For people with substantial risk of infection
Whooping cough	Killed cells or fragments of *Bordetella pertussis*	Children prior to school age
Tetanus	Purified tetanus toxoid	14-16 year olds with booster every 10 years
Meningitis caused by *Haemophilus influenzae* b	Polysaccharide from virus conjugated with protein to enhance effectiveness	Early childhood
Influenza	Killed virus (vaccines using genetically engineered antigenic fragments are also being developed)	For chronically ill people, especially with respiratory diseases, or for healthy people over 65 years of age
Measles	Attenuated virus	Early childhood
Mumps	Attenuated virus	Early childhood
Rubella	Attenuated virus	Early childhood; for females of child-bearing age who are not pregnant
Polio	Attenuated or killed virus (enhanced potency type)	Early childhood
Hepatitis B	Antigenic fragments of virus	Early childhood

1. After consulting your family doctor, medical centre or other medical authority, complete the table below, by:

    (a) Listing the vaccines administered to infants and young adults in your area.

    (b) Stating the diseases that each vaccine protects against.

    (c) Determine the ages at which each vaccine should be given. Place a tick (✔) in each age column as appropriate.

Vaccination Schedule								
Vaccine	**Diseases protected from**	**Age (months)**				**Age (years)**		

2. The graph at the top of the previous page illustrates how a person reacts to the injection of the same antibody on two separate occasions. This represents the initial vaccination followed by a booster shot.

    (a) State over what time period the antigen levels were monitored: _____

    (b) State what happens to the antibody levels after the first injection: _____

    _____

    (c) State what happens to the antibody levels after the booster shot: _____

    _____

    (d) Explain why the second injection has a markedly different effect: _____

    _____

3. The whole question of whether young children should be immunized has been a point of hot debate with some parents. The parents that do not want their children immunized have strongly held reasons for doing so. In a balanced way, explore the arguments for and against childhood immunization:

    (a) State clearly the benefits from childhood immunization: _____

    _____

    _____

    (b) Explain why some parents are concerned about immunizing their children: _____

    _____

    _____

4. Consult your family doctor or medical centre and list 3 vaccinations that are recommended for travellers to overseas destinations with high risk of infectious disease:

    (a) Country/region: _____ Vaccine required: _____

    (b) Country/region: _____ Vaccine required: _____

    (c) Country/region: _____ Vaccine required: _____

RA 3

Types of Vaccine

There are two basic types of vaccine: subunit vaccines and whole-agent vaccines. **Whole-agent vaccines** contain complete nonvirulent microbes, either **inactivated** (killed), or alive but **attenuated** (weakened). Attenuated viruses make very effective vaccines and often provide life-long immunity without the need for booster immunizations. Killed viruses are less effective and many vaccines of this sort have now been replaced by newer subunit vaccines. **Subunit vaccines** contain only the parts of the pathogen that induce the immune response. They are safer than attenuated vaccines because they cannot reproduce in the recipient, and they produce fewer adverse effects because they contain little or no extra material.

Subunit vaccines can be made using a variety of methods, including cell fragmentation (*acellular vaccines*), inactivation of toxins (*toxoids*), genetic engineering (*recombinant vaccines*), and combination with antigenic proteins (*conjugated vaccines*). In all cases, the subunit vaccine loses its ability to cause disease but retains its antigenic properties so that it is still effective in inducing an immune response. Some of the most promising types of vaccine under development are the DNA vaccines, consisting of naked DNA which is injected into the body and produces an antigenic protein. The safety of DNA vaccines is uncertain but they show promise for use against rapidly mutating viruses such as influenza and HIV.

Types of Vaccine

Whole-Agent Vaccine

Contains whole, nonvirulent microorganisms

Subunit Vaccine

Contains some part or product of microorganisms that can produce an immune response

Adjuvants

Many subunit vaccines are made with the addition of **adjuvants**: additional agents that increase the effectiveness of the vaccine. Adjuvants are not part of the pathogen but include substances such as detergent, oil, and dead non-pathogenic bacteria. Their purpose is to increase inflammation and therefore the level of immune response.

Inactivated (killed)

Viruses for vaccines may be inactivated with formalin or other chemicals. Inactivated vaccines present no risk of infection but many are being replaced by newer, more effective acellular vaccines. *Examples: most influenza vaccines, Salk polio vaccine, rabies vaccine.*

Attenuated (weakened)

Mutated DNA

Attenuated viruses are usually strains in which mutations have accumulated during long-term cell culture. One danger of such vaccines is that these **live viruses** can back-mutate to a virulent form. *Examples: Sabin polio vaccine, and the vaccines against measles, mumps, and rubella (MMR).*

Recombinant vaccines

Yeast makes viral proteins

Recombinant sub-unit vaccines can be made using genetic engineering techniques, where non-pathogenic microbes (yeast and bacteria) are programmed to make a desired antigenic fraction. *Example: hepatitis B vaccine.*

Toxoids

Heat, iodine or formaldehyde

Toxins from bacteria are inactivated

Toxoids are bacterial toxins that have been inactivated by heat or chemicals. When injected, the toxoid stimulates the production of antitoxins (antibodies) that neutralize any circulating toxin. *Examples: diphtheria vaccine, tetanus vaccine.*

Conjugated vaccines

Toxoid attached

Polysaccharide from pathogen

Some pathogens produce poly-saccharide capsules that are poorly antigenic, especially in young children. To enhance their effectiveness, they are combined with proteins such as toxoids from other pathogens. *Example: vaccine against Haemophilus influenzae b.*

Acellular vaccines

Pieces of bacterial cells

Involves the fragmentation of a conventional whole-agent vaccine and collecting only those portions that contain the desired antigens. Because the complete cells are not used, infection is not possible. *Examples: newer whooping cough and typhoid vaccines.*

1. Describe briefly **how** each of the following types of vaccine are made and name an **example** of each:

   (a) Whole-agent vaccine: _____

   _____

   (b) Subunit vaccine: _____

   _____

   (c) Inactivated vaccine: _____

   _____

   (d) Attenuated vaccine: _____

   _____

   (e) Recombinant vaccine: _____

   _____

   (f) Toxoid vaccine: _____

   _____

   (g) Conjugated vaccine: _____

   _____

   (h) Acellular vaccine: _____

   _____

2. **Attenuated viruses** provide long term immunity to their recipients and generally do not require booster shots. Suggest a possible reason why attenuated viruses provide such effective long-term immunity when inactivated viruses do not:

   _____

   _____

3. Bearing in mind the structure of viruses, explain why **heat** cannot be used to kill viruses to make **inactivated vaccines**:

   _____

   _____

4. Vaccines may now be produced using **genetic engineering techniques**.
   (a) Describe an advantage of creating vaccines using genetic engineering techniques (recombinant method):

   _____

   (b) Draw a simple **diagram** to illustrate the use of the recombinant method to manufacture a vaccine:

EA 3

Edible Vaccines

Although still a few years away, the development of edible vaccines produced by transgenic plants will overcome many of the problems faced when using traditional, injectable vaccines. Plants engineered to contain the vaccine can be grown locally, in the area where vaccination is required, overcoming the logistic and economic problems of transporting prepared vaccines over long distances. Most importantly, edible vaccines do not require syringes, saving money and eliminating the risk of infection from contaminated needles. One method used to generate edible vaccines relies on the bacterium *Agrobacterium tumefaciens* to deliver the genes for viral or bacterial antigens into plant cells. The diagram below illustrates this process using potatoes.

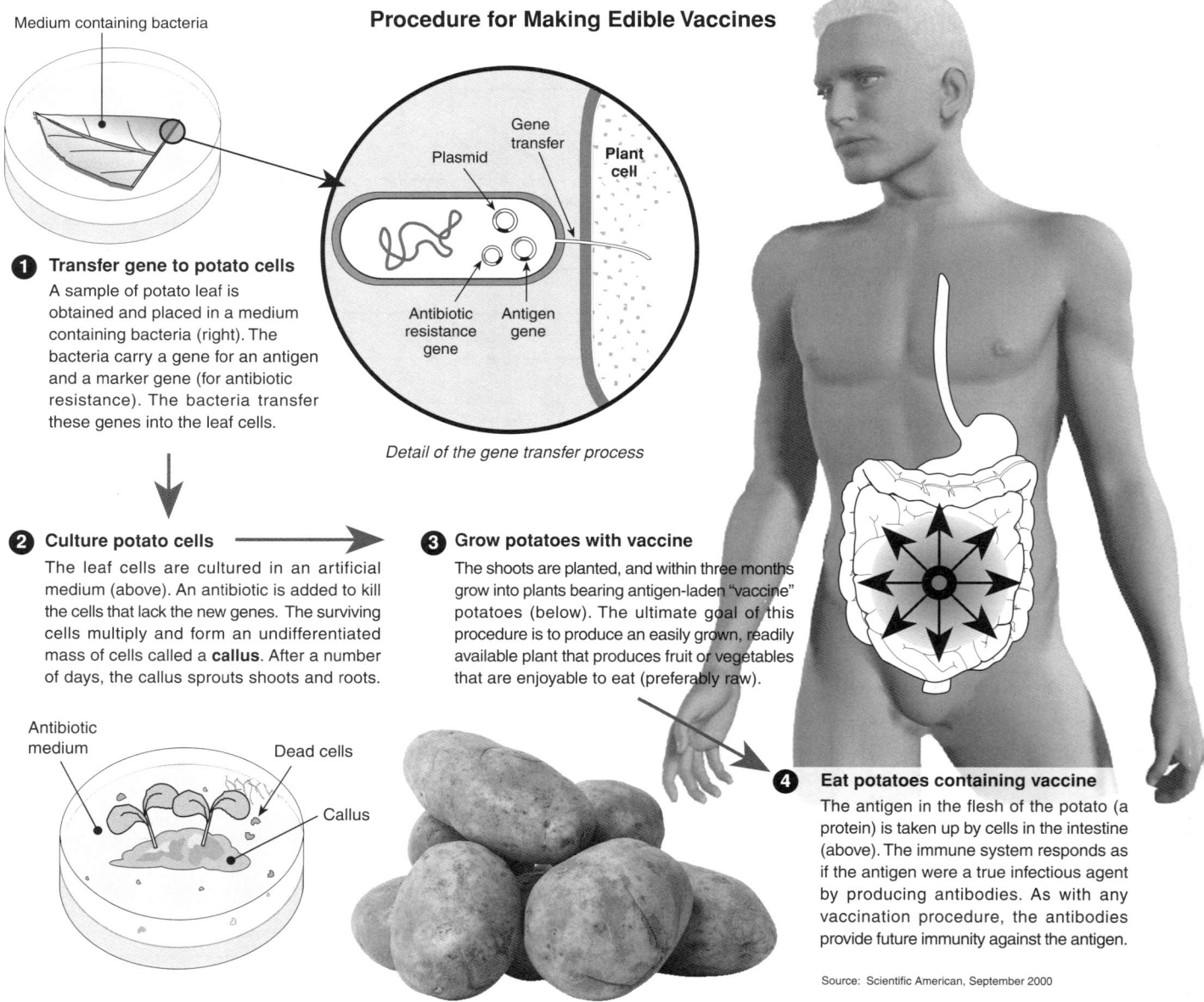

Procedure for Making Edible Vaccines

Medium containing bacteria

1 Transfer gene to potato cells

A sample of potato leaf is obtained and placed in a medium containing bacteria (right). The bacteria carry a gene for an antigen and a marker gene (for antibiotic resistance). The bacteria transfer these genes into the leaf cells.

Plasmid

Gene transfer

Plant cell

Antibiotic resistance gene

Antigen gene

Detail of the gene transfer process

2 Culture potato cells

The leaf cells are cultured in an artificial medium (above). An antibiotic is added to kill the cells that lack the new genes. The surviving cells multiply and form an undifferentiated mass of cells called a **callus**. After a number of days, the callus sprouts shoots and roots.

3 Grow potatoes with vaccine

The shoots are planted, and within three months grow into plants bearing antigen-laden "vaccine" potatoes (below). The ultimate goal of this procedure is to produce an easily grown, readily available plant that produces fruit or vegetables that are enjoyable to eat (preferably raw).

Antibiotic medium

Dead cells

Callus

4 Eat potatoes containing vaccine

The antigen in the flesh of the potato (a protein) is taken up by cells in the intestine (above). The immune system responds as if the antigen were a true infectious agent by producing antibodies. As with any vaccination procedure, the antibodies provide future immunity against the antigen.

Source: Scientific American, September 2000

1. Outline two **advantages** of using edible vaccines:

    (a) _____

    (b) _____

2. Outline one **disadvantage** of using edible vaccines: _____

3. Although potatoes are easy to propagate and are grown in many regions of the world, they are not particularly suitable for use as edible vaccines because cooking denatures the antigenic proteins. Giving a reason, suggest another fruit or vegetable that would be more suitable:

    _____

    _____

4. Explain why a gene for antibiotic resistance is added to the bacterium: _____

    _____

Monoclonal Antibodies

R 2

A **monoclonal antibody** is an artificially produced antibody that neutralizes only one specific protein (antigen). Monoclonal antibodies are produced in the laboratory by stimulating the production of B-lymphocytes in mice injected with the antigen. These B-lymphocytes produce an antibody against the antigen. When isolated and made to fuse with immortal tumor cells, they can be cultured indefinitely in a suitable growing medium (as illustrated below). Monoclonal antibodies are useful for three reasons: they are totally uniform (i.e. clones), they can be produced in large quantities, and they are highly specific. The uses of antibodies produced by this method have ranged from diagnostic tools to treatments for infections and cancer. The therapeutic use of monoclonal antibodies has been limited because the antibodies are currently produced by non-human cells. The immune systems of some people have reacted against the foreign proteins (the antibodies themselves). It is hoped in the future to produce monoclonal antibodies derived from human cells, which will probably cause fewer reactions.

Making Monoclonal Antibodies

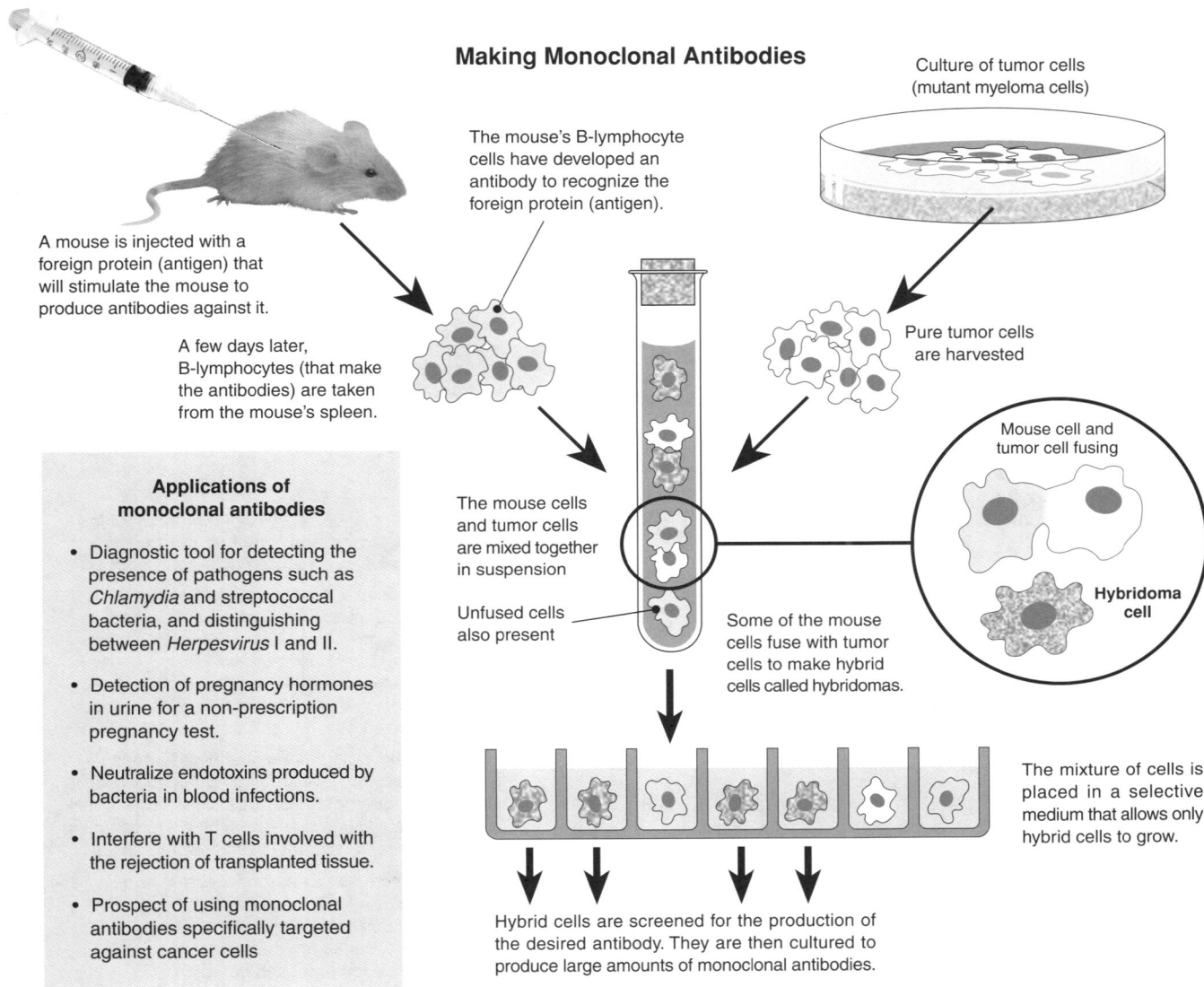

The mouse's B-lymphocyte cells have developed an antibody to recognize the foreign protein (antigen).

Culture of tumor cells (mutant myeloma cells)

A mouse is injected with a foreign protein (antigen) that will stimulate the mouse to produce antibodies against it.

A few days later, B-lymphocytes (that make the antibodies) are taken from the mouse's spleen.

Pure tumor cells are harvested

Mouse cell and tumor cell fusing

The mouse cells and tumor cells are mixed together in suspension

Unfused cells also present

Some of the mouse cells fuse with tumor cells to make hybrid cells called hybridomas.

Hybridoma cell

The mixture of cells is placed in a selective medium that allows only hybrid cells to grow.

Applications of monoclonal antibodies

- Diagnostic tool for detecting the presence of pathogens such as *Chlamydia* and streptococcal bacteria, and distinguishing between *Herpesvirus* I and II.

- Detection of pregnancy hormones in urine for a non-prescription pregnancy test.

- Neutralize endotoxins produced by bacteria in blood infections.

- Interfere with T cells involved with the rejection of transplanted tissue.

- Prospect of using monoclonal antibodies specifically targeted against cancer cells

Hybrid cells are screened for the production of the desired antibody. They are then cultured to produce large amounts of monoclonal antibodies.

1. Describe the characteristic of tumor cells that allows an ongoing culture of antibody-producing lymphocytes to be made:

_____

2. List four applications of monoclonal antibodies:

(a) _____

(b) _____

(c) _____

(d) _____

3. Describe a problem with the current method of producing monoclonal antibodies using mice:

_____

4. Name the mouse cells used to produce the monoclonal antibodies: _____

The Origin and Evolution of Life

IB SL

Not applicable
but see #27 (cross ref: Mechanisms of Evolution)

IB HL

Not applicable
but see #27 (cross ref: Mechanisms of Evolution)

IB Options

Complete nos:
Option D: SL/HL: 1-3, 5-8, 12, 14-15, 18-23, 27(a)-(d) HL only: 27 (d)-(e)

AP Biology

Complete nos:
*1-27
Some numbers extension as appropriate*

Learning Objectives

☐ 1. Compile your own glossary from the **KEY WORDS** displayed in **bold type** in the learning objectives below.

The origin of life on Earth

The prebiotic world *(pages 72-74)*

☐ 2. Outline the conditions of **prebiotic Earth**, including reference to the role of the following: *high temperature, lightning, ultraviolet light penetration, and reducing atmosphere.* Explain the probable events that lead to the formation of life on Earth.

☐ 3. Recognize major stages in the evolution of life on Earth. Summarize the main ideas related to where life originated: ocean surface, extraterrestrial (**panspermia**), and deep sea thermal vents.

☐ 4. Describe some of the geological and paleontological evidence that suggests when life originated on Earth.

☐ 5. Outline the experiments (in particular the experiments of **Miller** and **Urey**) that have attempted to simulate the **prebiotic environment** on Earth. Describe their importance in our understanding of the probable origin of organic compounds.

☐ 6. Discuss the hypothesis that the first catalysts responsible for **polymerization reactions** were clay minerals and RNA.

The first cells *(pages 72-73 also SB 1: page 323)*

☐ 7. Describe the possible role of RNA as the first self-replicating molecule. Discuss its role as an enzyme and its role in the origin of the first self-replicating cells.

☐ 8. Discuss the possible origin of membranes and the first prokaryotic cells.

☐ 9. Describe the evidence in the **geological record** for the first aquatic **prokaryotes**. Discuss the importance of these early organisms to the later evolution of diversity.

☐ 10. Distinguish between the **Eubacteria**, the **Archaea**, and the **Eukarya** with respect to their features and the environments in which they live. Explain what the current ecology of some bacterial groups tells us about the probable conditions of early life on Earth.

The origin of eukaryotes *(page 75)*

☐ 11. Recall how eukaryotes differ from prokaryotes. Explain why the evolution of eukaryotic cells is regarded as a milestone in the development of complexity in living things.

☐ 12. Discuss the **endosymbiotic** (endosymbiont) **theory** for the evolution of eukaryotic cells. Summarize the evidence in support of this theory.

☐ 13. Summarize the main ideas about the evolution of multicellular life. Describe the benefits gained by the evolution of multicellularity (multicellular life).

The Evidence for Evolution

Background: *The greatest obstacle to the establishment of evolutionary theory has been the difficulty in observing evolution in the time scales within which humans operate. Although more recently there have been direct observations made of populations evolving within observable time periods (flour beetles, bacteria, viruses, <u>Drosophila</u>), much of the evidence for evolution is indirect or circumstantial. The weight of accumulated evidence from many fields of science is overwhelmingly in support of evolution. The way in which organisms are classified reflects their evolutionary development (phylogeny) and degree of relatedness. Students should be aware that the scientific debate of evolution has centered on hypotheses for the evolutionary processes, <u>not</u> on the phenomenon of evolution itself.*

The fossil record *(pages 76-82)*

☐ 14. State the conditions under which different **fossils** form. Include reference to **petrified remains**, **prints** and **molds**, and preservation in **amber**, **tar**, **peat**, and **ice**.

☐ 15. Outline the methods for dating rocks and fossils using **radioisotopes**, with specific reference to ^{14}C and ^{40}K. Appreciate the degree of accuracy achieved by different dating methods and how the choice of isotope to use is made. Define the term: **half-life** and deduce the approximate age of materials based on a simple **decay curve** for a radioisotope.

☐ 16. Appreciate that the dating of the main fossil-bearing rocks has provided the data for dividing the history of life on Earth into **geological periods**, which collectively form the geological time scale. Explain the system used to describe the age of rock strata (*era, period, epoch*).

☐ 17. Explain what is meant by **transitional forms** and explain their significance. Offer an explanation for the apparent lack of transitional forms in the fossil record. Using examples, describe the trends that fossils indicate in the evolution of related groups.

☐ 18. Outline the **paleontological evidence** for evolution using one example e.g. evolution of horses or birds.

Comparative biochemistry *(pages 83-85)*

☐ 19. Explain the biochemical evidence by the universality of DNA, amino acids, and protein structures (e.g. cytochrome C) for the common ancestry of living organisms. Describe how comparisons of specific molecules between species are used as an indication of relatedness or phylogeny. Examples could include comparisons of DNA, amino acid sequences, or blood proteins (see #20).

☐ 20. Describe how **immunology** provides a method of quantifying the relatedness of species. Describe the basic principles and techniques involved.

☐ 21. Discuss how biochemical variations can be used as an **evolutionary** (molecular) **clock** to determine probable dates of divergence from a common ancestor.

Anatomical comparisons (pages 85-87)

☐ 22. In a general way, describe how **comparative anatomy**, **embryology**, and physiology have contributed to an understanding of evolutionary relationships.

☐ 23. Distinguish between **homologous** structures and **analogous structures** arising as a result of convergent evolution. Give examples of **homology**. Explain the evidence for evolution provided by homologous anatomical structures, including: the vertebrate pentadactyl limb and vertebrate embryos. NOTE: Recognize that although vertebrate embryos may pass through similar stages during their development, ontogeny does not recapitulate phylogeny; Haeckel's original drawings were inaccurate and misleading.

☐ 24. Giving appropriate examples, discuss the significance of **vestigial organs** as indicators of evolutionary trends in some groups.

Biogeography (pages 88-93)

☐ 25. Using named examples, explain how the geographical distribution of plants and animals (both living and extinct), provides evidence of dispersal of organisms from a point of origin across pre-existing barriers.

☐ 26. Outline the evidence for the occurrence of crustal movements by plate tectonics.

Modern examples of evolution (pages 100-105)

☐ 27. Outline two modern examples of observed evolution. For each example, identify the species involved, the selective pressures thought to be operating, common ancestor(s) if known, and (if appropriate) the species diversity that has arisen as a result of the evolution. One example must be the changes to the size and shape of the beaks of **Galapagos finches**. Other examples could include:

(a) Development of **antibiotic resistance** in bacteria.

(b) Development of **pesticide resistance** in insects.

(c) **Heavy metal tolerance** in plants.

(d) Selective predation on moths by birds (proposed as being the selective agent for **transient polymorphism** in peppered moths, although this has never been adequately demonstrated).

(e) The sickle cell trait as the basis for **balanced polymorphism** in regions where malaria is prevalent.

Cross reference with IB Core: 4.3 and Option D6: see the following topic: 'Mechanisms of Evolution'.

Textbooks

See the 'Textbook Reference Grid' on pages 8-9 for textbook page references relating to material in this topic.

Supplementary Texts

The following references for teachers provide excellent, detailed material on life's origins:

■ **The Molecular Origins of Life** (1998) Brack, A. (ed). Cambridge U.P. ISBN: 0-521-56475-1. *A thought provoking summary of this topic.*

■ **Biogenesis: Theories of Life's Origin** (1999) Lahav, N. Oxford University Press. ISBN: 0-19-511755-7. *A critical discussion of the study of the origin of life (detailed with good diagrams).*

Periodicals

See page 6 for details of publishers of periodicals:

STUDENT'S REFERENCE

Origins of life & eukaryote evolution

■ **The Rise of Life on Earth (series)** National Geographic, 193(3) March 1998, pp. 54-81. *Series of excellent, readable articles covering the theories for the origins of life on Earth, the evolution of life's diversity, and the origin of eukaryotic cells.*

■ **An RNA World** Biol. Sci. Rev., 11(3) January 1999, pp. 2-6. *An experiment to reproduce the prebiotic conditions on Earth suggests that RNA evolved before DNA as an early enzyme.*

■ **Other Worlds** New Scientist, 18 September 1999, pp. 24-47. *Articles in this special issue cover the conditions required for life to evolve and the organization of the first biological life.*

Geological history and fossil record

■ **The Geological Time Scale** New Scientist, 20 May 1995 (Inside Science). *Fossil dating and the construction of evolutionary time scales.*

■ **The Quick and the Dead** New Scientist, 5 June 1999, pp. 44-48. *Fossil formation, fossil types, and the preservation expected in certain environments.*

■ **Life Grows Up** National Geographic, 193(4) April 1998, pp. 100-115. *The evolution of life: ancient fossils reveal the rise of life on Earth.*

■ **Dinosaur Detectives** New Scientist, 18 April 1998, pp. 24-29. *The interpretation of fossils is a matter of piecing together a jigsaw of evidence.*

■ **How Old is...** National Geographic, 200(3) September 2001, pp. 79-101. *A comprehensive discussion of dating methods and their application.*

Comparative studies

■ **A Waste of Space** New Scientist, 25 April 1998, pp. 38-39. *Vestigial organs; how they arise in an evolutionary sense and what they may be for.*

■ **Computers, DNA, and Evolution** Biol. Sci. Rev., 11(5) May 1999, pp. 24-29. *Using computers to compare the DNA sequences of different species and establish phylogeny.*

TEACHER'S REFERENCE

Origins of life & eukaryote evolution

■ **Life's far Flung Raw Materials** Sci. American, July 1999, pp. 26-33. *The origins of life: how organic molecules arose and the lab simulations that have tried to replicate their creation.*

■ **Proof of Life** New Scientist, 22 Feb. 2003, pp. 28-31. *The most recent studies of microfossils suggest that life on Earth may be much younger than first thought.*

■ **Born Lucky** New Scientist, 12 July 2003, pp. 32-35. *This article discusses how, against odds, life established itself quickly on Earth, and suggests that this can tell us something about where life began. One of a series in this issue.*

■ **Life's Rocky Start** Sci. American, April 2001, pp. 62-71. *The origins of life: prebiotic experiments & the role of minerals in early reactions on Earth.*

■ **The Ice of Life** Sci. American, August 2001, pp. 37-41. *Space ice may promote organic molecules and may have seeded life on Earth.*

Fossils and comparative evidence

■ **Putting Together Fossil Collections for 'Hands On' Evolution Laboratories** The Am. Biology Teacher, 63(1), January 2001, pp. 16-19. *How to put together a fossil lab: types of fossils (species) and provides good photos and contact.*

■ **Biological Misfits as Evidence of Evolution** The American Biology Teacher, 59(7), Sept. 1997, pp. 392-394. *Adaptation, natural selection, and evolution: organisms are not always perfectly adapted. Examples provided are the Hawaiian goose, Arctic hare, and tree kangaroo.*

■ **Haeckel's Embryos and Evolution** The American Biology Teacher, 61(5), May 1999, pp. 345-349. *An article that sets the record straight about the flaws in Haeckel's work. It examines how to study embryology in the context of phylogeny.*

Case study in transitional fossils: birds

■ **Winging It** New Scientist, 28 Aug. 1999, pp. 28-32. *Update on the evidence for the origin of bird flight.*

■ **Dinosaurs and Birds** The American Biology Teacher, 61(9), Nov. 1999, pp. 701-705. *A look at the bird-dinosaur link and the origins of flight.*

■ **Dinosaurs take Wing** National Geographic, 194(1) July 1998, pp. 74-99. *The evolution of birds from small theropod dinosaurs. Explores the homology between the typical dinosaur limb and the wing of the modern bird. Excellent article.*

■ **The Origin of Birds and their Flight** Scientific American, Feb. 1998, pp. 28-37. *Excellent article on avian evolution. The central idea is that birds are as much dinosaurs as humans are mammals.*

■ **Birds Do It ..... Did Dinosaurs?** New Scientist 1 Feb. 1997, pp. 26-31. *Evolution of flight in the light of recent fossil finds. Includes an overview of the adaptations for flight. Excellent article.*

Comparative studies

■ **Ancient DNA** Scientific American, November 1993, pp. 60-66. *Although older, this is a valuable article covering the study of reconstituted DNA fragments and how it is used to make comparisons between existing and ancient species.*

■ **'New' Persuasive Evidence for Evolution** The American Biology Teacher, 60(9), Nov. 1998, pp. 662-70. *Investigating the molecular evidence for evolution: an account of how ancient 'errors' can persist in modern species.*

Internet

See pages 10-11 for details of how to access **Bio Links** from our web site: **www.thebiozone.com**. From Bio Links, access sites under the topics:

GENERAL BIOLOGY ONLINE RESOURCES > **Online Textbooks and Lecture Notes.**

EVOLUTION: • A history of evolutionary thought • BIO 414 evolution • Evolution • The Talk.Origins archive ... *and others* > **Evolution: Theory and Evidence:** • Continental drift and biogeography • Evolution for evolution: an eclectic survey • Transitional vertebrate fossils FAQ ... *and others* > **The Fossil Record:** • Geological time scale • Geology and geologic time • The age of the Earth • The Paleo ring ... *and others* > **The Origins of Life on Earth:** • From primordial soup to prebiotic beach • Miller/Urey experiment • Origin of life > **SPACE BIOLOGY > Exobiology:** • Archaea in space • Exobiology homepage ... *and others*

Software and video resources are now provided in the Teacher Resource Handbook

The Origin of Life on Earth

A 2

Recent discoveries of **prebiotic** conditions on other planets and their moons has rekindled interest in the origin of life on primeval Earth. Experiments demonstrate that both peptides and nucleic acids may form polymers naturally in the conditions that are thought to have existed in a primitive terrestrial environment. RNA has also been shown to have enzymatic properties (**ribozymes**) and is capable of self-replication. These discoveries have removed some fundamental obstacles to creating a plausible scientific model for the origin of life from a prebiotic soup. Much research is now underway. In the next few years, space probes will be sent to Mars, and probably also to some of the moons of Jupiter and Saturn. They will search for evidence of prebiotic conditions or primitive microorganisms. The study of life in such regions beyond our planet is called **exobiology**.

Steps Proposed in the Origin of Life

The appearance of life on our planet may be understood as the result of evolutionary processes that involve the following major steps:

1. Formation of the Earth (4600 mya) and its acquisition of volatile organic chemicals by collision with comets and meteorites, which provided the precursors of biochemical molecules.

2. Prebiotic synthesis and accumulation of amino acids, purines, pyrimidines, sugars, lipids, and other organic molecules in the primitive terrestrial environment.

3. Prebiotic condensation reactions involving the synthesis of polymers of peptides (proteins), and nucleic acids (most probably just RNA) with self-replicating and catalytic (enzymatic) abilities.

4. Synthesis of lipids, their self-assembly into double-layered membranes and liposomes, and the 'capturing' of prebiotic (self-replicating and catalytic) molecules within their boundaries.

5. Formation of a **protobiont**; an immediate precursor to the first living systems. Such protobionts would exhibit cooperative interactions between small catalytic peptides, replicative molecules, proto-tRNA, and protoribosomes.

An RNA World

RNA has the ability to act as both genes and enzymes and offers a way around the "chicken-and-egg" problem: genes require enzymes to form; enzymes require genes to form. The first stage of evolution may have proceeded by RNA molecules performing the catalytic activities necessary to assemble themselves from a nucleotide soup. At the next stage, RNA molecules began to synthesize proteins. There is a problem with RNA as a prebiotic molecule because the ribose is unstable. This has led to the idea of a pre-RNA world (PNA).

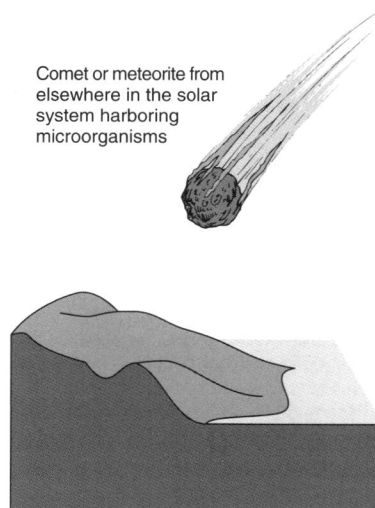

Photo: Ron Lind

These living **stromatolites** from a beach in Western Australia are created by mats of bacteria. Similar, fossilized stromatolites have been found in rocks dating back to 3500 million years ago.

Dynamics of an RNA world

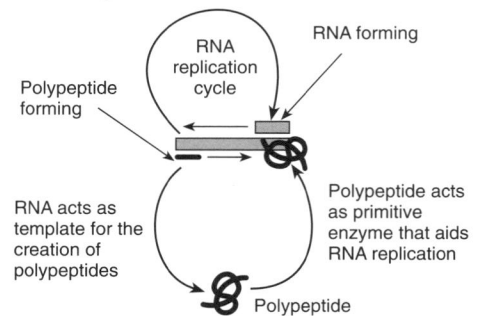

RNA forming

RNA replication cycle

Polypeptide forming

RNA acts as template for the creation of polypeptides

Polypeptide acts as primitive enzyme that aids RNA replication

Polypeptide

Scenarios for the Origin of Life on Earth

The origin of life remains a matter of scientific speculation. Three alternative views of how the key processes occurred are illustrated below:

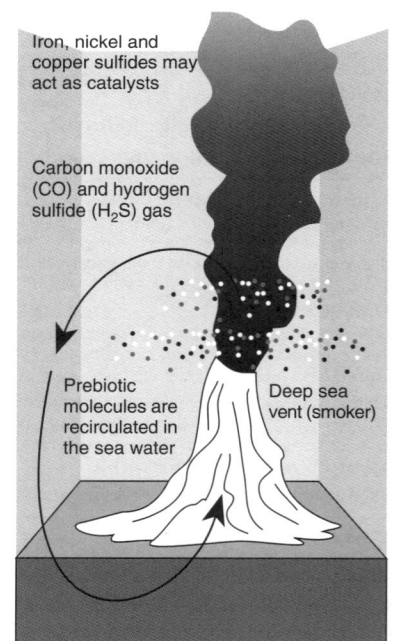

Volcanoes provide gases and heat energy

Ultraviolet light

Lightning

Froth (bubbles)

Prebiotic soup

Comet or meteorite from elsewhere in the solar system harboring microorganisms

Iron, nickel and copper sulfides may act as catalysts

Carbon monoxide (CO) and hydrogen sulfide (H_2S) gas

Prebiotic molecules are recirculated in the sea water

Deep sea vent (smoker)

Ocean surface (tidal pools)
This popular theory suggests that life arose in a tidepool, pond or on moist clay on the primeval Earth. Gases from volcanoes would have been energized by UV light or electrical discharges to form the prebiotic molecules in froth.

Panspermia
Cosmic ancestry (panspermia) is a serious scientific theory that proposes living organisms were 'seeded' on Earth as 'passengers' aboard comets and meteors. Such incoming organisms would have to survive the heat of re-entry.

Undersea thermal vents
A recently proposed theory suggests that life may have arisen at ancient volcanic vents (called smokers). This environment provides the necessary gases, energy, and a possible source of catalysts (metal sulfides).

Landmarks in the Origin and Evolution of Life

Geological column

Present day

Billions of years ago (bya)

1.0

2.0

3.0

4.0

4.6

Fossil history of large eukaryotic organisms is well documented.

0.55 bya: Fossils of more complex, multicelled creatures were thought to have first appeared here (but see below). Fossils 600-540 my old, reaching 1 meter across have been found in the Ediacara Hills, Flinders Ranges, South Australia.

1.1 bya: Grooves in sandstone from the Vindhyan Basin, central India, may be the burrows of ancient worm-like creatures. This is 500 million years earlier than any previous evidence for multicellular animals.

2.1 bya: First fossil imprints appear in the geological record that are so large they can only be eukaryotes.

2.5 bya: Molecular fossil of cyanobacteria, 2-methylhopane, is abundant in organic-rich sedimentary rocks from the Mount McRae shale in Western Australia.

2.7 bya: Compounds in the oily residue squeezed out of Australian shale suggest the presence of eukaryotic cells. It appears to push the beginnings of complex life on Earth a billion years earlier than scientists had first thought.

3.5 bya: The oldest microbial community now known is from the Apex chert of northwestern Western Australia. It is a diverse assemblage of cyanobacteria fossils, leaving behind big, layered mounds of fossil bacterial colonies (stromatolites).

A series of prebiotic steps that lead to the formation of the **protobiont**; an immediate precursor to the first living systems.

4.6 bya: Formation of the Earth and its acquisition of volatile organic chemicals by collision with comets and meteorites, which provided the precursors of biochemical molecules.

A black smoker: In 1977, a vent was discovered at the Galápagos spreading centre (mid-oceanic ridge), out of which gushed hot water laden with dissolved minerals. Since this discovery, hydrothermal venting has been found to be common along the length of the 55 000 km ridge crest system. Such black smokers are named after the dirty looking, high temperature water (350°C) that gushes from the chimney structures that they form. Such an environment is thought to be a possible site for prebiotic synthesis of life molecules.

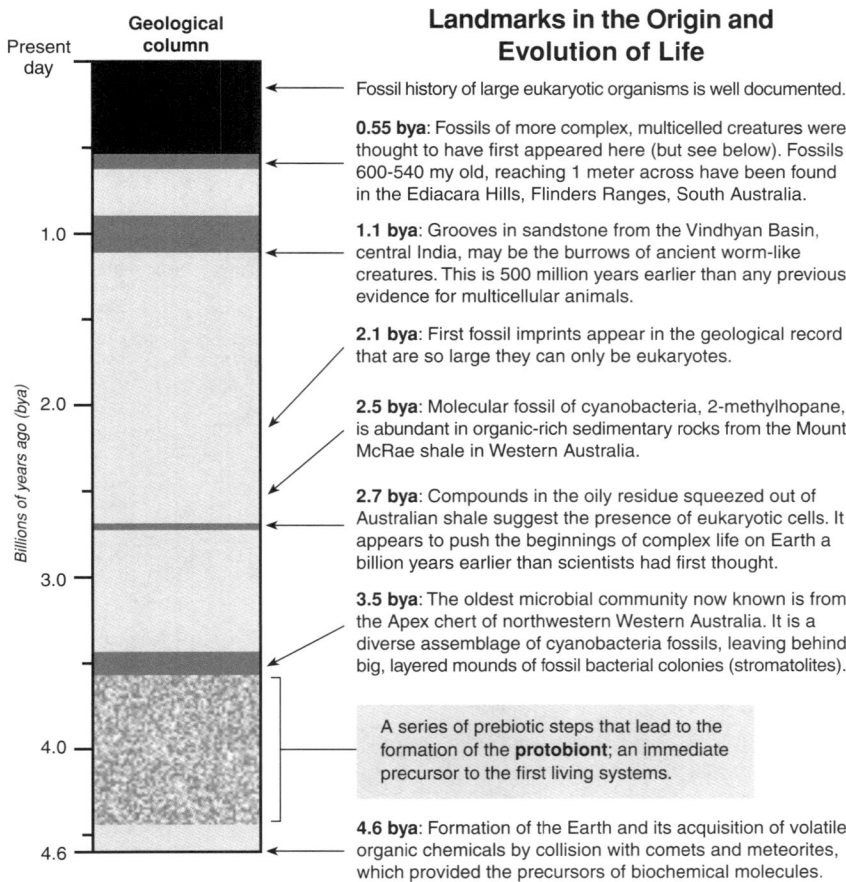

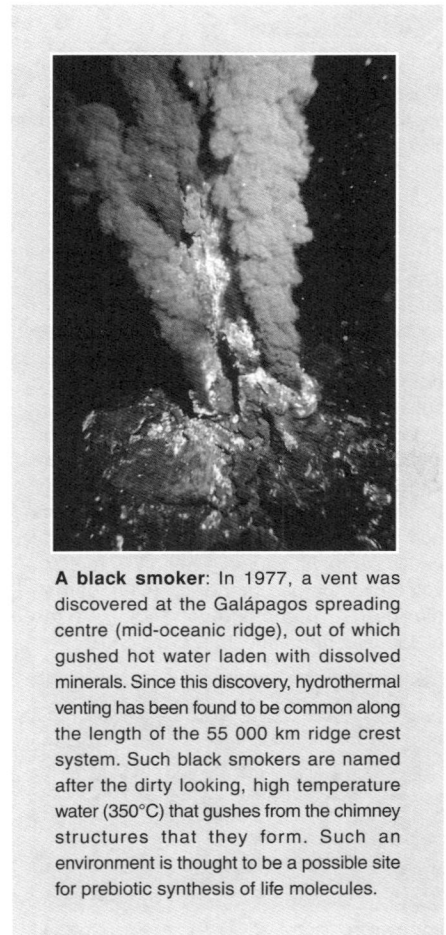

1. Summarize the three most accepted scientific models for the origin of life on Earth:

(a) Ocean surface: _____

_____

_____

(b) Panspermia: _____

_____

_____

(c) Undersea thermal vents: _____

_____

_____

2. Explain how the discovery of ribozymes has assisted in creating a plausible model for the prebiotic origin of life:

_____

_____

3. State how old the earliest fossils of microscopic life are known to be: _____

4. Scientists are seriously looking for evidence of life on other planets of our solar system, as well as some of their moons.

(a) Name a planet or a moon that are pending targets for such spacecraft missions: _____

(b) Explain how the discovery of life elsewhere in our solar system may affect the explanations for the origin of life:

_____

_____

Prebiotic Experiments

A 3

In the 1950s, Stanley Miller and Harold Urey used equipment (illustrated below) to attempt to recreate the conditions on the primitive Earth. They hoped that the experiment might give rise to the biological molecules that were forerunners to the development of the first living organisms. Researchers at the time believed that the Earth's early atmosphere was made up of methane, water vapor, ammonia, and hydrogen gas. Many variations on this experiment, using a variety of recipes, have produced similar results. It seems that the building blocks of life are relatively easy to create. Many types of organic molecules have even been detected in deep space.

The Miller-Urey Experiment

The experiment (right) was run for a week after which samples were taken from the collection trap for analysis. Up to 4% of the carbon (from the methane) had been converted to amino acids. In this and subsequent experiments, it has been possible to form all 20 amino acids commonly found in organisms, along with nucleic acids, several sugars, lipids, adenine, and even ATP (if phosphate is added to the flask). Researchers now believe that the early atmosphere may be similar to the vapors given off by modern volcanoes: carbon monoxide (CO), carbon dioxide (CO_2), and nitrogen (N_2). Note the absence of free atmospheric oxygen.

Iron pyrite, or 'fools gold' (above), has been proposed as a possible stabilizing surface for the synthesis of organic compounds in the prebiotic world.

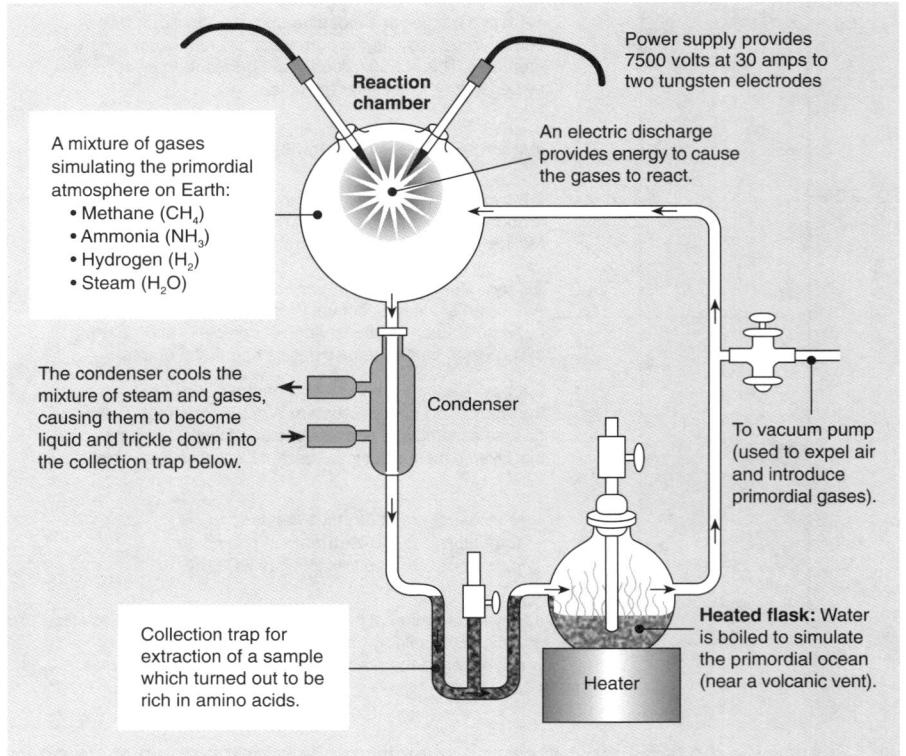

Reaction chamber

Power supply provides 7500 volts at 30 amps to two tungsten electrodes

A mixture of gases simulating the primordial atmosphere on Earth:
• Methane (CH_4)
• Ammonia (NH_3)
• Hydrogen (H_2)
• Steam (H_2O)

An electric discharge provides energy to cause the gases to react.

The condenser cools the mixture of steam and gases, causing them to become liquid and trickle down into the collection trap below.

Condenser

To vacuum pump (used to expel air and introduce primordial gases).

Collection trap for extraction of a sample which turned out to be rich in amino acids.

Heated flask: Water is boiled to simulate the primordial ocean (near a volcanic vent).

Heater

Some scientists envisage a global winter scenario for the formation of life. Organic compounds are more stable in colder temperatures and could combine in a lattice of ice. This frozen world could be thawed later.

Lightning is a natural phenomenon associated with volcanic activity. It may have supplied a source of electrical energy for the formation of new compounds (such as oxides of nitrogen) which were incorporated into organic molecules.

The early Earth was subjected to volcanism everywhere. At volcanic sites such as deep sea hydrothermal vents and geysers (like the one above), gases delivered vital compounds to the surface, where reactions took place.

1. In the Miller-Urey experiment simulating the conditions on primeval Earth, identify parts of the apparatus equivalent to:

   (a) Primeval atmosphere: _____

   (b) Primeval ocean: _____

   (c) Lightning: _____

   (d) Volcanic heat: _____

2. Name the organic molecules that were created by this experiment: _____

3. (a) Suggest a reason why the Miller-Urey experiment is not an accurate model of what happened on the primeval Earth:

   (b) Suggest changes to the experiment that could help it to better fit our understanding of the Earth's primordial conditions:

The Origin of Eukaryotes

RA 2

The first firm evidence of eukaryote cells is found in the fossil record at 540-600 mya. It is thought that eukaryote cells evolved from large prokaryote cells that ingested other free-floating prokaryotes. They formed a symbiotic relationship with the cells they engulfed (**endosymbiosis**). The two most important organelles that developed in eukaryote cells were mitochondria, for aerobic respiration, and chloroplasts, for photosynthesis in aerobic conditions. Primitive eukaryotes probably acquired mitochondria by engulfing purple bacteria. Similarly, chloroplasts

may have been acquired by engulfing primitive cyanobacteria (which were already capable of photosynthesis). In both instances the organelles produced became dependent on the nucleus of the host cell to direct some of their metabolic processes. The sequence of evolutionary change shown below suggests that the lines leading to animal cells diverged before those leading to plant cells, but the reverse could also be true. Animal cells might have evolved from plant-like cells which subsequently lost their chloroplasts.

The Origin of Eukaryotic Cells

Chloroplasts have an internal membrane structure that is nearly identical to that of modern cyanobacteria.

Chloroplasts possess a self-replicating circular chromosome. It uses a genetic code that contains prokaryotic features, supporting the probable origins of chloroplasts as endosymbionts.

Chloroplast DNA (cpDNA)

Mitochondrial DNA (mtDNA)

Mitochondria possess a self-replicating circular chromosome and use a genetic code identical to that used by prokaryotes. This supports the probable origins of mitochondria as endosymbionts.

Precursor prokaryotic cells

Aerobic bacterium (pre-mitochondrion)

To present-day aerobic bacteria

To present-day animal cells

Nucleated pre-prokaryote

pre-mitochondrion engulfed

Mitochondrion

Both mitochondria and chloroplast retain DNA of their own

To present-day plant cells

A cell that could engulf others and which had packaged its own genes inside a nucleus

Nucleus

pre-chloroplast engulfed

Photosynthetic prokaryote (pre-chloroplast)

1. Distinguish between the two possible sequences of evolutionary change suggested in the endosymbiosis theory:

_____

_____

_____

2. Explain how the endosymbiosis theory accounts for the origins of the following organelles in eukaryotic cells:

   (a) Mitochondria: _____

   _____

   (b) Chloroplasts: _____

   _____

3. Describe the evidence that is found in modern mitochondria and chloroplasts that supports the endosymbiosis theory:

   _____

   _____

4. Comment on how the fossil evidence of early life supports or contradicts the endosymbiotic theory: _____

   _____

   _____

The History of Life on Earth

A 2

Unlike the tales of folklore and religion, the scientific explanation the origin of life on Earth is based soundly on the extensive fossil record, as well as the genetic comparison of modern life forms. Together they clearly indicate that modern life forms arose from ancient ancestors that have long since become extinct. These ancient life forms themselves originally arose from primitive cells living some 3,500 million years ago in conditions quite different from those on Earth today. The earliest fossil records of living things show only simple cell types. It is believed that the first cells arose as a result of evolution at the chemical level in a 'primordial soup' (a rich broth of chemicals in a warm pool of water, perhaps near a volcanic vent). Life appears very early in Earth's history, but did not evolve beyond the simple cell stage until much later, (about 600 mya). This would suggest that the development of complex life forms required more difficult evolutionary hurdles to be overcome. The buildup of free oxygen in the atmosphere, released as a by-product from photosynthesizing organisms, was important for the evolutionary development of animal life.

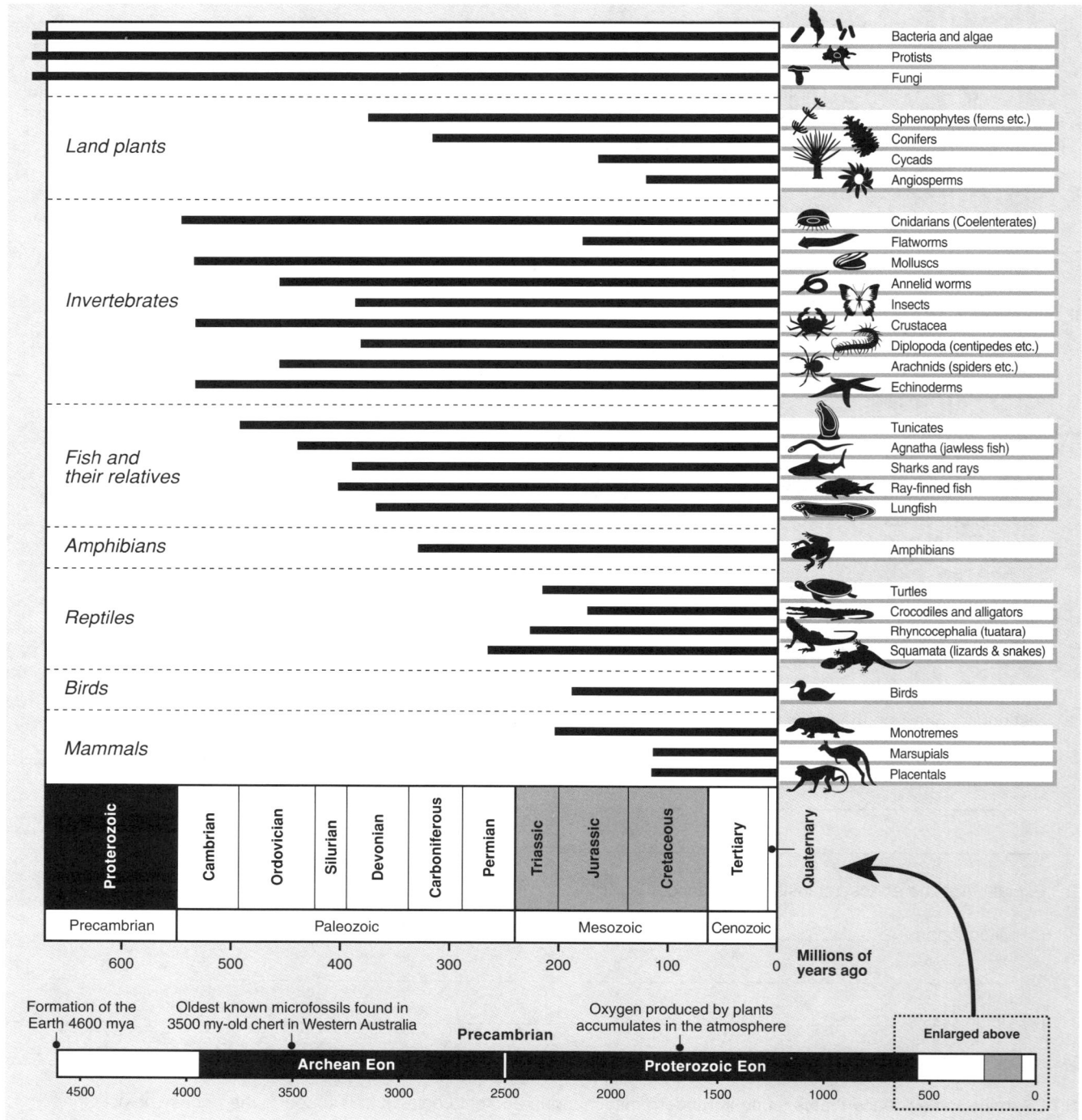

Bacteria and algae
Protists
Fungi

Land plants
Sphenophytes (ferns etc.)
Conifers
Cycads
Angiosperms

Invertebrates
Cnidarians (Coelenterates)
Flatworms
Molluscs
Annelid worms
Insects
Crustacea
Diplopoda (centipedes etc.)
Arachnids (spiders etc.)
Echinoderms

Fish and their relatives
Tunicates
Agnatha (jawless fish)
Sharks and rays
Ray-finned fish
Lungfish

Amphibians
Amphibians

Reptiles
Turtles
Crocodiles and alligators
Rhyncocephalia (tuatara)
Squamata (lizards & snakes)

Birds
Birds

Mammals
Monotremes
Marsupials
Placentals

Proterozoic | Cambrian | Ordovician | Silurian | Devonian | Carboniferous | Permian | Triassic | Jurassic | Cretaceous | Tertiary | Quaternary

Precambrian | Paleozoic | Mesozoic | Cenozoic

600   500   400   300   200   100   0   **Millions of years ago**

Formation of the Earth 4600 mya

Oldest known microfossils found in 3500 my-old chert in Western Australia

Precambrian

Oxygen produced by plants accumulates in the atmosphere

Enlarged above

Archean Eon | **Proterozoic Eon**

4500   4000   3500   3000   2500   2000   1500   1000   500   0

1. Explain the importance of the buildup of free oxygen in the atmosphere for the evolution of animal life:

_____

2. Using the diagram above, determine how many millions of years ago the fossil record shows the first appearance of:

(a) Invertebrates: _____

(b) Fish (ray-finned): _____

(c) Land plants: _____

(d) Reptiles: _____

(e) Birds: _____

(f) Mammals: _____

Cenozoic

1.65 mya: Modern humans evolve and their hunting activities, starting at the most recent ice age, cause the most recent mass extinction.

3-5 mya: Early humans arise from ape ancestors

65-1.65 mya: Major shifts in climate. Major adaptive radiations of angiosperms (flowering plants), insects, birds and mammals.

Diatryma
Deinotherium
Unitatherium
Glyptodon
Humans
Saber-tooth cats

Mesozoic

65 mya: Apparent asteroid impact causes mass extinctions of many marine species and all dinosaurs.

135-65 mya: Major radiations of dinosaurs, fishes, and insects. Origin of angiosperms.

181-135 mya: Major radiations of dinosaurs.

240-205 mya: Recoveries, adaptive radiation of marine invertebrates, dinosaurs and fishes. Origin of mammals Gymnosperms become dominant land plants.

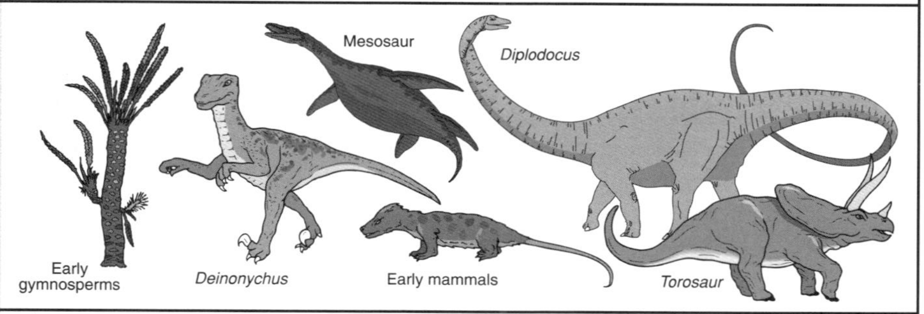

Mesosaur
Diplodocus
Early gymnosperms
Deinonychus
Early mammals
Torosaur

Later Paleozoic

240 mya: Mass extinction of nearly all species on land and in the sea.

435-280 mya: Vast swamps with the first vascular plants. Origin and adaptive radiation of reptiles, insects and spore bearing plants (including gymnosperms).

500-435 mya: Major adaptive radiations of marine invertebrates and early fishes.

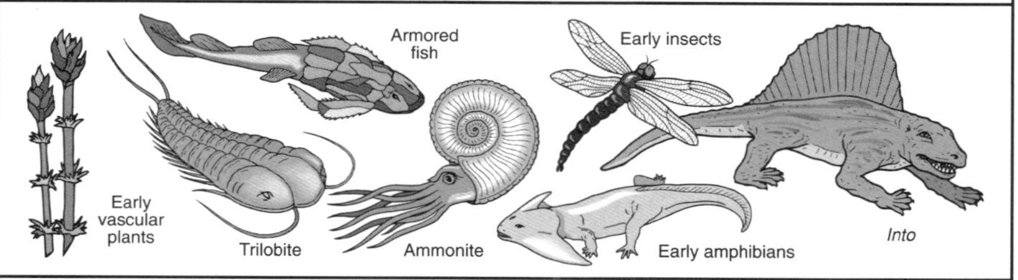

Armored fish
Early insects
Early vascular plants
Trilobite
Ammonite
Early amphibians
Into

Early Paleozoic (Cambrian)

550-500 mya: Origin of animals with hard parts (appear as fossils in rocks). Simple marine communities. A famous Canadian site with a rich collection of early Cambrian fossils is known as the Burgess Shale deposits; examples are shown on the right.

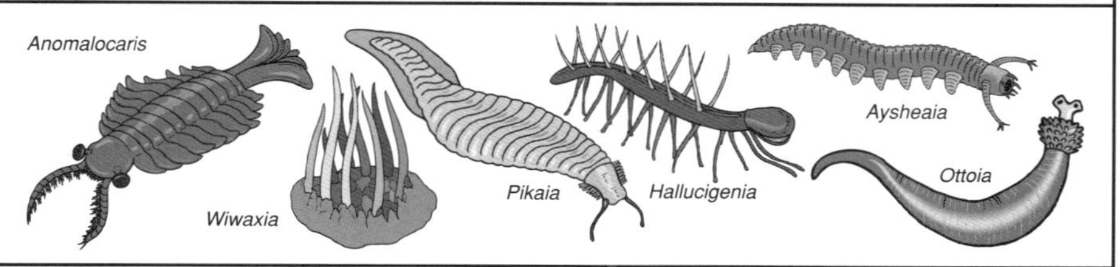

Anomalocaris
Aysheaia
Ottoia
Wiwaxia
Pikaia
Hallucigenia

Precambrian

2500–570 mya: Origin of protists, fungi, algae and animals.

3800–2500 mya: Origin of photosynthetic bacteria.

4600–3800 mya: Chemical and molecular evolution leading to origin of life; protocells to anaerobic bacteria.

4600 mya: Origin of Earth.

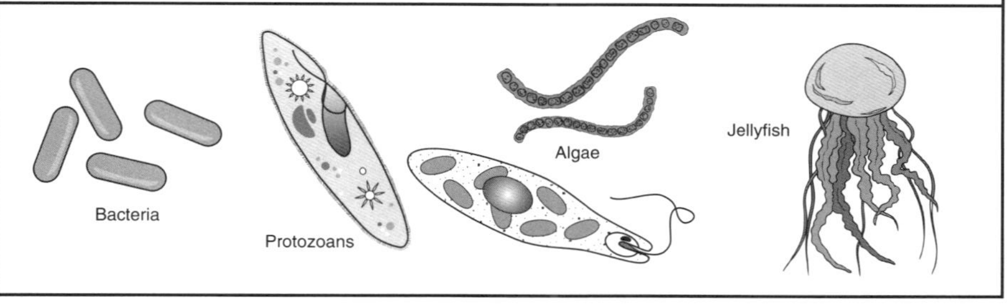

Jellyfish
Algae
Bacteria
Protozoans

3. An important feature of the history of life is that it has not been a steady progression of change. There have been bursts of evolutionary change as newly evolved groups undergo **adaptive radiations** and greatly increase in biodiversity. Such events are often associated with the sudden mass extinction of other, unrelated groups.

   (a) Explain the significance of mass extinctions in stimulating new biodiversity: _____

   _____

   _____

   _____

   (b) Briefly describe how the biodiversity of the Earth has changed since the origin of life:

   _____

   _____

   _____

   _____

Fossil Formation

K 1

Fossils are the remains of long-dead organisms that have escaped decay and have, after many years, become part of the Earth's crust. A fossil may be the preserved remains of the organism itself, the impression of it in the sediment (cast), or marks made by it during its lifetime (called trace fossils). For fossilization to occur, rapid burial of the organism is required (usually in water-borne sediment). This is followed by chemical alteration, where minerals are added or removed. Fossilization requires the normal processes of decay to be permanently arrested. This can occur if the remains are isolated from the air or water and decomposing microbes are prevented from breaking them down. Fossils provide a record of the appearance and extinction of organisms, from species to whole taxonomic groups. Once this record is calibrated against a time scale (by using a broad range of dating techniques), it is possible to build up a picture of the evolutionary changes that have taken place.

Modes of preservation

Silicification: Silica from weathered volcanic ash is gradually incorporated into partly decayed wood (also called petrification).

Phosphatization: Bones and teeth are preserved in phosphate deposits.

Pyritization: Iron pyrite replaces hard remains of the dead organism.

Tar pit: Animals fall into and are trapped in mixture of tar and sand.

Trapped in amber: Gum from conifers traps insects and then hardens.

Limestone: Calcium carbonate from the remains of marine plankton is deposited as a sediment that traps the remains of other sea creatures.

Brachiopod (lamp shell), Jurassic (New Zealand)

Cast: This impression of a lamp shell is all that is left after the original shell material was dissolved after fossilization.

All photos: RA

Polished amber

Ants

Insects in amber: The fossilized resin or gum produced by some ancient conifers trapped these insects (including the ants visible in the enlargement) about 25 million years ago (Madagascar).

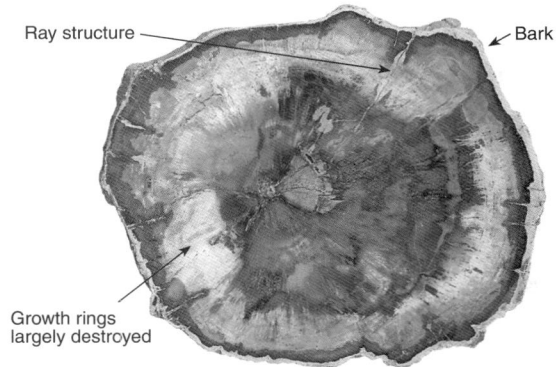

Ray structure — — Bark

Growth rings largely destroyed

Petrified wood: A cross-section of a limb from a coniferous tree (Madagascar).

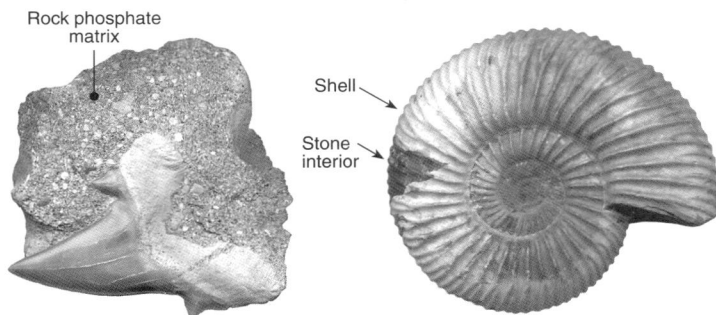

Rock phosphate matrix

Shark tooth: The tooth of a shark *Lamna obliqua* from phosphate beds, Eocene (Khouribga, Morocco).

Shell
Stone interior

Ammonite: This ammonite still has a layer of the original shell covering the stone interior, Jurassic (Madagascar).

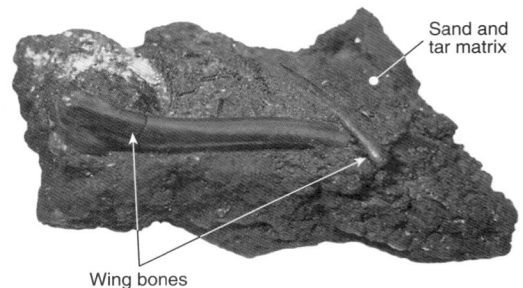

Sand and tar matrix

Wing bones

Bird bones: Fossilized bones of a bird that lived about 5 million years ago and became stuck in the tar pits at la Brea, Los Angeles, USA.

Shell and chambers replaced by iron pyrite

Ammonite: This ammonite has been preserved by a process called pyritization, late Cretaceous (Charmouth, England).

Fossil fern: This compression fossil of a fern leaf shows traces of carbon and wax from the original plant, Carboniferous (USA).

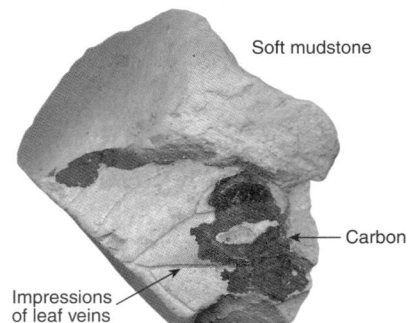

Soft mudstone

Carbon

Impressions of leaf veins

Sub-fossil: Leaf impression in soft mudstone (can be broken easily with fingers) with some of the remains of the leaf still intact (a few thousand years old, New Zealand).

Reptilian Features

Forelimb has three functional fingers with grasping claws.

Lacks the reductions and fusions present in other birds.

Breastbone is small and lacks a keel.

True teeth set in sockets in the jaws.

The hindlimb girdle is typical of dinosaurs, although modified.

Long, bony tail.

Suggested reconstruction of *Archaeopteryx*

Avian Features

Vertebrae are almost flat-faced.

Impressions of feathers attached to the forelimb.

Belly ribs.

Incomplete fusion of the lower leg bones.

Impressions of feathers attached to the tail.

Transitional Fossils

Transitional fossils possess a mixture of traits that are found in two different, but related, taxonomic groups. They suggest that one group may have given rise to the other by evolutionary processes. The fossil above is that of the prehistoric bird *Archaeopteryx* found in the Solnhofen limestone quarry, Germany. This crow-sized animal (50 cm length), which lived in the late Jurassic, possessed a large proportion of reptilian features, but also a number of avian (birdlike) features including feathers.

1. Explain how the each of the following preservation processes can result in fossil formation:

(a) Pyritization: _____

_____

(b) Amber: _____

_____

(c) Petrification: _____

_____

(d) Phosphatization: _____

_____

(e) Tar pit: _____

_____

2. Name the natural process that must be arrested in order for fossilization to take place: _____

3. Explain what is meant by a transitional fossil: _____

_____

RA ② The Fossil Record

The diagram below represents a cutting into the earth revealing the layers of rock. Some of these layers may have been laid down by water (sedimentary rocks) or by volcanic activity (volcanic rocks). Fossils are the actual remains or impressions of plants, animals, or other organisms that become trapped in the sediments after their death. Layers of sedimentary rock are arranged in the order that they were deposited, with the most recent layers near the surface (unless they have been disturbed).

Profile with Sedimentary Rocks Containing Fossils

Ground surface

Youngest sediments

Oldest sediments

Recent fossils are found in more recent sediments
The more recent the layer of rock, the more resemblance there is between the fossils found in it and living forms.

Numerous extinct species
The number of extinct species is enormously greater than the number living today.

Fossil types differ in each sedimentary rock layer
Fossils found in a given layer of sedimentary rock generally differ in significant respects from those in other layers.

Only primitive fossils are found in older sediments
Phyla are represented by more generalized forms in the older layers, and not by specialized forms (such as those alive today).

New fossil types mark changes in environment
In the rocks marking the end of one geological period, it is common to find many new fossils that become dominant in the next. Each geological period had an environment very different from those before and after. Their boundaries coincided with drastic environmental changes and the appearance of new niches. These produced new selection pressures resulting in new adaptive features in the surviving species, as they responded to the changes.

The rate of evolution can vary

According to the fossil record, rates of evolutionary change seem to vary. There are bursts of species formation and long periods of relative stability within species (stasis). The occasional rapid evolution of new forms apparent in the fossil record, is probably a response to a changing environment. During periods of stable environmental conditions, evolutionary change may slow down.

The Fossil Record of Proboscidea

African and Indian elephants have descended from a diverse group of animals known as **proboscideans** (named for their long trunks). The first pig-sized, trunkless members of this group lived in Africa 40 million years ago. From Africa, their descendants invaded all continents except Antarctica and Australia. As the group evolved, they became larger; an effective evolutionary response to deter predators. Examples of extinct members of this group are illustrated below:

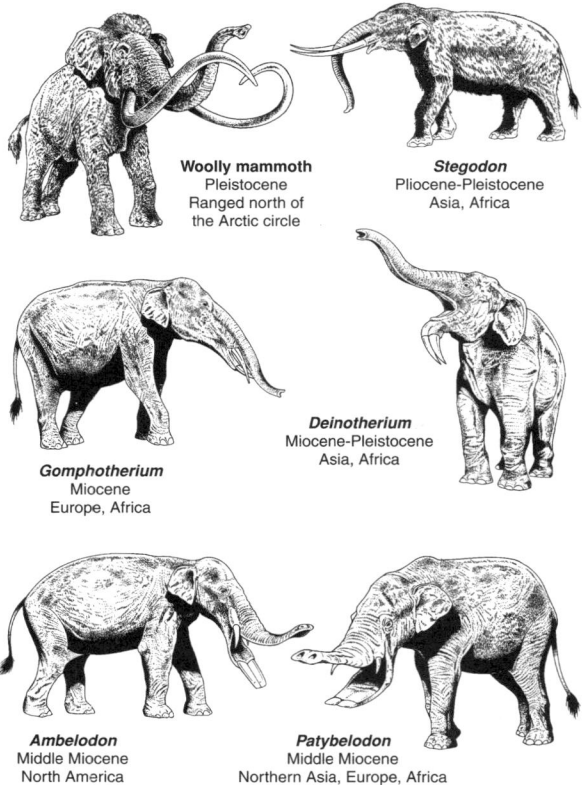

Woolly mammoth
Pleistocene
Ranged north of the Arctic circle

Stegodon
Pliocene-Pleistocene
Asia, Africa

Deinotherium
Miocene-Pleistocene
Asia, Africa

Gomphotherium
Miocene
Europe, Africa

Ambelodon
Middle Miocene
North America

Patybelodon
Middle Miocene
Northern Asia, Europe, Africa

- **Modern day species can be traced:** The evolution of many present-day species can be very well reconstructed. For instance, the evolutionary history of the modern elephants is exceedingly well documented for the last 40 million years. The modern horse also has a well understood fossil record spanning the last 50 million years.

- **Fossil species are similar to but differ from today's species:** Most fossil animals and plants belong to the same major taxonomic groups as organisms living today. However, they do differ from the living species in many features.

1. Name two animal groups for which there is a good fossil record showing their evolutionary development:

_____

2. Name an animal group that appears to have changed very little over the last 100 million years or so:

_____

3. Explain what a fossil is: _____

_____

_____

Rock profile at location 1

Rock profile at location 2

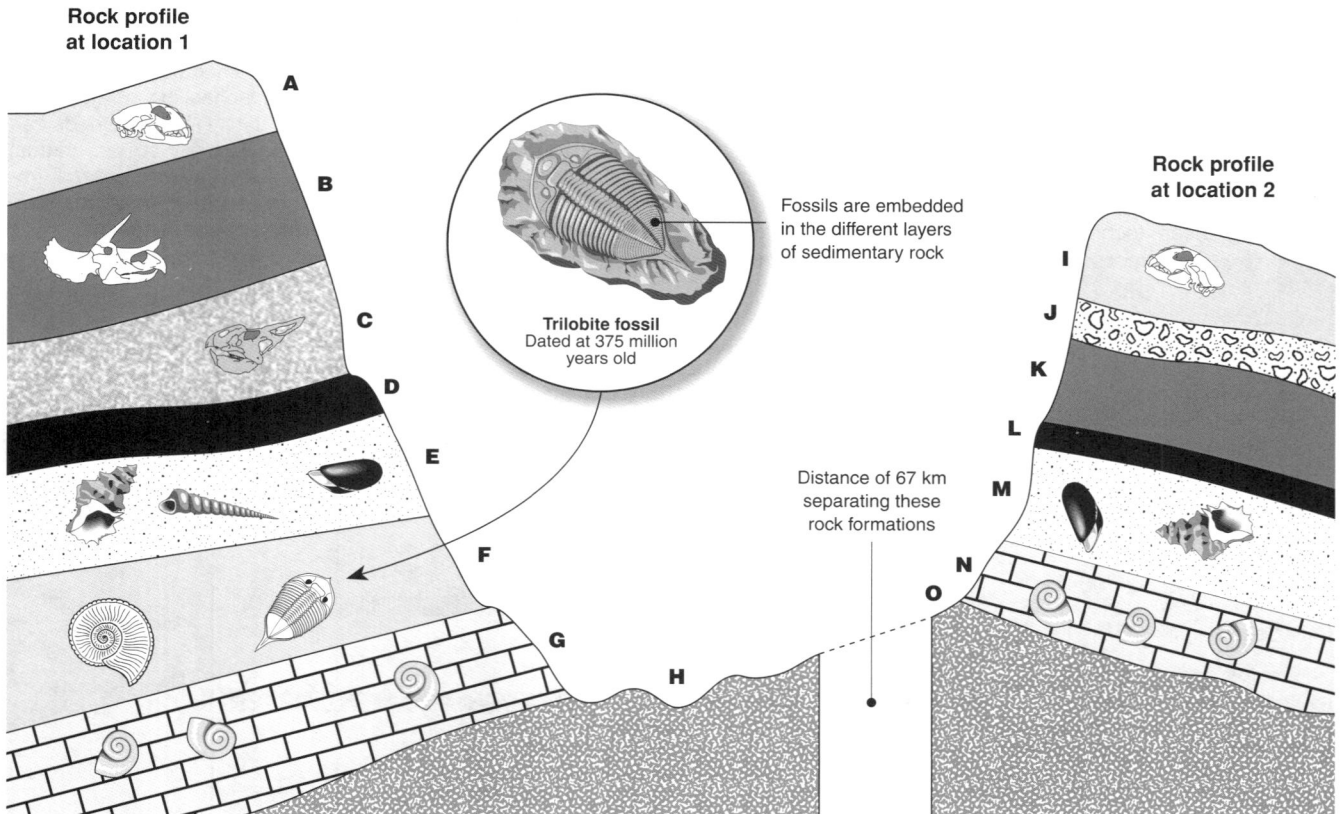

Fossils are embedded in the different layers of sedimentary rock

Trilobite fossil
Dated at 375 million years old

Distance of 67 km separating these rock formations

The questions below relate to the diagram above, showing a hypothetical rock profile from two locations separated by a distance of 67km. There are some differences between the rock layers at the two locations. Apart from layers D and L which are volcanic ash deposits, all other layers are comprised of sedimentary rock.

4. Assuming there has been no geological activity (e.g. tilting or folding), state in which rock layer (A-O) you would find:

   (a) The youngest rocks at Location 1: _____   (c) The youngest rocks at Location 2: _____

   (b) The oldest rocks at Location 1: _____   (d) The oldest rocks at Location 2: _____

5. (a) State which layer at location1 is of the same age as layer M at location 2: _____

   (b) Explain the reason for your answer above: _____

   _____

6. The rocks in layer H and O are sedimentary rocks. Explain why there are no visible fossils in layers:

   _____

   _____

7. (a) State which layers present at location 1 are missing at location 2: _____

   (b) State which layers present at location 2 are missing at location 1: _____

8. Name three methods of dating rocks: _____

   _____

   _____

9. Using radiometric dating, the trilobite fossil was determined to be approximately 375 million years old. The volcanic rock layer (D) was dated at 270 million years old, while rock layer B was dated at 80 million years old. Give the approximate **age range** (i.e. greater than, less than or between given dates) of the rock layers listed below:

   (a) Layer A: _____   (d) Layer G: _____

   (b) Layer C: _____   (e) Layer L: _____

   (c) Layer E: _____   (f) Layer O: _____

RDA2 Dating Fossils

Fossils themselves are rarely able to be dated directly. In general, it is the rocks in which they are found that are dated. The exception is the method of radiocarbon dating that can measure directly the age of the organic matter in a sample. Dating usually begins with an attempt to order past events in the rock profile, and to relate the fossils to rock layers that can be dated. During the past 50 years, many techniques for measuring the age of rocks and minerals have been established. In the early days of developing these techniques, there were some problems in producing dependable results. Nowadays, these methods are much refined and often provide dates with a high degree of certainty. Often, more than one dating method can be applied to a sample, providing an excellent cross-checking ability which provides further confidence in a given date. Dating methods can be grouped into two categories: those that rely on the gradual radioactive decay of an element (e.g. **radiocarbon, potassium-argon, fission-track**); and those that use other methods (e.g. **tree-rings, paleomagnetism, thermoluminescence**).

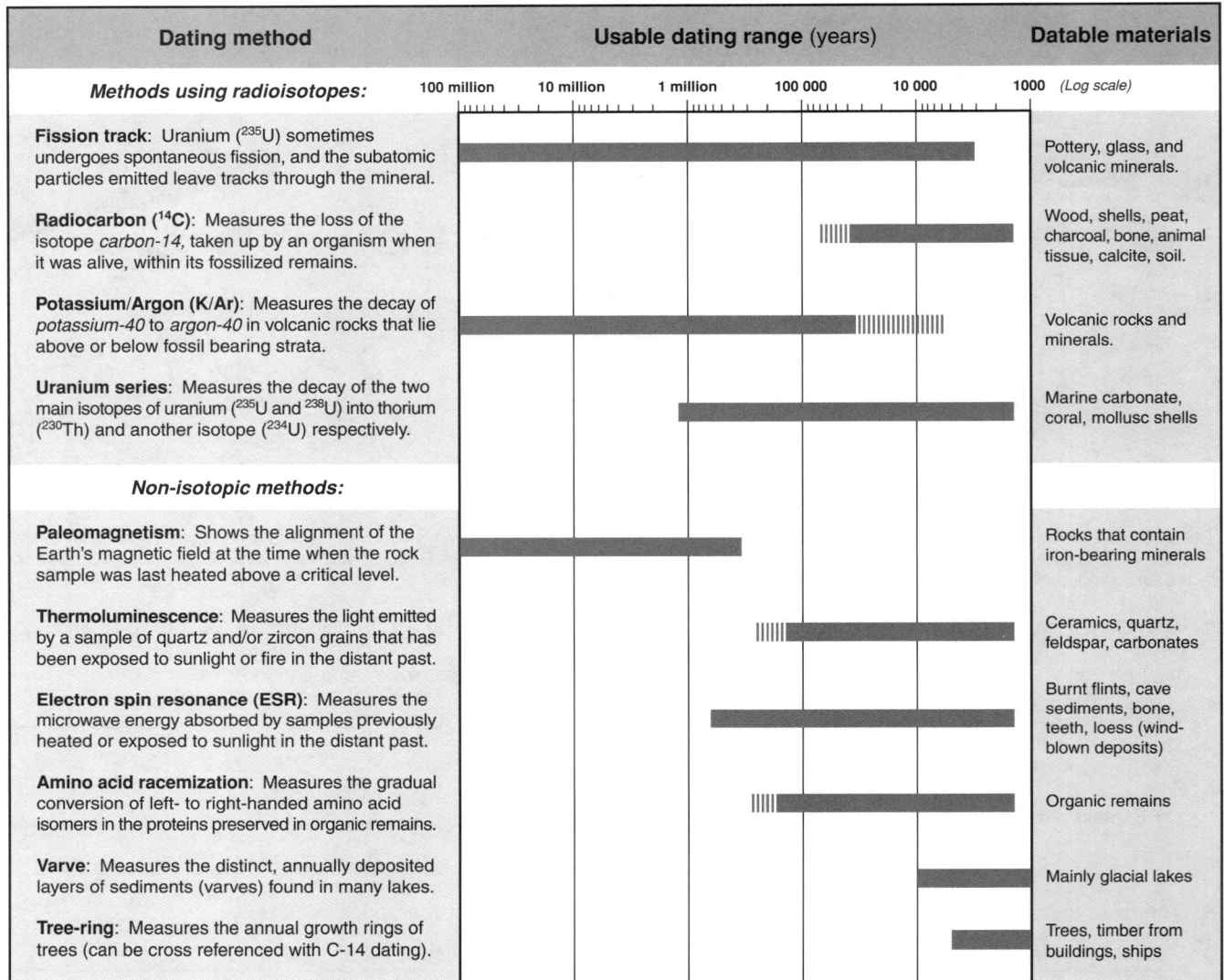

Dating method	Usable dating range (years)	Datable materials
Methods using radioisotopes:	100 million 10 million 1 million 100 000 10 000 1000 (Log scale)	
Fission track: Uranium (^{235}U) sometimes undergoes spontaneous fission, and the subatomic particles emitted leave tracks through the mineral.		Pottery, glass, and volcanic minerals.
Radiocarbon (^{14}C): Measures the loss of the isotope *carbon-14,* taken up by an organism when it was alive, within its fossilized remains.		Wood, shells, peat, charcoal, bone, animal tissue, calcite, soil.
Potassium/Argon (K/Ar): Measures the decay of *potassium-40* to *argon-40* in volcanic rocks that lie above or below fossil bearing strata.		Volcanic rocks and minerals.
Uranium series: Measures the decay of the two main isotopes of uranium (^{235}U and ^{238}U) into thorium (^{230}Th) and another isotope (^{234}U) respectively.		Marine carbonate, coral, mollusc shells
Non-isotopic methods:		
Paleomagnetism: Shows the alignment of the Earth's magnetic field at the time when the rock sample was last heated above a critical level.		Rocks that contain iron-bearing minerals
Thermoluminescence: Measures the light emitted by a sample of quartz and/or zircon grains that has been exposed to sunlight or fire in the distant past.		Ceramics, quartz, feldspar, carbonates
Electron spin resonance (ESR): Measures the microwave energy absorbed by samples previously heated or exposed to sunlight in the distant past.		Burnt flints, cave sediments, bone, teeth, loess (wind-blown deposits)
Amino acid racemization: Measures the gradual conversion of left- to right-handed amino acid isomers in the proteins preserved in organic remains.		Organic remains
Varve: Measures the distinct, annually deposited layers of sediments (varves) found in many lakes.		Mainly glacial lakes
Tree-ring: Measures the annual growth rings of trees (can be cross referenced with C-14 dating).		Trees, timber from buildings, ships

1. Examine the diagram above and determine the approximate dating range (note the logarithmic time scale) and datable materials for each of the methods listed below:

	Dating range	Datable materials
(a) Potassium-argon method:	_____	_____
(b) Radiocarbon method:	_____	_____
(c) Tree-ring method:	_____	_____
(d) Thermoluminescence:	_____	_____

2. When the date of a sample has been determined, it is common practice to express it in the following manner:
   Example: **1.88 ± 0.02** million years old. Explain what the **± 0.02** means in this case:

   _____

3. Suggest a possible source of error that could account for an incorrect dating measurement using a radioisotope method:

   _____

DNA Hybridization

The more closely two species are related, the fewer differences there will be in the exact sequence of bases. This is because there has been less time for the point mutations that will bring about these changes to occur. Modern species can be compared to see how long ago they shared a **common ancestor.** This technique gives a measure of 'relatedness', and can be calibrated as a **molecular clock** against known fossil dates. It is then possible to give approximate dates of common origin to species with no or poor fossil data. This method has been applied to primate DNA samples to help determine the approximate date of human divergence from the apes, which has been estimated to be between 10 and 5 million years ago.

DNA Hybridization

1. Blood samples from each species are taken, from which the DNA is isolated.

2. The DNA from each species is made to unwind into single strands by applying heat (both human and chimpanzee DNA unwinds at 86°C).

3. Enzymes are used to snip the single strands of DNA into smaller pieces (about 500 base pairs long).

4. The segments from human and chimpanzee DNA are combined to see how closely they bind to each other (single strand segments tend to find their complementary segments and rewind into a double helix again).

5. The greater the similarity in DNA base sequence, the stronger the attraction between the two strands and therefore they are harder to separate again. By measuring how hard this hybrid DNA is to separate, a crude measure of DNA 'relatedness' can be achieved.

6. The degree of similarity of the hybrid DNA can be measured by finding the temperature that it unzips into single strands again (in this case it would be 83.6°C).

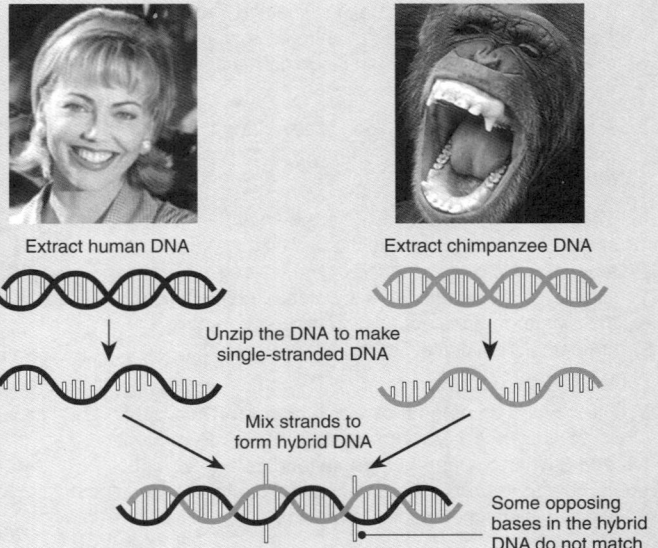

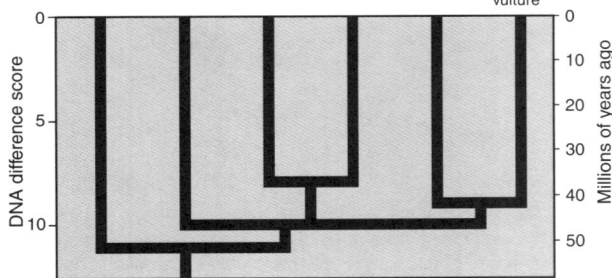

Extract human DNA   Extract chimpanzee DNA

Unzip the DNA to make single-stranded DNA

Mix strands to form hybrid DNA

Some opposing bases in the hybrid DNA do not match

Flamingo   Ibis   Shoebill   Pelican   Stork   New World vulture

Using DNA hybridization, the relationships among the **New World vultures** and **storks** has been determined. It has been possible to estimate how long ago various members of the group shared a common ancestor.

Similarity of human DNA to that of other primates

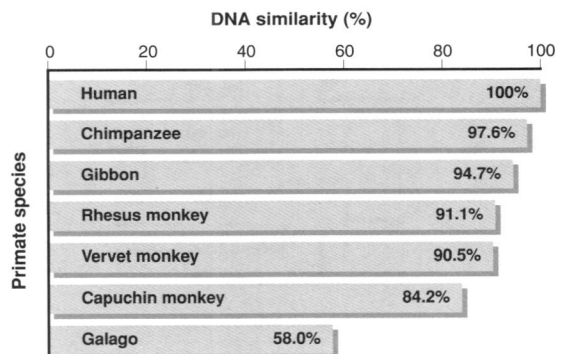

DNA similarity (%)

Primate species	DNA similarity
Human	100%
Chimpanzee	97.6%
Gibbon	94.7%
Rhesus monkey	91.1%
Vervet monkey	90.5%
Capuchin monkey	84.2%
Galago	58.0%

The genetic relationships among the **primates** has been investigated using DNA hybridization. Human DNA was compared with that of the other primates. It largely confirmed what was suspected from anatomical evidence.

1. Explain how DNA hybridization can give a measure of genetic relatedness between species:

_____

_____

_____

2. Study the graph showing the results of a DNA hybridization between human DNA and that of other primates.

   (a) State which is the most closely related primate to humans: _____

   (b) State which is the most distantly related primate to humans: _____

3. State the DNA difference score for: (a) Shoebills and pelicans: _____   (b) Storks and flamingos: _____

4. State how long ago, on the basis of DNA hybridization evidence, that the ibis and the New World vulture shared a common ancestor:

DA 2 Immunological Studies

Immunological studies provide a method of indirectly estimating the degree of similarity of proteins in different species. If differences exist in the proteins, then there must also be differences in the DNA that codes for them. The evolutionary relationships of a large number of different animal groups have been established on the basis of immunology. The results support the phylogenies developed from other areas: biogeography, comparative anatomy, and fossil evidence.

Method for Immunological Comparison

1. Blood serum (containing blood proteins but no cells) is collected from a human and is injected into a rabbit. This causes the formation of antibodies in the rabbit's blood. These identify human blood proteins, attach to them and render them harmless.

2. A sample of the rabbit's blood is taken and the rabbit's antibodies that recognize human blood proteins are extracted.

3. These anti-human antibodies are then added to blood samples from other species to see how well they recognize the proteins in the different blood. The more similar the blood sample is to original human blood, the greater the reaction (which takes the form of creating a precipitate, i.e. solids).

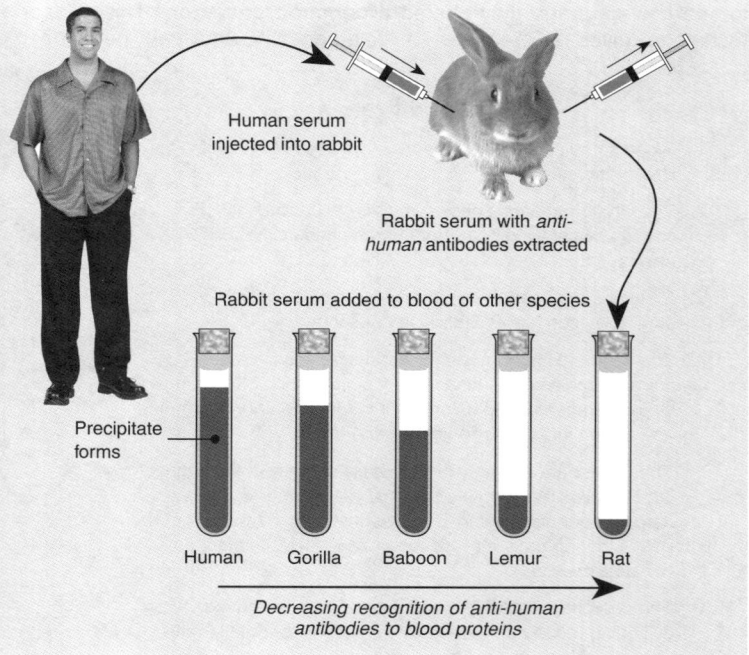

The five blood samples that were tested (on the right) show varying degrees of precipitate (solid) formation. Note that when the anti-human antibodies are added to human blood there is a high degree of affinity. There is poor recognition when added to rat blood.

Human serum injected into rabbit

Rabbit serum with *anti-human* antibodies extracted

Rabbit serum added to blood of other species

Precipitate forms

Human   Gorilla   Baboon   Lemur   Rat

Decreasing recognition of anti-human antibodies to blood proteins

Immunological Comparison of Tree Frogs

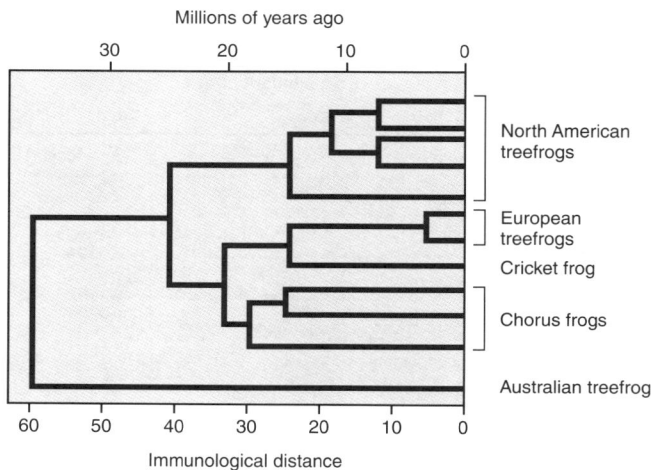

Millions of years ago

30   20   10   0

North American treefrogs

European treefrogs

Cricket frog

Chorus frogs

Australian treefrog

60   50   40   30   20   10   0

Immunological distance

The relationships among **tree frogs** have been established by immunological studies. The immunological distance is a measure of the number of amino acid substitutions between two groups. This, in turn, has been calibrated to provide a time scale showing when the various related groups diverged.

1. Briefly describe how immunological studies have contributed evidence that the process of evolution has taken place:

_____

_____

_____

_____

2. Study the graph above showing the immunological distance between tree frogs. State the immunological distance between the following frogs:

(a) Cricket frog and the Australian tree frog: _____ (b) The various chorus frogs: _____

3. Describe how closely the Australian tree frog is related to the other frogs shown:

_____

4. State when the North American tree frogs became separated from the European tree frogs: _____

RDA 2   Other Evidence for Evolution

Amino Acid Sequences

Each of our proteins has a specific number of amino acids arranged in a specific order. Any differences in the sequence reflect changes in the DNA sequence. The hemoglobin beta chain has been used as a standard molecule for comparing the precise sequence of amino acids in different species. Hemoglobin is the protein in our red blood cells that is responsible for carrying oxygen around our bodies. The hemoglobin in adults is made up of four polypeptide chains: two alpha chains and two beta chains. Each is coded for by a separate gene.

Example right: When the sequence of human hemoglobin, which is 146 amino acids long, was compared with that of five other primate species it was found that chimpanzees had an identical sequence while those that were already considered less closely related had a greater number of differences. This suggests a very close genetic relationship between humans, chimpanzees and gorillas, but less with the other primates.

Amino Acid Differences Between Humans and Other Primates

The *'position of changed amino acid'* is the point in the protein, composed of 146 amino acids, at which the **different** amino acids occurs

Primate	No. of amino acids different from humans	Position of changed amino acids
Chimpanzee	Identical	–
Gorilla	1	104
Gibbon	3	80 87 125
Rhesus monkey	8	9 13 33 50 76 87 104 125
Squirrel monkey	9	5 6 9 21 22 56 76 87 125

Comparative Embryology

By comparing the development of embryos from different species, Ernst von Bayer in 1828 noticed that animals are more similar during early stages of their embryological development than later as adults. This later led to Ernst Haeckel (1834-1919) to propose his famous principle: *ontogeny recapitulates phylogeny*. He claimed that the development of an individual (ontogeny) retraces the stages through which the individual species has passed during its evolution (phylogeny). This idea is now known to be an oversimplification and is misleading. Although early developmental sequences between all vertebrates are similar, there are important deviations from the general developmental plan in different species. Notice the gill slits that briefly appear in the human embryo (arrowed). The more closely related forms of the monkey and humans continue to appear similar until a later stage in development, compared to more distantly related species. From the study of foetal development it is possible to find clues as to how evolution generates the diversity of life forms through time, but 'ontogeny does not recapitulate phylogeny'.

Developmental stage	Amphibian	Bird	Monkey	Human
Fertilized egg				
Late cleavage				
Body segments				Gill slits
Limb buds				
Late foetal				

1. Study the table of data showing the differences in **amino acid sequences** for selected primates. Explain why chimpanzees and gorillas are considered most closely related to humans, while monkeys are less so:

_____

_____

_____

2. Briefly describe how **comparative embryology** has contributed evidence to support the concept of evolution:

_____

_____

3. Describe a commonly used biochemical method for precisely analyzing the genes in organisms to determine their evolutionary relationships:

_____

_____

Comparative Anatomy

The evolutionary relationships between groups of organisms is determined mainly by structural similarities called **homologous structures** (homologies), which suggest that they all descended from a common ancestor with that feature. The bones of the forelimb of air-breathing vertebrates are composed of similar bones arranged in a comparable pattern. This is indicative of a common ancestry. The early land vertebrates were amphibians and possessed a limb structure called the **pentadactyl limb**: a limb with 5 fingers or toes (below left). All vertebrates that descended from these early amphibians, including reptiles, birds and mammals, have limbs that have evolved from this same basic pentadactyl pattern. They also illustrate the phenomenon known as **adaptive radiation**, since the basic limb plan has been adapted to meet the requirements of different niches.

Generalized Pentadactyl Limb

The forelimbs and hind limbs have the same arrangement of bones but they have different names. In many cases bones in different parts of the limb have been highly modified to give it a specialized locomotory function.

Forelimb   **Hind limb**

Humerus (upper arm) — Femur (thigh)
Fibula
Tibia
Radius
Ulna
Carpals (wrist) — Tarsals (ankle)
Metacarpals (palm) — Metatarsals (sole)
Phalanges (fingers) — Phalanges (toes)

Specializations of Pentadactyl Limbs

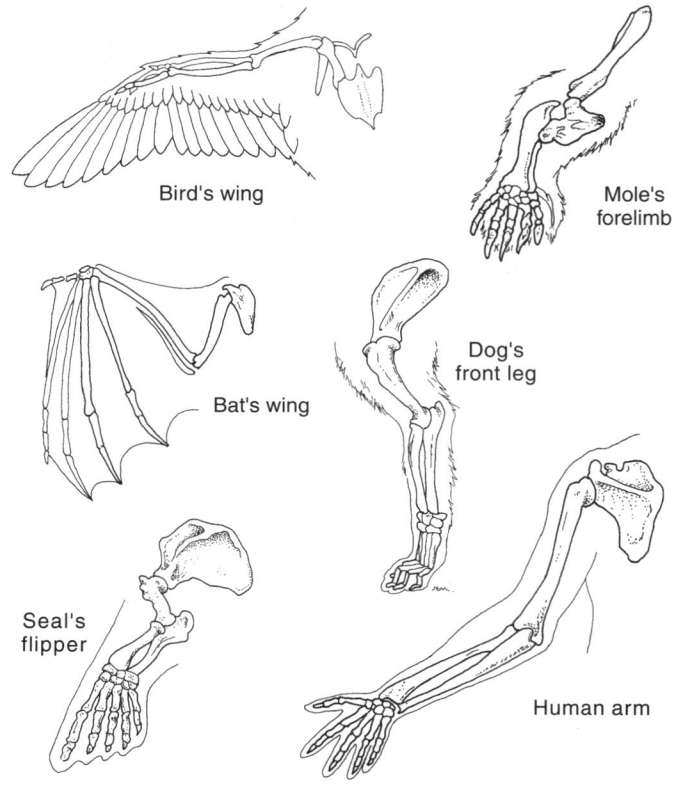

Bird's wing

Mole's forelimb

Bat's wing

Dog's front leg

Seal's flipper

Human arm

1. Briefly describe the purpose of the major anatomical change that has taken place in each of the limb examples above:

   (a) Bird wing: _Highly modified for flight. Forelimb is shaped for aerodynamic lift and feather attachment._

   (b) Human arm: _____

   (c) Seal flipper: _____

   (d) Dog foot: _____

   (e) Mole forelimb: _____

   (f) Bat wing: _____

2. Describe how homology in the pentadactyl limb is evidence for adaptive radiation: _____

   _____

   _____

   _____

3. Homology in the behavior of animals (for example, sharing similar courtship or nesting rituals) is sometimes used to indicate the degree of relatedness between groups. Suggest how behavior could be used in this way:

   _____

   _____

   _____

A 2

Vestigial Organs

Some classes of characters are more valuable than others as reliable indicators of common ancestry. Often, the less any part of an animal is used for specialized purposes, the more important it becomes for classification. Vestigial organs are an example of this. If vestigial features have no clear function and are no longer subject to natural selection, the common ancestry between different species is not clouded by later adaptation to particular purposes. It is sometimes argued that some vestigial organs are not truly vestigial, i.e. they may perform some small function. While this may be true in some cases, the features can still be considered vestigial if their new role is a minor one, unrelated to their original function.

Ancestors of Modern Whales

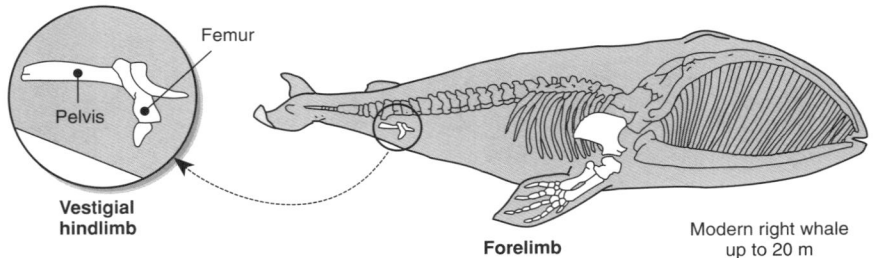

1.8 m long

Pakicetus (early Eocene) a carnivorous, four limbed, early Eocene whale ancestor, probably rather like a large otter. It was still partly terrestrial and not fully adapted for aquatic life.

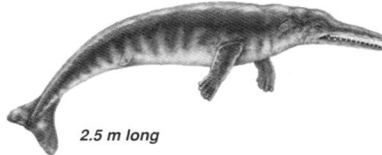

2.5 m long

Protocetus (mid Eocene). Much more whale-like than *Pakicetus*. The hindlimbs were greatly reduced and although they still protruded from the body (arrowed), they were useless for swimming.

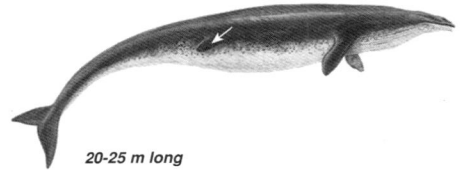

20-25 m long

Basilosaurus (late Eocene). A very large ancestor of modern whales. The hind limbs contained all the leg bones, but were vestigial and located entirely within the main body, leaving a tissue flap on the surface (arrowed).

Vestigial organs are common in nature. The vestigial hindlimbs of modern whales (right) provide anatomical evidence for their evolution from a carnivorous, four footed, terrestrial ancestor. The oldest known whale, *Pakicetus*, from the early Eocene (~54 mya) still had four limbs. By the late Eocene (~40 mya), whales were fully marine and had lost almost all traces of their former terrestrial life. For fossil evidence, see *Whale Origins* at: www.neoucom.edu/Depts/Anat/whaleorigins.htm

Femur

Pelvis

Vestigial hindlimb

Forelimb

Modern right whale up to 20 m

Vestigial organs in birds and reptiles

In all snakes (far left), one lobe of the lung is vestigial (there is not sufficient room in the narrow body cavity for it). In some snakes there are also vestiges of the pelvic girdle and hind limbs of their walking ancestors. Like all ratites, kiwis (left) are flightless. However, more than in other ratites, the wings of kiwis are reduced to tiny vestiges. Kiwis have evolved in the absence of predators to a totally ground dwelling existence.

1. In terms of natural selection explain how structures, that were once useful to an organism, could become vestigial:

_____

_____

_____

_____

2. Suggest why a vestigial structure, once it has been reduced to a certain size, may not disappear altogether:

_____

_____

3. Whale evolution shows the presence of **transitional forms** (fossils that are intermediate between modern forms and very early ancestors). Suggest how vestigial structures indicate the common ancestry of these forms:

_____

_____

_____

Biogeographical Evidence

A 2

The distribution of organisms around the world lends powerful support to the idea that modern forms evolved from ancestral populations. **Biogeography** is the study of the geographical distribution of species, both present-day and extinct. It stresses the role of dispersal of species from a point of origin across pre-existing barriers. Studies from the island populations (below) indicate that flora and fauna of different islands are more closely related to adjacent continental species than to each other.

Galapagos and Cape Verde islands

The expectation that the fauna and flora of tropical islands would be the same anywhere in the world was shattered when explorers last century began to bring back samples from their expeditions. It was found that the Galapagos Islands had species very similar to but distinct from the South American mainland. Similarly, in the Cape Verde Islands, species had close relatives on the West Africa mainland. This implied that ancestral forms found their way from the mainland to the islands where they then underwent evolutionary changes.

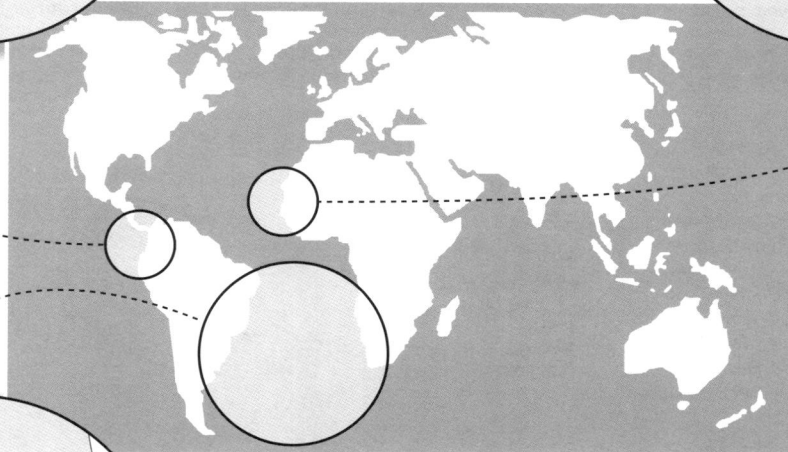

Galapagos Is
South America
800 km
Pacific Ocean

Cape Verde Is
Western Africa
450 km
Atlantic Ocean

South Atlantic Ocean
South America
Africa
4500 km
3000 km
Tristan da Cunha

Tristan da Cunha

The island of Tristan da Cunha in the South Atlantic Ocean is a great distance from any other land mass. Even though it is closer to Africa, there are more species closely related to South American species found there (see table on right). This is probably due to the predominant westerly trade winds from the direction of South America. The flowering plants of universal origin are found in both Africa and South America and could have been introduced to the island from either source.

South American origin	
7	Flowering plants
5	Ferns
30	Liverworts

African origin	
2	Flowering plants
2	Ferns
5	Liverworts

Universal origin	
19	Flowering plants

1. Define the term biogeography: _____

_____

2. The Galapagos Islands and the Cape Verde Islands are tropical islands close to the equator. These islands have plants and animals that are very different from each other. Explain why this is so:

_____

_____

3. The island of Tristan da Cunha is situated in the South Atlantic Ocean remote from any other land. State the origin of the majority of the plant species that are found there, and explain why this is so:

_____

_____

4. Describe how biogeography provides support for the theory of evolution: _____

_____

_____

Oceanic Island Colonizers

A 1

Oceanic islands have a **unique biota** because only certain groups of plants and animals tend to colonize them, while others are just not able to do so. The animals that successfully colonize oceanic islands have to be marine in habit, or able to survive long periods at sea or in the air. This precludes large numbers from ever reaching distant islands. Plants also have limited capacity to reach distant islands. Only some have fruits and seeds that are salt tolerant. Many plants are transferred to the islands by wind or migrating birds. The biota of the **Galapagos islands** provide a good example of the results of such a colonization process.

Land mammals: Few non-flying mammals colonize islands, unless these are very close to the mainland. Mammals have a higher metabolism, need more food and water than reptiles, and cannot sustain themselves on long sea journeys.

Reptiles: Reptiles probably reach distant islands by floating in driftwood or on mats of floating vegetation. A low metabolic rate enables them to survive the long periods without food and water.

Blown by strong winds

Oceanic island

Active flight

Small birds, bats, and insects: These animals are blown to islands by accident. They must adapt to life there or perish.

Seabirds: Seabirds fly to and from islands with relative ease. They may become adapted to life on land, as the flightless cormorant has done in the Galapagos Islands. Others, like the frigate bird, may treat the island as a stopping place.

Sea mammals: Seals and sea lions have little difficulty in reaching islands, but they return to the sea after the breeding season and do not colonize the interior.

Rafting on drifting vegetation

Swimming

Deep ocean

Amphibians: Cannot live away from fresh water. They seldom reach offshore islands unless that island is a continental remnant.

Planktonic larvae

Crustaceans: Larval stages drift to islands. Crabs often evolve novel forms on islands. Many are restricted to shore-line areas. Some crabs, such as coconut crabs, have adapted to an island niche.

The oldest islands making up the Galapagos archipelago appeared above sea level some 3-4 million years ago. The photographs on this page show some of the features typical of animals that colonize oceanic islands. The **flightless cormorant** (below left) is one of a number of bird species that have lost the power of flight once they had taken up residence on an island. The **giant tortoises** of the Galapagos (below center) are not unique. There were other, almost identical, giant tortoise subspecies living on islands in the Indian Ocean including the Seychelles archipelago, Reunion, Mauritius, Farquhar,

and Diego Rodriguez. These were almost completely exterminated by early Western sailors, although a small population remained untouched on the island of Aldabra. Another feature of oceanic islands is the 'adaptive radiation' (diversification) of colonizing species into different specialist forms. The two forms of Galapagos iguana almost certainly arose, through diversification, from a hardy traveler from the South American mainland. The **marine iguana** (below right) feeds on the seaweeds of the shoreline and is adept at swimming. The **land iguana** (right) feeds on cacti, which are numerous.

Land iguana feeding on cactus

Flightless cormorant

Giant Galapagos tortoise

Marine iguana feeding on seaweed

1. Explain why the flora and fauna of the Galapagos Archipelago must be relatively recent arrivals: _____

_____

2. Describe how the marine iguana and the land iguana have become different: _____

_____

PA③ Continental Drift and Evolution

The process of **continental drift** is not just a theory. It is still happening now and some of the continents' movements can be measured using laser technology. Movements of up to 2-11 cm a year have been recorded between continents. The movements of the Earth's 12 major crustal plates are driven by thermal convection currents in the mantle; a geological process known as **plate tectonics.** Some continents appear to be drifting apart while others are on a direct collision course. Various pieces of evidence have been collected to show that the modern continents were once joined together as 'supercontinents'. One supercontinent, called **Gondwana**, was made up of the southern continents some 200 million years ago. The diagram below shows some of the data collected that are used as evidence to indicate how the modern continents once fitted together.

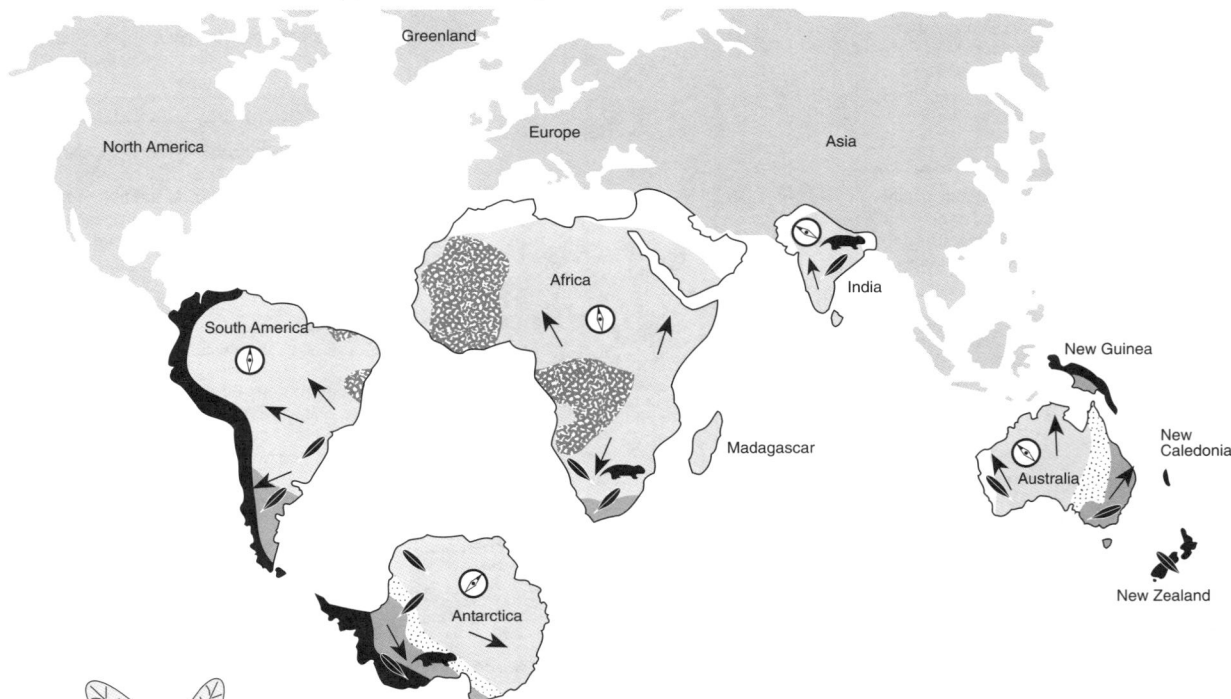

Glossopteris is a hardy plant that grew adjacent to the glacial ice sheets of Gondwana some 350-230 million years ago

Lystrosaurus is a primitive mammal-like reptile 1 m long, that was widely distributed throughout the southern continents about 240 million years ago

Key

Direction of ice sheet movement 350-230 million years ago	Geomagnetic pole direction 150 million years ago	Distribution of *Lystrosaurus*	Distribution of *Glossopteris*
Old Precambrian rocks (older than 650 mya)	Precambrian basement rocks (650-570 mya)	Early Paleozoic folding (570-350 mya)	Late Paleozoic–Early Mesozoic folding (350-160 mya)	Late Mesozoic folding (160-70 mya)

1. Name the modern landmasses (continents and large islands) that made up the super continent of Gondwana:

2. Cut out the southern continents on the facing page and arrange them to recreate the supercontinent of Gondwana. Take care to cut the shapes out close to the coastlines. When arranging them into the space showing the outline of Gondwana, take into account the following information:
   (a) The location of ancient rocks and periods of mountain folding during different geological ages.
   (b) The direction of ancient ice sheet movements.
   (c) The geomagnetic orientation of old rocks (the way that magnetic crystals are lined up in ancient rock gives an indication of the direction the magnetic pole was at the time the rock was formed).
   (d) The distribution of fossils of ancient species such as *Lystrosaurus* and *Glossopteris*.

3. Once you have positioned the modern continents into the pattern of the supercontinent, mark on the diagram:
   (a) The likely position of the South Pole 350-230 million years ago (as indicated by the movement of the ice sheets).
   (b) The likely position of the geomagnetic South Pole 150 million years ago (as indicated by ancient geomagnetism).

4. State what general deduction you can make about the position of the polar regions with respect to land masses:

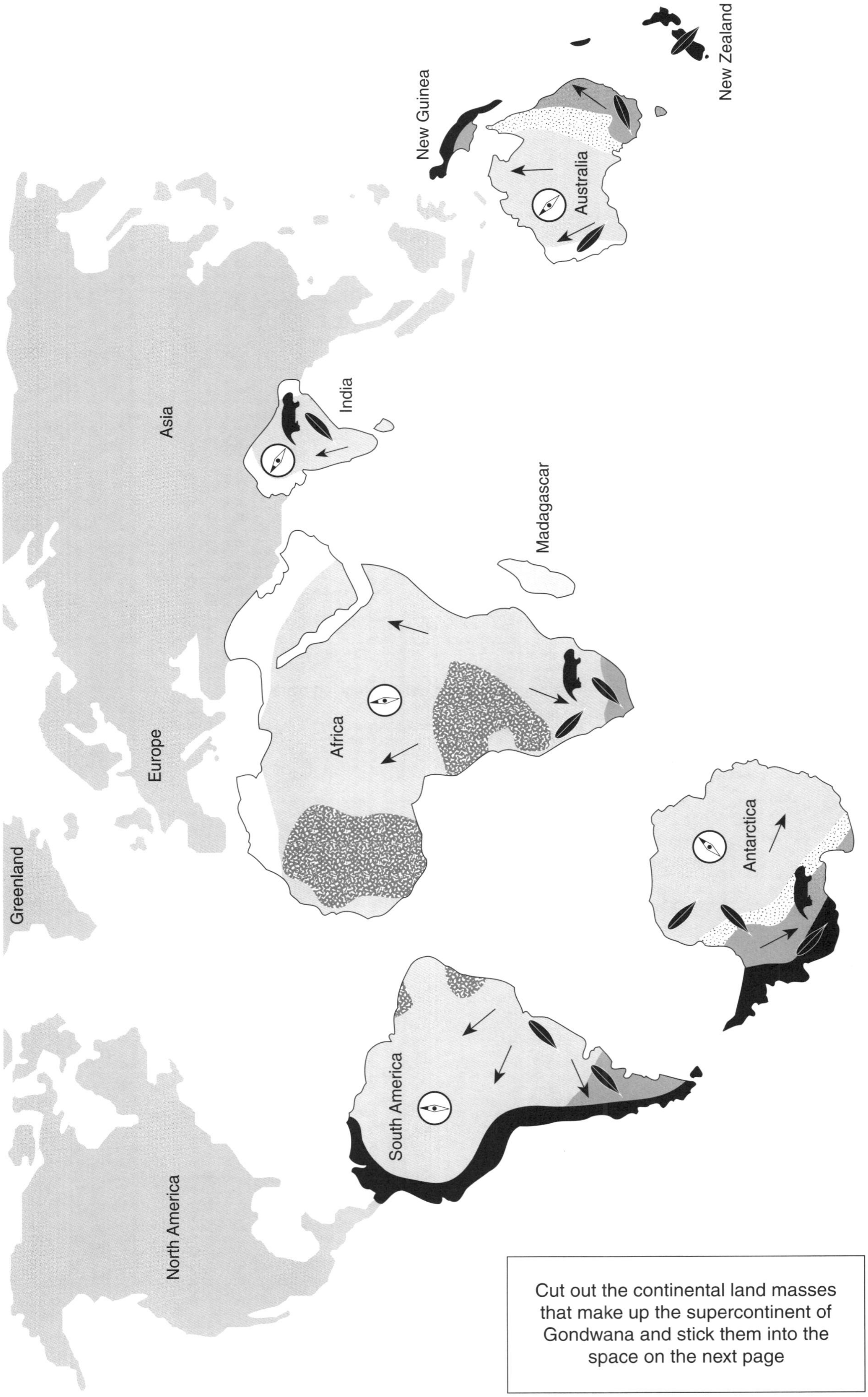

New Guinea

New Zealand

Australia

India

Asia

Madagascar

Europe

Africa

Greenland

Antarctica

North America

South America

Cut out the continental land masses that make up the supercontinent of Gondwana and stick them into the space on the next page

This page has been deliberately left blank

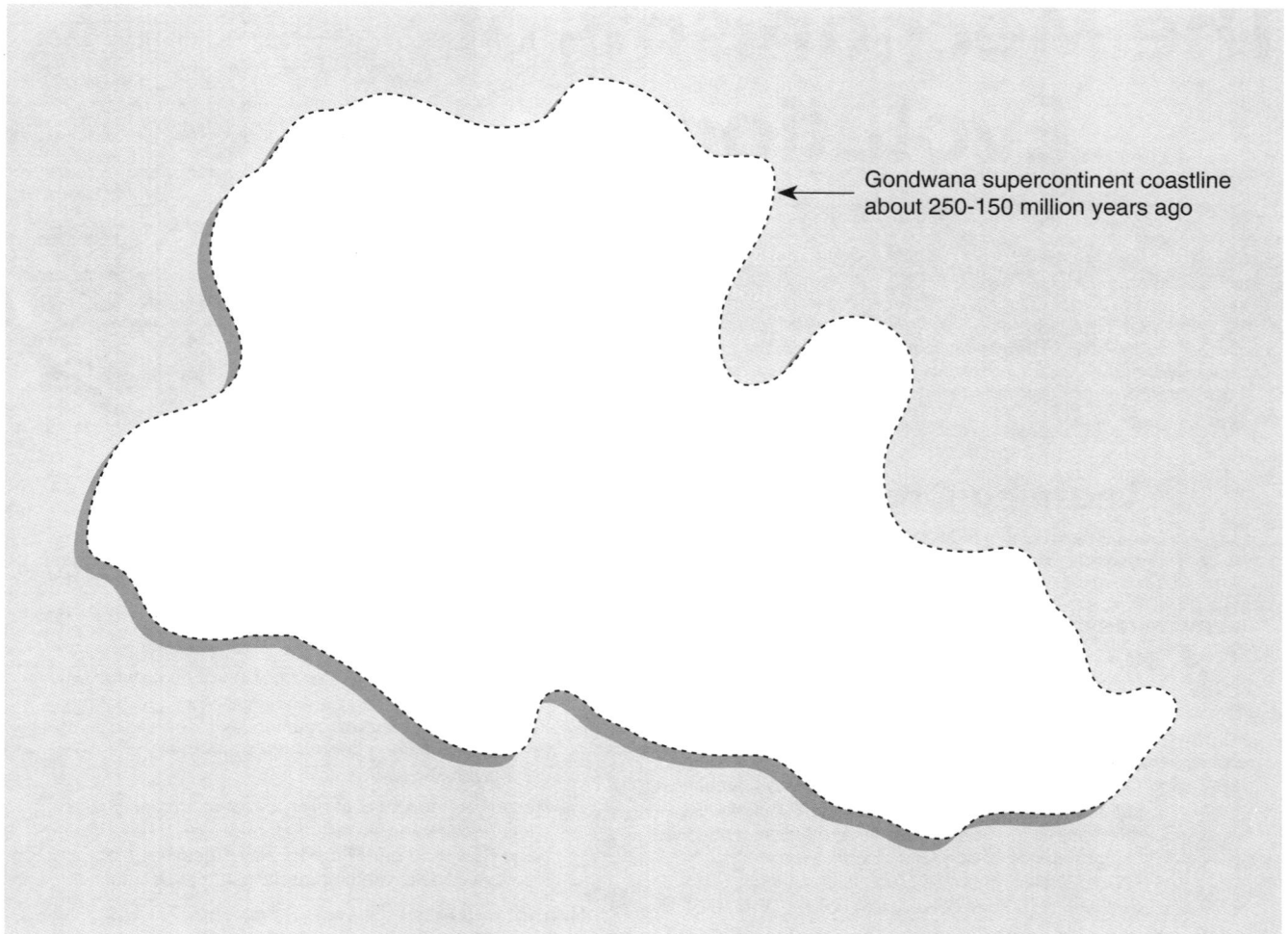

Gondwana supercontinent coastline about 250-150 million years ago

5. Fossils of *Lystrosaurus* are known from Antarctica, South Africa, India and Western China. With the modern continents in their present position, *Lystrosaurus* could have walked across dry land to get to China, Africa and India. It was not possible for it to walk to Antarctica, however. Explain the distribution of this ancient species in terms of continental drift:

_____

_____

6. The southern beech (*Nothofagus*) is found only in the southern hemisphere, in such places as New Caledonia, New Guinea, eastern Australia (including Tasmania), New Zealand, and southern South America. Fossils of southern beech trees have also been found in Antarctica. They have never been distributed in South Africa or India. The seeds of the southern beech trees are not readily dispersed by the wind and are rapidly killed by exposure to salt water.

(a) Suggest a reason why *Nothofagus* is not found in Africa or India: _____

_____

(b) Use a colored pen to indicate the distribution of *Nothofagus* on the current world map (on the previous page) and on your completed map of Gondwana above.

(c) State how the arrangement of the continents into Gondwana explains this distribution pattern:

_____

_____

7. The Atlantic Ocean is currently opening up at the rate of 2cm per year. At this rate in the past, calculate how long it would have taken to reach its current extent, with the distance from Africa to South America being 2,300 km (assume the rate of spreading has been constant):

_____

8. Explain how continental drift provides evidence to support evolutionary theory: _____

_____

_____

_____

The Mechanisms of Evolution

IB SL
Complete nos:
1-2, 5-6, 15, 17(d)-(e)
Extension: 7, 13-14, 16

IB HL
Complete nos:
1-2, 5-6, 15, 17(d)-(e)
Extension: 7, 13-14, 16

IB Options
Complete nos:
Option D: SL/HL: 3-4, 17(a), (c)-(e) HL: 8-15, 17(a)-(b), 24-26, 34
Ext: 16, 18-23, 27-33

AP Biology
Complete nos:
1-35
Some numbers extension as appropriate

Learning Objectives

1. Compile your own glossary from the **KEY WORDS** displayed in **bold type** in the learning objectives below.

A modern synthesis of evolution *(pages 72, 96-98)*

2. Give a precise definition of the term **evolution**, explaining how evolution is a feature of **populations** and not of individuals.

3. Identify some of the main contributors to the modern theory of evolution. Include:
   - An outline of Lamarck's theory of evolution by the inheritance of acquired characteristics. Include reference to the mechanism of, and lack of evidence for, inheritance of acquired characteristics.
   - An explanation of the Darwin-Wallace theory of evolution by natural selection (cross ref. with #5-6).

4. Discuss the evidence for various theories for the origin of species, including the theories of Darwin and Wallace, and Lamarck, and the theories of **panspermia** and evolution by special creation. Discuss the applicability of the scientific method to each.

5. Outline the fundamental ideas in Darwin's *"Theory of evolution by natural selection"*. Include reference to:
   - *The tendency of populations to overproduce.*
   - *The fact that overproduction leads to competition.*
   - *The fact that members of a species show variation, that sexual reproduction promotes variation, and that variation is (usually) heritable.*
   - *The differential survival and reproduction of individuals with favorable, heritable variations.*

6. Discuss the (Darwin-Wallace) theory that species evolve by natural selection.

7. Appreciate how Darwin's original theory has been modified in the **new synthesis** to take into account our understanding of genetics and inheritance.

8. Understand the term: **fitness** and explain how evolution, through **adaptation**, equips species for survival. Recognize structural and physiological adaptations of organisms to their environment.

The concept of the gene pool *(pages 106-114, 134)*

9. Understand the concept of the **gene pool** and explain the term **deme**. Recognize that populations may be of various sizes and geographical extent.

10. Explain the term **allele frequency** and describe how allele frequencies are expressed for a population.

11. State the Hardy-Weinberg principle (of **genetic equilibrium**). Understand the criteria that must be satisfied in order to achieve genetic equilibrium in a population. Identify the consequences of the fact that these criteria are rarely met in reality.

12. Explain how the **Hardy-Weinberg equation** provides a simple mathematical model of **genetic equilibrium** in a population. Demonstrate an ability to use the Hardy-Weinberg equation to calculate the allele, genotype, and phenotype frequencies from appropriate data.

Microevolution *(page 106)*

13. Recognize that changes occur in gene pools when any or all of the criteria for genetic equilibrium are not met. Identify **microevolution** as changes in the allele frequencies of gene pools. Appreciate that populations, not individuals, evolve.

14. Recognize the forces in microevolution that may alter allele frequencies: **natural selection**, **genetic drift**, **gene flow**, and **mutation**. Identify processes that increase genetic variation and those that decrease it.

Natural selection *(pages 97, 99-109)*

15. Recall that individuals within a species show **variation** and that heritable variation is the raw material for natural selection. Explain how **natural selection** is responsible for most evolutionary change by selectively changing genetic variation through differential survival and reproduction. Interpret data to explain how natural selection produces change in a population (see #17).

16. Describe three types of natural selection: **stabilizing**, **directional**, and **disruptive selection**. Describe the outcome of each type in a population exhibiting a normal curve in phenotypic variation.

17. As required, describe examples of evolution including:
   (a) **Transient polymorphism**, e.g. **industrial melanism** in peppered moths (*Biston betularia*).
   (b) The sickle cell trait as the basis for **balanced polymorphism** in malarial regions.
   (c) Changes to the size and shape of the beaks of **Galapagos finches** (cross ref. with the topic 'The Evidence for Evolution', Option D.3).
   (d) The development of **multiple antibiotic resistance** in bacteria and one other example of evolution in response to environmental change - refer to (e).
   (e) The development of **pesticide resistance** in insects or **heavy metal tolerance** in plants.

Genetic drift *(pages 106, 117)*

18. Define the term **genetic drift** and describe the conditions under which it is important. Explain, using diagrams or a gene pool model, how genetic drift may lead to loss or **fixation of alleles** (where a gene is represented in the population by only one allele).

Mutation *(pages 106, 109, and SB1 pages 169-181)*

19. Recognize **mutations** as the ultimate source of all new alleles. Use a diagram to explain how mutations alter the genetic equilibrium of a population. Recall that recombination during meiosis reshuffles alleles and increases variation, but it does not create new alleles.

Gene flow (pages 106, 109, 114)

□ 20. Explain, using diagrams or a gene pool model, how **migration** leads to **gene flow** between natural populations, and may affect allele frequencies.

Special events in gene pools (pages 106, 115-117)

□ 21. Explain the **founder effect**, including reference to its genetic and evolutionary consequences.

□ 22. Explain the **population bottleneck effect**, including reference to its genetic and evolutionary consequences.

□ 23. Appreciate how the founder effect and population (genetic) bottlenecks may accelerate the pace of evolutionary change. Explain the importance of **genetic drift** in populations that undergo these events.

Speciation (pages 118-123, also see page 390)

□ 24. Recall your definition of **evolution** and distinguish clearly between **microevolution** and **macroevolution**.

□ 25. Define **species**. Describe how the nature of some species can create problems for our definition.

□ 26. Recognize the role of **natural selection** and **isolation** in **speciation**. Discuss speciation in terms of migration, geographical or ecological isolation (also see # 27-28) and adaptation (see #8), leading to reproductive or genetic isolation of gene pools.

□ 27. Define the term: **reproductive isolation**. Describe how populations may become reproductively isolated through: *altered behavior or physiology, geographical isolation, polyploidy, or niche differentiation*. If required, distinguish between and describe **prezygotic** and **postzygotic** reproductive isolating mechanisms (RIMs).

□ 28. In more detail that in #26, explain the events occurring in **allopatric speciation**, identifying situations in which it is most likely to occur.

□ 29. Explain the events in **sympatric speciation** and describe the situations in which it is most likely to occur. Explain why RIMs tend to be more pronounced between sympatric (as opposed to allopatric) species. Explain the role of **polyploidy** in instant speciation (cross ref. with "Applied Plant and Animal Science").

□ 30. Recognize stages in species development, including reference to the reduction in gene flow as populations become increasingly isolated.

Patterns of evolution (pages 124-133)

□ 31. Describe the major stages in a **species life cycle** extending from origin to extinction.

□ 32. Providing examples, distinguish between the two species formation patterns: **sequential (phyletic) speciation** and **adaptive radiation**. Recognize adaptive radiation as a form of **divergent evolution**. Appreciate how evolution has resulted in a great diversity of forms among living organisms.

□ 33. Using examples, explain what is meant by **convergent evolution**. Distinguish clearly between **analogous** and **homologous structures**, recognizing that analogous structures may arise as a result of convergence. Appreciate that some biologists also recognize **parallel evolution** (as distinct from convergence) to indicate evolution along similar lines in closely related groups (as opposed to more distantly related groups).

□ 34. Distinguish between the two models for the pace of evolutionary change: **punctuated equilibrium** and **gradualism**. Discuss the evidence for each model.

□ 35. Explain what is meant by **extinction**. Describe the role of extinction in the process of evolution. Distinguish between **background** and **mass extinction**. If required, name some of the major **mass extinctions** and state when they occurred. Discuss some of the theories for the causes of such extinctions.

Textbooks

See the 'Textbook Reference Grid' on pages 8-9 for textbook page references relating to material in this topic.

Supplementary Texts

See pages 5-6 for additional details of these texts:

■ Adds, J., *et al.*, 2001. **Genetics, Evolution and Biodiversity**, (NelsonThornes), pp. 101-108.

■ Clegg, CJ., 1999. **Genetics and Evolution**, (John Murray), pp. 60-78.

■ Jones, N., *et al.*, 2001. **Essentials of Genetics**, pp. 190-232.

Periodicals

See page 6 for details of publishers of periodicals:

STUDENT'S REFERENCE

■ **The Species Enigma** New Scientist, 13 June 1998 (Inside Science). *The nature of species, ring species, and the status of hybrids.*

■ **The Hardy-Weinberg Principle** Biol. Sci. Rev., 15(4), April 2003, pp. 7-9. *A succinct explanation of the basis of the Hardy-Weinberg principle, and its uses in estimating genotype frequencies and predicting change in populations.*

■ **Polymorphism** Biol. Sci. Rev., 14(1), Sept. 2001, pp. 19-21. *An account of polymorphism in populations, with several case studies (including Biston moths) provided as illustrative examples.*

■ **Live and Let Live** New Scientist, 3 July 1999, pp. 32-36. *Hybrids are intact entities, subject to the same evolutionary pressures as pure species.*

■ **The Rise of Mammals** Nat. Geographic, 203(4), pp. April 2003, p. 2-37. *An account of the adaptive radiation of the mammals and the significance of the placenta in mammalian evolution.*

■ **The Cheetah: Losing the Race?** Biol. Sci. Rev., 14(2) Nov. 2001, pp. 7-10. *The evolutionary bottleneck experienced by cheetahs and its implications for the genetics of the species.*

■ **Mass Extinctions** New Scientist, 11 December 1999 (Inside Science). *The nature and causes of the five mass extinctions of the past. A discussion of the current sixth extinction is included.*

■ **The Sixth Extinction** Nat. Geographic, 195(2) Feb. 1999, pp. 42-59. *High rates of extinction have occurred five times in the past. The sixth extinction is on its way, driven by human impact.*

TEACHER'S REFERENCE

■ **15 Answers to Creationist Nonsense** Scientific American, July 2002, pp. 62-69. *A synopsis of the common arguments presented by Creationists and the answers offered by science.*

■ **The American Biology Teacher** contains many excellent articles covering the teaching of basic evolutionary principles. Examples are listed below:

Using Evolution as the Framework for Teaching Biology: 63(1), January 2001, pp. 20-23.

A Lab Exercise Explaining Hardy-Weinberg Equilibrium: 63(9), Nov. 2001, pp. 670-676.

Natural Selection Among Playing Cards: 64(4), April 2002, pp. 276-278.

Variability and Drift in Natural Populations...: 64(6), August 2002, pp. 455-463.

■ **Adaptation - A Question of Definitions** SSR 83(304), March 2002, pp. 97-101. *Proper and improper use of the term adaptation in biology.*

■ **Cichlids of the Rift Lakes** Scientific American, Feb. 1999, pp. 44-49. *An excellent account of the speciation events documented in cichlid fishes.*

■ **Listen, we're Different** New Scientist, 17 July 1999, pp. 32-35. *Speciation in cicadas as a result of behavioral and temporal isolating mechanisms.*

■ **Live and Let Live** New Scientist, 3 July 1999, pp. 32-36. *Recent research suggests that hybrids are intact entities subject to the same evolutionary pressures as pure species.*

■ **Which Came First?** Scientific American, Feb. 1997, pp. 12-14. *Who were the real ancestors of birds? Shared features among fossils may result from convergence rather than common ancestry.*

■ **Evolution: Five Big Questions** New Scientist, 14 June 2003, pp. 32-39, 48-51. *A discussion of the five most points of discussion regarding evolution and the mechanisms by which it occurs.*

■ **Replaying Life** New Scientist, 13 February 1999, pp. 29-33. *Rapid evolution in bacteria driven by habitat diversity and niche differentiation.*

■ **The Challenge of Antibiotic Resistance** Sci. American, March 1998, pp. 32-39. *Antibiotic resistance in bacteria and its selective advantage.*

Internet

See pages 10-11 for details of how to access **Bio Links** from our web site: **www.thebiozone.com**. From Bio Links, access sites under the topics:

EVOLUTION: • BIO 414 evolution • Evolution • • The Talk.Origins archive ... *and others* > **Charles Darwin**: • Darwin and evolution overview • What is Darwinism? *... and others*

Also see the sites listed under "*Evolution Theory and Evidence*" and "*The Fossil Record*".

GENETICS > **Population Genetics**: • Introduction to evolutionary biology • Micro-evolution and population genetics • Random genetic drift • Population genetics: lecture notes ... *and others*

Software and video resources are now provided in the Teacher Resource Handbook

RA③ The Modern Theory of Evolution

Although **Charles Darwin** is credited with the development of the theory of evolution by natural selection, there were many people that contributed ideas upon which he built his own. Since Darwin first proposed his theory, aspects that were problematic (such as the mechanism of inheritance) have now been explained. The theory has undergone refinement and has been expanded to incorporate the modern developments in biology. The development of the modern theory of evolution has a history going back at least two centuries. The diagram below illustrates the way in which some of the major contributors helped to form the currently accepted model, often referred to as the **new synthesis** (or the Neo-Darwinian theory). Some of the early contributors did not have the concept of evolution in their minds when they put forward their ideas, but their work contributed toward the development of a unifying theory explaining how species can change over time.

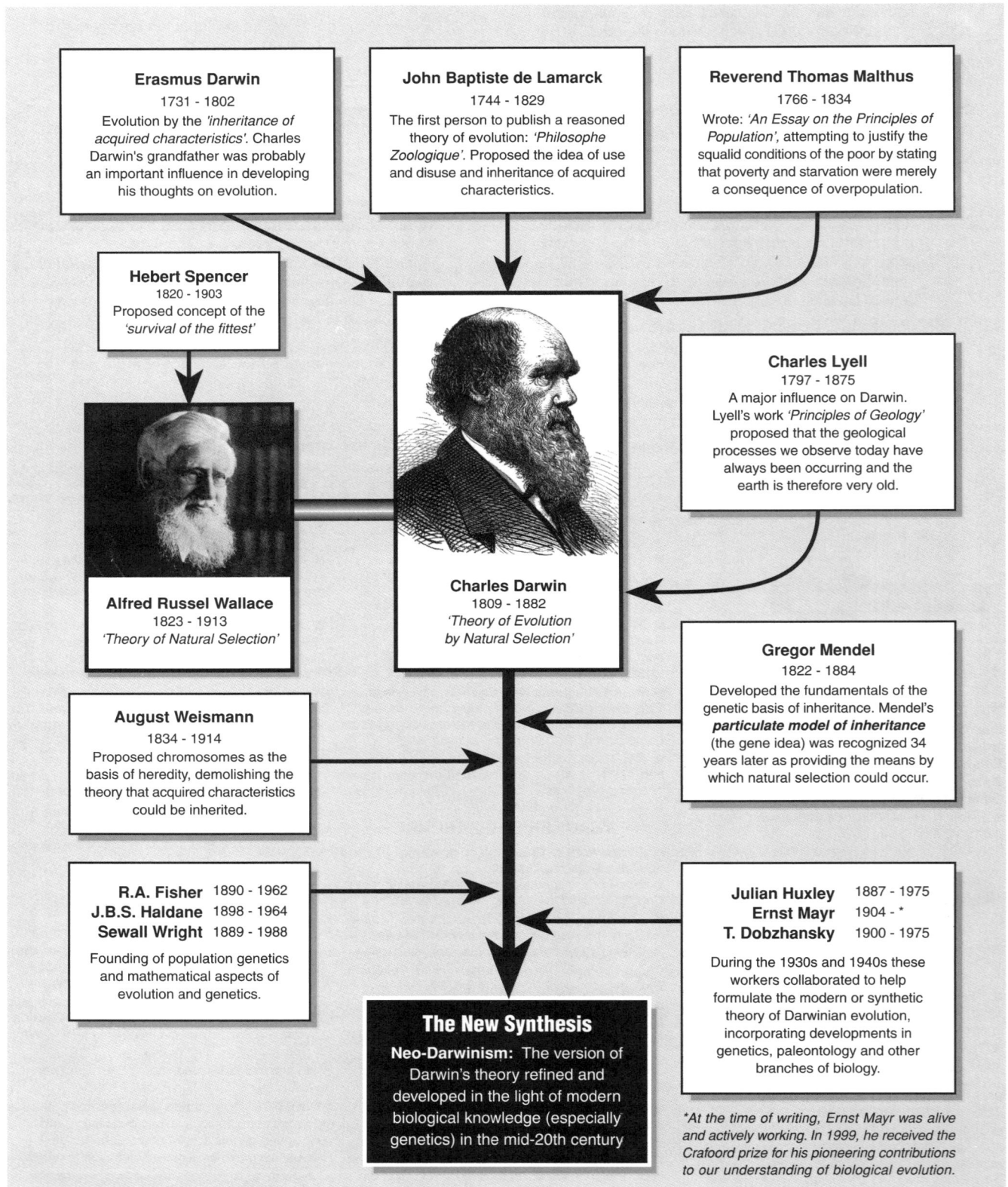

Erasmus Darwin
1731 - 1802
Evolution by the *'inheritance of acquired characteristics'*. Charles Darwin's grandfather was probably an important influence in developing his thoughts on evolution.

John Baptiste de Lamarck
1744 - 1829
The first person to publish a reasoned theory of evolution: *'Philosophe Zoologique'*. Proposed the idea of use and disuse and inheritance of acquired characteristics.

Reverend Thomas Malthus
1766 - 1834
Wrote: *'An Essay on the Principles of Population'*, attempting to justify the squalid conditions of the poor by stating that poverty and starvation were merely a consequence of overpopulation.

Hebert Spencer
1820 - 1903
Proposed concept of the *'survival of the fittest'*

Charles Lyell
1797 - 1875
A major influence on Darwin. Lyell's work *'Principles of Geology'* proposed that the geological processes we observe today have always been occurring and the earth is therefore very old.

Alfred Russel Wallace
1823 - 1913
'Theory of Natural Selection'

Charles Darwin
1809 - 1882
'Theory of Evolution by Natural Selection'

Gregor Mendel
1822 - 1884
Developed the fundamentals of the genetic basis of inheritance. Mendel's ***particulate model of inheritance*** (the gene idea) was recognized 34 years later as providing the means by which natural selection could occur.

August Weismann
1834 - 1914
Proposed chromosomes as the basis of heredity, demolishing the theory that acquired characteristics could be inherited.

R.A. Fisher 1890 - 1962
J.B.S. Haldane 1898 - 1964
Sewall Wright 1889 - 1988
Founding of population genetics and mathematical aspects of evolution and genetics.

Julian Huxley 1887 - 1975
Ernst Mayr 1904 - *
T. Dobzhansky 1900 - 1975
During the 1930s and 1940s these workers collaborated to help formulate the modern or synthetic theory of Darwinian evolution, incorporating developments in genetics, paleontology and other branches of biology.

The New Synthesis
Neo-Darwinism: The version of Darwin's theory refined and developed in the light of modern biological knowledge (especially genetics) in the mid-20th century

At the time of writing, Ernst Mayr was alive and actively working. In 1999, he received the Crafoord prize for his pioneering contributions to our understanding of biological evolution.

1. From the diagram above, choose one of the contributors to the development of evolutionary theory (excluding Charles Darwin himself), and write a few paragraphs discussing their role in contributing to Darwin's ideas. You may need to consult an encyclopedia or other reference to assist you.

Darwin's Theory

A 2

In 1859, Darwin and Wallace jointly proposed that new species could develop by a process of natural selection. Natural selection is the term given to the mechanism by which better adapted organisms survive to produce a greater number of viable offspring. This has the effect of increasing their proportion in the population so that they become more common. It is Darwin who is best remembered for the theory of evolution by natural selection through his famous book: '**On the origin of species by means of natural selection**', written 23 years after returning from his voyage on the Beagle, from which much of the evidence for his theory was accumulated. Although Darwin could not explain the origin of variation nor the mechanism of its transmission (this was provided later by Mendel's work), his basic theory of evolution by natural selection (outlined below) is widely accepted today. The study of population genetics has greatly improved our understanding of evolutionary processes, which are now seen largely as a (frequently gradual) change in allele frequencies within a population. Students should be aware that scientific debate on the subject of evolution centers around the relative merits of various alternative hypotheses about the nature of evolutionary processes. The debate is not about the existence of the phenomenon of evolution itself.

Darwin's Theory of Evolution by Natural Selection

Overproduction
Populations produce too many young: many must die

Populations tend to produce more offspring than are needed to replace the parents. Natural populations normally maintain constant numbers. There must therefore be a certain number dying.

Variation
Individuals show variation: some are more favorable than others

Individuals in a population vary in their phenotype and therefore, their genotype. Some variants are better suited to the current conditions than others and find it easier to survive and reproduce

Natural Selection
Natural selection favors the best suited at the time

The struggle for survival amongst overcrowded individuals will favor those variations which have the best advantage. This does not necessarily mean that those struggling die, but they will be in a poorer condition.

Inherited
Variations are Inherited. The best suited variants leave more offspring.

The variations (both favorable and unfavorable) are passed on to offspring. Each new generation will contain proportionally more descendents from individuals with favorable characters than those with unfavorable.

1. In your own words, describe how Darwin's theory of evolution by natural selection provides an explanation for the change in the appearance of a species over time:

_____

_____

_____

_____

Adaptations and Fitness

An **adaptation**, is any heritable trait that suits an organism to its natural function in the environment (its niche). These traits may be structural, physiological, or behavioral. The idea is important for evolutionary theory because adaptive features promote fitness. **Fitness** is a measure of how well suited an organism is to survive in its habitat and its ability to maximize the numbers of offspring surviving to reproductive age. Adaptations are distinct from *properties* which, although they may be striking, cannot be described as adaptive unless they are shown to be functional in the organism's natural habitat. Genetic adaptation must not be confused with *physiological adjustment* (acclimatization), which refers to an organism's ability to *adapt* during its lifetime to changing environmental conditions. The physiological changes that occur when a person spends time at altitude provide a good example of acclimatization. Examples of adaptive features arising through evolution are illustrated below.

Ear Length in Rabbits and Hares

The external ears of many mammals are used as important organs to assist in thermoregulation (controlling loss and gain of body heat). The ears of rabbits and hares native to hot, dry climates, such as the jack rabbit of south-western USA and northern Mexico, are relatively very large. The Arctic hare lives in the tundra zone of Alaska, northern Canada and Greenland, and has ears that are relatively short. This reduction in the size of the extremities (ears, limbs, and noses) is typical of cold adapted species.

Arctic hare: *Lepus arcticus*

Black-tail jackrabbit: *Lepus californicus*

Body Size in Relation to Climate

Regulation of body temperature requires a large amount of energy and mammals exhibit a variety of structural and physiological adaptations to increase the effectiveness of this process. Heat production in any endotherm depends on body volume (heat generating metabolism), whereas the rate of heat loss depends on surface area. Increasing body size minimizes heat loss to the environment by reducing the surface area to volume ratio. Animals in colder regions therefore tend to be larger overall than those living in hot climates. This relationship is know as **Bergman's rule** and it is well documented in many mammalian species. Cold adapted species also tend to have more compact bodies and shorter extremities than related species in hot climates.

Fennec fox

Arctic fox

The **fennec fox** of the Sahara illustrates the adaptations typical of mammals living in hot climates: a small body size and lightweight fur, and long ears, legs, and nose. These features facilitate heat dissipation and reduce heat gain.

The **Arctic fox** shows the physical characteristics typical of cold-adapted mammals: a stocky, compact body shape with small ears, short legs and nose, and dense fur. These features reduce heat loss to the environment.

Number of Horns in Rhinoceroses

Not all differences between species can be convincingly interpreted as adaptations to particular environments. Rhinoceroses charge rival males and predators, and the horn(s), when combined with the head-down posture, add effectiveness to this behavior. Horns are obviously adaptive, but it is not clear that the possession of one (Indian rhino) or two (black rhino) horns is necessarily related directly to the environment in which those animals live.

Great Indian rhino

African black rhino

1. Distinguish between adaptive features (genetic) and acclimatization:

_____

_____

2. Explain the nature of the relationship between the length of extremities (such as limbs and ears) and climate:

_____

_____

3. Explain the adaptive value of a larger body size at high latitude: _____

_____

_____

Natural Selection

A 3

Natural selection operates on the phenotypes of individuals, produced by their particular combinations of alleles. In natural populations, the allele combinations of some individuals are perpetuated at the expense of other genotypes. This differential survival of some genotypes over others is called **natural selection**. The effect of natural selection can vary; it can act to maintain the genotype of a species or to change it. **Stabilizing** selection maintains the established favorable characteristics and is associated with stable environments. In contrast, **directional selection** favors phenotypes at one extreme of the phenotypic range and is associated with gradually changing environments. **Disruptive selection** is a much rarer form of selection favoring two phenotypic extremes, and is a feature of fluctuating environments.

Stabilizing Selection

Extreme variations are culled from the population (there is selection against them). Those with the established (middle range) adaptive phenotype are retained in greater numbers. This reduces the variation for the phenotypic character. In the example right, light and dark snails are eliminated, leaving medium colored snails. Stabilizing selection can be seen in the selection pressures on human birth weights.

Directional Selection

Directional selection is associated with gradually changing conditions, where the adaptive phenotype is shifted in one direction and one aspect of a trait becomes emphasized (e.g. coloration). In the example right, light colored snails are eliminated and the population becomes darker. Directional selection was observed in peppered moths in England during the Industrial Revolution. They responded to the air pollution of industrialization by increasing the frequency of darker, melanic forms.

Disruptive or Diversifying Selection

Disruptive selection favors two extremes of a trait at the expense of intermediate forms. It is associated with a fluctuating environment and gives rise to **balanced polymorphism** in the population. In the example right, there is selection against medium colored snails, which are eliminated. There is considerable evidence that predators, such as insectivorous birds, are more likely to find and eat common morphs and ignore rare morphs. This enables the rarer forms to persist in the population.

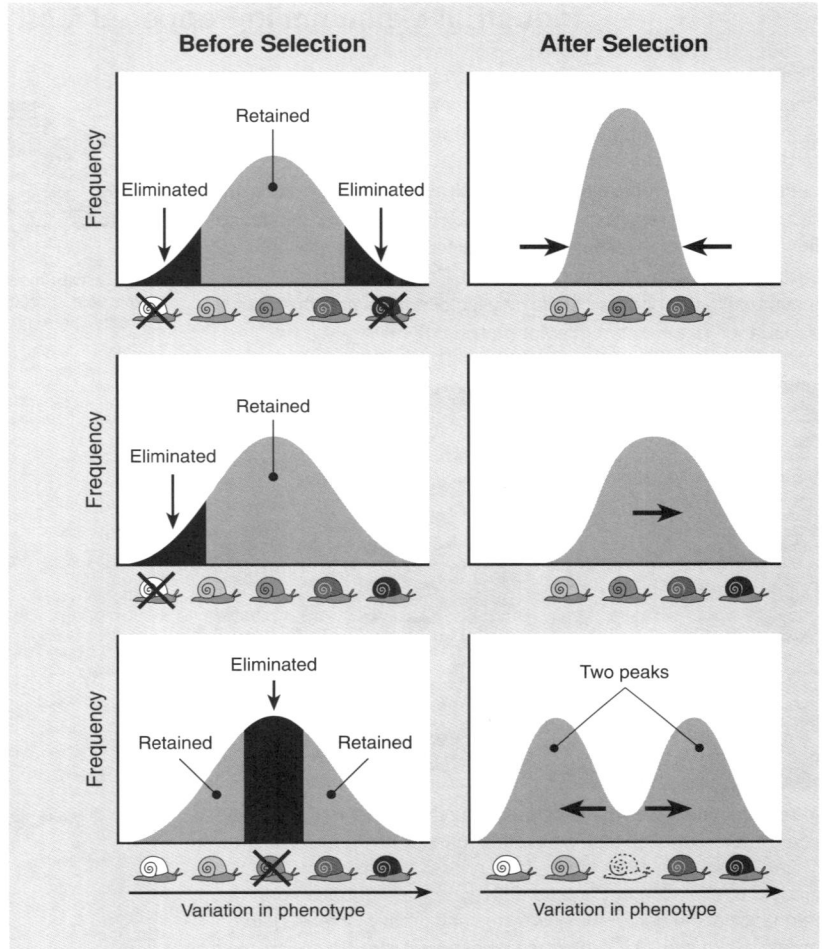

Before Selection | **After Selection**

1. (a) Distinguish between directional selection and disruptive selection, identifying when each is likely to operate:

_____

_____

_____

(b) State which of the three types of selection described above will lead to evolution, and explain why:

_____

_____

2. Explain how a change in environment may result in selection becoming directional rather than stabilizing:

_____

_____

3. Explain how, in a population of snails, through natural selection, shell color could change from light to dark over time:

_____

_____

_____

Industrial Melanism

Natural selection may act on the frequencies of phenotypes (and hence genotypes) in populations in one of three different ways (through stabilizing, directional, or disruptive selection). Over time, natural selection may lead to a permanent change in the genetic makeup of a population. The increased prevalence of melanic forms of the peppered moth, *Biston betularia*, during the

Industrial Revolution, is one of the best known examples of directional selection following a change in environmental conditions. Although the protocols used in the central experiments on *Biston*, and the conclusions drawn from them, have been queried, it remains one of the clearest documented examples of phenotypic change in a polymorphic population.

Industrial Melanism in Peppered Moths, *Biston betularia*

The **peppered moth**, *Biston betularia*, occurs in two forms (morphs): the gray mottled form, and a dark melanic form. Changes in the relative abundance of these two forms was hypothesized to be the result of selective predation by birds, with pale forms suffering higher mortality in industrial areas because they are more visible. The results of experiments by H.D. Kettlewell supported this hypothesis but did not confirm it, since selective predation by birds was observed but not quantified. Other research indicates that predation by birds is not the only factor determining the relative abundance of the different color morphs.

Gray or mottled morph: vulnerable to predation in industrial areas where the trees are dark.

Melanic or carbonaria morph: dark color makes it less vulnerable to predation in industrial areas.

Museum collections of the peppered moth made over the last 150 years show a marked change in the frequency of the melanic form. Moths collected in 1850 (above left), prior to the major onset of the industrial revolution in England. Fifty years later (above right) the frequency of the darker melanic forms had greatly increased. Even as late as the mid 20th century, coal-based industries predominated in some centers, and the melanic form occurred in greater frequency in these areas (see map, right).

Frequency of peppered moth forms in 1950

This map shows the relative frequencies of the two forms of peppered moth in the UK in 1950; a time when coal-based industries still predominated in some major centers.

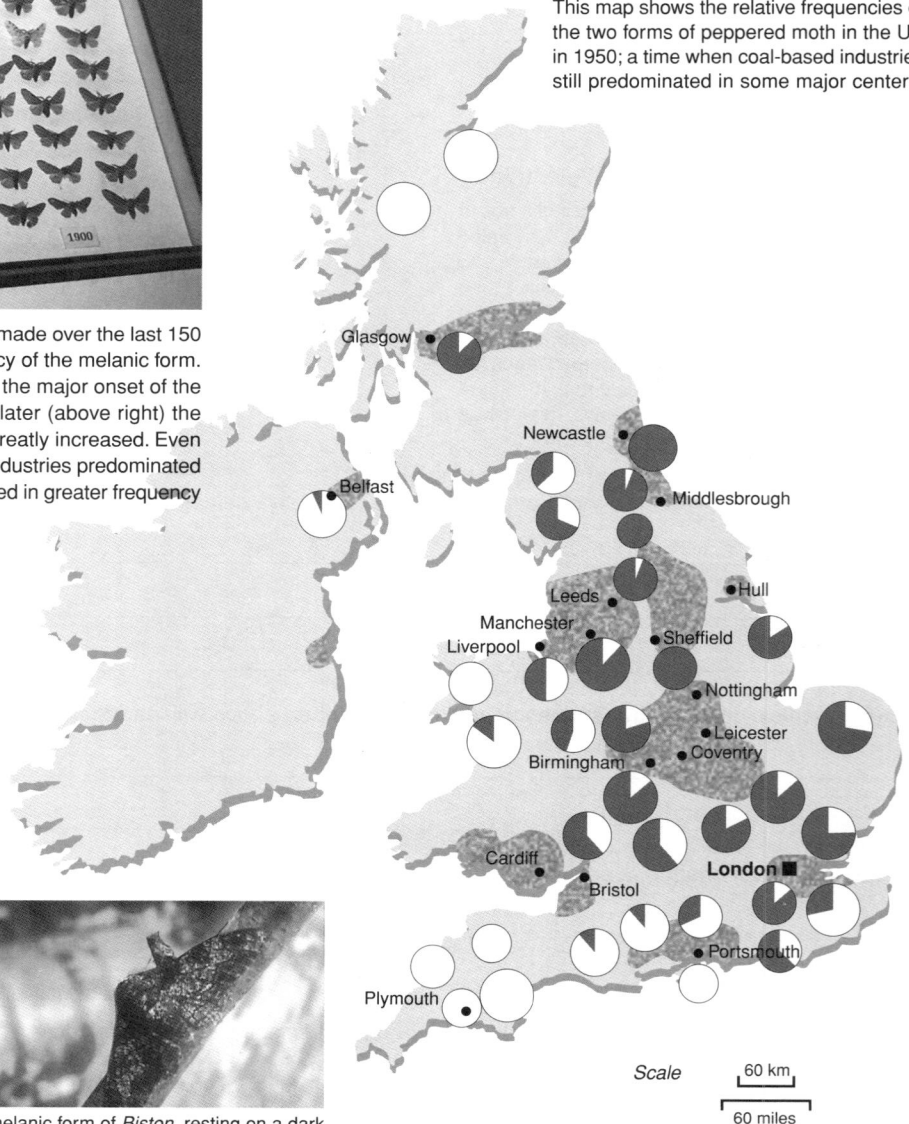

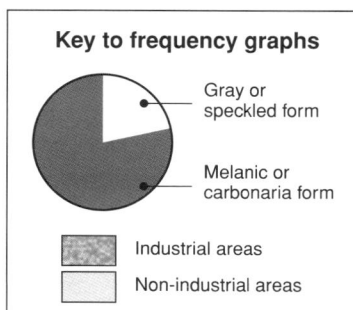

Key to frequency graphs

- Gray or speckled form
- Melanic or carbonaria form
- Industrial areas
- Non-industrial areas

A gray (mottled) form of *Biston*, camouflaged against a lichen covered bark surface. In the absence of soot pollution, mottled forms appear to have the selective advantage.

A melanic form of *Biston*, resting on a dark branch, so that it appears as part of the branch. Note that the background has been faded out so that the moth can be seen.

Scale   60 km
        60 miles

Changes in frequency of melanic peppered moths

In the 1940s and 1950s, coal burning was still at intense levels around the industrial centres of Manchester and Liverpool. During this time, the melanic form of the moth was still very dominant. In the rural areas further south and west of these industrial centers, the gray or speckled forms increased dramatically. With the decline of coal burning factories and the Clean Air Acts in cities, the air quality improved between 1960 and 1980. Sulfur dioxide and smoke levels dropped to a fraction of their previous levels. This coincided with a sharp fall in the relative numbers of melanic moths.

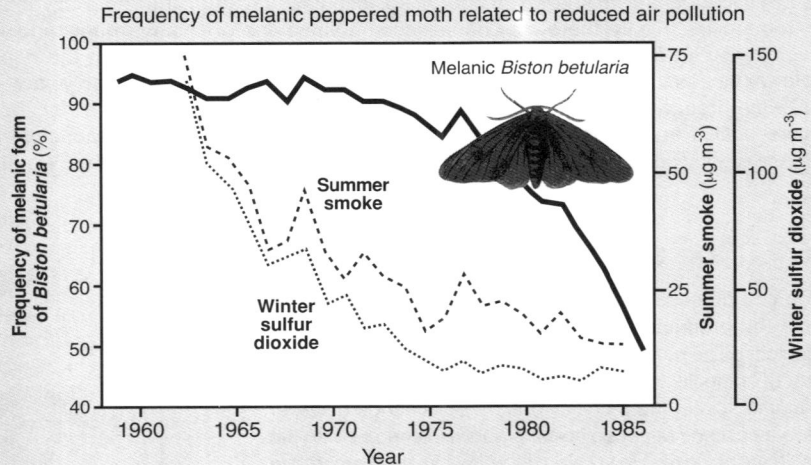

Frequency of melanic peppered moth related to reduced air pollution

1. The populations of peppered moth in England have undergone changes in the frequency of an obvious phenotypic character over the last 150 years. Describe the phenotypic character that changed in its frequency:

_____

2. (a) Identify the (proposed) selective agent for phenotypic change in *Biston*: _____

   (b) Describe how the selection pressure on the light colored morph has changed with changing environmental conditions over the last 150 years:

   _____

   _____

3. The industrial centers for England in 1950 were located around London, Birmingham, Liverpool, Manchester, and Leeds. Glasgow in Scotland also had a large industrial base. Comment on how the relative frequencies of the two forms of peppered moth were affected by the geographic location of industrial regions:

_____

_____

_____

_____

4. The level of pollution dropped around Manchester and Liverpool between 1960 and 1985.

   (a) State how much the pollution dropped by: _____

   (b) Describe how the frequency of the darker melanic form responded to this reduced pollution: _____

   _____

   _____

5. In the example of the peppered moths, state whether the selection pressure is disruptive, stabilizing, or directional:

_____

6. Outline the key difference between natural and artificial selection: _____

_____

7. Discuss the statement "the environment directs natural selection": _____

_____

_____

_____

EA ③ Heterozygous Advantage

There are two mechanisms by which natural selection can affect allele frequencies. Firstly, there may be selection against one of the homozygotes. When one homozygous type (for example, aa), has a lower fitness than the other two genotypes (in this case, Aa or AA), the frequency of the deleterious allele will tend to decrease until it is completely eliminated. In some situations, both homozygous conditions (aa **and** AA) have lower fitness than the heterozygote; a situation that leads to **heterozygous advantage** and may result in the stable coexistence of both alleles in the population (**balanced polymorphism**). There are remarkably few well-documented examples in which the evidence for heterozygous advantage is conclusive. The maintenance of the sickle cell mutation in malaria-prone regions is one such example.

The Sickle Cell Allele (HbS)

Sickle cell disease is caused by a mutation to a gene that directs the production of the human blood protein called hemoglobin. The mutant allele is known as **Hb^S** and produces a form of hemoglobin that differs from the normal form by just one amino acid in the β-chain. This minute change however causes a cascade of physiological problems in people with the allele. Some of the red blood cells containing mutated hemoglobin alter their shape to become irregular and spiky; the so-called **sickle cells**.

Sickle cells have a tendency to clump together and work less efficiently. In people with just one sickle cell allele plus a normal allele (the heterozygote condition **Hb^{S}Hb**), there is a mixture of both red blood cell types and they are said to have the sickle cell trait. They are generally unaffected by the disease except in low oxygen environments (e.g. climbing at altitude). People with two Hb^S genes (**Hb^{S}Hb^S**) suffer severe illness and even death. For this reason Hb^S is considered **a lethal gene**.

Heterozygous Advantage in Malarial Regions

Falciparum malaria is widely distributed throughout central Africa, the Mediterranean, Middle East, and tropical and semi-tropical Asia (Fig. 1). It is transmitted by the *Anopheles* mosquito, which spreads the protozoan *Plasmodium falciparum* from person to person as it feeds on blood.

SYMPTOMS: These appear 1-2 weeks after being bitten, and include headache, shaking, chills, and fever. Falciparum malaria is more severe than other forms of malaria, with high fever, convulsions, and coma. It can be fatal within days of the first symptoms appearing.

THE PARADOX: The Hb^S allele offers considerable protection against malaria. Sickle cells have low potassium levels, which causes plasmodium parasites inside these cells to die. Those with a normal phenotype are very susceptible to malaria, but heterozygotes (**Hb^{S}Hb**) are much less so. This situation, called **heterozygous advantage**, has resulted in the Hb^S allele being present in moderately high frequencies in parts of Africa and Asia despite its harmful effects (Fig. 2). This is a special case of balanced polymorphism, called a **balanced lethal system** because neither of the homozygotes produces a phenotype that survives, but the heterozygote is viable.

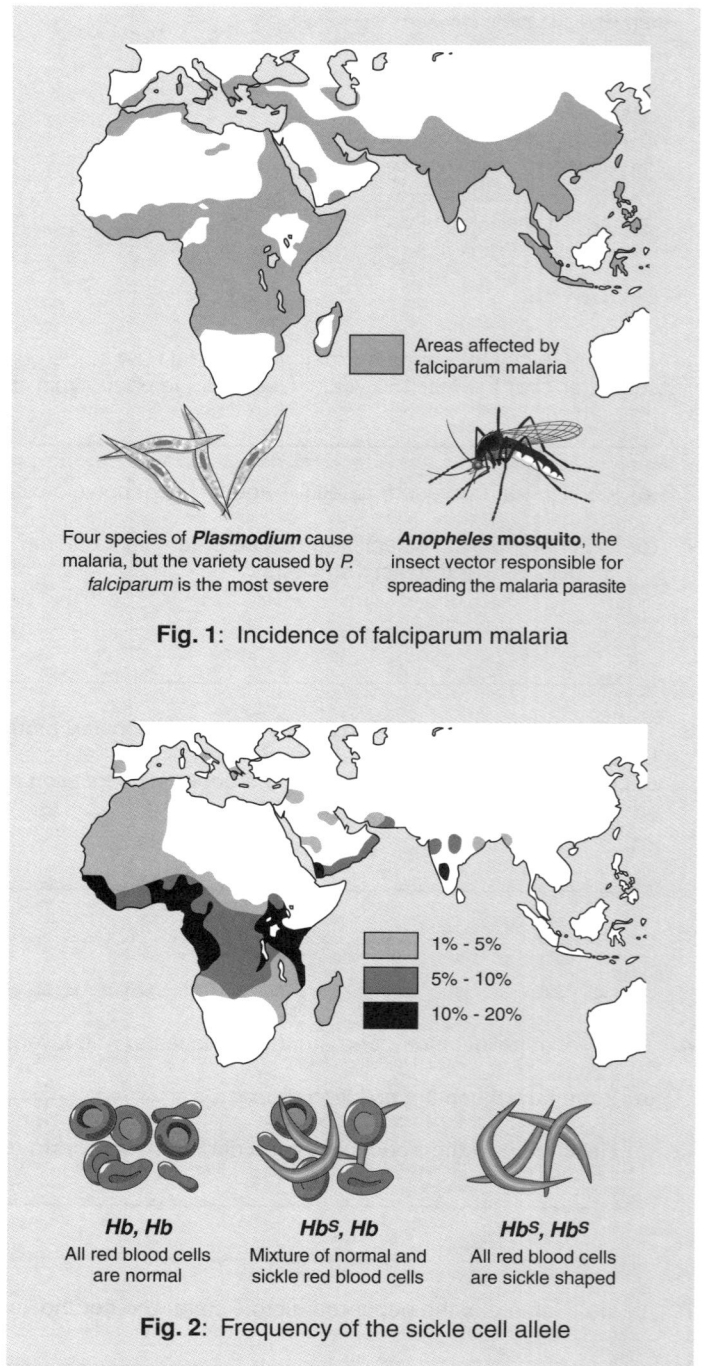

Areas affected by falciparum malaria

Four species of *Plasmodium* cause malaria, but the variety caused by *P. falciparum* is the most severe

Anopheles **mosquito**, the insect vector responsible for spreading the malaria parasite

Fig. 1: Incidence of falciparum malaria

1% - 5%
5% - 10%
10% - 20%

Hb, Hb
All red blood cells are normal

Hb^S, Hb
Mixture of normal and sickle red blood cells

Hb^S, Hb^S
All red blood cells are sickle shaped

Fig. 2: Frequency of the sickle cell allele

1. Define the term **heterozygous advantage**: _____

    _____

2   With respect to the sickle cell allele, explain how heterozygous advantage can lead to balanced polymorphism:

    _____

    _____

    _____

Selection for Human Birth Weight

PDA 2

This activity explores the selection pressures acting on the birth weight of human babies. Carry out the steps below:

Step 1: Collect the birth weights from 100 birth notices from your local newspaper (or 50 if you are having difficulty getting enough - this should involve looking back through the last 2-3 weeks of birth notices). If you cannot obtain birth weights in your local newspaper, a set of 100 sample birth weights is provided in the Model Answers booklet.

Step 2: Group the weights into each of the 12 weight classes (of 0.5 kg increments). Determine what percentage (of the total sample) fall into each weight class (e.g., 17 babies weigh 2.5-3.0 kg out of the 100 sampled = 17%)

Step 3: Graph these in the form of a **histogram** for the 12 weight classes (use the graphing grid provided below). Be sure to use the scale provided on the **left** vertical (y) axis.

Step 4: Create a second graph by plotting percentage mortality of newborn babies in relation to their birth weight. Use the scale on the **right** y axis and data provided (below right).

Step 5: Draw a **line** of 'best fit' through these points.

The size of the baby and the diameter and shape of the birth canal are the two crucial factors in determining whether a normal delivery is possible.

Mortality of newborn babies related to birth weight

Weight (kg)	Mortality (%)
1.0	80
1.5	30
2.0	12
2.5	4
3.0	3
3.5	2
4.0	3
4.5	7
5.0	15

Source: Biology: The Unity & Diversity of Life (4th ed), by Starr and Taggart

1. Describe the shape of the histogram for birth weights: _____

2. State the optimum birth weight in terms of the lowest newborn mortality rate: _____

3. Describe the relationship between the newborn mortality rate and the birth weights: _____

_____

4. Describe the selection pressures that are operating to control the range of birth weight: _____

_____

_____

5. Describe how medical intervention methods during pregnancy and childbirth may have altered these selection pressures:

_____

_____

A 2   Darwin's Finches

The Galapagos Islands, 920 km off the west coast of Ecuador, played a major role in shaping Darwin's thoughts about natural selection and evolution. While exploring the islands in 1835, he was struck by the unique and peculiar species he found there. In particular, he was intrigued by the island's finches. The Galapagos group is home to 13 species of finches in four genera. This variety has arisen as a result of evolution from one common ancestral species. Initially, a number of small finches, probably grassquits, made their way from South America across the Pacific to the Galapagos Islands. In the new environment, which was relatively free of competitors, the colonizers underwent an adaptive radiation, producing a range of species each with its own unique feeding niche. Although similar in their plumage, nest building techniques, and calls, the different species of finches can easily be distinguished by the size and shape of their beaks. The beak shape of each species is adapted for a different purpose, such as crushing seeds, pecking wood, or probing flowers for nectar. Between them, the 13 species of this endemic group fill the roles of seven different families of South American mainland birds. Modern methods of DNA (genetic) analysis have confirmed Darwin's insight and have shown that all 13 species evolved from a flock of about 30 birds arriving a million years ago.

The Evolution of Darwin's Finches

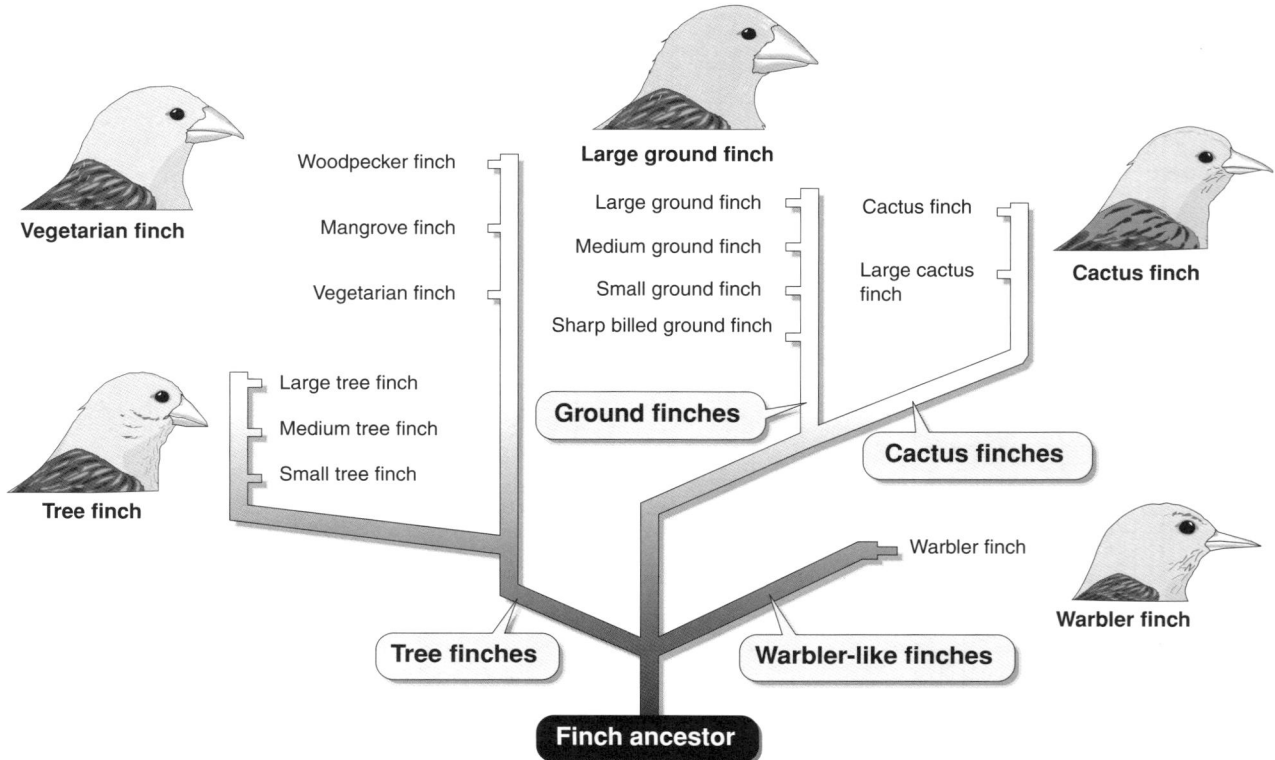

Vegetarian finch

Woodpecker finch

Mangrove finch

Vegetarian finch

Large ground finch

Large ground finch

Medium ground finch

Small ground finch

Sharp billed ground finch

Cactus finch

Large cactus finch

Cactus finch

Ground finches

Cactus finches

Tree finch

Large tree finch

Medium tree finch

Small tree finch

Tree finches

Warbler finch

Warbler-like finches

Warbler finch

Finch ancestor

Tree finches	Cactus finches	Ground finches	Warbler finches
As the name implies, tree finches are largely arboreal and feed mainly on insects. The bill is sharper than in ground finches and better suited to grasp insects. Paler than ground or cactus finches, they also have streaked breasts.	Probably descended from ground finches. Beak is probing. Males are mostly black, females are streaked, like ground finches. Found in arid areas on prickly pear cactus where they eat insects on the cactus, or the cactus itself.	Four species with crushing-type bills used for seed eating. On Wolf Island, they are called vampire finches because they peck the skin of animals to draw blood, which they then drink. Such behavior has evolved from eating parasitic insects off animals.	Named for their resemblance to the unrelated warblers, the beak of the warbler finch is the thinnest of the Galapagos finches. It is the most widespread species, found throughout the archipelago. Warbler finches prey on flying and ground dwelling insects.

1. Outline the main factors that have contributed to the adaptive radiation of Darwin's finches: _____

_____

_____

_____

Evolution in Bacteria

A 2

As a result of their short generation times, bacterial populations can show significant evolutionary change within relatively short periods of time. One such evolutionary change is the acquisition of **antibiotic resistance**. Antibiotics are drugs that fight bacterial infections. After being discovered in the 1940s, they rapidly transformed medical care and dramatically reduced illness and death from bacterial disease. With the increased and often indiscriminate use of antibiotics, many bacteria quickly developed drug resistance. The increasing number of multi-drug resistant bacterial strains is particularly worrying; resistant infections inhibit the treatment of patients and increase patient mortality. Moreover, antibiotic resistance adds considerably to the costs of treating disease and, as resistance spreads between bacterial strains, new drugs have an increasingly limited life span during which they are effective.

The Evolution of Drug Resistance in Bacteria

Susceptible bacterium

Slightly insensitive bacterium

Bacterium with greater resistance survives

Drug resistance genes can be transferred to non resistant strains

Within any population, there is genetic variation. In this case, the susceptibility of the bacterial strain is normally distributed, with some cells being more susceptible than others.

If the amount of antibiotic delivered is too low, or the full course of antibiotics is not completed, only the most susceptible bacteria will die.

Now a population of insensitive bacteria has developed. Within this population there will also be variation in the susceptibility to antibiotics. As treatment continues, some of the bacteria may acquire greater resistance.

A highly resistant population has evolved. The resistant cells can exchange genetic material with other bacteria, passing on the resistance genes. The antibiotic that was initially used against this bacterial strain will now be ineffective against it.

Observing Adaptive Radiation

Recently, scientists have demonstrated rapid evolution in bacteria. *Pseudomonas fluorescens* was used in the experiment and propagated in a simple heterogeneous environment consisting of a 25 cm^3 glass container containing 6 cm^3 of broth medium. Over a short period of time, the bacteria underwent morphological diversification, with a number of new morphs appearing. These morphs were shown to be genetically distinct. A striking feature of the evolved species is their niche specificity, with each new morph occupying a distinct habitat (below, left). In a follow up experiment (below, right), the researchers grew the same original bacterial strain in the same broth under identical incubation conditions, but in a homogenous environment (achieved by shaking the broth). Without the different habitats offered by an undisturbed environment, no morphs emerged. The experiment illustrated the capacity of bacteria to evolve to utilize available niches.

Heterogeneous environment

WS bacteria (wrinkly morphology) evolved to colonize the air-broth interface.

The FS species (fuzzy morphology) colonized the bottom of the container.

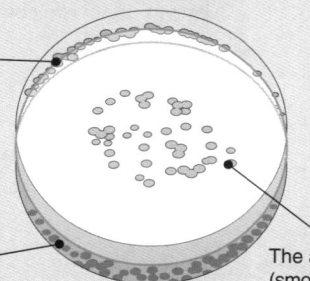

The ancestral SM species (smooth morphology) colonized the surface of the broth.

Homogenous environment

Because there is only one niche, no adaptive radiation occurs.

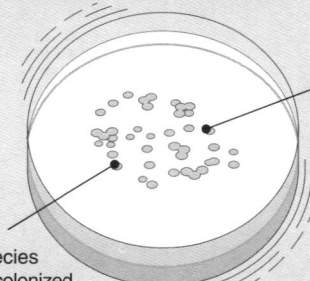

1. Using an illustrative example, explain why evolution of new properties in bacteria can be very rapid: _____

_____

_____

2. (a) In the example above, suggest why the bacteria evolved when grown in a heterogeneous environment:

_____

_____

(b) Predict what would happen if the FS morph was cultured in the homogeneous environment:

_____

_____

Gene Pools and Evolution

The diagram below illustrates the dynamic nature of **gene pools**. It portrays two imaginary populations of one beetle species. Each beetle is a 'carrier' of genetic information, represented here by the alleles (A and a) for a single **codominant gene** that controls the beetle's color. Normally, there are three versions of

the phenotype: black, dark, and pale. Mutations may create other versions of the phenotype. Some of the **microevolutionary processes** that can affect the genetic composition (**allele frequencies**) of the gene pool are illustrated below.

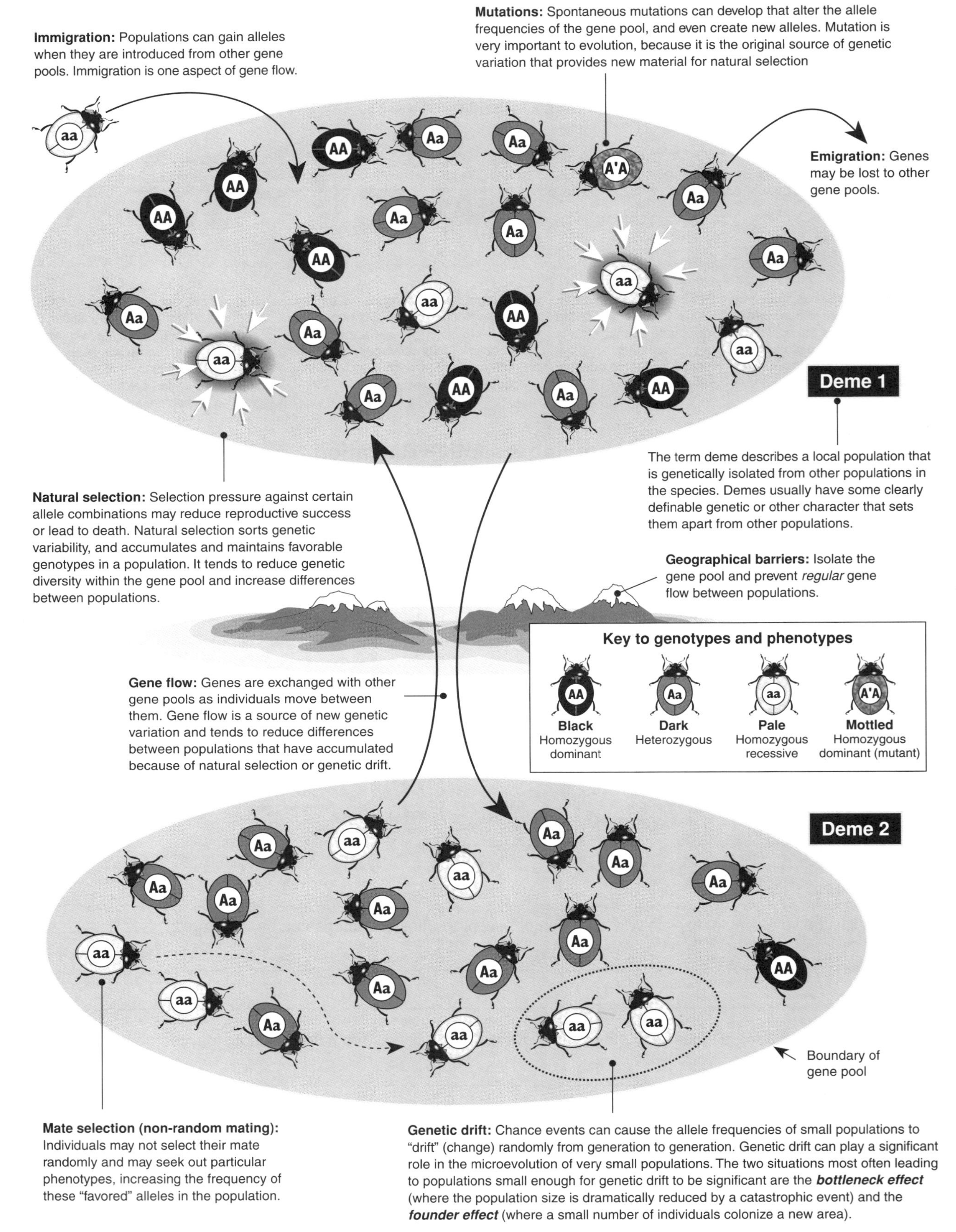

Immigration: Populations can gain alleles when they are introduced from other gene pools. Immigration is one aspect of gene flow.

Mutations: Spontaneous mutations can develop that alter the allele frequencies of the gene pool, and even create new alleles. Mutation is very important to evolution, because it is the original source of genetic variation that provides new material for natural selection

Emigration: Genes may be lost to other gene pools.

Deme 1

The term deme describes a local population that is genetically isolated from other populations in the species. Demes usually have some clearly definable genetic or other character that sets them apart from other populations.

Natural selection: Selection pressure against certain allele combinations may reduce reproductive success or lead to death. Natural selection sorts genetic variability, and accumulates and maintains favorable genotypes in a population. It tends to reduce genetic diversity within the gene pool and increase differences between populations.

Geographical barriers: Isolate the gene pool and prevent *regular* gene flow between populations.

Gene flow: Genes are exchanged with other gene pools as individuals move between them. Gene flow is a source of new genetic variation and tends to reduce differences between populations that have accumulated because of natural selection or genetic drift.

Key to genotypes and phenotypes

Black
Homozygous dominant

Dark
Heterozygous

Pale
Homozygous recessive

Mottled
Homozygous dominant (mutant)

Deme 2

Boundary of gene pool

Mate selection (non-random mating): Individuals may not select their mate randomly and may seek out particular phenotypes, increasing the frequency of these "favored" alleles in the population.

Genetic drift: Chance events can cause the allele frequencies of small populations to "drift" (change) randomly from generation to generation. Genetic drift can play a significant role in the microevolution of very small populations. The two situations most often leading to populations small enough for genetic drift to be significant are the **bottleneck effect** (where the population size is dramatically reduced by a catastrophic event) and the **founder effect** (where a small number of individuals colonize a new area).

Gene Pool Exercise

PA 2

Cut out each of the beetles on this page and use them to reenact different events within a gene pool as described in this topic (see *Gene Pools and Evolution, Changes in a Gene Pool, Founder Effect, Population Bottlenecks, Genetic Drift*).

This page has deliberately been left blank

A② **Factors Affecting Gene Pools**

One of the fundamental concepts for population genetics is stated as follows:

For a very large, randomly mating population, the proportion of dominant to recessive alleles remains constant from one generation to the next (the population is in genetic equilibrium).

In practical terms this means that, if a gene pool is to remain unchanged, it must satisfy all of the criteria listed on the left side of the diagram below (factors that favor gene pool stability). The fact that few populations can be identified as meeting all (or any) of these criteria means that they must be undergoing continual change in their genetic makeup.

For each of the five factors (numbers 1-5) below, state briefly **how** and **why** each would affect the allele frequency in a gene pool:

Factors That Favor Gene Pool Stability	Factors That Favor Gene Pool Change

1. Population size: _____

   _____

   _____

   _____

   _____

Large population

Small population

2. Mate selection: _____

   _____

   _____

   _____

   _____

Random mating

Assortative mating

3. Gene flow between populations: _____

   _____

   _____

   _____

   _____

Barrier to gene flow

No gene flow

Immigration

Emigration

Gene flow

4. Mutations: _____

   _____

   _____

   _____

   _____

No mutation

New recessive allele

Mutations

5. Natural selection: _____

   _____

   _____

   _____

   _____

No natural selection

Natural selection

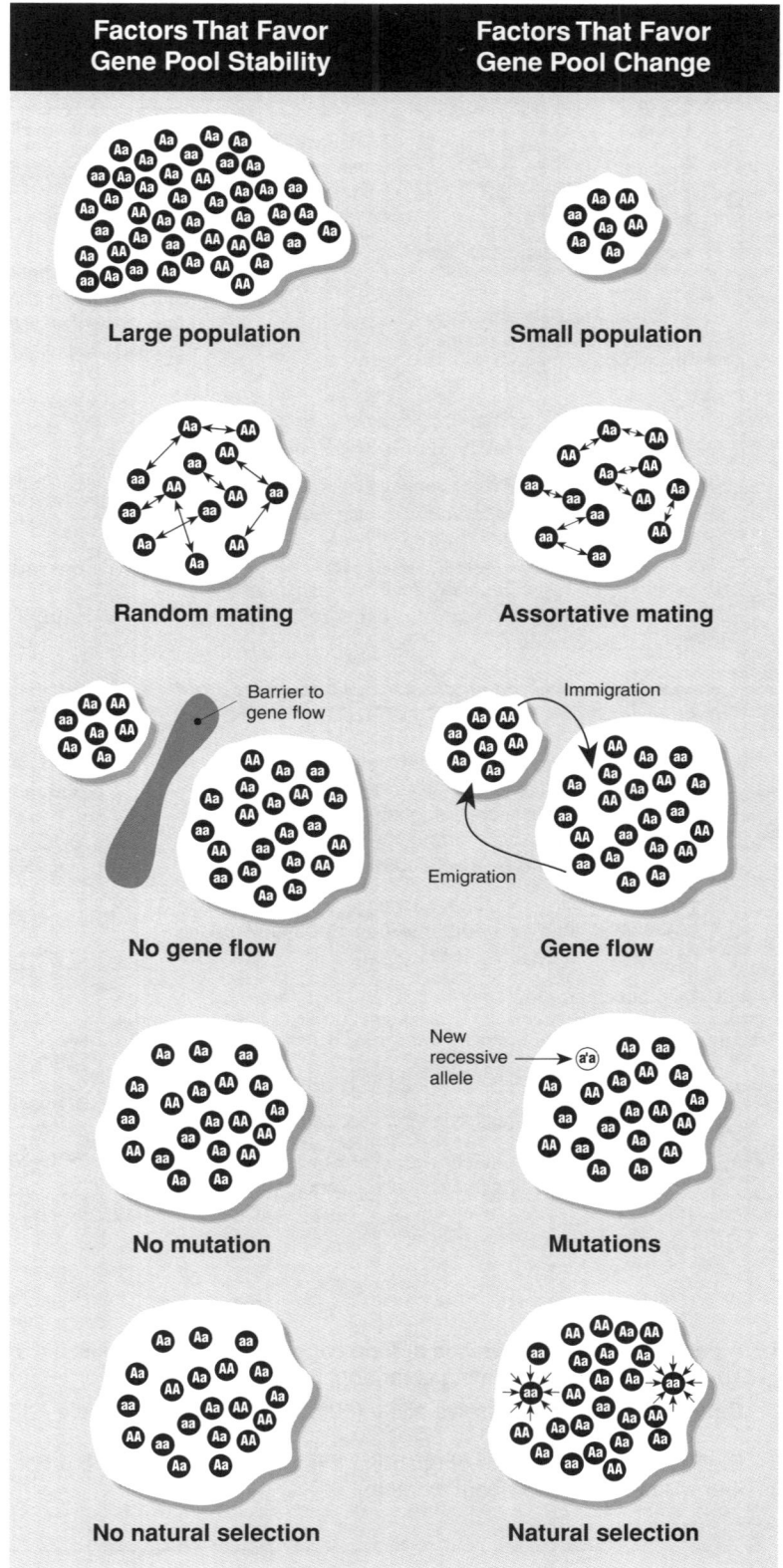

6. (a) List the factors that tend to increase genetic variation in populations: _____

   (b) List the factors that tend to decrease genetic variation in populations: _____

Population Genetics Calculations

The **Hardy-Weinberg equation** provides a simple mathematical model of genetic equilibrium in a gene pool, but its main application in population genetics is in calculating allele and genotype frequencies in populations, particularly as a means of studying changes and measuring their rate. The use of the Hardy-Weinberg equation is described below.

Punnett square

Frequency of allele combination **AA** in the population is represented as **p²**

Frequency of allele combination **aa** in the population is represented as **q²**

Frequency of allele combination **Aa** in the population (add these together to get **2pq**)

$$(p + q)^2 = p^2 + 2pq + q^2 = 1$$

Frequency of allele types

p = Frequency of allele A

q = Frequency of allele a

Frequency of allele combinations

p^2 = Frequency of AA (homozygous dominant)

2pq = Frequency of Aa (heterozygous)

q^2 = Frequency of aa (homozygous recessive)

The Hardy-Weinberg equation is applied to populations with a simple genetic situation: dominant and recessive alleles controlling a single trait. The frequency of all of the dominant (A) and recessive alleles (a) equals the total genetic complement, and adds up to 1 or 100% of the alleles present.

How To Solve Hardy-Weinberg Problems

In most populations, the frequency of two alleles of interest is calculated from the proportion of homozygous recessives (q^2), as this is the only genotype identifiable directly from its phenotype. If only the dominant phenotype is known, q^2 may be calculated (1 – the frequency of the dominant phenotype). The following steps outline the procedure for solving a Hardy-Weinberg problem:

Remember that all calculations must be carried out using proportions, NOT PERCENTAGES!

1. Examine the question to determine what piece of information you have been given about the population. In most cases, this is the percentage or frequency of the homozygous recessive phenotype q^2, or the dominant phenotype p^2 + 2pq (see note above).

2. The first objective is to find out the value of p or q, If this is achieved, then every other value in the equation can be determined by simple calculation.

3. Take the square root of q^2 to find q.

4. Determine p by subtracting q from 1 (i.e. p = 1 – q).

5. Determine p^2 by multiplying p by itself (i.e. p^2 = p x p).

6. Determine 2pq by multiplying p times q times 2.

7. Check that your calculations are correct by adding up the values for p^2 + q^2 + 2pq (the sum should equal 1 or 100%).

Worked example

In the American white population approximately 70% of people can taste the chemical phenylthiocarbamide (PTC) (the dominant phenotype), while 30% are non-tasters (the recessive phenotype).

Determine the frequency of: | **Answers**
(a) Homozygous recessive phenotype(**q²**). 30% - provided
(b) The dominant allele (**p**). 45.2%
(c) Homozygous tasters (**p²**). 20.5%
(d) Heterozygous tasters (**2pq**). 49.5%

Data: The frequency of the dominant phenotype (70% tasters) and recessive phenotype (30% non-tasters) are provided.

Working:
Recessive phenotype: **q²** = 30%
                                  use 0.30 for calculation

   therefore: **q** = 0.5477
                        square root of 0.30

   therefore: **p** = 0.4522
                        1 – q = p
                        1 – 0.5477 = 0.4523

Use p and q in the equation (top) to solve any unknown:

Homozygous dominant **p²** = 0.2046
                              (p x p = 0.4523 x 0.4523)

Heterozygous: **2pq** = 0.4953

---

1. A population of hamsters has a gene consisting of 90% M alleles (black) and 10% m alleles (gray). Mating is random.
   Data: Frequency of recessive allele (10% m) and dominant allele (90% M).

   Determine the proportion of offspring that will be black and the proportion that will be gray (show your working).

Recessive allele:	q	=	
Dominant allele:	p	=	
Recessive phenotype:	q²	=	
Homozygous dominant:	p²	=	
Heterozygous:	2pq	=	

2. You are working with pea plants and found 36 plants out of 400 were dwarf.
   Data: Frequency of recessive phenotype (36 out of 400 = 9%)

   (a) Calculate the frequency of the tall gene: _____

   (b) Determine the number of heterozygous pea plants:

   _____

   _____

Recessive allele:	q	=	
Dominant allele:	p	=	
Recessive phenotype:	q^2	=	
Homozygous dominant:	p^2	=	
Heterozygous:	$2pq$	=	

3. In humans, the ability to taste the chemical phenylthiocarbaminde (PTC) is inherited as a simple dominant characteristic. Suppose you found out that 360 out of 1 000 college students could not taste the chemical
   Data: Frequency of recessive phenotype (360 out of 1000).

   (a) State the frequency of the gene for tasting PTC:

   _____

   (b) Determine the number of heterozygous students in this population:

   _____

Recessive allele:	q	=	
Dominant allele:	p	=	
Recessive phenotype:	q^2	=	
Homozygous dominant:	p^2	=	
Heterozygous:	$2pq$	=	

4. A type of deformity appears in 4% of a large herd of cattle. Assume the deformity was caused by a recessive gene.
   Data: Frequency of recessive phenotype (4% deformity).

   (a) Calculate the percentage of the herd that are carriers of the gene:

   _____

   (b) Determine the frequency of the dominant gene in this case:

   _____

Recessive allele:	q	=	
Dominant allele:	p	=	
Recessive phenotype:	q^2	=	
Homozygous dominant:	p^2	=	
Heterozygous:	$2pq$	=	

5. Assume you placed 50 pure bred black guinea pigs (dominant allele) with 50 albino guinea pigs (recessive allele) and allowed the population to attain genetic equilibrium (several generations have passed).
   Data: Frequency of recessive allele (50%) and dominant allele (50%).

   Determine the proportion (%) of the population that becomes white:

   _____

Recessive allele:	q	=	
Dominant allele:	p	=	
Recessive phenotype:	q^2	=	
Homozygous dominant:	p^2	=	
Heterozygous:	$2pq$	=	

6. It is known that 64% of a large population exhibit the recessive trait of a characteristic controlled by two alleles (one is dominant over the other).
   Data: Frequency of recessive phenotype (64%).

   Determine the following:

   (a) The frequency of the recessive allele: _____

   (b) The percentage that are heterozygous for this trait: _____

   (c) The percentage that exhibit the dominant trait: _____

   (d) The percentage that are homozygous for the dominant trait: _____

   (e) The percentage that has one or more recessive alleles: _____

7. Albinism is recessive to normal pigmentation in humans. The frequency of the albino allele was 10% in a population.
   Data: Frequency of recessive allele (10% albino allele).

   Determine the proportion of people that you would expect to be albino:

   _____

   _____

Recessive allele:	q	=	
Dominant allele:	p	=	
Recessive phenotype:	q^2	=	
Homozygous dominant:	p^2	=	
Heterozygous:	$2pq$	=	

(DA❸) Analysis of a Squirrel Gene Pool

In Olney, Illinois, in the United States, there is a unique population of albino (white) and gray squirrels. Between 1977 and 1990, students at Olney Central College carried out a study of this population. They recorded the frequency of gray and albino squirrels. The albinos displayed a mutant allele expressed as an albino phenotype only in the homozygous recessive condition. The data they collected are provided in the table below. Using the **Hardy-Weinberg equation** for calculating genotype frequencies, it was possible to estimate the frequency of the normal 'wild' allele (G) providing gray fur coloring, and the frequency of the mutant albino allele (g) producing white squirrels. This study provided real, first hand, data that students could use to see how genotype frequencies can change in a real population.

Thanks to **Dr. John Stencel**, Olney Central College, Olney, Illinois, US, for providing the data for this exercise.

Gray squirrel, usual color form   Albino form of gray squirrel

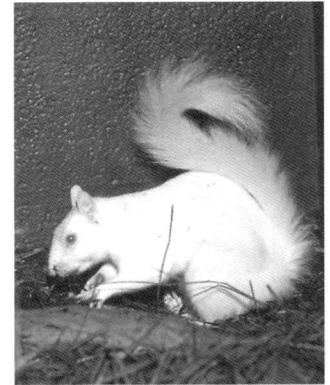

Population of gray and white squirrels in Olney, Illinois (1977-1990)

Year	Gray	White	Total	GG	Gg	gg	Freq. of g	Freq. of G
1977	602	182	784	26.85	49.93	23.21	48.18	51.82
1978	511	172	683	24.82	50.00	25.18	50.18	49.82
1979	482	134	616	28.47	49.77	21.75	46.64	53.36
1980	489	133	622	28.90	49.72	21.38	46.24	53.76
1981	536	163	699	26.74	49.94	23.32	48.29	51.71
1982	618	151	769	31.01	49.35	19.64	44.31	55.69
1983	419	141	560	24.82	50.00	25.18	50.18	49.82
1984	378	106	484	28.30	49.79	21.90	46.80	53.20
1985	448	125	573	28.40	49.78	21.82	46.71	53.29
1986	536	155	691	27.71	49.86	22.43	47.36	52.64
1987	No data collected this year							
1988	652	122	774	36.36	47.88	15.76	39.70	60.30
1989	552	146	698	29.45	49.64	20.92	45.74	54.26
1990	603	111	714	36.69	47.76	15.55	39.43	60.57

1. **Graph population changes**: Use the data in the first 3 columns of the table above to plot a line graph. This will show changes in the phenotypes: numbers of gray and white (albino) squirrels, as well as changes in the total population. Plot: **gray**, **white**, and **total** for each year:

   (a) By how much have total population numbers fluctuated over the sampling period (as a %):

   _____

   (b) Describe the overall trend in total population numbers and any pattern that may exist:

   _____

   _____

   _____

   _____

   _____

   _____

[Graph grid: y-axis "Number of squirrels" 0 to 800, x-axis "Year" 1977 to 1990]

2. **Graph genotype changes**: Use the data in the genotype columns of the table on the previous page to plot a line graph. This will show changes in the allele combinations (**GG**, **Gg**, **gg**). Plot: **GG**, **Gg**, and **gg** for each year:

Describe the overall trend in the frequency of:

(a) Homozygous dominant (**GG**) genotype:

_____

_____

(b) Heterozygous (**Gg**) genotype:

_____

_____

(c) Homozygous recessive (gg) genotype:

_____

_____

_____

Graph: y-axis labelled "Frequency of genotype" ranging 0% to 60%; x-axis labelled "Year" ranging 1977 to 1990.

3. **Graph allele changes**: Use the data in the last two columns of the table on the previous page to plot a line graph. This will show changes in the *allele frequencies* for each of the dominant (**G**) and recessive (**g**) alleles. **Plot**: the frequency of **G** and the frequency of **g**:

(a) Describe the overall trend in the frequency of the dominant allele (**G**):

_____

_____

_____

(b) Describe the overall trend in the frequency of the recessive allele (**g**):

_____

_____

_____

_____

Graph: y-axis labelled "Frequency of allele" ranging 0% to 70%; x-axis labelled "Year" ranging 1977 to 1990.

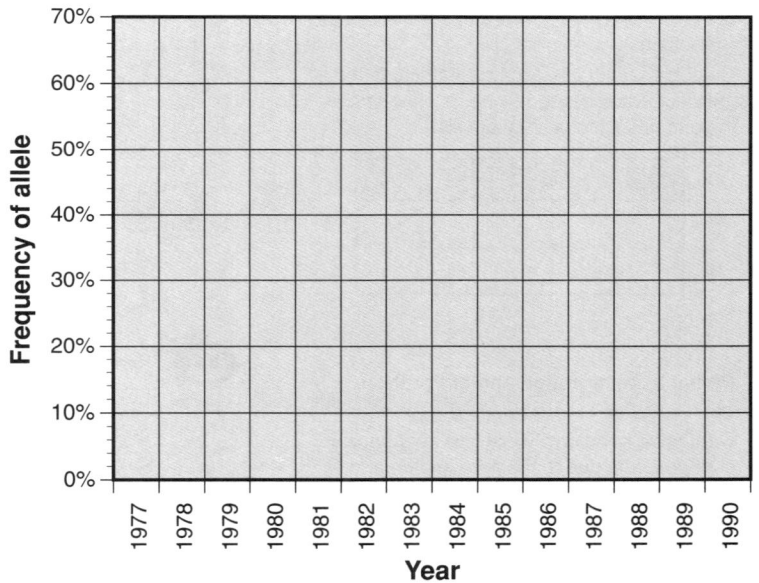

4. (a) State which of the three graphs best indicates that a significant change may be taking place in the gene pool of this population of squirrels:

_____

(b) Give a reason for your answer: _____

_____

_____

5. Describe a possible cause of the changes in allele frequencies over the sampling period: _____

_____

_____

_____

DA 3 # Changes in a Gene Pool

The diagram below shows an imaginary population of beetles undergoing changes as it is subjected to two 'events'. The three phases represent a progression in time, i.e. the same gene pool, undergoing change. The beetles have three phenotypes determined by the amount of pigment deposited in the cuticle. Three versions of this trait exist: black, dark, and pale. The gene controlling this character is represented by two alleles **A** and **a**. Your task is to analyze the gene pool as it undergoes changes.

Phase 1: Initial gene pool

Calculate the frequencies of the *allele types* and *allele combinations* by counting the actual numbers, then working them out as percentages.

Black   AA
Dark   Aa
Pale   aa

	A	a	AA	Aa	aa
No.	27		7		
%	54		28		

Allele types   Allele combinations

Phase 2: Natural selection

In the same gene pool at a later time there was a change in the allele frequencies. This was due to the loss of certain allele combinations due to natural selection. Some of those with a genotype of aa were eliminated (poor fitness).

Calculate as for above. Do not include the individuals surrounded by small white arrows in your calculations; they are dead!

	A	a	AA	Aa	aa
No.					
%					

Phase 3: Immigration and emigration

This particular kind of beetle exhibits wandering behavior. The allele frequencies change again due to the introduction and departure of individual beetles, each carrying certain allele combinations.

Calculate as above. In your calculations, include the individual coming into the gene pool (AA), but remove the one leaving (aa).

	A	a	AA	Aa	aa
No.					
%					

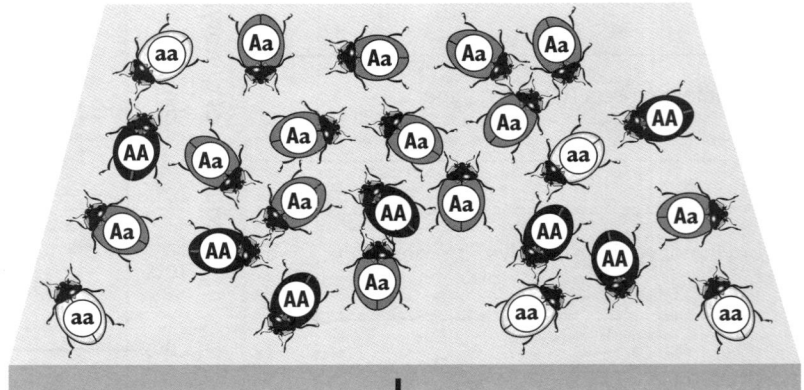

Two pale individuals died and therefore their alleles are removed from the gene pool.

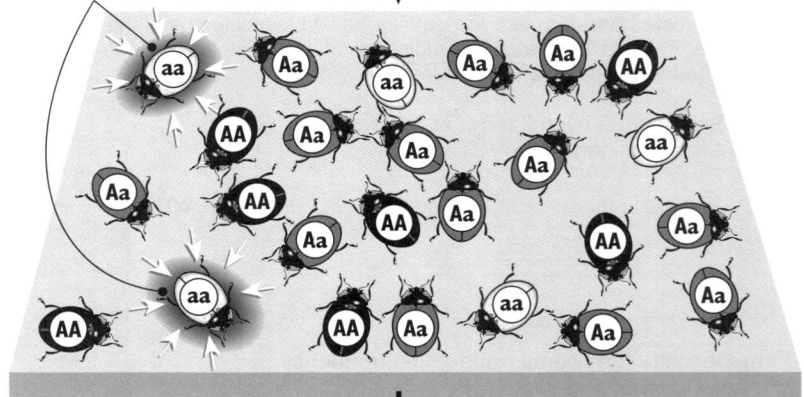

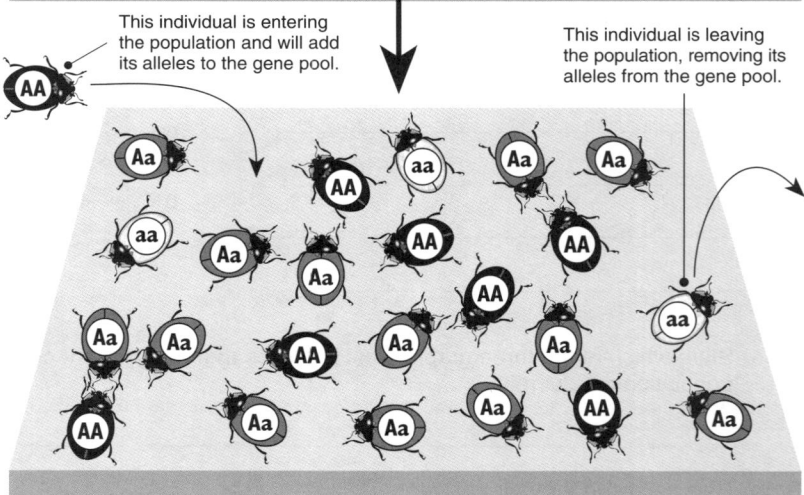

This individual is entering the population and will add its alleles to the gene pool.

This individual is leaving the population, removing its alleles from the gene pool.

1. Explain how the number of dominant alleles (A) in the genotype of a beetle affects its phenotype:

_____

_____

2. For each phase in the gene pool above (place your answers in the tables provided; some have been done for you):
   (a) Determine the relative frequencies of the two alleles: A and a. Simply total the **A** alleles and **a** alleles separately.
   (b) Determine the frequency of how the alleles come together as allele pair combinations in the gene pool (AA, Aa and aa). Count the number of each type of combination
   (c) For each of the above, work out the frequencies as percentages:
   Allele frequency = No. counted alleles ÷ Total no. of alleles x 100

DA③ The Founder Effect

Occasionally, a small number of individuals from a large population may migrate away, or become isolated from, their original population. If this colonizing or 'founder' population is made up of only a few individuals, it will probably have a *non-representative sample* of alleles from the parent population's gene pool. As a consequence of this **founder effect**, the

colonizing population may evolve differently from that of the parent population, particularly since the environmental conditions for the isolated population may be different. In some cases, it may be possible for certain alleles to be missing altogether from the individuals in the isolated population. Future generations of this population will not have this allele.

Some individuals from the mainland population are carried at random to the offshore island by natural forces such as strong winds.

This population may not have the same allele frequencies as the mainland population.

Mainland population

Island population

Mainland population

	Allele frequencies		Phenotype frequencies		
	Actual numbers	Calculate %	Black	Dark	Pale
Allele A					
Allele a					
Total					

Colonizing island population

	Allele frequencies		Phenotype frequencies		
	Actual numbers	Calculate %	Black	Dark	Pale
Allele A					
Allele a					
Total					

1. Compare the mainland population to the population which ended up on the island (use the spaces in the tables above):
   (a) Count the **phenotype** numbers for the two populations (i.e. the number of black, dark and pale beetles).
   (b) Count the **allele** numbers for the two populations: the number of dominant alleles (A) and recessive alleles (a).
       Calculate these as a percentage of the total number of alleles for each population.

2. Describe how the allele frequencies of the two populations are different: _____

_____

3. Describe some possible ways in which various types of organism can be **carried** to an offshore island:

   (a) Plants: _____

   (b) Land animals: _____

   (c) Non-marine birds: _____

4. Since founder populations are often very small, **describe** another process that may further alter the allele frequencies:

_____

_____

Population Bottlenecks

A 3

Populations may sometimes be reduced to low numbers by predation, disease, or periods of climatic change. A population crash may not be 'selective': it may affect all phenotypes equally. Large scale catastrophic events (e.g. fire or volcanic eruption) are examples of such non-selective events. Humans may severely (and selectively) reduce the numbers of some species through hunting and/or habitat destruction. These populations may recover, having squeezed through a 'bottleneck' of low numbers.

The diagram below illustrates how population numbers may be reduced as a result of a catastrophic event. Following such an event, the small number of individuals contributing to the gene pool may not have a representative sample of the genes in the pre-catastrophe population, i.e. the allele frequencies in the remnant population may be severely altered. Genetic drift may cause further changes to allele frequencies. The small population may return to previous levels but with a reduced genetic diversity.

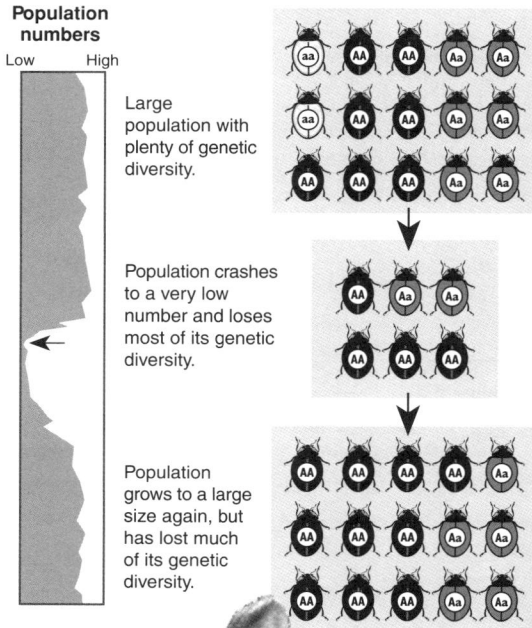

Population numbers

Low   High

Large population with plenty of genetic diversity.

Population crashes to a very low number and loses most of its genetic diversity.

Population grows to a large size again, but has lost much of its genetic diversity.

Time

The original gene pool is made up of the offspring of many lineages (family groups and sub-populations).

| Lineage A | Lineage B | Lineage C |

Extinction   *Extinction*   *Extinction*   *Extinction*   *Extinction*   *Extinction*

Only two descendents of lineage B survive the extinction event.

Genetic bottleneck

Extinction event such as a volcanic eruption.

All present day descendents of the original gene pool trace their ancestry back to individual B and therefore retain only a small sample of genes present in the original gene pool.

Population Bottleneck in Cheetahs

Until recently, the dwindling population of cheetahs in the wild was thought to be the result of over-hunting and habitat destruction. The world population of cheetahs has declined to fewer than 20 000. Recent genetic analysis has found that the total cheetah population has very little genetic diversity (they all have very similar genotypes). It appears that cheetahs may have narrowly escaped extinction at the end of the last ice age, about 10-20 000 years ago. The population crash may have been so severe that the total species may have been reduced to a single family group. If all modern cheetahs arose from a single surviving litter, this would explain the lack of genetic diversity. This is not a surprising finding, since 75% of all large mammals perished at this time (including well-known animals such as mammoths, cave bears and sabre-tooth tigers). The lack of genetic variation has led to a number of features that threaten the survival of the cheetah species, including: sperm abnormalities, decreased fecundity (number of offspring produced in its lifetime), high cub mortality, and sensitivity to disease.

1. Endangered species are often subjected to population bottlenecks. Explain how population bottlenecks affect the ability of a population of an endangered species to recover from its plight:

2. Explain why the lack of genetic diversity in cheetahs has increased their sensitivity to disease:

3. Describe the effect of a population bottleneck on the potential of a species to adapt to changes (i.e. its ability to evolve):

RA ❸

Genetic Drift

Not all individuals, for various reasons, will be able to contribute their genes to the next generation. **Genetic drift** (also known as the Sewell-Wright Effect) refers to the *random changes in allele frequency* that occur in all populations, but are much more pronounced in small populations. In a small population, the effect of a few individuals not contributing their alleles to the next generation can have a great effect on allele frequencies. Alleles may even become **lost** from the gene pool altogether (frequency becomes 0%) or **fixed** as the only allele for the gene present (frequency becomes 100%).

The genetic makeup (allele frequencies) of the population changes randomly over a period of time

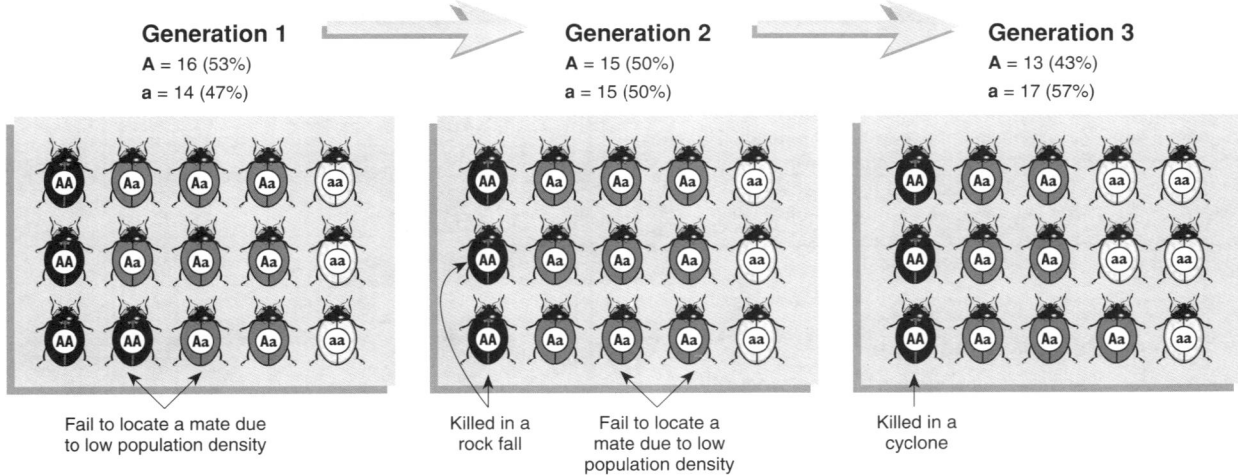

Generation 1
A = 16 (53%)
a = 14 (47%)

Generation 2
A = 15 (50%)
a = 15 (50%)

Generation 3
A = 13 (43%)
a = 17 (57%)

Fail to locate a mate due to low population density

Killed in a rock fall

Fail to locate a mate due to low population density

Killed in a cyclone

This diagram shows the gene pool of a hypothetical small population over three generations. For various reasons, not all individuals contribute alleles to the next generation. With the random loss of the alleles carried by these individuals, the allele frequency changes from one generation to the next. The change in frequency is directionless as there is no selecting force. The allele combinations for each successive generation are determined by how many alleles of each type are passed on from the preceding one.

Computer Simulation of Genetic Drift

Below are displayed the change in allele frequencies in a computer simulation showing random genetic drift. The breeding population progressively gets smaller from left to right. Each simulation was run for 140 generations.

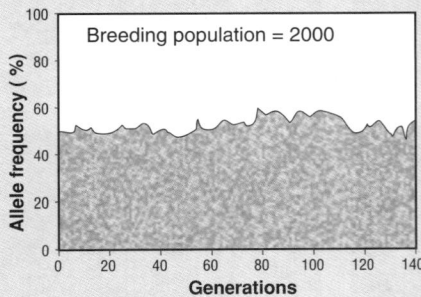

Breeding population = 2000

Breeding population = 200

Breeding population = 20

Allele lost from the gene pool

Large breeding population

Fluctuations are minimal in large breeding populations because the large numbers buffer the population against random loss of alleles. On average, losses for each allele type will be similar in frequency and little change occurs.

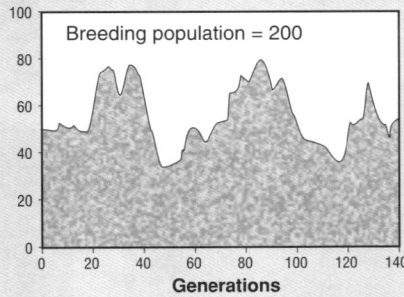

Small breeding population

Fluctuations are more severe in smaller breeding populations because random changes in a few alleles cause a greater percentage change in allele frequencies.

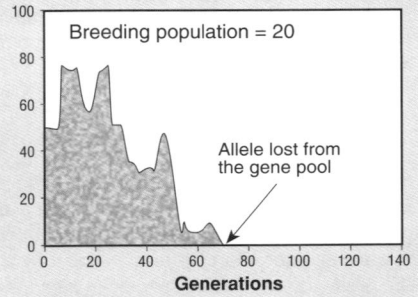

Very small breeding population

Fluctuations in very small breeding populations are so extreme that the allele can become fixed (frequency of 100%) or lost from the gene pool altogether (frequency of 0%).

1. Define the term **genetic drift**: _____

_____

2. Describe how genetic drift affects the amount of genetic variation within very small populations: _____

_____

_____

3. Name a small breeding population of animals or plants in your country in which genetic drift could be occurring:

_____

Reproductive Isolation

Any factor that prevents two species from producing fertile hybrids contributes to **reproductive isolation**. Reproductive isolating mechanisms are important in preserving the uniqueness of a gene pool. They prevent the dilution effect of **gene flow** *into* the pool from other populations. Such gene flow may detract from the good combinations already developed as a result of natural selection. Single barriers may not completely stop gene flow, so most species have more than one type of barrier. Geographical barriers are sometimes considered not to be isolating mechanisms because they are not part of the species' biology. Such barriers often precede the development of other isolating mechanisms, which can operate before or after fertilization.

Prezygotic Isolating Mechanisms (Before-Fertilization)

Spatial (geographical)

Includes physical barriers such as: mountains, rivers, altitude, oceans, isthmuses, deserts, ice sheets. There are many examples of speciation occurring as a result of isolation by oceans or by geological changes in lake basins (e.g. the proliferation of cichlid fish species in Lake Victoria). The many species of iguana from the Galapagos Islands are now quite distinct from the Central and South American species from which they arose.

Land iguana: Galapagos Is.

Galapagos Is

South America

800 km

Pacific Ocean

Temporal (including seasonal)

Timing of mating activity for an organism may prevent contact with closely related species: nocturnal, diurnal, spring, summer, fall, spring tide etc. Plants flower at different times of the year or even at different times of the day. Closely related animals may have quite different breeding seasons.

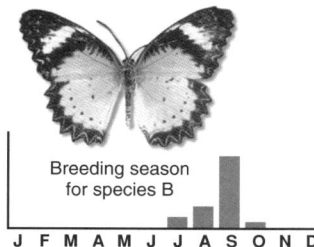

Breeding season for species B

J F M A M J J A S O N D

Breeding season for species A

J F M A M J J A S O N D

Ecological (habitat)

Closely related species may occupy different habitats even within the same general area. In the USA, geographically isolated species of antelope squirrels occupy different ranges either side of the Grand Canyon. The white tailed antelope squirrel inhabits the desert to the north of the canyon, while the smaller Harris's antelope squirrel has a much more limited range to the south of the canyon.

Grand Canyon

Harris's antelope squirrel

Gamete mortality

Sperm and egg fail to unite. Even if mating takes place, most gametes will fail to unite. The sperm of one species may not be able to survive in the reproductive tract of another species. Gamete recognition may be based on the presence of species specific molecules on the egg or the egg may not release the correct chemical attractants for sperm of another species.

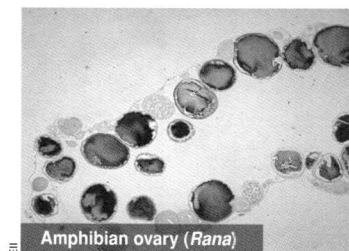

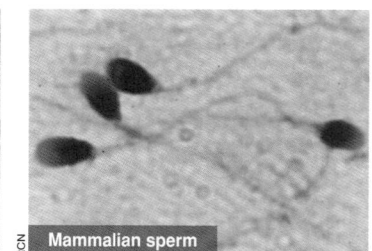

Amphibian ovary (*Rana*)

Mammalian sperm

Behavioral (ethological)

Animals attract mates with calls, rituals, dances, body language, etc. Complex displays, such as the flashes of fireflies, are quite specific. In animals, behavioral responses are a major isolating factor, preserving the integrity of mating within species. Birds exhibit a remarkable range of courtship displays that are often quite species-specific.

Peacock display of tail

Blue footed boobies courtship

Structural (morphological)

Shape of the copulatory (mating) apparatus, appearance, coloration, insect attractants. Insects have a lock-and-key arrangement for their copulatory organs. Pheromone chemical attractants, which may travel many kilometers with the aid of the wind, are quite specific, attracting only members of the same species.

Beetles mating

Damselflies mating

Postzygotic Isolating Mechanisms

Hybrid sterility

Even if two species mate and produce hybrid offspring that are vigorous, the species are still reproductively isolated if the hybrids are sterile (genes cannot flow from one species' gene pool to the other). Such cases are common among the horse family (such as the zebra and donkey shown on the right). One cause of this sterility is the failure of meiosis to produce normal gametes in the hybrid. This can occur if the chromosomes of the two parents are different in number or structure (see the **"zebronkey"** karyotype on the right). The **mule**, a cross between a donkey stallion and a horse mare, is also an example of **hybrid vigor** (they are robust) as well as **hybrid sterility**. Female mules sometimes produce viable eggs but males are infertile.

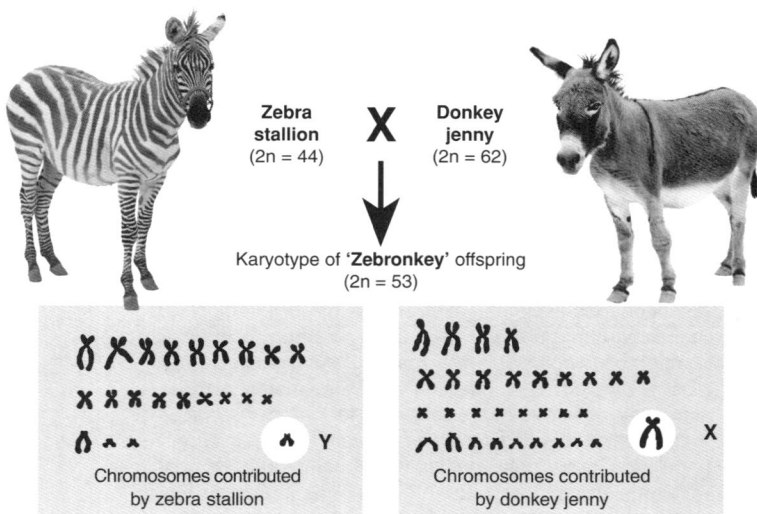

Zebra stallion (2n = 44) X Donkey jenny (2n = 62)

Karyotype of 'Zebronkey' offspring (2n = 53)

Chromosomes contributed by zebra stallion

Chromosomes contributed by donkey jenny

Hybrid inviability

Mating between individuals of two different species may sometimes produce a zygote. In such cases, the genetic incompatibility between the two species may stop development of the fertilized egg at some embryonic stage. Fertilized eggs often fail to divide because of unmatched chromosome numbers from each gamete (a kind of aneuploidy between species). Very occasionally, the hybrid zygote will complete embryonic development but will not survive for long.

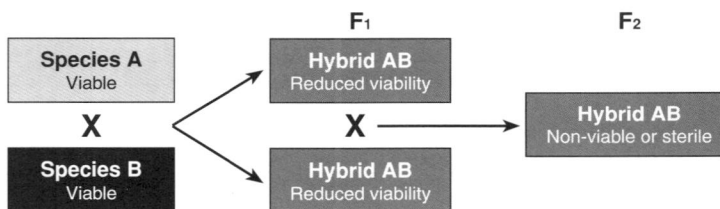

Zygote is formed   Gastrula fails to develop

Hybrid breakdown

First generation (F1) are fertile, but the second generation (F2) are infertile or inviable. Conflict between the genes of two species sometimes manifests itself in the second generation.

F_1 F_2

Species A Viable X Species B Viable → Hybrid AB Reduced viability → Hybrid AB Reduced viability X → Hybrid AB Non-viable or sterile

1. In general terms, explain the role of reproductive isolating mechanisms in maintaining the integrity of a species:

_____

_____

2. In the following examples, classify the reproductive isolating mechanism as either **prezygotic** or **postzygotic** and describe the mechanisms by which the isolation is achieved (e.g. temporal isolation, hybrid sterility etc.):

(a) Some different cotton species can produce fertile hybrids, but breakdown of the hybrid occurs in the next generation when the offspring of the hybrid die in their seeds or grow into defective plants:

Prezygotic / postzygotic (delete one)   Mechanism of isolation: _____

(b) Many plants have unique arrangements of their floral parts that stops transfer of pollen between plants:

Prezygotic / postzygotic (delete one)   Mechanism of isolation: _____

(c) Three species of orchid living in the same rainforest do not hybridize because they flower on different days:

Prezygotic / postzygotic (delete one)   Mechanism of isolation: _____

(d) Several species of the frog genus *Rana*, live in the same regions and habitats, where they may occasionally hybridize. The hybrids generally do not complete development, and those that do are weak and do not survive long:

Prezygotic / postzygotic (delete one)   Mechanism of isolation: _____

3. Postzygotic isolating mechanisms are said to reinforce prezygotic ones. Explain why this is the case:

_____

_____

Allopatric Speciation

Allopatric speciation is a process thought to have been responsible for a great many instances of species formation. It has certainly been important in countries which have had a number of cycles of geographical fragmentation. Such cycles can occur as the result of glacial and interglacial periods, where ice expands and then retreats over a land mass. Such events are also accompanied by sea level changes which can isolate populations within relatively small geographical regions.

Stage 1: Moving into new environments

There are times when the range of a species expands for a variety of different reasons. A single population in a relatively homogeneous environment will move into new regions of their environment when they are subjected to intense competition (whether it is interspecific or intraspecific). The most severe form of competition is between members of the same species since they are competing for identical resources in the habitat. In the diagram on the right there is a 'parent population' of a single species with a common gene pool with regular 'gene flow' (theoretically any individual has access to all members of the opposite sex for mating purposes).

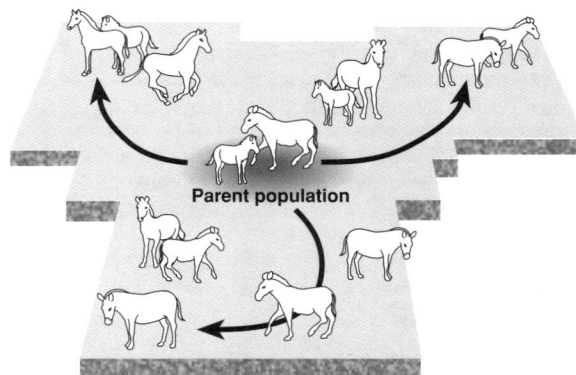

Parent population

Stage 2: Geographical isolation

Isolation of parts of the population may occur due to the formation of **physical barriers**. These barriers may cut off those parts of the population that are at the extremes of the species range and gene flow is prevented or rare. The rise and fall of the sea level has been particularly important in functioning as an isolating mechanism. Climatic change can leave 'islands' of habitat separated by large inhospitable zones that the species cannot traverse.

Example: In mountainous regions, alpine species are free to range widely over extensive habitat during cool climatic periods. During warmer periods, however, they may become isolated because their habitat is reduced to 'islands' of high ground surrounded by inhospitable lowland habitat.

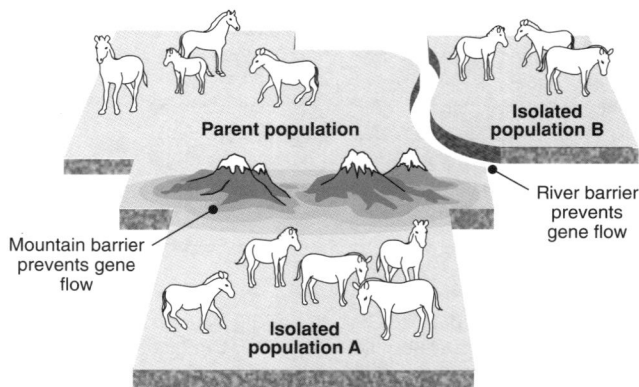

Parent population

Isolated population B

River barrier prevents gene flow

Mountain barrier prevents gene flow

Isolated population A

Stage 3: Different selection pressures

The isolated populations (A and B) may be subjected to quite different selection pressures. These will favor individuals with traits that suit each particular environment. For example, population A will be subjected to selection pressures that relate to drier conditions. This will favor those individuals with phenotypes (and therefore genotypes) that are better suited to dry conditions. They may for instance have a better ability to conserve water. This would result in improved health, allowing better disease resistance and greater reproductive performance (i.e. more of their offspring survive). Finally, as allele frequencies for certain genes change, the population takes on the status of a **subspecies**. Reproductive isolation is not yet established but the subspecies are significantly different genetically from other related populations.

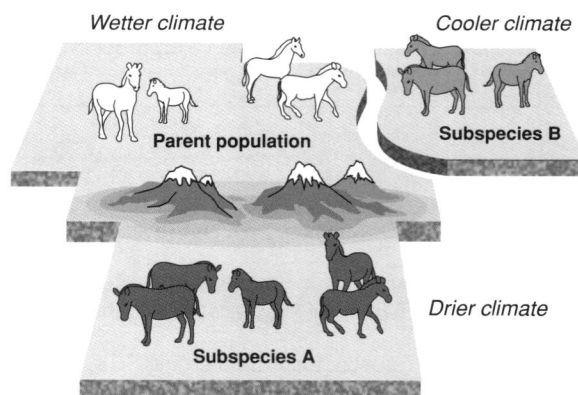

Wetter climate

Cooler climate

Parent population

Subspecies B

Drier climate

Subspecies A

Stage 4: Reproductive isolation

The separated populations (isolated subspecies) will often undergo changes in their genetic makeup as well as their behavior patterns. These ensure that the gene pool of each population remains isolated and 'undiluted' by genes from other populations, even if the two populations should be able to remix (due to the removal of the geographical barrier). Gene flow does not occur. The arrows (in the diagram to the right) indicate the zone of overlap between two species after the new Species B has moved back into the range inhabited by the parent population. Closely-related species whose distribution overlaps are said to be **sympatric species**. Those that remain geographically isolated are called **allopatric species**.

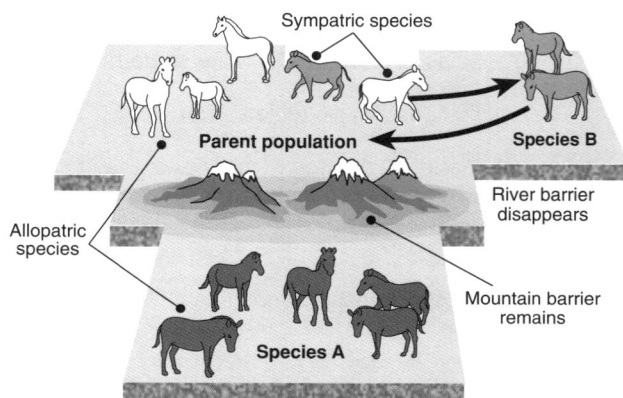

Sympatric species

Parent population

Species B

River barrier disappears

Allopatric species

Mountain barrier remains

Species A

1. Describe why some animals, given the opportunity, move into new environments: _____

_____

2. (a) Plants are unable to move. State how plants might disperse to new environments: _____

_____

   (b) Describe the amount of **gene flow** within the parent population prior to and during this range expansion:

_____

_____

3. Name the **process** that causes the formation of new **mountain ranges**: _____

4. Name the event that can cause large changes in **sea level** (up to 200 meters): _____

5. Identify six **physical barriers** that could isolate different parts of the same population: _____

_____

_____

_____

6. Describe the effect that physical barriers have on **gene flow**: _____

_____

_____

_____

7. (a) List **four** different types of **selection pressure** that could have an effect on a gene pool: _____

_____

_____

   (b) Describe briefly how these selection pressures affect the isolated gene pool in terms of **allele frequencies**:

_____

_____

_____

8. Describe two types of **prezygotic** and two types of **postzygotic** reproductive isolating mechanisms:

   (a) Prezygotic: _____

_____

_____

   (b) Postzygotic: _____

_____

_____

9. Define the term **sympatric species**: _____

_____

_____

10. Define the term **allopatric species**: _____

_____

_____

A 2 # Sympatric Speciation

New species may be formed even where there is no separation of the gene pools by physical barriers. Called **sympatric speciation**, it is rarer than allopatric speciation, although not uncommon in plants which form **polyploids**. There are two situations where sympatric speciation is thought to occur. These are described below:

Speciation Through Niche Differentiation

Niche isolation

In a heterogeneous environment (one that is not the same everywhere), a population exists within a diverse collection of **microhabitats**. Some organisms prefer to occupy one particular type of 'microhabitat' most of the time, only rarely coming in contact with fellow organisms that prefer other microhabitats. Some organisms become so dependent on the resources offered by their particular microhabitat that they never meet up with their counterparts in different microhabitats.

Reproductive isolation

Finally, the individual groups have remained genetically isolated for so long because of their microhabitat preferences, that they have become reproductively isolated. They have become new species that have developed subtle differences in behavior, structure, and physiology. Gene flow (via sexual reproduction) is limited to organisms that share a similar microhabitat preference (as shown in the diagram on the right).

Example: Some beetles prefer to find plants identical to the species they grew up on, when it is time for them to lay eggs. Individual beetles of the same species have different preferences.

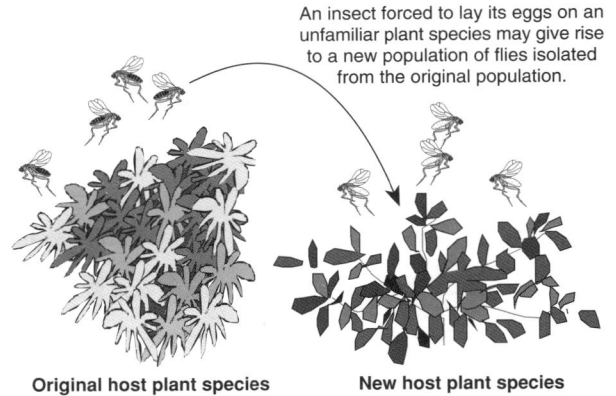

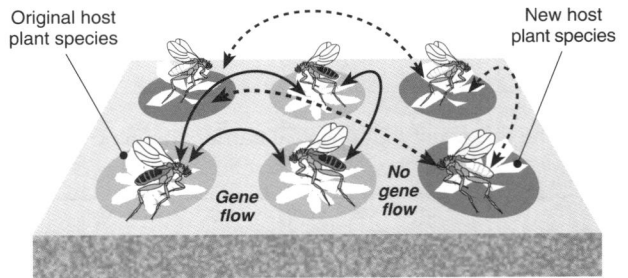

An insect forced to lay its eggs on an unfamiliar plant species may give rise to a new population of flies isolated from the original population.

Original host plant species   **New host plant species**

Original host plant species   New host plant species

Gene flow   No gene flow

Instant Speciation by Polyploidy

When polyploidy occurs, it is possible to form a completely new species without isolation from the parent species. This type of malfunction during the process of meiosis produces sudden reproductive isolation for the new group. Because the sex-determining mechanism is disturbed, animals are rarely able to achieve new species status this way (they are effectively sterile e.g. tetraploid XXXX). Many plants, on the other hand, are able to reproduce vegetatively, or carry out self pollination. This ability to reproduce on their own enables such polyploid plants to produce a breeding population.

Speciation by allopolyploidy

This type of polyploidy usually arises from the doubling of chromosomes in a hybrid between two different species. The doubling often makes the hybrid fertile.

Examples: Modern wheat. Swedes are polyploid species formed from a hybrid between a type of cabbage and a type of turnip.

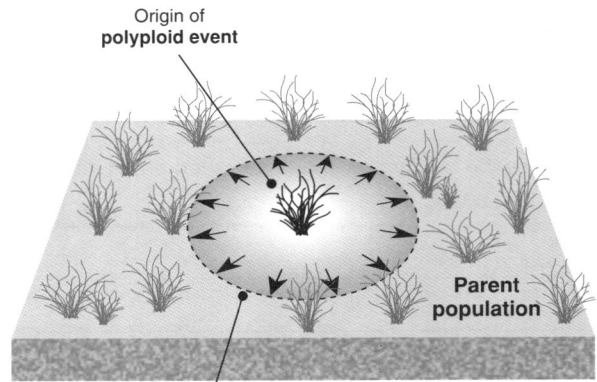

Origin of **polyploid event**

Parent population

New polyploid plant species spreads outwards through the existing parent population

---

1. Define the term **sympatric speciation** (do not confuse this with *sympatric species*):

_____

_____

2. Explain briefly how polyploidy may cause the formation of a new species: _____

_____

_____

3. Name an example of a species that has been formed by polyploidy: _____

4. Explain briefly how niche differentiation may cause the formation of a new species: _____

_____

_____

Stages in Species Development

The diagram below represents a possible sequence of genetic events involved in the origin of two new species from an ancestral population. As time progresses (from top to bottom of the diagram) the amount of genetic variation increases and each group becomes increasingly isolated from the other. The mechanisms that operate to keep the two gene pools isolated from one another may begin with **geographical barriers**. This may be followed by **prezygotic** mechanisms which protect the gene pool from unwanted dilution by genes from other pools. A longer period of isolation may lead to **postzygotic** mechanisms (see the page on reproductive isolating mechanisms). As the two gene pools become increasingly isolated and different from each other, they are progressively labeled: population, race, and subspecies. Finally they attain the status of separate species.

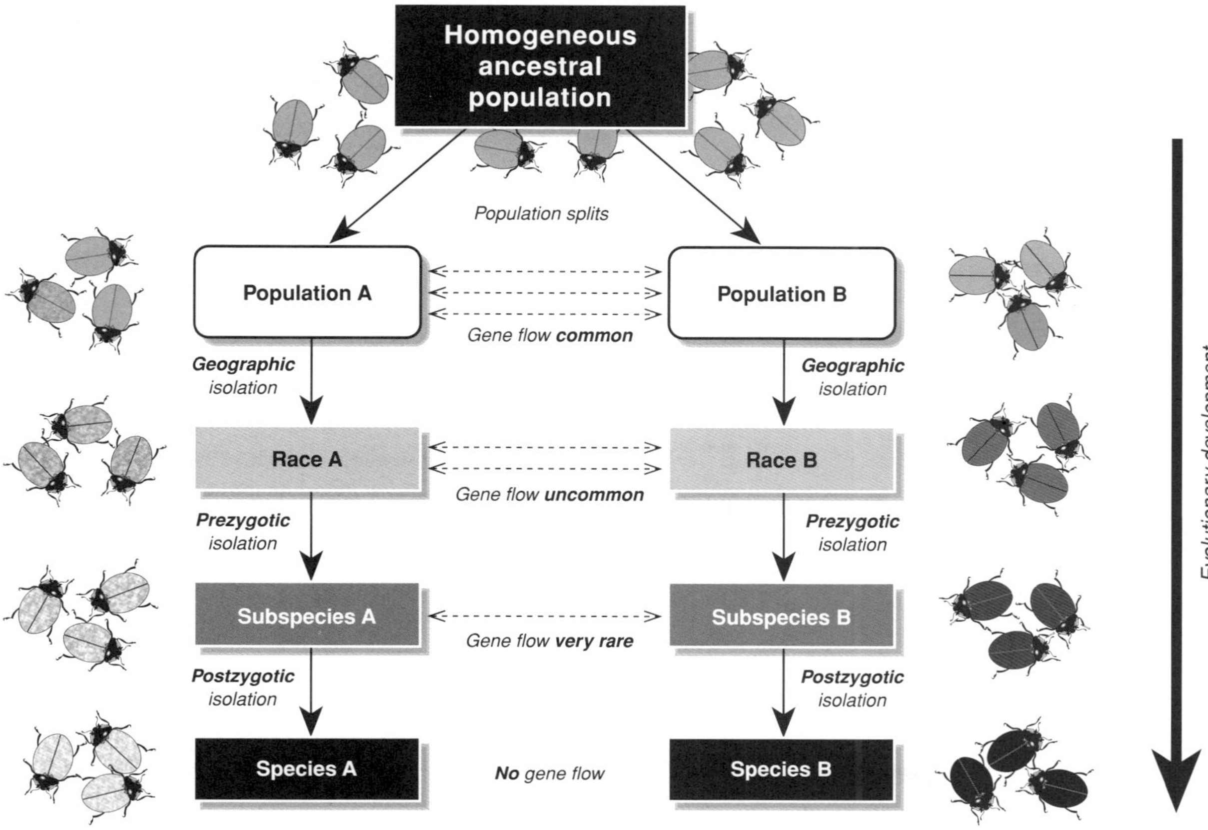

1. Explain what happens to the extent of gene flow between diverging populations as they gradually attain species status:

_____

_____

2. Early human populations about 500 000 ya were scattered across Africa, Europe, and Asia. This was a time of many regional variants, collectively called archaic *Homo sapiens*. The fossil skulls from different regions showed mixtures of characteristics, some modern and some 'primitive'. These regional populations are generally given subspecies status. Suggest reasons why gene flow between these populations may have been rare, but still occasionally occurred:

_____

_____

_____

3. In the USA, the species status of several duck species, including the black duck (*Anas rubripes*) and the mottled duck in Florida (*A. fulvigula*) is threatened by interbreeding with the now widespread and very adaptable mallard duck (*A. platyrhynchos*). Similar threatened extinction though hybridization has occurred in New Zealand, where the native gray duck has been virtually eliminated as a result of interbreeding with the introduced mallard.

   (a) Suggest why these hybrids threaten the species status of some native duck species: _____

   _____

   (b) Suggest what factor may deter mallards from hybridizing with other duck species: _____

   _____

Patterns of Evolution

A 2

The diversification of an ancestral group into two or more species in different habitats is called **divergent evolution**. This process is illustrated in the diagram below, where two species have diverged from a **common ancestor**. Note that another species budded off, only to become extinct. Divergence is common in evolution. When divergent evolution involves the formation of a large number of species to occupy different niches, this is called

an **adaptive radiation**. The example below (right) describes the radiation of the mammals that occurred after the extinction of the dinosaurs; an event that made niches available for exploitation. Note that the evolution of species may not necessarily involve branching: a species may accumulate genetic changes that, over time, result in the emergence of what can be recognized as a different species. This is known as **sequential evolution** (below).

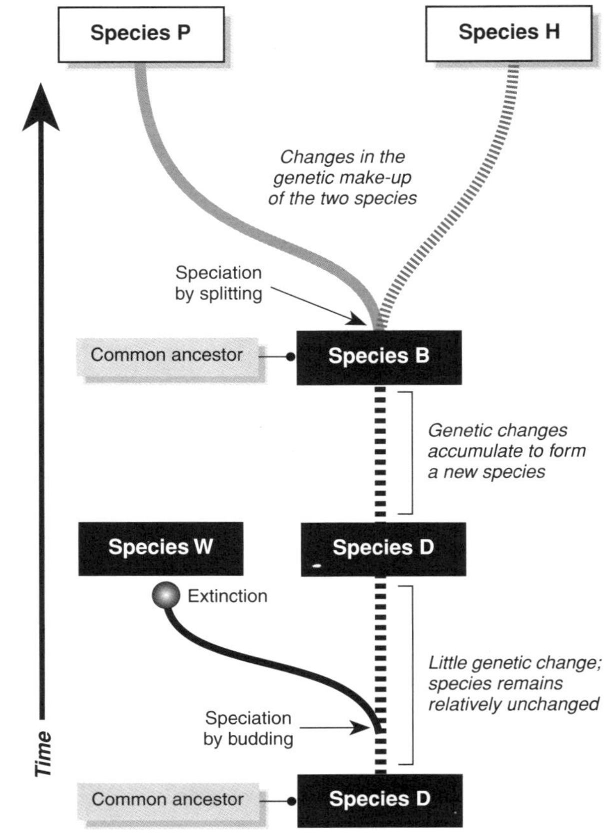

Mammalian Adaptive Radiation

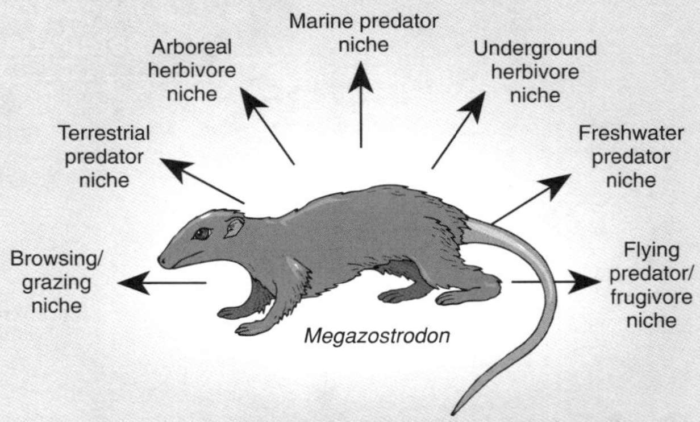

Arboreal herbivore niche · Marine predator niche · Underground herbivore niche · Terrestrial predator niche · Freshwater predator niche · Browsing/grazing niche · Flying predator/frugivore niche

Megazostrodon

Megazostrodon: one of the first mammals

Megazostrodon (above) is known from fossil remains in South Africa. This shrew-like animal first appeared in the Early Jurassic period (about 195 million years ago) and probably had an insectivorous diet.

The earliest true mammals evolved about 195 million years ago, long before they underwent their major adaptive radiation some 65-50 million years ago. These ancestors to the modern forms were very small (12 cm), many were nocturnal and fed on insects and other invertebrate prey. It was climatic change as well as the extinction of the dinosaurs (and their related forms) that suddenly left many niches vacant for exploitation by such an adaptable 'generalist'. All modern mammal orders developed very quickly and early.

Species P · **Species H**

Changes in the genetic make-up of the two species

Speciation by splitting

Common ancestor → **Species B**

Genetic changes accumulate to form a new species

Species W · **Species D**

Extinction

Little genetic change; species remains relatively unchanged

Speciation by budding

Common ancestor → **Species D**

Time

1. Provide brief definitions of the following terms, clearly distinguishing between them:

   (a) Divergent evolution: _____

   (b) Adaptive radiation: _____

   (c) Sequential evolution: _____

   (d) Common ancestor: _____

2. In the hypothetical example of divergent evolution illustrated above, left:

   (a) Classify the type of evolution that produced species B from species D: _____

   (b) Classify the type of evolution that produced species P and H from species B: _____

   (c) Name all species that evolved from: **Common ancestor D**: _____ **Common ancestor B**: _____

   (d) Suggest why species B, P, and H all possess a physical trait not found in species D or W: _____

RA② The Rate of Evolutionary Change

There has been debate in recent years over the pace of evolution, with two theories being proposed: **gradualism** and **punctuated equilibrium**. Some scientists believe that both mechanisms may operate: the pace of evolution may be gradual and steady in certain instances and abrupt in others.

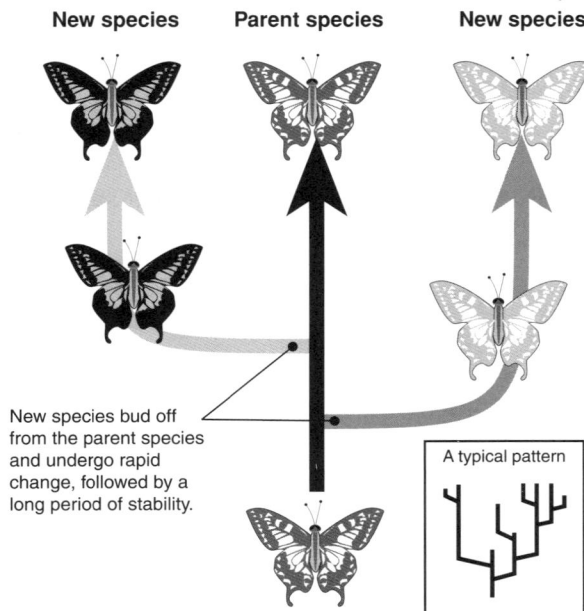

New species bud off from the parent species and undergo rapid change, followed by a long period of stability.

A typical pattern

Each species undergoes gradual changes in its genetic makeup and phenotype.

New species diverges from the parent species.

A typical pattern

Punctuated Equilibrium

There is abundant evidence in the fossil record that, instead of gradual change, species stayed much the same for long periods of time (called stasis). These periods were punctuated by short bursts of evolution which produce new species quite rapidly. According to the punctuated equilibrium theory, most of a species' existence is spent in stasis and little time is spent in active evolutionary change. The stimulus for evolution occurs when some crucial factor in the environment changes.

Gradualism

Gradualism assumes that populations slowly diverge from one another by accumulating adaptive characteristics in response to different selective pressures. If species evolve by gradualism, there should be transitional forms seen in the fossil record, as is seen with the evolution of the horse. Trilobites, an extinct marine arthropod, are another group of animals that have exhibited gradualism. In a study in 1987 a researcher found that they changed gradually over a 3 million year period.

1. Suggest the kinds of environments that would support the following paces of evolutionary change:

    (a) Punctuated equilibrium: _____

    _____

    _____

    (b) Gradualism: _____

    _____

    _____

2. In the fossil record of early human evolution, species tend to appear suddenly, linger for often very extended periods before disappearing suddenly. There are few examples of smooth inter-gradations from one species to the next. Which of the above models best describes the rate of human evolution:

    _____

3. Some species apparently show little evolutionary change over long periods of time (hundreds of millions of years).

    (a) Name two examples of such species: _____

    (b) State the term given to this lack of evolutionary change: _____

    (c) Suggest why such species have changed little over evolutionary time: _____

    _____

RA ② Convergent Evolution

Not all similarities between species are a result of common ancestry. Species from different evolutionary lines may come to resemble each other if they have similar ecological roles and natural selection has shaped similar adaptations. This is called **convergent evolution** (**convergence**). Analogous structures (below) may arise as result of convergence.

Convergence in Swimming Form

Although similarities in body form and function can arise because of common ancestry, it may also be a result of **convergent evolution**. Selection pressures in a particular environment may bring about similar adaptations in unrelated species. These selection pressures require the solving of problems in particular ways, leading to the similarity of body form or function. The development of succulent forms in unrelated plant groups (*Euphorbia* and the cactus family) is an example of convergence in plants. In the example (right), the selection pressures of the aquatic environment have produced a similar **streamlined** body shape in unrelated vertebrate groups. Icthyosaurs, penguins, and dolphins each evolved from terrestrial species that took up an aquatic lifestyle. Their general body form has evolved to become similar to that of the shark, which has always been aquatic. Note that flipper shape in mammals, birds, and reptiles is a result of convergence, but its origin from the pentadactyl limb is an example of **homology**.

Fish: Shark

Reptile: Icthyosaur (extinct)

Mammal: Dolphin

Bird: Penguin

Analogous Structures

Analogous structures are those that have the same function and often the same basic external appearance, but **quite different origins**. The example on the right illustrates how a complex eye structure has developed independently in two unrelated groups. The appearance of the **eye** is similar, but there is no genetic relatedness between the two groups (mammals and cephalopod molluscs). The **wings** of birds and insects are also an example of analogy. The wings perform the same function, but the two groups share no common ancestor. *Longisquama*, a lizard-like creature that lived about 220 million years ago, also had 'wings' that probably allowed gliding between trees. These 'wings' were not a modification of the forearm (as in birds), but highly modified long scales or feathers extending from its back.

Mammalian eye

Octopus eye

Mammalian eye: Iris, Lens, Cornea, Retina

Octopus eye: Iris, Lens, Cornea, Retina

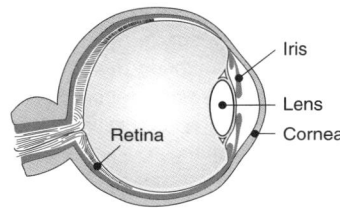

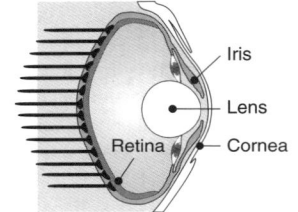

1. In the example above illustrating convergence in swimming form, describe two ways in which the body form has evolved in response to the particular selection pressures of the aquatic environment:

   (a) _____

   _____

   (b) _____

   _____

2. Describe two of the selection pressures that have influenced the body form of the swimming animals above:

   (a) _____

   (b) _____

3. Early taxonomists, when encountering new species in the Pacific region and the Americas, were keen to assign them to existing taxonomic families based on their apparent similarity to European species. In recent times, many of the new species have been found to be quite unrelated to the European families they were assigned to. Explain why the traditional approach did not reveal the true evolutionary relationships of the new species:

   _____

   _____

   _____

   _____

4. For each of the paired examples, briefly describe the adaptations of body shape, diet and locomotion that appear to be similar in both forms, and the likely selection pressures that are acting on these mammals to produce similar body forms:

Convergence between marsupial and placentals

Australia

Marsupials and **placental** mammals were separated from each other very early in mammalian evolution (about 120 mya). Marsupials were initially widely distributed throughout the ancient supercontinent of Gondwana, and there are some modern species still living in the American continent. Gondwana split up about 100 million years ago. As the placentals developed, they displaced the marsupials in most habitats around the world. The island continent of Australia, because of its early isolation by the sea, escaped this competition and placentals did not reach the continent until the arrival of humans 35 000 to 50 000 years ago. The Australian marsupials evolved into a wide variety of forms (below left) that bear a remarkable resemblance to ecologically equivalent species of North American placentals (below right).

North America

Marsupial mammals		Placental mammals
Wombat	(a) Adaptations: Both have rodent-like teeth, eat roots and above ground plants and excavate burrows Selection pressures: Diet requires chisel-like teeth for gnawing. The need to seek safety from predators on open grassland	Wood chuck
Flying phalanger	(b) Adaptations: Selection pressures:	Flying squirrel
Marsupial mole	(c) Adaptations: Selection pressures:	Mole
Marsupial mouse	(d) Adaptations: Selection pressures:	Mouse
Tasmanian wolf (tiger)	(e) Adaptations: Selection pressures:	Wolf
Long-eared bandicoot	(f) Adaptations: Selection pressures:	Jack rabbit

RDA③ Adaptive Radiation in Mammals

Adaptive radiation is diversification (both structural and ecological) among the descendants of a single ancestral group to occupy different niches. Immediately following the sudden extinction of the dinosaurs, the mammals underwent an adaptive radiation. Most of the modern mammal groups became established very early. The diagram below shows the divergence of the mammals into major orders; many occupying niches left vacant by the dinosaurs. The vertical extent of each gray shape shows the time span for which that particular mammal order has existed (note that the scale for the geological time scale in the diagram is not linear). Those that reach the top of the chart have survived to the present day. The width of a gray shape indicates how many species were in existence at any given time (narrow means there were few, wide means there were many). The dotted lines indicate possible links between the various mammal orders for which there is no direct fossil evidence.

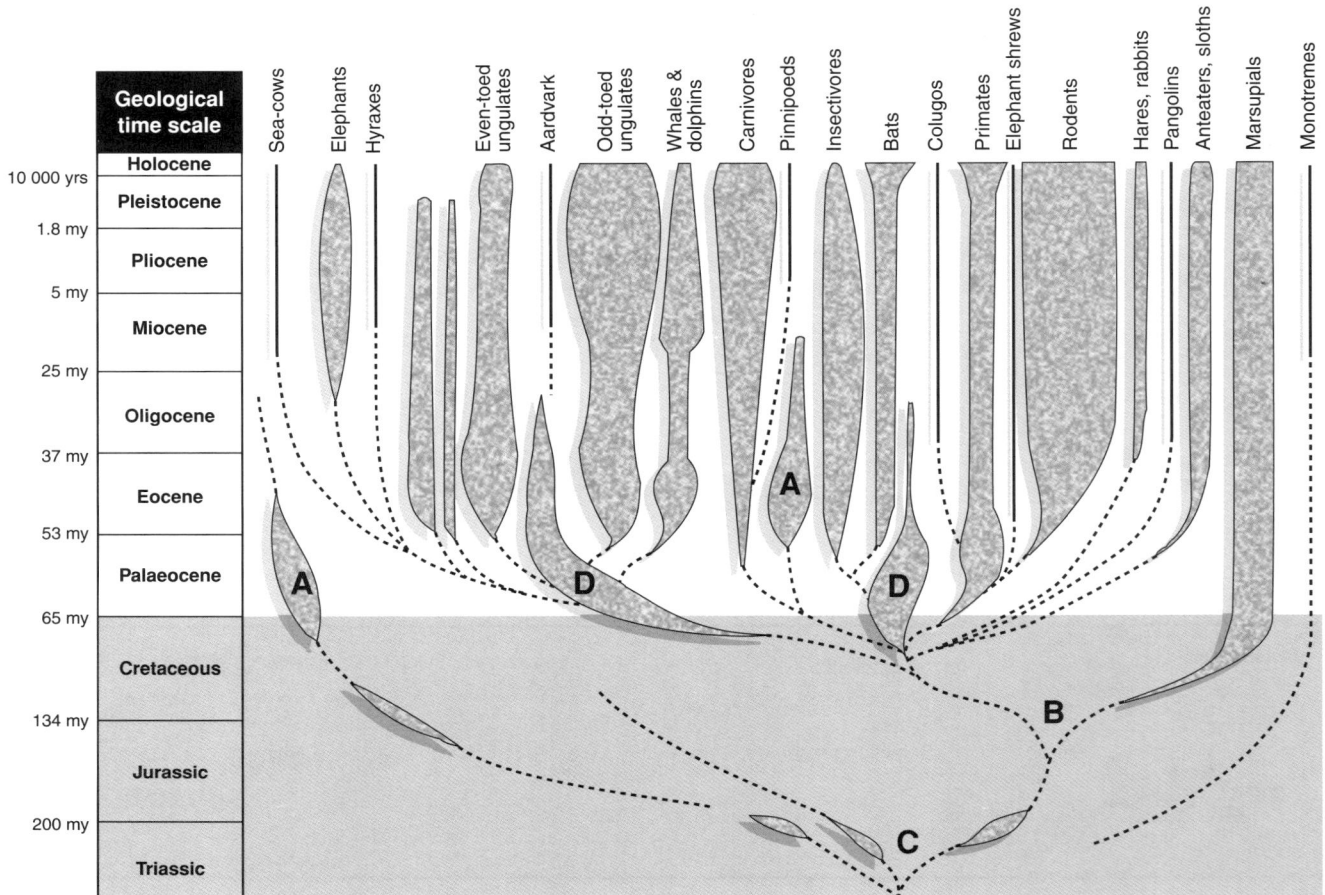

1. Define the term: adaptive radiation: _____

_____

_____

2. State the term used to describe the animal groups at point **C** in the diagram above: _____

3. Explain what occurred at point **B** in the diagram above: _____

_____

4. List two things that the animal orders labeled **D** in the diagram above have in common:

   (a) _____

   (b) _____

5. State which two orders appear to have been most successful in terms of the number of species produced:

_____

6. Explain what has happened to the mammal orders labeled **A** in the diagram above: _____

7. Name the time period (epoch) when there was the most adaptive radiation: _____

8. Describe two key features that distinguish mammals from other vertebrates:

    (a) _____ (b) _____

9. Describe the principal reproductive features that distinguish each of the major mammal groups:

    (a) Monotremes: _____

    (b) Marsupials: _____

    (c) Placentals: _____

10. There are 18 orders of placental mammals (or 17 in schemes that include the pinnipeds within the Carnivora). Their
    names and a brief description of the type of mammal belonging to each group is provided below. Identify and label each
    of the diagrams with the correct name of their Order:

Orders of Placental Mammals

Order	Description
Insectivora	Insect-eating mammals
Macroscelidae	Elephant shrews (formerly classified with insectivores)
Chiroptera	Bats
Cetacea	Whales and dolphins
Pholidota	Pangolins
Rodentia	Rodents
Probiscidea	Elephants
Sirenia	Sea-cows (manatees)
Artiodactyla	Even-toed hoofed mammals
Dermoptera	Colugos
Primates	Primates
Edentata	Anteaters, sloths, and armadillos
Lagomorpha	Pikas, hares, and rabbits
Carnivora	Flesh-eating mammals (canids, raccons, bears, cats)
Pinnipedia	Seals, sealions, walruses. (Often now included as a sub-order of Carnivora).
Tubulidentata	Aardvark
Hyracoidea	Hyraxes
Perissodactyla	Odd-toed hoofed mammals

1 _____

2 _____

3 _____

4 _____

5 _____

6 _____

7 _____

8 _____

9 _____

10 _____

11 _____

12 _____

13 _____

14 _____

15 _____

16 _____

17 _____

18 _____

11. For each of three named **orders** of placental mammal, describe one **adaptive feature** that allows it to exploit a different
    niche from other placentals, and state a **biological advantage** that the adaptation provides the organism.

    (a) Order: _____ Adaptive feature: _____

        Biological advantage: _____

    (b) Order: _____ Adaptive feature: _____

        Biological advantage: _____

    (c) Order: _____ Adaptive feature: _____

        Biological advantage: _____

RDA❸ Adaptive Radiation in Ratites

The **ratites** evolved from a single common ancestor (a monophyletic group) of birds that lost the power of flight very early on in their evolutionary development. Ratites possess two features that distinguish them from other birds – a *flat breastbone* (instead of the more usual keeled shape) and a *primitive palate* (roof to the mouth). Flightlessness in itself is not unique to this group. There are other examples of birds that have lost the power of flight, particularly on remote, predator-free islands. Fossil evidence indicates that the ancestors of ratites were flying birds living about 80 million years ago. These ancestors also had a primitive palate, but they possessed a keeled breastbone.

Elephantbird
Several species - Extinct
Madagascar

Ostrich
Struthio camelus
Africa

Emu
Dromaius novaehollandiae
Australia

Cassowary
3 species
Australia & New Guinea

Rhea
2 species
South America

Kiwi
3 species
New Zealand

Moa
11 species - Extinct
New Zealand

The geographical distribution of modern day and extinct ratite species can be partially explained in terms of continental drift. The ancestral ratite population existed at a time when the southern continents of South America, Africa and Australia (together with their major offshore islands) were joined as a single land mass called Gondwana. As the continents moved apart as a result of plate tectonics, the early ratite populations were carried with them. Subsequent speciation on each continent and some of the islands produced the variety of forms shown here. The 50 species of tinamou (see chart below) from South America, are considered a sister group to the ratites even though they can fly, because they possess the archaic palate. This relationship is confirmed by DNA sequence tests. The diagram below shows a possible phylogenetic tree based upon comparisons of mitochondrial DNA sequences. This view has been supported by the extensive comparison of skeletons from the different ratite species.

Mesozoic Era

Birds evolved from a saurischian (small theropod) dinosaur ancestor about 150 million years ago (below)

Ratites diverge from the line to the rest of the birds about 100 million years ago

Cenozoic Era

Fossil evidence suggests that **ratite ancestors** possessed a keeled breastbone and an archaic palate (roof of mouth)

A Letters indicate common ancestors

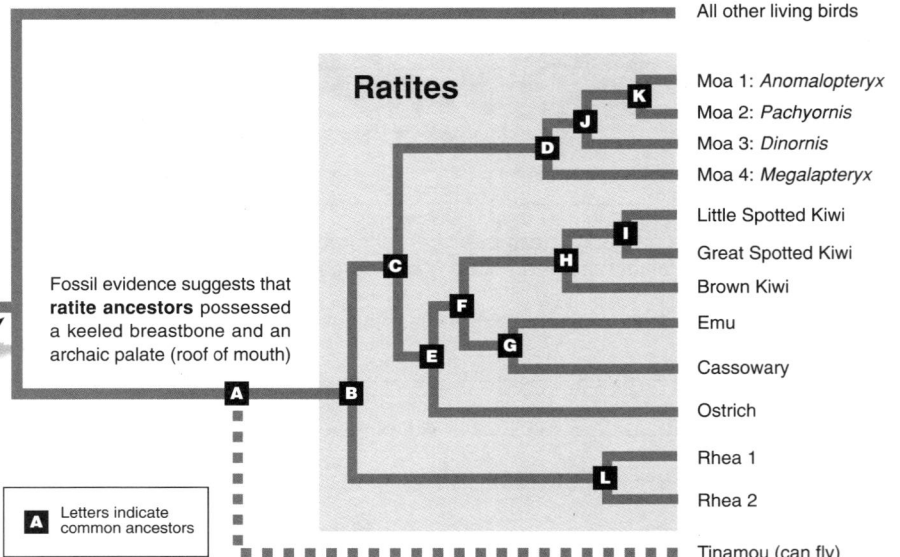

Ratites

All other living birds
Moa 1: *Anomalopteryx*
Moa 2: *Pachyornis*
Moa 3: *Dinornis*
Moa 4: *Megalapteryx*
Little Spotted Kiwi
Great Spotted Kiwi
Brown Kiwi
Emu
Cassowary
Ostrich
Rhea 1
Rhea 2
Tinamou (can fly)

1. (a) List three physical features that all ratites share that distinguishes them from most other birds:

    _____

    (b) What primitive feature do tinamou share with the ratites: _____

    _____

2. Describe two anatomical changes common to all ratite birds that have evolved as a result of flightlessness and state the selection pressures for those changes:

    (a) Anatomical change: _____

      Selection pressure: _____

      _____

    (b) Anatomical change: _____

      Selection pressure: _____

      _____

3. Name the ancient super-continent that the ancestral ratite population inhabited: _____

4. (a) The extinct elephantbird from Madagascar is thought to be very closely related to another modern ratite. Based purely on the **geographical distribution** of ratites, state which modern species is the most likely relative:

      _____

    (b) State the **reason** why you chose the modern ratite in your answer to (a) above: _____

      _____

    (c) **Draw** lines on the diagram at the bottom of the previous page to represent the divergence of the elephantbird from the modern ratite you have selected above.

5. (a) Name **two** other flightless birds that are **not ratites**: _____

    (b) Explain why these other flightless species are not considered part of the ratite group: _____

      _____

      _____

6. Eleven species of moa is an unusually large number compared to the species diversity of the kiwis – the other ratite group found in New Zealand. Moas comprise 5 genera while kiwis have only one genus. The diets of the moas and the kiwis are thought to have had a major influence on each group's capacity to diverge into separate species and genera. The moas were herbivorous, while kiwis are nocturnal feeders, feeding on worms and other invertebrates in the leaf litter. Suggest why, on the basis of their diet, moas were able to diverge into many species, while kiwis diverged little:

    _____

    _____

    _____

7. The DNA evidence suggests that New Zealand had two separate invasions of ratites; an early invasion from the moas (before the breakup of Gondwana) followed by a second invasion of the ancestors of the kiwis. Suggest a possible sequence of events that could account for this:

    _____

    _____

    _____

    _____

8. The common ancestors of divergent groups are labeled (A-L) on the diagram at the bottom of the previous page. State the **letter** indicating the **common ancestor** for:

    (a) The kiwis and the Australian ratites: _____   (b) The kiwis and the moas: _____

RA 2   Geographical Distribution

The camel family, Camelidae, consists of six modern-day species that have survived on three continents: Asia, Africa and South America. They are characterized by having only two functional toes, supported by expanded pads for walking on sand or snow. The slender snout bears a cleft upper lip. The recent distribution of the camel family is fragmented. Geophysical forces such as plate tectonics and the ice age cycles have controlled the extent of their distribution. South America, for example, was separated from North America until the end of the Pliocene, about 2 million years ago. Three general principles about the dispersal and distribution of land animals are:

■ When very closely related animals (as shown by their anatomy) were present at the same time in widely separated parts of the world, it is highly probable that there was no barrier to their movement in one or both directions between the localities in the past.
■ The most effective barrier to the movement of land animals (particularly mammals) was a sea between continents (as was caused by changing sea levels during the ice ages).
■ The scattered distribution of modern species may be explained by the movement out of the area they originally occupied, or extinction in those regions between modern species.

Origin and Dispersal of the Camel Family

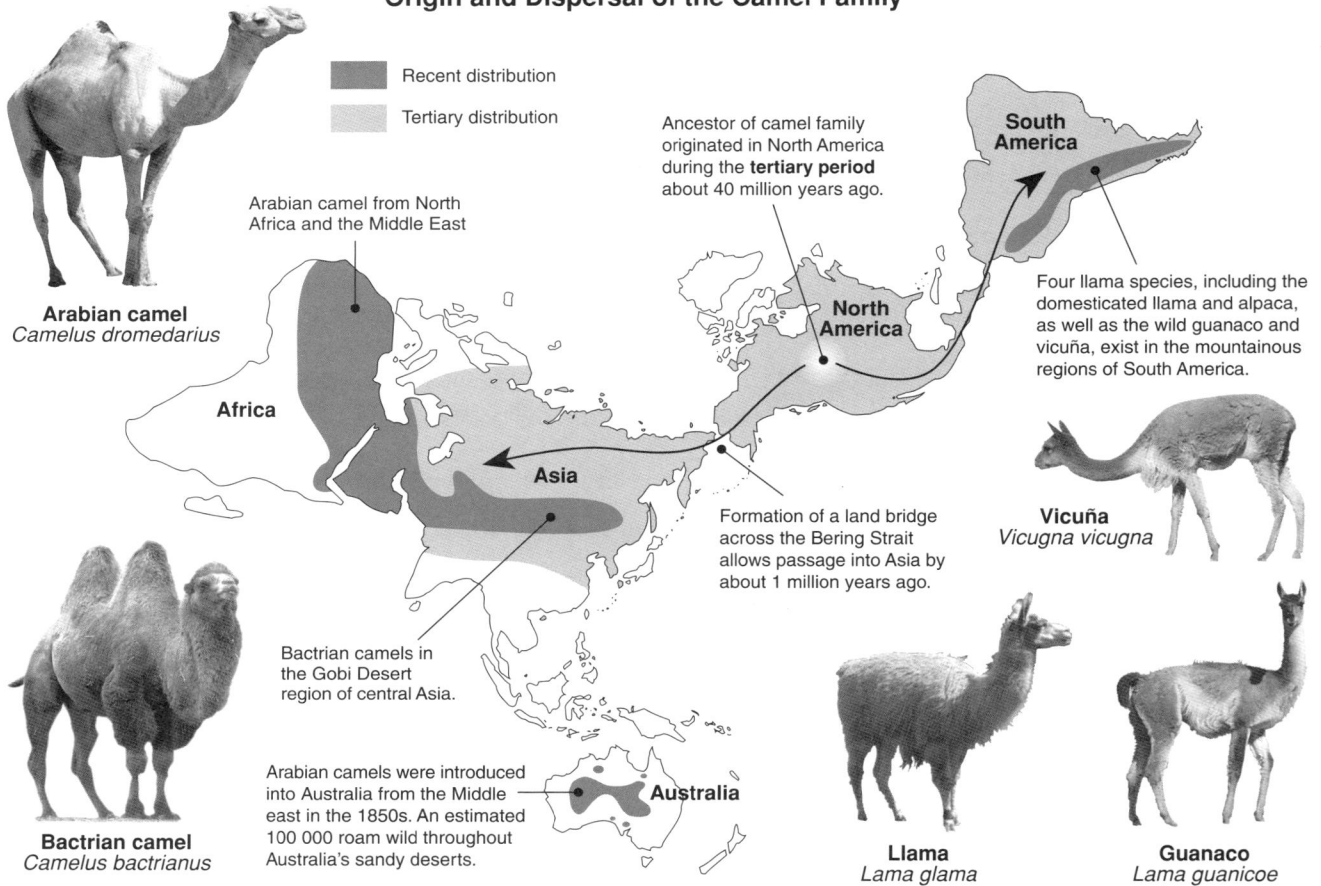

Recent distribution

Tertiary distribution

Ancestor of camel family originated in North America during the **tertiary period** about 40 million years ago.

Arabian camel from North Africa and the Middle East

South America

North America

Four llama species, including the domesticated llama and alpaca, as well as the wild guanaco and vicuña, exist in the mountainous regions of South America.

Arabian camel
Camelus dromedarius

Africa

Asia

Vicuña
Vicugna vicugna

Formation of a land bridge across the Bering Strait allows passage into Asia by about 1 million years ago.

Bactrian camels in the Gobi Desert region of central Asia.

Arabian camels were introduced into Australia from the Middle east in the 1850s. An estimated 100 000 roam wild throughout Australia's sandy deserts.

Australia

Bactrian camel
Camelus bactrianus

Llama
Lama glama

Guanaco
Lama guanicoe

1. The early camel ancestors were able to move into the tropical regions of Central and South America. Give a possible reason why this was prevented in southern Asia and southern Africa:

_____

2. Arabian camels are found wild in the Australian Outback. Explain how they got there and why they were absent during prehistoric times:

_____

3. The camel family originated in North America. Explain why there are no camels in North America now:

_____

4. Suggest how early camels managed to get to Asia from North America: _____

_____

5. Describe the present distribution of the camel family and explain why it is scattered (discontinuous):

_____

_____

Extinction

Extinction is an important process in evolution as it provides opportunities, in the form of vacant niches, for the development of new species. Most species that have ever lived are now extinct. The species alive today make up only a fraction of the total list of species that have lived on earth throughout its history. Extinction is a natural process in the life cycle of a species. Background extinction is the steady rate of species turnover in a taxonomic group (a group of related species). The duration of a species is thought to range from as little as 1 million years for complex larger organisms, to as long as 10-20 million years for simpler organisms. Superimposed on this constant background extinction are catastrophic events that wipe out vast numbers of species in relatively brief periods of time in geological terms. The diagram below shows how the number of species has varied over the history of life on Earth. The number of species is indicated on the graph by families – a taxonomic group comprising many genera and species. There have been five major extinction events and two of these have been intensively studied by paleontologists.

Major Mass Extinctions

The Permian extinction
(225 million years ago)
This was the most devastating mass extinction of all. Nearly all life on Earth perished, with 90% of marine species and probably many terrestrial ones also, disappearing from the fossil record. This extinction event marks the **Paleozoic-Mesozoic** boundary.

The Cretaceous extinction
(65 million years ago)
This extinction event marks the boundary between the Mesozoic and Cenozoic eras. More than half the marine species and many families of terrestrial plants and animals became extinct, including nearly all the dinosaur species (the birds are now known to be direct descendants of the dinosaurs).

Megafaunal extinction
(10 000 years ago)
This mass extinction occurred when many giant species of mammal died out. This is known as the 'Pleistocene overkill' because their disappearance was probably hastened by the hunting activities of prehistoric humans. Many large marsupials in Australia and placental species elsewhere became extinct.

The sixth extinction
(presenst day)
The current mass extinction is largely due to human destruction of habitats (e.g. coral reefs, tropical forests) and pollution. It is considered far more serious and damaging than some earlier mass extinctions because of the speed at which it is occurring. The increasing human impact is making biosphere recovery difficult.

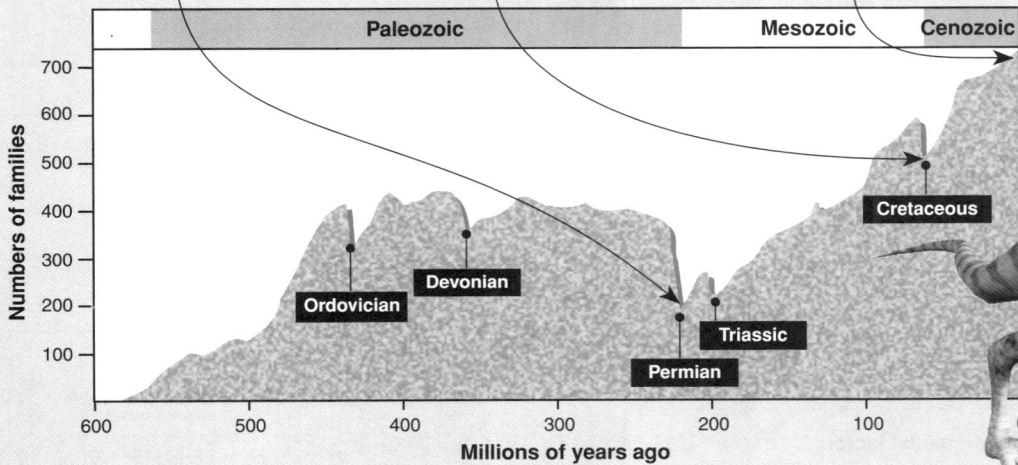

1. Describe the main features (scale and type of organisms killed off) of each of the following major extinction events:

   (a) Permian extinction: _____

   _____

   _____

   (b) Cretaceous extinction: _____

   _____

   _____

   (c) Megafaunal extinction: _____

   _____

   _____

2. Explain how human activity has contributed to the most recent mass extinction: _____

   _____

3. In general terms, describe the effect that past mass extinctions had on the way the surviving species **further evolved**:

   _____

   _____

Genes and Evolution

A 3

Each individual organism in a population is the carrier of its own particular combination of genetic material. Different combinations of genes come about because of the shuffling of the chromosomes during gamete formation. New combinations of alleles arise as a result of mate selection and the chance meeting of a vast range of different gametes from each of the two parents. Some combinations are well suited to particular environments, while others are not. Those organisms with an inferior collection of genes will have reduced reproductive success. This means that the genes (alleles) they carry will decrease in frequency and fewer will be passed on to the next generation's gene pool. Those individuals with more successful allele combinations will have higher reproductive success. The frequency of their alleles in the gene pool will increase.

The Importance of Genetic Processes in Evolution

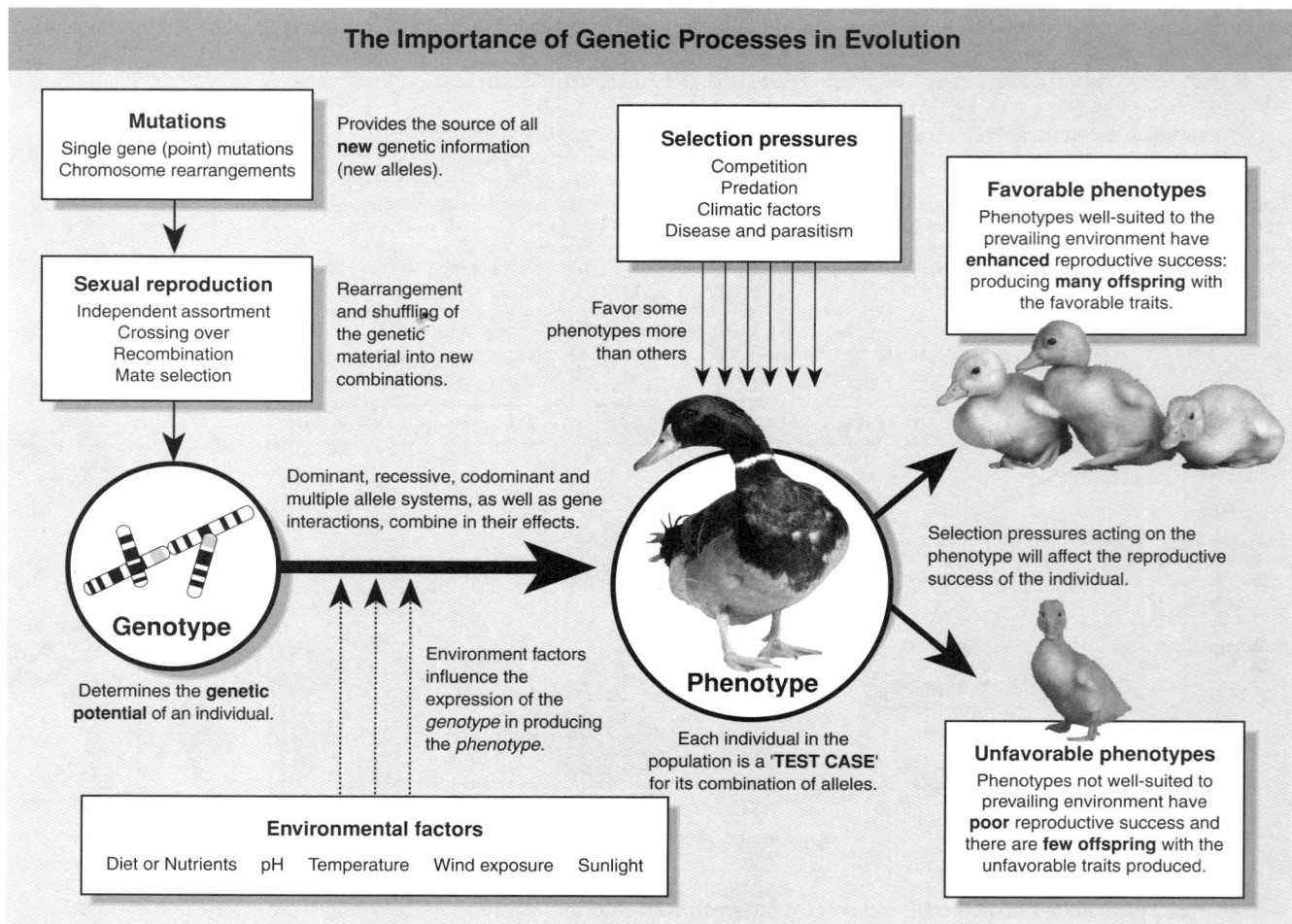

Mutations
Single gene (point) mutations
Chromosome rearrangements

Provides the source of all **new** genetic information (new alleles).

Selection pressures
Competition
Predation
Climatic factors
Disease and parasitism

Favorable phenotypes
Phenotypes well-suited to the prevailing environment have **enhanced** reproductive success: producing **many offspring** with the favorable traits.

Sexual reproduction
Independent assortment
Crossing over
Recombination
Mate selection

Rearrangement and shuffling of the genetic material into new combinations.

Favor some phenotypes more than others

Genotype

Dominant, recessive, codominant and multiple allele systems, as well as gene interactions, combine in their effects.

Selection pressures acting on the phenotype will affect the reproductive success of the individual.

Determines the **genetic potential** of an individual.

Environment factors influence the expression of the *genotype* in producing the *phenotype*.

Phenotype

Each individual in the population is a '**TEST CASE**' for its combination of alleles.

Unfavorable phenotypes
Phenotypes not well-suited to prevailing environment have **poor** reproductive success and there are **few offspring** with the unfavorable traits produced.

Environmental factors
Diet or Nutrients   pH   Temperature   Wind exposure   Sunlight

1. Study the diagram above. Explain the evolutionary significance of the following processes:

(a) Mutations: _____

_____

(b) Sexual reproduction: _____

_____

(c) Selection pressures: _____

_____

2. Describe the long-term effect on the gene pool of enhanced reproductive success for a particular phenotype:

_____

_____

3. Explain why each individual in a population is a **test case** for its combination of alleles: _____

_____

_____

The Evolution of Humans

IB SL
Not applicable to core

IB HL
Not applicable to core

IB Options
Complete nos:
Option D:
SL/HL: 1, 3, 5-10,
12-14, 17-18, 20-22
Extension: 11

AP Biology
Not applicable to AP Biology

Learning Objectives

☐ 1. Compile your own glossary from the **KEY WORDS** displayed in **bold type** in the learning objectives below.

Humans as primates *(pages 137-140)*

☐ 2. Describe the classification of the Primate order into the following groups, with examples: **prosimians, New World monkeys, Old World monkeys, apes, humans**.

☐ 3. State the full classification of modern humans from kingdom to sub-species. Identify the major physical features that define humans as primates.

☐ 4. Define the terms: **primate, prosimian, anthropoid, hominoid, pongid, hominid**. Identify the major physical features that all primates have in common, and that identify humans as primates.

☐ 5. Discuss the biochemical and anatomical evidence that supports the idea that humans evolved from a bipedal species of African ape. Discuss the **neoteny** of these early bipedal apes (i.e. delayed onset of puberty leading to an increased period of parental care).

☐ 6. Describe the regional climate changes in East Africa 7-5 million years ago, outlining their role in human evolutionary development. Relate the changes of climatic zones to alterations in habitats exploited by primates at the time (changes in zones of tundra, temperate forest, savannah, tropical forest).

Early hominid evolution *(pages 141-145, 148-151)*

Since the mid-1990s, new fossil finds have overturned earlier ideas about early hominid evolution. Altogether the picture is becoming more complicated as new finds uncover more information about early hominid evolution. Be aware that older textbooks will not reflect these recent developments.

☐ 7. Discuss the incomplete nature of the fossil record and how this leads to uncertainty about precise lineages.

☐ 8. Describe the anatomical features that are associated with **bipedalism**. Include reference to the length of the limbs, shape and orientation of the pelvis, **valgus** (carrying) **angle** of the knee, structure of the foot, position of the skull, and curvature of the spine.

☐ 9. Discuss the origin and consequences of **bipedalism** in human evolution, identifying when significant developments occurred.

☐ 10. Identify the **trends** and **main features** of the biological evolution of the following three early hominid species:

* *Australopithecus afarensis*
* *Australopithecus africanus*
* *Australopithecus (Paranthropus) robustus*

NOTE: There is a growing consensus that the robust **australopithecines** (which includes *A. robustus*) should be placed in a separate genus: *Paranthropus*.

☐ 11. Be aware that a complete listing of early hominid species appearing in the scientific literature includes:

* *Sahelanthropus tchadensis* ("Toumai")
* *Orrorin tugenensis* ("Millennium Man")
* *Ardipithecus ramidus* (2 subspecies)
* *Australopithecus anamensis, A. bahrelghazali,* **A. afarensis, A. africanus,** *A. garhi*
* *Kenyanthropus platyops*
* *Paranthropus boisei,* **Paranthropus robustus**

☐ 12. Explain the terms: **robust** and **gracile** used to describe early hominid body shapes. Explain how the evolution of the early hominids was a response to habitat change and a shift in the resources they exploited.

Genus *Homo* *(pages 141-148, 152-155)*

☐ 13. Identify **distinguishing characteristics** of the genus *Homo* (features that are unique to them).

☐ 14. Identify the **trends** and **main features** of the biological and cultural evolution of the genus *Homo*:

* **Homo habilis** *(also Homo rudolfensis)*
* **Homo erectus** *(also Homo ergaster)*
* **Homo neanderthalensis (Neanderthals)**
* **Homo sapiens** *(anatomically modern humans)*

☐ 15. Suggest reasons why all hominid species, apart from our own, became extinct.

☐ 16. Provide summaries of the two main hypotheses for the origin and dispersal of modern humans: **replacement** and **multiregional hypotheses**. Explain the evidence in support of each hypothesis. Identify trends in the dispersal of early humans from their probable region of origin in south-eastern Africa.

☐ 17. Discuss the trends in the development of brain size and intelligence during the course of human evolution and identify the selection pressures involved in this. Identify when significant developments in increasing brain size and intelligence occurred.

☐ 18. Identify **specific trends** and consequences of brain development such as continued brain expansion, the development of the **Broca's** (speech production) and **Wernicke's** (speech recognition) areas.

☐ 19. Provide possible reasons for the loss of body hair, increasing dependence on group cooperation and the development of a language.

☐ 20. Distinguish between **cultural evolution** and **biological evolution** (genetically transmitted changes) and their relative importance in the evolution of humans.

☐ 21. Discuss trends in cultural development, including tool use, the development of abstract thought – expressed in paintings and sculpture, and spiritual practices.

☐ 22. Discuss trends in the evolution of complex behaviors (namely the use of tools, fire, clothing, beliefs). Explain how the development of these behaviors was aided by a growing capacity for learning and communication.

Textbooks

See the 'Textbook Reference Grid' on pages 8-9 for textbook page references relating to material in this topic.

Supplementary Texts

■ **The Cambridge Guide to Prehistoric Man** Lambert, D. 1987. Cambridge University Press, London. ISBN: 0-521-33364-4.

■ **The First Humans** 1993.University of Queensland Press, St. Lucia, QL. *A superb text that has an excellent section on primate evolution covering some of the current ideas.* ISBN: 0-7022-2676-9.

■ **The Cambridge Encyclopedia of Human Evolution** 1992. Cambridge University Press, Cambridge. *An outstanding reference for teachers and keen students.* ISBN: 0-521-46786-1.

■ **Biological Anthropology** Park, M. A. 1996. Mayfield Publishing Co. *An excellent resource, pitched at an accessible level for most students. Highly recommended.* ISBN: 1-55934-424-5.

■ **Understanding Physical Anthropology and Archeology** Jurmain, R., H, Nelson, & W. A. Turnbaugh, 1990. West Publishing Co. *This teacher reference covers many aspects of human evolution in depth.* ISBN: 0-314-66758-X.

■ **Humans before Humanity** Foley, R. 1995. Blackwell Publishers Inc. *A teacher reference providing a modern view of human evolution and dispersal.* ISBN: 0-631-20528-4.

■ **African Exodus** Stringer, C & R. McKie. 1996. Pimlico. *A teacher reference clarifying the debate over human origins.* ISBN: 0-7126-7307-5.

■ **The Last Neanderthal** Tattersall, I. 1995. American Museum of Natural History. *An excellent, thorough resource that extends beyond the scope of the title subject.* ISBN: 0-02-860813-5.

Periodicals

See page 6 for details of publishers of periodicals:

TEACHER'S REFERENCE

■ **Teaching Human Evolution** The American Biology Teacher, May 2003, 65(5), pp. 333-339. *Teaching human evolution is easier than it looks: an overview of paleoanthropology.*

Scientific American **SPECIAL ISSUE: New Look at Human Evolution**. 13(2) July 2003. *A collection of twelve feature articles (some of which are new and some are updated from previous issues):*

■ **An Ancestor to Call Our Own** pp. 4-13. *Controversial new fossils may be close to origin of humanity (Sahelanthropus, Orririn, Ardipithecus).*

■ **Early Hominid Fossils from Africa** pp. 14-19. *A recently discovered species of Australopithecus anamensis pushes back origins of bipedalism.*

■ **Once We Were Not Alone** pp. 20-27. *For at least 4 million years, many hominid species have shared the planet, often at the same time and in the same region.*

■ **Who Were The Neandertals?** pp. 28-37. *Evidence that these hominids interbred with anatomically modern humans and may have had a more advanced culture than previously thought.*

■ **Out of Africa Again .... and Again?** pp. 38-45. *An update of the 1997 article by the same name. Africa is the birth place of humanity. There may have been several waves of hominid emigration out of the continent.*

■ **The Multiregional Evolution of Humans** pp. 46-53. *Both fossil and genetic clues argue that ancient ancestors of various human groups lived where they are found today.*

■ **The Recent African Genesis of Humans** pp. 54-61. *Genetic studies indicate that an African woman of 200,000 years ago was our common ancestor.*

■ **Food for Thought** pp. 62-71. *Dietary change was a driving force in human evolution.*

■ **Skin Deep** pp. 72-79. *Human skin color has developed to be dark enough to prevent UV from destroying folate, while still producing vitamin D.*

■ **The Evolution of Human Birth** pp. 80-85. *The difficulties of childbirth may have created selection pressures for seeking assistance during birth.*

■ **Once Were Cannibals** pp. 86-93. *The practice of cannibalism may be deep-rooted in our history.*

■ **If Humans Were Built to Last** pp. 94-100. *We would look a lot different (inside and out) if evolution had produced the body to function smoothly in both youth and old age.*

■ **East Side Story: The Origin of Humankind** Scientific American, May 1994, p. 62-69. *Africa's Rift Valley holds the secret to hominid divergence from apes and to the emergence of humans.*

■ **Late Ice Age Hunting Technology** Scientific American, July 1994, pp. 66-71. *Cro-Magnon artisans produced sophisticated hunting tools.*

■ **How We Came to be Human** Scientific American, Dec. 2001, pp. 42-49. *The evolution of human culture, intelligence, and brain size.*

■ **Neanderthal Notes** Scientific American, Sept. 1997, pp. 17-18. *Controversial discovery of a 43,000 year old flute at Neanderthal camp.*

STUDENT'S REFERENCE

Primates and primate evolution

■ **The Greatest Apes** New Scientist, 15 May 1999, pp. 26-30. *Account of the genetic differences and similarities between chimps and humans.*

■ **A Curious Kinship: Apes and Humans** National Geographic, 181(3) March 1992, pg. 2-45. *From awe to indifference, contradictions mark our attitudes towards our closest relatives, the Great Apes – orangutans, chimpanzees and gorillas.*

■ **Birth of a Tool Maker** New Scientist, 11 March 1995, pp. 38-41. *Tool use and sociality in chimps.*

Human origins and evolution

■ **Meet Kenya man** National Geographic, 200(4) Oct 2001, pp. 84-89. *Description of the recent discovery of Kenyanthropus platyops; a new candidate for humankind's ancestor.*

■ **Talking Heads** New Scientist, 14 Apr. 2001, pp. 26-29. *Description of fossil skull from Java that supports the multi-regional hypothesis for the origin of modern humans.*

■ **On the Origin of Races** New Scientist, 16 Jan. 1993, pp. 34-37. *Fossil skulls and ancient remains are providing important clues about the evolution of human races.*

■ **Family Secrets** New Scientist, 19 June 1999, pp. 42-46. *It has long been thought that modern humans wiped out Neanderthals. New evidence suggests this may not have been the case.*

■ **Human Origins: The Challenge of Java's Skulls** New Scientist, 7 May 1994, pp. 36-40. *Fossils of three ancient Indonesians could spell death for many theories about human origins.*

■ **Distant Cousins** New Scientist 19 July 1997, p.5. *DNA extracted from Neanderthal bones suggest that they last shared a common ancestor with modern humans some 600 000 years ago.*

■ **Rift: Where Humans Began** New Scientist, 4 June 1994, pp. 24-27. *Bipedalism and its association with climatic change in Africa.*

■ **Neanderthals** National Geographic, 189(1) January 1996, pp. 2-35. *A thorough exploration of Neanderthal ecology and evolution, including a discussion of fossil interpretation.*

■ **The Dawn of Humans: The Farthest Horizon** National Geographic, 188(3) Sept. 1995, pp. 38-51. *Recent fossils from East Africa are helping paint a portrait of a species on the cusp between apes and humans - Ardipithecus ramidus.*

■ **The Dawn of Humans: Face to Face with Lucy's Family** National Geographic, 189(3) March 1996, pp. 96-117. *A thorough account of the Australopithecines.*

■ **The Dawn of Humans: The First Steps** National Geographic, 191(2) Feb. 1997, pp. 72-99. *An examination of the current state of knowledge regarding early human evolution (discusses*

bipedalism and selection pressures for involved).

■ **The Dawn of Humans: Expanding Worlds** National Geographic, 191(5) May 1997, pp. 84-109. *Another article in this series on human evolution covering the significance of the Asian fossils and the expansion and evolution of Homo erectus.*

■ **The Dawn of Humans - Redrawing Our Family Tree?** National Geographic, 194(2) August 1998, pp. 90-99. *In the light of more fossil evidence, the relationships between species in the human evolutionary tree are changing.*

■ **The Dawn of Humans - People Like Us** National Geographic, 198(1) July 2000, pp. 90-117. *An excellent account documenting human evolution in the last phase of the ice age.*

■ **The Dawn of Humans - The First Americans** National Geographic, 198(6) December 2000, pp. 40-67. *A flood of new evidence has thrown the study of early Americans into exciting disarray. Includes an account of the application and reliability of dating techniques for recent material.*

■ **Australia's Date with Destiny** New Scientist, 7 Dec. 1996, pp. 28-31. *Startling archaeological finds indicate that the first people arrived in Australia more than 100 000 years earlier than thought.*

■ **The Human Story** New Scientist, 7 June 1997 (Inside Science). *A four page synopsis of the story of human evolution. A usefully brief overview without great detail in any particular area.*

■ **Stand Tall and Stay Cool** New Scientist, 12 May 1988, pg 62-65. *The first step on the road to human evolution was to move to an upright stance. Did our ancestors do it to keep cool?*

■ **Tracking the First of Our Kind** National Geographic, 192 (3) September 1997, pp. 92-99. *Explores the origins and dispersal of humans. The out of Africa theory is also discussed.*

Cultural evolution

■ **France's Magical Cave Art: Chauvet Cave** National Geographic, 200(2) August 2001, pp. 104-121. *Detailed description of a cave decorated with fabulous prehistoric artwork dated at 35 000 years.*

■ **Bigger ain't Better** New Scientist, 23 Feb. 2002, p. 15. *Based on the latest study of primates, brain size alone cannot explain human intelligence.*

■ **Hunted!** New Scientist, 13 April 2002, pp. 34-37. *Many basic human behaviors may have stemmed from our ancestral origins as prey.*

■ **Fired up** New Scientist, 20 May 2000, pp. 30-34. *New evidence suggests that hominids may have been using fire for longer than previously thought.*

■ **The Dawn of Humans: The First Europeans** National Geographic, 192(1) July 1997, pp. 96-113. *Human evolution in Europe based on fossils from early settlements.*

Internet

See pages 10-11 for details of how to access **Bio Links** from our web site: **www.thebiozone.com**. From Bio Links, access sites under the topics:

HUMAN EVOLUTION > **Cultural Evolution:** • Stone age reference collection • Stone pages • The Chauvet cave > **Human Fossil Record:** • A look at modern human origins • Becoming Human • Early Human Evolution • Fossil evidence for human evolution in China • Fossil hominids FAQ • Fossil shakes family tree • Hominid species • Human origins and evolution page • New human ancestor? • Peter Brown's Australian and Asian paleoanthropology • Prominent hominid fossils > **Primates:** • Bonobo sex and society • Chimpanzee hunting habits • Fossil primates • Intelligent chimps - toolmakers

Software and video resources are now provided in the Teacher Resource Handbook

General Primate Characteristics

A 2

The primates have a combination of features that are unique to their group. All primates have retained five digits in the hands and feet (pentadactyly) although some have one digit markedly reduced (e.g. thumb in spider monkeys). **Nails** are found on at least some digits in all modern primates. Climbing is achieved by grasping (not by using claws) and is aided by tactile pads at the end of the digits. Primates have flexible hands and feet with a good deal of **prehensility** (grasping ability). They have a tendency toward **erectness**, particularly in the upper body. This tendency is associated with sitting, standing, leaping, and (in some) walking. The **collarbone** (clavicle) has been retained, allowing more flexibility of the shoulder joint (the clavicle has been lost in many other quadrupedal mammals as an adaptation to striding). Primates have a generalized **dental pattern**, particularly in the back teeth (molars). Unspecialized teeth enabled primates to adopt a flexible omnivorous diet. The snout is reduced along with the olfactory regions of the brain. Baboons go against this trend, with a secondary increase in muzzle length. There is an emphasis on **vision**, with visual areas of the brain enhanced, and well developed binocular, stereoscopic vision to provide overlapping visual fields and good depth perception. Colour vision is probably present in all primates, except specialized nocturnal forms. The **brain** is large and generally more complex than in other mammals. Fetal nourishment is more efficient and **gestation** is longer than in most other mammals. Single births are the norm. Infancy is prolonged with longer periods of infant dependency and a large **parental investment** in each offspring. Life span is generally longer than most other mammals and there is a greater dependency on highly flexible **learned** behavior. Unusually for mammals, adult males of many primate species often associate permanently with the group. Label the diagram below with appropriate **key word summaries** to describe the general physical characteristics of all primates:

The primate pictured is a **white-fronted capuchin monkey** (*Cebus albifrons*) from northern South America. These monkeys inhabit the mid-canopy deciduous, gallery forests.

Brain size and specialization:

Vision:

Collarbone:

Face shape and snout:

Teeth shape and dental arrangement:

Posture:

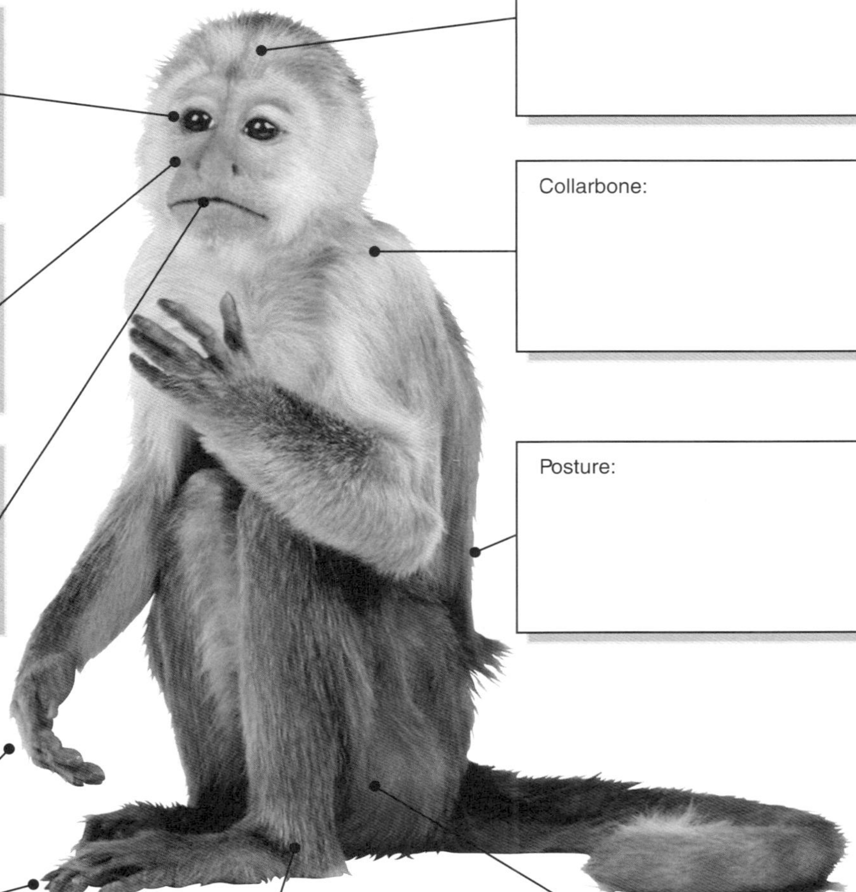

Hands and feet:

Limb joints:

Reproduction:

Social organization:

Primate Groups

Hominids

Homo neanderthalensis

Australopithecus afarensis

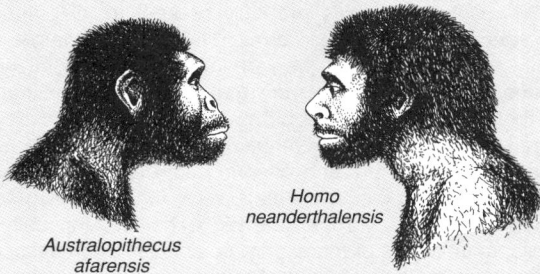

All hominids have the first 3 features, the rest are possessed to varying degrees:

1. Bipedal - modified feet, thigh bone, pelvis, spine
2. Large cerebral cortex (forebrain)
3. Reduced canines (and teeth in general)
4. Nose and chin are prominent, reduced eye ridges
5. Highly sensitive skin (assumed)
6. Body hair very reduced to assist cooling (assumed)
7. Complex social behavior

e.g. *Australopithecus*, *Homo*

Hominoids (apes and hominids)

Features common to all hominoids:

1. No tail
2. Semi-erect or fully erect posture
3. Broad chest, pelvis and shoulders
4. Relatively long arms and mobile shoulder joints
5. Larger brain

Apes

Orangutan

Gibbon

Lowland gorilla

Common chimpanzee

Features common to all apes (pongids):

1. Some brachiating (swing underneath from branch to branch)
2. Some mainly ground dwelling and quadrupedal
3. Flattened nose
4. Bony eye ridges

Old World Monkeys

Macaque

Olive baboon

Features common to all Old World monkeys:

1. Tail not prehensile
2. Quadrupedal (use all four limbs to move about)
3. Some are ground dwelling
4. Nostrils are close together and open downwards

New World Monkeys

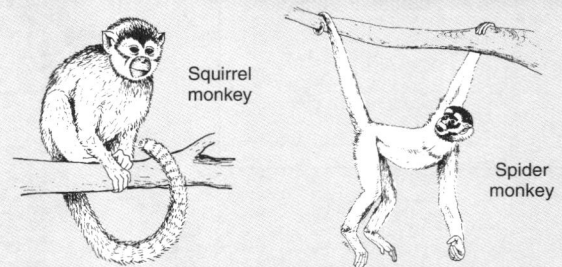

Squirrel monkey

Spider monkey

Features common to all New World monkeys:

1. Prehensile tail that can be used as a fifth limb
2. Quadrupedal (use all four limbs to move about)
3. Strictly arboreal (tree dwelling)
4. Widely separated nostrils

Prosimians

Features common to most prosimians:

1. Tooth comb and grooming claw
2. Wet naked nose with whiskers
3. Arboreal (tree dwelling)
4. Grasping hands and feet
5. Long, mobile limbs
6. Quadrupedal
7. Binocular vision
8. Upright sitting position
9. Nails instead of claws on most digits
10. Simpler placenta

Loris

Ringtailed lemur

Tarsiers

Tarsiers have traditionally been grouped with the prosimians. Recent opinion is that they have a number of distinctive features that set them apart. They exhibit some advanced features in common with the anthropoids (monkeys, apes and humans).

Features common to tarsiers and anthropoids:

1. Dry hairy nose
2. Whiskers reduced
3. No grooming claw
4. Entire upper lip
5. Complex placenta

Tarsier

Primate Classification

DA 3

There is much debate over how the classification of primates should be organized. There are various, new schemes proposed that attempt to interpret the probable evolutionary relationships of the primates. There is considerable evidence suggesting that modern tarsiers are more closely related to simians (monkeys, apes, and humans) than to other prosimians. The classification of the apes (hominoids) has its fair share of controversy. There is confusion over the distinction between the families Pongidae and Hominidae within the Hominoidea. Originally, all great apes were placed in the family Pongidae, and the family Hominidae was reserved for humans and their direct fossil relatives. It is now widely acknowledged that the African apes (gorillas and chimpanzees) are more closely related to humans than they are to the orangutans (from Asia), and there have been a number of attempts to reflect this in new classifications. A newly proposed classification of the superfamily Hominoidea (inset below) places the orangutans in the subfamily Ponginae and combines the African apes and humans in the subfamily Homininae.

Superfamily Hominoidea

Family Hylobatidae:	{various gibbon species}
Family Hominidae:	
Subfamily Ponginae	
Genus *Pongo*:	
Pongo pygmaeus	Bornean orangutan
Pongo abelii	Sumatran orangutan
Subfamily Homininae	
Tribe Gorillini	
Genus *Gorilla*:	
Gorilla gorilla	Western gorilla
Gorilla beringei	Eastern gorilla
Tribe Panini	
Genus *Pan*:	
Pan troglodytes	Common chimpanzee
Pan paniscus	Pygmy chimpanzee
Tribe Hominini	
Genus *Homo*:	
Homo sapiens	Human

Genetic relatedness of primates

The diagram below illustrates a new way of classifying the hominoids (apes and humans) based on genetic similarities. The percentages next to each of the points where a split occurs indicates the amount of difference in the total genetic makeup (genomes) of the two groups being considered. For example, the genome of the gibbons compared to the rest of the apes (orangutans, gorillas, chimpanzees) and humans differs by 5.7%. The resulting diagram based on successive splitting of divergent groups is calibrated according to these genetic differences. A large genetic difference between any two groups implies that they are distantly related, whereas small genetic differences suggest they share a recent common ancestor.

Split between humans and chimpanzees, with the gorillas

Split between humans and chimpanzees

Split between the group containing humans, chimpanzees, gorillas, with the orangutans

1.4%

Human

Pygmy chimpanzee (bonobo)

Common chimpanzee

1.8%

Western gorilla

Split between the great apes (Hominidae) and gibbons (Hylobatidae)

3.6%

Eastern lowland gorilla

Eastern mountain gorilla

Split between the apes (Hominoidea) and Old World monkeys (Cercopithecoidea)

5.7%

Bornean orangutan

Sumatran orangutan

Split between the New World monkeys (Catarrhini) and the group containing the apes and Old World monkeys (Platyrrhini)

7.9%

Gibbon

13.0%

Old World monkey

New World monkey

40   30   20   10   0

Millions of years ago

1. According to the diagram above, showing relatedness according to genetic similarity:

   (a) Name the hominoid group that is most closely related to the 2 chimpanzee species: _____

   (b) Name the 2 chimpanzee species: _____

2. Determine from the diagram how long ago:

   (a) The 2 species of chimpanzee split from a common ancestor: _____

   (b) The chimpanzees split from the line to humans: _____

   (c) The African apes (and humans) split from the Asian apes (orangutans and gibbons): _____

3. Explain what assumption must be made in order for the degree of genetic diversity to be used as a measure of evolutionary distance:

_____

RA ❷ Human Characteristics

Humans have features that set them apart from other primates. Looking at the differences between modern humans and apes helps to identify a progression of evolutionary changes in the fossils of human ancestors.

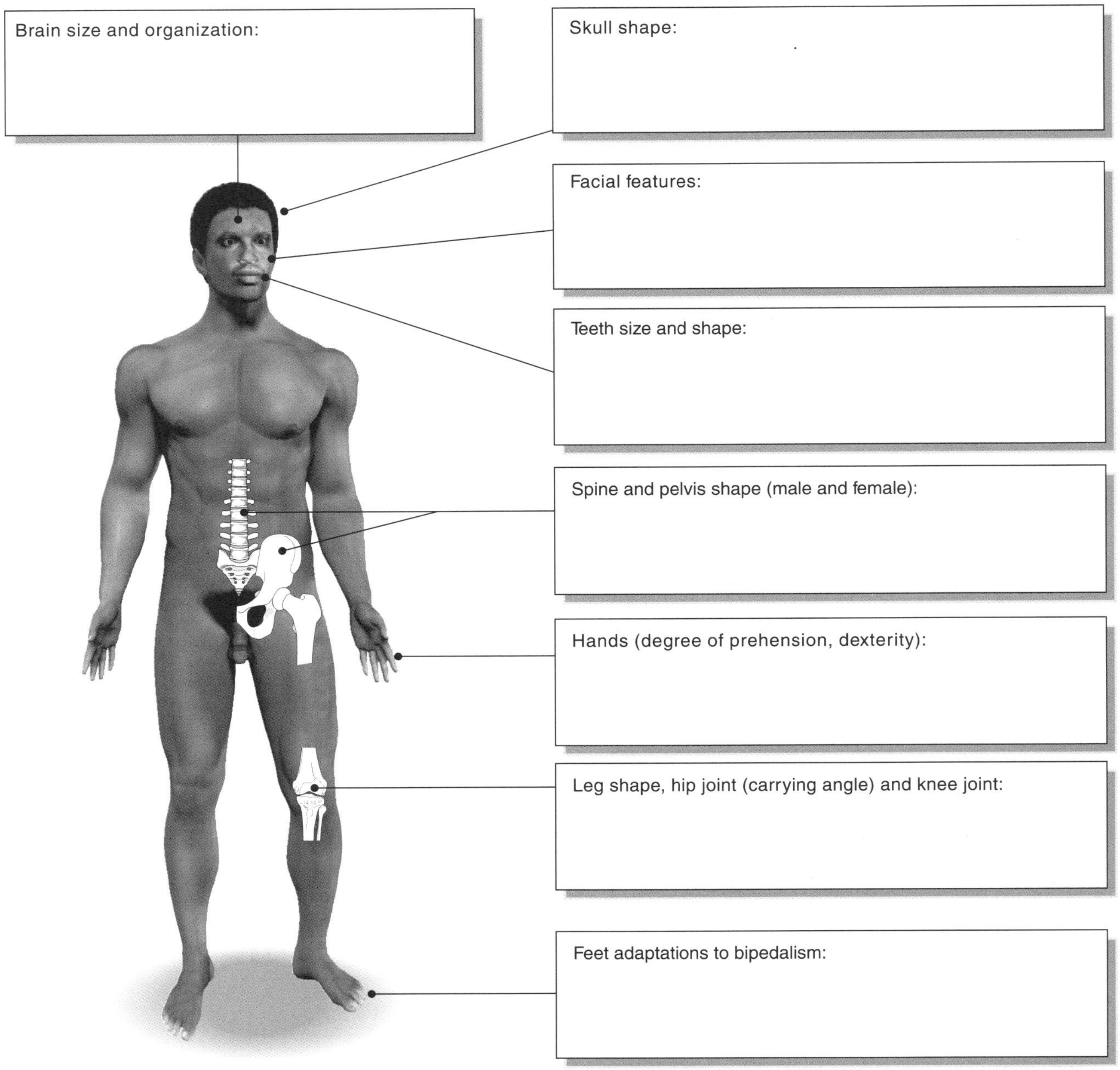

Brain size and organization:

Skull shape:

Facial features:

Teeth size and shape:

Spine and pelvis shape (male and female):

Hands (degree of prehension, dexterity):

Leg shape, hip joint (carrying angle) and knee joint:

Feet adaptations to bipedalism:

1. Fill in the spaces on the diagram above, the characteristics that distinguish humans from other primates.

2. Briefly comment on the following human attributes:

    (a) Culture: _____

    _____

    _____

    (b) Abstract thought: _____

    _____

    _____

    (c) Social organization: _____

    _____

    _____

Distinguishing Features of Hominids

The data below provide you with lists of features that distinguish the many hominid species from each other. In your reading, the 'known dates' provided may vary from those given below, mainly due to varying interpretations on the dating of sites by different researchers. Some early hominid species, including various australopithecines and *Kenyanthropus*, are not listed.

Distinguishing Features of Early Human Species

	Homo habilis (small)	Homo habilis (large)	Homo erectus	Archaic Homo sapiens	Homo neanderthalensis	Early Homo sapiens
Other name	None	*Homo rudolfensis*	*Homo ergaster* for older African forms	*Homo heidelbergensis*	*The Neanderthals*	Early anatomically modern humans
Known date (years ago)	2 – 1.6 million	2.4 – 1.6 million	1.8 – 0.3 million	400 000 - 100 000	150 000 - 30 000	160 000 - 60 000
Brain size	500-650 cc	600-800 cc	750-1250 cc	1100-1400 cc	1200-1750 cc	1200-1700 cc
Height	1.0 m	*c.* 1.5 m	1.3 - 1.5 m	?	1.5-1.7 m	1.6-1.85 m
Physique	Relatively long arms	Robust but 'human' skeleton	Robust but 'human' skeleton	Robust but 'human' skeleton	Robust but 'human' skeleton, adapted for cold	Modern skeleton possibly adapted for warmth
Skull shape	Small face with developed nose	Larger, flatter face	Flat, thick skull with sagittal 'keel' and large brow ridge	Higher cranium, face less protruding	Reduced brow ridge, midface projection, long low skull	Small or no brow ridge, shorter and higher skull
Teeth and jaws	Smaller, narrow molars; thinner jaw	Large narrow molars; robust jaw	Smaller teeth than *H. habilis*, robust jaw in larger individuals	Similar to *H. erectus* but smaller teeth	Similar to Archaic *H. sapiens*; except for incisors, smaller teeth	Teeth may be smaller; shorter jaws than Neanderthals; chin developed
Geographical distribution	Eastern, and possibly Southern Africa	Eastern Africa possibly? western Asia (Rep. Georgia)	Africa, Asia, Indonesia, and possibly Europe	Africa, Asia and Europe	Europe and western Asia	Africa and western Asia

Distinguishing Features of Early Hominids

	Orrorin tugenensis	Ardipithecus ramidus	Australopithecus anamensis	Australopithecus afarensis	Australopithecus africanus	Paranthropus robustus
Other name	"Millennium Man"	Two subspecies: *ramidus* & *kadabba*	None	None	None	*Australopithecus robustus*
Known date (years ago)	6.0 million	4.4 – 5.8 million	4.2 – 3.9 million	3.9 – 2.5 million	~3.0 – 2.3 million	2.2 – 1.5 million
Brain size	? cc	? cc	? cc	400 – 500 cc	400 – 500 cc	530 cc
Height	? m	*c.* 1.22 m	? m	1.07 – 1.52 m	1.1 – 1.4 m	1.1 – 1.3 m
Physique	Possibly bipedal forest dweller. Little else known	Possibly bipedal forest dweller. Little else known	Partial leg bones strongly suggest bipedalism; humerus extremely humanlike	Light build. Some apelike features: relatively long arms, curved fingers/toes, sexual dimorphism	Light build. Probably long arms, more 'human' features, probably less sexual dimorphism	Heavy build. Relatively long arms. Moderate sexual dimorphism.
Skull shape	Not yet described	Foramen magnum more forward than apes	Primitive features in the skull, possibly apelike	Apelike face, low forehead, bony brow ridge, flat nose, no chin	Brow ridges less prominent; higher forehead and shorter face	Long, broad, flat face; crest on top of skull; moderate facial buttressing
Teeth and jaws	Not yet described	Teeth are intermediate between those of *A. afarensis* and earlier apes. Smaller, narrow molars; thinner jaw	Very similar to those of older fossil apes, but canines vertical; teeth have thicker tooth enamel like in humans	Human-like teeth, canines smaller than apes, larger than humans. Jaw shape half way between an ape's and human.	Teeth and jaws much larger than in humans; tooth row fully parabolic like humans; canine teeth further reduced	Very thick jaws; small incisors and canines; large molar-like premolars; very large molars
Geographical distribution	Eastern Africa	Eastern Africa	Eastern Africa	Eastern Africa	Southern Africa	Southern Africa

RDA❸ # Hominid Evolution

The diagram below shows a provisional 'consensus' view of the family tree for the hominids (the group that includes the modern humans and pre-humans). There is much controversy over the interpretation of fossil data from the period 4-2 million years ago (mya). Some **paleo-anthropologists** (scientists who study fossil hominid remains) believe that more branches existed than are shown

here, with a number of adaptive radiations occurring over this period. It is almost certain that the early Australopithecines evolved into *Homo habilis*, which was ancestral to modern humans, by about 2 mya. A divergent branch, genus *Paranthropus*, coexisted with early *Homo*, but eventually became extinct about one million years ago. The diagram below does not attempt to show species relationships.

In 2001, the 6-7 my old remains of a nearly complete skull with gorilla-like features was unearthed in Chad. Nicknamed "Toumai" and assigned to a new genus, **Sahelanthropus tchadensis**, scientists debate whether the skull's features place it in the human family tree, or whether it represents the remains of a proto-gorilla.

The 6 my old remains of five chimpanzee-sized **Orrorin tugenensis** specimens were unearthed at Baringa in Kenya in 2000. The teeth are very humanlike and a perfectly preserved thigh bone clearly shows features associated with walking upright (bipedalism).

Ardipithecus ramidus was an ape with some humanlike features. Two subspecies have been identified: *A. r. ramidus* (4.4 my old) and the older *A. r. kadabba* (5.8 my old). Fossils suggest that it was at least partially bipedal with teeth that were also more humanlike.

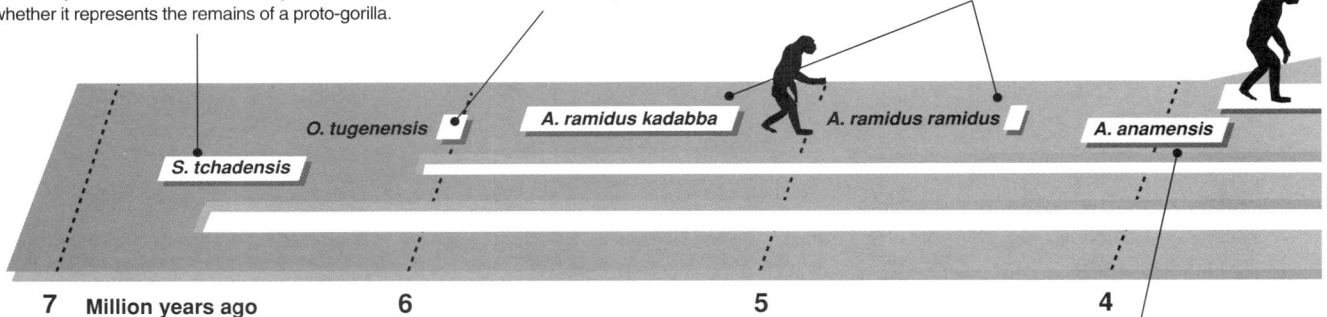

O. tugenensis — A. ramidus kadabba — A. ramidus ramidus — A. anamensis — S. tchadensis

7 Million years ago   **6**   **5**   **4**

New DNA and biochemical evidence suggests that the **last common ancestor** of hominids and apes occurred between 5 and 10 million years ago. The last common ancestor should have a combination of features reminiscent of both humans and apes.

There is a large gap in the fossil record that has until recently been very deficient in early hominid remains. The 1995 discovery of hominid fossils in Kenya, dated about 4 million years old have been named **Australopithecus anamensis**.

1. Define the term **hominid**: _____

   _____

2. (a) List the key identifying features of the (gracile) **australopithecines**: _____

   _____

   (b) List the species that are normally assigned to this group: _____

   _____

3. (a) Name the species considered to be the common ancestor to later australopithecines and also to genus *Homo*:

   _____

   (b) State the date range for this hominid: _____

4. People who do not understand hominid evolution often argue that:

   "If humans evolved from chimpanzees, then today's chimpanzees should be continuing to evolve into humans everyday"

   (a) State the date range paleoanthropologists believe hominids and chimpanzees last shared a common ancestor:

   _____

   (b) List two sources of evidence by which researchers have determined this date: _____

   _____

   (c) Rewrite the statement quoted above to correctly describe the evolutionary relationship between modern chimpanzees and humans:

   _____

   _____

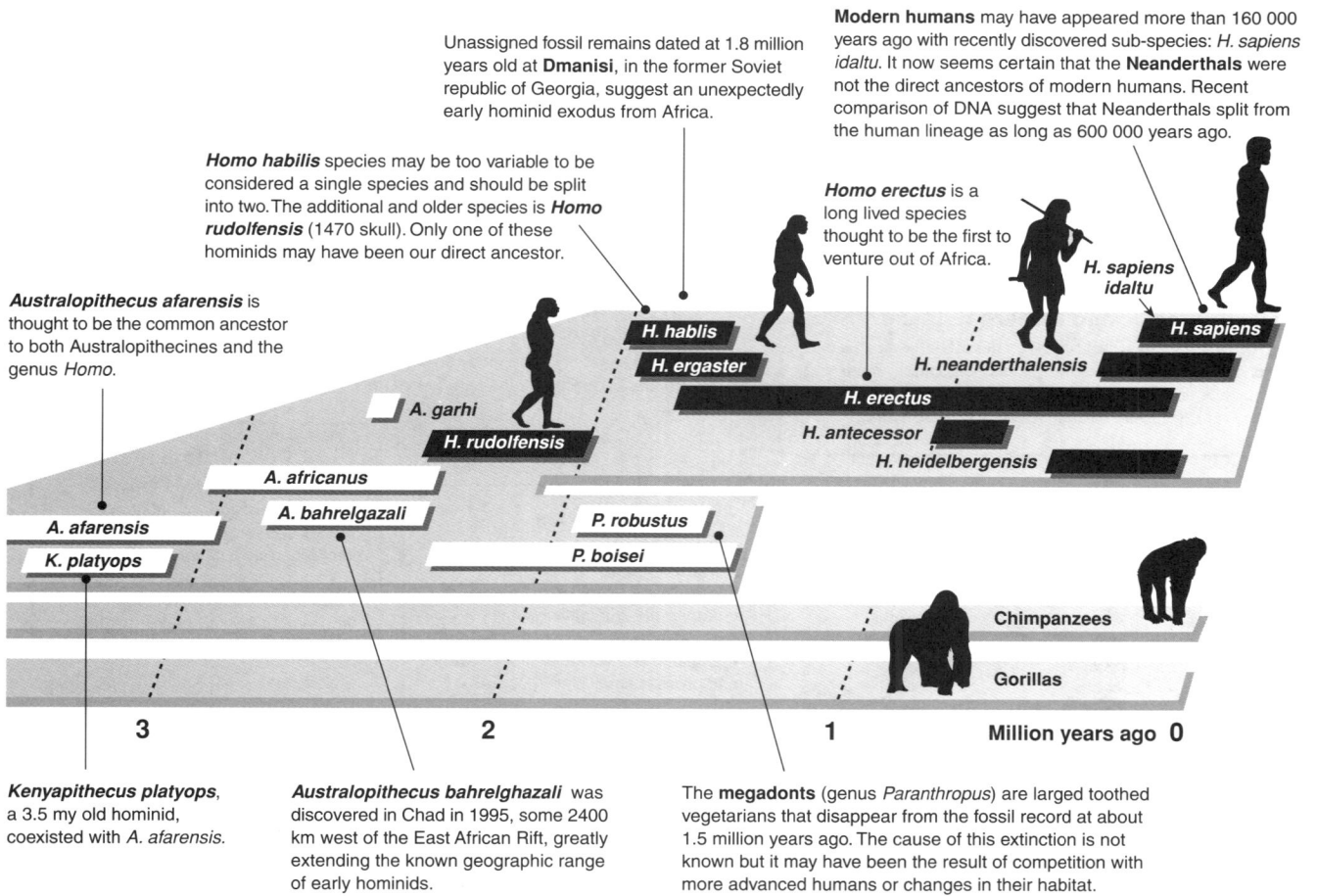

Modern humans may have appeared more than 160 000 years ago with recently discovered sub-species: *H. sapiens idaltu*. It now seems certain that the **Neanderthals** were not the direct ancestors of modern humans. Recent comparison of DNA suggest that Neanderthals split from the human lineage as long as 600 000 years ago.

Unassigned fossil remains dated at 1.8 million years old at **Dmanisi**, in the former Soviet republic of Georgia, suggest an unexpectedly early hominid exodus from Africa.

Homo habilis species may be too variable to be considered a single species and should be split into two. The additional and older species is *Homo rudolfensis* (1470 skull). Only one of these hominids may have been our direct ancestor.

Homo erectus is a long lived species thought to be the first to venture out of Africa.

Australopithecus afarensis is thought to be the common ancestor to both Australopithecines and the genus *Homo*.

H. sapiens idaltu

H. hablis

H. ergaster

H. neanderthalensis

H. sapiens

A. garhi

H. rudolfensis

H. erectus

A. africanus

H. antecessor

A. afarensis

A. bahrelgazali

H. heidelbergensis

K. platyops

P. robustus

P. boisei

Chimpanzees

Gorillas

3   2   1   Million years ago 0

Kenyapithecus platyops, a 3.5 my old hominid, coexisted with *A. afarensis*.

Australopithecus bahrelghazali was discovered in Chad in 1995, some 2400 km west of the East African Rift, greatly extending the known geographic range of early hominids.

The **megadonts** (genus *Paranthropus*) are larged toothed vegetarians that disappear from the fossil record at about 1.5 million years ago. The cause of this extinction is not known but it may have been the result of competition with more advanced humans or changes in their habitat.

5. (a) Describe what a **megadont** is: _____

    (b) List two species that belong to this group: _____

    (c) Suggest why they may have become extinct: _____

    _____

6. Using the diagram above determine:

    (a) The total number of hominid species (i.e. from 6 mya to the present day): _____

    (b) The number of hominid species that existed between 3 and 2 million years ago: _____

7. The recent discovery of the oldest hominid has yielded important information about that stage in human evolution.

    (a) Name the oldest, clearly described hominid fossil: _____

    (b) List two features of this species that suggest that it was not just an ancient chimpanzee: _____

    _____

    _____

8. Explain why it is most **unlikely** that the Neanderthals were ancestors to modern humans: _____

    _____

    _____

    _____

9. Suggest a possible reason why hominid fossils older than about 4.5 million years have been difficult to find:

    _____

    _____

DA 2   The Emerging View

The view of 'evolutionary tree' illustrated in the previous activity is simplified to make it easier to understand where the various hominid groups lie in relationship to each other. There has been a tendency over the last 40 years to try to fit the assembled fossil evidence into a **linear progression** of early, ape-like forms gradually evolving into more human-like intermediates until the modern human form was achieved in the last tens of thousands of years. In the late 1980s and early 1990s, a large number of new hominid fossils were discovered

and some of the previously discovered ones were also reassessed. This led to a change in thinking that acknowledged the **bushier** nature of the human evolutionary tree. Recently this later view has been further refined to harmonize the view of human evolution with the evidence gathered on the better understood evolution of other mammals. Human evolution can now be thought of as a succession of **adaptive radiations**, some of which were 'sidelines' to the modern human lineage and all but one species (our own) becoming **extinct**.

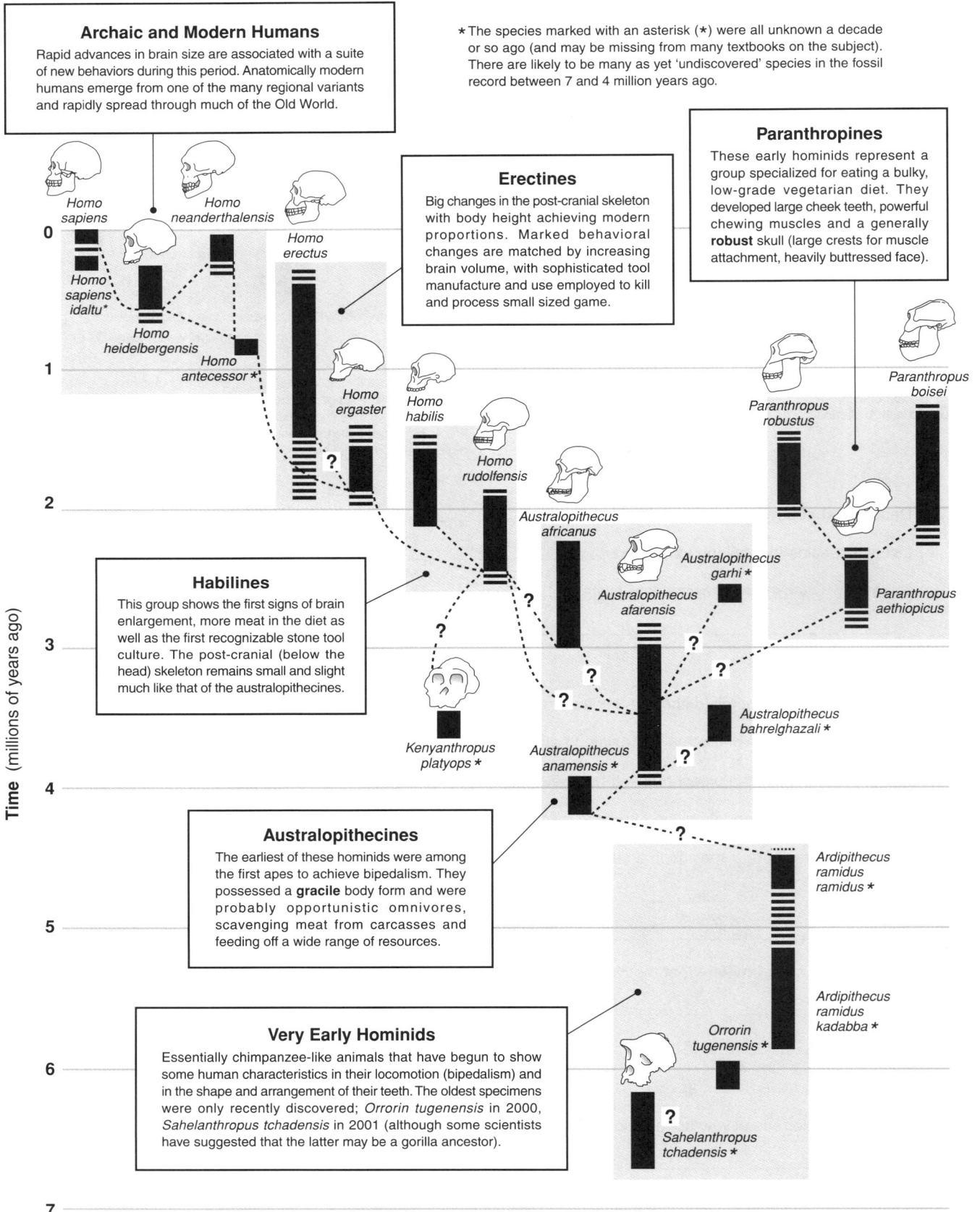

Archaic and Modern Humans

Rapid advances in brain size are associated with a suite of new behaviors during this period. Anatomically modern humans emerge from one of the many regional variants and rapidly spread through much of the Old World.

* The species marked with an asterisk (*) were all unknown a decade or so ago (and may be missing from many textbooks on the subject). There are likely to be many as yet 'undiscovered' species in the fossil record between 7 and 4 million years ago.

Paranthropines

These early hominids represent a group specialized for eating a bulky, low-grade vegetarian diet. They developed large cheek teeth, powerful chewing muscles and a generally **robust** skull (large crests for muscle attachment, heavily buttressed face).

Erectines

Big changes in the post-cranial skeleton with body height achieving modern proportions. Marked behavioral changes are matched by increasing brain volume, with sophisticated tool manufacture and use employed to kill and process small sized game.

Habilines

This group shows the first signs of brain enlargement, more meat in the diet as well as the first recognizable stone tool culture. The post-cranial (below the head) skeleton remains small and slight much like that of the australopithecines.

Australopithecines

The earliest of these hominids were among the first apes to achieve bipedalism. They possessed a **gracile** body form and were probably opportunistic omnivores, scavenging meat from carcasses and feeding off a wide range of resources.

Very Early Hominids

Essentially chimpanzee-like animals that have begun to show some human characteristics in their locomotion (bipedalism) and in the shape and arrangement of their teeth. The oldest specimens were only recently discovered; *Orrorin tugenensis* in 2000, *Sahelanthropus tchadensis* in 2001 (although some scientists have suggested that the latter may be a gorilla ancestor).

Time (millions of years ago)

Labels on chart: *Homo sapiens*, *Homo neanderthalensis*, *Homo sapiens idaltu* *, *Homo erectus*, *Homo heidelbergensis*, *Homo antecessor* *, *Homo ergaster*, *Homo habilis*, *Homo rudolfensis*, *Australopithecus africanus*, *Australopithecus garhi* *, *Australopithecus afarensis*, *Paranthropus robustus*, *Paranthropus boisei*, *Paranthropus aethiopicus*, *Kenyanthropus platyops* *, *Australopithecus bahrelghazali* *, *Australopithecus anamensis* *, *Ardipithecus ramidus ramidus* *, *Ardipithecus ramidus kadabba* *, *Orrorin tugenensis* *, *Sahelanthropus tchadensis* *

A 1960s view of human evolution

The illustration below was in common usage in the popular press 30 years ago to represent the **linear progression** from a primitive apelike ancestor to modern humans. It is still used as a visual metaphor for the idea of evolution in the world of advertising.

Evolving lineage with the accumulation of gradual genetic changes under the influence of natural selection

Predictions according to the linear progression model

- The fossil record should consistently show smooth intergradations from one species to the next.

Anatomically modern humans   African apes

Time (millions of years)

Homo

Megadonts

Early bipedal apes

Diversity

The actual evidence observed

- Few smooth intergradations from one species to the next.
- Species tend to appear suddenly in the fossil record.
- The species linger for varying but often very extended periods of time in the fossil record.
- The species disappear as suddenly as they arrived.
- They are replaced by other species which might or might not be closely related to them.

Source: Robert Foley, **Humans Before Humanity**, Blackwell Publishers (1995)

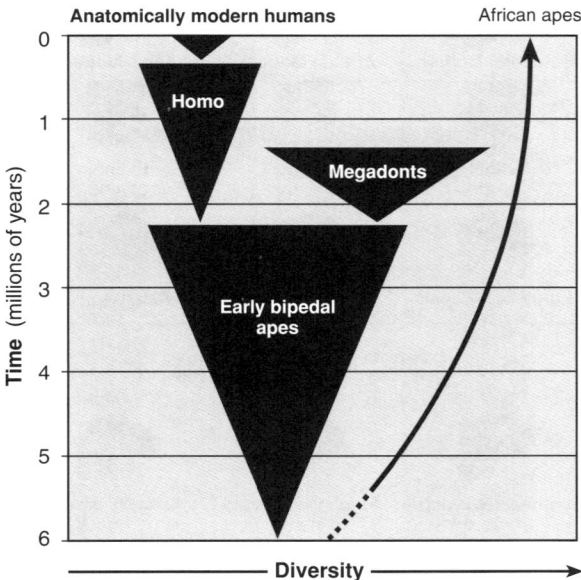

The current view of human evolution

The diagram on the left depicts human evolution as a series of adaptive radiations. The first radiation is that of the **early bipedal apes** – the australopithecines. The second radiation involves the genus *Paranthropus*, a group of species that exploited a coarse, low-grade vegetable food source (nuts, root tubers and seeds) resulting in **megadontic** adaptations (very large teeth). The third radiation is genus *Homo*, with the **habilines** and **erectines** developing a larger brain, diversifying and dispersing from Africa to other parts of the Old World. The last radiation does not involve any major evolutionary divergence, but reflects the dispersal of **modern humans** with considerable geographic separation.

Source: Ian Tattersall, *The Fossil Trail*, Oxford University Press (1995)

1. Explain why the 1960s **linear progression** view of human evolution is not an acceptable scientific model:

_____

_____

_____

2. Explain whether the *emerging view* (on the opposite page) and the data above support the **punctuated equilibrium** or **gradualism** models of evolutionary development and the origin of new species:

_____

_____

3. Describe the 4 main **adaptive radiations** that have occurred during hominid evolution over the last 4 million years:

(a) _____

(b) _____

(c) _____

(d) _____

DA③ The Origin of Modern Humans

There is great debate over the origins of "anatomically modern" humans – i.e., the first emergence of *Homo sapiens*. The two main contesting theories are called **multiregional** and **replacement** hypotheses, with the **assimilation** model (not shown) being a compromise between the other two. The "moderns" lack some of the features characteristic of earlier, archaic hominids, such as the protruding snout and heavy brow ridges. The modern skulls have an essentially flat face, are globular (rather than elongated), and have a more nearly vertical forehead. The face is narrower and smaller, and the jaw has a protruding chin. The rest of the skeleton is less robust.

Multiregional Hypothesis

Advocates: Milford Wolpoff, University of Michigan
            Alan Thorne, Australian National University

Based largely on the fossil evidence and the anatomical characteristics of modern populations, 'multiregional evolution' traces all modern populations back at least 1 million years to when early humans (*Homo erectus*) first left Africa. Modern *Homo sapiens* emerged gradually throughout the world, and as the populations dispersed, they remained in 'genetic contact'. This gene flow between neighboring populations ensured that the general 'modern human blueprint' was adopted by all. This limited gene flow still allowed for slight anatomical differences to be retained or develop in the regional populations. Wolpoff and Thorne who are advocates of this theory maintain that the mitochondrial DNA data can be interpreted in a way that supports the multi-regional Model.

> See *Scientific American* SPECIAL ISSUE: New Look at Human Evolution.
> August 25, 2003, pp 46-61, for two excellent articles on each of these models.

Replacement Hypothesis

Advocates: Christopher Stringer, Natural History Museum in London
            The late Alan C. Wilson

Also known as the "Out of Africa Hypothesis" and "Eve Hypothesis". This model keeps *Homo sapiens* as a separate species and states that modern humans evolved from archaics in only one location, Africa, and then spread, replacing the archaic populations when they came in contact. The extinction of these regional archaic populations occurred because the modern humans were better adapted. In support of this theory, the late Allan C. Wilson and colleagues carried out genetic studies on modern endemic human populations. They concluded that the evolutionary record of mitochondrial DNA could be traced back to a single female who lived in Africa some 200 000 years ago. This woman, real or hypothetical, has been dubbed 'Eve' by Wilson and his team. By implication, this theory maintains that all modern descendants contain mitochondrial DNA that can be traced directly back to Eve.

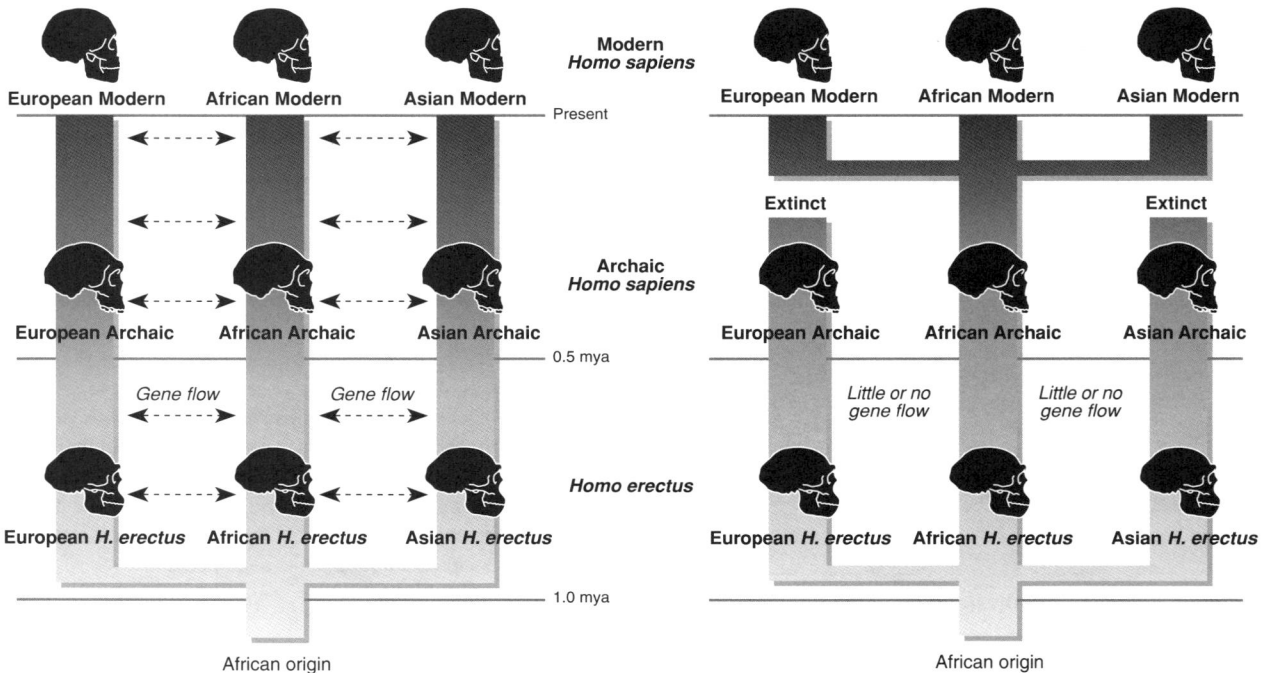

Predictions made by this model

1. Fossils that show the change from one stage to the next in all geographic regions (transitional forms).

2. Modern traits should appear in the fossil record somewhat simultaneously all over the Old World range of Archaic *Homo sapiens*.

3. Today's modern "racial" traits characteristic of a particular region can be traced back to ancient forms in that region.

4. The human species today should have a high degree of genetic diversity since it is an old species with distinct populations that have had a lot of time to accumulate genetic differences.

5. The amount of genetic variation within each modern human group is about the same since they have all been evolving together.

Source: Michael A. Park, Biological Anthropology, Mayfield Publishing, 1996

Predictions made by this model

1. Transitional forms would be found in only one place (in this case Africa) which is the area of origin for modern humans.

2. Modern traits should appear first in one location (Africa) and then later elsewhere as the modern population spread to other parts of the Old World.

3. Modern and archaic populations should overlap in time outside the area that moderns originated (the process of replacement would not be instantaneous).

4. Humans today should have relatively little genetic diversity since the species is young.

5. Today's modern populations should differ in the amount of genetic variation, the most diversity being found in the region where moderns first evolved (this would have been the oldest group and therefore the one that had the most time for genetic variation to accumulate).

The map below shows a probable origin and dispersal of modern humans throughout the world. An African origin is almost certain, with south eastern Africa being the most likely region. The dispersal was affected at crucial stages by the presence or absence of 'land bridges' formed during the drop in sea level that occurs with the onset of ice ages. The late development of boating and rafting technology slowed dispersal into Australia and the Pacific. New Zealand was one of the last places on Earth to be populated. (on the map, **ya** = years ago).

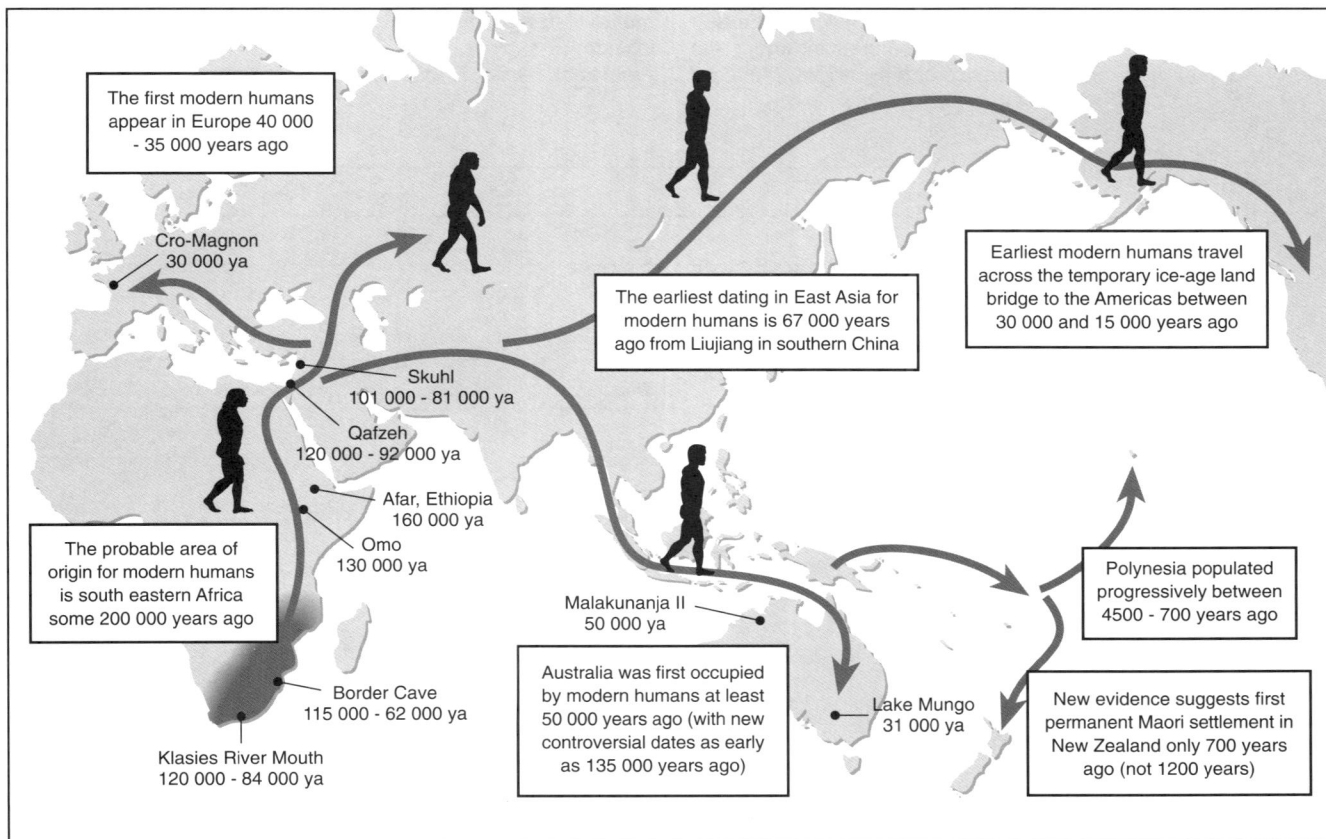

The first modern humans appear in Europe 40 000 - 35 000 years ago

Cro-Magnon 30 000 ya

The earliest dating in East Asia for modern humans is 67 000 years ago from Liujiang in southern China

Earliest modern humans travel across the temporary ice-age land bridge to the Americas between 30 000 and 15 000 years ago

Skuhl 101 000 - 81 000 ya

Qafzeh 120 000 - 92 000 ya

Afar, Ethiopia 160 000 ya

Omo 130 000 ya

The probable area of origin for modern humans is south eastern Africa some 200 000 years ago

Malakunanja II 50 000 ya

Polynesia populated progressively between 4500 - 700 years ago

Australia was first occupied by modern humans at least 50 000 years ago (with new controversial dates as early as 135 000 years ago)

Lake Mungo 31 000 ya

New evidence suggests first permanent Maori settlement in New Zealand only 700 years ago (not 1200 years)

Border Cave 115 000 - 62 000 ya

Klasies River Mouth 120 000 - 84 000 ya

1. State at what date the two models suggest that anatomically modern humans shared a common ancestry:

   (a) Replacement model: _____ years ago   (b) Multiregional model: _____ years ago

2. In 1992, paleoanthropologists (*Nature*, Vol. 357, page 404) recovered the remains of two *Homo erectus* skulls in China, that have modern faces but still possess a cranium typical of *Homo erectus*. State which of the two models this new evidence supports and why:

   _____

   _____

3. Mitochondrial DNA was used to compare the genetic relatedness of modern human endemic populations (i.e. native populations from around the world). Explain why it was used instead of DNA from the nucleus:

   _____

   _____

4. Explain the significance of the *gene flow* between early populations of humans in the 'multiregional model':

   _____

   _____

5. In the 'Out of Africa model', modern humans move out of Africa to populate the rest of the world. Describe the fate of the other human populations already inhabiting these regions, according to this theory:

   _____

   _____

6. Discuss the implications of an early (135 000 ya) arrival of modern humans into Australia:

   _____

   _____

Hominid Skull Identification

RA 2

This activity will help you identify particular skull types. Give the **name** of the species for each of the hominid skull shapes below. With reference to the following list, give a description of the **key features** that help in its identification. Features include: *the overall shape of the skull, the presence of brow ridges, the facial* *angle, the size (volume) of the brain case compared to the rest of the skull, the presence or absence of a snout, the robustness of the jaw, size of teeth, the presence of a sagittal crest.* Species include: *H. sapiens, H. neanderthalensis, Archaic H. sapiens, H. erectus, H. habilis, P. robustus, P. boisei, A. afarensis, A. africanus.*

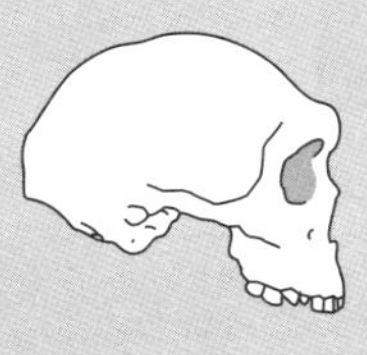

(a) Species: _____

   Features: _____

   _____

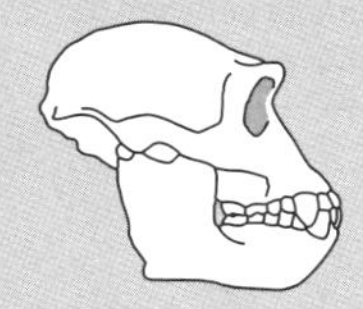

(b) Species: _____

   Features: _____

   _____

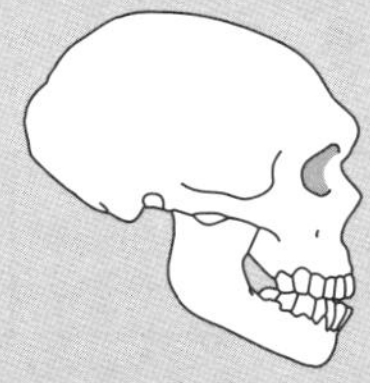

(c) Species: _____

   Features: _____

   _____

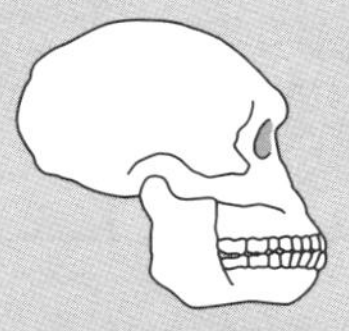

(d) Species: _____

   Features: _____

   _____

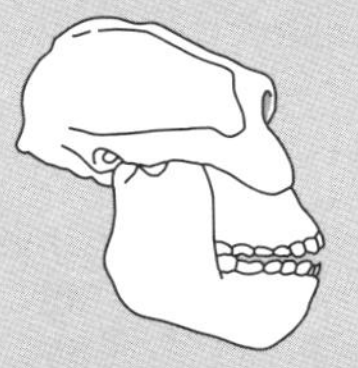

(e) Species: _____

   Features: _____

   _____

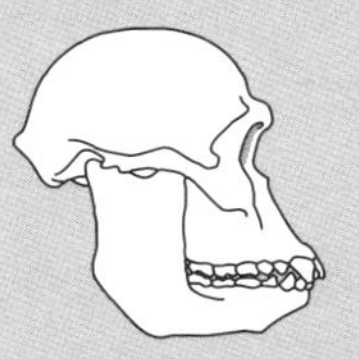

(f) Species: _____

   Features: _____

   _____

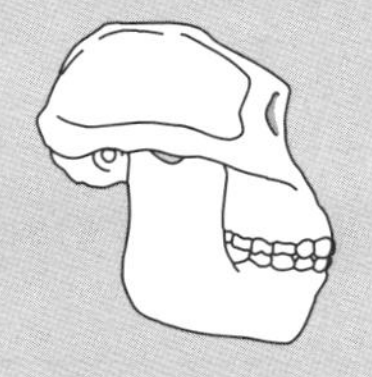

(g) Species: _____

   Features: _____

   _____

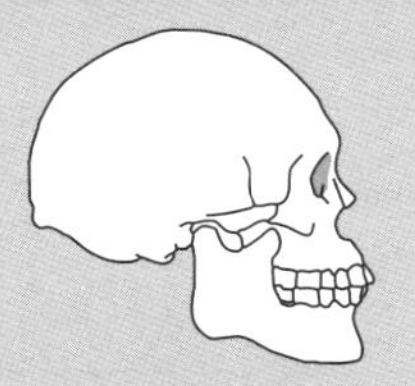

(h) Species: _____

   Features: _____

   _____

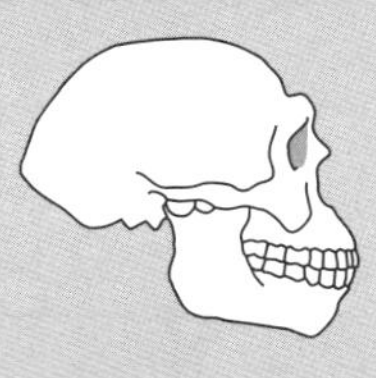

(i) Species: _____

   Features: _____

   _____

Bipedalism and Nakedness

The first major step in the development of humans as a distinct group from apes was their ability to adopt a habitually upright stance. Closely linked to this shift in the mode of locomotion was the reduction in body hair (we are the only 'naked ape'). A number of selection pressures for hair reduction are suggested below. Some experts have suggested that bipedalism and hair reduction were evolutionary responses to the changing climate of East Africa about 7-5 million years ago (see below). Numerous reasons have been offered for the development of bipedalism in hominids. The need to adjust to a newly emerging habitat was probably important, although the earliest hominids may still have been forest dwellers. Gone is the old image of bipedalism evolving as a result of a move into the savannah (open grassland). Current theories must explain how bipedalism may have emerged in a more forested environment. Animal and plant fossils at hominid sites have indicated that the earliest bipedal hominids frequented a variety of habitats, including **open woodland**, **gallery forest**, **closed woodland**, and **savannah**. The considerable number of early hominid species living at the same time may reflect local adaptations to different environments. As forests receded in Africa due to the drying of the global climate, vast areas of savannah became established. Many primate species were not able to adjust to the loss of trees since they were primarily adapted to tree-dwelling. These primates retreated with their shrinking range. Others met the challenge by successfully adopting new behavior patterns that resulted in anatomical adaptations. Baboons and the hominids succeeded in this, while others failed and became extinct.

Hair Reduction

Retention of head hair
Hair on the head (and to a lesser extent the shoulders) has been retained to reflect and radiate heat before it reaches the skin of the exposed part of the body.

Parasite control
With the reduction in body hair, control of parasites, such as fleas, ticks and lice, would have been improved. This became particularly important when early hominids began to use a 'home base' rather than continually wandering. Parasites, such as fleas, need to complete their life cycle at a single location so that hatching eggs can reinfect their host.

Lice   Ticks   Fleas

Thermoregulation
Shorter, finer hairs (not hair loss) in early hominids has allowed greater heat loss by radiating from the skin surface. Well developed sweat glands allow us to lose heat at an astounding 700 watts m^2 of skin (a capacity not approached by any other mammal).

Bipedalism

Seeing over the grass
Being upright may have helped to spot predators or locate carcasses at a distance.

Carrying food
The capacity to carry food away from a kill site or growing site to a position of safety would have had great survival advantage.

Carrying offspring
Walking upright enabled early hominids to carry their offspring while following the large game herds of the savannah on long seasonal migrations.

Hold tools and weapons
Tool use was probably a consequence of bipedalism, rather than a cause. Upright walking appears to have been established well before the development of hunting in early hominids.

Thermoregulation
Advantages of the upright walking are:
1. 60% less surface area presented to the sun at midday.
2. Greater air flow across the body when it is lifted higher off the ground. The air higher up is also less humid and cooler.

Efficient locomotion
With the change in habitat resulting from the cooling and drying of the Late Miocene a more efficient means of moving across the growing expanses of savannah was required. Bipedalism provides an energy efficient method that favors low speed, long distance movement – walking.

The changing climate of East Africa in the Miocene

As the climate and habitat changed, early hominids in the wooded savannah would have been forced to move across open ground to exploit their food resources amongst the trees. They would also have been under pressure to experiment with new food resources.

Near-continuous forest

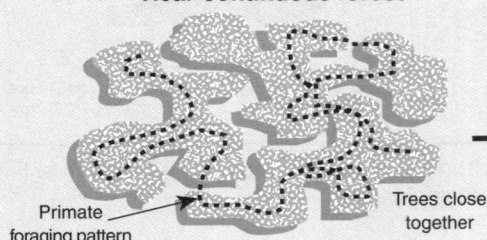

Habitat changes due to a cooling of the climate in the latter part of the Miocene

Wooded savannah

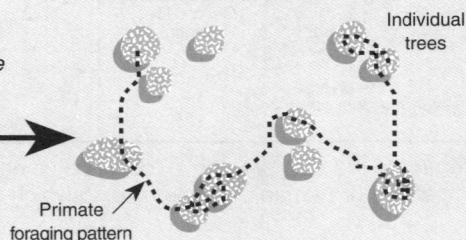

Individual trees

Primate foraging pattern

Trees close together

Primate foraging pattern

Pre-hominids foraged for food in nearly continuous forest; food resources were readily available. A near completely arboreal life was possible with only the occasional need to move on the ground.

By the late Miocene, some early hominids were faced with a very different habitat of widely separated trees. They were probably forced to experiment with savannah food resources.

RA ③ Adaptations for Bipedalism

Important modifications in the skeleton are associated with the move to bipedal locomotion in early hominids. The skeleton opposite is an example of an early bipedal hominid. It is a reconstruction of 'Lucy' (*Australopithecus afarensis*) dated at about 3 million years ago. While Lucy still possessed some ape-like characteristics, such as curved toes, she was a fully-bipedal hominid with all the modern adaptations associated with modern human walking. Lucy was a small individual, only 1.1 meters tall, about the height of a 5-6 year old child. Although there is no doubt that Lucy was habitually bipedal, a number of skeletal features suggest that tree climbing was still an important part of this hominid's niche. Such activities may have been associated with escape from predators, obtaining a secure sleeping place, and foraging for foods found in trees. The features that point to a link with **arboreal** (tree-dwelling) locomotion are indicated on the left of the diagram. *A. afarensis* forms an important link between the quadrupedal locomotion of apes and bipedalism in hominids.

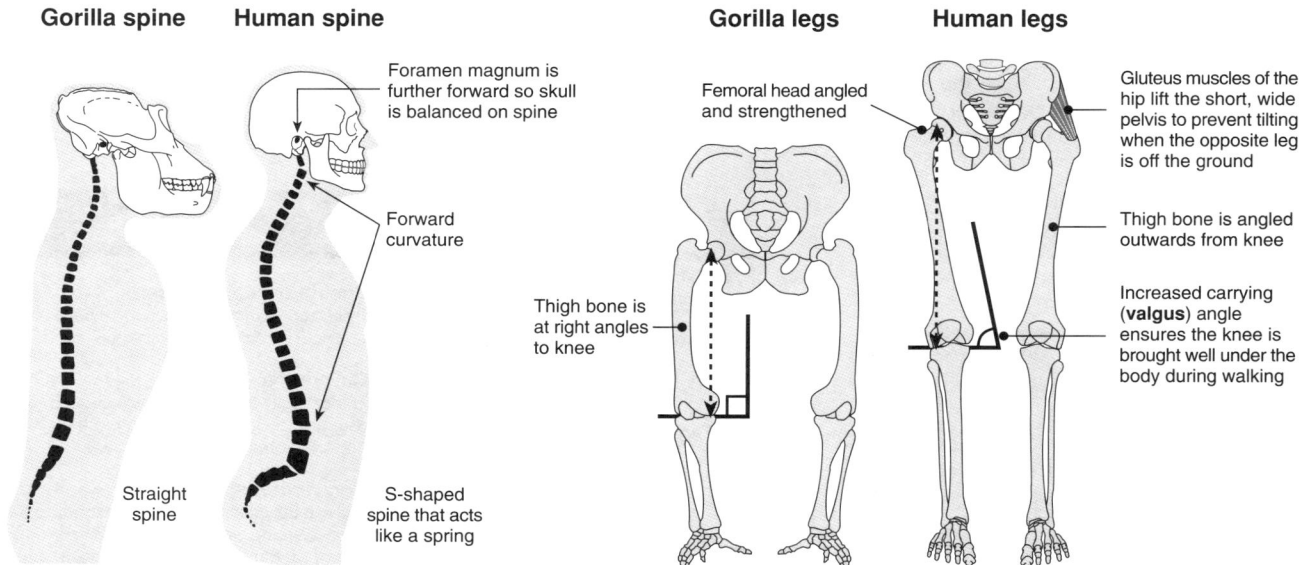

Gorilla spine   **Human spine**

Foramen magnum is further forward so skull is balanced on spine

Forward curvature

Straight spine

S-shaped spine that acts like a spring

Gorilla legs   **Human legs**

Femoral head angled and strengthened

Gluteus muscles of the hip lift the short, wide pelvis to prevent tilting when the opposite leg is off the ground

Thigh bone is angled outwards from knee

Thigh bone is at right angles to knee

Increased carrying (**valgus**) angle ensures the knee is brought well under the body during walking

Chimpanzee	Human	Australopithecine
Lower end of femur	**Lower end of femur**	**Lower end of femur**
Outer (lateral) condyle Inner (medial) condyle	Buttress of bone to prevent sideways deflection of leg muscles	
Chimpanzee foot	**Human foot**	**Australopithecine footprints**
Lighter shading represents points of contact with the ground	Lighter shading represents points of contact with the ground Direction of weight transmission in walking	Footprints thought to belong to an Australopithecine at Laetoli dated at 3.7 mya
Big toe diverges (separate from other toes) Curved toe bones	Big toe aligned with other toes	Heel bone missing from fossil Foot bones (OH8) from Bed I at Olduvai Gorge

1. Referring to the diagram above, describe whether each of the **australopithecine fossils** compare more closely to the *chimpanzee* or *human* examples (i.e. to which do they bear the closest resemblance):

(a) Lower end of femur: _____

(b) Foot prints: _____

(c) Foot skeleton: _____

Lucy's* ape-like characteristics

Shape of the tooth row (dental arcade) is half way between the straight-sided U-shape of an ape jaw and the more rounded, parabolic shape of a human jaw.

Shoulder joint that is orientated towards the head.

Chest (thorax) is funnel-shaped.

Relatively long arms compared to legs.

Wrist has high mobility.

Finger bones are curved.

Relatively short legs.

Toes are long and curved.

Ankle joint is highly mobile.

Redrawn from a photograph by © David L. Brill 1985

*Lucy is the name given to a specimen of *Australopithecus afarensis*

(a) Position of foramen magnum (where the spine enters the skull):

(b) Spine shape:

(c) Pelvis shape and gluteus muscles:

(d) Femur shape and length:

(e) Knee joint:

(f) Shape of foot and arrangement of toe bones:

2. Fill in the boxes, (a) to (f) above, describing the modifications required for habitual bipedal locomotion (walking upright).

3. List **six** possible selection pressures that may have encouraged the development of bipedalism in early hominids:

(a) _____   (d) _____

(b) _____   (e) _____

(c) _____   (f) _____

4. Imagine you are on an expedition to a well known hominid fossil site in east Africa. Name a part of a hominid fossil skeleton that you would wish to find that would be ideal in **clearly indicating bipedalism**:

_____

5. List two selection pressures that may have encouraged the retention of tree-climbing ability in *A. afarensis*:

_____

6. Explain the significance of the **carrying (valgus) angle** in bipedal locomotion of the hominids:

_____

_____

_____

DA 3 The Development of Intelligence

The human brain is an extraordinary organ and is responsible for our unique human behavioral qualities. Although it makes up just 2% of our body weight, it demands about 20% of the body's metabolic energy at rest. This makes the brain an expensive organ to maintain. The selection pressures for increased brain size must have been considerable for additional energy to be made available. The normal human adult brain averages around 1330 cc, but ranges in size between 1000 and 2000 cc. The modern brain contains as many as 10 000 million nerve cells, each of which has thousands of synaptic connections with other nerve cells. But intelligence is not just a function of **brain size**. There are large mammals, such as elephants and whales, with brain volumes greater than ourselves and yet they are not considered to be as intelligent. It appears that what is more important is the brain size relative to body size. Modern humans have a brain volume three times larger than that predicted for an average monkey or ape with our body size. Another important factor is the way in which the brain is organized. Two areas of the brain have become highly developed in modern humans – **Broca's area** concerned with speech and **Wernicke's area** concerned with comprehension of language. Coupled with the brain's evolutionary development is the increasingly complex behavior exhibited by hominids (see the diagram on the facing page).

Brain Volume for Hominid Species

This table provides a generalized summary of the changes in estimated brain volume recorded from fossil remains of hominids. The dates for each species are generally the middle of their time range for long-lived species or the beginning of their time range for short-lived species.

Hominid species	Years ago (mya)	Average brain Volume (cm³)
Australopithecus afarensis	3.5	440
Australopithecus africanus	2.5	450
Paranthropus robustus	2.0	520
Paranthropus boisei	1.5	515
Homo rudolfensis	2.0	700
Homo habilis	1.8	575
Homo ergaster	1.8	800
Homo erectus	0.5	1 100
Homo heidelbergensis	0.2	1 250
Homo neanderthalensis	0.05	1 550
Early Homo sapiens	0.08	1 450

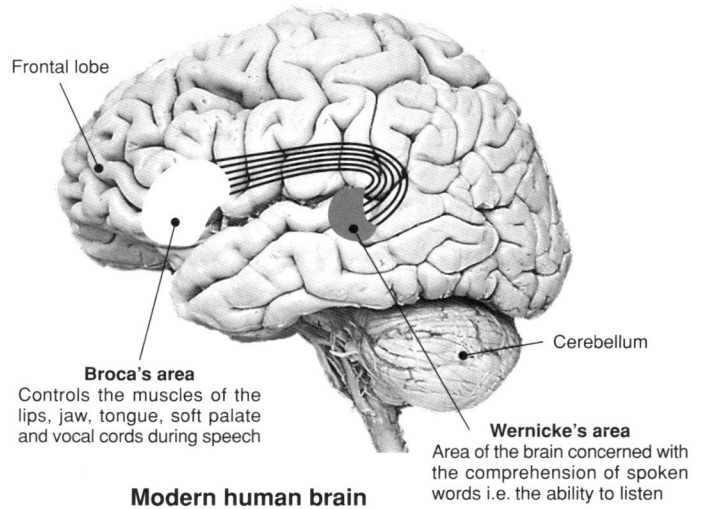

Frontal lobe

Broca's area
Controls the muscles of the lips, jaw, tongue, soft palate and vocal cords during speech

Cerebellum

Wernicke's area
Area of the brain concerned with the comprehension of spoken words i.e. the ability to listen

Modern human brain

Changes in Hominid Brain Volume Over Time

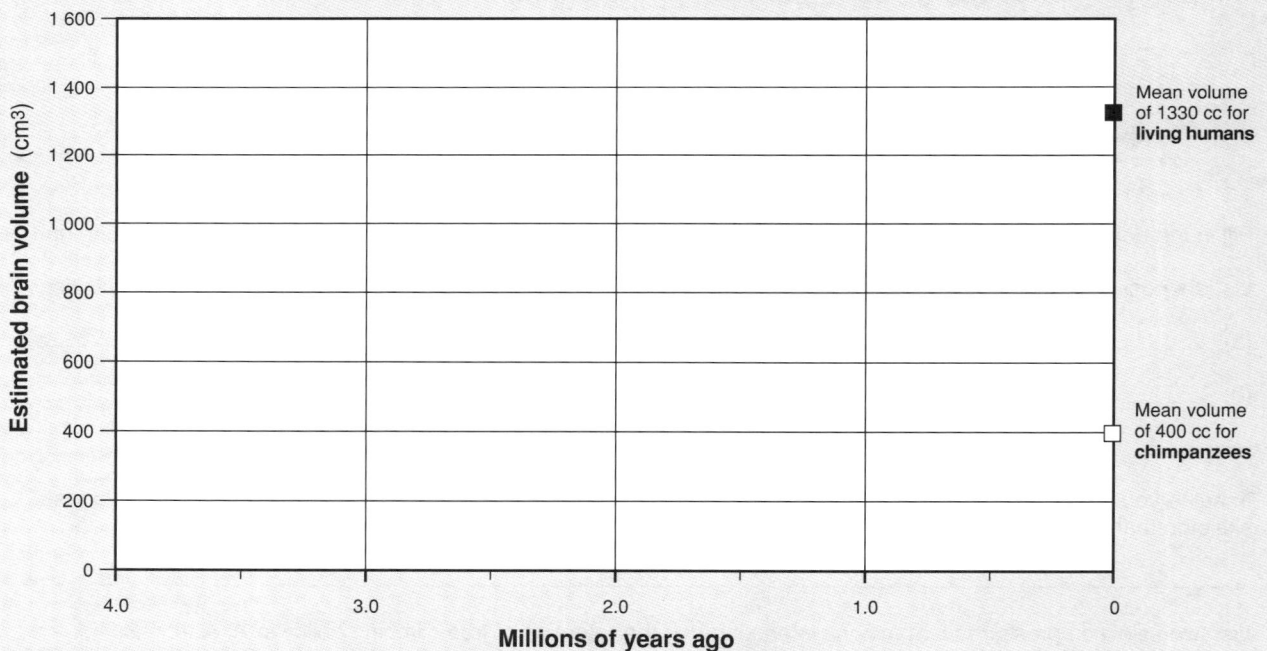

Estimated brain volume (cm³)

■ Mean volume of 1330 cc for **living humans**

□ Mean volume of 400 cc for **chimpanzees**

Millions of years ago

1. Plot the data in the table on the estimated *Brain Volume for Hominid Species* (above) onto the graph provided.

2. There were two 'bursts' (sudden increases) of brain expansion during human evolution. **Indicate on the graph** you have plotted where you think these two events occurred.

3. Explain why brain volume alone is not a good indicator of intelligence: _____

_____

Hunting large game animals

The Modern Human Mind
Creating artifacts and images with symbolic meanings as a means of communication. Using knowledge of animal habits, tools, advanced planning and communication to coordinate the hunting of large game.

Artistic expression of spiritual ideas

Natural History Intelligence
Being able to predict the future using current observations by understanding the habits of potential game, the rhythms of the seasons, and the geography of the landscape such as location of water sources and caves.

Social Intelligence
Language to communicate ideas, plan survival strategies, and coordinate group activities of resource gathering and hunting of increasingly larger game. Group bonding behavior improves survival opportunities for members.

Technical Intelligence
Producing artifacts from mental templates required an understanding of abstract ideas and physical processes: the fracturing behavior of stone, angles of striking stone and how hard to strike, and the trajectory of a thrown projectile.

Enhancing the natural protection of rock shelter

Caring for the elderly

Prolonged infant dependency

Making clothes from animal skins

Toolmaking using flint

Toolmaking using bone and antler

The photos above were taken at *Préhisto-Parc* near Les Eyzies, in southern France. **Top left**: A group of Neanderthals hunting a woolly mammoth by using a concealed pit. **Top Right**: A Cro-Magnon artist at work. **Bottom**: A Cro-Magnon family group at a rock shelter campsite. PHOTOS: Richard Allan

4. State why the brain is considered to be an 'expensive' organ to maintain by the body:

   _____

5. Name a **selection pressure** that might have been acting on early humans to encourage brain development:

   _____

   _____

6. Explain how each of the following areas of human intelligence may have improved the success of early humans:

   (a) Natural history intelligence:_____

   _____

   (b) Social intelligence:_____

   _____

   (c) Technical intelligence:_____

   _____

RA 2 Cultural Evolution

Natural selection acting on the expression of genes brought about considerable transformations in the anatomy of early humans. In addition, is was possible for ideas and behaviors that were learned to be passed on to offspring. This non-genetic means of adaptation, called **cultural evolution**, further enhanced the success of early humans.

Resulting physical features

The physical features that developed in response to selection pressures of the environment include:

Head balanced on the top of the backbone, instead of held up by large neck muscles. Large brain capable of learning, planning and passing on ideas. Very keen eyesight, capable of judging distances with eyes located high above the ground. Other senses are less well developed. Light but strong jaw, with teeth suitable for varied foods. Backbone slightly curved, allowing upright standing on two legs without getting tired, thus freeing hands, and giving eyes good all round vision. Hands able to grasp and manipulate objects in a very sensitive way. Legs that allowed efficient walking and running on two legs. Flexible ankle, but rigid and arched foot, allowing efficient walking on hard ground.

Environmental forces

Over many millions of years, the evolution of human ancestors has been directed by the forces of natural selection. Environmental forces such as climatic change causing alterations in habitat and food supply, as well as fierce predators, acted on the gene pool.

Climatic change

The climate became drier and the forests which were the homes of the earlier primates gradually disappeared. This not only reduced shelter but also meant that traditional food sources became scarce or disappeared. New food resources had to be experimented with.

Fierce predators

Many large and fierce predators made a ground dwelling lifestyle dangerous. Early humans would have to protect themselves from attack using smart behavioral solutions.

Adopted niche

An opportunist/scavenger that was able to live reasonably successfully on the ground. Able to exploit a number of varied habitats, early humans utilized a range of food resources.

Cultural forces

Because of the unique combination of brain and specialized physical features mentioned above, early humans very gradually began to direct the course of their own evolution. They began to control their environment; to use it to alter their way of life. At first they did this in small ways, and with little effect on other living things. The result was the development of efficient hunters living in organized groups. Their genes had been almost unchanged, but they now lived more comfortably, with a better survival rate, and more time to plan ahead.

Tool making
Tools made by chipping stones, or shaping bones or wood were used in a wide variety of ways. In some cases, the use of tools replaced the need to develop physical features.

Fire making
Fire is a powerful tool. It provided a means of keeping warm in cold periods, deterring predators from a camp site, and driving animals during a hunt. It was also used to cook, allowing difficult to digest food to be eaten more easily.

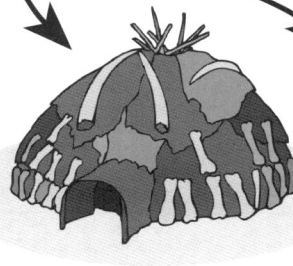

Shelter and clothing
The earliest shelters were probably natural ones, such as caves, overhangs and large trees. Creating artificial shelters allowed flexibility in where they were located. Clothing enhanced their ability to withstand cold.

Cooperative hunting
Working in organized groups requiring considerable coordination, early humans were able to tackle large game that would be impossible for a solitary hunter.

1. Explain what is meant by **cultural evolution:** _____

_____

_____

Development of Agriculture

People learned to plant and look after food plants, especially grains, and to domesticate animals. In the Middle East, about 8000 BC they learned to grow wheat, while in Mexico, about 500 BC they began to grow maize.

Maize
(Central America)

Rice (Asia)

Wheat
(Middle East)

Donkey

Bactrian camel

Goat

Sheep

Development of Stable Settlements

Communities of successful grain cultivators grew up, living in permanent, stable settlements of quite large size. Such people developed qualities such as patience, industry and a sense of property, and prepared the way for the next step.

Development of Cities

As communities became larger, trade and commerce began to develop. Large cities grew up where markets and trading systems developed. These were places where people could develop special skills - pottery, metal work, etc. It also resulted in rivalry between states and in wars.

The Present and the Future

Humankind's success has given us the two problems of over-population and pollution that threaten to destroy us. Not only can we modify our environment, but because of our knowledge of genetics, we are actually directing the evolution of other living things by selective breeding. It even seems likely that we may soon be able to direct our own evolution by actually altering genes. In fact we are reaching a stage where we have so much power to change that we need to think and act very carefully.

The Knowledge Explosion

The sharing of ideas, and more free time for some in the cities resulted in a great speeding up of cultural evolution. In the last 200 years there has been a very rapid development of science and technology. Humankind developed the power to dominate the environment completely. In particular, medical science has largely solved the problems of infectious disease, and technology has allowed us to produce material wealth at a staggering rate.

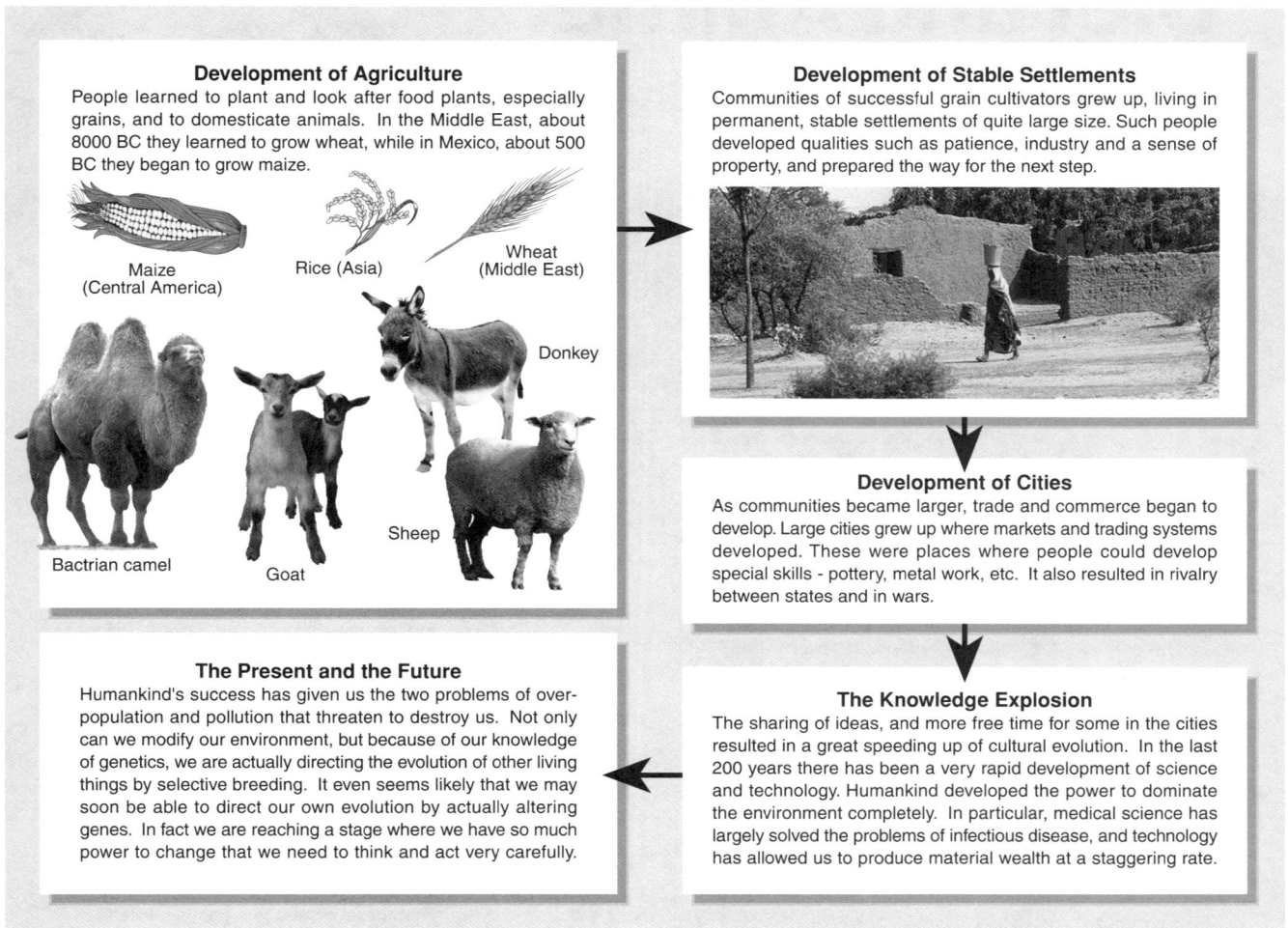

The move from opportunist scavenger to hunter/gatherer was a major stage in mankind's cultural evolution. It was taken in a series of small steps, over a very long time - perhaps a million years. A few human societies, such as the Australian aborigines last century, were still at this stage until very recently.

2. List 2 effects that a drying climate would have had on the selection pressures directing the evolution of early hominids:

_____

_____

_____

3. Explain briefly how each of the cultural developments listed below enhanced the survival capacity of early humans:

(a) Manufacture of bone and stone tools: _____

_____

(b) Shelters and clothing: _____

_____

(c) Use of fire: _____

_____

(d) Cooperative hunting: _____

_____

(e) Development of agriculture: _____

_____

(f) Commerce and communication: _____

_____

Diet and Animal Nutrition

IB SL

Complete nos:
1, 11-12, 15, 18, 20, 22, 25-26
Extension: 2-3

IB HL

Complete nos:
1, 11-12, 15, 18, 20, 22, 25-26
Extension: 2-3

IB Options

Complete nos:
Option A: 28-38
Option H: 13-14, 16-17, 19, 21 23-24, 26-27

AP Biology

Complete nos:
1-27
Some numbers extension as appropriate

Learning Objectives

□ 1. Compile your own glossary from the **KEY WORDS** displayed in **bold type** in the learning objectives below.

Modes of nutrition *(page 158)*

□ 2. Using named examples, distinguish between the broadly different modes of nutrition: **autotrophic**, chemoheterotrophic (=**heterotrophic**). Identify the source of energy and carbon in each case. Define **nutrient** and describe their general role.

Heterotrophic nutrition *(page 158)*

□ 3. Recall the terms: **heterotroph** and **heterotrophic nutrition**. Explain why animals need to feed. Describe the three principal modes of heterotrophic nutrition: **parasitic**, **saprophytic** (=**saprobiontic**), **holozoic**.

Saprophytic nutrition *(pages 158-159)*

□ 4. Describe **saprophytic nutrition** as illustrated by the bread mold *Rhizopus*. Identify the structural adaptations of the fungus, the type of food utilized, nutrients and other growth requirements, and the method by which the food is digested and absorbed.

Parasitic nutrition *(pages 158, 160)*

□ 5. Describe the **parasitic nutrition** of a typical cestode **parasite** as illustrated by the pork tapeworm *Taenia solium*. Identify the structural adaptations of the parasite, the type of food utilized, nutrients and other growth requirements, and the method by which the food is digested and absorbed.

Mutualistic nutrition *(pages 158, 161)*

□ 6. Explain what is meant by **mutualistic nutrition** as illustrated by the nutritional relationship between:
  • Nitrogen-fixing bacterium *Rhizobium* and members of the legume family.
  • Cellulose digesting bacteria and ruminants. Identify the location of the bacteria in the ruminant gut.

Holozoic nutrition *(pages 158, 162-173)*

□ 7. Define the term **holozoic nutrition**. Recognize that holozoic nutrition is the most common nutritional mode amongst animals. Providing examples, describe structural and functional diversity in the guts and feeding appendages of animals. In your descriptions, you may wish to compare different phyla, as well as making comparisions within the same order.

□ 8. Classify holozoic animals according to the type of food eaten: e.g. **carnivore**, **omnivore**, **herbivore**, and according to the form of the food they take in e.g. large or small particles, or fluid.

□ 9. Recognize diversity in **feeding methods** amongst holozoic animals by describing the structures and processes involved in: *fluid feeding, filter feeding, deposit feeding, cropping, bulk feeding.*

□ 10. Identify and describe the adaptations of mammalian **herbivores** and **carnivores**, as illustrated by a named **ruminant** and a named carnivore. Include reference to:
  • *Gut length and the relative capacity of gut regions.*
  • *The structure of the stomach (simple vs complex).*
  • *The digestive enzymes present and the role of microbial digestion in nutrition and protein intake.*
  • *The type and arrangement of teeth (the dentition).*

  In each case, explain the significance of the adaptation with reference to the processing of the food eaten.

□ 11. Briefly describe the four stages involved in processing food: **ingestion**, **digestion**, **absorption**, and **egestion**. On a simple diagram, summarize the location of these processes in a generalized **alimentary canal** (**gut**).

Digestion and absorption in humans

Enzymes and digestion *(pages 172-175, 178)*

□ 12. Explain the need for **enzymes** in digestion. Identify broad categories of digestive enzymes.

□ 13. Identify the digestive in humans and their secretions. Describe the composition of **saliva**, **gastric juice**, and **pancreatic juice**. Explain the role of these in providing the optimum pH for enzyme activity.

□ 14. Draw and explain the structural features of **exocrine glands** as seen using electron microscopy.

□ 15. Describe the sites of production (source), **substrate**, products (of digestion) and optimum pH conditions for (at least) one **amylase**, **protease**, and **lipase** enzyme.

□ 16. Explain why protein-digesting enzymes (e.g. pepsin and trypsin) are secreted as inactive precursors. State how they are activated at their site of action.

□ 17. Identify examples of membrane-bound enzymes in the epithelium of the small intestine and outline their role in digestion. Describe the action of **endopeptidases** and **exopeptidases**.

□ 18. Draw a diagram of the digestive system in humans. Include reference to: *mouth, esophagus, stomach, liver, small and large intestine, anus, pancreas, and gall bladder*. Separately, or by annotating your diagram, outline the function of the **stomach** and **small intestine**.

□ 19. Describe the composition and secretion of **bile**. Explain the problem of lipid digestion in a hydrophilic medium and the role of bile in overcoming this problem.

Absorption and transport *(pages 171-177, 179)*

□ 20. Distinguish between **absorption** and **assimilation**. Identify where each of the following is absorbed: water, small molecules (alcohol, glucose), breakdown products of carbohydrate, protein, and fat digestion.

□ 21. Draw a portion of the **ileum** in transverse section as seen using light microscopy. Your diagram should show the basic features including the **mucosa** and layers of **longitudinal** and **circular muscle**.

☐ 22. Describe the structure of a villus (including blood and lymph vessels). In general terms, describe how the structure is related to its role in absorption.

☐ 23. Explain the structural features of an epithelial cell of a villus as seen using electron microscopy. Include reference to the following: **microvilli, mitochondria, pinocytotic vesicles**, and **tight junctions**.

☐ 24. Describe the mechanisms by which various nutrients are absorbed in the ileum, including the roles of **diffusion, facilitated diffusion**, and **active transport** (including **endocytosis**). Appreciate the role of micelles and chylomicrons in lipid absorption and transport.

☐ 25. Separately, or on an annotated diagram (#18), outline the function of the **large intestine**.

☐ 26. List the materials that are not absorbed and are **egested** and, if required, explain why they remain undigested. Explain the role of the large intestine and rectum in feces formation and egestion.

☐ 27. Outline the control of digestive secretion by nerves and hormones. Identify the roles of *gastrin, secretin,* and/or *cholecystokinin* and include reference to the origin of the hormone, its action, and the stimulus for its release.

Diet and health *(pages 26, 44-45,180-183, 258-259, also see SB 1: The Chemistry of Life)*

☐ 28. Recall the definition of the term **nutrient**. List the constituents of a **diet**, explaining the functions of each. Describe the basis of a **balanced diet** and recognize the role of adequate nutrition in health.

☐ 29. Understand nutritional requirements with reference to total energy intake, total fat and proportion of saturated and unsaturated fat, dietary fiber, sodium, and sugars. Evaluate common packaged food items by interpreting the dietary information printed on them. Calculate, compare, and evaluate the nutritional content (including energy values) of named foods and diets.

☐ 30. Discuss how energy needs may vary according to age, gender, **activity** level and **basal metabolic rate**, and condition (e.g. **lean body mass**).

☐ 31. List two sources of each of the following in the diet: monosaccharides, disaccharides, and polysaccharides. Outline the uses of absorbed carbohydrates.

☐ 32. List three sources of lipids in the diet. Outline the uses of absorbed lipids. Discuss the significance of high-lipid diets in relation to **obesity** and **coronary heart disease**. Explain the significance of saturated and unsaturated lipids in relation to a healthy diet.

☐ 33. Understand that cholesterol is synthesized in the liver. Outline the role of cholesterol in the body (e.g. as a component of membranes and some hormones).

☐ 34. List four sources of protein in the diet. Outline the fate of ingested protein, including reference to **protein synthesis**, **essential amino acids**, and **deamination**.

☐ 35. Explain the general importance of vitamins, minerals, and **fiber** in the diet. For each of the following vitamins or minerals, state (at least) one function in the body. If required, also identify the result of deficiency, especially with respect to **vegan** and **vegetarian diets**.
   • **Retinol** (vitamin A), **ascorbic acid** (vitamin C), **tocopherol** (vitamin E), **iodine**, and **zinc**.
   • **Calciferol** (vitamin D) and **cyanocobalamin** (vitamin B_{12}), including disorders arising from deficiencies.
   • **Calcium** and **iron**, including the disorders arising from deficiencies (anemia and osteoporosis).

☐ 36. Discuss the ethical issues surrounding the eating of meat, fish, eggs, and dairy products, including the rationale for the vegetarian or vegan choice.

☐ 37. Define **malnutrition** and distinguish it from starvation. Suggest how malnutrition can be caused by any of a number of social, economic, cultural, or environmental factors, alone or in combination. Using published quantitative data, discuss one example of global malnutrition, e.g. obesity, marasmus, anorexia nervosa.

☐ 38. List and describe the role of chemical additives in food. Outline possible harmful effects of named food additives. Explain the importance of proper hygiene in food handling and preparation. *NOTE: This objective, and material for it, will be developed in future editions.*

Textbooks

See the 'Textbook Reference Grid' on pages 8-9 for textbook page references relating to material in this topic.

Supplementary Texts
See pages 5-6 for additional details of this text:

■ Clegg, C.J., 1998. **Mammals: Structure and Function** (John Murray), pp. 12-23.

Periodicals

See page 6 for details of publishers of periodicals:
STUDENT'S REFERENCE

■ **The Pancreas and Pancreatitis** Biol. Sci. Rev., 13(5) May 2001, pp. 2-6. *The structure and role of the pancreas, including acinar cell secretion.*

■ **Rumen Microbiology** Biol. Sci. Rev., 14 (4) April 2002, pp. 14-17. *An excellent account of the role of microorganisms in ruminant digestion.*

■ **Unknown Quantity** New Scientist, 27 February 1999, pp. 18-19. *The damaging effects of vitamin megadoses: what are safe maximum doses?*

■ **Vital Vitamins** Biol. Sci. Rev., 11(5) May 1999, pp. 32-35. *The role of dietary vitamins, including the details of various vitamin deficiencies.*

■ **Food Glorious Food** New Scientist, 18 Oct. 1997, (Inside Science). *Protective and high risk foods, the role of carbohydrates and fiber, and aspects of diet-related health and disease.*

■ **Minerals and Bioavailability** Biol. Sci. Rev., 12 (5) May 2000, pp. 38-40. *The role of minerals in the diet, including reference to how easily they become available for use.*

■ **The Happy Fat** New Scientist, 24 August 2002, pp. 34-37. *The right amount of the right type of fat in the diet is important in mood stability.*

■ **Obesity: A Weighty Problem** Biol. Sci. Rev., 10(1) Sept. 1997, pp. 17-20. *Human diet, the energy intake equation, and an examination of the genetic and environmental causes of obesity.*

■ **Eating Disorders: Myths and Misconceptions** Biol. Sci. Rev., 9(5) May 1997, pp. 25-27. *The causes and treatments of eating disorders.*

■ **Salt: the Origin of Hypertension** Biol. Sci. Rev., 12(5) May 2000, pp. 35-37. *The role of salt in hypertensive disorders in humans.*

TEACHER'S REFERENCE

■ **Rebuilding the Food Pyramid** Scientific American, January 2003, pp. 52-59. *A major revision of the basic nutritional guidelines provided for consumers and health professionals. A critique of dietary information and an analysis of what we should be eating now (a good topic for debate).*

■ **Cut the Carbs** New Scientist, 18 March 2000, pp. 26-31. *An analysis of human dietary fads, and an excellent synopsis of basic nutritional guidelines. A comparison of carnivore and herbivore guts is included.*

■ **Protein at a Price** New Scientist, 18 March 2000, pp. 32-36 and see p. 45. *Across the globe people are eating more meat. Are livestock eating grain that could be feeding the world's poor?*

Internet WWW

See pages 10-11 for details of how to access **Bio Links** from our web site: **www.thebiozone.com**. From Bio Links, access sites under the topics:

GENERAL BIOLOGY ONLINE RESOURCES > Online Textbooks and Lecture Notes • An on-line biology book • Learn.co.uk *... and others*

ANIMAL BIOLOGY: • Anatomy and physiology • Comparative vertebrate anatomy lecture notes • Human physiology lecture notes • Froguts.com • Web Anatomy *... and others* **Nutrition:** • Human anatomy online - Digestive system • Large intestine: Introduction and index • Nutrient requirements • The pancreas • Your digestive system and how it works *... & others*

BIODIVERSITY: • Will's skull page

HEALTH AND DISEASE > Human Health Issues: Eating disorders Food additives guide • Food safety and nutrition info *... and others*

Software and video resources are now provided in the Teacher Resource Handbook

Modes of Nutrition

A 2

The way in which living organisms obtain their source of energy and carbon is termed their nutritional mode. There is a great diversity in nutritional modes amongst different phyla, with the prokaryotes (bacteria) showing the greatest variety in terms of the range of organic and inorganic compounds used as energy sources. The diagram below illustrates the classification of nutritional modes in living organisms. The diagram simplifies the real situation and concentrates on the diversity within eukaryotic groups. Aspects of nutrition in a typical saprophyte and a specialized mammalian parasite are described later in this topic.

Nutritional Patterns in Organisms

Living organisms can be classified according to their source of energy and carbon. According to their **energy source**, organisms are classified as either **phototrophs** (using light as their main energy source) or **chemotrophs** (using inorganic or organic compounds for energy). As a **carbon source**, **autotrophs** (*self-feeders*) use carbon dioxide, and **heterotrophs** (*feeders on others*) need an organic carbon source. Most organisms are either photoautotrophs, chemoautotrophs, or chemoheterotrophs. Prokaryotes show a huge variety of nutritional modes. Many are photo- or chemoautotrophs (chemosynthetic) but a large number are chemoheterotrophs (as are animals and fungi). For many, the energy and carbon source is glucose.

Heterotrophic Nutrition (Chemoheterotrophs*)

Most of the bacteria with which we are familiar are chemoheterotrophs.

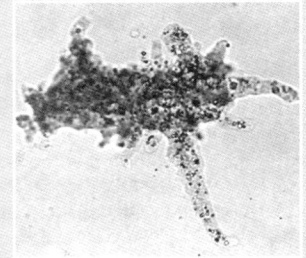

Protozoans, such as *Amoeba*, engulf food particles by phagocytosis.

* A few bacterial groups are photoheterotrophic.

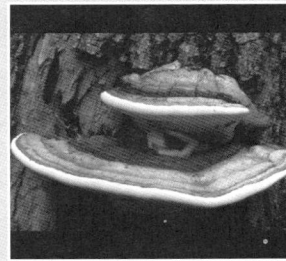

Autotrophic Nutrition

Photoautotrophs: Photosynthetic bacteria, cyanobacteria, algae, plants.

Chemoautotrophs: Sulfur, iron, hydrogen, and nitrifying bacteria.

Fungi may be saprophytic (see below), parasitic, or mutualistic.

Feeding provides animals with a carbon and energy source: glucose.

Nutritional Modes of Heterotrophs

Heterotrophic organisms feed on organic material in order to obtain the energy and nutrients they require. They depend either directly on other organisms (dead or alive), or their by-products (e.g., feces, cell walls, or food stores). There are three principal modes of heterotrophic nutrition: saprophytic (saprotrophic), parasitic, and holozoic. Within the animal phyla, holozoic nutrition is the most common nutritional mode.

Most fungi and many bacteria are saprophytes (also called saprotrophs). They are decomposer organisms feeding off dead or decaying matter.

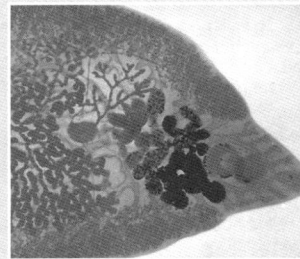

Parasites, e.g., flukes, live on or within their host for much or all of their life. Bacteria, fungi, protists, and animals all have parasitic representatives.

Holozoic means to feed on solid organic material from the bodies of other organisms. It is the main feeding mode of animals, although a few specialized plants may obtain some nutrients this way. Holozoic animals are classified according to the form of the food they take in: small or large particles, or fluid.

1. Explain what is meant by the following terms:

    (a) Photoautotroph: _____

    _____

    (b) Chemoautotroph: _____

    _____

    (c) Chemoheterotroph: _____

    _____

2. Give two examples of saprophytes: _____

Saprophytic Nutrition

A 2

All fungi lack chlorophyll and are **heterotrophic**, absorbing nutrients by direct absorption from the substrate. Many are **saprophytic** (=saprotrophic or saprobiontic), feeding on dead organic matter, although some are parasitic or live in a relationship with another organism (mutualistic). Parasitic fungi are common plant pathogens, invading plant tissues through stomata, wounds, or by penetrating the epidermis. Mutualistic fungi are very important: they form lichens in association with algae or cyanobacteria, and the mutualistic mycorrhizal associations between fungi and plant roots are essential to the health of many forest plants. Saprophytic fungi, together with bacteria, are the major decomposers of the biosphere. They contribute to decay and therefore to nutrient recycling. Like all fungi, the body is composed of rapidly growing filaments called **hyphae**, which are **usually** divided by incomplete compartments called **septa**. The hyphae together form a large mass called a **mycelium** (the feeding body of the fungus). The familiar mushroom-like structures that we see are the above-ground reproductive bodies that arise from the main mycelium. The nutrition of a typical saprophyte, *Rhizopus*, is outlined below.

Saprophytic Nutrition in *Rhizopus*

Saprophytes grow best in dark, moist environments, but are found wherever organic material is available. Much of a fungus is composed of water, so a moist environment is essential. Saprophytic fungi secrete enzymes from the hyphal tips. Digestion occurs outside the fungal body and the small molecules are then absorbed by the hyphae across the chitinous cell wall and the plasma membrane. Nutrients are then transported to all parts of the fungus. Excess nutrients are stored within the mycelium as glycogen.

Nutrients required by most saprophytes

An organic carbon source, e.g. starch, cellulose, glucose.   A source of nitrogen   Growth factors such as vitamins   Some ions, e.g. magnesium, phosphorus, trace elements

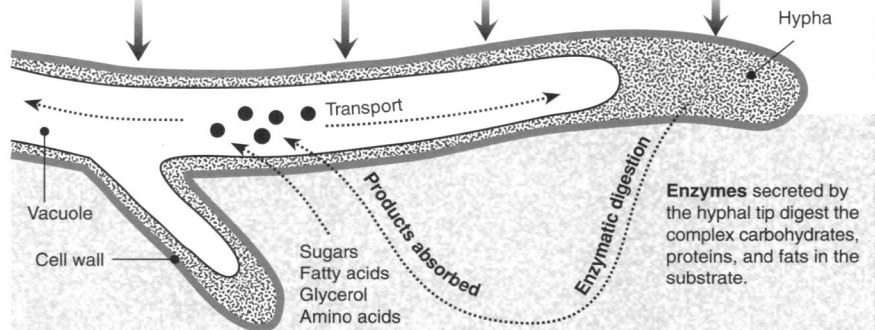

Bread mold (*Rhizopus*)

Rhizopus is a common fungus, found on damp, stale bread and rotting fruit. Unlike many fungi, *Rhizopus* has hyphae that are undivided by septa.

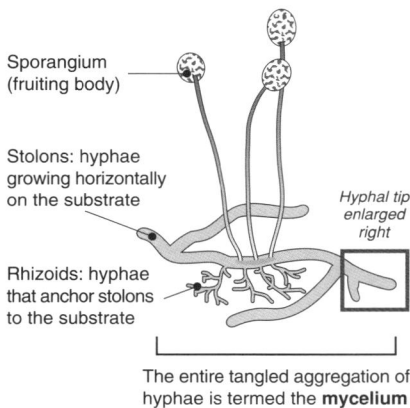

Sporangium (fruiting body)

Stolons: hyphae growing horizontally on the substrate

Hyphal tip enlarged right

Rhizoids: hyphae that anchor stolons to the substrate

The entire tangled aggregation of hyphae is termed the **mycelium**

Hypha

Transport

Vacuole

Cell wall

Sugars
Fatty acids
Glycerol
Amino acids

Products absorbed

Enzymatic digestion

Enzymes secreted by the hyphal tip digest the complex carbohydrates, proteins, and fats in the substrate.

Environmental requirements

The environmental requirements of fungi are met by the substrate on which they are growing:

■ Temperature between 5° and 25°C   ■ Oxygen (very few fungi are anaerobic)
■ Water (the fungal body is about 90% water)   ■ Neutral to slightly acid pH (pH 5.6-7) .

1. (a) Clearly describe the structure of the feeding body of a saprophytic fungus: _____

_____

(b) Explain why a moist environment is essential for fungal growth: _____

2. List four nutrients required by a saprophytic fungus:

(a) _____   (c) _____

(b) _____   (d) _____

3. State where these nutrients come from: _____

_____

4. **Describe** the way in which a saprophytic fungus obtains its nutrients: _____

_____

_____

5. Contrast digestion and absorption in a saprophytic fungus and a holozoic animal: _____

_____

_____

Parasitic Nutrition

RA 2

Parasitism is the most common of all symbiotic relationships. Here the host is always harmed by the presence of the parasite but is usually not killed. The main benefit derived by the parasite is obtaining nutrition, but there may be secondary advantages, such as protection. Many animal groups have members that have adopted a **parasitic** lifestyle, although parasites occur more commonly in particular taxa. Insects, some annelids (e.g. leeches), and flatworms have many parasitic representatives, and two classes of flatworms are entirely parasitic. Animal parasites are highly specialized carnivores, feeding off the body fluids or skin of host species. Parasites that attach to the outside of a host are called **ectoparasites** and have mouthparts specialized for piercing and sucking blood or tissue fluids. Those that live within the body of the host are called **endoparasites**. They may obtain nutrients by sucking or absorb simple food compounds directly from the host, as in the case of the pork tapeworm shown below. All 3,400 or so species of tapeworm are endoparasites and the majority are adapted for living in the guts of vertebrates. In all species, a primary host and one or more intermediate hosts are required to complete the life cycle.

Parasitic Nutrition in the Pork Tapeworm (*Taenia solium*)

Tapeworms (cestodes) are a specialized class of flatworms adapted to a parasitic lifestyle in the intestines of vertebrates. Features of the pork tapeworm, *Taenia solium*, illustrate adaptations to obtaining nutrition at the expense of the host. Humans are the only primary host (the host for the adult stage). When the eggs are passed from humans in the feces, they may be swallowed by a pig or other mammal, whereupon they hatch and can be reingested by the primary host when the pig flesh is eaten. Tapeworms have no mouth or digestive system, and they do not produce digestive enzymes. They are protected by the host's body and bathed in the host's digested food, which is absorbed over the tapeworm's entire body. The entire length of the worm is covered in a thick, enzyme-resistant cuticle, which protects it from the host's digestive enzymes.

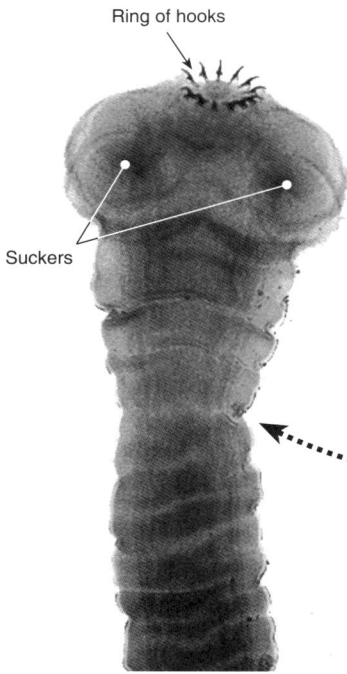

Ring of hooks

Suckers

Enlargement of scolex (head) of *Taenia solium*

Photo: CDC

Gut wall

New segments

Gut lumen

Ripe segments full of eggs are passed out with the feces to be ingested by a pig (the secondary or intermediate host).

Respiration is anaerobic as an adaptation to the low oxygen environment in the gut.

Up to 1000 segments (proglottids) make up the worm. Total length up to 8 meters.

The tapeworm is attached in the gut wall of a human (the primary host) by hooks and suckers on the scolex. Most of the body is floating free within the gut lumen.

1. Describe the way in which the pork tapeworm obtains its required nutrition: _____

_____

2. Briefly describe four adaptations of the pork tapeworm for its parasitic lifestyle (include two nutritional adaptations):

   (a) _____

   (b) _____

   (c) _____

   (d) _____

3. (a) Explain what is meant by a primary host: _____

   (b) Explain what is meant by an intermediate host: _____

   (c) Name the primary host for the pork tapeworm: _____

   (d) Name an intermediate host for the pork tapeworm: _____

4. Identify a similarity between the nutrition of a tapeworm and the nutrition of a saprophytic fungus (see previous page):

_____

5. Name another animal parasite and give its primary host: _____

Mutualistic Nutrition

Although nitrogen is an abundant element, making up about 80% of the Earth's atmosphere, biologically available nitrogen compounds are relatively scarce. Atmospheric nitrogen (N_2) is stable, and a lot of energy is required to break the dinitrogen bond and form organic compounds. However, many prokaryotes are able to do this, and plants that can use bacteria to fix nitrogen have a great nutritional advantage. Much of the nitrogen available to plants is supplied by nitrogen-fixing bacteria. These bacteria reduce atmospheric nitrogen to ammonium ions, combining them with organic acids to produce amino acids. The amino acids provide a nitrogen supply to plants. Nitrogen fixation in plants occurs within **root nodules** - unique associations or **symbioses** between plants and nitrogen fixing bacteria. The presence of nodules allows plants to grow successfully even when soil nitrate is low. When the plant dies, the nitrogen is returned to the soil through decomposition. For this reason, nitrogen fixing plants (particularly legumes) are important in soil management, and promote natural soil fertility when used in crop rotations.

Nitrogen Fixation in Root Nodules

Root nodules are a root **symbiosis** between a higher plant and a bacterium. The bacteria fix atmospheric nitrogen and are extremely important to the nutrition of many plants, including the economically important legume family. Root nodules are extensions of the root tissue caused by entry of a bacterium. In legumes, this bacterium is *Rhizobium*. Other bacterial genera are involved in the root nodule symbioses in non-legume species.

The bacteria in these symbioses live in the nodule where they fix atmospheric nitrogen and provide the plant with most, or all, of its nitrogen requirements. In return, they have access to a rich supply of carbohydrate. The fixation of atmospheric nitrogen to ammonia occurs within the nodule, using the enzyme **nitrogenase**. Nitrogenase is inhibited by oxygen and the nodule provides a low O_2 environment in which fixation can occur.

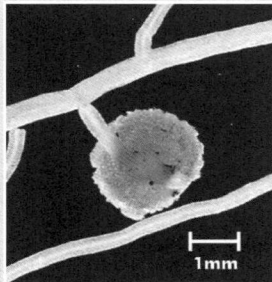

Two examples of legume nodules caused by *Rhizobium*. The photographs above show the size of a single nodule (left), and the nodules forming clusters around the roots of *Acacia* (right).

Root Nodules in Legumes

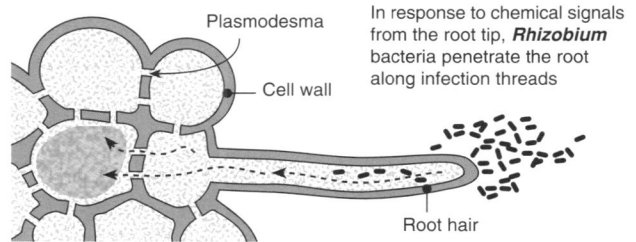

Plasmodesma

Cell wall

In response to chemical signals from the root tip, *Rhizobium* bacteria penetrate the root along infection threads

Root hair

After infecting a root, the bacteria produce a hormone-like chemical, which induces the formation of the enlarged nodule. *Rhizobium* bacteria are free living in the soil, but adopt a large bacteroid morphology when they invade a root and induce nodule formation.

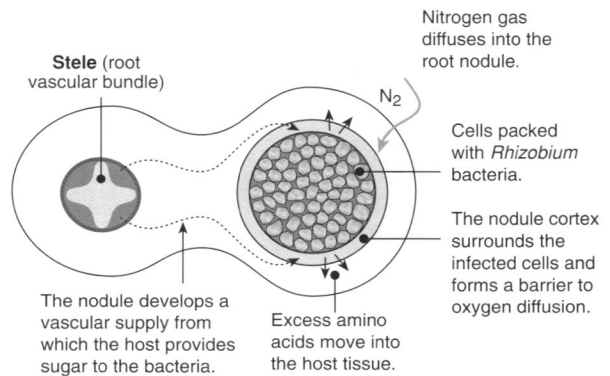

Stele (root vascular bundle)

Nitrogen gas diffuses into the root nodule.

N_2

Cells packed with *Rhizobium* bacteria.

The nodule cortex surrounds the infected cells and forms a barrier to oxygen diffusion.

The nodule develops a vascular supply from which the host provides sugar to the bacteria.

Excess amino acids move into the host tissue.

1. Define symbiosis in relation to plants and nitrogen fixing bacteria: _____

_____

2. Root nodules are a mutualistic relationship between a bacterium and a plant. Explain the benefits of the relationship to:

(a) The plant: _____

_____

(b) The bacterium: _____

_____

3. Name the bacterial genus involved in root nodule formation in legumes: _____

4. Explain the purpose of the following features of a root nodule:

(a) The nodule cortex: _____

(b) The vascular supply to the nodule: _____

5. List two examples of leguminous plants: _____

6. Identify the stimulus for the formation of the enlarged nodule: _____

Insect Mouthparts

RA 1

Insect mouthparts consist of the labrum and three sets of modified, paired appendages known as the mandibles, maxillae, and labium. They are variously adapted to tackle different diets and, in some cases, this has involved loss or fusion of some of the paired appendages. In chewing insects, the **labrum** forms an upper lip and helps pull food into the mouth. The **mandibles** form the first pair of mouthparts and are used as jaws to chew, cut, and tear food, and may also be used to carry things, fight (see right), or to mold wax. The **maxillae** (and palps) form the second pair of mouthparts and are used for food sensing and handling. The **labium**, with its palps, is a single structure and acts as a lower lip to close the mouth. The particular form of the mouthparts depends on the diet, and sometimes on the life stage. In many insects, metamorphosis from the larval to adult stage involves a structural and functional change in the mouthparts associated with a change in diet.

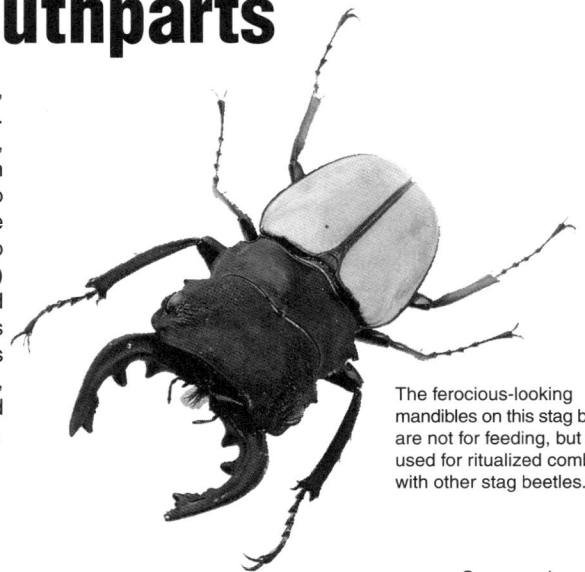

The ferocious-looking mandibles on this stag beetle are not for feeding, but are used for ritualized combat with other stag beetles.

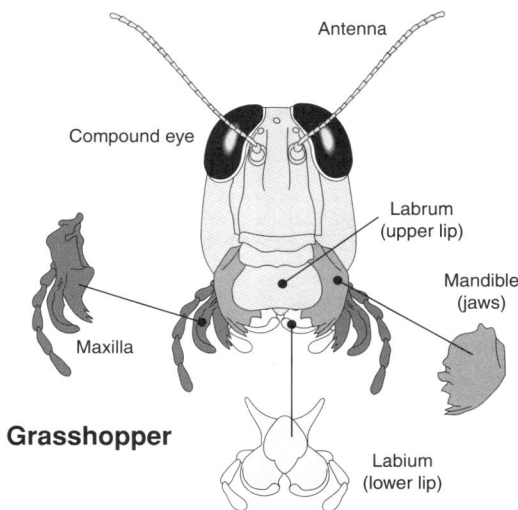

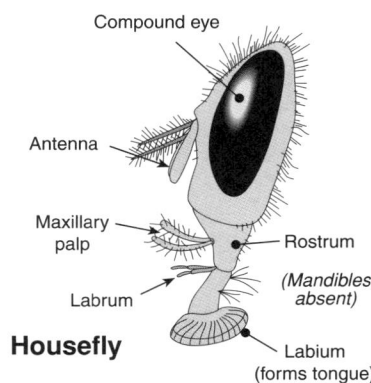

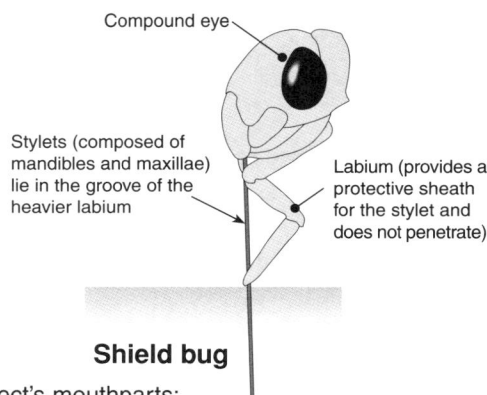

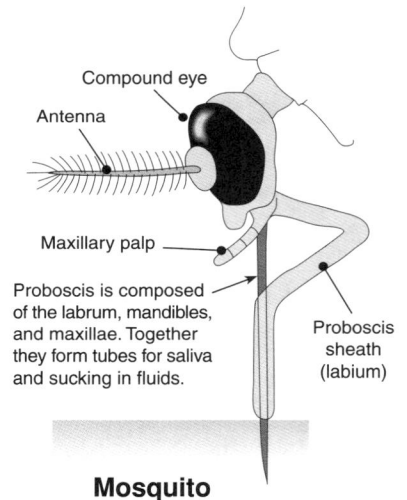

Grasshopper

Antenna
Compound eye
Labrum (upper lip)
Mandible (jaws)
Maxilla
Labium (lower lip)

Housefly

Compound eye
Antenna
Maxillary palp
Labrum
Rostrum
(Mandibles absent)
Labium (forms tongue)

Butterfly

Compound eye
Antenna
Labial palp
Maxillary proboscis

Honey bee (worker)

Compound eye
Antenna
Mandible
Maxillary palp
Galea (modified maxilla)
Glossa (tongue)
Labial palp

Shield bug

Compound eye
Stylets (composed of mandibles and maxillae) lie in the groove of the heavier labium
Labium (provides a protective sheath for the stylet and does not penetrate)

Mosquito

Compound eye
Antenna
Maxillary palp
Proboscis is composed of the labrum, mandibles, and maxillae. Together they form tubes for saliva and sucking in fluids.
Proboscis sheath (labium)

1. Name the four main parts of an insect's mouthparts:

_____

2. Name the four main modes of feeding carried out by the various insect groups: _____

_____

3. Match the following list of insects with their correct mode of feeding: *locust, bee, biting fly, moth, mosquito, beetle, cicada, housefly, flea, dragonfly, aphid, maggot*. There may be more than one example for each feeding mode.

   (a) Chewing: _____   (e) Sucking: _____

   (b) Sponging: _____   (f) Piercing/sponging: _____

   (c) Chewing/lapping: _____   (g) Piercing/sucking: _____

   (d) Seizing/chewing: _____   (h) Sucking with mouth hooks: _____

Insect A   Insect B   Insect C   Insect D   Insect E

4. For each of the photographs of insects above (A - E), identify the **type of insect** and the structures labeled (a)-(q). Note that some of the labeled structures are not mouthparts:

Identity of **insect A**:_____

    (a) _____   (c) _____

    (b) _____

Identity of **insect B**:_____

    (d) _____   (f) _____

    (e) _____

Identity of **insect C**:_____

    (g) _____   (i) _____

    (h) _____

Identity of **insect D**:_____

    (j) _____   (l) _____

    (k) _____

Identity of **insect E**:_____

    (m) _____   (p) _____

    (n) _____   (q) _____

    (o) _____

5. The diagrams on the right illustrate the arrangement of the mouthparts for various insects. Use highlighter pens to create a color key and color in each type of mouthpart.

6. Many insects undergo metamorphosis at certain stages in their life cycle. Butterflies start their active life as caterpillars, after which they pass through a pupal stage, to finally emerge as butterflies. Comment on the diets and changes to the mouthparts of caterpillars and their adult forms (butterflies):

    (a) Caterpillar diet: _____

        Mouthparts: _____

        _____

    (b) Butterfly diet: _____

        Mouthparts: _____

        _____

Cross-Section Through Insect Mouthparts

Mosquito — Labrum, Food tube, Salivary tube, Mandible, Maxilla (Stylets), Labium (proboscis sheath)

Shield bug — Maxilla, Food tube, Salivary tube, Mandible, Labium (proboscis sheath)

Honeybee — Glossa, Food tube, Galea (part of maxilla), Labial palp

Butterfly — Left galea, Right galea (part of maxilla), Food tube

Housefly — Labrum, Food tube, Salivary tube, Labium

Mouthparts key

[ ] Labrum [ ] Labium [ ] Maxilla [ ] Mandible

Note: salivary tubes in the housefly and mosquito are derived from hypopharynx

A 2 **Methods of Feeding**

Animals show great variety in their diets and their methods of obtaining food. Animals may feed on solid or fluid food and may suck, bite, lap, or swallow it whole. The adaptations of mouthparts and other feeding appendages reflects both the diet and the way in which they obtain their food. Different modes of feeding among animals are illustrated below.

Fluid feeding

Fluid feeders suck or lap up fluids such as blood, plant sap, or nectar. Many insects (flies, moths, butterflies, aphids), annelids, arachnids and some mammals exploit these food sources. Fluid feeders have mouthparts and guts that enable them to obtain and process a liquid diet. Many have piercing or tubular mouthparts to obtain fluids directly. Others, like spiders, secrete enzymes into the captured prey and then suck up their liquefied remains.

Filter feeding

An extraordinary range of animals from simple sponges to large marine vertebrates, like the baleen whales, feed by filtering suspended particles out of the water. Special cells lining the body of sponges create water currents and engulf the food particles that are brought in. Many filter feeding annelids, echinoderms, and molluscs, e.g. tubeworms and feather stars, rely on mucus and cilia to trap food particles and move them to the mouth.

Bulk feeding and cropping

A great number of animals feed on large food masses which may be caught (actively or otherwise) and ingested whole or in pieces. Examples include snakes and most mammalian predators. Most have fangs for holding prey and/or teeth for cutting flesh. Other animals are grazing or cropping herbivores (e.g. many insects and mammalian herbivores), cutting off pieces of vegetation and using their mouthparts to chew the vegetation into pieces.

Sieve and deposit feeding

Humpback and other baleen whales use comblike plates suspended from the upper jaw to sieve shrimps and fish from large volumes of water. Food is trapped against the plates when the mouth closes and water is forced out. Earthworms are nonselective deposit feeders, moving through the soil using a powerful muscular pharynx to suck in a mix of organic and inorganic material. The undigested residue is egested as castings at the soil surface.

1. Describe one **structural** adaptation for obtaining food in the following animals:

   (a) A blood sucking mosquito: _____

   (b) A filter feeding whale: _____

   (c) A mammalian predatory carnivore: _____

   (d) A leaf chewing grasshopper: _____

   (e) An ambush predator, such as a python: _____

   (f) A filter feeding marine invertebrate: _____

   (g) *Hydra*: _____

2. Describe one **behavioral** adaptation for obtaining food in the following animals:

   (a) A blood sucking mosquito: _____

   (b) A filter feeding whale: _____

   (c) A mammalian predator: _____

   (d) Chimpanzees hunting for monkeys: _____

   (e) An ambush predator, such as a python: _____

   (f) A filter feeding marine invertebrate: _____

   (g) Scavenging bird (gull or vulture): _____

Food Vacuoles and Simple Guts

The simplest form of digestion occurs inside cells **(intracellularly)** within food vacuoles. This process is relatively slow and digestion is exclusively intracellular only in protozoa and sponges. In animals with simple, sac-like guts, digestion begins extracellularly (with secretion of enzymes to the outside or into the digestive cavity) and is completed intracellularly.

Paramecium

A food vacuole (formed by endocytosis) circulates in the cytoplasm while intracellular digestion takes place

Oral groove sweeps food particles into the cytostome (mouth)

Undigested material is eliminated by exocytosis from the anal pore

Undigested residue ruptures out

Food vacuole forms

Nucleus

Food digested within vacuole

Meal

Amoeba

Pseudopodia engulf a small organism

Branched gastrovascular cavity increases the surface area for absorption of nutrients

Planarian: Dugesia

Muscular pharynx is everted. It penetrates prey releasing digestive enzymes

Partially digested food is sucked up

Digestive residue (waste)

Food in

Gland cells in the cavity lining secrete enzymes

Nutritive cells in the cavity lining absorb nutrients

Gastrovascular cavity

Sea anemone

Intracellular digestion in food vacuoles

EXAMPLES: *Protozoans (above), sponges*

The simplest digestive compartments are food vacuoles: organelles where a single cell can digest its food without the digestive enzymes mixing with the cell's own cytoplasm. Sponges and protozoans (e.g. *Paramecium* and *Amoeba*) digest food in this way. *Paramecium* sweeps food into a food groove, from where vacuoles form. *Amoeba* engulf food using cytoplasmic extensions called pseudopodia. Digestion is intracellular, occurring within the cell itself.

Digestion in a gastrovascular cavity

EXAMPLES: *Cnidarians, flatworms (above)*

Some of the simplest animals have a digestive sac or gastrovascular cavity with a single opening through which food enters and digested waste passes out. In organisms with this system, digestion is both extra- and intracellular. Digestion begins (using secreted enzymes) either in the cavity (in cnidarians) or outside it (flatworms). In both these groups, the digestion process is completed intracellularly within the vacuoles in cells.

1. Explain two ways in which simple saclike gastrovascular cavities differ from tubelike guts:

   (a) _____

   (b) _____

2. (a) Distinguish between intracellular and extracellular digestion: _____

   _____

   _____

   (b) Explain why intracellular digestion is not suitable as the only means of digestion for most animals:

   _____

   _____

   _____

Diversity in Tube Guts

Tube-like digestive tracts (guts) run through the body from the mouth to the anus. The gut can be divided into regions where different stages in the processing of food occur along its length. Tube guts are relatively uniform in their general structure: there are regions for storing, digesting, absorbing and eliminating the food. However the different specializations that occur in each gut region will depend both on the diet and the method of ingestion (prechewed, liquid, unchewed). Some variations on the structure and regional specializations of tube guts are shown below.

Digestion in Complete Tube Guts

EXAMPLES: *Most animals: nematodes, annelids, molluscs, arthropods, echinoderms, chordates*

In contrast to the sac-like cavities of cnidarians and flatworms, most animals have digestive tubes running between two openings: a mouth and an anus. The food moves along the tube in one direction so the gut can be organized into specialized regions that carry out digestion and absorption of nutrients in a stepwise fashion.

Usually, food ingested at the mouth and pharynx passes through an esophagus to a crop, gizzard or stomach. In the intestine, digestive enzymes break down the food molecules and nutrients are absorbed across the epithelium of the gut wall. Undigested wastes are passed out (egested) through the anus.

The degree of specialization within tube guts varies depending on the animal and the type of diet. Four examples of regional specialization to suit different diets are illustrated.

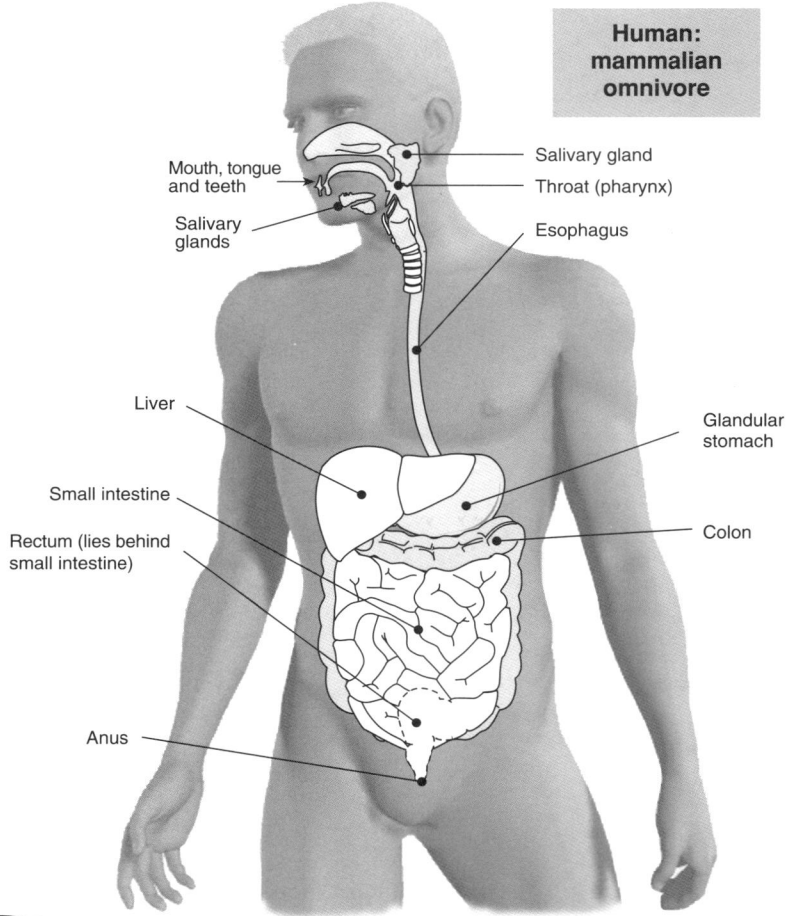

Human: mammalian omnivore

- Mouth, tongue and teeth
- Salivary glands
- Salivary gland
- Throat (pharynx)
- Esophagus
- Liver
- Glandular stomach
- Small intestine
- Colon
- Rectum (lies behind small intestine)
- Anus

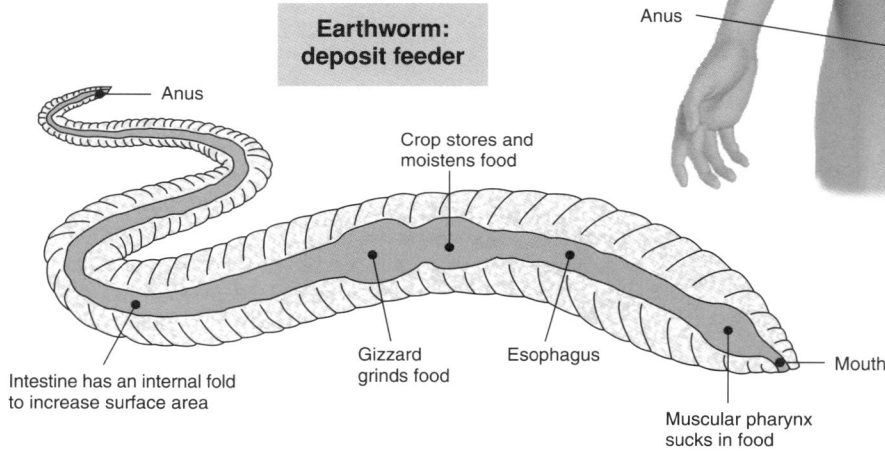

Earthworm: deposit feeder

- Anus
- Crop stores and moistens food
- Intestine has an internal fold to increase surface area
- Gizzard grinds food
- Esophagus
- Mouth
- Muscular pharynx sucks in food

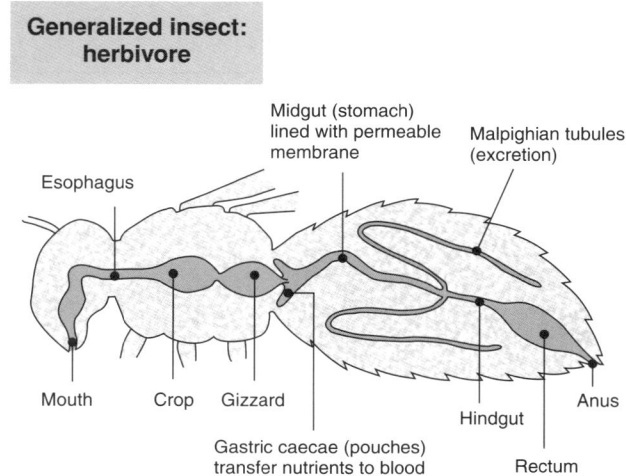

Generalized insect: herbivore

- Esophagus
- Midgut (stomach) lined with permeable membrane
- Malpighian tubules (excretion)
- Mouth
- Crop
- Gizzard
- Gastric caecae (pouches) transfer nutrients to blood
- Hindgut
- Rectum
- Anus

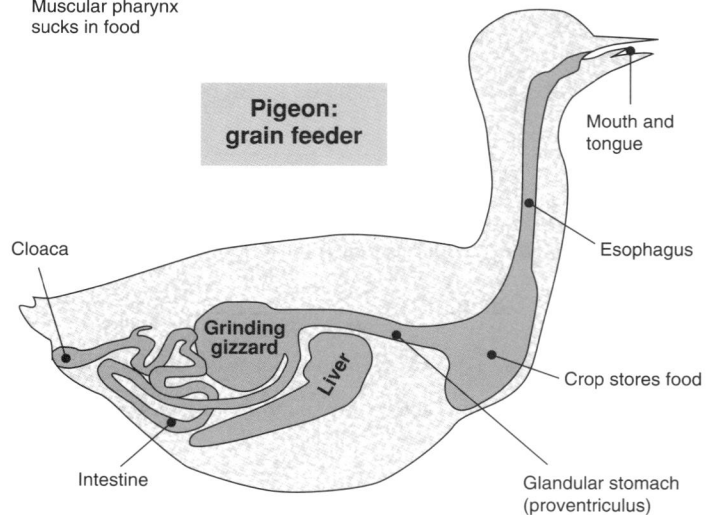

Pigeon: grain feeder

- Cloaca
- Mouth and tongue
- Grinding gizzard
- Liver
- Esophagus
- Crop stores food
- Intestine
- Glandular stomach (proventriculus)

Recognizing Digestive Organs in a Dissection

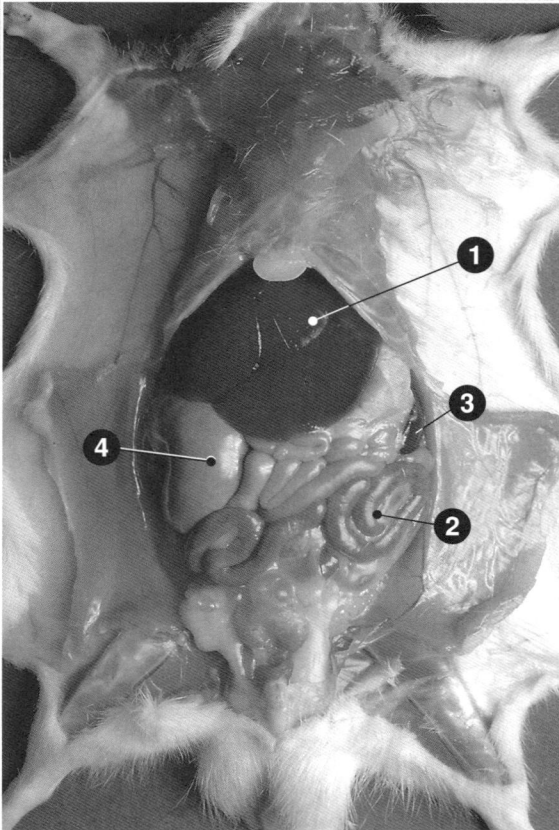

A: Rat abdominal organs *in situ*

B: Rat abdominal organs *partially dissected*

In your studies of anatomy, it is likely that you will be required to complete an actual, or virtual, dissection. The photographs (A and B) above show dissection of the body cavity of a laboratory white rat. A shows the organs *in situ*, as they appear undisturbed in the abdomen. B shows the organs after they have been partially dissected out. The numbers indicate structures to be labeled.

A. 1 _____   B. 1 _____

   2 _____   2 _____

   3 _____   3 _____

   4 _____   4 _____

                                                   5 _____

                                                 6 _____

1. Some structures have a similar function in different animals. State the general function of the following gut structures:

   (a) Gizzard: _____

   (b) Stomach or crop: _____

   (c) Intestine (midgut in insects): _____

2. (a) In the dissections of the rat (above), label each of the structures indicated in the spaces provided (photo A: 1-4, photo B: 1-6). Some structures are the same, but the same numbers do not necessarily indicate the same structure.

   (b) Of the various guts pictured opposite, which one does the rat gut most closely resemble: _____

   (c) Explain your answer to (b) in terms of the structures present and absent: _____

   _____

   _____

   (d) State one reason why you might expect this similarity: _____

Mammalian Guts

A 2

Among animals, bulky, high fiber diets are harder to digest than diets containing very little plant material. Herbivores therefore tend to have longer guts with larger chambers than carnivores. Grazing mammals are dependent on symbiotic microorganisms to digest plant cellulose for them. This microbial activity may take place in the stomach (foregut fermentation) or the colon and caecum (hindgut fermentation). Some grazers are ruminants; regurgitating and rechewing partially digested food, which is then reswallowed. The diagrams below compare gut structure in representative mammals. Further detail of the adaptations of carnivores and ruminant herbivores is provided opposite.

Omnivore
Human: *Homo sapiens*

Omnivorous diets can vary enormously and the specific structure of the gut varies accordingly. Some contain a lot of plant material, with animal flesh eaten occasionally. Pigs, bears, and some primates such as chimpanzees, are omnivores of this sort. Other omnivores forage for animal and vegetable foods about equally. The food predominating in the diet at any time will depend on seasonal availability and preference.

Carnivore
Dog: *Canis familiaris*

The guts of carnivores are adapted for processing animal flesh. The viscera (gut and internal organs) of killed or scavenged animals are eaten as well as the muscle, and provide valuable nutrients. Regions for microbial fermentation are poorly developed or absent. Some animals evolved as carnivores, but have since become secondarily adapted to a more omnivorous diet (bears) or a highly specialized herbivorous diet (pandas). Their guts retain the basic features of a carnivore's gut.

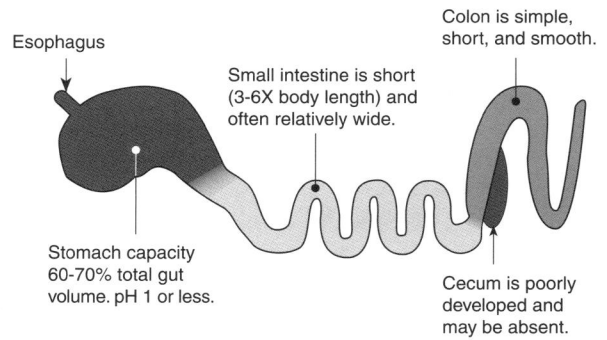

Herbivore: foregut digestion
Cattle: *Bos taurus*

Cattle, sheep, deer, and goats are ruminants. The stomach is divided into a series of large chambers, including a rumen, which contains bacteria and ciliates that digest the plant material in the diet. The division of the stomach into chambers means that the passage of food is slowed and there is time for the microorganisms to act on the plant cellulose. Volatile fatty acids released by the microbes provide energy, and digestion of the microbes themselves provides the ruminant with protein.

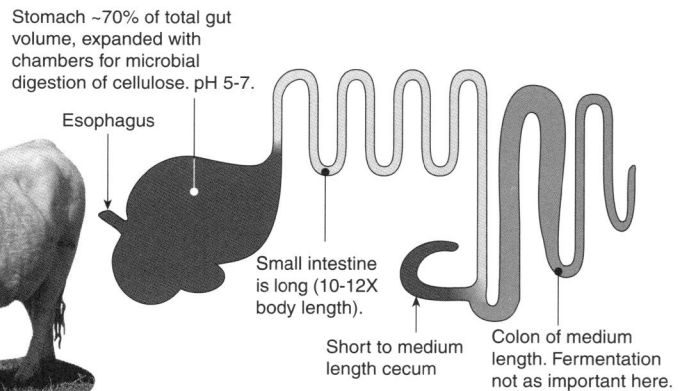

Herbivore: hindgut digestion
Rabbit: *Oryctolagus cuniculus*

Rabbits are specialized herbivores. The cecum is expanded into a very large chamber for digestion of cellulose. At the junction between the ileum and the colon, indigestible fibre is pushed into the colon where it forms hard feces. Digestible matter passes into the cecum where anaerobic bacteria ferment the material and more absorption takes place. Vitamins and microbial proteins from this fermentation are formed into soft fecal pellets, which pass to the anus and are reingested (coprophagy).

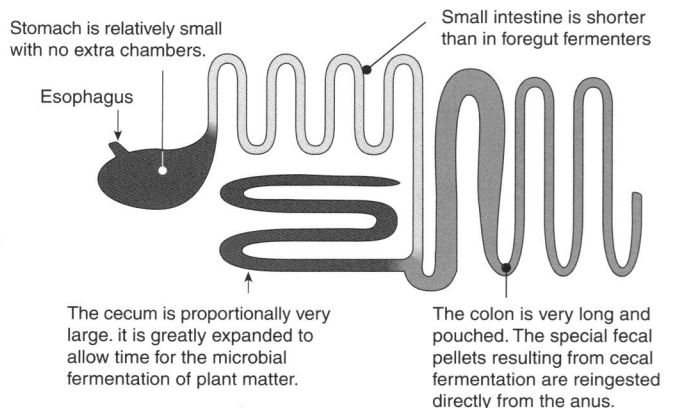

Small intestine is of medium length (10-11X body length in humans, but shorter in some other omnivores).

Colon is relatively long. The degree of pouching is related to fibre content of the diet. Usually some fermentation by gut bacteria occurs here.

Esophagus

Cecum: usually poorly developed

Stomach capacity in humans is 20-30% of total gut volume, but greater in some other omnivores. pH 2.

Appendix

Esophagus

Small intestine is short (3-6X body length) and often relatively wide.

Colon is simple, short, and smooth.

Stomach capacity 60-70% total gut volume. pH 1 or less.

Cecum is poorly developed and may be absent.

Stomach ~70% of total gut volume, expanded with chambers for microbial digestion of cellulose. pH 5-7.

Esophagus

Small intestine is long (10-12X body length).

Short to medium length cecum

Colon of medium length. Fermentation not as important here.

Stomach is relatively small with no extra chambers.

Small intestine is shorter than in foregut fermenters

Esophagus

The cecum is proportionally very large. it is greatly expanded to allow time for the microbial fermentation of plant matter.

The colon is very long and pouched. The special fecal pellets resulting from cecal fermentation are reingested directly from the anus.

Dental adaptations

Ruminant herbivore: Cattle (*Bos taurus*)

Ruminants are specialized herbivores with teeth adapted for chewing and grinding. Their nutrition is dependent on their mutualistic relationship with their microbial gut flora (bacteria and ciliates), which digest plant material and provide the ruminant with energy and protein. In return, the rumen provides the microbes with a warm, oxygen free, nutrient rich environment.

Carnivore: Lion (*Panthera leo*)

The teeth and guts of carnivores are superbly adapted for eating animal flesh. The canine and incisor teeth are specialized to bite down and cut, while the carnassials are enlarged, lengthened, and positioned to act as shears to slice through flesh. As meat is easier to digest than cellulose, the guts of carnivores are comparatively more uniform and shorter than those of herbivores.

Small temporalis muscle

Horny pad

Incisors

Masseter muscle is very large to assist in chewing.

Canine

Premolars

Diastema (toothless space)

Molars are large for grinding

Large temporalis muscle provides most of the biting force.

Canines

Incisors

In carnivores, the masseter muscle assists in stabilizing the jaw. Chewing is less important.

Carnassials (lower is hidden behind upper) are modified molars/premolars.

Premolars

Flow of food in the stomach

Regurgitation, rechewing, and reswallowing

Omasum: removes water

Passage of food

Abomasum: true stomach secretes gastric juices.

Esophagus

Powerful gastric juices (acid and pepsin enzyme) digest the proteins found in meat.

Passage of food

Reticulum: forms the cud which is returned to the mouth.

Rumen: contains bacteria for the digestion of cellulose and ciliates to digest starch.

To the duodenum

Strong muscular movements provide physical mixing.

1. For each of the following, summarize the **structural** differences between the guts of a carnivore and a named herbivore:

    (a) Size of stomach (relative to body size): _____

    (b) Relative length of small intestine: _____

    (c) Development of hind gut (cecum and colon): _____

2. (a) Explain the role of microbial fermentation in the nutrition of foregut fermenting herbivores: _____

    (b) Describe a herbivorous diet that would be less reliant on microbial fermentation: _____

3. Contrast the pH of the stomach contents in carnivores, omnivores, and herbivores, and explain the differences:

4. Identify and explain a structural difference between carnivores and ruminant herbivores with respect to:

    (a) The teeth: _____

    (b) The jaw musculature: _____

Digesting Different Diets

RA ②

During digestion, food is changed by physical and chemical means from its original state until its constituents are released as small, simple molecules that can be absorbed and assimilated. The content of animal diets is tremendously variable and the ways in which animals have evolved to process their food is similarly varied. Some foods, like egg and honey, are pure, concentrated nutriment. Other diets are of high nutritional value, but contain large volumes of water (e.g. blood) or are bulky and take a long time to digest (whole prey items). Other diets are not only bulky, but are also of low nutritional value (e.g. vegetation). Some adaptations for dealing with particular, specialized diets are explained below.

Animal	Diet and Problems	Adaptations to Diet

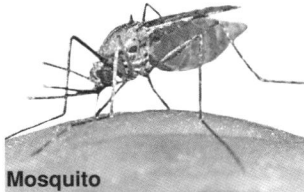

Mosquito
Others: leeches, spiders, ticks

High fluid diet: blood
Blood is a high protein, low bulk, fluid. The problems associated with processing it are:
- Preventing coagulation of blood and blockage of mouthparts during ingestion.
- Storage of a large quantity of fluid.
- Slowing passage of low bulk food through the gut so that it can be digested.

Powerful **anticoagulants** are injected using the piercing mouthparts. These keep the blood flowing.

A greatly **enlarged crop** stores the blood, releasing it slowly in smaller amounts into the stomach (midgut).

The **stomach is divided** into three sequential regions that absorb water to concentrate the blood, secrete protease enzymes for digestion, and absorb nutrients.

Bumble bee
Others: honeybees, aphids, butterflies

High fluid diet: plant sap and nectar
Plant sap is high volume sugary fluid. The problems associated with processing it are:
- Eliminating large volumes of water and obtaining sufficient protein and vitamins.
- Storage of a large quantity of fluid.
- Dilution of enzymes by the large volumes.
- In some cases, excessive sugar intake.

The **stomach is greatly dilated** and divided into three regions. The first and last parts are greatly coiled and actively remove water.

The **mid region** of the stomach is **specialized** for secretion of carbohydrase enzymes and absorption. It receives the sap only after most of the water is removed.

Unabsorbed sugars can be passed out of the hindgut in copious amounts known as "honeydew". This allows them to absorb enough food to meet protein needs.

Sheep
Others: All ruminants: e.g. cows

Bulky, high cellulose diet: grass
Plant material contains large amounts of cellulose. Problems with this diet include:
- Ingesting enough to meet protein and vitamin needs. Digesting the cellulose.
- Storing large volumes of bulky material.
- Coping with large amounts of gas produced by fermenting plant material.

Stomach is greatly expanded into several, large storage and fermentation chambers (e.g. the rumen) containing microorganisms (bacteria and ciliate Protozoa).

The **gut symbionts digest the cellulose**, producing volatile fatty acids, which are absorbed directly from the chambers and provide energy and nutrients. Digestion of the microorganisms themselves provides protein.

Some material is regurgitated and rechewed. Smaller particles pass onto the absorptive region of the stomach.

Koala

Toxic plants: *Eucalyptus* leaves
Problems with this diet are:
- The leaves contain toxins in the oils, waxes and resins, e.g. hydrocyanic acid.
- It is low in energy and quality (low protein).
- The diet is bulky and high volume.

Note: some insects e.g. monarch butterflies, eat toxic plants and use the toxins for defense

The **cecum** of the hindgut is **greatly expanded** to form a fermentation chamber containing microorganisms which digest the cellulose of the plant material.

They meet their protein needs by eating **large volumes**.

Koalas are able to **detoxify eucalypt poisons** by forming nontoxic compounds in the liver, which are then excreted.

Koalas are **fastidious** feeders and select only certain age leaves of certain species.

1. There are a number of disadvantages to a diet that consists of a toxic plant. Suggest ONE advantage of such a diet:

_____

2. Describe one common feature of the guts of fluid feeders: _____

_____

3. Suggest why it is so important for fluid feeders to reduce the volume of their ingested food by absorbing water:

_____

_____

4. (a) Explain how ruminant herbivores supplement the protein content of their diet: _____

_____

   (b) Suggest why koalas are less able to do this: _____

_____

🐾 RA② Adaptations for Absorption

In most animal phyla, the small products of enzymic digestion are absorbed through a gut lining. Absorption of the simple components of food (e.g. simple sugars, amino acids, fatty acids and glycerol) must take place before the nutrients can be assimilated (taken up by all the body's cells). In animals with a tubular gut, it is an advantage to maximize the uptake of nutrients from the intestine as the digested food passes through. There is great diversity amongst the invertebrate phyla in the way in which absorption is facilitated. In cnidarians, specialized cells lining the gut ingest food particles directly by phagocytosis. In other phyla, the inner surface area of the gut is increased by infolding so that the area over which nutrient uptake can occur is very large. This is the case in vertebrates also, as shown for mammals in the activity "*Stomach and Small Intestine*".

Cnidarian gastrovascular cavity

EXAMPLE: *Hydra*

In *Hydra*, specialized cells line the gastrovascular cavity. Some of these secrete enzymes into the cavity to begin digestion. Special nutritive cells (illustrated) take in the partly digested fragments by phagocytosis, to form food vacuoles where digestion is completed. These cells have beating hair-like flagella that create currents and improve the delivery of food to the cells.

Insect gastric ceca

EXAMPLE: Grasshopper or locust

In insects of the grasshopper family (and others), the gastric ceca are midgut pouches just behind the proventriculus. The ceca improve absorption by transferring nutrients into the blood. Secretion of enzymes and absorption of nutrients occurs in the midgut. Unlike the fore and hindgut (which are lined with chitin), the midgut is lined with a permeable peritrophic membrane which allows nutrient absorption.

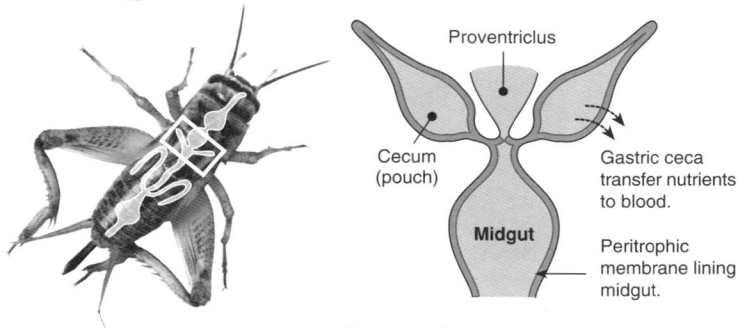

Annelid typhlosole

EXAMPLE: *Lumbricus* (earthworm)

In earthworms, the entire length of the small intestine is folded into a structure called the typhlosole. Secretion of enzymes, digestion and absorption all occur in the intestine and the typhlosole increases the amount of surface area for absorption of nutrients. Not all annelids have a typhlosole, although many have similar foldings to increase surface area.

Nutritive cell with food vacuoles

Food uptake

External environment

Proventriculus

Cecum (pouch)

Gastric ceca transfer nutrients to blood.

Midgut

Peritrophic membrane lining midgut.

Typhlosole lined with absorptive cells.

Absorption **Gut space**

1. Explain why animals increase the surface area of the inner gut surface: _____

_____

_____

2. With reference to a named example, describe how they do this: _____

_____

_____

3. Refer to the activity "*Stomach and Small Intestine*' and answer the following:

(a) Identify the features and structures in the mammalian gut that increase surface area: _____

_____

(b) Explain how the transport of nutrients from the gut is facilitated: _____

_____

(c) Compare the degree of infolding with that generally found in invertebrates and suggest a reason for the difference:

_____

_____

The Human Digestive Tract

RA 2

It is estimated that an adult consumes about 20 000 kg of food between the ages of 18 and 38 years; about a metric tonne a year. Although babies grow rapidly from birth, growth is not the most significant reason for our ongoing eating. Our bodies require a constant source of energy for the vast number of biochemical reactions that constitute **metabolism**. Food provides the source of this energy. Tube-like digestive tracts (guts) run through the

body from the mouth to the anus. The digestive tract prepares the food we eat for use by the body's cells through five basic activities: eating (ingestion), movement (of food through the gut), digestion (physical and chemical breakdown), absorption, and elimination. However the different specializations that occur in each region will depend both on the diet and the method of ingestion (prechewed, liquid, unchewed).

Feeding and satiety centers in the hypothalamus regulate eating

Structures of the Human Gut

Word list: *Liver, small intestine, gall bladder, stomach, salivary glands, colon (large intestine), esophagus, pancreas, mouth and teeth, anus, rectum, appendix.*

A G
B H
C I
D J
E K
F L

The Functions of Gut Structures

In the boxes provided, write the letter (A-L) that represents the part of the gut responsible for each of the functions summarized below:

(a) Main region for enzymatic digestion & nutrient absorption
(b) Consolidation of the feces before elimination
(c) Main function (humans) is water and mineral absorption
(d) Secretes acid and pepsin, stores and mixes food
(e) A gland which produces an alkaline, enzyme-rich fluid
(f) Produces bile and has many homeostatic functions
(g) Produces saliva which contains the enzyme amylase

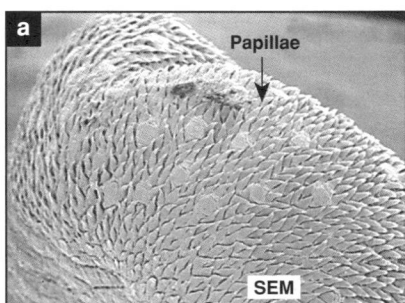

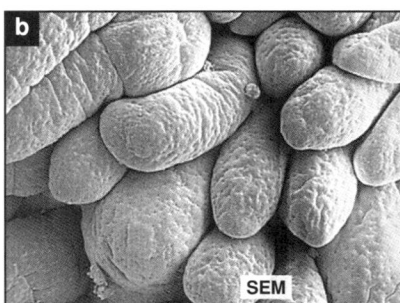

a — Papillae — SEM
b — SEM
c — Villi — Lumen
d — Gastric gland
e — Pulp cavity — Enamel
f — Bile ducts

© Biozone International 2001-2003

Processes in a Tube Gut

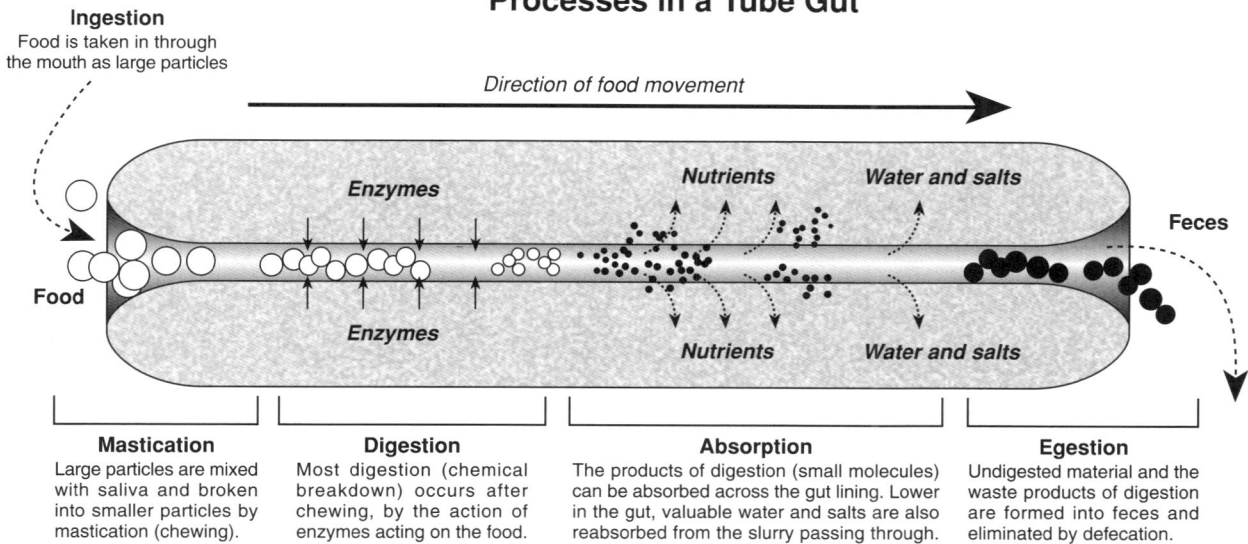

Ingestion
Food is taken in through the mouth as large particles

Direction of food movement

Enzymes

Nutrients   **Water and salts**

Feces

Food

Enzymes

Nutrients   **Water and salts**

Mastication	**Digestion**	**Absorption**	**Egestion**
Large particles are mixed with saliva and broken into smaller particles by mastication (chewing).	Most digestion (chemical breakdown) occurs after chewing, by the action of enzymes acting on the food.	The products of digestion (small molecules) can be absorbed across the gut lining. Lower in the gut, valuable water and salts are also reabsorbed from the slurry passing through.	Undigested material and the waste products of digestion are formed into feces and eliminated by defecation.

Peristalsis

When food is processed in a tube gut it is usually formed into small lumps (each is called a bolus). These are moved through the gut by waves of muscular contraction; a process called **peristalsis**. The wall of a gut tube has two layers of muscle: an inner layer of circular muscles which can squeeze the tube to a narrower diameter, and longitudinal muscles which can contract to shorten the tube. They work in opposite ways; one contracts while the other relaxes. They are said to be antagonistic pairs of muscles.

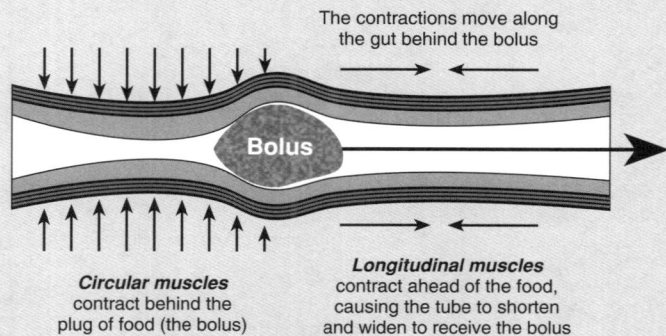

The contractions move along the gut behind the bolus

Bolus

Circular muscles
contract behind the plug of food (the bolus)

Longitudinal muscles
contract ahead of the food, causing the tube to shorten and widen to receive the bolus

1. In the spaces provided on the diagram (left), name the parts labeled A-L (choose from the word list provided). Match each of the **functions** described (a) – (g) with the letter that represents the corresponding structure on the diagram:

2. On the diagram, mark with lines and labels: anal sphincter (**AS**), pyloric sphincter (**PS**), cardiac sphincter (**CS**):

3. Identify the region of the gut illustrated by the photographs (a) – (f) on the previous page (e is mammalian but not human):

   (a) _____   (b) _____

   (c) _____   (d) _____

   (e) _____   (f) _____

4. Define the term **bolus**: _____

5. Describe how peristalsis moves material through a tube gut: _____

6. State an advantage of having a gut where food moves in only one direction: _____

7. Name one factor that would influence the length and specialization in the gut: _____

8. Briefly describe how the following processes are involved in processing food:

   (a) Mastication: _____

   (b) Absorption: _____

Stomach and Small Intestine

Digestion in the gut depends on both the physical movement of the food and its enzymatic breakdown into constituent components. Most digestion occurs in the stomach and small intestine. The digestive enzymes involved may be bound to the surfaces of the intestinal epithelial cells or occur as components of the secretions of digestive glands (e.g. pancreas). The structure and functions of the stomach and small intestines, and their enzymic secretions are shown on this and the next page.

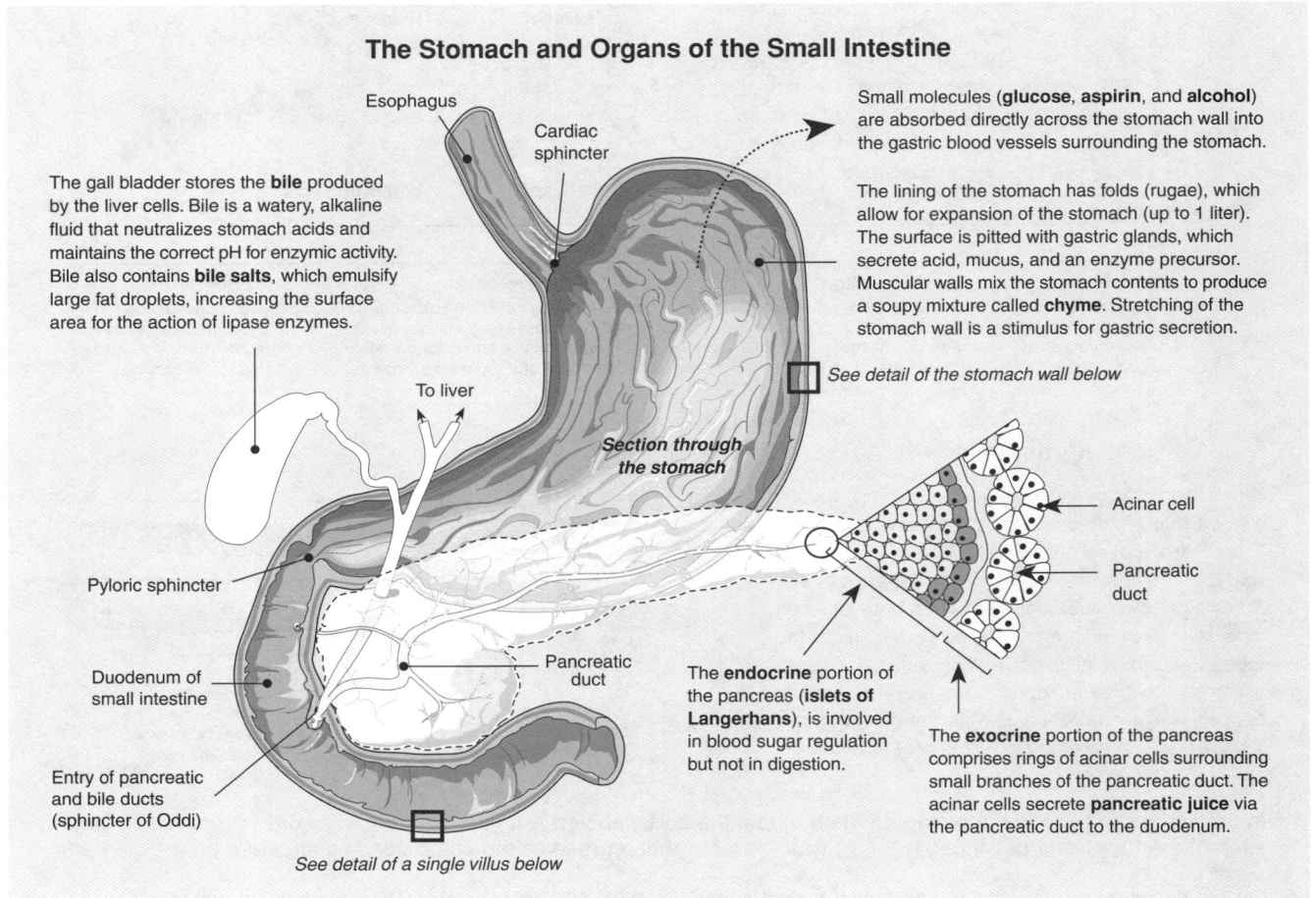

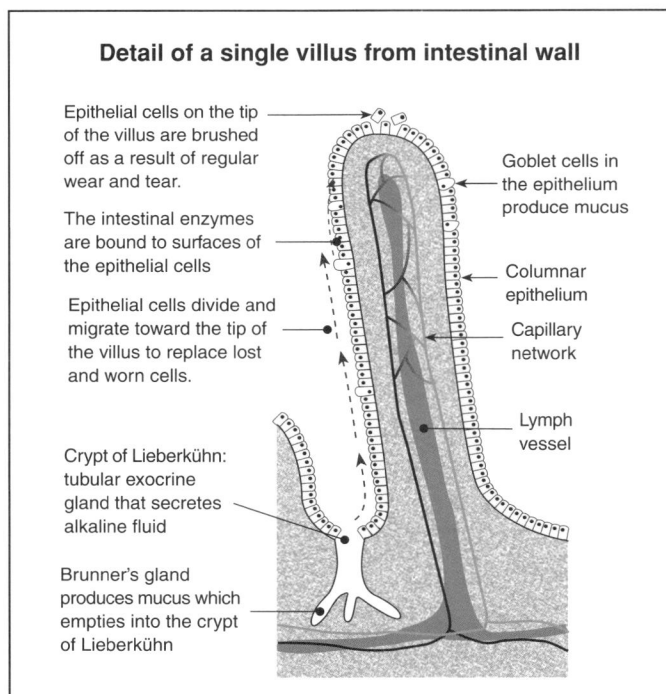

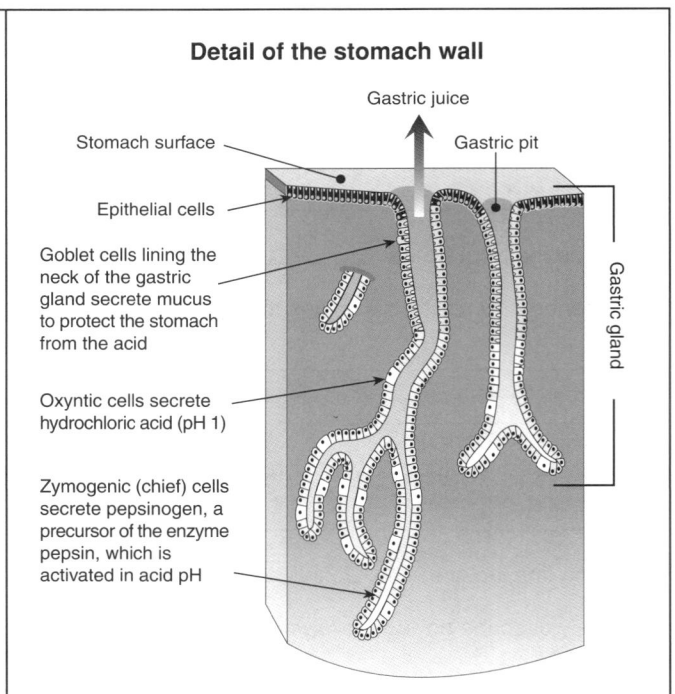

The Stomach and Organs of the Small Intestine

Esophagus

Cardiac sphincter

Small molecules (**glucose**, **aspirin**, and **alcohol**) are absorbed directly across the stomach wall into the gastric blood vessels surrounding the stomach.

The gall bladder stores the **bile** produced by the liver cells. Bile is a watery, alkaline fluid that neutralizes stomach acids and maintains the correct pH for enzymic activity. Bile also contains **bile salts**, which emulsify large fat droplets, increasing the surface area for the action of lipase enzymes.

The lining of the stomach has folds (rugae), which allow for expansion of the stomach (up to 1 liter). The surface is pitted with gastric glands, which secrete acid, mucus, and an enzyme precursor. Muscular walls mix the stomach contents to produce a soupy mixture called **chyme**. Stretching of the stomach wall is a stimulus for gastric secretion.

See detail of the stomach wall below

To liver

Section through the stomach

Acinar cell

Pancreatic duct

Pyloric sphincter

Duodenum of small intestine

Pancreatic duct

The **endocrine** portion of the pancreas (**islets of Langerhans**), is involved in blood sugar regulation but not in digestion.

The **exocrine** portion of the pancreas comprises rings of acinar cells surrounding small branches of the pancreatic duct. The acinar cells secrete **pancreatic juice** via the pancreatic duct to the duodenum.

Entry of pancreatic and bile ducts (sphincter of Oddi)

See detail of a single villus below

Detail of a single villus from intestinal wall

Epithelial cells on the tip of the villus are brushed off as a result of regular wear and tear.

The intestinal enzymes are bound to surfaces of the epithelial cells

Epithelial cells divide and migrate toward the tip of the villus to replace lost and worn cells.

Crypt of Lieberkühn: tubular exocrine gland that secretes alkaline fluid

Brunner's gland produces mucus which empties into the crypt of Lieberkühn

Goblet cells in the epithelium produce mucus

Columnar epithelium

Capillary network

Lymph vessel

Detail of the stomach wall

Gastric juice

Stomach surface

Gastric pit

Epithelial cells

Goblet cells lining the neck of the gastric gland secrete mucus to protect the stomach from the acid

Oxyntic cells secrete hydrochloric acid (pH 1)

Zymogenic (chief) cells secrete pepsinogen, a precursor of the enzyme pepsin, which is activated in acid pH

Gastric gland

---

1. Movements of the gut push food through the gut tube. State their other important role: _____

_____

Intestinal villi and microvilli

The photograph (left) shows a section through the ileum with the **intestinal villi** and **intestinal glands** (crypts of Lieberkühn) indicated. The intestinal glands secrete mucus and alkaline fluid. **Epithelial cells** lining the surface of the villi are regularly worn off and replaced by new cells migrating from the base of the intestinal glands. Each epithelial cell has many **microvilli** (microscopic projections called the brush border) which further increase the intestinal surface area.

Enzymes bound to the microvilli surfaces of the epithelial cells (peptidases, maltase, lactase, and sucrase) break down small peptides and carbohydrate molecules into their constituent parts. The breakdown products (monosaccharides, amino acids) are then absorbed into the underlying blood and lymph vessels. **Mucous cells** (white spots arrowed) produce mucus to protect the epithelial cells from enzymatic digestion. The **blood vessels** transport nutrients to the liver. **Lymph vessels** transport the products of fat digestion.

Enzyme secretions of the gut and their role in digestion

Secretion and source	Site of action	Active enzyme	Substrate and products	Control of secretion
Gastric juice: stomach	Stomach	Pepsin	Protein ⟶ peptides	Reflex stimulation, stretching of the stomach wall, and the hormone **gastrin**.
Pancreatic juice: pancreas (exocrine region only)	Duodenum	Pancreatic amylase Trypsin Chymotrypsin Pancreatic lipase	Starch ⟶ maltose Protein ⟶ peptides Protein ⟶ peptides Fats ⟶ fatty acids + glycerol	Control of pancreatic secretions is via release of the hormones **secretin** and **cholecystokinin**.
Intestinal juice and enzymes: small intestine	Small intestine	Maltase Peptidases	Maltose ⟶ glucose Polypeptides ⟶ amino acids	Reflex action and contact with intestinal wall.

2. Describe the three main functions of the stomach in humans:

(a) _____

(b) _____

(c) _____

3. Explain the significance of the pH with respect to the secretions of:

(a) The stomach: _____

(b) The intestine: _____

4. The effects of an alcoholic drink are felt soon after drinking, rapid pain relief can be gained from taking aspirin, and blood sugar rises shortly after sucking a glucose sweet. Explain why these substances have such a rapid effect when ingested:

_____

_____

5. Explain the general role of the following structures of the stomach:

(a) The cardiac sphincter: _____

(b) Internal stomach folds (rugae): _____

(c) Secreted mucus: _____

6. Explain how the villi and microvilli assist in the efficient absorption of nutrients: _____

_____

7. Protein-digesting enzymes (e.g. trypsin, chymotrypsin, and pepsin) are secreted in an inactive form and activated after release. Explain why it is necessary for these enzymes to be secreted in an inactive form:

_____

_____

_____

The Large Intestine

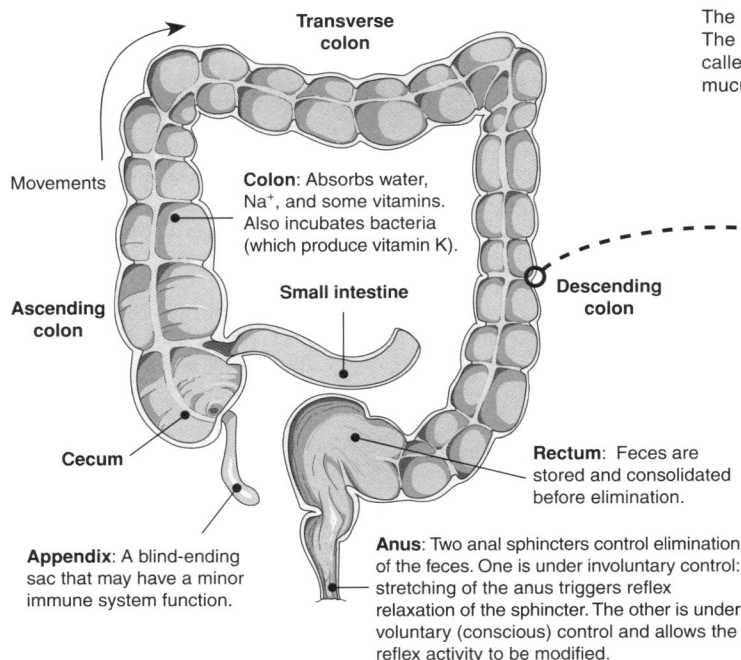

After most of the nutrients have been absorbed in the small intestine, the remaining fluid contents pass into the large intestine (appendix, cecum, and colon). The fluid comprises undigested or undigestible food, bacteria, dead cells sloughed off from the gut wall, mucus, bile, ions, and a large amount of water. In humans and other omnivores, the large intestine is concerned mainly with the reabsorption of water and electrolytes. Infection or disease can cause an increase in gut movements, resulting in insufficient reabsorption of water and diarrhea. Sluggish gut movements cause the reabsorption of too much water and the feces become hard and difficult to pass, a condition known as constipation. The semi-solid waste material (feces) passes from the **colon** to the rectum, where it is stored and consolidated before being expelled (egested). Egestion of feces is controlled by the activity of two sphincters in the **anus**, one being under involuntary reflex control.

The Large Intestine

Transverse colon

Movements

Colon: Absorbs water, Na$^+$, and some vitamins. Also incubates bacteria (which produce vitamin K).

Small intestine

Ascending colon

Descending colon

Cecum

Rectum: Feces are stored and consolidated before elimination.

Appendix: A blind-ending sac that may have a minor immune system function.

Anus: Two anal sphincters control elimination of the feces. One is under involuntary control: stretching of the anus triggers reflex relaxation of the sphincter. The other is under voluntary (conscious) control and allows the reflex activity to be modified.

A single crypt from the intestinal wall

The lining of the large intestine consists of a simple columnar epithelium. The epithelium is not folded into villi, but instead contains tubular glands called crypts containing numerous goblet cells. The goblet cells produce mucus, which lubricates the colon wall and aids formation of the feces.

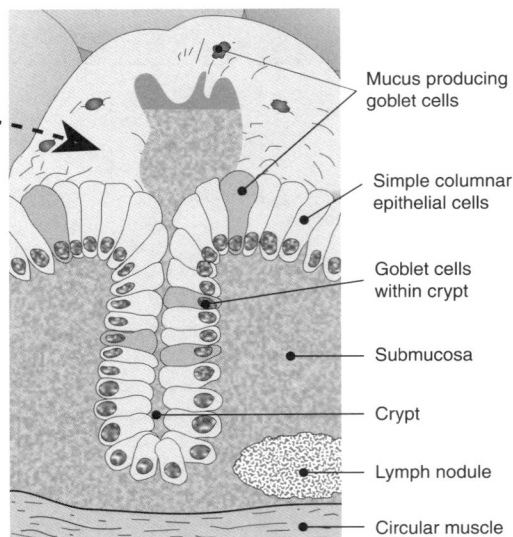

Mucus producing goblet cells

Simple columnar epithelial cells

Goblet cells within crypt

Submucosa

Crypt

Lymph nodule

Circular muscle

Appendicitis

Obstruction of the appendix by fecal matter or some other cause can lead to an inflammation called *appendicitis*. Appendicitis usually develops rapidly with little warning over a period of 6-12 hours. The usual symptom is abdominal pain, accompanied by nausea, vomiting and a slight fever. When severe, it can be life threatening. Acute appendicitis is treated by surgical removal of the appendix (**appendectomy**). The entire procedure usually takes about one hour and is performed in one of two ways: through what is called an open operation or through the laparoscopic technique.

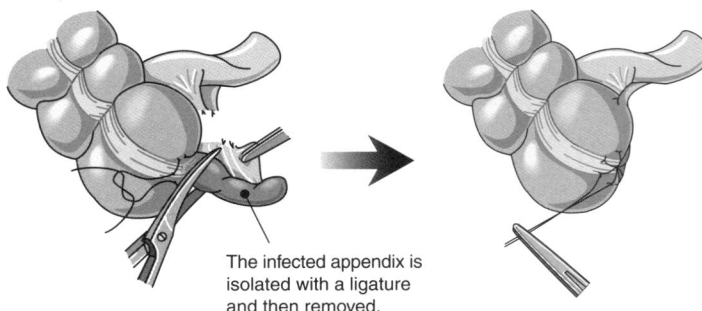

The infected appendix is isolated with a ligature and then removed.

1. Outline the main function of the large intestine: _____

2. Suggest why the lining of the large intestine consists of crypts as opposed to villi like projections: _____

_____

3. The photograph below shows a cross section through the colon wall. Using the diagram of the single crypt (above right) label the features indicated using the following word list: *circular muscle, submucosa, lymph nodule, epithelial cells*.

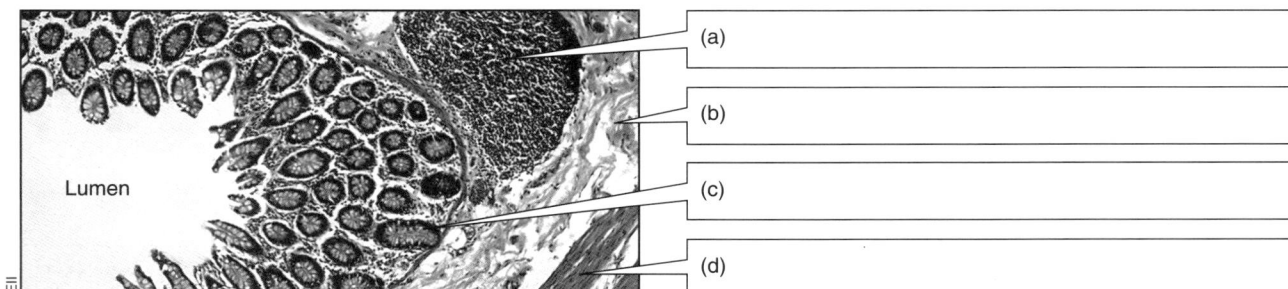

Lumen

(a)

(b)

(c)

(d)

The Control of Digestion

A 2

The majority of digestive juices are secreted only when there is food in the gut and both nervous and hormonal mechanisms are involved in coordinating and regulating this activity appropriately. The digestive system is innervated by branches of the **autonomic nervous system** (sympathetic and parasympathetic stimulation). Hormonal regulation is achieved through the activity of several hormones: **gastrin**, **secretin**, and **cholecystokinin** (formerly called **pancreozymin**). These are released into the bloodstream in response to nervous or chemical stimuli and influence the activity of gut and associated organs.

Hormonal and Nervous Control of Digestion

Salivation is entirely under nervous control. Some saliva is secreted continuously in response to **parasympathetic stimulation** via the vagus nerve. The presence of food in the mouth stimulates the salivary glands (and stomach) to increase their secretions. This response operates through a simple cranial reflex via the vagus nerve. The smell, sight, and thought of food also stimulates salivary (and gastric) secretion. These stimuli involve higher brain activity and learning (a conditioned reflex).

The feeding center of the brain

The **feeding center** in the hypothalamus is constantly active. It monitors metabolites in the blood and stimulates hunger when these metabolites reach low levels. After a meal, a neighboring region of the hypothalamus, **the satiety center**, suppresses the activity of the feeding center for a period of time. Impulses from these two centers travel via the vagus nerve to stimulate the secretion of particular digestive hormones.

The secretions and muscular activity of the gut are regulated by both nervous and hormonal mechanisms. **Parasympathetic stimulation** of the stomach and pancreas via the **vagus nerve** increases their secretion. Sympathetic stimulation has the opposite effect.

The entry of food into the small intestine, especially fat and gastric acid, stimulates the cells of the intestinal mucosa to secrete the hormones **cholecystokinin** (CCK) and **secretin**.

The presence of food in the stomach causes it to stretch. This mechanical stimulus results in secretion of the hormone **gastrin** from cells in the mucosa of the stomach. This activity is mediated through a simple **reflex**.

Cholecystokinin circulates in the blood and stimulates the pancreas to increase its secretion of enzyme-rich fluid. CCK also stimulates the release of bile into the intestine from the gall bladder. **Secretin** stimulates the pancreas to increase its secretion of alkaline fluid. This fluid neutralizes the acid entering the intestine. Secretin also stimulates the production of bile from the liver cells. **Both secretin and CCK** stimulate the secretion of intestinal juice but inhibit gastric secretion and general motility of the gastrointestinal tract.

Gastrin is secreted in response to eating food (particularly protein). Gastrin is released into the bloodstream where it acts back on the stomach to increase gastric secretion and motility. Gastrin also increases the motility of the gastrointestinal tract in general, and this helps to propel food through the gut.

Vagus nerve

Gastrin

CCK and secretin

1. Describe the role of each of the following stimuli in the control of digestion, identifying both the response and its effect:

(a) Presence of food in the mouth: _____

_____

(b) Presence of fat and acid in the small intestine: _____

_____

(c) Stretching of the stomach by the presence of food: _____

_____

2. Outline the role of the vagus nerve in regulating digestive activity: _____

_____

The Role of the Liver

A 2

The liver is a large organ, weighing about 1.4 kg, and is well supplied with blood. It carries out several hundred different functions and has a pivotal role in the maintenance of homeostasis. Its role in the digestion of food centers around the production of the alkaline fluid, **bile**, which is secreted at a rate of 0.8-1.0 liter per day. It is also responsible for processing absorbed nutrients, which arrive at the liver via the hepatic portal system. These functions are summarized below.

Digestive Functions of the Liver

The digestive role of the liver is in the production of **bile**. Bile is a yellow, brown, or olive-green alkaline fluid (pH 7.6–8.6), consisting of water and bile salts, cholesterol, lecithin, bile pigments, and several ions. The bile salts are used in the small intestine to break up (**emulsify**) fatty molecules for easier digestion and absorption. The high pH neutralizes the acid entering the small intestine from the stomach. Bile is also partly an excretory product; the breakdown of red blood cells in the liver produces the principal bile pigment, **bilirubin**. Bacteria act on the bile pigments, giving the brownish color to feces. The production and secretion of bile is regulated through nervous and hormonal mechanisms. The hormones (secretin and cholecystokinin) are released into the blood from the intestinal mucosa in response to the presence of food (especially fat) in the small intestine.

Liver Tissue

The liver tissue is made up of many lobules, each one comprising cords of liver cells (hepatocytes), radiating from a central vein (CV), and surrounded by branches of the hepatic artery, hepatic portal vein, and bile ductule. Bile is produced by the individual liver cells, which secrete it into canaliculi that empty into small bile ducts. The hepatocytes also process the nutrients entering the liver via the hepatic portal system.

Internal Gross Structure of the Human Liver

Vagus nerve stimulates bile production

Secretin stimulates bile production

Common bile duct transports bile from the gallbladder to the small intestine

Gallbladder stores bile, releasing it into the small intestine when required

Cholecystokinin (CCK) stimulates release of bile into the gut

Bile flows from small ductules into larger bile ducts

Hepatic duct

Pancreatic duct

Sphincter of Oddi relaxes to release bile into the small intestine. Sphincter relaxation is stimulated by the hormone CCK.

Cords of hepatocytes radiate from the central vein

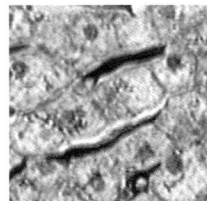

Individual liver cells

CV

1. The liver produces bile. Identify the two main functions of bile in digestion:

    (a) Function 1: _____

    (b) Function 2: _____

2. Describe the two primary functions of the liver related to the processing of digestion products arriving from the gut:

    (a) Function 1: _____

    (b) Function 2: _____

3. Explain the role of the gall bladder in digestion: _____

    _____

4. Describe in what way bile is an excretory product as well as a digestive secretion:

    _____

    _____

5. Name the two principal hormones controlling the production (secretion) and release of bile, and state the effect of each:

    (a) Hormone 1: _____ Effect: _____

    (b) Hormone 2: _____ Effect: _____

6. State the stimulus for hormonal stimulation of bile secretion: _____

    _____

Absorption and Transport

All the chemical and physical processes of digestion from the mouth to the small intestine are aimed at the breakdown of food molecules into forms that can pass through intestinal lining into the underlying blood and lymph vessels. These breakdown products include monosaccharides, amino acids, fatty acids, glycerol, and glycerides. Passage of these molecules from the gut into the blood or lymph is called **absorption**. After absorption, nutrients are transported directly or indirectly to the liver for storage or processing. Some of the features of nutrient absorption and transport are shown below. For simplicity, all nutrients are shown in the lumen of the intestine, even though some nutrients are digested on the epithelial cell surfaces.

The Hepatic Portal System

The liver obtains oxygenated blood from the hepatic artery, but it also receives deoxygenated blood containing newly absorbed nutrients via the hepatic portal vein. The **hepatic portal system** refers to all the blood flow from the digestive organs that passes through the liver before returning to the heart. Hepatic portal blood is rich in nutrients: the liver monitors and processes this load before the blood passes into general circulation.

To heart
Blood leaving the liver eventually enters the vena cava
Hepatic portal vein

Intestinal villus
Chylomicron
Area enlarged below left
Monosaccharide
Short chain fatty acid
Amino acid
Venule
Arteriole
Epithelium
Capillary
Lacteal (branch of lymph vessel)

Absorption: Most of the simple molecules that are the final products of food breakdown are absorbed by the epithelial cells of the villi into the blood vessels and are transported directly to the liver where they are processed.

Lumen of gut	Brush border of microvilli	Intestinal epithelial cell	Capillary of villus

To thoracic duct
Lymph vessel

Glucose and galactose — Active transport
Fructose — Facilitated diffusion
Diffusion
Amino acids — Active transport
Dipeptides
Tripeptides — Active transport
Amino acids
Diffusion
Short chain fatty acids — Diffusion
Diffusion
Long chain fatty acids — Diffusion (+ micelles)
Monoglycerides
Triglycerides
Fat soluble vitamins (A, D, E, K)
To lacteal of villus

Micelles are spherical aggregates of 20-50 molecules of bile salt. They aid the passage of lipids across the membrane of the epithelial cells.

Transport of lipids: Most lipids are long chain fatty acids. These and the monoglycerides reach the liver by a more indirect route than other molecules. Once within the epithelial cells (aided by micelles), long chain fatty acids and glycerol are recombined in the smooth endoplasmic reticulum to form triglycerides. The triglycerides aggregate into chylomicrons, which leave the epithelial cell and enter the lymphatic circulation. Eventually they enter the general circulation near the heart and arrive at the liver via the hepatic artery.

Chylomicrons are formed in the endoplasmic reticulum of the intestinal epithelial cells. Triglycerides aggregate with phospholipids and cholesterol and become coated with protein. The protein coat keeps the fat in suspension during transport.

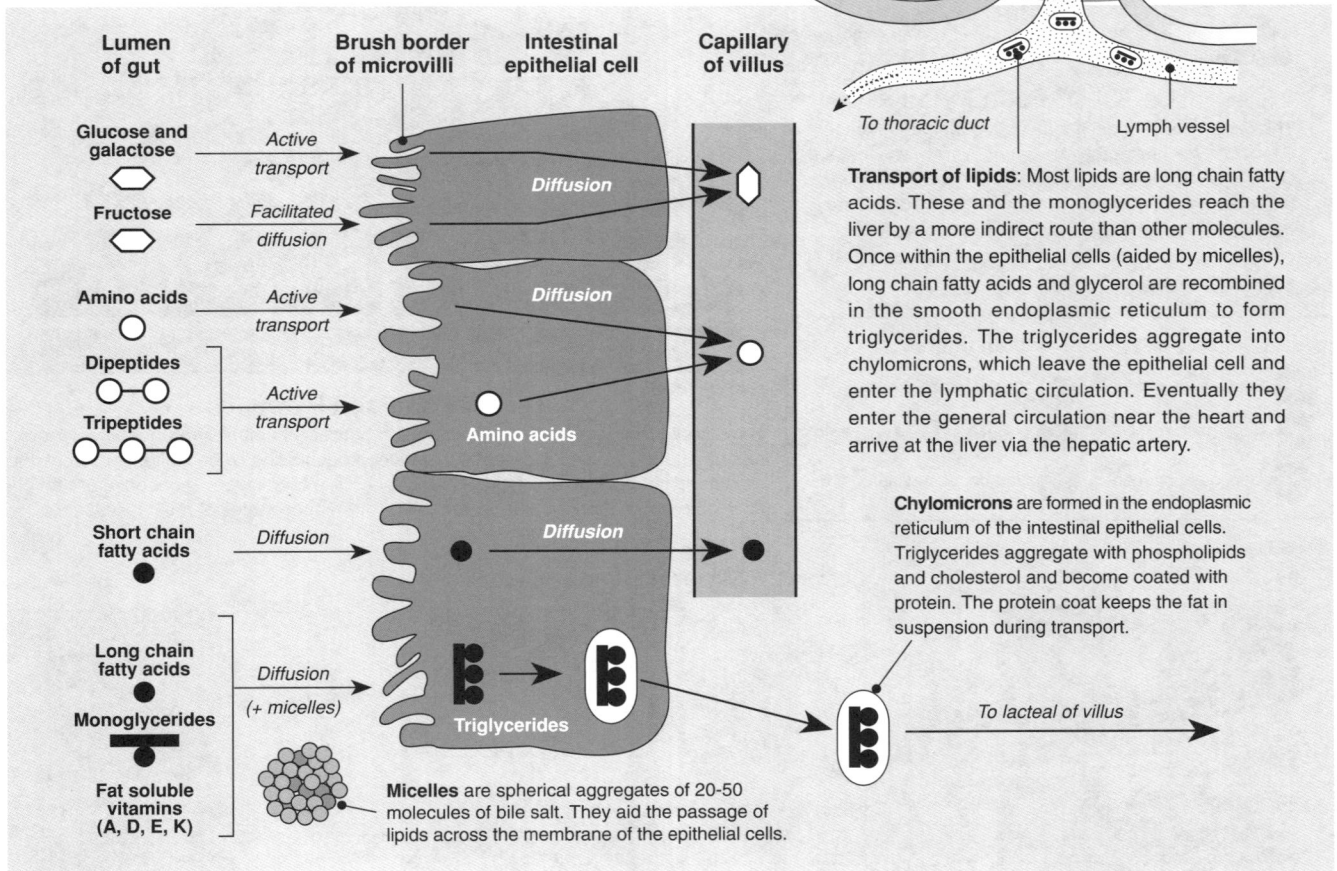

1. State the function of the following in fat digestion:

   (a) Micelles: _____

   (b) Chylomicrons: _____

2. Explain why it is important that venous blood from the gut is transported first to the liver via the hepatic portal circulation:

   _____

   _____

RDA❷   A Balanced Diet

Nutrients are required for metabolism, tissue growth and repair, and as an energy source. Good nutrition (provided by a **balanced diet**) is recognized as a key factor in good health. Conversely poor nutrition (malnutrition) may cause ill-health or **deficiency diseases**. A diet refers to the quantity and nature of the food eaten. While not all foods contain all the representative nutrients, we can obtain the required balance of different nutrients by eating a wide variety of foods. In a recent overhaul of previous dietary recommendations, the health benefits of monounsaturated fats (such as olive and canola oils), fish oils,

and whole grains have been recognized, and people are being urged to reduce their consumption of highly processed foods and saturated (rather than total) fat. Those on diets that restrict certain food groups (e.g., vegans) must take care to balance their intake of foods to ensure an adequate supply of protein and other nutrients (e.g., iron and B vitamins). Dietary information, including **Recommended Daily Amounts** (RDAs) for energy and nutrients, is provided to consumers through the food labeling. Such information helps individuals to assess their nutrient and energy intake and adjust their diet accordingly.

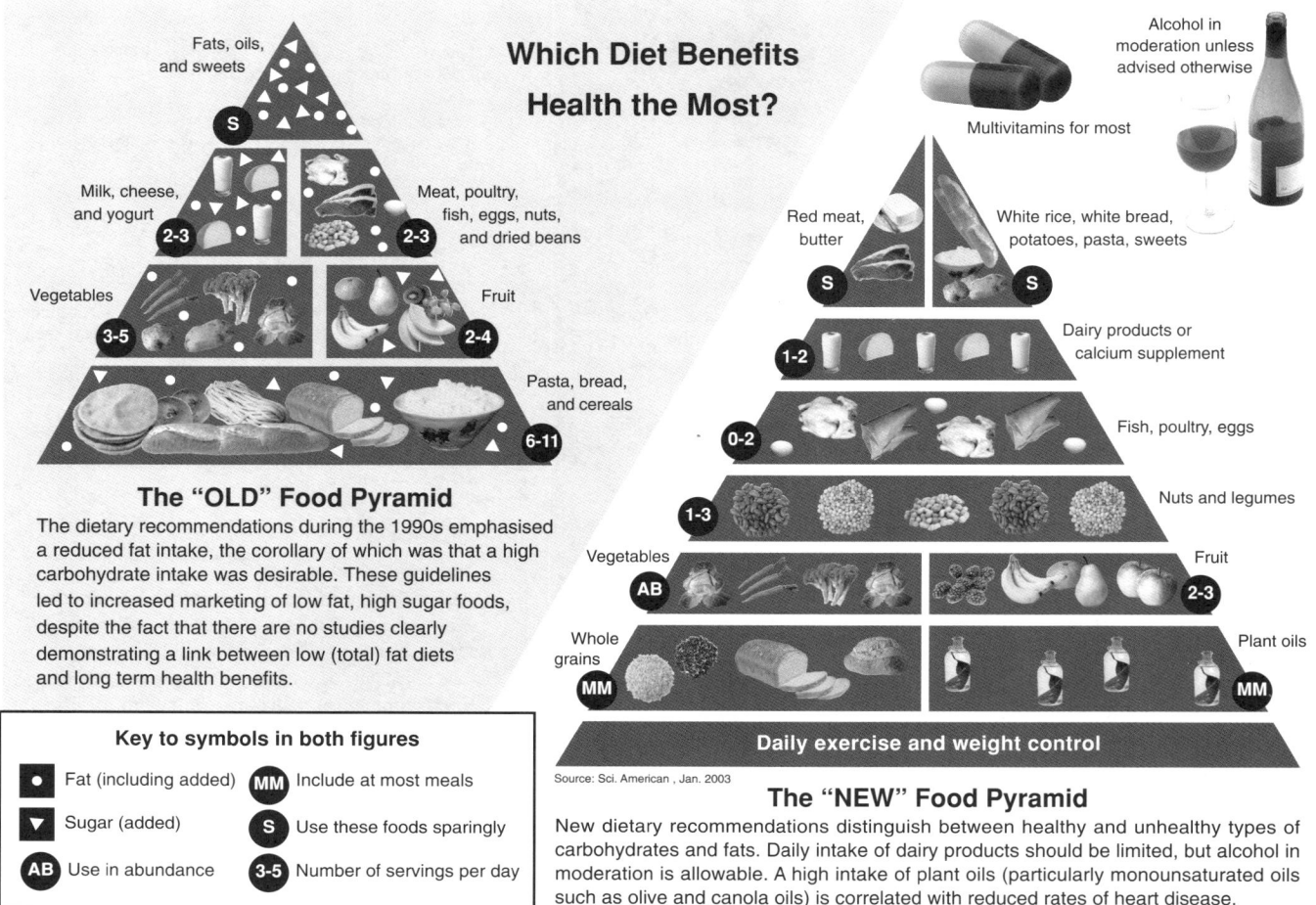

Which Diet Benefits Health the Most?

Fats, oils, and sweets — S

Milk, cheese, and yogurt — 2-3

Meat, poultry, fish, eggs, nuts, and dried beans — 2-3

Vegetables — 3-5

Fruit — 2-4

Pasta, bread, and cereals — 6-11

The "OLD" Food Pyramid

The dietary recommendations during the 1990s emphasised a reduced fat intake, the corollary of which was that a high carbohydrate intake was desirable. These guidelines led to increased marketing of low fat, high sugar foods, despite the fact that there are no studies clearly demonstrating a link between low (total) fat diets and long term health benefits.

Alcohol in moderation unless advised otherwise

Multivitamins for most

Red meat, butter — S

White rice, white bread, potatoes, pasta, sweets — S

Dairy products or calcium supplement — 1-2

Fish, poultry, eggs — 0-2

Nuts and legumes — 1-3

Vegetables — AB

Fruit — 2-3

Whole grains — MM

Plant oils — MM

Daily exercise and weight control

Source: Sci. American , Jan. 2003

Key to symbols in both figures

● Fat (including added)	MM Include at most meals		
▼ Sugar (added)	S Use these foods sparingly		
AB Use in abundance	3-5 Number of servings per day		

The "NEW" Food Pyramid

New dietary recommendations distinguish between healthy and unhealthy types of carbohydrates and fats. Daily intake of dairy products should be limited, but alcohol in moderation is allowable. A high intake of plant oils (particularly monounsaturated oils such as olive and canola oils) is correlated with reduced rates of heart disease.

Common Mineral Deficiencies

Fracture

Chin

Goiter on neck

Pregnant women may develop anemia

Calcium Deficiency

Calcium is required for enzyme function, formation of bones and teeth, blood clotting, and muscular contraction. Calcium deficiency causes poor bone growth and structure, increasing the tendency of bones to fracture and break. It also results in muscular spasms and poor blood clotting ability.

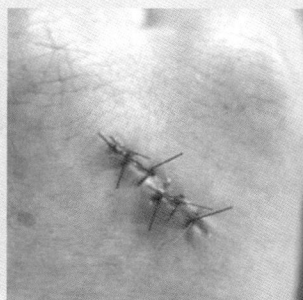

Zinc Deficiency

Zinc is found in red meat, poultry, fish, whole grain cereals and breads, legumes, and nuts. It is important for enzyme activity, production of insulin, making of sperm, and perception of taste. A deficiency in zinc causes growth retardation, a delay in puberty, muscular weakness, dry skin, and a delay in wound healing.

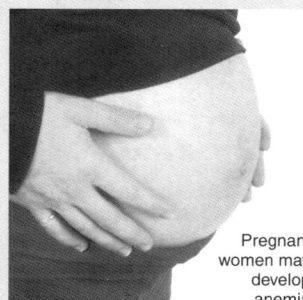

Iron Deficiency

Anemia results from lower than normal levels of hemoglobin in red blood cells. Iron from the diet is required to produce hemoglobin. People most at risk include women during pregnancy and those with an inadequate dietary intake. Symptoms include fatigue, fainting, breathlessness, and heart palpitations.

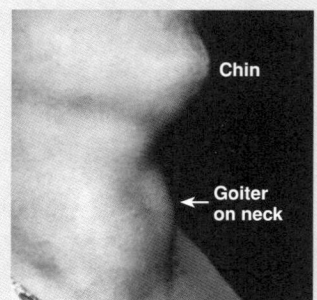

Iodine Deficiency

Iodine is essential for the production of thyroid hormones. These hormones control the rate of metabolism, growth, and development. Shortage of iodine in the diet may lead to **goiter** (thyroid enlargement as shown above). Iodine deficiency is also responsible for some cases of thyroid underactivity (**hypothyroidism**).

Labeling Food Products

Nutritional facts labels are used as a guide that consumers can use to determine if a particular food is a good source of a particular nutrient or to compare different brands of a similar type of food.

Calories provide a measure of how much energy is contained per serving.

These nutrients should be limited as they are usually consumed in adequate amounts during the day. Excessive consumption of some of these nutrients can lead to chronic diseases.

Eating enough of these nutrients can improve health and help reduce the risk of some diseases.

For labeling purposes, the US FDA set 2000 calories as the reference amount for calculating %DVs. 5% DV is considered low, whereas greater than 20% is considered high.

BBT's Cheesy Pasta Meal

Nutritional Facts

Serving size 1 cup (228 g)
Servings per container 2

Amount per serving
Calories 250   Calories from fat 110

	% Daily Value *
Total Fat 12 g	18%
Saturated Fat 3 g	15%
Cholesterol 30 mg	10%
Sodium 470 mg	20%
Total Carbohydrate 31 g	10%
Dietary Fibre 0 g	0%
Sugars 5 g	
Protein 5 g	
Vitamin A	4%
Vitamin C	2%
Calcium	20%
Iron	4%

Percentage Daily Values are based on a 2000 calorie diet. Your daily values may be higher or lower depending on your calorie needs.

	Calories	2000	2500
Total Fat	Less than	65 g	80 g
Sat Fat	Less than	20 g	25 g
Cholesterol	Less than	300 mg	300 mg
Sodium	Less than	2400 mg	2400 mg
Total Carbo	Less than	300 mg	375 mg
Dietary Fibre	Less than	25 mg	30 mg

Recommended Dietary Allowance (RDA) for selected nutrients

The RDA represents the establishment of a nutritional norm for planning and assessing dietary intake.

RDAs are the levels of intake of essential nutrients considered to be adequate to meet the known needs of practically all healthy people.

RDA figures were first published in 1943 and have been updated and expanded as more data became available and scientists developed a better understanding of nutritional requirements.

The table below shows RDAs (expressed as average daily intake) for selected nutrients for particular groups of the population.

Age range (years)	Protein (g)	Calcium (mg)	Iron (mg)	Folate (µg)	Vit. A (µg)	Vit. C (mg)
Males						
11 - 14	45	1300	12	150	1000	50
15 - 18	59	1300	12	200	1000	60
19 - 24	58	1000	10	200	1000	60
24 +	63	1200	10	200	1000	60
Females						
11 - 14	46	1300	15	150	800	50
15 - 18	44	1300	15	180	800	60
19 - 24	46	1000	15	180	800	60
24 +	50	1200	15	180	800	60
Pregnant*	60	1100	30	400	800	70
Lactating*	65	1200	15	280	1200	90

* RDA based on women 19-54 years.   Source: US FDA
* RDA for pregnancy is for the 2nd and 3rd trimester.

1. Identify two major roles of **nutrients** in the diet:

_____

2. (a) Compare the two food pyramids (opposite) and explain briefly how their recommendations for good nutrition differ:

_____

_____

(b) Based on the information on the graph (right), state the evidence that might support the revised recommendations:

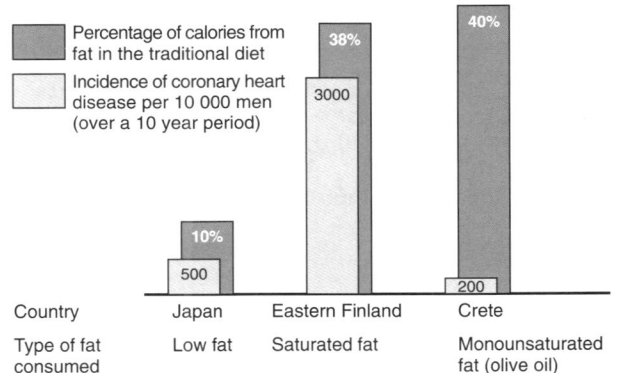

_____

_____

_____

_____

_____

_____

_____

Percentage of calories from fat in the traditional diet

Incidence of coronary heart disease per 10 000 men (over a 10 year period)

38%   40%

3000

10%

500   200

Country	Japan	Eastern Finland	Crete
Type of fat consumed	Low fat	Saturated fat	Monounsaturated fat (olive oil)

3. With reference to the table above, suggest why vegetarians must take particular care of their nutrition when pregnant:

_____

_____

4. Suggest how **RDAs** can be applied in the following situations:

(a) Dietary planning and assessment: _____

_____

(b) Food labeling and consumer information: _____

_____

RDA 1

Deficiency Diseases

Malnutrition is the general term for nutritional disorders resulting from not having enough food (starvation), not enough of the right food (deficiency), or too much food (obesity). Children under 5 are the most at risk from starvation and deficiency diseases because they are growing rapidly and are more susceptible to disease. Malnutrition is a key factor in the deaths of 6 million children each year, and in developing countries, dietary deficiencies are a major problem. In these countries malnutrition usually presents as **marasmus** or **kwashiorkor** (energy and protein deficiencies). Specific vitamin deficiencies in adults may lead to **beriberi** (vitamin B_1), **scurvy** (vitamin C), **rickets** (vitamin D) or **pellagra** (niacin). Vitamin deficiencies in childhood result in chronic, lifelong disorders. Deficiency diseases are rare in developed countries. People who do suffer from some form of dietary deficiency are either alcoholics, people with intestinal disorders that prevent proper nutrient uptake, or people with very restricted diets, such as strict vegetarians and vegans.

Vitamin D deficiency
Lack of vitamin D in children produces the disease rickets. In adults a similar disease is called osteomalacia. Sufferers typically show skeletal deformities (e.g. bowed legs, left) because inadequate amounts of calcium and phosphorus are incorporated into the bones. Vitamin D is produced by the skin when exposed to sunlight and it is vital for the absorption of calcium from the diet.

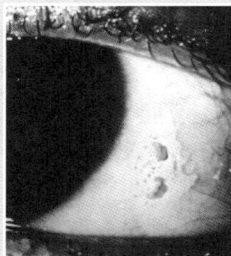

Vitamin A deficiency
Vitamin A (found in animal livers, eggs, and dairy products) is essential for the production of light-absorbing pigments in the eye and for the formation of cell structures. Symptoms of deficiency include loss of night vision, inflammation of the eye, **keratomalacia** (damage to the cornea), and the appearance of **Bitots spots** – foamy, opaque patches on the white of the eye (refer to photo).

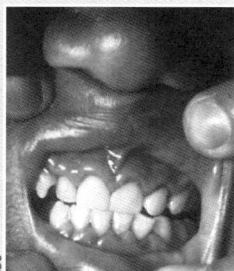

Vitamin C deficiency
Vitamin C deficiency causes a disease known as scurvy. It is now rare in developed countries because of increased consumption of fresh fruit and vegetables. Inadequate vitamin C intake disturbs the body's normal production of collagen, a protein in connective tissue that holds body structures together. This results in poor wound healing, rupture of small blood vessels (visible bleeding in the skin), swollen gums, and loose teeth.

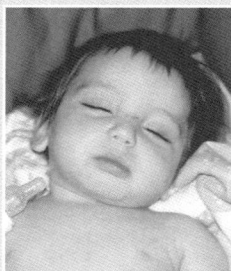

Vitamin B_{12} deficiency
Found primarily in meat, but also in eggs and dairy products. B_{12} is required for nucleic acid and protein metabolism, and for the maturation of red blood cells. It is essential for proper growth and for the proper nervous system function. Deficiency results in pernicious anemia, poor appetite, weight loss, growth failure, tiredness, brain damage, nervousness, muscle twitching, degeneration of the spinal cord, depression, and lack of balance.

Vitamin E deficiency
Found in nuts and seeds, vitamin E is a major antioxidant nutrient, retarding cellular aging due to oxidation. Vitamin E also strengthens capillary walls and promotes normal blood clotting. It has also been used by doctors in helping to prevent sterility, and to treat muscular dystrophy, calcium deposits in blood vessel walls, and heart conditions. Deficiency may lead to a rupture of red blood cells, loss of reproductive powers, abnormal fat deposits in the muscles, degenerative changes in the heart and other muscles, and dry skin.

Marasmus
Marasmus is the most common form of deficiency disease. It is a severe form of protein and energy malnutrition that usually occurs in famine or starvation conditions. Children suffering from marasmus are stunted and extremely emaciated. They have loose folds of skin on the limbs and buttocks, due to the loss of fat and muscle tissue. Unlike kwashiorkor, another form of malnutrition, marasmus does not cause abdominal bloating. However sufferers have no resistance to disease and common infections are typically fatal.

1. Define the term **malnutrition** and distinguish it from **starvation**: _____

_____

2. Identify the primary source and function of the following vitamins:

(a) Vitamin B_{12}: _____

_____

(b) Vitamin C: _____

_____

(c) Vitamin D: _____

_____

3. Discuss the likely reasons behind someone in a westernized society suffering from a vitamin deficiency: _____

_____

_____

DA ① Dietary Disorders

Most forms of malnutrition in western societies are the result of poorly balanced nutrient intakes rather than a lack of food *per se*. Dietary disorders may arise as a result of overeating (**obesity**), insufficient food intake (**anorexia nervosa**), or abnormally erratic eating habits (**bulimia nervosa**). Other health problems typically prevalent in western societies, including **cardiovascular diseases**, have been associated to varying degrees with the consumption of highly processed foods, high in cholesterol and saturated fats. Low fibre intake is a factor in the development of **colon cancer**, while high salt intake may lead to **hypertension**.

Anorexia Nervosa

An eating disorder characterized by an intense fear of being fat, severe weight loss, and a wilful avoidance of food. Clinically, anorexics are below 75% of the weight expected for their height and age. Anorexia most often affects teenage girls and young adult women (approximately 5% of sufferers are male). The exact cause of this form of self-starvation is not known, but research suggests that it is caused when emotional distress interacts with a physiological imbalance in a vulnerable individual. Anorexia is quite distinct from **bulimia**. Bulimics generally binge eat, and then purge their stomachs, rather than avoiding food altogether.

Obesity

Obesity is the most common form of malnutrition in affluent societies. It is a condition where there is too much body fat (not the same as being overweight). In the USA, nearly 25% of all adults are obese. Some genetic and hormonal causes are known, although obesity is a result of energy intake (eating) exceeding the **net energy expenditure**. Dieting is often ineffective for long-term weight loss because once normal eating is resumed the body responds by storing more fat in fat cells. Obesity increases the incidence of hypertension (high blood pressure), stroke, coronary artery disease, and adult onset diabetes mellitus.

Health risks associated with anorexia nervosa

Depression that can lead to suicide.

Swollen salivary glands.

Excessive downy hair on face, arms, legs and back.

Liver and kidney damage, even failure.

Anemia (low iron levels).

Permanent loss of bone mass, which increases the risk of fractures and leads to osteoporosis.

Deficiency in saliva results in cavities and tooth loss.

Ion imbalances lead to irregular heartbeat and cardiac arrest.

Constantly feeling cold (hypothermia).

Menstrual periods stop (amenorrhea).

Health risks associated with obesity

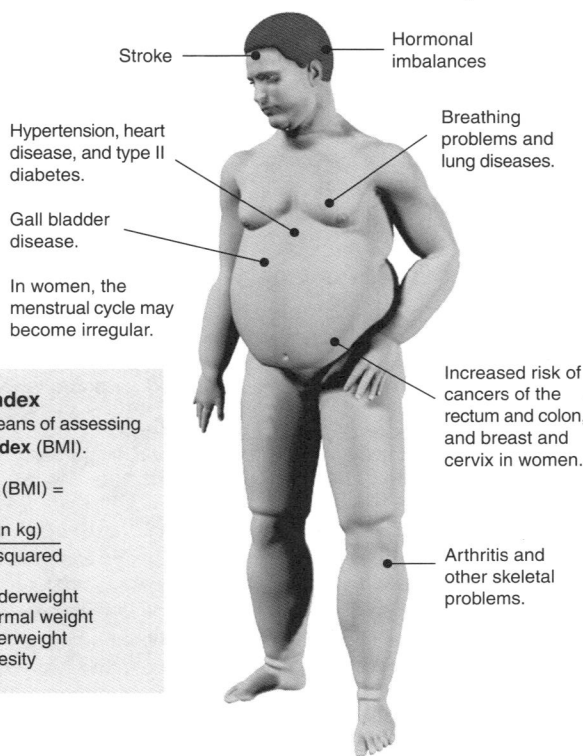

Stroke

Hormonal imbalances

Hypertension, heart disease, and type II diabetes.

Breathing problems and lung diseases.

Gall bladder disease.

In women, the menstrual cycle may become irregular.

Increased risk of cancers of the rectum and colon, and breast and cervix in women.

Arthritis and other skeletal problems.

Body Mass Index

The most widely accepted means of assessing obesity is the **body mass index** (BMI).

Body mass index (BMI) =

$$\frac{\text{weight of body (in kg)}}{\text{height (in meters) squared}}$$

A BMI of:
- 17 to 20 = underweight
- 20 to 25 = normal weight
- 25 to 30 = overweight
- over 30 = obesity

1. Describe the two basic energy factors that determine how a person's weight will change: _____

_____

2. Using the BMI, calculate the minimum and maximum weight at which a 1.85 m tall man would be considered:

   (a) Overweight: _____   (c) Obese: _____

   (b) Normal weight: _____   (d) Underweight: _____

3. State the possible health consequences of the following aspects of a diet:

   (a) High salt consumption: _____

   (b) Low fibre content: _____

   (c) High cholesterol content: _____

4. List the key differences between anorexia nervosa and bulimia nervosa: _____

_____

_____

Animal Transport Systems

IB SL	IB HL	IB Options	AP Biology
Complete nos: 1-3, 10, 16, 18, 20-21, 24 Extension: 4, 7, 9	Complete nos: 1-3, 10, 16, 18, 20-21, 24 Extension: 4, 7, 9	Complete nos: Option B: 27-30 Option H: 11-13, 22, 25, 31-33, extension: 23, 26	Complete nos: 1-30 Some numbers extension as appropriate

Learning Objectives

☐ 1. Compile your own glossary from the **KEY WORDS** displayed in **bold type** in the learning objectives below.

Background and required knowledge

☐ 2. Explain the need for **transport systems** in different organisms (e.g. multicellular plants, animals) in relation to size and **surface area to volume ratio**.

☐ 3. Recognize the relationship between the transport systems of larger organisms and their specialized exchange systems.

Animal transport systems (pages 186-188)

☐ 4. Explain why animals above a certain size require an internal transport system. Describe the components and functions of transport systems in animals, including the **blood vessels**, **heart**, and **blood** (or **hemolymph**).

Open and closed circulatory systems

☐ 5. Giving examples, and using schematic diagrams, describe the basic structure and function of the two types of circulatory system found in animals:
   ☐ **Open circulatory systems** (arthropods, most molluscs).
   ☐ **Closed circulatory systems** (vertebrates and some invertebrates, e.g. many annelids, cephalopods).
   For each type of system, consider the following:
   • The types of blood vessels present and whether or not these are continuous, closed channels.
   • How exchanges occur between the blood and tissues and the efficiency of these.
   • The basic structure of the heart.
   • The relative speed and pressure of fluid circulation.

☐ 6. Giving examples, describe the features of:
   ☐ Closed, **single circulatory systems**
   ☐ Closed, **double circulatory systems** in representative classes, e.g. amphibians, reptiles, and mammals.
   For each type of system, consider the following:
   • Whether or not the blood returns to the heart after being oxygenated at the gas exchange surface.
   • Whether the blood flows around the body at relatively low or relatively high pressure.
   • How the heart structure influences blood flow and the efficiency of the transport system as a whole.

The human circulatory system

☐ 7. In more detail than in #6, describe the **closed, double circulatory system** of a mammal, identifying: **carotid arteries**, **heart** and associated vessels, **liver** and **kidneys** and associated vessels. Indicate the direction of blood flow and the relative oxygen content of the blood at different points. Distinguish between the **pulmonary circulation** and the **systemic circulation**.

Vessels and body fluids (pages 189-195, 216-217)

☐ 8. Appreciate that all the **blood vessels** in the closed circulatory of vertebrates are lined with a thin endothelium, and the basic structure of each type of vessel is relatively uniform in all vertebrate classes.

☐ 9. Recognize the structure of **arteries**, **veins**, and **capillaries** using a light microscope.

☐ 10. Explain the relationship between the structure and functional role of **arteries**, **capillaries**, **veins**, and (if required) **arterioles**. If required, draw labeled diagrams to illustrate the salient features of these comparisons.

☐ 11. Explain the importance of **capillaries**. Draw a diagram to show the relative positions of blood vessels in a capillary network and their relationship to the **lymphatic vessels** (in humans). Distinguish between **blood**, **lymph**, **plasma**, and **tissue fluid**.

☐ 12. Describe the formation and roles of **tissue fluid** and **lymph** in humans. You should demonstrate an awareness of the role of pressure differences in forming tissue fluid, but calculations of these are not required.

☐ 13. Outline the transport functions of the lymphatic system, identifying how lymph is returned to the blood circulatory system. Recognize the lymphatic system as a network of vessels that parallels the blood system.

☐ 14. Using examples, describe the role of the **blood** and **hemolymph** in the transport systems of vertebrates and invertebrates respectively.

☐ 15. Describe the functional role of circulatory fluids and their associated **respiratory pigments** in transporting respiratory gases. Describe the structure and function of a named **respiratory pigment**. Appreciate that respiratory pigments are not universally present and animals in some taxonomic groups do not need them.

☐ 16. Describe the nature and/or composition of **blood** in humans, including the role of each of the following:
   Non-cellular components: **plasma** (water, mineral ions, blood proteins, hormones, nutrients, urea, vitamins).
   Cellular components: **erythrocytes**, **leukocyte** (**lymphocytes**, **monocytes**, **granulocytes**), **platelets**.

☐ 17. Identify the homeostatic roles of blood, and comment on the role of blood in modern medicine. Giving examples, discuss the difficulties involved in producing viable blood substitutes.

☐ 18. Identify the main substances transported by the blood. If required, state how each of the identified substances is transported (e.g. bound, free in plasma etc.) and/or the sites at which exchanges occur.

Heart structure and function (pages 187, 196-199)

☐ 19. Using schematic diagrams, compare the basic structure of a mammalian heart with the structure of the heart in any or all of the following: *fish, amphibian, reptile, bird.*

The human heart

☐ 20. Draw a diagram to describe the internal and external gross structure of a mammalian (e.g. human) **heart**. Identify: **atria**, **ventricles**, **atrioventricular valves**, and **semilunar valves**, as well the major vessels (**aorta**, **vena cava**, **pulmonary artery** and **vein**) and the coronary circulation. Relate the differences in the thickness of the heart chambers to their functions.

☐ 21. Describe the action of the heart in terms of collecting blood, pumping blood, and opening and closing valves. Clearly describe the passage of blood through the heart and describe the role of the valves in this.

☐ 22. Explain the events of the **cardiac cycle**, relating stages in the cycle (**atrial systole**, **ventricular systole**, and **diastole**) to the maintenance of blood flow through the heart. Describe the **heart sounds** and relate these to stages in the cardiac cycle. Analyze data showing pressure and volume changes in the left atrium, left ventricle, and the aorta during the cardiac cycle.

☐ 23. Understand the terms **systolic** and **diastolic blood pressure**. Describe typical values of these in the normal range and in a person with **hypertension**.

☐ 24. Outline the control of heartbeat in terms of the **pacemaker**, nerves, and **adrenaline**. Understand what is meant by the **myogenic** nature of the heartbeat,

☐ 25. In more detail than in #24 above, outline the mechanisms controlling heartbeat, including the role of the **sinoatrial node** (SAN), the **atrioventricular** (AV) **node**, and the conducting fibers in the ventricular walls (**bundle of His**, and the **Purkinje fibers**). Relate the activity of the SAN to the **intrinsic heart rate**.

☐ 26. Describe the extrinsic regulation of **heart rate** through **autonomic nerves** (vagus and cardiac nerves). Identify the role of the **medulla**, **baroreceptors** (pressure receptors), and **chemoreceptors** in the response of the heart to changing demands (e.g. exercise).

The effects of exercise (pages 200-201, 301-302)

☐ 27. Define the terms: **pulse** and **pulse rate** and explain how they relate to heart rate. Explain the significance of resting pulse rate in relation to physical **fitness**.

☐ 28. Investigate the effects of exercise on the body. List measurements that could be made to test fitness.

☐ 29. Explain how **training** affects the cardiovascular system (cross reference with the topic "Nerves, Muscles, and Movement"). Define the term: **cardiac output** and explain how it is calculated. Explain how **heart rate**, **stroke volume**, and cardiac output change with exercise (particularly aerobic exercise).

☐ 30. Discuss the short and long term physiological effects of aerobic exercise, including: appropriate redistribution of blood flow in response to exercise and adaptation of the cardiovascular and musculoskeletal system to regular exercise (effect on resting heart rate, stroke volume, endurance, and general health).

Cardiovascular diseases

☐ 31. Recognize the term **cardiovascular disease** (CVD), as a broad term encompassing a variety of diseases. Distinguish between CVDs that are congenital and those that are associated with a poor diet and lifestyle.

☐ 32. Outline the causes and features of **coronary thrombosis** and **atherosclerosis**, including the effect of the latter on blood flow and its relationship to **myocardial infarction**.

☐ 33. Describe **risk factors** in the development of cardiovascular diseases. Include reference to genetic factors, gender, and lifestyle factors (e.g. cigarette smoking, diet, and obesity). Distinguish between controllable and uncontrollable **risk factors** for the development of CVD, and give examples of each.

Textbooks

See the 'Textbook Reference Grid' on pages 8-9 for textbook page references relating to material in this topic.

Supplementary Texts

See pages 5-6 for additional details of these texts:

■ Adds, J. et al., 2000. **Exchange & Transport, Energy & Ecosystems** (NelsonThornes), pp. 43-56.

■ Clegg, C.J., 1998. **Mammals: Structure and Function** (John Murray), pp. 30-38.

■ Fullick, A., 1998. **Human Health and Disease** (Heinemann), pp. 74-82.

Periodicals

See page 6 for details of publishers of periodicals:

STUDENT'S REFERENCE

■ **Red Blood Cells** Bio. Sci. Rev. 11(2) Nov. 1998, pp. 2-4. *The structure and function of erythrocytes, including the details of oxygen transport.*

■ **Cunning Plumbing** New Scientist, 6 February 1999, pp. 32-37. *The arteries can actively respond to changes in blood flow, spreading the effects of mechanical stresses to avoid extremes.*

■ **ECGs: Getting to the Heart of the Matter** Biol. Sci. Rev., 10(1) Sept. 1997, pp. 21-24. *Monitoring the electrical activity of the heart, the cardiac cycle and medical diagnosis of heart disease.*

■ **Blood Pressure** Biol. Sci. Rev., 12(5) May 2000, pp. 9-12. *Blood pressure: its control, measurement, and significance to diagnosis.*

■ **A Fair Exchange** Biol. Sci. Rev., 13(1), Sept. 2000, pp. 2-5. *Formation and reabsorption of tissue fluid (includes disorders of fluid balance).*

■ **Fascinating Rhythm** New Scientist, 3 January 1998, pp. 20-25. *Cardiac rhythm and how changes in the rhythm can signify the onset of disease.*

TEACHER'S REFERENCE

■ **Breaking Out of the Box** The American Biology Teacher, 63(2), Feb. 2001, pp. 101-115. *Investigating cardiovascular activity: a web-based activity on the cardiac cycle.*

■ **Spectrophotometric Properties of Hemoglobin** The American Biology Teacher, 59(2), February 1997, pp. 104-107. *Measuring spectral absorption for oxyhemoglobin and carboxyhemoglobin, and the role of hemoglobin as an oxygen transport molecule in the blood.*

■ **Modeling Blood Flow in the Aorta** The American Biology Teacher, 59(9), Nov. 1997, pp. 586-588. *Modeling blood flow in the aorta as a way to investigate the fluid dynamics of the CVS.*

■ **Measuring How Elastic Arteries Function** The American Biology Teacher, 59(8), October 1997, pp. 513-517. *Investigating blood flow through elastic arteries, including: changes in blood pressure, the role of elastin and collagen, and the mechanical properties of arteries.*

■ **The Search for Blood Substitutes** Scientific American, February 1998, pp. 60-65. *Finding a successful blood substitute depends on being able to replicate to exact properties of blood.*

■ **Defibrillation: The Spark of Life** Scientific American, June 1998, pp. 68-73. *This article explains just how an electric shock resets the heart's rhythm after heart failure.*

■ **Atherosclerosis: The New View** Scientific American, May 2002, pp. 28-37. *The latest views on the pathological development and rupture of plaques in atherosclerosis. An excellent account.*

■ **On Two Hearts & Other Coronary Reflections** The American Biology Teacher, 60(1), Jan. 1998, pp. 66-69. *Heart disease: atherosclerosis and its effects on the health of the circulatory system.*

Internet

See pages 10-11 for details of how to access **Bio Links** from our web site: **www.thebiozone.com**. From Bio Links, access sites under the topics:

GENERAL BIOLOGY ONLINE RESOURCES > Online Textbooks and Lecture Notes: • S-Cool! A level biology revision guide • Learn.co.uk • Mark Rothery's biology web site ... *and others*

ANIMAL BIOLOGY: • Anatomy and physiology • Human physiology lecture notes ... *and others* > **Circulatory System:** • Animal circulatory systems • Cardiology compass • Heart diseases • How the heart works • The circulatory system • The heart: A virtual exploration • The matter of the human heart ... *and others*

HEALTH AND DISEASE > Non-infectious Disease: • American Heart Association • Cardiology compass • Heart disease • NOVA online: cut to the heart

Software and video resources are now provided in the Teacher Resource Handbook

Circulatory Systems

A ①

Two basic types of circulatory systems have evolved in animals. Many invertebrates have an **open circulatory system**, while vertebrates (including humans) have a **closed circulatory system**. The latter is often called a cardiovascular system because it consists of a heart and a network of tube-like vessels. The circulatory systems of arthropods are open but quite varied. Insects, unlike most other arthropods, do not use a circulatory system to transport oxygen around the body. Instead, oxygen is delivered directly to the tissues via a system of "air tubes" (the tracheal system) that carries oxygen directly to all tissues. In addition to its usual transport functions, the circulatory system may also be important in hydraulic movement (e.g. newly emerged butterflies expand their wings through hydraulic pressure).

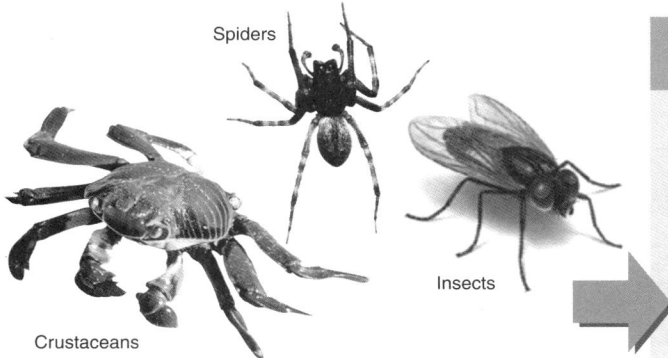

Types of Circulatory Systems

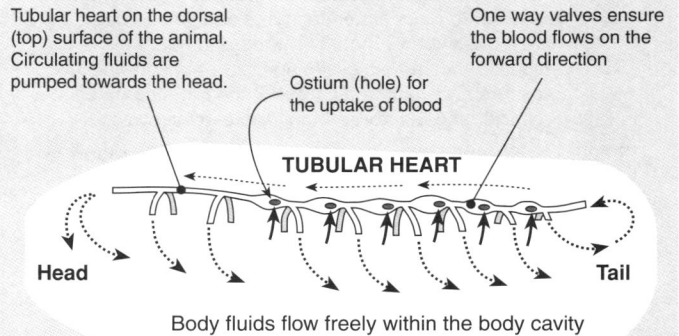

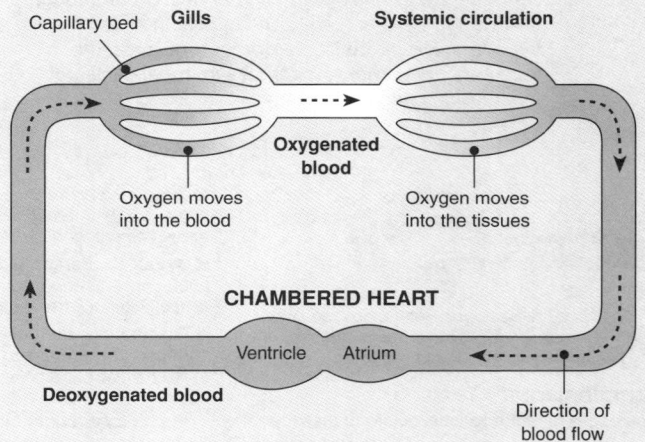

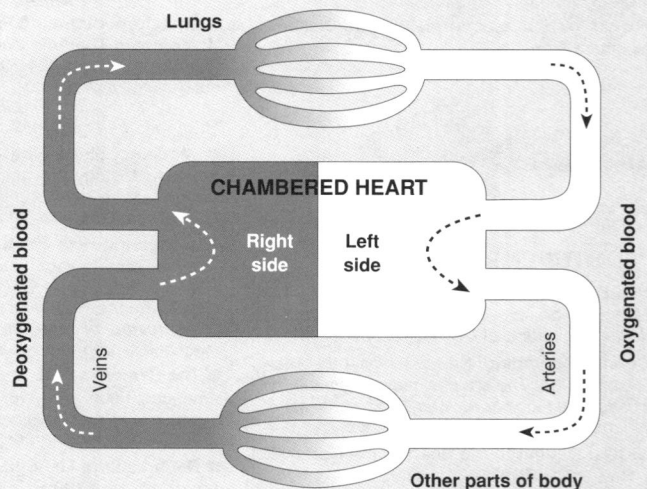

Spiders

Insects

Crustaceans

Open Circulation Systems

Arthropods and molluscs (except squid and octopus) have open circulatory systems in which the blood is pumped by a tubular, or sac-like, heart through short vessels into large spaces in the body cavity. The blood bathes the cells before reentering the heart through holes (**ostia**). Muscle action may assist the circulation of the blood.

Tubular heart on the dorsal (top) surface of the animal. Circulating fluids are pumped towards the head.

Ostium (hole) for the uptake of blood

One way valves ensure the blood flows on the forward direction

TUBULAR HEART

Head

Tail

Body fluids flow freely within the body cavity

Rays

Bony fish

Sharks

Closed, Single Circuit Systems

In closed circulation systems, the blood is contained within vessels and is returned to the heart after every circulation of the body. Exchanges between the blood and the fluids bathing the cells occur by diffusion across capillaries. In single circuit systems, typical of fish, the blood goes directly from the gills to the body. The blood loses pressure at the gills and flows at low pressure around the body.

Capillary bed   **Gills**   **Systemic circulation**

Oxygenated blood

Oxygen moves into the blood

Oxygen moves into the tissues

CHAMBERED HEART

Ventricle   Atrium

Deoxygenated blood

Direction of blood flow

Birds

Reptiles

Amphibians

Closed, Double Circuit Systems

Double circulation systems occur in all vertebrates other than fish. The blood is pumped through a pulmonary circuit to the lungs, where it is oxygenated. The blood returns to the heart, which pumps the oxygenated blood, through a systemic circuit, to the body. In amphibians and most reptiles, the heart is not completely divided and there is some mixing of oxygenated and deoxygenated blood. In birds and mammals, the heart is fully divided and there is no mixing.

Lungs

CHAMBERED HEART

Right side   **Left side**

Deoxygenated blood

Veins

Arteries

Oxygenated blood

Other parts of body

Fish Heart

The fish heart is linear, with a sequence of three chambers in series (the conus may be included as a fourth chamber). Blood from the body first enters the heart through the sinus venosus, then passes into the atrium and the ventricle. A series of one-way valves between the chambers prevents reverse blood flow. Blood leaving the heart travels to the gills.

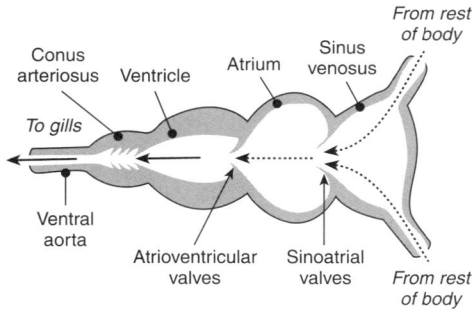

Amphibian Heart

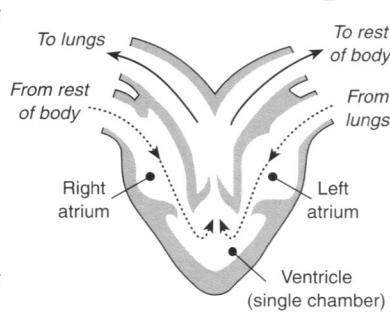

Amphibian hearts are three chambered. The atrium is divided into left and right chambers, but the ventricle lacks an internal dividing wall. Although this allows mixing of oxygenated and deoxygenated blood, the spongy nature of the ventricle reduces mixing. Amphibians are able to tolerate this because much of their oxygen uptake occurs across their moist skin, and not their lungs.

Mammalian Heart

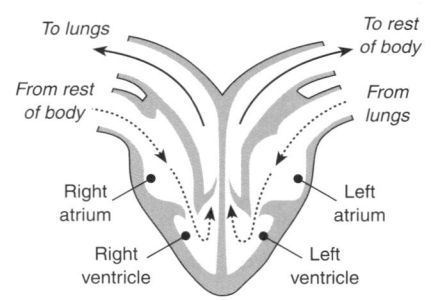

In birds and mammals, the heart is fully partitioned into two halves, resulting in four chambers. Blood circulates through two circuits, with no mixing of the two. Oxygenated blood from the lungs is kept separated from the deoxygenated blood returning from the rest of the body.

1. Explain the difference between closed and open systems of circulation: _____

   _____

   _____

2. When comparing the two types of closed circulatory systems, explain why a double is more efficient than a single circuit:

   _____

   _____

   _____

3. Vertebrate hearts have evolved from relatively simple structures (as in fish) to more complex organs such as those found in mammals. Describe the number and arrangement of heart chambers in:

   (a) Fish: _____

   _____

   _____

   (b) Amphibians: _____

   _____

   _____

   (c) Mammals: _____

   _____

   _____

4. Describe where the blood flows to after it passes through the gills in a fish:

   _____

   _____

Mammalian Transport

A 1

Animal cells require a constant supply of nutrients and oxygen, and continuous removal of wastes. Simple, small organisms (e.g. sponges, cnidarians, flatworms, nematodes) can achieve this through simple diffusion across moist body surfaces without requiring a specialized system. Larger, more complex organisms require a circulatory system to transport materials because diffusion is too inefficient and slow to supply all the cells of the body adequately. Circulatory systems transport nutrients,

oxygen, carbon dioxide, wastes, and hormones. They also help to maintain fluid balance, regulate body temperature, and assist in the defense of the body against invading microorganisms. Mammals have a double circulatory system: a pulmonary system, which carries blood between the heart and lungs, and a systemic system, which carries blood between the heart and the rest of the body. The diagram below illustrates the main vessels that make up the human circulatory system.

Schematic Overview of the Human Circulatory System

Deoxygenated blood (colored gray below) travels to the right side of the heart via the vena cavae. The heart pumps the deoxygenated blood to the lungs where it releases carbon dioxide and receives oxygen. The oxygenated blood (colored white below) travels via the pulmonary vein back to the heart from where it is pumped to all parts of the body. The **venous system** (figure, left) returns blood from the capillaries to the heart. The **arterial system** (figure right) carries blood from the heart to the capillaries. **Portal systems** carry blood between two capillary beds.

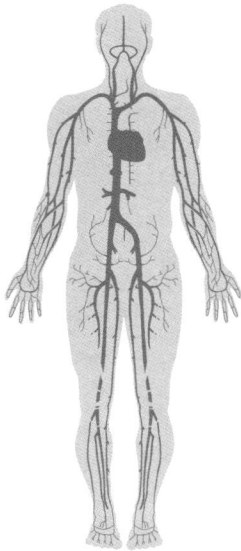

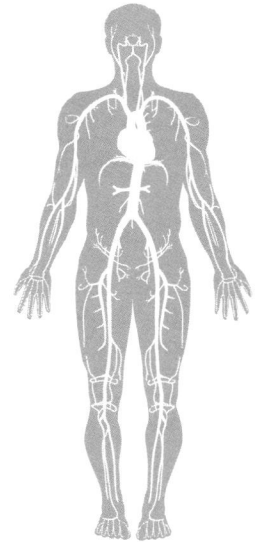

VENOUS SYSTEM

Superior vena cava:
receives deoxygenated blood from the head and body.

Right atrium:
receives deoxygenated blood via the superior and inferior vena cavae.

Right ventricle:
pumps deoxygenated blood to the lungs.

Inferior vena cava:
receives deoxygenated blood from the lower body and organs.

Hepatic vein:
carries deoxygenated blood from the liver.

Hepatic portal vein:
carries deoxygenated, nutrient rich blood from the gut for processing.

Renal vein:
carries deoxygenated blood from the kidneys.

ARTERIAL SYSTEM

...nary vein:
...ygenated
...to the heart.

Pulmonary artery:
carries deoxygenated blood to the lungs.

Left atrium:
receives oxygenated blood from the lungs.

Left ventricle:
pumps blood from the left atrium to the aorta.

Hepatic artery:
carries oxygenated blood to the liver.

Mesenteric artery:
carries oxygenated blood to the gut.

Renal artery:
carries oxygenated blood to the kidneys.

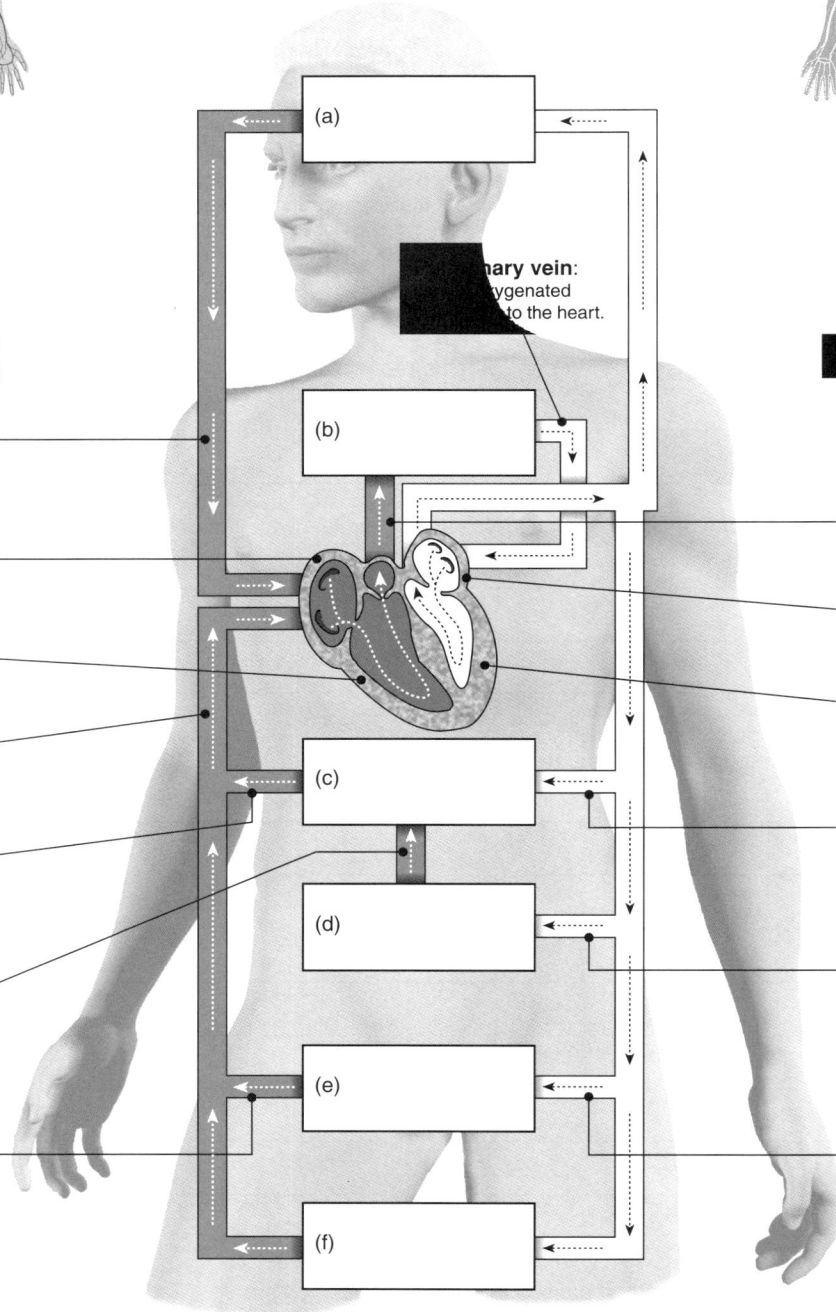

(a)
(b)
(c)
(d)
(e)
(f)

1. Complete the diagram above by labeling the boxes with the organs or structures they represent.

![hand icon] A1

Arteries

In vertebrates, arteries are the blood vessels that carry blood away from the heart to the capillaries within the tissues. The large arteries that leave the heart divide into medium-sized (distributing) arteries. Within the tissues and organs, these distribution arteries branch to form very small vessels called **arterioles**, which deliver blood to capillaries. Arterioles lack the thick layers of arteries and consist only of an endothelial layer wrapped by a few smooth muscle fibers at intervals along their length. Resistance to blood flow is altered by contraction (**vasoconstriction**) or relaxation (**vasodilation**) of the blood vessel walls, especially in the arterioles. Vasoconstriction increases resistance and leads to an increase in blood pressure whereas vasodilation has the opposite effect. This mechanism is important in regulating the blood flow into tissues.

Arteries

Arteries have an elastic, stretchy structure that gives them the ability to withstand the high pressure of blood being pumped from the heart. At the same time, they help to maintain pressure by having some contractile ability themselves (a feature of the central muscle layer). Arteries nearer the heart have more elastic tissue, giving greater resistance to the higher blood pressures of the blood leaving the left ventricle. Arteries further from the heart have more muscle to help them maintain blood pressure. Between heartbeats, the arteries undergo elastic recoil and contract. This tends to smooth out the flow of blood through the vessel.

Arteries comprise three main regions (right):

1. A thin inner layer of epithelial cells called the **endothelium** lines the artery.

2. A central layer (the **tunica media**) of elastic tissue and smooth muscle that can stretch and contract.

3. An outer connective tissue layer (the **tunica externa**) has a lot of elastic tissue.

Artery Structure

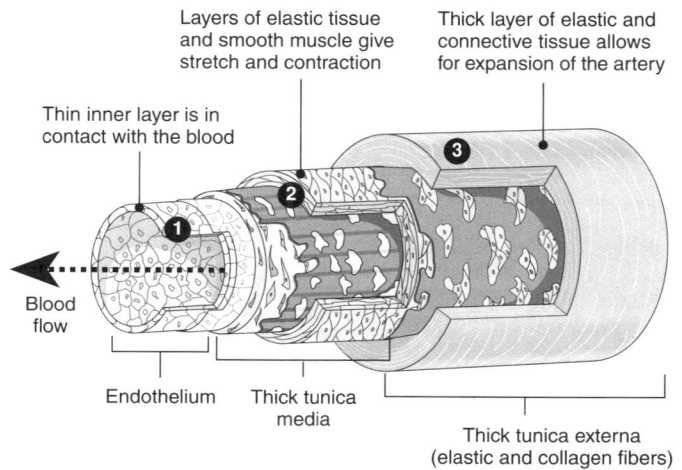

Layers of elastic tissue and smooth muscle give stretch and contraction

Thick layer of elastic and connective tissue allows for expansion of the artery

Thin inner layer is in contact with the blood

Blood flow

Endothelium

Thick tunica media

Thick tunica externa (elastic and collagen fibers)

Cross section through a large artery

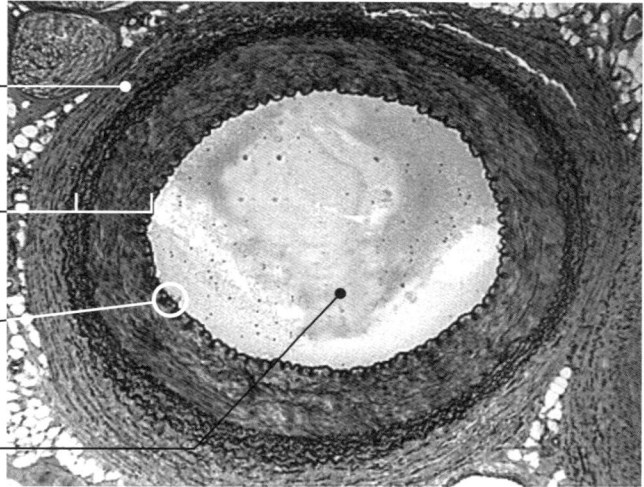

(a)

(b)

(c)

(d)

1. Using the diagram to help you, label the photograph of the cross section through an artery (above).

2. (a) Explain why the walls of arteries need to be thick with a lot of elastic tissue: _____

_____

(b) Explain why arterioles lack this elastic tissue layer: _____

_____

3. Explain the purpose of the smooth muscle in the artery walls: _____

_____

4. (a) Describe the effect of vasodilation on the diameter of an arteriole: _____

(b) Describe the effect of vasodilation on blood pressure: _____

Veins and Capillaries

Veins are the blood vessels that return blood to the heart from the tissues. The smallest veins (**venules**) return blood from the capillary beds to the larger veins. Veins and their branches contain about 59% of the blood in the body. The structural differences evident between veins and arteries is mainly associated with differences in the relative thickness of the vessel layers and the diameter of the lumen. These, in turn, are related to the vessel's functional role. In vertebrates, capillaries are very small vessels that connect arterial and venous circulation and allow efficient exchange of nutrients and wastes between the blood and tissues. Capillaries form networks or beds and are abundant where metabolic rates are high.

Veins

Veins are made up of essentially the same three layers as arteries but they have less elastic and muscle tissue. However they can still expand enough to adapt to changes in the pressure and volume of the blood passing through them. Blood flowing in the veins has lost a lot of pressure because it has passed through the narrow capillary vessels. If a vein is cut, the blood oozes out slowly, whereas arterial blood spurts rapidly. The low pressure in veins means that many veins, especially those in the limbs, need to have valves to prevent backflow of the blood as it returns to the heart.

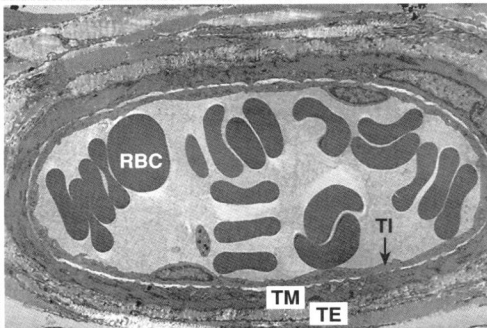

Above: TEM of a vein showing red blood cells (RBC) in the lumen, and the tunica intima (TI), tunica media (TM), and tunica externa (TE).

Capillaries

Blood passes from the arterioles into capillaries, the smallest blood vessels in the body. Capillaries have a diameter of 4-10 μm. Red blood cells are 7-8 μm and can only just squeeze through. The only tissue present is the endothelium of squamous epithelial cells. Capillaries form a vast network of vessels that penetrate all parts of the body and are so numerous that no cell is more than 25 μm from any capillary. It is in the capillaries that the exchange of materials between the body cells and the blood takes place.

The Structure of Veins

Inner thin layer of cells lining the vein (tunica intima)

Central thin layer of elastic and muscle tissue (tunica media)

Thin layer of elastic connective tissue (tunica externa)

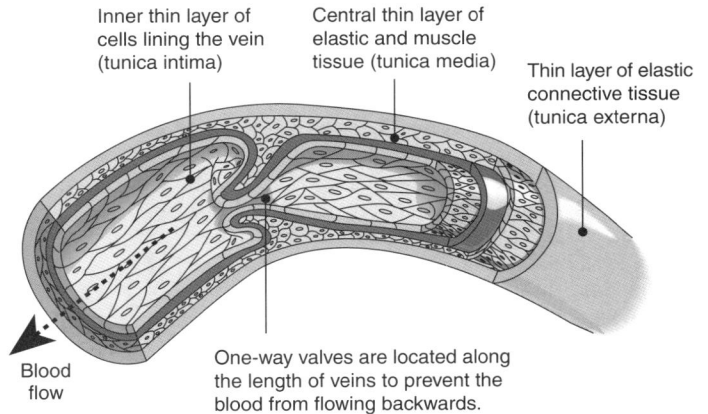

Blood flow

One-way valves are located along the length of veins to prevent the blood from flowing backwards.

Exchanges in Capillaries

Water and solutes pass back and forth with very little barrier.

The capillary walls are formed of a single layer of endothelial cells.

Blood flow is slow (<1 mm per second).

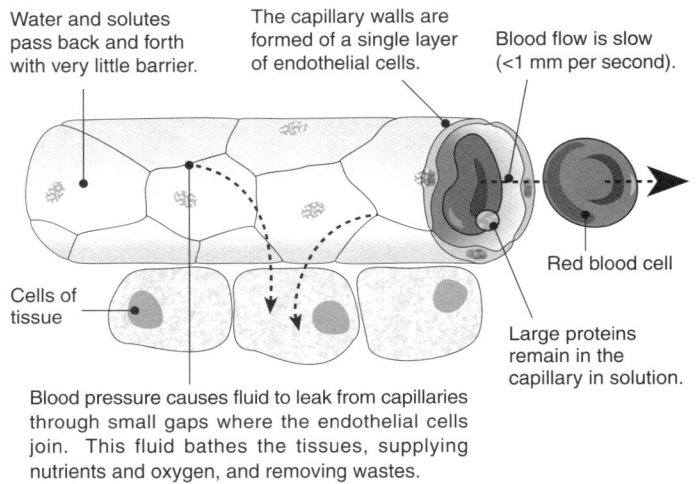

Red blood cell

Cells of tissue

Large proteins remain in the capillary in solution.

Blood pressure causes fluid to leak from capillaries through small gaps where the endothelial cells join. This fluid bathes the tissues, supplying nutrients and oxygen, and removing wastes.

1. Contrast the structure of veins and arteries with respect to the following:

   (a) Thickness of muscle and elastic tissue: _____

   (b) Size of the lumen (inside of the vessel): _____

   (c) With respect to their functional roles give a reason for these differences: _____

   _____

2. Explain the role of the valves in assisting the veins to return blood back to the heart: _____

   _____

3. (a) Explain what causes fluid to leak out of the capillaries: _____

   (b) Describe the purpose of this leakage: _____

   (c) Explain why exchanges between the blood and other body tissues occurs only through capillaries: _____

   _____

Lymph and Tissue Fluid

Fluid that leaks out of the capillaries has an essential role in bathing the tissues. Fluid movement into and out of capillaries depends on the balance between the blood (hydrostatic) pressure (HP) and the concentration of solutes (e.g. ions and proteins) at each end of a capillary bed (see below). Not all the fluid is returned to the capillaries and this extra fluid must be returned to the general circulation. This is the role of the **lymphatic system**; a system of vessels that parallels the system of arteries and veins. The

lymphatic system consists of the lymph and lymph vessels, and the lymphatic tissues and organs (e.g. spleen, lymph nodes). As well as collecting the tissue fluid that escapes from the capillaries and returning it into circulation, the lymphatic system also has a role in internal defense, and in transporting lipids absorbed from the digestive tract. *NOTE: Those wishing to cover this topic using **solute potential** terminology can download an alternative version of this page from:* **www.thebiozone.com/solutepotential.html**

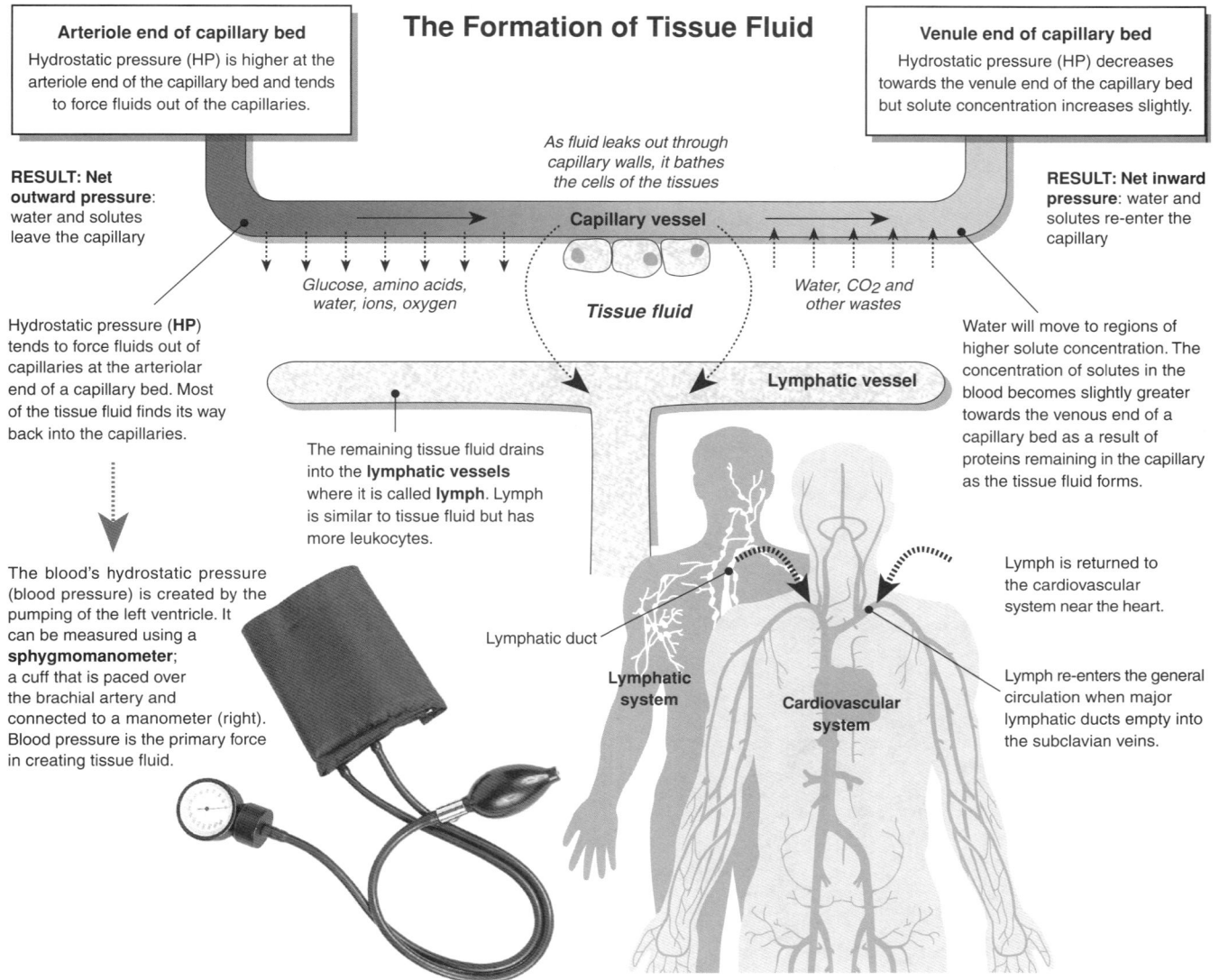

The Formation of Tissue Fluid

Arteriole end of capillary bed
Hydrostatic pressure (HP) is higher at the arteriole end of the capillary bed and tends to force fluids out of the capillaries.

Venule end of capillary bed
Hydrostatic pressure (HP) decreases towards the venule end of the capillary bed but solute concentration increases slightly.

RESULT: Net outward pressure: water and solutes leave the capillary

RESULT: Net inward pressure: water and solutes re-enter the capillary

As fluid leaks out through capillary walls, it bathes the cells of the tissues

Capillary vessel

Glucose, amino acids, water, ions, oxygen

Tissue fluid

Water, CO_2 and other wastes

Hydrostatic pressure (**HP**) tends to force fluids out of capillaries at the arteriolar end of a capillary bed. Most of the tissue fluid finds its way back into the capillaries.

Lymphatic vessel

The remaining tissue fluid drains into the **lymphatic vessels** where it is called **lymph**. Lymph is similar to tissue fluid but has more leukocytes.

Water will move to regions of higher solute concentration. The concentration of solutes in the blood becomes slightly greater towards the venous end of a capillary bed as a result of proteins remaining in the capillary as the tissue fluid forms.

The blood's hydrostatic pressure (blood pressure) is created by the pumping of the left ventricle. It can be measured using a **sphygmomanometer**; a cuff that is paced over the brachial artery and connected to a manometer (right). Blood pressure is the primary force in creating tissue fluid.

Lymphatic duct

Lymphatic system

Cardiovascular system

Lymph is returned to the cardiovascular system near the heart.

Lymph re-enters the general circulation when major lymphatic ducts empty into the subclavian veins.

1. In your own words, explain how hydrostatic pressure and solute concentration operate to cause fluid movement at:

   (a) The arteriolar end of a capillary bed: _____

   _____

   (b) The venous end of a capillary bed: _____

   _____

2. State the two ways in which tissue fluid is returned into the general circulation:

   (a) _____

   (b) _____

3. Suggest why women in the late stages of pregnancy often suffer from swelling in the lower limbs (edema):

   _____

   _____

Blood

Blood makes up about 8% of body weight. Blood is a complex liquid tissue comprising cellular components suspended in plasma. If a blood sample is taken, the cells can be separated from the plasma by centrifugation. The cells (formed elements) settle as a dense red pellet below the transparent, straw-colored plasma. Blood performs many functions: it transports nutrients, respiratory gases, hormones, and wastes; it has a role in thermoregulation through the distribution of heat; it defends against infection; and its ability to clot protects against blood loss.

Non-Cellular Blood Components

The non-cellular blood components form the plasma. Plasma is a watery matrix of ions and proteins and makes up 50-60% of the total blood volume.

Water
The main constituent of blood and lymph.
Role: Transports dissolved substances. Provides body cells with water. Distributes heat therefore has a central role in thermoregulation. Regulation of water content helps to regulate blood pressure and volume.

Mineral ions
Sodium, bicarbonate, magnesium, potassium, calcium, chloride.
Role: Osmotic balance, pH buffering, and regulation of membrane permeability. They also have a variety of other functions, e.g., Ca^{2+} is involved in blood clotting.

Plasma proteins
7-9% of the plasma volume.
Serum albumin
Role: Osmotic balance and pH buffering, Ca^{2+} transport.
Fibrinogen and prothrombin
Role: Take part in blood clotting.
Immunoglobulins
Role: Antibodies involved in the immune response.
α-globulins
Role: Bind/transport hormones, lipids, fat soluble vitamins.
β-globulins
Role: Bind/transport iron, cholesterol, fat soluble vitamins.
Enzymes
Role: Take part in and regulate metabolic activities.

Substances transported by non-cellular components
Products of digestion
Examples: sugars, fatty acids, glycerol, and amino acids.
Excretory products
Example: urea
Hormones and vitamins
Examples: insulin, sex hormones, vitamins A and B12.
Importance: These substances occur at varying levels in the blood. They are **transported** to and from **the cells** dissolved in the plasma or bound to plasma proteins.

Cellular Blood Components

The formed elements of blood float in the plasma and make up 40-50% of the total blood volume.

Erythrocytes (red blood cells or RBCs)
5-6 million per mm^3 blood; 38-48% of total blood volume.
Role: RBCs **transport oxygen** (O_2) and a small amount of carbon dioxide (CO_2). The oxygen is carried bound to hemoglobin (Hb) in the cells. Each Hb molecule can bind four molecules of oxygen.

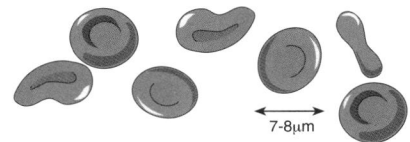

7-8μm

Platelets
Small, membrane bound cell fragments derived from bone marrow cells; about 1/4 the size of RBCs.
0.25 million per mm^3 blood.
Role: To start the blood clotting process.

2μm

Leukocytes (white blood cells)
5-10 000 per mm^3 blood
2-3% of total blood volume.
Role: Involved in internal defense. There are several types of white blood cells (below).

Lymphocytes
T and B cells.
24% of the white cell count.
Role: Antibody production and cell mediated immunity.

Neutrophils
Phagocytes.
70% of the white cell count.
Role: Engulf foreign material.

Eosinophils
Rare leukocytes; normally 1.5% of the white cell count.
Role: Mediate allergic responses such as hayfever and asthma.

Basophils
Rare leukocytes; normally 0.5% of the white cell count.
Role: Produce heparin (an anti-clotting protein), and histamine. Involved in inflammation.

The Examination of Blood

Different types of microscopy give different information about blood. An SEM (right) shows the detailed external morphology of the blood cells. A fixed smear of a blood sample viewed with a light microscope (far right) can be used to identify the different blood cell types present, and their ratio to each other. Determining the types and proportions of different white blood cells in blood is called a **differential white blood cell count**. Elevated counts of particular cell types indicate allergy or infection.

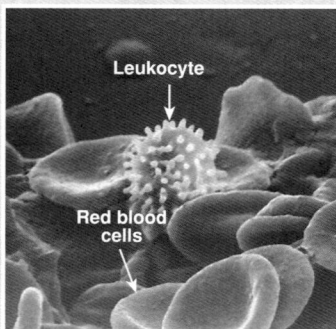

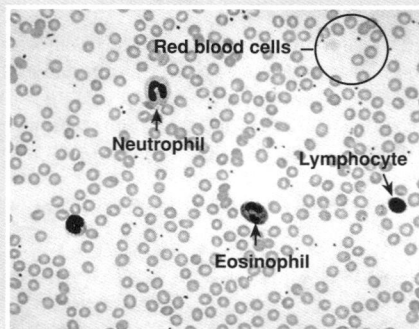

SEM of red blood cells and a leukocytes. **Light microscope** view of a fixed blood smear.

1. For each of the following blood functions, identify the component of the blood responsible and state how the function is carried out (the mode of action). The first one is done for you:

   (a) **Temperature regulation**. *Blood component:* Water component of the plasma

   Mode of action: Water absorbs heat and dissipates it from sites of production (e.g., organs)

   (b) **Protection against disease**. *Blood component:* _____

   Mode of action: _____

   (c) **Communication between cells, tissues, and organs**. *Blood component:* _____

   Mode of action: _____

   (d) **Oxygen transport**. *Blood component:* _____

   Mode of action: _____

   (e) **CO_2 transport**. *Blood component:* _____

   Mode of action: _____

   (f) **Buffer against pH changes**. *Blood component:* _____

   Mode of action: _____

   (g) **Nutrient supply**. *Blood component:* _____

   Mode of action: _____

   (h) **Tissue repair**. *Blood components:* _____

   Mode of action: _____

   (i) **Transport of hormones, lipids, and fat soluble vitamins**. *Blood components:* _____

   Mode of action: _____

2. Identify two features that distinguish red and white blood cells: _____

3. Explain two physiological advantages of red blood cell structure (lacking nucleus and mitochondria):

   (a) _____

   (b) _____

4. Suggest what each of the following results from a differential white blood cell count would suggest:

   (a) Elevated levels of eosinophils (above the normal range): _____

   (b) Elevated levels of neutrophils (above the normal range): _____

   (c) Elevated levels of basophils (above the normal range): _____

   (d) Elevated levels of lymphocytes (above the normal range): _____

The Search for Blood Substitutes

Blood's essential homeostatic role is evident when considering the problems encountered when large volumes of blood are lost. Transfusion of whole blood (see photograph below) or plasma is an essential part of many medical procedures, e.g. after trauma or surgery, or as a regular part of the treatment for some disorders (e.g. thalassemia). This makes blood a valuable commodity. A blood supply relies on blood donations; but as the demand for blood increases, the availability of donors continues to decline. This decline is partly due to more stringent screening of donors for diseases such as HIV/AIDS, hepatitis, and variant CJD. The inadequacy of blood supplies has made the search for a safe, effective blood substitute the focus of much research. Despite some possibilities, no currently available substitute reproduces all of blood's many homeostatic functions.

Essential criteria for a successful blood substitute

❑ The substitute should be non-toxic and free from diseases.

❑ It should work for all blood types.

❑ It should not cause an immune response.

❑ It should remain in circulation until the blood volume is restored and then it should be safely excreted.

❑ It must be easily transported and suitable for storage under normal refrigeration.

❑ It should have a long shelf life.

❑ It should perform some or all of blood tasks.

A shortfall in blood supplies, greater demand, and public fear of contaminated blood, have increased the need for a safe, effective blood substitute. Such a substitute must fulfil strict criteria (above).

A researcher displays a hemoglobin based artificial blood product, developed by Defense R&D Canada – Toronto and now produced under license by Hemosol Inc. Human testing and marketing has now progressed successfully into advanced trials. A human hemoglobin molecule is pictured in the background. Photo with permission from Hemosol inc.

Chemical based

These rely on synthetic oxygen-carrying compounds called **perfluorocarbons** (PFCs). PFCs are able to dissolve large quantities of gases. They do not dissolve freely in the plasma, so they must be emulsified with an agent that enables them to be dispersed in the blood.

Advantages: PFCs can transport a lot of oxygen, and transfer gases quickly.

Disadvantages: May result in oxygen accumulation in the tissues, which can lead to damage.

Examples: Oxygent™: Produced in commercial quantities using PFC emulsion technology; Perflubon (a PFC), water, a surfactant, and salts, homogenized into a stable, biologically compatible emulsion.

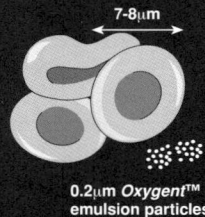

Oxygent™ is a PFC based blood substitute; the small particles travel in the plasma, through blocked capillaries, to deliver oxygen to oxygen depleted tissues.

7-8μm

0.2μm *Oxygent™* emulsion particles

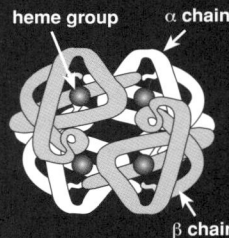

heme group   α chain

β chain

Hemoglobin (left) contains 2 alpha and 2 beta chains grouped together with 4 oxygen-carrying heme groups. It is toxic when free in the plasma unless it is carried bound to other compounds.

Hemoglobin based

These rely on hemoglobin (Hb), modified by joining it to a polymer (polyethylene glycol) to make it larger.

Advantages: Modified hemoglobin should better be able to approximate the various properties of blood.

Disadvantages: Hb is toxic unless carried within RBCs; it requires modification before it can be safely transported free in the plasma. Substitutes made from human Hb use outdated blood as the Hb source. Bovine Hb may transmit diseases (e.g. BSE).

Examples: Hemolink™, a modified human Hb produced by Hemosol Inc. in California. Research is focused on developing cell culture lines with the ability to produce Hb.

1. Describe two essential features of a successful blood substitute, identifying briefly why the feature is important:

   (a) _____

   (b) _____

2. Name the two classes of artificial blood substitutes: _____

3. Explain why it is difficult to reproduce blood's many functions: _____

   _____

4. Suggest why it is important to be able to produce modified hemoglobin from cultures (rather than from collected blood):

   _____

   _____

   _____

RA②   Respiratory Pigments

Regardless of the gas exchange system present, the amount of oxygen that can be carried in solution in the blood is small. The efficiency of gas exchange in animals is enhanced by the presence of **respiratory pigments**. All respiratory pigments consist of proteins complexed with iron or copper. They combine reversibly with oxygen and greatly increase the capacity of blood to transport oxygen and deliver it to the tissues. For example, the amount of oxygen dissolved in the plasma in mammals is only about 2 cm³ O₂ per liter. However the amount carried bound to haemoglobin is 100 times this. Hemoglobin is the most widely distributed respiratory pigment and is characteristic of all vertebrates and many invertebrate taxa. Other respiratory pigments include chlorocruorin, hemocyanin, and hemerythrin. Note that the precise structure and carrying capacity of any one particular pigment type varies between taxa (see the range of hemoglobins in the table below).

Respiratory Pigments

Respiratory pigments are colored proteins capable of combining reversibly with oxygen, hence increasing the amount of oxygen that can be carried by the blood. Pigments typical of representative taxa are listed below. Note that the polychaetes are very variable in terms of the pigment possessed.

Taxon	Oxygen capacity (cm³ O₂ per 100 cm³ blood)	Pigment
Oligochaetes	1 - 10	Hemoglobin
Polychaetes	1 - 10	Hemoglobin, chlorocruorin, or hemerythrin
Crustaceans	1 - 6	Hemocyanin
Molluscs	1 - 6	Hemocyanin
Fishes	2 - 4	Hemoglobin
Reptiles	7 - 12	Hemoglobin
Birds	20 - 25	Hemoglobin
Mammals	15 - 30	Hemoglobin

Mammalian Hemoglobin

Hemoglobin is a globular protein consisting of 574 amino acids arranged in four polypeptide sub-units: two identical **beta chains** and two identical **alpha chains**. The four sub-units are held together as a functional unit by bonds. Each sub-unit has an iron-containing heme group at its center and binds one molecule of oxygen.

Chemical formula:
$$C_{3032}H_{4816}O_{872}N_{780}S_8Fe_4$$

Beta chain: 146 amino acids

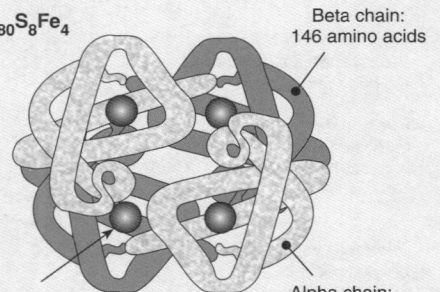

In hemoglobin, each polypeptide encloses an iron-containing heme group which binds one oxygen molecule.

Alpha chain: 141 amino acids

Aquatic polychaete fanworms e.g. *Sabella*, possess **chlorocruorin**.

Oligochaete annelids, such as earthworms, have **hemoglobin**.

Aquatic crustaceans e.g. crabs, possess **hemocyanin** pigment.

Vertebrates such as this fish have **hemoglobin** pigment.

Cephalopod molluscs such as *Nautilus* contain **hemocyanin**.

Birds, being vertebrates contain the pigment **hemoglobin**.

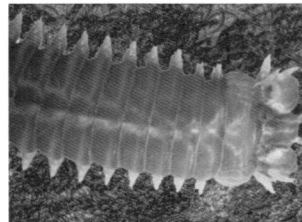

Many large active polychaetes, e.g. *Nereis,* contain **hemoglobin**.

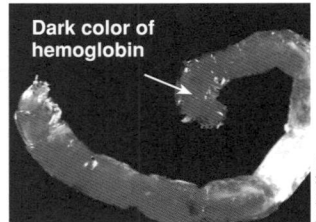

Dark color of hemoglobin

Chironomus is one of only two insect genera to contain a pigment.

1. (a) Explain how respiratory pigments increase the carrying capacity of the blood: _____

_____

(b) Identify which feature of a respiratory pigment determines its oxygen carrying capacity: _____

_____

2. With reference to hemoglobin, suggest how oxygen carrying capacity is related to metabolic activity: _____

_____

_____

3. Suggest why larger molecular weight respiratory pigments are carried dissolved in the plasma rather than within cells:

_____

The Human Heart

RA 2

The heart is the centre of the human cardiovascular system. It is a hollow, muscular organ, weighing on average 342 grams. Each day it beats over 100 000 times to pump 3780 liters of blood through 100 000 kilometers of blood vessels. The heart lies between the lungs, to the left of the body's midline. It comprises a system of four muscular chambers that alternately fill and empty of blood, acting as a double pump. The left side pumps blood to the body tissues. The right side pumps blood to the lungs. The two upper chambers are the atria (right and left). The two lower chambers are the right and left ventricles. Both upper and lower chambers are separated by a partition or **septum**. The coronary arteries branch from the aorta and provide the circulation for the heart muscle itself. It is these arteries that become blocked in many cases of heart disease.

Human Heart Structure

(sectioned, anterior view)

Aorta carries oxygenated blood to the head and body

Vena cava receives deoxygenated blood from the head and body

Pulmonary artery carries deoxygenated blood to the lungs

Bicuspid valve

RA

LA

Tricuspid valve prevents backflow of blood into right atrium

RV

Chordae tendinae non-elastic strands supporting the valve flaps

LV

Semi-lunar valve prevents the blood flow back into ventricle

Septum separates the ventricles

Key to abbreviations

RA   Right atrium; receives deoxygenated blood via anterior and posterior vena cavae

RV   Right ventricle; pumps deoxygenated blood to the lungs via the pulmonary artery

LA   Left atrium; receives blood returning to the heart from the lungs via the pulmonary veins

LV   Left ventricle; pumps oxygenated blood to the head and body via the aorta

Top view of a heart in section, showing valves

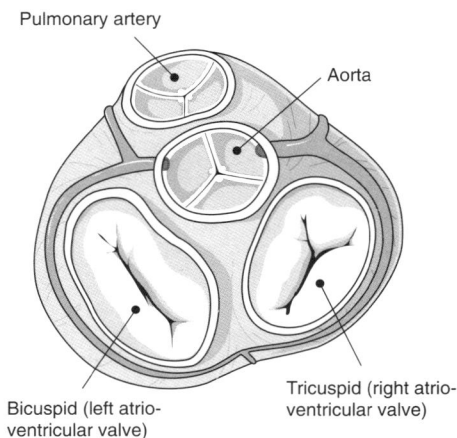

Pulmonary artery

Aorta

Bicuspid (left atrio-ventricular valve)

Tricuspid (right atrio-ventricular valve)

Posterior view of heart

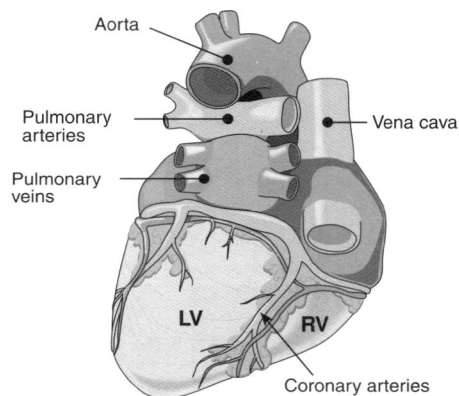

Aorta

Pulmonary arteries

Vena cava

Pulmonary veins

LV

RV

Coronary arteries

1. In the schematic diagram of the heart, below, label the four chambers and the main vessels entering and leaving them. The arrows indicate the direction of blood flow. Use large colored circles to mark the position of each of the four valves.

Schematic Diagram of Heart Structure

(a)

(b)

(c)

(d)

(e)

(f)

(g)

(h)

Septum separates the two halves of the heart

2. The wall of the left ventricle is thicker and more muscular than that of the right ventricle. Explain the reason for this:

The Cardiac Cycle

The cardiac cycle refers to the sequence of events of a heartbeat. The pumping of the heart consists of alternate contractions (systole) and relaxations (diastole). The entire cycle is divided into three stages (below). For a heart beating at 75 beats per minute, one cardiac cycle lasts about 0.8 seconds. Pressure changes generated by the cycle of contraction and relaxation cause the valves to open and close, preventing the backflow of blood. The noise of the blood when the valves open and close produces the heartbeat sound (lubb-dupp).

Heart during ventricular filling

The **pulse** results from the rhythmic expansion of the arteries as the blood spurts from the left ventricle. Pulse rate therefore corresponds to heart rate.

Stage 1: Atrial systole and ventricular filling The ventricles relax and blood flows into them from the atria. Note that 70% of the blood from the atria flows passively into the ventricles. It is during the last third of ventricular filling that the atria contract.

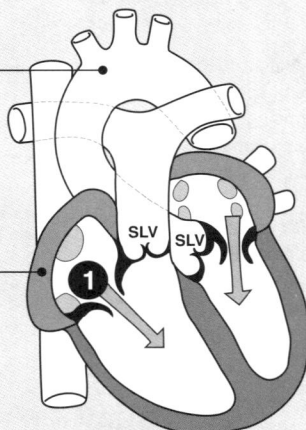

Heart during ventricular contraction

Stage 2: Ventricular systole The atria relax, the ventricles contract, and blood is pumped from the ventricles into the aorta and the pulmonary artery. The start of ventricular contraction coincides with the first heart sound.

Stage 3 (not shown): There is a short period of atrial and ventricular contraction. Semilunar valves (**SLV**) close to prevent backflow into the ventricles (see diagram, left). The cycle begins again.

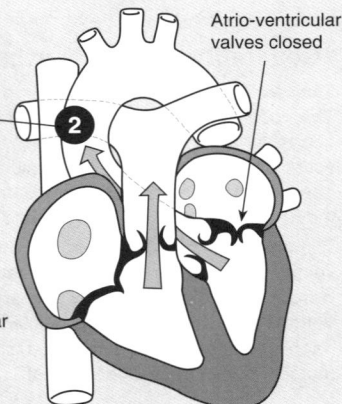

Atrio-ventricular valves closed

Note that some texts separate stage 1 into two distinct stages, with the full cycle ending on stage 4

The Normal Electrocardiogram (ECG)

The electrical impulses transmitted through the heart generate electrical currents that can be detected on the body surface. They can be recorded on a heart monitor as a trace, called an electrocardiogram or ECG. The ECG pattern is the result of the different impulses produced at each phase of the **cardiac cycle**. Each wave of electrical activity brings about a corresponding contraction in the part of the heart receiving the electrical impulse.

- The first wave of the ECG corresponds to stage 1 of the cardiac cycle (atrial contraction and ventricular filling).
- The second wave of the ECG corresponds to stage 2 of the cardiac cycle (ventricular contraction),
- The third wave corresponds to stage 3 of the cardiac cycle.

A normal ECG (right) shows a regular repeating pattern of electrical pulses. Heart disorders may be detected through changes in the electrical activity that appear on the ECG.

Second wave: The spread of the impulse through the ventricles, which contract.

Third wave: Recovery of the electrical activity of the ventricles, which are relaxed.

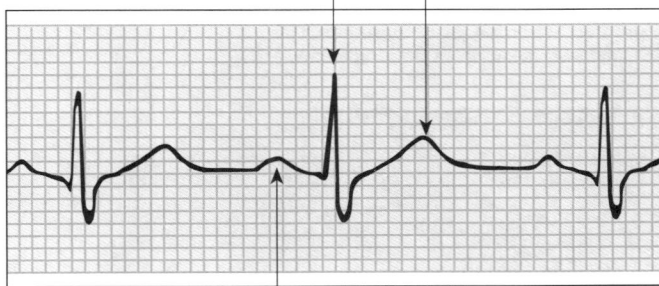

First wave: The spread of the impulse from the pacemaker through the atria, which then contract.

3. (a) Explain what is meant by the term diastole: _____

   (b) Explain what is meant by systole: _____

4. Explain the purpose of the valves in the heart: _____

_____

_____

5. Suggest the physiological reason for the period of electrical recovery experienced each cycle (ECG: third wave):

_____

_____

6. Explain why an ECG is an important medical tool: _____

_____

7. (a) Explain what you are recording when you take a pulse: _____

_____

   (b) Name a place where pulse rate could best be taken and briefly explain why: _____

_____

Control of Heart Activity

RA 2

When removed from the body the cardiac muscle continues to beat. Therefore, the origin of the heartbeat is **myogenic**: the contractions arise as an intrinsic property of the cardiac muscle itself. The heartbeat is regulated by a special conduction system consisting of the pacemaker (**sinoatrial node**) and specialized conduction fibers called **Purkinje fibers**. The pacemaker sets a basic rhythm for the heart, but this rate is influenced by the cardiovascular control centre in the medulla in response to sensory information from pressure receptors in the walls of the heart and blood vessels, and by higher brain functions. Changing the rate and force of heart contraction is the main mechanism for controlling cardiac output in order to meet changing demands.

Generation of the Heartbeat

The basic rhythmic heartbeat is **myogenic**. The nodal cells (SAN and atrioventricular node) spontaneously generate rhythmic action potentials without neural stimulation. The normal resting rate of self-excitation of the SAN is about 50 beats per minute.

The amount of blood ejected from the left ventricle per minute is called the **cardiac output**. It is determined by the **stroke volume** (the volume of blood ejected with each contraction) and the **heart rate** (number of heart beats per minute).

Cardiac output

= stroke volume × heart rate

Cardiac muscle responds to stretching by contracting more strongly. The greater the blood volume entering the ventricle, the greater the force of contraction. This relationship is known as **Starling's Law.**

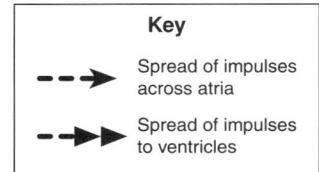

A TEM photo of cardiac muscle showing branched fibers (muscle cells). Each muscle fiber has one or two nuclei and many large mitochondria. **Intercalated discs** are specialized electrical junctions that separate the cells and allow the rapid spread of impulses through the heart muscle.

Sinoatrial node (SAN) is also called the **pacemaker**. It is a mass of specialized muscle cells near the opening of the superior vena cava. The pacemaker initiates the cardiac cycle, spontaneously generating action potentials that cause the atria to contract. The SAN sets the basic pace of the heart rate, although this rate is influenced by hormones and impulses from the autonomic nervous system.

Atrioventricular node (AVN) at the base of the atrium briefly delays the impulse to allow time for the atrial contraction to finish before the ventricles contract.

Bundle of His (atrioventricular bundle) containing Purkinje tissue. A tract of conducting fibers that distribute the action potentials over the ventricles causing ventricular contraction.

Key	
‑‑‑➤	Spread of impulses across atria
‑‑►►	Spread of impulses to ventricles

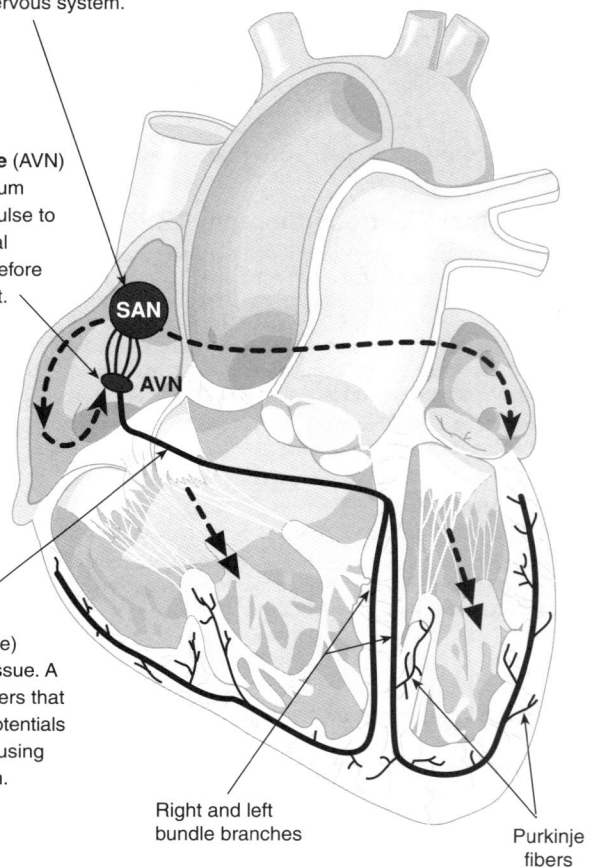

Right and left bundle branches

Purkinje fibers

1. Identify the role of each of the following in heart activity:

   (a) The sinoatrial node: _____

   (b) The atrioventricular node: _____

   (c) The bundle of His: _____

2. Explain the significance of the delay in impulse conduction at the AVN: _____

   _____

3. (a) Calculate the cardiac output when stroke volume is 70 cm³ and the heart rate is 70 beats per minute:

   _____

   (b) Trained endurance athletes have a very high cardiac output. Suggest how this is achieved: _____

   _____

Autonomic Nervous System
Control of Heartbeat

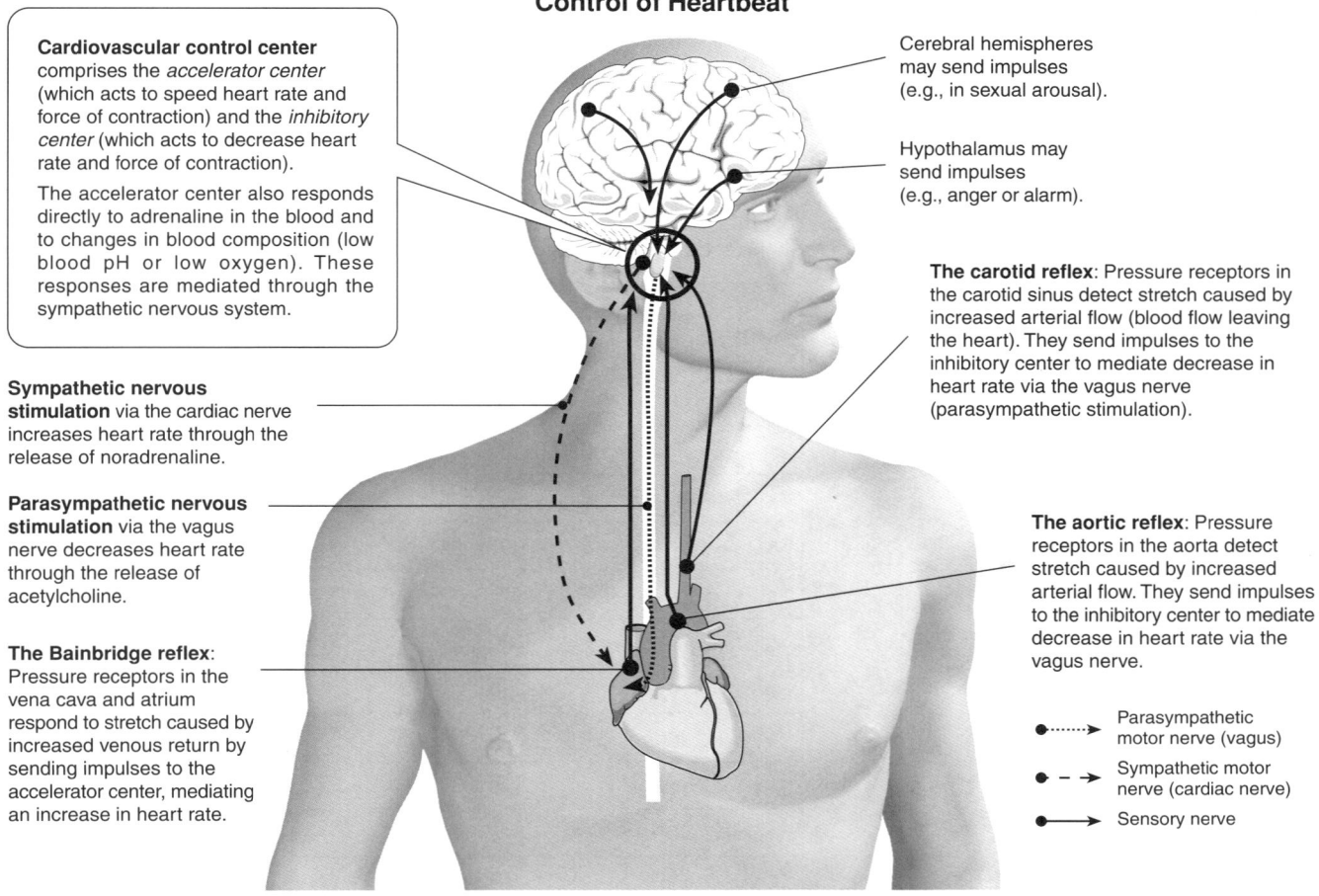

Cardiovascular control center comprises the *accelerator center* (which acts to speed heart rate and force of contraction) and the *inhibitory center* (which acts to decrease heart rate and force of contraction).

The accelerator center also responds directly to adrenaline in the blood and to changes in blood composition (low blood pH or low oxygen). These responses are mediated through the sympathetic nervous system.

Sympathetic nervous stimulation via the cardiac nerve increases heart rate through the release of noradrenaline.

Parasympathetic nervous stimulation via the vagus nerve decreases heart rate through the release of acetylcholine.

The Bainbridge reflex: Pressure receptors in the vena cava and atrium respond to stretch caused by increased venous return by sending impulses to the accelerator center, mediating an increase in heart rate.

Cerebral hemispheres may send impulses (e.g., in sexual arousal).

Hypothalamus may send impulses (e.g., anger or alarm).

The carotid reflex: Pressure receptors in the carotid sinus detect stretch caused by increased arterial flow (blood flow leaving the heart). They send impulses to the inhibitory center to mediate decrease in heart rate via the vagus nerve (parasympathetic stimulation).

The aortic reflex: Pressure receptors in the aorta detect stretch caused by increased arterial flow. They send impulses to the inhibitory center to mediate decrease in heart rate via the vagus nerve.

●·······▸ Parasympathetic motor nerve (vagus)

●‒ ‒▸ Sympathetic motor nerve (cardiac nerve)

●———▸ Sensory nerve

4. (a) With respect to the heart beat, explain what is meant by **myogenic**: _____

_____

(b) Describe the evidence for the myogenic nature of the heart beat: _____

_____

5. During heavy exercise, heart rate increases. Describe the mechanisms that are involved in bringing about this increase:

_____

_____

6. (a) Identify a stimulus for a decrease in heart rate: _____

(b) Explain how this change in heart rate is brought about: _____

_____

7. Identify two pressure receptors involved in control of heart rate and state what they respond to:

(a) _____

(b) _____

8. Guarana is a chemical found in many energy drinks. A group of students designed an experiment to test whether guarana stimulates a cardiovascular response. The test subjects had their pulses recorded before and after drinking an energy drink containing a known amount of guarana.

(a) Suggest two reasons why the test subjects may respond in different ways: _____

_____

(b) Describe a suitable control for this experiment: _____

_____

DA② Exercise and Blood Flow

Exercise promotes health by improving the rate of blood flow back to the heart (venous return). This is achieved by strengthening all types of muscle and by increasing the efficiency of the heart. During exercise blood flow to different parts of the body changes in order to cope with the extra demands of the muscles, the heart and the lungs.

1. The following table gives data for the **rate** of blood flow to various parts of the body at rest and during strenuous exercise. **Calculate** the **percentage** of the total blood flow that each organ or tissue receives under each regime of activity.
   HINT: Divide the rate for each organ/tissue by the total e.g. (700 ÷ 5000) x 100 = 14%.

Organ or tissue	At rest		Strenuous exercise	
	$cm^3 min^{-1}$	% of total	$cm^3 min^{-1}$	% of total
Brain	700	14 %	750	4.2 %
Heart	200	%	750	%
Lung tissue	100	%	200	%
Kidneys	1100	%	600	%
Liver	1350	%	600	%
Skeletal muscles	750	%	12 500	%
Bone	250	%	250	%
Skin	300	%	1900	%
Thyroid gland	50	%	50	%
Adrenal glands	25	%	25	%
Other tissue	175	%	175	%
TOTAL	5000	**100%**	17 800	**100%**

2. Explain how the body increases the rate of blood flow during exercise: _____

_____

_____

3. (a) State approximately how many times the total rate of blood flow increases between rest and exercise: _____

   (b) Explain why the increase is necessary: _____

   _____

   _____

4. (a) State which organs or tissues show no change in the rate of blood flow with exercise: _____

   _____

   (b) Explain why this is the case: _____

   _____

   _____

5. (a) State which organs or tissues show the most change in the rate of blood flow with exercise: _____

   _____

   (b) Explain why this is the case: _____

   _____

   _____

Endurance refers to the ability of the muscles and the cardiovascular and respiratory systems to carry out exercise. Muscular endurance allows sprinters to run fast for a short time or body builders and weight lifters to lift an immense weight and hold it for a few seconds. Cardiovascular and respiratory endurance refer to the body as a whole: the ability to endure a high level of activity over a prolonged period. This type of endurance is seen in marathon runners, and long distance swimmers and cyclists. Different sports ("short burst sports" compared with endurance type sports) require different training methods and the physiologies (muscle bulk and cardiovascular fitness) of the athletes can be quite different.

The human heart and circulatory system make a number of adjustments in response to aerobic or endurance training. These include:

- **Heart size**: Increases. The left ventricle wall becomes thicker and its chamber bigger.

- **Heart rate**: Heart rate (at rest and during exercise) decreases markedly from non-trained people.

- **Recovery**: Recovery after exercise (of breathing and heart rate) is faster in trained athletes.

- **Stroke volume**: The volume of blood pumped with each heart beat increases with endurance training.

- **Blood volume**: Endurance training increases blood volume (the amount of blood in the body).

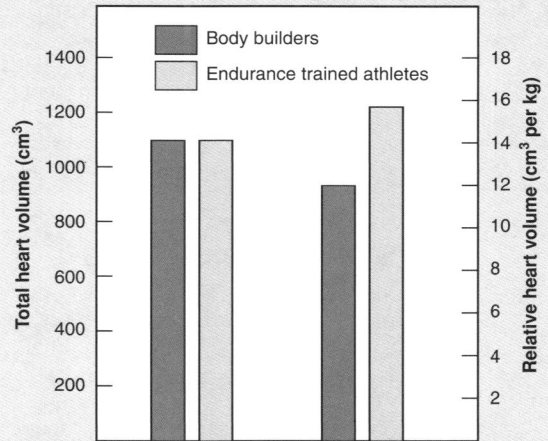

Difference in heart size of highly trained body builders and endurance athletes. Total heart volume is compared to heart volume as related to body weight. Average weights as follows: Body builders = 90.1 kg. Endurance athletes = 68.7 kg.

Weightlifters have good muscular endurance; they lift extremely heavy weights and hold them for a short time. Typical sports with high muscular endurance but lower cardiovascular endurance are sprinting, weight lifting, body building, boxing and wrestling.

Distance runners have very good cardiovascular and respiratory endurance; they sustain high intensity exercise for a long time. Typical sports needing cardiovascular endurance are distance running, cycling, and swimming (triathletes combine all three).

6. Suggest a reason why heart size increases with endurance activity: _____

_____

7. In the graph above right, explain why the relative heart volume of endurance athletes is greater than that of body builders, even though their total heart volumes are the same:

_____

8. Heart stroke volume increases with endurance training. Explain how this increases the efficiency of the heart as a pump:

_____

9. Resting heart rates are much lower in trained athletes compared with non-active people. Explain the health benefits of a lower resting heart rate:

_____

_____

Gas Exchange in Animals

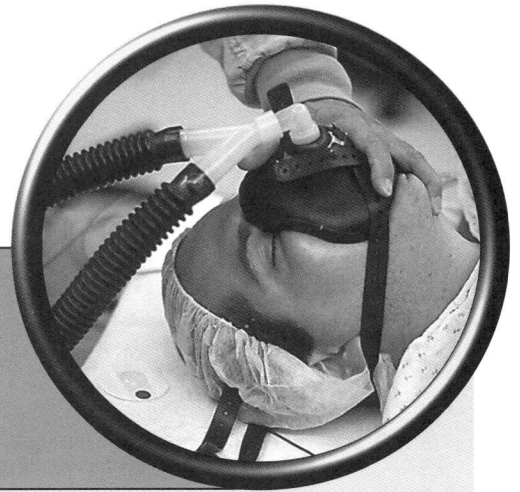

IB SL	**IB HL**	**IB Options**	**AP Biology**
Complete nos: 1-3, 8-9, 10(c), 14, 16, 18(a)-(c) Extension: 5-7, 15, 17, 18 (d)-(e)	Complete nos: 1-3, 8-9, 10(c), 14, 16, 18(a)-(c) Extension: 5-7, 15, 17, 18 (d)-(e)	Complete nos: Option B: 19-23 Option H: 19-28, 31-33, extension: 29-30	Complete nos: 1-33 Some numbers extension as appropriate

Learning Objectives

☐ 1. Compile your own glossary from the **KEY WORDS** displayed in **bold type** in the learning objectives below.

The need for gas exchange *(page 204)*

☐ 2. Recognize that organisms need to exchange materials with their environment: **respiratory gases**, nutrients, and excretory products.

☐ 3. Distinguish between **cellular respiration** and **gas exchange**. Explain how cellular respiration creates a constant demand for **oxygen** and a need to eliminate **carbon dioxide** gas.

☐ 4. Understand that the physical properties of an environment place particular constraints on the type of gas exchange system that can be used. Outline the **physical characteristics** of the following environments: *marine, freshwater, terrestrial*. Explain briefly how the structural features of organisms relate to the environment in which they are found.

☐ 5. Identify the process by which gases are exchanged across gas exchange surfaces. Describe the essential features of gas exchange surfaces. With reference to **Fick's law** explain the significance of these features.

☐ 6. Describe the relationship between an organism's size and its surface area (the **surface area: volume ratio** or **SA:V**). Explain the significance of this relationship to the exchange of gases with the environment.

☐ 7. Recognize that the development of gas exchange systems in larger organisms is an adaptation to facilitate adequate rates of gas exchange.

Gas exchange in animals *(pages 205-209)*

☐ 8. Recall the essential features of a gas exchange surface. Describe how the gas exchange surfaces of animals are maintained in a functional state.

☐ 9. Explain what is meant by **ventilation** and distinguish it from gas exchange. Explain the necessity for a ventilation system (or mechanism) in animals.

☐ 10. With reference to any of the examples below, identify the main features of animal gas exchange systems:
   (a) **Body surface** with (e.g. annelids) or without (e.g. protistans, flatworms) a circulatory system.
   (b) **Gills** (fish and aquatic arthropods). Describe the general features of the gas exchange system in bony fish. Relate the structure of gills to their suitability as gas exchange organs in water.
   (c) **Lungs** (vertebrates other than fish). Using a diagram, describe the general features of the ventilation system in a mammal (e.g. a human). Relate the structure of lungs to their suitability as gas exchange organs in air.
   (d) **Tracheal tubes** (e.g. insects). Describe the location and structure of tracheal tubes, including the role of the spiracles. Describe the way in which gases move into and out of the tracheae and the tissues.

Gas exchange in bony fish *(page 208)*

☐ 11. In more detail than in 10(b) above, describe the structure, location, adaptations, and function of the gas exchange surfaces and related structures in *bony fish* (**gill lamellae** and **filaments**).

☐ 12. Explain how gases are exchanged between the water and the blood. Explain the role of **countercurrent exchange** in fish **gills** in facilitating efficient gas exchange. Comment on the oxygen extraction rates achieved by gills (vs the rates achieved by lungs in air).

☐ 13. Describe ventilation in bony fish.

Gas exchange in humans *(pages 210-213)*
Humans can be used as a mammalian example

☐ 14. In more detail than in 10(c) above, describe the structure, location, adaptations, and function of the ventilation system in humans (**trachea, bronchi, bronchioles, lungs,** and **alveoli**).

☐ 15. Describe the distribution of the following tissues and cells in the trachea, bronchi, and bronchioles: **cartilage, ciliated epithelium, goblet cells,** and **smooth muscle cells**. Describe the function of the cartilage, **cilia,** goblet cells, smooth muscle, and **elastic fibers** in the gas exchange system.

☐ 16. List the features of the alveoli that are adaptations to their functional role in gas exchange, including reference to the total surface area provided, the single epithelial layer, moist lining, and capillary network.

☐ 17. Recognize the relationship between gas exchange surfaces (alveoli) and the blood vessels in the lung tissue. Draw a simple diagram of an **alveolus** (air sac) to illustrate the movement of O_2 and CO_2, into and out of the blood in the surrounding capillary.

☐ 18. Recall the structure of the thorax in humans and describe the mechanism of ventilation (**breathing**). Include reference to the following:
   (a) The role of the **diaphragm**, internal and external **intercostal muscles**, and the abdominal muscles in changing the air pressure in the lungs.
   (b) The distinction between **inspiration** (inhalation) as an active process and **expiration** (exhalation) as a passive process (during normal, quiet breathing).
   (c) The difference between quiet and forced breathing.
   (d) The role of **surfactant** in lung function.
   (e) The composition of inhaled and exhaled air.

The control of breathing in humans *(page 214)*

☐ 19. Explain how basic rhythm of breathing is controlled through the activity of the **respiratory center** in the medulla and its output via the **phrenic nerves** and the **intercostal nerves**.

☐ 20. Explain the role of the **stretch receptors** and the **vagus nerve** in ending inspiration during normal breathing. Identify this control as the **inflation reflex**.

☐ 21. Identify influences on the respiratory centre and comment on how these reflect changes in the body's demand for oxygen. Include reference to the activity of the **carotid** and **aortic bodies** (chemoreceptors in the carotid arteries and the aorta).

☐ 22. Distinguish between **involuntary** and **voluntary control** of breathing.

☐ 23. Explain how and why ventilation rate varies with **exercise**. Your explanation should include reference to the changes in blood composition that occur with exercise and the physiological effects of these changes. Understanding the mechanisms by which **ventilation rate** is adjusted to meet the demands of exercise requires a basic understanding of the mechanisms controlling breathing (see # 19-22).

Gas transport in humans *(pages 195, 216-217)*

☐ 24. Describe the general role of respiratory pigments (**myoglobin** and fetal and adult **hemoglobin**) in the transport and delivery of oxygen to the tissues.

☐ 25. Define the term **partial pressure** and understand its significance with respect to gas transport.

☐ 26. Explain the ways in which CO_2 is carried in the blood, including the action and role of the following: carbonic anhydrase, **chloride shift**, plasma proteins as blood buffers, and hydrogen-carbonate (bicarbonate) ions.

☐ 27. Describe the transport of oxygen in relation to the **oxygen-hemoglobin dissociation curve**. Explain the oxygen dissociation curves of adult and fetal **hemoglobin** and **myoglobin** and identify the significance of the differences described.

☐ 28. Describe the effect of pH (CO_2 level) on the oxygen-hemoglobin dissociation curve (the **Bohr effect**) and explain its significance.

Measuring ventilation rates *(pages 212-213)*

☐ 29. Explain how ventilation is measured in humans using a **spirometer**. Define the terms: **tidal volume, vital capacity, residual volume, dead space air**.

☐ 30. Explain how the breathing (ventilation) rate and **pulmonary ventilation** (PV) rate are calculated and expressed. Provide some typical values for **breathing rate, tidal volume**, and **PV**. Describe how each of these is affected by strenuous exercise.

Gas exchange and high altitude *(page 215)*

☐ 31. Explain the problem of gas exchange at **high altitude**. Describe the short and long term effects of high altitude on human physiology, and explain the way the body **acclimatizes**. Include reference to: *blood composition (red blood cell number, blood viscosity), density of capillaries, and breathing and heart rates*. Comment on the significance of these changes to the maintenance of adequate rates of exchange at altitude.

Respiratory disorders *(pages 218-219)*

☐ 32. Outline the possible causes of **lung cancer**, including the link between tobacco smoking and lung cancer. Briefly describe the effects of lung cancer on the gas exchange system, identifying detrimental changes to the alveolar epithelium, lung capacity, blood vessel walls, and composition of gases in the lung.

☐ 33. Outline the possible causes of **asthma**, including the role of allergens in triggering asthma attacks and, if required, the physiological basis of the response and the role of histamine. Explain the effects of asthma on the gas exchange system and appreciate why it can be such a debilitating disease.

Textbooks

See the 'Textbook Reference Grid' on pages 8-9 for textbook page references relating to material in this topic.

Supplementary Texts

See pages 5-6 for additional details of this text:
■ Clegg, C.J., 1998. **Mammals: Structure and Function** (John Murray), pp. 24-31.

Internet

See pages 10-11 for details of how to access **Bio Links** from our web site: **www.thebiozone.com**. From Bio Links, access sites under the topics:

GENERAL BIOLOGY ONLINE RESOURCES > Online Textbooks and Lecture Notes • An on-line biology book • Learn.co.uk ... *and others*

ANIMAL BIOLOGY: • Anatomy and physiology • Human physiology lecture notes ... *and others* > **Gas Exchange:** • The respiratory system • Gas exchange • Lesson 11: The respiratory system • Gas exchange in aquatic environments • Respiration in aquatic insects • Respiratory system

HEALTH AND DISEASE > Non-Infectious Diseases: • Asthma • Chemicals and human health • American Cancer Society ... *and others*

Periodicals

See page 6 for details of publishers of periodicals:
STUDENT'S REFERENCE
■ **Lungs and the Control of Breathing** Bio. Sci. Rev. 14(4) April 2002, pp. 2-5. *The mechanisms, control, and measurement of breathing in humans. This article includes good, clear diagrams and useful summaries of important points.*

■ **Gas Laws** Biol. Sci. Rev., 11(1) Sept. 1998, pp. 14-17. *The significance of the gas laws to gas exchange and diffusion of gases within tissues.*

■ **Countercurrent Exchange Mechanisms** Biol. Sci. Rev., 9(1) Sept. 1996, pp. 2-6. *The function of countercurrent multipliers, including fish gills.*

■ **A Breath of Fresh Air** Biol. Sci. Rev., 7(5) May 1995, pp. 22-25. *Breathing, including the biochemistry of gas exchange, oxygen dissociation curves and homeostatic control of breathing.*

■ **Red Blood Cells** Bio. Sci. Rev. 11(2) Nov. 1998, pp. 2-4. *The structure and function of red blood cells, including details of oxygen transport.*

■ **Humans with Altitude** New Scientist, 2 Nov. 2002, pp. 36-39. *The short term adjustments and (evolutionary) adaptations of those living at altitude.*

Respiratory diseases
■ **Smoking** Biol. Sci. Rev., 10(1) Sept. 1997, pp. 14-16. *Smoking related diseases and the effects of tobacco smoking on human physiology.*

■ **Dust to Dust** New Scientist, 21 Sept. 2002 (Inside Science). *A supplement that concentrates on dust pollution, but also examines the impact of this pollutant on respiratory health.*

■ **Environmental Lung Disease** New Scientist, 23 September 1995 (Inside Science). *Excellent supplement on lung disorders, with good diagrams illustrating lung functioning and gas transport.*

■ **Air Pollution and Asthma** Biol. Sci. Rev., 9(4) March 1997, pp. 32-36. *The link between air pollution and respiratory disorders such as asthma.*

TEACHER'S REFERENCE
■ **Breathless** New Scientist, 8 March 2003, pp. 46-49. *Adaptations for gas exchange in shark species able to withstand anoxia. A better understanding of the mechanisms for this may help with treatment of stoke and heart attack victims.*

■ **The Effect of Hyperventilation on the Ability to Hold one's Breath** The American Biology Teacher, 59(4), April, 1997, pp. 229-231. *Investigating the effects of hyperventilation and blood CO_2 and O_2 level on respiratory physiology.*

Software and video resources are now provided in the Teacher Resource Handbook

Introduction to Gas Exchange

K 1

Living cells require energy for the activities of life. Energy is released in cells by the breakdown of sugars and other substances in the metabolic process called **cellular respiration**. As a consequence of this process, gases need to be exchanged between the respiring cells and the environment. In most organisms (with the exception of some bacterial groups) these gases are carbon dioxide (CO_2) and oxygen (O_2). The diagram below illustrates this process for an animal. Plant cells also respire, but their gas exchange budget is different because they also produce O_2 and consume CO_2 in photosynthesis.

The Need for Gas Exchange

Gas exchange surfaces provide a means for gases to enter and leave the body. Some organisms use the body surface as the sole gas exchange surface, but many have specialized gas exchange structures (e.g. lungs, gills, or stomata). Amphibians use the body surface and simple lungs to provide for their gas exchange requirements.

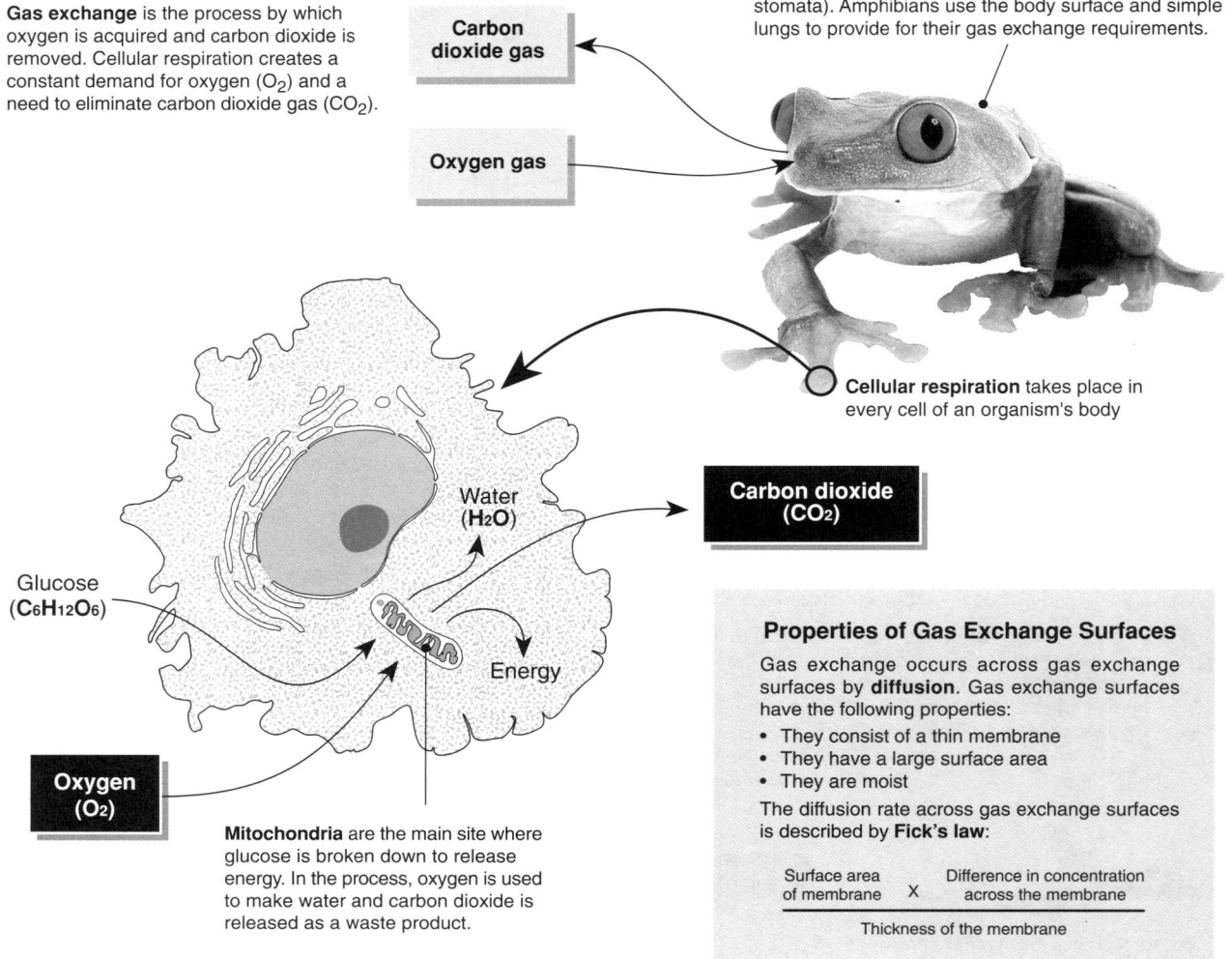

Gas exchange is the process by which oxygen is acquired and carbon dioxide is removed. Cellular respiration creates a constant demand for oxygen (O_2) and a need to eliminate carbon dioxide gas (CO_2).

Carbon dioxide gas

Oxygen gas

Cellular respiration takes place in every cell of an organism's body

Water (H$_2$O)

Carbon dioxide (CO$_2$)

Glucose ($C_6H_{12}O_6$)

Energy

Oxygen (O$_2$)

Mitochondria are the main site where glucose is broken down to release energy. In the process, oxygen is used to make water and carbon dioxide is released as a waste product.

Properties of Gas Exchange Surfaces

Gas exchange occurs across gas exchange surfaces by **diffusion**. Gas exchange surfaces have the following properties:

- They consist of a thin membrane
- They have a large surface area
- They are moist

The diffusion rate across gas exchange surfaces is described by **Fick's law**:

$$\frac{\text{Surface area of membrane} \times \text{Difference in concentration across the membrane}}{\text{Thickness of the membrane}}$$

---

1. Name the gases involved in cellular respiration: _____

2. Distinguish between cellular respiration and gas exchange: _____

_____

_____

3. Describe the main function of a gas exchange surface: _____

_____

4. List the **three** features that all gas exchange surfaces have in common: _____

_____

5. Explain the significance of Fick's Law to the functioning of gas exchange surfaces: _____

_____

_____

Gas Exchange in Freshwater

A 1

The availability of oxygen in water is very low relative to air: oxygen diffuses into water only very slowly and it is not very soluble (unlike CO_2). Moreover, as water temperature increases, the amount of oxygen that can be dissolved decreases. Despite these constraints, many invertebrate phyla, including the molluscs, annelids, and arthropods, have freshwater representatives. The majority of aquatic invertebrates are insects. As is the case in terrestrial insects, gases move to and from the tissues via the tracheae: the network of air-filled tubes that forms the insect respiratory system. What varies is the method by which oxygen enters this system. Like many aquatic invertebrates, aquatic insect larvae rely on **diffusion** across the body surface, with or without gills. Adult insects carry air with them when submerged. The air may be carried as a distinct bubble beneath the wings, or stay trapped by regions of unwettable (hydrofuge) hairs. A thin film of air trapped by hairs is called a **plastron**. It provides a source of oxygen and acts as a non-compressible diffusion gill, into which oxygen can diffuse from the water.

Adaptations of Aquatic Invertebrates for Gas Exchange

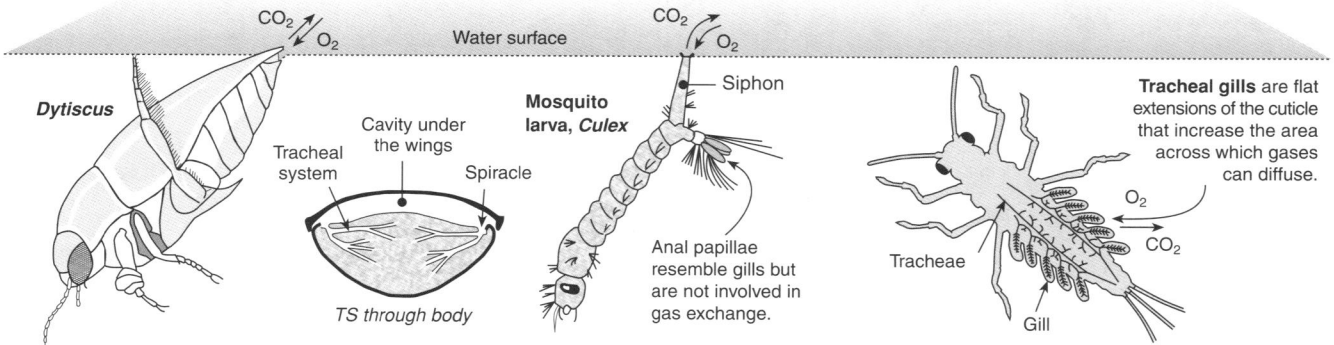

Surface air breathers

The **diving beetle**, *Dytiscus*, traps air from the surface beneath its wings where it forms a compressible gill. The spiracles open into the air space and lead to the tracheal tubes. As the submerged insect respires, the oxygen is gradually used up and the bubble decreases in size. A **mosquito larva** penetrates the water surface with a siphon extending from a spiracle at the tip of the abdomen. The larva hangs at the surface while gas exchange occurs by diffusion.

Tracheal gills

In the larvae of many aquatic insects, gas exchange occurs by diffusion across the body surface. This is enhanced by the presence of **tracheal gills** which may account for 20-70% of O_2 uptake depending on their surface area.

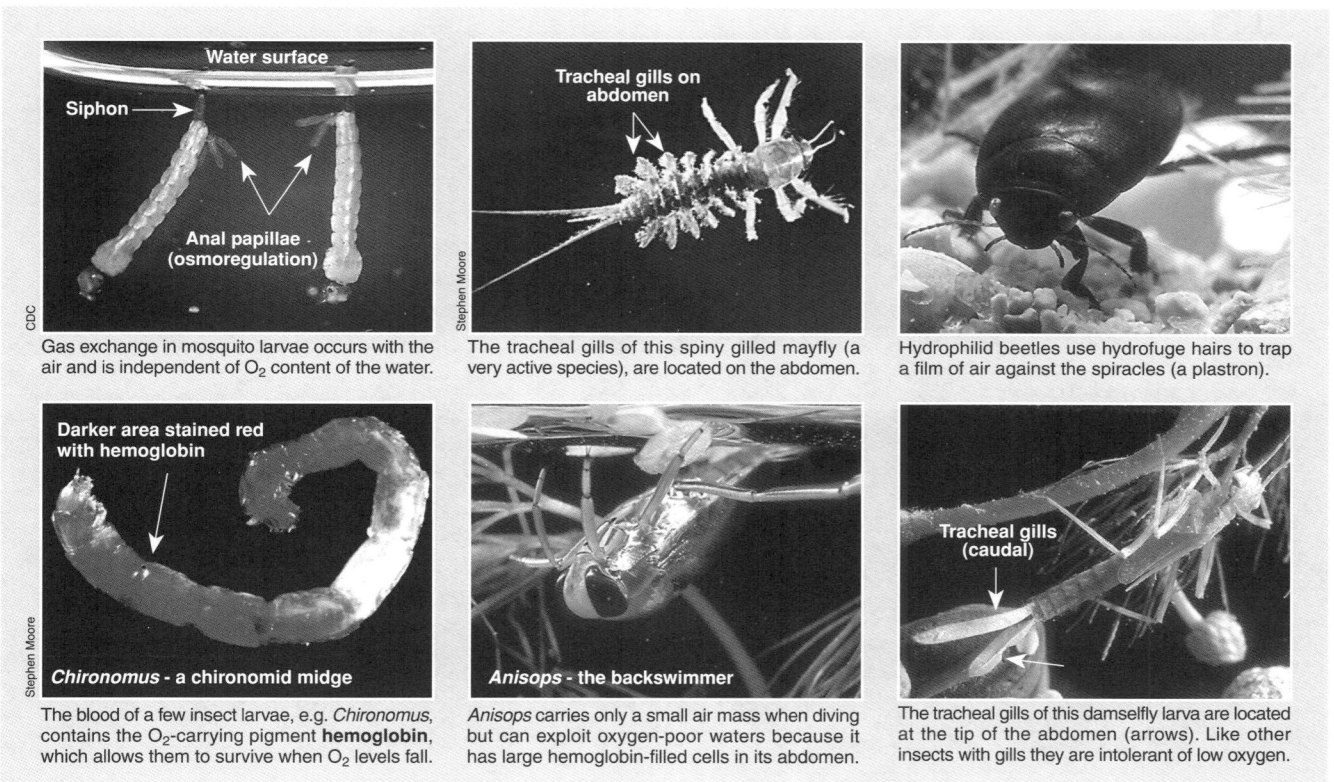

Gas exchange in mosquito larvae occurs with the air and is independent of O_2 content of the water.

The tracheal gills of this spiny gilled mayfly (a very active species), are located on the abdomen.

Hydrophilid beetles use hydrofuge hairs to trap a film of air against the spiracles (a plastron).

The blood of a few insect larvae, e.g. *Chironomus*, contains the O_2-carrying pigment **hemoglobin**, which allows them to survive when O_2 levels fall.

Anisops carries only a small air mass when diving but can exploit oxygen-poor waters because it has large hemoglobin-filled cells in its abdomen.

The tracheal gills of this damselfly larva are located at the tip of the abdomen (arrows). Like other insects with gills they are intolerant of low oxygen.

1. Giving an example for each, briefly describe two structural adaptations of freshwater invertebrates for gas exchange:

   (a) _____

   (b) _____

2. Describe one physiological adaptation of freshwater invertebrates for gas exchange: _____

   _____

Gas Exchange in Animals

RA2

The way in which gas exchange is achieved is influenced by the animal's general body form and by the environment in which the animal lives. Small, aquatic organisms such as **protozoans**, sponges, flatworms and cnidarians, require no specialized respiratory structures. Gases are exchanged between the surrounding water (or moist environment) and the body's cells by diffusion directly across the organism's surface. Larger animals require specialized gas exchange systems. The complexity of these is related to the efficiency of gas exchange required, which is determined by the oxygen demands of the organism.

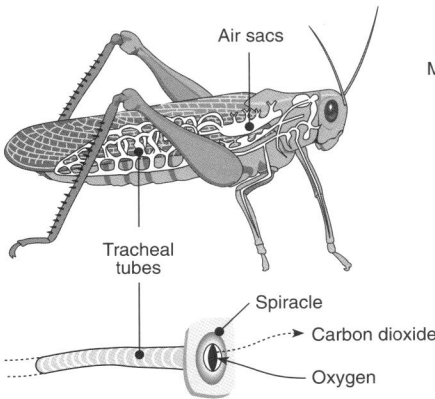

Air sacs

Tracheal tubes

Spiracle

Carbon dioxide

Oxygen

Carbon dioxide

Oxygen

Mucus

Pores

Skin surface enlarged

Bucco-pharynx

Lungs with intricate infoldings of the walls

Trachea

Anterior air sacs

Posterior air sacs

Lungs

Gas exchange in insects

Insects, and sometimes spiders, transport gases via a system of branching tubes called **tracheae** or **tracheal tubes**. The gases move by diffusion across the moist lining directly to and from the tissues. The end of each tube contains a small amount of fluid which regulates the movement of gases by changing the surface area of air in contact with the cells.

Gas exchange in amphibians

All amphibians make some use of surface gas exchange. There are even some salamanders (a type of amphibian) that have no lungs at all and rely completely on surface gas exchange. This is only possible if the surface is kept moist by secretions from mucous glands. Frogs carry out gas exchange through the skin and in the lungs. At times of inactivity, the skin alone is a sufficient surface with either water or air.

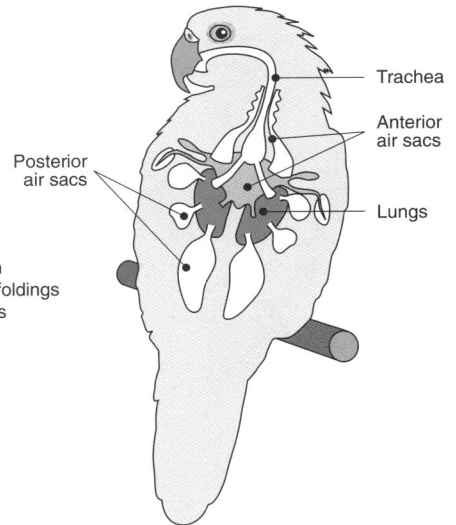

Gas exchange in birds

A bird has air sacs in addition to lungs. The air sacs function in ventilating the lungs, where gas exchange takes place. Together, the anterior and posterior air sacs function as bellows that keep air flowing through the lungs continuously and in one direction.

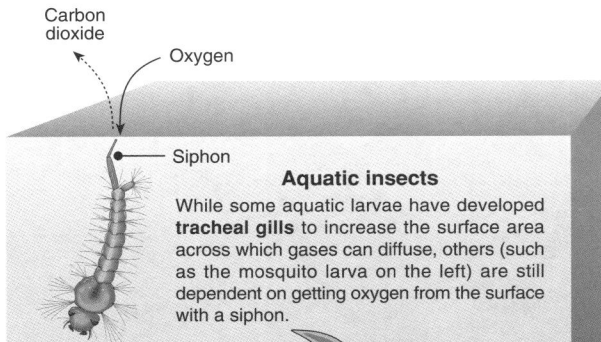

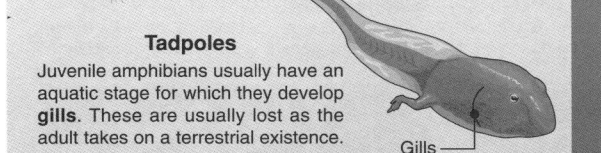

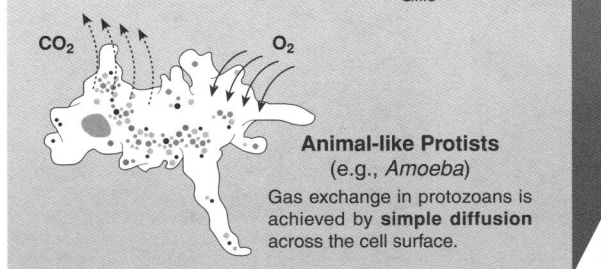

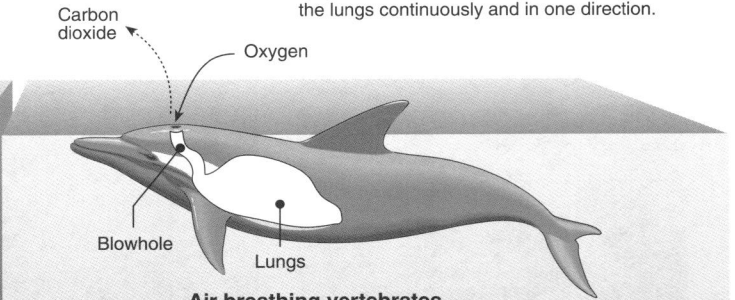

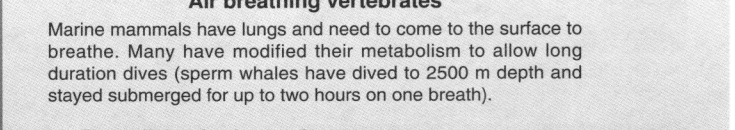

Carbon dioxide

Oxygen

Siphon

Carbon dioxide

Oxygen

Blowhole

Lungs

Aquatic insects

While some aquatic larvae have developed **tracheal gills** to increase the surface area across which gases can diffuse, others (such as the mosquito larva on the left) are still dependent on getting oxygen from the surface with a siphon.

Tadpoles

Juvenile amphibians usually have an aquatic stage for which they develop **gills**. These are usually lost as the adult takes on a terrestrial existence.

Gills

CO₂

O₂

Animal-like Protists
(e.g., *Amoeba*)

Gas exchange in protozoans is achieved by **simple diffusion** across the cell surface.

Air breathing vertebrates

Marine mammals have lungs and need to come to the surface to breathe. Many have modified their metabolism to allow long duration dives (sperm whales have dived to 2500 m depth and stayed submerged for up to two hours on one breath).

Bony fish, sharks, and rays

Fish breathe oxygen dissolved in water which they extract by using **gills**. Gills can achieve 80% extraction rates, over three times the rate of human lungs from air.

Oxygen

Carbon dioxide

Gills

Jellyfish

Ruffles

Jellyfish increase their surface area for gas exchange by having ruffles.

Gills

Nudibranch

Nudibranch snails have elaborate exposed gills to assist gas exchange.

Moist skin

Salamander

Some salamanders have no lungs and breathe solely through their skin.

Tube worms

Tube worms carry out gas exchange with feathery extensions in the water.

1. Suggest two reasons for the development, in animals, of gas exchange structures and systems:

    (a) _____

    (b) _____

2. (a) Explain why the air sacs of birds provide more efficient use of the air taken in with each breath:

    _____

    _____

    (b) Suggest a reason why birds require such an efficient method of gas exchange: _____

    _____

    _____

3. Complete the following list as a summary of the main features of the respiratory structures found in animals. Briefly state the **location in the body** of each system, name the animal group or groups that use each system, and state in which medium (air or water) each system is used:

    (a) **Body surface**: Location in the body: _____

    _____

    Animal groups: _____ Medium: _____

    (b) **Tracheal tubes**: Location in the body: _____

    _____

    Animal groups: _____ Medium: _____

    (c) **Gills**: Location in the body: _____

    _____

    Animal groups: _____ Medium: _____

    (d) **Lungs**: Location in the body: _____

    _____

    Animal groups: _____ Medium: _____

4. Suggest why the gas exchange structures in air breathers tend to be internal (e.g. lungs) rather than external (e.g. gills):

    _____

    _____

5. Describe two ways in which air breathers manage to keep their gas exchange surfaces moist:

    (a) _____

    (b) _____

6. Provide two reasons why gills do not function effectively on land:

    (a) _____

    (b) _____

7. Explain how amphibian skin achieves a large surface area: _____

    _____

8. Explain why organisms with gills are at risk when their water is polluted by large amounts of organic material:

    _____

    _____

Gas Exchange in Insects & Fish

RA 2

Aquatic and terrestrial environments present different problems for the exchange of gases. The availability of oxygen in water is very low relative to air, and water is a very dense and viscous medium. Most aquatic animals have respiratory systems comprising a water pumping mechanism and gills for gas exchange. These features are described below for bony fish. In contrast to water, air is a rich source of easily obtained oxygen, but it is also relatively dry. Systems for air breathing include the ventilation lungs of terrestrial vertebrates and the tracheal tubes of insects. Unlike gills, the gas exchange surface in these systems is internal, and therefore protected from desiccation.

Fish Gills

The gills of fish have a great many folds, which are supported and kept apart from each other by the water. This gives them a high surface area for gas exchange. The outer surface of the gill is in contact with the water, and blood flows in vessels inside the gill. Gas exchange occurs by diffusion between the water and blood across the gill membrane and capillaries. The operculum (gill cover) permits exit of water and acts as a pump, drawing water past the gill filaments. Fish gills are very efficient and can achieve an 80% extraction rate of oxygen from water; over three times the rate of human lungs from air.

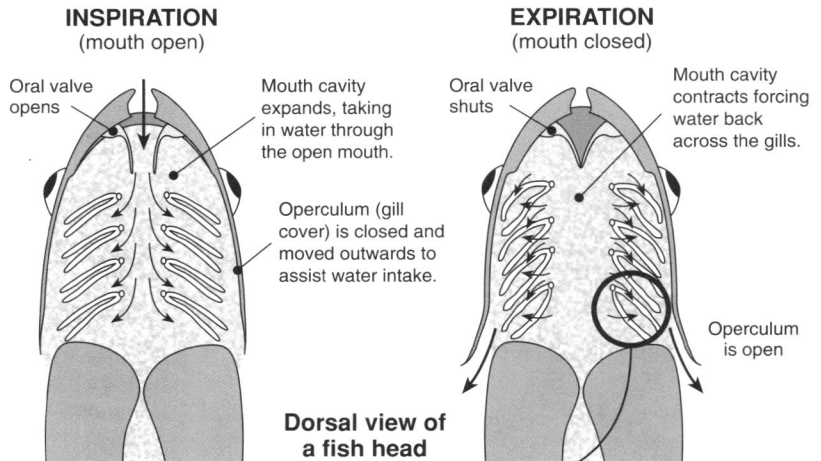

Operculum (gill cover)

INSPIRATION (mouth open)

Oral valve opens

Mouth cavity expands, taking in water through the open mouth.

Operculum (gill cover) is closed and moved outwards to assist water intake.

EXPIRATION (mouth closed)

Oral valve shuts

Mouth cavity contracts forcing water back across the gills.

Operculum is open

Dorsal view of a fish head

Bony bar (branchial arch)

Blood vessels

Gill lamella

Water flow

Direction of blood flow in gill lamellae.

Water flows in opposite direction to blood flow (countercurrent effect).

Detail of gill filament

Blood flow

Source: C.J. Clegg & D.G. McKean (1994)

Countercurrent Versus Parallel Current Flow

The structure of fish gills and their physical arrangement in relation to the blood flow ensure that gas exchange rates are maximized. A constant stream of oxygen-rich water flows over the gill filaments in the opposite direction to the direction of blood flow through the gills. This is termed **countercurrent flow**. Blood flowing through the gill capillaries therefore encounters water of increasing oxygen content. In this way, the concentration gradient (for oxygen uptake) across the gill is maintained across the entire distance of the gill lamella. A parallel current flow would not achieve the same oxygen extraction rates because the concentrations across the gill would quickly equalize.

Countercurrent flow

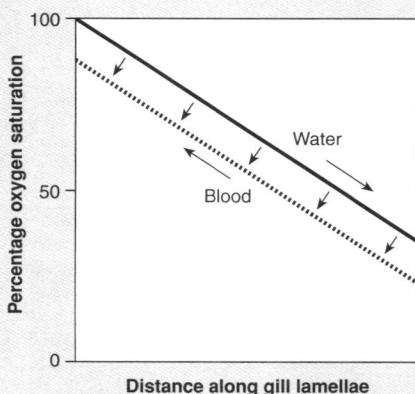

Percentage oxygen saturation

Water

Blood

Distance along gill lamellae

Countercurrent blood flow across a gill lamella

water

water

water

water

Blood

Parallel current flow

(Blood flow reversed on diagram at left)

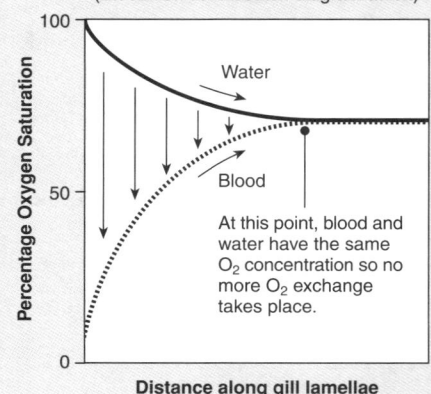

Percentage Oxygen Saturation

Water

Blood

At this point, blood and water have the same O_2 concentration so no more O_2 exchange takes place.

Distance along gill lamellae

Insect Tracheal Tubes

Insects, and some spiders, transport gases via a system of branching tubes called tracheae or tracheal tubes. The gases move by diffusion across the moist lining directly to and from the tissues. The end of each tube contains a small amount of fluid in which the respiratory gases are dissolved. The fluid is drawn into the muscle tissues during their contraction, and is released back into the tracheole when the muscle rests. Insects ventilate their tracheal system by making rhythmic body movements to help move the air in and out of the tracheae.

Spiracle openings on the abdomen

Spiracles are controlled valves that form the exit point of trachea from the body (an insect may have up to a maximum of 20 spiracles; eight abdominal pairs and two thoracic pairs).

Insect muscle fibers

Air sacs, present in some insects, act as bellows during vigorous body movements.

Tracheal tubes

Tracheoles

Tracheal tubes

Spiracle

Carbon dioxide

Oxygen

Detail of tracheole ending

Dissolved oxygen is delivered to muscle fibers by the fluid.

Fluid moves into the tracheoles when muscles are at rest; fluid is drawn into the tissue when muscles are contracting.

1. Animals with special gas exchange structures usually keep the air or water moving over the gas exchange surface:

   (a) State the term that describes this activity: _____

   (b) Explain why it is necessary: _____

   (c) Explain how this movement is achieved in:

   A bony fish: _____

   _____

   _____

   A terrestrial insect: _____

   _____

   _____

2. Explain how oxygen and CO_2 are exchanged between the air and body tissues at the end of tracheoles in insects:

   _____

   _____

   _____

3. Identify two features of a fish gas exchange system (gills and related structures) that facilitate gas exchange:

   (a) _____

   (b) _____

4. Explain why the countercurrent system in fish gills is more efficient than a parallel current flow: _____

   _____

   _____

   _____

The Human Respiratory System

Lungs are internal sac-like organs found in most amphibians, and all reptiles, birds, and mammals. The paired lungs of mammals are connected to the outside air by way of a system of tubular passageways: the trachea, bronchi, and bronchioles. Ciliated, mucus secreting epithelium lines this system of tubules, trapping and removing dust and pathogens before they reach the gas exchange surfaces. Each lung is divided into a number of lobes, each receiving its own bronchus. Each bronchus divides many times, terminating in the respiratory bronchioles from which arise 2-11 alveolar ducts and numerous **alveoli** (air sacs). These provide a very large surface area (70 m^2) for the exchange of respiratory gases by diffusion between the alveoli and the blood in the capillaries. The details of this exchange across the **respiratory membrane** are described opposite.

Morphology of the Respiratory System

Nasal passages warm and moisten the air entering through the nostrils. Each nostril has a border of hairs to trap particles and filter them out of the system.

Air entering the body through the mouth enters the pharynx and mixes with air from the nasal passages.

The **trachea** lies in front of the esophagus and extends into the thorax. It is strengthened with C-shaped bands of cartilage and lined with ciliated epithelium.

The trachea splits into two **bronchi**. These are also supported by cartilage bands.

Bronchioles branch off the bronchi and divide into progressively smaller branches. The cartilage is gradually lost as the bronchioles decrease in diameter.

Lung

Lung

Photograph left: The nasal epithelium produces large amounts of mucus, seen here as droplets.

Photograph below: The epithelium of the trachea has many cilia. Mucus is produced from goblet cells.

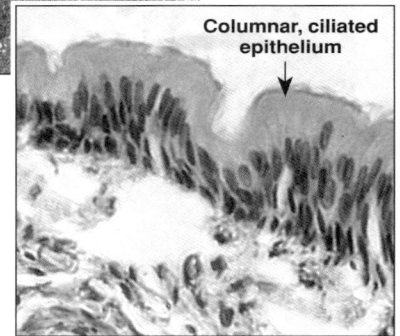

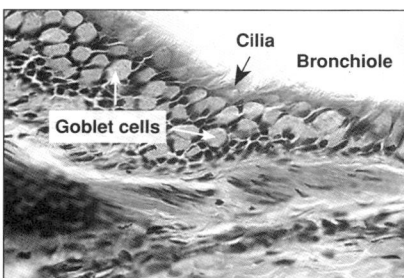

Columnar, ciliated epithelium

Cilia

Bronchiole

Goblet cells

All photos on this page: EII

Photograph above: The epithelial lining of the bronchioles is ciliated and lined with mucus-producing **goblet cells**.

Photograph right: Respiratory bronchiole and alveolar duct leading to alveoli. Note the thin alveolar walls.

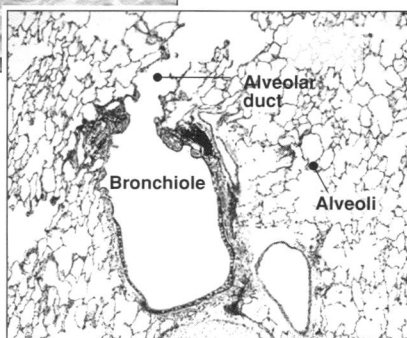

Alveolar duct

Bronchiole

Alveoli

Detail of a terminal bronchiole and its branches

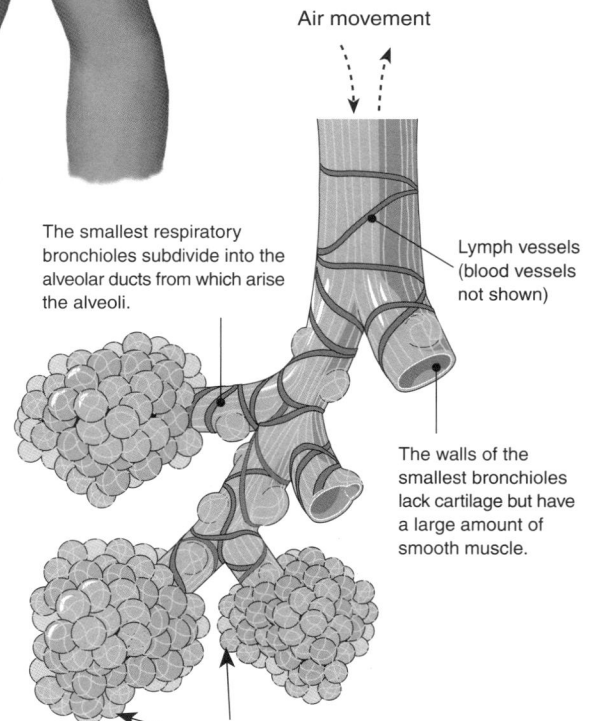

The smallest respiratory bronchioles subdivide into the alveolar ducts from which arise the alveoli.

Air movement

Lymph vessels (blood vessels not shown)

The walls of the smallest bronchioles lack cartilage but have a large amount of smooth muscle.

The alveolar ducts lead to the alveoli. The alveoli tend to recoil inward (deflate) after each breath out. A phospholipid **surfactant** helps to prevent this by decreasing surface tension in the lung.

Detail of an Alveolus

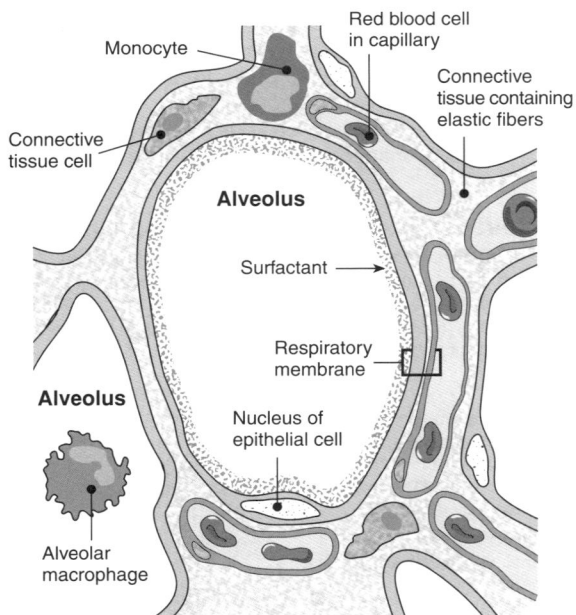

Monocyte
Red blood cell in capillary
Connective tissue containing elastic fibers
Connective tissue cell
Alveolus
Surfactant
Respiratory membrane
Alveolus
Nucleus of epithelial cell
Alveolar macrophage

The diagram above illustrates the physical arrangement of the alveoli to the capillaries through which the blood moves. Phagocytic monocytes and macrophages are also present to protect the lung tissue. Elastic connective tissue gives the alveoli their ability to expand and recoil.

Detail of the Respiratory Membrane

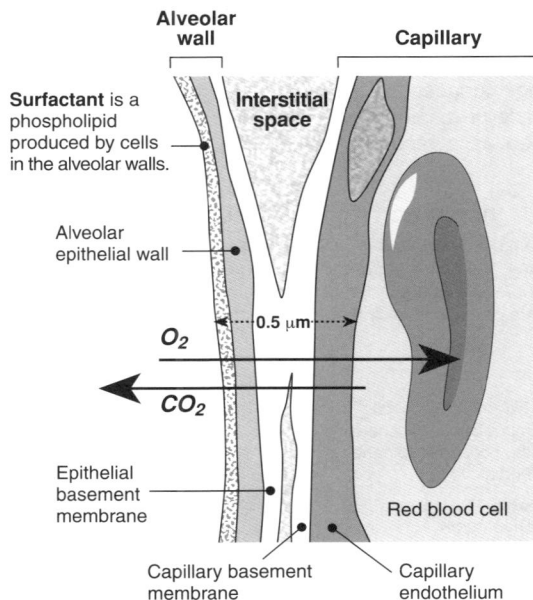

Alveolar wall
Capillary
Surfactant is a phospholipid produced by cells in the alveolar walls.
Interstitial space
Alveolar epithelial wall
0.5 μm
O_2
CO_2
Epithelial basement membrane
Red blood cell
Capillary basement membrane
Capillary endothelium

The **respiratory membrane** is the term for the layered junction between the alveolar epithelial cells, the endothelial cells of the capillary, and their associated basement membranes (thin, collagenous layers that underlie the epithelial tissues). Gases move freely across this membrane.

1. (a) Explain how the basic structure of the human respiratory system provides such a large area for gas exchange:

_____

_____

(b) Identify the general region of the lung where exchange of gases takes place:

2. Describe the structure and purpose of the respiratory membrane: _____

_____

_____

3. State the role of the surfactant in the alveoli: _____

_____

4. Using the information above and opposite, complete the table below summarising the **histology of the respiratory pathway**. Name each numbered region and use a tick or cross to indicate the presence or absence of particular tissues.

	Region	Cartilage	Ciliated epithelium	Goblet cells (mucus)	Smooth muscle	Connective tissue
1						✓
2						
3		gradually lost				
4	Alveolar duct		✗	✗		
5					very little	

5. Babies born prematurely are often deficient in surfactant. This causes respiratory distress syndrome; a condition where breathing is very difficult. From what you know about the role of surfactant, explain the symptoms of this syndrome:

_____

_____

Breathing in Humans

DA2

In mammals, the mechanism of breathing (ventilation) provides a continual supply of fresh air to the lungs and helps to maintain a large diffusion gradient for respiratory gases across the gas exchange surface. Oxygen must be delivered regularly to supply the needs of respiring cells. Similarly, carbon dioxide, which is produced as a result of cellular metabolism, must be quickly eliminated from the body. Adequate lung ventilation is essential to these exchanges. The cardiovascular system participates by transporting respiratory gases to and from the cells of the body. The volume of gases exchanged during breathing varies according to the physiological demands placed on the body (e.g. by exercise). These changes can be measured using spirometry.

Inspiration (inhalation or breathing in)

During quiet breathing, inspiration is achieved by increasing the space (therefore decreasing the pressure) inside the lungs. Air then flows into the lungs to fill the space. Inspiration is always an active process involving muscle contraction.

1a External intercostal muscles contract causing the ribcage to expand and move up

1b Diaphragm contracts and drops downwards

2 Thoracic volume increases, lungs expand, and the pressure inside the lungs decreases

3 Air flows into the lungs in response to the pressure gradient

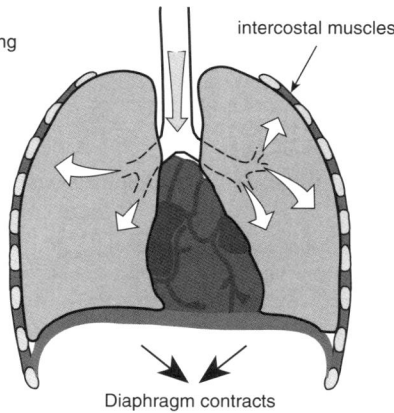

intercostal muscles

Diaphragm contracts

Expiration (exhalation or breathing out)

During quiet breathing, expiration is achieved passively by decreasing the space (thus increasing the pressure) inside the lungs. Air then flows passively out of the lungs to equalize with the air pressure. In active breathing, muscle contraction is involved in bringing about both inspiration and expiration.

1 In **quiet breathing**, external intercostal muscles and diaphragm relax. Elasticity of the lung tissue causes recoil.

In **forced breathing**, the internal intercostals and abdominal muscles also contract to increase the force of the expiration

2 Thoracic volume decreases and the pressure inside the lungs increases

3 Air flows passively out of the lungs in response to the pressure gradient

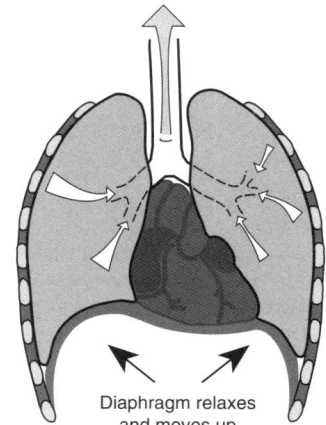

Diaphragm relaxes and moves up

Using spirometry to determine changes in lung volume

The apparatus used to measure the amount of air exchanged during breathing and the rate of breathing is a **spirometer** (also called a respirometer). A simple spirometer consists of a weighted drum, containing oxygen or air, inverted over a chamber of water. A tube connects the air-filled chamber with the subject's mouth, and soda lime in the system absorbs the carbon dioxide breathed out. Breathing results in a trace called a spirogram, from which lung volumes can be measured directly.

During inspiration
Air is removed from the chamber, the drum sinks, and an upward deflection is recorded on the paper on the rotating drum.

During expiration
Air is added to the chamber, the drum rises, and a downward deflection is recorded.

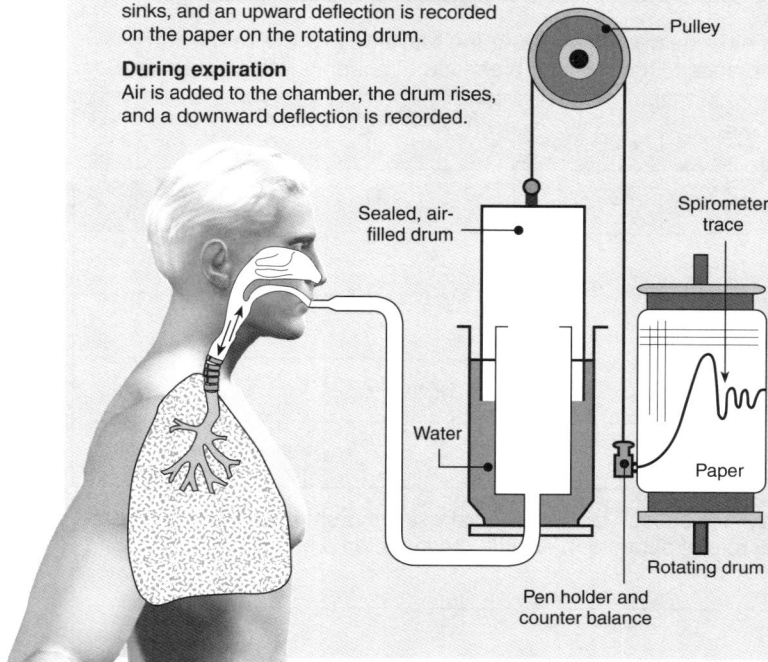

Pulley

Sealed, air-filled drum

Spirometer trace

Water

Paper

Pen holder and counter balance

Rotating drum

Lung Volumes and Capacities

The air in the lungs can be divided into volumes. Lung capacities are combinations of volumes.

Description of volume	Vol (liter)
Tidal volume (TV) Volume of air breathed in and out in a single breath	**0.5**
Inspiratory reserve volume (IRV) Volume breathed in by a maximum inspiration at the end of a normal inspiration	**3.3**
Expiratory reserve volume (ERV) Volume breathed out by a maximum effort at the end of a normal expiration	**1.0**
Residual volume (RV) Volume of air remaining in the lungs at the end of a maximum expiration	**1.2**
Description of capacity	
Inspiratory capacity (IC) = TV + IRV Volume breathed in by a maximum inspiration at the end of a normal expiration	**3.8**
Vital capacity (VC) = IRV + TV + ERV Volume breathed in by a maximum inspiration following a maximum expiration	**4.8**
Total lung capacity (TLC) = VC + RV The total volume of the lungs. Only a fraction of TLC is used in normal breathing	**6.0**

Only about 70% of the air that is inhaled reaches the alveoli. The rest remains in the air spaces of the nose, throat, larynx, trachea and bronchi. This air is unavailable for gas exchange and is called the **dead air volume (dead space air)**.

Measuring Changes in Lung Volume

Changes in lung volume can be measured using spirometry (see opposite). Total adult lung volume varies between 4 and 6 liters (dm^3) (it is greater in males). The **vital capacity** is somewhat less than this because of the residual volume of air that remains in the lungs even after expiration. The exchange between fresh air and the residual volume is a slow process and the composition of gases in the lungs remains relatively constant (table, right). Once measured, the **tidal volume** can be used to calculate the pulmonary ventilation rate or **PV**: the amount of air exchanged with the environment per minute. During exercise, the breathing rate, tidal volume, and PV increase up to a maximum (as indicated below).

Respiratory gas	Approximate percentages of O_2 and CO_2		
	Inhaled air	Air in lungs	Exhaled air
O_2	21.0%	13.8%	16.4%
CO_2	0.04%	5.5%	3.6%

Above: The percentages of respiratory gases in air (by volume) during normal breathing. The percentage volume of oxygen in the alveolar air (in the lung) is lower than that in the exhaled air because of the influence of the dead air volume in the airways (air unavailable for gas exchange).

Spirogram for a male during quiet and forced breathing, and during exercise

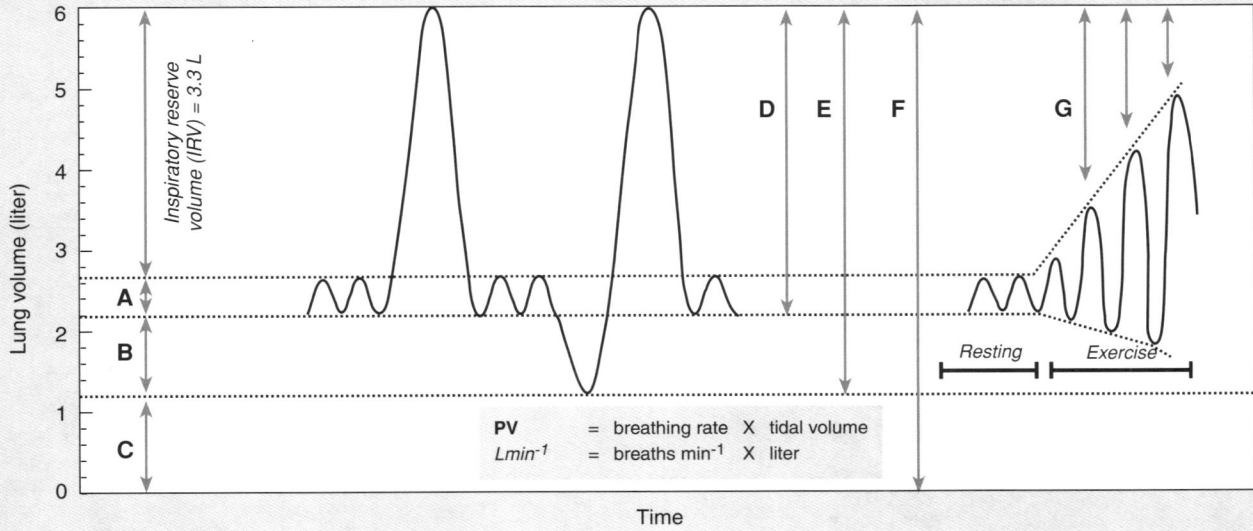

PV $= $ breathing rate $\times$ tidal volume
$Lmin^{-1}$ $= $ breaths min^{-1} $\times$ liter

1. (a) **Briefly** outline the sequence of events involved in **quiet breathing**: _____

_____

_____

(b) Explain the essential difference between this and the situation during heavy exercise or forced breathing:

_____

_____

2. Using the definitions given opposite, identify the volumes and capacities indicated by the letters A-F on the diagram of a spirogram above. For each, indicate the volume (vol) in liters. The inspiratory reserve volume has been identified for you:

(a) A: _____ Vol: _____ (d) D: _____ Vol: _____

(b) B: _____ Vol: _____ (e) E: _____ Vol: _____

(c) C: _____ Vol: _____ (f) F: _____ Vol: _____

3. Explain what is happening in the sequence indicated by the letter **G**: _____

_____

4. Calculate PV when breathing rate is 15 breaths per minute and tidal volume is 4.0 L: _____

5. The table above gives approximate percentages for respiratory gases during breathing. Study the data and:

(a) Calculate the difference in CO_2 between inhaled and exhaled air: _____

(b) Explain where this 'extra' CO_2 comes from: _____

(c) Explain why the dead air volume raises the oxygen content of exhaled air above that in the lungs: _____

A 2 Control of Breathing

The basic rhythm of breathing is controlled by the **respiratory center**, a cluster of neurons located in the medulla oblongata. This rhythm is adjusted in response to the physical and chemical changes that occur when we carry out different activities. Although the control of breathing is involuntary, we can exert some degree of conscious control over it. The diagram below illustrates these controls.

The Control of Breathing

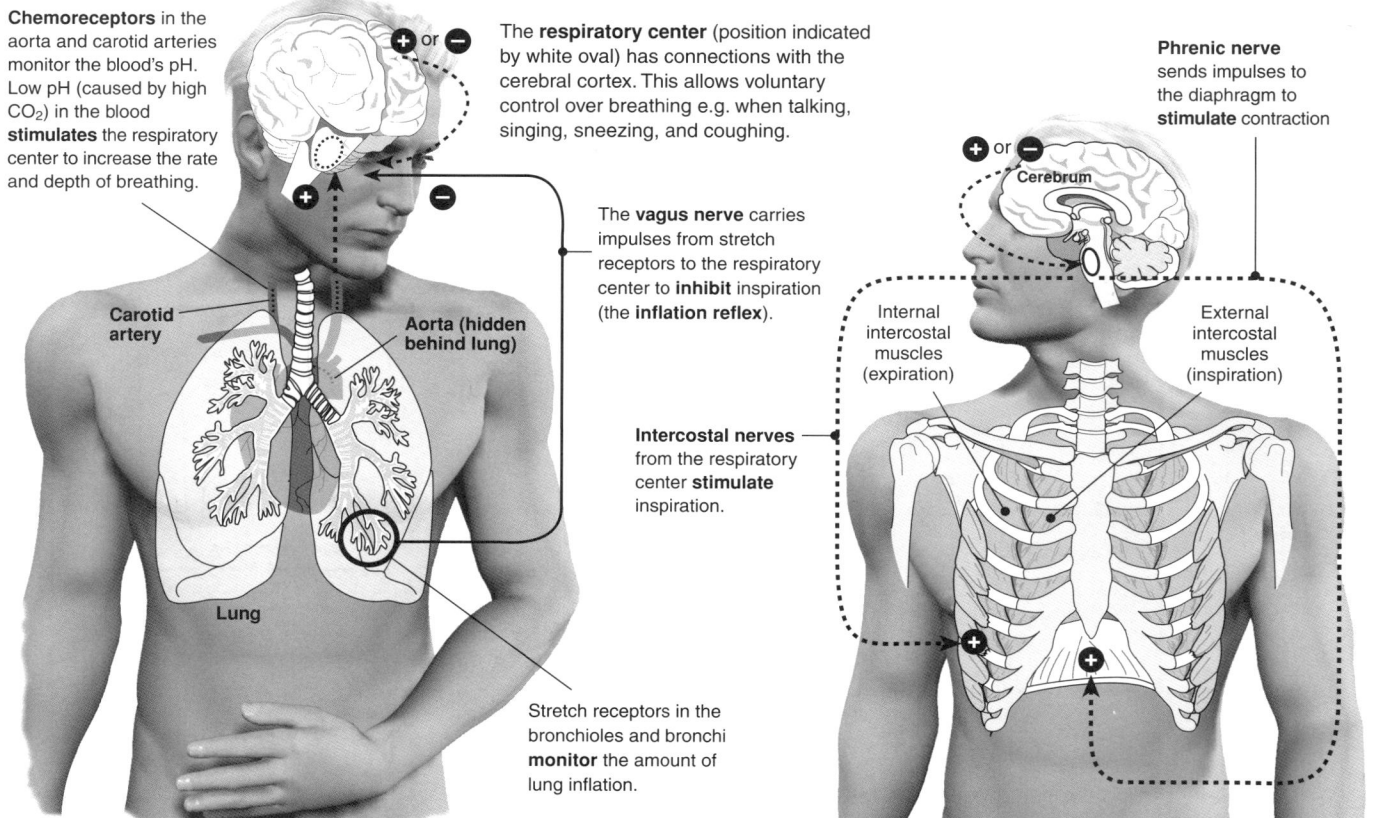

Chemoreceptors in the aorta and carotid arteries monitor the blood's pH. Low pH (caused by high CO_2) in the blood **stimulates** the respiratory center to increase the rate and depth of breathing.

The **respiratory center** (position indicated by white oval) has connections with the cerebral cortex. This allows voluntary control over breathing e.g. when talking, singing, sneezing, and coughing.

Phrenic nerve sends impulses to the diaphragm to **stimulate** contraction

Cerebrum

The **vagus nerve** carries impulses from stretch receptors to the respiratory center to **inhibit** inspiration (the **inflation reflex**).

Carotid artery

Aorta (hidden behind lung)

Internal intercostal muscles (expiration)

External intercostal muscles (inspiration)

Intercostal nerves from the respiratory center **stimulate** inspiration.

Lung

Stretch receptors in the bronchioles and bronchi **monitor** the amount of lung inflation.

Stretch receptors in the bronchioles monitor lung inflation and send impulses to inhibit the respiratory center and end the breath in. Feedback from sensory receptors and input from the higher brain centres influence the basic rhythm (left figure). The respiratory center sends rhythmic impulses to the intercostal muscles and the diaphragm to bring about normal breathing (right figure).

1. Explain how the basic rhythm of breathing is controlled: _____

_____

2. Identify the role of the following nerves in breathing:

   (a) Phrenic nerve: _____

   (b) Intercostal nerves: _____

   (c) Vagus nerve: _____

3. (a) State the purpose of the inflation reflex: _____

   (b) Explain how the inflation reflex operates: _____

_____

4. (a) Describe the effect of low blood pH on the rate and depth of breathing: _____

   (b) Explain how this effect is mediated: _____

_____

   (c) Suggest why blood pH is a good mechanism by which to regulate breathing rate: _____

_____

The Effects of High Altitude

A 2

The air at high altitudes contains less oxygen than the air at sea level. Air pressure decreases with altitude so the pressure (therefore amount) of oxygen in the air also decreases. Sudden exposure to an altitude of 2000 meters would make you breathless on exertion and above 7000 meters most people would become unconscious. The effects of altitude on physiology are related to this lower oxygen availability. Humans and other animals can make some physiological adjustments to life at altitude. Some of the adaptations of the cardiovascular and respiratory systems to high altitude are outlined below.

Mountain Sickness

Altitude sickness or mountain sickness is usually a mild illness associated with trekking to altitudes of 5000 meters or so. Common symptoms include headache, insomnia, poor appetite and nausea, vomiting, dizziness, tiredness, coughing and breathlessness. The best way to avoid mountain sickness is to ascend to altitude slowly (no more than 300 m per day above 3000 m). Continuing to ascend with mountain sickness can result in more serious illnesses: accumulation of fluid on the brain (cerebral edema) and accumulation of fluid in the lungs (pulmonary edema). These complications can be fatal if not treated with oxygen and a rapid descent to lower altitude.

People who live permanently at high altitude, e.g., Tibetans, Nepalese, and Peruvian Indians, have physiologies adapted (genetically, through evolution) to high altitude. Their blood volumes and red blood cell counts are high, and they can carry heavy loads effortlessly despite a small build. In addition, their metabolism uses oxygen very efficiently.

Physiological Adjustment to Altitude

Effect	Minutes	Days	Weeks
Increased heart rate	←——————→		
Increased breathing		←——————→	
Concentration of blood		←——→	
Increased red blood cell production			←——————→
Increased capillary density			←——→

The human body can make adjustments to life at altitude. Some of these changes take place almost immediately: breathing and heart rates increase. Other adjustments may take weeks (see above). These responses are all aimed at improving the rate of supply of oxygen to the body's tissues. When more permanent adjustments to physiology are made (increased blood cells and capillary networks) heart and breathing rates can return to normal.

Llamas, vicunas, and Bactrian camels are well suited to high altitude life. Vicunas and llamas, which live in the Andes, have high blood cell counts and their red blood cells live almost twice as long as those in humans. Their hemoglobin also picks up and offloads oxygen more efficiently than the hemoglobin of most mammals.

1. (a) Describe the general effects of high altitude on the body: _____

   _____

   (b) Name the general term given to describe these effects: _____

2. (a) Name one short term physiological adaptation that humans make to high altitude: _____

   _____

   (b) Explain how this adaptation helps to increase the amount of oxygen the body receives: _____

   _____

3. (a) Name one longer term adaptation that humans can make to living at high altitude: _____

   _____

   (b) Explain how this adaptation helps to increase the amount of oxygen the body receives: _____

   _____

Gas Transport in Humans

The transport of respiratory gases around the body is the role of the blood and its respiratory pigments. Oxygen is transported throughout the body chemically bound to the respiratory pigment **hemoglobin** inside the red blood cells. In the muscles, oxygen from hemoglobin is transferred to and retained by **myoglobin**, a molecule that is chemically similar to hemoglobin except that it consists of only one haem-globin unit. Myoglobin has a greater affinity for oxygen than hemoglobin and acts as an oxygen store within muscles, releasing the oxygen during periods of prolonged or extreme muscular activity. If the myoglobin store is exhausted, the muscles are forced into oxygen debt and must respire anaerobically. The waste product of this, lactic acid, accumulates in the muscle and is transported (as lactate) to the liver where it is metabolized under aerobic conditions.

Gas Exchange and Transport

Air movement

Bronchiole

Alveoli (air sacs): Each alveolus is a cup shaped pouch. The short airways from the alveoli merge with other airways forming small bronchioles and then larger bronchi.

Capillary

Alveoli

Area of contact with lung capillary enlarged below

Alveolar surface: the gas exchange membranes are only 0.5 μm thick. This allows for rapid diffusion.

CO_2 O_2

Lung capillary: The lung capillaries surround the alveoli very closely, allowing for diffusion of gases back and forth across the tiny space.

HbO_2

When oxygen levels are high (as occurs in the lungs and surrounding blood vessels) hemoglobin binds with a lot of oxygen (the hemoglobin is saturated).

Most of the oxygen in the blood (97%) is carried in the red blood cells by a protein called hemoglobin (**Hb**). Hemoglobin is a respiratory pigment: it increases the amount of oxygen the blood can carry by binding oxygen in a reversible reaction.

Body tissue capillary: The capillaries in the tissues are very close to the body cells, allowing for rapid diffusion of gases back and forth.

Most of the carbon dioxide in the blood (85%) is carried as bicarbonate (HCO_3^-), formed in the red blood cells from CO_2 and water in a reversible, enzyme driven, reaction. Bicarbonate diffuses out of the red blood cells and into the plasma where it contributes to the **buffer** capacity of the blood.

HCO_3^-

HbO_2

When carbon dioxide levels are high (as in the body tissues needing oxygen), hemoglobin releases the oxygen.

Carbon dioxide from body cells diffuses into the capillary.

CO_2 O_2

Oxygen diffuses into the body cells from capillaries.

Body cells

Transport of Carbon Dioxide in the Blood

5% dissolved in the plasma

75-85% as bicarbonate in cells and plasma

10-20% carried bound to Hb (HbCO$_2$); called **carbaminohemoglobin**

CO_2

Respiring body cell

Carbonic anhydrase   *Carbonic acid*   **Red blood cell**

$CO_2 + H_2O \rightleftharpoons H_2CO_3 \rightleftharpoons HCO_3^- + H^+$

Carried by Hb

H^+ is picked up by Hb. In this way, Hb acts as a blood buffer.

Chloride diffuses into the red blood cell to counter the loss of bicarbonate ions. This is called the **chloride shift**.

Cl^- $Na^+ + HCO_3^-$

NaCl in blood $NaHCO_3$

Bicarbonate diffuses into the plasma where it combines with sodium.

Oxygen does not easily dissolve in blood, but is carried in chemical combination with hemoglobin (Hb) in red blood cells. The most important factor determining how much oxygen is carried by Hb is the level of oxygen in the blood. The greater the oxygen tension, the more oxygen will combine with Hb. This relationship can be illustrated with an oxygen-hemoglobin dissociation curve as shown below (Fig. 1). In the lung capillaries, (high O_2), a lot of oxygen is picked up and bound by Hb. In the tissues, (low O_2), oxygen is released. In skeletal muscle, myoglobin picks up oxygen from hemoglobin and therefore serves as an oxygen store when oxygen tension begin to fall. The release of oxygen is enhanced by the Bohr effect (Fig. 2).

Respiratory Pigments and the Transport of Oxygen

Fig. 1: Dissociation curves for hemoglobin and myoglobin at normal body temperature for fetal and adult human blood.

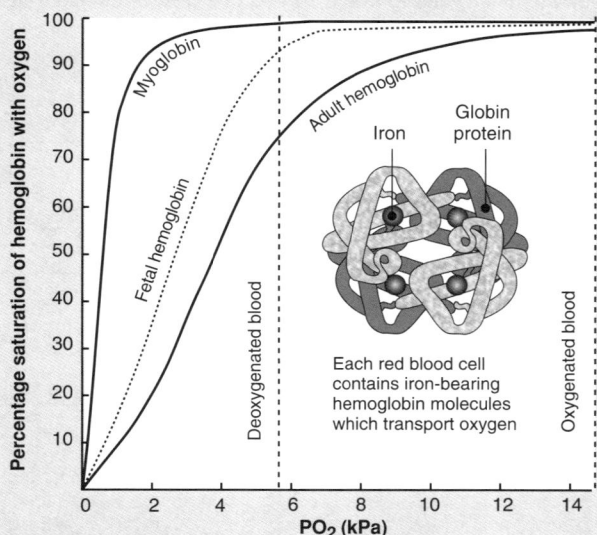

As oxygen level increases, more oxygen combines with hemoglobin (Hb). Hb saturation remains high, even at low oxygen tensions. Fetal Hb has a high affinity for oxygen and carries 20-30% more than maternal Hb. Myoglobin in skeletal muscle has a very high affinity for oxygen and will take up oxygen from hemoglobin in the blood.

Fig. 2: Oxygen-hemoglobin dissociation curves for human blood at normal body temperature at different blood pH.

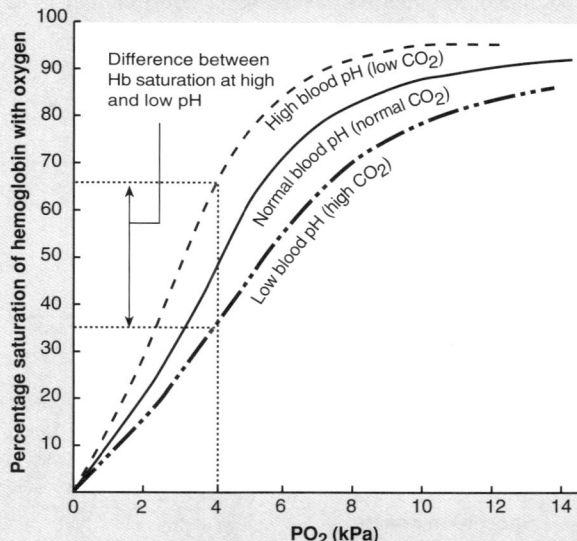

As pH increases (lower CO_2), more oxygen combines with Hb. As the blood pH decreases (higher CO_2), Hb binds less oxygen and releases more to the tissues (**the Bohr effect**). The difference between Hb saturation at high and low pH represents the amount of oxygen released to the tissues.

1. (a) Name two regions in the body where oxygen levels are very high: _____

   (b) Two regions where carbon dioxide levels are very high: _____

2. Explain the significance of the **reversible binding** reaction of hemoglobin (Hb) to oxygen:

   _____

3. (a) Hemoglobin saturation is affected by the oxygen level in the blood. Describe the nature of this relationship:

   _____

   (b) Comment on the significance of this relationship to oxygen delivery to the tissues:_____

   _____

4. (a) Describe how fetal Hb is different to adult Hb: _____

   (b) Explain the significance of this difference to oxygen delivery to the fetus: _____

   _____

5. At low blood pH, less oxygen is bound by hemoglobin and more is released to the tissues:

   (a) Name this effect:_____

   (b) Comment on its significance to oxygen delivery to respiring tissue: _____

   _____

6. Explain the significance of the very high affinity of myoglobin for oxygen: _____

   _____

7. Name the two main contributors to the buffer capacity of the blood: _____

RA2 Diseases Caused by Smoking

Tobacco smoking has only recently been accepted as a major health hazard, despite its practice in Western countries for more than 400 years, and much longer elsewhere. Cigarettes became popular at the end of World War I because they were cheap, convenient, and easier to smoke than pipes and cigars. They remain popular for the further reason that they are more addictive than other forms of tobacco. The milder smoke can be more readily inhaled, allowing **nicotine** (a powerful addictive poison) to be quickly absorbed into the bloodstream. **Lung cancer** is the most widely known and most harmful effect of smoking; 98% of cases are associated with cigarette smoking. Symptoms include chest pain, breathlessness, and coughing up blood. Tobacco smoking is also directly associated with a range of other respiratory and cardiovascular diseases. The damaging components of smoke include tar, carbon monoxide, nitrogen dioxide, and nitric oxide. Many of these chemicals occur in greater concentrations in sidestream smoke than in mainstream smoke (inhaled) due to the presence of a filter in the cigarette.

The Effects of Tobacco Smoking

Long term effects

Smoking damages the arteries of the brain and may result in a **stroke**.

All forms of tobacco-smoking increase the risk of **mouth cancer**, **lip cancer**, and **cancer of the throat** (pharynx).

Lung cancer is the best known harmful effect of smoking.

In a young man who smokes 20 cigarettes a day, the risk of **coronary artery disease** is increased by about three times over that of a nonsmoker.

Short term effects

- Reduction in capacity of the lungs.
- Increase in muscle tension and a decrease in steadiness of the hands.
- Raised blood pressure (10-30 points).
- Very sharp rise in carbon monoxide levels in the lungs contributing to breathlessness.
- Increase in pulse rate by up to 20 beats per minute.
- Surface blood vessel constriction drops skin temperature by up to 5°C.
- Dulling of appetite as well as the sense of smell and taste.

Smoking leads to severe constriction of the arteries supplying the extremities and leads to **peripheral vascular disease**.

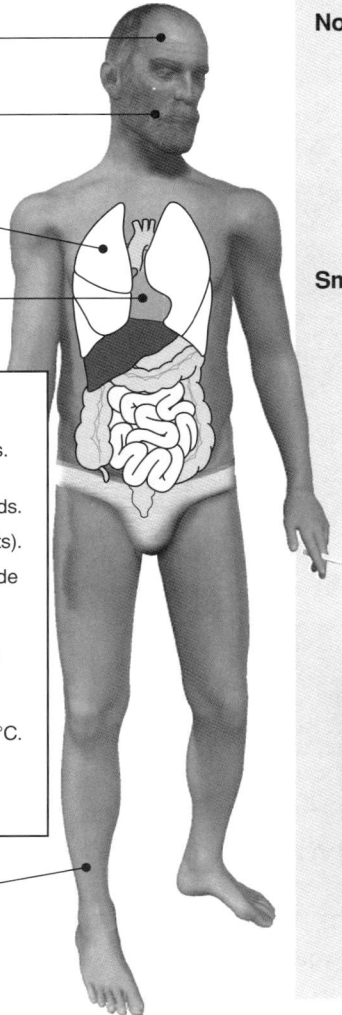

How Smoking Damages Lung Tissue

Non-smoker

Normal arrangement of alveoli

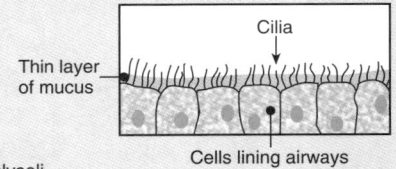

Thin layer of mucus

Cilia

Cells lining airways

Smoker

Coalesced alveoli

Extra mucus produced

Smoke particles

Cancerous cell

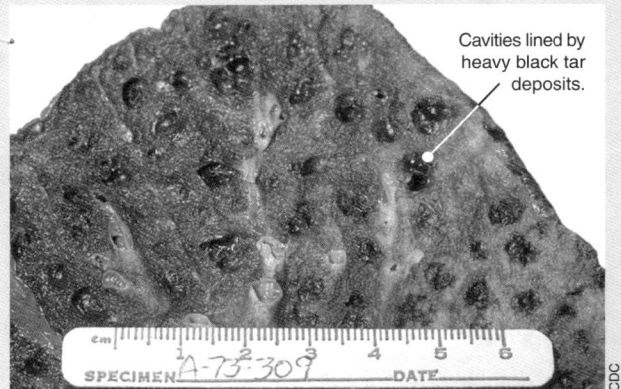

Smoke particles indirectly destroy the walls of the lung's alveoli.

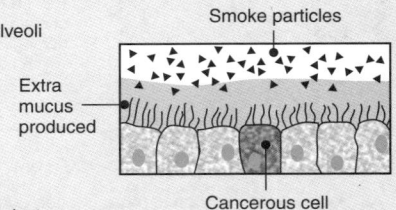

Cavities lined by heavy black tar deposits.

Gross pathology of lung tissue from a patient with emphysema. Tobacco tar deposits can be seen. Tar contains at least 17 known carcinogens.

---

1. Describe the effect of the following constituents of tobacco smoke when inhaled:

   (a) Tar: _____

   (b) Nicotine: _____

   (c) Carbon monoxide: _____

2. Describe two physical changes to the lung that result from long-term smoking: _____

   _____

3. List the symptoms of the following diseases associated with long-term smoking:

   (a) Emphysema: _____

   (b) Coronary artery disease: _____

   (c) Lung cancer: _____

(RA②) Hypersensitivity and Asthma

Hypersensitivity is a general term referring to a range of disorders involving an inappropriate immune response to an **allergen**. Hypersensitivity reactions include hayfever (allergic rhinitis) and **asthma**. They occur after a person has been **sensitized** to an antigen (the allergen) and are mediated by histamine. In some cases, the reaction causes only localized discomfort, as in the case of hayfever. More generalized reactions (such as anaphylaxis from drug injections), or localized reactions that affect essential body systems (such as asthma), can cause death through asphyxiation and/or circulatory shock.

Hypersensitivity

A person becomes **sensitized** when they form antibodies to harmless substances in the environment such as pollen or spores (steps 1-2 right). These substances, termed **allergens**, act as antigens to induce antibody production and an allergic response. Once a person is sensitized, the antibodies respond to further encounters with the allergen by causing the release of **histamine** from mast cells (steps 4-5). It is histamine that mediates the symptoms of hypersensitivity reactions such as hay fever and asthma. These symptoms include wheezing and airway constriction, inflammation, itching and watering of the eyes and nose, and/or sneezing.

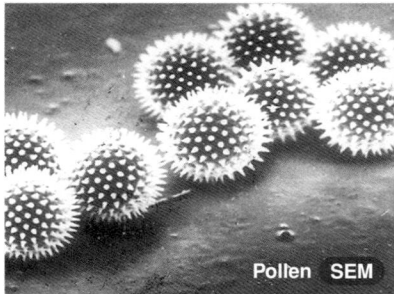

Pollen SEM | Ragweed

Hay fever (allergic rhinitis) is an allergic reaction to airborne substances such as dust, molds, pollens, and animal fur or feathers. Allergy to wind-borne pollen is the most common, and certain plants (e.g. ragweed and privet) are highly allergenic. There appears to be a genetic susceptibility to hay fever, as it is common in people with a family history of eczema, hives, and/or asthma. The best treatment for hay fever is to avoid the allergen, although anti-histamines, decongestants, and steroid nasal sprays will assist in alleviating symptoms.

Asthma is a common disease affecting more than 15 million people in the US. It usually occurs as a result of an allergic reaction to allergens such as house dust and the feces of house dust mites, pollen, and animal dander. As with all hypersensitivity reactions, it involves the production of histamines from mast cells (far right). The site of the reaction is the respiratory bronchioles where the histamine causes constriction of the airways, accumulation of fluid and mucus, and inability to breathe. During an attack, sufferers show labored breathing with overexpansion of the chest cavity (photo, right).

Asthma attacks are often triggered by environmental factors such as cold air, exercise, air pollutants, and viral infections. Recent evidence has also indicated the involvement of a bacterium: *Chlamydia pneumoniae*, in about half of all cases of asthma in susceptible adults.

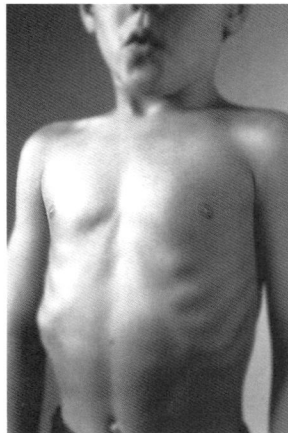

The Basis of Hypersensitivity

B cell

① B cell encounters the allergen and differentiates into plasma cells

Plasma cell

Antibodies

② The plasma cell produces antibodies

Mast cell

③ Antibodies bind to specific receptors on the surface of the mast cells

Vesicles with histamine

④ The mast cell binds the allergen when it encounters it again.

⑤ The mast cell releases histamine and other chemicals, which together cause the symptoms of an allergic reaction.

1. Explain the role of histamine in hypersensitivity responses: _____

_____

2. Explain what is meant by becoming **sensitized** to an allergen: _____

_____

3. Explain the effect of **bronchodilators** and explain why they are used to treat asthma: _____

_____

Reproduction and Development

IB SL

Complete nos:
1, 5, 8, 13, 21-24, 26, 30, 32, 35-37, 39
Extension: 2, 27

IB HL

Complete nos:
1, 5, 8, 13-23, 25-26, 28-32, 35-37, 39
Extension: 2, 28

IB Options

Not applicable to options

AP Biology

Complete nos:
1-23, 24 or 25, 26-40
Some numbers extension as appropriate

Learning Objectives

☐ 1. Compile your own glossary from the **KEY WORDS** displayed in **bold type** in the learning objectives below.

Principles of reproduction (pages 222-225, see Senior Biology 1 for coverage of meiosis)

☐ 2. Explain the need for **reproduction** and identify the risks, benefits, and energetic costs associated with it.

☐ 3. Distinguish between **sexual** and **asexual reproduction**. Discuss the consequences and advantages of each. Understand that **haploid** and **diploid** phases occur in the life cycles of sexually reproducing organisms. Giving examples, briefly describe features of the following types of reproduction: **budding, fragmentation, parthenogenesis, hermaphroditism,** and reproduction involving two **separate sexes**.

☐ 4. Explain the role of **gamete formation** and **fertilization** in **sexual reproduction**. Describe differences between male gametes (**sperm**) and female gametes (**eggs**) in terms of size, the number produced, and motility.

☐ 5. Recall the role of **meiosis** in producing gametes, identifying the significance of the reduction division. Explain how **fertilization** restores the diploid chromosome number in the zygote. Interpret **life cycles** of organisms in terms of **mitosis, meiosis, fertilization,** and **chromosome number**.

Sexual reproduction in animals

Reproductive patterns (pages 224-227, 321-323)

☐ 6. Distinguish between **internal** and **external fertilization** and describe the features associated with each. Describe the advantages and disadvantages of each method. Identify animals with each type of strategy.

☐ 7. Relate the evolution of vertebrate reproductive systems to the move to being land-living. Identify reproductive strategies in amphibians that reflect their partial adaptation to terrestrial lifestyles.

☐ 8. With respect to internal fertilization, define the term **copulation** and distinguish it from **fertilization**. Identify the structures that have developed in males and females to enable internal fertilization.

☐ 9. Using examples, distinguish between **internal** and **external development** of the **embryo** and describe the features associated with each method. Describe the advantages and disadvantages of each strategy. Explain the terms **oviparous** and **viviparous**, and give examples of animals with each type of reproduction.

☐ 10. Define the term **parental care**. Providing examples, describe some different strategies for parental care.

☐ 11. Describe diversity seen in the reproductive structures and strategies of animals (including **courtship** and **mating** behaviors). Useful comparisons can be made between amphibians, birds, and mammals, and between vertebrates and invertebrates.

☐ 12. Describe the structure of the reproductive system in at least two animals. Identify the location and function of: **gonad** (**testis, ovary**), **oviduct, penis** (if present), **vagina** (if present), **uterus** (if present). Identify any associated structures that have a role in reproduction.

Reproduction in humans

Reproductive organs (pages 228, 234-235)

☐ 13. Using a labeled diagram, identify and describe the structure and function of adult male and female reproductive systems in humans. Note the relative positions of the organs but do not include any histological details.

☐ 14. Draw the structure of **testis** tissue as seen using a light microscope. Include reference to: **seminiferous tubules**, blood capillaries, and **interstitial cells**. Draw a seminiferous tubule with adjacent interstitial cells in XS. Indicate the **Sertoli cells** and developing sperm.

☐ 15. Outline the processes involved in the production of male gametes (**spermatogenesis**) and their location. Include reference to mitosis, cell growth, meiosis, and cell differentiation. Outline the role of the hormones: follicle stimulating hormone (**FSH**), luteinizing hormone (**LH**), and **testosterone** in spermatogenesis.

☐ 16. Draw the structure of the ovary as seen using a light microscope. Include reference to the following: **primary oocytes, zona pellucida, Graafian follicles**.

☐ 17. Outline the processes involved in oogenesis, including reference to mitosis, cell growth, meiosis, the unequal division of the cytoplasm, and the degeneration of the **polar bodies**. If required, explain the role of **hormones** in **gametogenesis** in females.

☐ 18. Compare spermatogenesis and oogenesis with respect to the number of gametes formed and the timing of the gamete formation and release.

☐ 19. Draw the structure of mature **sperm** and **egg**, emphasizing the features of the gamete that are related to its functional role.

☐ 20. Outline the role of the **epididymis, seminal vesicle,** and **prostate gland** in the production of **semen**.

The menstrual cycle (pages 229-230)

☐ 21. Explain the main features of the human **menstrual cycle** including: the development of the ovarian **follicles** and **corpora lutea**, the cyclical changes to the **uterine endometrium**, and **menstruation**.

☐ 22. Relate the changes in the menstrual cycle to the changes in the hormones regulating the cycle: **progesterone, estrogen, FSH,** and **LH**. Emphasize the role of **feedback control** in the menstrual cycle.

Human development (pages 236-239, 242-245)

☐ 23. Explain what is meant by **puberty** and describe the physical changes associated with it. Identify **primary** and **secondary sexual characteristics** in males and females and the explain the role of **sex hormones** (**testosterone** and **estrogen**) in human development.

☐ 24. Recall the difference between copulation and **fertilization**. Appreciate how fertilization in humans is dependent on the timing of gamete transfer. In general terms, describe the events in fertilization.

☐ 25. In more detail than #24, describe fertilization, including reference to the timing and significance of the **acrosome reaction**, **penetration** of the egg membrane by the sperm, and the **cortical reaction**.

☐ 26. Describe early embryonic development up to the **implantation** of the **blastocyst** (including **cleavage**).

☐ 27. Outline the main events in **embryonic development** between implantation and 5-8 weeks. Include reference to the early development of both the nervous and circulatory systems.

☐ 28. Explain the role of **human chorionic gonadotropin** (also called human chorionic gonadotrophin or HCG) in early pregnancy. Identify the source of this hormone.

☐ 29. Draw a diagram of the uterus during **pregnancy** and identify the following: **uterus, placenta, umbilical cord, embryonic membranes, amniotic fluid, fetus**. Recognize pregnancy as the period of **gestation**.

☐ 30. Describe the role of the amniotic sac and amniotic fluid in supporting and protecting the fetus. Appreciate the role of **placenta** in the exchange of materials between the maternal and fetal blood.

☐ 31. Describe the structure and function of the **placenta**. Explain how the placenta is maintained during **pregnancy** and describe its functions in relation to the development of the embryo.

☐ 32. Outline the process of **birth** (parturition) and its control, including the role of **oxytocin** and **progesterone**. Recognize the role of positive feedback in birth.

☐ 33. Explain what is meant by **lactation** and explain its importance to early nutrition. Describe the function and regulation of **prolactin** and **oxytocin** in lactation.

☐ 34. Describe the changes that occur with aging, including the development of **degenerative diseases**. Describe the involvement of hormones in female **menopause**.

Contraception and reproductive technologies (pages 231-233, 240-241)

☐ 35. Define the terms: **family planning** and **contraception**. Describe four methods of contraception, including at least one method from each of the following: **mechanical, chemical,** and **behavioral**.

☐ 36. Discuss the ethics of family planning and contraception.

☐ 37. Outline the technique of **amniocentesis** and explain its role in the early detection of chromosomal disorders. Identify the risks and benefits of amniocentesis and outline when the procedure would be recommended.

☐ 38. Describe other pre- and post-natal methods for detecting abnormalities, including **chorionic villus sampling** and **ultrasound** (prenatal), and blood tests (post natal). State when these procedures are used and identify the risks (if any) involved.

☐ 39. Outline the process of **in vitro fertilization** (IVF). Explain when this technique is used and discuss the ethical issues associated with it.

☐ 40. Describe the procedures involved in some other reproductive technologies available to enhance human fertility, including **gamete intrafallopian transfer** (GIFT) and **artificial insemination** (AI).

Textbooks

See the 'Textbook Reference Grid' on pages 8-9 for textbook page references relating to material in this topic.

Supplementary Texts

See pages 5-6 for additional details of these texts:

■ Clegg, C.J., 1998. **Mammals: Structure and Function** (John Murray), pp. 78-86.

■ Murray, P. & N. Owens, 2001. **Behavior and Populations** (Collins), pp. 28-61.

Periodicals

See page 6 for details of publishers of periodicals:

STUDENT'S REFERENCE

■ **Animal Attraction** National Geographic, July 2003, pp. 28-55. *An engaging and expansive account of mating in the animal world.*

■ **Why we don't Lay Eggs** New Scientist, 12 June 1999, pp. 26-31. *Mammalian reproduction: the role of the placenta, the evolution of live birth, and mammalian exceptions to the usual pattern.*

■ **The Biology of Milk** Biol. Sci. Rev., 10(1) Sept. 1997, pp. 32-35. *The production and composition of milk and its role in the biology of mammals.*

Human reproduction (incl. technology)

■ **Spermatogenesis** Biol. Sci. Rev., 15(4) April 2003, pp. 10-14. *The process and control of sperm production in humans, with a discussion of the possible reasons for male infertility.*

■ **The Great Escape** New Scientist, 15 Sept. 2001, (Inside Science). *How the fetus is accepted by the mother's immune system during pregnancy.*

■ **Measuring Female Hormones in Saliva** Biol. Sci. Rev., 13(3) January 2001, pp. 37-39. *The female reproductive system, and the complex hormonal control of the female menstrual cycle.*

■ **Male Contraception** Biol. Sci. Rev., 13(2) Nov. 2000, pp. 6-9. *A new contraceptive technology involves the inhibition of spermatogenesis in males.*

■ **The Placenta** Biol. Sci. Rev., 12 (4) March 2000, pp. 2-5. *The structure and function of the human placenta (includes prenatal diagnoses).*

Human development and aging

■ **Menopause - Design Fault, or By Design** Biol. Sci. Rev., 14(1) Sept. 2001, pp. 2-6. *An excellent synopsis of the basic biology of menopause.*

■ **Aging** National Geographic, 192(5), Nov. 1997, pp. 2-31. *An account of the physiological aspects of ageing as well as the social issues of elderly care.*

■ **The Biology of Ageing** Biol. Sci. Rev., 10(3) January 1998, pp. 18-21. *The physiological basis of ageing, healthy ageing and prolonging life.*

■ **Age - Old Story** New Scientist, 23 Jan. 1999, (Inside Science). *The processes involved in ageing. An accessible, easy-to-read, but thorough account.*

TEACHER'S REFERENCE

■ **Pregnancy Tests** Scientific American, Nov. 2000, pp. 92-93. *Pregnancy tests: how they work and the role of HCG in signalling pregnancy.*

■ **The Evolution of Human Birth** Sci. American, Nov. 2001, pp. 60-65. *An examination of the unique aspects of human reproduction and how they arose.*

■ **Modeling Radial Holoblastic Cleavage** The American Biology Teacher, May 2000, pp. 362-364. *Making 3D models to help students understand the concepts behind embryological processes.*

■ **Boy or Girl** New Scientist, 14 Sept. 2002, pp. 42-45. *Conception and the determination of offspring gender: not a matter of chance alone.*

■ **The Timing of Birth** Scientific American, March 1999, pp. 50-57. *A hormone found in the human placenta influences the timing of delivery.*

■ **Let me Out** New Scientist, 10 January 1998, pp. 24-29. *Fetus and mother are in conflict and it is the fetus that determines the timing of birth.*

■ **Designing a Dilemma** New Scientist, 11 December 1999, pp. 18-19. *A short, but useful account of preimplantation and prenatal tests.*

Internet

See pages 10-11 for details of how to access **Bio Links** from our web site: **www.thebiozone.com**. From Bio Links, access sites under the topics:

GENERAL BIOLOGY ONLINE RESOURCES > Online Textbooks and Lecture Notes: • An on-line biology book • Learn.co.uk ... *and others*

ANIMAL BIOLOGY: • Anatomy and physiology • Human physiology lecture notes ... *and others* > **Reproduction and Development:** • Anatomical travelogue • Dynamic development • Learn.co.uk: Reproduction • Menstrual cycle and pregnancy • Fertility UK: Physiology ... *and others*

BIOTECHNOLOGY > Applications in Biotechnology > Reproductive Biotechnology: • Assisted reproductive technologies • Atlanta reproductive Health center • Frequently asked questions about infertility ... *and others*

Software and video resources are now provided in the Teacher Resource Handbook

Asexual Reproduction

A 1

In most forms of asexual reproduction, the parent splits, fragments, or buds to produce offspring identical to itself. Parthenogenesis is a special type of asexual reproduction where unfertilized eggs give rise to clones. Asexually reproducing organisms do not need to find a mate, so the energy that might otherwise be used for sexual activity can be used for other things. Asexual reproduction is rapid, but all the offspring are genetically identical. If conditions change there is little ability to adapt.

Binary Fission

Binary fission is a method of asexual reproduction that occurs in prokaryotes (bacteria and cyanobacteria) and protists (e.g., *Amoeba* and *Paramecium*). Binary fission occurs by division of a parent body into two, more or less equal, parts. The cell's DNA is replicated, followed by division of the nucleoplasm (in prokaryotes) or the cytoplasm (protists). The series (right) shows stages in the process of binary fission in *Amoeba*. The photograph below this series shows binary fission in *Paramecium*. The nucleus has divided and the cytoplasm is dividing. The arrows indicate where a constriction is developing in the cell.

Note that some life cycle stages of parasitic protozoans, such as the malarial parasite *Plasmodium*, undergo **multiple fission**. The nucleus divides repeatedly before the final division of the cytoplasm to produce many new cells. Repeated cycles of multiple fission produce large numbers of offspring very rapidly.

Amoeba undergoing fission

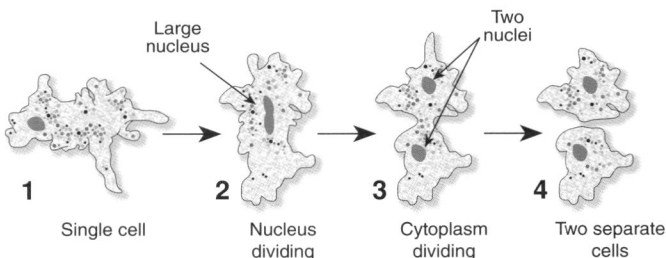

1	2	3	4
Single cell	Nucleus dividing	Cytoplasm dividing	Two separate cells

Large nucleus — Two nuclei

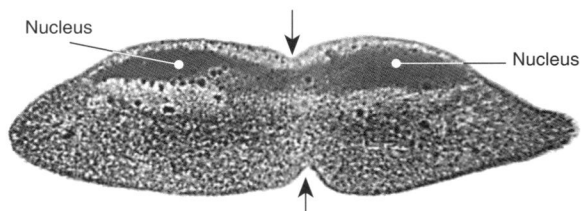

Nucleus   Nucleus

Paramecium (photo RCN)

Budding and Fragmentation

Sponges and most cnidarians (e.g., *Hydra*) can reproduce by **budding**. A small part of the parent body separates from the rest and develops into a new individual. This new individual may remain attached as part of the colony, or the budding offspring may constrict at its point of attachment (arrowed on the photograph) and eventually be released as an independent organism.

The photo (right) shows *Hydra* budding. The new individual is forming on the right of the animal. Cnidarians also undergo **fragmentation**. In this natural process, the organism spontaneously divides into fragments which then regenerate. Fragmentation also occurs in sponges and flatworms (platyhelminthes).

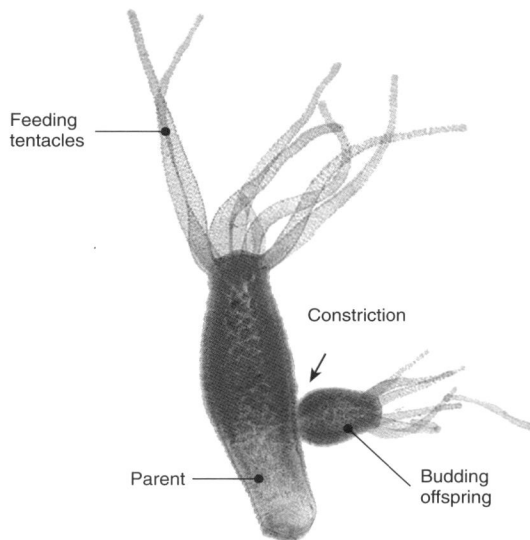

Feeding tentacles

Constriction

Parent

Budding offspring

Hydra (photo Ell)

1. Name the reproductive process occurring in the photograph of *Paramecium* above: _____

2. Name the reproductive process occurring in *Hydra*: _____

3. (a) Suggest why multiple fission produces offspring more rapidly than does simple binary fission: _____

_____

_____

_____

   (b) Explain the advantage of multiple fission to an intracellular parasite such as *Plasmodium*: _____

_____

_____

Alternating Asexual and Sexual Cycles of Reproduction

Some organisms combine several cycles of asexual reproduction by **parthenogenesis** (below, left) with periods when they reproduce sexually (producing gametes by meiosis which combine in fertilization). The parthenogenetic phase enables the rapid reproduction of a well adapted clone.

The sexual phase is induced when the environment becomes unfavorable for the clone. The new generation, produced by sexual reproduction, may include some individuals that are better adapted to a new set of environmental conditions.

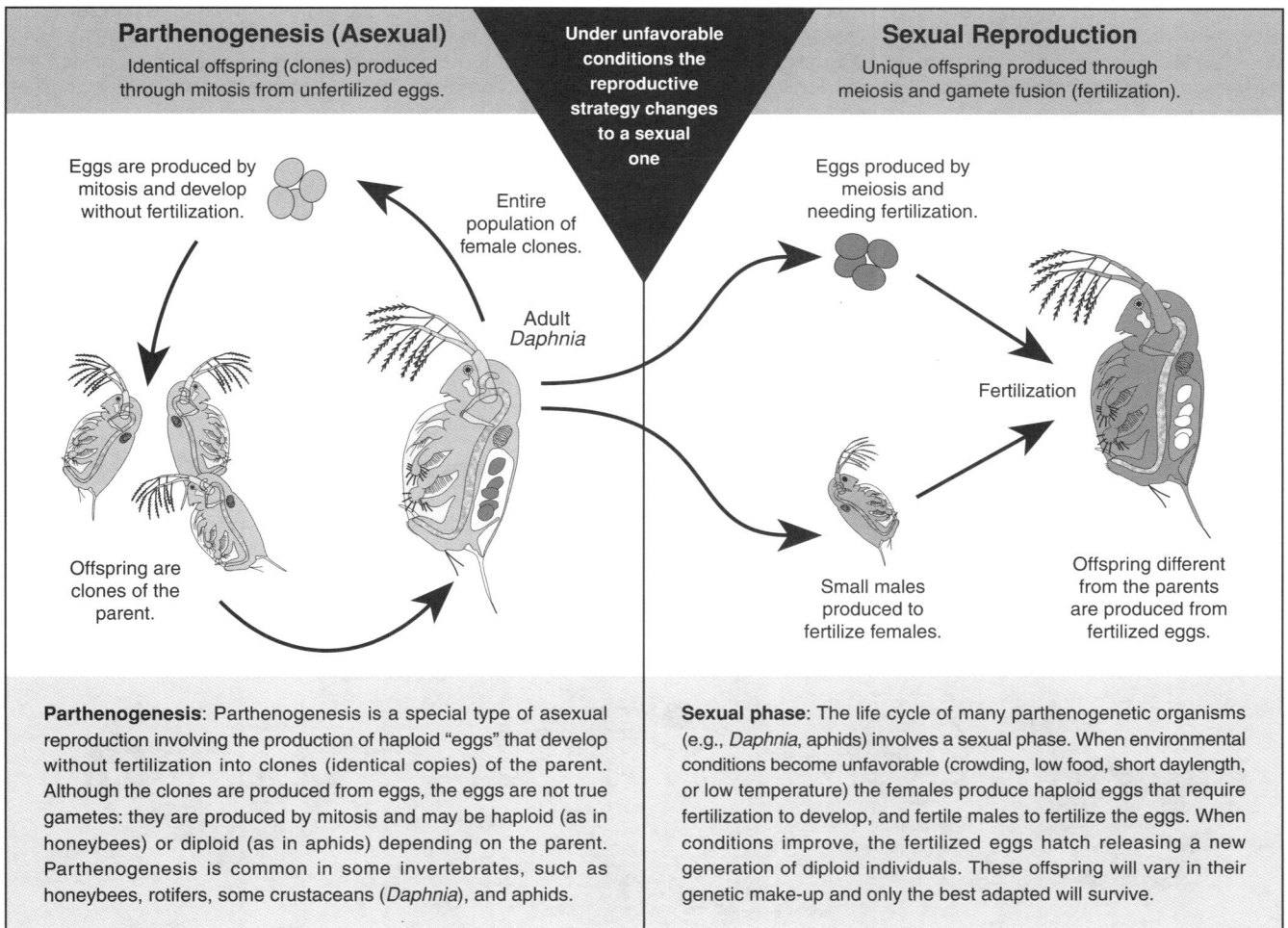

Parthenogenesis (Asexual)
Identical offspring (clones) produced through mitosis from unfertilized eggs.

Under unfavorable conditions the reproductive strategy changes to a sexual one

Sexual Reproduction
Unique offspring produced through meiosis and gamete fusion (fertilization).

Eggs are produced by mitosis and develop without fertilization.

Entire population of female clones.

Adult *Daphnia*

Offspring are clones of the parent.

Eggs produced by meiosis and needing fertilization.

Fertilization

Small males produced to fertilize females.

Offspring different from the parents are produced from fertilized eggs.

Parthenogenesis: Parthenogenesis is a special type of asexual reproduction involving the production of haploid "eggs" that develop without fertilization into clones (identical copies) of the parent. Although the clones are produced from eggs, the eggs are not true gametes: they are produced by mitosis and may be haploid (as in honeybees) or diploid (as in aphids) depending on the parent. Parthenogenesis is common in some invertebrates, such as honeybees, rotifers, some crustaceans (*Daphnia*), and aphids.

Sexual phase: The life cycle of many parthenogenetic organisms (e.g., *Daphnia*, aphids) involves a sexual phase. When environmental conditions become unfavorable (crowding, low food, short daylength, or low temperature) the females produce haploid eggs that require fertilization to develop, and fertile males to fertilize the eggs. When conditions improve, the fertilized eggs hatch releasing a new generation of diploid individuals. These offspring will vary in their genetic make-up and only the best adapted will survive.

4. Name one potential disadvantage of reproducing asexually: _____

_____

_____

5. Explain what is meant by parthenogenesis: _____

_____

_____

6. Describe two advantages of having a reproductive strategy where parthenogenesis (the asexual phase) is interrupted occasionally by a period of sexual reproduction:

(a) Advantage 1: _____

_____

(b) Advantage 2: _____

_____

7. Suggest why some organisms (e.g., *Daphnia*, rotifers, aphids) are stimulated by certain environmental conditions (e.g., crowding, low food, temperature or daylength changes), to enter a sexual phase of reproduction:

_____

_____

Animal Sexual Reproduction

All types of sexual reproduction involve the production of **gametes** (sex cells), produced by special sex organs called **gonads**. Female gametes (**eggs**) and male gametes (**sperm**) come together in **fertilization**. Animal sexual reproduction follows one of three main patterns, determined by the location of fertilization and embryonic development. These patterns are: external fertilization and development; internal fertilization followed by external development; internal fertilization and development. **External fertilization** is found in many aquatic invertebrates and most fish, where eggs and sperm are released into the surrounding water. Male and female parents usually release their gametes (spawn) at the same time and place in

order to increase the chances of successful fertilization. In other invertebrates, reptiles, sharks, birds, and mammals, sperm are transferred from the male to inside the female's genital tract during the act of **copulation**. This **internal fertilization** increases the chance that the gametes will meet successfully. In birds and most reptiles, one adaptation to life on land has been the evolution of the **amniote egg**: a structure that enables the embryo to complete its development outside the parent surrounded by a protective shell and nourished by a yolk sac. The pattern of internal development in mammals provides the most advantages for the embryo in terms of nourishment and protection during development.

Achieving Fertilization: The Mating Game

Many marine invertebrates release gametes into the sea. Fertilization and development are external to the parent. *Example: giant clam*

Insects often have elaborate courtship rituals. Fertilization is internal, but the eggs are laid and develop externally. *Example: dipteran flies*

In amphibians, a prolonged coupling, called amplexus, precedes gamete release and external fertilization. *Example: frogs*

In birds and reptiles gamete fertilization is internal but the eggs are laid (usually in nests) and develop externally. *Example: quail*

Mammals exhibit internal fertilization, a long period of internal development, and often prolonged parental care. *Example: African lions*

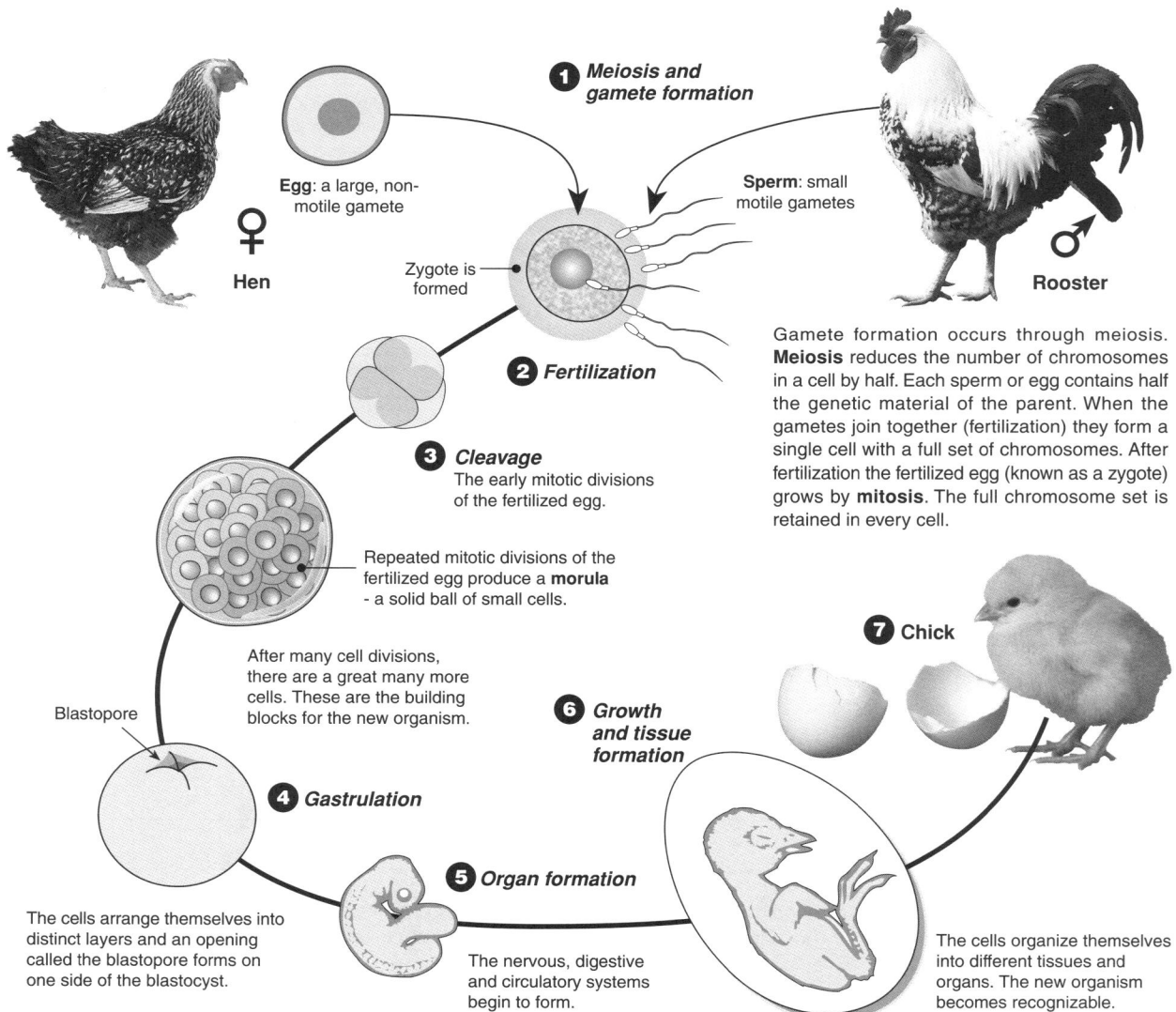

1 Meiosis and gamete formation

Egg: a large, non-motile gamete

Sperm: small motile gametes

Hen ♀

Rooster ♂

Zygote is formed

2 Fertilization

3 Cleavage
The early mitotic divisions of the fertilized egg.

Repeated mitotic divisions of the fertilized egg produce a **morula** - a solid ball of small cells.

After many cell divisions, there are a great many more cells. These are the building blocks for the new organism.

Blastopore

4 Gastrulation

The cells arrange themselves into distinct layers and an opening called the blastopore forms on one side of the blastocyst.

5 Organ formation

The nervous, digestive and circulatory systems begin to form.

6 Growth and tissue formation

7 Chick

The cells organize themselves into different tissues and organs. The new organism becomes recognizable.

Gamete formation occurs through meiosis. **Meiosis** reduces the number of chromosomes in a cell by half. Each sperm or egg contains half the genetic material of the parent. When the gametes join together (fertilization) they form a single cell with a full set of chromosomes. After fertilization the fertilized egg (known as a zygote) grows by **mitosis**. The full chromosome set is retained in every cell.

Hermaphroditism

Most animals have separate sexes (individuals are either male or female). However, in some animals both sperm and eggs can be produced in the same individual. Such animals are known as **hermaphrodites**. In earthworms (below), flatworms, and some molluscs (e.g. land snails), both male and female organs are active in the same animal and there is typically a reciprocal transfer of sperm (each receives sperm from the other during copulation). In this type of hermaphroditism, there is no self fertilization: a mate is necessary for any fertilization to occur. However, some specialized hermaphroditic animals, such as parasitic tapeworms, are capable of self-fertilization.

White patches are sperm being exchanged

The photo above shows two earthworms in a mating clasp. Each worm places its reproductive region (the clitellum) against the reproductive region of the other worm, and sperm is exchanged.

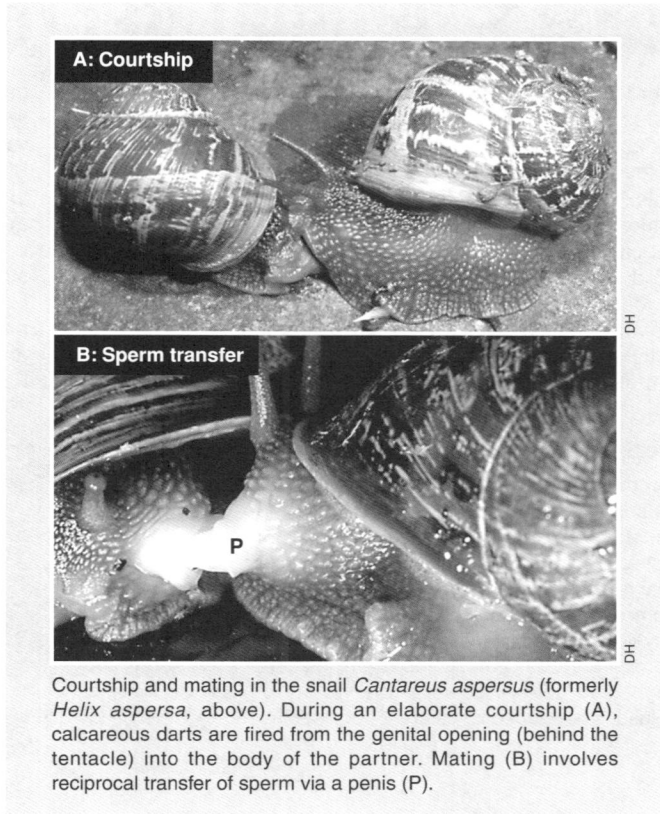

A: Courtship

B: Sperm transfer

Courtship and mating in the snail *Cantareus aspersus* (formerly *Helix aspersa*, above). During an elaborate courtship (A), calcareous darts are fired from the genital opening (behind the tentacle) into the body of the partner. Mating (B) involves reciprocal transfer of sperm via a penis (P).

1. Describe one advantage of sexual reproduction: _____

_____

2. Describe one potential disadvantage of sexual reproduction: _____

_____

3. Compare and contrast the key differences between male and female gametes in relation to:

   (a) The size of gametes: _____

   (b) Number of gametes produced: _____

   (c) Motility of gametes: _____

4. (a) Define the term **external fertilization**: _____

   (b) Describe the features of external fertilization: _____

   _____

5. (a) Define the term **internal fertilization**: _____

   (b) Describe the features of internal fertilization: _____

   _____

   (c) Name an animal group with internal fertilization but external development: _____

   (d) Name an animal group with internal fertilization and internal development: _____

   (e) Explain one benefit and one cost involved in providing for internal development of an embryo:

   Benefit: _____

   Cost: _____

6. Explain why each new individual produced from the fusion of the two gametes is unique: _____

_____

Animal Reproductive Strategies

RA 2

To reproduce sexually, animals must have systems to ensure that gametes meet and fertilization takes place. There is a huge range in the complexity of reproductive structures in animals: the least complex do not even have distinct gonads, whereas the most complex comprise numerous ducts, glands, and accessory structures to produce the gametes and protect the eggs and developing embryos. Diverse systems for reproduction have evolved amongst the invertebrates; some of the most complex are found in parasitic flatworms. Insects, which have separate sexes and highly developed reproductive systems, are illustrated in detail here. Insects frequently also have elaborate courtship and mating behaviors associated with successful transfer of

gametes. Amongst the vertebrates, the basic structures of the reproductive system are relatively uniform, but there is huge variation in the strategies shown by different vertebrate groups. Biologists distinguish **oviparous** (egg laying) animals from, **viviparous** (live bearing) animals. A small number of vertebrates are also **ovoviviparous**: the young are born live but their nutrition inside the mother is derived from stores within the egg. This strategy is typical of non-mammal species that bear live young. Here the contrast is made between the reproductive strategies of amphibians, which rely heavily on water for their reproduction, and the strategy of birds, in which the evolution of a shelled egg has freed them from their reproductive dependence on water.

Reproductive Strategies of Frogs

In most frogs and toads, fertilization is external. This is achieved when the male clasps the female. Called **amplexus**, this clasping may last several hours or even days until the female lays her eggs. Not all frogs lay eggs in water. Some frogs have adopted novel behavior and physiological strategies to avoid their eggs becoming an easy meal. The examples here (right and below) illustrate the variety of solutions developed by different frog species.

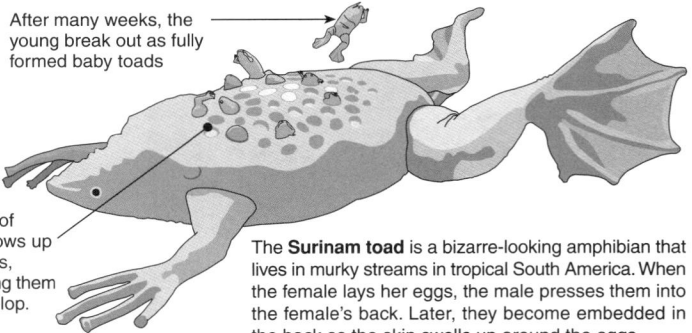

After many weeks, the young break out as fully formed baby toads

A special layer of spongy skin grows up around the eggs, completely hiding them while they develop.

The **Surinam toad** is a bizarre-looking amphibian that lives in murky streams in tropical South America. When the female lays her eggs, the male presses them into the female's back. Later, they become embedded in the back as the skin swells up around the eggs.

Male

Some frogs lay their eggs in a nest of foam either on land (attached to leaves) or floating on water. The foam not only hides the eggs from predators, but it keeps them moist and prevents them from drying out.

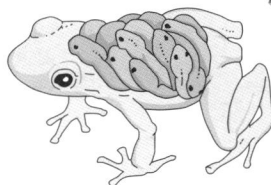

Some species of small frogs in both South America and Africa lay eggs that hatch into tadpoles on land. The tadpoles stick to the back of one of the parents with mouthparts modified to function as suckers. The parent carries the tadpoles to water.

Some frog species lay eggs on leaves or branches overhanging the water. In some of these species one of the parents remains with the eggs until they hatch. The tadpoles that emerge from the eggs drop into the water below to complete their development.

When a female midwife toad lays her string of eggs, the male winds them around his back legs. He carries the eggs for about a month, visiting puddles to keep them moist. When the eggs are ready to hatch he places them in a suitable pool.

The Structure and Physiology of a Bird's Egg

Both reptiles and birds (which evolved from reptilian ancestors) developed watertight shelled eggs, called **cleidoic eggs**. The egg is supplied with all the necessary food material as well as fats that yield water when metabolized. The shell enclosing the egg provides protection and reduces water loss, yet permits gas exchange. Waste materials from the developing chick embryo are stored in the egg.

Newly hatched chicken egg

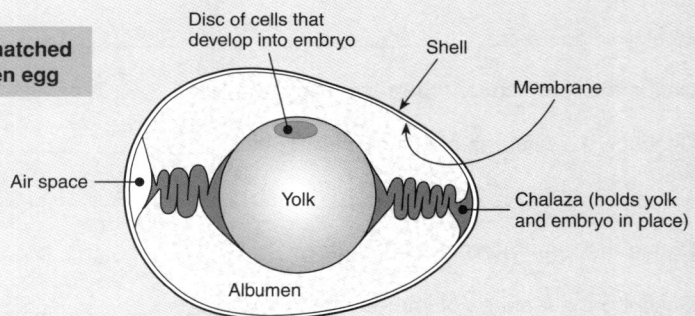

Disc of cells that develop into embryo

Shell

Membrane

Air space

Yolk

Chalaza (holds yolk and embryo in place)

Albumen

Ten-day old chicken egg

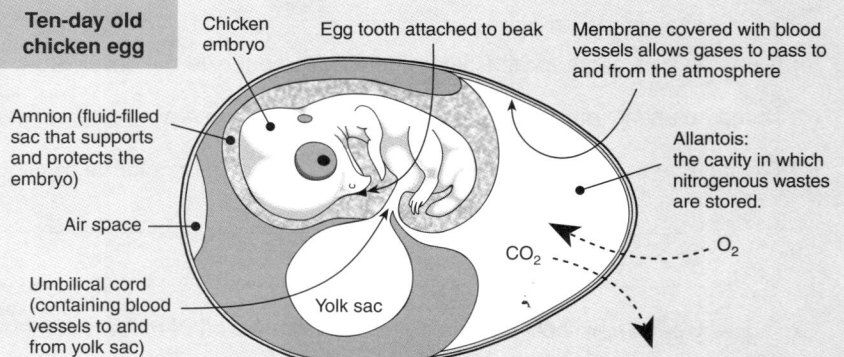

Chicken embryo

Egg tooth attached to beak

Membrane covered with blood vessels allows gases to pass to and from the atmosphere

Amnion (fluid-filled sac that supports and protects the embryo)

Allantois: the cavity in which nitrogenous wastes are stored.

Air space

CO_2

O_2

Umbilical cord (containing blood vessels to and from yolk sac)

Yolk sac

Reproductive Strategies of Insects

Insects reproduce sexually, mainly by internal fertilization followed by the production of yolk-filled eggs. A single pair of gonads is located in the abdomen. Most insects transfer sperm within small packets called **spermatophores**. Claspers at the end of the male's abdomen hold the female's abdomen during copulation. The terminal segments of the female's abdomen may form an **ovipositor**, often extendable or needle-like, with which they lay their eggs. Depending on the insect species, eggs may be buried in soil, animal dung, or rotting carcasses, injected into plant tissue or living hosts, or cemented to twigs or leaves.

Mating in Damselflies

The *Odonata* (damselflies and dragonflies) are unique amongst the insects in that the male copulatory apparatus is situated on abdominal segments close to its thorax. However the testes are located at the end of its abdomen so that, prior to mating, the male has to bend the abdomen round to transfer semen from the testes to the penis. The location of the male genitals also accounts for the unique "wheel position" adopted by *Odonata* as shown below.

Insect reproductive organs

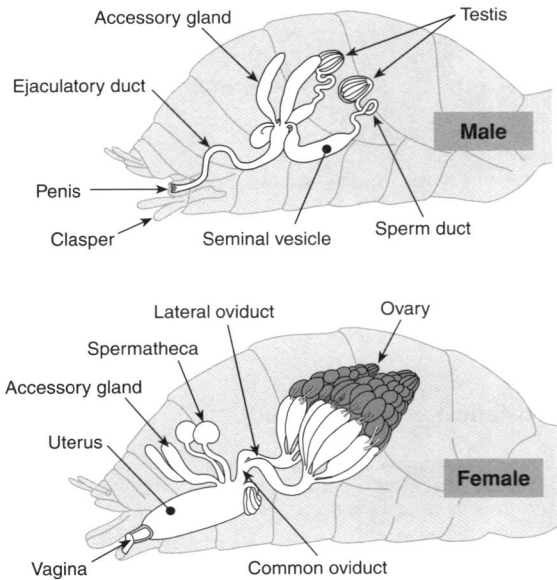

Male: Accessory gland, Testis, Ejaculatory duct, Penis, Clasper, Seminal vesicle, Sperm duct

Female: Lateral oviduct, Ovary, Spermatheca, Accessory gland, Uterus, Vagina, Common oviduct

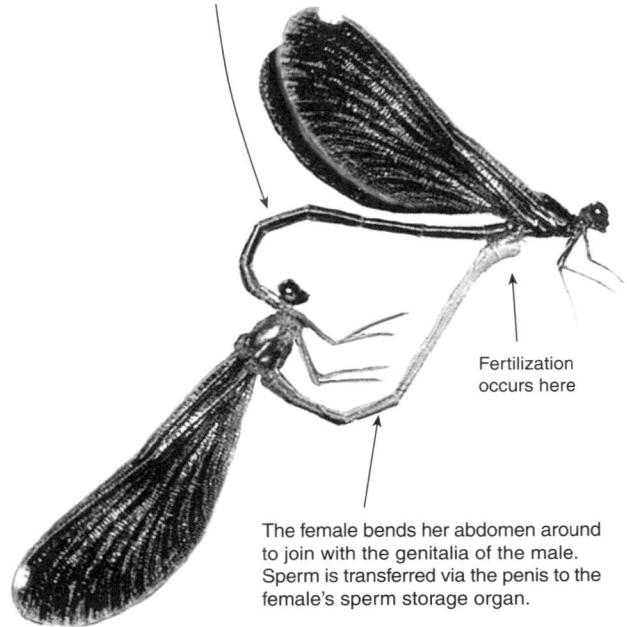

The male damselfly grips onto a twig with its front legs during mating while holding the female behind the head with clasping organs at the end of its abdomen.

Fertilization occurs here

The female bends her abdomen around to join with the genitalia of the male. Sperm is transferred via the penis to the female's sperm storage organ.

1. Define the following terms:

(a) **Oviparous**: _____

(b) **Viviparous**: _____

2. Some frogs and toads have evolved novel ways of enhancing the survival of their eggs.

(a) State the two main threats to the survival of frog/toad eggs: _____

(b) Describe how the **midwife toad** enhances the survival of its eggs: _____

(c) Describe how the **Surinam toad** enhances the survival of its eggs: _____

3. (a) Name two types of animal that produce **cleidoic eggs**: _____

(b) Describe the main feature of a cleidoic egg that has made it so successful: _____

(c) Explain how a cleidoic egg provides for the following needs of a developing embryo:

Elimination of wastes: _____

Gas exchange: _____

Nutrition (food supply): _____

RA 2 **Female Reproductive System**

The female reproductive system in mammals produces eggs, receives the penis and sperm during sexual intercourse, and houses and nourishes the young. Female reproductive systems in mammals are similar in their basic structure (uterus, ovaries etc.) but the shape of the uterus and the form of the placenta during pregnancy vary. The human system is described below.

Oogenesis

Oogenesis is the process by which mature ova (egg cells) are produced by the ovary. Oogonia are formed in the female embryo and undergo repeated mitotic divisions to form the primary oocyte. These remain in prophase of meiosis I throughout childhood. At this stage, all the eggs a female will ever have are present, but they remain in this resting phase until puberty. At puberty, meiosis resumes. Eggs are released, arrested in metaphase of meiosis II. This second division is only completed upon fertilization.

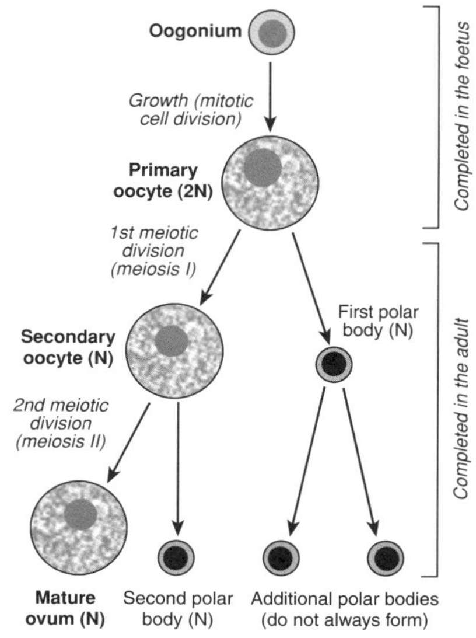

Oogonium

Growth (mitotic cell division)

Primary oocyte (2N)

Completed in the foetus

1st meiotic division (meiosis I)

Secondary oocyte (N)

First polar body (N)

Completed in the adult

2nd meiotic division (meiosis II)

Mature ovum (N) | Second polar body (N) | Additional polar bodies (do not always form)

The Female Reproductive System

(a)   (b)   (c)

Spine

Colon

Bladder

(d)

Pubis

(e)

Anus

Labia

(f)

Urethra

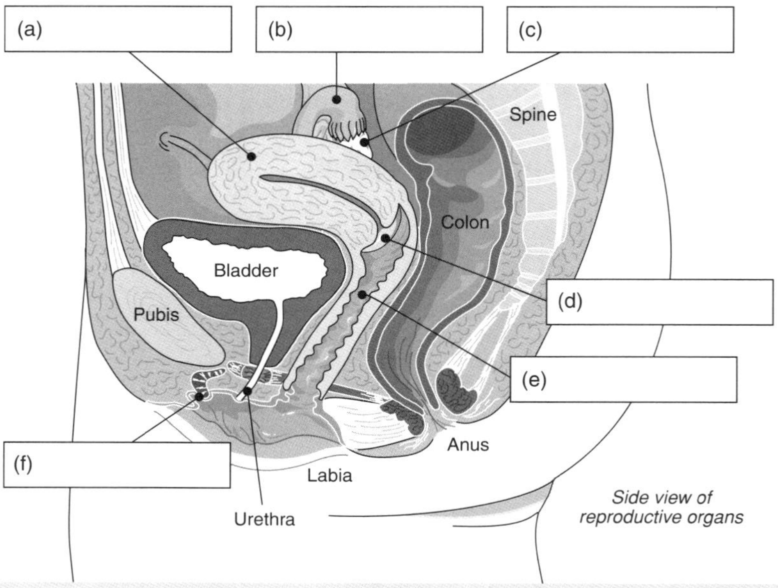

Side view of reproductive organs

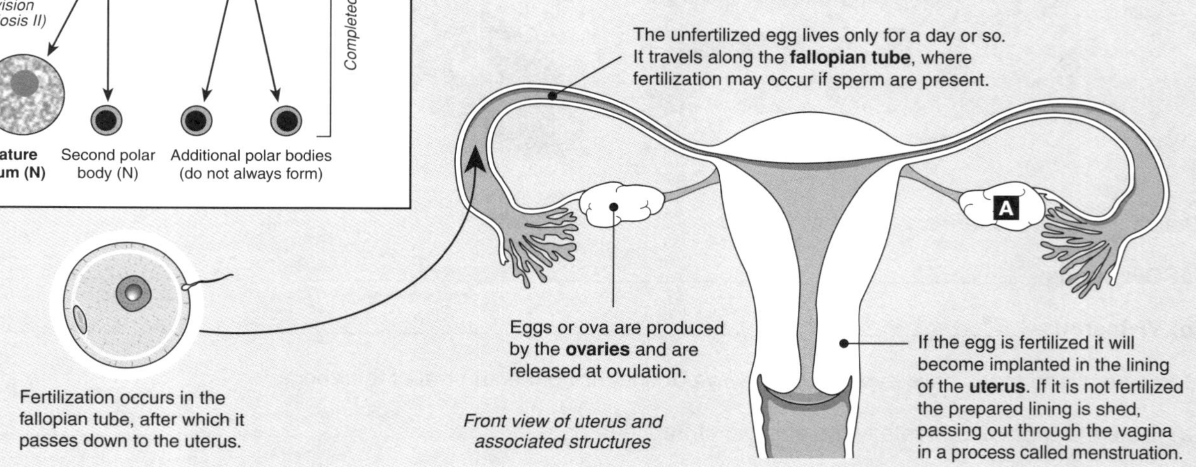

Ovulation and Implantation

The unfertilized egg lives only for a day or so. It travels along the **fallopian tube**, where fertilization may occur if sperm are present.

A

Eggs or ova are produced by the **ovaries** and are released at ovulation.

If the egg is fertilized it will become implanted in the lining of the **uterus**. If it is not fertilized the prepared lining is shed, passing out through the vagina in a process called menstruation.

Fertilization occurs in the fallopian tube, after which it passes down to the uterus.

Front view of uterus and associated structures

1. The female human reproductive system and associated structures are illustrated above. Using the word list, identify the labeled parts. **Word list**: *ovary, uterus (womb), vagina, fallopian tube (oviduct), cervix, clitoris.*

2. In a few words or a short sentence, state the function of each of the structures labeled (a) - (d) in the above diagram:

    (a) _____

    (b) _____

    (c) _____

    (d) _____

3. (a) Name the organ labeled (A) in the diagram: _____

    (b) Name the event associated with this organ that occurs every month: _____

    (c) Name the process by which mature ova are produced: _____

4. (a) Name the stage in meiosis at which the oocyte is released from the ovary: _____

    (b) State when in the reproductive process meiosis II is completed: _____

The Menstrual Cycle

In non-primate mammals the reproductive cycle is characterized by a **breeding season** and an **oestrous cycle** (a period of greater sexual receptivity during which ovulation occurs). In contrast, humans and other primates are sexually receptive throughout the year and may mate at any time. Like all placental mammals, their uterine lining thickens in preparation for pregnancy. However, unlike other mammals, primates shed this lining as a discharge through the vagina if fertilization does not occur. This event, called **menstruation**, characterizes the human reproductive or **menstrual cycle**. In human females, the menstrual cycle starts from the first day of bleeding and lasts for about 28 days. It involves a predictable series of changes that occur in response to hormones. The cycle is divided into three phases (see below), defined by the events in each phase.

The Menstrual Cycle

Luteinizing hormone (LH) and follicle stimulating hormone (FSH): These hormones from the anterior pituitary have numerous effects. FSH stimulates the development of the ovarian follicles resulting in the release of estrogen. Estrogen levels peak, stimulating a surge in LH and triggering ovulation.

Hormone levels: Of the follicles that begin developing in response to FSH, usually only one (the Graafian follicle) becomes dominant. In the first half of the cycle, estrogen is secreted by this developing Graafian follicle. Later, the Graafian follicle develops into the corpus luteum (below right) which secretes large amounts of progesterone (and smaller amounts of estrogen).

The corpus luteum: The Graafian follicle continues to grow and then (around day 14) ruptures to release the egg (ovulation). LH causes the ruptured follicle to develop into a corpus luteum (yellow body). The corpus luteum secretes progesterone which promotes full development of the uterine lining, maintains the embryo in the first 12 weeks of pregnancy, and inhibits the development of more follicles.

Menstruation: If fertilization does not occur, the corpus luteum breaks down. Progesterone secretion declines, causing the uterine lining to be shed (menstruation). If fertilization occurs, high progesterone levels maintain the thickened uterine lining. The placenta develops and nourishes the embryo completely by 12 weeks.

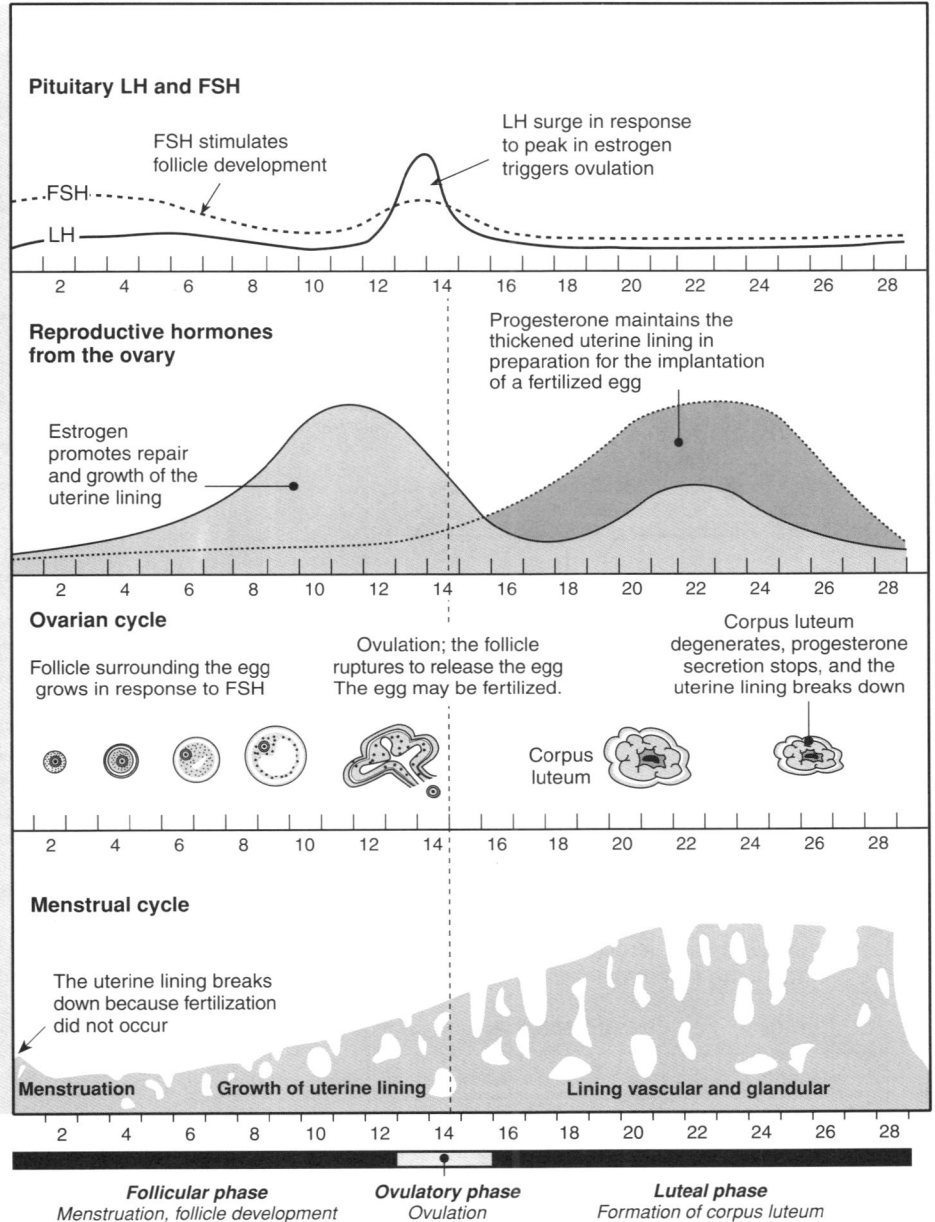

Pituitary LH and FSH

FSH stimulates follicle development

LH surge in response to peak in estrogen triggers ovulation

FSH
LH

Progesterone maintains the thickened uterine lining in preparation for the implantation of a fertilized egg

Reproductive hormones from the ovary

Estrogen promotes repair and growth of the uterine lining

Ovarian cycle

Follicle surrounding the egg grows in response to FSH

Ovulation; the follicle ruptures to release the egg. The egg may be fertilized.

Corpus luteum degenerates, progesterone secretion stops, and the uterine lining breaks down

Corpus luteum

Menstrual cycle

The uterine lining breaks down because fertilization did not occur

Menstruation   **Growth of uterine lining**   **Lining vascular and glandular**

Day of the cycle: 2   4   6   8   10   12   14   16   18   20   22   24   26   28

Follicular phase
Menstruation, follicle development

Ovulatory phase
Ovulation

Luteal phase
Formation of corpus luteum

1. Name the hormone responsible for:

    (a) Follicle growth: _____   (b) Ovulation: _____

2. Each month, several ovarian follicles begin development, but only one (the Graafian follicle) develops fully:

    (a) Name the hormone secreted by the developing follicle: _____

    (b) State the role of this hormone during the follicular phase: _____

    (c) Suggest what happens to the follicles that do not continue developing: _____

3. (a) Name the principal hormone secreted by the corpus luteum: _____

    (b) State the purpose of this hormone: _____

4. State the hormonal trigger for menstruation: _____

Control of the Menstrual Cycle

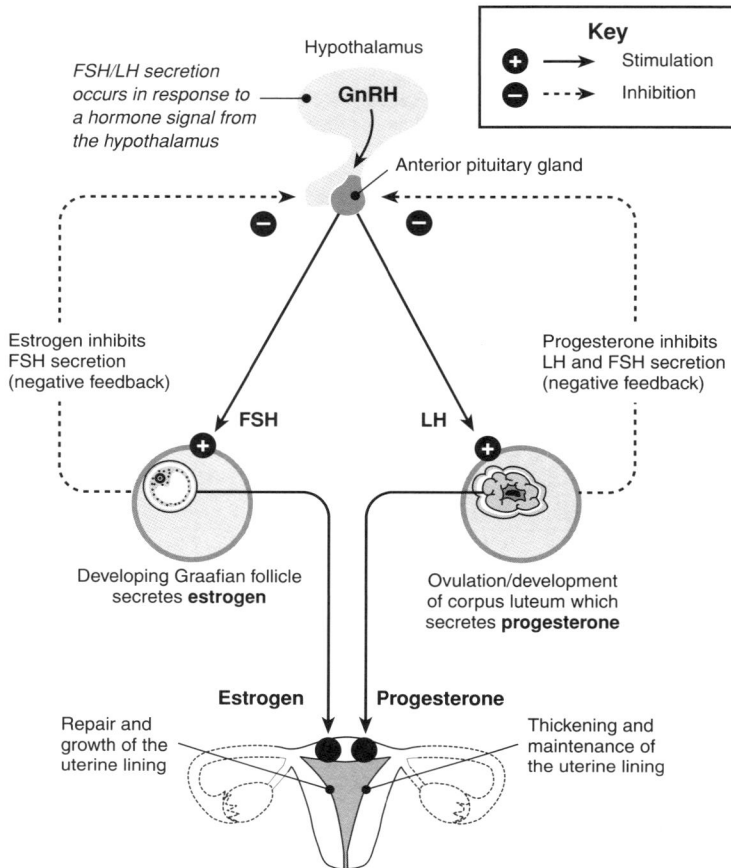

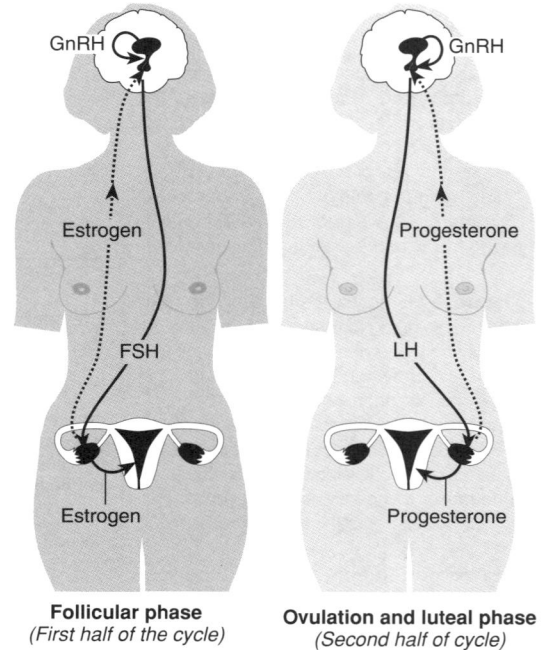

The female menstrual cycle is regulated by the interplay of several reproductive hormones. The main control centers for this regulation are the **hypothalamus** and the **anterior pituitary gland**. The hypothalamus secretes GnRH (gonadotrophin releasing hormone), a hormone that is essential for normal gonad function in males and females. GnRH is transported in blood vessels to the anterior pituitary where it brings about the release of two hormones: follicle stimulating hormone (FSH) and luteinizing hormone (LH). It is these two hormones that induce the cyclical changes in the ovary and uterus. Regulation of blood hormone levels during the menstrual cycle is achieved through **negative feedback** mechanisms. The exception to this is the mid cycle surge in LH (see previous page) which is induced by the rapid increase in estrogen secreted by the developing follicle.

Control of the Menstrual Cycle

Follicular phase
(First half of the cycle)

Ovulation and luteal phase
(Second half of cycle)

The diagrams above and left summarize the main hormonal controls during the two halves of the menstrual cycle. In the first half of the cycle, FSH stimulates follicle development in the ovary. The developing follicle secretes estrogen which acts on the uterus and, in the anterior pituitary, inhibits FSH secretion. In the second half of the cycle, LH induces ovulation and development of the corpus luteum. The corpus luteum secretes progesterone which acts on the uterus and also inhibits further secretion of LH (and also FSH).

1. Using the information above and on the previous page, complete the table below summarizing the role of hormones in the control of the menstrual cycle. To help you, some of the table has been completed:

Hormone	Site of secretion	Main effects and site of action during the menstrual cycle
GnRH		
		Stimulates the growth of ovarian follicles
LH		
		At high level, stimulates LH surge. Promotes growth and repair of the uterine lining.
Progesterone		

2. Briefly explain the role of negative feedback in the control of hormone levels in the menstrual cycle:

_____

_____

3. **FSH** and **LH** (called ICSH or interstitial cell stimulating hormone in males) also play a central role in male reproduction. Refer to the activity "Male Reproductive System" and state how these two hormones are involved **in male reproduction**:

_____

Contraception

Humans have many ways in which to manage their own reproduction. They may choose to prevent or assist fertilization of an egg by a sperm (conception). **Contraception** refers to the use of methods or devices that prevent conception. There are many contraceptive methods available including physical barriers (such as condoms) that prevent egg and sperm ever meeting. The most effective methods (excluding sterilization) involve chemical interference in the normal female cycle so that egg production is inhibited. This is done by way of **oral contraceptives** (below, left) or hormone implants. If taken properly, oral contraceptives are almost 100% effective at preventing pregnancy. The placement of their action in the normal cycle of reproduction (from gametogenesis to pregnancy) is illustrated in the flow diagram below. Other contraceptive methods are included for comparison.

Hormonal Contraception

The most common method by which to prevent conception using hormones is by using an oral contraceptive pill (OCP). These may be **combined OCPs**, or low dose mini pills.

Combined oral contraceptive pills (OCPs)

These pills exploit the feedback controls over hormone secretion normally operating during a menstrual cycle. They contain combinations of synthetic **estrogens** and **progesterone**. They are taken daily for 21 days, and raise the levels of these hormones in the blood so that FSH secretion is inhibited and no ova develop. Sugar pills are taken for 7 days; long enough to allow menstruation to occur but not long enough for ova to develop. Combined OCPs can be of two types:

Monophasic pills (left): Hormones (H) are all at one dosage level. Sugar pills (S) are usually larger and differently colored.

Triphasic pills (right): The hormone dosage increases in stages (1,2,3), mimicking the natural changes in a menstrual cycle.

Mini-pill (progesterone only)

The mini-pill contains 28 days of low dose progesterone; generally too low to prevent ovulation. The pill works by thickening the cervical mucus and preventing endometrial thickening.

The mini-pill is less reliable than combined pills and must be taken at a regular time each day. However, it is safer for older women and those who are breastfeeding.

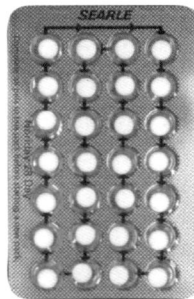

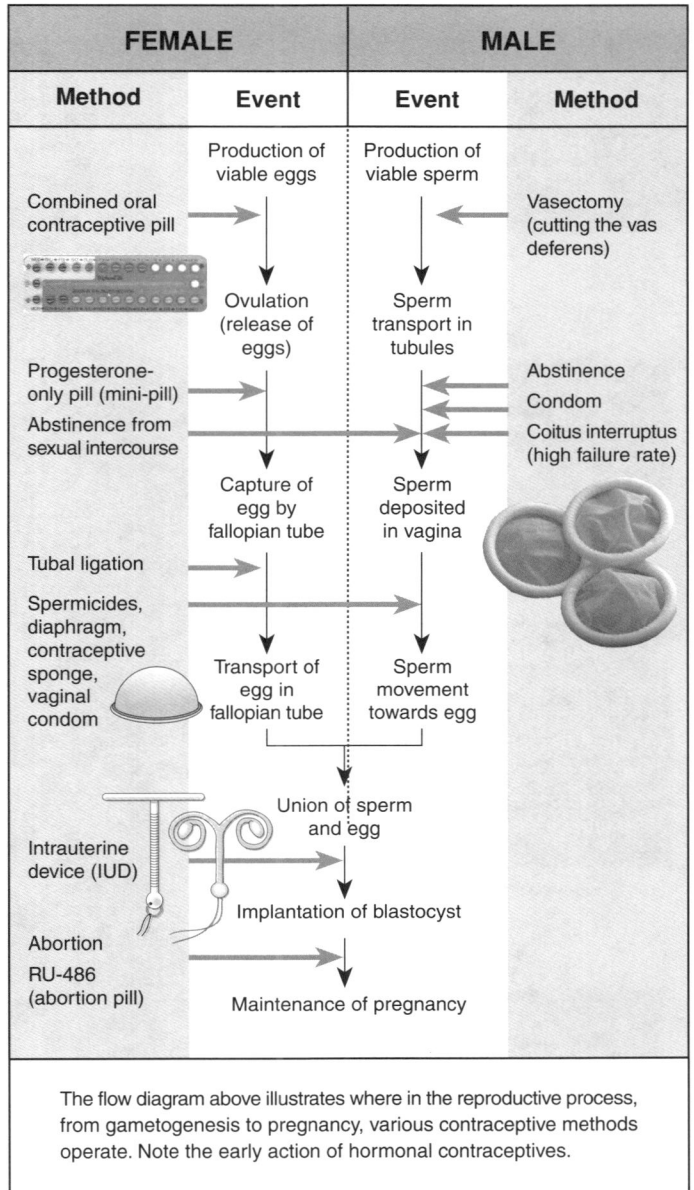

The flow diagram above illustrates where in the reproductive process, from gametogenesis to pregnancy, various contraceptive methods operate. Note the early action of hormonal contraceptives.

1. Explain briefly how the **combined oral contraceptive pill** acts as a contraceptive: _____

2. Contrast the mode of action of OCPs with that of the mini-pill, giving reasons for the differences:

3. Suggest why oral contraceptives offer such effective control over conception: _____

Treating Female Infertility

Failure to ovulate is one of the most common causes of female infertility. In most cases, the cause is hormonal, although sometimes the ovaries may be damaged or not functioning normally. Female infertility may also arise through damage to the fallopian tubes as a result of infection or scarring. These cases are usually treated with hormones, followed by IVF (see below and opposite). Most treatments for female infertility involve the use of synthetic female hormones, which stimulate ovulation, boost egg production, and induce egg release.

Treating Female Infertility

Cause of the infertility
Failure to ovulate because of low levels of GnRH, FSH, LH, or ovarian hormones.

Hormonal treatment successful?
Treatment may enable conception in the usual way.

Fallopian tubes blocked?
Eggs may be collected from the follicles using laparoscopy and fertilized *ex-vivo* in a glass dish (in-vitro fertilization or IVF).

Successful fertilization

At an early stage of cell division, the pre-embryo is transferred to the uterus. A pregnancy results if implantation is successful.

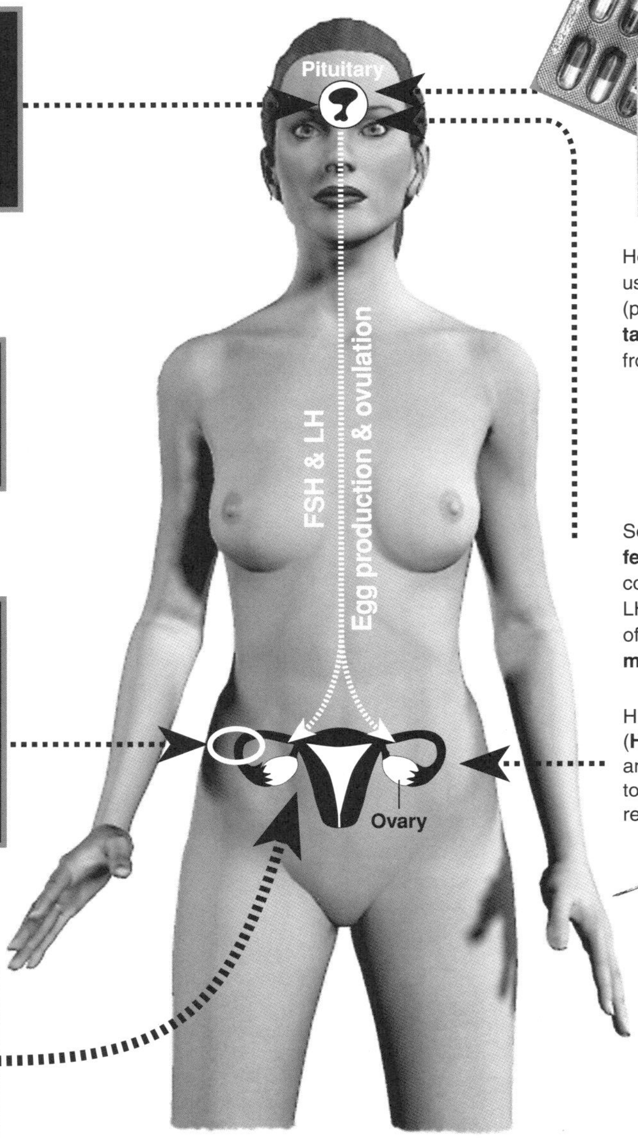

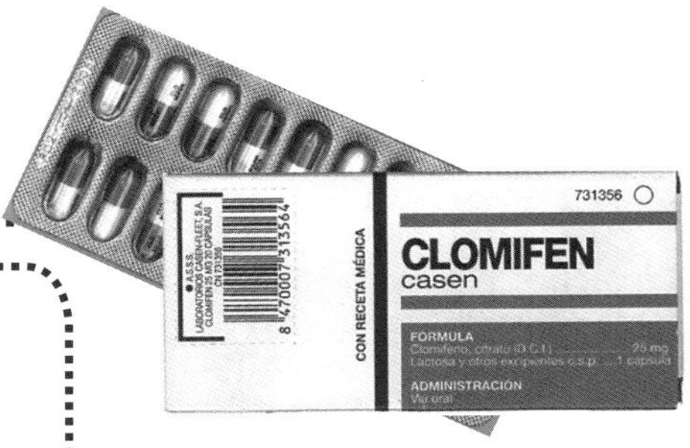

Hormone imbalance can be corrected using estrogen-like drugs, e.g. **clomiphene** (pictured here under a trade name) and **tamoxifen**, which induce release of FSH from the pituitary.

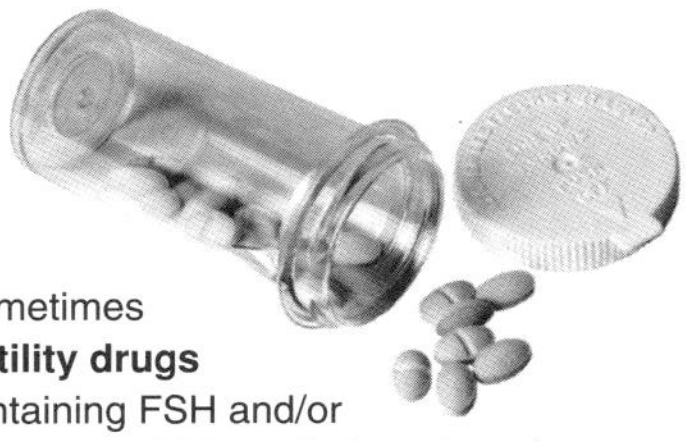

Sometimes **fertility drugs** containing FSH and/or LH are used. These induce the release of many ova, increasing the risk of a **multiple pregnancy.**

Human chorionic gonadotrophin (**HCG**) can replace LH and may be injected to induce egg release.

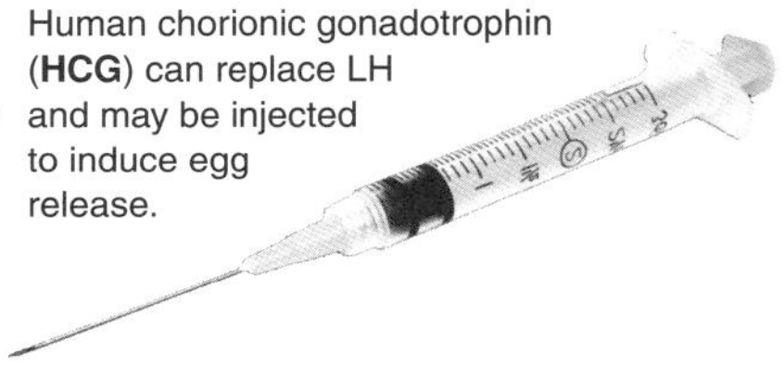

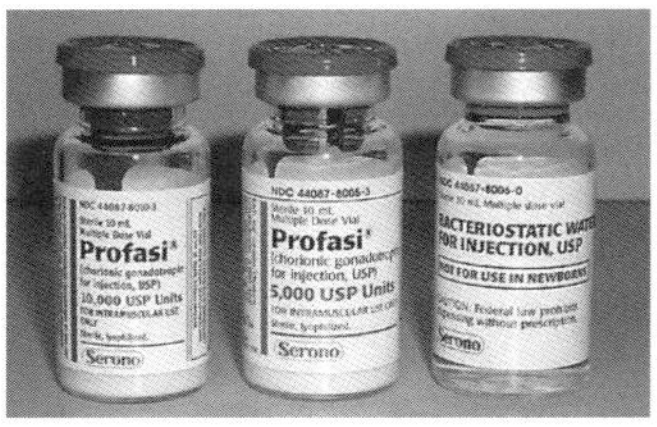

HCG is a hormone involved in the maintenance of early pregnancy.

1. Explain two ways in which the hormonal drugs used to enhance fertility operate:

    (a) _____

    _____

    (b) _____

    _____

2. Identify two examples of female infertility where treatment using IVF would be appropriate:

    (a) _____

    (b) _____

3. Identify one risk associated with the use of fertility drugs: _____

Human Reproductive Technology

Infertility may result from a disturbance of any of the factors involved in fertilization or embryonic development. Female infertility may be due to a failure to ovulate, requiring stimulation of the ovary, with or without hormone therapy. For couples with one or both partners incapable of providing suitable gametes, it may be possible for them to receive eggs and/or sperm from donors. **Artificial insemination** (AI) may be used to introduce selected sperm from the male partner or from a donor. **In vitro fertilization** (IVF) may be used for patients with irreparable damage to the fallopian tubes. The **gamete intrafallopian**

transfer (GIFT) technique is now widely accepted as a form of treatment for patients with one or more functioning fallopian tubes. **Surrogate mothers** may be used to 'incubate' the fetus in cases where the woman is incapable of sustaining a pregnancy. **Fertility drugs** may be used to treat ovulation failure, as well as to induce the production of many eggs for use in IVF or GIFT. Such drugs stimulate the pituitary gland and may induce the simultaneous release of numerous eggs; an event called *superovulation*. If each egg is allowed to be fertilized, the resulting embryos may then be frozen after 24-72 hours culture.

Causes of Infertility

Infertility is a common problem (as many as 1 in 6 couples require help from a specialist). The cause of the infertility may be inherited, due to damage caused by an infectious disease, or psychological.

Causes of male infertility:
- *Penis:* Fails to achieve or maintain erection; abnormal ejaculation.
- *Testes:* Too few sperm produced or sperm are abnormally shaped, have impaired motility, or too short lived.
- *Vas deferens:* Blockage or structural abnormality may impede passage of sperm.

Causes of female infertility:
- *Fallopian tubes:* Blockage may prevent sperm from reaching egg – one or both tubes may be damaged (disease) or absent (congenital).
- *Ovaries:* Eggs may fail to mature or may not be released.
- *Uterus:* Abnormality or disorder may prevent implantation of the egg.
- *Cervix:* Antibodies in cervical mucus may damage or destroy the sperm.

In Vitro Fertilization (IVF)

The woman is given hormone therapy (fertility drugs) causing a number of eggs to mature at the same time (superovulation).

Several eggs are removed from the ovary through a laparoscope.

Sperm

The eggs are mixed with sperm from her partner (or donor) and incubated in a culture medium until blastocysts are formed.

The blastocyst(s) is then implanted in the mother's uterus and the pregnancy is allowed to continue normally.

Gamete Intrafallopian Transfer (GIFT)

A procedure for assisting conception, suitable only for women with healthy fallopian tubes.

Using a needle for aspiration, under laparoscopic or ultrasound guidance, the eggs are removed from the ovary.

Sperm

After being mixed with the partner's sperm, the eggs are introduced into the fallopian tube, where fertilization takes place.

A fertilized egg can subsequently become implanted in the uterus.

Biological Origins of Gamete Donations

Both partners provide gametes for IVF or GIFT (they donate their own gametes).

Donor X

Male partner unable to provide sperm; sperm from male donor.

X Donor

Female partner unable to provide eggs; egg from female donor.

Donor X X Donor

Both partners unable to provide gametes; sperm and egg obtained from donors.

1. List three causes of infertility for men: _____

2. List three causes of infertility for women: _____

3. List the key stages of **IVF**: _____

_____

_____

4. List the key stages of **GIFT**: _____

_____

Male Reproductive System

RA 3

The reproductive role of the male is to produce the sperm and deliver them to the female. When a sperm combines with an egg, it contributes half the genetic material of the offspring and, in humans and other mammals, determines its sex. The reproductive structures in human males (shown below) are in many ways typical of other mammals.

(a)

(b)

(c)

(d)

Epididymis: Coiled tube where sperm mature

(e)

(f)

(g)

Vas deferens: Carries sperm to the urethra

Epididymis: Coiled tube where sperm develop motility

Seminiferous tubules: Bundles of coiled tubes (total length 500 m) leading to the epididymis.

Cutaway of a single testis

Cross Section Through Seminiferous Tubule

The photograph (below, left) shows maturing sperm (arrowed) with tails projecting into the tubule. Their heads are embedded in the Sertoli cells in the tubule wall and they are ready to break free and move to the epididymis where they complete their maturation. The same cross-section is illustrated diagrammatically (below, right).

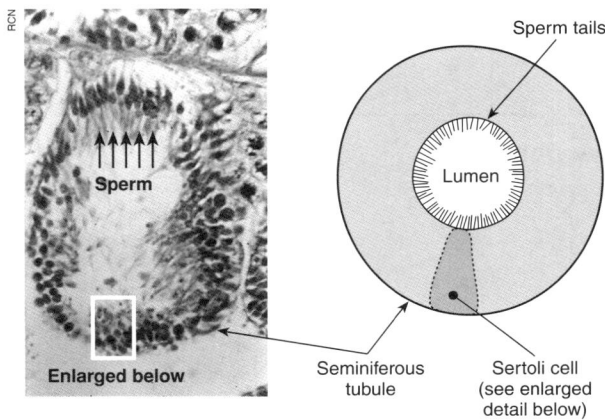

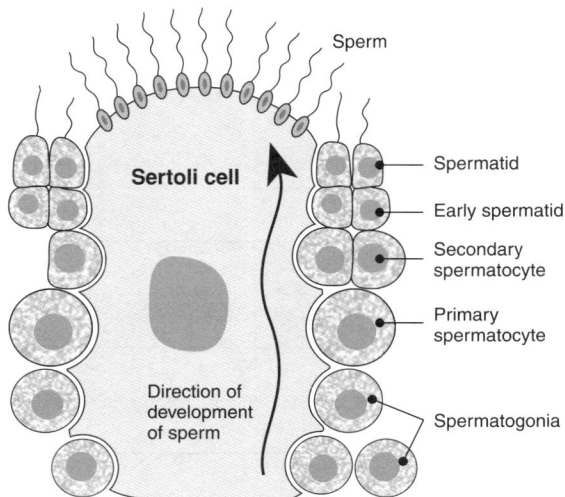

RCN

Sperm

Enlarged below

Sperm tails

Lumen

Seminiferous tubule

Sertoli cell (see enlarged detail below)

Sertoli cell

Sperm

Spermatid

Early spermatid

Secondary spermatocyte

Primary spermatocyte

Spermatogonia

Direction of development of sperm

Spermatogenesis

Spermatogenesis is the process by which mature spermatozoa (sperm) are produced in the testis. In humans, they are produced at the rate of about 120 million per day. Spermatogenesis is regulated by the hormones **FSH** (from the anterior pituitary) and testosterone (secreted from the testes in response to **ICSH** (LH) from the anterior pituitary). Spermatogonia, in the outer layer of the seminiferous tubules, multiply throughout reproductive life. Some of them divide by meiosis into spermatocytes, which produce spermatids. These are transformed into mature sperm by the process of spermiogenesis in the seminiferous tubules of the testis. Full sperm motility is achieved in the epididymis.

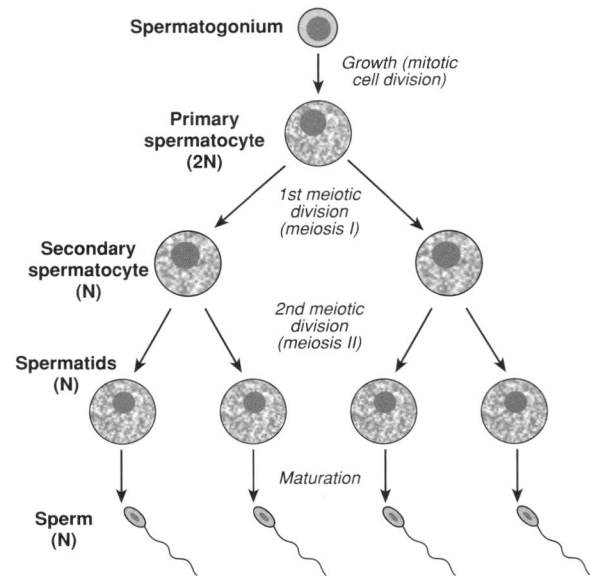

Spermatogonium

Growth (mitotic cell division)

Primary spermatocyte (2N)

1st meiotic division (meiosis I)

Secondary spermatocyte (N)

2nd meiotic division (meiosis II)

Spermatids (N)

Maturation

Sperm (N)

Sperm Structure

Mature spermatozoa (sperm) are produced by a process called spermatogenesis in the testes (see description of the process on the previous page). Meiotic division of spermatocytes produces spermatids which then differentiate into mature sperm. Sperm are quite simple in structure – their purpose is to swim to the egg and donate their genetic material. They are composed of three regions: headpiece, midpiece, and tail. Sperm do not live long (only about 48 hours), but they swim quickly and there are so many of them (millions per ejaculation) that some are able to reach the egg to fertilize it.

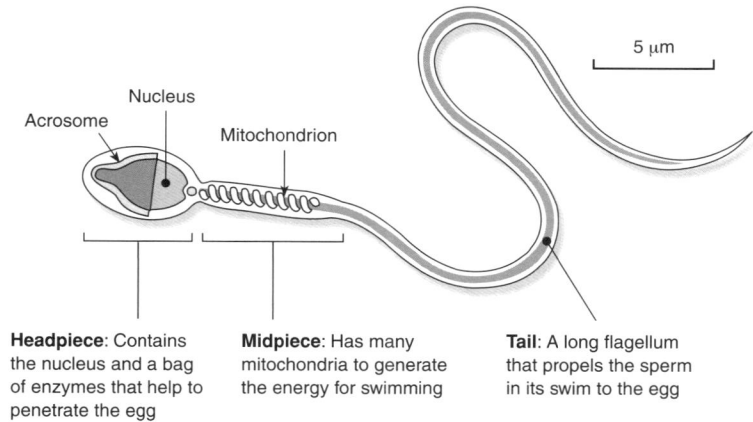

Acrosome Nucleus Mitochondrion 5 μm

Headpiece: Contains the nucleus and a bag of enzymes that help to penetrate the egg

Midpiece: Has many mitochondria to generate the energy for swimming

Tail: A long flagellum that propels the sperm in its swim to the egg

1. The male human reproductive system and associated structures are shown on the previous page. Using the following word list identify the labeled parts (write your answers in the spaces provided on the diagram).
   Word list: *bladder, scrotal sac, sperm duct (vas deferens), seminal vesicle, testis, urethra, prostate gland*

2. In a short sentence, state the function of each of the structures labeled (a) - (g) in the diagram on the previous page:

   (a) _____

   (b) _____

   (c) _____

   (d) _____

   (e) _____

   (f) _____

   (g) _____

3. (a) Name the process by which mature sperm are formed: _____

   (b) Name the hormones regulating this process: _____

   (c) State where most of this process occurs: _____

   (d) State where the process is completed: _____

4. In older men, the prostate gland sometimes enlarges. This causes a partial or nearly complete constriction of the urethra. Describe the symptoms of this disorder:

   _____

   _____

5. The secretions of the prostate gland (which make up a large proportion of the seminal fluid produced in an ejaculation) are of alkaline pH, while the secretions of the vagina are normally slightly acidic. With this information, explain the role the prostate gland secretions have in maintaining the viability of sperm deposited in the vagina.

   _____

   _____

6. Each ejaculation of a healthy, fertile male contains 100-400 million sperm. State why so many sperm are needed:

   _____

7. Recently, concern has been expressed about the level of synthetic estrogen-like chemicals in the environment. Explain the reason for this concern with regards to male fertility:

   _____

   _____

   _____

Fertilization and Early Growth

When an egg cell is released from the ovary it is arrested in metaphase of meiosis II and is termed a secondary oocyte. **Fertilization** occurs when a sperm penetrates an egg cell at this stage and the sperm and egg nuclei unite to form the zygote.

Fertilization is always regarded as time 0 in a period of gestation (pregnancy) and has five distinct stages (below). After fertilization, the zygote begins its **development** i.e. its growth and differentiation into a multicellular organism (opposite).

Fertilization (Time 0)

The stages in fertilization are represented below in a numbered sequence (1-5)

1. Capacitation

The surface of the sperm cell undergoes changes that are essential to enabling the acrosome reaction and sperm entry.

2. The Acrosome Reaction

Enzymes from the acrosome (an enzyme-filled bag at the tip of the sperm) are released and digest a pathway through the follicle cells (not shown) and the jelly-like zona pellucida surrounding the egg cell (secondary oocyte).

3. Fusion of Sperm Head

The plasma membranes of the sperm and egg fuse, and the nucleus of the sperm enters the egg cytoplasm. Fusion causes a sudden membrane depolarization that acts as a "fast block" to further sperm entry. The fusion of the two plasma membranes also triggers the completion of meiosis II in the egg cell and induces the cortical reaction (below).

4. The Cortical Reaction

The fusion of the two plasma membranes induces a permanent change in the egg surface that prevents further sperm entry. Cortical granules in the egg cytoplasm release their contents into the space between the plasma membrane and the vitelline layer. Substances released from the granules raise and harden the vitelline layer to form a slow (permanent) block to further sperm entry.

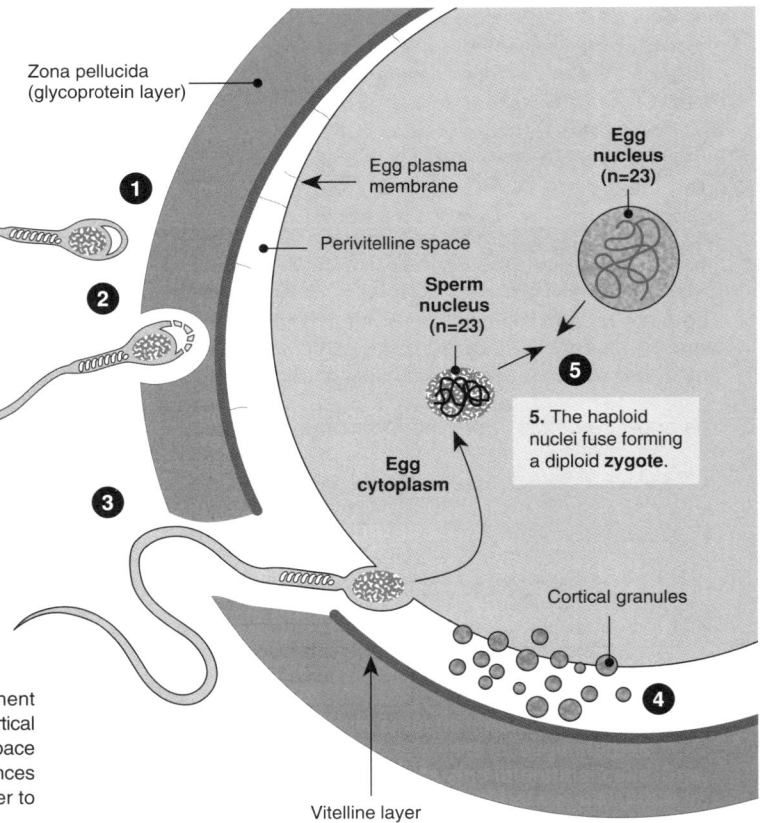

Zona pellucida (glycoprotein layer)

Egg plasma membrane

Perivitelline space

Egg nucleus (n=23)

Sperm nucleus (n=23)

5. The haploid nuclei fuse forming a diploid **zygote**.

Egg cytoplasm

Cortical granules

Vitelline layer

1. Briefly describe the significant events (and their importance) occurring at each of the following stages of fertilization:

   (a) Capacitation: _____

   _____

   (b) The acrosome reaction: _____

   _____

   (c) Fusion of egg and sperm plasma membranes: _____

   _____

   (d) The cortical reaction: _____

   _____

   (e) Fusion of egg and sperm nuclei: _____

   _____

2. Explain the significance of the blocks that prevent entry of more than one sperm into the egg (polyspermy):

   _____

   _____

3. (a) Explain why the egg cell, when released from the ovary, is termed a secondary oocyte:_____

   _____

   (b) State at which stage, its meiotic division is completed: _____

The first division of the zygote produces 2 cells

Zona pellucida

Morula

After 3 days

The **blastocyst**, a hollow ball of cells, embeds into the uterine wall using enzymes to digest and penetrate the lining.

The uterine lining provides nourishment for the embryo until the placenta develops.

The placenta develops from the fetal membranes and the maternal uterine lining.

The yolk sac is small in humans, although it provides the nourishment in some animals.

Umbilical cord

The fluid-filled amniotic sac encloses the embryo in the amniotic fluid.

5 week old embryo

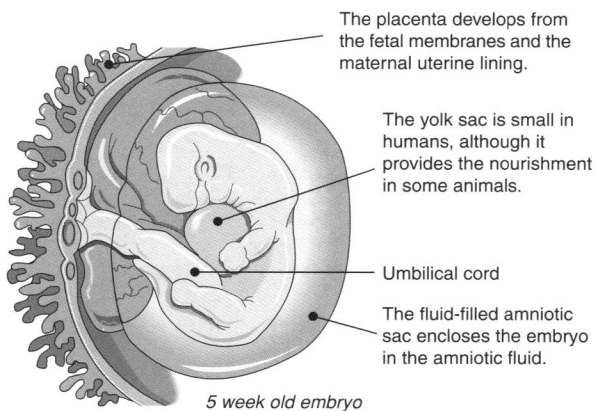

Early Growth and Development

Cleavage and Development of the Morula

Immediately after fertilization, rapid cell division takes place. These early cell divisions are called **cleavage** and they increase the number of cells, but not the size of the zygote. The first cleavage is completed after 36 hours, and each succeeding division takes less time. After 3 days, successive cleavages have produced a solid mass of cells called the **morula**, (left) which is still about the same size as the original zygote.

Implantation of the Blastocyst (after 6-8 days)

After several days in the uterus, the morula develops into the blastocyst. It makes contact with the uterine lining and pushes deeply into it, ensuring a close maternal-fetal contact. Blood vessels provide early nourishment as they are opened up by enzymes secreted by the blastocyst. The embryo produces **HCG** (human chorionic gonadotropin), which prevents degeneration of the corpus luteum and signals that the woman is pregnant.

Embryo at 5-8 Weeks

Five weeks after fertilization, the embryo is only 4-5 mm long, but already the central nervous system has developed and the heart is beating. The embryonic membranes have formed; the amnion encloses the embryo in a fluid-filled space, and the allanto-chorion forms the fetal portion of the placenta. From two months the embryo is called a fetus. It is still small (30-40 mm long), but the limbs are well formed and the bones are beginning to harden. The face has a flat, rather featureless appearance with the eyes far apart. Fetal movements have begun and brain development proceeds rapidly. The placenta is well developed, although not fully functional until 12 weeks. The umbilical cord, containing the fetal umbilical arteries and vein, connects fetus and mother.

4. State what contribution the sperm and egg cell make to each of the following:

   (a) The nucleus of the zygote: Sperm contribution: _____   Egg contribution: _____

   (b) The cytoplasm of the zygote: Sperm contribution: _____   Egg contribution: _____

5. Explain what is meant by cleavage and comment on its significance to the early development of the embryo:

   _____

   _____

6. Examine the diagram above showing early stages of embryonic development and answer the following:

   (a) Explain the importance of implantation to the early nourishment of the embryo: _____

   _____

   (b) Name the fetal tissues that contribute to the formation of the placenta: _____

   _____

   (c) Suggest a purpose of the amniotic sac and comment on its importance to the developing embryo:

   _____

   _____

   (d) Suggest why the heart is one of the very first structures to develop in the embryo: _____

   _____

The Placenta

RA 2

As soon as an embryo embeds in the uterine wall it begins to obtain nutrients from its mother and increase in size. At two months, when the major structures of the adult are established, it is called a fetus. It is entirely dependent on its mother for nutrients, oxygen, and elimination of wastes. The placenta is the specialized organ that performs this role, enabling exchange between fetal and maternal tissues, and allowing a prolonged period of fetal growth and development within the protection of the uterus. The placenta also has an endocrine role, producing hormones that enable the pregnancy to be maintained.

Section enlarged right

Cervix

Umbilical cord

Above: Fetus (near full term), showing placental attachment and position in the uterus.

Below: Photograph shows a 14 week old fetus. Limbs are fully formed, many bones are beginning to ossify, and joints begin to form. Facial features are becoming more fully formed.

Umbilical cord

10 mm

Schematic diagram showing part of the placenta in section

Sinus filled with maternal blood

Chorionic villus with fetal arterioles and venules

Chorionic tissue (fetal)

Umbilical vein

Umbilical cord

Umbilical arteries

Boundary between fetal and maternal tissues

Maternal endometrium

Maternal venule

Maternal arteriole

→ Blood flow

┈┈▶ Exchange of wastes and nutrients via diffusion

The placenta is a disc-like organ, about the size of a dinner plate and weighing about 1 kg. It develops when fingerlike projections of the fetal chorion (the chorionic villi) grow into the endometrium of the uterus. The villi contain the numerous capillaries connecting the fetal arteries and vein. They continue invading the maternal tissue until they are bathed in the maternal blood sinuses. The maternal and fetal blood vessels are in such close proximity that oxygen and nutrients can diffuse from the maternal blood into the capillaries of the villi. From the villi, the nutrients circulate in the umbilical vein, returning to the fetal heart. Carbon dioxide and other wastes leave the fetus through the umbilical arteries, pass into the capillaries of the villi, and diffuse into the maternal blood. Note that fetal blood and maternal blood do not mix: the exchanges occur via diffusion through thin walled capillaries.

1. In simple terms, explain the basic structure of the human placenta: _____

_____

_____

_____

2. The umbilical cord contains the fetal arteries and vein. Describe the status of the blood in each type of fetal vessel:

   (a) Fetal arteries: Oxygenated and containing nutrients / Deoxygenated and containing nitrogenous wastes (delete one)

   (b) Fetal vein: Oxygenated and containing nutrients / Deoxygenated and containing nitrogenous wastes (delete one)

3. Teratogens are substances that may cause malformations in embryonic development (e.g nicotine, alcohol):

   (a) Give a general explanation why substances ingested by the mother have the potential to be harmful to the fetus:

   _____

   (b) Explain why cigarette smoking is so harmful to fetal development: _____

   _____

The Hormones of Pregnancy

A 2

Human reproductive physiology occurs in a cycle (the menstrual cycle) which follows a set pattern and is regulated by the interplay of several hormones. Control of hormone release is brought about through feedback mechanisms: the levels of the female reproductive hormones, estrogen and progesterone, regulate the secretion of the pituitary hormones that control the ovarian cycle (see earlier pages). Pregnancy interrupts this cycle and maintains the corpus luteum and the placenta as endocrine organs with the specific role of maintaining the developing fetus for the period of its development. During the last month of pregnancy the peptide hormone oxytocin induces the uterine contraction that will expel the baby from the uterus.

Hormonal Changes During Pregnancy, Birth, and Lactation

During the first 12-16 weeks pregnancy, the corpus luteum secretes enough progesterone to maintain the uterine lining and sustain the developing embryo. After this, the placenta takes over as the primary endocrine organ of pregnancy. **Progesterone** and **estrogen** from the placenta maintain the uterine lining, inhibit the development of further ova (eggs), and prepare the breast tissue for **lactation** (milk production). At the end of pregnancy, the placenta loses competency, progesterone levels fall, and high estrogen levels trigger the onset of labor. After birth, the secretion of prolactin increases. Prolactin maintains lactation during the period of infant nursing.

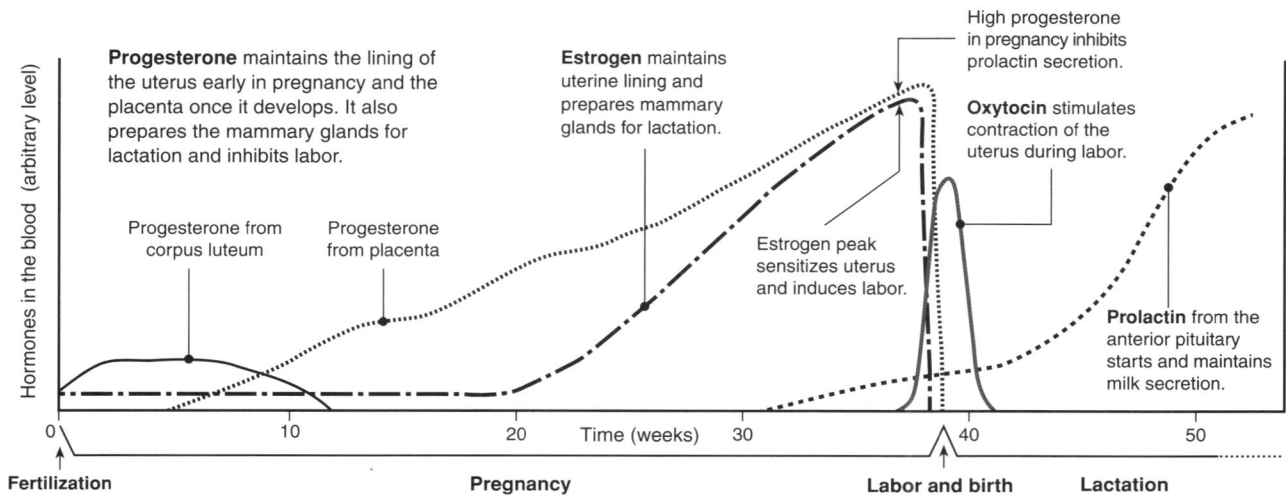

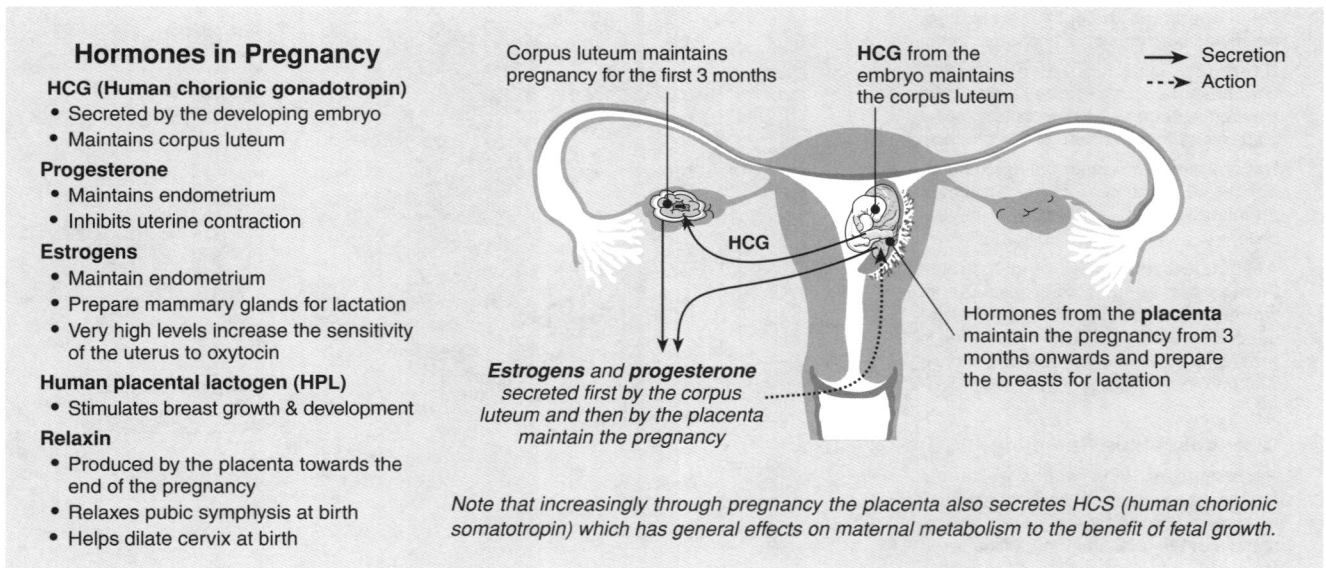

Graph labels: Hormones in the blood (arbitrary level) vs Time (weeks).

Progesterone maintains the lining of the uterus early in pregnancy and the placenta once it develops. It also prepares the mammary glands for lactation and inhibits labor.

Progesterone from corpus luteum

Progesterone from placenta

Estrogen maintains uterine lining and prepares mammary glands for lactation.

High progesterone in pregnancy inhibits prolactin secretion.

Oxytocin stimulates contraction of the uterus during labor.

Estrogen peak sensitizes uterus and induces labor.

Prolactin from the anterior pituitary starts and maintains milk secretion.

Fertilization   Pregnancy   Labor and birth   Lactation

Hormones in Pregnancy

HCG (Human chorionic gonadotropin)
- Secreted by the developing embryo
- Maintains corpus luteum

Progesterone
- Maintains endometrium
- Inhibits uterine contraction

Estrogens
- Maintain endometrium
- Prepare mammary glands for lactation
- Very high levels increase the sensitivity of the uterus to oxytocin

Human placental lactogen (HPL)
- Stimulates breast growth & development

Relaxin
- Produced by the placenta towards the end of the pregnancy
- Relaxes pubic symphysis at birth
- Helps dilate cervix at birth

Corpus luteum maintains pregnancy for the first 3 months

HCG from the embryo maintains the corpus luteum

→ Secretion
--→ Action

HCG

Hormones from the **placenta** maintain the pregnancy from 3 months onwards and prepare the breasts for lactation

Estrogens and *progesterone* secreted first by the corpus luteum and then by the placenta maintain the pregnancy

Note that increasingly through pregnancy the placenta also secretes HCS (human chorionic somatotropin) which has general effects on maternal metabolism to the benefit of fetal growth.

1. (a) Explain why the corpus luteum is the main source of progesterone in early pregnancy:

   _____

   (b) Name the hormones responsible for maintaining pregnancy: _____

2. (a) Name two hormones involved in labor (onset of the birth process): _____

   (b) Explain two physiological factors in initiating labor: _____

   _____

3. Explain why prolactin secretion increases markedly after birth: _____

   _____

Prenatal Diagnosis of Disease

Technological advances in recent decades have enabled greater control over conception, gestation, and birth. There are now a number of commonly used prenatal (before birth) diagnostic tests that can be used to investigate fetal health and development, and test for genetic abnormalities. Prenatal diagnoses vary a lot in terms of how invasive they are to the pregnancy and how much information they provide. Tests of the α-fetoprotein levels in the mother's blood serum can indicate **Down syndrome** (low α-fetoprotein) or **neural tube defects** (high α-fetoprotein) without risk to the fetus. Other prenatal procedures (e.g. **ultrasound**) carry a low risk and have become almost routine in some societies. **Amniocentesis** and **chorionic villus sampling** present a greater risk to both the mother and fetus and are usually reserved for the detection of chromosomal abnormalities in high risk pregnancies. All prenatal diagnostic procedures should involve supportive and accurate counseling regarding the benefits and risks of the procedure, and the choices available should the pregnancy prove to be abnormal.

Candidates for Diagnosis

Before costly and potentially high-risk prenatal tests involving chromosome analysis are carried out, there must be some clinical indication of a potential problem with either of the parents or with the pregnancy. Some **clinical indications** for chromosomal analysis are:

- Family history of inherited genetic disorders or malformities.

- History of infertility, miscarriage, stillbirth, or early neonatal death.

- First pregnancy at an older age or maternal age over 38.

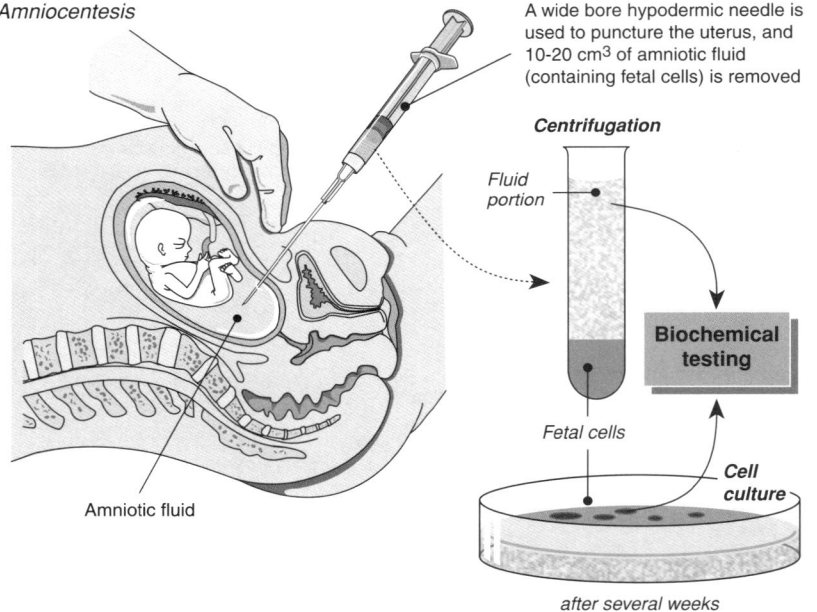

Genetic counseling

Chromosome (karyotype) analysis

Simple prenatal diagnoses (e.g. ultrasound, pictured opposite) are routinely performed in order to reassure parents that a pregnancy is normal, to check fetal growth, or to determine gender. More complex and higher risk prenatal tests involving chromosomal analysis (below and photo, above right) are not routinely performed. **Genetic counseling** (photo above, left) involves advising a patient of their risks and options and is usual practice where such tests are indicated. See the table left listing the clinical indications for chromosome analysis.

Amniocentesis

Performed at: 14-16 weeks into the pregnancy. The amniotic fluid (which naturally contains some fetal cells) is centrifuged, and the cells are cultured, examined biochemically, and karyotyped.

Used for: Detection of nearly 300 chromosomal disorders, such as Down syndrome, neural tube defects (e.g. spina bifida), and inborn errors of metabolism.

Recommended: A maternal age nearing or over 40, when parents are carriers of an inherited disorder or already have a child with a chromosomal disorder.

Associated risks: Risk of miscarriage through damage to fetus or placenta. In women younger than 35, the risk of miscarriage through the procedure is greater than the risk of carrying a child with chromosomal abnormalities.

Chorionic Villus Sampling (CVS)

Performed at: 8-10 weeks gestation. Using ultrasound guidance, a narrow tube is inserted through the cervix and a sample of the fetal chorionic villi is taken from the placenta. Compared with amniocentesis, more fetal cells are obtained so analysis can be completed earlier and more quickly.

Used for: As for amniocentesis: detection of chromosomal and metabolic disorders.

Recommended: Recommendations as for amniocentesis.

Associated risks: Risk of miscarriage is higher than for amniocentesis but, if abortion is recommended, this can be performed sooner. Note that both amniocentesis and CVS rely on the ultrasound to determine the position of the fetus and placenta in the uterus.

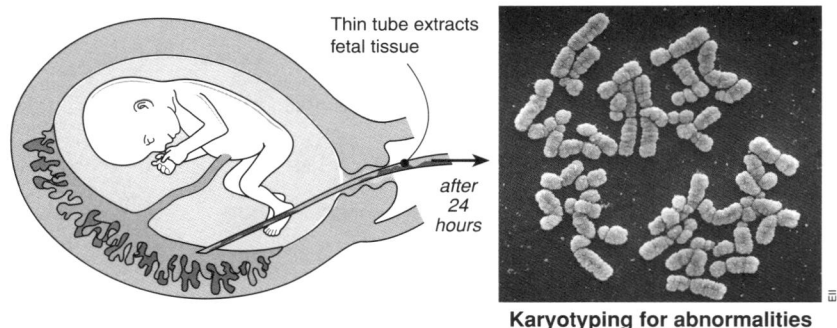

Amniocentesis

A wide bore hypodermic needle is used to puncture the uterus, and 10-20 cm³ of amniotic fluid (containing fetal cells) is removed

Centrifugation

Fluid portion

Biochemical testing

Fetal cells

Cell culture

Amniotic fluid

after several weeks

Chorionic villus sampling

Thin tube extracts fetal tissue

after 24 hours

Karyotyping for abnormalities

Diagnostic Ultrasound in Pregnancy

Ultrasound is commonly used to view the uterus and fetus during pregnancy. Scans are often performed at 18 to 20 weeks into a pregnancy, frequently as a routine procedure. They may also be performed earlier (at about 10-11 weeks) or later (after 34 weeks) if problems are indicated (e.g. severe vomiting in early pregnancy, gestational diabetes, or indications that the fetus is not growing normally). Ultrasound is used for the diagnosis of multiple pregnancies (twins) and gross fetal abnormalities (e.g. trisomy). It is also used to determine fetal age and growth, gender, conception date, and placental position. Such information aids pregnancy management. Ultrasound is *apparently* safe, but the risks associated with frequent scans are unknown.

The reflected sound waves give a visual echo of the fetus inside the uterus.

In this fetus, the general shape of the body and limbs can be discerned. The operator magnifies regions of interest in order to take more accurate measurements.

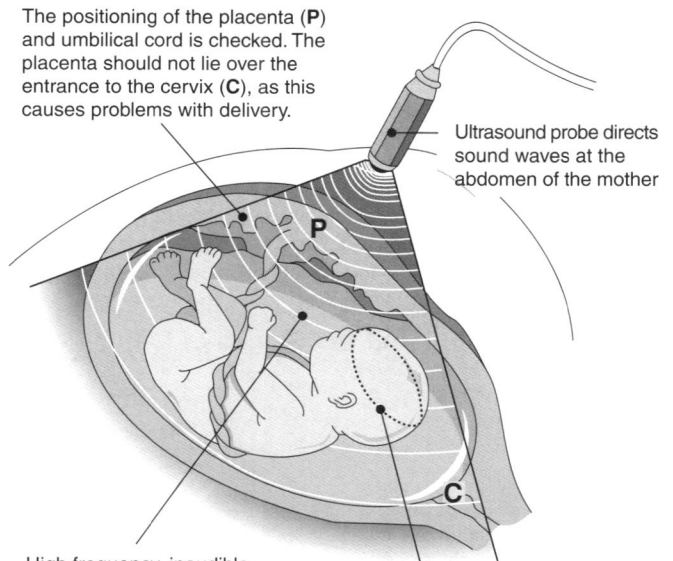

The positioning of the placenta (**P**) and umbilical cord is checked. The placenta should not lie over the entrance to the cervix (**C**), as this causes problems with delivery.

Ultrasound probe directs sound waves at the abdomen of the mother

High frequency, inaudible sound waves are reflected off the fetus and back to a receiver in the probe.

The operator takes specific measurements (on screen) of certain regions of the body e.g. limb length, head length and circumference. These are used to determine if development is normal and growth is within the expected range.

1. (a) Explain the medical reasons why an ultrasound scan might be used to examine a fetus:

(b) Name **one** other feature that may be detected with ultrasound: _____

(c) Explain why ultrasound scans are usually performed later in pregnancy (20 weeks): _____

2. Chorionic villus sampling (CVS), if performed very early in pregnancy (at 5-7 weeks) may cause limb abnormalities, probably via upsetting critical sites of fetal blood flow. Suggest why CVS might be performed at such an early stage:

3. Name **one** chromosomal disorder detectable through amniocentesis: _____

4. (a) Explain why amniocentesis is not usually recommended for women younger than 35:

(b) Suggest when amniocentesis might be recommended for younger women, in spite of the risk:

5. State **two** clinical indications for needing a prenatal test involving chromosome analysis:

(a) _____ (b) _____

6. Suggest why a history of infertility or miscarriage may indicate that a parent is carrying an inherited genetic disorder:

7. **List** some of the ethical concerns of the following information gained through prenatal diagnoses:

(a) Gender determination: _____

(b) Abortion of a viable fetus: _____

Birth and Lactation

A human pregnancy (the period of **gestation**) lasts, on average, about 38 weeks after fertilization. It ends in labor, the birth of the baby, and expulsion of the placenta. During pregnancy, progesterone maintains the placenta and inhibits contraction of the uterus. At the end of a pregnancy, increasing estrogen levels overcome the influence of progesterone and labor begins. Prostaglandins, factors released from the placenta, and the physiological state of the baby itself are also involved in

triggering the actual timing of labor onset. Labor itself comprises three stages (below), and ends with the delivery of the placenta. After birth, the mother provides nutrition for the infant through **lactation**: the production and release of milk from mammary glands. Breast milk provides infants with a complete, easily digested food for the first 4-6 months of life. All breast milk contains maternal antibodies, which give the infant protection against infection while its own immune system develops.

Birth and the Stages of Labor

Stage 1: Dilation

Duration: 2-20 hours

The time between the onset of labor and complete opening (dilation) of the cervix. The amniotic sac may rupture at this stage, releasing its fluid. The hormone **oxytocin** stimulates the uterine contractions necessary to dilate the cervix and expel the baby. It is these uterine contractions that give the pain of labor, most of which is associated with this first stage.

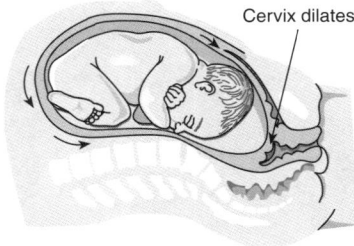

Cervix dilates

Stage 2: Expulsion

Duration: 2-100 minutes

The time from full dilation of the cervix to delivery. Strong, rhythmic contractions of the uterus pass in waves (arrows), and push the baby to the end of the vagina, where the head appears.

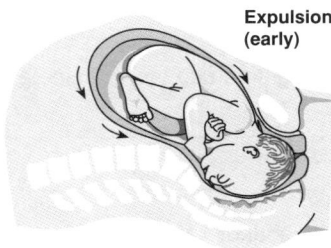

Expulsion (early)

As labor progresses, the time between each contraction shortens. Once the head is delivered, the rest of the body usually follows very rapidly. Delivery completes stage 2.

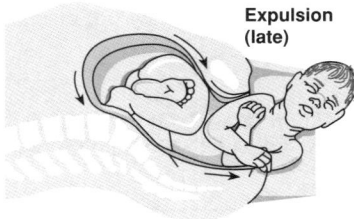

Expulsion (late)

Stage 3: Delivery of placenta

Time: 5-45 minutes after delivery

The third or **placental stage**, refers to the expulsion of the placenta from the uterus. After the placenta is delivered, the placental blood vessels constrict to stop bleeding.

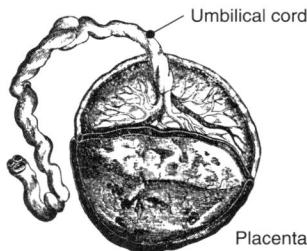

Umbilical cord

Placenta

Delivery of the Baby: The End of Stage 2

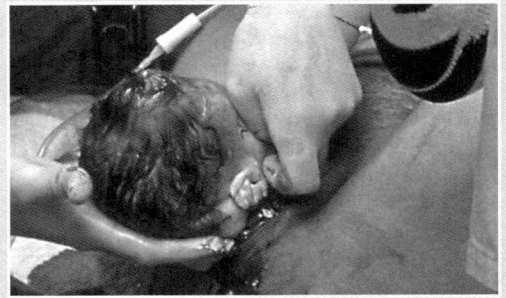

Delivery of the head. This baby is face forward. The more usual position for delivery is face to the back of the mother.

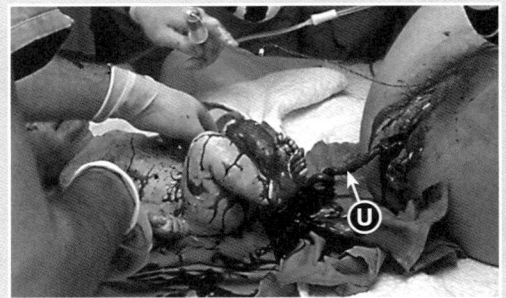

Full delivery of the baby. Note the umbilical cord (U), which supplies oxygen until the baby's breathing begins.

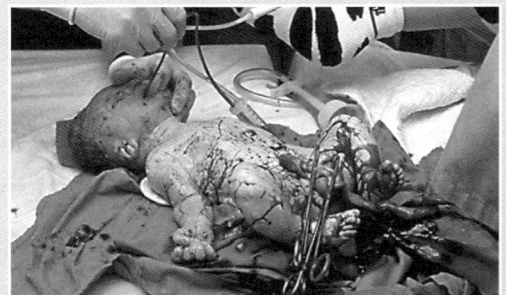

Post-birth check of the baby. The baby is still attached to the placenta and the airways are being cleared of mucus.

1. Name the three stages of birth, and briefly state the main events occurring in each stage:

    (a) Stage 1: _____

    (b) Stage 2: _____

    (c) Stage 3: _____

2. (a) Name the hormone responsible for triggering the **onset** of labor: _____

    (b) Describe two other factors that might influence the timing of labor onset: _____

    _____

    _____

Lactation and its Control

After birth, levels of the hormone **prolactin** (from the anterior pituitary) increase markedly. Prolactin stimulates milk production. **Suckling** by an infant maintains prolactin secretion and causes the release of **oxytocin** by the posterior pituitary. Oxytocin induces the milk ducts to contract, resulting in milk release.

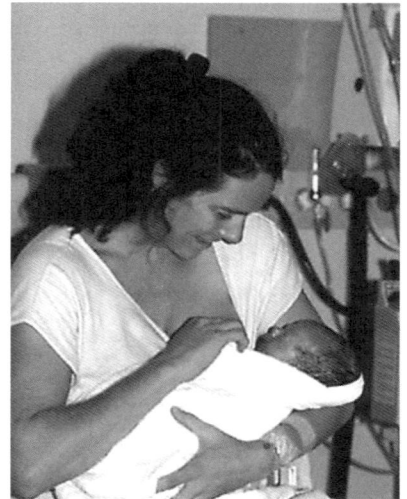

Stimulus to pituitary gland (circled)

Prolactin

Oxytocin

Alveolus

Mammary duct

+ Symbol indicating stimulation

IN THE LACTATING MAMMARY GLAND:

■ Alveoli of the mammary gland produce milk in response to prolactin.

■ Contraction of the mammary ducts ejects milk to the nipple in a reflex letdown (induced by oxytocin).

■ Suckling stimulates the pituitary gland to secrete prolactin and oxytocin.

It is essential to establish breast feeding soon after birth, as this is when infants exhibit the strong reflexes that enable them to learn to suckle effectively. The first formed milk, colostrum, has very little sugar, virtually no fat, and is rich in maternal antibodies. Breast milk that is produced later has a higher fat content, and its composition varies as the nutritional needs of the infant change during growth.

3. Explain why the umbilical cord continues to supply blood to the baby for a short time after delivery: _____

_____

4. For each of the following processes, state the primary controlling hormone and its site of production:

(a) Uterine contraction during labor: Hormone: _____ Site of production: _____

(b) Production of milk: Hormone: _____ Site of production: _____

(c) Milk ejection in response to suckling: Hormone: _____ Site of production: _____

5. State which hormone inhibits prolactin secretion during pregnancy: _____

6. Describe two benefits of breast feeding to the health of the infant:

(a) _____

(b) _____

7. (a) Describe the nutritional differences between the first formed milk (colostrum) and the milk that is produced later:

_____

_____

(b) Suggest a reason for these differences: _____

_____

8. Explain why the nutritional composition of breast milk might change during a six-month period of breast feeding:

_____

9. Infants exhibit marked growth spurts at six weeks and three months of age. At these time, their caloric (energy intake) requirements also increase sharply. With reference to what you know about the control of lactation, suggest how a breast-feeding mother could continue to provide for the increased energy requirements of her infant:

_____

_____

Sexual Development

Like many animals, humans differentiate into the male or female sex by the action of a combination of different hormones. The hormones testosterone (in males), and estrogen and progesterone (in females), are responsible for puberty (the onset of sexual maturity), the maintenance of gender differences, and the production of gametes. In females, estrogen and progesterone also regulate the menstrual cycle, and ensure the maintenance of pregnancy and nourishment of young.

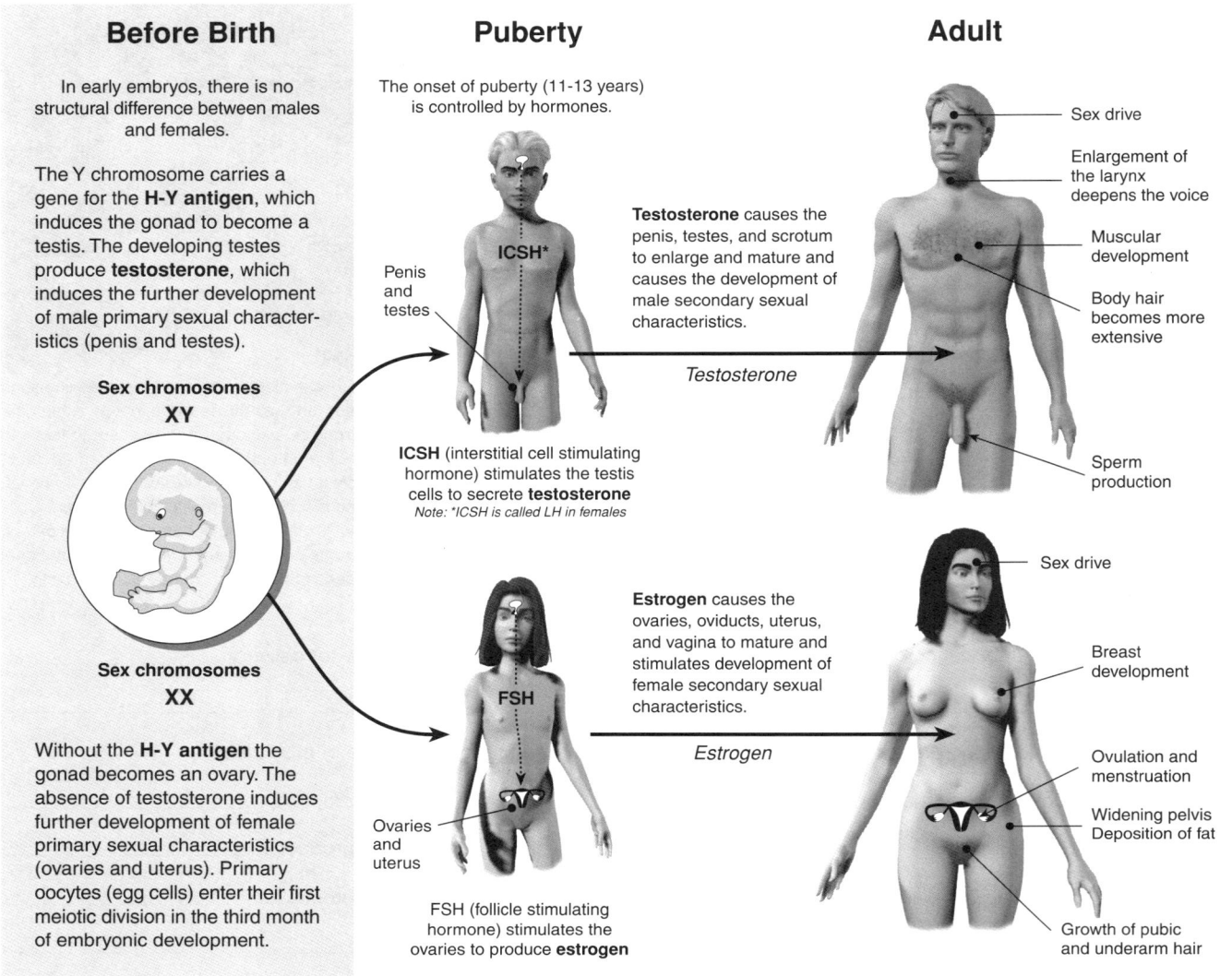

Before Birth

In early embryos, there is no structural difference between males and females.

The Y chromosome carries a gene for the **H-Y antigen**, which induces the gonad to become a testis. The developing testes produce **testosterone**, which induces the further development of male primary sexual characteristics (penis and testes).

Sex chromosomes
XY

Sex chromosomes
XX

Without the **H-Y antigen** the gonad becomes an ovary. The absence of testosterone induces further development of female primary sexual characteristics (ovaries and uterus). Primary oocytes (egg cells) enter their first meiotic division in the third month of embryonic development.

Puberty

The onset of puberty (11-13 years) is controlled by hormones.

ICSH*

Penis and testes

ICSH (interstitial cell stimulating hormone) stimulates the testis cells to secrete **testosterone**
Note: *ICSH is called LH in females*

Testosterone causes the penis, testes, and scrotum to enlarge and mature and causes the development of male secondary sexual characteristics.

Testosterone

FSH

Ovaries and uterus

FSH (follicle stimulating hormone) stimulates the ovaries to produce **estrogen**

Estrogen causes the ovaries, oviducts, uterus, and vagina to mature and stimulates development of female secondary sexual characteristics.

Estrogen

Adult

Sex drive

Enlargement of the larynx deepens the voice

Muscular development

Body hair becomes more extensive

Sperm production

Sex drive

Breast development

Ovulation and menstruation

Widening pelvis
Deposition of fat

Growth of pubic and underarm hair

1. Define what is meant by:

   (a) Primary sexual characteristics: _____

   (b) Secondary sexual characteristics: _____

2. Name the hormone responsible for determining sex (gender) in the fetus: _____

3. Describe the effects on a normal female if she were to take male hormones to enhance muscle development for sport:

   _____

4. (a) Explain the role of the extra fat deposits laid down by the female at puberty: _____

   _____

   (b) Describe a potential reproductive side effect of starvation or severe dieting for women of child-bearing age:

   _____

5. A second hormone, progesterone, is important in regulating female reproduction after puberty:

   (a) Name the site(s) of production of this hormone: _____

   (b) State its major roles: _____

   _____

RA 2
The Process of Aging

After physical maturity is attained the body undergoes **degenerative changes** known as senescence or aging. Aging is a progressive failure of the body's homeostatic responses, occurring as a result of cells dying and renewal rates slowing or stopping. It is a general response, producing observable changes in structure and physiology; there is a decline in skeletal and muscular strength, and reduced immune function. Aging increases susceptibility to stress and disease, and disease and aging often accelerate together.

Osteoarthritis of the knee joint

Osteoarthritis is a common degenerative disease aggravated by mechanical stress on bone joints. It is characterized by the degeneration of cartilage and the formation of osteophytes (bony outgrowths at the joint). This leads to pain, stiffness, inflammation, and full or partial loss of joint function. Osteoarthritis occurs in almost all people over the age of 60 and affects three times as many women as men. Weight bearing joints such as those in the knee, foot, hips, and spine are most commonly affected. Currently there is no cure for osteoarthritis, although symptoms can be relieved by painkillers and anti-inflammatory drugs.

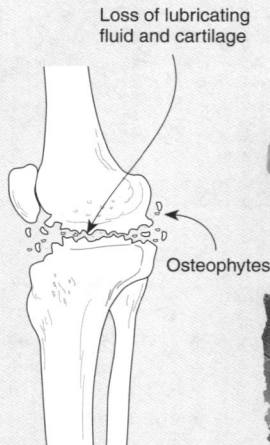

Loss of lubricating fluid and cartilage

Osteophytes

Osteoporosis of the spine

Osteoporosis is an age-related disorder where bone mass decreases, and there is a loss of height and an increased tendency for bones to break (fracture). Women are at greater risk of developing the disease than men because their skeletons are lighter and their estrogen levels fall after menopause (estrogen provides some protection against bone loss). Younger women with low hormone levels and/or low body weight are also affected. Osteoporosis affects the whole skeleton, but especially the spine, hips, and legs.

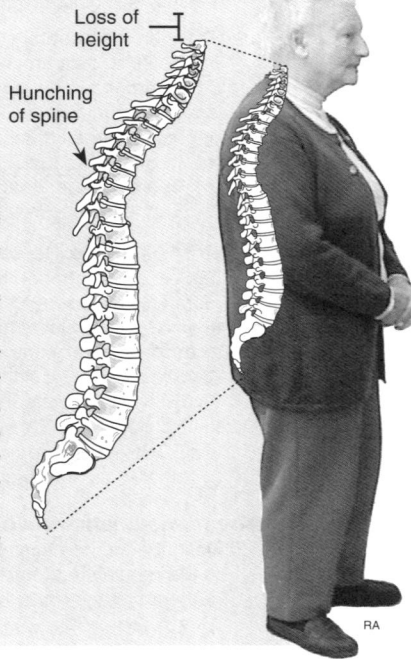

Loss of height

Hunching of spine

Age Related Changes

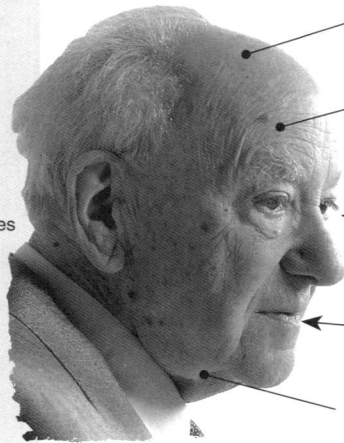

Graying and loss of hair.

Thousands of brain cells are lost each day; as a result there is a reduced ability to memorize and learn new skills. Incidence of Alzheimer's disease increases.

Loss of acuity in all senses (e.g., vision and hearing), mainly as a result of nerve cell loss. The eyes often develop **cataracts**.

Loss of teeth.

Loss of elastic connective tissue causes the skin to sag and wrinkle. Skin bruises easily and the malfunction of melanocytes causes liver spotting.

- Several cell types, including neurons, and skeletal and cardiac muscle cells cannot be replaced.
- Metabolic rate decreases. Digestive and kidney function declines.
- The arteries develop deposits associated with atherosclerosis.
- Muscle and bone mass decrease and fat deposits increase. There is a loss of height.
- Arthritis and other joint problems occur, particularly in the hands, feet, hips, elbows, and knees.
- Fertility declines. In women this happens with menopause, usually at about 45-55 years of age. In men, fertility declines more slowly.
- Cancers increase, e.g., prostate cancer in men, and breast and cervical cancer in women.

RA

RA

1. Briefly explain what causes aging of the body, carefully relating the physiological changes to the observable effects:

_____

_____

2. Suggest how weight-bearing exercise could delay the onset of aging: _____

_____

3. Name and describe two degenerative diseases or disorders, including reference to symptoms and physiological causes:

(a) _____

_____

(b) _____

_____

Homeostasis and Excretion

IB SL

Complete nos:
1-5, 7, 11-13, 19, 22(e)
Extension, 6, 8

IB HL

Complete nos:
1-5, 7, 11-13, 19-22(e), 23-31, 34
Extension, 6, 8

IB Options

Complete nos:
Option B: 15(c)
Option H (HL only): 7-10, 14-16, 18, 32
Extension: 17, 33

AP Biology

Complete nos:
1-34
Some numbers extension as appropriate

Learning Objectives

☐ 1. Compile your own glossary from the **KEY WORDS** displayed in **bold type** in the learning objectives below.

Principles of homeostasis (pages 248-250)

☐ 2. Understand the role of **homeostasis** in providing independence from the fluctuating external environment. Identify factors that require regulation in order for an organism to maintain a steady state.

☐ 3. Explain, using examples, the principle of **negative feedback**, identifying how it stabilizes systems against excessive change. Explain the role of **receptors**, **effectors**, and negative feedback in homeostasis. *Also see the topic, "Reproduction and Development", for the role of feedback mechanisms in regulating the levels of reproductive hormones.*

☐ 4. Appreciate the interdependence and general roles of the two regulatory systems (hormonal and nervous) with which mammals achieve homeostasis.

Nervous regulation (page 251)

☐ 5. Outline the general structure of the **nervous system**, relating the structure to the way in which animals receive **stimuli** and generate a **response**.

☐ 6. Appreciate the importance of negative feedback in nervous systems. Contrast the speed of nervous and endocrine responses.

Hormonal regulation (pages 252-255)

☐ 7. Understand what is meant by the terms: **endocrine gland**, **hormone**, and **target tissue**. Describe the general organization of the **endocrine system** and appreciate its role in the maintenance of homeostasis.

☐ 8. Explain how hormones act and why they have wide-ranging physiological effects. Contrast the speed of endocrine and nervous responses. Explain the role of feedback mechanisms in regulating hormone levels.

☐ 9. Describe the role of the **hypothalamus** and **pituitary gland** in homeostasis. On a diagram of the hypothalamus and pituitary, distinguish between the anterior and posterior pituitary and identify the position and role of the portal vein and **neurosecretory cells**.

☐ 10. Identify an example of each of the following types of hormones: **steroid hormones**, **peptide hormones**, and **tyrosine derivatives**. Distinguish between the mode of action of steroid and peptide hormones.

Case studies in homeostasis

Control of body temperature (page 257)

☐ 11. Describe the control of body temperature in humans with reference to the corrective mechanisms that come into play when body temperature rises or falls from the normal. Include reference to the following:

- The role of the blood in the transfer of heat.
- The role of the sweat glands and skin arterioles (vasoconstriction and vasodilation).
- The role of shivering in heat generation.

Identify the role of the **hypothalamus** (heat gain and heat loss centers), the autonomic nervous system, and **thermoreceptors** in the skin in monitoring and responding to temperature change.

Control of blood glucose (page 256)

☐ 12. Understand the factors that lead to variation in blood glucose levels. Understand the normal range over which blood glucose levels fluctuate.

☐ 13. Describe the general structure of the pancreas and outline its role as an **endocrine organ**. Explain, using a diagram, how the regulation of **blood glucose** level is achieved in humans, including reference to the role of each of the following:
   - (a) Negative feedback mechanisms.
   - (b) The hormones **insulin** and **glucagon**.
   - (c) The role of the liver in glucose-glycogen conversions.

Control of thyroxine secretion (page 255)

☐ 14. Explain the control of thyroxine secretion by negative feedback. Include reference to the secretion of **TRH** (thyrotropin-releasing hormone), transport to the **anterior pituitary** in the portal vein, secretion of **TSH** (thyroid stimulating hormone), and secretion of thyroxine. Appreciate the general metabolic effects of thyroid hormones. Describe the influence of thyroxine level, TSH level, and body temperature on the hypothalamus and the regulation of TRH secretion.

The homeostatic role of the liver (pages 258-259)

☐ 15. Describe the homeostatic role of the liver with respect to the regulation of nutrient levels in the blood and nutrient storage, including its role in:
   - (a) **Carbohydrate metabolism**: production of glucose from amino acids and storage of glucose.
   - (b) Protein metabolism, including **deamination**, **transamination**, and the formation of **plasma proteins** and **urea**.
   - (c) **Fat metabolism**, including the use of fats in respiration, the synthesis of triglycerides and **cholesterol**, and the transport of lipids.
   - (d) Storage of iron, retinol, and calciferol.
   - (e) Breakdown of red blood cells and hemoglobin.

☐ 16. Outline the circulation of the blood through the liver tissue. Include the flow through the **hepatic artery**, **hepatic portal vein**, **sinusoids**, and **hepatic vein**.

☐ 17. Outline the general structure and histology of the liver. Identify the following: *liver lobule, hepatocytes, portal triad, Küpffer cells, sinusoids, and central vein.*

☐ 18. Describe the process of bile secretion, including reference to the composition of bile, the roles of the bile canaliculi, the gall bladder, and the bile duct.

Excretion and water balance (pages 260-266)

☐ 19. Clearly explain what is meant by the terms: **excretion** and **osmoregulation**. Appreciate why organisms must regulate water balance and dispose of the toxic waste products of metabolism.

☐ 20. Identify the major **nitrogenous waste products** excreted by animals (e.g. mammals, birds, and fish) and identify their origin. Appreciate how the excretory product is related to life history and environment.

☐ 21. Understand that oxygen is excreted in plants when oxygen production from photosynthesis exceeds demand. Appreciate why plants do not face the same nitrogen excretion problems as animals.

☐ 22. Describe diversity in the principal organs of excretion and osmoregulation found in animals. Include reference to the basic structure and role of any of the following:
  (a) **Protonephridia** (flatworms) or **nephridia** (annelids).
  (b) **Malpighian tubules** (insects).
  (c) **Antennal glands** and **gills** (crustaceans).
  (d) **Gills** (fish).
  (e) **Kidneys** (all vertebrates).

☐ 23. Identify the non-nitrogenous excretory products in mammals. Name the organs involved in their disposal.

☐ 24. Describe the different homeostatic problems associated with living in salt and fresh water. Describe, with examples, the mechanisms by which animals in fresh and salt water regulate their water and ion balance.

Water budget in mammals (page 262)

☐ 25. Describe the control of water budget in a desert rodent with reference to the physiological mechanisms that minimize water loss, how water requirements are met without drinking, and behavioral adaptations that reduce the need for water.

☐ 26. Compare the water budget of a desert rodent and a mammal that is not desert adapted, such as a human. Discuss reasons for the differences.

The physiology of excretion (pages 266-269)

☐ 27. On a diagram, identify the main structures of the mammalian urinary system: **kidneys**, **ureters**, **renal blood vessels**, bladder, urethra (cross ref. with #22(e)).

☐ 28. Describe the gross structure of the mammalian kidney to include the **cortex**, **medulla**, and **renal pelvis**.

☐ 29. Using a labeled diagram, describe the structure and arrangement of a nephron and its associated blood vessels. Include reference to the structure of the **glomerulus**, and the location of the **convoluted tubules** and **collecting duct**.

☐ 30. Explain concisely how the kidney nephron produces urine. Include reference to:
  (a) The process of **ultrafiltration** in the **glomerulus**, with reference to the role of blood pressure and the ultrastructure of the glomerulus and renal capsule.
  (b) The **selective reabsorption** of water and solutes (e.g. glucose) in the **proximal convoluted tubule**.
  (c) The roles of the **loop of Henlé**, **medulla**, **collecting duct**, and ADH (anti-diuretic hormone) in the formation of urine and maintenance of water balance. Identify the role of the ionic gradient in the kidney in producing a concentrated urine.

☐ 31. Compare the composition of blood in the renal artery and renal vein, and compare the composition of glomerular filtrate and urine. Account for the differences.

☐ 32. Explain the control of **ADH** secretion. Include the role of hypothalamic **osmoreceptors**, synthesis of ADH by **neurosecretion** and its release from the **posterior pituitary**, the action of ADH on the kidney, and the role of **negative feedback** in regulating ADH output.

☐ 33. Recognize the role of **aldosterone** in promoting sodium reabsorption in the kidney.

☐ 34. Outline the principles involved in **kidney dialysis**. Outline the structure and action of kidney dialysis machines. Appreciate the role of kidney dialysis in the maintenance of homeostasis in cases of kidney failure.

Textbooks

See the 'Textbook Reference Grid' on pages 8-9 for textbook page references relating to material in this topic.

Supplementary Texts

See pages 5-6 for additional details of this text:
■ Clegg, C.J., 1998. **Mammals: Structure and Function** (John Murray), pp. 42-57, 70-71.

Periodicals

See page 6 for details of publishers of periodicals:

STUDENT'S REFERENCE

Homeostasis and excretion

■ **Homeostasis** Biol. Sci. Rev., 12(5) May 2000, pp. 2-5. *Homeostasis: what it is, the role of negative feedback and the autonomic nervous system, and the adaptations of organisms for homeostasis in extreme environments (excellent).*

■ **Metabolic Powerhouse** New Scientist, 11 November 2000 (Inside Science). *The myriad roles of the liver in metabolic processes, including discussion of amino acid and glucose metabolism.*

■ **The Liver in Health and Disease** Biol. Sci. Rev., 14(2) Nov. 2001, pp. 14-20. *The various roles of the liver: production of bile, and metabolism of protein, lipids, carbohydrates, and drugs.*

■ **Busy Doing Nothing** New Scientist, 25 April 1998, pp. 32-35. *The relationship between activity and metabolic rate in animals: they may appear idle but metabolically they may be in high gear.*

■ **Basement Membranes** Biol. Sci. Rev., 13(4) March 2001, pp. 36-39. *The structure, function, and diversity of basement membranes, with an account of their structural role in the glomerulus.*

■ **Diabetes** Biol. Sci. Rev., 15(2), Nov. 2002, pp. 30-35. *The homeostatic imbalance that results in diabetes. The role of the pancreas in the hormonal regulation of blood glucose is discussed.*

■ **Melatonin: Hormone of Darkness** Biol. Sci. Rev.,10(1) Sept. 1997, pp. 36-38. *Melatonin and its activity in the body in regulating natural rhythms.*

■ **Thyroxine** Biol. Sci. Rev., 12(2) Nov. 1999, pp. 19-21. *A good account of the structure of the thyroid, the physiological roles of its hormones, and their regulation through negative feedback.*

■ **Growth Hormone** Biol. Sci. Rev., 12 (4) March 2000, pp. 26-28. *Growth hormone, its secretion from the pituitary, and the consequences of growth hormone deficiencies in humans.*

■ **Nitrogen Excretion in Animals** Biol. Sci. Rev., 8(5) May 1996, pp. 27-31. *Excretory products in animals, including a discussion of the urea cycle.*

■ **Countercurrent Exchange Mechanisms** Biol. Sci. Rev., 9(1) Sept. 1996, pp. 2-6. *The role of countercurrent multipliers in biological systems: including operation in the kidney nephron.*

■ **Hormonal Manipulation by Athletes** Biol. Sci. Rev., 15(2) Nov. 2002, pp. 2-5. *The misuse of steroid hormones by athletes: the actions of the hormones (their anabolic effects) and how they are involved in the body's response to exercise.*

■ **Uric Acid - Life Saver and Liability** Biol. Sci. Rev., 9(1) Sept. 1996, pp. 22-24. *Nitrogen excretion and the situations in which uric acid is produced.*

TEACHER'S REFERENCE

■ **A Simple Temperature Gradient Apparatus to Determine Thermal Preference in *Daphnia*** The American Biology Teacher, 64(9), Nov. 2002, pp. 679-681. *In this simple experiment, students use a thermal gradient to investigate thermoregulatory behavior and thermal preference in an ectotherm.*

Internet

See pages 10-11 for details of how to access **Bio Links** from our web site: **www.thebiozone.com**. From Bio Links, access sites under the topics:

GENERAL BIOLOGY ONLINE RESOURCES > **Online Textbooks and Lecture Notes:** • S-Cool! A level biology revision guide • Learn.co.uk • Mark Rothery's biology web site ... *and others*

ANIMAL BIOLOGY > Excretion: • Comparative physiology of vertebrate kidneys • Excretory system • The kidney • Urinary system > **Homeostasis:** • Ask the experts: What is homeostasis? • Homeostasis • Homeostasis: general principles Physiological homeostasis • Temperature regulation

Software and video resources are now provided in the Teacher Resource Handbook

RA② Maintaining Homeostasis

The various organ systems of the body act to maintain homeostasis through a combination of hormonal and nervous mechanisms. In everyday life, the body must regulate respiratory gases, protect itself against agents of disease (pathogens), maintain fluid and salt balance, regulate energy and nutrient supply, and maintain a constant body temperature. All these must be coordinated and appropriate responses made to incoming stimuli. In addition, the body must be able to repair itself when injured and be capable of reproducing (leaving offspring).

Regulating Respiratory Gases

Oxygen demand changes with activity level and environment (e.g. altitude).

CO₂ production changes with activity level and environment.

Capacity for O₂ transport depends on blood hemoglobin.

Muscular activity increases oxygen demand and carbon dioxide production.

Oxygen must be delivered to all cells and carbon dioxide (a waste product of cellular respiration) must be removed. Breathing (inhalation and exhalation) brings in oxygen and expels CO₂. The rate of breathing is varied according to the oxygen requirement. Both gases are transported around the body in the blood; the oxygen mostly bound to hemoglobin.

Coping with Pathogens

Lymph tissue

Attack by pathogens inhaled or eaten with food and drink.

Infections of the reproductive system (STIs) from yeasts, viruses, and bacteria.

Attack on skin and mucous membranes from fungal pathogens.

All of us are under constant attack from pathogens (disease causing organisms). The body has a number of mechanisms that help to prevent the entry of pathogens and limit the damage they cause if they do enter the body. The skin, the digestive system and the immune system are all involved in limiting damage.

Maintaining Nutrient Supply

Digestion in the gut provides the building materials for the body to grow and repair tissue.

Food and drink provides energy and nutrients, but supply is pulsed at mealtimes with little in between.

Water must be reabsorbed from the digested material.

The solid waste products of digestion (feces) must be eliminated.

Food and drink must be taken in to maintain the body's energy supplies. Steady levels of energy (as glucose) is available to cells through hormonal regulation of blood sugar levels. Insulin, released by the endocrine cells of the pancreas, causes cells to take up glucose after a meal. Glucagon causes the release of glucose from the liver.

Repairing Injuries

Wounds result in bleeding. Clotting begins soon after and phagocytes prevent the entry of pathogens.

Muscle and tendon injuries through excessive activity.

Hernias can be caused by strain as in heavy lifting.

Bone fractures caused by falls and blows.

Damage to body tissues triggers the inflammatory response. There is pain, swelling, redness, and heat. Phagocytes and other white blood cells move to the injury site. The inflammatory response is started (and ended) by chemical signals (e.g. from histamine and prostaglandins) released when tissue is damaged.

Maintaining Fluid and Ion Balance

Water and ions taken in with food and drink.

Water loss through breathing.

Loss of water and ions via sweat.

Loss of water and ions via urine and feces.

Coordinating Responses

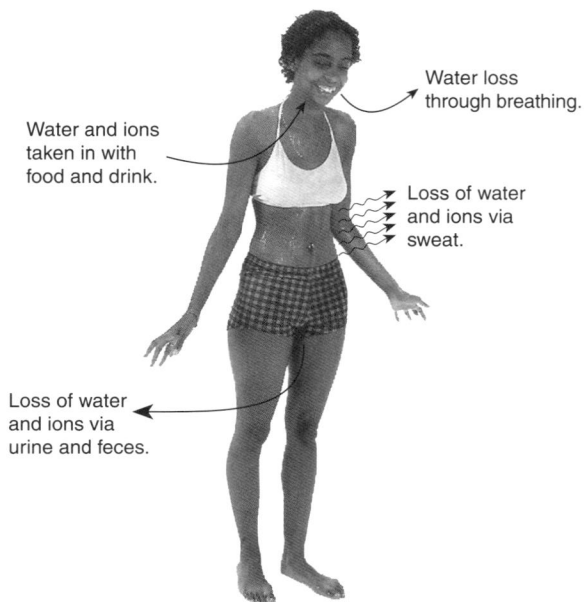

The brain monitors and regulates hormone levels and coordinates complex movements.

Glands (e.g. the adrenals) respond to messages from the brain to produce regulatory hormones.

Environmental stimuli bombard the senses through ears, nose, eyes, skin, and mouth.

Simple reflexes, such as pain withdrawal, allow rapid responses to stimuli.

The levels of water and ions in the body are maintained mainly by the kidneys, although the skin is also important. Osmoreceptors monitor the fluid and ion levels of the blood and bring about the release of regulatory hormones; the kidneys regulate reabsorption of water and sodium from blood in response to levels of the hormones ADH and aldosterone.

The body is constantly bombarded by stimuli from the environment. The brain sorts these stimuli into those that require a response and those that do not. Responses are coordinated via nervous or hormonal controls. Simple nervous responses (reflexes) act quickly. Hormonal responses take longer to produce a response and the response is more prolonged.

1. Describe two mechanisms that operate to restore homeostasis after infection by a pathogen:

(a) _____

_____

_____

(b) _____

_____

_____

2. Describe two mechanisms by which responses to stimuli are brought about and coordinated:

(a) _____

_____

(b) _____

_____

3. Explain two ways in which water and ion balance are maintained. Name the organ(s) and any hormones involved:

(a) _____

_____

(b) _____

_____

4. Explain two ways in which the body regulates its respiratory gases during exercise:

(a) _____

_____

(b) _____

_____

Principles of Homeostasis

A 2

Homeostasis is the condition where the body's internal environment remains relatively constant, within narrow limits. For the body's cells to survive and function properly, the composition and temperature of the fluids around the cells must remain much the same. An organism is said to be in homeostasis when the internal environment contains the optimal concentration of gases, nutrients, ions and water, at the optimal temperature. Negative *feedback mechanisms* are involved in the control of homeostasis. Feedback mechanisms provide information about the state of a system to its control centre. In negative feedback, movement away from an ideal state causes a return back to the ideal state (the set point). The intensity of the corrective action is reduced as the system returns to this set point. Using such control systems the body acts to counteract disturbances and restore homeostasis. The system operates through a combination of nervous and hormonal mechanisms (see below).

Negative Feedback and Regulatory Control Systems

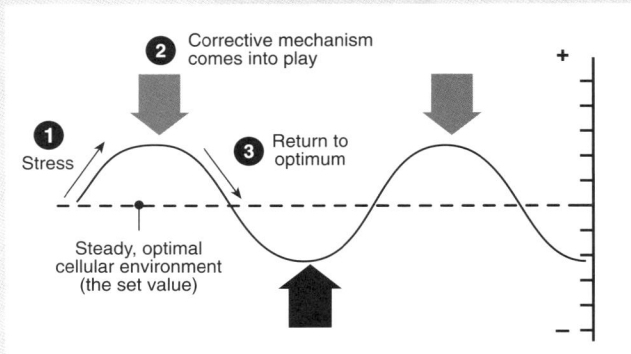

2 Corrective mechanism comes into play

1 Stress

3 Return to optimum

Steady, optimal cellular environment (the set value)

1 A stress or disturbance takes the internal environment away from optimum

2 Stress is detected by receptors and corrective mechanisms are activated

3 The corrective mechanisms act to restore conditions back to the set value

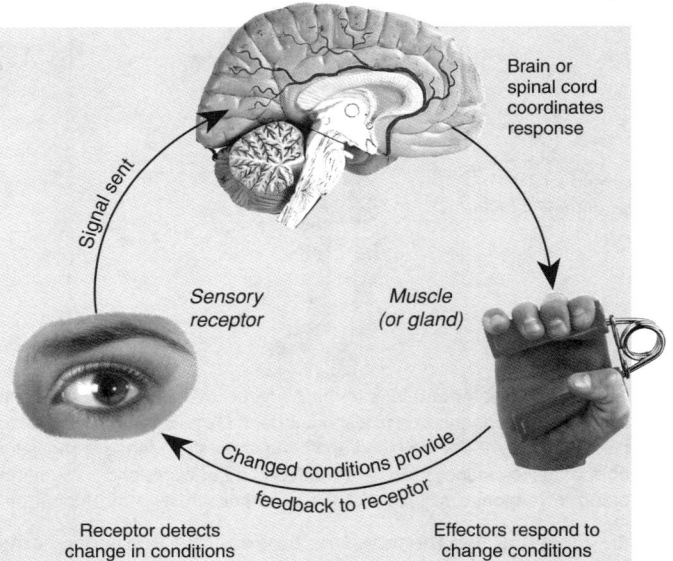

Brain or spinal cord coordinates response

Signal sent

Sensory receptor

Muscle (or gland)

Changed conditions provide feedback to receptor

Receptor detects change in conditions

Effectors respond to change conditions

Negative feedback acts to eliminate any deviation from preferred conditions. It is part of almost all the control systems in living things. The diagram (above left) shows how a stress or disturbance is counteracted by corrective mechanisms that act to restore conditions back to an optimum value. The diagram (above right) illustrates this principle for a biological system.

Internal environment
Fluctuations in ion composition, acidity (pH), temperature, nutrients, gases, and water content are **small**.

In *Paramecium*, two contractile vacuoles collect water and expel it to the outside.

Food vacuoles: Contain ingested food.

Paramecium
A single-celled protist found predominantly in freshwater.

External environment
Fluctuations in ion composition, acidity (pH), availability of water, gases, nutrients, and temperature can be **very large**.

The food groove collects food as a source of energy and nutrients.

80 µm

Factors varying across a membrane
Acidity (pH)
Ionic composition
Water potential
Temperature
Nutrient availability
Gas concentration

1. Identify the three main components of a regulatory control system in the human body: _____

_____

2. Briefly describe the effect of negative feedback mechanisms in biological systems: _____

_____

_____

Nervous Regulatory Systems

An essential feature of living organisms is their ability to coordinate their activities. In multicellular animals, such as mammals, detecting and responding to environmental change, and regulating the internal environment (homeostasis) is brought about by two coordinating systems: the nervous and endocrine systems. Although structurally these two systems are quite different, they frequently interact to coordinate behavior and physiology. The nervous system contains cells called neurons (or nerve cells). Neurons are specialized to transmit information in the form of electrochemical impulses (action potentials). The nervous system is a signalling network with branches carrying information directly to and from specific target tissues. Impulses can be transmitted over considerable distances and the response is very precise and rapid. Whilst it is extraordinarily complex, comprising millions of neural connections, its basic plan (below) is quite simple. Further detail on nervous system structure and function is provided in the topic: *Nerves, Muscles, and Movement*.

Coordination by the Nervous System

The vertebrate nervous system consists of the central nervous system (brain and spinal cord), and the nerves and receptors outside it (peripheral nervous system). Sensory input to receptors comes via stimuli. Information about the effect of a response is provided by feedback mechanisms so that the system can be readjusted. The basic organization of the nervous system can be simplified into a few key components: the sensory receptors, a central nervous system processing point, and the effectors which bring about the response (below):

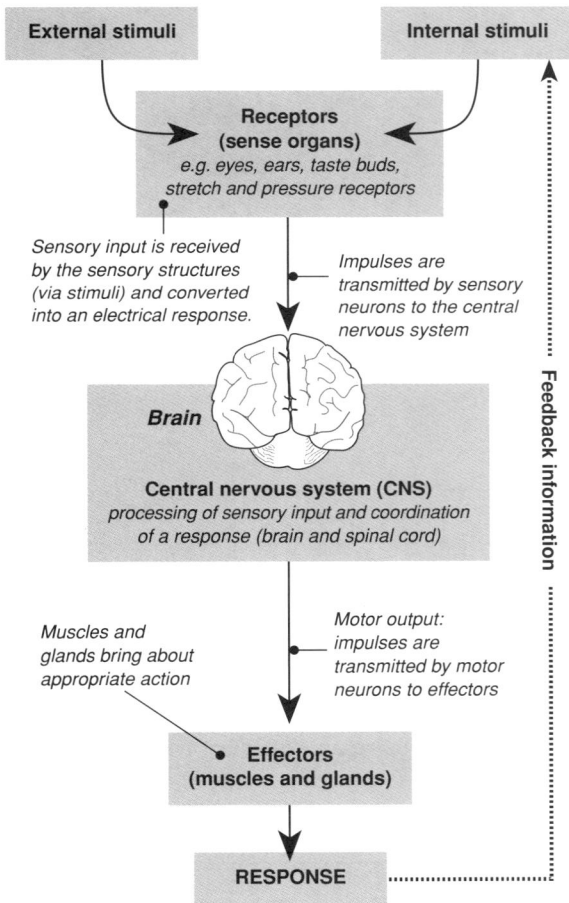

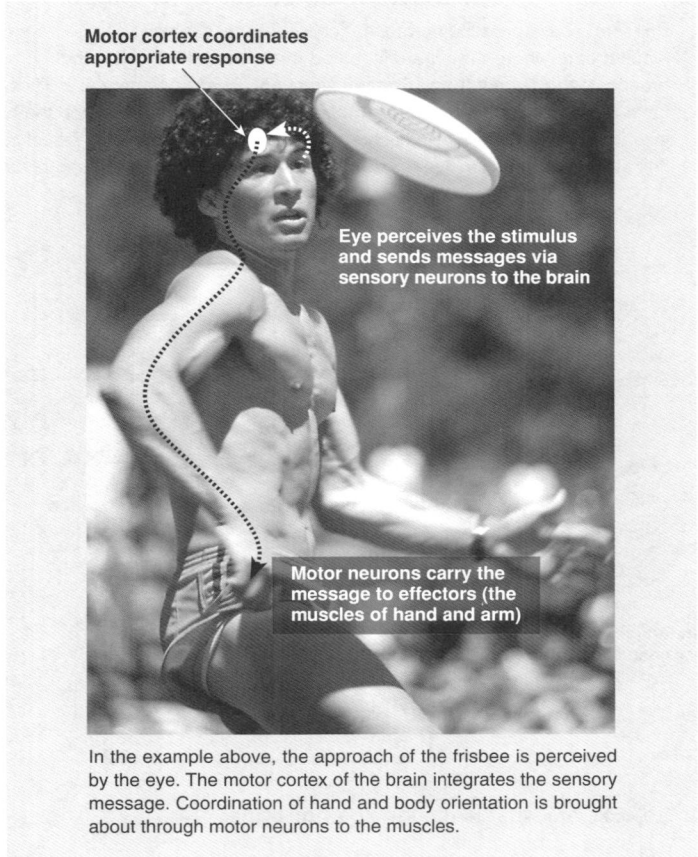

External stimuli **Internal stimuli**

Receptors (sense organs)
e.g. eyes, ears, taste buds, stretch and pressure receptors

Sensory input is received by the sensory structures (via stimuli) and converted into an electrical response.

Impulses are transmitted by sensory neurons to the central nervous system

Brain

Central nervous system (CNS)
processing of sensory input and coordination of a response (brain and spinal cord)

Feedback information

Muscles and glands bring about appropriate action

Motor output: impulses are transmitted by motor neurons to effectors

Effectors (muscles and glands)

RESPONSE

Motor cortex coordinates appropriate response

Eye perceives the stimulus and sends messages via sensory neurons to the brain

Motor neurons carry the message to effectors (the muscles of hand and arm)

In the example above, the approach of the frisbee is perceived by the eye. The motor cortex of the brain integrates the sensory message. Coordination of hand and body orientation is brought about through motor neurons to the muscles.

Comparison of nervous and hormonal control

	Nervous control	Hormonal control
Communication	*Impulses across synapses*	*Hormones in the blood*
Speed	*Very rapid (within a few milliseconds)*	*Relatively slow (over minutes, hours, or longer)*
Duration	*Short term and reversible*	*Longer lasting effects*
Target pathway	*Specific (through nerves) to specific cells*	*Hormones broadcast to target cells everywhere*
Action	*Causes glands to secrete or muscles to contract*	*Causes changes in metabolic activity*

1. Briefly state the role of the following basic components in a nervous system:

   (a) Sensory receptor: _____

   (b) Central nervous system: _____

   (c) Effector: _____

2. Describe two differences between nervous control and endocrine control of body systems:

   (a) _____

   (b) _____

K① Hormonal Regulatory Systems

The endocrine system regulates the body's processes by releasing chemical messengers (hormones) into the bloodstream. Hormones are potent chemical regulators: they are produced in minute quantities yet can have a large effect on metabolism. The endocrine system comprises endocrine cells (organized into endocrine glands), and the hormones they produce. Unlike exocrine glands (e.g., sweat and salivary glands), endocrine glands are ductless glands, secreting hormones directly into the bloodstream rather than through a duct or tube. Some organs (e.g., the pancreas) have both endocrine and exocrine regions, but these are structurally and functionally distinct. The basis of hormonal control and the role of negative feedback mechanisms in regulating hormone levels are described below.

The Mechanism of Hormone Action

Endocrine cells produce hormones (chemical messengers) and secrete them into the bloodstream where they are distributed throughout the body. Although hormones are broadcast throughout the body, they affect only specific target cells. These target cells have receptors on the plasma membrane which recognize and bind the hormone (see inset, below right). The binding of hormone and receptor triggers the response in the target cell. Cells are unresponsive to a hormone if they do not have the appropriate receptors.

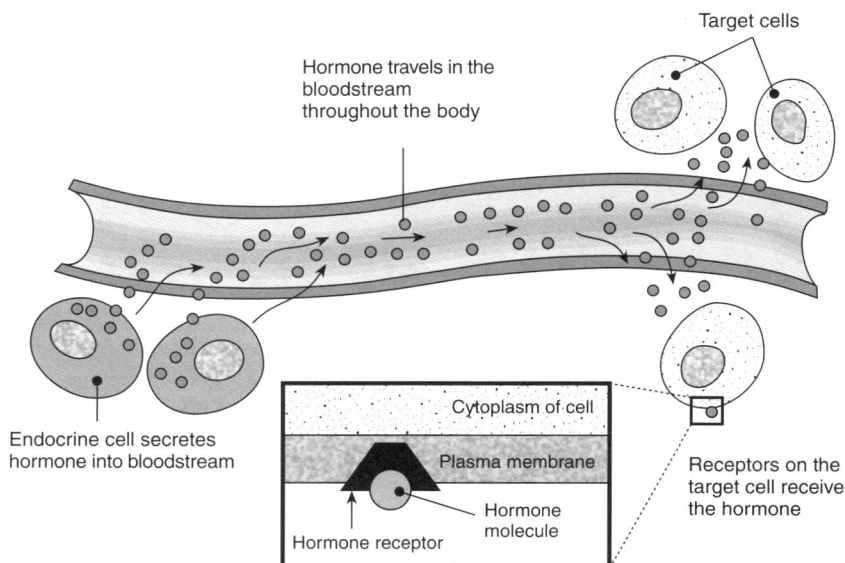

Target cells

Hormone travels in the bloodstream throughout the body

Endocrine cell secretes hormone into bloodstream

Cytoplasm of cell

Plasma membrane

Hormone receptor

Hormone molecule

Receptors on the target cell receive the hormone

Antagonistic Hormones

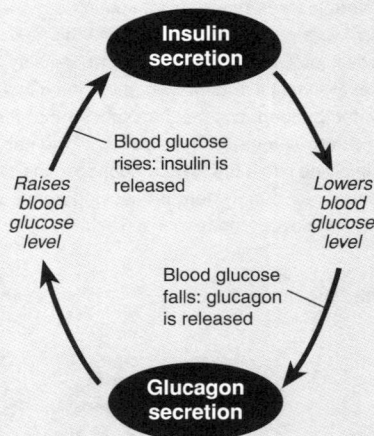

Insulin secretion

Blood glucose rises: insulin is released

Raises blood glucose level

Lowers blood glucose level

Blood glucose falls: glucagon is released

Glucagon secretion

The effects of one hormone are often counteracted by an opposing hormone. Feedback mechanisms adjust the balance of the two hormones to maintain a physiological function. Example: insulin decreases blood glucose and glucagon raises it.

1. (a) Explain what is meant by a **hormone**: _____

_____

(b) Explain what is meant by **antagonistic hormones** and provide an example of two such hormones:

_____

Example: _____

(c) Explain the role of feedback mechanisms in adjusting hormone levels (explain using an example if this is helpful):

_____

_____

2. Explain how a hormone can bring about a response in target cells even though all cells may receive the hormone:

_____

_____

3. Explain **why** hormonal control differs from nervous system control with respect to the following:

(a) The speed of hormonal responses is slower: _____

_____

(b) Hormonal responses are generally longer lasting: _____

_____

Mechanisms of Hormone Action

Once a hormone is released, it is carried in the blood to target cells that respond specifically to that hormone. Water soluble hormones are carried free in the blood, whilst steriod and thyroid hormones are carried bound to plasma proteins. Target cells contain receptors that bind the hormone so that it is able to exert its effect. The binding occurs in one of two ways. One involves an interaction of the hormone with plasma membrane receptors followed by activation of a second messenger. The other involves an interaction of the hormone with intracellular receptors, without the involvement of a second messenger. Once the target cells respond, the response is recognized by the hormone-producing cell through a feedback signal and the hormone is degraded.

Hormone Action Using a Second Messenger

Cyclic AMP is a **second messenger** linking the hormone to the cellular response. Cellular concentration of CAMP increases markedly once a hormone binds and the cascade of enzyme-driven reactions is initiated.

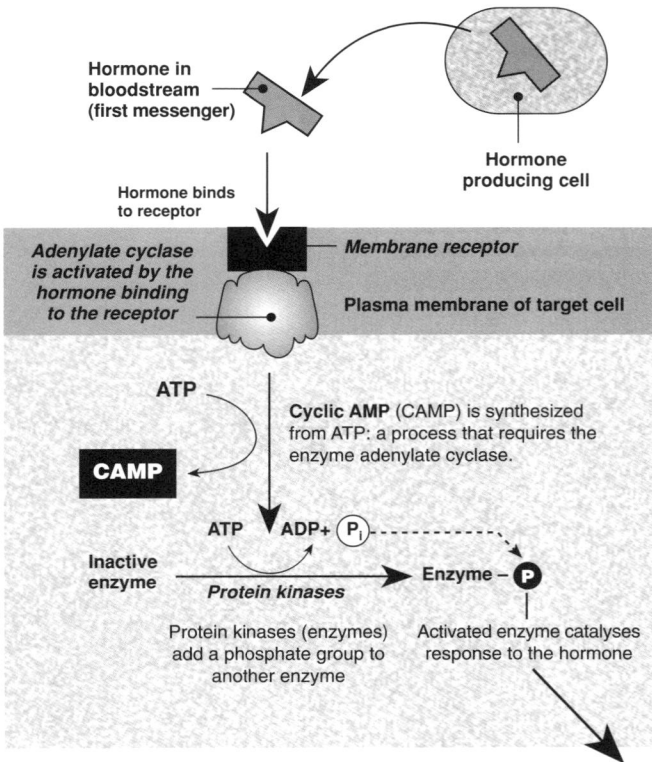

Activation of Genes by a Steroid Hormone

Steroid hormones alter cell function through direct activation of genes. Once inside the target cell, they bind to intracellular receptor sites, creating hormone-receptor complexes that activate specific genes.

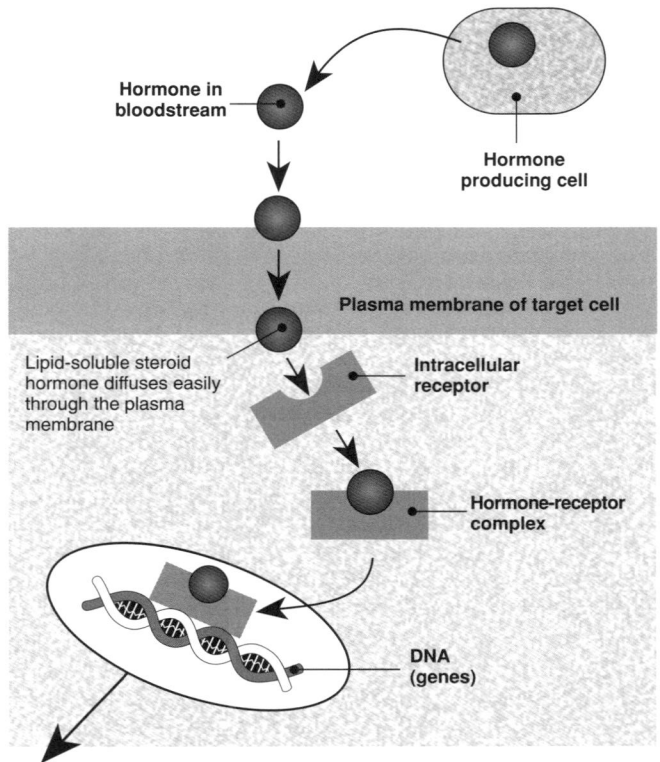

Hormone in bloodstream (first messenger)

Hormone producing cell

Hormone binds to receptor

Adenylate cyclase is activated by the hormone binding to the receptor

Membrane receptor

Plasma membrane of target cell

ATP

Cyclic AMP (CAMP) is synthesized from ATP: a process that requires the enzyme adenylate cyclase.

CAMP

ATP → ADP+ (Pᵢ)

Inactive enzyme

Enzyme – P

Protein kinases

Protein kinases (enzymes) add a phosphate group to another enzyme

Activated enzyme catalyses response to the hormone

Hormone in bloodstream

Hormone producing cell

Plasma membrane of target cell

Lipid-soluble steroid hormone diffuses easily through the plasma membrane

Intracellular receptor

Hormone-receptor complex

DNA (genes)

Action of Hormone: Alteration of Cell Function
• **Enzyme activation** • **Secretion from cell** • **Protein synthesis** • **Altered membrane permeability**

1. Explain the two mechanisms by which a hormone can bring about a cellular response:

    (a) _____

    _____

    (b) _____

    _____

2. State in what way these two mechanisms are alike: _____

    _____

3. Explain how a very small amount of hormone is able to exert a disproportionately large effect on a target cell:

    _____

    _____

4. Explain how the binding of a hormone to a target cell can be likened to an enzyme-substrate reaction: _____

    _____

    _____

The Endocrine System

RA 3

Homeostasis is achieved through the activity of the nervous and endocrine systems, which interact in the regulation of the body's activities. The nervous system is capable of rapid responses to stimuli. Slower responses, and long term adjustments of the body (growth, reproduction, and adaptation to stress), are achieved through endocrine control. The endocrine system comprises **endocrine glands** and their **hormones**. Endocrine glands are ductless glands that are distributed throughout the body. Under appropriate stimulation (see below), they secrete **hormones**: chemical messengers that are carried in the blood to **target** cells, where they have a specific metabolic effect. After exerting their effect, hormones are broken down and excreted from the body. Although a hormone circulates in the blood, only the targets will respond. Hormones may be amino acids, peptides, proteins (often modified), fatty acids, or steroids. Some basic features of the human endocrine system are explained below.

Hypothalamus
Coordinates nervous and endocrine systems. Secretes releasing hormones, which regulate the hormones of the anterior pituitary. Produces oxytocin and ADH, which are released from the posterior pituitary.

Parathyroid glands
On the surface of the thyroid, they secrete PTH (parathyroid hormone), which regulates blood calcium levels and promotes the release of calcium from bone. High levels of calcium in the blood inhibit PTH secretion.

Pancreas
Specialized α and β endocrine cells in the pancreas produce glucagon and insulin. Together, these control blood sugar levels.

Ovaries (in females)
At puberty the ovaries increase their production of estrogen and progesterone. These hormones control and maintain female characteristics (breast development and pelvic widening), stimulate the menstrual cycle, maintain pregnancy, and prepare the mammary glands for lactation.

Pituitary gland
The pituitary is located below the hypothalamus. It secretes at least nine hormones that regulate the activities of other endocrine glands.

Thyroid gland
Secretes thyroxine, an iodine containing hormone needed for normal growth and development. Thyroxine stimulates metabolism and growth via protein synthesis.

Adrenal glands (above kidneys)
The adrenal medulla produces adrenalin and noradrenalin; responsible for the fight or flight response.
The adrenal cortex produces various steroid hormones, including aldosterone (sodium regulation) and cortisol (response to stress).

Testes (in males)
At puberty (the onset of sexual maturity) the testes of males produce testosterone in greater amounts. Testosterone hormone controls and maintains "maleness" (muscular development and deeper voice), and promotes sperm production.

1. Explain what is meant by a target tissue: _____

_____

2. (a) Name an endocrine gland and identify a hormone that it produces: _____

   (b) Name the target tissue for this hormone: _____

   (c) Outline the homeostatic function of this hormone and explain how it controls the activity of the target tissue:

   _____

   _____

   (d) Briefly explain how the release of this hormone is regulated: _____

   _____

   _____

3. Explain why it is an advantage for hormones to be carried in the blood: _____

_____

RA 2   The Hypothalamus and Pituitary

The **hypothalamus** is located at the base of the brain, just above the pituitary gland. Information comes to the hypothalamus through sensory pathways from the sense organs. On the basis of this information, the hypothalamus controls and integrates many basic physiological activities (e.g. temperature regulation, food and fluid intake, and sleep), including the reflex activity of the **autonomic nervous system**. The pituitary gland comprises two regions: the **posterior pituitary**, which is neural in origin and is essentially an extension of the hypothalamus, and the **anterior**

pituitary, which is connected to the hypothalamus by blood vessels. The hypothalamus regulates pituitary activity and is the principal centre for coordinating the activity of the body's nervous and endocrine systems. The hypothalamus contains several distinct regions of neurosecretory cells. These are specialized neurons which are at the same time both nerve cells and endocrine cells. They produce hormones (usually peptides) in the cell body, which are transported down the axon and released into the blood in response to nerve impulses.

Hormones of the Hypothalamus and Pituitary

Neurosecretory cells in the hypothalamus produce **inhibiting** and **releasing factors** (hormones) into capillaries. These neurohormones control the release of other hormones from the anterior pituitary.

Hypothalamus monitors hormone levels and indirectly controls many functions e.g. body temperature, hunger, sleep.

Portal vein links two capillary networks (**CN**)

Anterior pituitary

Capillary network releases at least seven peptide hormones into the blood from simple secretory cells (see table below). Their release is controlled by the **releasing** and **inhibiting** factors from the hypothalamus.

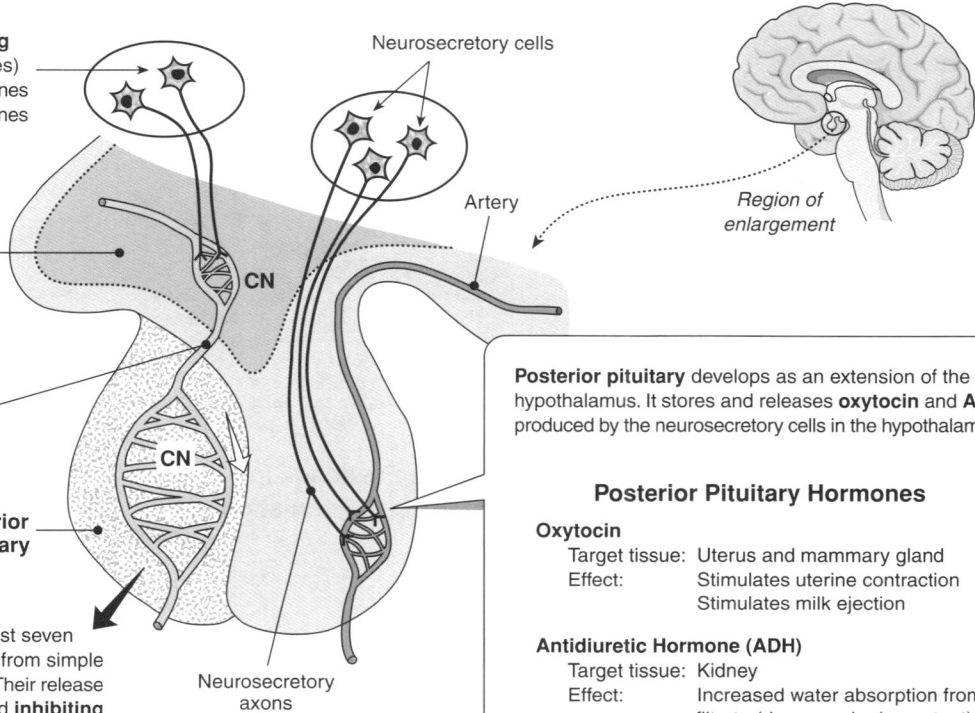

Neurosecretory cells

Artery

Region of enlargement

CN

CN

Neurosecretory axons

Posterior pituitary develops as an extension of the hypothalamus. It stores and releases **oxytocin** and **ADH** produced by the neurosecretory cells in the hypothalamus.

Posterior Pituitary Hormones

Oxytocin
Target tissue: Uterus and mammary gland
Effect: Stimulates uterine contraction
                       Stimulates milk ejection

Antidiuretic Hormone (ADH)
Target tissue: Kidney
Effect: Increased water absorption from
                       filtrate (decreased urine output)

Anterior Pituitary Hormone	Target tissue	Primary action
Growth hormone (GH)	All tissues	Stimulates general tissue growth and protein synthesis
Prolactin	Mammary gland	Stimulates synthesis of milk protein, growth of mammary gland
Thyroid stimulating hormone (TSH)	Thyroid gland	Increases synthesis and secretion of thyroid hormones
Follicle stimulating hormone (FSH)	Seminiferous tubules (male), ovarian follicles (female)	Increases sperm production (male), stimulates follicle maturation (female)
Luteinising hormone (LH)	Interstitial cells in ovary (female), interstitial cells in testis (male)	Secretion of ovarian hormones, ovulation, formation of corpus luteum (female), androgen synthesis and secretion (male)
Melanophore-stimulating hormone	Melanophores and melanocytes	Increases melanin synthesis and dispersal (skin darkening)
Adrenocorticotrophin (ACTH)	Adrenal cortex	Increases synthesis and secretion of hormones from the adrenal cortex

1. Explain how the anterior and posterior pituitary differ with respect to their relationship to the hypothalamus:

_____

_____

2. Explain how the differences between the two regions of the pituitary relate to the nature of their hormonal secretions:

_____

_____

3. Explain how the release of TSH is regulated: _____

_____

_____

Control of Blood Glucose

The endocrine portion of the **pancreas**, the α and β cells of the **islets of Langerhans**, produces two hormones, **insulin** and **glucagon**. Together, these hormones mediate the regulation of blood glucose, maintaining a steady state through **negative feedback**. Insulin promotes a decrease in blood glucose through synthesis of glycogen and cellular uptake of glucose. Glucagon promotes an increase in blood glucose through the breakdown of glycogen and the synthesis of glucose from amino acids. Restoration of normal blood glucose level acts through negative feedback to stop hormone secretion. Regulating blood glucose to within narrow limits allows energy to be available to cells as needed. Extra energy is stored, as glycogen or fat, and is mobilized to meet energy needs as required. The liver is pivotal in these carbohydrate conversions.

Effects of Insulin and Glucagon

The hormones insulin and glucagon together regulate blood glucose levels. When food is unavailable for long periods of time, glucose can be obtained firstly from the metabolism of stored glycogen in the liver and, when this becomes depleted, from stored fats. Data are based on a morning meal with no further food (fasting) for 12 hours or more.

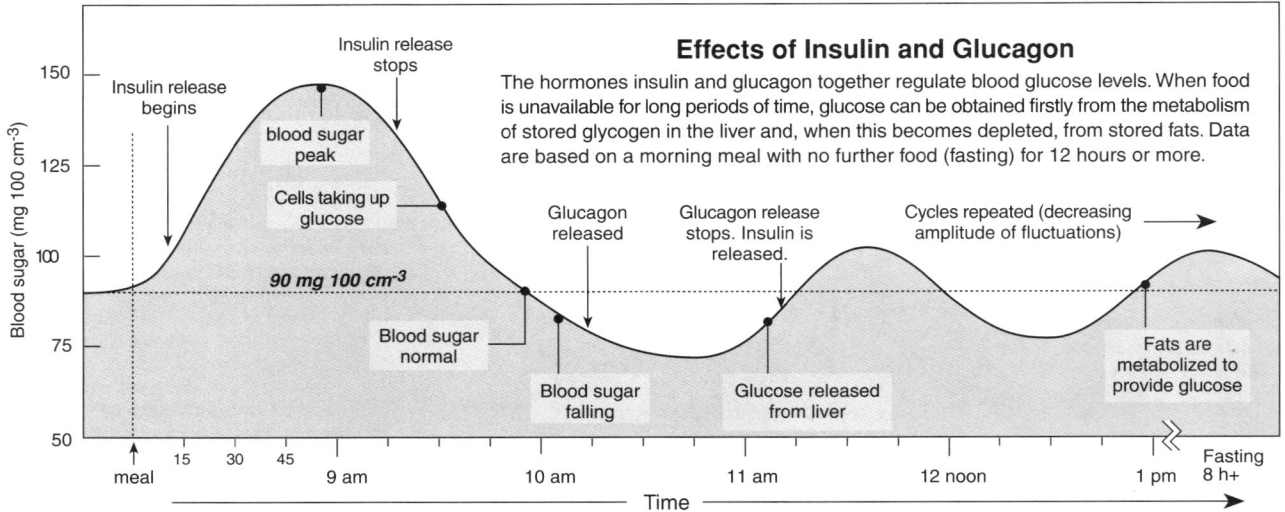

Negative Feedback in Blood Glucose Regulation

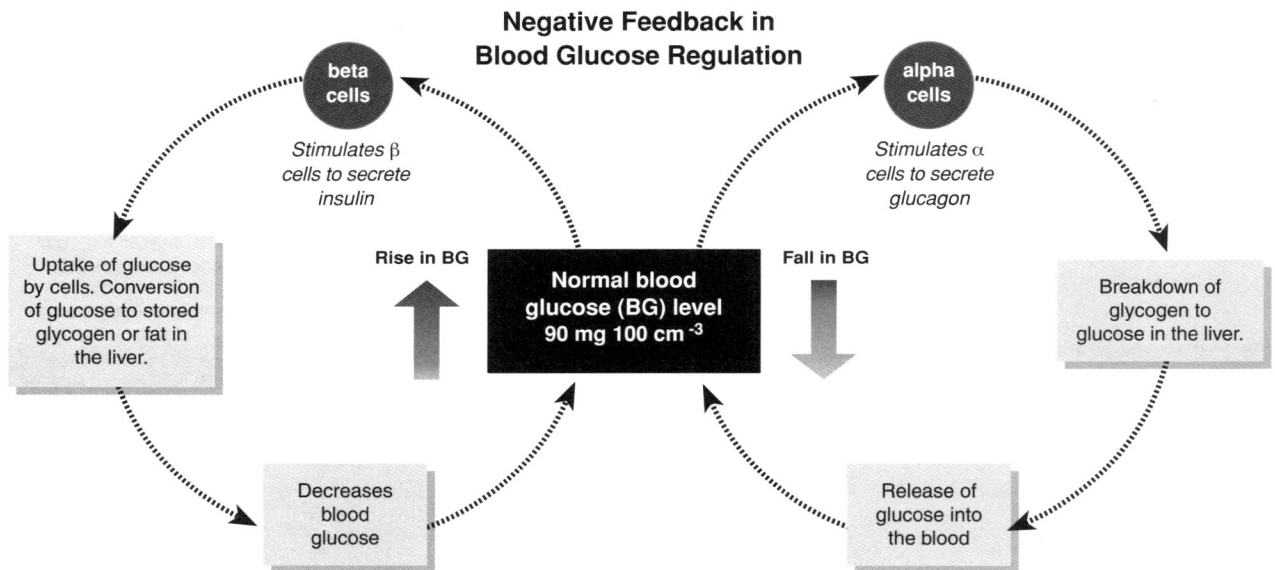

1. (a) Name the stimulus for the release of insulin: _____

   (b) Name the stimulus for the release of glucagon: _____

   (c) Explain how glucagon brings about an increase in blood glucose level: _____

   _____

   (d) Explain how insulin brings about a decrease in blood glucose level: _____

   _____

2. Outline the role of negative feedback in the control of blood glucose: _____

   _____

3. Explain why fats are metabolized after a long period without food: _____

   _____

A2 Thermoregulation in Mammals

In humans and other placental mammals, the temperature regulation centre of the body is in the **hypothalamus**. In humans, it has a 'set point' temperature of 36.7°C. The hypothalamus responds directly to changes in core temperature and to nerve impulses from receptors in the skin. It then coordinates appropriate nervous and hormonal responses to counteract the changes and restore normal body temperature. Like a thermostat, the hypothalamus detects a return to normal temperature and the corrective mechanisms are switched off (negative feedback). Toxins produced by pathogens, or substances released from some white blood cells, cause the set point to be set to a higher temperature. This results in fever and is an important defense mechanism in the case of infection.

Counteracting Heat Loss

Heat promoting center* in the hypothalamus monitors fall in skin or core temperature below 35.8°C and coordinates responses that generate and conserve heat. These responses are mediated primarily through the **sympathetic nerves** of the autonomic nervous system.

Thyroxine (together with adrenaline) **increases metabolic rate**.

Under conditions of *extreme* cold, adrenaline and thyroxine increase the energy releasing activity of the liver. Under normal conditions, the liver is thermally neutral.

Muscular activity (including *shivering*) produces internal heat.

Erector muscles of hairs contract to raise hairs and increase insulating layer of air. Blood flow to skin decreases (**vasoconstriction**).

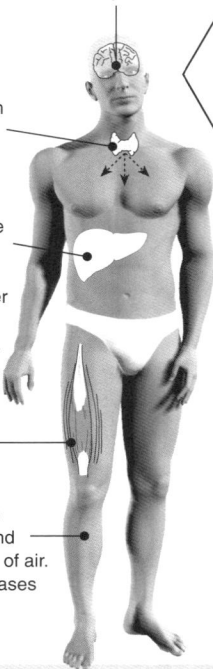

Factors causing heat loss
- Wind chill factor accelerates heat loss through conduction.
- Heat loss due to temperature difference between the body and the environment.
- The rate of heat loss from the body is increased by being wet, by inactivity, dehydration, inadequate clothing, or shock.

Factors causing heat gain
- Gain of heat directly from the environment through radiation and conduction.
- Excessive fat deposits make it harder to lose the heat that is generated through activity.
- Heavy exercise, especially with excessive clothing.

*NOTE: The heat promoting center is also called the "cold centre" and the heat losing center is also called the "hot centre". We have used the terminology descriptive of the activities promoted by the center in each case.

Counteracting Heat Gain

Heat losing center* in the hypothalamus monitors any rise in skin or core temperature above 37.5°C and coordinates responses that increase heat loss. These responses are mediated primarily through the **parasympathetic nerves** of the autonomic nervous system.

Sweating increases. Sweat cools by evaporation.

Muscle tone and **metabolic rate** are decreased. These mechanisms reduce the body's heat output.

Blood flow to skin (**vasodilation**) increases. This increases heat loss.

Erector muscles of hairs relax to flatten hairs and decrease insulating air layer.

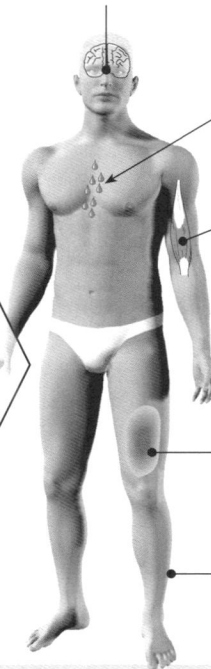

The Skin and Thermoregulation

Thermoreceptors in the dermis (probably free nerve endings) detect changes in skin temperature outside the normal range and send nerve impulses to the hypothalamus, which mediates a response. Thermoreceptors are of two types: **hot thermoreceptors** detect a rise in skin temperature above 37.5°C while the **cold thermoreceptors** detect a fall below 35.8°C. Temperature regulation by the skin involves **negative feedback** because the output is fed back to the skin receptors and becomes part of a new stimulus-response cycle.

Note that the thermoreceptors detect the temperature change, but the hair erector muscles and blood vessels are the **effectors** for mediating a response.

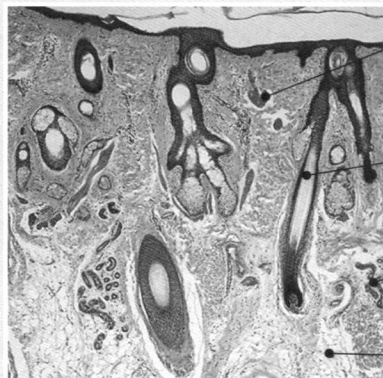

Cross section through the skin of the scalp.

Blood vessels in the dermis dilate (vasodilation) or constrict (vasoconstriction) to respectively promote or restrict heat loss.

Hairs raised or lowered to increase or decrease the thickness of the insulating air layer between the skin and the environment.

Sweat glands produce sweat in response to parasympathetic stimulation from the hypothalamus. Sweat cools through evaporation.

Fat in the subdermal layers insulates the organs against heat loss.

1. State two mechanisms by which body temperature could be reduced after intensive activity (e.g. hard exercise):

   (a) _____   (b) _____

2. Briefly state the role of the following in regulating internal body temperature:

   (a) The hypothalamus: _____

   (b) The skin: _____

   (c) Nervous input to effectors: _____

   (d) Hormones: _____

(🖐 RA②) # The Liver's Homeostatic Role

The liver, located just below the diaphragm and making up 3-5% of body weight, is the largest homeostatic organ. It performs a vast number of functions including production of bile, storage and processing of nutrients, and detoxification of poisons and metabolic wastes. The liver has a **unique double blood supply** and up to 20% of the total blood volume flows through it at any one time. This rich vascularization makes it the central organ for regulating activities associated with the blood and circulatory system. In spite of the complexity of its function, the liver tissue and the liver cells themselves are structurally relatively simple. Features of liver structure and function are outlined below. The histology of the liver in relation to its role is described opposite.

Homeostatic Functions of the Liver

The liver is one of the largest and most complex organs in the body. It has a central role as an organ of homeostasis and performs many functions, particularly in relation to the regulation of blood composition. General functions of the liver are outlined below. Briefly summarized, the liver:

1. Secretes bile, important in emulsifying fats in digestion.
2. Metabolizes amino acids, fats, and carbohydrates (below).
3. Synthesizes glucose from non-carbohydrate sources when glycogen stores are exhausted (gluconeogenesis).
4. Stores iron, copper, and some vitamins (A, D, E, K, B_{12}).
5. Converts unwanted amino acids to urea (urea cycle).
6. Manufactures heparin and plasma proteins (e.g. albumin).
7. Detoxifies poisons or turns them into less harmful forms.
8. Some liver cells phagocytose worn-out blood cells.
9. Synthesizes cholesterol from acetyl coenzyme A.

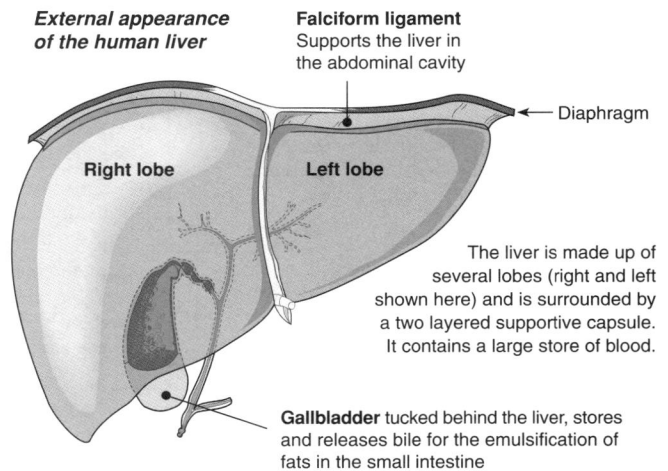

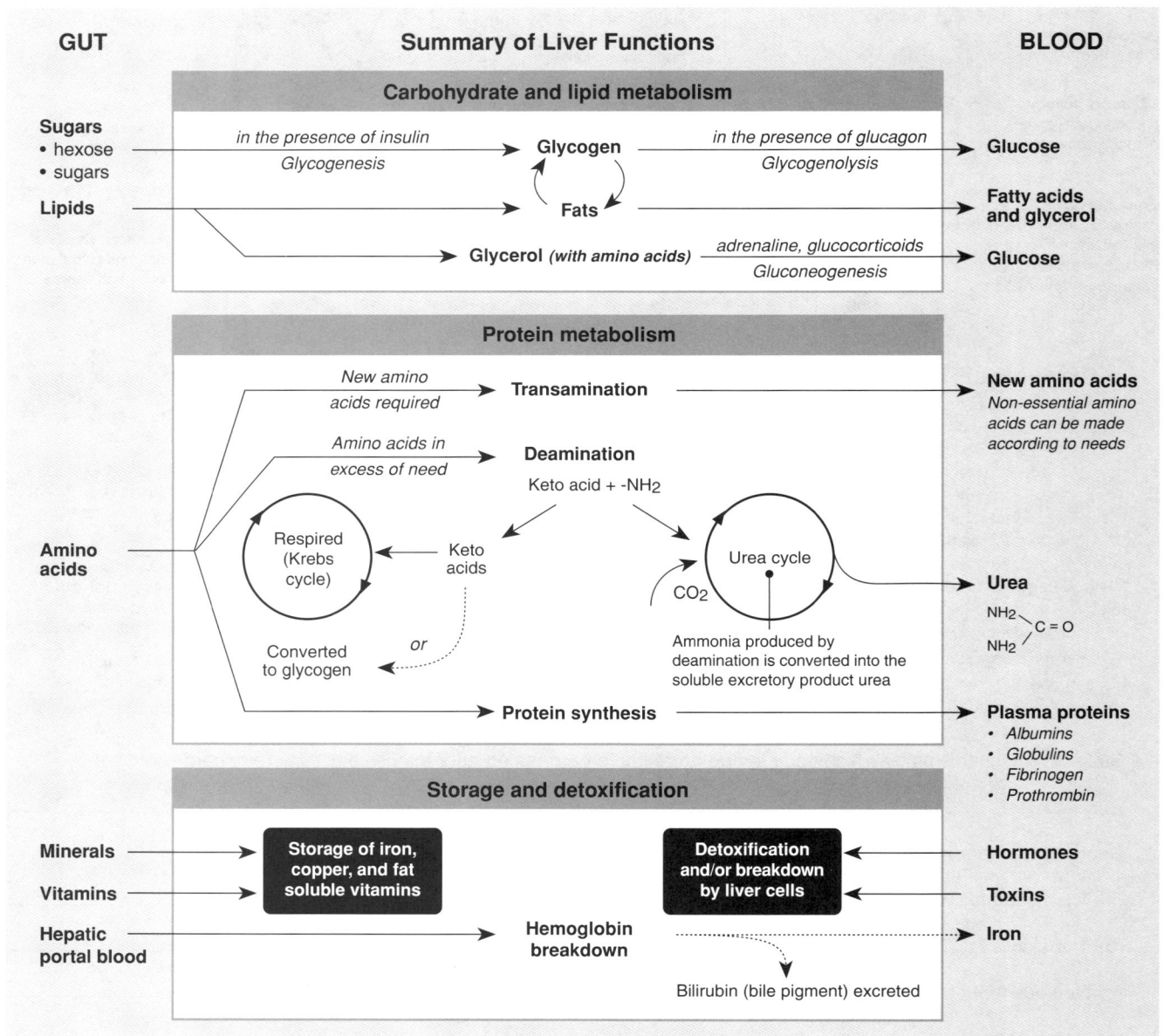

External appearance of the human liver

Falciform ligament
Supports the liver in the abdominal cavity

← Diaphragm

Right lobe   **Left lobe**

The liver is made up of several lobes (right and left shown here) and is surrounded by a two layered supportive capsule. It contains a large store of blood.

Gallbladder tucked behind the liver, stores and releases bile for the emulsification of fats in the small intestine

GUT   Summary of Liver Functions   BLOOD

Carbohydrate and lipid metabolism

Sugars
• hexose
• sugars

in the presence of insulin   *in the presence of glucagon*
Glycogenesis   **Glycogen**   *Glycogenolysis*   → **Glucose**

Lipids   **Fats**   → **Fatty acids and glycerol**

→ **Glycerol** *(with amino acids)* *adrenaline, glucocorticoids* → **Glucose**
                                      Gluconeogenesis

Protein metabolism

New amino acids required → **Transamination** → **New amino acids**
                                                      Non-essential amino acids can be made according to needs

Amino acids in excess of need **Deamination**
                                  Keto acid + -NH_2

Amino acids

Respired (Krebs cycle) ← Keto acids   Urea cycle
                                             CO_2

Converted to glycogen   *or*   → **Urea**
                                             NH_2 — C = O NH_2

Ammonia produced by deamination is converted into the soluble excretory product urea

→ **Protein synthesis** → **Plasma proteins**
                            • Albumins
                            • Globulins
                            • Fibrinogen
                            • Prothrombin

Storage and detoxification

Minerals → **Storage of iron, copper, and fat soluble vitamins**   **Detoxification and/or breakdown by liver cells** ← **Hormones**

Vitamins   ← **Toxins**

Hepatic portal blood → **Hemoglobin breakdown**   → **Iron**

Bilirubin (bile pigment) excreted

The Internal Structure of the Liver

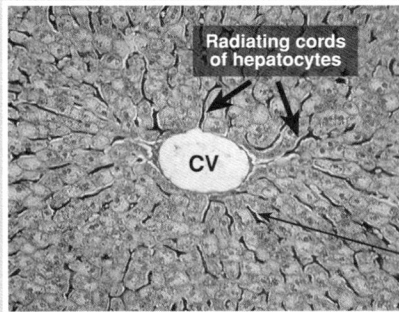

Radiating cords of hepatocytes

CV

Bile ductule

Branch of hepatic portal vein

Branch of hepatic artery

Blood flows towards the central vein

Schematic illustration of the arrangement of lobules and portal tracts in liver tissue

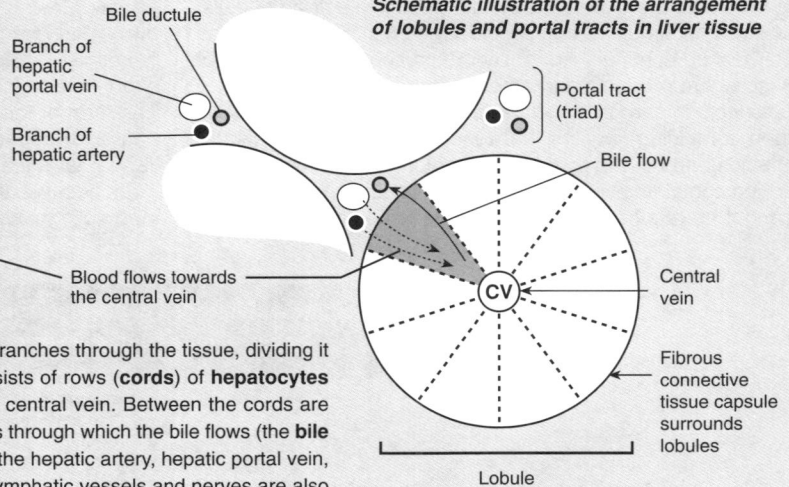

Portal tract (triad)

Bile flow

Central vein

CV

Fibrous connective tissue capsule surrounds lobules

Lobule

The connective tissue capsule covering the liver branches through the tissue, dividing it into functional units called **lobules**. A lobule consists of rows (**cords**) of **hepatocytes** (liver cells) arranged in a radial pattern around a central vein. Between the cords are blood spaces called **sinusoids** and small channels through which the bile flows (the **bile canaliculi**). Between the lobules are branches of the hepatic artery, hepatic portal vein, and bile duct. These form a **portal tract** (triad). Lymphatic vessels and nerves are also found in this area (not shown). **The photograph above** shows most of a liver lobule in a human, illustrating the central vein, the cords of liver cells, and sinusoids (dark spaces).

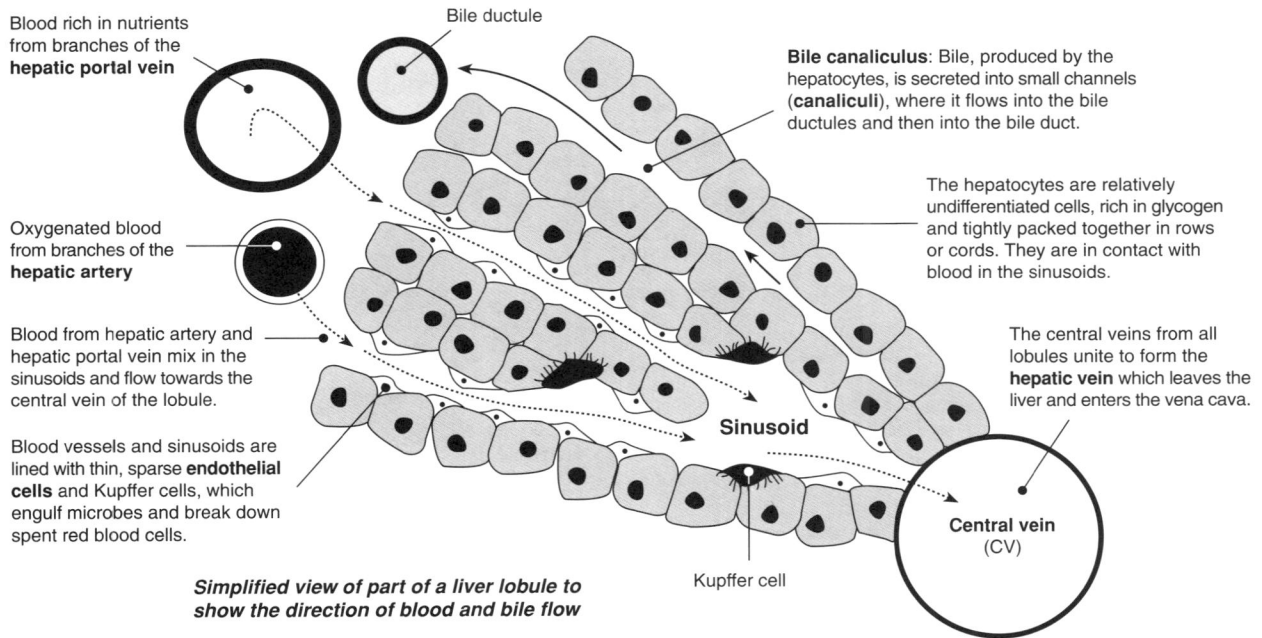

Blood rich in nutrients from branches of the **hepatic portal vein**

Bile ductule

Bile canaliculus: Bile, produced by the hepatocytes, is secreted into small channels (**canaliculi**), where it flows into the bile ductules and then into the bile duct.

Oxygenated blood from branches of the **hepatic artery**

The hepatocytes are relatively undifferentiated cells, rich in glycogen and tightly packed together in rows or cords. They are in contact with blood in the sinusoids.

Blood from hepatic artery and hepatic portal vein mix in the sinusoids and flow towards the central vein of the lobule.

The central veins from all lobules unite to form the **hepatic vein** which leaves the liver and enters the vena cava.

Blood vessels and sinusoids are lined with thin, sparse **endothelial cells** and Kupffer cells, which engulf microbes and break down spent red blood cells.

Sinusoid

Central vein (CV)

Simplified view of part of a liver lobule to show the direction of blood and bile flow

Kupffer cell

1. State the two sources of blood supply to the liver, describing the primary physiological purpose of each supply:

    (a) Supply 1: _____ Purpose: _____

    (b) Supply 2: _____ Purpose: _____

2. Briefly describe the role of the following structures in liver tissue:

    (a) Bile canaliculi: _____

    (b) Phagocytic Kupffer cells: _____

    (c) Central vein: _____

    (d) Sinusoids: _____

3. Briefly explain three important aspects of **either** protein metabolism **or** carbohydrate metabolism in the liver:

    (a) _____

    (b) _____

    (c) _____

Nitrogenous Wastes in Animals

Waste materials are generated by the metabolic activity of cells. If allowed to accumulate, they would reach toxic concentrations and so must be continually removed. Excretion is the process of removing waste products and other toxins from the body. Waste products include carbon dioxide and water, and the nitrogenous (nitrogen containing) wastes that result from the breakdown of amino acids and nucleic acids. The simplest breakdown product of nitrogen containing compounds is ammonia, a small molecule that cannot be retained for long in the body because of its high

toxicity. Most aquatic animals excrete ammonia immediately into the water where it is washed away. Other animals convert the ammonia to a less toxic form that can remain in the body for a short time before being excreted via special excretory organs. The form of the excretory product in terrestrial animals (urea or uric acid) depends on the type of organism and its life history. Terrestrial animals that lay eggs produce uric acid rather than urea, because it is non-toxic and very insoluble. It remains as an inert solid mass in the egg until hatching.

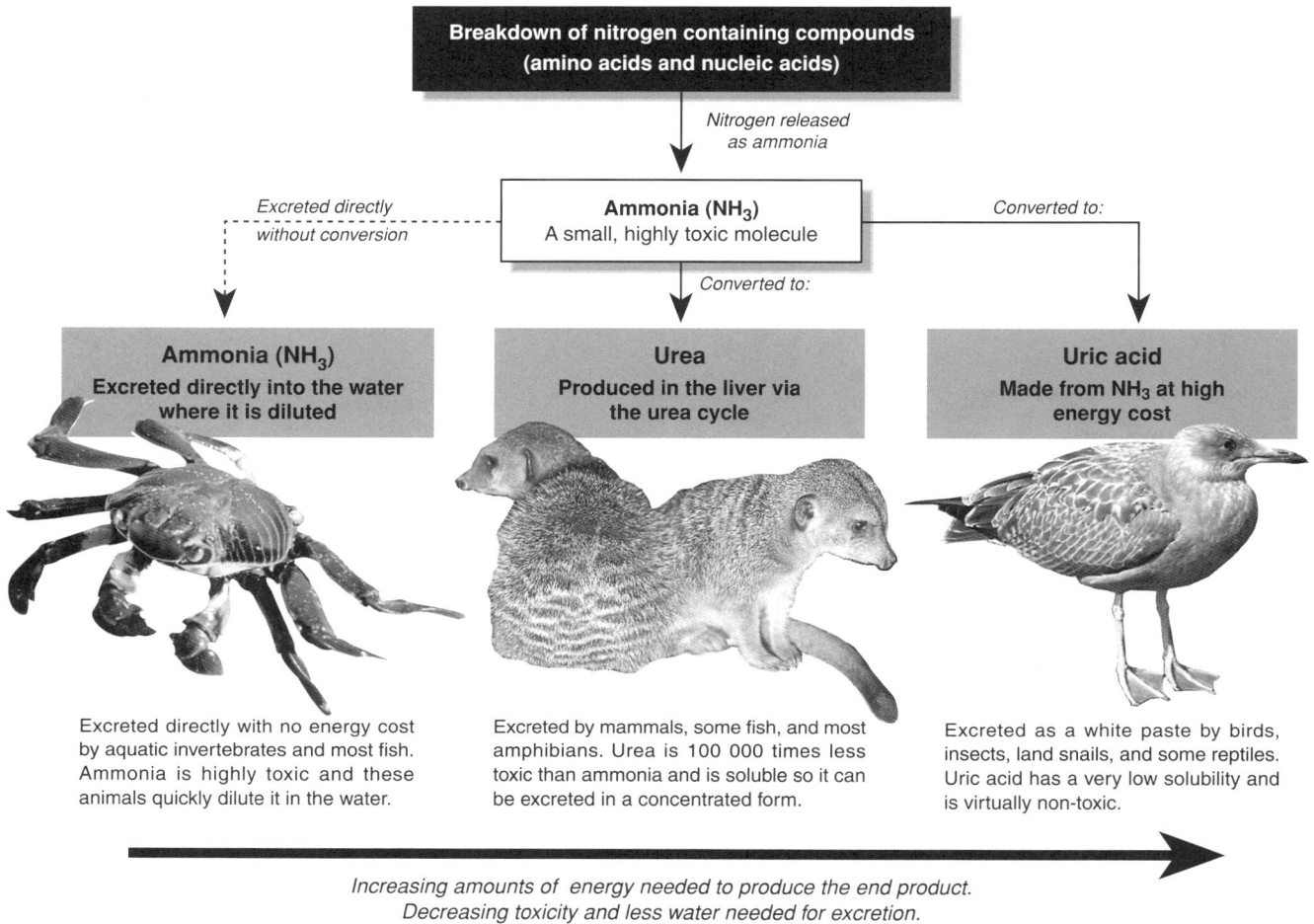

Breakdown of nitrogen containing compounds (amino acids and nucleic acids)

Nitrogen released as ammonia

Ammonia (NH_3)
A small, highly toxic molecule

Excreted directly without conversion

Converted to:

Converted to:

Ammonia (NH_3)
Excreted directly into the water where it is diluted

Urea
Produced in the liver via the urea cycle

Uric acid
Made from NH_3 at high energy cost

Excreted directly with no energy cost by aquatic invertebrates and most fish. Ammonia is highly toxic and these animals quickly dilute it in the water.

Excreted by mammals, some fish, and most amphibians. Urea is 100 000 times less toxic than ammonia and is soluble so it can be excreted in a concentrated form.

Excreted as a white paste by birds, insects, land snails, and some reptiles. Uric acid has a very low solubility and is virtually non-toxic.

Increasing amounts of energy needed to produce the end product.
Decreasing toxicity and less water needed for excretion.

1. Name the main source of nitrogen containing wastes in animals: _____

_____

2. Explain why organisms in aquatic environments excrete ammonia directly, without first converting it to a less toxic form:

_____

_____

3. Explain the advantages in having an excretory product that is both soluble and of low toxicity (e.g. urea):

_____

_____

4. Uric acid is very energy expensive to make. Explain the advantage it has over urea as an excretory product:

_____

_____

_____

RA ③ Invertebrate Excretory Systems

Metabolism produces toxic by-products. The most troublesome of these to eliminate from the body is nitrogenous waste from the metabolism of proteins and nucleic acids. The simplest and most common type of excretory organs, widely distributed in invertebrates, are simple tubes (**protonephridia** and **nephridia**) opening to the outside through a pore. The **malpighian tubules** of insects are highly efficient, removing nitrogenous wastes from the blood, and also functioning in **osmoregulation**. Note that all three forms of nitrogenous waste are represented here: ammonia (flatworms, annelids), urea (annelids), and uric acid (insects).

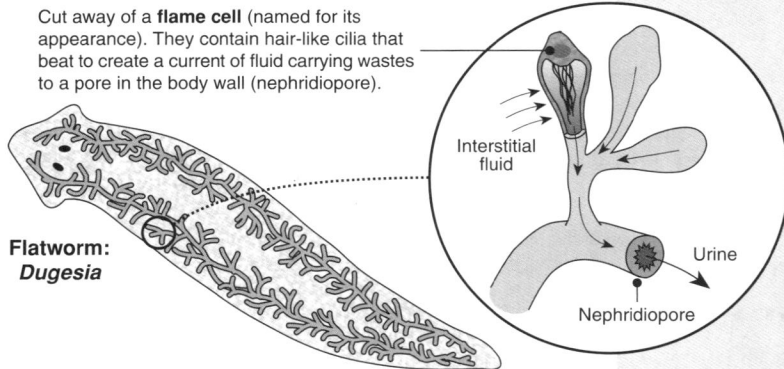

Cut away of a **flame cell** (named for its appearance). They contain hair-like cilia that beat to create a current of fluid carrying wastes to a pore in the body wall (nephridiopore).

Interstitial fluid

Urine

Nephridiopore

Flatworm: *Dugesia*

Platyhelminthes (flatworms)

Excretory system: **protonephridia**

Protonephridia are very simple excretory structures. Each protonephridium comprises a branched tubule ending in a number of blind capillaries called **flame cells**. **Ammonia** is excreted directly into the moist environment. Flatworms do not have a circulatory system or fluid-filled inner body spaces. They use their branching network of flame cells to regulate the composition of the fluid bathing the cells (interstitial fluid). Interstitial fluid enters the flame cell and is propelled along the tubule, away from the blind end, by beating cilia. Tubules merge into ducts that expel the urine through **nephridiopores**.

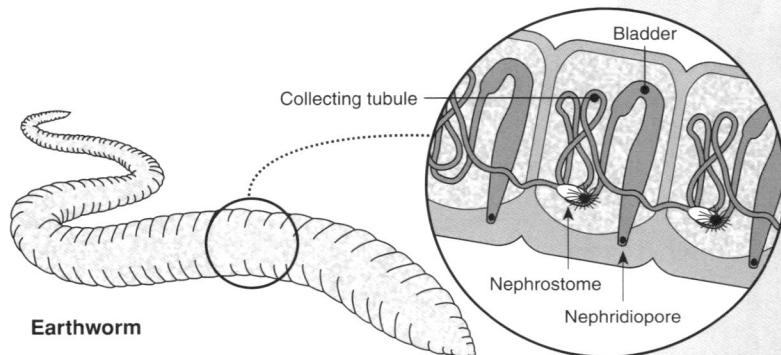

Bladder

Collecting tubule

Nephrostome

Nephridiopore

Earthworm

Annelids (segmented worms)

Excretory system: **nephridia**

In earthworms, each segment has a pair of excretory organs called **nephridia**, which drain the next segment in front. Fluid enters the nephrostome and passes through the collecting tubule. These tubules are surrounded by a capillary network of blood vessels (not shown here) which recover valuable salts from the developing urine. The collecting tubule empties into a storage bladder which expels the dilute urine (a mix of **ammonia** and **urea**) to the outside through the nephridiopore.

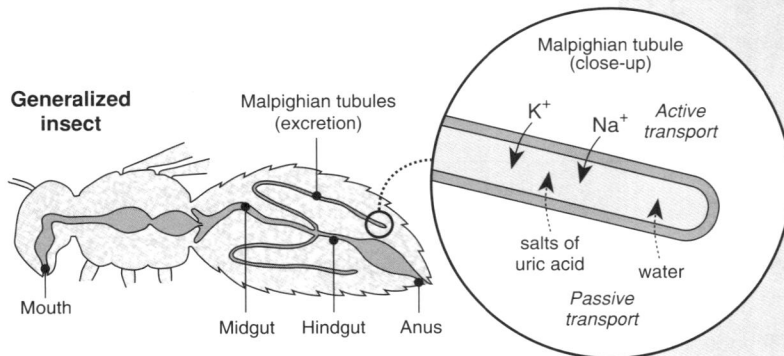

Malpighian tubule (close-up)

Generalized insect

Malpighian tubules (excretion)

K^+

Na^+ Active transport

salts of uric acid

water

Passive transport

Mouth

Midgut Hindgut Anus

Insects

Excretory system: **malpighian tubules**

Insects have two to several hundred **malpighian tubules** projecting from the junction of the midgut and hindgut. They bathe in the clear fluid (hemolymph) of the insect's body cavity where they actively pump K^+ and Na^+ into the tubule. Water, uric acid salts, and several other substances follow by passive transport. Water and some ions are reabsorbed in the hindgut, while **uric acid** precipitates out as a paste and is passed out of the anus along with the fecal material. The ability to conserve water by excreting solid uric acid has enabled insects to colonize very arid environments.

1. For each of the following, name the organs for excreting nitrogenous waste and state the form of the waste product:

   (a) Flatworm: _____ Waste: _____

   (b) Insect: _____ Waste: _____

   (c) Earthworm: _____ Waste: _____

2. Explain briefly how insects concentrate their nitrogenous waste into a paste: _____

   _____

   _____

3. For one of the above animals, relate the form of the excretory product to the environment in which the animal lives:

   _____

   _____

Waste Products in Humans

A 3

In humans and other mammals, a number of organs are involved in the excretion of the waste products of metabolism: mainly the kidneys, lungs, skin, and gut. The liver is a particularly important organ in the initial treatment of waste products. particularly the breakdown of hemoglobin and the formation of urea from ammonia. Excretion should not be confused with the elimination or egestion of undigested and unabsorbed food material from the gut. Note that the breakdown products of hemoglobin (blood pigment) are excreted in bile and pass out with the feces, but they are not the result of digestion.

CO$_2$
Water

Lungs
Excretion of carbon dioxide with some loss of water.

Liver
Produces urea from ammonia in the urea cycle. Breakdown of hemoglobin in the liver produces the bile pigments e.g. bilirubin.

Gut
Excretion of bile pigments in the feces. Also loses water, salts, and carbon dioxide.

Bladder
Storage of urine before it is expelled to the outside.

Skin
Excretion of water, carbon dioxide, hormones, salts and ions, and small amounts of urea as sweat.

All cells
All the cells that make up the body carry out cellular respiration; they break down glucose to release energy and produce the waste products, carbon dioxide and water.

Excretion In Humans

In mammals, the kidney is the main organ of excretion, although the skin, gut, and lungs also play important roles. As well as ridding the body of nitrogenous wastes, the kidney is also able to excrete many unwanted poisons and drugs that are taken in from the environment. Usually these are ingested with food or drink, or inhaled. As long as these are not present in toxic amounts, they can usually be slowly eliminated from the body.

Kidney
Filtration of the blood to remove urea. Unwanted ions, particularly hydrogen (H$^+$) and potassium (K$^+$), and some hormones are also excreted by the kidneys. Some poisons and drugs (e.g. penicillin) are also excreted by active secretion into the urine. Water is lost in excreting these substances and extra water may be excreted if necessary.

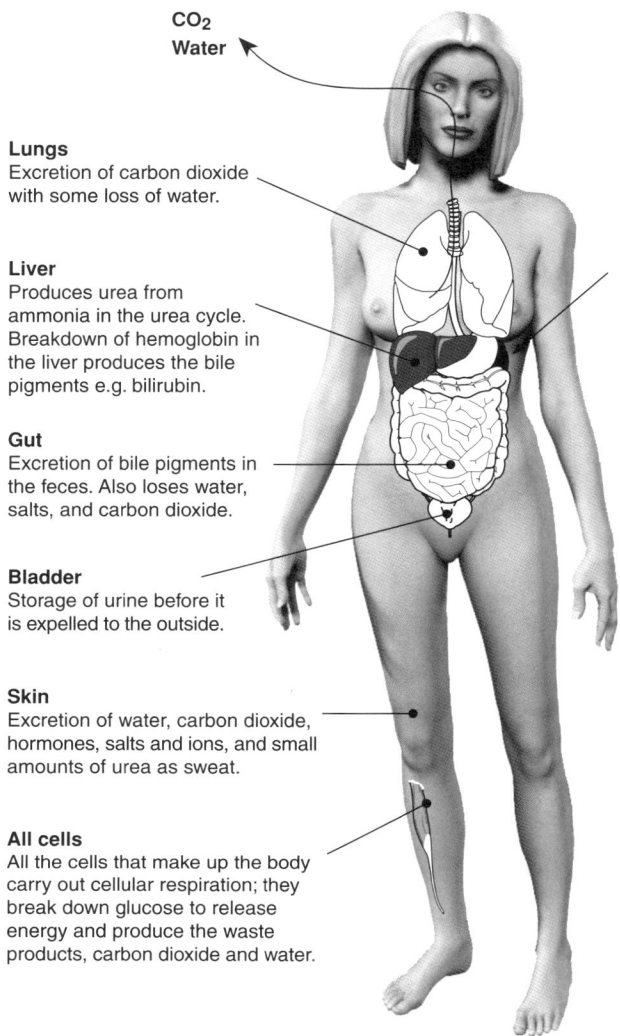

Substance	Origin*	Organ(s) of excretion
Carbon dioxide		
Water		
Bile pigments		
Urea		
Ions (K+, H+)		
Hormones		
Poisons		
Drugs		

* Origin refers to from where in the body each substance originates

1. In the diagram above, complete the table summarizing the origin of excretory products and the main organ or organs of excretion involved for each substance.

2. Explain the role of the liver in excretion, even though it is not an excretory organ itself: _____

_____

_____

3. Tests for pregnancy are sensitive to an excreted substance in the urine. Suggest what this substance might be:

_____

4. People sometimes suffer renal (kidney) failure, where the kidneys cease to operate and can no longer produce urine. Given that the kidney rids the body of excessive ions and water, as well as nitrogenous wastes, describe the probable effects of kidney failure. You may wish to discuss this as a group. HINT: Consider the effects of salt and water retention, and the effect of high salt levels on blood pressure and on the heart.

_____

_____

_____

Water Budget in Mammals

DA 2

Water loss is a major problem for most mammals. The degree to which urine can be concentrated (and water conserved) depends on the number of nephrons present in the kidney and the length of the loop of Henle. The highest urine concentrations are found in mammals from desert environments, such as kangaroo rats (below). Under normal conditions these animals will not drink water, obtaining most of their water from the metabolic break down of food instead.

Regulation of Water Balance in Humans

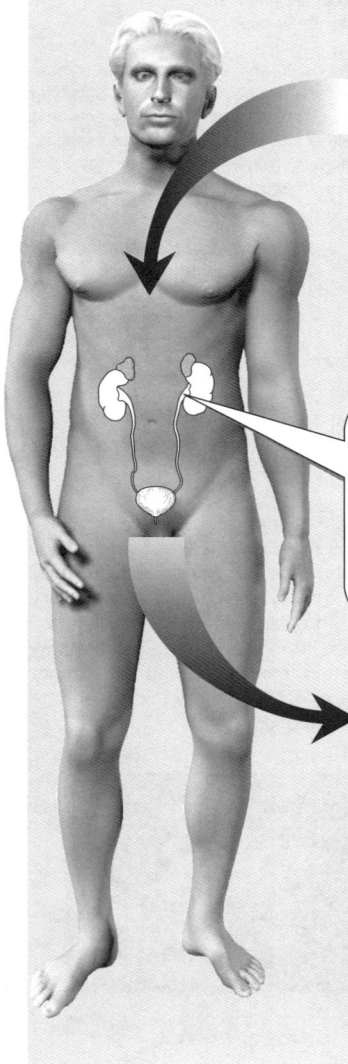

Water gains

A typical 70 kg male human requires 2.4 liters of water daily. Of this, 63% is obtained through drinking fluids, 21% from food, and the remaining 16% as a result of metabolism.

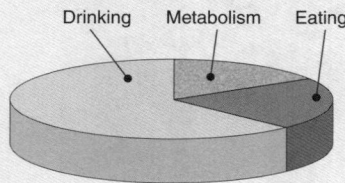

Drinking   Metabolism   Eating

The water content and solute concentration of the body fluids is maintained at a relatively constant level by **osmoregulation**. Osmoregulation is achieved primarily by regulating the volume and composition of the urine.

Water losses

The same adult male will lose 63% of body water through urination, 16.5% as a result of breathing, 16.5% through the skin, and 4% in feces.

Urine/plasma concentration ratio = 4

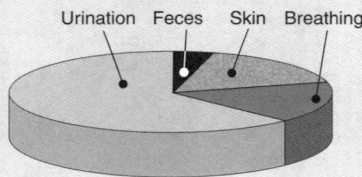

Urination   Feces   Skin   Breathing

Adaptations of Arid Adapted Rodents

Most desert-dwelling mammals are adapted to tolerate a low water intake. Arid adapted rodents, such as jerboas and kangaroo rats, conserve water by reducing losses to the environment and obtain the balance of their water needs from the oxidation of dry foods (respiratory metabolism). The table below shows the water balance in a kangaroo rat after eating 100 g of dry pearl barley. Note the high urine to plasma concentration ratio relative to that of humans.

Water balance in a kangaroo rat *(Dipodomys spectabilis)*	
Water gains	**Water losses**
Absorbed from food 6.0 cm³	Breathing 43.9 cm³
From metabolism 54.0 cm³	Urination 13.5 cm³
	Defecation 2.6 cm³

Urine/plasma concentration ratio = 17

Adaptations of kangaroo rats

Kangaroo rats, and other arid-adapted rodents, tolerate long periods without drinking, meeting their water requirements from the metabolism of dry foods. They dispose of nitrogenous wastes with very little output of water and they neither sweat nor pant to keep cool.

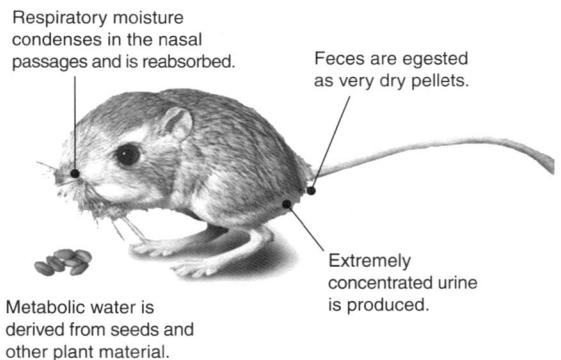

Respiratory moisture condenses in the nasal passages and is reabsorbed.

Feces are egested as very dry pellets.

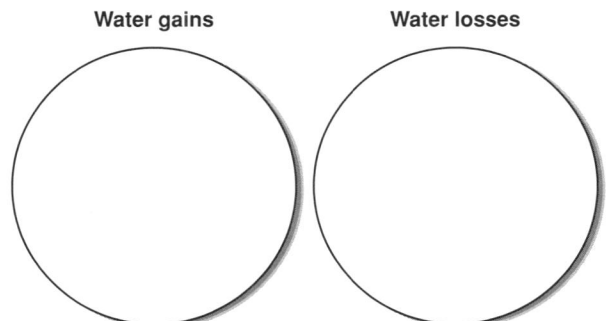

Metabolic water is derived from seeds and other plant material.

Extremely concentrated urine is produced.

---

1. Explain why most mammals need to drink regularly: _____

   _____

2. Using the tabulated data for the kangaroo rat (above), graph the water gains and losses in the space provided below.

3. Describe three physiological adaptations of desert adapted rodents to low water availability:

   (a) _____

   _____

   (b) _____

   _____

   (c) _____

   _____

Water gains   **Water losses**

Excretion and Osmoregulation

A 2

Many aspects of metabolism e.g. enzyme activity, membrane transport, and nerve conduction, are dependent on particular concentrations of ions and metabolites. To achieve this balance, the salt and water content of the internal environment must be regulated. The mechanisms for obtaining, retaining and eliminating water and solutes (*osmoregulation* and *excretion*) in marine, freshwater and terrestrial organisms vary considerably. These differences reflect not only the constraints of the particular environment but the evolutionary inheritance of the organism.

Mechanisms against water loss

- Behavior and habitat choice
- Waxy cuticle of insects
- Oily secretion from glands in the skin
- Insulating fur or feathers
- Dry, scaly skin of reptiles

Large losses from airways except in arthropods.

Metabolism of stored fat (as in the camel's hump) can be used to provide water. In camels, the hump disappears as the fat is used up.

Drinks water
Eats food

The efficient kidneys of mammals produce a concentrated urine containing **urea**. Most reptiles, birds, insects and land snails excrete nitrogenous waste as uric acid (requires very little water but more energy in its excretion).

Stomach

Water is extracted from the diet, even when this is dry food (e.g. seeds).

Some insects, frogs, and arachnids (e.g. scorpions) can take up water directly from the atmosphere.

Water loss by evaporation from skin or exoskeleton.

Water lost in feces and urine.

Animals adapted to arid regions and those that hibernate can tolerate large losses of body weight as they metabolize their fat reserves to produce water.

····▶ Losses
——▶ Gains

The primary water balance problem for terrestrial animals is water loss. Water is required for all metabolism, including the metabolism of food and the disposal of waste products. Mammals must **drink water** regularly, although some are able to survive for long periods without drinking by generating water from the metabolism of fats. Mammals have efficient **kidneys** and produce a concentrated urine high in urea. In most land arthropods, water is conserved by limiting losses to the environment. The **chitinous exoskeleton** itself does not reduce water loss much but the waxy cuticle of insects retards water loss very effectively. The respiratory structures of arthropods are chitinous, internal tubes and there is little loss from these. All animals show behavioral adaptations to limiting water loss by seeking out damper environments. This is particularly important for desert animals and for arthropods with little resistance to dehydration.

Tolerance of water loss and burrowing behavior in desert frogs.

Behavioral adaptations, efficient kidneys, and thick fur in kangaroos

Humidity seeking behavioral adaptations in woodlice.

Chitinous exoskeleton with waxy, waterproof cuticle in insects.

1. (a) Explain the role of the waxy cuticle on the exoskeleton of insects: _____

_____

(b) Explain why aquatic arthropods lack this cuticle: _____

_____

2. Explain the role of behavior in preventing water loss in some animals: _____

_____

3. Explain the advantages to a desert animal of retreating to a burrow during the day: _____

_____

4. In terms of water balance in aquatic vertebrates, explain the difference between marine and freshwater environments:

_____

_____

Marine Environments

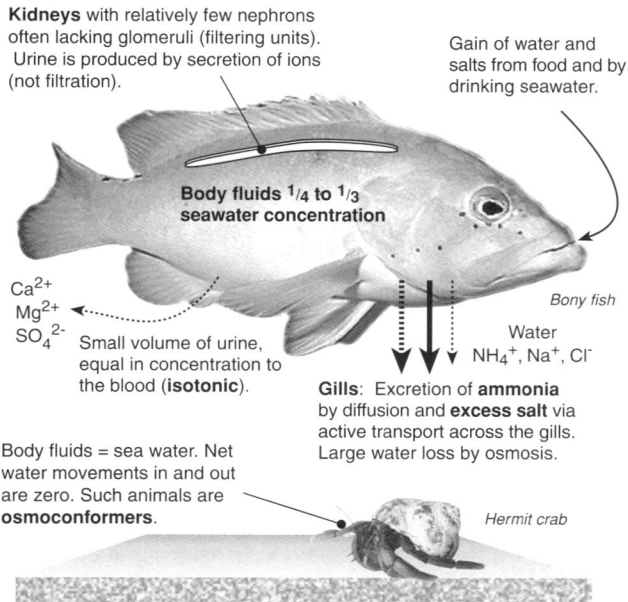

Kidneys with relatively few nephrons often lacking glomeruli (filtering units). Urine is produced by secretion of ions (not filtration).

Gain of water and salts from food and by drinking seawater.

Body fluids $1/4$ to $1/3$ seawater concentration

Ca^{2+}
Mg^{2+}
SO_4^{2-} Small volume of urine, equal in concentration to the blood (**isotonic**).

Bony fish

Water
NH_4^+, Na^+, Cl^-

Gills: Excretion of **ammonia** by diffusion and **excess salt** via active transport across the gills. Large water loss by osmosis.

Body fluids = sea water. Net water movements in and out are zero. Such animals are **osmoconformers**.

Hermit crab

Freshwater Bony Fish

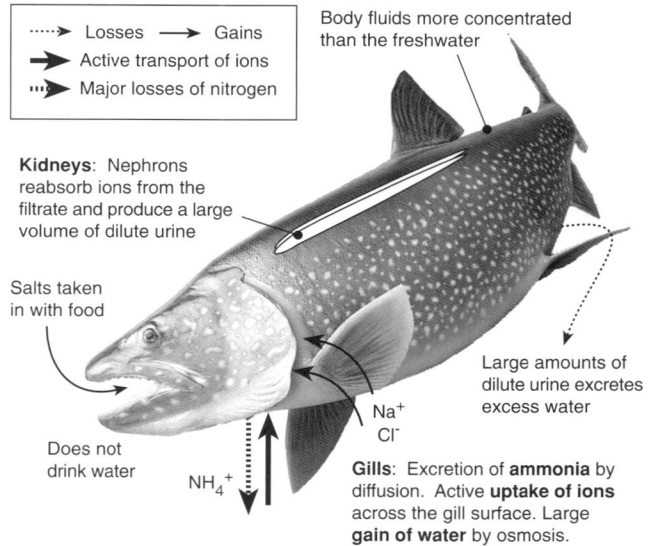

-----> Losses ——> Gains
——> Active transport of ions
····> Major losses of nitrogen

Body fluids more concentrated than the freshwater

Kidneys: Nephrons reabsorb ions from the filtrate and produce a large volume of dilute urine

Salts taken in with food

Large amounts of dilute urine excretes excess water

Does not drink water

Na^+
Cl^-
NH_4^+

Gills: Excretion of **ammonia** by diffusion. Active **uptake of ions** across the gill surface. Large **gain of water** by osmosis.

Most marine invertebrates do not regulate salt and water balance; they are **osmoconformers** and their body fluids fluctuate with changes in the environment. Animals, such as fish and marine mammals, that regulate their salt and water fluxes are termed **osmoregulatory**. Bony fish lose water osmotically and counter the loss by drinking salt water and excreting the excess salt. Marine elasmobranchs generate osmotic concentrations in their body fluids similar to seawater by tolerating high urea levels. Excess salt from the diet is excreted via a salt gland in the rectum. Marine mammals produce a urine that is high in both salt and urea. Some intertidal animals tolerate frequent dilutions of normal seawater and may actively take up salts across the gill surfaces to compensate for water gain and salt loss.

Freshwater animals have body fluids that are osmotically more concentrated than the water they live in. Water tends to enter their tissues by osmosis and must be expelled to avoid flooding the body. Simple protozoans use contractile vacuoles to collect the excess water and expel it. Other invertebrates expel water and nitrogenous wastes using simple nephridial organs. Bony fish and aquatic arthropods produce dilute urine (containing ammonia) and actively take up salts across their gills (in aquatic insects these are often non-respiratory, anal gills). The kidneys of freshwater bony fish also reabsorb salts from the filtrate through active transport mechanisms. These ion gains are important because some loss of valuable ions occurs constantly as a result of the high urine volume.

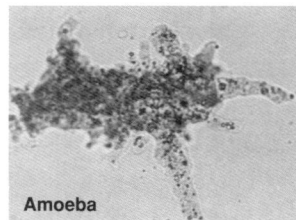

Most marine invertebrates, like these sea anemones, are osmoconformers.

Elasmobranchs maintain an osmotic concentration similar to seawater.

Contractile vacuoles in protozoans collect excess water and expel it.

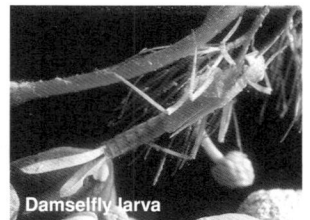

In aquatic insect larvae, the gills actively take up salts from the water.

5. Describe how freshwater animals can compensate for salt losses that occur when they excrete large amounts of water:

_____

6. (a) Explain what is meant by an **osmoregulator** and give an example: _____

_____ **Example**: _____

(b) Explain what is meant by an **osmoconformer** and give an example: _____

_____ **Example**: _____

7. Freshwater and marine bony fish have contrasting excretion and osmoregulation problems. Explain why:

(a) Marine bony fish drink vast quantities of salt water: _____

(b) Freshwater bony fish do not drink water at all: _____

8. Describe the salt and water balance problems faced by migrating fish as they move from a marine environment to freshwater (as happens during spawning runs in salmon):

_____

_____

The Human Urinary System

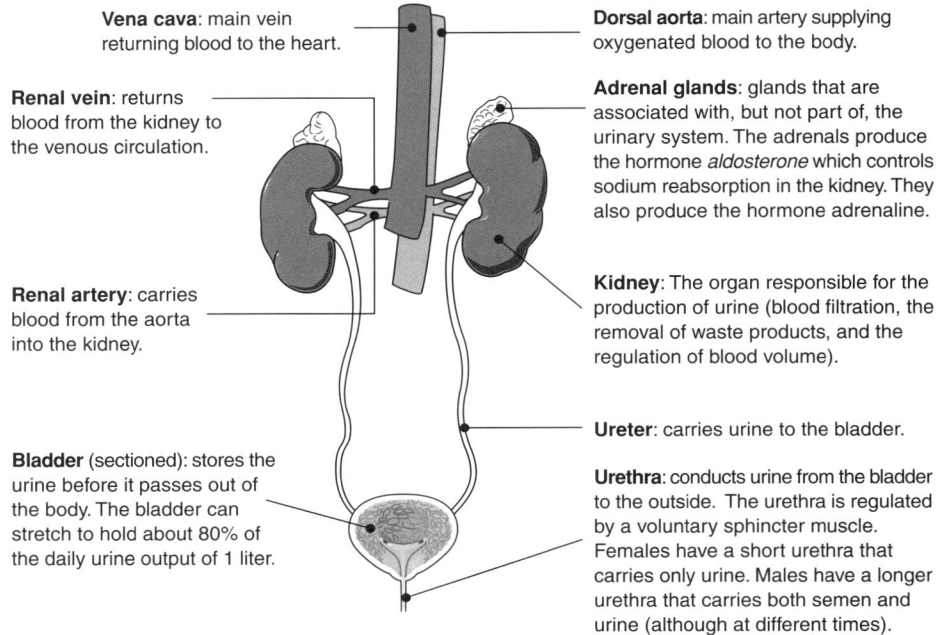

A 2

The human urinary system consists of the kidneys and bladder, and their associated blood vessels and ducts. The kidneys have a plentiful blood supply from the renal artery which branches off the aorta. The blood is filtered by the kidneys to form urine. Urine is produced continuously, passing along the ureters to the bladder, a hollow muscular organ lined with smooth muscle and special, stretchable epithelium. Each day the kidneys filter about 180 liters of fluid. Most of this is reabsorbed, leaving a daily urine output of about 1 liter. By adjusting the amount of water, ions, and other materials excreted, the kidneys help to maintain the body's internal chemical balance. All vertebrates have kidneys, but their efficiency in producing a concentrated urine varies considerably. Fish cannot produce a urine that is more concentrated than their blood, whereas mammalian kidneys are very efficient, producing a urine that is concentrated to varying degrees depending on requirements.

The Human Urinary System

Position of the urinary system in a human.

Vena cava: main vein returning blood to the heart.

Renal vein: returns blood from the kidney to the venous circulation.

Renal artery: carries blood from the aorta into the kidney.

Bladder (sectioned): stores the urine before it passes out of the body. The bladder can stretch to hold about 80% of the daily urine output of 1 liter.

Dorsal aorta: main artery supplying oxygenated blood to the body.

Adrenal glands: glands that are associated with, but not part of, the urinary system. The adrenals produce the hormone *aldosterone* which controls sodium reabsorption in the kidney. They also produce the hormone adrenaline.

Kidney: The organ responsible for the production of urine (blood filtration, the removal of waste products, and the regulation of blood volume).

Ureter: carries urine to the bladder.

Urethra: conducts urine from the bladder to the outside. The urethra is regulated by a voluntary sphincter muscle. Females have a short urethra that carries only urine. Males have a longer urethra that carries both semen and urine (although at different times).

Internal structure of the human kidney

Nephrons are arranged with all the collecting ducts pointing towards the ureter.

Outer **cortex**

Inner **medulla**

The urine collects in a space near the ureter called the **renal pelvis** before flowing out of the kidney via the ureter.

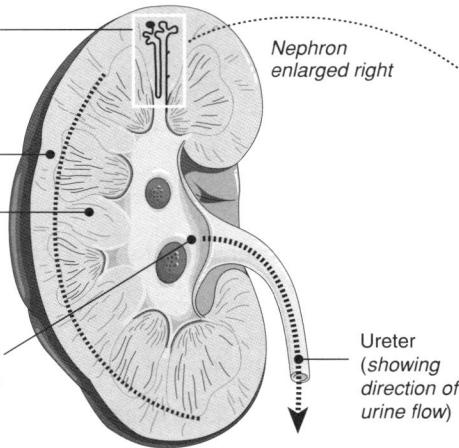

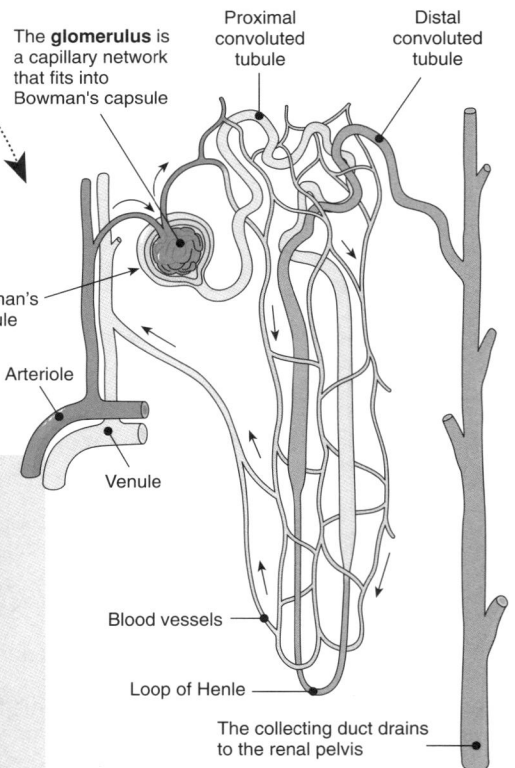

Nephron enlarged right

Ureter (*showing direction of urine flow*)

The **glomerulus** is a capillary network that fits into Bowman's capsule

Bowman's capsule

Arteriole

Venule

Proximal convoluted tubule

Distal convoluted tubule

Blood vessels

Loop of Henle

The collecting duct drains to the renal pelvis

Nephron structure

Human kidneys are about 100-120 mm long and 25 mm thick. Each kidney is surrounded by a layer of fatty tissue and two layers of fibrous connective tissue. These layers protect the kidneys and anchor them in position. The inner tissue appears striated (striped), due to alignment of the **nephrons** and surrounding blood vessels. It is the precise alignment of the nephrons in the kidney that makes it possible to fit in all the filtering units required.

Each kidney contains more than 1 million nephrons. They are **selective filter elements**, which regulate blood composition and excrete wastes. The initial urine is formed by **filtration** in the glomerulus. Blood enters the capillaries of the glomerulus, where water and solutes are forced through the capillary walls to form the filtrate. The filtrate is modified as it passes through the tubules of the nephron and the final urine passes out the ureter.

Fluid is forced through the capillaries of the **glomerulus**, forming a filtrate similar to blood but lacking cells and proteins.

Summary of activities in the kidney nephron

Urine is formed in the kidney nephron by ultrafiltration of the blood and subsequent modification of the filtrate to add or remove substances (e.g. ions). The processes involved in urine formation are summarized below for each region of the nephron: glomerulus, proximal convoluted tubule, loop of Henle, distal convoluted tubule, and collecting duct.

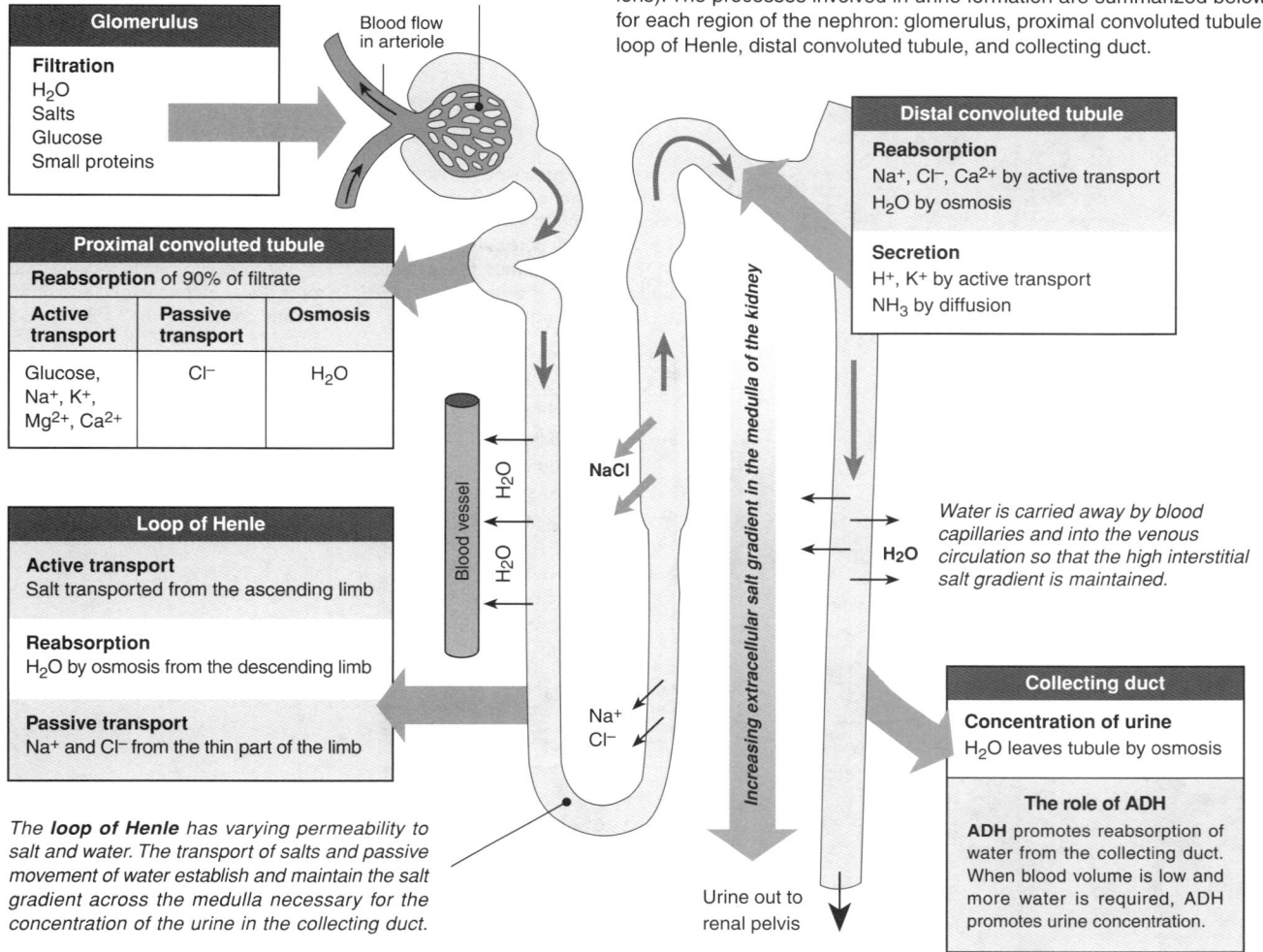

Glomerulus

Filtration
H_2O
Salts
Glucose
Small proteins

Blood flow in arteriole

Distal convoluted tubule

Reabsorption
Na^+, Cl^-, Ca^{2+} by active transport
H_2O by osmosis

Secretion
H^+, K^+ by active transport
NH_3 by diffusion

Proximal convoluted tubule

Reabsorption of 90% of filtrate

Active transport	Passive transport	Osmosis
Glucose, Na^+, K^+, Mg^{2+}, Ca^{2+}	Cl^-	H_2O

Blood vessel

H_2O

H_2O

NaCl

Increasing extracellular salt gradient in the medulla of the kidney

Water is carried away by blood capillaries and into the venous circulation so that the high interstitial salt gradient is maintained.

H_2O

Loop of Henle

Active transport
Salt transported from the ascending limb

Reabsorption
H_2O by osmosis from the descending limb

Passive transport
Na^+ and Cl^- from the thin part of the limb

Na^+
Cl^-

Collecting duct

Concentration of urine
H_2O leaves tubule by osmosis

The role of ADH
ADH promotes reabsorption of water from the collecting duct. When blood volume is low and more water is required, ADH promotes urine concentration.

The **loop of Henle** has varying permeability to salt and water. The transport of salts and passive movement of water establish and maintain the salt gradient across the medulla necessary for the concentration of the urine in the collecting duct.

Urine out to renal pelvis

1. Give a concise definition of a nephron and summarize its role in excretion: _____

_____

2. Explain the importance of the following in the production of urine in the kidney nephron:

   (a) Filtration of the blood at the glomerulus: _____

   _____

   (b) Active secretion: _____

   _____

   (c) Reabsorption: _____

   _____

   (d) Osmosis: _____

   _____

3. (a) Identify the purpose of the salt gradient in the kidney: _____

   _____

   (b) Explain how this salt gradient is produced: _____

   _____

RA 2 **Control of Kidney Function**

Variations in salt and water intake, and in the environmental conditions to which we are exposed, contribute to fluctuations in blood volume and composition. The primary role of the kidneys is to regulate blood volume and composition (including the removal of nitrogenous wastes), so that homeostasis is maintained. This is achieved through varying the volume and composition of the urine. Two hormones, antidiuretic hormone and aldosterone, are involved in the process.

Brain

ADH
ACTS ON KIDNEY

Variation in urine output

Control of Blood Volume

Osmoreceptors in the hypothalamus of the brain detect a fall in the concentration of water in the blood. They stimulate **neurosecretory cells in the hypothalamus** to synthesize and secrete the hormone ADH (antidiuretic hormone).

ADH passes from the hypothalamus to the posterior pituitary where it is released into the blood. ADH increases the permeability of the kidney collecting duct to water so that more water is reabsorbed and urine volume decreases.

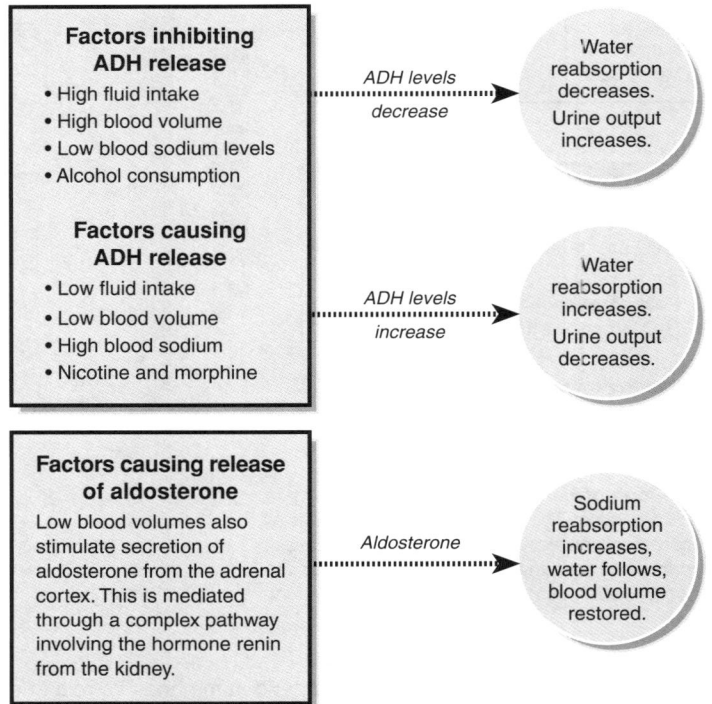

Factors inhibiting ADH release
• High fluid intake
• High blood volume
• Low blood sodium levels
• Alcohol consumption

ADH levels decrease ·······▶

Water reabsorption decreases. Urine output increases.

Factors causing ADH release
• Low fluid intake
• Low blood volume
• High blood sodium
• Nicotine and morphine

ADH levels increase ·······▶

Water reabsorption increases. Urine output decreases.

Factors causing release of aldosterone
Low blood volumes also stimulate secretion of aldosterone from the adrenal cortex. This is mediated through a complex pathway involving the hormone renin from the kidney.

Aldosterone ·······▶

Sodium reabsorption increases, water follows, blood volume restored.

1. (a) *Diabetes insipidis* is a type of diabetes, caused by a lack of ADH. Based on what you know of the role of ADH in kidney function describe the symptoms of this disease:

_____

_____

(b) Suggest how this disorder might be treated: _____

_____

2. Explain why alcohol consumption (especially to excess) causes dehydration and thirst: _____

_____

_____

3 (a) State the effect of aldosterone on the kidney nephron:_____

(b) Explain the net result of this effect: _____

4. Explain how negative feedback mechanisms operate to regulate blood volume and urine output:

_____

_____

_____

Kidney Dialysis

A ②

A dialysis machine is a machine designed to remove wastes from the blood. It is used when the kidneys fail, or when blood acidity, urea, or potassium levels increase much above normal. In kidney dialysis, blood flows through a system of tubes composed of semi-permeable membranes. Dialysis fluid (dialysate) has a composition similar to blood except that the concentration of wastes is low. It flows in the opposite direction to the blood on the outside of the dialysis tubes. Consequently, waste products like urea diffuse from the blood into the dialysis fluid, which is constantly replaced. The dialysis fluid flows at a rate of several 100cm^3 per minute over a large surface area. For some people dialysis is an ongoing procedure, but for others dialysis just allows the kidneys to rest and recover.

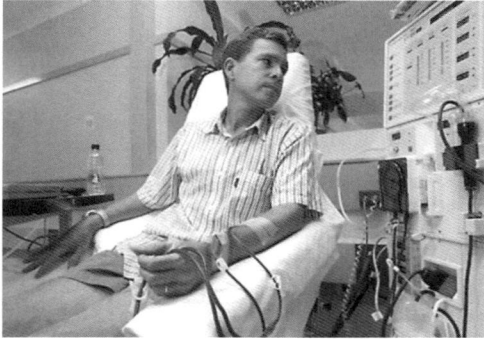

A patient undergoing kidney dialysis at a hospital.

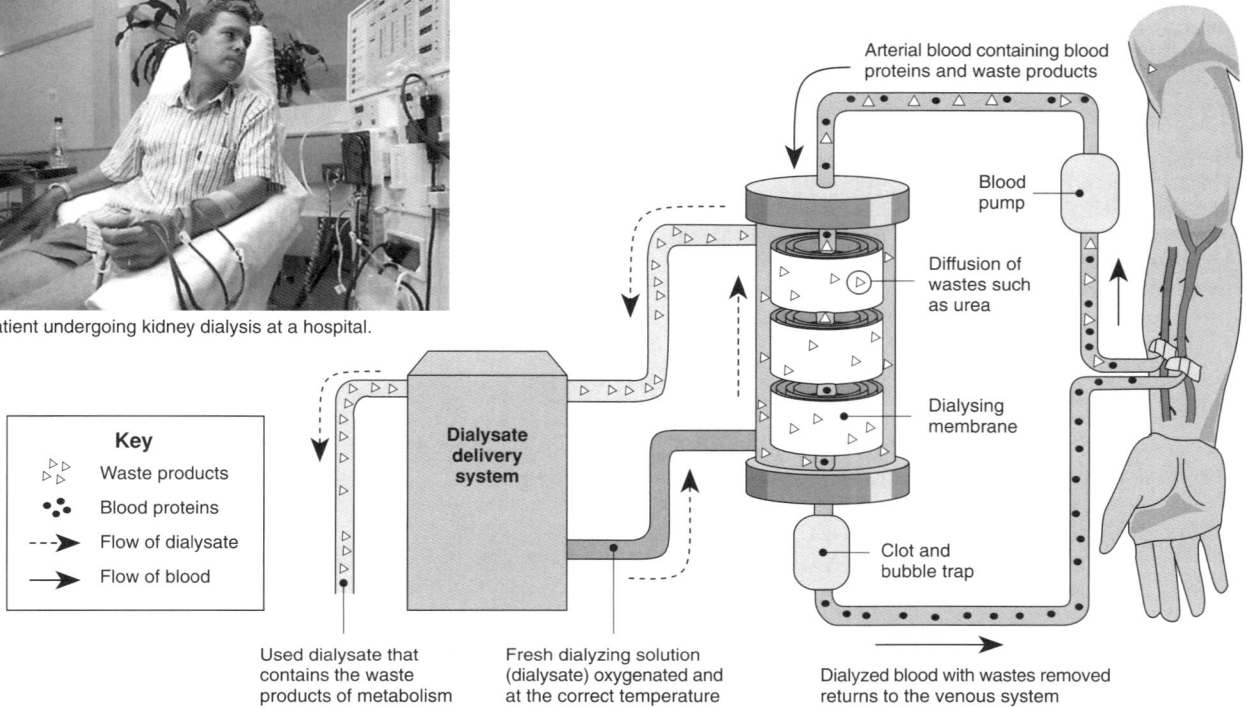

Arterial blood containing blood proteins and waste products

Blood pump

Diffusion of wastes such as urea

Dialysing membrane

Clot and bubble trap

Dialyzed blood with wastes removed returns to the venous system

Key

▷ ▷ Waste products

•:• Blood proteins

- - -> Flow of dialysate

——> Flow of blood

Dialysate delivery system

Used dialysate that contains the waste products of metabolism

Fresh dialyzing solution (dialysate) oxygenated and at the correct temperature

1. In kidney dialysis, explain why the dialyzing solution is constantly replaced rather than being recirculated:

_____

_____

2. Explain why ions such as potassium and sodium, and small molecules like glucose do not diffuse rapidly from the blood into the dialyzing solution along with the urea:

_____

_____

3. Explain why the urea passes from the blood into the dialyzing solution: _____

_____

4. Describe the general transport process involved in dialysis: _____

_____

5. Give a reason why the dialyzing solution flows in the opposite direction to the blood: _____

_____

_____

6. Explain why a clot and bubble trap is needed after the blood has been dialyzed but before it re-enters the body:

_____

_____

_____

Nerves, Muscles, and Movement

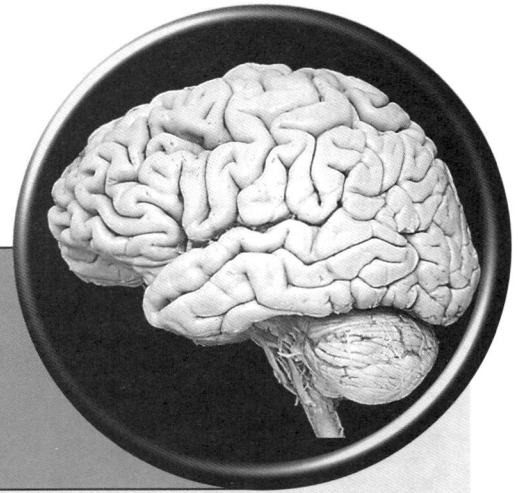

IB SL
Complete nos:
1, 5

IB HL
Complete nos:
1, 5-6, 11, 13-14, 16-
17, 19, 31-32, 35,
38-39 Extension:
15, 36-37

IB Options
Complete nos:
OPT B: 5, 11, 17, 19, 33-
35, 38-46 OPT E: SL/HL:
7-8, 12, 23-25, 27-30 HL:
9-10, 18, 20, 22

AP Biology
Complete nos:
1-46
Some numbers
extension as
appropriate

Learning Objectives

☐ 1. Compile your own glossary from the **KEY WORDS** displayed in **bold type** in the learning objectives below.

Animal nervous systems (pages 272-274)

☐ 2. Describe the structure of nervous systems in some invertebrates, including cnidarians (nerve net), echinoderms (nerve ring with radial nerves), flatworms (nerve ladders), and annelids and arthropods (ventral nerve cord and segmental ganglia).

☐ 3. Describe the trend towards increasing **cephalization** in the taxa listed above and relate it to increasingly complex behavior and greater sensory development.

☐ 4. Compare the **brain structure** of different vertebrates and relate any differences to the animal's evolutionary history, its environment, and its sensory requirements.

The mammalian nervous system (page 275)

☐ 5. Recall that the nervous system consists of the **central nervous system** (CNS) and the **peripheral nerves,** and is composed of specialized **neurons** that carry electrical impulses rapidly around the body.

The central nervous system (pages 275-276)

☐ 6. Outline the general organization of the human nervous system, distinguishing between the **central nervous system** (CNS) and the **peripheral nervous system** (PNS). Identify the functional role of each division.

☐ 7. Draw the gross structure of the **brain**, including the **medulla oblongata, cerebellum, hypothalamus, pituitary gland,** and **cerebral hemispheres**. State one function for each of these named parts.

The peripheral nervous system (pages 275, 277)

☐ 8. Recognize the two divisions of the PNS: **sensory division** and **motor division**. Know that the motor division of the PNS is divided into **autonomic** and **somatic nervous systems** and state the role of each.

☐ 9. Recognize the components of the autonomic nervous system (**ANS**): the **sympathetic** and **parasympathetic neurons** (nervous systems). Describe their roles and recognize that they have generally **antagonistic** effects.

☐ 10. Explain the effects of the sympathetic and parasympathetic systems with reference to:
(a) Control of pupil diameter and/or tear production.
(b) Control of bladder emptying or anal control.
(c) Control of heart rate and force of contraction.
Understand that some reflex autonomic activity can be modified by conscious control, and provide an example.

Neuron structure and function (pages 278-280)

☐ 11. Describe, using diagrams, the structure and function of different types of **neurons**: **motor** (**effector**) and **sensory neurons**, and **relay neurons** (**interneurons**).

☐ 12. Define the term **reflex** and describe the adaptive value of reflexes. Using an annotated diagram, describe the functioning of a simple spinal **reflex arc** involving three neurons. Outline examples of reflexes, including the **pain withdrawal reflex** and one other spinal reflex, and the pupil reflex and one other **cranial reflex**. Discuss the use of the pupil reflex in testing for brain death.

☐ 13. Explain how the **resting potential** of a neuron is established. Include reference to the movement of Na^+ and K^+, the differential permeability of the membrane, and the generation of an **electrochemical gradient**.

☐ 14. Describe the generation of the **nerve impulse** with reference to the change in **membrane permeability** of the nerve leading to **depolarization**.

☐ 15. Describe how an **action potential** is propagated along a myelinated nerve by **saltatory conduction**. Include reference to the **all-or-nothing** nature of the impulse, and role of **myelin** and the **nodes of Ranvier**.

☐ 16. Describe impulse conduction in a **non-myelinated** nerve. Appreciate the difference in speed of conduction between myelinated and non-myelinated fibers.

Synapses (pages 281-283)

☐ 17. Identify the role of synapses in the mammalian nervous system. Describe the basic features of a **cholinergic synapse** (as seen using electron microscopy).

☐ 18. With reference to **acetylcholine** and **noradrenaline**, recognize that the synapses of the PNS are classified according the **neurotransmitter** involved.

☐ 19. Explain the principles of synaptic transmission, e.g. at a **cholinergic synapse**. Include reference to the arrival of the **action potential** at the **presynaptic terminal**, the role of Ca^{2+} and **neurotransmitter** (e.g. acetylcholine), the depolarization of the **post-synaptic neuron**, and subsequent removal of the neurotransmitter.

☐ 20. Explain how presynaptic neurons can encourage or inhibit postsynaptic transmission. Appreciate the role of synapses in **unidirectionality**, allowing the interconnection of nerve pathways, and **integration** through **summation** and **inhibition**.

☐ 21. Describe the basic structure and function of the **neuromuscular junction**. Recognize the neuro-muscular junction as a specialized cholinergic synapse.

☐ 22. Describe the effects of neurotransmitters and **psycho-active** drugs on the nervous system and behavior, as illustrated by pain and the action of **endorphins** and **enkephalins**, and Parkinson's and the role of excitatory and inhibitory psychoactive drugs and **dopamine**.

Perception of stimuli (pages 284-287)

☐ 23. Identify internal and external **stimuli** and describe examples of sensory receptors that respond to these, as illustrated by: **mechanoreceptors, photoreceptors, chemoreceptors,** and **thermoreceptors**.

□ 24. Describe the way in which sensory receptors act as **biological transducers**.

□ 25. Describe the structure and function of the photo-receptor cells (**rods** and **cones**) in the retina, including:
(a) The role of the photosensitive pigments.
(b) Use in bright and dim light.
(c) The basis of monochromatic and trichromatic vision.
(d) The neural basis for differences in **sensitivity** and **acuity** between rods and cones.

□ 26. Using examples, describe how a range of senses is used to provide an animal with information about its environment. Identify the **stimulus** to which each of these senses responds.

The human eye *(pages 288-289)*

□ 27. Using a diagram, describe the basic structure and function of the human **eye**. Include reference to the transmission and refraction of light and the focusing of the image (including **accommodation**).

□ 28. Annotate a diagram of the **retina**, including identification of the **rods**, **cones**, **bipolar neurons**, **ganglion cells**, and the direction of light movement.

□ 29. Describe the structure and function of the photo-receptor cells (**rods** and **cones**) in the retina, including the role of the photosensitive pigments, photoreception in bright and dim light, the basis of monochromatic and trichromatic vision, and the neural basis for differences in **sensitivity** and **acuity** between rods and cones.

□ 30. Outline how visual stimuli are processed in the retina, including reference to generator potentials in the rod or cone cells and action potentials in the **optic nerve**. In as much detail as required, explain the role of the **visual cortex** in processing visual information.

Animal locomotion *(pages 290-291)*

□ 31. Outline the diversity of locomotion in animals as illustrated by: *movement in an earthworm, swimming in bony fish, flying in birds, and walking in an arthropod.*

The human skeleton *(pages 292-294)*

□ 32. Describe the roles of the **nerves**, (skeletal) **muscles**, and **bones** in producing movement or locomotion.

□ 33. Identify the components of the **musculoskeletal system** and the main regions of the human skeleton, including reference to **axial** and **appendicular** parts.

□ 34. Describe the structure of a **long bone**, including the features conferring strength and shock absorption.

□ 35. Using an annotated diagram, describe the structure

and function of the **elbow joint**, including reference to: **cartilage**, **synovial fluid**, **tendons**, **ligaments**, and named **bones** and **antagonistic muscles**.

□ 36. Describe the ultrastructure of compact (hard) bone, identifying the following: *periosteum, osteoblasts, osteocytes, matrix, lacunae,* and *Haversian canals.*

Muscle and movement *(pages 295-297, 300-301)*

□ 37. Distinguish between **cardiac muscle**, **skeletal** (striated) **muscle**, and **smooth muscle**, with reference to their gross structure, physiology, and functional role.

□ 38. Describe the structure of **skeletal muscle fibers**, as seen with electron microscopy. Identify the **sarcomere** and **myofibrils,** and describe the composition and arrangement of the (**myo**)**filaments**.

□ 39. Explain how skeletal muscle contracts. As required, discuss the role of **actin** and **myosin filaments**, **ATP**, the **sarcoplasmic reticulum**, and **calcium ions**.

□ 40. Explain the differences in **speed** and **stamina** of **fast twitch** and **slow twitch** (**tonic**) **fibers**.

□ 41. Describe how movement is achieved in terms of **antagonistic muscle action**. Identify the role of reflex inhibition in the movement of antagonistic muscle pairs.

Muscles and energy *(pages 298-299)*

□ 42. Identify sources of energy for muscle contraction. With respect to the energy yield and waste products, compare **aerobic** and **anaerobic** pathways as sources of ATP for muscle contraction.

□ 43. Explain **muscle fatigue** and relate it to the increase in **blood lactate**, depletion of carbohydrate supplies, and decreased pH. Explain how these changes provide the stimulus for increased breathing (and heart) rates.

□ 44. Explain what is meant by **oxygen debt**. Describe the ultimate fate of blood lactate and explain how the oxygen debt is repaid after intense exercise.

Fitness and training *(pages 200-201, 300-302)*

□ 45. Describe the principles of **training** with reference to: **specificity**, **progressive overload**, **intensity**, and **duration**. Describe measures of **fitness**. Discuss the causes, prevention, and treatment of **injuries**. Debate the use of performance enhancing drugs in sport.

□ 46. Explain the effects of training on human physiology:
• *The effect on the cardiovascular system: blood flow, heart (pulse) rate,* **stroke volume**, **cardiac output**.
• *The effect on the respiratory system: breathing rate,* **tidal volume**, *residual volume, ventilation efficiency.*
• *The muscles: development of specific fiber types.*

Textbooks

See the 'Textbook Reference Grid' on pages 8-9 for textbook page references relating to material in this topic.

Supplementary Texts

See pages 4-6 for additional details of these texts:
■ Adds, J. *et al.* 2001. **Respiration and Coordination** (NelsonThornes), pp. 14-33, 140-157.
■ Clegg, C.J., 1998. **Mammals: Structure and Function** (John Murray), pp. 58-69, 72-77.

Internet

See pages 10-11 for details of how to access **Bio Links** from our web site: **www.thebiozone.com**. From Bio Links, access sites under the topics: **ANIMAL BIOLOGY**: • Anatomy and physiology • WebAnatomy *... & others* **Neuroscience**: • Basic

neural processes • The human eye *... & others* **Support & Movement**: • Bone and joint sources • Energy production during physical activity • Exercise physiology • Muscles *... & others*

Periodicals

See page 6 for details of publishers of periodicals:
STUDENT'S REFERENCE

■ **Skeletal Muscle: Is Bigger Always Better?** Biol. Sci. Rev., 11(2) Nov. 1998, pp. 36-39. *The structure of muscle and physiology of contraction.*
■ **A Pacinian Corpuscle** Biol. Sci. Rev., 12(3) Jan. 2000, pp. 33-34. *An account of the structure and operation of a common pressure receptor.*
■ **Before your Very Eyes** New Scientist 15 March 1997 (Inside Science). *Eye structure, and the perception and processing of visual information.*
■ **Making the Connection** Biol. Sci. Rev.,13(3) January 2001, pp. 10-13. *The central nervous system, neurotransmitters, and synapses.*

■ **The Autonomic Nervous System** Bio. Sci. Rev. 11(4) March 1999, pp. 30-34. *The structure and function of the autonomic nervous system.*
■ **The Nervous System** (series) New Scientist, 10 June 1989, 11 Nov. 1989, 29 June 1991 (Inside Science). *Nervous system structure and function.*
■ **Roots of Fatigue** New Scientist, 21 May 1994, (Inside Science). *Muscle contraction, fatigue, and the role of ATP and calcium in muscle function.*

TEACHER'S REFERENCE

■ **Bodyworks** New Scientist, 13 December 1997, pp. 38-41. *The physiology of muscles and microtubules: what makes our muscles move.*
■ **Acting Out Muscle Contraction** The Am. Biology Teacher, 65(2), Feb. 2003, pp. 128-132. *An experiment to demonstrate muscle contraction.*
■ **Demonstrating the Stretch Reflex** The Am. Biology Teacher, 62(7), Sept., 2000, pp. 503-507. *Demonstrating muscular coordination and control.*

Software and video resources are now provided in the Teacher Resource Handbook

Invertebrate Nervous Systems

Animals respond to stimuli in order to survive. In one-celled organisms the entire cell surface is sensitive to stimuli and the cell responds by moving towards or away from the stimulus. More sophisticated responses require more complex nervous control. Some invertebrates (e.g. *Hydra*) have only a loosely organized nervous system. Others have more complex systems with a nerve cord, a brain, and usually a head with sensory structures. The nerve cord is on the ventral (lower) surface in arthropods and annelids whereas it is on the dorsal (upper surface) in vertebrates. In insects and vertebrates, the nervous and endocrine systems work together to regulate many activities. This allows both rapid and slower, longer lasting responses.

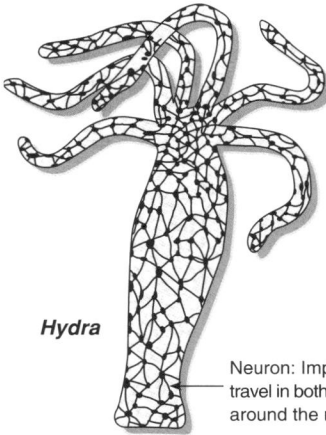

Hydra

Neuron: Impulses travel in both directions around the net

Nerve Net (left)

EXAMPLES: *Cnidarians, e.g. Hydra*

A loosely organized system of nerves with no central control (no central nervous system). The neurons are located in the outer ectoderm and mesoglea (middle jelly-like layer). The strength of the nervous system response to a stimulus depends directly on the stimulus strength. The sensory receptors are cells within the outer body layer, the effectors that bring about body movement are the contractile elements of individual cells.

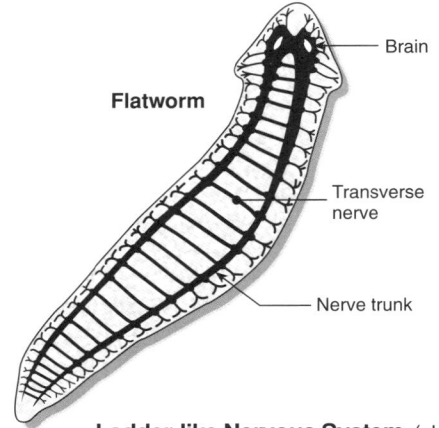

Flatworm

Brain

Transverse nerve

Nerve trunk

Ladder-like Nervous System (above)

EXAMPLE: *Platyhelminthes (flatworms)*

Flatworms are the simplest animals to show the development of a central nervous system, with a simple brain and nerve trunks that act as thoroughfares for information. Transverse nerves connect the main nerve trunks.

Radial Nervous System (right)

EXAMPLES: *Echinoderms, e.g. starfish*

Radial nerves run through each arm from the central nerve ring around the mouth. Branches of the radial nerves form an interconnected network similar to the nerve net of *Hydra*. It is believed that a nerve center exists at the junction of each radial nerve with the nerve ring, and that this nerve center allows one or other arm to dominate during directional movement.

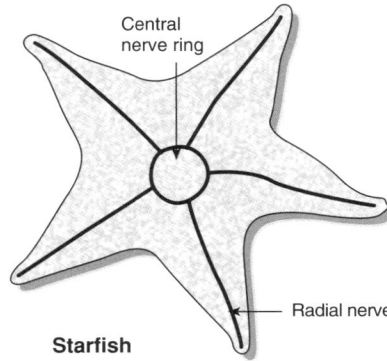

Central nerve ring

Radial nerve

Starfish

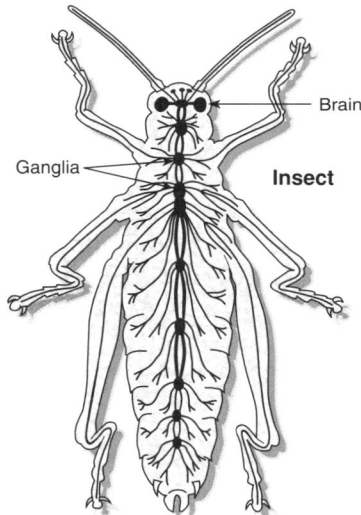

Brain

Ganglia

Insect

Ventral Nerve Cord and Brain (left and right)

EXAMPLES: *Annelids (earthworms, leeches), arthropods (crustaceans, insects, spiders, scorpions)*

The nerve cords of these segmented animals often contain ganglia (clumps of nerve cells) in each segment. These ganglia coordinate the actions of each segment. The brains are larger and more complex than in flatworms. In insects, there has been an even greater trend towards concentration of ganglia in the head, thorax and abdomen, associated with the fusion of segments and different activities in these regions. In insects, there is also prominent **cephalization**; formation of a distinctive head and brain.

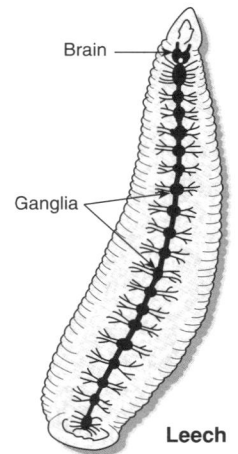

Brain

Ganglia

Leech

Annelid: earthworm

Arthropod: grasshopper

Cnidarian: sea anemone

Echinoderm: sea star

The more highly organized nervous systems of annelids and arthropods are associated with a number of sensory organs of varying complexity. Those in annelids are generally very simple structures in the epidermis, consisting of individual cells or small groups of cells that are sensitive to touch, pressure, chemical stimuli, and temperature. Insect sense organs include simple eyes (ocelli), complex compound eyes, and a number of epidermal sense organs.

The sensory receptors of cnidarians are restricted largely to the outer (ectoderm) layers. They are simple sensory cells, concentrated around the mouth and on the tentacles, and are used for prey detection and capture.

The primary sensory receptors of sea stars and other echinoderms are contained within the epidermis. They are simple sensory cells and function in the reception of light, contact, and chemical stimuli.

1. Briefly describe the arrangement of the nervous system in the following invertebrates:

   (a) Cnidarians e.g. *Hydra*, sea anemone: _____

   _____

   _____

   (b) Platyhelminthes: _____

   _____

   _____

   (c) Echinoderms: _____

   _____

   _____

   (d) Annelids: _____

   _____

   _____

   (e) Arthropods: _____

   _____

   _____

2. (a) Contrast the speed and efficiency of nerve impulse transmission in cnidarians and arthropods:

   _____

   _____

   (b) Explain a reason for these differences: _____

   _____

   _____

3. (a) Explain what is meant by **cephalization**: _____

   _____

   (b) Comment on the significance of cephalization to the type of responses and behavior possible in invertebrates:

   _____

   _____

   (c) Describe the general trend seen in nervous system organization, from cnidarians through to insects:

   _____

   _____

   (d) State what you would regard as the main evolutionary (selection) pressure for the development of a brain:

   _____

4. Describe the advantages of combining segmental nervous control (via ganglia) with control via a distinctive brain:

   _____

   _____

   _____

The Vertebrate Brain

The vertebrate brain develops as an expansion of the anterior end of the neural tube in embryos. The forebrain, midbrain, and hindbrain can be seen very early in development, with further differentiation as development continues. The brains of fish and amphibians are relatively unspecialized, with a rudimentary cerebrum and cerebellum. The reptiles show the first real expansion of the cerebrum, with the gray matter external in the cortex. In the birds and mammals, the brain is relatively large,

with well developed cerebral and cerebellar regions. In primitive vertebrates, the cerebral regions act primarily as olfactory centers. In higher vertebrates, the cerebrum takes over the many of the functions of other regions of the brain (e.g. the optic lobes), becoming the primary integration center of the brain. The cerebellum also becomes more important as locomotor and other muscular activities increase in complexity. The relative sizes of different regions of vertebrate brains are shown below.

Vertebrate Brains

All vertebrates, from fish and amphibians, to humans and other mammals, have brains with the same basic structure. The brain develops from a hollow tube and comprises the forebrain, midbrain, and hindbrain (which runs into the spinal cord). During the course of vertebrate evolution some parts of the brain (e.g. the medulla) have remained largely unchanged, retaining their primitive functions. Other parts (e.g. the cerebrum of the forebrain) have expanded and taken on new functions.

Key to Brain Regions and their Functions

Olfactory bulb: receives and processes olfactory signals.

Cerebrum: Behavior, complex thought and reasoning.

Cerebellum: Center for controlling movement and balance.

Medulla: Reflex functions and relay for sensory information.

Optic lobe: Receives and processes visual information.

The medulla (part of the hindbrain) in fish, amphibians, and reptiles is prominent. It relays sensory information to or from parts of the brain associated with sensory processing. In these groups both the optic lobe (visual processing) and the centers associated with processing olfactory information (in the thalamus) are also large.

In vertebrates other than mammals, a major part of the midbrain is associated with the analysis of vision, and the optic lobes are very large. In mammals, the analysis of vision is a function of the forebrain. The forebrain itself has changed dramatically in size during vertebrate evolution. In birds most of the cerebrum is associated with complex behavior. In mammals, there has been an progressive increase in the size and importance of the cerebrum; particularly the parts associated with complex thought, reasoning, and communication.

1. (a) Describe one major difference between the brain structure of mammals and other vertebrates:

(b) Suggest what brain structure can tell us about the sensory perception of an animal:

2. Discuss the trends in brain development during the course of vertebrate evolution and relate these to changes to changes in lifestyle and behavior:

The Mammalian Nervous System

A 2

The **nervous system** is the body's control and communication center. It has three broad functions: detecting stimuli, interpreting them, and initiating appropriate responses. Its basic structure is outlined below. Further detail is provided in the following pages.

The Human Nervous System

The **central nervous system** comprises the brain and spinal cord. The spinal cord is a cylinder of nervous tissue extending from the base of the brain down the back, protected by the spinal column. It transmits messages to and from the brain, and controls spinal reflexes.

The **peripheral nervous system** (right, far right) comprises all the nerves and sensory receptors outside the central nervous system.

■ Brain (see below)
▨ Spinal cord
▨ Peripheral nerves

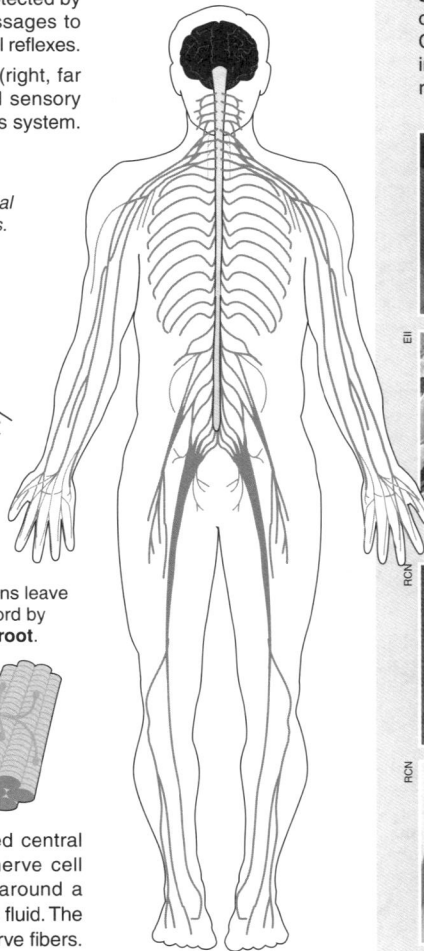

Below: cross sections through the spinal cord to show entry and exit of neurons.

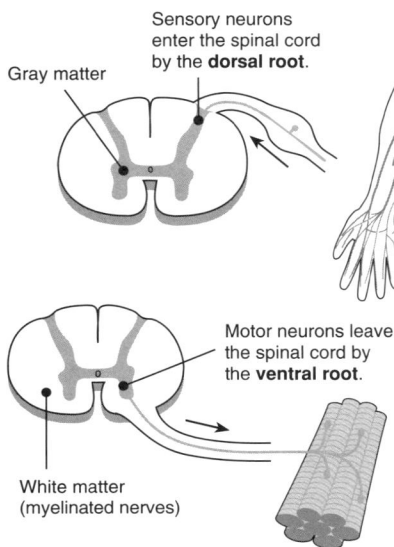

Sensory neurons enter the spinal cord by the **dorsal root**.

Gray matter

Motor neurons leave the spinal cord by the **ventral root**.

White matter (myelinated nerves)

The **spinal cord** has an H shaped central area of gray matter, comprising nerve cell bodies, dendrites, and synapses around a central canal filled with cerebrospinal fluid. The area of white matter contains the nerve fibers.

The Peripheral Nervous System (PNS)

The PNS comprises **sensory** and **motor divisions**. Peripheral nerves all enter or leave the CNS, either from the spinal cord (the spinal nerves) or the brain (cranial nerves). They can be **sensory** (from sensory receptors), **motor** (running to a muscle or gland), or **mixed** (containing sensory and motor neurons). Cranial nerves are numbered in roman numerals, I-XII. They include the vagus (X), a mixed nerve with an important role in regulating bodily functions, including heart rate and digestion.

Sensory Division

Sensory nerves arise from **sensory receptors** (left) and carry messages to the central nervous system for processing.

The sensory system keeps the central nervous system aware of the external and internal environments. This division includes the familiar sense organs such as ears, eyes (A), and taste buds (B) as well as internal receptors that monitor internal state (e.g. thirst, hunger, body position, movement, pain).

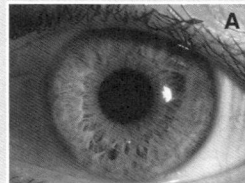

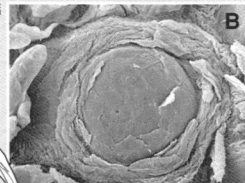

Motor Division

Motor nerves carry impulses from the CNS to **effectors**: muscles (left) and glands. The motor division comprises two parts:

Somatic nervous system: the neurons that carry impulses to voluntary (skeletal) muscles (C).

Autonomic nervous system: regulates visceral functions over which there is generally no conscious control, e.g. heart rate, gut peristalsis involving smooth muscle (D), pupil reflex, and sweating.

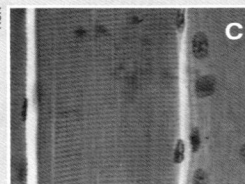

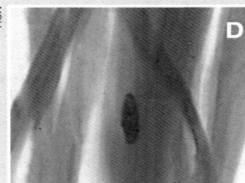

1. List and briefly describe the three main functions of the nervous system:

   (a) _____

   (b) _____

   (c) _____

2. In the human nervous system, briefly explain the structure and role of each of the following:

   (a) The central nervous system: _____

   _____

   (b) The peripheral nervous system: _____

   _____

3. Explain the significance of the separation of the motor division of the PNS into somatic and autonomic divisions:

   _____

   _____

   _____

The Human Brain

The brain is one the largest organs in the body. It is protected by the skull, the meninges (membranous coverings), and the cerebrospinal fluid (CSF). The brain is the control center for the body. It receives a constant flow of information from the senses, but responds only to what is important at the time. Some responses are very simple (e.g. cranial reflexes), whilst others require many levels of processing. The human brain is noted for its large, well developed cerebral region, and the region responsible for complex thought and reasoning. Each cerebral hemisphere is divided into four lobes by deep sulci or fissures. These lobes: temporal, frontal, occipital, and parietal, correspond to the bones of the skull under which they lie.

Primary Structural Regions of the Brain

Cerebrum: Divided into two cerebral hemispheres. Many, complex roles. It contains sensory, motor, and association areas, and is involved in memory, emotion, language, reasoning, and sensory processing.

Ventricles: Cavities containing the CSF, which absorbs shocks and delivers nutritive substances.

Thalamus is the main relay center for all sensory messages that enter the brain, before they are transmitted to the cerebrum.

Hypothalamus controls the autonomic nervous system and links nervous and endocrine systems. Regulates appetite, thirst, body temperature, and sleep.

Midbrain
Pons
Medulla

Cerebellum coordinates body movements, posture, and balance.

Brainstem: Relay center for impulses between the rest of the brain and the spinal cord. Controls breathing, heartbeat, and the coughing and vomiting reflexes.

MRI scan of the brain viewed from above. The visual pathway has been superimposed on the image. Note the crossing of sensory neurons to the opposite hemisphere and the fluid filled ventricles (V) in the center.

Sensory and Motor Regions in the Cerebrum

General sensory area receives sensations from receptors in the skin, muscles and viscera. Sensory information from receptors on one side of the body crosses over to the opposite side of the cerebral cortex where conscious sensations are produced. The size of the sensory region for different body parts depends on the number of receptors in that particular body part.

Visual areas within the occipital lobe receive, interpret, and evaluate visual stimuli. In vision, each eye views both sides of the visual field but the brain receives impulses from left and right visual fields separately (see photo caption above). The visual cortex combines the images into a single impression or **perception** of the image.

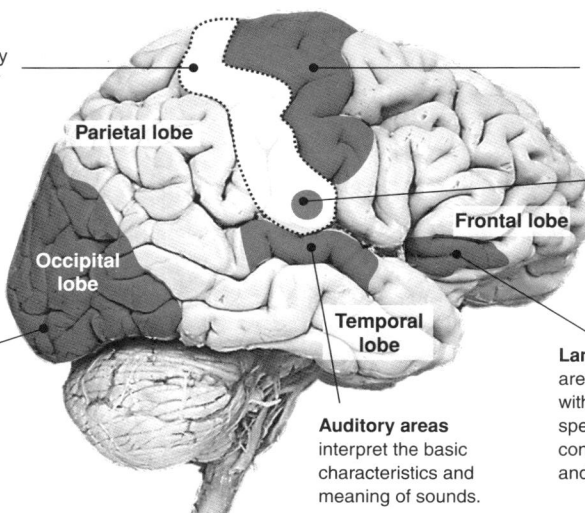

Primary motor area controls muscle movement. Stimulation of a point one side of the motor area results in muscular contraction on the opposite side of the body.

Primary gustatory area interprets sensations related to taste.

Language areas: The motor speech area (Broca's area) is concerned with speech production. The sensory speech area (Wernicke's area) is concerned with speech recognition and coherence.

Auditory areas interpret the basic characteristics and meaning of sounds.

Parietal lobe

Occipital lobe

Frontal lobe

Temporal lobe

1. For each of the following bodily functions, state the region(s) of the brain involved in its control:

   (a) Breathing and heartbeat: _____

   (b) Memory and emotion: _____

   (c) Posture and balance: _____

   (d) Autonomic functions: _____

   (e) Visual processing: _____

   (f) Body temperature: _____

   (g) Language: _____

   (h) Muscular contraction: _____

2. Describe the likely effect of a loss of function (through injury) to the primary motor area in the left hemisphere:

   _____

   _____

RA 2 The Autonomic Nervous System

The **autonomic nervous system** (ANS) regulates involuntary visceral functions by means of **reflexes**. Although most autonomic nervous system activity is beyond our conscious control, voluntary control over some basic reflexes (such as bladder emptying) can be learned. Most visceral effectors have dual innervation, receiving fibers from both branches of the ANS. These two branches, the **parasympathetic** and **sympathetic** divisions, have broadly opposing actions on the organs they control (excitatory or inhibitory). Nerves in the parasympathetic division release acetylcholine. This neurotransmitter is rapidly deactivated at the synapse and its effects are short lived and localized. Most sympathetic postganglionic nerves release noradrenaline, which enters the bloodstream and is deactivated slowly. Hence, sympathetic stimulation tends to have more widespread and long lasting effects than parasympathetic stimulation. Aspects of autonomic nervous system structure and function are illustrated below. The arrows indicate nerves to organs or ganglia (concentrations of nerve cell bodies).

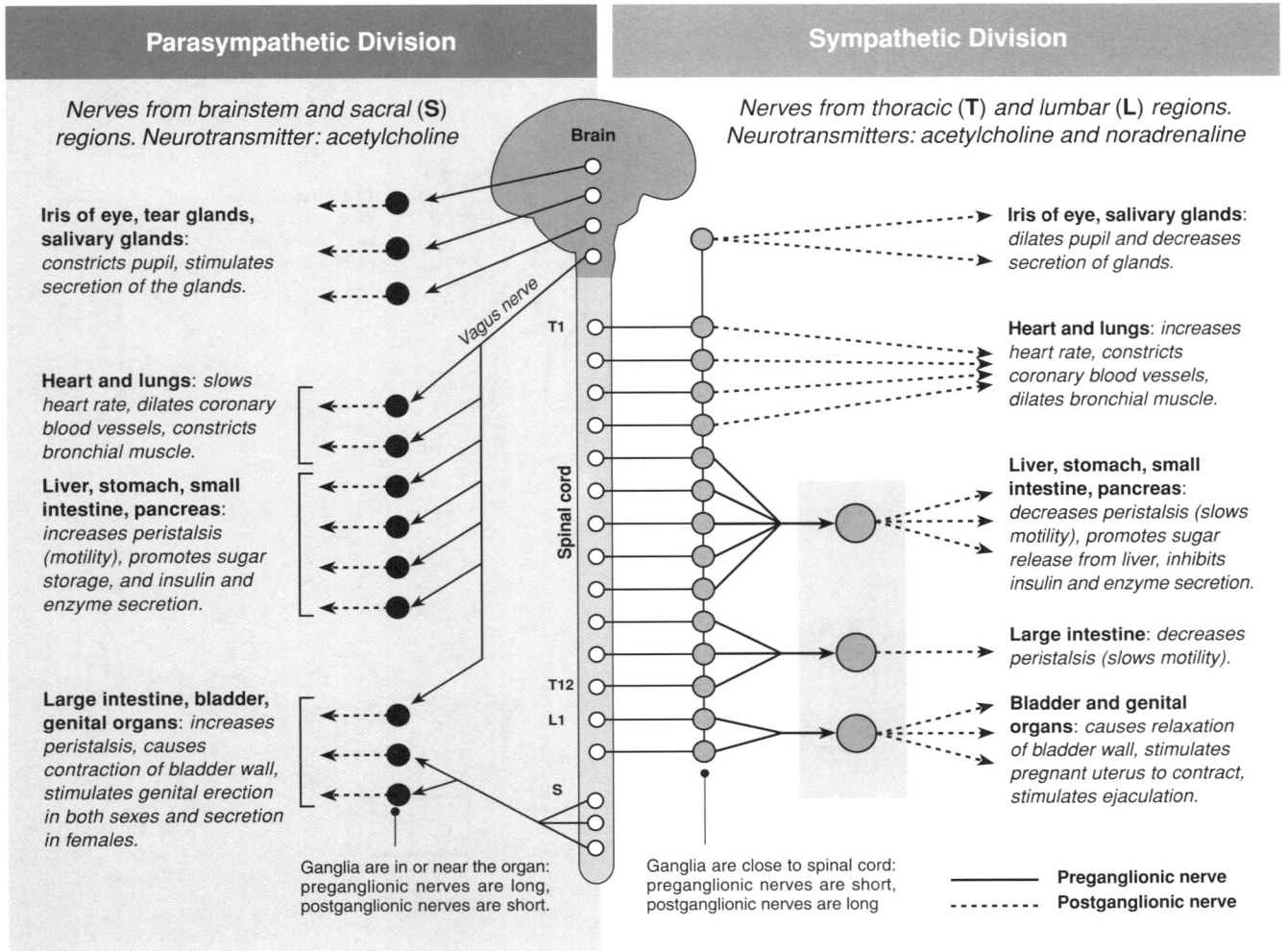

Parasympathetic Division	Sympathetic Division

Nerves from brainstem and sacral (S) regions. Neurotransmitter: acetylcholine

Brain

Nerves from thoracic (T) and lumbar (L) regions. Neurotransmitters: acetylcholine and noradrenaline

Iris of eye, tear glands, salivary glands: constricts pupil, stimulates secretion of the glands.

Iris of eye, salivary glands: dilates pupil and decreases secretion of glands.

Heart and lungs: slows heart rate, dilates coronary blood vessels, constricts bronchial muscle.

Heart and lungs: increases heart rate, constricts coronary blood vessels, dilates bronchial muscle.

Vagus nerve

T1

Liver, stomach, small intestine, pancreas: increases peristalsis (motility), promotes sugar storage, and insulin and enzyme secretion.

Spinal cord

Liver, stomach, small intestine, pancreas: decreases peristalsis (slows motility), promotes sugar release from liver, inhibits insulin and enzyme secretion.

Large intestine: decreases peristalsis (slows motility).

T12

Large intestine, bladder, genital organs: increases peristalsis, causes contraction of bladder wall, stimulates genital erection in both sexes and secretion in females.

L1

S

Bladder and genital organs: causes relaxation of bladder wall, stimulates pregnant uterus to contract, stimulates ejaculation.

Ganglia are in or near the organ: preganglionic nerves are long, postganglionic nerves are short.

Ganglia are close to spinal cord: preganglionic nerves are short, postganglionic nerves are long

——— **Preganglionic nerve**

- - - - - - - **Postganglionic nerve**

1. Explain the structure and role of each of the following divisions of the autonomic nervous system:

    (a) The sympathetic nervous system: _____

    _____

    (b) The parasympathetic nervous system: _____

    _____

2. Using an example (e.g. pupil reflex or control of heart rate), describe the role of reflexes in the functioning of the autonomic nervous system:

    _____

    _____

3. With reference to the emptying of the bladder, explain how a reflex activity can be modified by learning:

    _____

    _____

Neuron Structure and Function

RA 2

The nervous and endocrine systems are the body's regulatory and coordinating systems. Homeostasis depends on the ability of the nervous system to detect, interpret, and respond to, internal and external conditions. Sensory receptors relay information to the central nervous system (CNS) where it is interpreted and responses are coordinated. The information is transmitted along nerve cells (**neurons**) as electrical impulses. The speed of impulse conduction depends primarily on the axon diameter and whether or not the axon is myelinated (see below). Within the tolerable physiological range, an increase in temperature also increases the speed of impulse conduction: in cool environments, impulses travel faster in endothermic than in ectothermic vertebrates. Neurons typically consist of a cell body, dendrites, and an axon. Basic types are described below.

The Structure of Neurons

Sensory neuron
Transmits impulses from sensory receptors to other neurons.

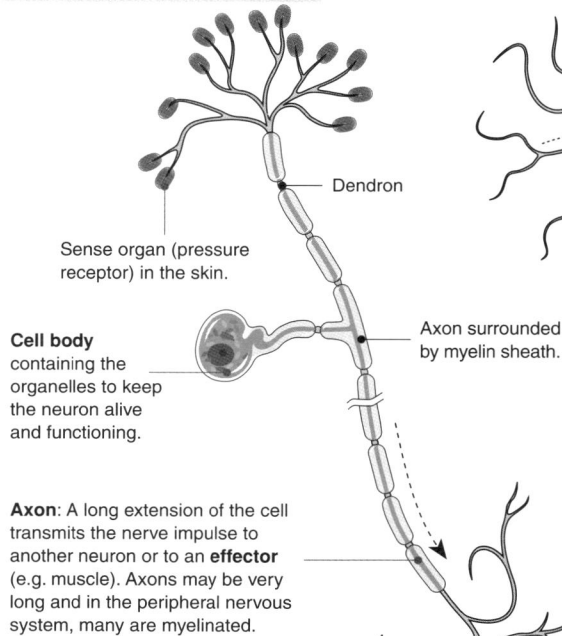

Dendron

Sense organ (pressure receptor) in the skin.

Cell body containing the organelles to keep the neuron alive and functioning.

Axon: A long extension of the cell transmits the nerve impulse to another neuron or to an **effector** (e.g. muscle). Axons may be very long and in the peripheral nervous system, many are myelinated.

Axon surrounded by myelin sheath.

Relay neuron
Also called association or interneurons. Located in the CNS and carry impulses from sensory to motor neurons (as in reflexes).

Dendrites: Bushy extensions of the cell body, specialized to receive stimuli.

Axon branches

Axon

Axon branches

Cell body

Dendrites

Impulse direction

Myelin sheath

Area enlarged below

Motor neuron
Transmits impulses from the CNS to muscles or glands.

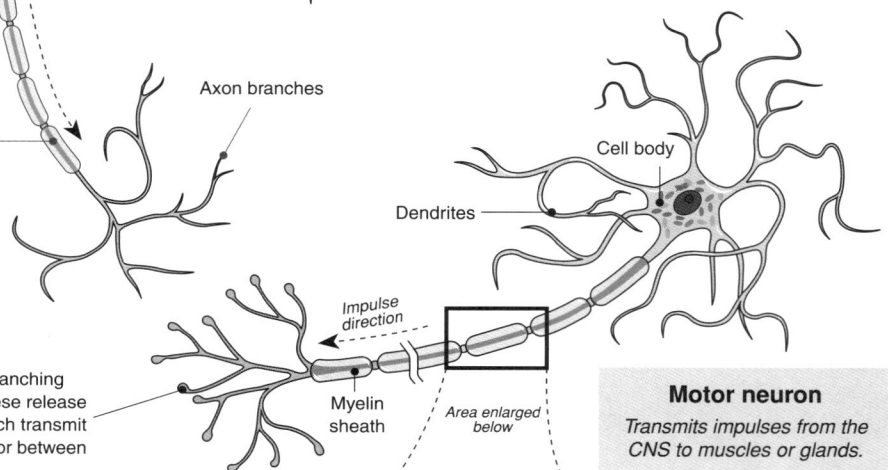

Axon branches: Extensively branching with tiny knobs at each end. These release neurotransmitter chemicals which transmit the message between neurons or between a neuron and a muscle cell.

The Myelin Sheath
Many nerves outside the CNS are **myelinated**. Specialized **Schwann cells** form a tightly wrapped **myelin sheath** around the axon of the nerve. Myelin is rich in lipid and forms an electrical insulation layer around the axon. This increases the speed of impulse conduction.

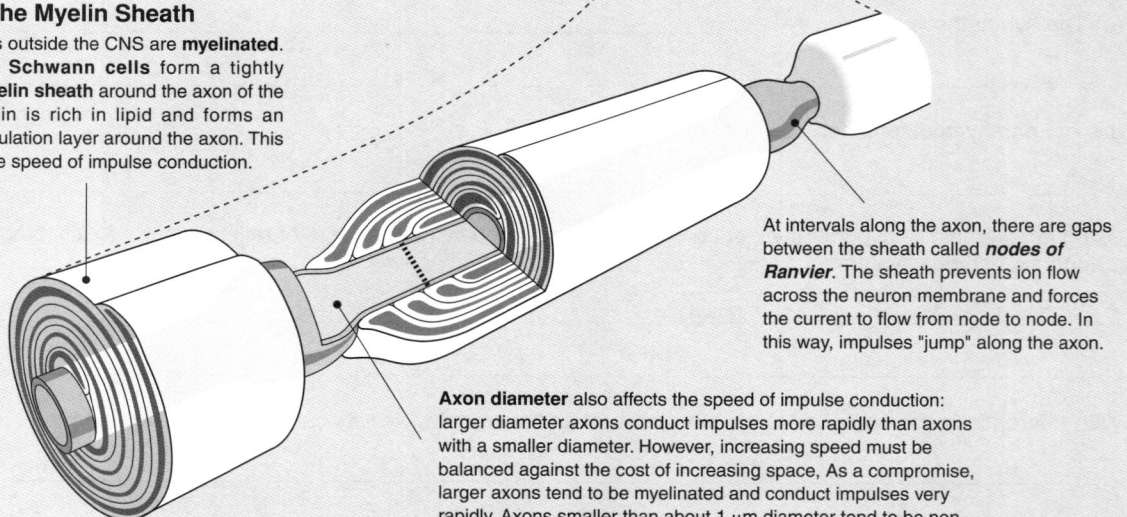

At intervals along the axon, there are gaps between the sheath called **nodes of Ranvier**. The sheath prevents ion flow across the neuron membrane and forces the current to flow from node to node. In this way, impulses "jump" along the axon.

Axon diameter also affects the speed of impulse conduction: larger diameter axons conduct impulses more rapidly than axons with a smaller diameter. However, increasing speed must be balanced against the cost of increasing space, As a compromise, larger axons tend to be myelinated and conduct impulses very rapidly. Axons smaller than about 1 μm diameter tend to be non-myelinated and operate where conduction speed is less important.

Pain Withdrawal: A Polysynaptic Reflex Arc

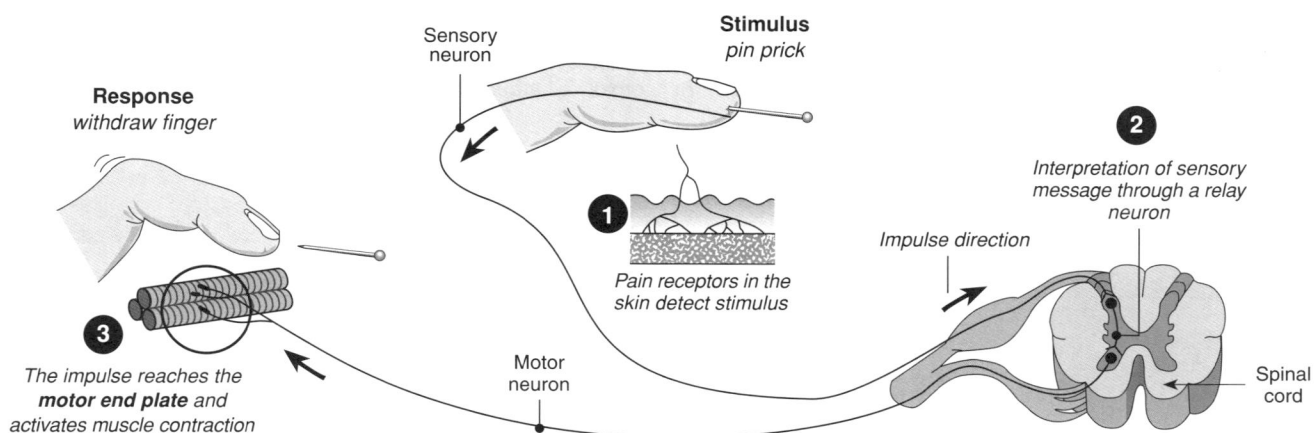

Stimulus
pin prick

Sensory
neuron

Response
withdraw finger

2

*Interpretation of sensory
message through a relay
neuron*

Impulse direction

1

*Pain receptors in the
skin detect stimulus*

3

*The impulse reaches the
motor end plate and
activates muscle contraction*

Motor
neuron

Spinal
cord

A reflex is an automatic response to a stimulus involving a small number of neurons and a central nervous system (CNS) processing point (usually the spinal cord, but sometimes the brain stem). This type of circuit is often called a **reflex arc**. Reflexes permit rapid responses to stimuli. They are classified according to the number of CNS synapses involved; **monosynaptic reflexes** involve only one CNS synapse (e.g. knee jerk), **polysynaptic reflexes** involve two or more (e.g. pain withdrawal reflex). Both are spinal reflexes. The pupil reflex (opening and closure of the pupil) is an example of a cranial reflex.

1. (a) Describe a structural difference between a motor and a sensory neuron: _____

   _____

   (b) Describe a functional difference between a motor and a sensory neuron: _____

   _____

2. (a) Predict what would happen to the part of an axon if it is cut so that it is no longer connected to its nerve cell body:

   _____

   (b) Explain your prediction: _____

   _____

3. (a) Describe one way (other than insulation of the axon) in which impulse conduction speed could be increased:

   _____

   (b) Name one animal that uses this method: _____

   (c) Describe the adaptive advantage of faster conduction of nerve impulses: _____

   _____

4. (a) Briefly, describe the cause of the disorder, multiple sclerosis (MS): _____

   _____

   (b) Explain why MS impairs nervous system function even though axons are undamaged: _____

   _____

5. (a) Explain why higher reasoning or conscious thought are not necessary or desirable features of reflexes:

   _____

   (b) Explain when it might be adaptive for conscious thought to intervene and modify a reflex action: _____

   _____

6. Distinguish between a spinal and a cranial reflex and give an example of each: _____

RA② Transmission of Nerve Impulses

Neurons, like all cells, contain ions or charged atoms. Those of special importance include sodium (Na^+), potassium (K^+), and negatively charged proteins. Neurons are **electrically excitable** cells: a property that results from the separation of ion charge either side of the neuron membrane. They may exist in either a resting or stimulated state. When stimulated, neurons produce electrical impulses that are transmitted along the axon. These impulses are transmitted between neurons across junctions called **synapses**. Synapses enable the transmission of impulses rapidly all around the body.

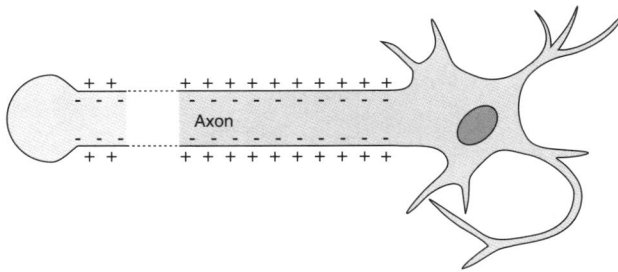

The Resting Neuron

When a neuron is not transmitting an impulse, the inside of the cell is negatively charged compared with the outside of the cell. The cell is said to be electrically polarized, because the inside and the outside of the cell are oppositely charged. The potential difference (voltage) across the membrane is called the resting potential and for most nerve cells is about -70 mV. Nerve transmission is possible because this membrane potential exists.

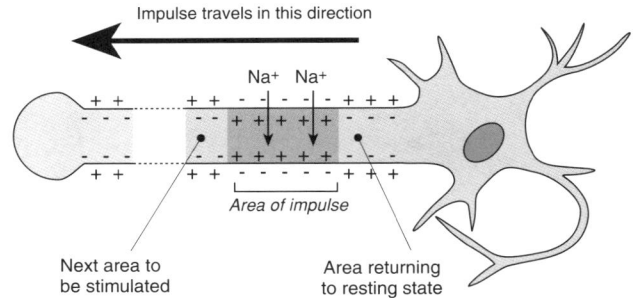

The Nerve Impulse

When a neuron is stimulated, the distribution of charges on each side of the membrane changes. For a millisecond, the charges reverse. This process, called **depolarization**, causes a burst of electrical activity to pass along the axon of the neuron. As the charge reversal reaches one region, local currents depolarize the next region. In this way the impulse spreads along the axon. An impulse that spreads this way is called an **action potential**.

The Action Potential

The depolarization described above can be illustrated as a change in membrane potential (in millivolts). In order for an action potential to be generated, the stimulation must be strong enough to reach the **threshold** potential; this is the potential (voltage) at which the depolarization of the membrane becomes "unstoppable" and the action potential is generated. The action potential is **all or none** in its generation. Either the **threshold** is reached and the action potential is generated or the nerve does not fire. The resting potential is restored by the movement of potassium ions (K^+) out of the cell. During this **refractory period**, the nerve cannot respond.

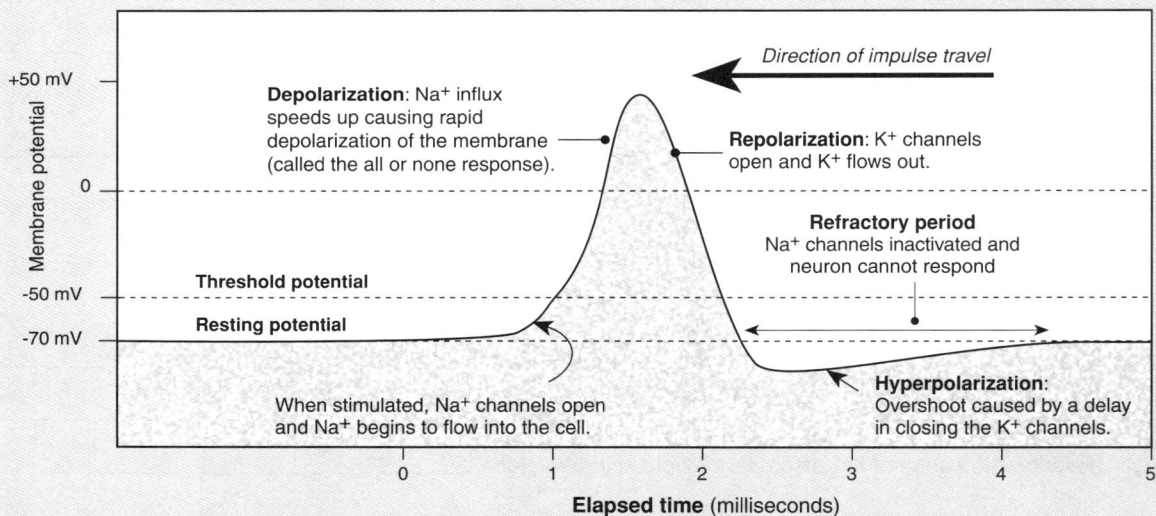

1. Explain how an action potential is able to pass along a nerve: _____

_____

2. Explain how the refractory period influences the direction in which an impulse will travel: _____

_____

3. Action potentials themselves are indistinguishable from each other. Explain how the nervous system is able to interpret the impulses correctly and bring about an appropriate response:

_____

_____

RA 2 Chemical Synapses

Action potentials are transmitted between neurons across synapses: junctions between the end of one axon and the dendrite or cell body of a receiving neuron. **Chemical synapses** are the most widespread type of synapse in nervous systems. The axon terminal is a swollen knob, and a small gap separates it from the receiving neuron. The synaptic knobs are filled with tiny packets of chemicals called **neurotransmitters**. Transmission involves the diffusion of the neurotransmitter across the gap, where it interacts with the receiving membrane and causes an electrical response. The response of a receiving cell to the arrival of a neurotransmitter depends on the nature of the cell itself, on its location in the nervous system, and on the neurotransmitter involved. Synapses that release ACh are termed **cholinergic**. In the example below, acetylcholine (ACh) causes membrane depolarization and the generation of an action potential (excitation).

A Cholinergic Synapse

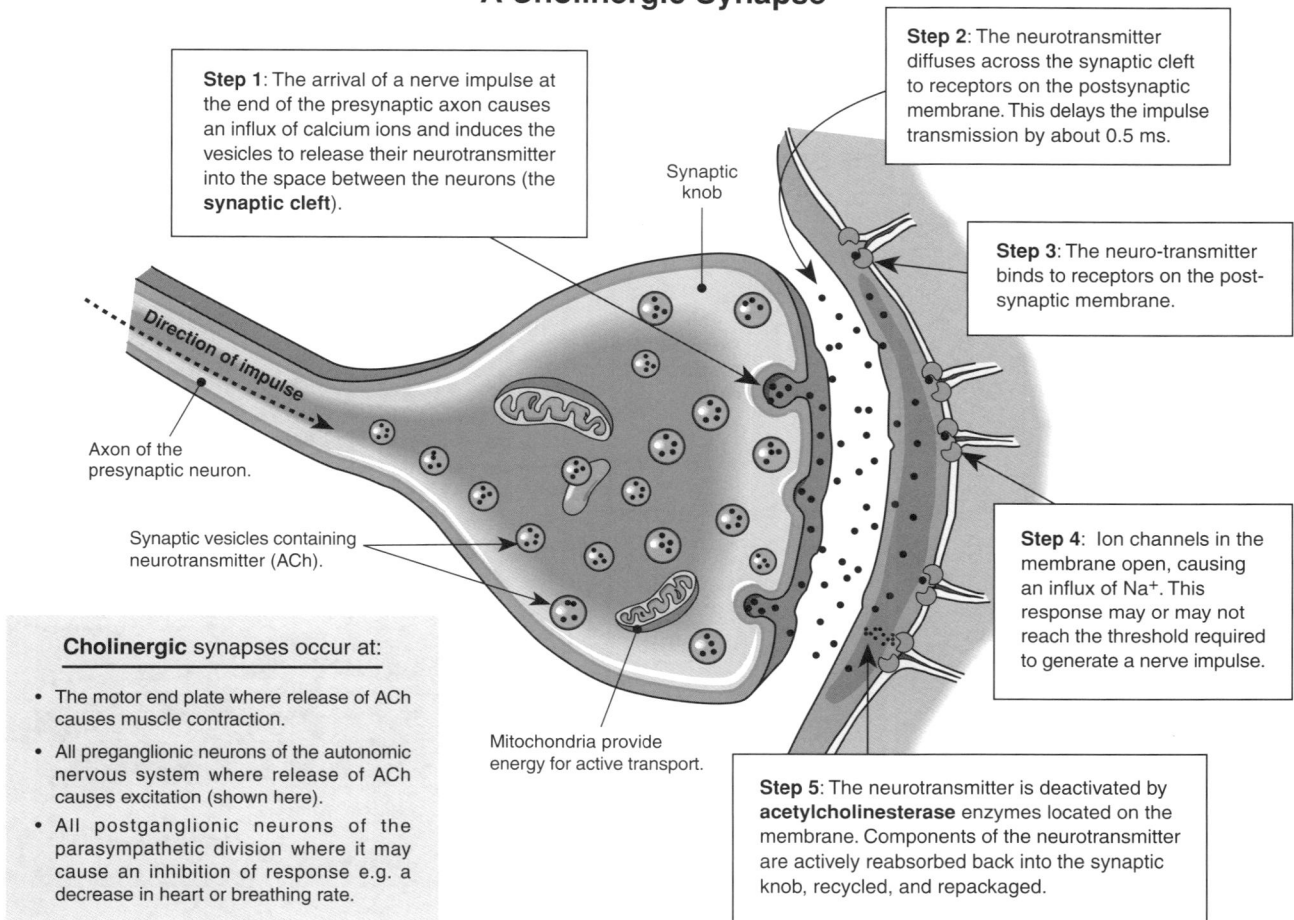

Step 1: The arrival of a nerve impulse at the end of the presynaptic axon causes an influx of calcium ions and induces the vesicles to release their neurotransmitter into the space between the neurons (the **synaptic cleft**).

Step 2: The neurotransmitter diffuses across the synaptic cleft to receptors on the postsynaptic membrane. This delays the impulse transmission by about 0.5 ms.

Step 3: The neuro-transmitter binds to receptors on the post-synaptic membrane.

Step 4: Ion channels in the membrane open, causing an influx of Na^+. This response may or may not reach the threshold required to generate a nerve impulse.

Step 5: The neurotransmitter is deactivated by **acetylcholinesterase** enzymes located on the membrane. Components of the neurotransmitter are actively reabsorbed back into the synaptic knob, recycled, and repackaged.

Synaptic knob

Direction of impulse

Axon of the presynaptic neuron.

Synaptic vesicles containing neurotransmitter (ACh).

Mitochondria provide energy for active transport.

Cholinergic synapses occur at:

- The motor end plate where release of ACh causes muscle contraction.
- All preganglionic neurons of the autonomic nervous system where release of ACh causes excitation (shown here).
- All postganglionic neurons of the parasympathetic division where it may cause an inhibition of response e.g. a decrease in heart or breathing rate.

1. Explain what is meant by a synapse: _____

2. Explain what causes the release of neurotransmitter into the synaptic cleft: _____

_____

3. State why there is a brief delay in transmission of an impulse across the synapse: _____

_____

4. (a) State how the neurotransmitter is deactivated: _____

   (b) Explain why it is important for the neurotransmitter substance to be deactivated soon after its release:

   _____

5. Consult a reference source to identify one function of acetylcholine in the nervous system: _____

_____

6. Suggest one factor that might influence the strength of the response in the receiving cell: _____

_____

Integration at Synapses

RA 3

Synapses play a pivotal role in the ability of the nervous system to respond appropriately to stimulation and to adapt to change. The nature of synaptic transmission allows the **integration** (interpretation and coordination) of inputs from many sources. These inputs need not be just excitatory (causing depolarization). Inhibition results when the neurotransmitter released causes negative chloride ions (rather than sodium ions) to enter the

postsynaptic neuron. The postsynaptic neuron then becomes more negative inside (hyperpolarized) and an action potential is less likely to be generated. At synapses, it is the sum of **all** inputs (excitatory and inhibitory) that leads to the final response in a postsynaptic cell. Integration at synapses makes possible the various responses we have to stimuli. It is also the most probable mechanism by which learning and memory are achieved.

Synapses and Summation

Nerve transmission across chemical synapses has several advantages, despite the delay caused by neurotransmitter diffusion. Chemical synapses transmit impulses in one direction to a precise location and, because they rely on a limited supply of neurotransmitter, they are subject to fatigue (inability to respond to repeated stimulation). This protects the system against overstimulation.

Synapses also act as centers for the **integration** of inputs from many sources. The response of a postsynaptic cell is often graded; it is not strong enough on its own to generate an action potential. However, because the strength of the response is related to the amount of neurotransmitter released, subthreshold responses can sum to produce a response in the post-synaptic cell. This additive effect is termed **summation**. Summation can be **temporal** or **spatial** (below). A neuromuscular junction (photo below) is a specialized form of synapse between a motor neuron and a skeletal muscle fiber. Functionally, it is similar to any excitatory cholinergic synapse.

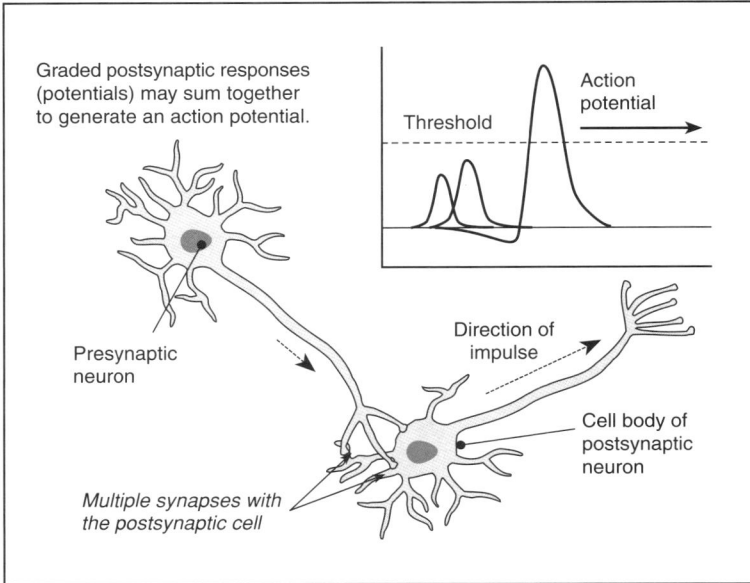

Graded postsynaptic responses (potentials) may sum together to generate an action potential.

Threshold
Action potential

Presynaptic neuron

Direction of impulse

Cell body of postsynaptic neuron

Multiple synapses with the postsynaptic cell

❶ Temporal summation

Presynaptic neuron

Action potential

Postsynaptic cell

Several impulses may arrive at the synapse in quick succession from a single axon. The individual responses are so close together in time that they sum to reach threshold and produce an action potential in the postsynaptic neuron.

❷ Spatial summation

Presynaptic neurons

Neurotransmitter

Individual impulses from spatially separated axon terminals may arrive **simultaneously** at different regions of the same postsynaptic neuron. The responses from the different places sum to reach threshold and produce an action potential.

❸ Neuromuscular junction

Axons

Motor end plate

Muscle fiber (cell)

The arrival of an impulse at the neuromuscular junction causes the release of acetylcholine from the synaptic knobs. This causes the muscle cell membrane (sarcolemma) to depolarize, and an action potential is generated in the muscle cell.

1. Explain the purpose of nervous system integration: _____

_____

2. (a) Explain what is meant by summation: _____

_____

(b) In simple terms, distinguish between temporal and spatial summation: _____

_____

_____

3. Describe two ways in which a neuromuscular junction is similar to any excitatory cholinergic synapse:

(a) _____

(b) _____

Drugs at Synapses

Synapses in the peripheral nervous system are classified according to the neurotransmitter they release; **cholinergic** synapses release acetylcholine (**Ach**) while **adrenergic** synapses release adrenaline or noradrenaline. The effect produced by these neurotransmitters depends, in turn, on the type of receptors present on the postsynaptic membrane. Ach receptors are classified as nicotinic or muscarinic according to their response to nicotine or muscarine (a fungal toxin).

Adrenergic receptors are also of two types, alpha (α) or beta (β), classified according to their particular responses to specific chemicals. **Drugs** exert their effects on the nervous system by mimicking (**agonists**) or blocking (**antagonists**) the action of neurotransmitters at synapses. Because of the small amounts of chemicals involved in synaptic transmission, drugs that affect the activity of neurotransmitters, or their binding sites, can have powerful effects even in small doses.

Drugs at Cholinergic Synapses

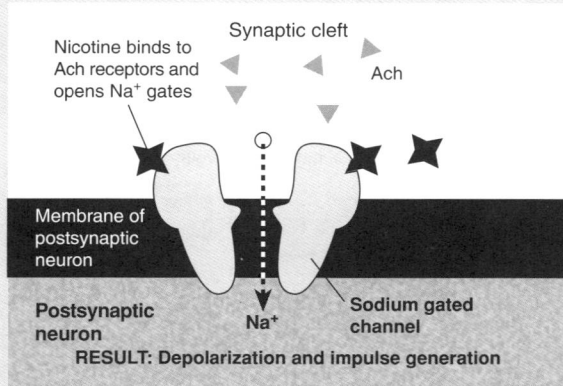

Nicotine binds to Ach receptors and opens Na$^+$ gates

Synaptic cleft

Ach

Membrane of postsynaptic neuron

Postsynaptic neuron

Na$^+$

Sodium gated channel

RESULT: Depolarization and impulse generation

Nicotine acts as a **direct agonist** at nicotinic synapses. Nicotine binds to and activates acetylcholine (Ach) receptors on the postsynaptic membrane. This opens sodium gates, leading to a sodium influx and membrane depolarization. Some agonists work indirectly at the synapse by preventing Ach breakdown. Such drugs are used to treat elderly patients with Alzheimer's disease.

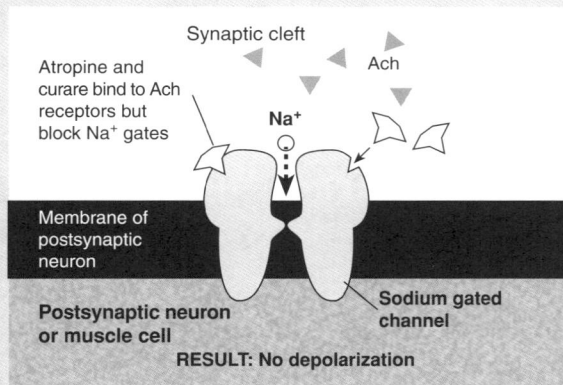

Atropine and curare bind to Ach receptors but block Na$^+$ gates

Synaptic cleft

Ach

Na$^+$

Membrane of postsynaptic neuron

Postsynaptic neuron or muscle cell

Sodium gated channel

RESULT: No depolarization

Atropine and **curare** act as antagonists at some cholinergic synapses. These molecules compete with Ach for binding sites on the postsynaptic membrane, and block sodium influx so that impulses are not generated. If the postsynaptic cell is a muscle cell, muscle contraction is prevented. In the case of curare, this causes death by flaccid paralysis.

Drugs at Adrenergic Synapses

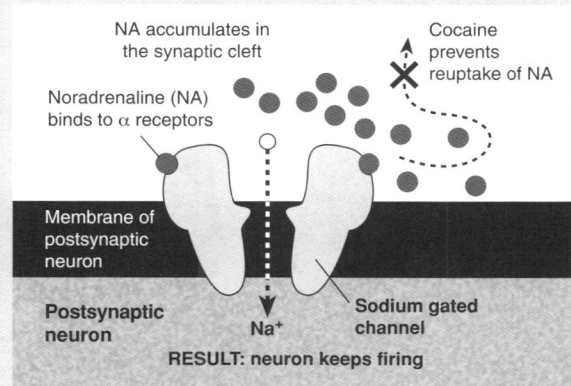

NA accumulates in the synaptic cleft

Noradrenaline (NA) binds to α receptors

Cocaine prevents reuptake of NA

Membrane of postsynaptic neuron

Postsynaptic neuron

Na$^+$

Sodium gated channel

RESULT: neuron keeps firing

Under normal circumstances, the continued activity of the neurotransmitter noradrenaline (NA) at the synapse is prevented by reuptake of NA by the presynaptic neuron. **Cocaine** and **amphetamine** drugs act indirectly as agonists by preventing this reuptake. This action allows NA to linger at the synapse and continue to exert its effects.

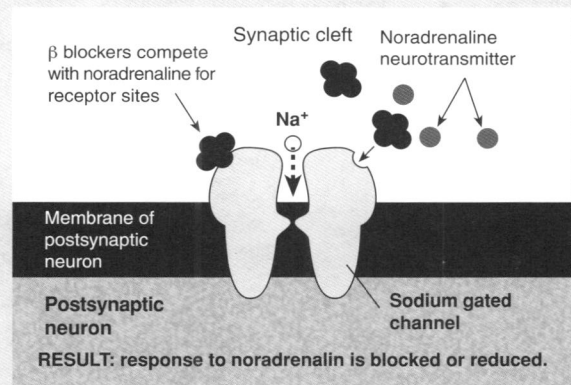

β blockers compete with noradrenaline for receptor sites

Synaptic cleft

Noradrenaline neurotransmitter

Na$^+$

Membrane of postsynaptic neuron

Postsynaptic neuron

Sodium gated channel

RESULT: response to noradrenalin is blocked or reduced.

Therapeutic drugs called **beta** (β) **blockers** act as direct antagonists at adrenergic synapses (sympathetic nervous system). They compete for the adrenergic β receptors on the postsynaptic membrane and block impulse transmission. Beta blockers are prescribed primarily to treat hypertension and heart disorders because they slow heart rate and reduce the force of contraction.

1. Providing an example of each, outline two ways in which drugs can act at a cholinergic synapse:

(a) _____

(b) _____

2. Providing an example, outline one way in which drugs can operate at adrenergic synapses:

_____

3. Explain why atropine and curare are described as direct antagonists:

_____

4. Suggest why curare (carefully administered) is used during abdominal surgery:

_____

Detecting Changing States

A stimulus is any physical or chemical change in the environment that is capable of provoking a response in an organism. Animals respond to stimuli in order to survive. Stimuli may be either external (outside the organism) or internal (within its body). Some of the stimuli to which animals respond are detailed below. The sense organs that detect and respond to these stimuli in humans are also described, together with some examples of sensory perception in other animal groups. Note that sensory receptors respond only to specific stimuli. The sense organs an animal possesses therefore determine how it perceives the world.

Hair cells in the vestibule of the inner ear respond to **gravity** by detecting the rate of change and direction of the head and body. Other hair cells in the cochlea of the inner ear detect **sound** waves. The sound is directed and amplified by specialized regions of the outer and middle ear (pinna, canal, middle ear bones).

Photoreceptor cells in the eyes detect color, intensity, and movement of **light**.

Olfactory receptors in the nose detect airborne **chemicals**. The human nose has about 5 million of these receptors, a bloodhound nose has more than 200 million. The taste buds of the tongue detect dissolved chemicals (gustation). Tastes are combinations of five basic sensations: sweet, salt, sour, bitter, and savoury (umami receptor).

Chemoreceptors in certain blood vessels, e.g. carotid arteries, monitor carbon dioxide levels (and therefore pH) of the blood. Breathing and heart rate increase or decrease (as appropriate) to adjust blood composition.

Baroreceptors in the walls of some arteries, e.g. aorta, monitor blood pressure. Heart rate and blood vessel diameter are adjusted accordingly.

Proprioreceptors (stretch receptors) in the muscles, tendons, and joints monitor limb position, **stretch**, and **tension**. The muscle spindle is a stretch receptor that monitors the state of muscle contraction and enables muscle to maintain its length.

Pressure deforms the skin surface and stimulates sensory receptors in the dermis. These receptors are especially abundant on the lips and fingertips.

Pain and temperature are detected by simple nerve endings in the skin. Deep tissue injury is sometimes felt on the skin as referred pain.

Humans rely heavily on their hearing when learning to communicate; without it, speech and language development are more difficult.

The vibration receptors in the limbs of arthropods are sensitive to movement: either sound or vibration (as caused by struggling prey).

The chemosensory Jacobson's organ in the roof of the mouth of reptiles (e.g. snakes) enables them to detect chemical stimuli.

Breathing and heart rates are regulated in response to sensory input from chemoreceptors.

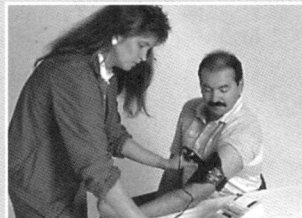

Baroreceptors and osmoreceptors act together to keep blood pressure and volume within narrow limits.

Many insects, such as these ants, rely on chemical sense for location of food and communication.

Jacobson's organ is also present in mammals and is used to detect sexual receptivity in potential mates.

1. Provide a concise definition of a stimulus: _____

_____

2. (a) Name one external stimulus and its sensory receptor: _____

   (b) Name one internal stimulus and its sensory receptor: _____

The Basis of Sensory Perception

RA 2

All sensory receptors operate on the same basis: a **stimulus** is detected by the receptor cell, which triggers a change in the receptor membrane and the generation of an electrical response (below, left). The simplest sensory receptors consist of a single sensory neuron capable of detecting a stimulus and producing a nerve impulse (e.g. free nerve endings). More complex sense cells form synapses with their sensory neurons (e.g. taste buds). Sensory receptors are classified according to the stimuli to which they respond. The response of a **mechanoreceptor**, the Pacinian corpuscle, to a stimulus (pressure) is described below, right.

The Nature of Sensory Reception

Sensory receptors are specialized to detect stimuli and respond by producing an electrical discharge. In this way they act as **biological transducers**, converting the energy from a stimulus into an electrochemical signal. Stimulation of a sensory receptor cell results in an electrical response with certain, specific properties. These properties (outlined below) govern how receptors respond and adapt to stimuli, and how they encode information for interpretation by the central nervous system. The example below illustrates these properties in a stretch receptor.

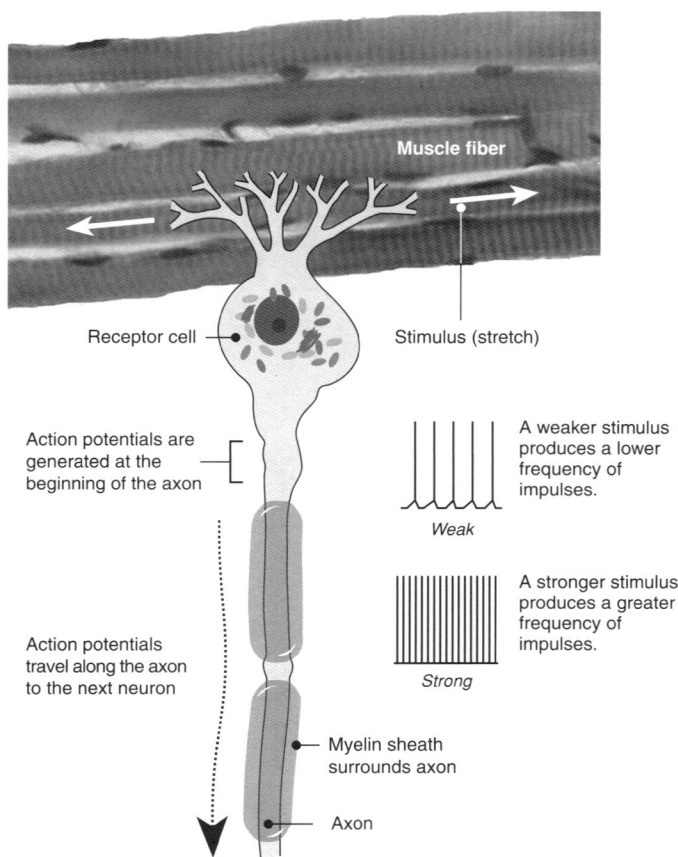

Muscle fiber

Receptor cell

Stimulus (stretch)

Action potentials are generated at the beginning of the axon

A weaker stimulus produces a lower frequency of impulses.

Weak

A stronger stimulus produces a greater frequency of impulses.

Strong

Action potentials travel along the axon to the next neuron

Myelin sheath surrounds axon

Axon

Properties of the Receptor Response

■ The frequency of impulses in the receptor cell is directly proportional to the strength of the stimulus.

■ Impulse frequency therefore provides information about the stimulus strength.

■ Sensory receptors show **sensory adaptation** and will stop responding to a constant stimulus of the same intensity.

The Pacinian Corpuscle

Pacinian corpuscles are pressure receptors that occur deep within the skin all over the body. They are relatively large and simple in structure, consisting of a sensory nerve ending (dendrite) surrounded by a capsule of layered connective tissue. When pressure is applied to the skin, the capsule is deformed. The deformation stretches the nerve ending and leads to a localized depolarization, called a **generator potential**. Once the generator potential reaches or exceeds a **threshold** value, it causes an **action potential** to flow along the sensory pathway (axon).

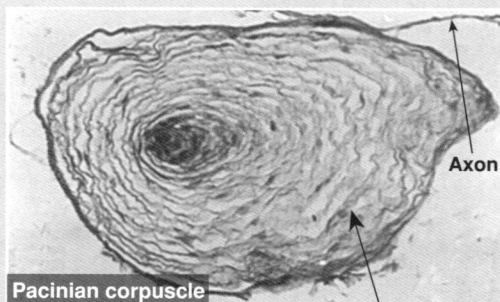

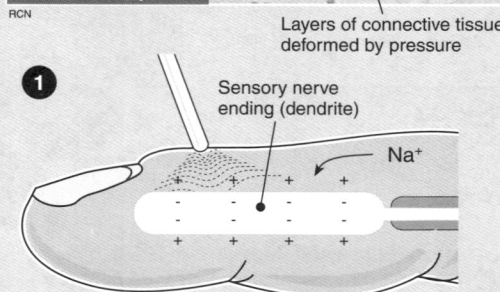

Pacinian corpuscle
RCN

Axon

Layers of connective tissue deformed by pressure

1

Sensory nerve ending (dendrite)

Na^+

Deforming the corpuscle leads to an increase in the permeability of the nerve to sodium. Na^+ diffuses into the nerve ending creating a localized depolarization.

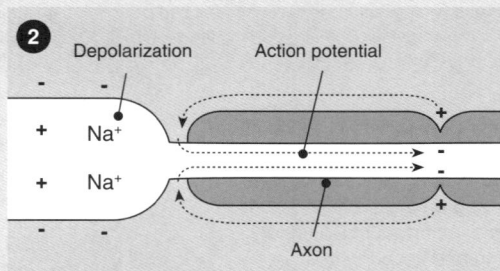

2

Depolarization   Action potential

Na^+

Na^+

Axon

When the depolarization (generator potential) reaches threshold, a volley of **action potentials** is triggered. These action potentials are conducted along the sensory axon.

---

1. Explain why sensory receptors are termed 'biological transducers': _____

_____

2. Explain the significance of linking the magnitude of a sensory response to stimulus intensity: _____

_____

3. Explain the physiological importance of sensory adaptation: _____

_____

Sensory Systems

A 3

Animal senses range in complexity from simple nerve endings to complex sense organs. The sensory systems present in any particular species are appropriate to its environment, and its requirements in terms of feeding, locomotion, reproduction, and predator avoidance. Consequently, many organisms respond to stimuli of which we may be unaware. This activity describes several senses, including various kinds of **mechanoreception**, a sense that is universal in the animal kingdom and involved in detection of sound and vibration, gravity, touch, pressure, and stretch. All mechanoreceptors operate on the same principle; deformation of the sensory structure by pressure, or by fluid or air displacement, leads to a nerve response. The diagram of the senses of the great white shark (*Carcharodon carcharias*), below, shows how senses work together to provide information about the environment. The use of sound (both its production and reception) in different animal phyla is illustrated opposite.

Senses in the Great White Shark

CHEMICAL SENSE - OLFACTION
Olfaction is a shark's most acute sense. The olfactory sacs lie under the snout. A flap of skin covers each sac and channels water into the chamber and across the sensory lamellae. About 70% of a shark's brain is devoted to sensing 'odors' dissolved in the water. A shark can determine the location of food from the presence of minute particles of flesh or blood in the water more than 0.5 km away.

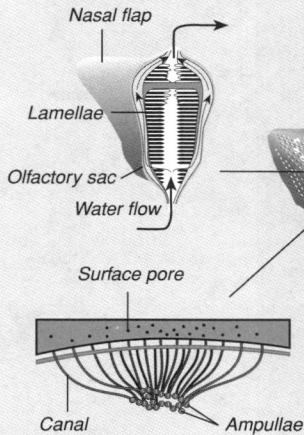

Nasal flap

Lamellae

Olfactory sac

Water flow

Surface pore

Canal   Ampullae

VISION
Sharks have excellent vision. The retina has both rods and cones, and the presence of a reflective tapetum lucidum improves vision in low light. Seawater has a density almost the same as that of the corneal tissue, so most of the refraction of light is done by the lens.

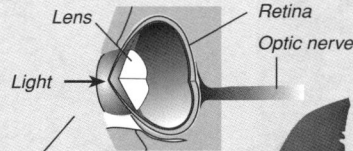

Lens   Retina

Optic nerve

Light

MECHANORECEPTION - LATERAL LINE
A system of small water-filled canals below the skin surface. Neuromasts in the canal detect the fluid displacement, and are used to assess water current direction and velocity. Together, the lateral line and the inner ear are called the **acoustico-lateralis system**.

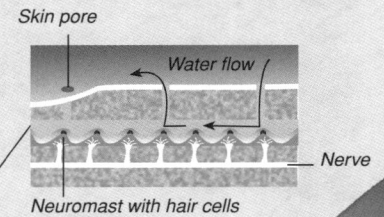

Skin pore

Water flow

Nerve

Neuromast with hair cells

ELECTRORECEPTION
Jelly-filled structures, called the **ampullae of Lorenzini**, detect weak electrical currents. Each ampulla is a small chamber lined with hair cells and attached to a canal filled with conductive jelly. The canals open as pores and are clustered around the eyes and snout. Sharks use the ampullae to sense prey and to navigate using geomagnetic field lines.

Taste bud

Nerve

CHEMICAL SENSE - TASTE BUDS
Taste receptors cells are on small taste buds in the mouth. They are best stimulated by direct contact, and are used to determine palatability.

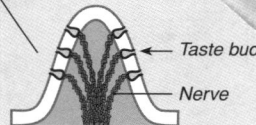

MECHANORECEPTION - HEARING
The ears are fluid filled structures (not visible here) at the top of the head. Their structure is similar to that of the mammalian ear, with a sac like base for detection of sound waves and three D-shaped tubes for the detection of acceleration and orientation. Sensitivity to sound is restricted to the low frequency range, particularly less than 375 Hz.

Potential prey (a fish) is sensed from up to 0.5 km away. The prey is first sensed through olfaction then, as the shark approaches, different senses become important in accurately locating and securing it.

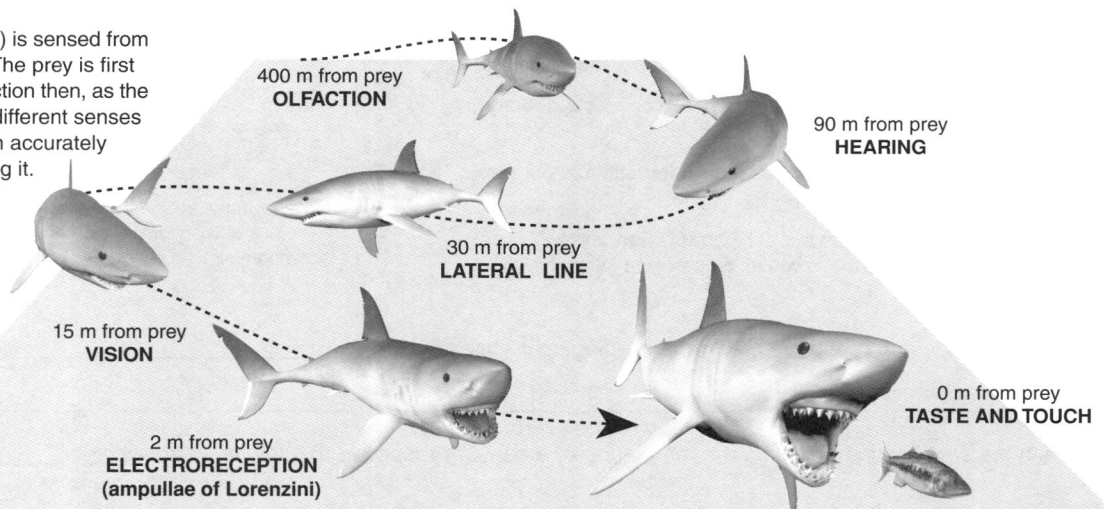

400 m from prey
OLFACTION

90 m from prey
HEARING

30 m from prey
LATERAL LINE

15 m from prey
VISION

2 m from prey
ELECTRORECEPTION
(ampullae of Lorenzini)

0 m from prey
TASTE AND TOUCH

Sensory systems involved in prey detection and capture in great white sharks

Sound and Hearing

Ears and the auditory organs of insects are also mechanoreceptors. Reception of mechanical stimuli (e.g. sound or vibration) is universal throughout animal phyla; sound waves travel through various media largely unimpeded and the production and reception of sound allows animals to navigate, communicate, and forage effectively. As indicated in the figure below, there is a wide range of frequencies for both sound production and reception amongst animal phyla. The dark bars in the figure indicate sound production and the lighter bars sound reception. Most fishes produce sound of various sorts, but these have been little studied in cartilaginous species such as sharks.

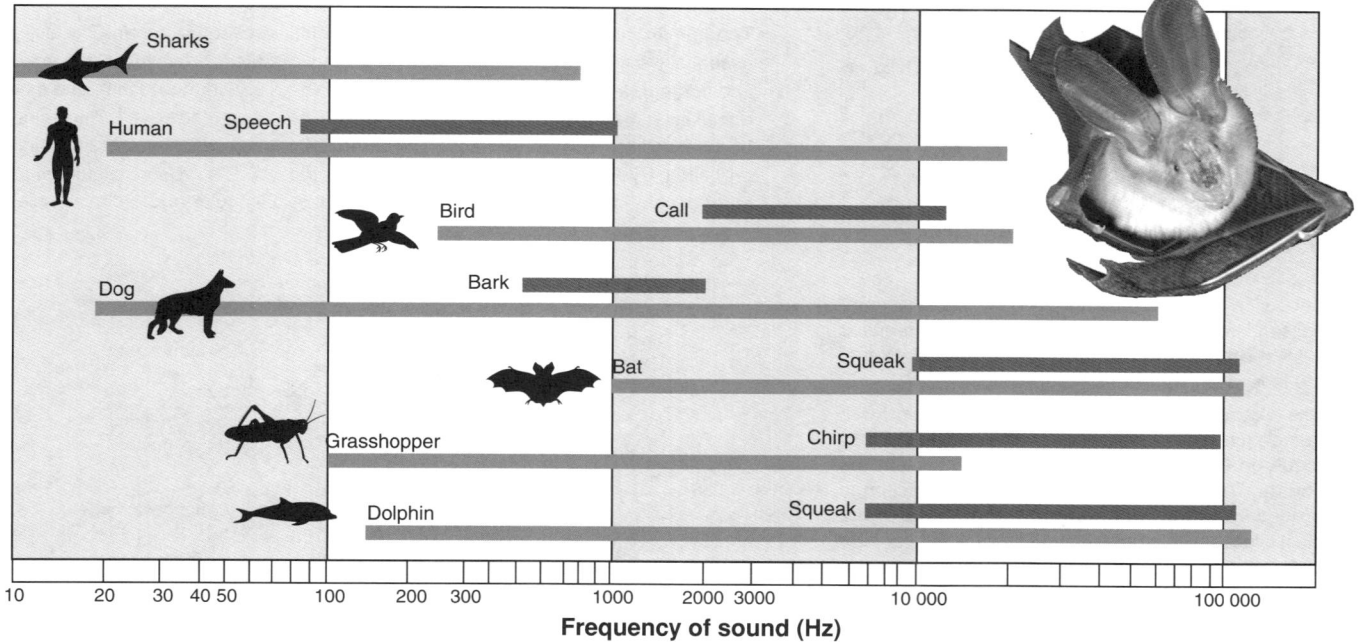

Sharks

Human Speech

Bird Call

Dog Bark

Bat Squeak

Grasshopper Chirp

Dolphin Squeak

10 20 30 40 50 100 200 300 1000 2000 3000 10 000 100 000

Frequency of sound (Hz)

1. Identify three types of mechanoreceptors and the stimuli to which they respond:

   (a) _____

   (b) _____

   (c) _____

2. State why you might suppose that sharks have color vision: _____

3. (a) In a general way, comment on the range of sound frequencies made by animals relative to what they can hear:

   _____

   _____

   (b) Comment on the adaptive value of this difference: _____

   _____

4. Suggest why the lateral line is an excellent organ for mechanoreception in water: _____

   _____

   _____

5. (a) Suggest why sensitivity to sound or vibration is so widespread amongst animal phyla: _____

   _____

   (b) Identify three uses animals make of their ability to perceive sound and vibration: _____

   _____

6. Discuss the benefits of using a range of different senses to gather information about the environment: _____

   _____

   _____

   _____

Vision

Eyes, such as the human eye detailed below, are sense organs specialized to detect light. The light is absorbed by the photosensitive pigments associated with the membranes of the photoreceptor cells.

The pigment molecules are altered by the absorption of light in such a way as to lead to the generation of nerve impulses. The impulses are then conducted via nerve fibers to a visual processing center.

The Mammalian Eye

The human eye is a complex and highly sophisticated sense organ. The eye is essentially a three layered structure comprising an outer fibrous layer (the sclera and cornea), a middle vascular layer (the choroid, ciliary body, and iris), and inner retinal layer (neurons and photoreceptor cells). The shape of the eye is maintained by the fluid filled cavities (aqueous and vitreous humors), which also assist in light refraction. Eye color is provided by the pigmented iris. The iris also regulates the entry of light into the eye through the contraction of circular and radial muscles.

Forming a Visual Image

For vision to occur, light reaching the photoreceptor cells must form an image on the retina. This requires **refraction** of the incoming light, **accommodation** of the lens, and **constriction** of the pupil.

The anterior part of the eye is concerned mainly with refracting (bending) the incoming light rays so that they focus on the retina. Most refraction occurs at the cornea. The lens adjusts the degree of refraction to produce a sharp image. Altering the shape of the elastic lens (accommodation) adjusts the eye for near or far objects. Constriction of the pupil narrows the diameter of the hole through which light enters the eye, preventing light rays entering from the periphery.

The point at which the nerve fibers leave the eye as the optic nerve, is the **blind spot** (where there are no photoreceptor cells). Nerve impulses travel along the optic nerves to the visual processing areas in the cerebral cortex. Images on the retina are inverted and reversed by the lens but the brain interprets the information it receives to correct for this image reversal.

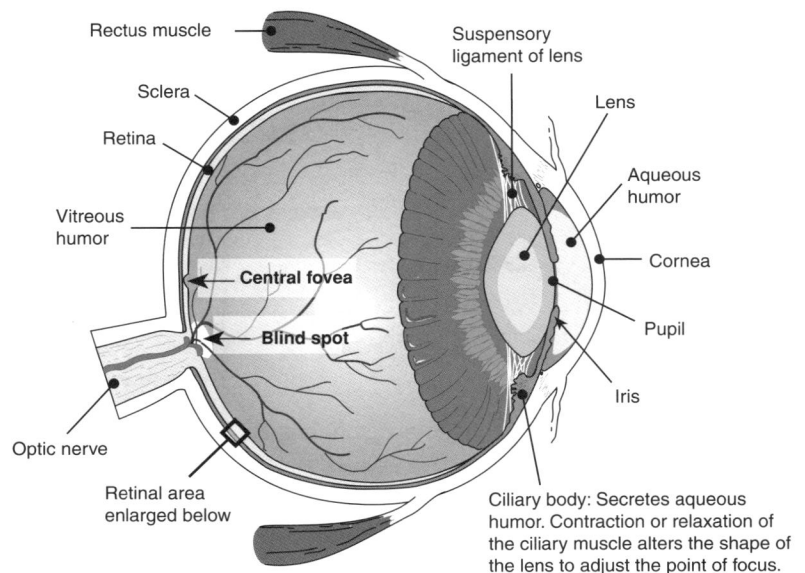

Ciliary body: Secretes aqueous humor. Contraction or relaxation of the ciliary muscle alters the shape of the lens to adjust the point of focus.

The Structure and Arrangement of Photoreceptors in the Retina

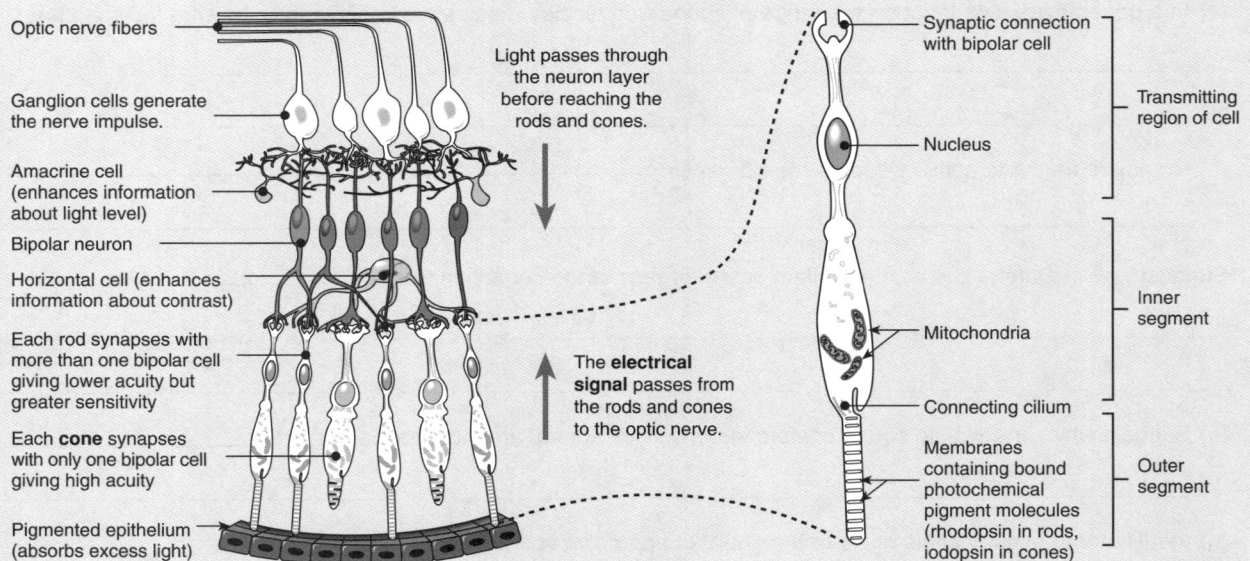

Arrangement of photoreceptors and neurons in the retina

Structure of a rod photoreceptor cell

The photoreceptor cells of the mammalian retina are the **rods** and **cones**. Rods are specialized for vision in dim light, whereas cones are specialized for color vision and high visual acuity. Cone density and visual acuity are greatest in the central fovea (rods are absent here). Light induces structural changes in the photochemical pigments of the rod and cone membranes, opening ion channels and leading to generator potentials (graded changes in membrane conductance), which spread through the photoreceptor cell. Each photoreceptor makes synaptic connection with a bipolar neuron, which transmits the potentials to the ganglion cells. These become depolarized and initiate nerve impulses. The frequency and pattern of impulses in the optic nerve conveys information about the changing visual field.

The Basis of Trichromatic Vision

There are three classes of **cones**, each with a maximal response in either short (blue), intermediate (green) or long (yellow-green) wavelength light (below). The yellow-green cone is also sensitive to the red part of the spectrum and is often called the red cone. The differential responses of the cones to light of different wavelengths provides the basis of trichromatic color vision.

Cone response to light wavelengths

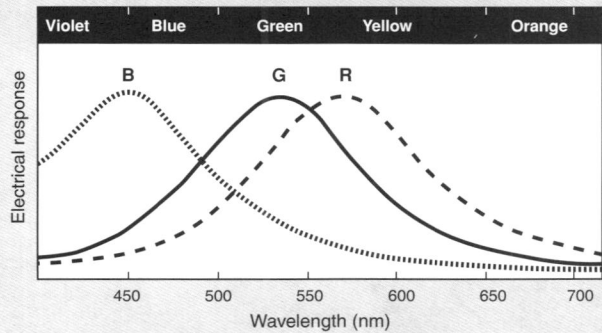

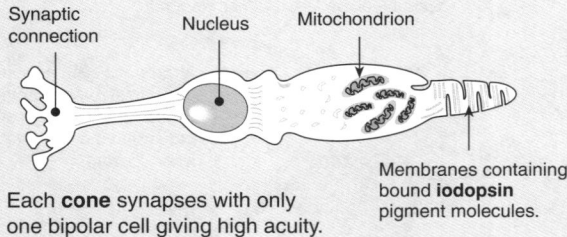

Synaptic connection
Nucleus
Mitochondrion

Membranes containing bound **iodopsin** pigment molecules.

Each **cone** synapses with only one bipolar cell giving high acuity.

1. Briefly describe the function of the following structures in the mammalian eye:

(a) The lens: _____

(b) The cornea: _____

(c) The photoreceptor cells: _____

2. (a) Explain the term: accommodation: _____

(b) Explain how accommodation is achieved: _____

_____

_____

3. In simple terms, explain how light is able to produce a nerve impulse in the ganglion cells: _____

_____

_____

4. Contrast the structure of the blind spot and the central fovea: _____

_____

_____

5. Complete the table below, comparing the features of rod and cone cells:

Feature	Rod cells	Cone cells
Visual pigment(s):		
Visual acuity:		
Overall function:		

6. (a) Explain the physiological basis for color vision in humans: _____

_____

_____

(b) State why cones are less sensitive than rods to low light levels: _____

_____

_____

Animal Support and Movement

Most animals support themselves in their environment and move around. In animals, support systems (skeletons) are adapted to methods of locomotion and feeding. Movement in water and on land requires different adaptations because of the very different properties of these two media. In vertebrates, limbs are usually modified for different modes of locomotion. Invertebrate methods of propulsion are more diverse, partly a reflection of their more diverse range of support systems.

Movement on Land

The spine, composed of individual vertebrae, provides a strong but flexible structure for supporting the body weight.

Muscles and bones act as levers to produce forward thrust. Ligaments join bones and provide extra support during movement.

Pillar-like legs transfer the body weight to the ground.

Specially adapted feet (e.g. hooves) provide friction against the ground.

Terrestrial animals have evolved numerous solutions to the problem of moving around. Movement on land requires that animals support their weight against gravity and develop motion by pushing against the surrounding medium (air) or the ground. They do this through the combined action of muscles and bones. Bone is heavy, so large bones (e.g. leg bones) are hollow to reduce weight. Birds have very light bones and many are fused together as an adaptation to flight. To move forward, land animals must overcome the forces (such as inertia) that act to keep them stationary. These forces are often called drag. For terrestrial animals drag is important when motion is at high speeds such as during flight.

Walking and Running

Heavy land mammals have short thick bones to support their weight, although they are not adapted for speed. Fast running mammals, e.g. antelope, have long, thin bones with flexible joints supported by strong ligament slings. In fast running land mammals, all four feet may leave the ground for part of each stride. Stability is maintained because of the forward momentum.

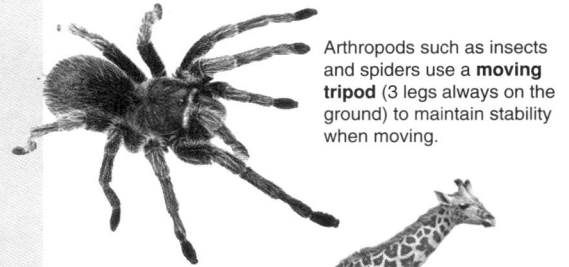

Arthropods such as insects and spiders use a **moving tripod** (3 legs always on the ground) to maintain stability when moving.

Some vertebrates use a moving tripod during slow walking.

Gliding flight   *Hovering flight*

Jumping and Leaping

Jumping animals have relatively long, powerful hindlimbs. In mammals the forelimbs are often reduced in size and used for slow movement and food handling. Jumping mammals need a long tail to help to centre the weight over the back legs. Jumping results in rapid acceleration and is often used for prey capture or escape. For some animals (e.g. kangaroos), jumping is also an energy efficient means of sustained locomotion.

Flying

Birds, some mammals, and many insects have mastered flight. Flying is a very rapid but energy expensive mode of locomotion. Flying animals have wings shaped like an airfoil (curved up on the top surface and thicker in the front). This reduces drag and increases lift. Wings have different origins: arthropod wings are extensions of the thorax exoskeleton, while vertebrate wings are modifications of the limbs.

Climbing

Amphibians, reptiles, birds, and most orders of mammals have climbing representatives. Adaptations for climbing involve structures and mechanisms for maximizing grip on surfaces, e.g. foot pads, claws, and grasping feet. Many of the expert climbers, such as primates, have elongated, flexible limbs for reaching and swinging. Others, e.g. rodents such as squirrels, combine agile climbing with leaping.

1. Briefly explain the reasons for the difference in bone length and thickness between the following land animals:

    (a) Large, slow land animals: _____

    _____

    (b) Smaller, faster land animals: _____

    _____

2. (a) Explain the advantages of flight to a land animal: _____

    _____

    (b) Name three broad groups of animal that fly: _____

    (c) Describe two main problems that need to be overcome by an animal if it is to fly: _____

    _____

    (d) Explain how the shape of a wing assists in this: _____

Movement in Water

Fins and flippers can be used for control, maneuvering and braking.

Some aquatic invertebrates have jelly filled bodies and/or gas filled floats to provide buoyancy.

Gas filled swim bladder

The backward displacement of water generates forward movement.

Fat, oil and gas filled structures are lighter than water and give buoyancy.

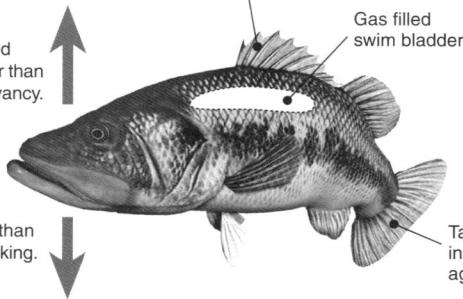

Path of the tail through the water

Bone, cartilage and muscle are denser than water and cause sinking.

Tail fins are important in generating thrust against the water.

Streamlined body shape reduces drag through the water.

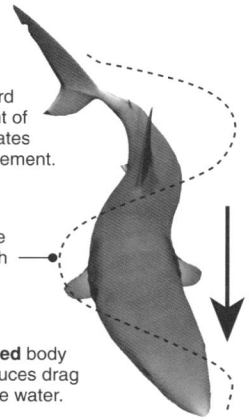

Animals show a wide range of adaptations to movement through water. In **invertebrates** propulsion can be generated by a huge range of mechanisms, from jointed limbs to adhesive tube feet (below). Where movement is across a substrate, a hard skeleton (external in arthropods, internal in echinoderms) or shell provides weight. Where buoyancy is required, air or gas chambers are usually used. **Vertebrates** have adapted to movement underwater by adapting limbs into paddles or fins. Birds have webbed feet to provide propulsion in water while also allowing for reasonable mobility on land. The fastest vertebrate swimmers (dolphins, whales and fish) use a powerful tail to provide thrust against the water.

Backswimmer
Feathered limbs in aquatic insects give effective rowing with paddles.

Marine snail
A large muscular foot allows snails to glide smoothly over the substrate.

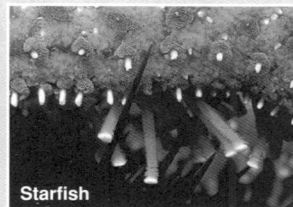

Starfish
Adhesive tube feet in echinoderms provide slow but strong movement.

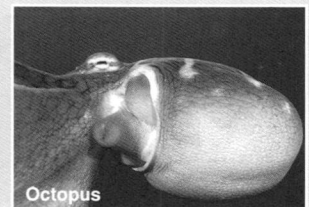

Octopus
Water jet propulsion in cephalopods allows rapid escape from danger.

Green sea turtle
Broad flippers and breast stroke action in turtles provide propulsion.

Fish
Powerful tail fin in fish gives thrust, other fins provide lift and control.

Penguin
Webbed feet and flightless, paddle like wings in penguins provide thrust.

Dolphins
Strong fins and horizontal tail fluke in dolphins give strong propulsion.

3. State in which situation jumping is normally used and why:

_____

4. Water provides most of the support for aquatic animals. Describe the main problem for animals moving through water:

_____

_____

5. (a) Explain what is meant by streamlining a body shape: _____

_____

(b) Explain why streamlining is a characteristic of the fastest swimmers: _____

_____

6. Outline some of the methods by which animals remain buoyant in the water: _____

_____

_____

_____

7. Many marine invertebrates (e.g. snails, starfish) do not require a buoyancy mechanism. Explain why this is the case:

_____

_____

The Human Skeleton

A 1

The skeletal system consists of bones and their associated connective tissues (cartilage, tendons, and ligaments). The skeletal system performs five basic functions: it provides support and protection; it allows for movement; and it is involved in storing minerals and producing red blood cells. It also has a role in the conduction of sound in the middle ear. The human skeleton consists of two main divisions: the **axial skeleton**, which comprises the bones of the head and torso (skull, spine, sternum, and ribs), and the **appendicular skeleton** (the limbs and limb girdles).

Word list: *humerus, patella, scapula, tibia, clavicle, sternum, vertebra, femur, phalanges, mandible, metacarpals, rib, ilium, fibula.*

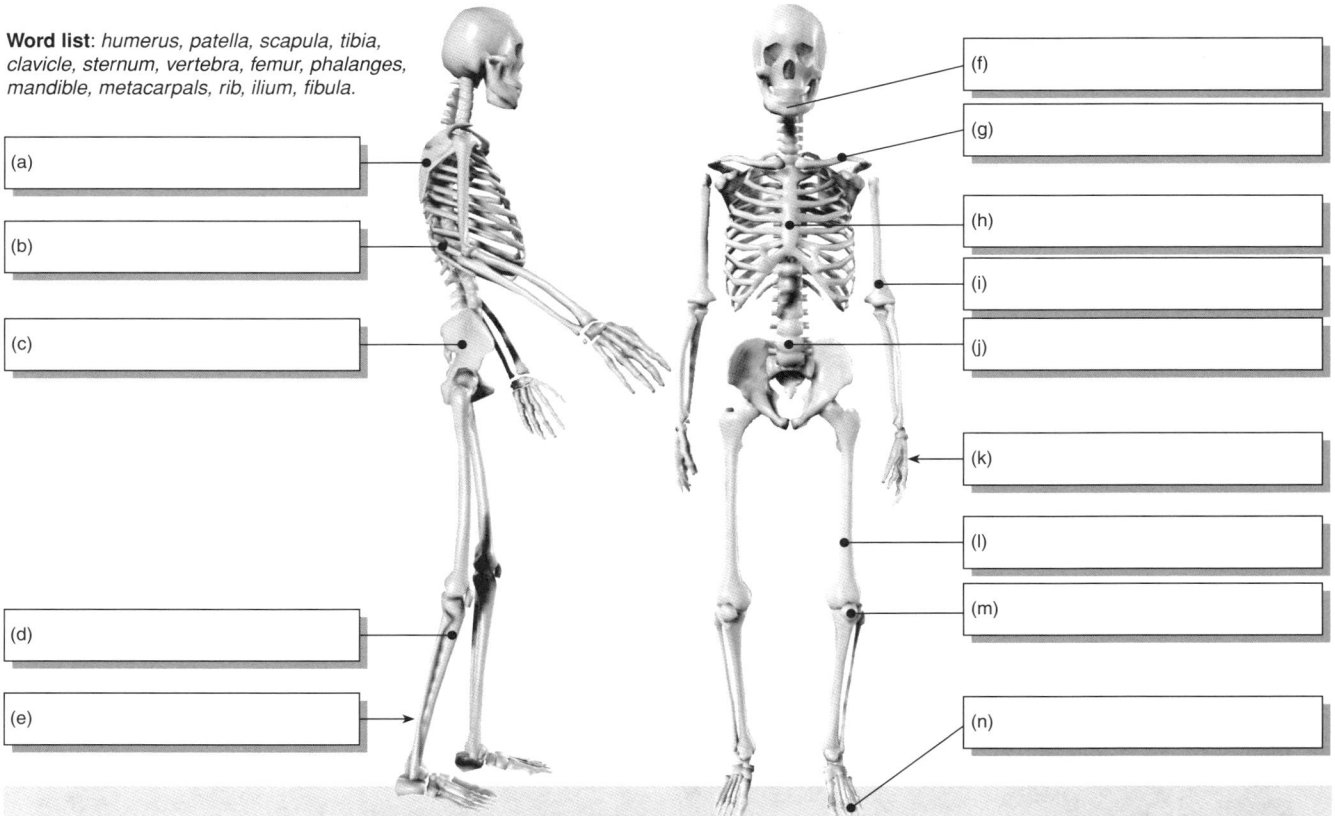

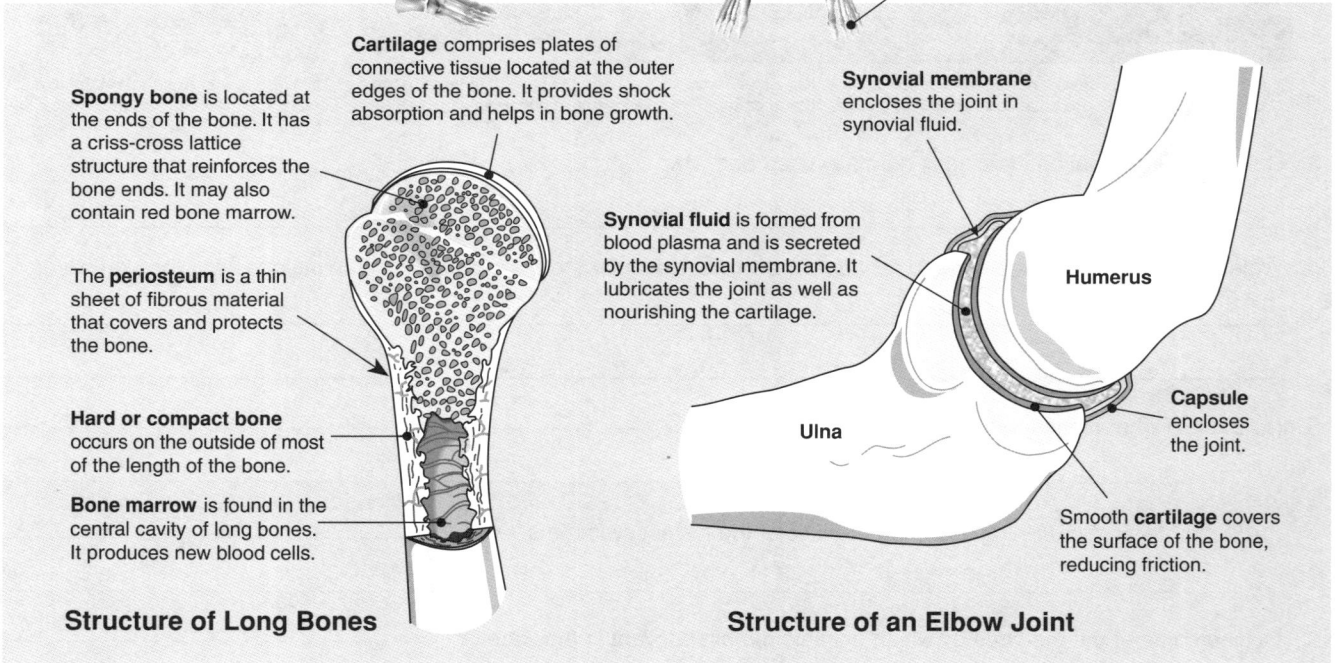

(a)

(b)

(c)

(d)

(e)

(f)

(g)

(h)

(i)

(j)

(k)

(l)

(m)

(n)

Spongy bone is located at the ends of the bone. It has a criss-cross lattice structure that reinforces the bone ends. It may also contain red bone marrow.

The **periosteum** is a thin sheet of fibrous material that covers and protects the bone.

Hard or compact bone occurs on the outside of most of the length of the bone.

Bone marrow is found in the central cavity of long bones. It produces new blood cells.

Cartilage comprises plates of connective tissue located at the outer edges of the bone. It provides shock absorption and helps in bone growth.

Synovial fluid is formed from blood plasma and is secreted by the synovial membrane. It lubricates the joint as well as nourishing the cartilage.

Synovial membrane encloses the joint in synovial fluid.

Humerus

Ulna

Capsule encloses the joint.

Smooth **cartilage** covers the surface of the bone, reducing friction.

Structure of Long Bones

Structure of an Elbow Joint

1. On the diagram above, use the word list provided to label the bones of the skeleton.

2. Briefly describe the functions of a mammalian skeleton (bone tissue) under the following headings:

(a) Movement: _____

_____

(b) Protection: _____

_____

The Ultrastructure of Bone

The cells that produce the bone are called **osteoblasts**. They secrete the matrix of calcium phosphate and collagen fibers that forms the rigid bone. Once mature and embedded within the matrix, the bone cells are called **osteocytes**. Dense bone has a very regular structure, composed of repeating units called *Haversian systems*. Each Haversian system has concentric rings of hard material enclosing the bone cells. Haversian canals running through the bone contain blood vessels and nerves so that the bone cells can be supplied with oxygen and nutrients, and wastes can be removed.

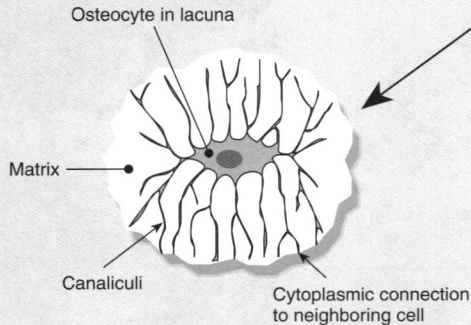

Haversian canal

Strands of tissue link bone cells

Outer surface of bone

Periosteum

Osteocyte in lacuna

Matrix

Canaliculi

Cytoplasmic connection to neighboring cell

Section through bone tissue

Inner surface of bone

Haversian canal through which veins, arteries, and nerves service surrounding bone tissue.

Osteocytes (mature bone cells)

Osteocyte (bone cell) embedded in a lacuna within the matrix (mainly calcium phosphate and collagen). The osteocytes maintain the bone tissue.

(c) Hearing: _____

_____

(d) Mineral storage: _____

_____

(e) Gas exchange: _____

_____

3. Explain the role that synovial fluid and cartilage play in a synovial joint: _____

_____

_____

4. Describe the structural role of osteocytes (bone cells): _____

_____

_____

5. Describe the function of the Haversian canal system in hard bone tissue: _____

_____

_____

_____

6. Define the following terms:

(a) Axial skeleton: _____

(b) Torso: _____

(c) Limb girdles: _____

The Mechanics of Locomotion

RA 2

Bones are too rigid to bend without damage. To allow movement, the skeletal system consists of many bones held together at **joints** by flexible connective tissues called **ligaments**. All movements of the skeleton occur at joints: points of contact between bones, or between cartilage and bones. Joints may be classified according to the amount of movement they permit: none (sutures); slight movement (symphyses), and free movement in one or more planes (e.g. **synovial joints**). Bones are made to move about a joint by the force of muscles acting upon them. The muscles are attached to bone by **tendons**. Many muscles act in **antagonistic** pairs, one set causing the joint to

move one way, the other set causing its return. The skeleton of an animal works as a system of levers. The joint acts as a fulcrum, the muscles exert the force, and the weight of the bone being moved represents the load. Contraction causes a muscle to shorten and this shortening moves attached bones. When only a few fibers in a muscle contract, the muscle will tighten but not produce movement. This partly contracted state is responsible for **muscle tone** and is important in maintaining **posture**. The amount of muscle contraction is monitored by sensory receptors in the muscle called **muscle spindle organs**. These provide the sensory information necessary to adjust movement as required.

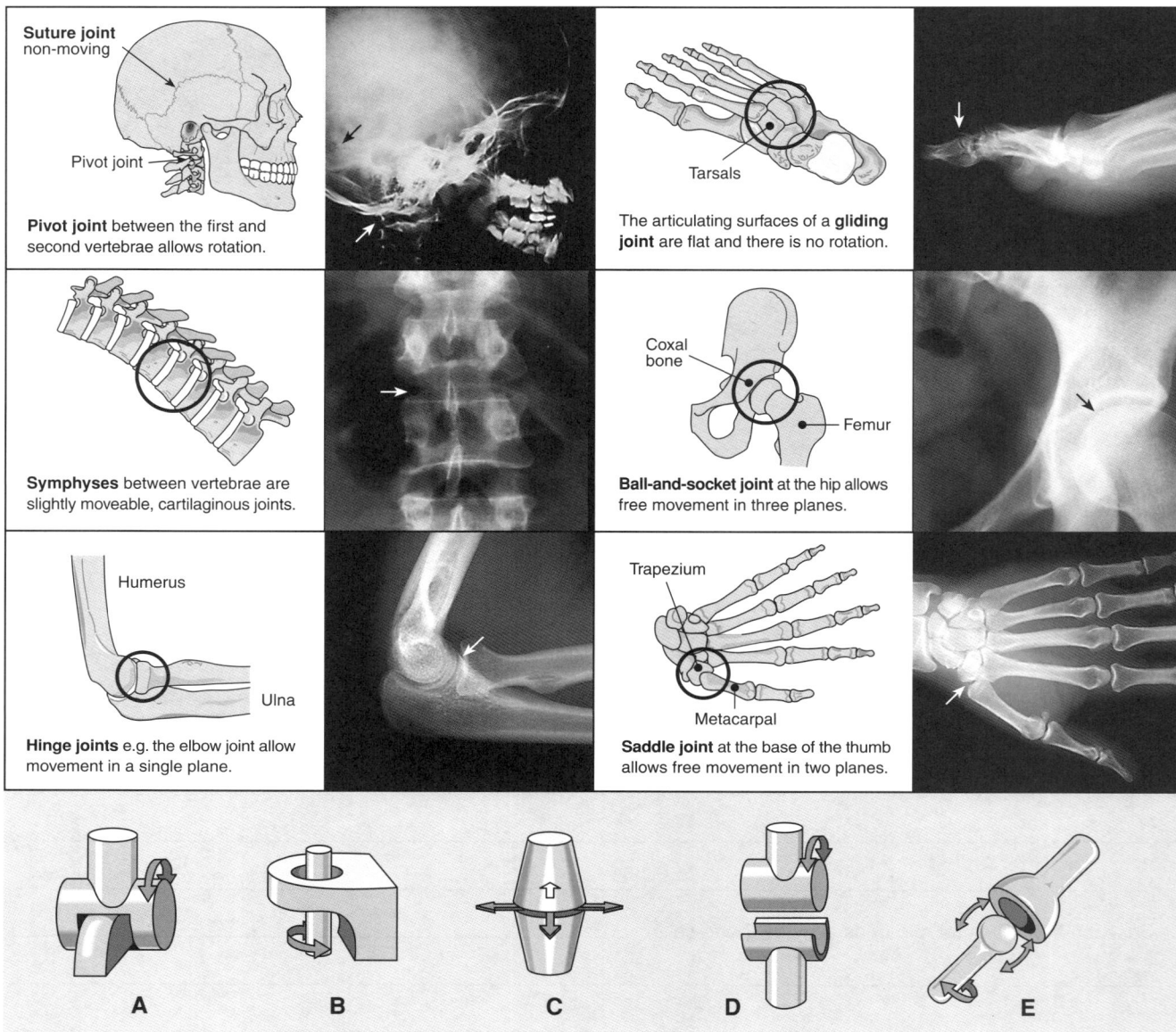

Suture joint non-moving

Pivot joint

Pivot joint between the first and second vertebrae allows rotation.

Symphyses between vertebrae are slightly moveable, cartilaginous joints.

Humerus

Ulna

Hinge joints e.g. the elbow joint allow movement in a single plane.

Tarsals

The articulating surfaces of a **gliding joint** are flat and there is no rotation.

Coxal bone

Femur

Ball-and-socket joint at the hip allows free movement in three planes.

Trapezium

Metacarpal

Saddle joint at the base of the thumb allows free movement in two planes.

A   B   C   D   E

1. Classify each of the models illustrating movement in synovial joints (A-E above), according to the labels given below:

   (a) Pivot: _____ (b) Hinge: _____ (c) Ball-and-socket: _____ (d) Saddle: _____ (e) Gliding: _____

2. Briefly state the role of each of the following in human locomotion:

   (a) Ligament: _____

   (b) Tendon: _____

   (c) Antagonistic muscles: _____

   (d) Bones: _____

   (e) Joints: _____

The Action of Antagonistic Muscles

The flexion (bending) and extension (unbending) of limbs is caused by the action of **antagonistic muscles**; muscles that work in pairs and whose actions oppose each other. Every coordinated movement in the body requires the application of muscle force. This is accomplished by the action of agonists, antagonists, and synergists. The opposing action of agonists and antagonists also produces muscle tone. Note that either muscle in an antagonistic pair can act as the prime mover, depending on the movement (flexion or extension).

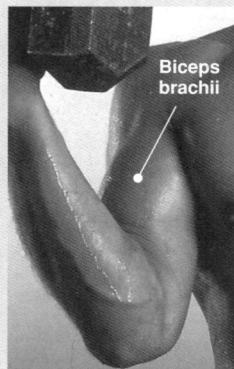

Biceps brachii

Agonists or prime movers: muscles that are primarily responsible for the movement and produce most of the force required.

Antagonists: muscles that oppose the prime mover. They may also play a protective role by preventing overstretching of the prime mover.

Synergists: muscles that assist the prime movers and may be involved in fine-tuning the direction of the movement.

During flexion of the forearm at the elbow, (left) the **biceps brachii** acts as the prime mover, and the antagonist, the **triceps brachii** at the back of the arm, is relaxing. During extension, their roles are reversed.

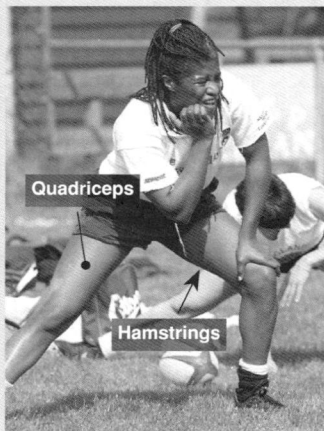

Quadriceps

Hamstrings

Movement of the leg is accomplished through the action of several large groups of muscles, collectively called the **quadriceps** and the **hamstrings**.

The hamstrings are actually a collection of three muscles, which act together to flex the leg. The quadriceps at the front of the thigh (a collection of four large muscles) opposes the motion of the hamstrings and extends the leg. When the prime mover contracts very forcefully, the antagonist also contracts very slightly. This prevents any overstretching and allows greater control over thigh movement.

The Role of the Muscle Spindle

Changes in length of a muscle are monitored by the **muscle spindle organ**, a stretch receptor located within skeletal muscle, parallel to the muscle fibers themselves. The muscle spindle is stimulated in response to sustained or sudden stretch on the central region of its specialized intrafusal fibers. Sensory information from the muscle spindle is relayed to the spinal cord. The motor response brings about adjustments to the degree of stretch in the muscle. These adjustments help in the coordination and efficiency of muscle contraction. Muscle spindles are important in the maintenance of muscle tone, postural reflexes, and movement control, and are concentrated in muscles that exert fine control over movement.

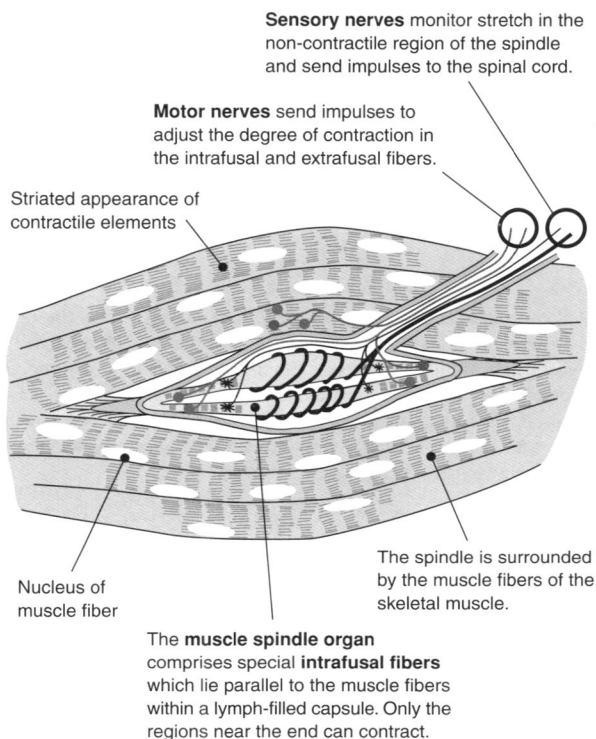

Sensory nerves monitor stretch in the non-contractile region of the spindle and send impulses to the spinal cord.

Motor nerves send impulses to adjust the degree of contraction in the intrafusal and extrafusal fibers.

Striated appearance of contractile elements

Nucleus of muscle fiber

The spindle is surrounded by the muscle fibers of the skeletal muscle.

The **muscle spindle organ** comprises special **intrafusal fibers** which lie parallel to the muscle fibers within a lymph-filled capsule. Only the regions near the end can contract.

3. Using appropriate terminology, explain how antagonistic muscles act together to raise and lower a limb:

_____

_____

_____

_____

_____

4. (a) Explain the role of the muscle spindle organ: _____

_____

   (b) With reference to the following, describe how the structure of the muscle spindle organ is related to its function:

   Intrafusal fibers lie parallel to the extrafusal fibers: _____

_____

   Sensory neurons are located in the non-contractile region of the organ: _____

_____

   Motor neurons synapse in the extrafusal fibers and the contractile region of the intrafusal fibers: _____

_____

A2 Muscle Structure and Function

There are three kinds of muscle: **skeletal, cardiac**, and **smooth** muscle, each with a distinct structure. The muscles used for posture and locomotion are skeletal (striated) muscles. Their distinct striped appearance is the result of the regular arrangement of contractile elements within the muscle cells. Muscle fibers are innervated by motor neurons, each of which terminates in a specialized cholinergic synapse called the **motor end plate**. A motor neuron and all the fibers it innervates is called a **motor unit**.

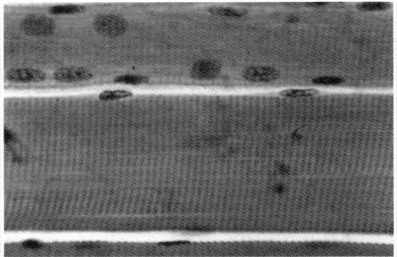

Skeletal muscle
Also called striated or striped muscle. It has a banded appearance under high power microscopy. Sometimes called voluntary muscle because it is under conscious control. The cells are large with many nuclei at the edge of each cell.

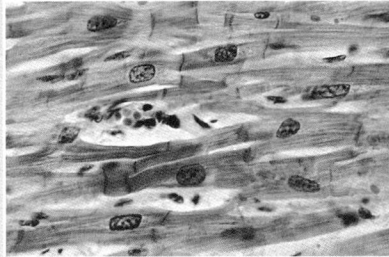

Cardiac muscle
Specialized striated muscle that does not fatigue. Cells branch and connect with each other to assist the passage of nerve impulses through the muscle. Cardiac muscle is not under conscious control (it is involuntary).

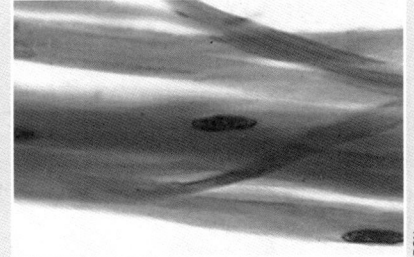

Smooth muscle
Also called involuntary muscle because it is not under conscious control. Contractile filaments are irregularly arranged so the contraction is not in one direction as in skeletal muscle. Cells are spindle shaped with one central nucleus.

Structure of Skeletal Muscle

Skeletal muscle is organized into bundles of muscle cells or **fibers**. Each fiber is a single cell with many nuclei and each fiber is itself a bundle of smaller **myofibrils** arranged lengthwise. Each myofibril is in turn composed of two kinds of **myofilaments** (thick and thin), which overlap to form light and dark bands. It is the alternation of these light and dark bands which gives skeletal muscle its striated or striped appearance. The **sarcomere**, bounded by the dark z-lines, forms one complete contractile unit.

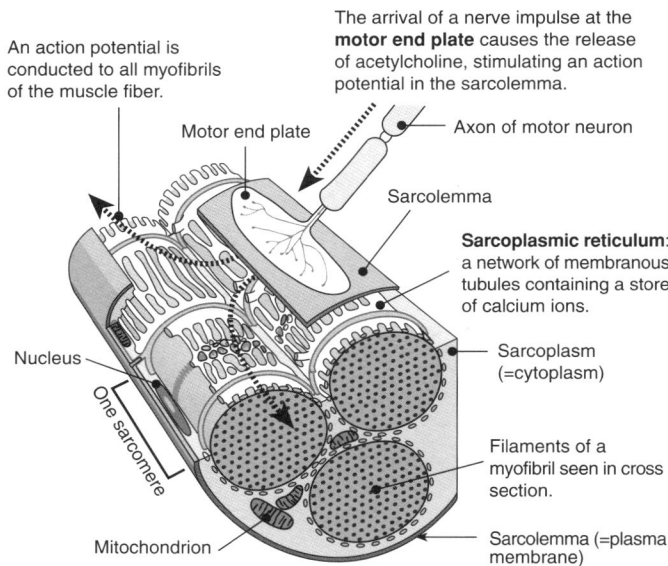

An action potential is conducted to all myofibrils of the muscle fiber.

The arrival of a nerve impulse at the **motor end plate** causes the release of acetylcholine, stimulating an action potential in the sarcolemma.

Motor end plate

Axon of motor neuron

Sarcolemma

Sarcoplasmic reticulum: a network of membranous tubules containing a store of calcium ions.

Sarcoplasm (=cytoplasm)

Nucleus

One sarcomere

Filaments of a myofibril seen in cross section.

Mitochondrion

Sarcolemma (=plasma membrane)

Several myofibrils of a muscle fiber

Longitudinal section of a sarcomere

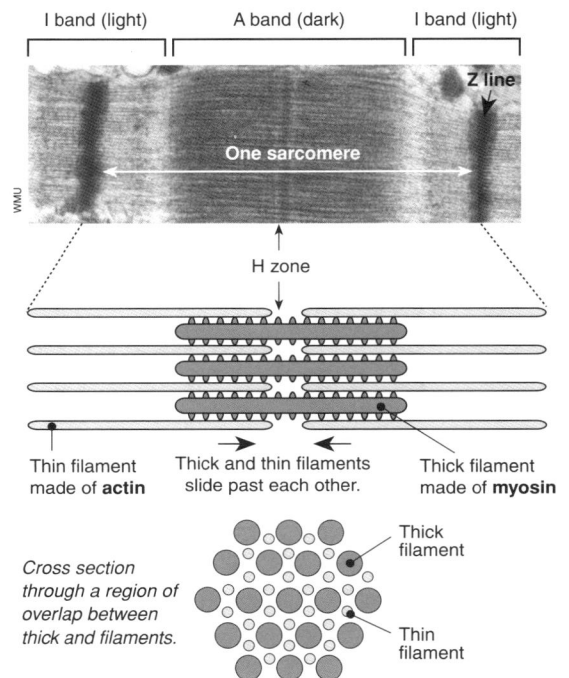

I band (light)   A band (dark)   I band (light)

Z line

One sarcomere

H zone

Thin filament made of **actin**

Thick and thin filaments slide past each other.

Thick filament made of **myosin**

Cross section through a region of overlap between thick and filaments.

Thick filament

Thin filament

The photograph of a sarcomere (above) illustrates the distinctive banding pattern of skeletal muscle. The pattern, which arises because of the arrangement of thin and thick filaments, is shown in schematic form below the photograph. A representation of the region of overlap is also illustrated.

The Banding Pattern of Myofibrils

Within a myofibril, thin filaments, held together by the **Z lines**, project in both directions. The arrival of a nerve impulse sets in motion a series of events that cause the thick and thin filaments to slide past each other. This **contraction** results in shortening of the muscle and is accompanied by a visible change in the appearance of the myofibril: the I band and the sarcomere shorten and H zone shortens or disappears.

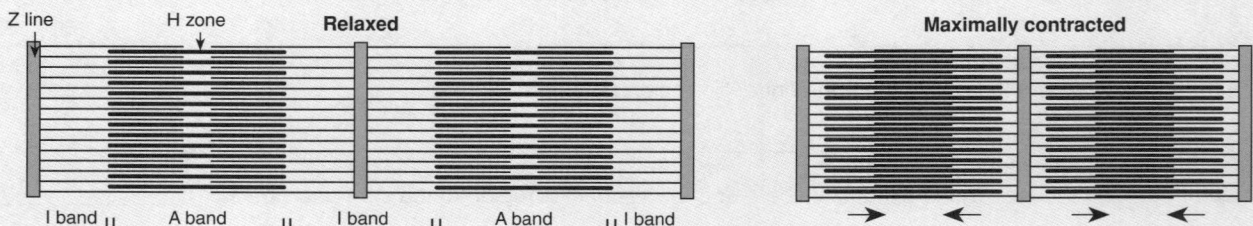

Z line   H zone   **Relaxed**

Maximally contracted

I band   A band   I band   A band   I band

The Sliding Filament Hypothesis

Muscle contraction requires calcium ions (Ca^{2+}) and energy (in the form of ATP) in order for the thick and thin filaments to slide past each other. The steps are:

1. The binding sites on the **actin** molecule (to which myosin 'heads' will locate) are blocked by a complex of two molecules: tropomyosin and troponin.

2. Prior to muscle contraction, ATP binds to the heads of the myosin molecules, priming them in an erect high energy state. Arrival of an action potential causes a release of Ca^{2+} from the sarcoplasmic reticulum. The Ca^{2+} binds to the troponin and causes the blocking molecules to move so that the myosin binding sites on the actin filament become exposed.

3. The heads of the cross-bridging myosin molecules attach to the binding sites on the actin filament. Release of energy from the hydrolysis of ATP accompanies the cross bridge formation.

4. The energy released from ATP hydrolysis causes a change in shape of the myosin **cross bridge**, resulting in a bending action (*the power stroke*). This causes the actin filaments to slide past the myosin filaments towards the centre of the sarcomere.

5. (Not illustrated). Fresh ATP attaches to the myosin molecules, releasing them from the binding sites and repriming them for a repeat movement. They become attached further along the actin chain as long as ATP and Ca^{2+} are available.

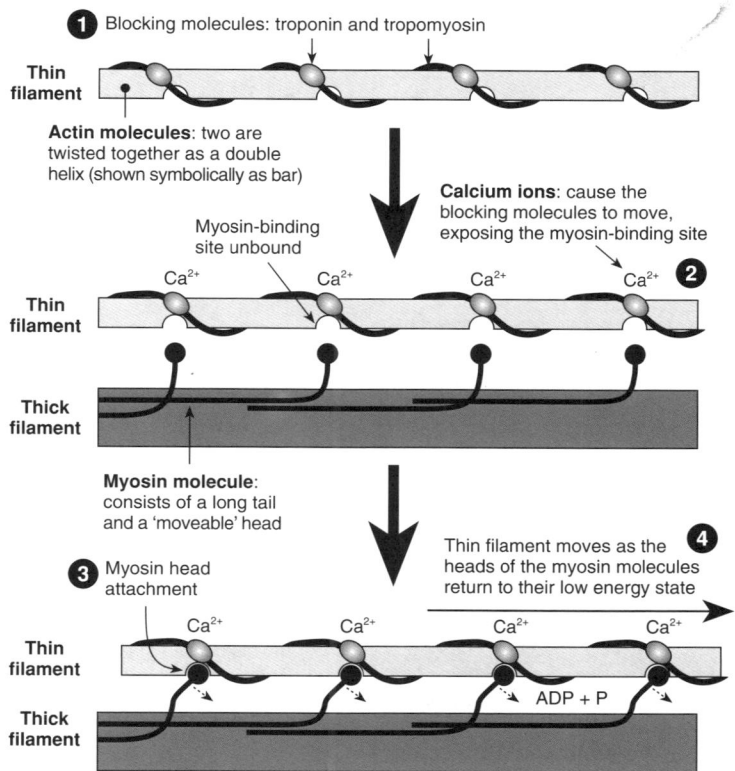

1. **Blocking molecules: troponin and tropomyosin**

Thin filament

Actin molecules: two are twisted together as a double helix (shown symbolically as bar)

Calcium ions: cause the blocking molecules to move, exposing the myosin-binding site

Myosin-binding site unbound

Ca^{2+} Ca^{2+} Ca^{2+} Ca^{2+} **2**

Thin filament

Thick filament

Myosin molecule: consists of a long tail and a 'moveable' head

3 Myosin head attachment

4 Thin filament moves as the heads of the myosin molecules return to their low energy state

Ca^{2+} Ca^{2+} Ca^{2+} Ca^{2+}

Thin filament

Thick filament

ADP + P

1. Summarize the features that distinguish each of the following muscle types:

   (a) Smooth muscle: _____

   (b) Striated muscle: _____

   (c) Cardiac muscle: _____

2. Match the following chemicals with their functional role in muscle movement (draw a line between matching pairs):

   (a) Myosin • Bind to the actin molecule in a way that prevents myosin head from forming a cross bridge

   (b) Actin • Supplies energy for the flexing of the myosin 'head' (power stroke)

   (c) Calcium ions • Has a moveable head that provides a power stroke when activated

   (d) Troponin-tropomyosin • Two protein molecules twisted in a helix shape that form the thin filament of a myofibril

   (e) ATP • Bind to the blocking molecules, causing them to move and expose the myosin binding site

3. (a) Explain the cause of the banding pattern visible in striated muscle: _____

   (b) **Explain** the change in appearance of a myofibril during contraction with reference to the following:

   The I band: _____

   The H zone: _____

   The sarcomere: _____

4. **Rigor mortis** is a state of partial contraction of the muscle that occurs after death. During rigor mortis, the muscles are locked and the body is stiff. From what you understand of muscle contraction, suggest why the muscle enters this state:

   _____

   _____

DA 2
Energy and Exercise

Exercise places an immediate demand on the body's energy supply systems. During exercise, the metabolic rate of the muscles increases by up to 20 times and the body's systems must respond appropriately to maintain homeostasis. The high energy compound, adenosine triphosphate (ATP) provides the immediate energy for exercise. Energy is released when the terminal phosphate group is split from the ATP molecule and this hydrolysis is coupled to muscular contraction. The ability to exercise for any given length of time depends on maintenance of adequate supplies of ATP to the muscles. There are three energy systems operating to do this: the ATP-CP system, the glycolytic system, and the oxidative system. The ultimate sources of energy for ATP generation in muscle via these systems are glucose, and stores of glycogen and triglycerides.

CP provides enough energy to fuel about 10 s of maximum effort (e.g., a 100 m race).

The ATP-CP System

The simplest of the energy systems is the **ATP-CP system**. CP or **creatine phosphate** is a high energy compound that stores energy sufficient for brief periods of muscular effort. Energy released from the breakdown of CP is not used directly to accomplish cellular work. Instead it rebuilds ATP to maintain a relatively constant supply. This process is anaerobic, occurs very rapidly, and is accomplished without any special structures in the cell. CP levels decline steadily as it is used to replenish depleted ATP levels. The ability of the ATP-CP system to maintain energy levels is limited to 3-15 seconds during an all out sprint. Beyond this, the muscle must rely on other processes for ATP generation.

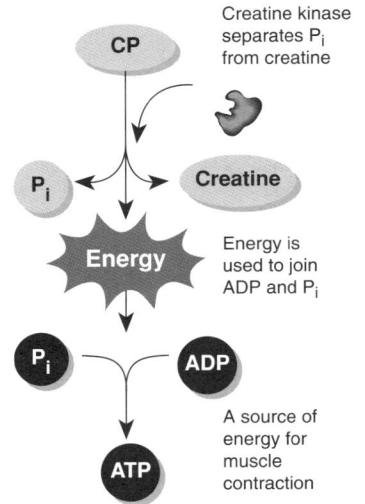

Creatine kinase separates P_i from creatine

Energy is used to join ADP and P_i

A source of energy for muscle contraction

Rugby and other field sports demand brief intense efforts with recovery in-between.

The Glycolytic System

ATP can also be provided by glycolysis: the first phase of cellular respiration. The ATP yield from glycolysis is low, only a net of 2ATP per molecule of glucose, but it produces ATP rapidly and does not require oxygen. The fuel for the glycolytic system is glucose, in the blood, or glycogen, which is stored in the muscle or liver and broken down to glucose-6-phosphate. Glycolysis provides ATP for exercise for only a few minutes. Its main limitation is that it causes lactic acid ($C_3H_6O_3$) to accumulate in the body tissues. It is the accumulation of lactic acid in the muscles that gives the feeling of muscle fatigue. The lactic acid must transported to the liver and respired aerobically. The extra oxygen needed for this is the **oxygen debt**.

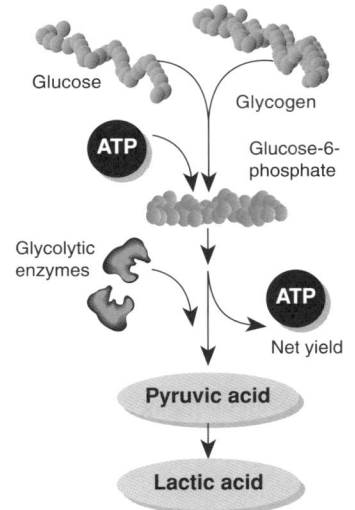

Glucose

Glycogen

Glucose-6-phosphate

Glycolytic enzymes

ATP

Net yield

Pyruvic acid

Lactic acid

Prolonged aerobic effort (e.g., distance running) requires a sustained ATP supply.

The Oxidative System

In the oxidative system, glucose is completely broken down to yield (about) 36 molecules of ATP. This process uses oxygen and takes place within the mitochondria. Aerobic metabolism has a high energy yield and is the primary method of energy production during sustained high activity. It is reliant on a continued supply of oxygen and therefore on the body's ability to deliver oxygen to the muscles. The fuels for aerobic respiration are glucose, stored glycogen, or stored **triglycerides**. Triglycerides provide free fatty acids, which are oxidized in the mitochondria by the successive removal of 2-carbon fragments (a process called β-oxidation). These 2 carbon units enter the Krebs cycle as acetyl coenzyme A (acetyl CoA).

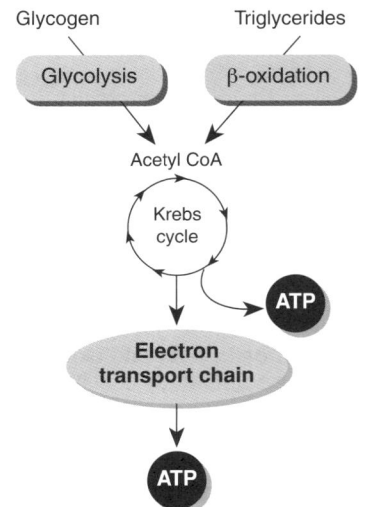

Glycogen

Triglycerides

Glycolysis

β-oxidation

Acetyl CoA

Krebs cycle

ATP

Electron transport chain

ATP

Oxygen Uptake During Exercise and Recovery

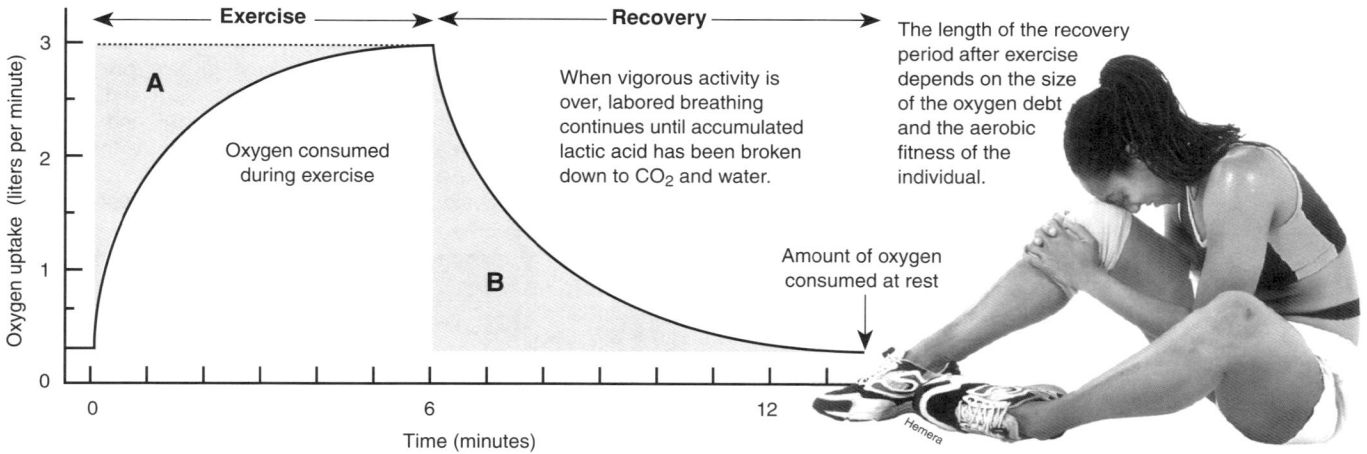

The graph above illustrates the principle of oxygen debt. In the graph, the energy demands of aerobic exercise require 3 liters (dm^3) of oxygen per minute. The rate of oxygen uptake increases immediately exercise starts, but the full requirement is not met until six minutes later. The **oxygen deficit** is the amount of oxygen needed (for aerobic energy supply) but not supplied by breathing. During the first six minutes, the energy is supplied largely from anaerobic pathways: the ATP-CP and glycolytic systems (opposite). After exercise, the oxygen uptake per minute does not drop immediately to its resting level. Extra oxygen is taken in despite the drop in energy demand (the **oxygen debt**). The oxygen debt is used to replace oxygen reserves in the body, restore creatine phosphate, and break down the lactic acid (through various intermediates) to CO_2 and water.

1. Explain why the supply of energy through the glycolytic system is limited:

   _____

   _____

2. Summarize the features of the three energy systems in the table below:

	ATP-CP system	Glycolytic system	Oxidative system
ATP supplied by:			
Duration of ATP supply:			

3. Study the graph and explanatory paragraph above, then **identify** and **describe** what is represented by:

   (a) The shaded region A: _____

   _____

   (b) The shaded region B: _____

   _____

4. With respect to the graph above, explain why the rate of oxygen uptake does not immediately return to its resting level after exercise stops:

   _____

   _____

5. The rate of oxygen uptake increases immediately exercise starts. Explain how the oxygen supply from outside the body to the cells is increased during exercise:

   _____

   _____

6. Lactic acid levels in the **blood** continue to rise for a time after exercise has stopped. Explain why this occurs:

   _____

   _____

The Effects of Training

RA 2

The body has an immediate response to an exercise bout but also, over time, responds to the stress of repeated exercise (**training**) by adapting and improving both its capacity for exercise and the efficiency with which it performs. Training causes tissue damage and depletes energy stores, but the body responds by repairing the damage, replenishing energy stores, and adjusting its responses so as to minimize the impact of exercise in the future. Five basic principles of training apply, although the extent to which each of these applies is dependent on the type and purpose of the training. Training must be **specific** to the particular demands of the sport or activity involved and must involve **progressive overload** of muscle in order to develop strength and stamina. Training should also be at a **frequency**, **intensity**, and **duration** that promotes changes in physiology appropriate to the activity and performance level required. The general effects of aerobic training on the physiology are described below and opposite.

Muscle Physiology and Performance

Regardless of the type of training, some of our ability to perform different types of activity depends on our genetic make-up. This is particularly true of aspects of muscle physiology, such as the relative proportions of different fiber types in the skeletal muscles.

Muscle fibers are primarily of two types: fast twitch (FT) or slow twitch (ST). Fast twitch fibers predominate during anaerobic, explosive activity, whereas slow twitch fibers predominate during endurance activity. In the table below, note the difference in the degree to which the two fiber types show **fatigue** (decreased capacity to do work). Training can increase fiber size but not the proportion of ST to FT, which is genetically determined.

Feature	Fast twitch	Slow twitch
Color	White	Red
Diameter	Large	Small
Contraction rate	Fast	Slow
ATP production	Fast	Slow
Metabolism	Anaerobic	Aerobic
Rate of fatigue	Fast	Slow
Power	High	Low

The Effects of Aerobic Training on Muscle

Overall result
Improved function of the oxidative system and better endurance.

Improved oxidation of glycogen: Training increases the capacity of skeletal muscle to generate ATP aerobically.

Increased myoglobin content. Myoglobin stores oxygen in the muscle cells and aids oxygen delivery to the mitochondria. Endurance training increases muscle myoglobin by 75%-80%.

Increase in lean muscle mass and consequent decrease in body fat. Trained endurance athletes typically have body fat levels of 15-19% (women) or 6-18% (men) compared with 26% (women) and 15% (men) for non-athletes.

The size of the slow twitch fibers increases. This change is associated with increased aerobic capacity.

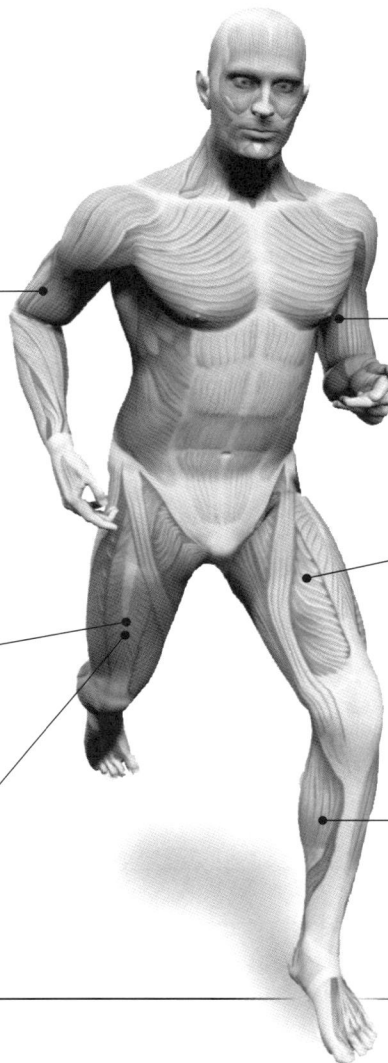

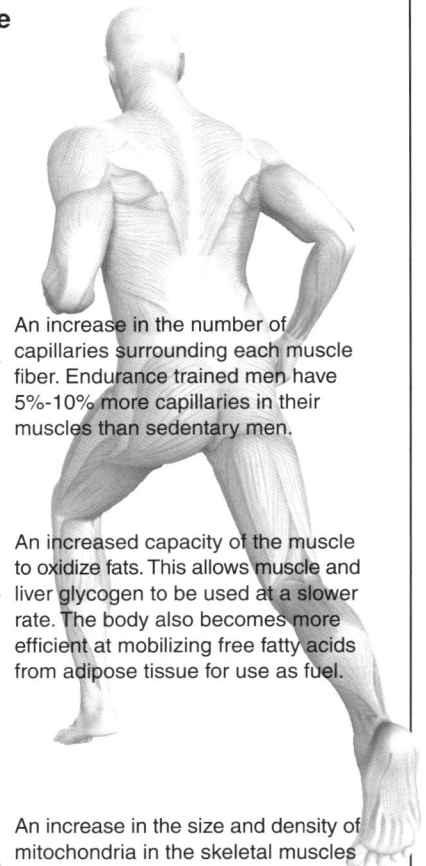

An increase in the number of capillaries surrounding each muscle fiber. Endurance trained men have 5%-10% more capillaries in their muscles than sedentary men.

An increased capacity of the muscle to oxidize fats. This allows muscle and liver glycogen to be used at a slower rate. The body also becomes more efficient at mobilizing free fatty acids from adipose tissue for use as fuel.

An increase in the size and density of mitochondria in the skeletal muscles and an increase in the activity and concentration of Krebs cycle enzymes.

1. (a) State what you understand by the term training: _____

_____

(b) In general terms, explain how training forces a change in physiology: _____

_____

The Effects of Aerobic Training

The Pulmonary System

Ventilation rate: The rate and depth of breathing increases during exercise. Training improves the efficiency of lung ventilation: for any given exercise level, the ventilation response to exercise is reduced.

Training improves the ventilation rhythm, so that breathing is in tune with the exercise rhythm. This promotes efficiency.

Overall result: Improved exchange of gases.

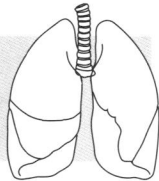

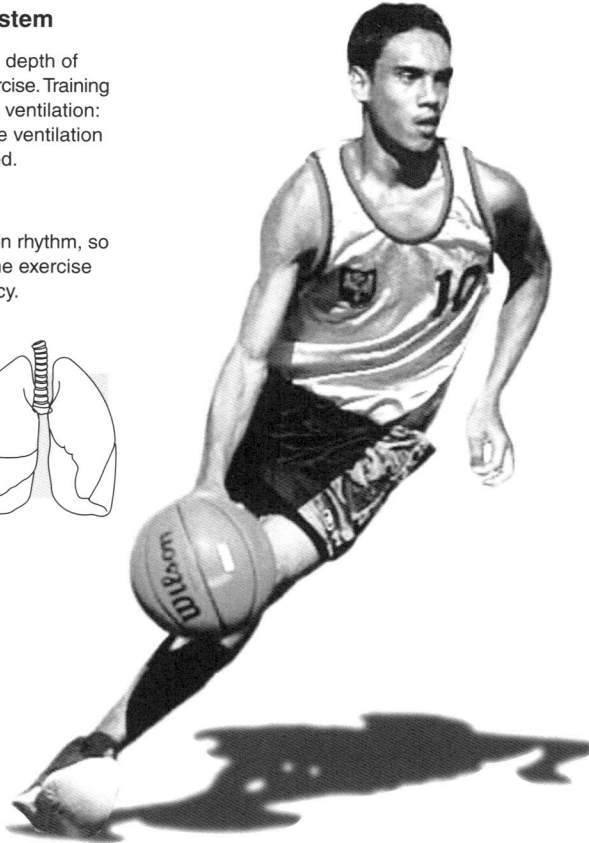

Cardiovascular Performance

Exercise lowers blood plasma volume by as much as 20% and the cellular portion of the blood becomes concentrated. With training, blood volume at rest increases to compensate.

Heart rate: Heart rate increases during exercise but aerobic training leads to a lower steady state heart rate overall for any given level of work.

Stroke volume (the amount of blood pumped with each beat) increases with aerobic training. This is related to an increased heart capacity, an increase in the heart's force of contraction, and an increase in venous return.

The increase in stroke volume results in an increased cardiac output.

During exercise, systolic blood pressure increases as a result of increased cardiac output. In response to training, the resting systolic blood pressure is lowered.

Blood flow changes during exercise so that more blood is diverted to working muscles and less is delivered to the gut.

Overall result: Meets the increased demands of exercise most efficiently.

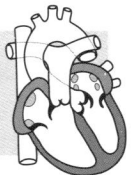

2. With respect to increasing functional efficiency, describe the role of each of the following effects of aerobic training:

   (a) Increase in stroke volume and cardiac output: _____

   _____

   _____

   (b) Increased ventilation efficiency: _____

   _____

   _____

   (c) Increase in the diameter of slow twitch fibers: _____

   _____

   _____

   (d) Increase in myoglobin level and in the size and density of mitochondria in the muscle fibers: _____

   _____

   _____

3. State which fibers predominate in each of the following activities, giving a brief reason for your answer:

   (a) Sprint activities: _____

   (b) Endurance running: _____

4. Explain the benefits of having muscles containing both fiber types (fast and slow twitch): _____

   _____

   _____

Types of Training

A 2

The adaptations made by the body to repeated exercise tend to be specific to the type of training involved. Regardless of variation in individual response, specific types of training have specific, relatively predictable effects on the body. The systems most involved are the musculoskeletal, pulmonary, cardiovascular, and energy supply systems. The precise effect of any training regime will depend on whether the training is aimed primarily at improving strength and power (the domain of anaerobic conditioning), or aerobic capacity and endurance (largely the domain of aerobic or endurance training).

Aerobic Training

Aerobic training is training that improves the efficiency of the aerobic energy-producing systems, as well as cardiovascular and respiratory endurance and efficiency. The improvements in endurance that accompany daily aerobic training, such as running, result from **general adaptation** to the training stimulus.

Aerobic endurance is developed primarily through the use of **regular endurance exercise** of appropriate duration and intensity to improve maximum rate of oxygen uptake (the $VO_{2\ max}$). Individuals will vary in their capacity to withstand high workloads and in their need for rest and ability to recover from training.

Distance running is a form of endurance exercise.

Anaerobic Conditioning

Anaerobic conditioning is training that improves the efficiency of the anaerobic energy-producing systems. Anaerobic training is of short duration. Each **interval** of exercise lasts only a few minutes and intervals are spaced by brief recovery periods during which the muscle energy stores are partially replenished.

The aim of anaerobic conditioning is to train the body to tolerate the increased lactic acid in the muscle. It is predominant in sports of short duration, such as weightlifting, but most training programs use some anaerobic conditioning to increase muscle tolerance to lactic acid.

Weightlifting is an anaerobic activity of short duration.

Nutrition During Training

During training, there must be an adequate and balanced intake of fluid and nutrients. Individuals vary in their nutritional requirements during training; the type, intensity, and duration of training, as well as body size and gender, will determine energy and nutrient demands. The summary below gives some general features of recommended sports nutrition:

Kilojoule (energy) **intake**:
Must increase to compensate for the energy expended and the increase in metabolic rate. Stable weight and good recovery after training are indications of adequate caloric intake.

Protein intake:
A modest increase is required to provide the raw materials to build and repair tissue.

Fluid intake:
Fluids are required to replenish fluids lost in sweating and restore blood volume. Intake must be adequate before, during, and after exercise.

Much of poor athletic performance can be attributed to dehydration during an event or inadequate replenishment of fluids and fuel following exercise.

Carbohydrate intake:
Carbohydrates should form 60%-70% of the diet. Carbohydrate provides fuel for oxidative metabolism; adequate intake therefore speeds recovery. Isotonic sports drinks containing a mix of electrolytes and carbohydrates replace fluids and ions lost through sweating and provide sugars to replenish glycogen stores.

1. Explain the essential difference between aerobic and anaerobic training: _____

_____

_____

2. With reference to the graph (right), explain the role of carbohydrate intake as part of a training program:

_____

_____

_____

_____

The role of diet in the recovery of muscle fuel stores

High carbohydrate diet

Low carbohydrate diet

Muscle glycogen (arbitrary units)

Training   Training   Training

3. State which factor would best determine an athlete's ability to perform anaerobic, explosive activities, such as sprinting:

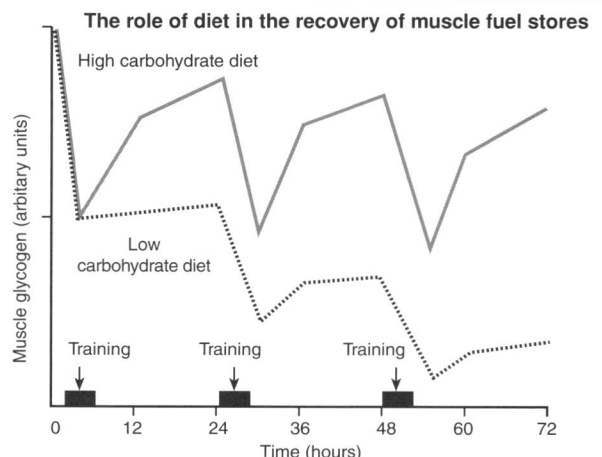

_____

| 0 | 12 | 24 | 36 | 48 | 60 | 72 |

Time (hours)

Animal Behavior

IB SL
Not applicable to core

IB HL
Not applicable to core

IB Options
Complete nos:
*Option E: SL/HL: 1-21, 23, 25, 28-30, 34-35
Extension: 22, 24, 26-27, 31, 33*

AP Biology
Complete nos:
*1-35
Some numbers extension as appropriate*

Learning Objectives

☐ 1. Compile your own glossary from the **KEY WORDS** displayed in **bold type** in the learning objectives below.

Introduction to behavior *(pages 305-306)*

☐ 2. Appreciate that the behavior of animals is related to the **environmental context**. Explain the role of **natural selection** in the development of behavior patterns; behavior is fine-tuned by microevolutionary processes in the same way as structure and physiology.

☐ 3. Contrast the dependence (or otherwise) of **innate** and **learned behavior** on the environmental context.

☐ 4. Describe, using species of birds or non-human mammals, specific examples of each of the following types of behavior. See the objective numbers provided for activities and details to help with your explanation:
   • **Migration** *see numbers 11-14*
   • **Grooming** *see number 36*
   • **Courtship** *see numbers 30-31*
   • **Communication** *see numbers 22, 25, 29, 36*
   • **Mate selection** *see numbers 32, 37*

☐ 5. Explain the need for **quantitative data** in studies of behavior. Suggest how these data could be obtained.

Innate behavior *(page 305)*

☐ 6. Distinguish **innate** from **learned behavior**. With respect to innate behavior, explain the terms **stereotyped, fixed action pattern**, and **sign stimuli**.

☐ 7. Explain the role of **orientation behaviors** in the survival of an organism. Distinguish between **migration** and orientation behavior, and other innate behaviors.

Taxes and kineses *(page 307)*

☐ 8. Define the terms: **taxis** (*pl.* taxes) and **kinesis** (*pl.* kineses), distinguishing clearly between them, Distinguish between **positive** and **negative** responses.

☐ 9. Explain, using named examples, the adaptive value of **taxes** and **kineses**. Typical examples of **taxes** include the response of *Euglena* toward light, flatworms towards food, and blowfly larvae away from light. Typical examples of **kineses** include the response of woodlice to humidity and body lice to temperature.

Migration and dispersal *(pages 308-311)*

☐ 10. Clearly define the term **migration**. Distinguish between a true migration and a **dispersal**. Identify examples of animals exhibiting each of these behaviors.

☐ 11. Identify the broad environmental cues important for migratory and dispersal behaviors. Identify how and why they might be different.

☐ 12. Define the term **navigation**. Describe how migratory birds navigate and identify the internal and external stimuli that trigger the migration.

☐ 13. Explain an example of migratory behavior, e.g. *Arctic tern, swallow, white stork, blue whale* (see #4). Identify the adaptive value of the behavior and the environmental cues involved in each case.

Learned behavior *(pages 312-313)*

☐ 14. Recall the difference between innate and **learned behaviors**. Name examples of learned behaviors, identifying their adaptive role in each case.

☐ 15. Explain what is meant by **habituation** and distinguish it clearly from *sensory adaptation*. Understand the basic characteristics of habituation and its adaptive value.

☐ 16. Define the term: **imprinting**, identifying its basic characteristics (including the critical period) and its adaptive value. Outline **Lorenz**'s experiments on imprinting in geese. Include reference to the role of **sign stimuli**, **species-specific behavior**, and **innate releasing mechanisms** in the imprinting behavior.

☐ 17. Explain what is meant by **classical conditioning**, and outline the work of **Pavlov** that illustrates this. Include reference to the following in your explanation: **unconditioned stimulus**, **conditioned stimulus**, **unconditioned response** and **conditioned response**. Discuss, using appropriate examples, how this form of learning improves the chances of survival.

☐ 18. Explain what is meant by **operant conditioning** and distinguish it from classical conditioning. Outline the work of **Skinner** that investigated this type of learning. Include reference to the following in your explanation: **operant response**, **reinforcement**, and **reward**.

Sociality and communication *(pages 314-317)*

☐ 19. Describe the benefits and problems associated with **social behavior**. Appreciate that most social behaviors are innate but may be modified by experience (learning).

☐ 20. Identify some important social behaviors, identifying the role of the behavior in each case. List examples of social animals and describe the behavior involved.

☐ 21. Define the terms: **communication** and **display**. Describe the types of auditory, visual, and olfactory signals used by animals to communicate. Distinguish between the types of communication displays and their purposes. Describe the role of communication in reproduction and in maintaining social systems.

Social organization *(pages 316-317)*

☐ 22. Outline the benefits to survival of **group behavior** and balance these against the disadvantages of such behavior. Distinguish between true **social organization** and large, rather loose groupings or **aggregations** (such as occur in flocks and schools).

Altruistic behavior *(page 318)*

☐ 23. Define the term: **altruistic behavior (altruism)**. Discuss the role of altruistic behavior in social organizations, using two examples (examples below):

Helpers at the nest: Describe altruism in birds (e.g. some species of jays), where helper birds (non-parents, but usually siblings) assist in rearing the offspring of a single pair. Discuss the benefits of this behavior to the helpers and the parents, and suggest how the behavior might be explained in an evolutionary sense.

Alarm calls in Belding's ground squirrel: Belding's ground squirrels will stare at a predator while giving an alarm call, even though this increases their chance of being attacked. Females with female relatives in the area are more likely to give these alarm calls. Explain the selective benefits of this behavior and identify any disadvantage to the individual.

Other cooperative behaviors *(pages 318-320)*

☐ 24. In general terms, describe the survival value of group cooperative behavior in: detection and defense against danger, food acquisition, and reproduction.

☐ 25. Describe social organization of honey bee colonies as an example of sociality in insects. Include reference to the **caste systems** and methods of **communication**. Appreciate why (in terms of the genetics of the individuals in the group) a social insect colony is sometimes termed a super-organism.

☐ 26. Describe various organizations within groups where **cooperative defense** reduces the chance of predation (e.g. baboon troops, musk oxen herds). Explain how bird breeding colonies may reduce predation, and identify the disadvantages of large scale nesting sites.

☐ 27. Describe an example of a species that exhibits **cooperative hunting** behavior, identifying the advantages to the individual and to the group. If appropriate, include reference to the role of **communication** and social position in the behavior.

Courtship and pair bonding *(page 314, 322-324)*

☐ 28. Define the term: **breeding behavior** and name examples. Explain how breeding behaviors achieve a suspension of the aggressive behaviors that normally accompany resource competition.

☐ 29. Identify the role of **courtship** behaviors in breeding. Describe courtship (and pair bonding if appropriate) in a named example e.g. mallard duck, peacock, grebes. Include reference to the following: **male display**, **stereotyped** fixed action patterns, duration of display. Discuss whether the behaviors are learned or innate.

☐ 30. Using a named example, explain the basis of **mate selection**. Include reference to the aspects of male behavior important in female choice and what they indicate about mate suitability. Recognize the role of **territories**, **male displays**, or **combat** in this process.

Parental care *(page 321)*

☐ 31. Define the term: **parental care** and appreciate that it is not considered to be altruism. Account for the variability observed in the degree of parental care in different species. Describe the nature of parental care in named examples to show this variation.

☐ 32. Describe examples of **sign stimuli** used by offspring to elicit parental care behaviors in the adults.

Aggressive behavior *(pages 314-315, 324)*

☐ 33. Distinguish between **aggression** and **agonistic behavior**. Identify examples of agonistic behavior in the following behaviors: *sexual, parental, parent-offspring, territorial, competitive, sibling, dominance.*

Hierarchies and territories *(pages 316, 323, 325)*

☐ 34. Identify the purpose and advantage of **hierarchies** and describe an example of an animal with a hierarchical social structure. In your example, identify behaviors used to maintain **rank** and consolidate relationships in the hierarchy (e.g. **grooming**, **displays**, **appeasement behavior**, vocalizations, or **ceremonies** that may be **aggressive** or **submissive**). Appreciate the role of auditory or visual signals in recognition of individuals and maintenance of social position in the hierarchy.

☐ 35. Distinguish between **territory** and **home range**. Describe the benefits and disadvantages of territories and explain how territorial behavior may change seasonally. Describe the types of auditory, visual, and olfactory signals used to mark and maintain territories.

Textbooks

See the 'Textbook Reference Grid' on pages 8-9 for textbook page references relating to material in this topic.

Supplementary Texts

See pages 4-6 for additional details of these texts:
■ Murray, P. and N. Owens, 2001. **Behavior and Populations** (Collins), pp. 6-27.

Internet

See pages 10-11 for details of how to access **Bio Links** from our web site: **www.thebiozone.com**. From Bio Links, access sites under the topics:
ANIMAL BEHAVIOR: • Animal behavior • Animal behavior glossary • Innate behavior • Ken's bioweb resources: Animal behavior • Pavlovian conditioning ... *and many others*

Software and video resources are now provided in the Teacher Resource Handbook

Periodicals

See page 6 for details of publishers of periodicals:

STUDENT'S REFERENCE

■ **Migration** New Scientist 12 September 1992 (Inside Science). *An excellent overview of migration in a number of different animal species.*

■ **Covert Observations of Nesting Sparrows** Sci. American, July 1996, pp. 76-77. *Techniques for studying and recording behavioral data (good).*

■ **No Way Out** New Scientist, 26 January 2002, pp. 34-38. *A study of repetitive behaviors in captive animals indicates a high level of frustration.*

■ **All for One** New Scientist, 13 June 1998, pp. 32-35. *Social insects such as ants and termites all show cooperative behavior: workers are altruistic and the colony functions as a superorganism.*

■ **The Social Life of Foxes** Biol. Sci. Rev., 13(2) Nov. 2000, pp. 15-18. *Social organization in a canid, including an examination of dominance relationships and the benefits of cooperative care.*

TEACHER'S REFERENCE

■ **Oh Brother!** New Scientist, 19 Feb. 2000, pp. 36-39. *This article looks at the reason for siblicide in animal species and suggests it is a mechanism for manipulating sex ratios in the offspring.*

■ **Divided We Fall: Cooperation Among Lions** Scientific American, May 1997, pp. 32-39. *Lions cooperate for both group and individual benefit.*

■ **Mating Strategies of Spiders** Sci. American, Nov. 1998, pp. 68-73. *The courtship rituals of spiders illustrate stereotyped behaviors.*

■ **Kin Recognition** Sci. American, June 1995, pp. 68-73. *Recognizing relatives: kinship is the organizing principle of all animal societies.*

■ **A Directed Research Project Investigating Territoriality and Aggression in Crickets** The Am. Biology Teacher 63(1), Jan. 2001, pp. 44-47. *The outline of an animal behavior experiment investigating aggression in crickets.*

■ **Africa's Wild Dogs** National Geographic, May 1999, pp. 36-63. *The ecology and behavior of wild dogs, including the role of territoriality.*

■ **How Females Choose their Mates** Scientific American, April 1998, pp. 46-51. *The methods by which females choose their reproductive mates.*

■ **The Economics of Fair Play** Scientific American, January 2002, pp. 80-85. *Fairness and cooperation in animal behavior. This article examines the economics of cooperation and how this can drive the evolution of sociality.*

■ **Playing Fair** New Scientist, 10 March 2001, pp. 38-42. *An examination of sharing and generosity in human societies: how do these behaviors evolve and what are the benefits? A good starting point for student discussion.*

The Components of Behavior

RA 2

Behavior in animals can be attributed to two components: **innate behavior** that has a genetic basis, and **learned behavior**, which results from the experiences of the animal. Together they combine to produce the total behavior exhibited by the animal. It should also be noted that experience may modify certain innate behaviors. Animals behave in fixed, predictable ways in many situations. The innate behavior follows a classical pathway called a **fixed-action pattern** (FAP) where an innate behavioral program is activated by a stimulus or **releaser** to direct some kind of behavioral response. Innate behaviors are generally adaptive and are performed for a variety of reasons. Learning, which involves the modification of behavior by experience, occurs in various ways.

Innate Behaviors

Reflex behavior
Simplest type of animal behavior. A sudden stimulus induces an automatic, involuntary and stereotyped response. Many reflexes are protective.

Kinesis
Random movement of an animal in which the rate of movement is related to the intensity of the stimulus, but not to its direction.

Taxis
A movement in response to the direction of a stimulus. Movement towards a stimulus are positive while those away from a stimulus are negative.

Stereotyped behavior
Occurs when the same response is given to the same stimulus on different occasions. This behavior shows fixed patterns of coordinated movements called fixed action patterns.

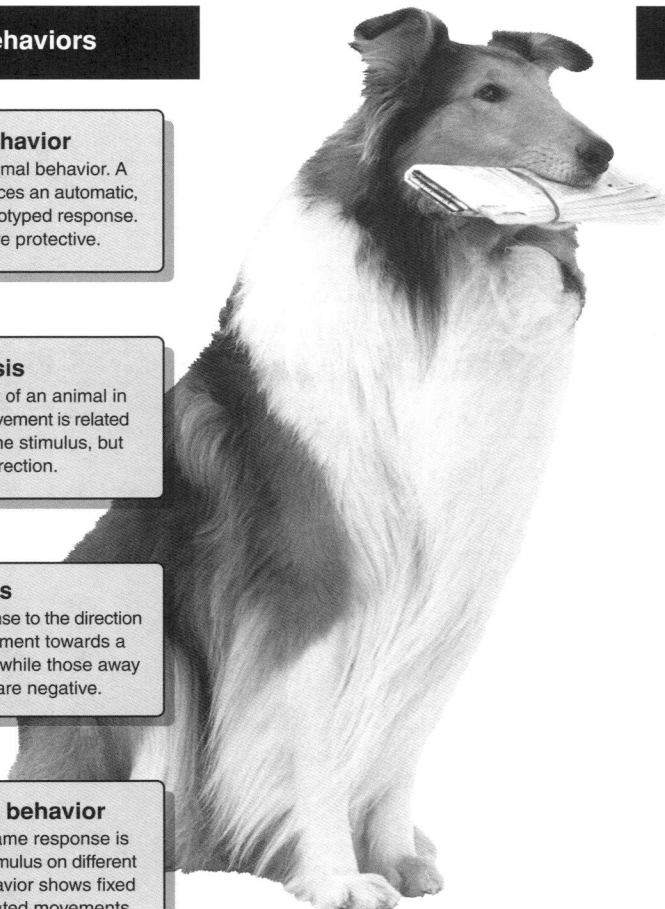

The complex behavior patterns exhibited by an animal

Learned Behaviors

Classical conditioning
Also called associative learning. Animals come to associate one stimulus with another.

Habituation
Response to a stimulus wanes when it is repeated with no apparent effect.

Insight behavior
Correct behavior on the first attempt where the animal has no prior experience.

Imprinting behavior
During a critical period, an animal can adopt a behavior by latching on to its first stimulus.

Operant conditioning
Also called trial and error learning, an animal is rewarded or punished after chance behavior.

Fixed Action Pattern

A **releaser** (sign stimulus) triggers the operation of an **innate behavioral program** in the brain that results in a **fixed-action pattern** (FAP): a predictable, stereotyped behavioral response.

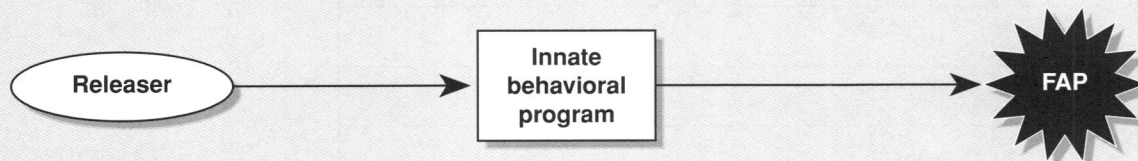

Releaser → Innate behavioral program → FAP

1. Distinguish between innate and learned behaviors: _____

_____

2. (a) Explain the role of releasers in innate behaviors: _____

_____

(b) Name a releaser for a fixed action pattern and the animal involved, and describe the behavior elicited: _____

_____

Animal Behavior Record

DA②

Observe and gather data on social interactions between animals of the same species. Bird species such as sparrows, ducks, hens, or seagulls are ideal, especially when resource competition is increased by feeding. Zoo animals such as primates provide excellent subjects. As a means of gathering semi-quantitative data about an animal's behavior it is possible to use a record sheet. Using a watch, a 'sample' of a single animal's behavior is taken at regular time intervals (e.g. every minute, on the minute). Select a time interval that suits the nature of the behavior and the time available to you have for taking the sample. It is useful for a number of people to study a group at the same time, each observing a different animal, to allow comparisons and provide a total picture of group interactions. Use the codes listed to classify the types of behavior shown by the animal. You may wish to present the results in table and/or graph format.

Species: _____ Date: _____ Time: _____

Sex: _____ Weather: _____

Age: _____ Season: _____

Behavior Chart		
1	21	41
2	22	42
3	23	43
4	24	44
5	25	45
6	26	46
7	27	47
8	28	48
9	29	49
10	30	50
11	31	51
12	32	52
13	33	53
14	34	54
15	35	55
16	36	56
17	37	57
18	38	58
19	39	59
20	40	60

Behavior Codes

R	resting
F	feeding
Dr	drinking
Pr	preening/grooming
Fl	flying
Su	sunning
Wl	walking
Fo	floating
Sw	swimming
Dp	display (eg singing)
Ag	aggression (eg fighting)
Sb	submission
OS	other social interaction

Location Codes

A	airborne
T	in a tree
TT	on a tree trunk
TB	on a tree branch
TL	on leaves
G	on ground
GG	on ground - grass
GL	on ground - leaf litter
GS	on ground - soil
GM	on ground - marsh
W	in the water
Wu	under water

Comments: _____

_____

_____

Simple Behaviors

RA 2

Taxes and kineses are examples of **orientation behaviors**. Such behaviors describe the way in which motile organisms (or gametes) **position** themselves and move in response to external cues (stimuli). Common stimuli are gravity, light, chemicals, and temperature. Some animals and many protozoa respond to certain stimuli simply by changing their rate of movement or by randomly turning without actually orientating to the stimulus. These movements are called **kineses**. In contrast, taxes involve orientation and movement directly

to or away from one or more stimuli, such as temperature. Taxes often involve moving the head (which carries the sensory receptors) from side to side until the sensory input from both sides is equal (a klinotaxic response). Note that many taxic responses are complicated by a simultaneous response to more than one stimulus. For example, fish orientate dorsal side up by responding to both light and gravity. Male moths orientate positively to pheromones but use the wind to judge the direction of the odor source (the female moth).

A When confronted with a vertical surface, snails will reorientate themselves so that they climb vertically upwards.	**B** Female moth / Male moth A flying male moth, encountering an odor (pheromone) trail left by a female, will turn and fly upwind until it reaches the female.	**C** 35°C 30°C Human body louse In a circular chamber, lice make relatively few turns at 30°C, but many random turns at 35°C.
D Spiny lobsters will back into tight crevices so that their body is touching the crevice sides. The antennae may be extended out.	**E** At close range, mosquitoes use the temperature gradient generated by the body heat of a host to home in on exposed flesh.	**F** Directional sunlight Blowfly maggots will turn and move rapidly away from a directional light source.

1. Define the following terms used to describe orientation responses in animals.

   (a) Kinesis: _____

   _____

   (b) Taxis: _____

   _____

2. Comment on the adaptive (survival) value of simple behaviors such as kineses: _____

   _____

   _____

3. Name the physical stimulus for each of the following **prefixes** used in naming orientation responses:

   (a) Geo- _____   (b) Hydro- _____   (c) Thigmo- _____

   (d) Photo- _____   (e) Chemo- _____   (f) Thermo- _____

4. For each of the above examples (A-F), describe the orientation response. Indicate whether the response is positive or negative (e.g. positive phototaxis):

   (a) **A:** _____   (b) **B:** _____

   (c) **C:** _____   (d) **D:** _____

   (e) **E:** _____   (f) **F:** _____

5. Suggest what temperature body lice "prefer", given their response in the chamber (in C): _____

Animal Migrations

There are many animals that move great distances at different times of the year or at certain stages in their life cycle. Genetically programmed behavior causes them to seek out more favorable conditions when triggered by an environmental cue (e.g. change of season). The cycles are often linked to breeding activity and the location of plentiful food resources at different times of the year. Migration is not without costs: migrating animals must expend huge amounts of energy and the journey itself is often hazardous.

Migratory locusts are found in desert regions such as northern and eastern Africa, the Middle East and Australia. When the locust populations expand but food is limited, the developing insects change into the voracious migrating form of the species. Their migration is, more correctly, a dispersal.

3000 km

Caribou spend the winter feeding in the coniferous forests in central Canada. In the spring they begin the northward trek to the tundra of the Barren Lands, within the Arctic Circle – a distance of some 1000 km. There they give birth to their calves in the relative safety of the open tundra.

750 to 1000 km

A number of **shearwater** species (including mutton birds) breed in Australia and islands around New Zealand, then migrate northwards with the onset of the southern winter to the north and northeast Pacific. The return journey across the eastern Pacific is assisted directly by the NE Trade winds.

11 000 to 13 500 km

Polar bears can cover distances of up to 1600 km walking across ice from Alaska, USA to set up winter dens across the Bering Strait in Siberia.

1600 km

Green turtles swim vast distances showing amazing navigational skills. They return from the coasts of South America to the beach of their own spawning on Ascension Island to lay eggs.

3000 km

Monarch butterflies have one of the longest of all insect migrations. Five or more generations are needed to complete one migration cycle. In North America, the insects overwinter in mass roosts in trees in warm southern California or near Mexico City. In spring they migrate north with some even reaching Canada by late summer - then return south for winter.

2000 to 4000 km

The **European swift** is one of 140 species of bird that follow one of Europe's most important migratory routes from northern Spain to North Africa and beyond. Migrating flocks of about 6 billion birds stream across the Strait of Gibraltar, but unfortunately, because of this predictability, as many as 900 million birds are killed each year by hunters.

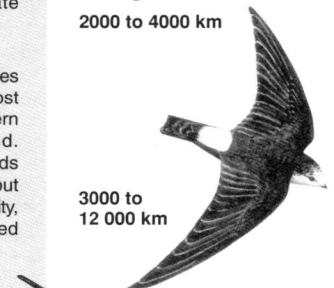

3000 to 12 000 km

A number of **whale** species that include the **humpback** and **gray whales** follow an annual migration pattern. In summer the whales feed in the krill-rich waters of the polar regions. In winter they move closer to the equator to give birth to young conceived the previous year and to mate again. They seldom feed in transit.

7000 km

European eels undertake an outstanding migration across the northern Atlantic ocean to spawn in the Sargasso Sea off the coast of Florida. The larvae that hatch from the eggs gradually drift back across to Europe, a migration which takes several years. Eventually they enter estuaries and move upriver where they feed, grow and mature.

3000 km

In New Zealand and elsewhere, **spiny lobsters** periodically make migrations of many hundreds of kilometers. The movement is predominantly against the prevailing current. It is thought to be an attempt to compensate for the long-term down stream movement of the population as planktonic larvae are swept in one direction by the ocean currents.

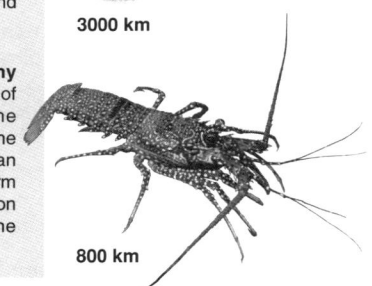

800 km

1. Match up the 10 **migration routes** on the previous page with each of the animals below:

   (a) Migratory locust: _____   (f) Monarch butterfly: _____

   (b) Caribou: _____   (g) European swift: _____

   (c) Shearwater: _____   (h) Humpback whale: _____

   (d) Polar bear: _____   (i) European eels: _____

   (e) Green turtle: _____   (j) Spiny lobster: _____

2. Suggest a **biological advantage** of the migrations for each of the organisms listed below.

   (a) Migratory locusts: _____

   _____

   (b) Monarch butterflies: _____

   _____

   (c) Humpback whale: _____

   _____

   (d) Spiny lobster: _____

   _____

3. Briefly describe two general disadvantages (to the individual) of long distance migration:

   (a) _____

   (b) _____

4. It has been suggested that both **continental drift** and the succession of **ice ages** have been major influences in the evolution of long distance migratory behavior in many animals (particularly birds).

   Continental drift: About 50 million years ago the pattern of the continents was different, with some closer (e.g. Africa and Eurasia) with others further apart. Many of the bird species present at this time, at least at the group (family) level, would be identifiable today. The movement of the continents to their present day positions takes place at speeds of several centimeters a year.

   Ice ages: There have also been half a dozen ice ages over the last 2 million years, two of which occurred in the last 150 000 years. The cycle of ice ages affected the geographical distribution of habitats, causing them to expand and contract, as well as moving them further away from the polar regions and then back again with each cycle. The speed of some of the temperature changes associated with the cycles may have been quite rapid – over tens of years, rather than hundreds. This must have benefited those species most that had a flexibility in their migratory strategy.

   Suggest how each of these events may have influenced the development of migratory behavior:

   (a) Continental drift: _____

   _____

   _____

   _____

   _____

   _____

   (b) Ice ages: _____

   _____

   _____

   _____

   _____

Migratory Navigation in Birds

RA②

Navigation is the process by which an animal uses various cues to determine its position in reference to a particular goal. Migrating birds must be able to know their flight direction and when they have reached their destination (goal). They use a wide range of environmental stimuli to provide navigational cues.

These include stellar and solar cues, visible landscape features, prevailing wind direction, low frequency sounds generated by winds, polarized light, the Earth's magnetic field, gravitational 'contours', and the smell of pungent sea bird colonies or the sweet smell of meadows. Some of these are examined below:

European starling migration

An experiment with starlings investigated the roles of **genetics** and **experience** in navigating during migration. Birds caught in the autumn leg of their migration were caught in the Netherlands and taken to Switzerland and released. The juveniles, which had not migrated before, flew to Spain. The more experienced birds reached their winter homes in France, Britain and Ireland.

Blackcap migration

Blackcaps are divided in their migration paths. Birds breeding in eastern Europe fly via Turkey to eastern Africa. Those from western Europe fly across the Strait of Gibralta to north Africa. In an experiment to test their genetic memory for navigation, birds from both populations were crossed. The hybrids tried to fly south but on a course that takes them over the Alps and the widest part of the Mediterranean.

Sun compass

Experiments have been carried out to investigate the existence of a sun compass and its importance for daytime migrations. Caged birds were placed in circular enclosures with four windows. Mirrors were used to alter the angle at which light entered the enclosures. At migration time, in natural conditions, these birds clearly showed a preferred flight direction (left). When mirrors bent the suns rays through 90°, the birds turned their preferred direction (middle and right).

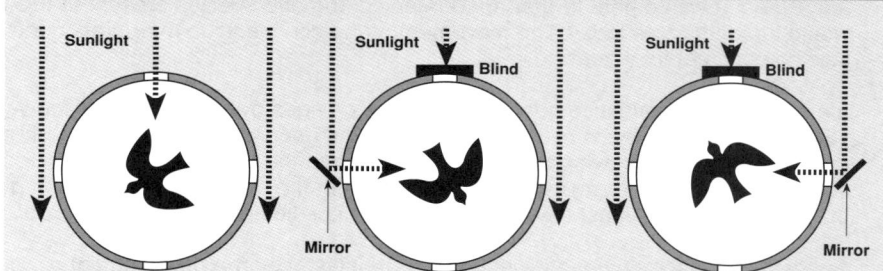

Magnetic compass

An experiment that investigated the possibility of a magnetic compass being used by migratory birds used magnetic coils to mimic the Earth's magnetic field. The birds detect magnetic north, the direction of their spring migration. When the magnetic field was twisted so that north was in the east-southeast position, the birds kept their original path for the first two nights. By the third night, they had detected the change and altered their path accordingly.

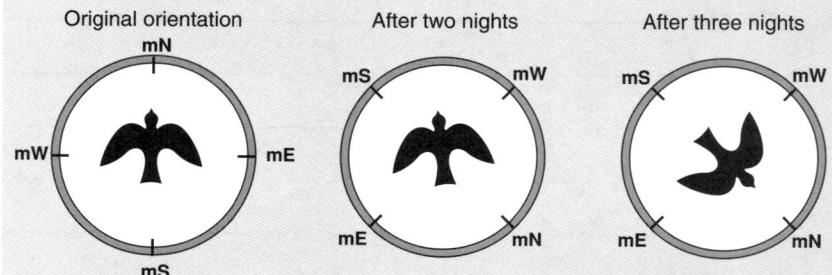

Star compass

An experiment that investigated the use of star positions in the night sky used an ink pad at the base of a cone of blotting paper. Nocturnal migrants flutter in their preferred direction of travel and the amount of ink shows. In a planetarium that projected the real sky, Indigo Buntings located the Pole Star and used it to find north, the direction of their spring migration. When the sky in the planetarium was rotated 90° counter-clockwise the birds altered their direction accordingly. Simulating a cloudy night, the obscured sky confused the birds.

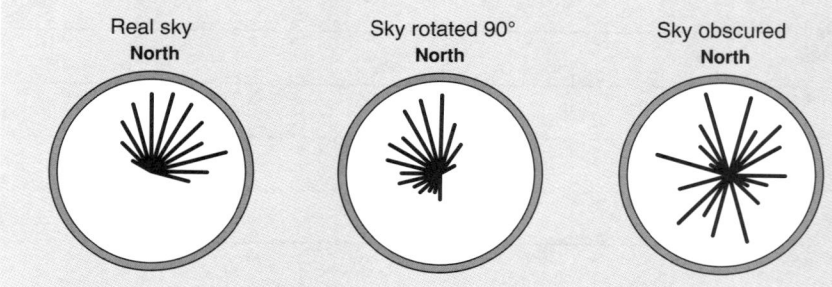

1. Making reference to the information on the **European starling** and **blackcap** migrations on the previous page, comment on the contributions that innate behavior (genetic programming) and learned behavior have on navigation in these migratory birds:

_____

_____

_____

_____

_____

_____

_____

2. The experiments on the previous page investigate three possible compass mechanisms used by migratory birds in the long distance migration flights. Discuss the results of each experiment to explain whether the experiment **effectively demonstrated** the operation of the compass:

(a) Sun compass: _____

_____

_____

_____

_____

_____

_____

(b) Magnetic compass: _____

_____

_____

_____

_____

_____

_____

(c) Star compass: _____

_____

_____

_____

_____

_____

_____

3. Birds that rely on a **sun compass** to navigate by use the position of the sun in the sky as a reference point to determine north. Because the earth rotates on its axis once a day, the position of the sun in the sky is constantly changing. Briefly describe an **essential mechanism** that the birds must have in order to make use of this type of compass:

_____

_____

_____

Learned Behavior

A 1

Imprinting occurs when an animal learns to make a particular response only to one type of animal or object. Imprinting differs from most other kinds of learned behavior in that it normally can occur only at a specific time during an animal's life. This **critical period** is usually shortly after hatching (about 12 hours) and can last for several days. While a critical period and the resulting

imprinted behavior are normally irreversible, they are not considered rigidly fixed. There are examples of animals that have had abnormal imprinted behaviors revert to the 'wild type'. There are two main types of imprinting using visual and auditory stimuli: filial and sexual imprinting. Breeding ground imprinting uses olfactory (smell) stimuli.

Filial (Parent) Imprinting

Filial imprinting is the process by which animals develop a social attachment. It differs from most other kinds of learning (including other types of imprinting), in that it normally can occur only at a specific time during an animal's life. This **critical period** is usually shortly after hatching (about 12 hours) and may last for several days. Ducks and geese have no innate ability to recognize *mother* or even their own species. They simply respond to, and identify as mother, the first object they encounter that has certain characteristics.

Breeding Ground Imprinting

Salmon undertake long migrations in the open ocean where they feed, grow and mature after hatching in freshwater streams. Some species remain at sea for several years, after which each fish returns to its exact home stream to spawn. Research has shown that this ability is based on **olfactory imprinting** where the fish recognize the chemical odors of their specific stream and swim towards its source. Other animals (bears, humans, etc.) have learned to exploit this behavior.

Sexual Identity Imprinting

Individuals learn to direct their sexual behavior at some stimulus objects, but not at others. Termed **sexual imprinting**, it may serve as a species identifying and species isolating mechanism. The mate preferences of birds have been shown to be imprinted according to the stimulus they were exposed to (other birds) during early rearing. Sexual imprinting generally involves longer periods of exposure to the stimulus than filial imprinting (*see left*).

Habituation

Habituation is a very simple type of learning involving a loss of a response to a repeated stimulus when it fails to provide any form of reinforcement (reward or punishment). Habituation is different to fatigue, which involves loss of efficiency in a repeated activity, and arises as a result of the nature of sensory reception itself. An example of habituation is the waning response of a snail attempting to cross a platform that is being tapped at regular time intervals. At first, the snail retreats into its shell for a considerable period after each tap. As the tapping continues, the snail stays in its shell for a shorter duration, before resuming its travel.

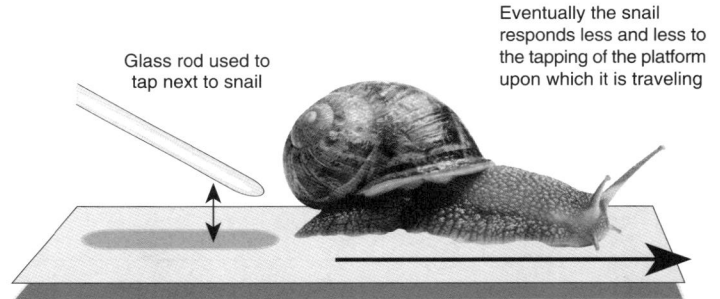

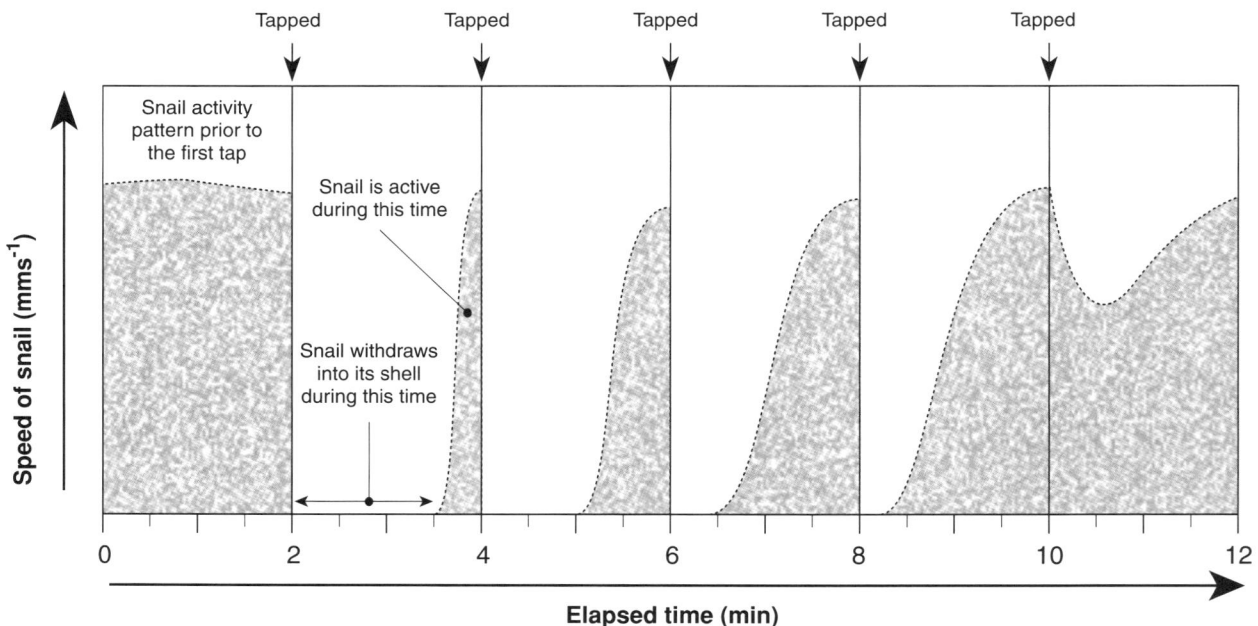

Glass rod used to tap next to snail

Eventually the snail responds less and less to the tapping of the platform upon which it is traveling

Snail activity pattern prior to the first tap

Snail is active during this time

Snail withdraws into its shell during this time

Tapped Tapped Tapped Tapped Tapped

Speed of snail (mms⁻¹)

Elapsed time (min)

Classical (Pavlovian) Conditioning

Classical conditioning, founded by **Ivan Pavlov**, describes a type of **associative learning** in which behavior that is normally triggered by a certain stimulus comes to be triggered by a substitute stimulus that previously had no effect on the behavior. Between 1890 and 1900, Pavlov noticed that the dogs he was studying would salivate when they knew they were to be fed. It was determined that the dogs were alerted by a bell that rung every time the door into the lab was opened. Through experimentation, Pavlov discovered that the ringing of the bell initially brought about no salivation, but the dogs could be **conditioned** to relate the ringing of the bell to the presentation of food. Eventually the ringing of the bell elicited the same salivation response as the presentation of food, indicating that the dog was conditioned to associate the two stimuli.

1 A bell is rung, immediately prior to feeding. The bell alone produces no salivary response in the dog.

2 Food is introduced after the bell has rung. Steps one are two are repeated a number of times (association of bell and food).

3 Eventually the dog becomes conditioned to salivate whenever the bell is rung, even when no food is presented.

Operant Conditioning

Operant conditioning is used to describe a situation where an animal learns to associate a particular behavioral act with a **reward** (as opposed to a stimulus in classical conditioning). This behavior determines whether or not the reward appears. **Burrhus Skinner** studied operant conditioning using an apparatus he invented called a **Skinner box** *(see right)*. Skinner designed the box so that when an animal (usually a pigeon or rat) pushed a particular button it was rewarded with food. The animals learned to associate the pushing of the button with obtaining food (the reward). The behavioral act that leads the animal to push the button in the first place is thought to be generated spontaneously (by accident or curiosity). This type of learning is also called **instrumental learning** because the spontaneous behavior is instrumental in obtaining the reward. Operant conditioning is the predominant learning process found in animals.

A Skinner box typically contains one or more buttons, which can be pressed to obtain a reward.

Food is dispensed when the correct button is pushed.

1. Explain what **filial imprinting** is: _____

_____

_____

2. For the example of **filial imprinting** (opposite), identify which parts of the behavior can be attributed to:

   (a) Innate behavior: _____

   (b) Learned behavior: _____

3. In relation to human behavior, describe an example of the following:

   (a) Habituation: _____

   _____

   (b) Imprinting: _____

   _____

   (c) Classical conditioning: _____

   _____

   (d) Operant conditioning: _____

   _____

DA 2 Animal Communication

Communication (the transmission of (understood) information) between animals of the same species is essential to the survival and reproductive success of animals. Effective communication enables animals to avoid predators, coordinate foraging and hunting activity, maintain social behaviors, and attract mates.

Messages can be passed between animals using a range of signals that commonly include visual, chemical, auditory, and tactile perception. Which of these signals is adopted will depend on the activity pattern and habitat of the animal. Visual displays, for example, are ineffective at night or in heavy undergrowth.

Channel
The medium in which the signal is transmitted:
visual; chemical/olfactory; tactile or auditory

Signal
The message conveyed from one individual to another:
Aggression; submission; courting; social bonding

Code

Code

Sender
The individual who transmits the signal

Rules by which the sender must transmit the signal

Rules which enable the receiver to decipher the signal

Receiver
The individual who detects the signal

PHOTO: The two male baboons on the right are engaged in a dominance display. Both animals are acting as senders and receivers of a message.

Context
The setting in which the communication occurs: *dominance display; courtship; predator alert; food gathering*

Olfactory Messages
Some animals produce special scents that are carried considerable distance by the wind. This may serve to advertise for a potential mate, or warn neighboring competitors to keep out of a territory. In some cases, mammals use their urine and feces to mark territorial boundaries. Sniffing genitals is common among mammals.

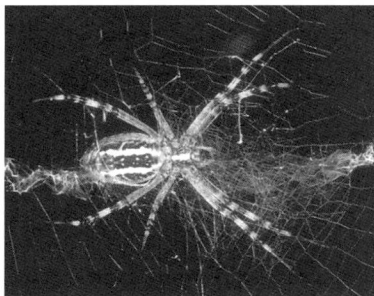

Tactile Messages
The touching of one animal by another may be a cooperative interaction or an aggressive one. Grooming behavior between members of a primate group communicates social bonding. Vibrations sent along a web by a male spider communicates to a potential female mate not to eat him.

Auditory Messages
Sound may be used to communicate over great distances. Birds keep rivals away and advertise for mates with birdsong. Fin whales are able to send messages over thousands of kilometers of ocean. Calls made by mammals may serve to attract mates, keep in touch with other members of a group or warn away competitors.

Visual Messages
Many animals convey information to other members of the species through their body coverings and adornment, as well as through gestures and body language. Through visual displays, it is possible to deliver threat messages, show submission, attract a mate and even exert control over a social group.

Warning
Animals may communicate a warning to other animals through visual displays. Many wasp species (like those above) have brightly colored black and yellow markings to tell potential predators that they risk being stung if attacked.

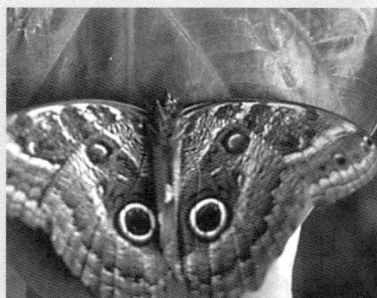

Deception
Animals may seek to deceive other animals about their identity. As an alternative to camouflage, animals may use visual markings that startle or deter potential predators. The eye spots on this moth may confuse a predator.

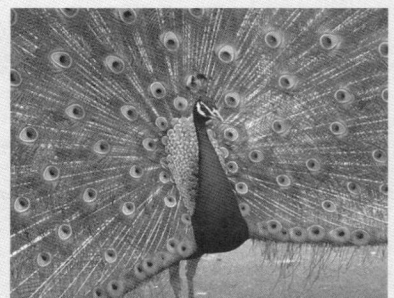

Attraction
Some animals produce a stunning visual display in order to attract a mate. The plumage of some bird species can be extremely colorful and elaborate, such as the peacock (above), the birds of paradise, and the lyrebird.

1. Name a **benefit** an animal may receive as a result of being able to communicate information that facilitates:

   (a) Maintaining social structures: _____

   (b) Coordinating foraging and hunting: _____

   (c) Advertising suitability as a mate: _____

   (d) Sending and receiving alarm signals: _____

2. List the kind of communication methods best suited to animals that are active at night in a forest habitat:

3. List the communication methods most effective for diurnal animals (active during the day) living in open grassland:

4. Postures provide a very important form of communication between animals. The drawings below (collectively called an ethogram) illustrate the various postures exhibited by the **purple swamphen** (*Porphyrio porphyrio*), a wetland bird belonging to the rail family. Social behaviors can often be graded from those that display overt aggression to those that are submissive. The purpose of the following exercise is to recognize that the swamphen has a ***graded range*** of display behaviors of increasing aggression or submission. By using the symbols (+, – and 0) at the bottom of the page, indicate the degree of aggressiveness, submissiveness or neutral body language. Use the spaces provided:

Ethogram for Swamphen Behavior

1A 1B — Fighting. One bird jumping with feet ready for clawing and beak open for pecking.

2A 2B — Fighting. One bird in aggressive upright posture with wings and tail raised and feet raised. The other bird is in the aggressive upright but not attacking.

3 — Full bow. Submissive wings and tail fully up.

4A 4B — Fighting. Both birds in aggressive uprights and using feet to attack.

5A 5B — Facing away. Submissive display to an aggressive upright bird.

6A 6B — Fighting. Both birds jumping with feet ready for clawing and beak open for pecking.

7 — Aggressive upright. Wings down. Tail horizontal.

8 — Move away. Submissive display. Wings exaggerated. Tail fully up to uncover white feathers.

9A 9B — Crouch. Submissive display to an aggressive upright bird.

10 — Horizontal forward. Aggressive display but not as aggressive as an upright.

11A 11B — Head flagging. Submissive display. Head held low and moved from side to side.

12 — Head flick. Submissive display. Usually at end of encounter. Wings exaggerated, tail fully up. Beak held too high to peck at other bird.

Range of aggressive/submissive behaviors

| ++ very aggressive | + slightly aggressive | 0 neutral | – slightly submissive | – – very submissive |

Social Organization

DA❷

All behavior appears to have its roots in the underlying genetic program of the individual. These innate behaviors may be modified by interactions of the individual with its environment, such as the experiences it is exposed to and its opportunities for learning. The behavioral adaptations of organisms affect their fitness (their ability to survive and successfully reproduce) and so are the products of natural selection. A behavior that leads to greater reproductive success should become more common in a species over time. Few animal species lead totally solitary lives. Many live in cooperative groups for all or part of their lives. Social animals comprise groups of individuals of the same species, living together in an organized fashion. They divide resources and activities between them and have a mutual dependence (i.e. they do not survive or successfully reproduce outside the group).

Tigers are solitary and territorial animals, living and hunting alone. A male will remain with a female for 3-5 days during the mating season. A female may have 3 or 4 cubs which will stay with their mother for more than 2 years.

Many invertebrates (e.g. hermit crabs) are solitary animals, with occasional, random encounters. Some animals may be drawn together at feeding sites. Wind or currents may also cause aggregations.

Schooling fish and herds of mammals are examples of animals that form groups of a loose association. There is no set structure or hierarchy to the group. The grouping is often to provide mutual protection.

Family groups may consist of one or more parents with offspring of various ages. The relationship between parents may be a temporary, seasonal one or may be life-long.

Some insects (e.g. ants, termites, some wasp and many bee species) form colonies. The social structure of these colonies ranges from simple to complex, and may involve castes that provide for division of labor.

Primates such as chimpanzees and baboons have evolved complex social structures. Organized in terms of dominance hierarchies, higher ranked animals within the group have priority access to food and other resources.

Advantages of Social Groups

1. Protection from physical factors
2. Protection from predators
3. Assembly for mate selection
4. Locating and obtaining food
5. Defense of resources against other groups
6. Division of labor amongst specialists
7. Richer learning environment
8. Population regulation

Disadvantages of Social Groups

1. Increased competition between group members for resources as group size increases.
2. Increased chance of the spread of diseases and parasites.
3. Interference with reproduction (e.g. cheating in parental care; infanticide by non-parents).

1. Briefly describe **two** ways in which behavior may be passed on between generations:

   (a) _____

   (b) _____

2. Explain briefly how large social groupings confer an advantage by providing:

   (a) Richer learning environment: _____

   _____

   _____

The effect of the number of adults in the family on pup survival for black-backed jackals

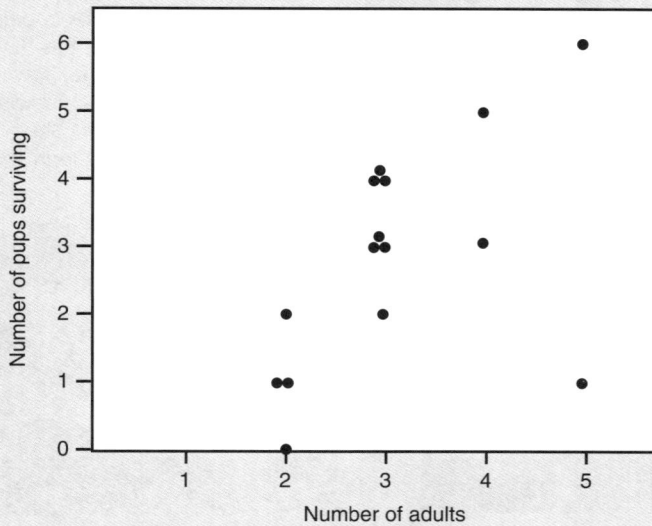

SOURCE: Drickamer & Vessey, Animal behavior (3rd Ed) PWS, 1992

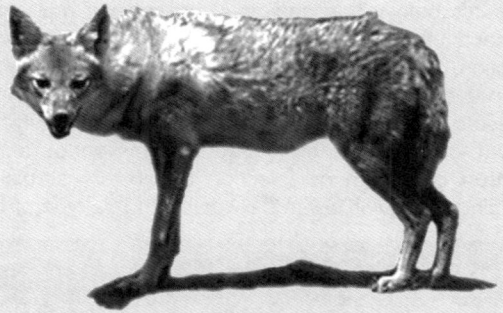

Black-backed jackal *(Canis mesomelas)*

Black-backed jackals live in the brushland of Africa. Monogamous pairs (single male and female parents) hunt cooperatively, share food and defend territories. Offspring from the previous year's litter frequently help rear their siblings by regurgitating food for the lactating mother and for the pups themselves. The pup survival results of 15 separate jackal groups are shown in the graph on the left.

(b) Division of labor among specialists: _____

_____

_____

_____

(c) Assembly for mate selection: _____

_____

_____

_____

3. The graph at the top of this page shows how the survival of black-backed jackal pups is influenced by the number of adult helpers in the group.

(a) Draw an approximate 'line of best fit' on the graph (by eye) and describe the general trend: _____

_____

(b) State two ways in which additional adult helpers may increase the survival prospects of pups:

_____

_____

_____

_____

4. Explain how a social behavior that is beneficial to individuals in a species may become more common over time:

_____

_____

_____

_____

_____

Cooperative Behavior

Individuals both within and between species may cooperate with each other for many reasons: for mutual defense and protection, to enhance food acquisition, or to rear young. To explain the evolution of cooperative behavior, it has been suggested that individuals benefit their own survival or the survival of their genes (offspring) by cooperating. **Kin selection** is a form of selection that favors altruistic (self-sacrificing) behavior towards relatives. In this type of behavior an individual will sacrifice its own opportunity to reproduce for the benefit of its close relatives. Individuals may also cooperate and behave altruistically if there is a chance that the "favor" may be returned at a later time. **Altruistic behavior** towards non-relatives is usually explained in terms of trade-offs, where individuals weigh up the costs and benefits of helpful behavior. Cooperation will evolve in systems where, in the long term, individuals all derive some benefit.

Many mammalian predators live in well organized social groups. These are formed for the purposes of cooperative hunting and defense and they facilitate offspring survival. In the gray wolves above, territories are marked by scent. Howling promotes group bonding and helps to keep neighboring packs away.

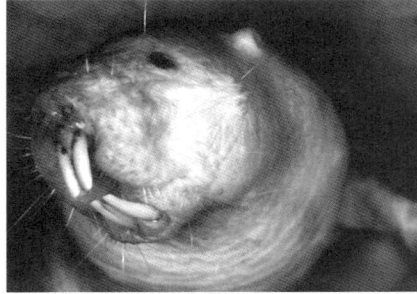

Naked mole rats, from the arid regions of Kenya, are unique among mammals in having a social organization similar to that of social insects. Up to 300 of the rodents spend their lives underground in a **colony** with a **caste system**, with workers, soldiers, infertile females, and one breeding queen.

The males of many species help their mates collect enough food to meet reproductive needs. In some species, especially amongst birds, non-breeding individuals e.g. older siblings, may assist in rearing the offspring by protecting or feeding them. This type of altruism may arise through **kin selection**.

Herding is an effective defensive behavior, providing a great number of eyes to detect approaching predators. Although they have horns for defense, when wildebeest (above) detect danger, their first reaction is to run as a group (at up to 80 kmh^{-1}).

South African meerkats live in communities in earth burrows. They are vulnerable to attack from land and aerial predators (especially vultures). The group maintains a constant surveillance by posting sentinels to warn the rest of the group of danger.

Cooperative (mutualistic) associations can occur between different species. Cape buffalos are warned of approaching predators by cattle egrets and maribou storks which in turn feed on insects disturbed by the buffalo as it grazes.

1. Define the following terms, making clear the distinction between them:

   (a) Altruistic behavior: _____

   _____

   (b) Kin selection: _____

   _____

2. Explain (in evolutionary terms) why an animal would raise the offspring of a close relative rather than their own:

   _____

   _____

   _____

3. Describe two ways in which members of a herd or a shoal reduce their likelihood of being attacked by a predator:

   (a) _____

   _____

   (b) _____

   _____

A2 Cooperative Defense and Attack

Young safely protected in centre

Attack pattern by wolves

Circular defense with heads facing outwards

Group defense in musk oxen: In the Siberian steppes, which are extensive grasslands, large grazing animals, such as musk oxen, must find novel ways of protecting themselves from predators. There is often no natural cover to help with defense, so they must make their own barrier in the form of a defensive circle. When wolves (their most common predator) attack, they shield the defenseless young inside the circle. Lone animals have little chance of surviving an attack as wolves hunt in packs.

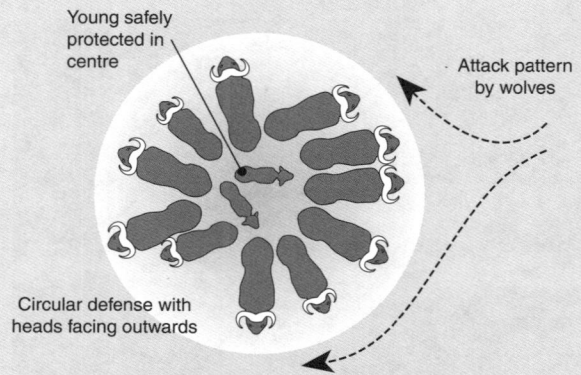

Multiple advancing fronts

Single, broad advancing front

Food caches

Food caches

Temporary nest

Temporary nest

Column raider

Swarm raider

Army ants foraging: There are two species of army ant that have quite different raiding patterns: *Eciton hamatum* whose columns go in many directions and *Eciton burchelli*, which is a swarm-raider, forming a broad front. Both species cache food at various points along the way (dark patches above). Through group cooperation, the tiny ants are able to subdue prey much larger than themselves, even managing to kill and devour animals such as lizards and small mammals. This would not be possible if they hunted as individuals.

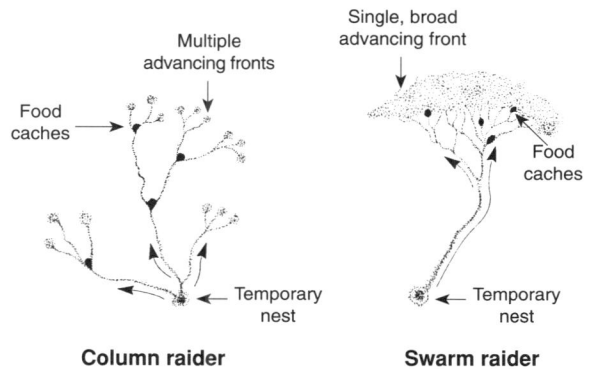

1. State a benefit of the cooperative interaction for each of the species (described above):

   (a) Musk oxen: _____

   _____

   _____

   (b) Army ants: _____

   _____

   _____

2. Sheep need to spend most of their day feeding on grass. They form mobs both naturally in the wild as well as on farms.

   (a) State why sheep form mobs: _____

   _____

   _____

   (b) Explain how this might enhance an individual sheep's ability to feed: _____

   _____

   _____

Cooperative Food Gathering

K 1

Humpback whales: The two whales pictured above are feeding near the surface. They swim below a school of fishes and confuse them by emitting a stream of small bubbles. They then swim upward in a spiral pattern with the mouth open, closing it as they break the surface. Water is squeezed out of the mouth, through a sieve of baleen plates, trapping the fish. By fishing cooperatively in this way, several whales herd the fish more effectively.

Pelicans fishing: Group hunting behavior in pelicans enables the birds to herd together large quantities of fish and facilitates the scoop-beak fishing method. Groups of 5 to 10 birds gather in shallow water. They swim in a horseshoe formation closing to an almost complete circle to trap the fish. They plunge their beaks into the water exactly at the same time to catch the fish. When pelicans fish alone, their fishing success may not be as good.

Ordinary worker ant exchanging sugary saliva with a 'replete' worker ant

A particular caste of honey ant spends most of its life serving as a living reservoir of honey.

'Replete' worker ant

Honeypot ant

Swollen abdomen

Honeypot ants: Honeypot ants of central Australia have a special group of workers called 'repletes'. These never leave the nest, but stay in underground galleries where they serve as vessels for storing a rich food supply. Regular workers that have been foraging for honey-dew and nectar return to the nest where they regurgitate food from their crops to feed the replete. The replete will continue to accept these offerings until its abdomen has swollen to the size of a pea (normally it is the size of a grain of rice). The repletes become so swollen that their movements are restricted to clinging to the gallery ceiling where many hundreds of them hang in a row. When the dry season arrives and food supplies become scarce, workers return to the repletes, coaxing them to regurgitate droplets of honey.

Lions hunting: Lions hunt on the savannah grasslands of East Africa. In this terrain, the sparse distribution of trees creates a great advantage for the fast moving prey of the lions (e.g. antelope). They can detect approaching lions easily, raise the alarm, and escape. Unlike solitary big cats, such as the leopard, that hunt in forest environments, lions must work as a team to use a strategy to trap the prey. Solitary lions have poor hunting success. When lions sight a herd of prey, several lionesses hide downwind. Others circle upwind and stampede the herd towards the lionesses waiting to attack. Lions must be careful not get injured in the hunt. A solitary, injured lion that cannot hunt will almost certainly starve. Cooperation when hunting reduces the risk of injury, and provides group support when it does.

1. State a benefit of the cooperative interaction for each of the species (described above):

(a) Humpback whales: _____

_____

(b) Pelicans: _____

_____

(c) Honeypot ants: _____

_____

(d) Lions: _____

_____

Parental Care

As with mating systems, there is a wide variation in the degree to which animals care for their young. Animals have a certain amount of energy that they are prepared to put into reproduction. This is called the **reproductive effort**. The amount of care given by parent(s) will depend on how much of this reproductive effort is allocated before birth (in producing the young) and how much is allocated to the period after the young are born (the parental care period). Some animals, such as birds, fish, and reptiles, give birth to their young in eggs with a supply of food in the form of yolk. This provides some nourishment during the early stages of development. Mammals carry young internally until they have reached a more developed stage. After birth or hatching, the parents of many mammals and birds care for their young by providing food, protection, and warmth.

Giant clam

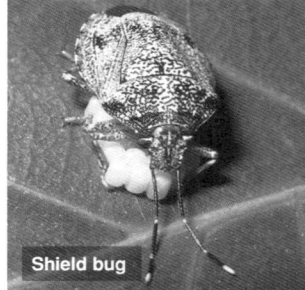
Shield bug

Canada geese

Sheep

Many invertebrates offer no parental care whatsoever. The giant clam (above left) is in the process of releasing millions of eggs into the surrounding water (arrowed). These will be fertilized by sperm released by other clams in the area. The massive numbers of resulting planktonic larvae will be severely reduced by plankton feeding animals. The shield bug (above right) is in the process of laying eggs. It will then abandon them to an uncertain future, risking their loss to predators.

Both mammals and birds are well known for their high levels of parental care. Other vertebrates, such as some amphibians, fish, and reptiles also provide intensive care until the offspring are capable of fending for themselves. Bird parents are required to incubate their eggs in a nest and then feed the chicks until they are independent. Although most mammals give birth to well developed offspring, they are dependent on their mother for nourishment via suckling milk, as well as learning valuable behaviors.

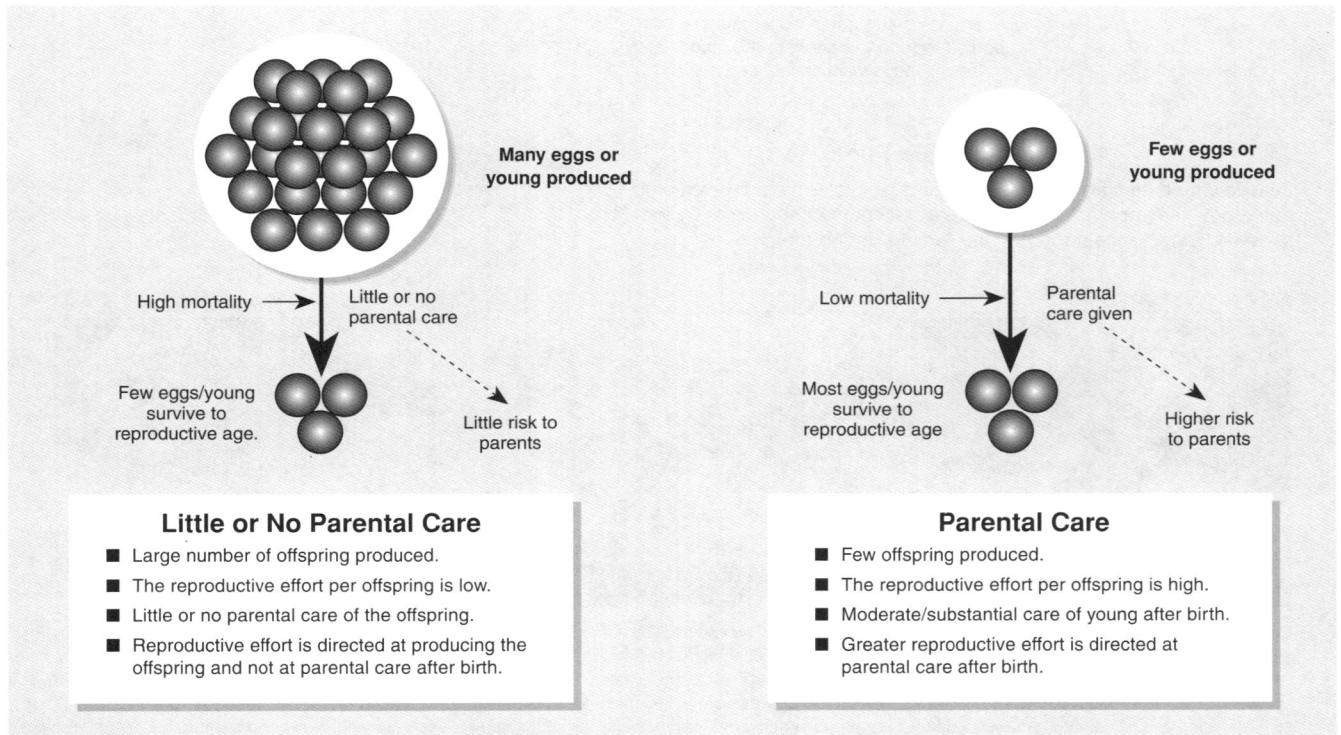

Many eggs or young produced

High mortality → Little or no parental care

Few eggs/young survive to reproductive age.

Little risk to parents

Few eggs or young produced

Low mortality → Parental care given

Most eggs/young survive to reproductive age

Higher risk to parents

Little or No Parental Care

■ Large number of offspring produced.
■ The reproductive effort per offspring is low.
■ Little or no parental care of the offspring.
■ Reproductive effort is directed at producing the offspring and not at parental care after birth.

Parental Care

■ Few offspring produced.
■ The reproductive effort per offspring is high.
■ Moderate/substantial care of young after birth.
■ Greater reproductive effort is directed at parental care after birth.

1. Explain how animals with little or no parental care compensate for not caring for their young:

_____

_____

2. Name 2 quite different animals that exhibit **little** or **no** parental care: _____

3. Name 2 quite different animals that exhibit **considerable** parental care: _____

4. List 3 specific ways that a young bird may benefit by having a high degree of parental care:

   (a) _____

   (b) _____

   (c) _____

RA ② **Breeding Behavior**

Many of the behaviors observed in animals are associated with reproduction, reflecting the importance of this event in an individual's life cycle. Many types of behavior are aimed at facilitating successful reproduction. These include **courtship** behaviors, which may involve attracting a mate to a particular breeding site (often associated with high availability of resources such as food or nesting sites). Courtship behaviors are aimed at reducing conflict between the sexes and are often **stereotyped** or ritualistic. They rely on **sign stimuli** to elicit specific responses in potential mates. Other reproductive behaviors are associated with assessing the receptivity of a mate, defending mates against others, and rearing the young.

Courtship gift
The male gives the female a meal (an insect wrapped up in a cocoon) to keep her occupied while he mates.

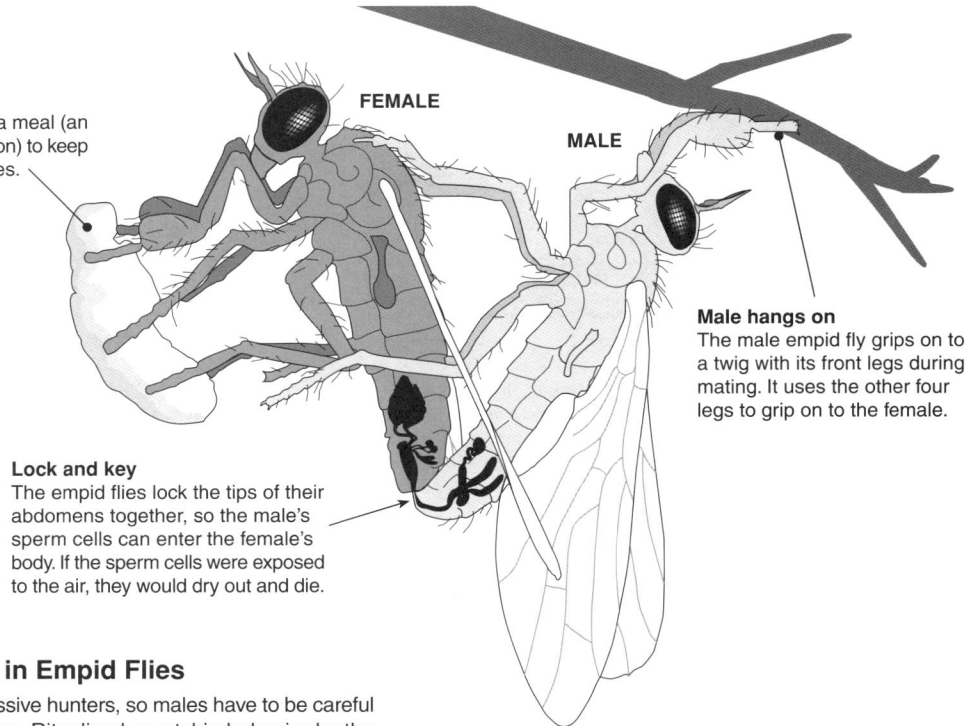

FEMALE

MALE

Male hangs on
The male empid fly grips on to a twig with its front legs during mating. It uses the other four legs to grip on to the female.

Lock and key
The empid flies lock the tips of their abdomens together, so the male's sperm cells can enter the female's body. If the sperm cells were exposed to the air, they would dry out and die.

Mating in Empid Flies

Female **empid flies** are aggressive hunters, so males have to be careful about how they approach them. Ritualized courtship behavior by the male facilitates acceptance by the female during attempts to mate.

Courtship behavior occurs as a prelude to mating and is most common in vertebrates and insects. One function of courtship is to synchronize the behaviors of the male and female so that mating can occur, and to override attack or escape behavior. Here, a male greater frigatebird calls, spreads its wings, and inflates its throat pouch to court a female.

It is common in some birds (and many arthropod) for the male to provide an offering, such as food or nesting material, to the female. These **rituals** reduce aggression in the male and promote appeasement behavior by the female. For some **monogamous** species, e.g. the blue-footed boobies mating above, the pairing begins a long term breeding partnership.

Many marine birds, such as the emperor penguins above, form breeding colonies where large numbers of birds come together to lay their eggs and raise their young. The adults feed at sea, leaving the young unattended for varying lengths of time. Penguin chicks congregate in large, densely packed groups to conserve body heat while their parents are away.

1. (a) Explain what is meant by **courtship behavior**: _____

_____

(b) Suggest a reason why courtship behavior may be necessary prior to mating: _____

_____

(c) Explain why courtship behavior is often ritualized and involves stereotyped displays: _____

_____

(d) Name one example of a courtship behavior: _____

Territorial Behavior

A territory is any area that is defended against members of the same species. Territoriality is generally widespread amongst the animal kingdom and serves many purposes:

- The population becomes spread out in relation to the food supply (resource availability often determines territory size).

- Territories provide enhanced protection from other males during courtship and mating.

- Because of the increased distance between pairs, the risk of infectious diseases spreading amongst a population is reduced.

Territories are usually defended by clear acts of aggression or ritualized signals (e.g. vocal, visual or chemical signals).

Gannet territories are relatively small with hens defending only the area they can reach while sitting on their nest.

Territoriality in Great Tits (*Parus major*)

Six breeding pairs of great tits were removed from an oak woodland (*below, left*). Within 3 days, four new pairs had moved into the unoccupied areas (*below, right*) and some residents had expanded their territories. The new birds moved in from territories in hedgerows, considered to be suboptimal habitat. This type of territorial behavior limits the density of breeding animals in areas of optimal habitat.

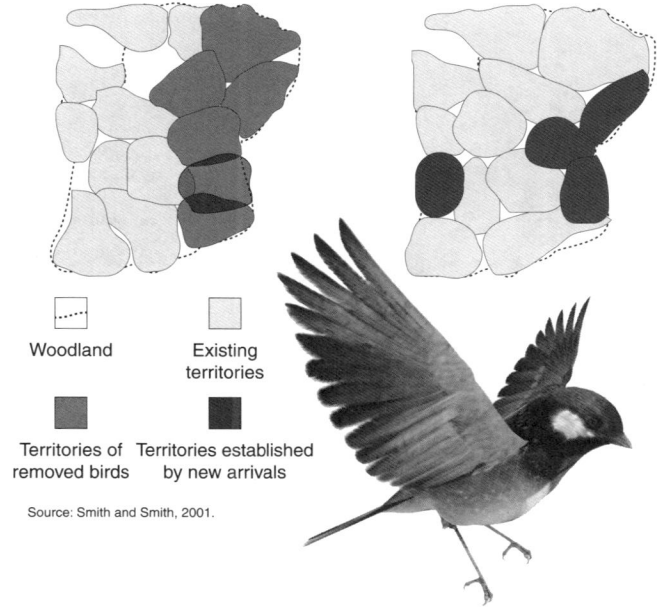

Woodland   Existing territories

Territories of removed birds   Territories established by new arrivals

Source: Smith and Smith, 2001.

2. In the courtship of empid flies:

    (a) Explain the nature and purpose of the courtship display: _____

    (b) Identify the **sign stimulus** in this behavior: _____

3. Define the term **territory**: _____

4. (a) Explain why a male will defend a particular breeding territory against other males: _____

    (b) Suggest how a female in this situation would select a mate: _____

5. Explain how a bird (such as the great tit) establishes and maintains its territory: _____

6. Describe two advantages and two disadvantages of maintaining a territory: _____

7. (a) Give one example of an animal that maintains a territory year round: _____

    (b) Give an example of an animal that maintains a territory only during the breeding season: _____

Aggressive Behavior

RA 2

Aggression is a complex phenomenon often associated with competition for resources but also including predatory behavior (hunting for prey). An associated but more precise term is **agonistic behavior**: behavior that is associated with **conflict** situations among members of the same species. Agonistic behavior includes all aspects of conflict, such as threats, submissions, chases and physical combat, but it specifically excludes predatory aggression for obtaining food. Conflicts between members of the same species are usually resolved without serious injury. Often, ritualized behavior (e.g. submissive behavior or ritualized threat) within a hierarchy will resolve conflict without physical combat being necessary.

Two male African elephants (above) are fighting. Confrontations like this seldom end in very serious physical injury and the contest is more one of establishing strength than inflicting wounds.

Aggression can occur between different species when they are competing for the same resources. In the photograph above, vultures are competing with hyenas for a carcass. The hyenas may also have been competing with lions and jackals.

Competing for the right to mate with a harem of females, two stags are locked antler to antler. While the antlers provide effective weapons to repel predator attacks and protect the herd, they seldom inflict serious injury on other stags.

Two wave albatrosses are engaged in ritualized aggression with wings spread to provide an intimidating display. These encounters may include a few harmless pecks.

The New Zealand sealion forms breeding colonies on several subantarctic islands. A bull will set up a territory on one of the breeding beaches, defend it against challenges from other bulls, and attract females as mates to the site.

Disputes between zebra stallions can get serious. The fighting is less ritualized than in many species and the force of the kick from the hind legs can cause serious injury. Face to face fighting may also result in serious bite injuries.

1. Distinguish between aggressive behavior and agonistic behavior: _____

_____

_____

_____

2. In social species, aggression between groups (e.g one group invading another's territory) is usually less ritualized and more inclined to lead to injury than aggression within the same social grouping. Explain why this is the case:

_____

_____

_____

3. Describe how the following behaviors reduce the risk of injury to individuals in a population:

(a) Dominance hierarchies: _____

_____

_____

(b) Ritual aggression: _____

_____

_____

(RA 2) **Home Ranges and Resources**

Olive baboons (*Papio anubis*) live in the African savannah and have a highly organized social structure. Within each troop there is an orderly hierarchy. The hierarchy promotes division of labor and maximizes the efficiency with which the troop can search for food and defend itself against predators and other troops. Each of the different baboon troops occupies a distinct **home range**. This is the area regularly utilized by the troop, and it provides all the resources the troop needs for its survival. Home ranges differ from territories in that they may overlap in places and are not necessarily defended exclusively.

Baboon Home Ranges in Nairobi Park

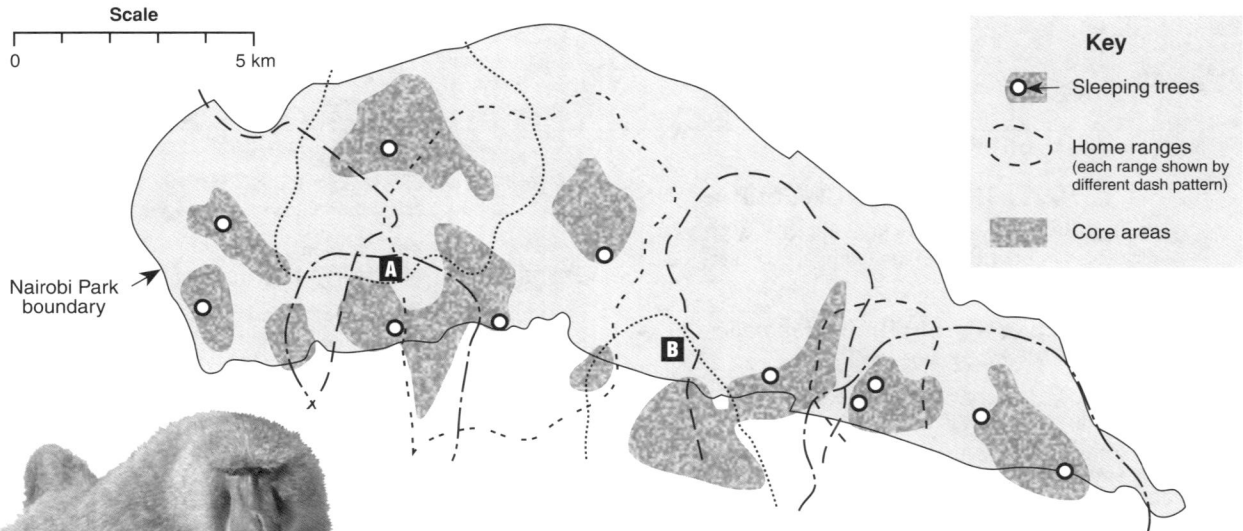

Scale
0 ———————— 5 km

Nairobi Park boundary

Key
○◄— Sleeping trees

- - - Home ranges (each range shown by different dash pattern)

Core areas

The map above shows the home ranges for baboon troops in Nairobi Park, Kenya. The size of each home range depends on the resources available in the area and the number of baboons in the troop (each troop can number from 20-80 baboons). Savannah-dwelling baboons spend more time on the ground than do most other primates and have one of the largest home ranges, averaging 20 km². They may travel up to 4 km a day in search of food. Most of the troop's activity is concentrated in the core area (which is like a territory). This area contains the best food sources, and more importantly, water holes and trees for sleeping in at night. Although olive baboons spend nearly all the day on the ground, they always return to the safety of the trees before dusk to sleep.

1. Describe one advantage to a baboon troop in having a troop hierarchy:

    _____

2. State which features might determine the size of the home range in any given area: _____

    _____

3. Distinguish between a territory and a home range: _____

    _____

4. Baboons defend the core areas aggressively. Suggest why they would do this: _____

    _____

5. (a) State how many home ranges are represented on the map: _____

    (b) State how many home ranges overlap at the following points on the map: Point A: _____ Point B: _____

    (c) Contrast the distribution of **home ranges** and **core areas** of neighboring troops: _____

    _____

6. Provide an example of a territorial animal and suggest a purpose for the territoriality: _____

    _____

    _____

Plant Science

IB SL

Not applicable

IB HL

Complete nos:
1-6, 9-15, 17-22, 25,
29, 32, 36, 39-40
Extension: 7-8, 16,
23-24, 28, 33, 37

IB Options

Complete nos:
Option F:
HL only: 30-31
Extension: 26

AP Biology

Complete nos:
1-40
Some numbers
extension as
appropriate

Learning Objectives

☐ 1. Compile your own glossary from the **KEY WORDS** displayed in **bold type** in the learning objectives below.

The role and diversity of plants *(see page 328 and Senior Biology 1: page 327)*

☐ 2. Recall the pivotal role of plants as producers in ecosystems and in the global carbon budget.

☐ 3. Outline plant diversity as illustrated by the structural differences between **bryophytes** (mosses and liverworts), **filicinophytes** (ferns), **coniferophytes** (conifers), and **angiospermophytes** (flowering plants).

Basic plant structure *(pages 329, 332-334, 337-338)*

☐ 4. Describe, using a diagram, the external structure of a named dicotyledonous (dicot) plant. Identify the **root**, **stem**, **leaf**, and **axillary** and **terminal buds**, and describe the function of each of these.

☐ 5. Using labeled **plan diagrams**, describe the distribution of tissues in the **stem**, **root**, and **leaf** of a generalized dicot plant. Define the term: **vascular bundle**. *Note that plan diagrams show regions of tissues (e.g. **xylem**, **phloem**) and NOT individual cells.*

☐ 6. Explain the relationship between the distribution of tissues (e.g. phloem, xylem, parenchyma) in a leaf and the functions of these tissues. Include reference to: *light absorption, gas exchange, support, water conservation, and transport of water and solutes.*

The leaf and gas exchange *(pages 339-341)*

☐ 7. Recall the need for gas exchange between the plant tissues and the environment and appreciate the role of the leaf as the primary gas exchange organ in plants. In more detail than in #6 above, describe the role of **stomata** and explain the movement of gases into and out of the **spongy mesophyll** of the leaf.

☐ 8. Describe the role of the stomata and their associated guard cells in controlling the entry and exit of gases to the gas exchange surface. Recognize the role of lenticels in gas exchange in woody plants.

Plant adaptations *(pages 347-350)*

☐ 9. Understand that species are adapted to survive in particular environments. Describe four structural and/or physiological adaptations in **xerophytes**. Examples could include: *C_4 photosynthetic metabolism, adaptations of the leaves and stems, adaptation of growth form, or life cycle adaptations.* Explain how these adaptations reduce **transpiration rate** and thereby enhance survival in dry conditions.

☐ 10. Describe two structural adaptations of **hydrophytes** with respect to their survival in an aquatic habitat.

Transport in flowering plants *(pages 330-331)*

☐ 11. Recognize that plants with transport tissues utilize these same tissues for support. Relate the presence of structural tissues in plants to the presence of an organized transport system. State the role of **cellulose**, **cell turgor**, and **xylem** in supporting the plant body.

Transport tissues *(pages 335-337)*

☐ 12. Recall the structure and function of the transport tissues in angiosperms: **xylem** (**vessels**, **tracheids**, **fibers**, **xylem parenchyma**) and **phloem** (**companion cells**, **sieve elements**, **fibers**, **phloem parenchyma**).

Uptake in roots *(pages 338, 346)*

☐ 13. Recall the structure of a dicot **primary root**. Explain how the root system provides a large surface area for uptake of water and mineral ions, identifying the role of the **root hairs** and the cell walls of the **root cortex**.

☐ 14. Describe the mechanism and pathways for water uptake in plant roots. Include reference to the role of **osmosis**, gradients in **solute concentration** and **pressure**, and the **symplastic** and **apoplastic pathways** through the root. Explain the role of the **endodermis** in movement of water into the **symplast**.

☐ 15. Describe the ways in which mineral uptake occurs in plant roots: passively as a result of water uptake and using active transport mechanisms.

☐ 16. Describe the function of some of the mineral ions important to plants, including: nitrate (NO_3^-), phosphate (PO_4^{3-}), and magnesium (Mg^{2+}) ions.

Transpiration *(pages 342-343)*

☐ 17. Define the terms **transpiration** and **transpiration stream**. Recognize transpiration as an inevitable consequence of gas exchange and identify the role of **stomata** in these processes. Identify two benefits of transpiration to plants.

☐ 18. Draw a labeled diagram to show the transpiration stream in a flowering plant. Explain how water and dissolved minerals are moved up the plant from the roots to the leaves, identifying the roles of each of:
   (a) Xylem (with particular reference to the structural features that facilitate water movement).
   (b) **Cohesion-tension** (capillary action)
   (c) **Transpiration pull** and **evaporation**
   (d) **Root pressure**

☐ 19. Explain the effect of abiotic factors e.g. humidity, light, air movement, temperature, and water availability, on transpiration rate in a typical terrestrial **mesophyte**.

☐ 20. Describe how the factors affecting transpiration could be investigated experimentally.

Transport in the phloem *(pages 344-345)*

☐ 21. Recall the role of **phloem** in the **translocation** of biochemicals and identify translocation as an **active** (energy requiring) process.

☐ 22. Draw a labeled diagram to show the movement of dissolved biochemicals (e.g. sucrose) in the phloem. Identify **sources** and **sinks** in phloem transport.

☐ 23. Describe the **mass flow (pressure-flow) hypothesis** for the mechanism of translocation in plants. Evaluate the evidence for and against the mass flow hypothesis.

☐ 24. With respect to the movement of substances in transport systems, explain what is meant by **mass (bulk) flow**. Explain the role of mass flow in the efficient supply of materials to tissues.

☐ 25. Describe an example of food storage in a named plant. State the role of food storage organs in perennials and identify different types of food storage organs.

Plant life cycles *(pages 351-353)*

☐ 26. Describe methods of **asexual reproduction** in angiosperms: *vegetative structures, cuttings, grafts*.

☐ 27. With reference to angiosperm life cycles, describe **alternation of generations**. Identify the life cycle stages, and the nature and significance of the **haploid (gametophyte)** and **diploid (sporophyte)** generations.

☐ 28. Contrast the relative importance of the sporophyte and gametophyte generations in non-angiosperms: *mosses, ferns, gymnosperms*. Appreciate the differences as part of the diversity of the plant kingdom.

The angiosperm flower *(pages 354-355)*

☐ 29. Using a labeled diagram, describe the structure of a typical (i.e. **monoecious**), **insect-pollinated** dicotyledonous **flower**, including: **sepal**, calyx, **petal**, corolla, **anther**, **filament**, stamen, **stigma**, **style**, **ovary**, carpel. State the function of each labeled part.

☐ 30. Using a labeled diagram, describe the structure and function of the principal parts of a typical monocotyledonous **wind pollinated** flower, as seen with the naked eye and a hand lens. Examples could include a cereal plant (e.g. wheat, rice) or a grass.

☐ 31. Distinguish between the typical adaptations of wind-pollinated and insect-pollinated flowers, identifying the significance of the differences.

Pollination and fertilization *(pages 351, 356)*

☐ 32. Define the term **pollination**, and distinguish between pollination, **fertilization**, and **seed dispersal**.

☐ 33. With the aid of diagrams, describe **pollination** and the events leading to **fertilization**. Include reference to the development of the pollen tube, the role of the **polar nuclei**, and the significance of the **double fertilization**.

☐ 34. Explain what is meant by **cross pollination** and explain its significance. Describe mechanisms in angiosperms for ensuring cross pollination: **protandry**, **protogyny**, and **dioecious flowers**.

Fruits and seeds *(pages 357-358)*

☐ 35. Identify stages in the development of a **fruit**. Explain two purposes of the fruit. Name the structure from which the fruit usually develops and discuss variations on this usual pattern.

☐ 36. Explain the purpose of a **seed**. Using a diagram, describe the external and internal structure of a named dicotyledonous, non-endospermic seed. Include reference to: the **testa**, **micropyle**, **embryo shoot (plumule)**, **embryo root (radicle)**, and **cotyledons**.

☐ 37. Briefly explain the function of each of the structures identified in #36.

☐ 38. List and describe the four common methods of **seed dispersal**. Using examples, compare different plants in their methods of seed dispersal and the pattern and efficiency of their seed dispersal method.

☐ 39. Describe the metabolic events in the **germination** of a typical starchy seed. You should include reference to: *the absorption of water and the purpose of this, the formation of gibberellin in the cotyledon, the production of amylase and the purpose of this*.

☐ 40. Explain the environmental conditions important in triggering **germination** in a typical seed.

Textbooks

See the 'Textbook Reference Grid' on pages 8-9 for textbook page references relating to material in this topic.

Supplementary Texts

See page 6 for additional details of this text:
■ Clegg, C.J., 2003. **Green Plants: The Inside Story**, (John Murray), entire text as required.

Periodicals

See page 6 for details of publishers of periodicals:

STUDENT'S REFERENCE

■ **High Tension** Biol. Sci. Rev., 13(1), Sept. 2000, pp. 14-18. *Cell specialization and transport in plants: an excellent account of the mechanisms by which plants transport water and solutes.*

■ **Plants in the Greenhouse World** New Scientist, 6 May 1989 (Inside Science). *Covers photosynthesis in plants, and how growth, stomatal opening, photosynthesis, and respiration are affected by water availability.*

■ **Water, Water, Everywhere...** Biol. Sci. Rev., 7(5) May 1995, pp. 6-9. *The role of water in plants, including turgor, mass flow and water potential.*

■ **Plants, Water and Climate** New Scientist, 25 February 1989 (Inside Science). *An excellent supplement covering important aspects of plant transport: osmosis and turgor, transport from the root to the leaf, transpiration, and stomatal control.*

■ **Flower Power** New Scientist, 9 January 1999, pp. 22-26. *Pollination and fertilization in angiosperms, and the place of pollen competition.*

TEACHER'S REFERENCE

■ **Supermarket Botany** The American Biology Teacher, 61(2), February, 1999, pp.128-131. *Use of produce in supermarkets to study plant form and function: stems, root types, leaves, flowers, types of fruits (provides a list and descriptions of these).*

■ **A Transpiration Experiment Requiring Critical Thinking Skills** The American Biology Teacher, 60(1), Jan. 1998, pp. 46-49. *The practical examination of transpiration in plants: designing and setting up a potometer to record water uptake.*

■ **Experiments with Corn to Demonstrate Plant Growth and Development** The American Biology Teacher, 62(4) April 2000, pp. 297-302. *Student investigation of germination, growth, and tropisms.*

■ **Temperature and Wind Effect on Plant Transpiration** The American Biology Teacher, 63(6) August 2001, pp. 420-421. *A how-to-do-it lab for students on plant transpiration.*

■ **A Learning Cycle Enquiry into Plant Nutrition** The American Biology Teacher, 65(2) Feb. 2003, pp. 136-141. *Using plant nutrition as a working example on experimental design, set-up and procedure, and data analysis.*

Internet

See pages 10-11 for details of how to access **Bio Links** from our web site: **www.thebiozone.com**. From Bio Links, access sites under the topics:

GENERAL BIOLOGY ONLINE RESOURCES: See sites under **Online Textbooks and Lecture Notes**.

PLANT BIOLOGY: • Kimball's plant biology lecture notes • Plant hormones and nutrition • Plant biology for non-science majors ... *and others* > **Classification and Diversity:** • Flowering plant diversity • Vascular plant families ... *and others* > **Structure and Function:** • Angiosperm structure and function tutorials • Lab I: Plant structure • Plant structure • Plant structure II ... *and others* > **Nutrition and Gas Exchange:** • Gas exchange in plants • Mineral requirements ... *and others* > **Support and Transport:** • Plant structure and growth • Plant transport lecture > **Reproduction:** • Asexual reproduction biology: Pearson College • Flower structure • Flowers and reproduction • Seed germination

Software and video resources are now provided in the Teacher Resource Handbook

Plants as Producers

RA 2

Life on earth is solar-powered – it runs on energy from the sun. Plants, algae, and some bacteria capture this solar energy and convert it into sugars. They achieve this through a process called **photosynthesis**. Each year these organisms produce more than 200 billion tonnes of food. The chemical energy stored in this food fuels the reactions that sustain life (metabolism). Producers are **autotrophs** (self-feeding). Organisms that cannot make their own food are **heterotrophs** and rely on producers either directly or indirectly for their energy. The photosynthesis that occurs in the oceans is vital to the Earth's functioning, providing oxygen and absorbing carbon dioxide. The oceans cover nearly three quarters of the globe. The evaporation from oceans provides most of the Earth's rainfall and ocean temperatures have a major effect on the world's climate. Despite its importance, humans have harvested the ocean heavily and used it to dump waste. Only in recent years have we realized the consequences of this.

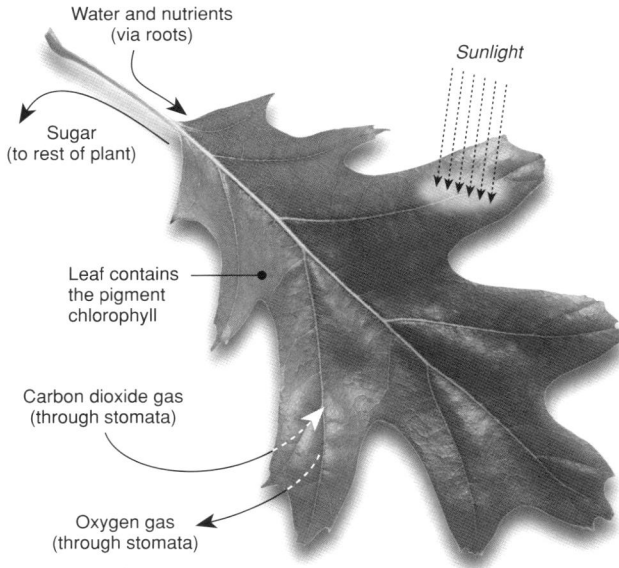

Water and nutrients (via roots)

Sunlight

Sugar (to rest of plant)

Leaf contains the pigment chlorophyll

Carbon dioxide gas (through stomata)

Oxygen gas (through stomata)

Requirements for Photosynthesis

In order to produce their own food, plants need only a few raw materials, light energy from the sun, and the pigment chlorophyll, which is contained in chloroplasts (in the leaves and stems of higher plants). Photosynthesis is summarized in the chemical equation below. It is important to note that this equation is a deceptively simple summary of a more involved process. Photosynthesis is not a single process but two complex processes (the light dependent and light independent reactions) each with multiple steps.

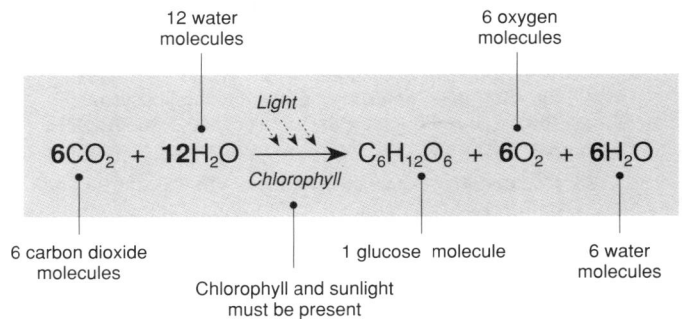

12 water molecules

6 oxygen molecules

$$6CO_2 + 12H_2O \xrightarrow[Chlorophyll]{Light} C_6H_{12}O_6 + 6O_2 + 6H_2O$$

6 carbon dioxide molecules

Chlorophyll and sunlight must be present

1 glucose molecule

6 water molecules

The photosynthesis of marine algae supplies a substantial portion of the world's oxygen. The oceans also act as sinks for the absorption of large amounts of carbon dioxide.

Macroalgae, like this giant kelp, are important marine producers. Algae living near the ocean surface get access to light used in photosynthesis (the red wavelength).

On land, vascular plants (such as trees with transport vessels) are the main producers of food. Plants at different levels in a forest receive different intensity and quality of light.

1. Write the overall chemical equation for photosynthesis using:

   (a) Words: _____

   (b) Chemical symbols: _____

2. Explain the role of producers to the functioning of the Earth's ecosystems: _____

   _____

   _____

3. Explain how light limits the distribution of algae in the ocean: _____

   _____

4. Describe ONE effect of deforestation on the Earth's climate and/or level of the gases oxygen and carbon dioxide:

   _____

   _____

RA① The General Structure of Plants

The support and transport systems in plants are closely linked - many of the same tissues are involved in both systems. Primitive plants (e.g. mosses and liverworts) are small and low growing, and have no need for support and transport systems. If a plant is to grow to any size, it must have ways to hold itself up against gravity and to move materials around its body. The body of a flowering plant has three parts: **roots** anchor the plant and absorb nutrients from the soil, **leaves** produce sugars by photosynthesis, and **stems** link the roots to the leaves and provide support for the leaves and reproductive structures. Vascular tissues (xylem and phloem) link all plant parts so that water, minerals, and manufactured food can be transported between different regions. All plants rely on fluid pressure within their cells (turgor) to give some support to their structure.

Food produced in the leaves must be transported around the plant.

The great heights reached by some trees presents problems for support and transport of materials.

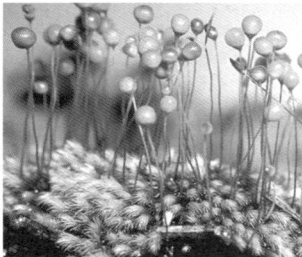

Mosses lack true vascular tissue. This limits their size and the kind of environments they are able to live in.

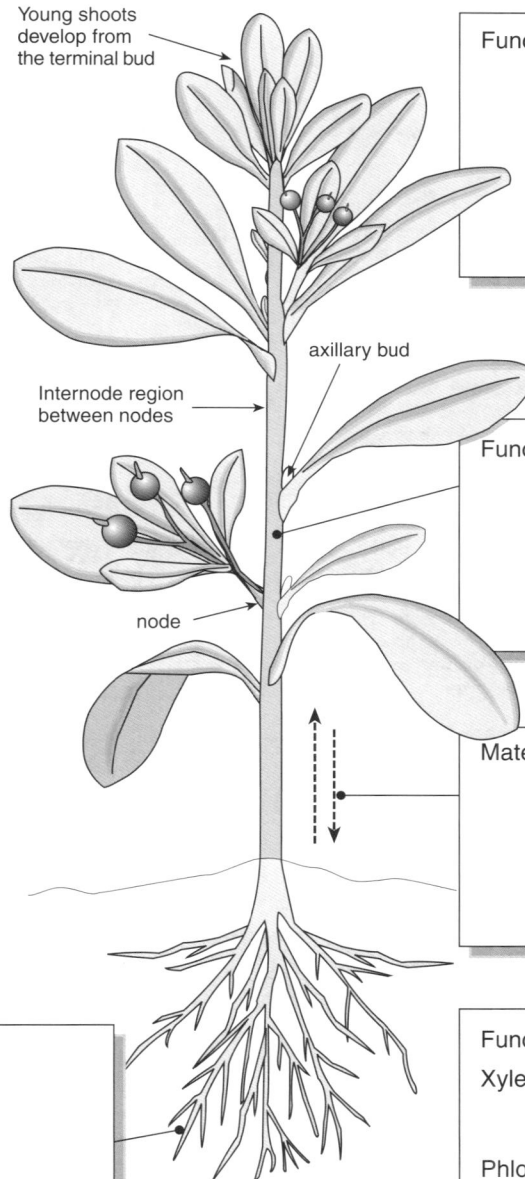

Young shoots develop from the terminal bud

axillary bud

Internode region between nodes

node

Functions of the leaves:

Functions of the stems:

Materials transported around the plant:

Functions of specific transport tissues:
Xylem:

Phloem:

Functions of the roots:

1. In the boxes provided in the diagram above:

    (a) List the main functions of the leaves, roots and stems (remember that the leaves themselves have leaf veins).

    (b) List the materials that are transported around the plant body.

    (c) Describe the functions of the transport tissues: xylem and phloem.

2. Name the solvent for all the materials that are transported around the plant: _____

3. State what processes are involved in the transport of sap in the following tissues:

    (a) The xylem: _____

    (b) The phloem: _____

Support in Plants

A 1

Plants support themselves in their environment and maintain the positions that enable them to carry out essential processes. All plants are provided some support by **cell turgor**. For very small plants, this is sufficient. Terrestrial vascular plants have strengthening tissues that may be hardened with lignin, and many also produce secondary growth (wood). For aquatic plants the water provides support, and adaptations are primarily to maintain the plant in the photic zone and to remain anchored.

Aquatic Environment

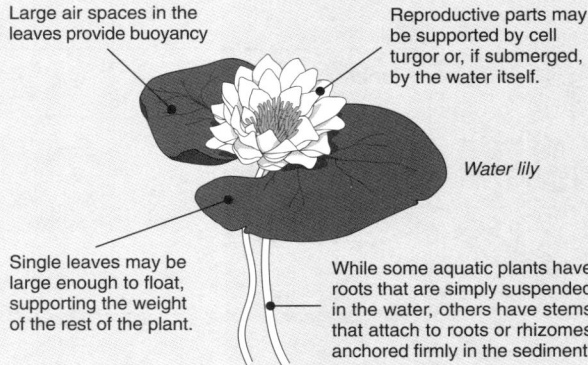

Large air spaces in the leaves provide buoyancy

Reproductive parts may be supported by cell turgor or, if submerged, by the water itself.

Water lily

Single leaves may be large enough to float, supporting the weight of the rest of the plant.

While some aquatic plants have roots that are simply suspended in the water, others have stems that attach to roots or rhizomes anchored firmly in the sediment.

Some aquatic plants, like **water hyacinth**, have swollen petioles that act as floats. Many form floating mats which block water ways and are serious weeds e.g. *Salvinia* and alligator weed.

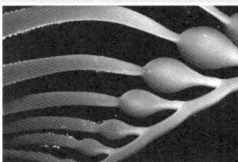

Marine and freshwater **algae** are not plants but have plant like qualities (e.g. chlorophyll). They lack vascular tissue and are supported by the water. Buoyancy may be assisted by airfilled floats or projections of the cell wall, which increase surface area (as in the case of diatoms).

Many floating or semi-aquatic plants, such as **water lilies**, have expanded leaves that provide a large surface area for flotation and photosynthesis. Such floating leaves support the submerged parts of the plant. These plants have roots that are attached to the bottom sediment.

Terrestrial Environment

Vascular plants with secondary thickening (woody tissue) can reach an enormous size. The Australian *Eucalyptus regnans* is reputed to grow to over 140 m in height. Their structural tissues (e.g. **xylem** and **wood**) provide support against gravity. Leaves and reproductive parts are supported by **cell turgor**.

Roots anchor the plant in the ground, forming a stable base for growth. The roots of large hardwood trees can form **buttresses**, providing extra support in poor soils.

Moss

Liverwort

Fern

Bryophytes (mosses and liverworts) lack any vascular tissue: the plant body is supported by **cell turgor**. As a consequence, they are small and their upward growth is restricted. Although there are no true roots, filamentous rhizoids anchor the plant in the ground.

Liverworts are simpler in structure than mosses. The gametophyte (the main plant body) is a flattened structure that may be a lobed thallus or leaf-like, depending on the species. The plant lies flat against the substrate, rising just a centimeter or two above the ground.

Ferns are tracheophytes (vascular plants). They have well developed vascular tissues that provide support and allow transport of nutrients and water around the plant. Because of this, they are able to grow to considerable heights (e.g. tree ferns).

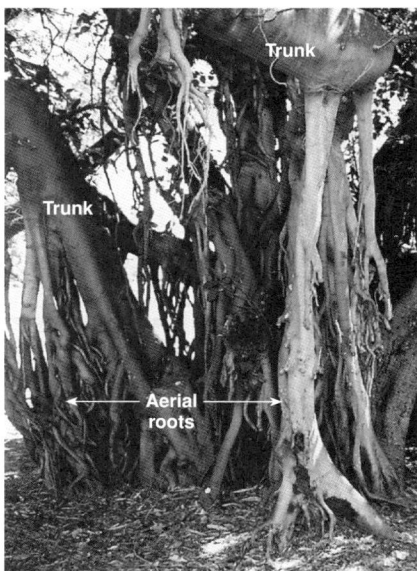

Trunk
Trunk
Aerial roots

Strangler fig
Host tree

Pneumatophores

The **Lord Howe Island fig** has ten or more trunks that develop and form aerial roots. These grow downwards and once anchored in the ground, they provide extra support for the heavy weight of the trunks, allowing them to cover a wide area. Without such support, the trunks would collapse.

Strangler figs begin life high in the forest canopy as epiphytes. They develop roots that grow towards the forest floor. Once rooted in the soil they grow rapidly, embracing the trunk of a host tree with roots and shading it. As the host tree increases in girth, the fig cuts off the sap supply to its roots, killing it.

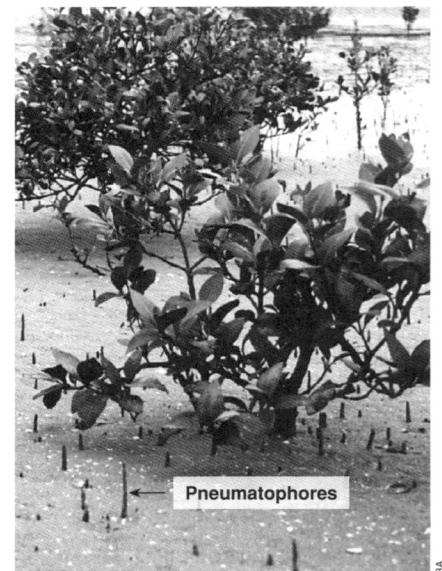

Mangroves grow on mudflat shorelines. The root system cannot penetrate far into the mud due to the lack of oxygen. Support is provided by roots that are sent out in all directions just below the surface. Pneumatophores or breathing roots, (seen above) arise from these shallow lateral roots.

Support in Woody Plants

Secondary xylem which consists of massed xylem vessels and fibers, makes up the bulk of the stem as **wood**, providing considerable strength.

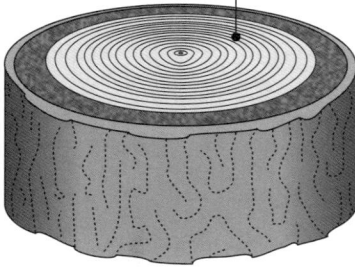

The strengthening of cells with lignin gives support to stems in all vascular plants. Lignin, together with cell turgor, is particularly important in non-woody (herbaceous) plants.

Xylem vessel with spiral thickening produced as a result of **lignin** deposition.

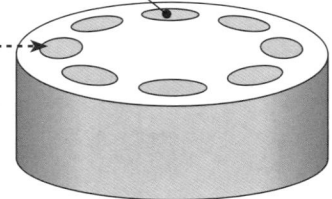

Support in Herbaceous Plants

Turgor pressure inside the parenchyma cells provides a strong inflating force that pushes against the epidermal layer.

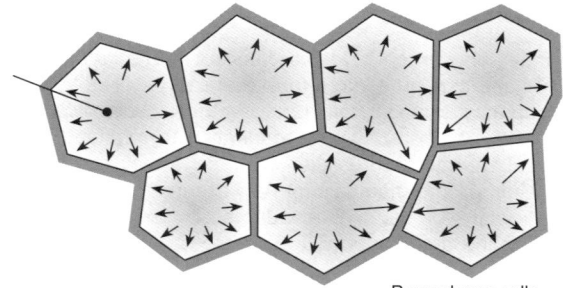

Parenchyma cells

Vascular bundles (comprising xylem and phloem) enhance the ability of herbaceous stems to resist tension and compression.

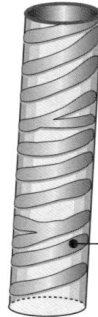

1. In terms of support, explain the main problem experienced by:

    (a) Aquatic plants: _____

    _____

    (b) Terrestrial (land) plants: _____

    _____

2. Describe how the following are achieved in the aquatic protists and plants named below:

    (a) Maintaining a stationary position in **seaweeds**: _____

    (b) Keeping the fronds of **kelp** near the surface: _____

    (c) Keeping **water lily** pads floating on the surface: _____

3. Describe the function of **buttresses** on the trunks of large rainforest hardwood trees:

    _____

    _____

4. Explain the role of the following in providing support for vascular plants:

    (a) Lignin: _____

    _____

    (b) Turgor pressure: _____

    _____

    (c) Vascular bundles: _____

    _____

    (d) Secondary xylem: _____

    _____

5. State how strangler fig trees overcome support problems during the early stage of their development:

    _____

    _____

    _____

Leaf Structure

RA 1

The main function of leaves is to collect the radiant energy from the sun and convert it into a form that can be used by the plant. The sugars produced from photosynthesis have two uses: (1) they can be broken down by respiration to release the stored chemical energy to do cellular work or (2) they can provide the plant with building materials for new tissues (growth and repair). The structure of the leaf is adapted to carry out the job of collecting the sun's energy. To an extent, a leaf is also able to

control the amount of carbon dioxide entering and the amount of water leaving the plant. Both the external and internal morphology of leaves are related primarily to habitat, especially availability of light and water. Regardless of their varying forms, foliage leaves comprise epidermal, mesophyll, and vascular tissues. The mesophyll (the packing tissue of the leaf) may be variously arranged according to the particular photosynthetic adaptations of the leaf.

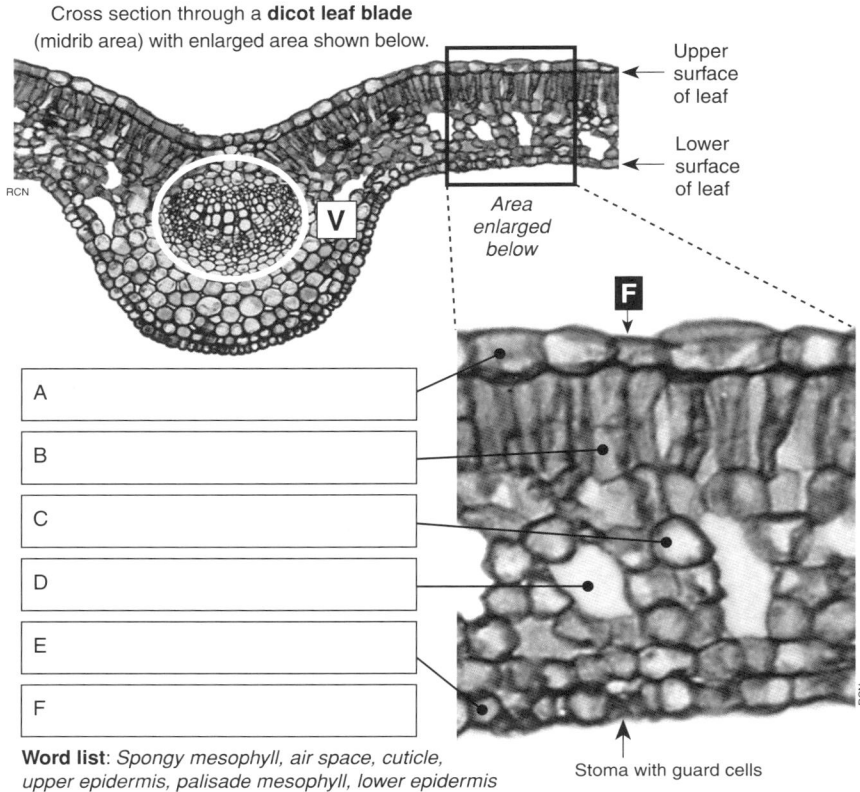

Cross section through a **dicot leaf blade** (midrib area) with enlarged area shown below.

Upper surface of leaf

Lower surface of leaf

Area enlarged below

V

F

A

B

C

D

E

F

Word list: *Spongy mesophyll, air space, cuticle, upper epidermis, palisade mesophyll, lower epidermis*

Stoma with guard cells

1. The internal arrangement of cells and tissues in a typical dicot leaf blade is illustrated in the photographs, above left. Use a text and the word list provided to identify the parts labeled (A)-(F) on the enlarged section.

2. Name the structure enclosed by the white circle (in the photo above) indicated by the letter **V**: _____

3. (a) Explain the purpose of the waxy cuticle that coats the leaf surface: _____

   (b) Explain why the leaf epidermis is transparent: _____

   (c) Explain why leaves are usually broad and flat: _____

4. (a) State the region of the leaf where most of the chloroplasts are found: _____

   (b) Name the important process that occurs in the chloroplasts: _____

5. Explain the purpose of the air spaces in the leaf: _____

6. (a) The panel of photographs, above right, illustrates morphological diversity in monocot /dicot leaves (delete one):

   (b) Explain your reason for this answer: _____

Sun plant

A **sun leaf**, when exposed to high light intensities, can absorb much of the light available to the cells.

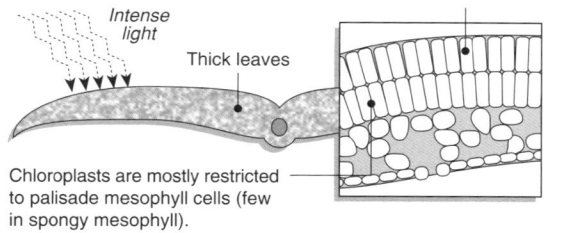

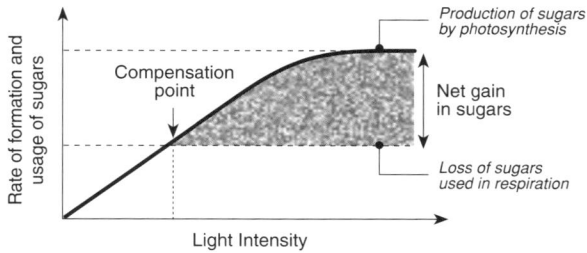

Intense light

Thick leaves

Palisade mesophyll layer often 2 or 3 cells thick

Chloroplasts are mostly restricted to palisade mesophyll cells (few in spongy mesophyll).

Sun leaves

Production of sugars by photosynthesis

Compensation point

Net gain in sugars

Loss of sugars used in respiration

Rate of formation and usage of sugars

Light Intensity

Plants adapted for full sunlight have higher levels of respiration and much higher *compensation points*. **Sun plants** include many weed species found on open ground. They expend much more energy on the construction and maintenance of thicker leaves than do shade plants. The benefit of this investment is that they can absorb the higher light intensities available and grow more quickly.

Shade plant

A **shade leaf** can absorb the light available at lower light intensities. If exposed to high light, most would pass through.

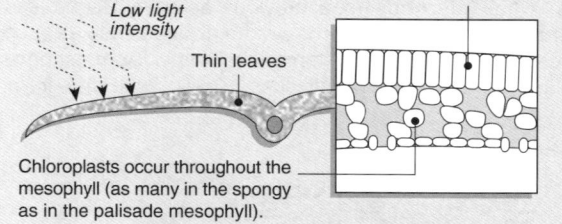

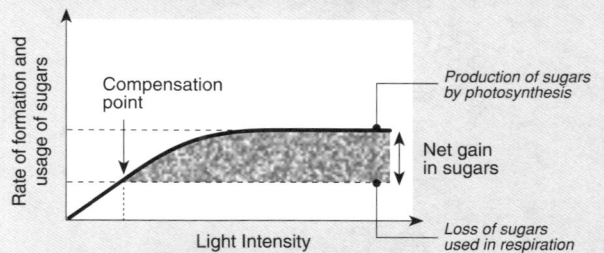

Low light intensity

Thin leaves

Palisade mesophyll layer only 1 cell thick

Chloroplasts occur throughout the mesophyll (as many in the spongy as in the palisade mesophyll).

Shade leaves

Production of sugars by photosynthesis

Compensation point

Net gain in sugars

Loss of sugars used in respiration

Rate of formation and usage of sugars

Light Intensity

Shade plants typically grow in forested areas, partly shaded by the canopy of larger trees. They have lower rates of respiration than sun plants, mainly because they build thinner leaves. The fewer number of cells need less energy for their production and maintenance. As a result, shade plants reach their *compensation point* at a low light intensity; much sooner than sun plants do.

7. List three features of leaves found on a **sun plant** :

(a) _____

(b) _____

(c) _____

8. List three features of leaves found on a **shade plant** :

(a) _____

(b) _____

(c) _____

9. (a) From the diagrams above, determine what is meant by the **compensation point** in terms of sugar production:

_____

_____

_____

(b) State which type of plant (sun or shade adapted) has the highest level of respiration: _____

(c) Explain how the plant compensates for the higher level of respiration: _____

_____

_____

Stem Structure

RA 2

The stems of most plants are the primary organs for supporting the plant. Stems have distinct points, called **nodes**, at which leaves and buds attach. The region of the stem between two nodes is the **internode** (see previous activity). Regardless of their shape or location, all stems can be distinguished as such by the presence of nodes and internodes. Stems, like most parts of the plant, contain vascular tissues. These take the form of

bundles containing the xylem and phloem and strengthening fibers. The arrangement of these bundles in the stem depends on the plant type (e.g. monocot or dicot). The growth that leads to the young, flexible stem is called **primary growth**. The increase in the girth (diameter) of the stem is the result of **secondary growth** and is caused by the production of wood. All plants have primary growth but only some plants show secondary growth.

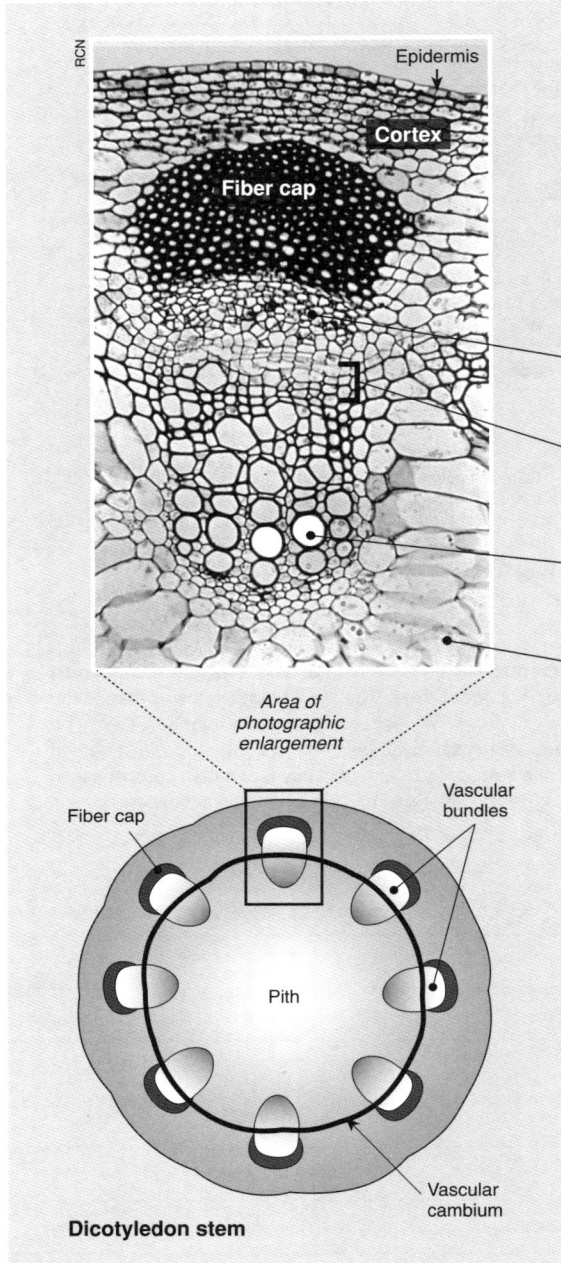

The Structure of Stems in Dicotyledons

The stems of all plants are covered with a thin layer of epidermal cells. The vascular tissue occurs in discrete units, called **vascular bundles**. In dicots, each vascular bundle contains **xylem** (to the inside) and **phloem** (to the outside). Between the phloem and the xylem is the **vascular cambium**; a layer of cells that divide to produce the thickening of the stem. The middle of the stem, called the **pith**, is filled with thin-walled parenchyma cells. The vascular bundles in dicots are arranged in an orderly way around the periphery of the stem, as shown in the diagram, below, left.

(a)

(b)

(c)

(d)

Word list: *xylem, pith, cambium, phloem*

The Structure of Stems in Monocotyledons

The main features of monocot stem structure are illustrated in the photograph to the right. The pith comprises large parenchyma cells. Note how the vascular bundles are scattered randomly through the stem. Contrast this with the orderly arrangement of the vascular bundles in the dicot stem.

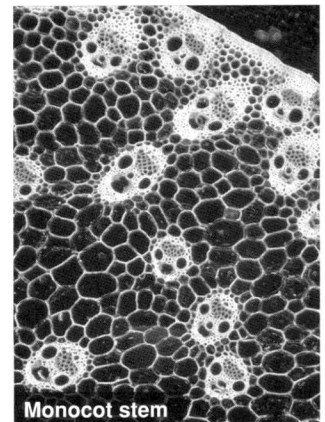

1. Use the information provided to label the photograph of the dicot stem (above).

2. Identify the feature that distinguishes stems from other parts of the plant: _____

3. Explain what is meant by a vascular bundle: _____

4. (a) Identify a distinguishing feature of stem structure in dicots: _____

   (b) Contrast the arrangement of the vascular bundles in monocots and dicots: _____

5. State the role of the vascular cambium: _____

Xylem

A 2

Xylem is the principal **water conducting tissue** in vascular plants. It is also involved in conducting dissolved minerals, in food storage, and in supporting the plant body. As in animals, tissues in plants are groupings of different cell types that work together for a common function. Xylem is a **complex tissue**. In angiosperms, it is composed of five cell types: tracheids, vessels, xylem parenchyma, sclereids (short sclerenchyma cells), and fibers. The tracheids and vessel elements form the bulk of the tissue. They are heavily strengthened and are the conducting cells of the xylem. Parenchyma cells are involved in storage, while fibers and sclereids provide support. When mature, xylem is dead.

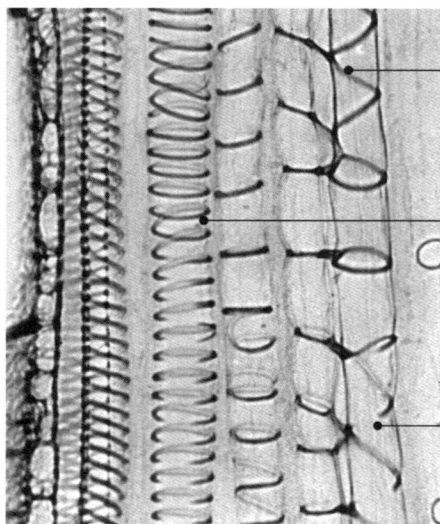

Xylem vessels form continuous tubes throughout the plant.

Spiral thickening of **lignin** around the walls of the vessel elements give extra strength allowing the vessels to remain rigid and upright.

Xylem is dead when mature. Note how the cells have lost their cytoplasm.

The Structure of Xylem Tissue

Xylem   Pith

This cross section through the stem, *Helianthus* (sunflower) shows the central pith, surrounded by a peripheral ring of vascular bundles. Note the xylem vessels with their thick walls.

Vessel element

Secondary walls are laid down and lignified to add strength

The end walls are perforated to allow rapid water transport

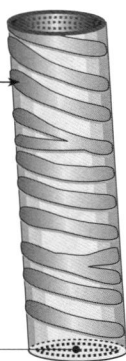

Tip of tracheid

Pits and bordered pits that allow transfer of water between cells

No cytoplasm or nucleus in mature cell

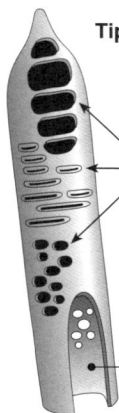

Vessel elements and tracheids are the two conducting cells types in xylem. Tracheids are long, tapering hollow cells. Water passes from one tracheid to another through thin regions in the wall called **pits**. Vessel elements have pits, but the end walls are also perforated and water flows unimpeded through the stacked elements.

Fibers are a type of sclerenchyma cell. They are associated with vascular tissues and usually occur in groups. The cells are very elongated and taper to a point and the cell walls are heavily thickened. Fibers give mechanical support to tissues, providing both strength and elasticity.

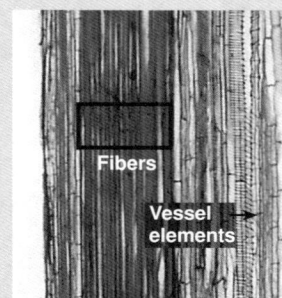

Fibers

Vessel elements

Vessel elements are found only in the xylem of angiosperms. They are large diameter cells that offer very low resistance to water flow. The possession of vessels (stacks of vessel elements) provides angiosperms with a major advantage over gymnosperms and ferns as they allow for very rapid water uptake and transport.

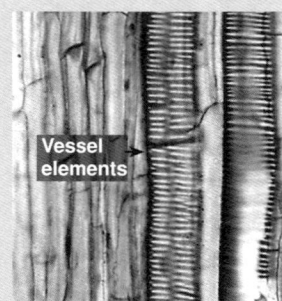

Vessel elements

1. Explain the function of xylem: _____

   _____

2. Identify the four main cell types in xylem and explain their role in the tissue:

   (a) _____

   (b) _____

   (c) _____

   (d) _____

3. Describe one way in which xylem is strengthened in a mature plant: _____

4. Describe a feature of vessel elements that increases their efficiency of function: _____

   _____

Phloem

Like xylem, **phloem** is a complex tissue, comprising a variable number of cell types. Phloem is the principal **food (sugar) conducting tissue** in vascular plants, transporting dissolved sugars around the plant. The bulk of phloem tissue comprises the **sieve tubes** (sieve tube members and sieve cells) and their companion cells. The sieve tubes are the principal conducting cells in phloem and are closely associated with the **companion cells** (modified parenchyma cells) with which they share a mutually dependent relationship. Other parenchyma cells, concerned with storage, occur in phloem, and strengthening fibers and sclereids (short sclerenchyma cells) may also be present. Unlike xylem, phloem is alive when mature.

LS through a sieve tube end plate

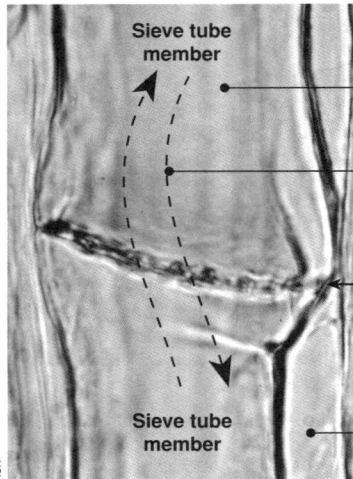

Sieve tube member

The sieve tube members lose most of their organelles but are still alive when mature

Sugar solution flows in both directions

Sieve tube end plate
Tiny holes (arrowed in the photograph below) perforate the sieve tube elements allowing the sugar solution to pass through.

Sieve tube member

Companion cell: a cell adjacent to the sieve tube member, responsible for keeping it alive

TS through a sieve tube end plate

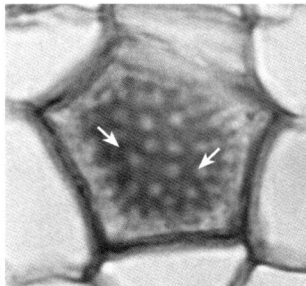

Adjacent sieve tube members are connected through **sieve plates** through which phloem sap flows.

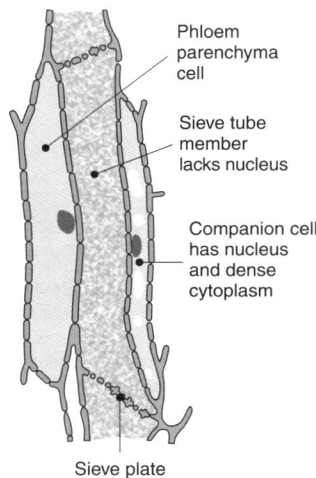

Phloem parenchyma cell

Sieve tube member lacks nucleus

Companion cell has nucleus and dense cytoplasm

Sieve plate

The Structure of Phloem Tissue

Phloem is alive at maturity and functions in the transport of sugars and minerals around the plant. Like xylem, it forms part of the structural vascular tissue of plants.

Fibers are associated with phloem as they are in xylem. Here they are seen in cross section where you can see the extremely thick cell walls and the way the fibers are clustered in groups. See the previous page for a view of fibers in longitudinal section.

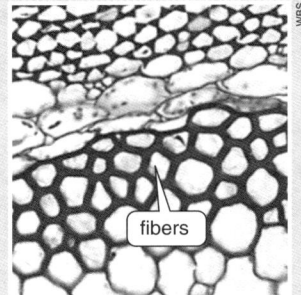

fibers

In this cross section through a buttercup root, the smaller companion cells can be seen lying alongside the sieve tube members. It is the sieve tube members that, end on end, produce the **sieve tubes**. They are the conducting tissue of phloem.

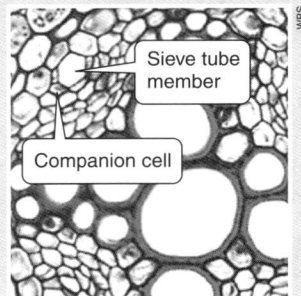

Sieve tube member

Companion cell

In this longitudinal section of a buttercup root, each sieve tube member has a thin **companion cell** associated with it. Companion cells retain their nucleus and control the metabolism of the sieve tube member next to them. They also have a role in the loading and unloading of sugar into the phloem.

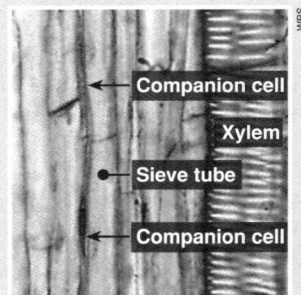

Companion cell

Xylem

Sieve tube

Companion cell

1. State the function of phloem: _____

2. Describe two differences between xylem and phloem: _____

    _____

3. Explain the purpose of the **sieve plate** at the ends of each sieve tube member: _____

    _____

4. (a) Name the conducting cell type in phloem: _____

    (b) Explain two roles of the companion cell in phloem: _____

    _____

5. State the purpose of the phloem parenchyma cells: _____

6. Name a type of cell that provides strengthening in phloem: _____

Root Structure

Roots are essential plant organs. They anchor the plant in the ground, absorb water and minerals from the soil, and transport these materials to other parts of the plant body. Roots may also act as storage organs, storing excess carbohydrate reserves until they are required by the plant. Roots are covered in an epidermis but, unlike the leaf epidermis, the root epidermis has only a very thin cuticle, which presents no barrier to water entry. Young roots are also covered with **root hairs**. Minerals and water must move from the soil into the xylem before they can be transported around the plant. Compared with stems, roots are relatively simple and uniform in structure. The structure of a dicot root is explained below. Monocot roots vary from dicot roots in having a prominent, heavily thickened endodermis and a central pith inside a prominent ring of vascular tissue.

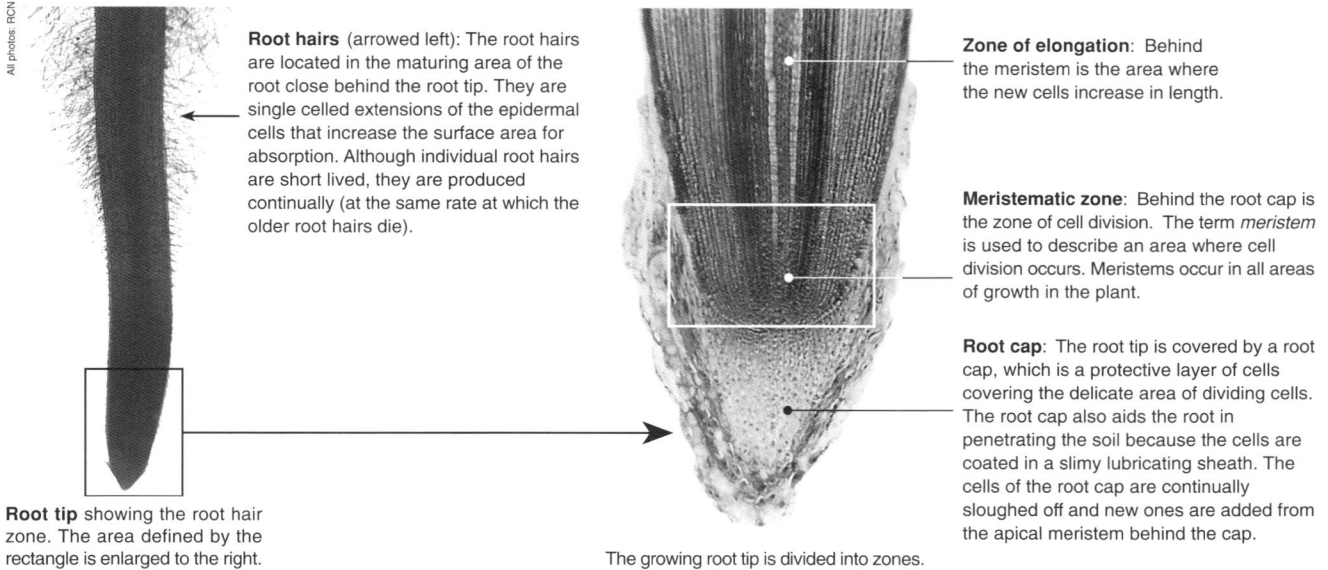

Root hairs (arrowed left): The root hairs are located in the maturing area of the root close behind the root tip. They are single celled extensions of the epidermal cells that increase the surface area for absorption. Although individual root hairs are short lived, they are produced continually (at the same rate at which the older root hairs die).

Root tip showing the root hair zone. The area defined by the rectangle is enlarged to the right.

Zone of elongation: Behind the meristem is the area where the new cells increase in length.

Meristematic zone: Behind the root cap is the zone of cell division. The term *meristem* is used to describe an area where cell division occurs. Meristems occur in all areas of growth in the plant.

Root cap: The root tip is covered by a root cap, which is a protective layer of cells covering the delicate area of dividing cells. The root cap also aids the root in penetrating the soil because the cells are coated in a slimy lubricating sheath. The cells of the root cap are continually sloughed off and new ones are added from the apical meristem behind the cap.

The growing root tip is divided into zones.

The Structure of a Dicot Root

These photographs show cross sections through a young dicot root. Note the large area of the root occupied by the cortex in the photograph to the left. The parenchyma (packing) cells of the cortex store starch and other substances. The air spaces between the cells are essential for aeration of the root tissue, which is non-photosynthetic. The vascular tissue, xylem (X) and phloem (P), is enlarged below. The vascular tissue is surrounded by the pericycle, a ring of cells from which lateral roots arise. The primary xylem of dicot roots forms a star shape in the centre of the vascular cylinder with usually 3 or 4 points.

Root hairs

Cortex of parenchyma cells

Air space

Vascular tissue (vascular cylinder or **stele***) is enlarged in the photo on the right.*

Cortex

Pericycle

Endodermis

1. Identify two structural features of roots that facilitate uptake of water and ions:

   (a) _____

   (b) _____

2. Describe the purpose of the protective cap of cells on the root tip: _____

3. Describe two distinguishing features of a dicot root:

   (a) _____

   (b) _____

Uptake in the Root

Plants need to take up water and minerals constantly. They must compensate for the continuous loss of water from the leaves and provide the materials they need for the manufacture of food. The uptake of water and minerals is mostly restricted to the younger, most recently formed cells of the roots and the root hairs. Some water moves through the plant tissues via the plasmodesmata of the cells (the **symplastic route**), but most passes through the free spaces between cell walls (the **apoplast**). Water uptake is assisted by root pressure, which arises because the soil and root tissue has a lower solute concentration than other plant tissues. Two processes are involved in water and ion uptake: diffusion (osmosis in the case of water) and active transport. ***NOTE***: *Those wishing to cover this topic using* **water potential** *terminology can download an alternative version from*: **www.thebiozone.com/waterpotential.html**

Schematic cross-section through a root

Root hair

Cortex cells of root

Some dissolved minerals enter passively with water, some by active transport.

Stele (vascular cylinder)

Xylem

Epidermal cell

Water moves by osmosis

Endodermis: a single layer of cells bearing a band of waterproof suberin (the **Casparian strip**)

Mineral Uptake

Many minerals are absorbed passively along with the water they are dissolved in. However, some minerals are in such low concentration in the soil that they must be taken up actively by the root. This active transport requires energy and is therefore "expensive" for the plant.

Root hairs **increase the surface area** for absorption of water and nutrients by many times. The root hairs are extensions of the root epidermal cells, extending out to make intimate contact with the film of water on the soil particles. Unlike older roots, the root hairs have no waterproof suberin layer and a very thin cuticle, so they present little barrier to water entry.

Enlargement of root cells

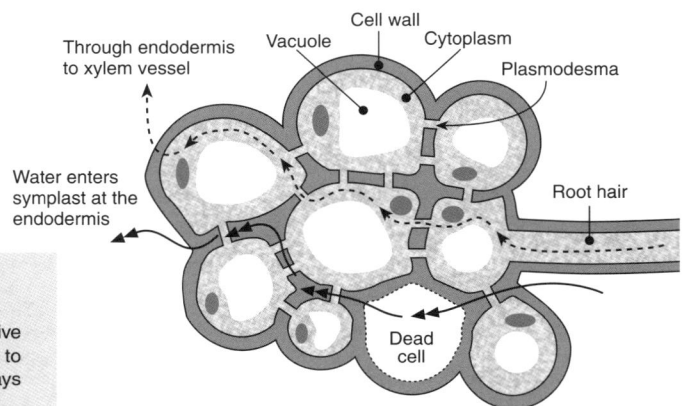

Through endodermis to xylem vessel

Vacuole

Cell wall

Cytoplasm

Plasmodesma

Root hair

Water enters symplast at the endodermis

Dead cell

Zone of higher solute concentration
May be due to: less turgid cells, lower wall pressure or more dissolved substances

Zone of lower solute concentration
May be due to: fully turgid cells, higher wall pressure or less dissolved substances

◄◄─── Apoplast pathway (cell wall)
◄- - - - Symplast pathway (cytoplasm)

Water Uptake

The uptake of water through the roots occurs by **osmosis** – the passive diffusion of water from where there is a lower solute concentration to where there is a higher solute concentration. Three different pathways of water transport are known to exist in flowering plants:

Apoplast pathway: About 90% of water moves through the tissues via the spaces within the cellulose cell walls, the water-filled spaces of dead cells and the hollow tubes of xylem vessels.

Symplast pathway: Some water also moves through the living contents of cells. Water enters the cytoplasm and moves between cells through the cytolasmic connections called *plasmodesmata* (*sing.* plasmodesma) that cross the cell walls through pits.

Vacuolar pathway: A small amount of water passes into the cell vacuoles by osmosis. This vacuolar pathway is the route by which individual cells absorb water. It is not shown on the diagram.

1. (a) Name the two mechanisms that plants use to absorb nutrients: _____

   (b) Describe the two principal pathways by which water moves through a plant: _____

   _____

2. Plants take up water constantly to compensate for transpirational loss. Describe a benefit of a large water uptake:

   _____

3. (a) Describe the consequence of the Casparian strip to the route water takes into the stele: _____

   _____

   (b) Suggest why this feature might be advantageous in terms of selective mineral uptake: _____

   _____

   _____

Gas Exchange in Plants

Respiring tissues require oxygen, and the photosynthetic tissues of plants also require carbon dioxide in order to produce the sugars needed for their growth and maintenance. The principal gas exchange organs in plants are the leaves, and sometimes the stems. In most plants, the exchange of gases directly across the leaf surface is prevented by the waterproof, waxy cuticle layer. Instead, access to the respiring cells is by means of **stomata**, which are tiny pores in the leaf surface. The plant has to balance its need for carbon dioxide (keeping stomata open) against its need to reduce water loss (stomata closed).

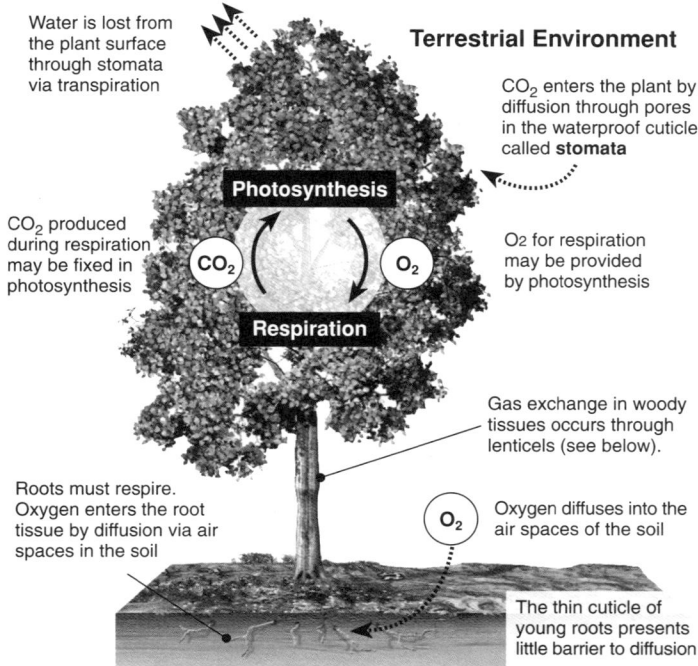

Terrestrial Environment

Water is lost from the plant surface through stomata via transpiration

CO_2 enters the plant by diffusion through pores in the waterproof cuticle called **stomata**

Photosynthesis

CO_2 produced during respiration may be fixed in photosynthesis

CO₂

O₂

O_2 for respiration may be provided by photosynthesis

Respiration

Gas exchange in woody tissues occurs through lenticels (see below).

Roots must respire. Oxygen enters the root tissue by diffusion via air spaces in the soil

O₂ Oxygen diffuses into the air spaces of the soil

The thin cuticle of young roots presents little barrier to diffusion

Most gas exchange in plants occurs through the leaves, but some also occurs through the stems and the roots. The shape and structure of leaves (very thin with a high surface area) assists gas exchange by diffusion.

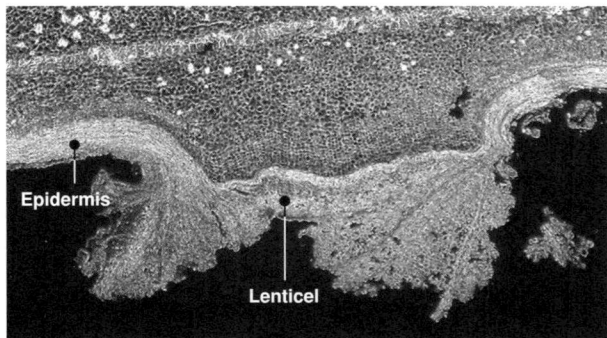

Epidermis

Lenticel

In woody plants, the wood prevents gas exchange. A lenticel is a small area in the bark where the loosely arranged cells allow entry and exit of gases into the stem tissue underneath.

Aquatic Environment

The aquatic environment presents special problems for plants. Water loss is not a problem, but CO_2 availability is often very limited because most of the dissolved CO_2 is present in the form of bicarbonate ions, which is not directly available to plants. Maximizing uptake of gaseous CO_2 by reducing barriers to diffusion is therefore important.

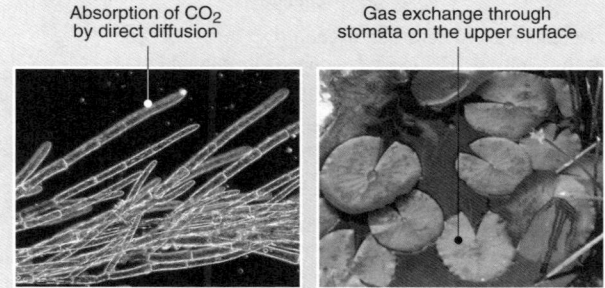

Absorption of CO_2 by direct diffusion

Gas exchange through stomata on the upper surface

Algae lack stomata but achieve adequate gas exchange through simple diffusion into the cells.

Floating leaves, such as the water lilies above, generally lack stomata on their lower surface.

With the exception of liverworts, all terrestrial plants and most aquatic plants have stomata to provide for gas exchange. CO_2 uptake is aided in submerged plants because they have little or no cuticle to form a barrier to diffusion of gases. The few submerged aquatics that lack stomata altogether rely only on diffusion through the epidermis. Most aquatic plants also have air spaces in their spongy tissues (which also assist buoyancy).

Transitional Environment

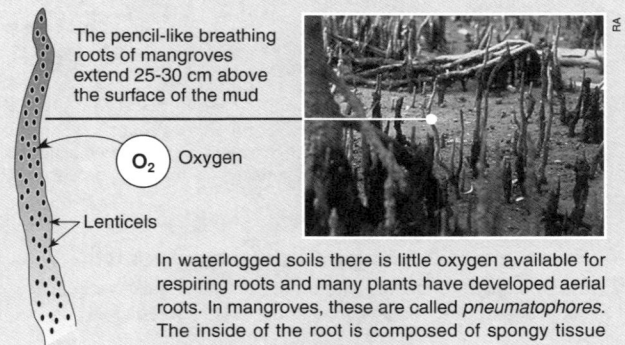

The pencil-like breathing roots of mangroves extend 25-30 cm above the surface of the mud

O₂ Oxygen

Lenticels

In waterlogged soils there is little oxygen available for respiring roots and many plants have developed aerial roots. In mangroves, these are called *pneumatophores*. The inside of the root is composed of spongy tissue filled with air from lenticels in the bark.

---

1. Name the gas produced by cellular respiration that is also a raw material for photosynthesis: _____

2. Describe the role of lenticels in plant gas exchange: _____

_____

3. Name the two properties of leaves that assist gas exchange: _____

4. With respect to gas exchange and water balance, describe the most important considerations for:

   (a) Terrestrial plants: _____

   (b) Aquatic plants: _____

5. Describe an adaptation for gas exchange in the following plants:

   (a) A submerged aquatic angiosperm: _____

   (b) A mangrove in a salty mudflat: _____

Gas Exchange and Stomata

The leaf epidermis of angiosperms is covered with tiny pores, called **stomata**. Angiosperms have many air spaces between the cells of the stems, leaves, and roots. These air spaces are continuous and gases are able to move freely through them and into the plant's cells via the stomata. Each stoma is bounded by

two **guard cells**, which together regulate the entry and exit of gases and water vapor. Although stomata permit gas exchange between the air and the photosynthetic cells inside the leaf, they are also the major routes for water loss through transpiration.

Gas Exchanges and the Function of Stomata

Gases enter and leave the leaf by way of stomata. Inside the leaf (as illustrated by a dicot, right), the large air spaces and loose arrangement of the spongy mesophyll facilitate the diffusion of gases and provide a large surface area for gas exchanges.

Respiring plant cells use oxygen (O_2) and produce carbon dioxide (CO_2). These gases move in and out of the plant and through the air spaces by diffusion.

When the plant is photosynthesizing, the situation is more complex. Overall there is a net consumption of CO_2 and a net production of oxygen. The fixation of CO_2 maintains a gradient in CO_2 concentration between the inside of the leaf and the atmosphere. Oxygen is produced in excess of respiratory needs and diffuses out of the leaf. These **net** exchanges are indicated by the arrows on the diagram.

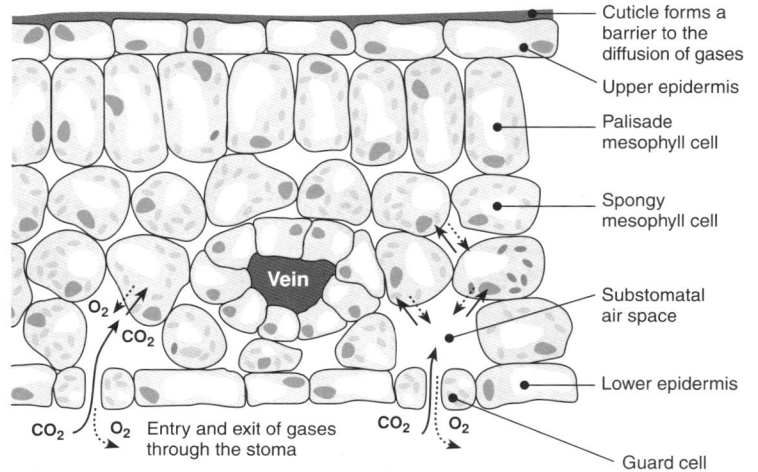

Net gas exchanges in a photosynthesizing dicot leaf

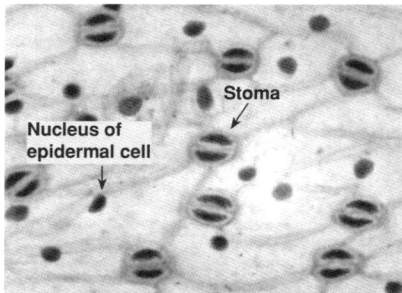

A surface view of the leaf epidermis of a dicot (above) illustrating the density and scattered arrangement of stomata. In dicots, stomata are usually present only on the lower leaf surface.

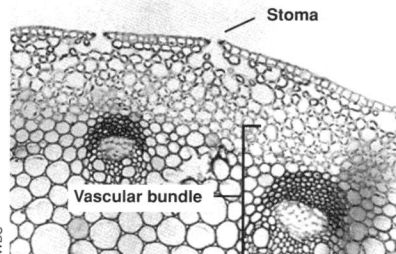

The stems of some plants (e.g. the buttercup above) are photosynthetic. Gas exchange between the stem tissues and the environment occurs through stomata in the outer epidermis.

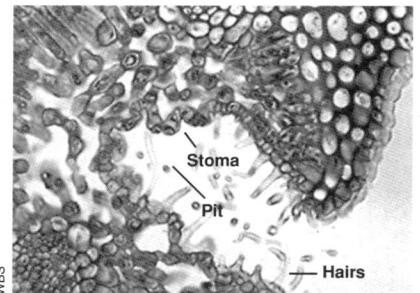

Oleander (above) is a xerophyte with many water conserving features. The stomata are in pits on the leaf underside. The pits restrict water loss to a greater extent than they reduce CO_2 uptake.

The cycle of opening and closing of stomata
The opening and closing of stomata shows a daily cycle that is largely determined by the hours of light and dark.

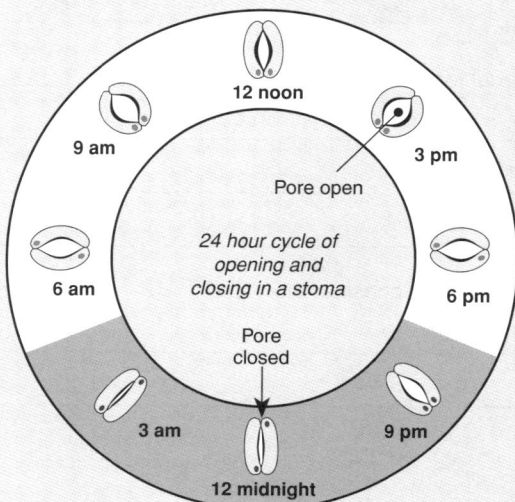

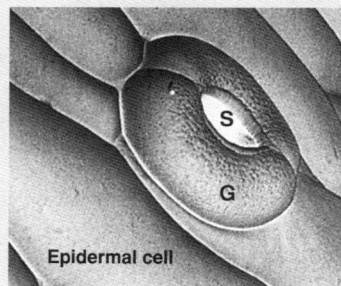

The image left shows a scanning electron micrograph (SEM) of a single stoma from the leaf epidermis of a dicot.

Note the guard cells (G), which are swollen tight and open the pore (S) to allow gas exchange between the leaf tissue and the environment.

Factors influencing stomatal opening

Stomata	Guard cells	Daylight	CO$_2$	Soil water
Open	Turgid	Light	Low	High
Closed	Flaccid	Dark	High	Low

The opening and closing of stomata depends on environmental factors, the most important being light, carbon dioxide concentration in the leaf tissue, and water supply. Stomata tend to open during daylight in response to light, and close at night (left and above). Low CO_2 levels also promote stomatal opening. Conditions that induce water stress cause the stomata close, regardless of light or CO_2 level.

The guard cells on each side of a stoma control the diameter of the pore by changing shape. When the guard cells take up water by osmosis they swell and become turgid, making the pore wider. When the guard cells lose water, they become flaccid, and the pore closes up. By this mechanism a plant can control the amount of gas entering, or water leaving, the plant. The changes in turgor pressure that open and close the pore result mainly from the reversible uptake and loss of potassium ions (and thus water) by the guard cells. **NOTE**: *Those wishing to cover this material using water potential terminology can download an alternative version from:* **www.thebiozone.com/waterpotential.html**

Stomatal Pore Open

K+ enters the guard cells from the epidermal cells (active transport coupled to a proton pump).

H_2O
K^+

Thickened ventral wall

Water follows K+ by osmosis.

H_2O
H_2O
K^+

Guard cell swells and becomes turgid.

Pore opens

K^+
H_2O
K^+
H_2O

Nucleus of guard cell

Stomata open when the guard cells actively take up K+ from the neighboring epidermal cells. The ion uptake increases the solute concentration in the guard cells. As a consequence, water is taken up by the cells and they swell and become turgid. The walls of the guard cells are thickened more on the inside than the outside wall, so that when the cells swell they buckle outward, opening the pore.

Stomatal Pore Closed

K+ leaves the guard cell and enters the epidermal cells.

Water follows K+ by osmosis.

H_2O

The guard cells become flaccid.

H_2O
K^+

H_2O
K^+

Pore closes

H_2O

K^+

Stomata close when K+ leaves the guard cells. The loss of these ions decreases the solute concentration in the guard cells. As a consequence, water moves out of the guard cells by osmosis and the cells sag together and close the pore. The K+ movements in and out of the guard cells are thought to be triggered by blue-light receptors in the cell membrane, which activate the active transport mechanisms involved.

1. With respect to a mesophytic, terrestrial flowering plant:

    (a) Describe the **net** gas exchanges between the air and the cells of the mesophyll in the dark (no photosynthesis):

    _____

    (b) Explain how this situation changes when a plant is photosynthesizing: _____

    _____

    _____

2. Identify two ways in which the continuous air spaces through the plant facilitate gas exchange:

    (a) _____

    (b) _____

3. Briefly outline the role of stomata in gas exchange in an angiosperm: _____

    _____

    _____

4. Summarize the mechanism by which the guard cells bring about:

    (a) Stomatal opening: _____

    _____

    _____

    _____

    (b) Stomatal closure: _____

    _____

    _____

    _____

Transipiration

DA 3

Plants lose water all the time, despite the adaptations they have to help prevent it (e.g. waxy leaf cuticle). Approximately 99% of the water a plant absorbs from the soil is lost by evaporation from the leaves and stem. This loss, mostly through stomata, is called **transpiration** and the flow of water through the plant is called the **transpiration stream**. Plants rely on a gradient in solute concentration from the roots to the air to move water through their cells. Water flows passively from soil to air along a gradient of increasing solute concentration. This gradient is the driving force in the ascent of water up a plant. A number of processes contribute to water movement up the plant: transpiration pull, cohesion, and root pressure. Transpiration may seem wasteful, but it has benefits; evaporative water loss cools the plant and the transpiration stream helps the plant to maintain an adequate mineral uptake, as many essential minerals occur in low concentrations in the soil. **NOTE**: *Those wishing to cover this topic using* **water potential** *terminology can download an alternative version from*: **www.thebiozone.com/waterpotential.html**

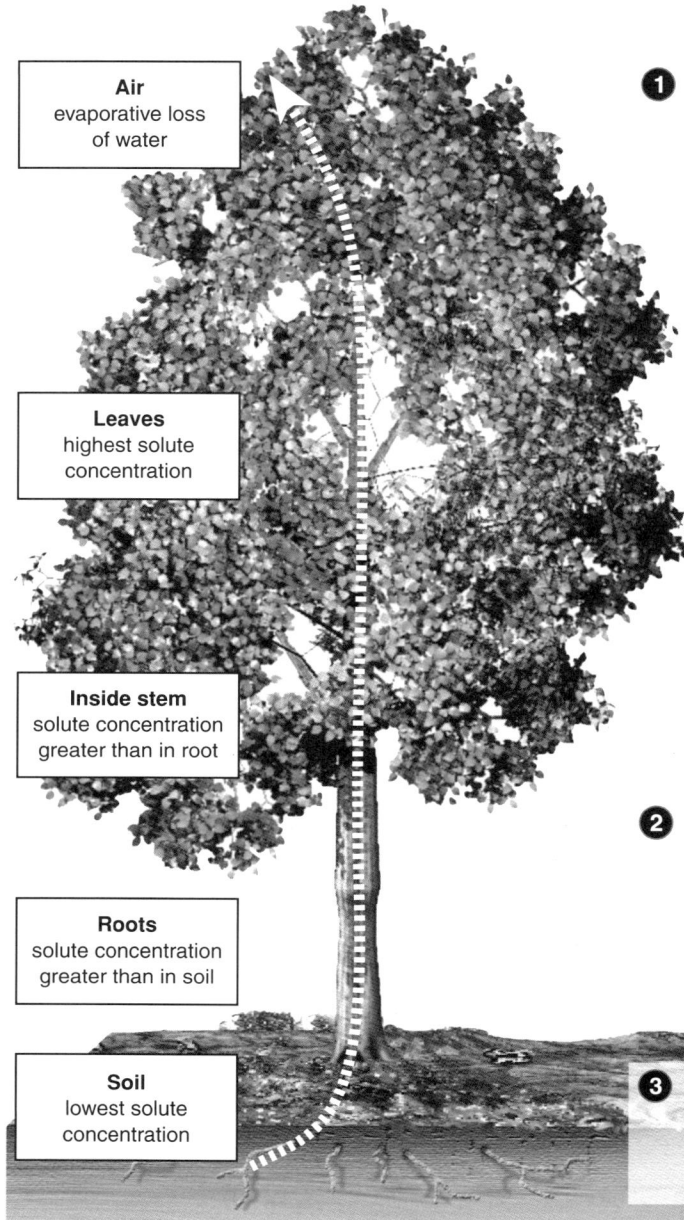

Air
evaporative loss of water

Leaves
highest solute concentration

Inside stem
solute concentration greater than in root

Roots
solute concentration greater than in soil

Soil
lowest solute concentration

1 **Transpiration pull** Water lost from the air spaces by evaporation through stomata is replaced by water from the mesophyll cells. The constant loss of water to the air (and production of sugars) creates a solute concentration in the leaves that is higher than elsewhere in the plant. Water is pulled through the plant along a **increasing gradient in solute concentration**.

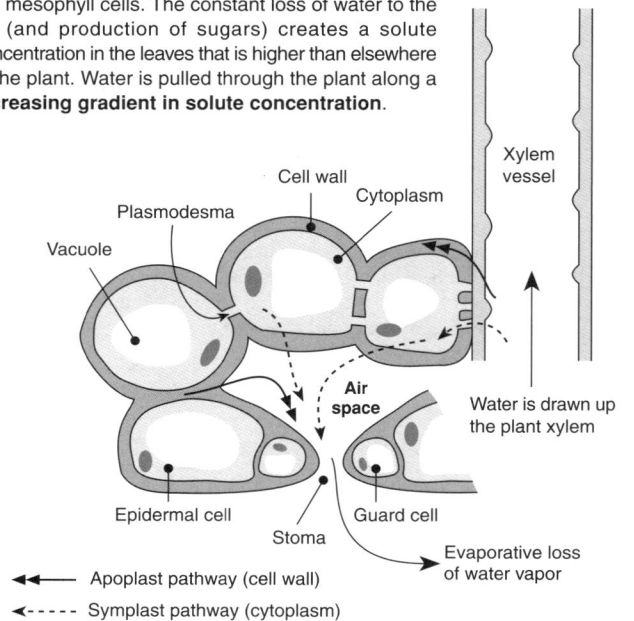

Cell wall
Cytoplasm
Plasmodesma
Vacuole
Xylem vessel
Air space
Water is drawn up the plant xylem
Epidermal cell
Stoma
Guard cell
Evaporative loss of water vapor

◄◄──── Apoplast pathway (cell wall)
◄----- Symplast pathway (cytoplasm)

2 **Cohesion** The transpiration pull is assisted by the special **cohesive** properties of water. Water molecules cling together as they are pulled through the plant and they **adhere** to the walls of the xylem. This creates one unbroken column of water through the plant. The upward pull on the cohesive sap creates a tension (a negative pressure). This facilitates water uptake and movement through the plant.

3 Water entering the stele from the soil creates a **root pressure;** a weak 'push' effect for the water's upward movement through the plant. Root pressure can force water droplets from some small plants under certain conditions (**guttation**), but generally it is plays a minor part in the ascent of water.

1. (a) Plants constantly lose water by transpiration. Explain how plants compensate for this:

_____

   (b) Describe one benefit of the transpiration stream for a plant: _____

_____

2. Briefly describe three processes that assist the transport of water from the roots of the plant upward:

   (a) _____

   (b) _____

   (c) _____

The Potometer

A potometer is a simple instrument for investigating transpiration rate (water loss per unit time). The equipment is simple and easy to obtain. A basic potometer, such as the one shown right, can easily be moved around so that transpiration rate can be measured under different environmental conditions

Some of the physical conditions investigated are:

- Humidity or vapor pressure (high or low)
- Temperature (high or low)
- Air movement (still or windy)
- Light level (high or low)
- Water supply

It is also possible to compare the transpiration rates of plants with different adaptations e.g. comparing transpiration rates in plants with rolled leaves vs rates in plants with broad leaves. If possible, experiments like these should be conducted simultaneously using replicate equipment. If conducted sequentially, care should be taken to keep the environmental conditions the same for all plants used.

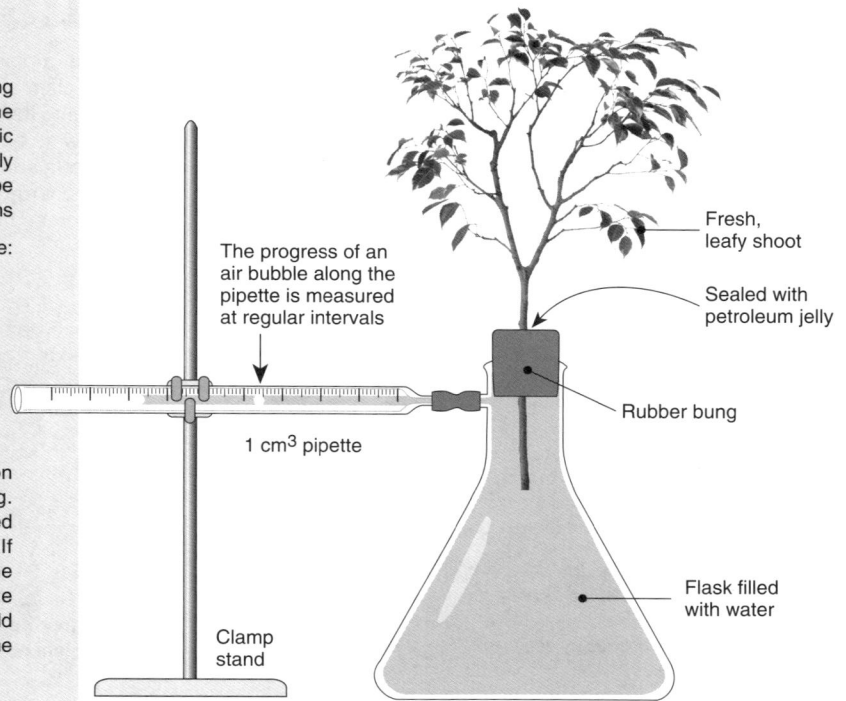

The progress of an air bubble along the pipette is measured at regular intervals

1 cm³ pipette

Clamp stand

Fresh, leafy shoot

Sealed with petroleum jelly

Rubber bung

Flask filled with water

3. Identify three environmental conditions that increase the rate of transpiration in plants, and explain how they operate:

(a) _____

(b) _____

(c) _____

4. The **potometer** (above) is an instrument used to measure transpiration rate. Briefly explain how it works:

_____

_____

5. An experiment was conducted on transpiration from a hydrangea shoot in a potometer. The experiment was set up and the plant left to stabilize (environmental conditions: still air, light shade, 20°C). The plant was then subjected to different environmental conditions and the water loss was measured each hour. Finally, the plant was returned to original conditions, allowed to stabilize and transpiration rate measured again. The data are presented below:

Experimental conditions	Temperature (°C)	Humidity (%)	Transpiration (gh⁻¹)
(a) Still air, light shade, 20°C	18°C	70	1.20
(b) Moving air, light shade, 20°C	18°C	70	1.60
(c) Still air, bright sunlight, 23°C	18°C	70	3.75
(d) Still air and dark, moist chamber, 19.5°C	18°C	100	0.05

(a) Name the control in this experiment: _____

_____

(b) State which factors increased transpiration rate, explaining how each has its effect: _____

_____

_____

(c) Suggest a possible reason why the plant had such a low transpiration rate in humid, dark conditions:

_____

_____

Translocation

RA 2

Phloem transports the organic products of photosynthesis (sugars) through the plant in a process called **translocation**. In angiosperms, the sugar moves through the sieve elements, which are arranged end-to-end and perforated with sieve plates. Apart from water, phloem sap comprises mainly sucrose (up to 30%). It may also contain minerals, hormones, and amino acids, in transit around the plant. Movement of sap in the phloem is from a **source** (a plant organ where sugar is made or mobilized) to a **sink** (a plant organ where sugar is stored or used). Loading sucrose into the phloem at a source involves energy expenditure; it is slowed or stopped by high temperatures or respiratory inhibitors. In some plants, unloading the sucrose at the sinks also requires energy, although in others, diffusion alone is sufficient to move sucrose from the phloem into the cells of the sink organ.

Transport in the Phloem by Pressure-Flow

Phloem sap moves from source (region where sugar is produced or mobilized) to sink (region where sugar is used or stored) at rates as great as 100 m h^{-1}: too fast to be accounted for by cytoplasmic streaming. The most acceptable model for phloem movement is the **pressure-flow** (bulk flow) hypothesis. Phloem sap moves by bulk flow, which creates a pressure (hence the term "pressure-flow"). The key elements in this model are outlined below and in steps 1-4 right. For simplicity, the cells that lie between the source (and sink) cells and the phloem sieve-tube have been omitted.

1. Loading sugar into the phloem from a source (e.g. leaf cell) increases the solute concentration inside the sieve-tube cells. This causes the sieve-tubes to take up water from the surrounding tissues by osmosis.

2. The water absorption creates a hydrostatic pressure that forces the sap to move along the tube (bulk flow), just as pressure pushes water through a hose.

3. The gradient of pressure in the sieve tube is reinforced by the active unloading of sugar and consequent loss of water by osmosis at the sink (e.g. root cell).

4. Xylem recycles the water from sink to source.

Measuring phloem flow

Experiments investigating flow of phloem often use aphids. Aphids feed on phloem sap (left) and act as natural **phloem probes**. When the mouthparts (stylet) of an aphid penetrate a sieve-tube cell, the pressure in the sieve-tube force-feeds the aphid. While the aphid feeds, it can be severed from its stylet, which remains in place in the phloem. The stylet serves as a tiny tap that exudes sap. Using different aphids, the rate of flow of this sap can be measured at different locations on the plant.

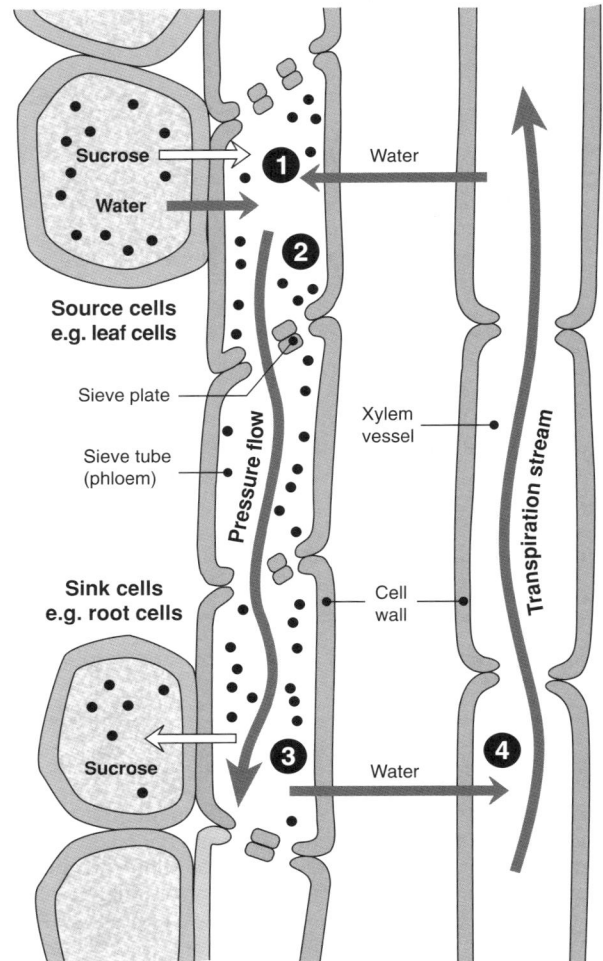

Modified after Campbell *Biology* 1993

1. (a) Explain what is meant by *source to sink* flow in phloem transport: _____

   (b) Name the usual **source** and **sink** in a growing plant:

   Source: _____   Sink: _____

   (c) Name another possible **source** region in the plant and state when it might be important: _____

   (d) Name another possible **sink** region in the plant and state when it might be important: _____

2. Explain why energy is required for translocation and where it is used: _____

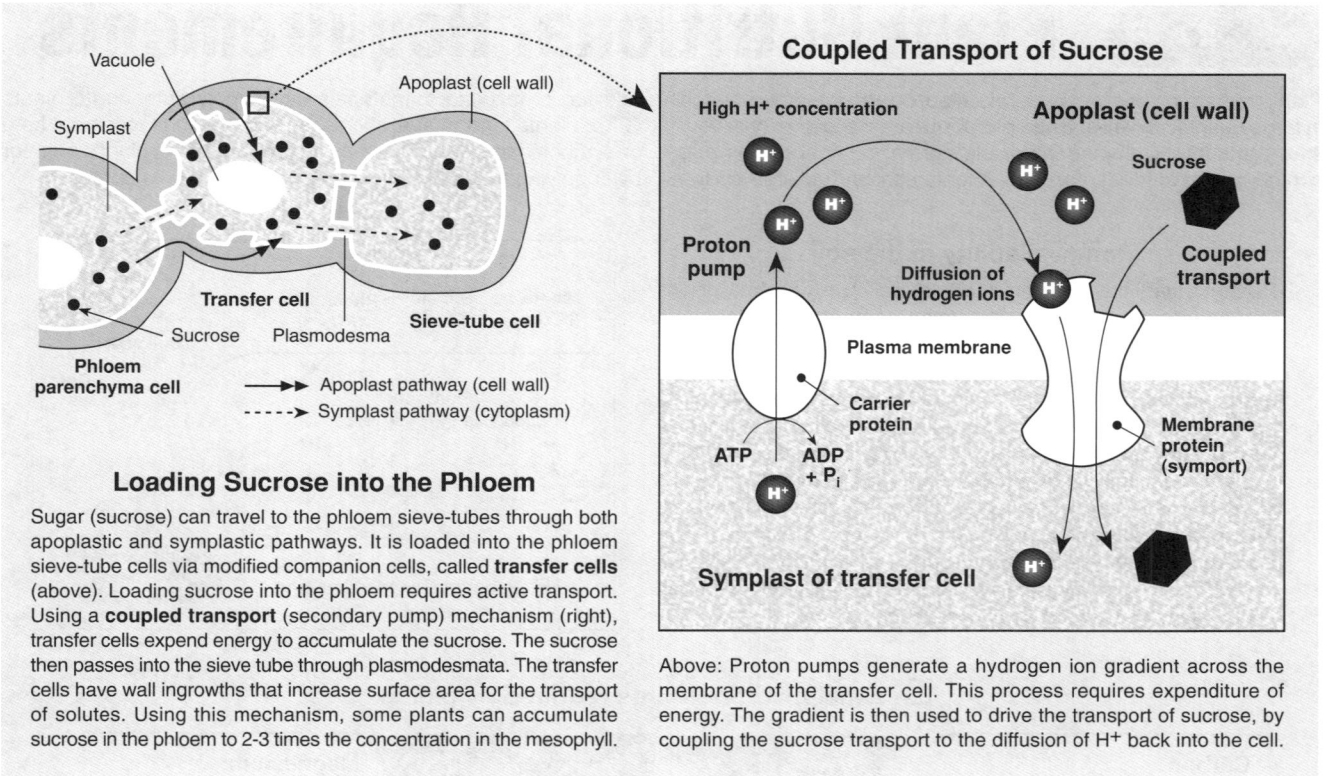

Loading Sucrose into the Phloem

Sugar (sucrose) can travel to the phloem sieve-tubes through both apoplastic and symplastic pathways. It is loaded into the phloem sieve-tube cells via modified companion cells, called **transfer cells** (above). Loading sucrose into the phloem requires active transport. Using a **coupled transport** (secondary pump) mechanism (right), transfer cells expend energy to accumulate the sucrose. The sucrose then passes into the sieve tube through plasmodesmata. The transfer cells have wall ingrowths that increase surface area for the transport of solutes. Using this mechanism, some plants can accumulate sucrose in the phloem to 2-3 times the concentration in the mesophyll.

Above: Proton pumps generate a hydrogen ion gradient across the membrane of the transfer cell. This process requires expenditure of energy. The gradient is then used to drive the transport of sucrose, by coupling the sucrose transport to the diffusion of H^+ back into the cell.

3. In your own words, describe what is meant by the following:

   (a) Translocation: _____

   _____

   (b) Pressure-flow movement of phloem: _____

   _____

   (c) Coupled transport of sucrose: _____

4. Briefly explain why water follows the sucrose as the sucrose is loaded into the phloem sieve-tube cell:

   _____

   _____

5. Explain the role of the companion (transfer) cell in the loading of sucrose into the phloem: _____

   _____

   _____

6. Contrast the composition of phloem sap and xylem sap (see the activities on xylem and phloem if you need help):

   _____

   _____

7. Explain why it is necessary for phloem to be alive to be functional, whereas xylem can function as a dead tissue:

   _____

   _____

8. The sieve plate represents a significant barrier to effective mass flow of phloem sap. Suggest why the presence of the sieve plate is often cited as evidence against the pressure-flow model for phloem transport:

   _____

   _____

   _____

Plant Nutritional Requirements

RA 2

Plants require a variety of minerals. **Macronutrients** are required in large quantities, whilst **trace elements** are needed in only very small amounts. Cropping interrupts normal nutrient cycles and contributes to nutrient losses. Nutrients can be replaced by the addition of **fertilizers**: materials that supply nutrients to plants. Other plants form mutualistic associations with mycorrhizal fungi or symbiotic bacteria. These associations aid the plant's nutrition by supplying a nutrient directly or by improving its uptake.

Ion availability in the soil

Plants normally obtain minerals from the soil. The availability of ions to plant roots depends on soil texture, since this affects the permeability of the soil to air and water. Mineral ions may be available to the plant in the soil water, adsorbed on to clay particles, or via release from humus and soil weathering. Plant **macronutrients** (e.g. nitrogen, sulfur, and phosphorus) are required in large amounts for building basic constituents like proteins. Trace elements (e.g. manganese, copper, and zinc) are required in smaller amounts. Many are necessary components of, or activators for, enzymes. After being absorbed by epidermal cells mineral ions diffuse down a concentration gradient to the endodermis. From the cytoplasm of the endodermis, the minerals may diffuse or be actively transported to the xylem for transport around the plant.

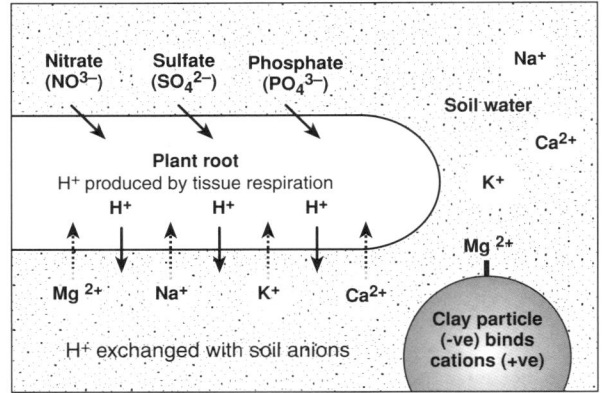

Nitrate (NO_3^-) Sulfate (SO_4^{2-}) Phosphate (PO_4^{3-}) Na^+

Soil water

Ca^{2+}

Plant root
H^+ produced by tissue respiration

K^+

H^+ H^+ H^+

Mg^{2+}

Mg^{2+} Na^+ K^+ Ca^{2+}

Clay particle (-ve) binds cations (+ve)

H^+ exchanged with soil anions

Essential macronutrients required by plants

Carbon:

Magnesium:

Nitrogen:

Potassium:

Calcium:

Sulfur:

Phosphorus:

Micronutrients: *generally serve as cofactors, electron carrier molecules and enzyme activators. Micronutrients include iron, boron, manganese, copper, zinc and molybdenum.*

1. Complete the diagram above, outlining the role the stated macronutrients play in plant development.

2. Name three sources of minerals for plants, apart from artificially applied fertilizers:

(a) _____

(b) _____

(c) _____

Photosynthesis in C₄ Plants

A 2

When photosynthesis takes place, the first detectable compound which is made by a plant is usually a 3-carbon compound called GP (glycerate 3-phosphate). Plants which do this are called C_3 plants. In some plants, however, a 4-carbon molecule called oxaloacetate, is the first to be made. Such plants, which include cereals and tropical grasses, are called C_4 plants. These plants have a high rate of photosynthesis, thriving in environments with high light levels and warm temperatures. Their yield of photosynthetic products is higher than that of C_3 plants, giving them a competitive advantage in tropical climates. The high productivity of the C_4 system is also an important property of crop plants such as sugar cane and maize.

Structure of a Leaf from a C₄ Plant

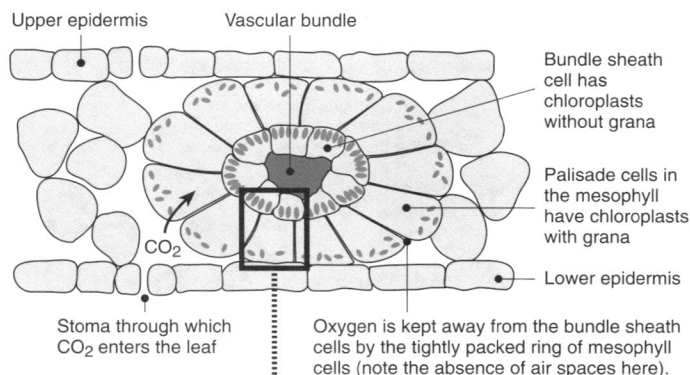

Upper epidermis
Vascular bundle
Bundle sheath cell has chloroplasts without grana
Palisade cells in the mesophyll have chloroplasts with grana
CO_2
Lower epidermis
Stoma through which CO_2 enters the leaf
Oxygen is kept away from the bundle sheath cells by the tightly packed ring of mesophyll cells (note the absence of air spaces here).

Calvin cycle
C_3 + CO_2
Pyruvate
C_4 Malate
Hatch-Slack pathway
C_3 PEP
C_4 Oxaloacetate
CO_2

A low oxygen environment is essential for the enzyme **ribulose bisphosphate carboxylase** (Rubisco) to function at maximum efficiency in the Calvin cycle.

Bundle sheath cells
Malate moves from the palisade cells to the inner bundle sheath cells where it is broken down to pyruvate, releasing free carbon dioxide. This is used as a raw material to feed into the Calvin cycle.

Palisade mesophyll cells
Photosynthesis in these cells fixes carbon dioxide in the cytoplasm and captures light energy in the chloroplasts. The enzyme **PEP carboxylase** has an extremely high affinity for CO_2 even when the latter is in low concentration. This allows the plant to fix large quantities of CO_2 rapidly.

Examples of C₄ plants
• Sugar cane *(Saccharum officinale)*
• Maize *(Zea mays)*
• Sorghum *(Sorghum bicolor)*
• Sun plant *(Portulaca grandifolia)*

Distribution of grasses using C₄ mechanism in North America

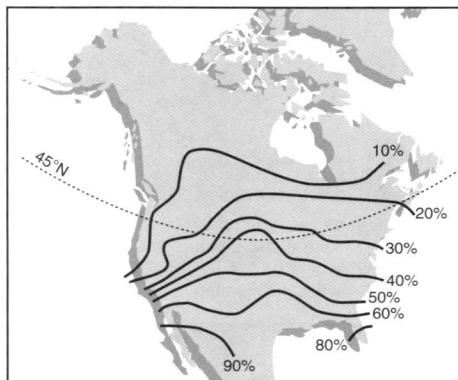

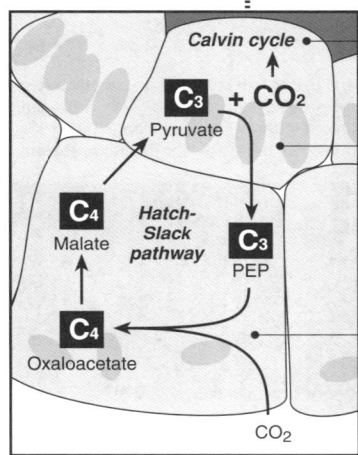

45°N
10%
20%
30%
40%
50%
60%
80%
90%

The photosynthetic strategy that a plant possesses is an important factor in determining where it lives. Because many of the enzymes of C_4 plants have optimum temperatures well above 25°C, they thrive in hot tropical and sub-tropical climates. Under these conditions, they can out-compete most C_3 plants because they achieve faster rates of photosynthesis. The proportion of grasses using the C_4 mechanism in North America is greatest near the tropics and diminishes northwards.

1. Explain why C_4 plants have a competitive advantage over C_3 plants in the tropics:

2. Explain why the bundle sheath cells are arranged in a way that keeps them isolated from air spaces in the leaf:

3. Study the map of North America above showing the distribution of C_4 plants. Explain the distribution pattern in terms of their competitive advantage and the environmental conditions required for this advantage:

4. In C_3 plants, the rate of photosynthesis is enhanced by higher atmospheric CO_2 concentrations. Explain why this is not the case for C_4 plants:

Adaptations of Xerophytes

Without sufficient water plant cells lose **turgor** and the tissue wilts. If a plant passes its **permanent wilting point** it will die. Water is lost from the plant by **transpiration**: the loss of water vapor, primarily through the stomata. Water balance is not a problem for aquatic plants; they allow water to flow in by osmosis until the cell wall stops further expansion. Plants adapted to dry conditions are called **xerophytes** and they show structural (xeromorphic) and physiological adaptations for water conservation. Some of these are outlined below. Halophytes (salt tolerant plants) and alpine species may also show xeromorphic features in response to the scarcity of obtainable water and high transpirational losses in these environments.

Tropical Forest Plant

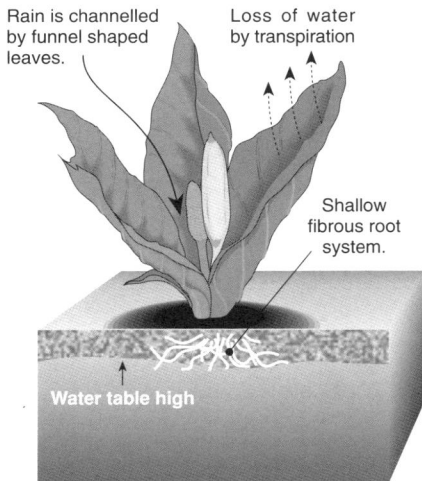

Rain is channelled by funnel shaped leaves.

Loss of water by transpiration

Shallow fibrous root system.

Water table high

Tropical plants live in areas of often high rainfall. There is also a corresponding high transpiration rate. Water availability is not a problem in this environment.

Dry Desert Plant

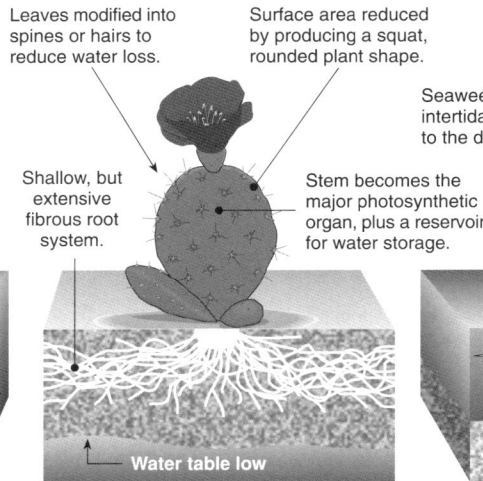

Leaves modified into spines or hairs to reduce water loss.

Surface area reduced by producing a squat, rounded plant shape.

Shallow, but extensive fibrous root system.

Stem becomes the major photosynthetic organ, plus a reservoir for water storage.

Water table low

Desert plants e.g. cacti, cope with low rainfall and high transpiration rates. Plants develop strategies to reduce water loss, store water, and access available water supplies.

Ocean Margin Plant

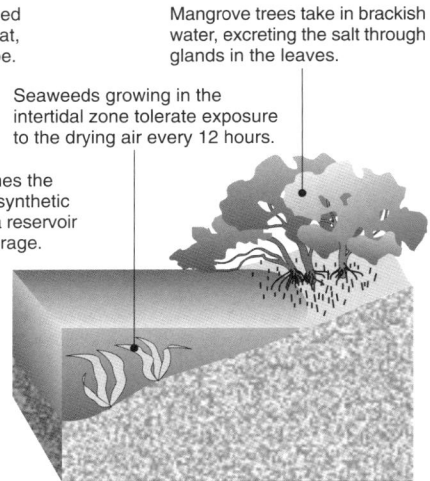

Mangrove trees take in brackish water, excreting the salt through glands in the leaves.

Seaweeds growing in the intertidal zone tolerate exposure to the drying air every 12 hours.

Land plants that colonize the shoreline (e.g. mangroves) must cope with high salt content in the water. Seaweeds below low tide do not have a water balance problem.

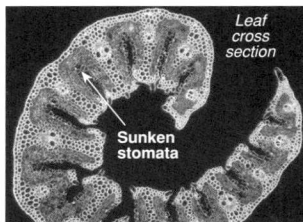

Leaf cross section

Sunken stomata

Grasses living in dry areas curl their leaves and have sunken stomata.

Mosses are poor at obtaining and storing water, restricting distribution.

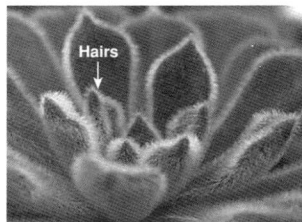

Hairs

Hairs on leaves trap air close to the surface, reducing transpiration rate.

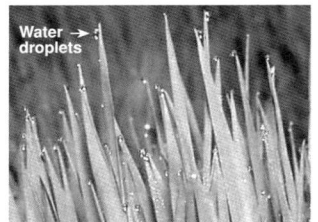

Water droplets

Excess water is forced from leaves (guttation) during high humidity.

Methods of water conservation in various plant species

Adaptation for water conservation	Effect of adaptation	Example
Thick, waxy cuticle to stems and leaves	Reduces water loss through the cuticle.	*Pinus* sp. ivy (*Hedera*), sea holly (*Eryngium*), prickly pear (*Opuntia*).
Reduced number of stomata	Reduces the number of pores through which water loss can occur.	Prickly pear (*Opuntia*), *Nerium* sp.
Stomata sunken in pits, grooves, or depressions Leaf surface covered with fine hairs Massing of leaves into a rosette at ground level	Moist air is trapped close to the area of water loss, reducing the diffusion gradient and therefore the rate of water loss.	**Sunken stomata**: *Pinus* sp., *Hakea* sp. **Hairy leaves**: lamb's ear. **Leaf rosettes**: dandelion (*Taraxacum*), daisy.
Stomata closed during the light, open at night	Carbon dioxide is fixed during the night, water loss during the day is minimized.	**CAM plants**, e.g. American aloe, pineapple, *Kalanchoe*, *Yucca*.
Leaves reduced to scales, stem photosynthetic Leaves curled, rolled, or folded when flaccid	Reduction in surface area from which transpiration can occur.	**Leaf scales**: broom (*Cytisus*). **Rolled leaf**: marram grass (*Ammophila*), *Erica* sp.
Fleshy or succulent stems Fleshy or succulent leaves	When readily available, water is stored in the tissues for times of low availability.	**Fleshy stems**: *Opuntia*, candle plant (*Kleinia*). **Fleshy leaves**: *Bryophyllum*.
Deep root system below the water table	Roots tap into the lower water table.	Acacias, oleander.
Shallow root system absorbing surface moisture	Roots absorb overnight condensation.	Most cacti

Adaptations in halophytes and drought tolerant plants

Ice plant (*Carpobrotus*): The leaves of many desert and beach dwelling plants are fleshy or succulent. The leaves are triangular in cross section and crammed with water storage cells. The water is stored after rain for use in dry periods. The shallow root system is able to take up water from the soil surface, taking advantage of any overnight condensation.

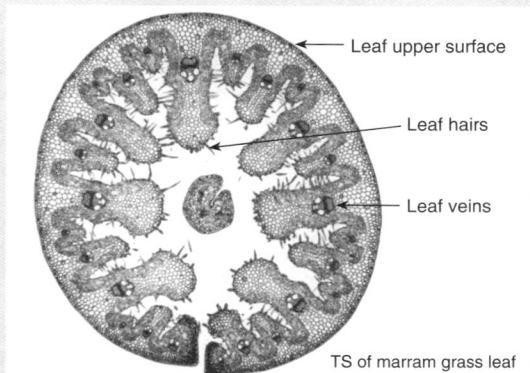

- Leaf upper surface
- Leaf hairs
- Leaf veins

TS of marram grass leaf

Marram grass (*Ammophila*): The long, wiry leaf blades of this beach grass are curled downwards with the stomata on the inside. This protects them against drying out by providing a moist microclimate around the stomata. Plants adapted to high altitude often have similar adaptations.

Ball cactus (*Delosperma saturatum*): In cacti, the leaves are modified into long, thin spines which project outward from the thick fleshy stem (see close-up above right). This reduces the surface area over which water loss can occur. The stem takes over the role of producing the food for the plant and also stores water during rainy periods for use during drought. As in succulents like ice plant, the root system in cacti is shallow to take advantage of surface water appearing as a result of overnight condensation.

1. Define the term xeromorphic: _____

   _____

2. Describe three xeromorphic adaptations of plants:

   (a) _____

   (b) _____

   (c) _____

3. Describe a physiological mechanism by which plants can reduce water loss during the daylight hours:

   _____

   _____

4. Explain why creating a moist microenvironment around the areas of water loss reduces transpiration rate:

   _____

5. Explain why seashore plants (halophytes) exhibit many desert-dwelling adaptations: _____

   _____

   _____

Adaptations of Hydrophytes

A 3

Hydrophytes are a group of plants which have adapted to living either partially or fully submerged in water. Survival in water poses different problems to those faced by terrestrial plants. Hydrophytes have a reduced root system, a feature that is often related to the relatively high concentration of nutrients in the sediment and the plant's ability to remove nitrogen and phosphorus directly from the water. The leaves of submerged plants are thin to increase the surface area of photosynthetic tissue and reduce internal shading. Hydrophytes typically have no cuticle (waterproof covering) or the cuticle is very thin. This enables the plant ability to absorb minerals and gases directly from the water. In addition, being supported by the water, they require very little in the way of structural support tissue.

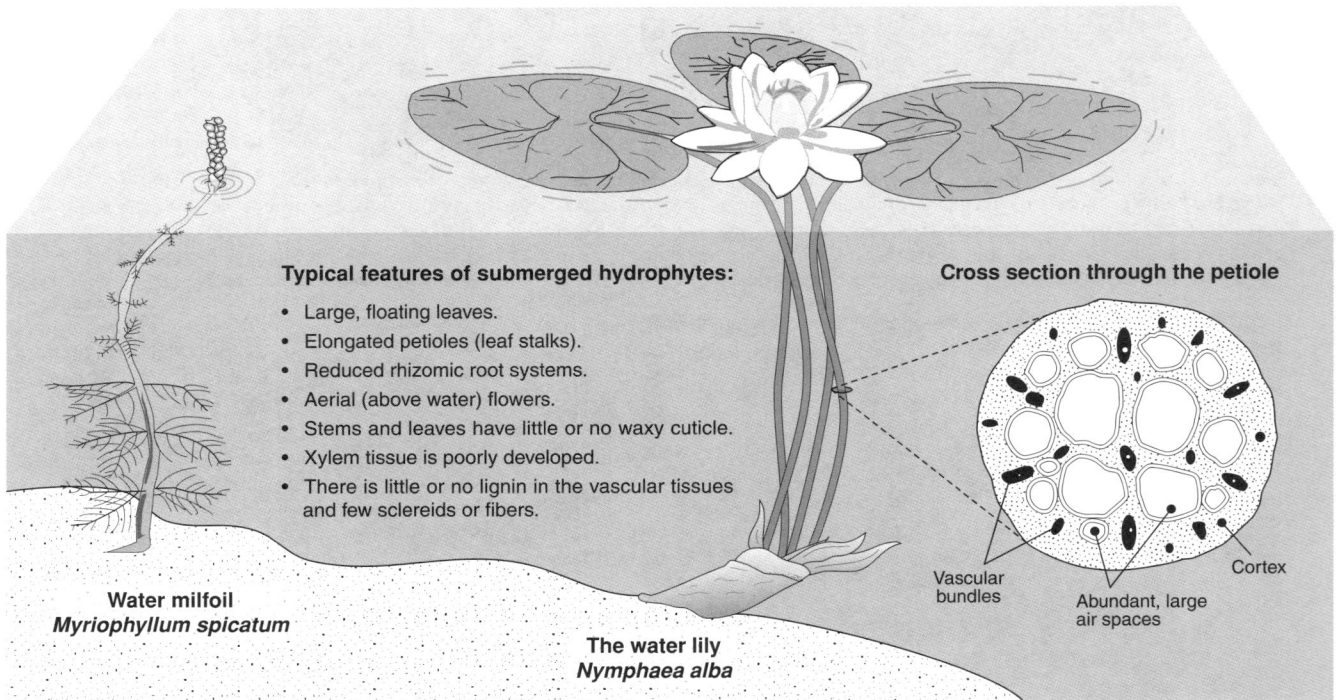

Typical features of submerged hydrophytes:

- Large, floating leaves.
- Elongated petioles (leaf stalks).
- Reduced rhizomic root systems.
- Aerial (above water) flowers.
- Stems and leaves have little or no waxy cuticle.
- Xylem tissue is poorly developed.
- There is little or no lignin in the vascular tissues and few sclereids or fibers.

Cross section through the petiole

Vascular bundles

Cortex

Abundant, large air spaces

Water milfoil
Myriophyllum spicatum

The water lily
Nymphaea alba

Myriophyllum's submerged leaves are well spaced and taper towards the surface to assist with gas exchange and distribution of sunlight.

The floating leaves of water lilies (*Nymphaea*) have a high density of stomata on the upper leaf surface so they are not blocked by water.

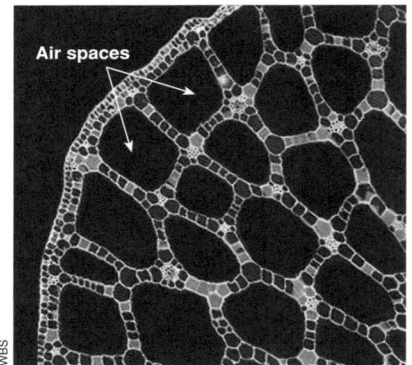

Air spaces

Cross section through *Potamogeton*, showing massive air spaces which assist with flotation and gas exchange.

1. Explain how the following adaptations assist hydrophytes to survive in an aquatic environment:

   (a) Large air spaces within the plants tissues: _____

   _____

   (b) Thin cuticle: _____

   _____

   (c) High stomatal densities on the upper leaf surface: _____

   _____

2. Explain why hydrophytic plants have retained an aerial (above water) flowering system: _____

   _____

Reproduction in Seed Plants

The primary method of reproduction for flowering plants is by seeds, which develop after fertilization of the female parts of the flower, and contain the protected plant embryo together with a store of food. The typical life cycle of a flowering plant such as the bean (below) involves the formation of gametes (egg and sperm) from the haploid gametophytes, the fertilization of the egg by a sperm cell to form the zygote, the production of fruit housing the seed, and the germination of the seed and its growth by mitosis. The eggs and sperm are housed within the female and male gametophytes (embryo sac and pollen grain respectively). The leafy plant bearing the flowers represents the sporophyte generation of the life cycle.

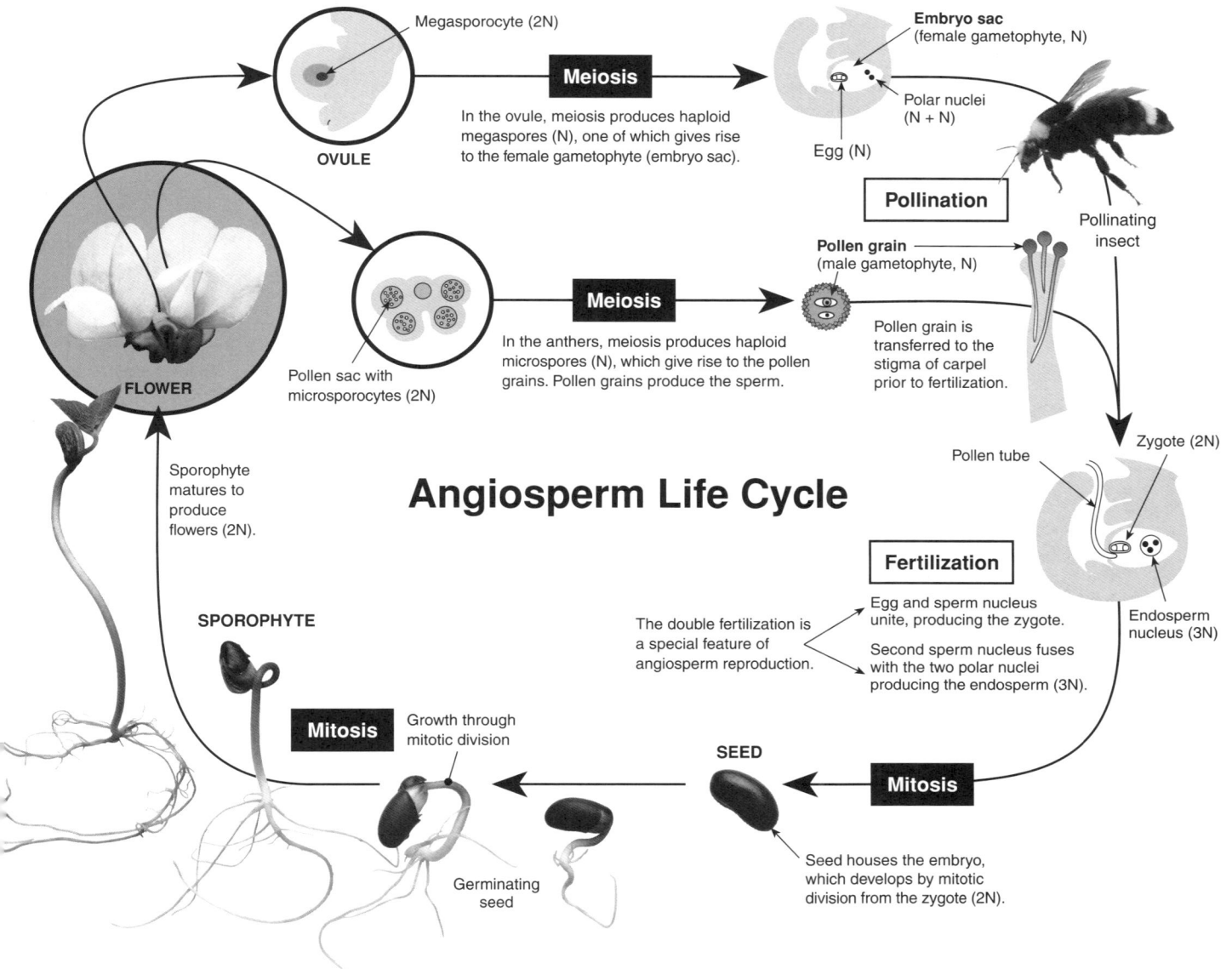

Angiosperm Life Cycle

Megasporocyte (2N)

Meiosis

In the ovule, meiosis produces haploid megaspores (N), one of which gives rise to the female gametophyte (embryo sac).

OVULE

Embryo sac (female gametophyte, N)

Polar nuclei (N + N)

Egg (N)

Pollination

Pollinating insect

Pollen grain (male gametophyte, N)

Meiosis

In the anthers, meiosis produces haploid microspores (N), which give rise to the pollen grains. Pollen grains produce the sperm.

Pollen sac with microsporocytes (2N)

FLOWER

Pollen grain is transferred to the stigma of carpel prior to fertilization.

Sporophyte matures to produce flowers (2N).

Pollen tube

Zygote (2N)

Fertilization

The double fertilization is a special feature of angiosperm reproduction.

Egg and sperm nucleus unite, producing the zygote.

Second sperm nucleus fuses with the two polar nuclei producing the endosperm (3N).

Endosperm nucleus (3N)

SPOROPHYTE

Mitosis

Growth through mitotic division

Germinating seed

SEED

Mitosis

Seed houses the embryo, which develops by mitotic division from the zygote (2N).

1. Explain the role of the fleshy fruit containing the seed: _____

    _____

2. Explain the role of the seed in the life cycle of flowering plants: _____

    _____

3. (a) State the purpose of meiosis in the plant life cycle: _____

    (b) Name the products of the meiotic divisions: _____

    (c) Briefly state the advantage of seed production over vegetative propagation: _____

    _____

    _____

4. Explain the purpose of mitosis in the plant life cycle: _____

    _____

Alternation of Generations

The life cycles of all plants include a gametophyte generation (haploid or n phase) and a sporophyte generation (diploid or 2n phase). The two generations alternate, each giving rise to the other (commonly termed **alternation of generations**). The two plant forms (sporophyte and gametophyte) are named for the type of reproductive cells they produce. Gametophytes produce gametes by mitosis, whereas sporophytes produce spores by meiosis. Spores develop directly into organisms. Gametes (egg and sperm) unite during fertilization to form a zygote which gives rise to an organism.

Algae

The sea lettuce *Ulva*, a green alga, has a life cycle alternating between two generations that seem to be the same. Although they appear identical, the cells of the sporophyte generation contain **26** chromosomes, while the gametophyte cells contain only **13** chromosomes. The sporophyte produces spores that settle on rock surfaces to grow into male and female gametophytes. These in turn mature and release gametes into the water. In fertilization, two gametes fuse and grow into a sporophyte.

Sporophyte　　　　**Gametophyte**

13　Spores

26

13

26　Two gametes fuse to form a zygote

13

Zygote　　　Gametes

Moss

Most moss species have separate male and female gametophytes. A sperm swims through a film of moisture to the female gametophyte (archegonium) and fertilizes an egg. The resulting zygote develops into an embryonic sporophyte on top of the female gametophyte. It grows a long stalk that has a spore-producing capsule (sporangium) at the tip. When the sporangium matures, it bursts, scattering the spores. Those landing on moist soil will germinate to form a new gametophyte.

Sporophyte　　　　**Gametophyte**

Spores

Sporophyte

Spore capsule

Sperm

Gametophyte

Sporophyte grows out of the top of a female gametophyte

Archegonium (female)　　Antheridium (male)

Fern

Ferns are sporophytes. Spores are formed on the back of the fronds and are released into the air to be dispersed by the wind. If a spore lands on moist soil, it will germinate into a very small **prothallus**. On this flat, heart-shaped gametophyte, male and female organs develop, but at different times. As with mosses, fern sperm use flagella to swim through moisture to the female cells to fertilize them. A new sporophyte grows out of the female organ (archegonium) and matures into a fern.

Sporophyte　　　　**Gametophyte**

Mature sporophyte

Spores

Archegonium (female organ)

Sperm

New sporophyte

Antheridium (male organ)

Gametophyte (mature prothallus)

Gymnosperm

Trees are sporophytes. Most gymnosperm species produce both pollen cones and ovulate (female) cones. Male cones produce hundreds of pollen grains (male gametophytes). A female cone contains many scales, each with two ovules. Wind blown pollen falls on the female cone and is drawn into the ovule through a tiny opening called the micropyle. The pollen grain germinates in the ovule and grows a pollen tube that seeks out the female gametophyte and fertilizes the egg cell within it.

Sporophyte　　Male (pollen) cone　　　**Gametophyte**

Pollen grain carried to female cone by wind

Female cone

Pollen grain grows a tube to reach the female gametophyte

Single scale from female cone

Mature sporophyte　　Seedling　　　Ovule

Angiosperm

Angiosperms, or flowering plants, are the most successful plants on Earth today. They reproduce sexually by forming flowers, fruits, and seeds. The sporophyte generation is clearly dominant, and the gametophyte generation is reduced in size to just a small number of cells (there are no archegonia or antheridia). Anthers develop an immature gametophyte in the form of a pollen grain. Most often, pollen is transferred between flowers by wind or animal activity; angiosperms and their animal pollinators exhibit coevolution. Some plants are self-pollinating.

1. The table below summarizes the main features of plant life cycles. Using brief explanations, complete the table (the first example has been completed for you):

Life cycle feature	Group				
	Algae	Mosses	Ferns	Gymnosperms	Angiosperms
Dominant generation	Gametophyte				
Alternate generation	Sporophyte (zygospore)				
Movement of sperm	Needs water				
Gametophyte reliance on sporophyte	None				
Sporophyte reliance on gametophyte	None				
Ecological niche with respect to reproduction	Water needed				

2. One of the principal trends evident in plant life cycles is the increasing independence on water for reproduction. Explain what feature of the male gamete (sperm or pollen) illustrates this:

_____

_____

3. State which generation increases in dominance from the algae to the angiosperms: _____

4. In the schematic diagram below, label: **the spores, the gametes, the zygote**. Beside each, indicate the chromosome state (haploid, **N**) or diploid, **2N**). Label each side of the diagram (gray and white) with haploid or diploid as appropriate:

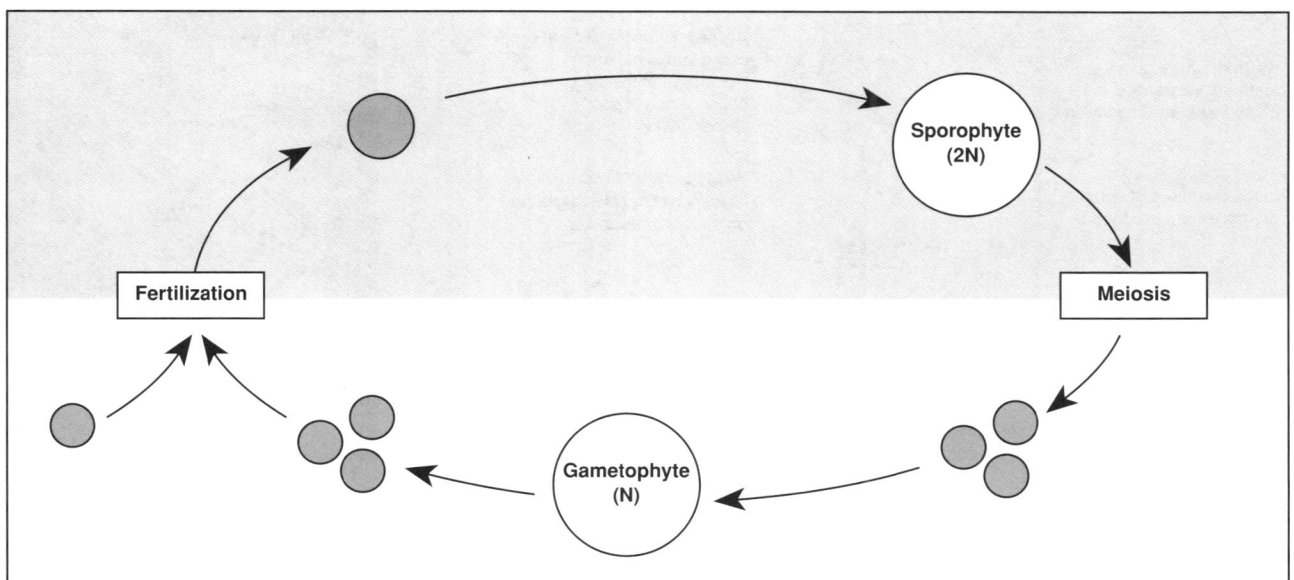

Angiosperm Reproduction

Flowering plants (**angiosperms**) are highly successful organisms. The egg cell is retained within the flower of the parent plant and the male gametes (contained in the **pollen**) must be transferred to it by **pollination** in order for fertilization to occur. Most angiosperms are **monoecious**, with male and female parts on the same plant. Some of these plants will self-pollinate, but most have mechanisms that make this difficult or impossible. The female and male parts may be physically separated in the flower, or they may mature at different times (in **protandrous** plants the

male matures first, whereas in **protogynous** plants the female matures first). **Dioecious plants** avoid this problem by carrying the male and female flowers on separate plants. Different methods of pollination (animal, wind, and water pollination) also help to ensure that **cross-pollination** occurs. Common animal pollinators include insects, bats, birds, and small reptiles. Animals are able to transfer pollen between plants very effectively and often over large distances, so much so that many plants have come to depend on only one or two animal pollinators.

Insect Pollinated Flowers

In most angiosperms the flower has both male and female parts. The flowers are temporary structures, often produced in large numbers. Those that are pollinated by insects typically offer an attraction such as nectar or edible flower parts and their pollen is relatively large and heavy. In

general, each flower consists of a stem, bearing sepals, petals, stamens, and carpels. Such flowers may be able to self pollinate although there are often mechanisms to prevent this. In **dioecious** plants, the male and female flowers occur on separate plants and cross pollination is assured.

Flower cross section

Stigma: The receptive part of the carpel. Pollen grains will germinate only if they land here.

Style: The structure that supports the stigma.

Ovary: The base of the carpel where the ovules develop.

Ovules: These are eggs and once fertilized, become the seeds. The ovule skin becomes the seed coat or testa.

An entire female part is the **carpel**. There may be one or more **carpels** per flower.

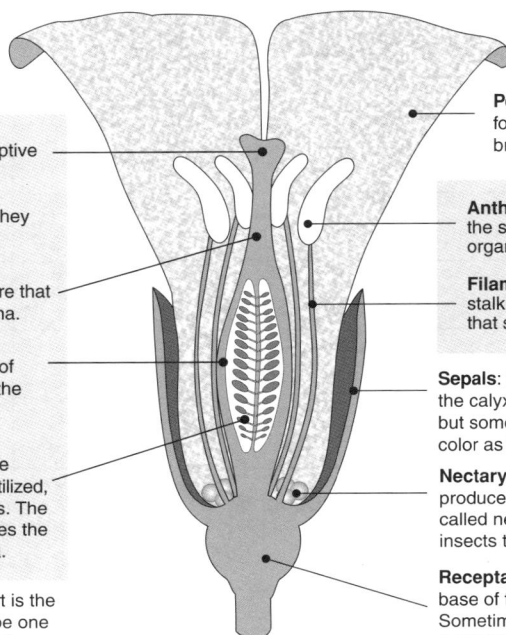

Petals: collectively form the corolla. Often brightly colored.

Anther: Top portion of the stamen – the male organ of reproduction.

Filament: The slender stalk part of the stamen that supports the anther.

Sepals: Collectively called the calyx. Usually green, but sometimes the same color as the petals.

Nectary: Plants produce a sugary liquid called nectar to attract insects to the flower.

Receptacle: The swollen base of the flower. Sometimes it forms the succulent tissue of the fruit.

Petals form 'guides' for insects that visit for nectar or pollen. In this way, wandering insects transfer pollen.

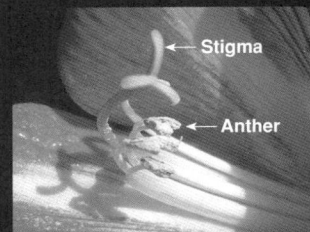

Stigma
Anther

Here, the stigma and anthers are separated to reduce self-pollination.

Pollen on bee leg

Pollen can be transported from flower to flower on the hairs of insects.

Wind Pollinated Flowers

Stigma: Large and feathery, suspended clear of the flower by long styles.

Large quantities of smooth, dry pollen are produced.

Bract: Protective leaf scale covers the flowers inside.

No scent or nectar is produced.

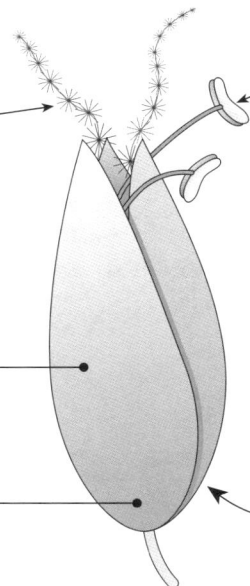

Anther: Hangs well clear of the leaf scale and produces light-weight pollen which is easily carried away.

Wind pollinated flowers typically have many tiny flowers grouped on a stalk or spikelets.

Most grasses are wind pollinated. The feathery appearance of their flowers is typical of wind pollinated plants.

1. Using the diagram opposite to help you, identify the parts of the flower labeled (a) to (g) on the cross section below.

(a)	**Flower cross section**	(d)
(b)		(e)
(c)		(f)
		(g)

RCN

2. (a) Name the male structures on a flower: _____

   (b) Name the female structures on a flower: _____

3. Define the following terms:

   (a) Protandry: _____

   _____

   (b) Protogyny: _____

   _____

   (c) Monoecious: _____

   _____

   (d) Dioecious: _____

   _____

4. Describe two adaptations of insect pollinated flowers:

   (a) _____

   (b) _____

5. Describe two adaptations of wind pollinated flowers:

   (a) _____

   (b) _____

6. Describe one advantage and one cost to the plant of insect pollination:

   (a) Advantage: _____

   (b) Cost: _____

7. Describe two ways in which plants manage to attract animal pollinators:

   (a) _____   (b) _____

8. Contrast the efficiency of wind and animals as pollinating agents, giving a reason for your answer: _____

   _____

   _____

9. Outline the main advantage of cross pollination: _____

   _____

RA❷ Pollination and Fertilization

Before the egg and sperm can fuse in fertilization, the pollen (which contains the male gametes) must be transferred from the male anthers to the female stigma in **pollination**. Most often the stigma of one plant receives pollen from other plants, often from a considerable distance away. Once pollination has occurred, the sperm nuclei can enter the ovule and fertilization can occur. In angiosperms, there is a double fertilization: one to produce the embryo and the other to produce the endosperm nucleus. The endosperm nucleus gives rise to the endosperm: the food store for the embryonic plant within the seed.

Growth of the pollen tube and double fertilization

Pollen grains are immature male gametophytes, formed by meiosis in the microspore mother cells within the pollen sac. Pollination is the actual transfer of the pollen from the stamens to the stigma. Pollen grains cannot move independently. They are usually carried by wind (**anemophily**) or animals (**entomophily**). After landing on the sticky stigma, the pollen grain is able to complete development, germinating and growing a pollen tube that extends down to the ovary. Directed by chemicals (usually calcium), the pollen tube enters the ovule through the micropyle, a small gap in the ovule. A **double fertilization** takes place. One sperm nucleus fuses with the egg to form the zygote. A second sperm nucleus fuses with the two polar nuclei within the embryo sac to produce the endosperm tissue (3N). There are usually many ovules in an ovary, therefore many pollen grains (and fertilizations) are needed before the entire ovary can develop.

Different pollens are variable in shape and pattern, and genera can be easily distinguished on the basis of their distinctive pollen. This feature is exploited in the relatively new field of forensic botany; the tracing of a crime through botanical evidence. The species specific nature of pollen ensures that only genetically compatible plants will be fertilized. Some species, such as *Primula*, produce two pollen types, and this assists in cross pollination between different flower types.

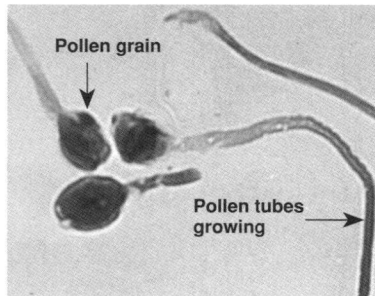
Germinating pollen grains

- Pollen grain
- Pollen tubes growing

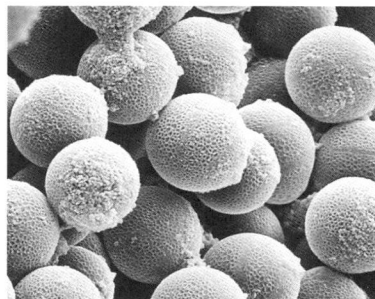
SEM: Primula (primrose) pollen

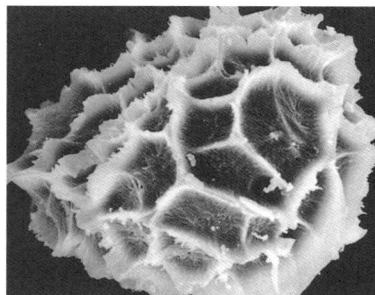
SEM: Dandelion pollen

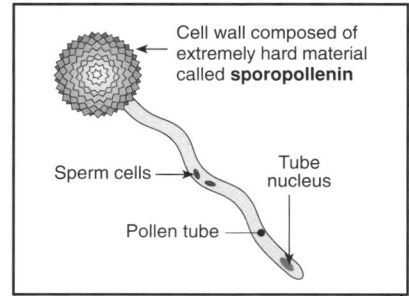

- Cell wall composed of extremely hard material called **sporopollenin**
- Sperm cells
- Tube nucleus
- Pollen tube

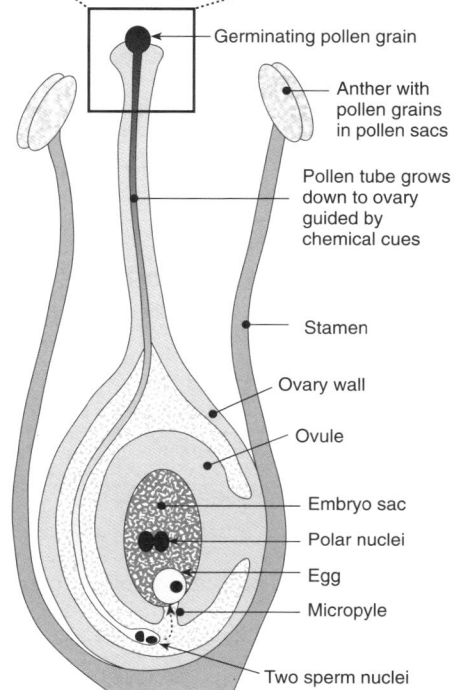

- Germinating pollen grain
- Anther with pollen grains in pollen sacs
- Pollen tube grows down to ovary guided by chemical cues
- Stamen
- Ovary wall
- Ovule
- Embryo sac
- Polar nuclei
- Egg
- Micropyle
- Two sperm nuclei

1. Define the term **pollination**: _____

   _____

2. (a) With respect to plants, define the term **fertilization**: _____

   _____

   (b) Describe the role of the double fertilization in angiosperm reproduction: _____

   _____

3. Name the main chemical responsible for pollen tube growth: _____

4. Suggest a reason for the great variability seen in the structure of pollen grains: _____

   _____

   _____

5. Pollen can be used as an indicator of past climates and vegetation. Give two reasons why pollen is well suited to this use:

   (a) _____

   (b) _____

Fruits

R ②

A **fruit** is a mature, ripened ovary, although other plant parts, in addition to the ovary, may contribute to the fleshy parts of what we call the fruit. As a seed develops, the ovary wall around it enlarges and changes to become the fruit wall or **pericarp**. The pericarp has three regions: the outer exocarp, central mesocarp, and inner endocarp. Fruits may open to release the seeds or they may retain the seeds and be dispersed whole. They are classified according to the number of ovaries involved in their formation and the nature of the fruit wall (dry or fleshy). Succulent fruits are usually dispersed by animals and dry fruits by wind, water, or mechanical means. Fruits occur only in angiosperms. Their development has been a central feature of angiosperm evolution.

Type of fruit	Description	Type of fruit	Description
Berry	A fleshy fruit with soft tissues throughout. The single seed or seeds are scattered through flesh.	Aggregate fruit	Formed from a single flower that has many carpels (ovaries) fused to form a single fruit.
Drupe	The fruit wall is fleshy but the endocarp surrounding the single seed forms a hard stone.	Multiple fruit	Formed from the ovaries of many flowers, fused together at maturity (e.g., fig, pineapple).
Legume	A simple fruit. Fruit wall is dry when mature and splits open along two seams to release the seeds.	False fruit	The fleshy part is formed from tissues other than the ovary, often the flower base.
Grain	A simple dry, one seeded fruit. The fruit wall and seed coat are joined and can not be separated.	Nut	A simple, one-seeded dry fruit with a hard fruit wall (the nut shell). The nut is the seed.

Seeds
Flesh is swollen flower stalk
Ovary wall
False fruit (pseudocarp), e.g., apple

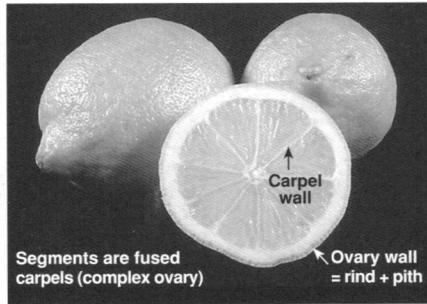
Carpel wall
Segments are fused carpels (complex ovary)
Ovary wall = rind + pith
Specialized berry, e.g., citrus fruits

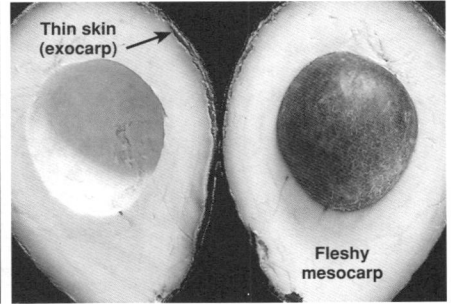
Thin skin (exocarp)
Fleshy mesocarp
Drupe, e.g., avocado

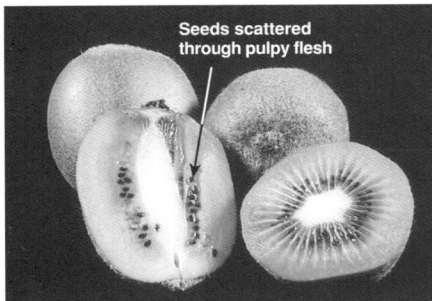
Seeds scattered through pulpy flesh
Berry, e.g., kiwifruit

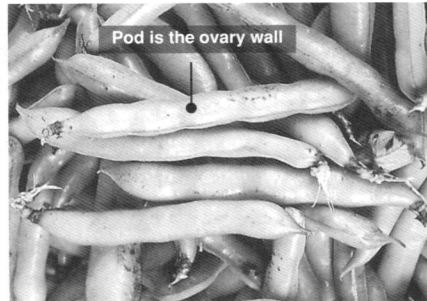
Pod is the ovary wall
Legume or pod, e.g., bean

Hard endoocarp (stone) enclosing the single seed
Drupe: fleshy with a single seed, e.g., peach

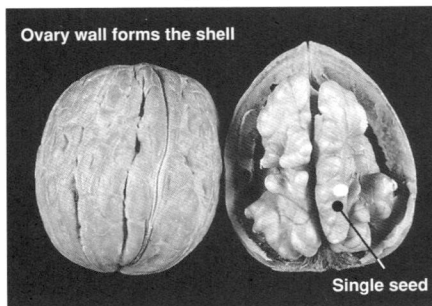
Ovary wall forms the shell
Single seed
Nut: a dry, hardshelled fruit, e.g., walnut

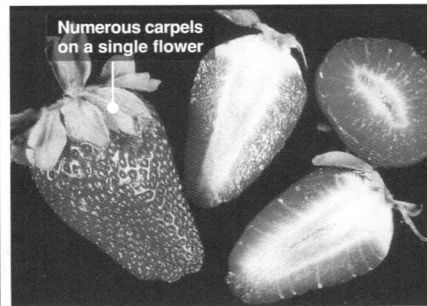
Numerous carpels on a single flower
Aggregate fruit, e.g., strawberry

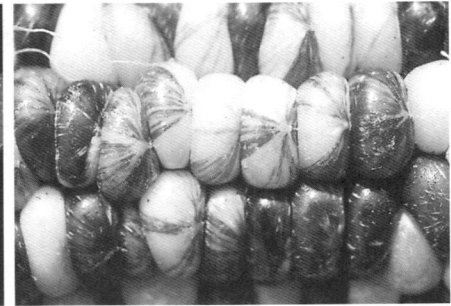
Grain: a dry, single seeded fruit, e.g., corn

1. Describe the two main purposes of fruits in the life cycle of flowering plants:

   (a) _____

   (b) _____

2. Using the table and the examples above to help you, classify the following fruits:

   (a) Plum: _____   (b) Pea: _____

   (c) Raspberry: _____   (d) Watermelon: _____

Seed Structure and Germination

After fertilization has occurred, the ovary develops into the fruit and the ovules within the ovary become the **seeds**. Recall that in plants there is double fertilization. One sperm fertilizes the egg to form the embryo, but another sperm combines with the diploid endosperm nucleus to form a large triploid cell which gives rise to the endosperm. The development of the endosperm is important and begins before embryonic development in order to produce a nutrient store for the young plant. A seed is an entire reproductive unit, housing the embryonic plant in a state of dormancy. During the last stages of maturing, the seed dehydrates until its water content is only 5-15% of its weight. The embryo stops growing and remains **dormant** until the seed germinates. At germination, the food store is mobilized to provide the nutrients for plant growth and development.

Dicot seeds: soy (above) cashew (below)
There are two fleshy cotyledons. These store food that was absorbed from the endosperm.

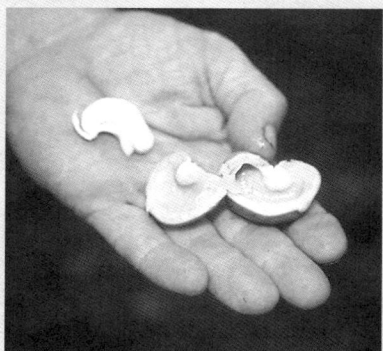

Germination requires rehydration of the seed and reactivation of the metabolism. The seed absorbs water through the seed coat (testa) and micropyle. As the dry substances in the seed tissue take up water, the cells expand, metabolism is reactivated, and embryonic growth begins. Activation begins with the release of gibberellin (GA) from the embryo. GA enhances cell elongation, making it possible for the root to penetrate the testa. It also stimulates the synthesis of enzymes, which hydrolyze the starch to produce sugars. The mobilized food stores are then delivered to the developing roots and shoots.

Seed Structure and Formation

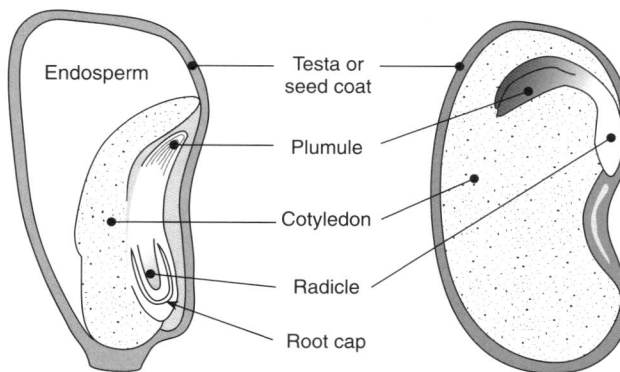

Monocot seed
(maize: *Zea mays*)

Dicot seed
(garden bean: *Phaseolus vulgaris*)

Every seed contains an embryo comprising a rudimentary shoot (plumule), root (radicle), and one or two cotyledons (seed leaves). The embryo and its food supply are encased in a tough, protective seed coat or **testa**. In monocots, the endosperm provides the food supply, whereas in most dicot seeds, the nutrients from the endosperm are transferred to the large, fleshy cotyledons.

Germination in a dicot seed
(garden bean: *Phaseolus vulgaris*)

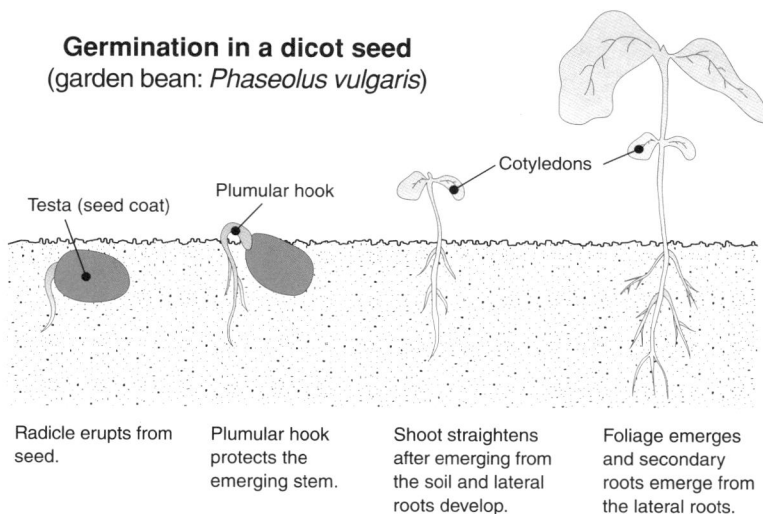

Radicle erupts from seed.

Plumular hook protects the emerging stem.

Shoot straightens after emerging from the soil and lateral roots develop.

Foliage emerges and secondary roots emerge from the lateral roots.

1. Give a brief definition of a **seed**: _____

_____

2. (a) State the purpose of the endosperm in angiosperms: _____

   (b) State how the endosperm is derived: _____

3. Explain the purpose of the testa in seeds: _____

4. Explain why the seed requires a food store: _____

_____

5. Explain why stored seeds must be kept dry: _____

Applied Plant and Animal Science

IB SL	IB HL	IB Options	AP Biology
Not applicable to core	Not applicable to core	Complete nos: *Option F: SL/HL: 1-10(a)-(c), 11-17, 19-27, 31-35 HL: 28-30*	Complete nos: *23-28*

Learning Objectives

☐ 1. Compile your own glossary from the **KEY WORDS** displayed in **bold type** in the learning objectives below.

Applied plant science

The role of plants *(page 361)*

☐ 2. Outline the importance of plants to people, with specific reference to each of the following: *food, fuel, clothing, building materials,* and *aesthetic values*. Provide examples to illustrate each of these uses.

Plant productivity *(pages 362-363)*

☐ 3. *Background*: Recognize measures of rates of production: **gross primary productivity** and **net primary productivity**. Relate net primary productivity to the **yield** (generally synonymous with **harvest**).

☐ 4. Explain how **plant (primary) productivity** can be measured in terms of **relative growth rate**, **harvestable dry biomass**, and **net assimilation rate**.

☐ 5. Outline how each of the following factors affect plant productivity: *light, water availability, carbon dioxide concentration, temperature, availability of nutrients, diseases, predators, plant genotype*.

☐ 6. Appreciate that humans can control the abiotic environment for plant growth and identify some of the general ways in which this can be done.

☐ 7. Explain how plant productivity can be optimized in controlled environments such as **greenhouses** (glasshouses). Include specific reference to the regulation of the abiotic factors that limit plant growth. Evaluate the economic factors associated with the enhancement of growth in controlled environments.

☐ 8. Explain the principles of crop production using **hydroponics**, and identify benefits of this technique.

Cereal crop plants *(pages 368-369)*

☐ 9. Identify some of the most important cereal crops (in a global sense) and appreciate their importance in the human diet. Identify the regions where these crops are grown and their relative importance in those regions.

☐ 10. Describe the **cultivation** of a plant of economic importance using one of the following examples: (a) **Wheat** (b) **Rice** (c) **Maize** (d) **Sorghum**. With respect to your chosen example, describe features that make it well suited to its region and method of cultivation.

Agricultural systems *(pages 364-365, 370-373)*

☐ 11. Appreciate the implications of **intensive farming** with respect to its environmental impact and its contribution to world food production. Recall the relationship between **diversity** and **ecosystem stability** and state how intensive agricultural systems differ from natural systems with respect to these features.

☐ 12. Recognize the effects of **harvesting** on the soil and explain the role of **fertilizers** in soil management. Providing examples, distinguish between **organic** and **inorganic fertilizers** and discuss the advantages and disadvantages of each. Consider: *availability of nutrient to plants, cost of production,* and *environmental impact*.

☐ 13. Appreciate the need for sustainable management of the soil resource. Discuss methods by which this could be achieved and comment on the feasibility of these.

☐ 14. Explain how **intensive monoculture** can lead to:
  • **Nutrient depletion** of soils and susceptibility to **pest invasion**, and the subsequent need for pesticides and fertilizers in these systems.
  • **Increased crop production** in terms of efficient use of available land, timing of interventions (e.g. for pest control), and harvest.

☐ 15. Discuss the biological and ethical issues surrounding **organic farming** and **non-organic farming** methods. Consider the following:
  • *Use of organic vs inorganic fertilizers (see #13)*
  • *Crop and land management practices*
  • *Use of pesticides, growth regulators, feed additives*
  • *Energy inputs required to maintain yield*
  • *Amount of land used*
  • *Pollution through fertilizer and pesticide run off*
  • *Soil degradation and loss*
  • *Long term sustainability of the farming practices*

Pesticides and pest control *(pages 371, 374-376)*

☐ 16. Appreciate the crop losses attributed to **pests** in terms of quantifiable harvest. Appreciate the means by which pests and **weeds** reduce crop yields:
  • *Weeds: Compete with crops for water and nutrients.*
  • *Insect pests: Damage and consume plant tissues, reduce photosynthesis, act as vectors for disease.*

☐ 17. Distinguish clearly between **biological** and **chemical pest control**. Discuss the biological and ethical issues surrounding these two methods of pest control. Consider the following: *efficacy of the control, the environmental risks, economic costs, long term sustainability, availability of alternatives*. With respect to the environmental effects of chemical pest controls, understand the terms: **persistence**, **toxicity**, **bioaccumulation** (biomagnification), and **specificity**.

☐ 18. Define the term **integrated pest management** (IPM). Discuss the biological and ethical issues involved in the use of IPM. Evaluate this type of pest control against alternative controls available.

Applied animal science *(page 392)*
NOTE: material for this area is still under development

☐ 19. Appreciate that animals have been domesticated for centuries to produce breeds suited to different uses. Using appropriate examples, describe the uses to which humans put animals.

□ 20. Describe the **rearing** of an animal of economic importance, using cattle, sheep, or chickens as an example. Examine the biological and ethical issues associated with its rearing for commercial purposes.

□ 21. With reference to #20 if appropriate, discuss intensive rearing techniques in terms of **yield** and ethical (including welfare) issues. Include reference to the use and misuse of antibiotics and growth hormones.

□ 22. Explain how veterinary techniques can be employed to improve the health and fecundity of (farmed) animals. Include reference to the use of **artificial insemination**, vaccination, and nutrient supplementation of the diet.

Plant growth regulators (pages 377-383)

□ 23. With reference to their role, distinguish between **plant growth regulators** (plant hormones) and fertilizers.

□ 24. Define the term **tropism**. Identify different types of plant tropism and the stimulus involved in each case. Distinguish between negative and positive tropisms.

□ 25. Explain the role of auxin in phototropism as an example of the control of plant growth by plant growth regulators. Evaluate the experimental evidence for the role of auxin in the regulation of plant growth.

□ 26. Describe the role of auxins in **apical dominance**, explaining how pruning promotes bushiness in plants.

□ 27. Explain the various commercial applications of plant growth regulators. Consider: *promotion of rooting (rooting powders), use as selective herbicides, use to induce fruit ripening, and production of seedless fruits.*

□ 28. Explain how flowering is controlled in **long-day** and **short-day plants**, explaining the role of **phytochrome** in this. Explain how daylength can be manipulated in the production of flowers.

Plant propagation (pages 384-387)

□ 29. Appreciate that plants can reproduce asexually by forming **tubers**, **runners**, and **bulbs**, and that plants can be propagated asexually by taking **cuttings**, **grafting**, and **layering**.

□ 30. Discuss the use of asexual reproduction in the artificial propagation of plants, emphasizing the benefits gained by rapid propagation of valuable clones, and the drawbacks (and benefits) of genetic uniformity.

□ 31. Explain the techniques used in cloning plants by **micropropagation** (tissue culture), including reference to: *growth media, aseptic technique,* and *use of plant growth regulators* (auxins, cytokinins, and gibberellins). Appreciate the applications of micropropagation in modern horticulture.

Plant and animal breeding (pages 388-391)

□ 32. Define the terms: **inbreeding**, **outbreeding**, **interspecific hybridization**, **polyploidy**, and **F_1 hybrid vigor**, providing examples to illustrate each. In your definitions, demonstrate an understanding of how these terms relate to livestock and crop breeding.

□ 33. Discuss why there is a need to maintain the biodiversity (species and genetic) of wild plant and animal stocks. Identify how this could be feasibly achieved.

□ 34. Explain, using wheat (or maize) as an example, how plant breeding programs have led to an improvement in **crop yield**. Suggest how this increase in yield has been achieved (e.g. though faster growth).

□ 35. Outline how animal breeding programs have led to an improvement in one of the following: *milk yield in cattle, meat yield in sheep, egg yield in poultry.*

Textbooks

See the 'Textbook Reference Grid' on pages 8-9 for textbook page references relating to material in this topic.

Periodicals

See page 6 for details of publishers of periodicals:

Animal breeding and rearing issues

■ **Biotechnology in the Dairy** Biol. Sci. Rev., 11(1) Sept. 1998, pp. 24-28. *The ethics of using bST to promote milk production in cattle.*
■ **Animal Diets** Biol. Sci. Rev., 12 (2) Nov. 1999, pp. 16-18. *Providing adequate nutrition to livestock: what do they need and how is it best delivered?*

Plant hormones and propagation

■ **Rainbow Growing** New Scientist, 24 October 1998, pp. 34-37. *Plant growth can be manipulated using exploitation of phytochrome's action.*
■ **Sending Plants around the Bend** Biol. Sci. Rev., 12(4) March 2000, pp. 14-17. *This excellent account details how plants perceive and respond to stimuli around them. Tropisms are fully covered.*
■ **Fast Tissue Culture** Biol. Sci. Rev., 10(3) January 1998, pp. 2-6. *The techniques and applications of simple tissue culture in plants.*
■ **Plant Breeding** Biol. Sci. Rev., 7(3) January 1995, pp. 32-34. *The principles of plant breeding and the role of selective breeding in crop evolution.*

Agriculture and pest control

■ **Food / How Altered?** National Geographic, May 2002, pp. 32-50. *An account of biotech foods; what are they, how altered are they, and how safe?*

■ **Beyond Organics** New Scientist, 18 May 2002, *Part of 4 issue series, this article examines the organic vs intensive farming debate (excellent).*
■ **Farming Revolution: Sustainable Agriculture** National Geographic, 188(6), Dec. 1995, pp. 60-89. *An excellent account of organic farming practices, with the emphasis being on US systems.*
■ **The Adaptations of Cereals** Biol. Sci. Rev., 12(3) Jan. 2001 pp. 30-33. *The adaptations of selected crop plants and their role.*
■ **Pastures New** New Scientist, 17 January 1998, pp. 30-33 *The impact of agriculture: grain production and issues relating to soil degradation.*
■ **Time to Rethink Everything** New Scientist, 27 April-18 May 2002 (4 issues). *Globalization, the impact of humans, & the sustainability of our future.*
■ **Follow that Food** New Scientist, 27 May 2000, pp. 28-31. *Studies of plant growth activity has led to a rethink of standard agricultural practices.*
■ **Roots of History** New Scientist, 13 Nov. 1999, (Inside Science). *A very good introduction to the role and importance of crops to human diets and culture. Includes: cereals, oils, teas, coffee, & fiber.*
■ **When Good Bugs Turn Bad** New Scientist, 15 January 2000, pp. 30-33. *The risks associated with biological control agents. Examples are provided.*
■ **Microbial Proteins Working for Man** Biol. Sci. Rev., 11(4) March 1999, pp. 6-7. *Microbial applications including the use of bacteria and fungi as biological control agents against insects.*

TEACHER'S REFERENCE

■ **Experiments with Corn to Demonstrate Plant Growth and Development** The American Biology Teacher, 62(4), April, 2000, pp. 297-302. *Practical investigation of growth and tropisms in corn.*
■ **Multiple Shoot Tip Cultures in Peas** The American Biology Teacher, 59(4), April, 1997, pp. 236-240. *An investigation of plant tissue culture.*
■ **Plant Tissue Culture in a Bag** The American Biology Teacher, 62(9), Nov. 2000, pp. 652-653. *Introductory investigation of plant tissue culture.*

■ **Potato Types: Their Characteristics and Uses** The American Biology Teacher, 59(1), January, 1997, pp. 26-29. *A discussion of the features of this valuable food crop (includes biodiversity issues).*

Internet

See pages 10-11 for details of how to access **Bio Links** from our web site: **www.thebiozone.com**. From Bio Links, access sites under the topics:
GENERAL BIOLOGY ONLINE RESOURCES: > **Online Textbooks and Lecture Notes**.
BIOTECHNOLOGY > **Applications of Biotechnology** > **Cloning and Tissue Culture**: • Tissue culture in the classroom > **Food Technology and GM Foods**: • ENN: genetically modified foods • Food for our future : *and others*
PLANT BIOLOGY: • Kimball's plant biology lecture notes • Plant hormones, nutrition, and transport > **Hormones & Responses**: • Plant hormones and growth regulators • Plant hormones and directional growth ... *and others*
RESOURCE MANAGEMENT & AGRICULTURE > **Resource Management - General** • World Resources Institute ... *and others* > **Agriculture**: • Sustainable agriculture educational page • What is sustainable agriculture? ... *and others* > **Crop Production**: • CO₂ enrichment methods • Crop and grasslands service (see rice, sorghum, maize) • Texas greenhouse management handbook > **Livestock Management and Improvement**: • Breeds of livestock: Oklahoma State University • Genetics Australia ... *and others* > **Biological and Pest Control**: • Biological Control • IPM • Defenders: Natural biological control ... *and others*

Software and video resources are now provided in the Teacher Resource Handbook

RA 1 The Importance of Plants

Via the process of photosynthesis, plants provide oxygen and are also the ultimate source of food and metabolic energy for nearly all animals. Besides foods (e.g. grains, fruits, and vegetables), plants also provide people with shelter, clothing, medicines, fuels, and the raw materials from which innumerable other products are made.

Plant tissues provide the energy for almost all heterotrophic life. Many plants produce delicious fruits in order to spread their seeds.

Plant tissues can be utilized to provide shelter in the form of framing, cladding, and roofing.

Many plants provide fibers for a range of materials including cotton (above), linen (from flax), and coir (from coconut husks).

Plant extracts, including rubber from rubber trees (above), can be utilized in many ways as an important manufacturing material.

Coal, petroleum, and natural gas are fossil fuels which were formed from the dead remains of plants and other organisms. Together with wood, they provide important sources of fuel.

Plants produce many beneficial and not so beneficial substances. Over 25% of all modern medicines are derived from plant extracts.

1. Using examples, describe how plant species are used by people for each of the following:

   (a) Food: _____

   _____

   (b) Fuel: _____

   _____

   (c) Clothing: _____

   _____

   (d) Building materials: _____

   _____

   (e) Aesthetic value: _____

   _____

   (f) Drugs: _____

   _____

   (g) Medicine: _____

   _____

2. Outline three reasons why the destruction of native forests is of concern:

   (a)_____

   (b)_____

   (c)_____

Plant Productivity

DA 2

The energy entering ecosystems is fixed by producers in photosynthesis. The rate of photosynthesis is dependent on factors such as temperature and the amount of light, water, and nutrients. The total energy fixed by a plant though photosynthesis is referred to as the **gross primary production** (GPP) and is usually expressed as Jm^{-2} (or kJm^{-2}), or as gm^{-2}. However, a portion of this energy is required by the plant for respiration. Subtracting respiration from GPP gives the **net primary production** (NPP). The **rate** of biomass production, or net primary productivity, is the biomass produced per area per unit time.

Measuring Productivity

Primary productivity of an ecosystem depends on a number of interrelated factors (light intensity, nutrients, temperature, water, and mineral supplies), making its calculation extremely difficult. Globally, the least productive ecosystems are those that are limited by heat energy and water. The most productive ecosystems are systems with high temperatures, plenty of water, and non-limiting supplies of soil nitrogen. The primary productivity of oceans is lower than that of terrestrial ecosystems because the water reflects (or absorbs) much of the light energy before it reaches and is utilized by producers. The table below compares the difference in the net primary productivity of various ecosystems.

Ecosystem Type	Net Primary Productivity	
	kcal m^{-2} y^{-1}	kJ m^{-2} y^{-1}
Tropical rainforest	15 000	63 000
Swamps and marshes	12 000	50 400
Estuaries	9000	37 800
Savanna	3000	12 600
Temperate forest	6000	25 200
Boreal forest	3500	14 700
Temperate grassland	2000	8400
Tundra/cold desert	500	2100
Coastal marine	2500	10 500
Open ocean	800	3360
Desert	< 200	< 840

* Data compiled from a variety of sources.

Leaf Area Index (LAI)

Leaf area index is a measure of the total leaf area of a given plant.

Harvestable Dry Biomass

Used for commercial purposes, it is the dry mass of crop available for sale or use.

Relative Growth Rate (R)

Relative growth rate is the gain in mass of plant tissue per unit time.

$$R = \frac{\text{Increase in dry mass in unit time}}{\text{Original dry mass of the plant}}$$

Net Assimilation Rate (NAR)

NAR is the increase in plant weight per unit of leaf area per unit time. Essentially it is the balance between carbon gain from photosynthesis and carbon loss from respiration.

$$NAR = \frac{\text{Increase in dry mass in unit time}}{\text{Leaf area}}$$

Net Primary Productivity of Selected Ecosystems (figures are in kJ m^{-2} y^{-1})

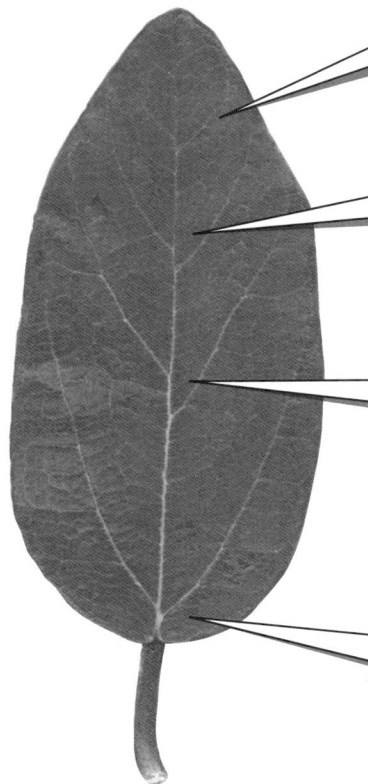

< 2500 — Arid desert

< 12 500 – 42 000 — Temperate forest

< 42 000 – 105 000 — Tropical rain forest

2500 – 42 000 — Continental shelf waters

Polar tundra and ice desert

Grassland agriculture

Intensive horticulture

Open ocean

1. Briefly describe three factors that may affect the primary productivity of an ecosystem:

   (a) _____

   (b) _____

   (c) _____

2. Explain the difference between **productivity** and **production** in relation to plants: _____

_____

3. Suggest how the LAI might influence the rate of primary production:

_____

_____

4. Using the data table opposite, choose a suitable graph format and plot the differences in the net primary productivity of various ecosystems (use either of the data columns provided, but not both). Use the graph grid provided, right.

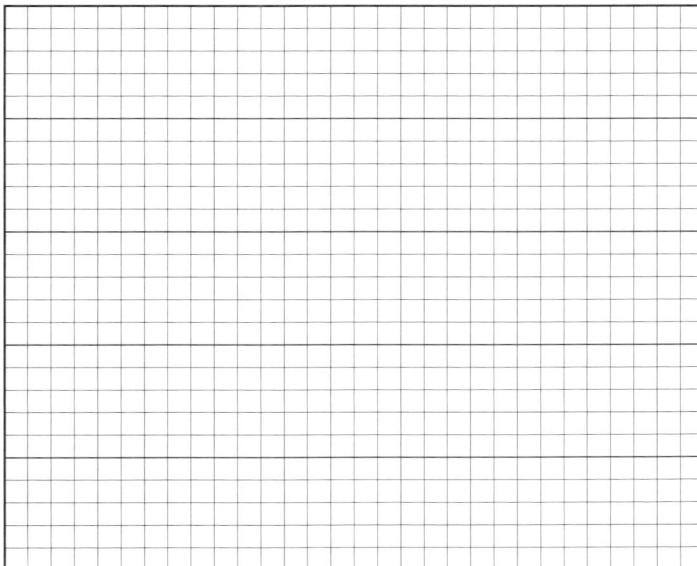

5. With reference to the graph:

(a) Suggest why tropical rainforests are among the most productive terrestrial ecosystems, while tundra and desert ecosystems are among the least productive:

_____

_____

_____

_____

_____

_____

(b) Suggest why, amongst aquatic ecosystems, the NPP of the open ocean is low relative to that of coastal systems:

_____

_____

_____

6. Estimating the NPP is relatively simple: all the plant material (including root material) from a measured area (e.g. 1 m^2) is collected and dried (at 105°C) until it reaches a constant mass. This mass, called the **standing crop**, is recorded (in kg m^{-2}). The procedure is repeated after some set time period (e.g. 1 month). The difference between the two calculated masses represents the *estimated* NPP:

(a) Explain why the plant material was dried before weighing: _____

_____

(b) Define the term: standing crop: _____

(c) Suggest why this procedure only provides an estimate of NPP: _____

_____

(d) State what extra information would be required in order to express the standing crop value in kJ m^{-2}:

_____

(e) Suggest what information would be required in order to calculate the GPP:

_____

7. Intensive horticultural systems achieve very high rates of production (about 10X those of subsistence systems).

(a) Outline the means by which these high rates are achieved: _____

_____

(b) Comment on the sustainability of these high rates (summary of a group discussion if you wish):

_____

_____

_____

Fertilizers and Plant Nutrition

A variety of minerals are required by plants. **Macronutrients** are required in large quantities, whilst **trace elements** are needed in only very small amounts. Harvesting interrupts the normal recycling of nutrients and contributes to nutrient losses. These nutrients can be replaced by the addition of fertilizers: materials that supply nutrients to plants. Some plants form symbiotic associations that aid in their nutrition. Legumes in particular (e.g. peas, beans, clover), are well known for their association with nitrogen-fixing bacteria that share their rich source of fixed nitrogen with their host plants. Legumes have been extensively used to maintain pasture productivity for grazing livestock, as well as in crop rotation to rejuvenate nitrogen-depleted soils. Historically, crop rotation was an important method to manage soil exhaustion on farms (see facing page). Such systems have become relatively obsolete as demand for production during the 1980s and early 1990s increased. The availability of low cost artificial fertilizers and pesticides (agrichemicals) have made continuous single-crop farms economically viable.

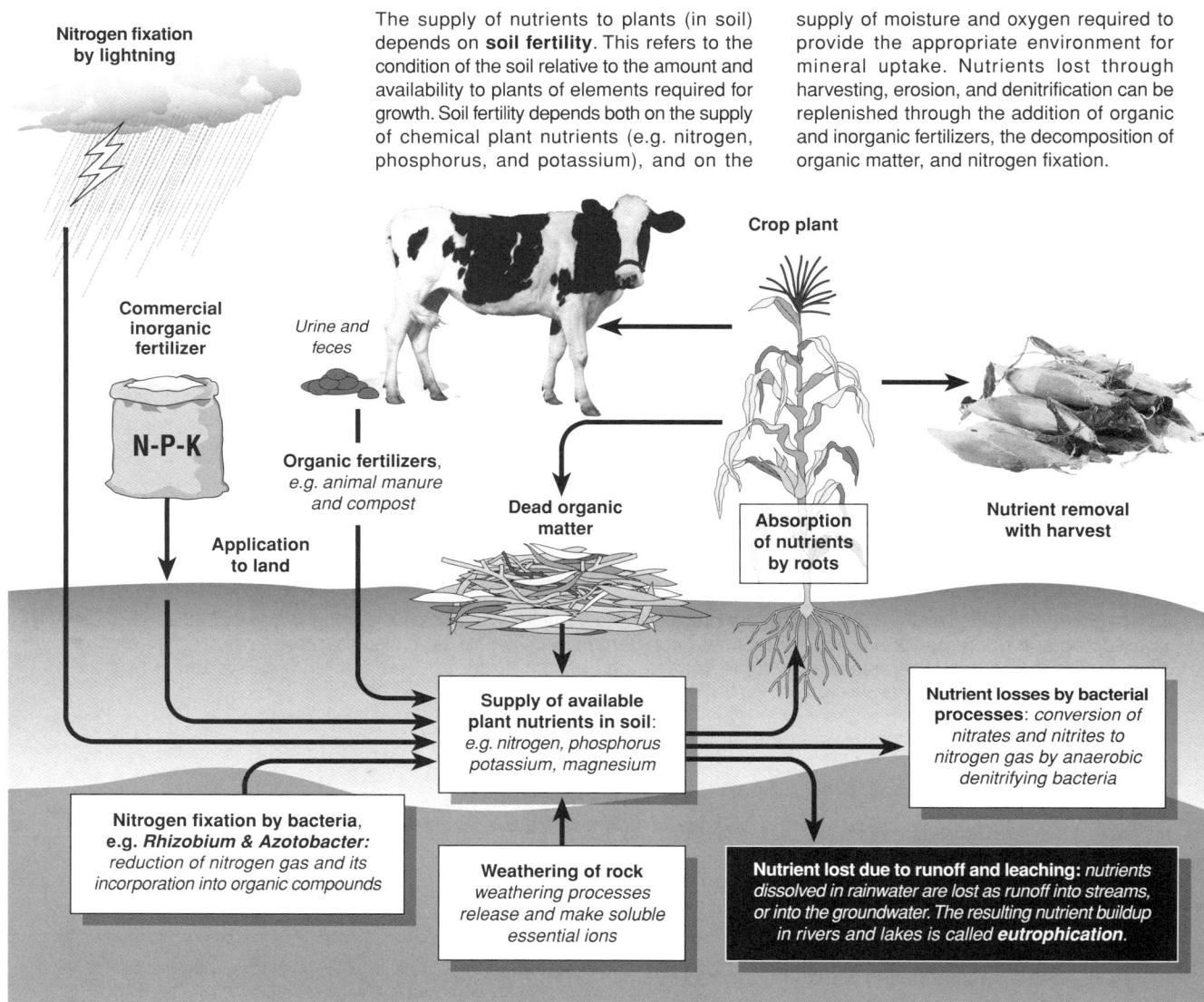

The supply of nutrients to plants (in soil) depends on **soil fertility**. This refers to the condition of the soil relative to the amount and availability to plants of elements required for growth. Soil fertility depends both on the supply of chemical plant nutrients (e.g. nitrogen, phosphorus, and potassium), and on the supply of moisture and oxygen required to provide the appropriate environment for mineral uptake. Nutrients lost through harvesting, erosion, and denitrification can be replenished through the addition of organic and inorganic fertilizers, the decomposition of organic matter, and nitrogen fixation.

The harvesting of commercial crops from agricultural land removes considerable amounts of nutrients. If left unreplenished, the soil will become nutrient deficient. The addition of organic fertilizers (animal manure and compost) and inorganic fertilizers (chemically synthesized) returns the soil's fertility. The production of inorganic fertilizers consumes considerable amounts of fossil fuel (e.g. urea may be made from natural gas).

The tractor above is **tilling** a field in preparation for sowing a new crop. Sometimes, the residue from the previous crop is left on the ground and mixed into the surface layers of the soil. This improves soil structure through aeration as well as returning minerals back into the soil for uptake by the next crop. Such a conservation **tillage** system is much better suited to crop rotations than to continuous cropping systems (see next page).

Crop Rotation

Crop rotation is an agricultural practice in which different crops are cultivated in succession on the same ground in successive years. Its purpose is to maintain soil fertility and reduce the adverse effects of pests. Legumes (peas, beans, clover, and vetch) are important in the rotation as they are a source of nitrogen for the soil. Other crops that may be included in a typical rotation are wheat, barley, and root crops. By contrast, continuous cropping systems require greater use of pesticides to control the recurring infestations of established pests.

Positive reasons for crop rotation

1. The yield advantages of crops being rotated has been proven to be much higher than that of continuous crops (unless the production of the latter is boosted by applying agrochemicals).

2. Conservation tillage systems, which incorporate **residues** from the previous crop into the soil, improve soil structure, drainage and aeration. This tillage system is better suited to crop rotations than to continuous crops, and contributes to greater crop yields.

3. Rotating crops can reduce the potential for serious insect and disease infestations associated with specific crop residues. By contrast, continuous crops produced under conservation tillage leave residues on the surface all year round that harbor insect pests and disease.

The practice of crop rotation has substantially declined in recent years it does not accommodate the shift to large-scale farming practices and the specialization of farms in a single crop.

Growing Crops in Alternative Media

Soil-less cultures provide a very controlled environment for crop production. Artificial soil media may consist of sand or mica flakes. These media are attractive because they can be made to start off in a sterile state (no pests or diseases), but they are totally devoid of nutrients, which must be added. Plants may also be grown in water alone, a technique known as **hydroponics**.

A technician at the US South Pole station, in Antarctica, monitors the hydroponic system growing lettuces and tomatoes. Here, they have to provide thermal insulation as well as nutrients.

1. Suggest why plant yield gradually declines over several harvests if the soil is regularly cropped but not fertilized:

_____

_____

2. Describe two ways in which the problem of declining crop yields could be prevented (or alleviated):

   (a) _____

   (b) _____

3. (a) Define the term fertilizer: _____

   (b) Explain the difference between an organic fertilizer and an inorganic fertilizer: _____

   _____

   (c) State which of these two types of fertilizer provides nutrients most readily to the plant and why: _____

   _____

   _____

4. (a) Outline the basic principles involved in the cultivation of crops using hydroponics: _____

   _____

   _____

   _____

   (b) State two advantages of this method: _____

   _____

5. Explain one disadvantage of fertilizer overuse: _____

_____

_____

Human Control of Plant Growth

Humans have learned that they may provide conditions that can maximize crop yield. Simple modification of the abiotic environment for growing conditions is possible in open field cultivation. Farmers may cover the soil with black plastic sheeting not only to reduce weed growth, but to increase soil temperature and so boost production. **Tunnel enclosures,** consisting of a shade cloth draped over wire hoops, may reduce light intensity, reduce airflow, prevent frost damage, and reduce damage by animal pests. A more complete control of the abiotic conditions is achieved by growing crops in a **glasshouse** (greenhouse) environment. Temperature, carbon dioxide concentration, and light intensity may be optimized to maximize the rate of photosynthesis, and therefore growth. Glasshouses allow the

manipulation of specific abiotic factors to trigger a change in the growing behavior of some crops (e.g. flowering). **Carbon dioxide enrichment** will dramatically increase the growth of glasshouse crops providing that other important abiotic factors are not limiting. Levels of CO_2 in normal air are generally between 300 and 400 ppm. Equipment is available to bleed minute amounts of CO_2 into the foliage of individual plants during the light cycle and maintain an increased concentration of 1500 ppm. Enrichment should commence at sunrise or when photoperiod begins and cease during dark hours. The **economic viability** of such control measures is determined by the increased production it provides compared with the capital cost of the equipment and the ongoing operating costs.

Plan View of a Typical Commercial Glasshouse

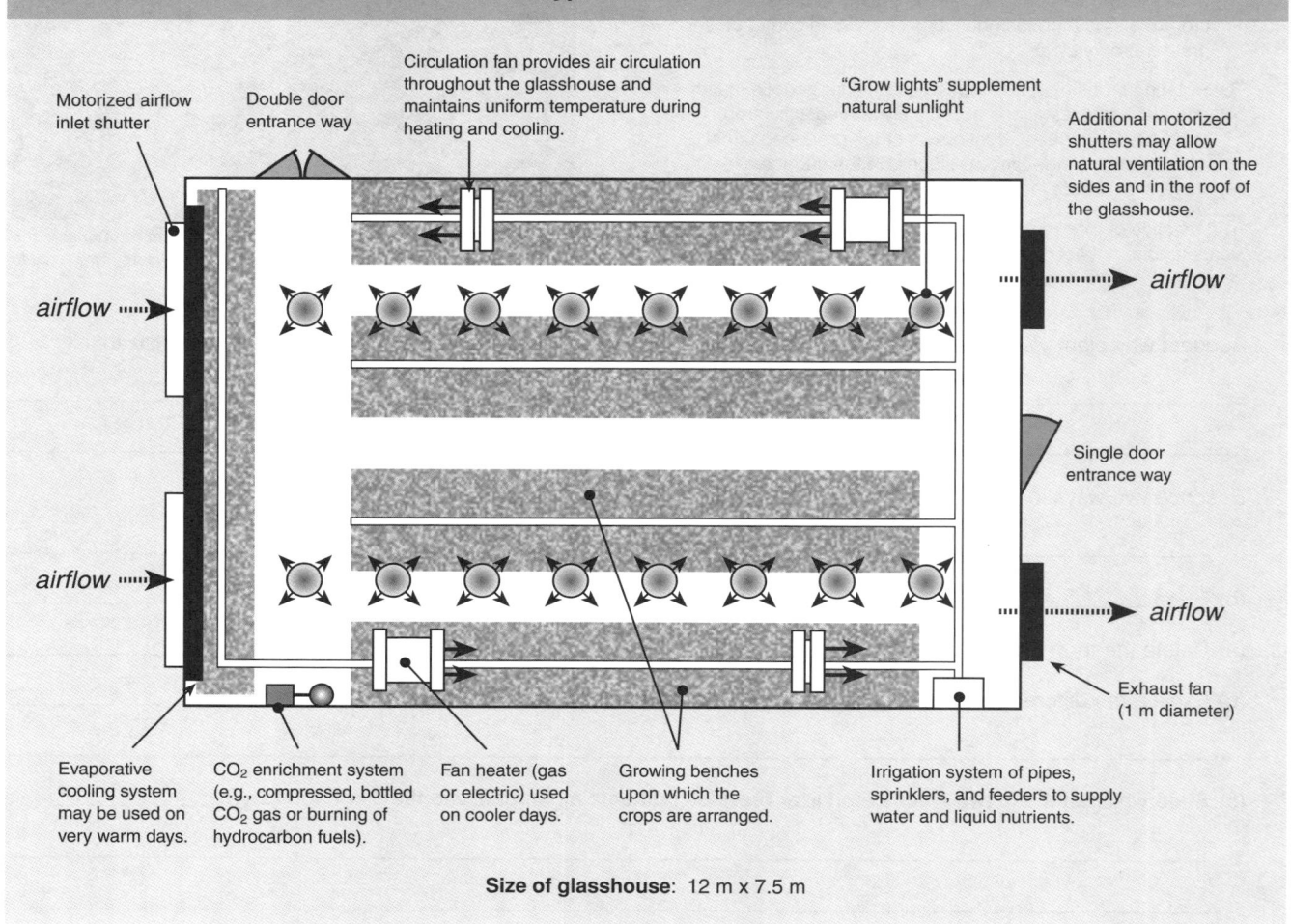

Motorized airflow inlet shutter

Double door entrance way

Circulation fan provides air circulation throughout the glasshouse and maintains uniform temperature during heating and cooling.

"Grow lights" supplement natural sunlight

Additional motorized shutters may allow natural ventilation on the sides and in the roof of the glasshouse.

airflow

airflow

airflow

Single door entrance way

airflow

Exhaust fan (1 m diameter)

Evaporative cooling system may be used on very warm days.

CO_2 enrichment system (e.g., compressed, bottled CO_2 gas or burning of hydrocarbon fuels).

Fan heater (gas or electric) used on cooler days.

Growing benches upon which the crops are arranged.

Irrigation system of pipes, sprinklers, and feeders to supply water and liquid nutrients.

Size of glasshouse: 12 m x 7.5 m

The degree to which the growing environment may be controlled and modified by enclosures varies. Simple black plastic sheeting may be laid over the soil to control weeds and absorb extra solar heat. Tunnel enclosures (such as those being used by the Asian farmers above), may be used to reduce light intensity, reduce airflow, prevent frost damage, and reduce damage by pests.

Large, commercial glasshouses have elaborate watering systems controlled by a microprocessor. The microprocessor unit is usually linked to sensors that may measure soil moisture content, air temperature, and humidity. Coupled with a timer, they are able to deliver optimum water conditions for plant growth by operating electric solenoid valves attached to the irrigation system.

Airflow through a glasshouse is essential to provide a homogeneous air temperature. It is also necessary to ensure that carbon dioxide gas (necessary for photosynthesis) is evenly distributed throughout the enclosure. A general airflow from one end of the enclosure to the other is maintained by a large number of fans all blowing in the same direction.

Carbon Dioxide Enrichment

Carbon dioxide (CO_2) is a raw material used in photosynthesis. If the supply of carbon dioxide is cut off or reduced, plant growth and development are curtailed. The amount of CO_2 in air is normally 0.03% (250-330 ppm). Most plants will stop growing when the CO_2 level falls below 150 ppm. Even at 220 ppm, a slow-down in plant growth is noticeable (see graph on right).

Controlled CO_2 atmospheres, which boost the CO_2 concentration to more than 1000 ppm, significantly increase the rate of formation of dry plant matter and total yield (e.g. of flowers or fruit). In glasshouse environments, boosting CO_2 levels also guards against localized fluctuations in CO_2 levels. These occur as a result of CO_2 depletion near the glasshouse center, relative to the edge.

The positive effect of CO_2 enrichment arises primarily because high CO_2 inhibits photorespiration, which normally occurs at high temperature and low CO_2. Up to 50% of photosynthetically fixed carbon may be reoxidized to CO_2 during photorespiration; inhibiting photorespiration is therefore beneficial to yield.

Five common methods of generating extra carbon dioxide are burning hydrocarbon fuels, compressed, bottled CO_2, dry ice, fermentation, and decomposition of organic matter.

Tests have been conducted with carnations and other flowers in controlled CO_2 atmospheres ranging from 200 to 550 ppm (see table right). The higher CO_2 concentrations significantly increased the rate of formation of dry plant matter, total flower yield, and market value.

Sources: Roger H. Thayer, Eco Enterprises; Hydroponic Society of America; Home Harvest at www.homeharvest.com

The effect of CO_2 concentration on plant growth

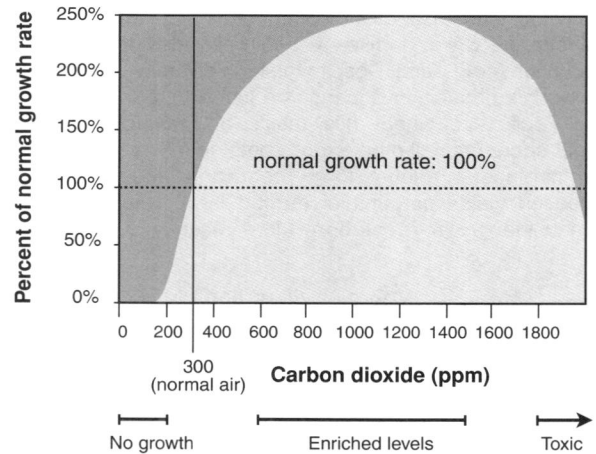

Sample results from CO_2 enrichment studies

Crop	Yield increase	Other improvements
Lettuce	40%	Larger heads of better quality.
Carnations	>30%	Earlier flowering (up to 2 weeks).
Roses	40%	Improvement in blossom quality, number and yield.
Tomatoes	29%	More desirable firmness, more uniform ripening.

1. List the equipment in a typical glasshouse that may control the following **abiotic factors**:

   (a) Temperature: _____

   (b) Humidity: _____

   (c) Light: _____

   (d) Water availability: _____

   (e) Soil nutrients: _____

   (f) Air flow: _____

2. Explain why **carbon dioxide enrichment** has the capacity to radically increase crop production:

   _____

   _____

3. Describe the two primary considerations influencing the **economic viability** of using equipment (such as that illustrated on the previous page) for controlling temperature, light intensity, carbon dioxide concentration, and humidity:

   _____

   _____

4. List two methods that are used commercially to increase the carbon dioxide content of air in horticultural glasshouses:

   _____

5. Explain the importance of circulation fans in maintaining optimum growing conditions in glasshouses:

   _____

   _____

Cereal Crop Production

Agricultural ecosystems may be industrialized (high-input) or traditional. Industrialized agriculture uses large amounts of fossil fuel energy, water, fertilizers, and pesticides to increase net production (crop yield). Despite the high diversity of edible plants, the world's population depends on just 30 crops for 95% of its food. Four crops: wheat, rice, maize, and potato, account for a bigger share than all other crops combined. Since 1950, most of the increase in global food production has resulted from increased yields per unit of farmed land. This increase was termed the **green revolution**. More recently, a second green revolution has being taking place, with the use of fast growing, high yielding varieties of rice, corn, and wheat, specially bred for tropical and subtropical climates. Producing more food from less land increases the per capita food production while at the same time protecting large areas of potentially valuable agricultural land from development. Although food production has nearly tripled since the 1950s, the rate of this increase has started to slow, and soil loss and degradation are taking a toll on formerly productive land. Sustainable farming practices (see page 370) provide one way in which to reduce this loss of productivity.

Wheat (*Triticum* spp.)

Wheat is the most important world cereal crop and is extensively grown in temperate regions. Bread (common) wheat is a soft wheat with a high gluten (protein) content. It is cultivated for the grain, which is used both whole or ground. Durum wheat is a hard (low gluten) wheat used primarily for the manufacture of pasta. Key areas for wheat production are the prairies of Canada and the USA, Europe, and Russia (the former Soviet wheat belt). The economic stability of many nations is affected by the trade in wheat and related commodities. ***New developments***: Wheat cultivars are selected for particular nutritional qualities or high yield in local conditions. Research focuses on breeding hardy, disease resistant, and high yielding varieties.

Maize (corn, *Zea mays*)

Maize is a widely cultivated tropical and subtropical C_4 cereal crop, second only to wheat in international importance as a food grain. The USA corn belt produces nearly half the world's maize. Some is exported, but now 85% is used within the USA as animal feed (as grain and silage). Maize is also a major cereal crop in Africa but is second to rice in importance in Asian countries. Nutritionally, maize is poor in the essential amino acids tryptophan and lysine. Recent breeding efforts have been aimed at addressing these deficiencies. ***New developments***: Plant breeding has produced high lysine hybrid varieties with better disease resistance and higher yields. Most countries have cultivars suited to local conditions.

Rice (*Oryza sativa*)

Rice is the basic food crop of monsoon Asia. It is highly nutritious and requires relatively little post-harvest processing. The most common paddy (*japonica*) varieties are aquatic and are often grown under irrigation. Its cultivation is labor intensive. Upland (*indica*) varieties have similar requirements to other cereal crops. Most rice is grown in China, mainly for internal consumption. Other major producers include India, Pakistan, Japan, Thailand and Vietnam. ***New developments***: Much effort has gone into producing fast growing, disease resistant, high yielding cultivars which will crop up to 3 times a season. Genetic engineering to increase tolerance to high salinity is extending the range for cultivation in the upland varieties of rice.

Sorghum (*Sorghum bicolor*)

Sorghum is a frost-sensitive, tropical C_4 plant, well adapted to arid conditions. It has low soil nutrition and water requirements, reflecting its origin in the sub-Saharan Sudan region of Africa. Sorghum is now widely cultivated in Africa, the middle East to India and Burma, and parts of Australia, the Americas and Southern Europe. It is nutritious and is used as a human foodstuff in Asia and Africa. In other regions, it is used mainly as animal feed and as an industrial raw material (for oil, starch, and fiber). ***New developments***: New hybrids are high yielding, low-growing, and ripen uniformly. Further breeding aims to improve grain quality, and combine high yield properties with the disease resistance of the African wild stocks.

World Production of Major Food Crops

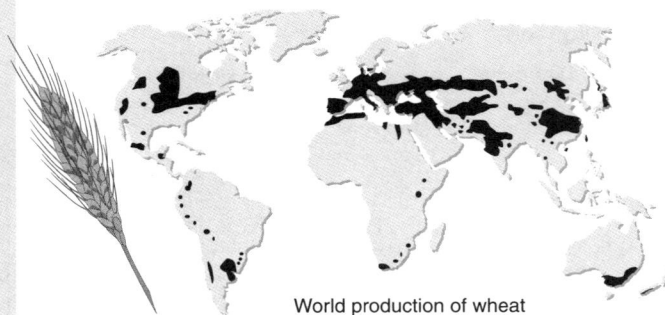

World production of wheat

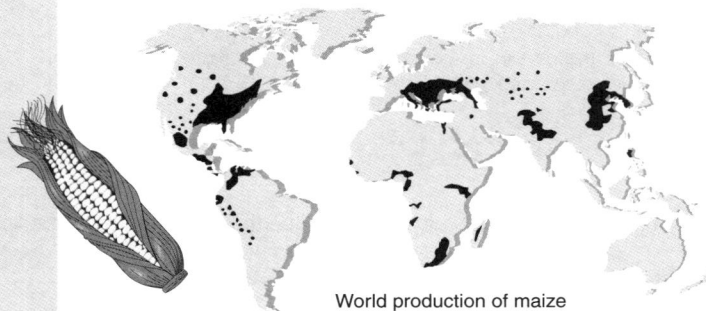

World production of maize

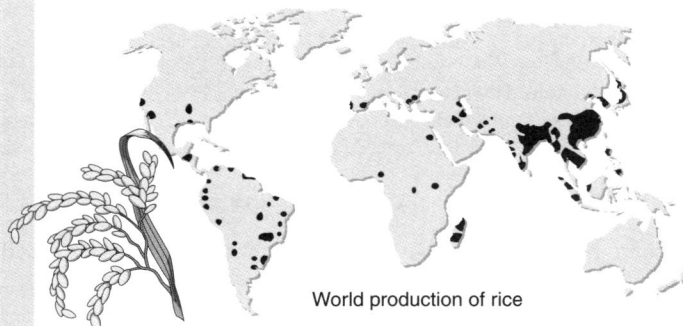

World production of rice

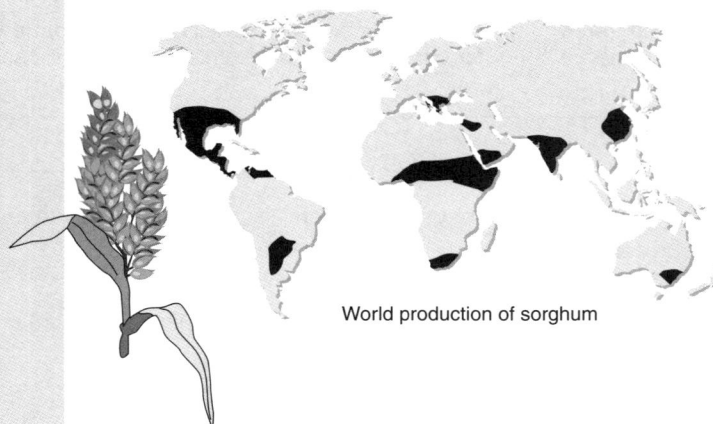

World production of sorghum

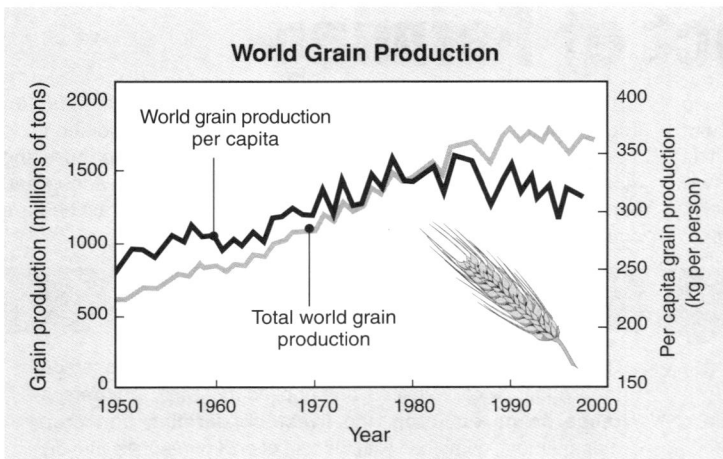

World Grain Production

Grain production (millions of tons)
- World grain production per capita
- Total world grain production

Per capita grain production (kg per person)

Year: 1950 1960 1970 1980 1990 2000

Cropping properties of major world crop plants

Crop plant	Yield (kg grain ha⁻¹)	Specific requirements for growth
Maize	1000 - 4000	Warm, frost free climate, fertile soil, drought intolerant
Wheat	1000 - 14 500	Adapted to a wide range of temperate climates and soils
Rice	4500 (paddy) 1500 (indica)	Tropical, paddy varieties are aquatic, drought intolerant
Sorghum	300 - 2000. As high as 6500 for irrigated hybrids	Wide range of soils. Drought tolerant. Grown in regions too dry for maize.

Sorghum is able to grow well in the very hot, dry regions of tropical Africa and central India. Adaptations include:

- A **dense root system** that is very efficient at extracting water from the soil.
- A thick **waxy cuticle** that prevents evaporative water loss through the leaf surface.
- The presence of special cells (called **motor cells**) on the underside of the leaf that cause the leaf to roll inwards in dry conditions. This traps moist air in the rolled leaf and reduces water loss.
- Reduced number of sunken stomata on leaves.

Maize grows well where temperature and light intensity are high. Adaptations include:

- A slightly different biochemical pathway for photosynthesis than that in most cooler climate plants. Called the **C₄ pathway**, the plant can fix carbon dioxide at low levels as a four-carbon molecule. This molecule is used to boost CO_2 in the regular C_3 pathway. This mechanism allows photosynthesis to continue at high rates (primarily through the inhibition of photorespiration).
- The roots are shallow, so maize often has small **aerial roots** at the base of the stem to increase their ability to withstand buffeting by wind.

Most of the **rice** in southeast Asia is grown partly submerged in paddy fields. Adaptations include:

- The stem of a rice plant has **large air spaces** (hollow aerenchyma) running the length of the stem. This allows oxygen to penetrate through to the roots which are submerged in water.
- The roots are also very shallow, allowing access to oxygen that diffuses into the surface layer of the waterlogged soil.
- When oxygen levels fall too low, the root cells respire anaerobically, producing ethanol. Ethanol is normally toxic to cells, but the root cells of rice have an unusually high tolerance to it.

1. Explain how crop yields were increased in:

   (a) The first green revolution: _____

   (b) The second green revolution (in the last 30 years): _____

2. Suggest a reason for the decline in per capita production of grain in the last decade: _____

3. Comment on the importance of wheat as a world food crop: _____

4. (a) Explain **when** sorghum is a preferable crop to maize: _____

   (b) Suggest why rice is less important as an export crop than wheat or maize: _____

5. Briefly describe TWO adaptive features of each of the cereal crops below:

   (a) Rice: _____

   (b) Maize: _____

The Impact of Farming

RA 2

The survival of all life depends on the soil, yet soil loss via erosion and chemical pollution threatens ecosystems throughout the world. As the world population grows and more land is cultivated for agriculture, sustainable farming practices will become essential to our continued survival. Current intensive farming practices are unsustainable; the over-use of inorganic fertilizer, the erosion of top soil, and the huge demand for irrigation are the leading causes of this. Finding solutions to these problems is not easy; if farmers suddenly stopped using inorganic fertilizers the world would experience widespread famine. The implications of two contrasting farming practices are outlined below.

Intensive Farming

Intensive farming techniques flourished after World War II. Using **high-yielding hybrid cultivars** and large inputs of **inorganic fertilizers**, **chemical pesticides**, and **farm machinery**, crop yields increased to 3 or 4 times those produced using the more extensive (low-input) methods of 5 decades ago. Large areas planted in monocultures (single crops) are typical. Irrigation and fertilizer programs are often extensive to allow for the planting of several crops per season. Given adequate irrigation and continued fertilizer inputs, yields from intensive farming are high. Over time, these yields decline as soils are eroded or cannot recover from repeated cropping.

Intensive agriculture relies on the heavy use of irrigation, inorganic fertilizers (produced using fossil fuels), pesticides, and farm machinery. Such farms may specialize in a single crop for many years.

Impact on the Environment

- Pesticide use is escalating yet pesticide effectiveness is decreasing. This causes a reduction in species diversity, particularly among the invertebrates.

- Mammals and birds may be affected by **bioaccumulation** of pesticides in the food chain and loss of food sources as invertebrate species diminish.

- Fertilizer use is increasing, resulting in a continued decline in soil and water quality.

- More fertilizer leaches from the soil and enters groundwater as a pollutant, relative to organic farming practices.

- Large fields lacking hedgerows or vegetated borders create an impoverished habitat and cause the isolation of remaining wooded areas.

- A monoculture regime leads to reduced biodiversity.

Sustainable Agricultural Practices

Organic farming is a sustainable form of agriculture based on the avoidance of chemicals and applied *inorganic* fertilizers. It relies on mixed (crop and livestock) farming and crop management, combined with the use of environmentally friendly pest controls (e.g. biological controls and flaming), and livestock and green manures. Organic farming uses **crop rotation** and **intercropping**, in which two or more crops are grown at the same time on the same plot, often maturing at different times. If well cultivated, these plots can provide food, fuel, and natural pest control and fertilizers on a sustainable basis. Yields are typically lower than on intensive farms, but the produce can fetch high prices, and pest control and fertilizer costs are reduced.

Some traditional farms use low-input agricultural practices similar to those used in modern organic farming. However, many small farming units find it difficult to remain economically viable.

Impact on the Environment

- Pesticides do not persist in the environment nor accumulate in the food chain.

- Produce is pesticide free and produced in a sustainable way.

- Alternative pest control measures, such as using natural predators and pheromone traps, reduce the dependence on pesticides.

- The retention of hedgerows or vegetated borders increases habitat diversity and produces corridors for animal movement between forested areas.

- Crop rotation (alternation of various crops, including legumes) prevents pests and disease species building up to high levels.

- Conservation tillage (ploughing crop residues into the topsoil) as part of the crop rotation cycle improves soil structure.

1. Explain how intensive monoculture can lead to nutrient depletion and pest invasion: _____

_____

_____

_____

Pesticides and Bioaccumulation

Certain substances in the environment are harmful when absorbed in high concentrations. Substances, such as pesticides, radioactive isotopes, heavy metals, and industrial chemicals such as PCBs can be taken up by organisms via their food or simply absorbed from the surrounding medium. The **toxicity** of a pesticide is a measure of how poisonous the chemical is, not only to the target organisms, but to non-target species as well. The **specificity** (broad or narrow spectrum) of a pesticide describes how selective it is in targeting a pest. An important issue relating to the use of a pesticide is its **persistence**; how long it remains in the environment. A pesticide may be *biodegradable* or resistant to biological breakdown. Many highly persistent pesticides cannot be metabolized or excreted. Instead, they are stored in fatty tissues and have the potential for **bioaccumulation** (biomagnification); progressive concentration with increasing trophic level. Higher order consumers (e.g. predatory birds and mammals) may ingest harmful or lethal quantities of a chemical because they eat a large number of lower order consumers.

Pesticide type	Examples	Environmental persistence	Biomag-nification
Insecticides			
Organochlorines	*DDT*, aldrin, dieldrin	2-15 yrs	Yes
Organophosphates	*Malathion, diazinon*	1-2 weeks/years	No
Carbamates	*Aldicarb, carbaryl, zineb, maneb*	Days to weeks	No
Botanicals	*Rotenone, pyrethrum, camphor*	Days to weeks	No
Microbials	*Various bacteria, fungi, protozoa*	Days to weeks	No
Fungicides			
Various chemicals	*Captan, zeneb, carbon sulfide, pentachlorphenol, methyl bromide*	Days	No
Herbicides			
Contact§ chemicals	*Paraquat, atrazine, simazine*	Days to weeks	No
Systemic¶ chemicals	*2,4-D, 2,4,5-T, Silvex, diruon, glyphosphate (Roundup)*	Days to weeks	No
Soil sterilants	*Tribualin, dalapon, butylate*	Days	No
Fumigants			
Various chemicals	*Carbon tetrachloride, ethylene dibromide, methyl bromide*	Years	Yes

* Now banned in most developed countries
¶ Systemic chemicals: Effective when it enters the general circulation of the plant or animal
§ Contact chemicals: Effective when it comes in contact with surface tissue

Biomagnification of DDT in an aquatic ecosystem

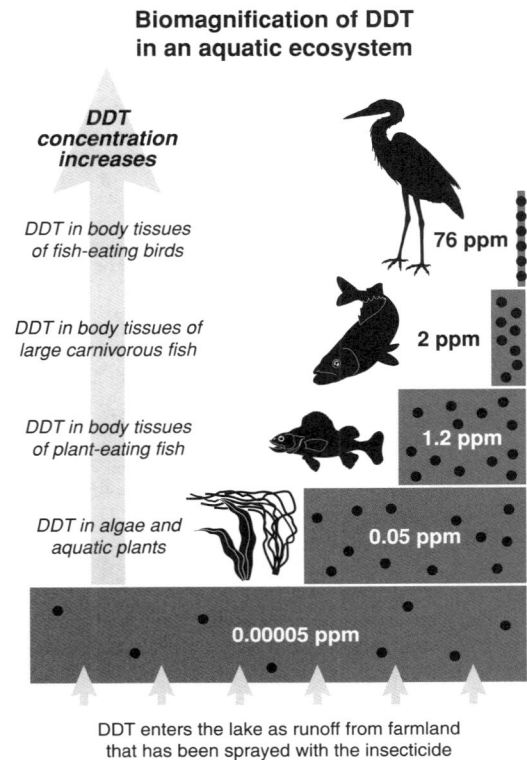

DDT concentration increases

DDT in body tissues of fish-eating birds — 76 ppm

DDT in body tissues of large carnivorous fish — 2 ppm

DDT in body tissues of plant-eating fish — 1.2 ppm

DDT in algae and aquatic plants — 0.05 ppm

0.00005 ppm

DDT enters the lake as runoff from farmland that has been sprayed with the insecticide

Source of data: G. Tyler Miller, Jr., 2000. Living in the Environment (11th Ed.), Brooks/Cole Publishing.

1. Define the following terms as they relate to the characteristics and use of pesticides:

(a) Toxicity: _____

(b) Specificity: _____

(c) Biodegradable: _____

(d) Bioaccumulation: _____

(e) Contact chemical: _____

(f) Systemic chemical: _____

2. Calculate the increase in DDT concentration between each step in the food chain:

(a) Water to algae: *0.05 ÷ 0.00005 = 1 000 times*   (c) Herbivorous fish to carnivorous fish: _____

(b) Algae to herbivorous fish: _____   (d) Carnivorous fish to fish-eating birds: _____

3. Suggest why many insecticides fail to provide long term control of their target species: _____

4. Suggest why some **organochlorine** pesticides have been banned in most developed countries: _____

5. State briefly why top consumers are most at risk from bioaccumulation: _____

Soil Degradation

Soil is a rather fragile resource and can be easily damaged or lost by inappropriate farming practices. Soil loss is termed **erosion**. Some erosion occurs naturally, but some is the result of human activities such as deforestation, foot traffic, farming of marginal land, and overgrazing. In some countries, especially in tropical regions, overgrazing, overcultivation, poor irrigation practices, and deforestation may cause **desertification** and **salinization**. Intensive agricultural practices, which call for ever-increasing doses of herbicides, pesticides, and fertilizer, result in a gradual deterioration of soil quality. Over time, the ability of the land to support crops is greatly reduced. Healthy soils are 'alive' with a diverse community of beneficial organisms whose activities help to improve soil structure and add organic material in the soil (the **humus**). Repeated application of chemicals kills these soil organisms and results in a soil that is hard, lacking in organic material, and unproductive.

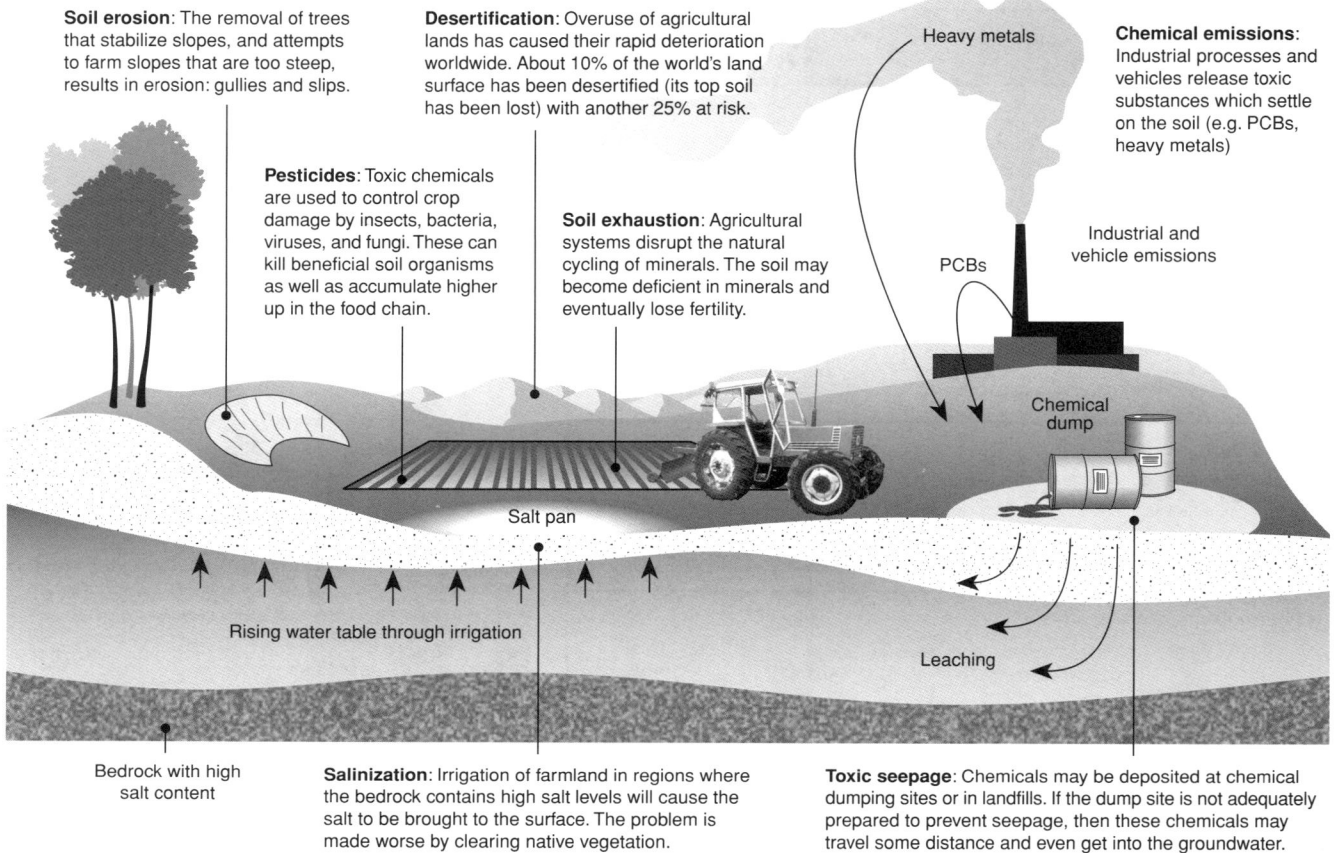

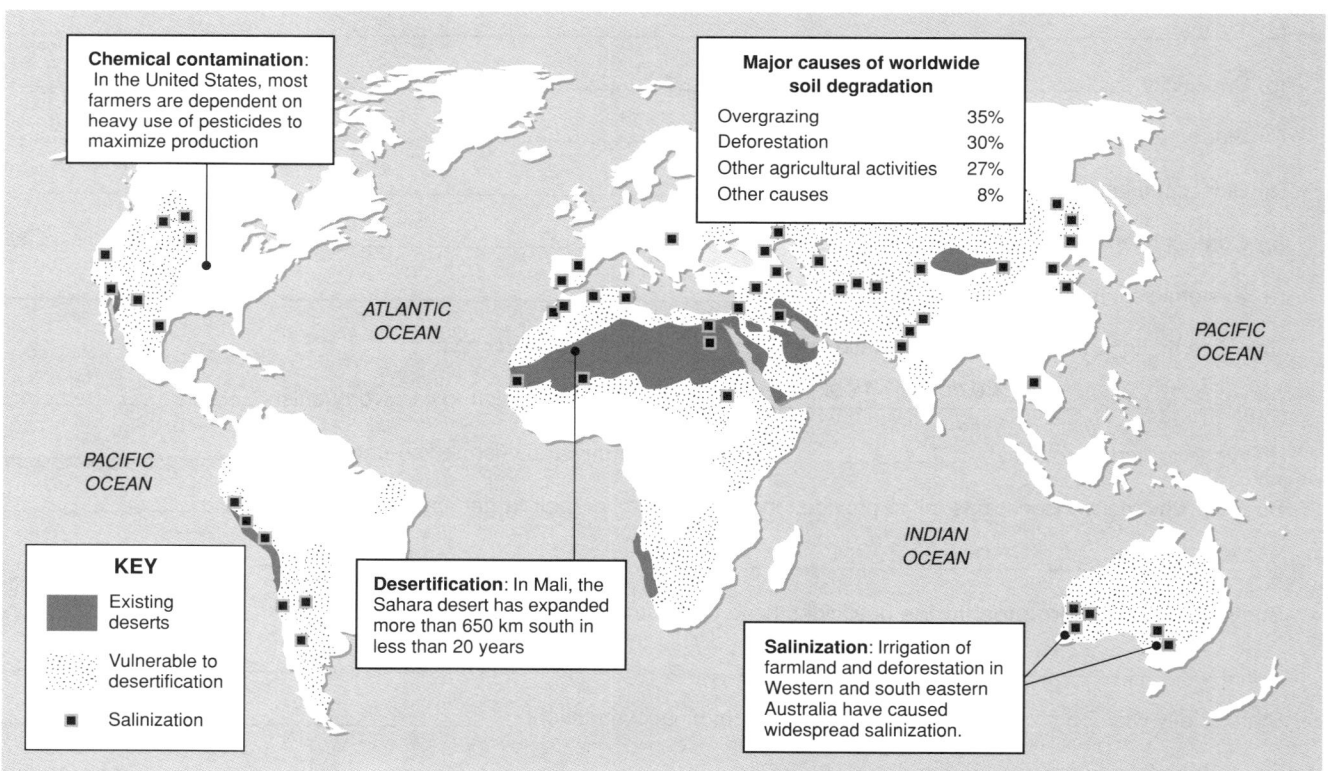

Soil erosion: The removal of trees that stabilize slopes, and attempts to farm slopes that are too steep, results in erosion: gullies and slips.

Pesticides: Toxic chemicals are used to control crop damage by insects, bacteria, viruses, and fungi. These can kill beneficial soil organisms as well as accumulate higher up in the food chain.

Desertification: Overuse of agricultural lands has caused their rapid deterioration worldwide. About 10% of the world's land surface has been desertified (its top soil has been lost) with another 25% at risk.

Soil exhaustion: Agricultural systems disrupt the natural cycling of minerals. The soil may become deficient in minerals and eventually lose fertility.

Heavy metals

Chemical emissions: Industrial processes and vehicles release toxic substances which settle on the soil (e.g. PCBs, heavy metals)

Industrial and vehicle emissions

PCBs

Chemical dump

Salt pan

Rising water table through irrigation

Leaching

Bedrock with high salt content

Salinization: Irrigation of farmland in regions where the bedrock contains high salt levels will cause the salt to be brought to the surface. The problem is made worse by clearing native vegetation.

Toxic seepage: Chemicals may be deposited at chemical dumping sites or in landfills. If the dump site is not adequately prepared to prevent seepage, then these chemicals may travel some distance and even get into the groundwater.

Chemical contamination: In the United States, most farmers are dependent on heavy use of pesticides to maximize production

Major causes of worldwide soil degradation	
Overgrazing	35%
Deforestation	30%
Other agricultural activities	27%
Other causes	8%

ATLANTIC OCEAN

PACIFIC OCEAN

PACIFIC OCEAN

INDIAN OCEAN

KEY

Existing deserts

Vulnerable to desertification

Salinization

Desertification: In Mali, the Sahara desert has expanded more than 650 km south in less than 20 years

Salinization: Irrigation of farmland and deforestation in Western and south eastern Australia have caused widespread salinization.

The problem of disposing of unwanted agricultural chemicals has reached major proportions in developed countries. Chemical dumps (such as the one illustrated above) suffer from deterioration, with the contents spilling from rusting drums and entering the ground water system.

The high use of pesticides in developed countries is claimed to be necessary by growers to maintain high levels of production. This often comes at the cost of destroying the natural predators of pest species. Pesticides can accumulate in the soil and enter the ground water system.

Human activities such as overgrazing livestock on pasture and deforestation may cause regional climate changes and a marked reduction in rainfall. This in turn may lead to the formation of a desert environment or the encroachment of an existing desert onto formerly arable land.

1. Explain how human induced salinization develops: _____

_____

_____

_____

2. Describe alternative farming practices that do not use chemically intensive methods for:

   (a) Nutrient enrichment: _____

   _____

   _____

   (b) Pest control: _____

   _____

   _____

3. Describe the two main causes of worldwide soil degradation: _____

   _____

   _____

4. (a) Explain what is meant by desertification: _____

   _____

   _____

   (b) List the main causes of desertification: _____

   _____

   (c) Describe a way in which desertification may be averted or reversed:

   _____

   _____

   _____

   _____

   _____

   _____

RA② Biological Control of Pests

Biological control (biocontrol) is a management tool for controlling pests using parasites, predators, pathogens, and weed feeders. Some control agents with a botanical or microbial origin (e.g. the Bt toxin) are called **biopesticides**. Others, such as pheromone traps, are also sometimes included as biocontrols. Biological control serves as an important alternative to conventional pesticide use, and it is an important component of **integrated pest management**. It is not risk free and not all attempts have been successful. Thorough investigation of a biocontrol agent is required in order to predict its behavior in a new environment. Some biological control agents may even become pests themselves. Some biocontrol programs attempt total elimination of a pest species, while others aim only to maintain pest numbers at acceptably low numbers.

Biological Control Agent	Pest Species

Whitefly *(Trialeurodes vaporariorum)*

Adult whiteflies resemble tiny moths and are about 3 mm long. Their young appear as scales on the undersides of many glasshouse plants where they feed by sucking the sap. They excrete a sticky "honeydew" upon which sooty molds develop, reducing the amount of light reaching the leaves.

Two biocontrol agents are in common use: the ladybird *Delphastus,* which feeds on eggs and larvae of whitefly, and the tiny parasitic wasp *Encarsia*.

Delphastus

Controls →

Whitefly

Biological control agent: Both the larvae and adults of the ladybird *Delphastus* feed on eggs and larvae of whitefly, consuming up to 150 whitefly eggs in a day.

Pest species: Whitefly can over-winter in a glasshouse on crops or weeds and the scales can withstand the occasional frost.

Mealybug *(various species)*

Mealybugs are often found in clusters on stems, leaves and roots. They produce honeydew which often leads to sooty mold growth. Large colonies can weaken the plant because of the amount of sap being taken which can result in yellowing leaves and defoliation.

Commonly used biocontrol agents are the ladybird *Cryptolaemus*, which feeds on mealybug larvae, and the tiny wasp *Leptomastix,* which is parasitic on the citrus and vine mealybug species.

Leptomastix

Controls →

Long-tailed mealybug

Biological control agent: Adult female *Leptomastix* wasps lay their eggs in nearly fully grown mealybugs. The parasitized mealybug becomes "mummified".

Pest species: The most common species found in glasshouses are the citrus mealybug, the vine mealybug, and the long-tailed mealybug (pictured above).

Prickly pear cactus *(Opuntia stricta)*

The prickly pear cactus was introduced to Australia as an ornamental plant in the 1800s. It dispersed rapidly to cover an estimated 250 000 square kilometers by 1925, much of it so densely that the land could not be used.

Evaluation of success: The biocontrol agent succeeded in clearing the 250 000 km² of prickly pear over several years. Now only scattered populations of the cactus occur.

Cactoblastis cactorum

Controls →

Prickly pear cactus

Biological control agent: The caterpillar of the moth *(Cactoblastis cactorum)*, which is a natural enemy of the prickly pear cactus is a voracious feeder.

Pest species: In the absence of natural predators, the prickly pear cactus thrived in regions of Australia with low rainfall.

White-spotted tussock moth
(Orgyia thyellina)

A relative of the gypsy moth, tussock moths have been accidentally introduced from Asia to Canada, the USA and, more recently, New Zealand. The caterpillars eat crops and ornamentals, and are a serious threat to forests.

Evaluation of success: Biocontrols gave mixed results in North America. Early aggressive control measures in New Zealand in 1997 appear to have successfully eradicated the pest.

Bacillus thuringiensis

Controls →

Tussock moth

Biological control agent: Affected areas are sprayed with Foray 48B, containing the toxin of the naturally occurring soil bacteria Btk (*Bacillus thuringiensis variety kurstaki*).

Pest species: The larvae from the tussock moth have the potential to destroy forestry and horticultural industries in areas where they become established.

Case study: Cascade effects following a biological control program

European rabbit: *Oryctolagus cuniculus*

Rabbits were successfully introduced into Britain by the Normans for their meat and fur. By the 1950s numbers were high enough for them to be considered an agricultural pest. The unauthorized introduction of myxomatosis caused a devastating loss of 99% of Britain's rabbits. Populations have stabilized in the presence of the disease, but the losses had unforeseen ecological effects still evident today.

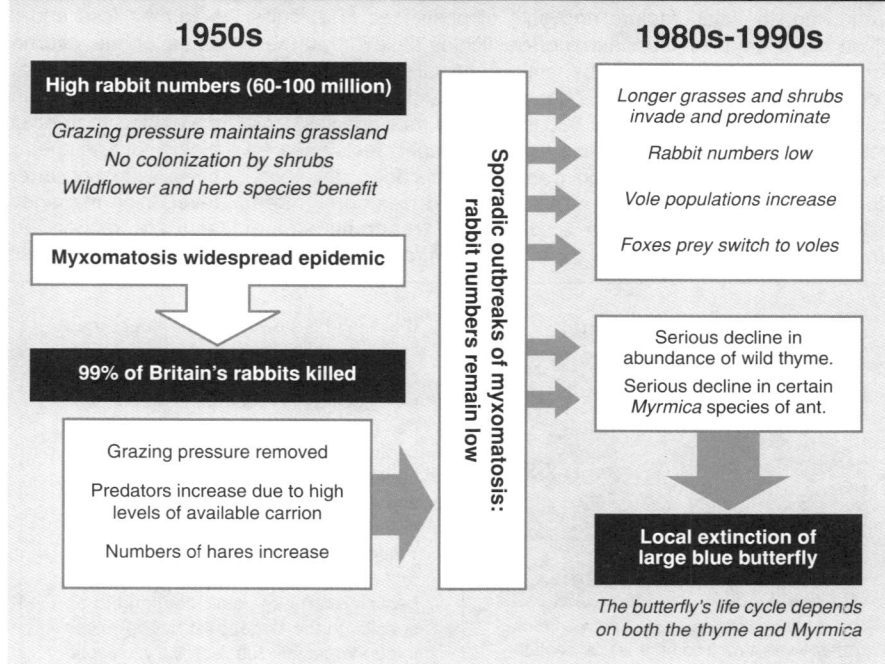

1950s

High rabbit numbers (60-100 million)

Grazing pressure maintains grassland
No colonization by shrubs
Wildflower and herb species benefit

Myxomatosis widespread epidemic

99% of Britain's rabbits killed

Grazing pressure removed

Predators increase due to high levels of available carrion

Numbers of hares increase

Sporadic outbreaks of myxomatosis: rabbit numbers remain low

1980s-1990s

Longer grasses and shrubs invade and predominate

Rabbit numbers low

Vole populations increase

Foxes prey switch to voles

Serious decline in abundance of wild thyme.
Serious decline in certain *Myrmica* species of ant.

Local extinction of large blue butterfly

The butterfly's life cycle depends on both the thyme and Myrmica

1. Explain the general principle of **biological control of pests**: _____

_____

_____

2. When a biological control agent is successful in controlling a pest population, it does not usually completely eradicate it. The pest population survives at a lower and acceptable level. Explain why the pest is not completely wiped out:

_____

_____

3. (a) Suggest why introduced species often become pests in a new country when they are not pests in their native habitat:

_____

_____

(b) The introduction of the natural control agent seems like the best option for controlling an introduced pest. Explain why extreme care must be exercised before introducing a biological pest control agent into a new country:

_____

_____

4. (a) In the case study above, suggest why the numbers of hares and voles increased after the decline of the rabbits:

_____

(b) Give a reason why prey switching occurred in foxes: _____

_____

5. Suggest what could have been done to predict the cascade effects of the myxomatosis epidemic:

_____

_____

6. Identify an agent for biological control of the following pests found in glasshouses:

(a) Mealybug: _____

(b) Whitefly: _____

Integrated Pest Management

Worldwide, the manufacture and sale of pesticides is a multi-billion dollar industry. Opponents of pesticides believe that their harmful effects outweigh the benefits, especially in the face of increasing genetic resistance to pesticides by their target organisms. Since 1950 at least 520 insect and mite species, 273 weeds, and 150 plant pathogens have developed resistance to one or more pesticides. When pesticide resistance develops, more frequent applications and larger doses are often recommended. This leads to a **pesticide treadmill**, where farmers pay more and more for a pest control program that becomes less and less effective. Today, experts recognize the value of the alternative approach known as **Integrated Pest Management** (IPM). In IPM, each crop and its pests are evaluated as part of an ecological system. A control program is developed that includes a sequence of crop management, and biological and chemical controls. The aim is not pest eradication but a reduction in crop damage to an **economically tolerable level**. Well managed IPM programs have outstanding success and are recognized as being economically and ecologically sound (see Indonesia's success story below).

Crop monitoring (ongoing)

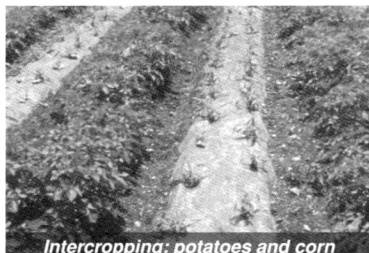

Intercropping: potatoes and corn

Careful crop management and monitoring of pest levels. When damage is unacceptable, farmers implement control measures.

IPM may be slower to take effect than conventional controls and for a program to work, expert knowledge of crop and pest ecology is required. However, well designed programs can reduce pest control costs and pesticide use and by 50-90%. IPM can also reduce crop losses and the need for fertilizers, and slow the development of pesticide resistance. Where chemical pesticide use is required, IPM attempts to use ecologically sensitive pesticides. These pesticides tend to be specific to the target pest but harmless to non-target species, less likely to cause resistance, non- persistent, and low-cost.

An International Success Story

- In 1986, the Indonesian government banned the use of 57 of 66 pesticides used on rice and phased out pesticide subsidies over two years.

- The money saved from subsidy reduction was used to launch a nationwide program of integrated pest management.

- Between 1987 and 1992, pesticide use fell by 65%, rice production rose by 15%, and 250 000 farmers were trained in IPM.

- By 1993 the program had saved the Indonesian government over $1.2 billion in pesticide costs; enough to fund IPM.

Stage 1: Cultivation controls

Cultivation controls e.g. vacuuming up pests, and hand, hot water, or flame weeding, start the pest and weed control program.

Stage 2: Biological controls

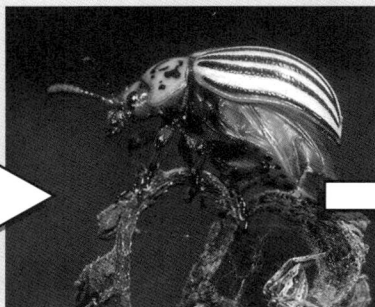

Sex attractants and biological controls e.g. natural predators, are used to reduce pest populations. The Colorado potato beetle pest (above) is controlled using a fungal pathogen combined with release and conservation of the beetle's natural predators.

Stage 3: Targeted pesticide use

Small amounts of narrow spectrum pesticides are applied as a last resort if other methods do not achieve adequate control. A variety of chemicals may be used at different times to slow the development of pest resistance and preserve natural predator populations.

1. State the aim of IPM: _____

2. IPM utilizes careful use of pesticides when necessary. Describe three features of an ideal chemical pesticide:

_____

_____

3. Outline the main features of an IPM program, briefly stating the importance of each:

   (a) _____

   (b) _____

   (c) _____

   (d) _____

4. Explain the biological and economic benefits of a well managed IPM program: _____

_____

_____

RA 1

Tropisms

Even though most plants are firmly rooted in the ground, they are still capable of growth responses to environmental stimuli such as light or gravity. These responses may involve a relatively sudden physiological change, as occurs in flowering, or a steady growth response, such as a tropism. **Tropisms** are plant growth responses to external stimuli, where the stimulus direction determines the direction of the growth response. Tropisms may be positive or negative depending on whether the plant moves towards or away from the stimulus. They can be distinguished from **nastic responses**, which are independent of stimulus direction.

Summary of Plant Tropic Responses

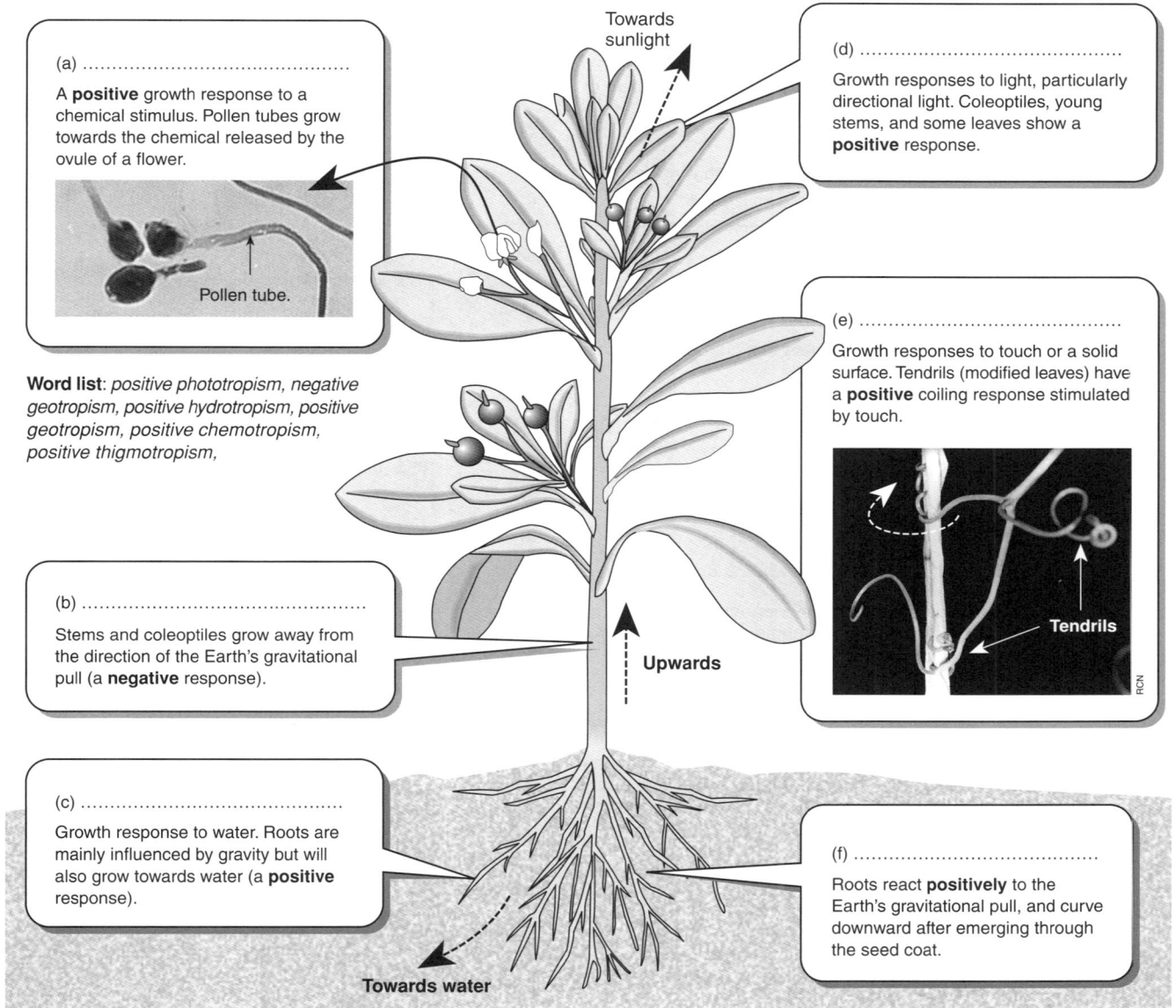

(a) ....

A **positive** growth response to a chemical stimulus. Pollen tubes grow towards the chemical released by the ovule of a flower.

Pollen tube.

Word list: *positive phototropism, negative geotropism, positive hydrotropism, positive geotropism, positive chemotropism, positive thigmotropism,*

(b) ....

Stems and coleoptiles grow away from the direction of the Earth's gravitational pull (a **negative** response).

(c) ....

Growth response to water. Roots are mainly influenced by gravity but will also grow towards water (a **positive** response).

Towards sunlight

(d) ....

Growth responses to light, particularly directional light. Coleoptiles, young stems, and some leaves show a **positive** response.

(e) ....

Growth responses to touch or a solid surface. Tendrils (modified leaves) have a **positive** coiling response stimulated by touch.

Tendrils

Upwards

(f) ....

Roots react **positively** to the Earth's gravitational pull, and curve downward after emerging through the seed coat.

Towards water

1. In the diagram above, identify the plant tropism involved in (a)-(f), according to the explanation provided.

2. (a) Define the term **tropism**: _____

   _____

   (b) Distinguish between a tropism and a nastic response: _____

   _____

3. Explain the adaptive value of the following tropisms:

   (a) Positive geotropism in roots: _____

   (b) Positive phototropism in coleoptiles: _____

   (c) Positive thigmotropism in weak stemmed plants: _____

   (d) Positive chemotropism in pollen grains: _____

Investigating Phototropism

Phototropism in plants was linked to a growth promoting substance in the 1920s. A number of classic experiments, investigating phototropic responses in severed coleoptiles, gave evidence for the hypothesis that **auxin** was responsible for the tropic responses of stems. Auxins promote cell elongation. Stem curvature in response to light can therefore result from the differential distribution of auxin either side of a stem. However, the mechanisms of hormone action in plants are still not well understood. Auxins increase cell elongation only over a certain concentration range and, at certain levels, auxins stop inducing elongation and begin to inhibit it. Note that there is *some* experimental evidence to contradict the original auxin hypothesis and the early experiments have been criticized for oversimplifying the real situation. Outlined below are some experiments investigating the phototropic response, and the role of hormone(s) in controlling it.

1. **Directional light:** A pot plant is exposed to direct sunlight near a window and as it grows, the shoot tip turns in the direction of the sun. If the plant was rotated, it adjusted by growing towards the sun in the new direction.

    (a) Name the hormone that regulates this growth response:

    _____

    (b) Give the full name of this growth response:

    _____

    (c) State how the cells behave to cause this change in shoot direction at:

    Point A: _____

    Point B: _____

    (d) State which side (A or B) would have the highest concentration of hormone:

    _____

    (e) Draw a diagram of the cells as they appear across the stem from point A to B (in the rectangle on the right).

    _____

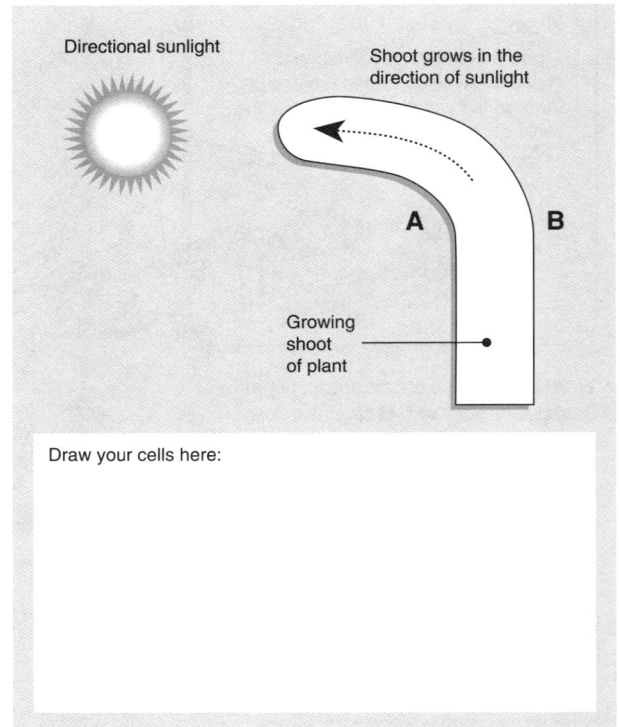

Draw your cells here:

2. **Light excluded from shoot tip:** With a tin foil cap placed over the top of the shoot tip, light is prevented from reaching it. When growing under these conditions, the direction of growth does not change towards the light source, but grows straight up. State what conclusion can you come to about the source and activity of the hormone that controls the growth response:

    _____

    _____

    _____

    _____

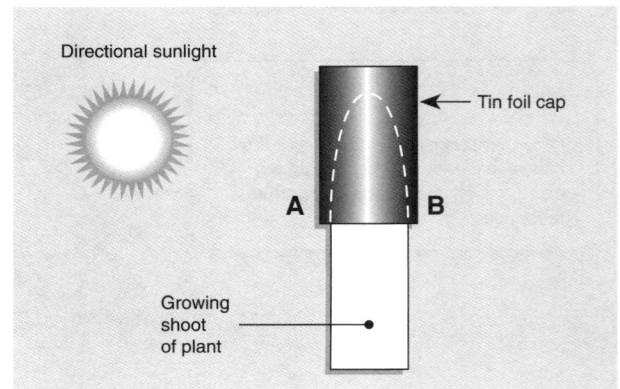

3. **Cutting into the transport system:** Two identical plants were placed side-by-side and subjected to the same directional light source. Razor blades were cut half-way into the stem, thereby interfering with the transport system of the stem. Plant A had the cut on the same side as the light source, while Plant B was cut on the shaded side. Predict the growth responses of:

    Plant A: _____

    _____

    Plant B: _____

    _____

    _____

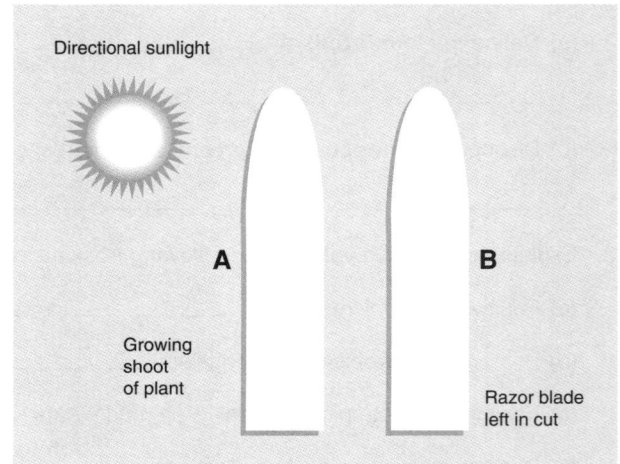

Investigating Geotropism

A2

Although the response of shoots and roots to gravity is well known, the mechanism behind it is not at all well understood. The importance of auxin as a plant growth regulator, as well as its widespread occurrence in plants, led to it being proposed as the primary regulator in the geotropic response. The basis of auxin's proposed role in geotropism is outlined below. The mechanism is appealing in its simplicity but, as noted below, has been widely criticized, and there is not a great deal of evidence to support it. Many of the early plant growth experiments (including those on phototropism) involved the use of coleoptiles. Their use has been criticized because the coleoptile (the sheath surrounding the young shoot of grasses) is a specialized and short-lived structure and is probably not representative of plant tissues generally.

Auxins and Geotropic Responses

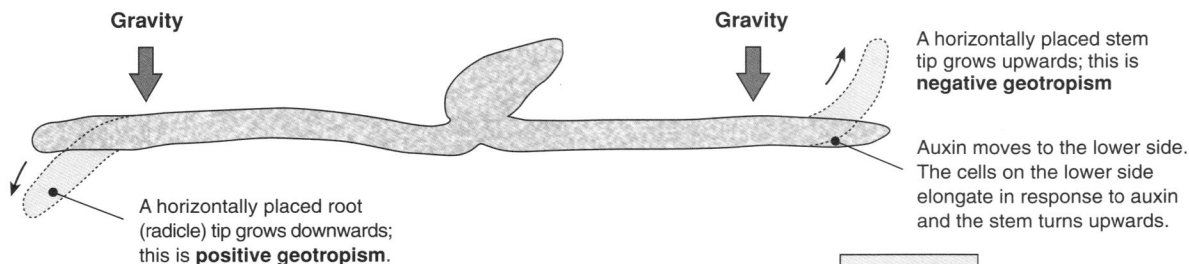

Gravity

Gravity

A horizontally placed stem tip grows upwards; this is **negative geotropism**

A horizontally placed root (radicle) tip grows downwards; this is **positive geotropism**.

Auxin moves to the lower side. The cells on the lower side elongate in response to auxin and the stem turns upwards.

Experiments on isolated shoot tips provide some evidence that geotropism (like phototropism) is due to different growth rates of upper and lower sides of the stem or root in response to the redistribution of auxin. In a horizontally placed shoot tip (see diagram, right), more auxin accumulates on the lower side than on the uppermost side. In stems, this causes elongation of the cells on the lower surface and the stem tip turns up. The root grows down because root elongation is inhibited by the high levels of auxin on the lower surface (see graph below).

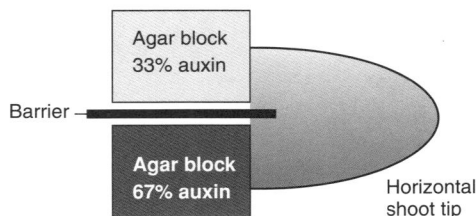

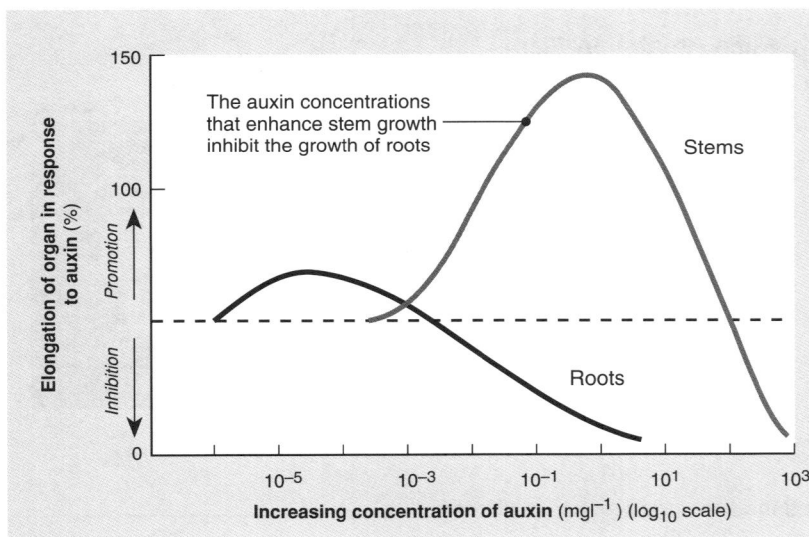

Agar block 33% auxin

Barrier

Agar block 67% auxin

Horizontal shoot tip

The auxin concentrations that enhance stem growth inhibit the growth of roots

Stems

Roots

Elongation of organ in response to auxin (%)

Promotion

Inhibition

150

100

0

10^{-5} 10^{-3} 10^{-1} 10^1 10^3

Increasing concentration of auxin (mgl^{-1}) (log$_{10}$ scale)

Auxin Concentration and Root Growth

In a horizontally placed seedling, auxin moves to the lower side of the organ in both the stem and root. Whereas the stem tip grows upwards, the root tip responds by growing down. Root elongation is inhibited by the same level of auxin that stimulates stem growth (see graph left). The higher auxin levels on the lower surface cause growth inhibition there. The most elongated cells are then on the upper surface and the root turns down. This simple auxin explanation for the geotropic response has been much criticized: the concentrations of auxins measured in the upper and lower surfaces of horizontal stems and roots are too small to account for the growth movements observed. Alternative explanations suggest that growth inhibitors are also somehow involved in the geotropic response.

1. Explain the mechanism proposed for the role of auxin in the geotropic response in:

   (a) Shoots (stems): _____

   _____

   (b) Roots: _____

   _____

   _____

2. (a) From the graph above, state the auxin concentration at which root growth becomes inhibited: _____

   (b) State the response of stem at this concentration: _____

3. Briefly state a reason why the geotropic response in stems or roots is important to the survival of a seedling:

   (a) Stems: _____

   (b) Roots: _____

Plant Rhythms

DA 2

Plants exhibit a number of growth responses and movements that are linked to environmental rhythms. Some plant movements, such as the daily opening of flowers, follow **circadian rhythms**. These responses to environmental cues are adaptive and benefit the plants in some way. **Photoperiodism** is the term used to describe the

cycles of plants in response to daylength. Seeds from the same species may grow into mature plants over a period of several months. Even though their germination dates may vary considerably, they all flower at about the same time. The exact onset of flowering varies depending on whether the plant is a short-day or long-day type.

Long-day plants

When subjected to the light regimes on the right, the 'long-day' plants below flowered as indicated:

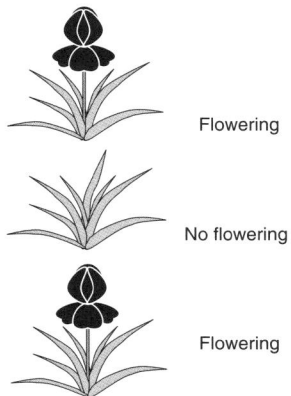

Flowering

No flowering

Flowering

Examples: *lettuce, clover, delphinium, gladiolus, beetscorn, coreopsis*

Photoperiodism in Plants

An experiment was carried out to determine the environmental cue that triggers flowering in 'long-day' and 'short-day' plants. The diagram below shows 3 different light regimes to which a variety of long-day and short-day plants were exposed.

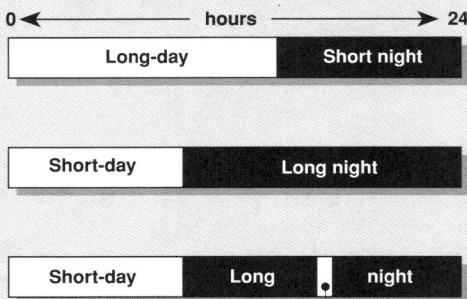

0 ◄─────────── hours ───────────► 24

| Long-day | Short night |

| Short-day | Long night |

| Short-day | Long | night |

Long night interrupted by a short period exposed to light

Short-day plants

When subjected to the light regimes on the left, the 'short-day' plants below flowered as indicated:

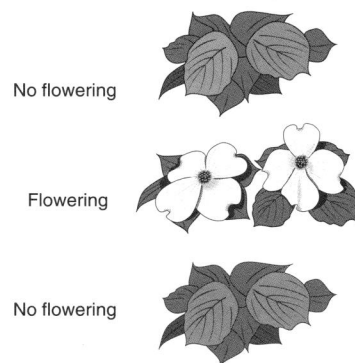

No flowering

Flowering

No flowering

Examples: *potatoes, asters, dahlias, cosmos, chrysanthemums, pointsettias*

Circadian Rhythm in Plants

The photographs below were taken of a single **tulip** flower over a single 12 hour period during spring

| 7.00 am | 9.30 am | 11.00 am | 5.00 pm | 7.00 pm |

1. Name the environmental cue that synchronizes the flowering process in plants: _____

2. Describe one biological advantage of this synchronization to the plants:_____

_____

3. Study the three light regimes above and the responses of short-day and long-day flowering plants to that light. From this observation, state the most important factor controlling the onset of flowering in:

   (a) Short-day plants: _____

   (b) Long-day plants: _____

4. For the series of photographs of the tulip flower above:

   (a) Describe the kind of behavior exhibited by the flower: _____

   _____

   (b) Name the environmental cue that synchronizes this cycle:_____

   (c) Describe one biological advantage to the plants of this kind of behavior: _____

   _____

Flowering and Dormancy

A 2

Photoperiodism is the response of a plant to the relative lengths of daylight and darkness. Flowering is one of the activities of plants that is photoperiodic, and plants can be classified according to how light affects their flowering. Photoperiodism is controlled through the action of a pigment called **phytochrome**, which acts like an alarm button for some biological clocks in plants. Phytochrome is also involved in other light initiated responses in plants, such as seed germination, leaf growth, and chlorophyll synthesis. Plants do not grow at the same rate all of the time. In temperate regions, many perennial and biennial plants start to shut down growth as autumn approaches and the days grow shorter. During the unfavorable seasons, they limit their growth or cease to grow altogether. This condition of arrested growth, or **dormancy**, enables plants to survive periods of water shortage or low temperature. The plant's buds will not resume growth until there is a convergence of environmental cues in early spring. Short days and long, cold nights (as well as dry, nitrogen deficient soils) are strong cues for dormancy. Seasonal changes in temperature also influence many plant responses, including seed germination and flowering. In many plants the dormancy breaking process and flowering are triggered by a specific period of exposure to low winter temperatures. This low-temperature stimulation of flowering or seed germination is called **vernalization**.

Photoperiodism

Photoperiodism is based on a system that monitors the day/night cycle. The photoreceptor involved in this, and a number of other light-initiated plant responses, is a blue-green pigment called **phytochrome**. Phytochrome is universal in vascular plants and has two forms: active and inactive. On absorbing light, it readily converts from the inactive form (P_r) to the active form (P_{fr}). P_{fr} predominates in daylight, but reverts spontaneously back to the inactive form in the dark. The plant measures daylength (or rather night length) by the amount of phytochrome in each form.

Summary of phytochrome related activities in plants

Process	Effect of daylight	Effect of darkness
Conversion of phytochrome	Promotes $P_r \rightarrow P_{fr}$	Promotes $P_{fr} \rightarrow P_r$
Seed germination	Promotes	Inhibits
Leaf growth	Promotes	Inhibits
Flowering - long day plants	Promotes	Inhibits
Flowering - short day plants	Inhibits	Promotes
Chlorophyll synthesis	Promotes	Inhibits

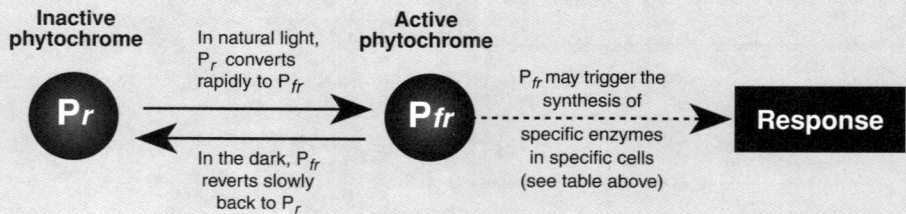

Inactive phytochrome P_r

In natural light, P_r converts rapidly to P_{fr}

Active phytochrome P_{fr}

In the dark, P_{fr} reverts slowly back to P_r

P_{fr} may trigger the synthesis of specific enzymes in specific cells (see table above)

Response

Day length and life cycle in plants (Northern Hemisphere)

The cycle of active growth and dormancy shown by temperate plants is correlated with the number of daylight hours each day (right). In the southern hemisphere, the pattern is similar, but is six months out of phase. The duration of the periods may also vary on islands and in coastal regions because of the moderating effect of nearby oceans.

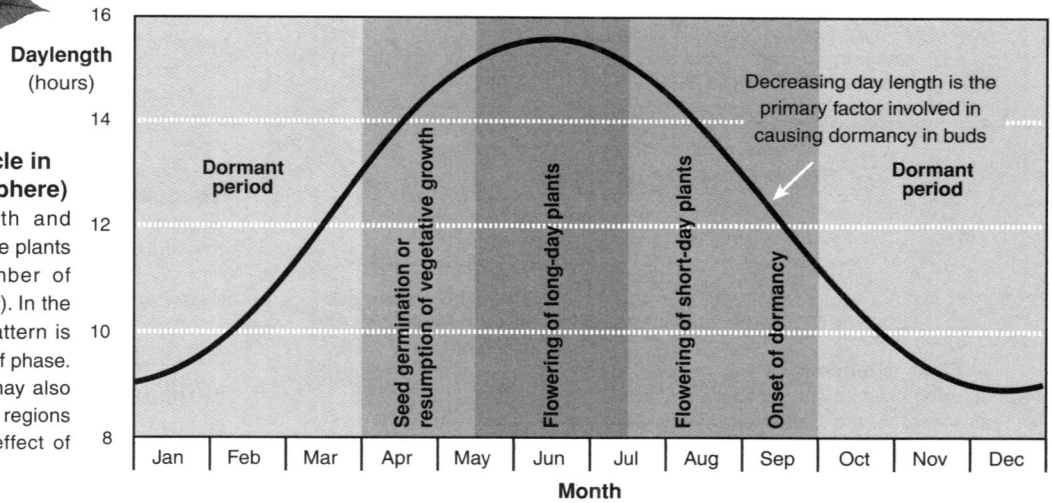

Daylength (hours)

Dormant period

Seed germination or resumption of vegetative growth

Flowering of long-day plants

Flowering of short-day plants

Onset of dormancy

Decreasing day length is the primary factor involved in causing dormancy in buds

Dormant period

Jan | Feb | Mar | Apr | May | Jun | Jul | Aug | Sep | Oct | Nov | Dec

Month

1. List three plant responses initiated by exposure to light that are thought to involve the action of phytochrome:

_____

2. State what causes phytochrome to change from its inactive to active form: _____

3. Define the term **dormancy**:_____

4. Define the term **vernalization**: _____

5. Suggest why dormancy is advantageous to plants living in temperate climates: _____

_____

6. Describe three strong environmental cues that may cause the onset of dormancy in plants:_____

_____

Plant Hormones and Applications

Like animals, plants use hormones to regulate their growth and development. Plant hormones (**phytohormones**) are organic compounds produced in one part of the plant and transported to another part, where they produce a growth response. Hormones are effective in extremely small amounts. There are five groups of phytohormones: **auxins** (indolacetic acid or IAA), **cytokinins**,

gibberellins, **ethene**, and **abscisic acid** (ABA). Together they control growth and development of the plant at various stages. Synthetic analogues of IAA have been produced for commercial use and are applied as growth promoters in rooting powders, and as inducers for fruit production. Some analogues (e.g. 2-4-5-T) even act as growth inhibitors and are used as selective herbicides.

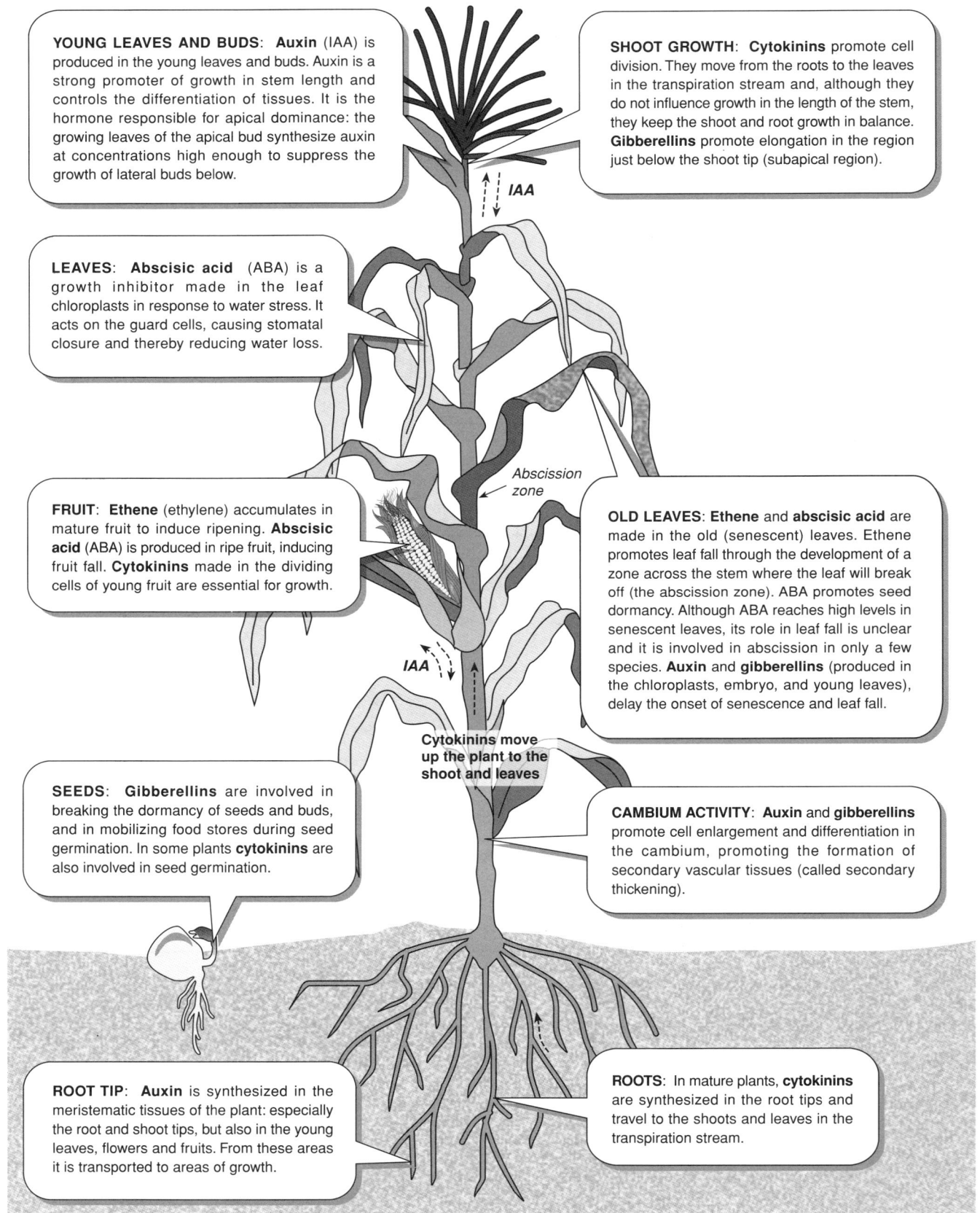

YOUNG LEAVES AND BUDS: **Auxin** (IAA) is produced in the young leaves and buds. Auxin is a strong promoter of growth in stem length and controls the differentiation of tissues. It is the hormone responsible for apical dominance: the growing leaves of the apical bud synthesize auxin at concentrations high enough to suppress the growth of lateral buds below.

SHOOT GROWTH: **Cytokinins** promote cell division. They move from the roots to the leaves in the transpiration stream and, although they do not influence growth in the length of the stem, they keep the shoot and root growth in balance. **Gibberellins** promote elongation in the region just below the shoot tip (subapical region).

IAA

LEAVES: **Abscisic acid** (ABA) is a growth inhibitor made in the leaf chloroplasts in response to water stress. It acts on the guard cells, causing stomatal closure and thereby reducing water loss.

Abscission zone

FRUIT: **Ethene** (ethylene) accumulates in mature fruit to induce ripening. **Abscisic acid** (ABA) is produced in ripe fruit, inducing fruit fall. **Cytokinins** made in the dividing cells of young fruit are essential for growth.

OLD LEAVES: **Ethene** and **abscisic acid** are made in the old (senescent) leaves. Ethene promotes leaf fall through the development of a zone across the stem where the leaf will break off (the abscission zone). ABA promotes seed dormancy. Although ABA reaches high levels in senescent leaves, its role in leaf fall is unclear and it is involved in abscission in only a few species. **Auxin** and **gibberellins** (produced in the chloroplasts, embryo, and young leaves), delay the onset of senescence and leaf fall.

IAA

Cytokinins move up the plant to the shoot and leaves

SEEDS: **Gibberellins** are involved in breaking the dormancy of seeds and buds, and in mobilizing food stores during seed germination. In some plants **cytokinins** are also involved in seed germination.

CAMBIUM ACTIVITY: **Auxin** and **gibberellins** promote cell enlargement and differentiation in the cambium, promoting the formation of secondary vascular tissues (called secondary thickening).

ROOT TIP: **Auxin** is synthesized in the meristematic tissues of the plant: especially the root and shoot tips, but also in the young leaves, flowers and fruits. From these areas it is transported to areas of growth.

ROOTS: In mature plants, **cytokinins** are synthesized in the root tips and travel to the shoots and leaves in the transpiration stream.

1. Explain the difference between plant hormones and animal hormones: _____

_____

_____

2. Outline one major effect of each of the hormones listed below:

   (a) Gibberellins: _____

   _____

   (b) Cytokinins: _____

   _____

   (c) Ethene: _____

   _____

   (d) Abscisic acid: _____

   _____

3. Explain the role of auxin (IAA) in the following plant growth processes:

   (a) Apical dominance: _____

   _____

   (b) Stem growth: _____

   _____

   (c) Secondary growth: _____

   _____

4. Outline why pruning (removing the central leader) induces bushy growth in plants: _____

   _____

5. Describe how a horticulturist could utilize hormones in each of the following situations:

   (a) To promote root development in plant cuttings: _____

   _____

   _____

   (b) To induce ripening in fruit: _____

   _____

   _____

   (c) To act as weed killer: _____

   _____

   _____

   (d) To promote seed germination: _____

   _____

   _____

   (e) To encourage seed dormancy prior to storage: _____

   _____

   _____

Plant Propagation

Large numbers of flowering plants are able to reproduce asexually by **vegetative propagation**. Humans exploit this ability and many successful strains of crop plants are hardly ever grown from seed. Plants can spread quickly by vegetative means when conditions are favorable. By doing this they do not need to produce flowers, pollen or seeds; processes with large energy costs to the plant. Vegetative propagation by artificial means (opposite) results in genetically identical plants (clones) year after year. Clones are produced for several reasons, such as

when uniformity of plant performance is desirable (e.g. in fruit trees), to multiply sterile or seedless species, or to propagate species with flowers in which the stamens have changed to petals and there is no pollen produced. In general, artificial propagation is a more efficient way to multiply certain kinds of plants because it produces a larger plant faster than one raised from seed and it avoids seed dormancy. New varieties can be developed by grafting, which combines the favorable characteristics of two existing varieties.

Examples of Natural Vegetative Structures

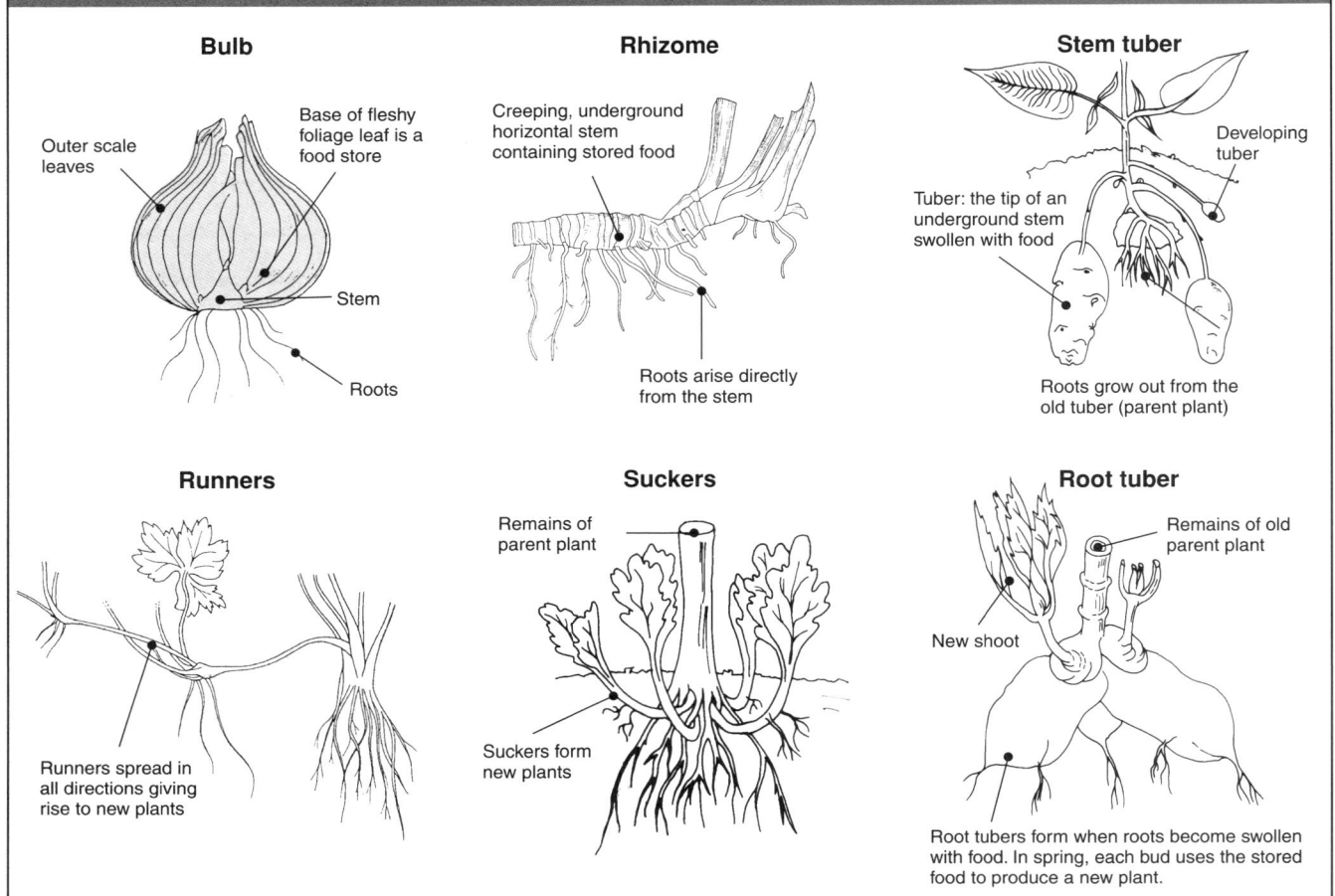

Bulb

Outer scale leaves

Base of fleshy foliage leaf is a food store

Stem

Roots

Rhizome

Creeping, underground horizontal stem containing stored food

Roots arise directly from the stem

Stem tuber

Developing tuber

Tuber: the tip of an underground stem swollen with food

Roots grow out from the old tuber (parent plant)

Runners

Runners spread in all directions giving rise to new plants

Suckers

Remains of parent plant

Suckers form new plants

Root tuber

Remains of old parent plant

New shoot

Root tubers form when roots become swollen with food. In spring, each bud uses the stored food to produce a new plant.

Garlic propagates via a bulb. Axillary buds (called cloves) form beside the existing bulb.

Ginger is a rhizome from which new growth will eventually lead to the formation of independent plants.

Tussock grasses propagate from horizontal stems that grow from buds at the tip of the rhizomes.

The roots growing out of this potato will form new tubers and eventually independent plants.

1. Explain what is meant by **vegetative propagation**: _____

_____

_____

Artificial Vegetative Propagation

Cutting

Cutting is a method of propagation where a vegetative structure is removed from a parent plant and grown as a new individual. Cuttings are successfully used to propagate herbaceous plants, but can be used on woody plants with the use of hormones that promote root growth.

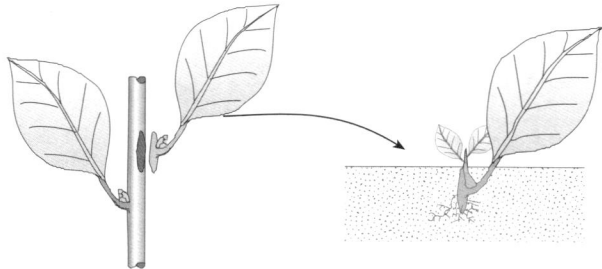

1 A leaf and axial bud is cut from the parent stock

2 The cutting is placed in a growth medium containing rooting hormones.

Grafting *(see photo series below)*

Grafting is a procedure by which the structures of two or more plants are joined. Typically a twig section (scion) from one plant is joined to the shoot of another (the rootstock). Grafting is used for many fruit and landscape trees because it avoids juvenility, and the special properties of the rootstock and the scion are able to be incorporated in the same plant.

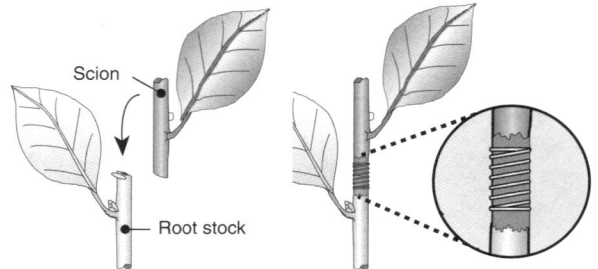

Scion

Root stock

1 A **scion** is prepared by taking a cutting. The scion is then grafted to another plant (root stock).

2 The graft is covered in wax to prevent infection and held together with twine or raffia.

A scion is removed from the parent plant prior to grafting.

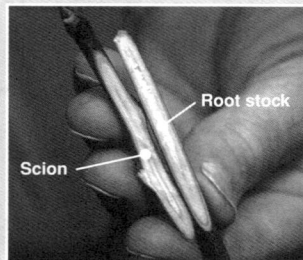

Scion

Incision into parent plant

Scion being grafted onto the stem of the root stock.

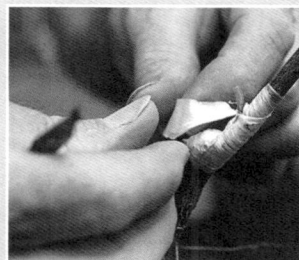

Root stock

Scion

The graft is sealed and covered to prevent water loss and infection.

The graft is then labelled for future reference and monitoring.

2. Describe how plants benefit by reproducing vegetatively: _____

_____

_____

3. Discuss how humans have benefited from the vegetative propagation of plants. Include reference to both biological and economic benefits:

_____

_____

_____

_____

4. Discuss the role of vegetative structures as food stores in plants: _____

_____

_____

_____

5. Distinguish between **cutting** and **grafting**: _____

_____

_____

_____

Plant Tissue Culture

A 2

Plant tissue culture, or **micropropagation**, is a method used for **cloning** plants. It is used widely for the rapid multiplication of commercially important plant species with superior genotypes, as well as in the recovery programs for endangered plant species. Plant productivity and quality may be rapidly improved, and resistance to disease, pollutants, and insects increased. Continued culture of a limited number of cloned varieties leads to a change in the genetic composition of the population (genetic variation is reduced). New genetic stock may be introduced into cloned lines periodically to prevent this reduction in genetic diversity. Micro-propagation is

possible because differentiated plant cells have the potential to give rise to all the cells of an adult plant. It has considerable advantages over traditional methods of plant propagation (see table below), but it is very labor intensive. In addition, the optimal conditions for growth and regeneration must be determined and plants propagated in this way may be genetically unstable or infertile, with chromosomes structurally altered or in unusual numbers. The success of tissue culture is affected by factors such as selection of **explant** material, the composition of the culturing media, plant hormone levels, lighting, and temperature.

❶ Stock plants are kept as free from pests and pathogens as possible.

Explant (in this case an axial bud)

❷ Small pieces are cut (excised) from the plant. Called **explants**, they may be stem tissue with nodes, flower buds, leaves or tiny sections of shoot tip meristems.

❸ The surfaces of the explants are sterilized using solutions such as sodium hypochlorite.

❹ The explants are transferred to a culture vessel under sterile conditions.

Advantages of Tissue Culture

- Possible to create large numbers of clones from a single seed or explant.

- Selection of desirable traits is possible directly from the culturing setup *(in vitro)*, decreasing the amount of space required for field trials.

- Reproduction of plants is possible without having to wait for the onset of seed production.

- Rapid propagation is possible for species that have long generation times, low levels of seed production, or seeds that do not readily germinate.

- Enables the preservation of pollen and cell collections from which plants may be propagated (like a seed bank).

- Allows the international exchange of sterilized plant materials (eliminating the need for quarantine).

- Helps to eliminate plant diseases through careful stock selection and sterile techniques during propagation.

- Overcomes seasonal restrictions for germination.

- Enables cold storage of large numbers of viable plants in a small space.

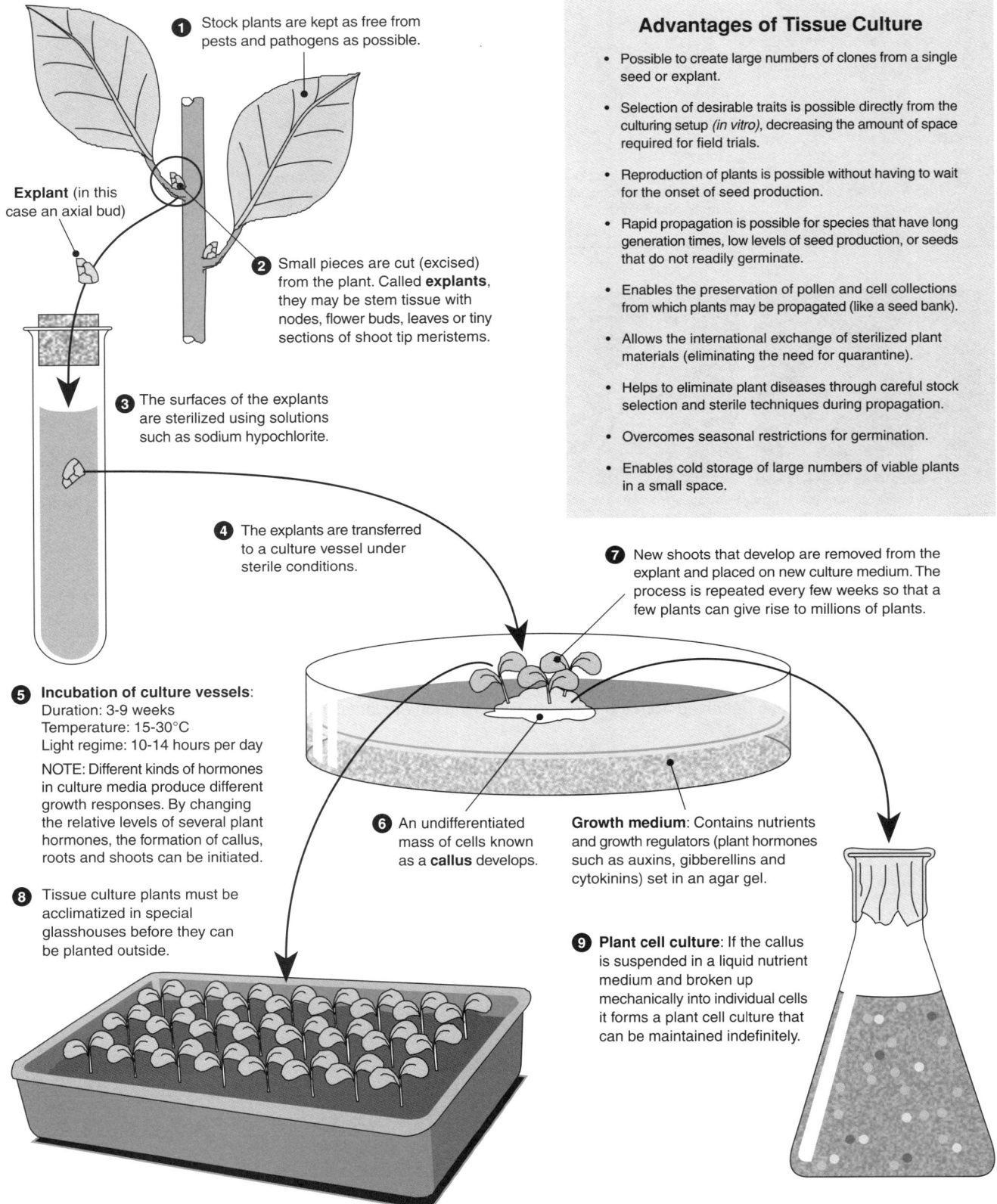

❼ New shoots that develop are removed from the explant and placed on new culture medium. The process is repeated every few weeks so that a few plants can give rise to millions of plants.

❺ **Incubation of culture vessels**:
Duration: 3-9 weeks
Temperature: 15-30°C
Light regime: 10-14 hours per day

NOTE: Different kinds of hormones in culture media produce different growth responses. By changing the relative levels of several plant hormones, the formation of callus, roots and shoots can be initiated.

❽ Tissue culture plants must be acclimatized in special glasshouses before they can be planted outside.

❻ An undifferentiated mass of cells known as a **callus** develops.

Growth medium: Contains nutrients and growth regulators (plant hormones such as auxins, gibberellins and cytokinins) set in an agar gel.

❾ **Plant cell culture**: If the callus is suspended in a liquid nutrient medium and broken up mechanically into individual cells it forms a plant cell culture that can be maintained indefinitely.

Micropropagation of the Tasmanian blackwood tree *(Acacia melanoxylon)*

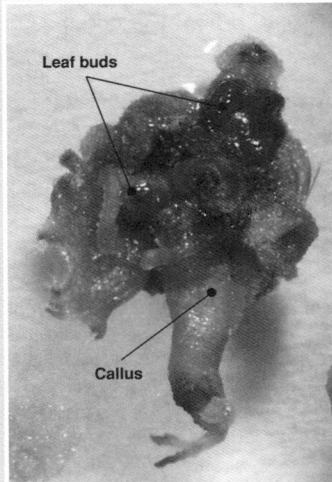

Greening and formation of leaf buds on a callus growing on culturing medium.

Normal shoots with juvenile leaves growing from a callus on media. They appear identical to those produced directly from seeds.

Seedling with juvenile foliage six months after transfer to greenhouse.

Micropropagation is increasingly used in conjunction with genetic engineering to propagate transgenic plants. Genetic engineering and micropropagation achieve similar results to conventional selective breeding but more precisely, quickly, and independently of growing season. The **Tasmanian blackwood** (above) provides a good example of a plant suited to this type of manipulation. It is a versatile hardwood tree now being extensively trialled in some countries as a replacement for tropical hardwoods. The timber is of high quality, but genetic variations between individual trees invariably lead to differences in timber quality and color. Tissue culture allows the multiple propagation of trees with desirable traits (e.g. uniform timber color). Tissue culture could also facilitate solutions to other problems that cannot be solved by forestry management. When combined with genetic engineering (introduction of new genes into the plant) problems of pest and herbicide susceptibility may be resolved. Genetic engineering may also be used to introduce a gene for male sterility, thereby stopping pollen production. This would improve the efficiency of conventional breeding programs by preventing self-pollination of flowers (the manual removal of stamens is difficult and very labor intensive).

Information courtesy of Raewyn Poole, University of Waikato (Unpublished Msc. thesis).

1. Explain the general purpose of tissue culturing plants: _____

_____

2. (a) Explain what a **callus** is: _____

_____

(b) Explain how a callus may be stimulated to initiate root and shoot formation: _____

_____

3. Describe two **advantages** of using micropropagation over traditional propagation methods:

(a) _____

_____

(b) _____

_____

4. Describe two **disadvantages** of using micropropagation over traditional propagation methods:

(a) _____

_____

(b) _____

_____

5. Discuss a potential problem with micropropagation in terms of long term ability to adapt to environmental changes:

_____

_____

Artificial Selection

RA 2

The ability of people to control the breeding of domesticated animals and crop plants has resulted in an astounding range of phenotypic variation over relatively short time periods. Most livestock, pets, and cultivated crops have undergone **artificial selection** (selective breeding), whereby people select breeding stock, based on (superior) phenotype. The aim of this process is to alter the average phenotype and genotype of the progeny. The dog is a striking example of artificial selection, with an enormous number and variety of breeds (400 or so). The dog thought to have descended from a single wild species - the wolf **Canis lupus**, and was probably first domesticated at least 14 000 years ago. All breeds are **interfertile**, although some crosses are prevented by large size differences. Five ancient dog breeds are recognized, from which all other breeds are thought to have descended by artificial selection over the last 14 000 years.

Gray wolf *Canis lupus pallipes*

The gray wolf is distributed throughout Europe, North America, and Asia. Amongst members of this species, there is a lot of variation in coat coloration. This accounts for the large variation in coat colors of dogs today.

Gray Wolf: Ancestor of Domestic Dogs

Until recently, it was unclear whether the ancestor to the modern domestic dogs was the desert wolf of the Middle East, the woolly wolf of central Asia, or the gray wolf of Northern Hemisphere. Recent genetic studies (mitochondrial DNA comparisons) now provide strong evidence that the ancestor of domestic dogs throughout the world is the gray wolf. It seems likely that this evolutionary change took place in a single region, most probably China.

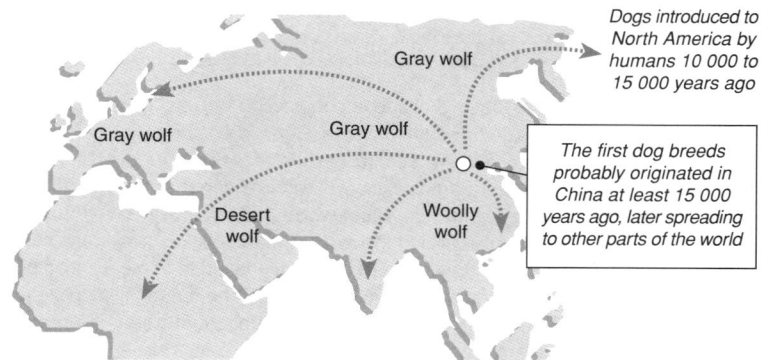

Dogs introduced to North America by humans 10 000 to 15 000 years ago

Gray wolf

Gray wolf

Gray wolf

Desert wolf

Woolly wolf

The first dog breeds probably originated in China at least 15 000 years ago, later spreading to other parts of the world

Mastiff-type
Canis familiaris inostranzevi
Originally from Tibet, the first records of this breed of dog go back to the Stoneage.

Greyhound
Canis familiaris leineri
Drawings of this breed on pottery dated from 8000 years ago in the Middle East make it one of the oldest.

Pointer-type
Canis familiaris intermedius
Probably derived from the greyhound breed for the purpose of hunting small game.

Sheepdog
Canis familiaris metris optimae
Originating in Europe, this breed has been used to guard flocks from predators for thousands of years.

Wolf-like
Canis familiaris palustris
Found in snow covered habitats in northern Europe, Asia (Siberia), and North America (Alaska)

1. Define the term artificial selection: _____

_____

2. Name the methods used to control the breeding process in dogs (in particular, to prevent unwanted offspring):

_____

3. Describe the behavioral tendency of wolves that predisposed them to becoming a domesticated animal:

_____

4. List the physical and behavioral traits that would be desirable (selected for) in the following uses of a dog:

   (a) Hunting large game (e.g. boar and deer): _____

   (b) Game fowl dog: _____

   (c) Stock control (sheep/cattle dog): _____

   (d) Family pet (house dog): _____

   (e) Guard dog: _____

Cauliflower
(flower)

Cabbage
(terminal buds)

Broccoli
(inflorescence)

Brussels sprout
(lateral buds)

Kale
(leaf)

Domestication of *Brassica*

At about 3750 BC in China, the cabbage was probably the first domesticated variety of its wild form to be developed. Artificial selection by humans has produced six separate vegetables from this single species: ***Brassica oleracea***. The wild form of this species is shown in the centre of this diagram. Different parts have been developed by human selection. In spite of the enormous visible differences, if allowed to flower, all six can cross-pollinate. Kale is closer to the wild type than the other related breeds.

Wild form
Brassica oleracea

Kohlrabi
(stem)

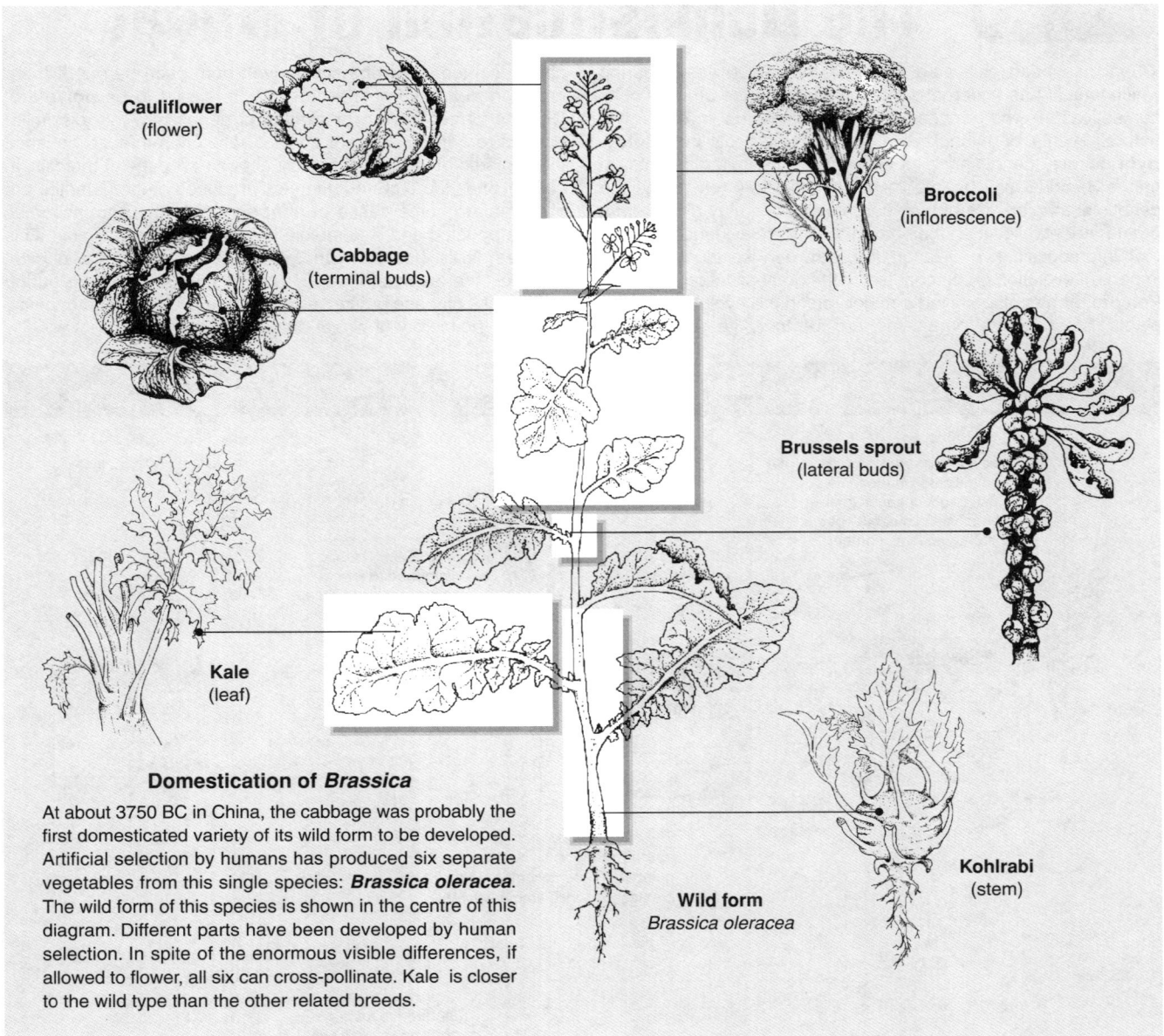

5. Study the diagram above and **name** which part of the plant has been *selected for* to produce each of the vegetables:

(a) Cauliflower: _____

(d) Brussels sprout: _____

(b) Kale: _____

(e) Cabbage: _____

(c) Broccoli: _____

(f) Kohlrabi: _____

6. State the feature of these vegetables that suggests they are members of the same species: _____

_____

7. Human artificial selection pressures can also influence the development of characteristics in 'unwanted' species. Explain how human weed control measures may inadvertently select for weed plants that have a resistance to the measures:

_____

_____

_____

8. Explain how a farmer thousands of years ago was able to improve the phenotypic character of a cereal crop:

_____

_____

_____

The Domestication of Wheat

A 2

Wheat has been cultivated for more than 9000 years, during which time it has undergone many changes in the process of its domestication. The process of wheat evolution involved two natural events of hybridization, accompanied by **polyploidy**. **Hybrids** are the offspring of genetically dissimilar parents. In nature, hybrids may be important because they recombine the genetic characteristics of their parents and this may give them a greater adaptability than their parents. There is evidence to show that interspecific hybridization (i.e. between species) was an important evolutionary mechanism in the domestication of wheat. **Polyploidy** has also played a major role in the evolution of crop plants. Most higher organisms are **diploid**, i.e. two set of

chromosomes (2N), one set derived from each parent. If there are more than two sets the organism is said to be **polyploid**. Diploids formed from hybridization of genetically very dissimilar parents, e.g. from different species, are often infertile because the two sets of chromosomes do not pair properly at meiosis. In such hybrids there are no gametes produced or the gametes are abnormal. In some cases of **allopolyploidy** the chromosomes can be doubled and a tetraploid is formed from the diploid. This restores fertility to a hybrid, because each of the original chromosome sets can pair properly with each other during meiosis. All of these processes are outlined in the diagram below showing the history of wheat domestication.

Polyploidy Events in the Evolution of Wheat

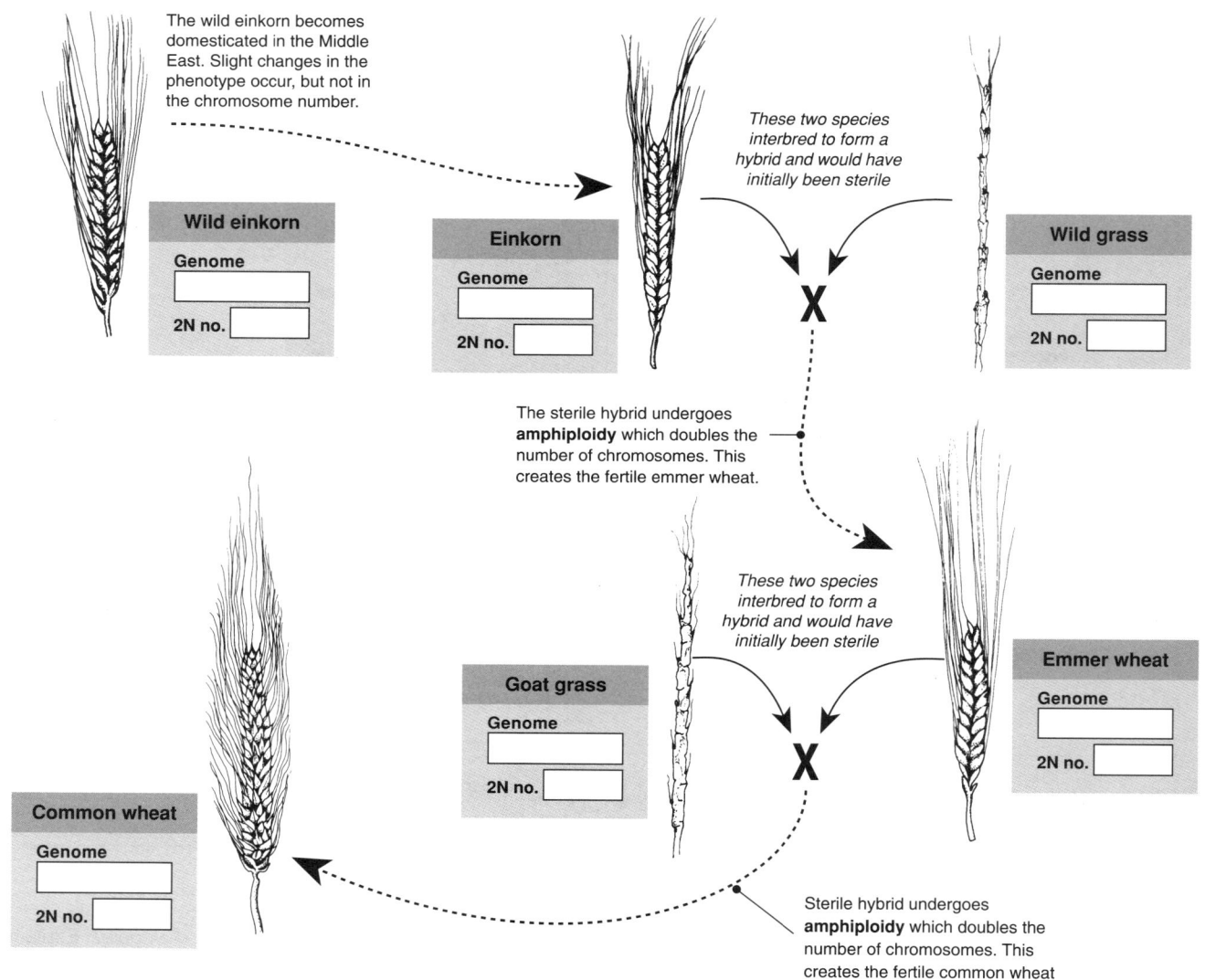

The wild einkorn becomes domesticated in the Middle East. Slight changes in the phenotype occur, but not in the chromosome number.

Wild einkorn
Genome
2N no.

Einkorn
Genome
2N no.

These two species interbred to form a hybrid and would have initially been sterile

Wild grass
Genome
2N no.

The sterile hybrid undergoes **amphiploidy** which doubles the number of chromosomes. This creates the fertile emmer wheat.

These two species interbred to form a hybrid and would have initially been sterile

Goat grass
Genome
2N no.

Emmer wheat
Genome
2N no.

Common wheat
Genome
2N no.

Sterile hybrid undergoes **amphiploidy** which doubles the number of chromosomes. This creates the fertile common wheat

The table on the right and the diagram above show the evolution of the common wheat. Common wheat is thought to have resulted from two sets of crossings between different species to produce hybrids. Wild einkorn (7 chromosomes, genome AA) evolved into einkorn, which crossed with a wild grass (7 chromosomes, genome BB) and gave rise to emmer wheat (14 chromosomes, genome AABB). Common wheat arose when emmer wheat was crossed with another type of grass (goat grass).

Common name	Taxonomic name	Genome	Chromosomes (1N)	(2N)
Wild einkorn	*Triticum aegilopiodes*	**AA**	7	14
Einkorn	*Triticum monococcum*	**AA**	7	14
Wild grass	*Aegilops speltoides*	**BB**	7	14
Emmer wheat	*Triticum dicoccum*	**AABB**	14	28
Goat grass	*Aegilops squarrosa*	**DD**	7	14
Common wheat	*Triticum aestivum*	**AABBDD**	21	42

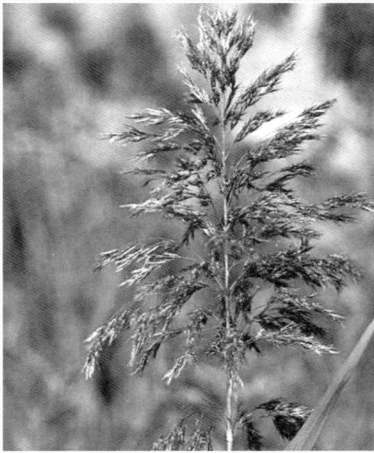

Ancient cereal grasses had heads which shattered readily so that seeds would be scattered widely.

Modern wheat has been selected for its non shattering heads, high yield, and high gluten content.

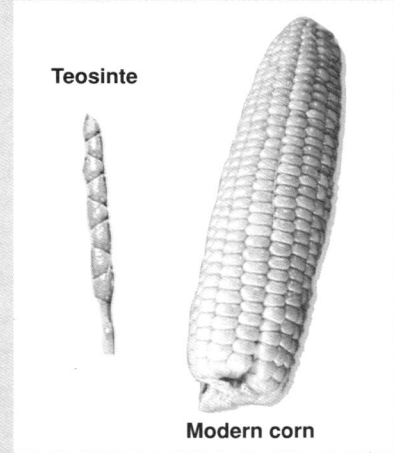

Teosinte

Modern corn

Corn has also evolved during its domestication. Teosinte is thought to be the ancestor to both corn and maize.

1. Using the table on the left, label each of the wheats and grasses in the diagram with the correct **genome** and **2N** chromosome number for each plant.

2. Define the following terms:

   (a) **Interspecific hybridization**: _____

   _____

   (b) **F₁ hybrid vigour**: _____

   _____

3. Explain how polyploidy has been involved in the evolution of wheat: _____

   _____

   _____

   _____

4. Cultivated wheat arose from wild, weedy ancestors through the selection of certain characters:

   (a) List the phenotypic traits that are desirable in modern wheat cultivars: _____

   _____

   (b) Suggest how ancient farmers would have carried out a selective breeding program: _____

   _____

   _____

5. Cultivated American cotton plants have a total of 52 chromosomes (2N = 52). In each cell there are 26 large chromosomes and 26 small chromosomes. Old World cotton plants have 26 chromosomes (2N = 26), all large. Wild American cotton plants have 26 chromosomes, all small. Briefly explain how cultivated American cotton may have originated from Old World cotton and wild American cotton:

   _____

   _____

   _____

   _____

6. Discuss the need to maintain the biodiversity of wild plants and ancient farm breeds: _____

   _____

   _____

   _____

Livestock Improvement

The domestication of livestock has a long history dating back at least 8000 years. Modern sheep and cattle breeds have been developed over centuries of breeding for particular qualities, e.g. milk or meat production, tolerance to climate or terrain, or as draught animals. Furthermore, different countries have different criteria for selection, based on their local environments and consumer preferences. Cattle breeding in today's society centers around selection for milk or meat production, with particular breeds being suited to different uses. Sheep are bred for meat,

wool, and/or milk production. Traditional **selective breeding** involves choosing breeding stock with desirable qualities. This method produces a steady but slow gain in the desired qualities of the line. This **genetic gain** has accelerated in recent times with the advent of more reliable ways in which to assess genetic value and assist reproduction. New technologies refine the selection process and increase the rate at which stock improvements are made. Rates are predicted to accelerate further, as technologies improve and become less costly.

Artificial Selection and Genetic Gain in Cattle

Cattle are selected on the basis of particular desirable traits. Some breeds are selected primarily for milk production and others primarily for beef. Most of the genetic improvement in dairy cattle has relied on selection of high quality progeny from proven stock and extensive use of superior sires through artificial insemination (AI). In beef cattle, AI

is useful for introducing new breeds. Consumer demand has led to the shift towards continental breeds such as the Charolais because they are larger, with a higher proportion of lean muscle. Many mixed breeds, e.g. Hereford-Friesian crosses, combine the favorable qualities of two breeds and are suitable for mixed dairying/beef production.

Beef breeds: Aberdeen-Angus, Hereford (above), Simmental, Galloway, Charolais. **Desirable traits**: high muscle to bone ratio, rapid growth and weight gain, hardy, easy calving, docile temperament.

Dairy breeds: Jersey, Friesian (above), Holstein, Aryshire. **Desirable traits**: high yield of milk with high butterfat, milking speed, docile temperament, and udder characteristics such as teat placement.

Special breeds: Humped (zebu) cattle like the Brahman (above) are well suited to hot climates. They may be crossed with traditional dairy or beef breeds to increase production from marginal land.

Genetic Gain

A breed is defined as a group of animals that, through selection and breeding, have come to resemble one another and pass on their traits reliably to their offspring. Improved breeding techniques accelerate the genetic progress or **genetic gain** (the gain toward a desirable phenotype).

The graph (right) illustrates the **predicted** gains based on artificial insemination and standard selection techniques (based on criteria such as production or temperament). These are compared with the predicted gains using breeding values and reproductive technologies e.g. embryo multiplication and transfer (EMT) of standard and transgenic stock, marker (gene) assisted selection, and sib-selection (selecting bulls on the basis of their sisters' performance).

A **breeding value** is a score assigned to a stud animal, derived from the sum of individual scores for different characteristics e.g. milk yield or temperament. Accurate assessment of breeding values makes the selection process less subjective and more value based.

Sources of data and breed information: Breeds of Livestock - Oklahoma State University web site and Genetics Australia web site (access both from www.thebiozone.com/links.html)

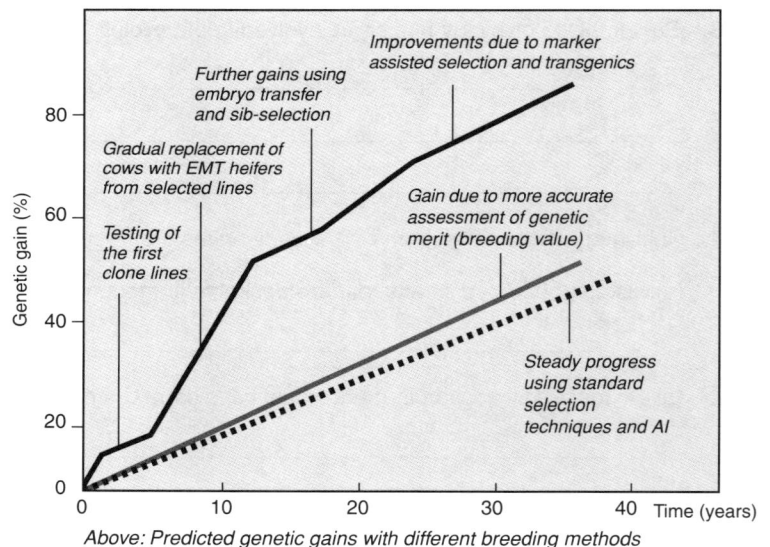

Above: Predicted genetic gains with different breeding methods

1. Identify the two methods by which most of the genetic progress in dairy cattle has been achieved:

   (a) _____ (b) _____

2. Explain what is meant by the term *genetic gain* as it applies to livestock breeding: _____

   _____

3. Describe the contribution that new reproductive technologies are making to the selective breeding in cattle:

   _____

4. Describe two desirable features of:

   (a) A dairy breed: _____

   (b) A beef breed: _____

Index

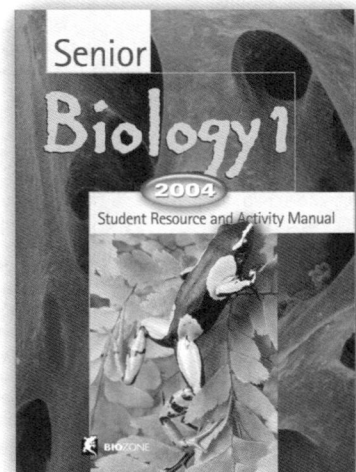